AF770930

CIVIL PROCEDURE

FIFTH EDITION

By

FLEMING JAMES, JR.
Late Sterling Professor of Law,
Yale University

GEOFFREY C. HAZARD, JR.
Trustee Professor of Law,
University of Pennsylvania

JOHN LEUBSDORF
Professor of Law and Frederick Lacey Distinguished Scholar,
Rutgers University

From the library of
Wolf, Greenfield & Sacks
600 Atlantic Avenue
Boston, MA 02210

New York, New York
FOUNDATION PRESS
2001

Foundation Press, a division of West Group, has created this publication to provide you with accurate and authoritative information concerning the subject matter covered. However, this publication was not necessarily prepared by persons licensed to practice law in a particular jurisdiction. Foundation Press is not engaged in rendering legal or other professional advice, and this publication is not a substitute for the advice of an attorney. If you require legal or other expert advice, you should seek the services of a competent attorney or other professional.

COPYRIGHT © 2001 By FOUNDATION PRESS
395 Hudson Street
New York, NY 10014
Phone Toll Free 1–877–888–1330
Fax (212) 367–6799
fdpress.com

All rights reserved
Printed in the United States of America

ISBN 1–56662–981–0 (hard cover)
ISBN 1–56662–982–9 (soft cover)

TEXT IS PRINTED ON 10% POST CONSUMER RECYCLED PAPER

From GCH, Jr. to his daughter, Katherine Hazard

From JL to his wife, Lynn B. Montz

*

PREFACE AND ACKNOWLEDGMENTS

This is a revision of the text on civil procedure first published by Professor James in 1965. Its aim is the same as the first edition: an explanatory companion for the basic law school course in civil procedure. It covers the matters included in most casebooks on the subjects, which in most law school curricula is the foundation course for procedure in general, including criminal procedure and administrative agency adjudication.

Civil procedure as a "subject" descends from the study of the common law forms of action. In the nineteenth century, the code pleading reforms simplified and standardized the common law forms of action, thereby distinguishing between what the legal grievance might be ("substantive" law) and how it should be presented and adjudged ("procedure"). Civil procedure in law school curricula was generally called "code pleading."

The adoption of the Federal Rules of Civil Procedure in 1938 resulted in a fundamental redefinition of the subject, especially as these rules have since become adopted or closely emulated in virtually all the states. The Federal Rules further simplified the rules governing the way in which legal grievances might be stated; they greatly liberalized the rules on joinder of claims and joinder of parties; and they established a far-reaching set of procedures for developing evidence prior to trial ("discovery"). The Federal Rules were elaborated in an era of legal history often characterized as the "legal explosion." This explosion involved an expansion of the types of interests protected by judicial remedies (such as consumer interests, civil rights and civil liberties, and "public" interests), a more thorough search for correct results (freer access to evidence, complex remedies, the growth of class actions), and more exacting regulation of the fairness of the adjudicative process (discretion of trial judges to prescribe procedures, broad appealability, and some tentative steps toward making legal assistance more widely available).

Recent decades have seen something of a retrenchment, as groups ranging from "tort reformers" to judges confronting expanding dockets have sought to limit overelaborate litigating and discourage baseless claims and defenses. The Federal Rules ideals have become a bit tarnished, yet no broadly accepted replacement has appeared. Meanwhile, such developments as alternative dispute resolution and multinational litigation have expanded the problems and possibilities of procedure.

In dealing with the subject matter, we have tried to provide both historical background and a critical perspective contemplating the course of future development in procedural law. We have sought to state what the law "is," to explain the problems to which the rules have been supplied as answers, and to suggest better answers where appropriate.

PREFACE AND ACKNOWLEDGMENTS

In preparing this edition, we reiterate acknowledgments to those mentioned in the previous editions. Antonio Gidi and Professor Melvyn Zarr have contributed useful suggestions for this edition. The Dean's Research Fund of Rutgers School of Law-Newark provided funding. We renew thanks to the following legal periodicals for permission to use material previously published in the first edition: Duquesne Law Review, Howard Law Journal, University of Miami Law Review, Vanderbilt Law Review, Virginia Law Review, and Yale Law Review.

GEOFFREY C. HAZARD, JR.
JOHN LEUBSDORF

March 2001

SUMMARY OF CONTENTS

*

TABLE OF CONTENTS

CHAPTER 2. PROPER COURT IN CIVIL ACTIONS

CHAPTER 5. DISCOVERY AND OTHER PRETRIAL DEVICES

CHAPTER 7. THE TRIAL

A. STRUCTURE OF A TRIAL

B. BASIC CONCEPTS OF JURY TRIAL PROCEDURE

C. CONTROLLING THE JURY: PREVERDICT DEVICES

D. CONTROLLING THE JURY: POSTVERDICT DEVICES

CHAPTER 8. RIGHT TO A JURY TRIAL

A. THE CONSTITUTIONAL RIGHT

CIVIL PROCEDURE

*

Chapter 1

INTRODUCTION

§ 1.1 Distinction Between Substance and Procedure; Functions of Procedure

Rules for adjudicating

This is a book about "procedure." A distinction is drawn between substantive law and procedural law or, as it is sometimes called, adjective law. The distinction is made in many different contexts, the line being drawn at one point in one context and elsewhere in another. No universal distinction is possible. For present purposes it is enough to say that the rules of substantive law define rights, duties, and powers of persons and institutions in their out-of-court relationships, while procedural rules govern the decision-making process by which substantive legal interests are maintained or redressed through courts. The rules of procedure in courts are the model for procedural rules of other tribunals such as quasi-judicial administrative agencies and arbitration proceedings.

Enforcing the law

In its day-to-day application, the law of procedure implements substantive law. As Hepburn says, "As its name 'adjective' imports, it exists for the sake of something else—for the sake of the substantive law."[1] It implements substantive law and thereby augments other inducements that persons have for conducting their relations in conformity with the substantive law's prescriptions. These other inducements include the admonitory effect of the substantive law (duty to obey rules emanating from a recognized authority) and lawful coercion or retaliation by the other party through refusing to continue a business or other relationship or invoking the disapproval of persons not directly involved in the controversy. The law of procedure provides a mechanism by which authority of the state, and its coercive powers, can be brought to bear, on a carefully examined basis, to secure compliance with the law when these inducements fail.

Procedural and substantive law influence each other. What procedures we prefer may depend on what law we are trying to enforce and in what way. A system designed for collecting debts may not be good for desegregating schools. At the same time, by affecting how, when, by whom and at what expense the substantive law can be enforced, procedural law inevitably modifies that law.[2]

Dispute resolution

Considered as a continuously functioning system, procedural law is more than "adjective." It implements a political ideal about resolving serious disputes over power, money, and personal standing in the community. It is a model—though not the only one—of dispute resolution. It involves both an appraisal by disinterested persons (the court and jurors) of the conflict situation in its objectively ascertainable aspects (the evidence) and a resolution according to principles applicable regardless of the identity of the specific disputants (rules of law).

These elements of procedure express social and political values concurrent with those expressed in substantive legal rules and are

§ 1.1

1. Hepburn, The Historical Development of Code Pleading 19, 20 (1897).

2. *See* Cover, Violence and the Word, 95 Yale L.J. 1601 (1986).

deemed worthy independent of the substantive law. The law of procedure is thus a branch of constitutional law in the broad sense.[3] The main problems of procedure revolve around trying to insure that these elements are realized in practice while giving effect to the goals implicit in the rules of substantive law.

Other goals

Other objectives of procedure, though secondary, also loom large. First, procedure should give all the parties to a dispute the assurance that they are being fairly dealt with, that each is given a reasonable chance to present his or her side before a reasonably convenient tribunal.[4] Second, procedure should not be unduly costly in time and money.[5] Finally, procedure should yield final and lasting adjudications so that people may enjoy repose and security in their legal relationships.[6]

These objectives will often compete and even conflict with one another. The full pursuit of the facts and applicable law in any dispute may be limited, for example, by the need for efficiency and finality. The hardest and most important job of a procedural system is to strike a wise balance throughout the various points of conflict.

Justice

In the discussion so far we have tacitly assumed that substantive justice is to be equated with the body of substantive rules that exist in the jurisdiction at any given time. This is obviously an oversimplification. There may be competing notions of justice, such as some abstract moral or ethical ideal ("natural law"), expediency in terms of social or economic goals, or the prevailing community sense of fairness. If one or more of these is accepted as the proper test, then clearly the corpus juris of a state may not coincide completely with it. Indeed it is a commonplace that some substantive rules are out of date and yield arbitrary results, at least occasionally, as measured by widely accepted standards of justice.

When that is the case, a question arises: To *what* justice should procedure be a handmaiden? In applying procedural law the court is unlikely to repudiate openly the substantive rules even when they produce unfortunate results. Of course, the courts have always transformed substantive rules in the process of applying them and, particularly at the appellate level, have a pervasive if marginal authority to overrule prior decisions. Not infrequently, however, the courts seek to

3. *See* Leubsdorf, Constitutional Civil Procedure, 63 Tex. L. Rev. 579 (1984).

4. *See* Lind, MacCoun, Ebener, Felstiner, Hensler, Resnik, and Tyler, The Perception of Justice: Tort Litigants' Views of Trial, Court-Annexed Arbitration, and Judicial Settlement Conferences, and bibliography therein (RAND Inst. for Civil Justice 1989).

5. *See* Posner, The Economics of Justice (1983).

6. Restatement (Second) of Judgments ch. 1.

accomplish substantial justice by adhering to established substantive law while manipulating procedural rules in favor of the "right" party. This causes some of the worst procedural rulings, which may bring some kind of substantive justice in the case at hand but which produce language and reasoning that vex other courts, where an application of them may thwart both procedural efficiency and substantive justice as measured by any test. Yet later courts in turn sometimes manipulate or disregard such rulings to produce what they consider good results.

The objectives we have mentioned are common to all systems of procedure, at least in societies that value the worth of the individual. Other objectives also have importance in our institutional framework. Chief among these is the proper allocation of functions and powers between judge and jury, between trial and appellate courts, and between state and nation.

§ 1.2 The Adversary System

A leading characteristic of the Anglo–American procedural system is its adversarial nature. In civil disputes it is generally up to the parties, not the court, to initiate and prosecute litigation, investigate the pertinent facts, and present proof and legal argument to the tribunal. The court's function is generally limited to adjudicating the issues raised by the parties on the proof they have presented and applying appropriate procedural sanctions on motion of a party.[1]

Party roles

Two separate principles are involved in the above statement—party-presentation and party-prosecution. Party-presentation concerns "content of the cause" and assumes that both sides (or all sides when the litigation involves more than two parties) have a balanced opportunity to investigate and present proof and legal argument. The principle is an expression of the interrelated ideas that parties should be masters of their own rights, free to press or waive claims or defenses, and that the social interest in securing legal rights is sufficiently served by leaving their enforcement to the self-interest of the parties directly affected. In the Anglo–American tradition, this principle has governed litigation involving not only private disputes but also public agencies (as when regulatory agencies sue to enforce their regulations) and legal questions of general public concern (such as "test cases"). Historically, even criminal prosecutions were considered proceedings by the king and were brought in his name (and in the eighteenth century many were brought by the injured party).

§ 1.2

1. *See generally* Millar, The Formative Principles of Civil Procedure, 18 Ill. L. Rev. 1 (1923). For critical analysis, see Freedman, Lawyers' Ethics in an Adversary System (1975); Hazard, Ethics in the Practice of Law ch. 9 (1978); Luban, Lawyers and Justice (1988); Frankel, The Search for Truth: An Umpireal View, 123 U. Pa. L. Rev. 1031 (1975); Simon, The Ideology of Advocacy, 1978 Wis. L. Rev. 30.

Party-prosecution is a kind of corollary: The parties move the case forward through its investigatory and decisional stages; the case stops or expires except as one or the other party requests the court to compel the opponent to take the next step.

Truth and acceptance

Uniting these two principles is an underlying concept of the relative roles of the *parties* and the *court.* The concept is that presentation and prosecution should be by a party, with the court acting as an essentially passive arbiter. Hence, even in judicial enforcement of rights of the public at large (as in the enforcement of the criminal law) or of individuals protected by laws such as those governing civil rights or the rights of children, the presentation and prosecution of enforcing litigation is in the hands, not of the court, but of an official or agency who appears as a party and is treated for most procedural purposes as an ordinary private litigant. This approach represents two judgments: (1) that truth is likely to emerge more from bilateral investigation and presentation, motivated by the strong pull of self-interest, than from judicial investigation motivated only by official duty;[2] and (2) that the moral force and acceptability of a decision will be greatest when it is made by one who does not have, and does not appear to have, the kind of psychological commitment to the result that is implied in initiating and conducting the presentation of a case. Yet the prerogatives of a party go beyond what is likely to elicit either truth or acceptability; they include the rights to fight and maneuver over evidentiary and procedural decisions, to seek decision makers likely to be favorable, and to attempt to persuade those decision makers by a variety of suggestive ploys.

Although the adversary system's stress on litigant autonomy and truth through struggle is very much at home in the culture of this nation, some other nations find it less acceptable. Civil law systems—that is, those tracing their law back to the Romans–usually follow the inquisitorial rather than the adversarial approach in criminal cases. That approach assigns to judges rather than prosecution and defense lawyers the central role in searching for the truth. On the other hand, in civil matters some of the same systems carry the logic of the adversary system even further than the United States, at least in one way: parties must find their own evidence, with little or no opportunity to compel opposing parties or neutrals to testify or produce documents.[3]

2. Morgan, Some Problems of Proof Under the Anglo–American System of Litigation 3 (1956); Millar, The Formative Principles of Civil Procedure, 18 Ill. L. Rev. 1, 16 (1923).

3. *See* Leubsdorf, Man In His Original Dignity: Legal Ethics in France ch. 7(2001); Damaska, The Faces of Justice and State Authority (1986); Langbein, The German Advantage in Civil Procedure, 52 U. Chi. L. Rev. 823 (1985).

Judge's responsibility

Even here, the principles of party-presentation and party-prosecution have never been given unqualified application, nor need they be fully equated with due process. The principle of party-prosecution has been modified in modern judicial administration by the proposition that the court has an affirmative responsibility to move a case along to settlement or trial.[4] The party-presentation principle is modified by the strong common law tradition that the judge who conducts the trial should play an active part in directing it so that, within the issues made by the parties, the true facts of claims and defenses will emerge and the appropriate law be applied to them.[5] To this end, the judge can exercise considerable initiative. In "public question" litigation such as school desegregation and prison administration cases, the judge's role is necessarily more active and, it is argued, should be assimilated to that of a program administrator.[6]

Other themes sustain the concept of the judge as a passive arbiter. One theme emphasizes the role of the jury and considers a strong role for the judge an infringement of the jury's province. Another theme is that procedural law should, as it were, speak for itself and not be manipulated by the judge.[7] These themes contradict each other and are inconsistent with the concept of the judge as interventionist. There is wide disagreement as to which theme should govern; individual judges have styles running from highly active to nearly supine. The only fair generalization is that federal judges traditionally are much more directive than state judges. Neither the passive nor the active style, however, violates any foundational principle of the adversary system when the counsel involved are reasonably competent. Indeed, the most serious weakness in the adversary system is that lawyers may bumble in presenting their case.[8]

Limits on scope of controversy

Whether the values served by the adversary system require the judge to stay within the issues framed by the parties is not a simple question. The ultimate control over what is submitted for decision should rest with the parties rather than the court. Surely the parties should be free to submit a dispute for adjudication without opening up all their affairs to judicial scrutiny and decision. A wife who sues her

4. *See* ABA Standards Relating to Trial Courts 2.50 (1976); Resnik, Managerial Judges, 96 Harv. L. Rev. 376 (1982); Symposium, Litigation Management, 53 U. Chi. L. Rev. 305 (1986).

5. Schwarzer, Dealing with Incompetent Counsel: The Trial Judge's Role, 93 Harv. L. Rev. 633 (1980).

6. *See* Chayes, The Role of the Judge in Public Law Litigation, 89 Harv. L. Rev. 1281 (1976); Fiss, Against Settlement, 93 Yale L.J. 1073 (1984).

7. *See* Resnik, Managerial Judges, 96 Harv. L. Rev. 374 (1987).

8. Chief Justice Burger's disparagement of trial lawyer competence, The Special Skills of Advocacy, 42 Fordham L. Rev. 227 (1973), was widely criticized as unscientific, but that does not mean it was inaccurate. *Compare* Federal Judicial Center, The Quality of Advocacy in the Federal Courts (1978), indicating the difficulty of measuring competence.

husband for breach of an express trust, for example, should be able to do so without conferring authority on the court to decree a divorce. Moreover, the parties should have substantial control even within the area of the dispute. If a party, fully realizing the consequences, wishes to repudiate a claim, defense, or contention, the court should be bound by that repudiation. Usually, however, a party is willing to take the best relief obtainable or to rely on any theory that will in fact help his or her cause.

Adequacy of representation

The assumed fairness of adjudication through party-presentation—the adversary system—rests on a network of debatable assumptions. One is that the parties are roughly equal in their ability to develop and present their respective positions. This assumption is plainly untrue as a universal proposition if we think of the parties themselves and consider the poor, ignorant, and fearful on the one extreme and an aggressive private organization or prosecutorial agency on the other.

Because the assumption is false, a substitute assumption is made—that the parties are represented by effective counsel. Giving life to this substitute assumption is the aim of systems of legal aid and defenders in criminal cases[9] and of rules of professional responsibility for lawyers.[10] Enormous gaps remain in these systems, however, and they do not remedy the situation in which one party, though represented, lacks resources for developing evidence and legal argument comparable to the opposing party's. Nor does the fact that both sides are represented mean that they have equally competent counsel; legal practitioners vary widely in acuity, tenacity, ability to organize and express ideas simply and vividly, and diligence in preparation. Also, aside from the counsels' skill, financial and other incentives may lead lawyers to disregard their clients' interests.[11]

Adversarial excess

A further assumption is that the parties will be substantially honorable in telling the truth, or at least in forbearing from outright perjury, and in revealing adverse evidence (such as documents or witnesses) when asked to do so, and that counsel will, as officers of the court, effectively induce their clients to so behave. In operation, the rules of procedure and those governing counsel's responsibility often fall far short of overcoming the strong incentives that a party has to distort the case. As feminists and others have observed, the adversary system

9. Cappelletti, Gordley, and Johnson, Toward Equal Justice: A Comparative Study of Legal Aid in Modern Societies (1975).

10. Model Rules of Professional Conduct, Rules 1.1–1.16; Wolfram, Modern Legal Ethics (1986).

11. Rosenthal, Lawyer and Client: Who's in Charge? (1974); Clermont and Currivan, Improving on the Contingent Fee, 63 Cornell L. Rev. 529 (1978).

encourages parties and lawyers to regard litigation as a war or sport in which winning is all that counts.[12] Party-presentation, moreover, offers no assurance that parties will present to the court evidence and argument vital to protect the concerns of nonparties, whose interests a case may affect.

Recognition of the weaknesses in this network of assumptions helps to explain the tendency of modern American procedure away from the extreme position that would render the judge a passive umpire—one who "merely keeps the ring"[13]—and this is probably a good thing. Anything that the law of procedure or the judge's role can do to equalize opportunity and put a faulty presentation on the right track so that the disputes are settled on their merits will, in the long run, bolster rather than destroy the adversary system and will increase the moral force of decisions. It is one thing for the court to be limited to deciding disputes raised by the parties and to be warned off from other areas. It is quite a different thing for the court to be limited to deciding the dispute before it in an inferior way simply because of inferior presentation.

Competence of judge

In this connection, however, two other matters must be kept in mind. One is that judges are not perfect. Judges, no less than lawyers, vary in their activity, ability to grasp ideas, diligence, and even in their sense of disinterestedness and objectivity. The fact that the office of judge in this country has important political dimensions—in selection of judges and in making policy through decisional law once they reach the bench—accentuates these personal factors. Trial lawyers frequently express fear of a judge who "takes over" a case while being either oblivious of its complexities or convinced that one side must be in the right. The other matter is that some lawsuits are a quest for justice by neither side but rather a mutual vendetta by parties who are civilized only insofar as they refrain from physical violence. When this appears to be the case, wise judges may well assume that their proper role is only that of referee.[14]

§ 1.3 Lawyers in the Adversary System

Because the acts of the parties make the adversary system run and because court procedures are too complex for most parties to operate them, lawyers play a crucial role in civil proceedings. That is not the only way in which a procedural system can work. Some societies lack paid

12. Wolfram, Client Perjury: The Kutak Commission and the Association of Trial Lawyers on Lawyers, Lying Clients, and the Adversary System, 1980 Am. B. Found. Res. J. 964; Thornburg, Metaphors Matter: How Images of Battle, Sports and Sex Shape the Adversary System, 10 Wis. Women's L.J. 225 (1995).

13. L.C.J. Hewart in Rex v. Harris, 2 K.B. 587, 590 (Crim. App. 1927).

14. Wyzanski, A Trial Judge's Freedom and Responsibility, 65 Harv. L. Rev. 1281 (1952).

lawyers; during the Colonial period, and in some modern revolutionary regimes, attempts have been made to prohibit parties from employing paid lawyers. In some nations, notably Japan and Great Britain, many civil litigants prosecute their claims without counsel, at least in cases involving modest amounts. In the United States, individuals (but not corporations) are free to represent themselves,[1] but they rarely do so successfully except in small claims courts and other relatively informal tribunals.

Because the adversary system gives lawyers such an important role, how lawyers behave goes far in determining whether the system will work properly. Ever since paid lawyers appeared, disgruntled clients, opposing parties, and commentators have charged them with abusive practices.

Constraints on lawyers

Today a variety of constraints on lawyers seek to prevent such practices. The court in which an action is pending may sanction lawyers for violations of procedural rules or the rules of professional ethics. Authority to impose such sanctions is conferred by statute and procedural rule and by the court's inherent power to control proceedings.[2] In appropriate circumstances, the court may require a lawyer to withdraw from a case, require the lawyer to pay an opposing party's attorney fees, report the lawyer to the bar disciplinary authorities, or fine or imprison the lawyer for contempt of court. Every state has adopted rules governing lawyers' behavior.[3] When the authorities initiate disciplinary proceedings, the courts may censure, suspend, or disbar a lawyer who violates these rules. Clients (and occasionally nonclients) may sue lawyers for professional malpractice and other torts.[4] Comprehensively, these legal sources constitute the law governing lawyers.[5] Finally, a lawyer's own values help shape what the lawyer makes of his or her professional life.

Effective representation

One major goal of the law governing lawyers is to ensure effective representation of clients. Lawyers must, for example, render diligent and competent service.[6] They must comply with client decisions about impor-

§ 1.3

1. *E.g.*, 28 U.S.C. § 1654; *see* Merco Construction Engrs. v. Municipal Court, 21 Cal.3d 724, 147 Cal.Rptr. 631, 581 P.2d 636 (1978) (corporation may appear only through counsel).

2. *E.g.*, 28 U.S.C. § 1927; Fed. R. Civ. P. 11; Roadway Express v. Piper, 447 U.S. 752, 100 S.Ct. 2455, 65 L.Ed.2d 488 (1980).

3. *E.g.*, Model Rules of Professional Conduct (1983) (adopted, with varying changes, by most states); Model Code of Professional Responsibility (1969) (still in force in some states); Hazard and Hodes, The Law of Lawyering (3d ed. 2000); Wolfram, Modern Legal Ethics (1986).

4. Mallen and Smith, Legal Malpractice (4th ed. 2000).

5. *See* Restatement of the Law Governing Lawyers (2000).

6. *E.g.*, Model Rules of Professional Conduct, Rules 1.1, 1.3 (1983).

tant matters such as settlement of litigation and must inform and consult with their clients—although lawyers can make many litigation decisions on the spot without consultation, decisions that generally will bind their clients.[7] Lawyers must keep confidential information they acquire while representing their clients unless disclosure is required to comply with the law, to prevent certain crimes, or for specified other reasons.[8] They may not accept a case when it raises an unacceptable conflict of interest that might lead to half-hearted representation or misuse of client confidence. Such a conflict might arise when, for example, a new case is brought against someone the lawyer's firm formerly represented in a suit involving overlapping facts.[9]

Overzealous representation

Another goal of the law regulating lawyers in civil proceedings is to prevent overzealous representation that can harm others and misuse the adversary system. For example, a lawyer may not assert a claim or defense without a foundation in fact and law.[10] A lawyer may not use evidence the lawyer knows to be false.[11] A lawyer may not help to destroy or withhold evidence sought by a valid subpoena or discovery request.[12] A lawyer may not make certain types of argument to a jury, such as those appealing to racial prejudice or asserting that the lawyer believes or disbelieves witnesses.[13] A party's lawyer may not contact another party who has a lawyer without that lawyer's permission[14] and, of course, must not bribe or threaten parties, witnesses, jurors, or judges.

The goals of these two bodies of law—ensuring effective representation of clients and avoiding abuse of nonclients and of the court system—are different. Sometimes the same act, such as researching the law before trial, furthers realization of both goals. But these goals imply conflicting incentives for the lawyer. Lawyers often are tempted to push representation of a client to the point at which it unjustifiably harms others. Because the rules limiting representation are as unclear as most legal rules, lawyers often do not know how far they may lawfully go.

7. *See* Maute, Allocation of Decision Making Authority Under the Model Rules of Professional Conduct, 17 U.C. Davis L. Rev. 1049 (1984); Mazor, Power and Responsibility in the Attorney–Client Relation, 20 Stan. L. Rev. 1120 (1968).

8. Model Rules of Professional Conduct, Rules 1.6, 3.3 (1983); Restatement of the Law Governing Lawyers ch. 5 (2000).

9. Model Rules of Professional Conduct Rules 1.7–11 (1983); Restatement of the Law Governing Lawyers ch. 8 (2000).

10. *E.g.*, Fed. R. Civ. P. 11; Model Rules of Professional Conduct, Rule 3.1 (1983); *see* § 3.13 *infra*.

11. *E.g.*, Model Rules of Professional Conduct, Rule 3.3 (1983); Wolfram, Client Perjury, 50 S. Cal. L. Rev. 809 (1977).

12. Model Rules of Professional Conduct Rule 3.4(a) (1983) (lawyer may be disciplined for unlawfully destroying evidence).

13. Model Rules of Professional Conduct Rule 3.4(e) (1983); Carlson, Argument to the Jury: Passion, Persuasion, and Legal Controls, 33 St. Louis L.J. 787 (1989).

14. Model Rules of Professional Conduct Rule 4.2 (1983); Leubsdorf, Communicating with Another Lawyer's Client: The Lawyer's Veto and the Client's Interest, 127 U. Pa. L. Rev. 683 (1979).

Limits of the law

Many lawyers would reply that there is a simple answer to conflicts between vigorous representation and the concerns of nonclients: The lawyer is to advance the client's interests by all means not plainly unlawful.[15] The adversary system itself provides one rationale for this approach: The opposing party will object to any arguably objectionable act, and the court will uphold the better view. Such optimism, of course, is warranted only when both parties are represented with equal effectiveness.[16] Even then, some tactics, such as waging elaborate disputes over the discoverability of marginally significant material, are likely to cause delay and waste resources, misfortunes that the adversary system will not prevent. An opposing party, moreover, may have no effective way to counteract other tactics, such as subtle appeals to a jury's prejudice, and yet it is impossible to write rules that clearly ban all undesirable appeals while allowing proper ones. In short, the adversary system cannot itself control all abuses of adversarial behavior.[17]

Proponents of uninhibited advocacy also defend it as protecting the clients' legal rights. On this basis it is argued that lawyers should do for their clients whatever their clients might lawfully do for themselves. Any blame for the lawyers' acts falls on their clients, for whom the acts were performed, or the legislature, which did not prohibit them.[18] Yet this argument begs the question when, as is so often the case, the legality of the lawyers' acts is dubious. The argument also assumes that clients invariably wish their lawyers to press every legal right to its arguable limit and thus to disregard the impact on others or on the legal system. This assumption is appropriate only when lawyers secure their clients' informed decision before acting. In any event, the clients' interest in taking every legally tenable step in the prosecution or defense of lawsuits does not always outweigh the concerns of other parties or the lawyers' own interest in a good reputation and a life with which they can feel content.

These problems, treated at length in professional responsibility courses, are also important for students of civil procedure. The actual functioning of the adversary system, and ultimately its defensibility, depends not merely on procedural rules but also on the behavior of lawyers. The subjects of professional responsibility and civil procedure are related in other ways as well. The law and institutions that shape the delivery of legal services help determine, for example, whether less

15. *See generally* on this problem The Good Lawyer (Luban ed. 1984); Luban, Lawyers and Justice (1988).

16. *See* § 1.2 *supra.*

17. *See* Hazard, Quis custodiet ipsos custodes?, 95 Yale L.J. 1523 (1986).

18. Pepper, The Lawyer's Amoral Ethical Role: A Defense, A Problem, and Some Possibilities, 1986 Am. B. Found. Res. J. 613.

wealthy civil litigants will receive adequate representation and hence whether the procedural system will function as it should.[19]

A. HISTORICAL BACKGROUND OF ANGLO-AMERICAN LAW

Studying the history of our civil procedure is dangerous. Often, the tale carries a moral: in the bad old days, they had the bad old common law, but now history has reached its goal in the Federal Rules, so there is no need to consider further change. Often too, the history law students receive is oversimplified, squashing together hundreds of years of procedure into a single system.

Nevertheless, some historical background is needed to understand today's procedure and its goals. Indeed, some of today's rules incorporate historical learning: when a party is entitled to trial by jury still depends on the ancient division between common law and equity. And ideally, historical study, like comparative law, can give perspective by teaching us that things could be different.

§ 1.4 Rise of King's Courts and Growth of Formulary System

At the time of the Norman conquest, 1066, justice was dispensed in England largely by local courts, some of them communal, others private or franchise courts having some characteristics of feudal courts. The king, too, had a court, the witan, but this was of and for men of high degree and did not administer justice generally throughout the country.[1]

Royal authority

The Norman kings did not destroy or immediately displace this system. Rather, they worked through existing institutions and subverted them gradually so as to bring about an entirely different system in the course of time. In that system the bulk of the justice in the country was dispensed by king's courts, which became regularized institutions with the jury trial as the standard method of resolving questions of fact and with a formalized system of pleading and procedure.[2] The system, with

19. *E.g.,* Mallard v. United States District Court, 490 U.S. 296, 109 S.Ct. 1814, 104 L.Ed.2d 318 (1989) (no legal duty of lawyer to accept federal court appointment of indigent civil plaintiff); In re Primus, 436 U.S. 412, 98 S.Ct. 1893, 56 L.Ed.2d 417 (1978) (solicitation by unpaid public interest lawyer constitutionally protected); Bates v. Arizona, 433 U.S. 350, 97 S.Ct. 2691, 53 L.Ed.2d 810 (1977) (price advertising constitutionally protected).

§ 1.4

1. 1 Holdsworth, A History of English Law ch. 1 (7th ed. 1956); Morgan, Introduction to the Study of Law 2–4 (2d ed. 1948); Adams, Origins of the English Constitution chs. 1, 2 (1931).

2. For general treatments of the formulary system, see Morgan, Introduction to the Study of Law chs. 5, 6 (2d ed. 1948); Maitland, The Forms of Action (1936 ed.); Shipman, Common Law Pleading ch. 2 (3d ed. 1923); Stephen, Principles of Pleading (1824).

its forms of action, became nationwide and endured, more or less, for six centuries;[3] it is the basis of much of what we have today.

In addition to his role in the feudal hierarchy, the king was traditionally vested with a prerogative power that derived not from feudal concepts but from his peculiar role as preserver of the peace of the realm, protector of the weak, and dispenser of justice. "It was by the help of these prerogative powers, which were regarded as inherent in the office of king, and as belonging to them as the successors of Edward the Confessor, that the Norman and Angevin kings so developed the powers of the feudal curia regis that they made it the most efficient organ of centralized government that existed in Western Europe."[4]

Writs

The Norman kings exploited and enlarged the prerogative power of the king and the notion of the king's peace. In this process the issuance of writs—written orders that some specific thing be done or not done, or that the order's addressee state why he had not complied—loomed large.[5] Originally these had no set forms, and the greatest flexibility was used in framing them so that royal commands were tailored to meet the varying needs of different situations, much the way an injunction is today.[6] Resort to the king's writs and the king's justice with its jury became popular, partly at least because it was better justice.

Writs were actually issued for and in the name of the king by the chancery, a department of government with the chancellor at its head.[7] That officer was "the secretary of state for all departments"[8] and keeper of the king's great seal. In the early days he usually was an ecclesiastic.

Forms of writs

The growing use of writs under the Norman kings interfered with the local and feudal courts and cut athwart the normal processes of feudal institutions. This was resented by those interested in maintaining these institutions, and during the thirteenth century both the expansion of royal authority and the practice of inventing new writs were curbed. By this time, however, the forms of writs issued to redress the more common complaints had become crystallized and were known as "writs of course" (*de cursu*); the issuance of such writs was not checked but

3. Milsom, Historical Foundations of the Common Law (1969).

4. 1 Holdsworth, A History of English Law 34 (7th ed. 1956).

5. Richardson and Sayles, The Governance of Medieval England from the Conquest to Magna Carta (1963); Stenton, English Justice Between the Norman Conquest and the Great Charter (1964); Van Caenegem, Royal Writs in England from the Conquest to Glanvill (1959); Watkin, The Significance of "In Consimili Casu," 23 Am. J. Legal Hist. 283 (1979).

6. 1 Holdsworth, A History of English Law 47–49 (7th ed. 1956); Morgan, Introduction to the Study of Law 10 (2d ed. 1948); Walsh, A Treatise on Equity ch. 1 (1930).

7. Morgan, Introduction to the Study of Law 10 (2d ed. 1948).

8. 1 Holdsworth, A History of English Law 37 (7th ed. 1956).

continued freely. Already these writs had brought many of the common disputes (which ordinarily would have been heard by local or feudal courts) before some delegate of the council (*curia regis*) for his judgment. In the course of time these king's justices became members of regular courts with regular sessions—the Court of Common Pleas, the Court of King's Bench, the Court of Exchequer.[9] The justices of a court sat together in London during the four yearly terms; at other times they rode circuit, trying cases with the help of local juries.

Forms of action

The writs that commenced actions in the king's courts ("original writs") contained a capsular and highly stylized statement of the grievance and were looked on as conferring authority or jurisdiction on the king's justice to try that case. Each of the writs de cursu became associated with its own form of action with its peculiar procedural incidents and its own substantive law. Thus the declaration (or *complaint,* as we would call it today) had to follow the form of the writ, every declaration called for its peculiar form of plea, and so on. Each form of action also had its own kind of *mesne* (pretrial) process and its own form of judgment and execution. Each action had to be sustained in terms of the law applicable to that form of action. The inquiry was not whether plaintiff should recover under the law of the land, but whether plaintiff had proved a case *in trespass*, or *in covenant,* or in whatever form the action had been brought. If not, plaintiff lost the case without consideration of the merits, although remaining free to try again using another kind of writ. As Henry Maine later said, "So great is the ascendancy of the Law of Actions in the infancy of Courts of Justice, that substantive law has at first the look of being gradually secreted in the interstices of procedure."[10]

Common Law

The substantive and procedural law we have been describing came to be called "common law" because they were common to all of England, unlike the customary law followed in local courts. The term common law came to have other meanings as well. It denoted the law and procedure of the "common law courts" (King's Bench, Common Pleas, and part of Exchequer), by contrast to those of the equity courts such as Chancery, to be described below. "Common law" can also be used to describe law created by judicial precedents, as opposed to legislation. And it can be used to describe legal systems such as our own stemming largely from England, as opposed to civil law systems descending from Roman law. (So much for the notion that legal terminology is clear and consistent.)

9. 1 Holdsworth, A History of English Law 37 (7th ed. 1956); Morgan, Introduction to the Study of Law 2–9 (2d ed. 1948); Adams, Origins of the English Constitution 136–143 (1931).

10. Hepburn, The Historical Development of Code Pleading 43–51 (1897); Maine, Dissertations on Early Law and Custom 389 (1883).

Early remedies

By the time the forms of action were fixed, the appropriate judgment in most of them was one for money damages or for the possession of land or a chattel. Likewise the writ of execution was one empowering the sheriff to seize and sell defendant's property to pay the damages or to deliver possession to the plaintiff.[11] Earlier writ forms commanding specific performance or reparation by the defendant had not become customary when the system crystallized and thereafter (with a few exceptions) were not available in connection with proceedings in the king's court.[12]

Juries

The adoption of jury trial early in the thirteenth century vitally influenced common law procedure. It led to trials at which witnesses presented oral testimony, while courts on the European continent relied instead on judges sifting written evidence. Because lawyers pleaded their cases in London before the full court but trials occurred throughout England before judges riding circuit, pleading and trial became sharply distinguished stages of litigation. Judges evolved many procedural methods of controlling juries: pleading requirements to narrow the issues presented to jurors, rules of evidence to determine what jurors could hear, instructions to tell jurors what law to apply, new trials to redress clear juror error.

The judges, lawyers and court clerks ran the common law courts, sometimes for their own benefit. There was little legislation or rulemaking. Courts developed procedure through precedent, which accumulated its distinctions over the centuries. Lawyers and clerks were paid for each procedural step they took, so they had no incentive to simplify procedures. Neither did judges, who sold clerkships in their courts and therefore benefitted if those clerkships were remunerative. On the other hand, the different common law courts competed for business with each other, striving to attract plaintiffs by expanding their jurisdictions.

Expanding forms of action

As a result of the developments sketched above, the writ system administered by the king's courts became formally rigid and closed by the end of the thirteenth century, with a limited number of fixed forms of action. With the reinvigoration of royal authority during and following the civil wars of the fourteenth century, the scope of the common law actions expanded. No new writs were devised, but the old forms of action, especially trespass, were construed to reach situations previously

11. Shipman, Common Law Pleading 26 (3d ed. 1923). Execution might also consist in seizing the person of the debtor and imprisoning him or her.

12. Sources cited *supra* note 6.

considered outside their terms.[13] The process of expansion was self-conscious but gradual, resembling the later expansion of federally defined rights in this country through evolving interpretation of the Due Process Clause. The expansion involved forced reasoning and fictionalizations that, as an intellectual style, took possession of the common law. By the nineteenth century many of the writs in common use were ones unknown in 1400,[14] and many of those used in 1400 had fallen by the wayside.[15] Nevertheless, the system failed in many ways to adapt itself to the needs of society; this failure led to the origin and growth of the competing—and complementary—system of equity.

§ 1.5 Rise of Equity

Inadequate remedy at law

Even as the common law actions enlarged in scope, large areas of legal right remained beyond their reach. Redress fell short either because such areas involved transactions not contemplated in the forms of action (particularly land transactions as land tenure was transformed from feudal to a privately proprietary form), or because common law procedure did not permit testimony by the parties and had no device for compelling production of documents such as deeds, or because the writ system generally did not embrace multiparty or multi-issue controversies. When these situations occurred, resort could be made by petition (or *bill*) directly to the king and his council, invoking the traditional prerogative power to do justice.[1] The council frequently referred these petitions to the chancellor, who was keeper of the king's great seal, had a staffed department under him, and was already in many ways the law member of the council.

Chancellor's decree

In handling these petitions the chancellor had in some way to bring the parties before him, sift out the facts, and implement his decisions. Unlike the common law courts, which usually tried to narrow the scope of disputes, chancellors sought to render complete justice by joining all related parties and claims. The procedures that were formulated made extensive use of the direct personal order to a party, of the contempt power as a sanction against disobedience, and of sworn pleadings,

13. Milsom, Historical Foundations of the Common Law (1969); Prichard, Scott v. Shepherd and the Emergence of the Tort of Negligence (1976); Shipman, Common Law Pleading ch. 4 (3d ed. 1923); Watkin, The Significance of "In Consimili Casu," 23 Am. J. Legal Hist. 283 (1979).

14. *E.g.,* ejectment, assumpsit (general and special), and trover. *See* Maitland, The Forms of Action, lect. 5 (1936 ed.).

15. *E.g.,* the real actions described in Maitland, The Forms of Action, lect. 3 (1936 ed.).

§ 1.5

1. For a fuller account of the events sketched in this paragraph and the remainder of the section, see 1 Holdsworth, A History of English Law ch. 5 (7th ed. 1956); Maitland, Equity, lect. 1 (2d ed. 1936); Walsh, Equity ch. 2 (1930).

affidavits, and depositions to develop the facts.[2] Thus defendant was summoned by a subpoena (*ad respondendum*) commanding the respondent to appear and answer under penalty. The answer had to contain a response under oath to each charge made in the plaintiff's bill of complaint.[3] The chancellor found the facts without a jury, although in some circumstances he could arrange for a jury trial in a common law court.

The chancellor's final decree was a personal order to the defendant to do, or not to do, a specific thing, with imprisonment the penalty for disobedience.[4] These were powerful and usually effective weapons, but they depended for their effectiveness on obedience and were occasionally set at naught by stubborn defendants or by those who could place themselves beyond the reach of punishment. In such cases the decree was impotent since it was denied the in rem effect of vesting title or warranting execution by its own force.

Trusts, contracts, fraud

The chancellor's remedies were nevertheless of great practical importance, particularly in enforcement of trusts.[5] A trust was a device by which land was conveyed to certain persons (trustees) but "to the use of" certain other persons (beneficiaries or *cestuis que use*) designated by the grantor. Its purpose was largely to effect the transfer of land without incurring the feudal restrictions and burdens that impeded traditionally recognized methods of transfer but that no longer served any useful purpose and were increasingly regarded as anachronistic and not morally binding. The law courts recognized the conveyance to the trustee but not the interest or estate of the beneficiary (*cestui*); the latter thus was completely at the mercy of the trustee so far as legal rights went. Equity did, however, recognize the cestui's interest and used its in personam control to compel the trustee to fulfill his or her trust and render to the cestui the beneficial interest accorded him or her by the terms of the grant. Equity also came to take jurisdiction in contract cases (developing the remedy of specific performance when the remedy at law was inadequate),[6] in cases of fraud, accident, and mistake,[7] and in cases where relief was sought against unreasonable penalties provided in instruments[8] (bonds, later mortgages, and so on) that would be enforceable at law.

2. *See* Jones, The Elizabethan Court of Chancery (1967).

3. For a description of equity procedures, see 3 Blackstone, Commentaries *442–455; Kerly, An Historical Sketch of the Equitable Jurisdiction of the Court of Chancery ch. 8 (1890); Macnair, The Law of Proof in Early Modern Equity (1999); *cf.* St. German's Doctor and Student (Plucknett and Barton eds. 1975).

4. Walsh, Equity § 9 (1930). *Cf. id.* at 10.

5. Maitland, Equity (2d ed. 1936); Walsh, Equity 18–22 (1930).

6. Walsh, Equity § 4(c), ch. 12 (1930).

7. Maitland, Equity 7 (2d ed. 1936); Walsh, Equity 4(e), chs. 20, 21 (1930).

8. Walsh, Equity § 4(f) (1930).

Substantive equitable principles

The chancellors developed principles of substantive law in the types of cases coming before them. These principles came to be regarded as a separate body of doctrine known as "equity."[9] The chancellors also evolved procedure to deal with these problems. Both became stabilized in established practices called "the course of the court."[10] Notwithstanding the regularization of equity so that certain recurring types of wrong could ordinarily be redressed by a routine bill, in theory equity jurisdiction remained extraordinary and in some sense extralegal. One consequence of this conception was that little consideration was given to harmonizing rights recognized "at law" with those "in equity" so that well into the twentieth century it was appropriate to speak of "legal" and "equitable" rights as though they were different though concurrent bodies of governing norms.[11]

Another consequence was that equitable redress was regarded as a privilege awarded at the chancellor's discretion rather than a right available on the basis of precedent. The tradition manifests itself in the perhaps obsolete precept that an injunction is an extraordinary remedy.[12] As Blackstone put it: "the suitor when he thought himself aggrieved found a desultory and uncertain remedy, according to the private opinion of the Chancellor."[13] And there was the famous quip of Selden that likened this measure "according to the conscience of him that is Chancellor" to "the measure of a Chancellor's foot,"[14] which would vary in its dimensions with each chancellor. Selden's dictum was an overstatement in the seventeenth century, and certainly is today,[15] but in the issuance of injunctive relief there remains a substantial place for the exercise of judicial discretion in the light of "reason and conscience."[16]

§ 1.6 Struggle Between Law and Equity and Subsequent Coexistence of the Systems

Law and equity: competition

The extensive jurisdiction of equity described in the last section was not attained without a struggle. Opposition to the extension came from Parliament and later from the law courts. The struggle was fanned by

9. The concept of distinct substantive principles remained in full force through the 1930s. *See id.*

10. *See* Yale, Nottingham's Chancery Cases vol. I (1957), vol. II (1961); *cf.* St. German's Doctor and Student (Plucknett and Barton eds. 1975).

11. *See* Langdell, Summary of Equity Pleading (1877); Hanbury, Modern Equity (3d ed. 1943); Morse, The Substantive Equity Historically Applied by the U.S. Courts, 54 Dick. L. Rev. 10 (1949).

12. Fiss, The Civil Rights Injunction (1978); Laycock, The Death of the Irreparable Injury Rule (1991). For historical background, see Rasck, A History of Injunctions in England before 1700, 61 Ind. L.J. 539 (1986).

13. 3 Blackstone, Commentaries *53.

14. 1 Holdsworth, A History of English Law 467–468 (7th ed. 1956).

15. Fiss, Injunctions 74–93 (1972).

16. *See, e.g.,* Weinberger v. Romero–Barcelo, 456 U.S. 305, 102 S.Ct. 1798, 72 L.Ed.2d 91 (1982).

equity's assertion of the right to implement its decisions by issuing injunctions restraining suitors at law from prosecuting their actions where the chancellor determined that successful prosecution of the lawsuit would bring an inequitable result because of the existence of an equitable defense that the law court would not recognize. Matters came to a head during the reign of James I over equitable injunctions issued for similar reasons against enforcements of judgments already rendered at law. In this case the common law position was bolstered by two statutes: Praemunire, 1353, 27 Edw. III, c.1, which denounced with severe penalties those "who ... sue in any other court to defeat or impeach the judgment given in the King's Court," and Prohibition, 1402, 4 Hen. IV, c.23, which provided that after judgment given in the king's courts, "the parties ... shall be thereof in peace until the judgment be undone by attaint or by error."[1]

A typical situation in this struggle involved an action at law on a specialty (that is, bond under seal) that had been obtained from the defendant by "fraud in the inducement," such as misrepresentation concerning the value or quality of something sold by plaintiff to defendant on credit where the bond in a large penal sum was given to secure payment of the purchase price. If the defendant had indeed executed the bond, knowing it was a bond, then the kind of fraud by which the defendant was induced to execute it was not recognized in the law courts as a defense to an action on the bond. Equity, however, did recognize this kind of fraud and would entertain a suit by the debtor against the creditor (obligee on the bond) for a rescission of the bond. If the debtor succeeded in showing the fraud, the chancellor would order the obligee to deliver the bond up for cancellation or to give a release of it under seal, on condition that the debtor restore to the creditor whatever benefit was received in the course of the transaction. Equity would, in short, try to put the parties back into the position they occupied before the fraudulent transaction took place.[2]

If the debtor discovered the fraud and brought a bill in equity before the creditor obtained a judgment at law, then the chancellor would enjoin the creditor from pursuing an action at law pending determination of the issue of fraud. If the chancellor found fraud, he would make this temporary injunction a permanent one as part of his final decree. If he found no fraud, he would dissolve the temporary injunction and the creditor would be free to continue prosecuting the action at law.

§ 1.6

1. Accounts of the famous struggle may be found in 1 Holdsworth, A History of English Law 459–465 (7th ed. 1956); Maitland, Equity 9–10 (2d ed. 1936). *But see* Jones, Conflict or Collaboration? Chancery Attitudes in the Reign of Elizabeth I, 5 Am. J. Legal Hist. 12 (1961).

2. *See, e.g.,* J.R. v. M.P., 37 Y.B. Hen. VI, fo. 13, pl. 3 (C.P. 1459); Heath v. Ridley, Cro. Jac. 335, 79 Eng. Rep. 286 (K.B. 1614); Walsh, Equity 26 (1930).

Supremacy of equity

If a judgment at law had already been obtained, effective equitable relief would necessarily involve interference with a law court's judgment. This happened in *Courtney v. Glanvil*[3] when Courtney, a young gentleman who had been defrauded in the sale of a jewel to him by Glanvil, found himself faced with a judgment on the bond he had given to secure the sale price. He exhibited his bill in chancery and the chancellor, finding fraud, decreed that Glanvil should take again his jewel and £ 100 (the value of other jewels sold) and give Courtney a satisfaction of the judgment at law, that is, a written discharge of the judgment. Glanvil was imprisoned for not performing this decree and he sought a writ of habeas corpus from the King's Bench, which found that the decree violated the statute Praemunire and issued the writ.

Lord Edward Coke, who was then chief justice of the King's Bench and had given the judgment in Glanvil's case, and some colleagues persuaded creditors in similar cases to secure indictments against their opponents for attacking judgments of the king's courts. The chancellor, Lord Ellsmere, appealed to the king, who referred the question to a body of lawyers with Francis Bacon at its head. This commission found that the statutes invoked (Praemunire and Prohibition) were not leveled against the chancery but against foreign ecclesiastical courts. Moreover the report "adroitly inflated the wind-ball that has ever since gone bouncing down the ages, that the chancery '*does not assume to undo the judgment,* but *only to restrain the corrupt conscience of the party.*' "[4] King James's stamp of approval on this judgment decisively established the supremacy of equity in those situations where its rules and those of the common law came into practical conflict.

Supreme though it might be, equity would only act when the remedy at law was inadequate. The inadequacy might result from substantive gaps in the common law, such as its failure to enforce trusts. Or it might result from procedural gaps, such as the common law's inability to hear class actions or obtain certain evidence.

Procedural confusion

The dual system, with equity in the ascendancy, lasted for the next two-and-a-half centuries.[5] There was some growth on each side and an increasing field of overlap. Equity, for example, developed remedies that were no longer dependent on coerced obedience but had a direct in rem effect of their own.[6] On its part, the law developed remedies that depended on equitable principles and let in defenses formerly cognizable only in equity.[7]

3. Cro. Jac. 345, 79 Eng. Rep. 294 (K.B. 1615).

4. Phelps, Falstaff and Equity 45–46 (1901).

5. 1 Holdsworth, A History of English Law 428 *et seq.* (7th ed. 1956).

6. Huston, Enforcement of Equitable Decrees (1915); Walsh, Equity 10, 11 (1930).

7. 3 Blackstone, Commentaries *432; Abbott, Fraud as a Defense at Law in the Federal Courts, 56 U. Pa. L. Rev. 289

Inconveniences of the dual system persisted. Suitors in equity continued to be dismissed because their proper remedy was at law. Plaintiffs and defendants at law could not in the law action establish equitable claims or defenses pertaining to the same occurrence. In many situations two or more suits growing out of a single transaction had to be brought to adjust properly the rights and remedies of the same parties. Too often, mistakes of form led to loss of a suit by the party entitled to win on the merits.[8]

Equity in American colonies

The dual system prevailed in many American colonies on the eve of the Revolution and persisted through the first half of the nineteenth century. During the eighteenth century, the colonies imported much of the English procedure, albeit with considerable simplification. States such as Delaware, New Jersey, and New York had separate courts of law and equity as in England. Others, such as Connecticut and New Hampshire, did not have separate courts, but the single court administered law and equity with just as rigid a separation as though there were separate courts. Massachusetts and Pennsylvania, however, largely repudiated equity (with its flavor of the hated royal prerogative) and had a different early history.[9] When Congress created the federal court system in 1789, it followed the pattern of states having a single court system that administered law and equity separately.[10]

By 1800 civil procedure in England and in many American jurisdictions retained two obsolescent technical characteristics: the forms of common law action, requiring that legal grievances be fitted into distinct molds 600 years old; and the division between those proceedings and proceedings in equity. Both divisions had become blurred by overlaps in the forms of action and partial integration of law and equity, but their vestiges remained strong, perhaps even more so in concept than in practice.

It is still not clear how badly the system worked and whose interests it promoted or frustrated. In the late sixteenth century, litigation seems to have been relatively affordable and popular, but this was no longer true by the end of the eighteenth century. Well before then, calls for

(1908); Cook, Equitable Defenses, 32 Yale L.J. 645 (1923); Hinton, Equitable Defenses Under Modern Codes, 18 Mich. L. Rev. 717 (1920).

8. *See* New York, First Report of Commissioners on Practice and Pleadings 67–87 (1848) [hereinafter First Report of Commissioners]; Baron Bowen, Progress in the Administration of Justice During the Victorian Period, in 2 Select Essays in Anglo–American Legal History 517–530 (1907).

9. *See* 5 The Papers of John Marshall xxxiii-li (Hobson ed. 1987); The Papers of Daniel Webster, Legal Papers, vol. 1: The New Hampshire Practice 63–65, 260–95 (Konefsky & King ed. 1982); Fisher, The Administration of Equity Through Common Law Forms in Pennsylvania, 1 L.Q. Rev. 455 (1885); Woodruff, Chancery in Massachusetts, 5 L.Q. Rev. 370 (1889).

10. Clark, Code Pleading § 9 (2d ed. 1947); *cf.* Wolfram, The Constitutional History of the Seventh Amendment, 57 Minn. L. Rev. 639 (1973).

reform began.[11] By the nineteenth century, most plaintiffs seem to have been commercial creditors suing other businesses or consumers, and the disaffection of such plaintiffs may have joined with the critiques of Jeremy Bentham and his followers[12] to overturn common law procedure.

§ 1.7 The American Codes and English Judicature Acts

Merger of law and equity

The hardships, delays, and injustices that resulted finally led to reform, first in New York State. The movement for it, led by David Dudley Field, culminated in the constitution of 1846 and the Field Code of 1848. The former abolished the court of chancery and paved the way for the merger of law and equity. The code sought to effectuate this merger and abolish the distinctions among the forms of action. It created the civil action in which the parties were to plead the facts constituting the cause of action or defense. The court then was to give judgment according to the law applicable to the facts found.

One form of action

The code was not intended to change substantive rights or alter the substantive showing formerly needed for given remedy. Unlike the subsequent Federal Rules, it sought to confine narrowly judicial discretion and to preserve the importance of pleading, nor did it greatly expand discovery. But it was intended to authorize a single court in a single action to draw on the properly applicable rules whether they were formerly denominated legal or equitable and, if legal, without regard to distinctions among actions. And it was intended to make available *all* the appropriate remedies in that action, even if separate proceedings in law and equity formerly would have been needed for full relief. The code also sought to liberalize the provisions for joinder of causes and parties.[1]

By 1900, twenty-seven states, particularly west of the Mississippi, had adopted codes having all or some of these features. Others kept the outline of the old system but modified its rigors by various devices such as allowing joinder of different forms of action, or amendment from form to form, or free transfer of cases between law and equity dockets.[2]

11. Brooks, Pettyfoggers and Vipers of the Commonwealth chs. 4, 5 (1986); Brooks, Lawyers, Litigation and English Society Since 1450, at 27–62, 91–95 (1998); Veall, The Popular Movement for Law Reform 1640–1660 (1970); Francis, Practice, Strategy and Institution: Debt Collection in the English Common-Law Courts, 1740–1840, 80 Nw. U.L. Rev. 807 (1986).

12. *E.g.,* Bentham, Rationale of Judicial Evidence (J.S. Mill ed. 1827).

§ 1.7

1. For the reasons for and aims of the codes, see First Report of Commissioners 67–87, 137–147; Subrin, David Dudley Field and the Field Code: A Historical Analysis of an Earlier Procedural Vision, 6 Law & Hist. Rev. 311 (1988). *See also* Hepburn, The Historical Development of Code Pleading (1897); Clark, Code Pleading 21–31 (2d ed. 1947).

2. Clark, *supra* note 1, at § 8; Hepburn, *supra* note 1, at 142–152; .

English Judicature Acts

Parallel reform occurred in England.[3] The common law procedure acts (1852–1860) and chancery reform acts of the same period introduced partial reforms such as joinder of different forms of action and use of equitable defenses in actions at law. Sweeping change came with the Judicature Acts of 1873 and 1875. These had the same essential features as the American codes but went even further. They created a single Supreme Court of Judicature, unified the substantive law, and provided for simplified pleading. Stylistically, however, they were different from the American codes. The latter were statutes that sought to prescribe each procedural step in detail; the English procedural rules contained relatively broad directions and contemplated broad discretion by the trial court.

Court rules

The English provisions were influential in this country in two respects. In content, their liberality in joinder of parties and claims was later emulated here. Of perhaps greater significance, they were promulgated under authority of the courts rather than being cast as legislation. The proposition that procedural rules should be court-made rules was subsequently adopted in our federal courts and in many states.[4]

§ 1.8 Federal Rules of Civil Procedure

Federal procedure before 1938

Before 1938 federal procedure was a strange mixture. Although in early days the U.S. Supreme Court was given substantial rulemaking power, and although this power was extensively exercised in equity and admiralty,[1] it had little scope in actions at law. In the procedure governing actions at law in the federal courts, congressional policy favored the principle of conformity to state practice. After experimenting with static conformity (that is, conformity with the state practice of a given date in the past), Congress provided in the Conformity Act of 1872 that "the practice, pleadings, and forms and modes of proceeding in civil causes, other than equity and admiralty causes, shall conform, as near as may be, to the practice, pleadings, and forms and modes of proceeding existing at the time in like causes in the courts of record in the State within which such district courts are held."[2] This was the governing

3. Clark, *supra* note 1, at § 6; Hepburn, *supra* note 1, at 177–194.

4. American Jud. Socy., The Rule–Making Power in State Court Systems (1967). For criticisms of rulemaking by the courts, see Levin and Amsterdam, Legislative Control over Judicial Rule–Making: A Problem in Constitutional Revision, 107 U. Pa. L. Rev. 1 (1958); Lesnick, The Federal Rule–Making Process, 61 A.B.A.J. 579 (1975); Burbank, The Rules Enabling Act of 1934, 130 U. Pa. L. Rev. 1015 (1982). *See also* ABA Standards Relating to Court Organization § 1.31.

§ 1.8

1. *See* Bator, Meltzer, Mishkin, and Shapiro, The Federal Courts and the Federal System 664–667 (3d ed. 1988).

2. Act of June 1, 1872, ch. 255, § 5, 17 Stat. 197.

principle until 1938. It caused great disuniformity in practice among the federal courts, which varied widely from the archaic to the relatively modern, depending on the varying practices among the states.

Federal equity procedure

On the equity side the picture was different. Here the practice was governed largely by Supreme Court rules from the beginning and was uniform throughout the nation. The original rules were modeled largely after English chancery practice, but rules adopted in 1912 liberalized the old procedure. The Law and Equity Act of 1915 advanced a substantial step toward merging the two systems by permitting equitable defenses to be interposed in actions at law.

Enabling Act of 1934

Pressure for further reform of federal procedure persisted. In 1886 David Dudley Field had urged the adoption of a federal code of procedure. A group within the American Bar Association became strong champions of a rulemaking statute that would set the stage for a procedural system built on Supreme Court rules, as the equity procedure already was. Some have viewed these lawyers as elitist conservatives, seeking to secure convenient procedures for their corporate clients, boost the prestige of federal judges, and deflect claims for change in the substantive law. Others claim that (whatever proponents may have expected) the rule-makers emphasized such New Deal virtues as legislation by experts, national uniformity, and reform. In any event, the movement finally led to the Enabling Act of 1934, now 28 U.S.C. § 2072, giving the Supreme Court "power to prescribe by general rules the forms of process, writs, pleadings, and motions, and the practice and procedure of the district courts and courts of appeals."[3]

Adoption of the Federal Rules

Acting under this statute, Chief Justice Hughes in 1935 appointed fourteen lawyers and law teachers as the Advisory Committee for the Federal Rules of Civil Procedure, with William D. Mitchell, former Attorney General, as chairman, and Charles E. Clark, then dean of the Yale Law School, as reporter, to recommend a draft of rules uniting law and equity. The committee proposed a system of rules that was approved by the Court with certain changes. In accordance with the Enabling Act, the rules were submitted to Congress for its acquiescence and, Congress having taken no exception to them, they became effective September 16, 1938.[4]

3. Burbank, The Rules Enabling Act of 1934, 130 U. Pa. L. Rev. 1015 (1982); Purcell, Brandeis and the Progressive Constitution: *Erie*, the Judicial Power, and the Politics of the Federal Courts in Twentieth-Century America (2000); Walker, The End of the New Deal and the Federal Rules of Civil Procedure, 82 Iowa L. Rev. 1269 (1997). *See* Clark and Moore, A New Federal Civil Procedure, 44 Yale L.J. 387 (1935).

4. *See* 308 U.S. 642, 645–766 (1939); Judge Charles Edward Clark (Petruck ed. 1991).

The rules thus produced bear the unmistakable imprint of the reporter, Charles E. Clark, and represent the largest single accomplishment in American civil procedure since the Field Code of 1848. Although they were not perfect and have been amended many times,[5] experience with them has on the whole been satisfactory, and more than half of the states have adopted them in their entirety or in large part.[6]

Basic principles of Federal Rules

The principal features of the Federal Rules of Civil Procedure are as follows:

- the union (or "merger") of law and equity to produce one procedural system for all claims, with retention of jury trial in actions formerly "at law";
- simplicity and liberal amendment in pleading and motion practice;
- liberal provisions for joinder of claims and parties, with devices of counterclaim, cross-claim, third-party claim, and intervention to permit additional claims and parties to be joined;
- comprehensive discovery procedures, permitting examination of witnesses and compulsory production of evidence in the possession of an opposing party;
- reliance on the discretion of trial judges, who were given broad power to modify procedure to meet the needs of each case; and
- simple provisions for appeal.

These various parts are integrated to promote the decision of disputes on their merits. All will receive extended treatment in the course of this book.

Although the Federal Rules swept away much of the old procedural systems, much remains. Indeed, the Rules' provisions for multiparty and multiclaim litigation, discovery, and generally the pursuit of perfect justice themselves derive from the old equity system.[7] The common law right to jury trial has not been repealed, and could not be without repealing the Seventh Amendment. With it remain much procedural law related to the jury, such as the law of evidence, judicial instructions to juries, and procedures for taking clear cases away from juries. Although some of the rule-makers sought to turn away from the "sporting theory

5. Of the various amendments the most far-reaching were those of 1966. *See* Kaplan, Continuing Work of the Civil Committee: 1966 Amendments of the Federal Rules of Civil Procedure, 81 Harv. L. Rev. 356, 591 (1967, 1968). Congress has also amended the Federal Rules, Pub. L. No. 96–481, Title II, § 205(a), 94 Stat. 2330 (1980); Pub. L. No. 97–462, 96 Stat. 2527 (1983).

6. McCormick, Chadbourn, and Wright, Federal Courts (8th ed. 1988); Oakley and Coon, The Federal Rules in State Courts: A Survey of State Court Systems of Civil Procedure, 61 Wash. L. Rev. 1367 (1986); Symposium, The 50th Anniversary of the Federal Rules of Civil Procedure, 137 U. Pa. L. Rev. 1873 (1989).

7. Subrin, How Equity Conquered the Common Law: The Federal Rules of Civil Procedure in Historical Perspective, 135 U. Pa. L. Rev. 909 (1987).

of justice," adversary tactics and the adversary system remain fundamental in civil procedure.

§ 1.9 Beyond the Federal Rules

The Federal Rules have been in effect for more than sixty years. During that time the number of civil actions filed each year in the federal courts has increased about sevenfold; it is now at least 250,000. (Many states have far more civil filings, with California approaching two million.) The number of District Judges has more than tripled, with each judge's caseload far greater than in 1938. As the Rules grow older, calls for further change have multiplied, although would-be reformers disagree about what kinds of changes are called for.[1]

How well have the Federal Rules fulfilled the purpose stated in Rule 1 "to secure the just, speedy, and inexpensive determination of every action?" If justice means deciding cases on their legal merits after full exploration of the facts, the Federal Rules have promoted justice. Under them, litigants have been able to use discovery to unearth evidence, and to receive a second chance to correct procedural missteps. New kinds of litigation such as employment discrimination cases, which often depend both on discovery and on novel equitable remedies, might be impractical without today's procedural system.

The Federal Rules' record for speed is more equivocal. The average time between the filing of a federal civil action and its disposition sharply declined in the decades before the Rules went into effect, but stabilized at about one year a few years later. (This is an average: there is more delay in some districts and some actions, and less in others.) Considering the huge increase in filings, and the smaller increase in judges, that is not a bad record.[2]

Expense is the Federal Rules' weak spot, although it is hard to know to what extent because there is little information on the cost of litigation before the Rules. One should not assume that all litigants engage in expensive discovery, for example.[3] The Rules also provided a new way to end baseless litigation without a trial by moving for summary judgment. Nevertheless, for those who have the will and the means, the Federal Rules provide many ways to multiply pretrial proceedings and lengthen trials.

§ 1.9

1. Marcus, Malaise of the Litigation Superpower, in Civil Justice in Crisis 71 (Zuckerman ed. 1999); Administrative Office of the U.S. Courts, Statistical Tables for the Federal Judiciary December 31, 1999 (2000); Report of the Commission on the Future of the California Courts, Justice in the Balance 2020, at 134 (1993).

2. Clark, Adjudication to Administration: A Statistical Analysis of Federal District Courts in the Twentieth Century, 55 S. Cal. L. Rev. 64 (1981); Johnson, Rocket Dockets: Reducing Delay in Federal Civil Litigation, 85 Calif. L. Rev. 225 (1997).

3. Willging, et al., Discovery and Discovery Practice, Problems, and Proposals for Change (1997). *See* § 6.3, *infra*.

Whatever their actual impact, the Rules enjoyed much popularity during their first decades. Such changes as were made tended to promote their original goal of broadening access to justice, for example by easing documentary discovery and facilitating class actions.[4] But with the end of the sixties, more restrictive trends appeared in civil procedure as well as elsewhere. The caseload growth likewise fostered calls for change, which have resulted in rule changes intended to restrict excessive discovery and baseless claims.[5]

Increased judicial effort to keep cases moving and promote their settlement has been a major feature of recent decades. The Federal Rules as well as other reforms increased the discretion of trial judges to set schedules, control discovery, join and sever claims, and generally control cases in their courts. Gradually, judges have become more like administrators, keeping watch over populations of cases and delegating some of their functions to magistrates. Through such means as pretrial conferences and court-ordered mediation, they have joined with the burgeoning movement for alternative dispute resolution to find new ways to encourage parties to resolve their disputes without going to trial.[6]

Creeping changes have also endangered the single procedural system for all civil actions and all federal district courts that the Federal Rules sought to institute. By the 1980s, district courts had promulgated 5000 local rules, many of them inconsistent with the Federal Rules or other law. After acting in 1988 to rein in local rules, Congress reversed itself two years later with legislation stimulating local experimentation.[7] Congress has since passed several laws mandating special procedures for securities class actions, employment discrimination class actions, and prison reform suits.[8]

As these Congressional interventions imply, civil procedure has become more politicized–or at least its political aspects have been more openly recognized. Precisely because civil litigation has increasingly affected the real world, interest groups have asked Congress to promote their substantive ends through procedural changes. The rulemaking process too has become more politicized, with different groups taking advantage of new rulemaking provisions that grant those outside the rulemaking committees the opportunity to comment on proposals. Often,

4. Fed. R. Civ. P. 23 (1966 amendments) and 26 and 34(1946 and 1970 amendments).

5. Fed. R. Civ. P. 11 (1983 and 1993 amendments) and 26 (1983 amendments).

6. Yeazell, The Misunderstood Consequences of Modern Civil Process, 1994 Wis. L. Rev. 631; Resnik, Trial as Error, Jurisdiction as Injury: Transforming the Meaning of Article III, 113 Harv. L. Rev. 924 (2000); §§ 5.19–21, *infra.*

7. Committee on Rules of Practice & Procedure, Judicial Conf. Of the U.S., Report of the Local Rules Project: Local Rules on Civil Practice (1989); Tobias, Improving the 1988 and 1990 Judicial Improvements Acts, 46 Stan. L. Rev. 1589 (1994).

8. Leubsdorf, Class Actions at the Cloverleaf, 39 Ariz. L. Rev. 453 (1997).

the main lobbyists have been plaintiffs' lawyers on the one hand and corporate defendants on the other. Often but not always, opposing groups have neutralized each other, discouraging the rulemakers from approving significant changes.[9]

Meanwhile, a few researchers have begun to investigate the actual working of discovery, pretrial conferences and other procedures. Some of their findings will be mentioned later in this book. In general, they have fostered skepticism (at least among academics) of sweeping changes implemented without previous testing. The results of procedural changes are hard to predict, and those who complain the most loudly are not necessarily aware of what is happening in the great bulk of cases.[10]

B. GENERAL ANALYSIS OF REMEDIES

§ 1.10 Classic Distinction Between *In Rem* and *In Personam* Relief

Traditionally, the relief that courts could award was classified into two kinds: *in rem* relief, conceived as affecting property, and *in personam* relief, conceived as directing a person to do something or refrain from doing so. The division between in rem and in personam remedies "exists" because of its historical significance in Anglo–American law and because it has become conventional in professional habits of thought. It should be recognized, however, that the meaning of these concepts has been different in various historical periods and varies in contemporary legal contexts.

Judgments at law

Historically, judgments at law were referred to as being in rem and equity decrees as being in personam. As we have seen,[1] judgments at law, as they crystallized in the thirteenth century, were not commands directed to one of the parties personally but were declarations of rights (that plaintiff recover of the defendant a stated sum of money, or possession of specific land, or the like), on the basis of which a writ of execution would issue empowering the sheriff to seize and sell defendant's goods, to put plaintiff into possession of the land, and so on.[2] Such judgments are said to afford in rem relief because the satisfaction of the judgment requires no act on defendant's part: The judgment itself may

9. 28 U.S.C. §§ 2071(b), 2073; Mullenix, Hope Over Experience: Mandatory Informal Discovery and the Politics of Rulemaking, 69 N.C.L. Rev. 795 (1991); Bone, The Process of Making Process: Court Rulemaking, Democratic Legitimacy, and Procedural Efficiency, 87 Geo. L.J. 887 (1999).

10. Symposium, Empirical Studies of Civil Procedure, 51 L. & Contemp. Probs. nos. 3, 4 (1998).

§ 1.10

1. Section 1.3 *supra.*

2. Shipman, Common Law Pleading 48 (3d ed. 1923); Stephen, Principles of Pleading 138–140 (1824).

pass title to land or to some other thing or may authorize the law's officer to do what is needed to satisfy a judgment for money or for possession.

Equitable decrees

Equitable decrees, in contrast, were characteristically in the form of personal commands to defendants and originally did not have an in rem effect.[3] Thus, if the chancellor found that a bond had been procured by fraud, he did not purport to adjudicate that the bond itself was void but rather directed defendant to deliver it up for cancellation or to execute a release under seal. Even remedies that we now consider as in rem, such as a mortgage foreclosure or a decree removing a cloud on title to land, began as purely in personam orders. To secure their compliance with such directives, defendants might be jailed until they obeyed or (later) their goods might be sequestered.[4]

Equivalence of decrees and judgments

All this was often summed up in the maxim that equity acts in personam, the law in rem.[5] By the course of legal evolution, this distinction became largely obliterated. Concepts of due process established that one could not be subjected to judgment concerning one's property without having been personally summoned to court. In this respect, all remedies are "in personam," whether legal or equitable. The legal effect of equitable decrees, however, has changed in two important respects. First, statutes and judicial decisions give direct determinative effect to most kinds of equitable decrees. Thus, a decree directing a defendant to convey land will itself be an effective transfer of title without the defendant's executing a deed in compliance with the decree ordering him or her to do so. Decrees foreclosing a mortgage or quieting title are given like effect. Second, a decree in equity is now binding not merely in the sense of requiring the defendant to do something but also in the sense that the adjudication on which a decree is based is as conclusive as an adjudication leading to a judgment "at law."

Jurisdiction terminology

Moreover, in contemporary legal usage the terms "in personam" and "in rem" are used to refer to the basis on which a court may exercise personal jurisdiction, as distinct from the kind of remedy it may grant when it exercises jurisdiction.[6] The line of demarcation between in personam and in rem for jurisdictional purposes is not the same as the distinction between remedies being considered here. The use of a single

3. J.R. v. M.P., Y.B. 37 Hen. VI, fo. 13, pl. 3 (C.P. 1459); Walsh, Equity 9 (1930). *Cf.* Maitland, Equity 9, 16–19 (2d ed. 1936).

4. Walsh, Equity §§ 9, 10 (1930).

5. *See* Cook, The Powers of Courts of Equity, 15 Colum. L. Rev. 37 (1915). *See generally* Friedell and Healy, An Introduction to *in rem* Jurisdiction and Procedure in the United States, 20 J. Mar. L. & Com. 55 (1989).

6. *See* Chapter 2.

pair of terms to refer to two different concepts of judicial authority has been the source of endless, and continuing, confusion.

Discretion in equity

There is, to be sure, a residue of the old distinction between in rem and in personam relief in the concept and purpose of an injunction, a remedy that originated with equity. An injunction accomplishes relief from a legal wrong by requiring the person to whom it is directed either to refrain prospectively from legally wrongful conduct or to repair a situation created by his or her past conduct. For example, one may be required not to participate in a threatened strike that is illegal[7] or may be required to remedy a past practice of racial discrimination by altering future practices.[8] In contrast, the remedy of damages permits the confiscation of property (through execution proceedings) to compensate the injured person for the past, or past and future, consequences of illegal conduct.[9] Also, a court has always had some discretion to refuse an injunction even when violation of a legal right is clear and continuing.[10] Thus, it is useful to differentiate these kinds of remedies, but it is not useful to do so by using the terms "in rem" and "in personam."

§ 1.11 Other Classifications of Relief

Adjudicating status

For analytic purposes it is more helpful, though less conventional in Anglo–American legal parlance, to think of the forms of relief as being in three categories[1] while noting the interrelation among them.

The first category is a judgment that simply transforms a legal relationship. Judgments of this character include those determining personal status such as divorce, annulment of marriage, parentage, and citizenship. They also include judgments that confirm, redefine, or reshape a person's interests in specific property, whether real estate or tangible or intangible property (such as shares of stock).[2] Proceedings leading to judgments of this kind include the common law actions of ejectment and trespass to try title (concerning real property) and replevin (to obtain possession of tangible personal property) and the equitable

7. *See* United States v. United Mine Workers, 330 U.S. 258, 67 S.Ct. 677, 91 L.Ed. 884 (1947).

8. *See* Franks v. Bowman Transp. Co., 424 U.S. 747, 96 S.Ct. 1251, 47 L.Ed.2d 444 (1976).

9. *See* Leubsdorf, Remedies for Uncertainty, 61 B.U.L. Rev. 132 (1981); Restatement (Second) of Judgments § 31.

10. *See* Weinberger v. Romero–Barcelo, 456 U.S. 305, 102 S.Ct. 1798, 72 L.Ed.2d 91 (1982) (discretion in issuing permanent injunction); Lawson Prods. v. Avnet, Inc., 782 F.2d 1429 (7th Cir.1986); Hamilton Watch Co. v. Benrus Watch Co., 206 F.2d 738 (2d Cir.1953) (discretion in issuing preliminary injunction).

§ 1.11

1. *Compare* Dobbs, Remedies § 1.1 (1973).

2. *See* Restatement (Second) of Judgments § 30.

suit to quiet title. The relief given in actions challenging the legality of governmental action is often of this type.[3]

The judgment is transformational in the sense that the persons whose interests are determined must either conduct themselves in a way that recognizes the new legal relationship or risk the possibility of further legal sanctions. Thus, persons who ignore a judgment determining that they have no interest in specific land and who continue to use it as their own would be subject to actions for damages and perhaps injunctions to compel them to vacate the property.

Perform specific act

The second category is a judgment creating an obligation to perform a specific act or to refrain from doing so. The most commonly encountered form of such a judgment is an injunction, but the remedies of specific performance (requiring performance of a contract) and of equitable replevin (requiring restoration of possession of personal property) also are of this character.[4] If persons against whom such a judgment is rendered do not conduct themselves in accordance with it, they may be subject to the further sanctions of civil contempt, including the possibility of being put in jail until they agree to comply, and criminal contempt, which is the imposition of punishment for ignoring the court's order.[5] But because it may be impossible to induce recalcitrant parties to comply with such a decree, courts will sometimes go no further than seeking to induce compliance by sequestering the parties' property.

Money judgment

The third category is a judgment creating an obligation to pay money.[6] This remedy, that of a judgment for damages, was the only one available in most common law actions and is still the kind of relief usually sought in litigation between private parties. A money judgment makes the property of the person against whom it is rendered liable to execution at the hands of the sheriff or marshal. Of equal practical importance, the judgment is an obligation that persons having custody of property owned by the defendant, such as a bank in which he or she keeps an account, must recognize if execution proceedings are brought to

3. *See* Davis, Administrative Law Text §§ 23.01–23.05 (3d ed. 1972).

4. *See* Restatement (Second) of Torts §§ 933 *et seq.*; Restatement (Second) of Contracts 358 *et seq.*; Ulen, The Efficiency of Specific Performance: Toward a Unified Theory of Contract Remedies, 83 Mich. L. Rev. 341 (1984); Schwartz, The Case for Specific Performance, 89 Yale L.J. (1979).

5. *See* Rendleman, Compensatory Contempt: Plaintiff's Remedy When a Defendant Violates an Injunction, 1980 U. Ill. L.F. 971. *Compare* Walker v. City of Birmingham, 388 U.S. 307, 87 S.Ct. 1824, 18 L.Ed.2d 1210 (1967), *with* In re Berry, 68 Cal.2d 137, 436 P.2d 273, 65 Cal.Rptr. 273 (1968). *See also* Greenawalt, A Contextual Approach to Disobedience, 70 Colum. L. Rev. 48 (1970).

6. *See* Restatement (Second) of Torts §§ 901–932; Restatement (Second) of Contracts §§ 327–346; Dobbs, Remedies ch. 3 (1973).

enforce the judgment.[7] Some money judgments, notably child support orders in some states, are also enforceable by jailing the debtor.

Compliance

Several observations may be made about these forms of remedies. First, in many circumstances a transformational remedy is sufficient for practical purposes. Second, courts are reluctant to direct a person to perform an act, through the remedy of injunction, when some other remedy will probably suffice.[8] They are particularly reluctant to resort to the sanction of jailing a person who violates a court order, even when the violation is flagrant. Third, the procedure for enforcing money judgments is, and always has been, relatively cumbersome, at least as against a person determined to obstruct enforcement. Fourth, and as a consequence of the foregoing, a judgment usually achieves effect through voluntary compliance. The efficacy of judgments thus depends chiefly on the moral authority of the adjudication itself, rather than the prospect it holds for the subsequent use of enforcing sanctions. From this perspective the most important aspect of any judgment is its transformational effect, defining legal rights that ordinarily will be observed and only occasionally will require supplemental resort to the expensive and uncertain machinery of coercive enforcement.

§ 1.12 Declaratory Relief

Uncertainty about legal rights

As we have seen in the preceding section, relief through compensatory damages was traditionally associated with actions at law, and relief through injunction was associated with equity. Transformational relief—that is, simply determining or confirming the parties' legal relationship to each other—was not a part of the traditional scheme of remedies, although it was an ingredient of each of them. Transformational relief eventually became recognized as a form of judicial redress of great utility, one that could be of still greater utility if it were available without technical limitations such as the "adequacy test" required for an injunction.[1] Moreover, in some situations persons could fall into dispute over their legal relationships but be unable to bring present suit because no wrong had yet been committed or even threatened. In such a

7. *See generally* Campbell and Lynn, Creditors' Rights Handbook (1985).

8. This reluctance traditionally was expressed in terms of the jurisdiction of a court of equity: that jurisdiction could be invoked to obtain an injunction only if the remedy of damages would be "inadequate." *See* Restatement (Second) of Torts § 933. The approach has survived the merger of law and equity in situations in which compelling a defendant to act would be oppressive or difficult to enforce or would contravene some other policy. Today, however, while courts are still more likely to grant an injunction that forbids a defendant to act, they are usually willing to require performance when it is practical and the plaintiff wants it. *See* Fiss, The Civil Rights Injunction (1978); Laycock, The Death of the Irreparable Injury Rule (1991).

§ 1.12

1. *See* § 1.11 note 8 *supra*.

situation, parties to the dispute could take action that would change the status quo only by acting at their legal peril, for example incurring liability for damages.[2]

Federal Declaratory Judgment Act

In response, the statutory remedy of a declaratory judgment was created.[3] These statutes, now in effect in all but one or two jurisdictions, typically provide that an action may be brought "to declare rights, status, and other legal relations whether or not further relief is or could be claimed."[4] The Federal Declaratory Judgment Act[5] has qualifying language that such an action may be brought only "in a case of actual controversy." For a long time doubt existed over the validity of these statutes. The source of the doubt was that, under the federal and most state constitutions, judicial power extended only to the decision of an actual "case or controversy," coupled with a belief that actual cases and controversies were confined to disputes involving accomplished or threatened wrongs calling for coercive relief.[6] The "case or controversy" doctrine will be addressed later in this book.[7]

Declaratory effects of judgments

The decisions casting doubt on declaratory judgments failed to realize that such relief could be provided in many situations where it was most needed without threatening or impairing the principle that courts should decide only actual cases or controversies.[8] It was also not recognized that all coercive relief is declaratory or transformational in two senses: A determination of legal relationships is implicit in a judgment awarding damages or an injunction, and a judgment of any kind is enforceable, not by the court as such, but by the parties' acceptance of its authority or by executive authority in the person of a sheriff or marshal. After an initial period of uncertainty, the validity and propriety of the declaratory remedy became fully established.

2. The classic example is presented by the facts in Willing v. Chicago Auditorium Assn., 277 U.S. 274, 48 S.Ct. 507, 72 L.Ed. 880 (1928). The lessee under a 99-year lease found that the building originally erected on the leased premises had become unprofitable and wished to replace it with a new and larger building. A dispute ensued over whether the lease permitted this without the landlord's consent.

3. *See generally* 6A Moore, Federal Practice and Procedure ¶ 57.03 *et seq.*; Restatement (Second) of Judgments § 33. For historical background, see Borchard, Declaratory Judgments (2d ed. 1941). *See also* Duernberg and Mushlin, History Comes Calling, 37 UCLA L. Rev. 139 (1989); Duernberg and Mushlin, The Trojan Horse, 36 UCLA L. Rev. 529 (1989) (two articles on the origins and effect of the Declaratory Judgment Act).

4. Uniform Declaratory Judgments Act, 12 U.L.A. 109.

5. 28 U.S.C. §§ 2201–2202. *See also* Fed. R. Civ. P. 57.

6. *See* Willing v. Chicago Auditorium Assn., 277 U.S. 274, 48 S.Ct. 507, 72 L.Ed. 880 (1928); Liberty Warehouse Co. v. Grannis, 273 U.S. 70, 47 S.Ct. 282, 71 L.Ed. 541 (1927); Anway v. Grand Rapids R.R., 211 Mich. 592, 179 N.W. 350 (1920).

7. *See* § 2.26 *infra.*

8. *See* Duke Power Co. v. Carolina Envtl. Study Group, 438 U.S. 59, 98 S.Ct. 2620, 57 L.Ed.2d 595 (1978).

Today, declaratory relief poses several questions. In the field of public law, uncertainty may still exist over whether a suit for declaratory relief is subject to special "case or controversy" or "ripeness" requirements that do not also apply to injunction suits. The Supreme Court decisions concerning "ripeness" are almost impossible to reconcile, but they appear no longer to impose special requirements on declaratory judgment suits.[9] In the field of private law, the questions concern the extent to which a dispute must have matured before the remedy is available, whether the remedy is available after the dispute has matured, and how much discretion the court has to deny the declaratory remedy.

Ripeness

As for the problem of maturity, the difference between an abstract question and a "controversy" is necessarily one of degree, and no precise test can be fashioned to tell when the requisite degree is reached.[10] A controversy may exist before the last irrevocable step is taken that will call for coercive relief, and the fact that a desired but challenged course of action will be taken only if it is adjudged legitimate does not make the question of legitimacy abstract. So if a party to a contract contends that performance by that party has been excused, and the other party insists to the contrary, the controversy is drawn well enough so that either should be able to sue for a declaratory judgment on the question.[11]

If the dispute has progressed to the point of full maturity before suit so that coercive relief is presently available, different questions arise. In some situations, injunctive relief for a threatened wrong may be prohibited, and the question is whether declaratory relief—which often has the same effect—may nevertheless be obtained.[12] Furthermore, when the declaratory plaintiff would be entitled to coercive relief if the allegations were sustained, a question arises whether he or she may seek the "milder" declaratory relief and abjure the claim for coercive relief. The argument against letting plaintiff do so is based on the possibility of

9. *See, e.g.*, Webster v. Reproductive Health Servs., 492 U.S. 490, 109 S.Ct. 3040, 106 L.Ed.2d 410 (1989) (suit for declaratory judgment and injunction against enforcement of abortion control legislation); Regional Rail Reorganization Act Cases, 419 U.S. 102, 95 S.Ct. 335, 42 L.Ed.2d 320 (1974). But see Calderon v. Ashmus, 523 U.S. 740, 118 S.Ct. 1694, 140 L.Ed.2d 970 (1998)(Constitution does not permit declaratory judgment resolving one issue of controversy that will be decided in habeas corpus proceeding). Declaratory judgments are not available in controversies over federal taxes, 28 U.S.C. § 2201, and the federal courts are admonished to use them sparingly in controversies over state taxes. Wright, Law of Federal Courts 100 (4th ed. 1983); Annot., 11 A.L.R.2d 359 (tax controversies).

10. Maryland Casualty Co. v. Pacific Coal & Oil Co., 312 U.S. 270, 61 S.Ct. 510, 85 L.Ed. 826 (1941); American Mach. & Metals v. De Bothezat Impeller Co., 166 F.2d 535, 536 (2d Cir.1948). *Compare* Sticker Indus. Supply Corp. v. Blaw–Knox Co., 367 F.2d 744 (7th Cir.1966) (ripeness for declaratory relief), *with* American Needle & Novelty Co. v. Schuessler Knitting Mills, 379 F.2d 376 (7th Cir.1967).

11. *E.g.*, Annots., 10 A.L.R.2d 743, 32 A.L.R.2d 970.

12. *See* note 9 *supra; compare* Great Lakes Dredge & Dock Co. v. Huffman, 319 U.S. 293, 63 S.Ct. 1070, 87 L.Ed. 1407 (1943).

piecemeal litigation if coercive relief turns out later to be needed, but supplemental relief seems seldom to have been necessary in practice.[13]

Suit by alleged wrongdoer

Where a matured claim is asserted and the putative defendant initiates an action to declare the claim invalid, different questions are presented. The pendency of the claim may involve tangible disadvantage to the putative defendant that would justify seeking to have it judicially settled.[14] Balanced against this is the strong tradition giving the injured party the choice of time and forum for bringing suit, and this choice carries substantial tactical advantages. If the injured party has already brought suit, or announced an intention immediately to do so, and the issues tendered for declaratory judgment would be settled in that suit, little justification would exist for letting the putative wrongdoer deprive the injured party of the traditional tactical advantages by bringing an independent action for declaratory judgment.[15]

Court's discretion

It is now settled that the court has an area of discretion to deny declaratory judgment even under the federal act, which makes no express mention of it.[16] The discretion cannot properly be exercised to deny relief when a case for it is made out and no valid countervailing considerations exist,[17] but dismissal is warranted when the relief "would not terminate the uncertainty or controversy giving rise to the proceeding"[18] or when the issues may more appropriately be determined in another proceeding in the light of considerations already mentioned.[19]

§ 1.13 Changing the Law

Since the 1950s, particularly since the momentous decision in *Brown v. Board of Education*,[1] civil litigation has been overtly recognized as a means of changing the law. The strategy of the litigants is often called "social advocacy" and the role of the courts commonly called—with both positive and negative connotations—"judicial activism." The remedial

13. *See* Restatement (Second) of Judgments § 33, Comment *c*. If the court permits the litigation to go forward "piecemeal," the rules of res judicata properly should not later be invoked if a claim for supplemental relief is brought. *Id.*

14. *See, e.g.,* Aetna Life Ins. Co. v. Haworth, 300 U.S. 227, 57 S.Ct. 461, 81 L.Ed. 617 (1937).

15. *See* Brillhart v. Excess Ins. Co., 316 U.S. 491, 62 S.Ct. 1173, 86 L.Ed. 1620 (1942); *cf.* Beacon Theatres v. Westover, 359 U.S. 500, 79 S.Ct. 948, 3 L.Ed.2d 988 (1959).

16. 6A Moore, Federal Practice and Procedure ¶ ¶ 57.07–57.08; 10 Wright and Miller, Federal Practice and Procedure §§ 2757–2759.

17. *See* Columbia Pictures Corp. v. De Toth, 26 Cal.2d 753, 161 P.2d 217 (1945).

18. Uniform Declaratory Judgments Act § 6, 12 U.L.A. 455.

19. Wilton v. Seven Falls Co., 515 U.S. 277, 115 S.Ct. 2137, 132 L.Ed.2d 214 (1995); State Auto Ins. Cos. v. Summy, 234 F.3d 131 (3d Cir.2000).

§ 1.13

1. 347 U.S. 483, 74 S.Ct. 686, 98 L.Ed. 873 (1954).

mechanism is essentially twofold: Change is sought in the substantive law through judicial decision, and specific enforcement of legal obligations—particularly obligations of public officials—is sought through injunctions implemented under court supervision. Change in substantive law also can result from criminal litigation such as *Miranda v. Arizona,*[2] which governs the rights of criminal suspects. In criminal cases, however, the advocates of legal change are usually on the defensive, while in civil litigation the champion of a social cause can assume the offensive and thereby have a larger set of options in selecting the time, the case, and the court.[3]

"Normal" legal evolution

Effecting changes in the law through litigation is a process as old as the law itself. The law, whether substantive or procedural, is not static but is continually open to change in connotation and formulation. Until the nineteenth century, however, the metamorphic nature of the law could not clearly be discerned except from the historian's perspective; even in the early twentieth century its plasticity was denied. Professor Arthur Corbin, writing of his legal education at the turn of the century, said:

> If we heard of such a thing as "evolution of the law," it meant nothing to us. And that the judges had any part in making and remaking the common law was a preposterous idea. "Judge-made law" was anathema. Even in 1914 ... Judge Baldwin [of the Yale Law School faculty] told the Lawyers' Club ... that there were only two instances of judge-made law in the history of Connecticut.[4]

Normally lawyers still advance their legal arguments on the pretence that they are explicating what the law "is," and judges generally compose opinions to suggest that their decisions are compelled by precedent. Nevertheless, American judges do make new law, are expected to make law, and sometimes acknowledge that fact. What is different today is that the judicial lawmaking function is more openly acknowledged.[5]

Law reform litigation

There are various ways by which an initiative to change the law can be launched in a civil case. The initiative may be presented by a

2. 384 U.S. 436, 86 S.Ct. 1602, 16 L.Ed.2d 694 (1966).

3. The larger initiatives potentially available in civil litigation are exhibited in cases where federal courts have abstained from interfering with pending state criminal cases. *See e.g.,* Huffman v. Pursue, Ltd., 420 U.S. 592, 95 S.Ct. 1200, 43 L.Ed.2d 482 (1975); Younger v. Harris, 401 U.S. 37, 91 S.Ct. 746, 27 L.Ed.2d 669 (1971).

4 Corbin, The Law School Under 10 Deans and 5 Presidents, 1 Yale L. Rep. 5 (1955).

5. *See, e.g.,* Bickel, The Least Dangerous Branch (1962); Ely, Democracy and Distrust: A Theory of Judicial Review (1980); Brest, The Fundamental Rights Controversy: The Essential Contradictions of Normative Constitutional Scholarship, 90 Yale L.J. 1063 (1981). *But see* Bork, The Tempting of America (1989).

plaintiff's complaint alleging that the defendant did or failed to do something and demanding relief accordingly; when defendant responds that the conduct was lawful according to the precedents, plaintiff argues that the precedents should be reconsidered and the law pronounced to be otherwise than it was before. The initiative may also be taken by a defendant who argues that his or her conduct, admittedly wrongful according to precedent, nevertheless ought to be regarded as lawful. The initiative may arise during an intermediate procedural stage of litigation, for example, in discovery of evidence before trial.

Example: law of privilege

The decision in *Upjohn Co. v. United States*[6] illustrates judicial lawmaking that results from issues raised during an intermediate procedural stage. *Upjohn* involved an Internal Revenue Service investigation of suspected illegal payments by an American corporation to foreign officials. After beginning an administrative investigation, the IRS issued a summons demanding that the company produce certain records relating to the payments. The company refused on the ground that the records in question contained confidential attorney work-product of the company's counsel and confidential attorney-client communications. A fair argument could be made for the company's position, but, at least as to parts of the records, the weight of authority was adverse to the company's position. The IRS then commenced a statutory action in the federal district court, seeking to compel the company to produce the records. The company in effect demurred[7] to the IRS petition (complaint), saying in essence: "Although we have documents such as those you describe, we have no legal obligation to surrender them because according to the law (as it ought to be) those documents are privileged." The company's contention was rejected by the district court and court of appeals but sustained by the Supreme Court, which thereby made new law in the law of privilege.[8]

Procedure to facilitate judicial lawmaking

Judicial lawmaking is inevitably controversial in a representative democracy whose Constitution does not expressly confer authority for that function. One of the mysteries of American politics remains the tacit acceptance of judicial lawmaking, even while its legitimacy is continually debated.[9]

Whatever the political justification for this form of social redress, as legal technique it has become a fixture. The large majority of civil cases

6. 449 U.S. 383, 101 S.Ct. 677, 66 L.Ed.2d 584 (1981).

7. *See* § 4.1 *infra.*

8. *See, e.g.,* Nath, *Upjohn*: A New Prescription for the Attorney–Client Privilege and Work Product Defense in Administrative Investigations, 30 Buffalo L. Rev. 11 (1981); Sexton, A Post-*Upjohn* Consideration of Corporate Attorney–Client Privilege, 57 N.Y.U. L. Rev. 443 (1982); The Supreme Court 1980 Term, 95 Harv. L. Rev. 270 (1981).

9. *See* sources cited *supra* note 5.

do not involve new legal issues, only questions of fact or application of settled legal principles. Any case, however, has potential to be the occasion of reshaping the law.

In general, the system of civil procedure does not facilitate the courts' lawmaking function. Even a "test case" expressly seeking a pronouncement of law from the appellate courts is almost always begun and prosecuted as though it involved only a question of fact or an interpretation of existing law.[10] This process often results in long delay and superfluous procedural maneuvering to get the case to the appellate level.[11]

A more serious defect is the lack of an official mechanism for marshalling the relevant information about the legal question involved and the practical and political implications of resolving it one way or another.[12] Fortunately, most appellate judges have had long years of experience in practical affairs and are as well qualified as most legislators to gauge the political climate and the movement of social forces. Both methods of lawmaking have their drawbacks. Procedures to facilitate judicial lawmaking in civil litigation, however, remain almost nonexistent, although expert witnesses and organizations submitting briefs as amici curiae (friends of the court) sometimes draw the attention of judges to the implications of a case. This gap can perhaps best be explained by the common unwillingness to accept openly the legitimacy of this form of judicial remedy and the fear of more openly politicizing the appellate courts.

§ 1.14 Institutional Decrees

During the decades following *Brown v. Board of Education,*[1] the courts, particularly the federal courts, became engaged in granting injunctions whose purpose and scope have led them to become known as "institutional decrees." The practice of issuing these decrees began when many school districts, especially in the South, refused to accept the law of desegregation announced in *Brown* and related cases. Citizens and officials normally accept the law as pronounced by the courts and voluntarily comply with it. Controversy in the school desegregation cases, however, was so pronounced that state officials would not comply with the law of their own accord until confronted with the immediate

10. *See, e.g.,* Grove City College v. Bell, 465 U.S. 555, 104 S.Ct. 1211, 79 L.Ed.2d 516 (1984), *overruled by* Civil Rights Restoration Act of 1987, Pub. L. No. 100–259, 102 Stat. 28 (1988).

11. *Compare* the expedited treatment given the appeals in United States v. Nixon, 418 U.S. 683, 94 S.Ct. 3090, 41 L.Ed.2d 1039 (1974), *and* Dames & Moore v. Regan, 453 U.S. 654, 101 S.Ct. 2972, 69 L.Ed.2d 918 (1981).

12. *See, e.g.,* Roe v. Wade, 410 U.S. 113, 93 S.Ct. 705, 35 L.Ed.2d 147 (1973); Brown v. Board of Education, 347 U.S. 483, 74 S.Ct. 686, 98 L.Ed. 873 (1954).

§ 1.14

1. 347 U.S. 483, 74 S.Ct. 686, 98 L.Ed. 873 (1954).

risk of contempt of court. President Eisenhower finally made it clear in the Little Rock showdown that military force would be used if necessary to overcome violent defiance of the court.[2] The courts were thus assured that their school desegregation decrees eventually would be enforced by physical coercion, but resisting school districts came to understand that they could postpone desegregation until faced with a direct court order.

Implementing desegregation

In addition to direct confrontation of judicial authority, evasion and pretense were used by school districts attempting to sidestep desegregation.[3] The courts responded to these evasive tactics by issuing decrees of increasing detail and appointing special officials to monitor and, in some instances, to administer the decrees. The administration of desegregation often involved other aspects of school administration and in some cities, notably Boston, the federal court became a virtual adjunct to the school board.[4] This kind of detailed and closely administered decree has also been used to enforce new legal rights for inmates of prisons and for patients at psychiatric hospitals and at other institutions.[5]

The institutional decree is a remedy far removed from the doctrine that equity will not enjoin the affirmative performance of a contract or other obligation requiring personal services.[6] The willingness of the courts to issue such decrees repudiates the traditional proposition that equity will act only when the remedy at law is plainly inadequate.[7] Given the reluctance of the federal executive to enforce desegregation in the absence of a judicial decree, however, the courts in the desegregation cases had no other course if they were to preserve their authority. And since then, in discrimination and other cases involving prospective wrongs the mandatory injunction has become a standard remedy.

2. *See, e.g.,* Muse, Ten Years of Prelude (1964); Sarratt, The Ordeal of Desegregation: The First Decade (1966); Wasby, D'Amato, and Metrailer, Desegregation from *Brown* to *Alexander*: An Exploration of Supreme Court Strategies (1977). Later, procedures to end federal funding of noncomplying school districts helped to end resistance. Orfield, The Reconstruction of Southern Education (1969).

3. See, for example, the desegregation plans contested in Swann v. Charlotte–Mecklenburg Bd. of Educ., 402 U.S. 1, 91 S.Ct. 1267, 28 L.Ed.2d 554 (1971); Green v. County School Bd., 391 U.S. 430, 88 S.Ct. 1689, 20 L.Ed.2d 716 (1968); Goss v. Board of Educ., 373 U.S. 683, 83 S.Ct. 1405, 10 L.Ed.2d 632 (1963). *See also* Limits of Justice: The Courts' Role in School Desegregation (Kalodner and Fishman eds. 1978); Sarratt, *supra* note 2; Wasby, D'Amato, and Metrailer, *supra* note 2.

4. In eight years the district court issued 400 rulings on the administration of the Boston school system. N.Y. Times, June 6, 1982, at A22, col. 1. The court subsequently reduced its role in administering the school system. Morgan v. McDonough, 554 F.Supp. 169 (D.Mass.1982).

5. *See, e.g.,* Fiss, The Civil Rights Injunction (1978); Leubsdorf, Completing the Desegregation Remedy, 57 B.U.L. Rev. 39 (1977); Rendleman, The Inadequate Remedy at Law as a Prerequisite for an Injunction, 33 U. Fla. L. Rev. 346 (1981); Note, Implementation Problems in Institutional Reform Litigation, 91 Harv. L. Rev. 428 (1977).

6. *See* Dobbs, Remedies 933 *et seq.* (1973).

7. *See* Fiss, The Civil Rights Injunction (1978); Laycock, The Death of the Irreparable Injury Rule (1991).

Effectiveness and legitimacy

Yet the difficulty of securing compliance with a mandatory decree in the face of resistance has not been eliminated, though it often fades from public view. And that difficulty in turn casts doubt on the authority of courts issuing such decrees. The effectiveness in practice of institutional decrees has been mixed and often depends on the specific circumstances, the institution involved, and the diplomatic skills of the judges, parties, and lawyers. Doubtless having these problems in mind, the Supreme Court has strongly implied disapproval of broad institutional decrees in situations other than discrimination.[8] Considered historically, the experience with institutional decrees indicates both that it is possible to govern a subsector of society by judicial decree and that doing so creates practical difficulties and involves losses as well as gains in the political and moral capital of the legal process.

C. AMERICAN COURT SYSTEMS

§ 1.15 State Court Systems[1]

Every state in the United States has its own court system created by its constitution or statutes. Most of the judicial business of the country is carried on in the state courts, including much business over which federal courts have concurrent jurisdiction.

Trial courts

Every state has a trial court of general original jurisdiction—"general" meaning that it can hear any kind of case except those specifically committed to some other court or administrative tribunal (such as probate court or the workers' compensation board). This court is called by various names in different states—superior court, district court, circuit court, and, in New York, supreme court. Many states also have courts of "limited," "special," or "inferior" jurisdiction that have authority restricted to cases within specified monetary limits (for example, $5,000), or of specified subject matter (such as housing violations, probate, and juvenile proceedings), often including minor criminal matters (notably traffic violations). Many states have consolidated these into a set of courts uniform throughout the state and known as the district or county court.[2] A few states and the District of Columbia have a unified

8. *See, e.g.,* City of Los Angeles v. Lyons, 461 U.S. 95, 103 S.Ct. 1660, 75 L.Ed.2d 675 (1983); Rizzo v. Goode, 423 U.S. 362, 96 S.Ct. 598, 46 L.Ed.2d 561 (1976). Both cases involved police practices. Courts have been more willing to grant institutional relief reforming prisons and, in some instances, mental hospitals. Hutto v. Finney, 437 U.S. 678, 98 S.Ct. 2565, 57 L.Ed.2d 522 (1978); Thomas S. by Brooks v. Flaherty, 699 F.Supp. 1178 (W.D.N.C.1988); Yackle, Reform and Regret (1989). *But see* 18 U.S.C. § 1836 (limiting prison reform remedies).

§ 1.15

1. *See* ABA Standards Relating to Court Organization § 1.10; Pound, Organization of Courts (1940).

2. *See* American Jud. Soc'y, An Assessment of the Courts of Limited Jurisdiction (1968).

trial court, that is, one trial court with specialized divisions that hears all cases except those committed to administrative tribunals.

Appellate courts

Every state has at least one appellate court.[3] Some have only one, but the large majority of states have an intermediate appellate court between the trial courts and the court of last resort, such as the California Court of Appeal and the Appellate Division of the Supreme Court in New York. Where there is such an intermediate appellate court, there is commonly provision for an appeal to it as of right (if the proper procedural steps are taken), with further review being a matter of discretion in all except select types of important cases. The highest appellate tribunal thus is viewed not so much as a court for the correction of routine errors as the final arbiter in cases that have peculiar importance either in themselves (such as a sentence of death in criminal cases) or for the state's system of jurisprudence.[4]

§ 1.16 Federal Court System[1]

District courts

The trial court in the federal judicial system is the district court. The territory of the nation is divided into ninety-one districts. With one exception no district crosses state lines. In each state and in the District of Columbia, there is at least one district; in some states there are more than one, the maximum number being four (New York and Texas). There is a district court for each district, and also one each for Puerto Rico, the Canal Zone, Guam, and the Virgin Islands. Each district has at least one judge, most of them two or more.

Courts of appeals

There are thirteen courts of appeals: one for the District of Columbia, eleven numbered circuits, and the Court of Appeals for the Federal Circuit. The numbered circuits have a jurisdiction defined by state and territorial boundaries, each containing from three to ten states and territories. For example, the Third Circuit includes the states of Delaware, New Jersey, and Pennsylvania, and the Virgin Islands. Each circuit court has five or more judges and ordinarily sits in panels of three judges each. The principal function of the numbered courts of appeals and that of the District of Columbia is reviewing cases tried in the district courts within the circuit. These courts also have jurisdiction to

3. *See* ABA Standards Relating to Appellate Courts §§ 3.00, 3.01; American Jud. Soc'y, Intermediate Appellate Courts (1968).

4. *See* ABA Standards Relating to Appellate Courts § 3.10.

§ 1.16

1. *See generally* Bator, Melzer, Mishkin, and Shapiro, The Federal Courts and the Federal System 1–63 (3d ed. 1988); 13 Wright and Miller, Federal Practice and Procedure §§ 3501 *et seq.;* 1 Moore, Federal Practice and Procedure ¶ ¶ 0.1 *et seq.*

review orders of designated administrative agencies (such as the National Labor Relations Board) and to issue original writs in appropriate cases. The jurisdiction of the Federal Circuit includes appeals from the district courts throughout the country in patent cases; certain copyright and trademark cases; certain tax cases; appeals from the United States Court of Claims; and certain other classes of cases.[2]

Supreme Court

The Supreme Court of the United States is the only federal court created directly by the Constitution.[3] Since 1869 it has consisted of one chief justice and eight associate justices. Before that, the number varied from six (the original number) to ten (from 1864 to 1869).

The Supreme Court has limited original jurisdiction[4] and appellate jurisdiction over the lower federal courts[5] and the highest state courts.[6] Although a few types of cases may be taken to the Supreme Court by appeal of right, most may be presented to it only in the Court's discretion, exercised by granting writ of certiorari or allowing an appeal to be heard on its merits.

Other federal courts

Special federal courts have jurisdiction over specific subject matters.[7] The United States Claims Court has jurisdiction over certain claims against the government. The Federal Circuit Court of Appeals has appellate jurisdiction over certain customs and patent matters. The Court of International Trade reviews certain administrative decisions by customs officials. There is a Tax Court and a Court of Military Appeals. There is also a Bankruptcy Court attached to each District Court.[8]

D. LIFE HISTORY OF A LAWSUIT

In the United States and other common law jurisdictions, actions are divided into clearly defined stages: the filing and service of pleadings defining the scope of the dispute; pretrial proceedings to uncover facts, dispose of baseless claims, and prepare for trial; a trial at which evidence is presented and findings are made; and subsequent appellate review. This division is not inevitable. In Germany, for example, one court

2. 28 U.S.C. § 1291 *et seq.*

3. U.S. Const. art. III, 1. *See generally* Frankfurter and Landis, The Business of the Supreme Court (1928).

4. U.S. Const. art. III, 2: "In all Cases affecting Ambassadors, other Public Ministers and Consuls, and those in which a state shall be a party, the Supreme Court shall have original jurisdiction." *See* 28 U.S.C. § 1251.

5. 28 U.S.C. §§ 1253, 1254.

6. 28 U.S.C. § 1257. The power of review of state court judgments is limited to questions of federal law involved therein. *See* Chemerinsky, Federal Jurisdiction ch. 10 (3d ed. 1999); Wright, Law of the Federal Courts 107 (4th ed. 1983).

7. Wright, Law of the Federal Courts 5 (4th ed. 1983).

8. 28 U.S.C. § 1471.

hearing could include the presentation of evidence, the redefinition of issues, and arrangements for future hearings.[1] Even in the United States, the great majority of suits are settled before trial, and a few develop unusual and colorful histories.[2]

§ 1.17 Commencement of Action; Summons and Complaint

The procedures for starting an action involve service of process (summons) on the defendant and, at some point, return of that process to court with an endorsement or certificate by the person who served the process describing the way in which it was served. The procedures generally provide for the service of the initial pleading (complaint) on the defendant either with the summons or in a prescribed time thereafter. But the order in which these steps occur and the precise point at which the action is deemed to be commenced (for example, for the purpose of tolling a statute of limitations) vary.

Rule 3

Under Rule 3 of the Federal Rules of Civil Procedure the first step is the filing of the complaint with the court (that is, the clerk's office).[1] On the filing of the complaint the clerk must forthwith issue a summons and deliver it to the plaintiff for service.[2] The summons and the complaint are to be served together by a person who is not a party to the action[3] and must ordinarily be served within 120 days of the filing of the complaint.[4]

Rule 4: commencing action

In some states the clerk issues the summons on a written demand for it, called a "praecipe," and the complaint is served on the party (often by a sheriff or constable) before being filed in court. In other states the plaintiff's attorney prepares and issues the summons and neither the court nor the clerk has anything to do with the action until the summons and complaint are returned to the court either on or before a regular return day (as in Connecticut[5]) or until a ruling of the court is desired or the case is ready to be placed on the docket (as in New York[6]).

1. Kaplan, von Mehren, and Schaefer, Phases of German Civil Procedure I, II, 71 Harv. L. Rev. 1193, 1443 (1958).

2. *E.g.,* Stern, The Buffalo Creek Disaster (1976); Harr, A Civil Action (1995). Many students find that reading case histories like these helps them understand how civil procedure works in the real world.

§ 1.17

1. Fed. R. Civ. P. 3.

2. *Id.* 4(b).

3. *Id.* 4(c).

4. *Id.* 4(m). *See* § 2.11 *infra.*

5. Conn. Gen. Stat. 53–46–52–48 (1958). *See* Taylor v. Judd, 41 Conn. 483, 485 (1874).

6. N.Y. Civ. Prac. L. & R. 304, 320, 2103, 3012. Under New York law, a claim may be "interposed" to toll the statute of limitations before service of summons under some circumstances. *Id.* at 203.

Under the federal system the action is deemed commenced when the complaint is filed in court, but under many state procedures the action begins when process is served.[7]

Jurisdiction and venue

Before taking any of these steps, the plaintiff must select a proper court for the action. One choice that must be made is whether to file in a state or federal court system.[8] Having made this choice, the plaintiff must then choose from *among* the federal or the state courts (as the case may be). In addition to considerations of individual preference and convenience, the plaintiff filing in the federal system must take into account (1) which court can assume jurisdiction over the defendant or, for an in rem action, over the res; and (2) federal venue requirements. For the state systems plaintiff must consider (1) which state can get jurisdiction over the parties or the res, (2) which court of an eligible state is given jurisdiction over the subject matter of the action, and (3) state venue requirements.

These questions will be explored in Chapter 2.

§ 1.18 Parties, Pleading, and Pretrial Procedures

Before suit can be started plaintiff must also choose the parties to it. Plaintiff must find out whether he or she is the proper party to file suit and whether anyone else may or must be associated as a plaintiff. And of course plaintiff must find out who may, and who must, be sued. The rules governing these choices are examined in Chapter 10.

Claims and defenses

When the parties and the court are chosen and the action is commenced, there follow the pleadings[1] in the action—the written statements of claim or defense and objections to the action or to a pleading. The rules governing these steps are examined in subsequent chapters.

Written pleadings and objections are of ancient lineage; there was a time when they constituted nearly the only ways in which a party was entitled to find out about his or her adversary's claim or defense until the actual trial. In the twentieth century, pretrial deposition and discovery procedures (which have an ancient lineage in equity) have permitted full, mutual pretrial disclosure of the facts relevant to the dispute. A

7. Fed. R. Civ. P. 3. *See* Walker v. Armco Steel Corp., 446 U.S. 740, 100 S.Ct. 1978, 64 L.Ed.2d 659 (1980), holding that a diversity action in federal court is not "commenced" until service of process on defendant in accordance with an Oklahoma statutory provision that the court found was an integral part of the state statute of limitations. *Compare* West v. Conrail, 481 U.S. 35, 107 S.Ct. 1538, 95 L.Ed.2d 32 (1987) (different result in federal question case).

8. *See* § 2.2 *infra.*

§ 1.18

1. Sometimes the filing of the complaint plays a part in the beginning of the action, as we saw in § 1.15 *supra.* The rules governing the complaint as a pleading are examined in Chapter 3.

pretrial conference of the court and counsel also enjoys wide use. These procedures are the subject of Chapter 5.

§ 1.19 Trial

After the pleadings are closed and discovery completed, the case finally comes to trial. This may be before a judge and jury or a judge without a jury. The rules for determining whether there is a right to jury trial and, if so, what should be done to enjoy that right are the subject of Chapter 8.

The rules governing the taking of evidence and conduct of examinations at trial are not extensively examined in this book.[1] Other rules governing the relationship between judge and jury and the allocation of functions between them are, however, dealt with at some length in Chapter 7. There we shall examine the rules governing the burdens of proof and sufficiency of the evidence as well as the various mechanical devices (such as motions) by which these rules are implemented. We shall also learn the difference between general and special verdicts and the various kinds of attacks that may be directed against verdicts.

§ 1.20 Judgments

The lawsuit itself culminates in a judgment; this has important results for the future relationships between the parties and may to some extent affect nonparties. The extent to which a judgment will preclude further litigation between the parties is a matter treated extensively in Chapter 11; Chapter 12 deals with methods of reviewing and otherwise attacking a judgment.

Some judgments are largely self-executing. Thus a valid decree of divorce itself terminates the marriage; a judgment quieting title or removing a cloud from title may itself make the title marketable, at least if properly recorded where that is required. Declaratory judgments will often have like effect.

Decrees requiring action or inaction

Other judgments or decrees, as we have seen,[1] involve personal orders to a defendant and depend for their effectiveness on the contempt power. This is the case with most injunctions and orders for the specific performance of contracts. The personal order is sometimes available also for compelling the payment of money, either because the duty to pay it derives from equitable principles (as in the case of alimony or an amount found due on a trustee's accounting) or because equitable principles or a

§ 1.19

1. A good introduction to the law of evidence is Strong et al., McCormick on Evidence (4th ed. 1999). The classic and compendious work on evidence is Wigmore, Evidence in Trials at Common Law (new revision in progress). Weinstein and Berger, Weinstein's Evidence (1975), analyzes and annotates the Federal Rules of Evidence.

§ 1.20

1. *See* §§ 1.8–1.10 *supra*.

statute give an auxiliary remedy for the collection of an ordinary money judgment out of assets that cannot be reached by ordinary legal process. Such a personal order will not generally issue without a finding that defendant has the ability to comply with it.

Execution of judgments

For the most part, judgments for money or for the possession of property are enforced by writs of execution, today as at common law.[2] Such a writ is not a command to the defendant but an authorization to the proper officer (usually a sheriff or marshal) to do something. In the case of a money judgment this will be to seize defendant's nonexempt property, sell it on execution sale, and apply the proceeds toward the satisfaction of the judgment. In some states the writ of execution authorizes the officer to take the defendant's body (that is, jail him or her) under certain circumstances on certain kinds of money judgments. This "body execution" comes from the common law and is to be distinguished from the use of the contempt power available only after a personal order to pay has been issued and disobeyed. Many defendants, of course, pay judgments against them without need for coercive measures, but many do not. Recent efforts have been made, for example, to raise the low payment level for child support payments.[3]

Many states also provide that a money judgment becomes a lien on real property of the defendant subject to certain limitations (such as territorial ones) and conditions (recording of the judgment) that vary with each state. This means that the plaintiff can still obtain an execution against the property even if the defendant sells it after the lien attaches.

If the judgment is for the possession of property, the writ of execution authorizes the officer to take possession from the defendant and put the plaintiff into possession. If this is impossible, equity would sometimes issue an injunction ordering defendant to yield possession, as by removing an encroaching structure, and under similar circumstances a court may issue such an order today.

Federal court judgments

Rule 69 covers execution of federal court judgments, providing that "process to enforce them ... [shall be] a writ of execution"[4] in accord with state law. The district court that renders the judgment ordinarily issues the writ, and it has ancillary jurisdiction to enforce the judgment.[5]

2. The law governing enforcement of money judgments is conventionally known as "creditors' rights" or "creditors' remedies." It is highly technical, in many respects obsolete, and considerably variant from one jurisdiction to another. *See generally* Moore and Phillips, Debtors' and Creditors' Rights (4th ed. 1975).

3. 42 U.S.C. §§ 651–669; Chambers, Making Fathers Pay (1979).

4. Fed. R. Civ. P. 69(a).

5. Skevofilax v. Quigley, 810 F.2d 378 (3d Cir.1987); Blackburn Truck Lines v. Francis, 723 F.2d 730 (9th Cir.1984).

In *Argento v. Village of Melrose Park,*[6] for instance, a plaintiff recovered judgment in a civil rights action against two police officers. Plaintiff was given enforcement of the award against the village that employed the police and its insurer inasmuch as state law made public entities liable for the torts of their employees without a separate action.

Historically, a judgment of a federal district court in one state was considered a "foreign" judgment in any other state; as such it could be enforced only by a separate suit in the second state. This archaic requirement was abrogated by the Federal Registration of Judgments Act.[7] Under the statute, a judgment entered in one district may be registered in any other district by filing a certified copy of the judgment. The Enforcement of Foreign Judgments Act[8] provides a similar procedure for state judgments in sister state courts. A federal judgment may also be registered in state courts if the applicable state law so permits. In *Keeton v. Hustler Magazine,*[9] for example, the plaintiff's $2 million judgment in a libel action in a federal court in New Hampshire was then registered in New York State court pursuant to a New York statute, the procedure being upheld against the contention that the New York law was preempted by the federal registration of judgments statute.

§ 1.21 Appeals

A final judgment, once entered, is generally subject to appeal to and review by an appellate court. The rules governing appeal and review are treated in Chapter 12. One very important rule should be noted here, however. That is the "final judgment rule," which is the generally—but not universally—prevailing rule governing American state and federal appellate procedure.

Final judgment rule

The rule provides that an appeal be taken only from a final judgment or order, not from an interlocutory ruling or order. This does not mean that interlocutory rulings are unreviewable, but rather that an appeal cannot be taken when the order or ruling is made but must wait until the final judgment. When appeal is taken from a final judgment many interlocutory rulings that were not *appealable* will become *reviewable.* Rulings at trial excluding or admitting evidence or giving or denying requests for instructions to the jury are typical examples. So are many rulings made on the pleadings or in the course of the pretrial discovery and deposition procedure.

Interlocutory appeals

In many states, such as New York, the final judgment rule is considerably relaxed so that interlocutory review by the intermediate

6. 838 F.2d 1483 (7th Cir.1988).

7. 28 U.S.C. § 1963.

8. 13 U.L.A. 152.

9. 815 F.2d 857 (2d Cir.1987).

appellate court is available in a range of circumstances. No system, however, permits appeal from orders made during the course of trial.[1] Federal statutes make appealable interlocutory orders granting, continuing, modifying, denying, or dissolving an injunction[2] or appointing a receiver. The Interlocutory Appeals Act grants discretion to the courts of appeals to review an interlocutory ruling by a district court if the latter in making the order states in writing that it involves a controlling question of law on which substantial ground exists for difference of opinion and that an immediate appeal may materially advance the ultimate termination of the litigation.[3] Furthermore, the rigors of the final judgment rule have always been subject to circumvention in exceptional cases by resort to the prerogative writs (prohibition and mandamus).[4]

The practical impact of the final judgment rule on a procedural system is very great. It often means that extensive areas of procedure are largely trial-court law. This is true to a considerable extent for the law governing pretrial procedures (deposition, discovery, pretrial conference practice) and the law governing the granting of new trials. Even theoretically, much of the law in these and other areas is wisely committed to the discretion of the trial court. But the point made here goes beyond that. The final judgment rule makes many rulings so unlikely to remain alive as subjects of effective appellate review that relatively little appellate court law exists to mark the limits of trial court discretion.

E. ALLOCATING LITIGATION EXPENSES

Litigants have always complained of the expense of litigation. Although the procedural reforms of the twentieth century often have been supported on the ground that they would reduce litigation expense, today the cost of bringing or defending against a civil suit concerning a small sum is often more than the amount in dispute.[5] Civil litigation is a handmade luxury product whose expense has fostered calls for arbitration, mediation, and other forms of alternative dispute resolution. Inasmuch as civil litigation is very expensive, the allocation of litigation expenses between winner and loser is important. The basic rule in the American system is that each party pays his or her own litigation expenses. There are, however, many important qualifications and exceptions to this general proposition.

§ 1.22 Costs and Interest

The prevailing plaintiff or defendant normally recovers some expenses, known as "costs," from the losing party.[1] Costs include such

§ 1.21

1. N.Y. Civ. Prac. L. & R. 5701.

2. 28 U.S.C. § 1292(a).

3. 28 U.S.C. § 1292(b). Fed. R. Civ. Pr. 23(f) and 54(b) permit other discretionary interlocutory appeals.

4. *See* Chapter 12.

5. *See* § 6.3 *infra*.

items as court filing fees, court reporter charges, statutory witness fees, and certain copying costs.[2] Often a court clerk awards costs on the basis of a documented request by the prevailing party. The judge has some discretion to deny costs to a successful party or to apportion them when the party was only partially successful. A poor person proceeding *in forma pauperis* need not pay costs.[3]

A prevailing plaintiff (but not a prevailing defendant) also receives interest on any damage award as compensation for the delay expenses that litigation imposes. Interest for the period after the court enters its judgment is awarded virtually automatically.[4] A plaintiff is much less likely to receive interest for the period between the defendant's wrongful act and the judgment. Although the law governing such prejudgment interest varies from state to state,[5] interest is usually available when the parties contracted for it or when the sum due was "liquidated," that is, readily ascertainable. The rate for calculating interest was formerly fixed and low, but some jurisdictions now allow it to vary with other interest rates.[6]

§ 1.23 Attorney Fees: The American Rule

Under what we commonly call the "American Rule," a prevailing plaintiff does not normally recover from the loser its litigation expenses other than those classified as costs or interest. Thus the winning party must bear the costs of hiring expert witnesses and investigators. Nor will the party be reimbursed for time devoted to maintaining the case. And the winning party will be left to pay its own attorney's fees, which usually constitute by far the largest expense of litigation.

Comparison to English Rule

Almost all civil litigation systems, except in the United States and Japan, reject the American Rule and follow the "English Rule," under which a prevailing party recovers all or most of its attorney's fees from the loser.[1] (Under a third rule, followed in some instances, the government bears the attorney's fees as part of the costs of the judicial system.)

§ 1.22

1. *E.g.,* Fed. R. Civ. P. 54(d); § 12.5 *infra.*

2. *E.g.,* 28 U.S.C. § 1920.

3. *E.g.,* 28 U.S.C. § 1915; Duniway, The Poor Man in the Federal Courts, 18 Stan. L. Rev. 1271 (1966); *see* Boddie v. Connecticut, 401 U.S. 371, 91 S.Ct. 780, 28 L.Ed.2d 113 (1971).

4. *E.g.,* 28 U.S.C. § 1961.

5. *Compare, e.g.,* R.I. Gen. Laws 9–21–10 (12 percent interest from accrual of cause of action) *with* Prime Management Co. v. Steinegger, 904 F.2d 811 (2d Cir. 1990) (under Connecticut law, prejudgment interest is within court's discretion); *see* Note, The Availability of Prejudgment Interest in Personal Injury and Wrongful Death Cases, 16 U.S.F. L. Rev. 325 (1982).

6. *E.g.,* 28 U.S.C. § 1961.

§ 1.23

1. Pfennigstorf, The European Experience with Attorney Fee Shifting, 47 Law & Contemp. Probs. 37 (1984). Alaska has adopted a version of the English Rule. Alaska R. Civ. P. 82.

Proponents of the English Rule argue that someone whose claim or defense the courts reject should reimburse the prevailing party's expenses of securing vindication. The American Rule's advocates reply that seeking a court ruling on one's claim or defense is not a wrongful act even if one ultimately loses, but a socially desirable course of conduct for which one should not be penalized. They also point out that in a system like ours, in which attorney's fees are large and not prescribed by statute, the English Rule would lead to elaborate disputes about what attorney's fees a prevailing party was entitled to recover. These policy considerations were not the inspiration for the American Rule, which apparently arose from lawyers' struggle to escape regulation of the fees they could charge their own clients.[2] They do, however, help to sustain the continuing adherence to the American Rule.

Several scholars have analyzed the probable effects of the American Rule on what suits are brought or defended. These analyses indicate that, by comparison with the English Rule, the American Rule encourages those with weaker claims or defenses to bring them to court while discouraging those with stronger claims or defenses. It also probably encourages parties who expect their attorney's fees to be smaller than those of their adversaries and parties who would find paying an adversary's fees particularly burdensome. Some analysts also believe the American Rule tends to reduce the expense of litigation because it eliminates as a disputable issue the appropriate attorney's fee award that the prevailing party should receive.[3]

Whatever its justification or impact, the American Rule is well entrenched. In recent decades, some corporate tort reformers advocated importing the English Rule, presumably to discourage potential plaintiffs with questionable cases. As the previous paragraph should suggest, the effects of such an import would be complex and hard to predict. One study, for example, indicates that defendants are not satisfied with the version of the English Rule followed in Alaska, because they have to pay attorney fees when they lose cases, but when they win find it hard to recover them from all but the few wealthy plaintiffs. In any event, proponents of the English Rule have made little headway.[4]

Contingent fees

2. Leubsdorf, Toward a History of the American Rule on Attorney Fee Recovery, 47 Law & Contemp. Probs. 9 (1984).

3. *E.g.,* Rowe, Predicting the Effects of Attorney Fee Shifting, 47 Law & Contemp. Probs. 139 (1984); Shavell, Suit, Settlement, and Trial: A Theoretical Analysis Under Alternative Methods for the Allocation of Legal Costs, 11 J. Legal Stud. 55 (1982). *See* §§ 6.3, 6.4 *infra.* Some empirical evidence supports these analyses. Hughes and Snyder, Litigation and Settlement under the English and American Rules: Theory and Evidence, 38 J.L. & Econ. 225 (1995); Snyder & Hughes, The English Rule for Allocating Legal Costs: Evidence Confronts Theory, 6 J.L. Econ. & Org. 345 (1990).

4. Cox, Hope of the Tort System: Congressional Proposals for Reform, 19 Harv. J.L. & Pub. Pol'y 667 (1996); Di Pietro & Carns, Alaska's English Rule: Attorney's Fee Shifting in Civil Cases, 13 Alaska L. Rev. 33 (1996).

The American Rule operates in special ways for personal injury tort plaintiffs, almost all of whom have contingent fee arrangements with their lawyers. Under a contingent fee arrangement, a plaintiff who loses typically is liable for nothing but court costs (as defined above) and the lawyer's out-of-pocket disbursements. If plaintiff wins or gets a settlement, plaintiff's lawyer receives a substantial fraction of the plaintiff's recovery. Most frequently, this is one third, but it is also common to provide that the lawyer will receive an increasing percentage depending on whether the case settles before trial, is tried, or is appealed.[5] This arrangement encourages potential plaintiffs to sue but makes their lawyers wary of accepting cases unlikely to yield a recovery.

In effect, the contingent fee turns a plaintiffs' lawyer into an entrepreneur who invests in the portfolio of cases most likely to maximize his clients' overall recovery, and hence the lawyer's own income. Because of its entrepreneurial implications, almost all nations but the United States have traditionally forbidden contingent fees as encouraging lawyer over-reaching and greed. Recently, however, England and France have legalized variants of the contingent fee. The argument for contingent fees is that, especially where the American Rule prevails, they provide access to the courts for plaintiffs unable to pay their lawyers in advance, and that they align the incentives of client and lawyer. The alignment of incentives is not complete: contingent fee lawyers can sometimes profit by settling a client's case rather than invest the time needed to increase the recovery. But lawyers' interests can diverge from those of their clients under any fee system: an hourly fee lawyer is tempted to put in too many hours on the case, and one on a salary too few. In practice, the behavior of lawyers receiving different kinds of fees seems to differ less than economists might predict.[6]

§ 1.24 Exceptions to the American Rule

Statutory exceptions

Since the American Rule was recognized during the nineteenth century, state and federal legislatures have passed thousands of statutes creating exceptions to it.[1] Many of these make it much easier for one party—usually the plaintiff—to recover its attorney's fees when it prevails than for the other party. This is commonly called a "one-way fee shifting" rule. Legislatures have done this to encourage plaintiffs to

5. Mackinnon, Contingent Fees (1964); Kritzer, The Wages of Risk: The Returns of Contingency Fee Legal Practice, 47 DePaul L. Rev. 267 (1998).

6. Clermont & Currivan, Improving on the Contingent Fee, 63 Cornell L. Rev. 529 (1927); Kritzer, et al., The Impact of Fee Arrangement on Lawyer Effort, 19 L. & Soc'y Rev. 251 (1985). England: Access to Justice Act 1999 (c. 22), § 27. France: Law No. 91-647, July 10, 1991, art. 72.

§ 1.24

1. 3 Newberg, Class Actions § 7040 (1985); Note, State Attorney Fee Shifting Statutes: Are We Quietly Repealing the American Rule?, 47 Law & Contemp. Probs. 321 (1984).

enforce valued rights, for example in civil rights litigation,[2] and sometimes to balance out inequality in litigating resources.[3]

Attorney's fee statutes have given rise to many questions.[4] When does a party "prevail"? How should courts assess the "reasonable attorney fees" that most statutes award? May a party bargain away a lawyer's fee award for a better settlement?[5] May a lawyer contract with a client in advance for a fee larger than what the court awards?[6] Fee award disputes usually arise after the merits of the case have been resolved and often develop into a suit within a suit. The Federal Rules and decisional law provide procedures for resolving these disputes. Fee claimants must provide documentation of lawyer hours and other items; discovery and evidentiary hearings are discouraged but sometimes allowed; and judges enter written findings explaining their reasoning when they pass on fee claims for more than a small amount.[7]

Other exceptions

Courts have recognized other exceptions to the American Rule even in the absence of a statute. Many contracts provide that the party writing the contract—such as a bank or landlord—may recover its attorney's fees from the other party if it must sue to enforce its rights. Contractual provisions of this kind are generally enforceable according to their terms, but many states regulate the size of the allowable fee recovery. Again, courts have allowed a plaintiff whose success confers a monetary or nonmonetary benefit on others (for example, by means of a class action) to make the others pay their share of the expenses when that can easily be done, for example, by taking the payment out of a "common fund" in the court's control.[8] Occasionally, a plaintiff recovers attorney's fees as part of its damages, as when the defendant's malicious prosecution of the plaintiff forces the plaintiff to pay for criminal defense counsel.[9]

Fees as sanctions

Courts recently have become more willing to make a party pay all or part of its opponent's attorney's fees as a sanction for litigation misconduct. The Federal Rules, for example, authorize judges to require a fee

2. *E.g.,* 42 U.S.C. § 1988; Christiansburg Garment Co. v. Equal Employment Opportunity Commission, 434 U.S. 412, 98 S.Ct. 694, 54 L.Ed.2d 648 (1978).

3. *E.g.,* 28 U.S.C. § 2412 (certain suits against federal government).

4. *See generally* Derfner and Wolf, Court Awarded Attorney Fees (1990).

5. Evans v. Jeff D., 475 U.S. 717, 106 S.Ct. 1531, 89 L.Ed.2d 747 (1986) (yes).

6. Venegas v. Mitchell, 495 U.S. 82, 110 S.Ct. 1679, 109 L.Ed.2d 74 (1990) (yes).

7. *See* Fed. R. Civ. P. 54(d); Hensley v. Eckerhart, 461 U.S. 424, 103 S.Ct. 1933, 76 L.Ed.2d 40 (1983); Larson, Federal Court Awards of Attorney's Fees 241–283 (1981).

8. *E.g.,* Boeing Co. v. Van Gemert, 444 U.S. 472, 100 S.Ct. 745, 62 L.Ed.2d 676 (1980); Hall v. Cole, 412 U.S. 1, 93 S.Ct. 1943, 36 L.Ed.2d 702 (1973).

9. *See* Leubsdorf, Recovering Attorney Fees as Damages, 38 Rutgers L. Rev. 439 (1986).

payment when a party files an unfounded pleading or resists discovery without justification.[10] Courts in some jurisdictions have a general power to sanction bad faith litigation.[11] Lawyers as well as clients may be required to pay.[12]

The increase in various kinds of attorney's fee award provisions has profoundly affected civil litigation. We seem to be moving toward a new regime, neither the American Rule nor the English Rule, under which courts award fees in many situations to implement many policies. Fee awards encourage some claims and defenses and discourage others. An award increases the power of the judge who awards the fee over the litigants or lawyers who pay or receive the fee. That in turn creates new tensions between litigants and their lawyers.

10. Fed. R. Civ. P. 11, 37. *See* §§ 3.13, 5.14 *infra*.

11. *E.g.,* Chambers v. NASCO, Inc., 501 U.S. 32, 111 S.Ct. 2123, 115 L.Ed.2d 27 (1991); Cal. Civ. Proc. Code § 128.5.

12. 28 U.S.C. § 1917; Roadway Express v. Piper, 447 U.S. 752, 100 S.Ct. 2455, 65 L.Ed.2d 488 (1980).

Chapter 2

PROPER COURT IN CIVIL ACTIONS

§ 2.1 Introduction

In this chapter we deal with rules that determine in which court an action may be brought. These rules fall into two general categories: rules of jurisdiction and rules of venue. Rules of jurisdiction comprise two subcategories: rules of personal jurisdiction and rules governing subject matter jurisdiction. These bodies of rules are similar to each other in that they define the court or courts in which a civil action may be properly maintained. They are also similar in that some rules of jurisdiction and all rules of venue are formulated in terms of the geographical location of the court in which the action may be maintained. They differ from each other, however, in several important respects.

Jurisdiction

Rules of jurisdiction in a sense speak from a position outside the court system and prescribe the authority of the courts within the system. They are to a large extent constitutional rules. The provisions of the U.S. Constitution specify the outer limits of the subject matter jurisdiction of the federal courts and authorize Congress, within those limits, to establish by statute the organization and jurisdiction of the federal courts. Thus, Article III of the Constitution defines the judicial power of the United States to include cases arising under federal law and cases between parties of diverse state citizenship as well as other categories.[1] The U.S. Constitution, particularly the Due Process Clause,[2] also establishes limits on the jurisdiction of the state courts. These due process limitations traditionally operate in two areas: jurisdiction of the subject matter and jurisdiction over persons. Within each state, the court system is established by state constitutional provisions or by a combination of such provisions and implementing legislation, which together define the authority of the various courts within the system.[3]

§ 2.1

1. U.S. Const. art. III, 1, 2. *See* Chemerinsky, Federal Jurisdiction ch. 3 (3d ed.1999); *compare* Amar, A Neo–Federalist View of Article III: Separating the Two Tiers of Federal Jurisdiction, 65 B.U.L. Rev. 205 (1985); Clinton, A Mandatory View of Federal Court Jurisdiction: A Guided Quest for the Original Understanding of Article III, 132 U. Pa. L. Rev. 741 (1984). *See also* Glidden Co. v. Zdanok, 370 U.S. 530, 82 S.Ct. 1459, 8 L.Ed.2d 671 (1962).

2. U.S. Const. amend. XIV, 1. *See* § 2.3 *infra.*

3. *See* U.S. Dept. of Justice, Law Enforcement Assistance Administration, National Survey of Court Organization (1973).

Rules of jurisdiction have the following characteristics:

1. They are formulated in terms of either the territorial extent of the court's authority or the subject matter of the action,[4] or both.
2. They regulate the authority of the court to hear and determine particular types of actions.
3. Because these rules govern the authority of the court, noncompliance with them results in the judgment in the action being, under some circumstances, vulnerable to legal attack even after it has apparently become final.[5]

Venue

Rules of venue are usually prescribed by statute,[6] although in some states they may be found in constitutional provisions. Venue rules presuppose that within the court system to which they apply, *some* court will have authority to hear the case—that is, have jurisdiction of the case. They prescribe which court within the system ought to hear the case based on conceptions of fairness to the parties and convenience of trial. Thus, they address the internal operation of the court system, as rules of fair and efficient judicial administration. Venue rules have the following characteristics:

1. They are formulated in terms of the relationship between the subject matter of the action and the territorial location of the court.[7]
2. They confer a privilege on the defendant to object to the action's being maintained in a court in which the venue is improper.
3. Because they involve a privilege of the defendant rather than the authority of the court, noncompliance with venue rules is an

4. For example, the subject matter jurisdiction of the federal courts includes actions between persons who are citizens of different states and actions involving claims based on federal law. *See* § 2.5 *infra*. The jurisdiction of a state court may be defined in terms of the monetary amount in controversy or some other attribute of a controversy, such as the fact that it involves divorce or probate or a dispute over title to land. *See* § 2.22 *infra*.

5. *See* § 12.17 *infra*.

6. *See, e.g.*, 28 U.S.C. § 1391. *See* N.Y. Temp. Commn. on the Courts, Advisory Committee on Practice and Procedure, First Preliminary Report 497: Venue Statutes in the Forty-Eight States (1957).

7. Thus, 28 U.S.C. § 1391(a) provides that an action in which jurisdiction is "founded only on diversity of citizenship" may be brought only in:

1. a judicial district where any defendant resides if all defendants reside in the same state,
2. a judicial district in which a substantial part of the events or omissions giving rise to the claim occurred, or a substantial part of property that is the subject of the action is situated, or
3. a judicial district in which any defendant is subject to personal jurisdiction at the time the action is commenced if no other district is available.

objection that must be taken at the threshold of the litigation and is waived if not so taken.[8]

Significance of "jurisdiction"

Two other points should be mentioned. First, the rules of venue refer to trial courts, not appellate courts. There is no concept of "venue" as applied to appellate courts, only a concept of jurisdiction. The jurisdiction of an appellate court is defined in terms of the lower courts from which appeals may be taken to that court.[9] Second, it is sometimes difficult to determine whether a rule specifying the proper trial court is a rule of venue or of jurisdiction. State constitutional or statutory provisions typically provide, for example, that actions concerning real property shall be brought in the county where the land is located.[10] Is this a rule of venue or of jurisdiction? Important consequences follow from the classification. If it is considered a rule of venue, then several results follow: (1) any objection to the court's hearing the case must be made at the threshold of the litigation; (2) if the objection is made and sustained, the action must be transferred to or recommenced in the proper county; (3) if the objection is not made at the threshold of the proceeding, it is waived and the judgment is not subsequently challengeable on the ground that the action was in the wrong court. If, however, it is considered a rule of jurisdiction, under conventional doctrine the objection may be taken at any time, even on appeal, and the judgment may be subject to still later attack on the ground that it is "void" because the court lacked jurisdiction.[11]

§ 2.2 Allocation of Judicial Business Between State and Federal Courts: In General

As noted in Chapter 1, each state has two parallel court systems, one state and the other federal. The problem of allocating business between them is part of the greater problem of allocating legal authority between the national and state governments in our complex federal system. That is a complicated subject itself, but identifying its principal aspects is important here because problems of jurisdiction often intersect problems of procedure, especially in federal courts.

8. *See* Fed. R. Civ. P. 12(h)(1); Note, Waiver of Federal Venue Privilege, 4 Ala. L. Rev. 127 (1951); *see, e.g.,* Cal. Civ. Proc. Code § 396b; Newman v. Sonoma County, 56 Cal.2d 625, 15 Cal.Rptr. 914, 364 P.2d 850 (1961).

9. *See, e.g.,* Korn, Civil Jurisdiction of the New York Court of Appeals and Appellate Divisions, 16 Buffalo L. Rev. 307 (1967); Sales and Cliff, Jurisdiction in the Texas Supreme Court and Courts of Civil Appeals, 26 Baylor L. Rev. 501 (1974).

10. *See* Annot., 115 A.L.R. 504.

11. *See, e.g.,* Fed. R. Civ. P. 12(h); Barquis v. Merchants Collection Assn., 7 Cal.3d 94, 101 Cal.Rptr. 745, 496 P.2d 817 (1972); §§ 4.2, 4.3, 12.7 *infra.*

Federal courts

The federal courts have restricted jurisdiction in that they are authorized to hear only those cases specified in Section 2, Article III of the Constitution and, within those limitations, only the cases that Congress by statute authorizes them to hear. A case not within such an authorized category can be brought only in a state court. Three categories include the vast bulk of federal district court litigation: cases to which the United States is a party (including prosecution of federal crimes);[1] cases between citizens of different states ("diversity of citizenship"); and cases arising under the Constitution, laws, and treaties of the United States ("federal question"). At the appellate level, the United States Courts of Appeals have jurisdiction of appeals from the federal district courts, but none over state courts even in cases involving questions of federal law; the Supreme Court has appellate jurisdiction over the lower federal courts, and over state courts with regard to questions of federal law.[2] Under Article III, the judicial power of the courts extends only to actual "cases" or "controversies." One necessary aspect of a "case" or "controversy" is that "the litigant is entitled to have the court decide the merits of the dispute or of particular issues."[3]

Diversity jurisdiction

The federal courts' diversity jurisdiction includes cases between citizens of different states (a corporation is treated as a citizen of the state of its incorporation and the state where its principal place of business is located) in which the amount in controversy exceeds $75,000, exclusive of interest and costs.[4] In such cases, however, federal and state courts have concurrent jurisdiction; the plaintiff has the choice of bringing such a case either in an appropriate federal court or an appropriate state court. But this choice is subject to the defendant's power, if defendant is a nonresident of the state where suit is brought, to remove the case from the state court to the federal court for the district in which the state court is located.[5]

Federal question jurisdiction

The federal district courts have federal question jurisdiction in cases where the plaintiff's claim is based on federal law ("general federal question")[6] and in specified types of federal question cases including

§ 2.2

1. Although Article III confers jurisdiction on the federal courts in cases to which the United States is a party, the United States may not be sued except as statute permits. Williams v. United States, 289 U.S. 553, 53 S.Ct. 751, 77 L.Ed. 1372 (1933). Statutes permitting such suits include the Tucker Act, 28 U.S.C. § 1346(a), 1491 (contract actions), and the Federal Tort Claims Act, 28 U.S.C. § 1346(b). *See* Bator, Meltzer, Mishkin, and Shapiro, The Federal Courts and the Federal System 1090–1158 (3d ed. 1988); § 2.16 *infra.*

2. *See* § 1.15 note 6 *supra.*

3. Warth v. Seldin, 422 U.S. 490, 498, 95 S.Ct. 2197, 2205, 45 L.Ed.2d 343, 354 (1975). *See also* Animal Legal Defense Fund v. Quigg, 932 F.2d 920 (Fed.Cir.1991); § 2.26 *infra.*

4. 28 U.S.C. § 1332; see § 2.24 *infra.*

5. 28 U.S.C. § 1441; see § 2.31 *infra.*

6. 28 U.S.C. § 1331; see § 2.27 *infra.*

actions under congressional statutes regulating commerce[7] (such as securities regulation) and actions based on certain constitutional protections and statutory protections of equal rights.[8] In a few types of federal question cases (such as the antitrust laws and patent infringement cases), the jurisdiction of the federal courts is exclusive,[9] but otherwise the plaintiff may enforce a federal claim in state court.[10] This choice is subject to the power of the defendant (regardless of his or her residence) to remove the action if it is within the federal court's original jurisdiction, except in a few situations where plaintiff's choice of forum may not be overridden.[11] A special form of federal question jurisdiction is admiralty jurisdiction; here the governing federal law is a blend of admiralty procedure and substantive maritime law.[12]

Division of jurisdiction between state and federal courts

Whether this division of jurisdiction makes sense is debatable.[13] Some legal analysts think the federal courts' diversity jurisdiction should be either abolished or confined to cases involving multiple parties of diverse citizenship. It is also argued that the federal courts should have jurisdiction of all cases in which a substantial federal question is presented, whether in the complaint or by way of defense or counterclaim, and that many types of federal cases presently within the jurisdiction of the federal courts should be consigned to administrative agencies. These proposals have not yet commanded enough support to bring about congressional amendment of the governing statutes.

The role of the federal courts in the administration of justice is imperiled by the interaction of three forces. First, the volume of litigation in the federal courts has been steadily increasing over the past decades; the increase in the number of criminal cases has been accelerat-

7. 28 U.S.C. § 1337.

8. 28 U.S.C. § 1343.

9. The exclusivity of federal jurisdiction in patent and copyright infringement cases and other instances is made express by statute, 28 U.S.C. § 1338(a); exclusivity in antitrust actions is by judicial interpretation of the statute. *See* Blumenstock Bros. v. Curtis Publishing Co., 252 U.S. 436, 440, 40 S.Ct. 385, 386, 64 L.Ed. 649, 652 (1920). *See* Note, Exclusive Jurisdiction of the Federal Courts in Private Civil Actions, 70 Harv. L. Rev. 509 (1957).

10. Gulf Offshore Co. v. Mobil Oil Corp., 453 U.S. 473, 101 S.Ct. 2870, 69 L.Ed.2d 784 (1981). The state courts have a constitutional obligation to entertain federally created rights of action. *See* Testa v. Katt, 330 U.S. 386, 67 S.Ct. 810, 91 L.Ed. 967 (1947).

11. 28 U.S.C. § 1441. *See* Chemerinsky, Federal Jurisdiction § 5.5 (3d ed. 1999). On the classes of cases not removable, see Wright, Law of the Federal Courts § 38 (4th ed. 1983).

12. *See* Gilmore and Black, The Law of Admiralty (2d ed. 1975); Currie, Unification of the Civil and Admiralty Rules, 17 Me. L. Rev. 1 (1965). By the terms of the jurisdictional statute, 28 U.S.C. § 1333, a claimant may enforce a claim based on admiralty and maritime law in state court if the claim is one that can be enforced through state remedies.

13. *See generally* American Law Inst., Study of the Division of Jurisdiction Between State and Federal Courts (1968); Currie, The Federal Courts and the American Law Institute, 36 U. Chi. L. Rev. 1, 268 (1968, 1969); Friendly, Federal Jurisdiction: A General View (1973); Posner, The Federal Courts: Crisis and Reform (1985).

ed by the "war on drugs" of the 1980s, which in turn has cramped the civil dockets. Second, strong constituencies resist withdrawing from the federal courts any matters within their jurisdiction. For example, civil rights groups want to maintain federal court jurisdiction in that field and corporate lawyers want diversity jurisdiction to extend to major corporate litigation. Third, many groups, including the federal judiciary itself, want the federal courts to remain relatively small, elite, and nonbureaucratic. It is obviously impossible to meet all these demands. The definition of federal district court jurisdiction therefore tends to become politically entrenched. There seems little prospect of consensus for significant change.[14] Hence, federal district court jurisdiction is likely to remain much as it is—primarily claims based on federal law and diversity cases.

A. STATE PERSONAL JURISDICTION RULES

§ 2.3 Federal Constitutional Limitations on State Court Authority

Legislative jurisdiction

Each state has comprehensive legal authority to govern matters within its jurisdictional limits, subject to the limiting or superseding effect of federal law and the limitations on the powers of the states as specified in the Constitution. General governing authority may be described as the state's legislative authority, meaning the authority to prescribe the rules of law governing the conduct of persons in the affairs of ordinary life.[1] An aspect of this authority is the power to apply such rules even to matters of "multistate" character—that is, events and transactions crossing state lines or affecting persons in more than one state.

Adjudicative jurisdiction

Roughly coextensive with its legislative jurisdiction, each state has legal authority to adjudicate controversies arising out of the affairs of ordinary life. This authority is usually referred to as judicial jurisdiction over the person. The exercise of judicial jurisdiction implies the authority to enter legally binding judgments and to use the coercive powers of executive agencies (for example, the sheriff) to compel compliance with those judgments.[2] In this sense, judicial jurisdiction is dependent on the "power" of the state.

14. *See* Federal Courts Study Comm., Tentative Recommendations for Public Comment (1989).

§ 2.3

1. *See generally* Hart, The Relations Between State and Federal Law, 54 Colum. L. Rev. 489 (1954); Allstate Ins. Co. v. Hague, 449 U.S. 302, 101 S.Ct. 633, 66 L.Ed.2d 521 (1981).

2. *See generally* Brilmayer, An Introduction to Jurisdiction in the American System (1986). Corresponding concepts in international law provide analogy to state court jurisdiction. *See* Restatement (Third) of the

This constellation of state authority is not expressly conferred by the Constitution, except by the general reference in Amendment X.[3] Rather, the Constitution presupposes that the states have this authority. This presupposition is drawn from three factors: the historical fact that the states existed as independent political units before adoption of the Constitution; the legal circumstance that the states commissioned the delegates to the Constitutional Convention and ratified the Constitution itself; and an analogy of the states to independent nations.[4] It is from this analogy that the states are spoken of as "sovereign." But they are sovereign only in a qualified sense because the Constitution imposes important limitations on their authority, including their authority to exercise judicial jurisdiction.

The principal constitutional limitations on the judicial authority of the states are as follows:

Constitutional limitations

- The judicial power of the federal government, conferred in Article III, is exercised through acts of Congress creating the federal courts. One aspect of this power is that the U.S. Supreme Court has authority to review and determine questions of federal law decided by the state courts in cases heard by them.[5] Another federal constraint on the autonomy of state courts is that judgments rendered in federal courts must be respected by the states even when the judgments are in diversity cases where state law applies.[6] (The state courts are, however, not bound for purposes of *stare decisis*—that is, the principle of respect for precedents—by federal decisions of state law questions.) Another aspect of the federal judicial power is the federal courts' exclusive jurisdiction created by the Constitution (as in admiralty)[7] or by federal statute;[8] in such cases the state courts have no authority to adjudicate.

- The Full Faith and Credit Clause of Article IV and its implementing statute impose obligations on each state concerning the legal authority of sister states. This clause requires that states respect judgments rendered in sister states by giving effect to the legal rights established by such judgments.[9]

Foreign Relations Law of the United States pt. IV (1987).

3. U.S. Const. amend. X: "The powers not delegated to the United States by the Constitution, nor prohibited by it to the States, are reserved to the States respectively, or to the people."

4. Pennoyer v. Neff, 95 U.S. 714, 24 L.Ed. 565 (1878). *See also* Hanson v. Denckla, 357 U.S. 235, 78 S.Ct. 1228, 2 L.Ed.2d 1283 (1958).

5. Martin v. Hunter's Lessee, 14 U.S. (1 Wheat.) 304, 4 L. Ed. 97 (1816).

6. Semtek Int'l Inc. v. Lockheed Martin Corp., ___ U.S. ___, 121 S.Ct. 1021, ___ L.Ed.2d ___ (2001).

7. *See* U.S.C. § 1333.

8. Note, Exclusive Jurisdiction of the Federal Courts in Private Civil Actions, 70 Harv. L. Rev. 509 (1957).

9. U.S. Const. art. IV, 1: "Full Faith and Credit shall be given in each State to the public Acts, Records, and Judicial Proceedings of every other State"; 28 U.S.C. § 1738. *See* Scoles and Hay, Conflict of Laws §§ 24.8 *et seq.* (1982).

• The Privileges and Immunities Clause of Article IV[10] requires a state to give citizens of sister states access to its courts on the same terms as the state's own citizens have such access.[11]

• The Supremacy Clause of Article VI provides that the Constitution, federal laws, and treaties of the United States are the supreme law of the land and that state judges are bound to apply them in cases where they are applicable.

• The Commerce Clause requires that a state give access to its courts to persons (that is, both citizens and corporations) from other states who undertake to bring actions based on transactions in interstate commerce.[12]

Due Process Clause

• The Due Process Clause of Amendment XIV, adopted in 1868, has been construed to impose limitations on (1) the circumstances under which a state court may validly summon before it a person who is situated outside the state;[13] (2) the transactions over which a state court may exercise jurisdiction, particularly concerning property located in another state and concerning the status of persons resident in another state;[14] and (3) the circumstances under which a state may apply its own law to a transaction occurring entirely or substantially outside of its borders.[15] The clause also imposes requirements concerning the giving of reasonable notice to a party against whom a proceeding is brought in state court.[16]

• The Equal Protection Clause of Amendment XIV limits, to an ill-defined extent, the respects in which a state may treat persons from

10. U.S. Const. art. IV, 2: "The Citizens of each State shall be entitled to all Privileges and Immunities of Citizens in the Several States."

11. *See generally* Currie and Schreter, Unconstitutional Discrimination in the Conflict of Laws: Privileges and Immunities, in Currie, Selected Essays on the Conflict of Laws (1963).

12. *See* Allenberg Cotton Co. v. Pittman, 419 U.S. 20, 95 S.Ct. 260, 42 L.Ed.2d 195 (1974). *Cf.* Bendix Autolite Corp. v. Midwesco Enters., 486 U.S. 888, 108 S.Ct. 2218, 100 L.Ed.2d 896 (1988). It seems clear that Congress could, if it wished, enact statutory limitations on the extent to which state courts might exercise jurisdiction over corporations doing interstate business. In fact, Congress has done so only in the form of a statute governing the venue of actions against national banks, which has been interpreted as limiting state court jurisdiction. *See* National Bank of N. Am. v. Associates of Obstetrics and Female Surgery, Inc., 425 U.S. 460, 96 S.Ct. 1632, 48 L.Ed.2d 92 (1976); *cf.* Dr. Ing. H.C.F. Porsche v. Superior Court, 123 Cal.App.3d 755, 177 Cal.Rptr. 155 (1981) (limitations on jurisdiction provided in a treaty). It seems equally clear that Congress could establish such limitations in cases not involving interstate commerce through its power to give effect to the Due Process Clause.

13. *See* § 2.4 *infra.*

14. *See, e.g.,* Hanson v. Denckla, 357 U.S. 235, 78 S.Ct. 1228, 2 L.Ed.2d 1283 (1958); May v. Anderson, 345 U.S. 528, 73 S.Ct. 840, 97 L.Ed. 1221 (1953).

15. Home Ins. Co. v. Dick, 281 U.S. 397, 50 S.Ct. 338, 74 L.Ed. 926 (1930); Phillips Petroleum Co. v. Shutts, 472 U.S. 797, 105 S.Ct. 2965, 86 L.Ed.2d 628 (1985). The Due Process Clause also entitles litigants to an adequate hearing before an impartial tribunal. *See, e.g.,* Aetna Ins. Co. v. Lavoie, 475 U.S. 813, 106 S.Ct. 1580, 89 L.Ed.2d 823 (1986).

16. *See* § 2.10 *infra.*

other states differently from local persons with regard to access to court and application of governing law.[17]

Federalism

In the following discussion we will be concerned chiefly with the limitations of the Due Process Clause.[18] But it is important that the Due Process Clause limitations be considered with an eye to these other limitations as well. Taken together, the Constitution's limitations on the states make clear that the legal position of a state in the federal system is anything but "sovereign" in the sense of being essentially like that of an independent nation in the world of international law. It is true, as we shall see, that historically the decisions concerning the judicial authority of the states evolved from the premise that they were much like sovereign nations. The premise introduces difficulties that could be avoided if state judicial authority were viewed as a problem not of quasi-international law but of allocation of authority among coordinate units of a federal system. In broad terms, the evolution of the law on this subject has been a gradual and halting process of replacing the "sovereignty" theory of state court authority with a theory based on federalism.[19]

§ 2.4 Territoriality and Due Process

A basic idea of state court personal jurisdiction is that a state court has authority to enter judgment against a person who is in the state, and served with process, against property located in the state and involved in a transaction in the state, and against one who consents to jurisdiction.[1] The leading case on the problem of state judicial jurisdiction is *Pennoyer v. Neff*,[2] decided by the Supreme Court in 1878. This was the first case in which the limitations on state court jurisdiction were held to be derived from the Due Process Clause, which had then recently been adopted. But in deciding the case the Court relied substantially on much older doctrines and decisions. These had evolved in cases arising in two contexts: (1) where the plaintiff tried to invoke the jurisdiction of a state court, and it was argued that the state lacked authority to exercise

17. *See* Currie, Unconstitutional Discrimination in the Conflict of Laws: Equal Protection, 28 U. Chi. L. Rev. 1 (1960); *cf.* Sosna v. Iowa, 419 U.S. 393, 95 S.Ct. 553, 42 L.Ed.2d 532 (1975).

18. *See* text at notes 13–17 *supra.*

19. *See generally* von Mehren and Trautman, Jurisdiction to Adjudicate: A Suggested Analysis, 79 Harv. L. Rev. 1121 (1966); Hazard, Interstate Venue, 74 Nw. U.L. Rev. 711 (1979); Transgrud, The Federal Common Law of Personal Jurisdiction, 57 Geo. Wash. L. Rev. 849 (1989); Kogan, A Neo-Federalist Tale of Personal Jurisdiction, 63 S. Cal. L. Rev. 257 (1990). For revival of the "sovereignty" concept, see World-Wide Volkswagen Corp. v. Woodson, 444 U.S. 286, 100 S.Ct. 559, 62 L.Ed.2d 490 (1980).

§ 2.4

1. *See* Burnham v. Superior Court, 495 U.S. 604, 110 S.Ct. 2105, 109 L.Ed.2d 631 (1990).

2. 95 U.S. 714, 24 L.Ed. 565 (1878). For the history of this case, see Perdue, Sin, Scandal, and Substantive Due Process: Personal Jurisdiction and *Pennoyer* Reconsidered, 62 Wash. L. Rev. 479 (1987).

jurisdiction;[3] and, (2) where the plaintiff had obtained a judgment in one state and sought to rely on the judgment in another state, and in the second proceeding it was argued that the judgment was not entitled to recognition because the state rendering the judgment lacked legal authority to do so.[4]

Comity among states

In the first of these contexts, the court's jurisdiction was considered before *Pennoyer* to be a question of limitations resulting from the mutual respect that the states ought to show one another, similar to the mutual respect among independent nations. The idea was that state *A* should not attempt to exercise jurisdiction over persons or property in state *B* without their consent because that would disturb relations between the states. The roles expressing these limitations were considered a kind of domestic American international law;[5] they were not necessarily considered to be a legal implication of federalism and thereby governed by the Constitution.

Full Faith and Credit

In the second context (the recognition of sister state judgments), however, the rule was that the judgment had to be recognized under the Full Faith and Credit Clause *if* the state that rendered it had jurisdiction.[6] Hence, application of the full faith and credit rule could involve the question whether the state that rendered the judgment had jurisdiction. In this context, the question of state court jurisdiction was clearly a matter of constitutional law. These two streams of doctrine both flowed alongside of and mixed with each other. As a result, doctrines and decisions concerning state judicial jurisdiction that evolved up to *Pennoyer v. Neff* peculiarly combined the incompatible ideas that the states were independent sovereigns and that their judicial jurisdiction was subject to constitutional requirements.

State sovereignty

Pennoyer v. Neff established the proposition that constitutional requirements operated in both contexts in which the question of jurisdiction might arise, that is, a state's original rendition of judgment and the situation of subsequent recognition of judgment in another state. If a state court entered judgment in a case in which *Pennoyer*'s personal jurisdiction requirements were lacking, it both denied the defendant due process in that court, and was not entitled to full faith and credit in another state's courts. Since constitutional limits operated in both contexts, the result has been that the scope of state court jurisdiction is

3. *See* Hazard, A General Theory of State Court Jurisdiction, 1965 Sup. Ct. Rev. 241, 253–256, 261.

4. *Id.* at 256–258.

5. Pennoyer v. Neff, 95 U.S. 714, 730, 24 L.Ed. 565, 571 (1878).

6. *Id.*, 95 U.S. at 731, 24 L. Ed. at 571.

controlled by federal constitutional law. On the other hand, the scope of that jurisdiction was conceived in terms of the states being independent sovereigns. As the Supreme Court said:

> The several States of the Union are not, it is true, in every respect independent.... But, except as restrained and limited by [the Constitution], they possess and exercise the authority of independent States, and the principles of public law ... are applicable to them. One of these principles is, that every State possesses exclusive jurisdiction and sovereignty over persons and property within its territory.[7]

Persons and property within the territory

The rule that a state has jurisdiction over persons and property who are within its territorial limits or consent to jurisdiction seems simple enough, especially when compared to today's personal jurisdiction law. Thus, if a person is in a state and is served with process, the court may enter a money judgment against him or her that is valid in the state where rendered and is entitled to recognition in other states. A judgment based on such service of process is called an in personam judgment because jurisdiction is based on the state's having legal authority over the defendant's person. If property is in a state and is "seized" at the commencement of the action, the court may enter a judgment determining rights in the property; the judgment generally was valid under *Pennoyer* in the state where rendered and was entitled to recognition in other states, although we shall see later that the Supreme Court has drastically restricted jurisdiction based on property.[8] A judgment based on this kind of exercise of jurisdiction is called an in rem judgment.

The conventional doctrine of jurisdiction developing from *Pennoyer* distinguished three types of in rem proceedings, although all began with the idea that the state has legal authority over the property involved. These three types are as follows:

Three types of in rem jurisdiction

In rem, against-all-the-world: The action concerns disputed claims to particular property (for example, a tract of land or a bank account), is accompanied by an appropriate form of notice (such as mail to record the owner's notice) addressed to all persons who may have claims to the property, and has the effect of determining the interests of all persons who might have claims to it.[9]

7. *Id.*, 95 U.S. at 722, 24 L. Ed. at 568.

8. *See, e.g.*, Pennington v. Fourth Natl. Bank, 243 U.S. 269, 37 S.Ct. 282, 61 L.Ed. 713 (1917); Weintraub, Commentary on the Conflict of Laws 140–141 (1971); *cf.* Western Union Tel. Co. v. Pennsylvania, 368 U.S. 71, 82 S.Ct. 199, 7 L.Ed.2d 139 (1961); § 2.7 *infra*.

9. Restatement (Second) of Judgments § 30, Comment *a;* Restatement (Second) of Conflict of Laws §§ 56–58; Weintraub, Commentary on the Conflict of Laws 140 (1971); von Mehren and Trautman, Jurisdiction to Adjudicate: A Suggested Analysis, 79 Harv. L. Rev. 1121 (1966).

Quasi in rem, against specific persons: The action concerns the claims to particular property of specifically named persons who are made parties to the proceeding; it has the effect of determining the interests of those persons but not others.[10]

Quasi in rem, attachment: The action concerns a claim that does *not* relate to the property. Through attachment or sequestration, property concededly owned by defendant is seized at the beginning of the action and held with a view to giving it to the plaintiff if the claim against the defendant is sustained on its merits.[11] For example, plaintiff may attach a bank account of the defendant in the state where the bank is located, plead a claim for tort or contract, and, if judgment is for plaintiff on the claim, then obtain an order directing the bank to pay the account (up to the amount of the judgment) to the plaintiff.

Historical weakness

Although *Pennoyer* asserts its territorial theory of personal jurisdiction with great confidence, the careful reader will note that few supporting authorities are provided. In fact, the theory was created by American judges during the nineteenth century. It diverged, for example, from English practice, under which a domiciliary could be sued without personal service, while *quasi in rem* jurisdiction had been abolished.[12] It diverged even more from practice that obtains today in some Continental nations, which reject jurisdiction based on personal service while allowing jurisdiction based on the plaintiff's citizenship (as in France) or permitting (as in Germany) the presence of the defendant's property to support a judgment not limited by that property's value.[13] The promulgation by the Supreme Court of the *Pennoyer* scheme provided a way of reining in exorbitant assertions of jurisdiction by state courts, while implementing the belief of judges of that era in clear Constitutional boundaries demarcating the proper spheres of state and federal governments.

Difficulties with "sovereignty" theory

Whatever its pedigree, the concept of states as sovereigns in our federal system is a source of unavoidable confusion. It involves the

10. Sources cited in note 9 *supra*.

11. Restatement (Second) of Judgments § 32; Restatement (Second) of Conflict of Laws §§ 66–68. *See* Carrington, The Modern Utility of Quasi in Rem Jurisdiction, 76 Harv. L. Rev. 303 (1962).

12. Korn, The Development of Judicial Jurisdiction in the United States: Part I, 65 Brook. L. Rev. 935 (1999); Weinstein, The Early American Origins of Territoriality in Judicial Jurisdiction, 37 St. Louis U.L.J. 1 (1992); Hazard, n. 3 *supra*; Ehrenzweig, The Transient Rule of Personal Jurisdiction: The "Power" Myth and Forum Conveniens, 65 Yale L.J. 289 (1956).

13. Lowenfeld, International Litigation and the Quest for Reasonableness ch. 4 (1996); Juenger, Federalism: Judicial Jurisdiction in the United States and in the European Communities: A Comparison, 82 Mich. L. Rev. 1195 (1984). The Brussels Convention now prevents members of the European Union from asserting such jurisdictional grounds against each others' nationals, but leaves them free to do so against Americans and others. *See* § 2.21 *infra*.

contradiction of saying both that the states are sovereigns, that is, legal worlds of their own independent of other authority, and that the scope of their jurisdictional authority is governed by the superior law of the federal Constitution. In modern times, when the United States has become as economically and socially united as France, for example, the idea that the states are sovereigns rather than provinces is both quaint and misleading.

Pennoyer's own facts and holding demonstrate the weakness of its sovereignty rationale. The Court held invalid a state court judgment because the defendant had been given only service by publication in a newspaper rather than personal service, and because the plaintiff attached the land used to pay the resulting default judgment after that judgment was entered rather than at the outset of the action. But the attached land was located within the state of Oregon, whose court rendered and enforced the judgment. Under the Supreme Court's own territorial logic, seizing land within the state was clearly within Oregon's powers as a sovereign, so it should have been upheld. Indeed, there was and is authority upholding post-judgment attachment.[14] The Supreme Court's holding, unlike its language, probably reflected considerations of procedural fairness rather than of territorial power.

Pennoyer v. Neff contains another anomaly in its observation that a state may grant a divorce to its inhabitant even though the other spouse is outside the state. The Court justified this jurisdiction as reflecting the state's power over the status, here the marital status, of its inhabitants. Apparently it thought of this status as located within the state. But a valid divorce clearly reaches outside the state: both spouses are divorced, including the one outside the state. The *Pennoyer* court bent its territorial principles a bit in order to deal with the plight of spouses, usually women, whose spouses had deserted them, could not be served in the state, and often could not be located at all.[15]

A final ambivalence in *Pennoyer* concerns its declaration that an out of state defendant may consent to personal jurisdiction. Consent may occur in different ways–by appearing in a case without objecting to jurisdiction, by agreeing in advance, by filing a suit that exposes one to counterclaims, or by engaging in activities that the state conditions on consent–some of which verge on legal fiction.[16] But even when consent is

14. Tocklin, *Pennoyer v. Neff:* The Hidden Agenda of Stephen J. Field, 28 Seton Hall L. Rev. 75 (1997); Note, The Requirement of Seizure in the Exercise of Quasi in Rem Jurisdiction: Pennoyer v. Neff Re-examined, 63 Harv. L. Rev. 657 (1950).

15. *See* Hartog, Man and Wife in America: A History (2000); Friedman, Rights of Passage: Divorce Law in Historical Perspective, 63 Oregon L. Rev. 649 (1984). Whether *Pennoyer* allowed the abandoning spouse as well as the abandoned one to obtain a divorce was long in dispute. *See* Maynard v. Hill, 125 U.S. 190, 8 S.Ct. 723, 31 L.Ed. 654 (1888); Haddock v. Haddock, 201 U.S. 562, 26 S.Ct. 525, 50 L.Ed. 867 (1906); § 2.7 *infra.*

16. *See* §§ 2.5, 2.9, 2.12, 4.7, 9.13 *infra*; National City Bank v. Republic of China, 348 U.S. 356, 75 S.Ct. 423, 99 L.Ed. 389 (1955).

genuine, how can a defendant's consent waive the sovereign rights of the state in which the defendant resides? If an Idaho farmer consents that the laws and government of Mississippi shall prevail on his farm, surely Idaho's sovereignty will nevertheless be violated if Mississippi proceeds to run courthouses and police stations on the farm. Obviously, the Court was not prepared to push to its logical conclusion its assertion that every state possesses exclusive sovereignty over persons and property within its territory.

Due process and state jurisdiction

Nevertheless, some limit on the powers of the states is essential to the logic of the law of state court jurisdiction. The logical relationship between due process and the scope of state court jurisdiction is as follows:

1. By fundamental principle of law, a person may not be required to answer in court, or be subjected to judgment by a court, if that court lacks legal authority to subject the person to its jurisdiction. This principle was established long before *Pennoyer* and is a premise in that decision.

2. A court lacks legal authority to subject a person to its jurisdiction unless the person is present within the territory of the political entity (state or nation) that constituted the court, or has property within that territory, or has some other recognized relationship on which it is appropriate to predicate the exercise of judicial authority. This proposition also is a premise in *Pennoyer*.

3. Proposition (1) above is a matter of due process under the Fourteenth Amendment. This is the critical step taken in *Pennoyer*:

> Since the adoption of the Fourteenth Amendment to the Federal Constitution, the validity [of a court's exercise of jurisdiction] may be directly questioned ... on the ground that proceedings in a court of justice to determine the personal rights and obligations of persons over whom the court has no jurisdiction do not constitute due process of law.[17]

Hence, if a state lacks the required legal authority to exercise jurisdiction over a person or property, then its purported effort to exercise such authority is a denial of due process.

The foregoing logic forms the basis of due process limitations on state court jurisdiction. This logic, however, has sometimes been disregarded by the Supreme Court. Thus, in *Insurance Corp. of Ireland v. Compagnie des Bauxites*,[18] the Court stated:

> The restriction on state sovereign power ... must be seen as ultimately a function of the individual liberty interest preserved by the Due Process Clause. That Clause is the only source of the personal jurisdic-

17. 95 U.S. at 733, 24 L. Ed. at 572.

18. 456 U.S. 694, 102 S.Ct. 2099, 72 L.Ed.2d 492 (1982).

tion requirement and the Clause itself makes no mention of federalism concerns.[19]

This statement is historically, analytically, and functionally questionable. Historically, some limits on state court jurisdiction evolved before the adoption of the Fourteenth Amendment. Hence, objections based on limitations on state power could be made before there was a Due Process Clause, for example as a defense to the enforcement of a state court judgment in another state. Analytically, the Due Process Clause presupposes other provisions of our constitutional structure, specifically the existence of the separate states to which the clause itself speaks. The clause does not "mention" federalism concerns; it takes them for granted in imposing constitutional limits on the states. Functionally, if only a citizen "liberty interest" were involved, then it would seem the *federal* government likewise would be precluded from infringing that interest. Yet it is settled that Congress can provide for nationwide service of process, even in private party disputes.[20]

Although the relevance of the states is thus built into the constitutional law of personal jurisdiction, it by no means follows that there is no alternative to *Pennoyer v. Neff*'s territorial theory, or its attempt to confine jurisdiction to cases instituted by the seizure of persons or property within the forum state's borders. Indeed, *Pennoyer*'s superficial simplicity concealed both intellectual and practical difficulties that ultimately led to its substantial modification. These difficulties can be grouped into the following problems: (1) What is meant by "presence" of a person or property within a state? (2) What are the effects on out-of-state property when jurisdiction is in personam and the effects on out-of-state persons when jurisdiction is in rem? and (3) How can persons outside a state be given legally effective notice of a proceeding, and if notice is given, what effect does it have?

§ 2.5 To *International Shoe* and Beyond

The rise of the business corporation tested the law of personal jurisdiction. The concept of jurisdiction over a person, leading to an in personam judgment, runs immediately into difficulty if the defendant is a corporation rather than a "flesh and blood" person. Since a corporation is not a physical entity, it cannot actually be present. Moreover, since the corporation is the creature of law, how can it have legal existence outside the state of its incorporation? By the late nineteenth century, corporations were spreading their business throughout the nation and beginning to dominate its economy. Claims by state citizens against corporations incorporated in other states multiplied. It could not be considered unfair to subject a large, multistate corporation to suit in a

19. 456 U.S. at 702 n.10, 102 S.Ct. at 2104 n.10, 72 L.Ed.2d at 501 n.10.

20. *See, e.g.*, State Farm Fire & Casualty Co. v. Tashire, 386 U.S. 523, 87 S.Ct. 1199, 18 L.Ed.2d 270 (1967) (interpleader); § 2.34 *infra*.

state where it did business, especially as railroads and telephones made it easier to reach the forum.

Presence of corporations

The courts solved this problem through three successively fashioned concepts. First, a corporation created by the law of one state could not have legal existence in another state unless the latter was willing to recognize that existence.[1] On this premise, the state could establish as a condition of giving recognition to a foreign corporation that the corporation appoint a person within the state to serve as an agent on whom process could be served.[2] The state statutes commonly provided, and still provide, that if the corporation fails to appoint its own specific agent, then a state official such as the Secretary of State shall be deemed the corporation's agent for service of process.[3]

This approach, involving presence conditioned on consent, subsequently encountered difficulty as applied to foreign corporations engaged in interstate business. It had been held that the Commerce Clause created a constitutionally protected right to engage in interstate business;[4] since the state could not refuse to allow the foreign corporation to conduct the local aspects of that business, it could not coerce the corporation into appointing an agent to receive service of process. This dilemma was solved by adopting a second concept, namely, that the corporation was "present" in the form of the presence of its employees, an office, maintenance of bank accounts, and so on, and that process could be served on its employee or, if none could be found, on that state's Secretary of State.[5] Over the course of time, this concept gave way to a third: The transactions themselves were considered a "presence."[6]

Presence of individuals

A parallel evolution of doctrine occurred concerning flesh-and-blood individuals. The original idea was that a person was present in a state and subject to its jurisdiction when he or she was physically present. The concept of actual physical presence was enlarged to include not only being present at the moment of service of process but also having some connection with the state. One such connection was domicile, so that

§ 2.5

1. Bank of Augusta v. Earle, 38 U.S. (13 Pet.) 519, 10 L. Ed. 274 (1839).

2. Lafayette Ins. Co. v. French, 59 U.S. (18 How.) 404, 15 L. Ed. 451 (1856).

3. *See* Restatement (Second) of Conflict of Laws § 41, Comment *c*; Note, Jurisdiction over Foreign Corporations: An Analysis of Due Process, 104 U. Pa. L. Rev. 381 (1955).

4. Sioux Remedy Co. v. Cope, 235 U.S. 197, 35 S.Ct. 57, 59 L.Ed. 193 (1914).

5. International Harvester Co. v. Kentucky, 234 U.S. 579, 34 S.Ct. 944, 58 L.Ed. 1479 (1914). *See also* Note, "Doing Business": Defining State Control over Foreign Corporations, 32 Vand. L. Rev. 1105 (1979).

6. Hutchinson v. Chase & Gilbert, 45 F.2d 139 (2d Cir.1930).

persons domiciled in a state were regarded as present even though they were physically absent.[7]

Another type of connection was established when a person came into the state, engaged in some transaction resulting in a legal dispute, and departed before having been served with process. Evolution of this concept began with the problem of motorists involved in accidents outside their home state. Courts held that since the state owned the roads, their use by an out-of-state motorist could be conditioned on the motorist's appointing someone as agent for service of process in any litigation rising from operation of the automobile in the state. State laws usually provided that the agent be the state's Secretary of State or Commissioner of Motor Vehicles.[8]

Of course, the consent of motorists to this procedure was more or less fictitious. It is highly dubious that the Privileges and Immunities Clause would allow a state to exclude outsiders from public roads freely accessible to its own residents, and motorists who have not studied civil procedure are unlikely to know the jurisdictional consequences of entering another state's roads. By upholding jurisdiction, the courts were recognizing that one who creates havoc within a state should be subject to suit there by local victims, regardless of whether the motorist can be served with legal process before driving out of the state.

International Shoe

The strands of doctrine concerning foreign corporations and nonresident individuals were drawn together in 1945 in *International Shoe Co. v. Washington*, where the Supreme Court said:

> Historically the jurisdiction of courts to render judgments in personam is grounded on their de facto power over the defendant's person.... But now ... due process requires only that in order to subject a defendant to a judgment in personam, if he be not present within the territory of the forum, he have certain minimum contacts with it such that the maintenance of the suit does not offend "traditional notions of fair play and substantial justice."
>
> The terms "present" or "presence" are used merely to symbolize those activities of the corporation's agent within the state which courts will deem to be sufficient to satisfy the demands of due process.... Those demands may be met by such contacts ... as make it reasonable, in context of our federal system of government, to require the corporation to defend the particular suit which is brought there.[9]

7. Milliken v. Meyer, 311 U.S. 457, 61 S.Ct. 339, 85 L.Ed. 278 (1940). *See* Restatement (Second) of Conflict of Laws § 29.

8. Hess v. Pawloski, 274 U.S. 352, 47 S.Ct. 632, 71 L.Ed. 1091 (1927).

9. 326 U.S. 310, 316–317, 66 S.Ct. 154, 158, 90 L.Ed. 95, 101–102 (1945). For an analysis and synthesis of the decisions leading from Pennoyer v. Neff to the "minimum contacts" rule of *International Shoe,* see Kurland, The Supreme Court, the Due Process Clause and the In Personam Jurisdiction of State Courts, 25 U. Chi. L. Rev. 569 (1958).

Specific jurisdiction

International Shoe thus established "minimum contacts" related to a claim as an alternative to "presence" as a basis of state court jurisdiction over that claim. Such jurisdiction is sometimes called "specific" jurisdiction because it is limited to a particular claim arising out of the defendant's contacts with the state, as opposed to "general" jurisdiction reaching *any* claim against a defendant.[10] The case arose from the state of Washington's attempt to bring suit in its own courts against the International Shoe Company to recover contributions that state law required employers to make to an unemployment compensation fund. The company had at least eleven salesmen who lived and sold shoes in Washington and reaped substantial income from their activities, but it was incorporated elsewhere and carefully avoided establishing a permanent office in Washington or allowing the salesmen to enter contracts there. Under previous law, it could argue with some hope of success that it was not "present" in Washington and was hence not subject to personal jurisdiction there. But the Supreme Court upheld jurisdiction because the state's claim for unemployment contributions arose out of the shoe company's contacts with the state.

Notice

In addition to recognizing specific jurisdiction, *International Shoe* also recognized new methods of giving notice as alternatives to the traditional service within the state. *Pennoyer v. Neff* had treated the service of process as a sovereign act that could take place only within the state's borders. *International Shoe* dispensed with the necessity of that kind of service. What it required was notice reasonably calculated to apprise the defendant of the suit–in the case before it, by registered mail to the defendant's headquarters and by service within the state on one of the shoe salesmen. The Court thus distinguished the acts of the plaintiff required to give notice from the acts of the defendant subjecting it to the jurisdiction of the Washington Court. Providing the latter were present, the plaintiff could sue a defendant located outside the state. At the same time, the Court made clear that the means of giving notice would have to be constitutionally adequate, and that meaningless formalities such as publishing notice in a newspaper would not necessarily suffice. Subsequent decisions have developed this point.[11]

Expanding jurisdiction

In addition to resolving these points, *International Shoe* raised many new questions or, to put it in other words, opened the way to further development. The opinion's concepts of "reasonable in the context of our federal system" and of "certain minimum contacts" consistent with

10. Von Mehren & Trautman, Jurisdiction to Adjudicate: A Suggested Analysis, 79 Harv. L. Rev. 1121 (1966).

11. *See* § 2.10 *infra*.

" 'traditional notions of fair play and substantial justice' " were a useful way to summarize earlier decisions applying the concept of "presence" to corporations and to specific activities such as the involvement of an out-of-state motorist in a local automobile accident. As a formula to govern future jurisdictional issues of nearly infinite variety, however, the formula is essentially question-begging. What is "reasonable in the context of our federal system"? The resolution of concrete problems is difficult, to say the least, through a formula that says essentially that jurisdiction exists if jurisdiction is reasonable. Courts have now been seeking for more than fifty years to give specific content to the concept of reasonableness.[12]

In retrospect, *International Shoe* can be seen as a New Deal or Progressive decision. This is clearly true of its immediate holding making it possible for Washington to enforce its unemployment compensation statute, but it is also true in other ways. The decision upheld governmental power to deal with social needs, and in particular to help underdogs. It recognized that the creation of a national economy required innovations reaching beyond state borders. And it sought to balance the relevant concerns of the people, corporations and governments involved flexibly and pragmatically, rather than laying down formal rules of limitation.

In jurisdictional law, this New Deal or Progressive tendency continued at least through 1957, when the Court decided *McGee v. International Life Insurance Co.*[13] The insurance company there had written to a California resident, offering to continue insuring him on the same terms as had a precursor insurer and had then received his premiums, but had no agent or office in California and was not shown to have engaged in any other business there. Nevertheless, the Court allowed the insured's mother and beneficiary to sue the insurer in California because of that state's interest in protecting its residents from the severe disadvantages of suing the insurer in its home state, Texas. This remains the most dramatic Supreme Court illustration of the use of long arm jurisdiction to protect the underdog and remedy comparative inconvenience.

Limiting jurisdiction

When the Supreme Court returned to the jurisdictional arena after a twenty year pause, it was with a different orientation. During the late 1970s and the 1980s, the Court handed down more than a dozen decisions, most of them upholding defendants' objections to jurisdiction. Perhaps this more restrictive view reflected for some Justices skepticism

12. *See* Symposium, Fifty Years of *International Shoe*: The Past and Future of Personal Jurisdiction, 28 U.C. Davis L. Rev. 513 (1995).

13. 355 U.S. 220, 78 S.Ct. 199, 2 L.Ed.2d 223 (1957); see also Travelers Health Ass'n v. Virginia, 339 U.S. 643, 70 S.Ct. 927, 94 L.Ed. 1154 (1950); Mullane v. Central Hanover Bank & Trust, 339 U.S. 306, 70 S.Ct. 652, 94 L.Ed. 865 (1950); Perkins v. Benguet Consol. Mining Co., 342 U.S. 437, 72 S.Ct. 413, 96 L.Ed. 485 (1952). But see Hanson v. Denckla, 357 U.S. 235, 78 S.Ct. 1228, 2 L.Ed.2d 1283 (1958).

about the benefits of litigation, especially tort litigation. Alternatively, one can see the Court as maintaining the basic thrust of *International Shoe* while trimming what it considers excesses and confronting new issues to which *International Shoe*'s generalities provide little guidance. Certainly the lower courts, while heeding the Supreme Court's cautions, nevertheless continued to uphold new assertions of jurisdiction.[14]

Whatever its goals, the Court during this period faced difficult problems and found it hard to develop consistent doctrine. It is difficult to reconcile statements in its opinions about such basic issues as the roles of tradition and development in jurisdiction law,[15] the relevance of state sovereignty,[16] and the bearing of litigants' inconvenience.[17] In the Court's most recent cases, one must count up the votes of Justices adhering to various opinions to ascertain just what a majority has decided.[18]

Although the Court has again been quiescent since 1990, no doubt it will eventually confront new jurisdictional disputes. Among the problems now looming on the horizon are actions against corporations from outside the United States, and suits arising from internet transactions.

§ 2.6 Long-Arm Jurisdiction

In response to *International Shoe*'s recognition of jurisdiction over claims arising from a defendant's contacts with a state, many states adopted "long arm" statutes. These statutes specify various types of events or transactions as minimum contacts and provide that a person involved in such a transaction can be served with process wherever he or she may be.[1] This is "special jurisdiction," limited to claims arising out of the defendant's contacts. As cases have been brought under the long arm statutes, courts have been required to evolve Constitutional limits for this kind of jurisdiction.

California and other states have adopted statutes simply providing that the state's "long arm" reaches as far as the Constitution will

14. Solimine, The Quiet Revolution in Personal Jurisdiction, 73 Tul. L. Rev. 1 (1998).

15. *Compare* Shaffer v. Heitner, 433 U.S. 186, 97 S.Ct. 2569, 53 L.Ed.2d 683 (1977) *with* Burnham v. Superior Court, 495 U.S. 604, 110 S.Ct. 2105, 109 L.Ed.2d 631 (1990).

16. *Compare* World–Wide Volkswagen Corp. v. Woodson, 444 U.S. 286, 100 S.Ct. 559, 62 L.Ed.2d 490 (1980) *with* Insurance Corp. of Ireland v. Compagnie des Bauxites, 456 U.S. 694, 702 n. 10, 102 S.Ct. 2099, 72 L.Ed.2d 492 (1982)(discussed in § 2.4 *supra*).

17. *Compare* World–Wide Volkswagen Corp. v. Woodson, 444 U.S. 286, 100 S.Ct. 559, 62 L.Ed.2d 490 (1980) *with* Asahi Metal Industry Co. v. Superior Court, 480 U.S. 102, 107 S.Ct. 1026, 94 L.Ed.2d 92 (1987).

18. Asahi Metal Industry Co. v. Superior Court, 480 U.S. 102, 107 S.Ct. 1026, 94 L.Ed.2d 92 (1987); Burnham v. Superior Court, 495 U.S. 604, 110 S.Ct. 2105, 109 L.Ed.2d 631 (1990).

§ 2.6

1. *See* Uniform Interstate and International Procedure Act, 13 U.L.A. 1980 (now withdrawn); Casad & Richman, Jurisdiction in Civil Actions (3d ed. 1998); Casad, Long Arm and Convenient Forum, 20 Kan. L. Rev. 1 (1971); Currie, The Growth of the Long Arm, 1963 U. Ill. L.F. 533.

permit: "A court of this state may exercise jurisdiction on any basis not inconsistent with the Constitution of this state or of the United States."[2] In other states, courts have construed variously phrased statutes to extend to the Constitutional limit, so that every long-arm case raises a Constitutional question but no issue of state law.[3]

Some statutes, without simply adopting the Constitutional standard, enumerate specific types of contacts: "The transaction of any business within this State," "the commission of a tortious act," "the ownership, use, or possession of any real estate,"[4] and so on. The legislatures adopting these statutes and the courts construing them presumably do not wish to reach the Constitutional limit, either to encourage outsiders to transact business involving the state without fear of local litigation, or to reduce their court caseloads, or in the hope of providing statutory standards easier to apply than Supreme Court caselaw. Under these statutes, nevertheless, two questions must be answered: Does the transaction constituting the contact come within the terms of the statute? If so, is applying the statute in the particular circumstances valid under the constitutional contacts rule?[5]

Statutory interpretation

The juxtaposition of these two questions is illustrated in *Gray v. American Radiator & Standard Sanitary Corp.*[6] In that case, Titan Valve Manufacturing Company, a corporation located in Ohio, made valves that were incorporated into water heaters made by American Radiator at a factory outside Ohio; the water heaters were in turn sold through normal distributional channels. One of them was installed in Illinois and there exploded, allegedly as a result of a defect in the valve, and injured the plaintiff. The court held that (1) the vending of a defective valve that could through normal commerce find its way into Illinois was the "commission of a tortious act within" Illinois, one of the categories in the Illinois long-arm statute; and that (2) as so interpreted and applied, the statute did not exceed the judicial jurisdiction of Illinois under the limitations imposed by the U.S. Constitution. This constitutional ruling, as we shall see, may no longer be valid.[7]

2. Cal. Civ. Proc. Code 410.10. *See* Symposium: California Jurisdiction, 21 Hast. L.J. 1104 (1970); *cf.* Comment, Constitutional Limitations on State Long Arm Jurisdiction, 49 U. Chi. L. Rev. 156 (1982).

3. Walkowitz, Going to the Limits of Due Process: Myth, Mystery and Meaning, 28 Duq. L. Rev. 233 (1990).

4. *See, e.g.,* Ill. Civ. Prac. Act § 17; N.Y. Civ. Prac. L. & R. 302(a).

5. *See, e.g.,* Ingraham v. Carroll, 90 N.Y.2d 592, 665 N.Y.S.2d 10, 687 N.E.2d 1293 (1997).

6. 22 Ill.2d 432, 176 N.E.2d 761 (1961).

7. Asahi Metal Industry Co. v. Superior Court, 480 U.S. 102, 107 S.Ct. 1026, 94 L.Ed.2d 92 (1987).

Lower courts have generally interpreted the long-arm statutes in favor of sustaining jurisdiction, as in *Gray,* and have applied the contacts rule of *International Shoe* with similar liberality.[8] When the contacts analysis is added to the previously recognized bases of state court jurisdiction, the result can be summarized as in the Restatement (Second) of Conflict of Laws § 27. According to the Restatement, jurisdiction to render an in personam judgment may be based, if the state statute so authorizes, on "presence, domicile, residence, ... doing business in the state, an act done in the state, causing an effect in the state by an act done elsewhere, ownership or possession of a thing in the state, [or] other relationships to the state which make the exercise of judicial jurisdiction reasonable."

Competing theories of federalism

But whether a connection between a transaction and a particular state makes that state's exercise of jurisdiction "reasonable" depends on the framework in which the problem is considered. One view considers the United States as a unitary community having subdivisions, historical in origin, called States, in which all manner of transactions occur without much regard for state lines. The participants in these transactions are free under the Privileges and Immunities, Due Process, and Equal Protection Clauses to perambulate, do business, engage in behavior involving possibilities for tort liability, and generally to incur obligations as though they were residents and citizens of a single political community. In such a community, the question of state court jurisdiction would be conceived as one of interstate venue and be based on the same principles for choice of court as are found in each state's venue rules.[9] The plaintiff could sue where a defendant resides or where a significant part of the transaction occurred, assuming the transaction occurred in the normal course of events. This view was reflected as early as 1914 in such cases as *International Harvester Co. v. Kentucky,*[10] in which a manufacturer selling in the national market was held subject to jurisdiction in a suit based on a transaction occurring in one of the states where it sold its goods. Other Supreme Court cases have reinforced this view, and state courts often use it to justify a long reach for their long-arm statutes.[11]

8. *See* Comment, In Personam Jurisdiction over Nonresident Manufacturers in Product Liability Actions, 63 Mich. L. Rev. 1028 (1965). *See also* Foster, Long-Arm Jurisdiction in Federal Courts, 1969 Wis. L. Rev. 9; Note, "Doing Business": Defining State Control over Foreign Corporations, 32 Vand. L. Rev. 1105 (1979).

9. *See* Hazard, Interstate Venue, 74 Nw. U.L. Rev. 711 (1979).

10. 234 U.S. 579, 34 S.Ct. 944, 58 L.Ed. 1479 (1914).

11. *E.g.,* International Shoe Co. v. Washington, 326 U.S. 310, 66 S.Ct. 154, 90 L.Ed. 95 (1945); McGee v. International Life Ins. Co., 355 U.S. 220, 78 S.Ct. 199, 2 L.Ed.2d 223 (1957); Burger King Corp. v. Rudzewicz, 471 U.S. 462, 105 S.Ct. 2174 85 L.Ed.2d 528 (1985); Buckeye Boiler Co. v. Superior Court, 71 Cal.2d 893, 80 Cal.Rptr. 113, 458 P.2d 57 (1969).

An alternate approach adheres to the historical conception of our system as a federal union of independent states: Each state has general authority within its territorial limits and only indirect authority outside those limits. The question of jurisdiction is accordingly one of "sovereignty" in which defendants are subject to jurisdiction only if they are present or have done an act that would indicate a temporary presence, such as entering a business transaction in the state. This view also appears frequently and is used by the Supreme Court when it holds that a state's jurisdictional reach has exceeded its constitutional grasp.[12]

Despite the Supreme Court's tendency to waver between these approaches, it has evolved three principles for assessing the Constitutional adequacy of long arm jurisdiction.

Purposeful availment

First, jurisdiction requires "some act by which the defendant purposefully avails itself of the privilege of conducting activities within the forum State."[13] The act is typically but not always one yielding benefit for the actor, such as selling goods or providing services.[14] In one case, however, the Court upheld jurisdiction over the editor of a defamatory article that inflicted harm within the forum state.[15] The purposeful availment requirement implements the federalism aspect of jurisdiction, although falling short of the territorial sovereignty logic of *Pennoyer v. Neff.* Rather, it reflects the belief that an outsider's voluntary involvement with a state provides a fair basis for subjecting that outsider to litigation arising out of that basis.[16]

Often, the requirement of purposeful availment singles out defendants who engage in interstate activities, and who are therefore able to defend in a foreign forum without disproportionate inconvenience. That is not always so, however, as witness *Burger King Corp. v. Rudzewicz,*[17] in which the Supreme Court allowed Burger King to drag to its Florida headquarters a far smaller Michigan franchisee that applied for its franchise through Burger King's Michigan office.

Another weakness of the requirement is that the purpose of a business organization is often unclear or irrelevant. For example, when a

12. *E.g.,* Helicopteros Nacionales de Colombia, S.A. v. Hall, 466 U.S. 408, 104 S.Ct. 1868, 80 L.Ed.2d 404 (1984); World-Wide Volkswagen Corp. v. Woodson, 444 U.S. 286, 100 S.Ct. 559, 62 L.Ed.2d 490 (1980).

13. Hanson v. Denckla, 357 U.S. 235, 253, 78 S.Ct. 1228, 2 L.Ed.2d 1283 (1958). Many other decisions quote this language.

14. *E.g.,* Keeton v. Hustler Magazine, 465 U.S. 770, 104 S.Ct. 1473, 79 L.Ed.2d 790 (1984).

15. Calder v. Jones, 465 U.S. 783, 104 S.Ct. 1482, 79 L.Ed.2d 804 (1984); see Redish, Of New Wine and Old Bottles: Personal Jurisdiction, the Internet, and the Nature of Constitutional Evolution, 38 Jurimetrics 575 (1998).

16. Perdue, Personal Jurisdiction and the Beetle in the Box, 32 B.C.L. Rev. 529 (1991) criticizes this theory of fairness.

17. 471 U.S. 462, 105 S.Ct. 2174, 85 L.Ed.2d 528 (1985); see Louis, Jurisdiction Over Those Who Breach Their Contracts: The Lessons of *Burger King*, 72 N.C.L. Rev. 55 (1993).

supplier sells components to another manufacturer who incorporates them into products that it sells in a state, as occurred in the *Gray* case, the supplier clearly benefits from the sale, but is this purposeful or merely knowing, and why does that matter? In *Asahi Metal Industry Co. v. Superior Court,*[18] four Supreme Court Justices said that jurisdiction over such a supplier is constitutionally forbidden, four said that it is proper, and Justice Stevens, the ninth Justice, reasoning more practically but less specifically, concluded that the acceptability of jurisdiction should depend on the volume and value of the supplier's sales.

Internet cases strain the "purposeful availment" test still more severely. One can think of the proprietor of a commercial website as dispatching sales information around the world in the hope of receiving orders, or as remaining at home where prospective customers may visit if they choose. The first reading would support jurisdiction outside the proprietor's home state under the "purposeful availment" approach, but the second would not. Some courts have therefore made jurisdiction turn on whether the defendant's site was "active" or "passive."[19] This unsatisfying distinction will presumably prevail unless cybercourts become available, or the Supreme Court follows Justice Stevens by upholding jurisdiction against internet proprietors engaged in substantial interstate business.[20]

Relation between claim and defendant's contacts

Second, long arm jurisdiction extends only over claims arising out of the defendant's contacts with the forum state, assuming those contacts to be adequate. This is what is meant by calling long arm jurisdiction specific jurisdiction, by contrast to general jurisdiction over all claims against the defendant. The relationship between the claim and the defendant's contacts has some slight tendency to promote the selection of a convenient forum, because it makes it more likely that relevant evidence will exist in the forum state. The requirement's main justification, however, derives from the theory under which the defendant's contacts with a state make it fair to require defense in that state of a claim arising from those contacts. Courts have disagreed as to whether a claim is sufficiently related if it would not have arisen but for the defendant's contacts, or if more is required,[21] another example of the

18. 480 U.S. 102, 107 S.Ct. 1026, 94 L.Ed.2d 92 (1987). For conflicting interpretations of the result, *compare* Barone v. Rich Bros., 25 F.3d 610 (8th Cir.1994) *with* Boit v. Gar–Tec Products, Inc., 967 F.2d 671 (1st Cir.1992).

19. *E.g.,* Cybersell, Inc. v. Cybersell, Inc., 130 F.3d 414 (9th Cir.1997); CompuServe, Inc. v. Patterson, 89 F.3d 1257 (6th Cir.1996); Zippo Mfg. Co. v. Zippo Dot Com, Inc., 952 F.Supp. 1119 (W.D.Pa.1997).

20. *See* Inset Systems, Inc. v. Instruction Set, Inc., 937 F.Supp. 161 (D.Conn. 1996); Maritz, Inc. v. Cybergold Inc., 947 F.Supp. 1328 (E.D.Mo.1996); *cf.* Carrington, Virtual Civil Litigation: A Visit to John Bunyan's Celestial City, 98 Colum. L. Rev. 1516 (1998).

21. Nowak v. Tak How Investments, Ltd., 94 F.3d 708 (1st Cir.1996); Shoppers Food Warehouse v. Moreno, 746 A.2d 320 (D.C.App.2000); Twitchell, The Myth of General Jurisdiction, 101 Harv. L. Rev. 610

tendency of long arm law to focus on factors having little to do with whether a given forum is a good place to resolve a dispute.

Inconvenience

Third, even when a claim arises from the out-of-state defendant's purposeful contacts with the forum state, the Constitution forbids the state's courts to hear the case if the defendant can show that doing so would be fundamentally unfair. This calls for evaluation of factors such as the burden on the defendant, the forum state's interests, the plaintiff's interest in obtaining relief, and the judicial system's interest in efficiency. Apparently, the defendant must bear a substantial burden of showing that the forum is inconvenient.[22]

This rather grudging formulation of the bearing of forum convenience, which most litigants would consider the most important factor in selecting the proper court, is a relatively recent development. *International Shoe* and its successors, as we have seen, placed a high value on counteracting inequalities between the resources of litigants.[23] More broadly, a unifying theme of the Supreme Court's jurisprudence has been that businesses engaged in operations that regularly involve ramifications in other states are generally subject to suit where those ramifications are felt, but an individual is subject to jurisdiction only for more intense spatial-temporal involvement. Since 1960 the Supreme Court has sustained state assertions of jurisdiction over interstate businesses involved in local transactions[24] but has reversed states' attempts to assert jurisdiction over nonresident persons such as a motorist for an accident occurring outside the state[25] and an automobile dealer who had been joined with the manufacturer in a products liability action brought in a jurisdiction halfway across the country from where the car was sold.[26]

Because assessments of inconvenience vary from case to case, any jurisdictional system relying on them is likely to be flexible, which also means that its results will sometimes be hard to predict. Often, convenience and inconvenience are reciprocal: a forum that is convenient for one party is inconvenient for the other, and vice versa. But often one party will have greater resources and interstate involvements than the other, and courts should take that into account.[27] And sometimes there is

(1988). What if one of a plaintiff's claims arises out of the defendant's contacts but another does not? *See* ESAB Group v. Centricut Inc., 126 F.3d 617 (4th Cir.1997) (court may decide both claims).

22. Asahi Metal Industry Co. v. Superior Court, 480 U.S. 102, 107 S.Ct. 1026, 94 L.Ed.2d 92 (1987); Burger King Corp. v. Rudzewicz, 471 U.S. 462, 105 S.Ct. 2174, 85 L.Ed.2d 528 (1985).

23. *See* § 2.5 *supra.*

24. *E.g.,* Keeton v. Hustler Magazine, 465 U.S. 770, 104 S.Ct. 1473, 79 L.Ed.2d 790 (1984).

25. Rush v. Savchuk, 444 U.S. 320, 100 S.Ct. 571, 62 L.Ed.2d 516 (1980).

26. World-Wide Volkswagen Corp. v. Woodson, 444 U.S. 286, 100 S.Ct. 559, 62 L.Ed.2d 490 (1980).

27. *E.g.,* McGee v. International Life Ins. Co., 355 U.S. 220, 78 S.Ct. 199, 2 L.Ed.2d 223 (1957). *Contra,* Burger King Corp. v. Rudzewicz, 471 U.S. 462, 105 S.Ct.

only one forum in which it may be possible to join all the parties involved in a controversy, so that failing to recognize jurisdiction over one party condemns another to litigate in several different forums or abandon its claims. Here too, courts should pay heed, and sometimes have done so.[28]

Kulko v. Superior Court[29] exemplifies the unfortunate consequences of disregarding the convenience factor. The plaintiff was a divorced wife who moved from New York to California, where both of the couple's children later decided to join her with the former husband's consent and, in one case, assistance. The Supreme Court refused to let the former wife sue for child support because the former husband had not purposefully availed himself of the privilege of conducting activities in California. (Having his children brought up there with his consent was not enough, although it is hard to think the Court would have thought so had he agreed to let them enroll in a California private school and had the school sued him for their tuition.) Yet California was the most convenient forum, since one spouse and both children were there. Moreover, the wife's suit also sought custody of the children, a claim that the California courts concededly had jurisdiction to hear. The Constitution should have been construed to allow litigation in the superior forum.

Overseas defendants

By contrast, in *Asahi Metal Industry Co. v. Superior Court*[30] the Court properly relied on convenience factors to reach a desirable result. The plaintiff there brought and later settled a California personal injury suit against the Taiwanese manufacturer of an allegedly defective motorcycle tire and the Japanese supplier of its valve. Before the settlement, the manufacturer brought a cross-claim against the supplier. It was this cross-claim that the Supreme Court held could not be pursued after the settlement before of the inconvenience to the Japanese defendant. Of course, California was also an inconvenient forum for the Taiwanese manufacturer, which presumably wished to litigate there rather in Japan for reasons other than convenience. The Court slightly clouded the issue by relying on the fact that the original plaintiff's claim had been settled and dismissed as part of its inconvenience analysis, since that implied that personal jurisdiction over a defendant can exist at the start of an

2174, 85 L.Ed.2d 528 (1985); Helicopteros Nacionales de Colombia, S.A. v. Hall, 466 U.S. 408, 104 S.Ct. 1868, 80 L.Ed.2d 404 (1984); see Weinberg, The Helicopter Case and the Jurisprudence of Jurisdiction, 58 So. Cal. L. Rev. 913 (1985).

28. Mullane v. Central Hanover Bank & Trust, 339 U.S. 306, 70 S.Ct. 652, 94 L.Ed. 865 (1950); see Phillips Petroleum Co. v. Shutts, 472 U.S. 797, 105 S.Ct. 2965, 86 L.Ed.2d 628 (1985); Helicopteros Nacionales de Colombia, S.A. v. Hall, 466 U.S. 408, 104 S.Ct. 1868, 80 L.Ed.2d 404 (1984). But see World-Wide Volkswagen Corp. v. Woodson, 444 U.S. 286, 100 S.Ct. 559, 62 L.Ed.2d 490 (1980).

29. 436 U.S. 84, 98 S.Ct. 1690, 56 L.Ed.2d 132 (1978); see Wasserman, Parents, Partners, and Personal Jurisdiction, 1995 U. Ill. L. Rev. 813.

30. 480 U.S. 102, 107 S.Ct. 1026, 94 L.Ed.2d 92 (1987).

action but disappear later, perhaps even in the middle of the trial. Nevertheless, dismissing the manufacturer's claim made sense.

Asahi is one of an increasing number of suits involving defendants from outside the United States that are now confronting the courts with new jurisdictional problems. Such suits may involve unusual inconvenience for the defendant, although requiring the plaintiff to sue overseas may only transfer the inconvenience from defendant to plaintiff. In the international context, moreover, the problems of governmental sovereignty that have long ebbed among the states take on new life. Many foreign nations object to aspects of international litigation brought in United States courts, for example because it involves service of process or discovery activities within their borders, the assertion of alien jurisdictional theories, or sometimes the application of United States law to their nationals. Many foreign nationals are only too glad to assert such objections, so that litigation may lead to procedural objections here, countersuits abroad, or judgments that foreign courts will not enforce.[31] Some also fear that too enthusiastic application of American long arm statutes will discourage foreign enterprises from doing business with Americans.[32] To some extent, these problems may be avoided by contracting in advance for arbitration of disputes in international transactions, or through treaties governing such matters as jurisdiction, service of pleadings, discovery, and enforcement of judgments.[33] To the extent this does not occur, United States courts will increasingly be urged to inflect jurisdictional law in response to the special features of international disputes.

§ 2.7 Presence of Property and Persons

Long arm jurisdiction is only one of the forms of personal jurisdiction consistent with due process. *Pennoyer v. Neff*[1] also recognized jurisdiction based on the presence of property in the state, the status of a citizen, personal service in the state, and consent.[2] Over the years, judicial treatment of these other kinds of jurisdiction has evolved.

Tangible and intangible property

The concept of jurisdiction over property, leading to an in rem or quasi in rem judgment, was not difficult to apply in real property cases, which have a definite situs (location).[3] The real property is situated in

31. *E.g.,* British Airways Bd. v. Laker Airways Ltd., [1984] 3 All E.R. 39 (H.L. 1984)(Eng.); see generally Lowenfeld, International Litigation and the Quest for Reasonableness (1996).

32. In Helicopteros Nacionales de Colombia, S.A. v. Hall, 466 U.S. 408, 104 S.Ct. 1868, 80 L.Ed.2d 404 (1984), the Solicitor General filed a brief advancing this argument.

33. *See* §§ 2.9, 2.11, 2.21, 5.15.

§ 2.7

1. 95 U.S. 714, 24 L.Ed. 565 (1878); see § 2.4 *supra.*

2. For consent, see § 2.9 *infra.* For a general survey, see Casad & Richman, Jurisdiction in Civil Actions (3d ed. 1998).

3. *See, e.g.,* Arndt v. Griggs, 134 U.S. 316, 10 S.Ct. 557, 33 L.Ed. 918 (1890); Martin v. Better Taste Popcorn Co., 89 F.Supp. 754 (S.D.Iowa 1950).

one state, and that state should adjudicate claims to the property through in rem proceedings and can seize the property to pay creditors through quasi in rem attachment proceedings. The concept of presence of property runs into difficulty, however, when applied to movables, which may be in one state at one time and elsewhere some other time,[4] and even greater difficulty as applied to intangibles (bank accounts, shares of stock) because they have no physical existence anywhere. The courts undertook to resolve this problem by attributing a permanent situs to movables and intangibles. One way to do so was to say that the "situs" of movables and intangibles was the place where their owner was domiciled. This solution had its most frequent application in proceedings to determine rights of succession in the property of a decedent, and when employed for such purposes it usually worked satisfactorily. But the domicile-as-situs theory was not satisfactory if there was a dispute over whether a certain kind of property interest was real property (having situs where the land was located) or movable property (having situs where its owner was domiciled) or if there was a dispute over the state in which the owner was domiciled.[5] Moreover, domicile was not the only theory used for attributing situs of intangibles. Debts owed to a person could be regarded as having situs, not where the owner of the debt (that is, the creditor) was domiciled, but where the debtor was located;[6] shares of stock in a corporation could be regarded as having situs where the share certificate was located or where the corporation kept its list of shareholders.[7]

Situs problems

The problem of locating a situs for property went to the foundation of the theory of in rem jurisdiction.[8] If, in a subsequent attack on the judgment, it is found that the property was not "in" the state that rendered the judgment, then there was no basis for jurisdiction and the judgment is void.[9] The inconsistencies in the concepts of situs thus

4. *See* Note, The Use of Maritime Attachment as a Jurisdictional Device, 12 Cornell Intl. L.J. 329 (1979); Note, The Power of a State to Affect Title in a Chattel Atypically Removed to It, 47 Colum. L. Rev. 767 (1947).

5. *See* Scoles and Hay, Conflict of Laws § 6.5 (2d ed. 1982).

6. Harris v. Balk, 198 U.S. 215, 25 S.Ct. 625, 49 L.Ed. 1023 (1905).

7. *See* Shaffer v. Heitner, 433 U.S. 186, 97 S.Ct. 2569, 53 L.Ed.2d 683 (1977); Note, Attachment of Corporate Stock: The Conflicting Approaches of Delaware and the Uniform Stock Transfer Act, 73 Harv. L. Rev. 1579 (1960); *cf.* McCarthy, Jurisdiction over Chattels the Title to Which Is Embodied in a Document, 31 N.D.L. Rev. 160 (1955). In Texas v. New Jersey, 379 U.S. 674, 85 S.Ct. 626, 13 L.Ed.2d 596 (1965), the Court faced no less than four ways of attributing situs to a kind of intangible property, funds sent by telegraphic money order.

8. *See* Alfred Dunhill of London, Inc. v. Republic of Cuba, 425 U.S. 682, 96 S.Ct. 1854, 48 L.Ed.2d 301 (1976), for a situation involving the problem in international context. *See also* United States v. First Nat. City Bank, 379 U.S. 378, 85 S.Ct. 528, 13 L.Ed.2d 365 (1965).

9. New York Life Ins. Co. v. Dunlevy, 241 U.S. 518, 36 S.Ct. 613, 60 L.Ed. 1140 (1916). *See also* Hanson v. Denckla, 357 U.S. 235, 78 S.Ct. 1228, 2 L.Ed.2d 1283 (1958).

resulted in uncertainty over the validity of an in rem judgment. Some decisions used the minimum contacts approach, attributing situs to a state that has some substantial connection with the transaction from which the dispute over the property arose;[10] other decisions settled rather arbitrarily on one theory or another for application to various types of property;[11] and some decisions seemed to select among theories with an eye to whether the theory chosen would render the judgment valid or invalid and thus whether it would be binding on the parties.[12] The result was ironic. The types of transactions involved—settlement of trusts, decedents' estates, interests in pension funds—are ones that particularly need consistent resolution through a single proceeding whose determination will be universally recognized. Yet the inconsistent rules regarding situs made that objective sometimes impossible to attain.

Shaffer v. Heitner

In 1977, the Supreme Court removed most of these problems by removing most of in rem and quasi in rem jurisdiction. In *Shaffer v. Heitner*,[13] the Court ruled that assertions of such jurisdiction are subject to the same Constitutional standard as long arm jurisdiction: the defendant's contacts with the state, which of course may include contacts relating to the attached property, must be sufficient to warrant jurisdiction over the claim in question. The Court noted the arbitrary results of assigning movable and intangible property a situs where its owner could then be forced to defend even claims unrelated to the property. It reasoned that, despite *Pennoyer*'s treatment of in rem and quasi in rem jurisdiction proceedings as suits against the attached property itself, it is the defendant who faces loss of that property. In practical effect, such proceedings (notwithstanding the limitation of the judgment to the value of the attached property) are thus indistinguishable from in personam suits seeking a money judgment, and should be subject to the same long arm standard.

Focusing in this way on the suit's impact on the defendant of course reflects *International Shoe*'s precept that the central issue in jurisdictional cases is not the state's power over the defendant or property in question but the fairness to the defendant of requiring him or her to defend against a particular claim in a particular forum. The Court indeed declared that all assertions of jurisdiction must comply with *International Shoe*'s standard of traditional notions of fair play and

10. Atkinson v. Superior Court, 49 Cal.2d 338, 316 P.2d 960 (1957); Danov v. ABC Freight Forwarding Corp., 266 Minn. 115, 122 N.W.2d 776 (1963).

11. *See* Texas v. New Jersey, 379 U.S. 674, 85 S.Ct. 626, 13 L.Ed.2d 596 (1965).

12. *Compare* Hanson v. Denckla, 357 U.S. 235, 78 S.Ct. 1228, 2 L.Ed.2d 1283 (1958), *with* United States v. First Nat. City Bank, 379 U.S. 378, 85 S.Ct. 528, 13 L.Ed.2d 365 (1965).

13. 433 U.S. 186, 97 S.Ct. 2569, 53 L.Ed.2d 683 (1977); see Rush v. Savchuk, 444 U.S. 320, 100 S.Ct. 571, 62 L.Ed.2d 516 (1980); Silberman, *Shaffer v. Heitner*: The End of an Era, 53 N.Y.U.L. Rev. 33 (1978); Casad, *Shaffer v. Heitner*: An End to Ambivalence in Jurisdiction Theory, 26 Kan. L. Rev. 61 (1977).

substantial justice. That declaration opened up tantalizing prospects of a general reworking of jurisdictional law, which has in fact not materialized.

Relevance of property

Shaffer recognizes that, in many situations, owning property within a state might be a purposeful contact supporting a suit against its owner on a claim arising out of that contact. For example, the owner of land in a state may constitutionally be required to defend there a claim that a dump on the land is emitting toxic chemicals, or a suit on a contract to sell the land. The claim in *Shaffer* itself was very different, which is why the Court found jurisdiction lacking. It was against officers and directors of the Greyhound Corp., which (although incorporated in Delaware) had its headquarters in Arizona and had violated the law in Oregon. Neither the plaintiff nor the defendants were from Delaware, where the suit was brought. Jurisdiction was based solely on the fact that the defendants owned shares in Greyhound, and on Delaware law providing that the stock of a Delaware corporation is deemed to be located in Delaware, a principle followed by no other state. Admittedly, the claim against the defendants arose from their activities as officers and directors of a Delaware corporation, but Delaware did not assert that as a ground of jurisdiction, so the Court disregarded it. (Immediately after the Supreme Court decision, Delaware passed a statute that did make being an officer or director of a Delaware corporation a basis of jurisdiction, thus retaining much corporate litigation in the Delaware courts.[14])

Even when possessing property in a state will not, under *Shaffer,* support jurisdiction, attaching property still performs an important role in litigation. Plaintiffs often try to attach a defendant's assets at the outset of an action in which jurisdiction has been obtained in some other way in order to be sure that any judgment will be collectible. A defendant may not dispose of assets that have been attached. Under a series of Supreme Court decisions, attachment must be accompanied by procedural safeguards to ensure that the defendant will not suffer an improper deprivation of property during the action.[15]

The *Shaffer* opinion also leaves open several ways in which jurisdiction based on attachment of property may perhaps still be constitutionally viable. If there is no other forum in which all the defendants to a claim may be joined, the principle of "jurisdiction by necessity" may allow jurisdiction based on attachment.[16] Relying on this possibility,

14. *See* Armstrong v. Pomerance, 423 A.2d 174 (Del.1980).

15. *See* §§ 5.17–18 *infra.*

16. *See* Shaffer, 433 U.S. at 211 n. 37; Helicopteros Nacionales de Colombia, S.A. v. Hall, 466 U.S. 408, 419 n. 13, 104 S.Ct. 1868, 80 L.Ed.2d 404 (1984); Amoco Overseas Oil Co. v. Compagnie Nationale Algerienne de Navigation, 605 F.2d 648 (2d Cir. 1979); Louring v. Kuwait Boulder Shipping Co., 455 F.Supp. 630 (D.Conn.1977).

lower courts have upheld the traditional admiralty procedure for starting an action by attaching a vessel before it can leave United States waters.[17]

Attachment may also be permissible to preserve a defendant's assets in one forum while litigation proceeds in another forum to which the defendant has stronger ties.[18] English courts frequently grant comparable relief, which they call *Mareva* or freezing injunctions.[19] Two Justices even suggested in *Shaffer* that quasi in rem jurisdiction may be acceptable when the attached assets are permanently fixed within the state, as is the case with land, a suggestion that lower courts apparently have not followed.[20] Lastly, when jurisdiction over a party is constitutionally proper under a long arm theory because of the defendant's acts, a state may nevertheless use attachment of property as a procedure for asserting that jurisdiction.[21]

Divorce jurisdiction

Within the *Pennoyer v. Neff* system, domestic relations proceedings could be conceptualized as being in rem, in personam, or both.[22] Paradoxically, under the decisions of the Supreme Court, the marriage tie itself was treated as a status that may be terminated by a state in which only one of the parties was domiciled, while the financial concomitants of marriage (alimony and division of property) were treated as in personam claims that can be determined only by a state in which the defendant can be personally served with process.[23] The logic of *Shaffer* would have supported challenges to these rules. Why, for example, should the fact that one spouse moves to a state warrant that state's courts in granting a divorce binding on the other spouse who lacked any other contacts with the state?[24]

17. Trans-Asiatic Oil Ltd. v. Apex Oil Co., 743 F.2d 956 (1st Cir.1984). *See* 15 U.S.C. § 1125(d)(2)(A) (allowing in rem suit to cancel internet registration when in personam jurisdiction unavailable in United States).

18. *See* Shaffer, 433 U.S. at 209; Carolina Power & Light Co. v. Uranex, 451 F.Supp. 1044 (N.D.Cal.1977); Barclays Bank, S.A. v. Tsakos, 543 A.2d 802 (D.C.App.1988).

19. Mareva Compania Naviera SA v. International Bulk Carriers SA, 2 Lloyd's Rep. 509, 1980 WL 149429 (CA1975)(Eng.). But see Grupo Mexicano de Desarrollo S.A. v. Alliance Bond Fund, 527 U.S. 308, 119 S.Ct. 1961, 144 L.Ed.2d 319 (1999).

20. *See* Shaffer, 433 U.S. at 217, 218 (Powell & Stevens, JJ., concurring).

21. Banco Ambrosiano, S.P.A. v. Artoc Bank & Trust Ltd., 62 N.Y.2d 65, 476 N.Y.S.2d 64, 464 N.E.2d 432 (1984).

22. *See* Restatement (Second) of Conflict of Laws §§ 69–79; Restatement (Second) of Judgments § 31; Weintraub, Commentary on the Conflict of Laws 168–199 (1971).

23. *See* Vanderbilt v. Vanderbilt, 354 U.S. 416, 77 S.Ct. 1360, 1 L.Ed.2d 1456 (1957); Estin v. Estin, 334 U.S. 541, 68 S.Ct. 1213, 92 L.Ed. 1561 (1948); Williams v. North Carolina, 325 U.S. 226, 65 S.Ct. 1092, 89 L.Ed. 1577 (1945). *But cf.* Simons v. Miami Beach First Natl. Bank, 381 U.S. 81, 85 S.Ct. 1315, 14 L.Ed.2d 232 (1965). *See* Currie, Suitcase Divorce in the Conflict of Laws, 34 U. Chi. L. Rev. 26 (1966); Comment, Divorce ex Parte Style, 33 U. Chi. L. Rev. 837 (1966). *Compare* May v. Anderson, 345 U.S. 528, 73 S.Ct. 840, 97 L.Ed. 1221 (1953) (child custody), *and* Hartford v. Superior Court, 47 Cal.2d 447, 304 P.2d 1 (1956) (proceeding to determine filial status).

24. Wasserman, Divorce and Domicile: Time to Sever the Knot, 39 Will. & Mary L. Rev. 1 (1997).

But *Shaffer* itself disclaimed any purpose to modify the "particularized rules governing adjudications of status," and courts have continued to follow the old rules, even when they foster separate suits for divorce and child support.[25] So far as divorce is concerned, issues of jurisdiction have become less important now that almost all states grant no-fault divorce, rendering unnecessary the former practice of establishing a domicile in Nevada in order to obtain an easy divorce there. Child custody and support continue to be controverted, and Congress has legislated some new "particularized rules" governing jurisdiction over them in order to prevent child kidnaping, evasion of support obligations, conflicting decisions in different states, and other abuses.[26]

Personal service

Shaffer v. Heitner appeared to open jurisdiction based on service within the state to constitutional challenge: why should a defendant's brief presence within a state warrant jurisdiction on an entirely unrelated claim? The Court rejected such a challenge in *Burnham v. Superior Court*,[27] upholding jurisdiction over a defendant served with a child support claim during a visit to California during which he visited his children.[28] Four Justices found the history of in-state service sufficient to support its constitutionality, apparently in all cases, and three of these were willing to construe out of existence *Shaffer*'s statements that all assertions of state court jurisdiction are subject to *International Shoe* standards. Four other Justices said only that service on a defendant voluntarily present in a state[29] "as a rule" supports jurisdiction, while the ninth Justice committed himself to no general rule. It may be, therefore, that service based on personal service will yet be held unconstitutional in extreme cases, such as when the defendant is served while flying across a state.[30] But don't hold your breath.

25. Shaffer, 433 U.S. at 209 n. 30; see Kulko v. Superior Court, 436 U.S. 84, 98 S.Ct. 1690, 56 L.Ed.2d 132 (1978); Wasserman, Parents, Partners, and Personal Jurisdiction, 1995 U. Ill. L. Rev. 813.

26. 28 U.S.C. §§ 1738A, 1738B. *See* Revised Uniform Reciprocal Enforcement of Support Act, 9B U.L.A. 567; Uniform Interstate Family Support Act, 9 U.L.A. 229.

27. 495 U.S. 604, 110 S.Ct. 2105, 109 L.Ed.2d 631 (1990); see Symposium, The Future of Personal Jurisdiction: A Symposium on *Burnham v. Superior Court*, 22 Rutgers L.J. 559 (1991).

28. In the absence of personal service, the Court had previously declined to find personal jurisdiction on similar facts. Kulko v. Superior Court, 436 U.S. 84, 98 S.Ct. 1690, 56 L.Ed.2d 132 (1978), discussed, § 2.6 *supra*.

29. Compare United States v. Alvarez-Machain, 504 U.S. 655, 112 S.Ct. 2188, 119 L.Ed.2d 441 (1992), upholding jurisdiction in a criminal case over a defendant kidnaped into the United States.

30. Grace v. MacArthur, 170 F.Supp. 442 (E.D.Ark.1959)(upholding jurisdiction). Such situations are relatively rare and may be governed by the rule of forum non conveniens. *See* § 2.20 *infra*; Maltz, Sovereign Authority, Fairness, and Personal Jurisdiction: The Case for the Doctrine of Personal Jurisdiction, 66 Wash. U.L.Q. 671 (1988).

General jurisdiction

Jurisdiction based on service within the state is general jurisdiction, that is, jurisdiction over any claim against the defendant, whether or not it arises out of the defendant's contacts with the state.[31] Now that *Burnham* has found service during a visit enough to support general jurisdiction, there can be little doubt that a defendant's domicile in the state will also continue to be considered sufficient to support such jurisdiction.[32] Thus, a plaintiff who cannot track down a defendant to serve process personally may sue in the state of the defendant's domicile, leaving the summons and complaint at that domicile.[33]

When the defendant is a corporation, it continues to be subject to general jurisdiction in any state where it has continuous and systematic contacts.[34] This would include, for example, any state where the corporation is incorporated, has its headquarters, or runs a factory or comparable establishment. Even a permanent office may be enough to support general jurisdiction over a corporation that solicits business in the state, and some courts have recognized jurisdiction over a corporation that solicits and obtains substantial business from an establishment just across the border.[35]

§ 2.8 Effects Out-of-State

A plaintiff who has obtained a judgment in a court of competent jurisdiction still has to enforce it. If the defendant fails to pay up and lacks sufficient assets within the jurisdiction that are subject to judicial execution, the plaintiff's only recourse may be to seek enforcement in another state or overseas. At that point, further problems arise.

Recognition of judgments in other states

As we have already noted, the Full Faith and Credit Clause and its implementing statute require each state to give full faith and credit to the "public Acts, Records, and judicial proceedings of every other State."[1] A state court's money judgment does not have immediate legal effect in a sister state; rather, the plaintiff, having obtained the judg-

31. *See* von Mehren & Trautman, Jurisdiction to Adjudicate: A Suggested Analysis, 79 Harv. L. Rev. 1121 (1966).

32. Milliken v. Meyer, 311 U.S. 457, 61 S.Ct. 339, 85 L.Ed. 278 (1940); Restatement, Second, Conflict of Laws § 29.

33. *E.g.*, Fed. R. Civ. P. 4(e)(2).

34. Perkins v. Benguet Consol. Mining Co., 342 U.S. 437, 72 S.Ct. 413, 96 L.Ed. 485 (1952); see Helicopteros Nacionales de Colombia, S.A. v. Hall, 466 U.S. 408, 104 S.Ct. 1868, 80 L.Ed.2d 404 (1984); Twitchell, The Myth of General Jurisdiction, 101 Harv. L. Rev. 610 (1988); § 2.5 *supra*.

35. *E.g.*, Wiwa v. Royal Dutch Petroleum Co., 226 F.3d 88 (2d Cir.2000); see 1 Casad & Richman, Jurisdiction in Civil Actions § 3–2 (3d ed. 1998); *cf.* Metropolitan Life Ins. Co. v. Robertson–Ceco Corp., 84 F.3d 560 (2d Cir.1996)(general jurisdiction existed, but its exercise was unreasonable where defendant barely met standard, claim was unrelated to forum, and plaintiff was multistate business).

§ 2.8

1. U.S. Const. art. IV, § 1; *see* 28 U.S.C. § 1738. Because the Clause extends to "acts" (statutes), it also sometimes requires a state to apply another state's law to a dispute. *E.g.*, Phillips Petroleum Co. v. Shutts, 472 U.S. 797, 105 S.Ct. 2965, 86 L.Ed.2d 628 (1985).

ment in one state, must bring a new action on it in the state where he or she wants to reach the defendant's property, obtain a judgment in the latter state, and execute on *that* judgment.[2] The enforcing state may not deny enforcement to judgments based on claims contravening its own public policy[3] or, with exceptions to be considered, relitigate the merits of the original judgment.

Exceptions

We have already encountered the major exception to full faith and credit: a state need not recognize the judgment of a court that lacked personal jurisdiction over the defendant.[4] But the only defendant that can take advantage of this option is one that did not appear or participate in the original action. Any defendant that did appear will be bound by the original court's resolution of the jurisdictional issue, which it can overturn only by persuading the U.S. Supreme Court to review that court's decision.[5] The defendant's situation will be no better if it litigates the merits in the original court without objecting to personal jurisdiction, because that will count as a waiver of the objection.[6] The defendant must therefore choose between appearing to litigate the merits and jurisdiction, knowing it will be bound by the result, and staying out of the original action, letting a default judgment be entered against it, and then challenging the original court's personal jurisdiction when the plaintiff seeks to enforce the judgment in another state. If the defendant's challenge prevails, the second court will not enforce the judgment. If it fails, the judgment will be enforced and the defendant will have no chance to dispute the merits of the underlying claim.

A state court need give the judgments of another state's court only the full faith and credit that "they have by law or usage in the courts" of the original state.[7] In other words, the second, enforcing state must

2. McElmoyle v. Cohen, 38 U.S. (13 Pet.) 312, 325, 10 L.Ed. 177 (1839); Paulsen, Enforcing the Money Judgment in a Sister State, 42 Iowa L. Rev. 202 (1957). The Uniform Enforcement of Foreign Judgments Act, 13 U.L.A. 171, considerably simplifies the procedure for suing on a foreign judgment in states that have adopted the act. *See* Leflar, The New Uniform Foreign Judgment Act, 24 N.Y.U. L. Rev. 336 (1949), discussing an earlier version of that Act. *See also* Revised Uniform Reciprocal Enforcement of Support Act, 9B U.L.A. 567; Uniform Interstate Family Support Act, 9 U.L.A. 229. In the federal court system, a judgment rendered in one district may be registered in another district, thereupon becoming as legally effective as if rendered in the latter originally. 28 U.S.C. § 1963. *See* Note, Registration of Federal Judgments, 42 Iowa L. Rev. 285 (1957).

3. Fauntleroy v. Lum, 210 U.S. 230, 28 S.Ct. 641, 52 L.Ed. 1039 (1908); see Milwaukee County v. M.E. White Co., 296 U.S. 268, 56 S.Ct. 229, 80 L.Ed. 220 (1935).

4. *E.g.*, McGee v. International Life Ins. Co., 355 U.S. 220, 78 S.Ct. 199, 2 L.Ed.2d 223 (1957); Pennoyer v. Neff, 95 U.S. 714, 722, 24 L.Ed. 565, 568 (1878). The defendant may usually challenge as well the subject matter jurisdiction of the original court. Restatement, Second, Judgments §§ 12, 69.

5. Baldwin v. Iowa State Traveling Men's Ass'n, 283 U.S. 522, 51 S.Ct. 517, 75 L.Ed. 1244 (1931); see Durfee v. Duke, 375 U.S. 106, 84 S.Ct. 242, 11 L.Ed.2d 186 (1963).

6. *See* § 2.12 *infra.*

7. 28 U.S.C. § 1738.

apply the first, rendering state's law of claim preclusion, whatever it may be, to the rendering state's judgments.[8] Thus, the Supreme Court has held that, when a judgment for child support, alimony, or child custody is subject to revision in the rendering state–which it almost always is–the enforcing state is equally free to modify it, and possibly even to treat it as a nonfinal judgment and deny it any recognition at all.[9] As applied to child custody rulings, this principle encouraged parents to "kidnap" their children and bring them to a state where they hoped to obtain custody. Congress has therefore passed legislation specifying which states' courts may grant or modify child custody orders.[10] Comparable legislation limits the power of one state's courts to modify or deny enforcement to child support orders issued in another state.[11]

Judgments affecting title to property

As these examples indicate, the Full Faith and Credit Clause can give rise to conflicts between states, or at least between individuals using the courts of different states for their own purposes. The effect of the Clause is to give the judgments of a state court a nationwide reach. This can easily clash with the notion, exemplified in *Pennoyer v. Neff,*[12] that each state controls persons and property within its territorial limits. The history of equity courts complicates the problem. These courts claimed the power to compel a defendant within their jurisdiction to perform acts elsewhere, but their only enforcement method was to coerce the defendant before them. Hence, it was long unclear whether injunctions and other equitable relief are entitled to full faith and credit in other states.[13]

For these reasons, courts limited the credit owed to a state court judgment resolving a dispute about the ownership of property in another state. Suppose *P* serves *D* with process in state *X* in a suit in which *P* claims to be the owner of property in state *Y*, a claim that *D* disputes.

8. Restatement, Second, Conflicts §§ 94, 95; Erichson, Interjurisdictional Preclusion, 96 Mich. L. Rev. 946 (1998). Whether a state must apply issue preclusion principles to another state's judgments is unclear. *See* Baker v. General Motors Corp., 522 U.S. 222, 118 S.Ct. 657, 139 L.Ed.2d 580 (1998); Scoles, Interstate Preclusion by Prior Litigation, 74 Nw. U.L. Rev. 742 (1979); Casad, Interstate Preclusion and the Restatement (Second) of Judgments, 66 Cornell. L. Rev. 510 (1981). On claim and issue preclusion, see ch. 11 *infra.*

9. *See* Ford v. Ford, 371 U.S. 187, 83 S.Ct. 273, 9 L.Ed.2d 240 (1962); New York *ex rel.* Halvey v. Halvey, 330 U.S. 610, 67 S.Ct. 903, 91 L.Ed. 1133 (1947); Barber v. Barber, 323 U.S. 77, 65 S.Ct. 137, 89 L.Ed. 82 (1944); Sistare v. Sistare, 218 U.S. 1, 30 S.Ct. 682, 54 L.Ed. 905 (1910).

10. 28 U.S.C. § 1738A.

11. 28 U.S.C. § 1738B; see also Revised Uniform Reciprocal Enforcement of Support Act, 9B U.L.A. 567 (amended 1968); Uniform Interstate Family Support Act, 9 U.L.A. 229 (amended 1996). More controversial legislation provides that a state need not give effect to gay and lesbian marriages in other states. 28 U.S.C. § 1738C; *compare* Strasser, Baker and Some Recipes for Disaster: On DOMA, Covenant Marriages, and Full Faith and Credit Jurisprudence, 64 Brook. L. Rev. 307 (1998) *with* Borchers, Baker v. General Motors: Implications for Inter-Jurisdictional Recognition of Non-Traditional Marriages, 32 Creighton L. Rev. 147 (1998).

12. 95 U.S. 914, 24 L.Ed. 565 (1878); § 2.4 *supra.*

13. Price, Full Faith and Credit and the Equity Conflict, 84 Va. L. Rev. 747 (1998).

This looks like an in personam action, an exercise of state *X*'s jurisdiction over the person of *D*. But if the judgment is treated as conclusive of the title to the property as between *P* and *D*, then the judgment could be said "directly" to affect property in state *Y*, a consequence that would conflict with the theory that state *Y* has exclusive authority over such property. If the property is movable or intangible, the judgment may be sustained on the theory that, since *D* was in state *X*, the property followed *D* and therefore was also in state *X*. If the property is realty, however, this approach is incompatible with the theory of situs and the exclusive jurisdiction of the state of that situs. And according to old authority, which may still hold, the judgment between *P* and *D* would not be required to be recognized by state *Y* if the property was real property even though it was binding as between the parties.[14]

Baker v. General Motors Corp.

In *Baker v. General Motors Corp.*,[15] the Supreme Court recently confronted another state court order affecting behavior in another state. General Motors, alleging that its former employee had broken a confidentiality agreement, secured a Michigan court injunction barring the employee from testifying against it in "any litigation." When the Bakers sought to use the employee's testimony in their products liability suit brought against General Motors in Missouri, General Motors contended that the Full Faith and Credit Clause required the court to enforce its Michigan injunction against the employee. The Supreme Court rejected that contention, primarily because "a Michigan court cannot, by entering the injunction . . . , dictate to a court in another jurisdiction that evidence relevance to the Bakers' case–a controversy to which Michigan is foreign–shall be inadmissible."

It is easier to accept the Court's ruling than to analyze it. Plainly, it is intolerable that litigation between two parties in one state should bar a third party from using otherwise admissible evidence in another state. It follows that an injunction against testifying should receive less faith and credit than, say, a state court judgment for damages against a former employee who broke a confidentiality agreement. But is the decisive point the fairness point (in which case, the same result might follow as a matter of due process even if the second suit were in the same state) or the intrusion on the second state's court system, or some combination of the two? And what is the bearing of the Court's explanation that, although equity decrees are entitled to full faith and credit, the

14. *See* Fall v. Eastin, 215 U.S. 1, 30 S.Ct. 3, 54 L.Ed. 65 (1909); Clarke v. Clarke, 178 U.S. 186, 20 S.Ct. 873, 44 L.Ed. 1028 (1900). *See generally* Weintraub, Commentary on the Conflict of Laws 296–338 (1971); Hancock, Conceptual Devices for Avoiding the Land Taboo in Conflict of Laws, 20 Stan. L. Rev. 1 (1967).

15. 522 U.S. 222, 118 S.Ct. 657, 139 L.Ed.2d 580 (1998); see Pearson, Common Law Preclusion, Full Faith and Credit, and Consent Judgments: The Analytical Challenge, 48 Cath. U.L. Rev. 419 (1999).

enforcing court need not follow the rendering court's practices regarding the time, manner, and mechanisms for enforcing judgments? These questions remain open.

State and federal courts

The principles of full faith and credit have been applied to all the combinations of state and federal courts within the United States, although the Clause itself is directly applicable only when a state court is asked to enforce the judgment of another state's court. The Supreme Court has read the statute that implements the Clause to require federal courts to give full faith and credit to state courts, absent another federal statute saying the contrary.[16] Thus, the Court applied full faith and credit principles in the *Baker* case discussed in the two previous paragraphs, even though the second court in that case was not a Missouri state court but a federal court located in Missouri. Supreme Court precedent also requires state courts to honor the judgments of federal courts.[17]

Judgments from foreign nations

When we turn to judgments rendered by courts outside the United States, neither the Full Faith and Credit Clause nor other federal law requires states to grant recognition. Indeed, some states still will not enforce the judgments of nations that deny reciprocal enforcement to United States judgments.[18] Most states, however, will enforce at least some foreign judgments, and many states have adopted the Uniform Foreign Money–Judgments Recognition Act.[19]

Courts considering judgments from foreign nations, unlike those considering domestic judgments, will deny enforcement when the foreign court failed to provide procedures compatible with due process of law or applied law violating domestic public policy.[20] For example, courts have

16. 28 U.S.C. § 1738, as construed in, *e.g.*, Marrese v. American Academy of Orthopaedic Surgeons, 470 U.S. 373, 105 S.Ct. 1327, 84 L.Ed.2d 274 (1985); Matsushita Electric Indus. Co. v. Epstein, 516 U.S. 367, 116 S.Ct. 873, 134 L.Ed.2d 6 (1996).

17. Deposit Bank v. Frankfort, 191 U.S. 499, 24 S.Ct. 154, 48 L.Ed. 276 (1903); Embry v. Palmer, 107 U.S. 3, 2 S.Ct. 25, 27 L.Ed. 346 (1883). Whether state courts should give federal judgments the same effect as federal courts would has been disputed. *Compare* Degnan, Federalized Res Judicata, 85 Yale L.J. 741 (1976) *with* Burbank, Interjurisdictional Preclusion, Full Faith and Credit and Federal Common Law: A General Approach, 71 Corn. L. Rev. 733 (1986); see Erichson, Interjurisdictional Preclusion, 96 Mich. L. Rev. 945 (1998). *See* Semtek Int'l Inc. v. Lockheed Martin Corp., ___ U.S. ___, 121 S.Ct. 1021, ___ L.Ed.2d ___ (2001) (effect of federal judgment ordinarily governed by preclusion law of state where federal court located).

18. *Compare* Hilton v. Guyot, 159 U.S. 113, 16 S.Ct. 139, 40 L.Ed. 95 (1895); Banque Libanaise Pour Le Commerce v. Khreich, 915 F.2d 1000 (5th Cir.1990)(requiring reciprocity) *with* Nicol v. Tanner, 310 Minn. 68, 256 N.W.2d 796 (1976); Restatement, Third, Foreign Relations Law § 481 (not requiring reciprocity).

19. 13 U.L.A. 263; see Teitz, Transnational Litigation ch. 8 (1996).

20. Uniform Money–Judgments Recognition Act, 13 U.L.A. 263, § 4; Restatement, Third, Foreign Relations § 482. *See* Society of Lloyd's v. Ashenden, 233 F.3d 473 (7th Cir.2000).

refused to enforce a judgment from a nation where civil law had disrupted the local courts, as well as an English libel judgment considered incompatible with the First Amendment.[21]

In appraising the foreign court's personal jurisdiction, moreover, a court in this country will consider both whether the foreign court had jurisdiction under its own law and whether its assertion of jurisdiction was compatible with United States principles of fairness, which are approximately the same as the Constitutional law of personal jurisdiction. Because foreign courts do not apply the Due Process Clause, this means that a United States court will consider whether due process standards were satisfied before enforcing a foreign judgment even when the defendant appeared before the foreign court. Unlike an appearing defendant in another state's court, an appearing defendant in a foreign court will thus not be considered wholly bound by that court's decision that it has jurisdiction.[22]

The extent to which foreign courts will enforce United States judgments varies from nation to nation, but at least some nations are less receptive to other nations' judgments than are courts here.[23] Germany, for example, has used public policy grounds to deny enforcement of United States judgments for punitive damages, while France enforced no foreign judgments at all until 1964.[24] The Brussels Convention now entitles nationals of European Union nations to enforce the decisions of a court in one such nation in any other such nation; at the same time, the Convention limits the jurisdictional grounds that any European Union member's courts may assert against a national of any other member.[25] The United States, not being a member of the Union, is not a party to the Brussels Convention, and attempts to negotiate a multinational judgment recognition treaty including the United States have so far not succeeded.[26] The United States has, however, joined the New York Convention, which provides for court enforcement of arbitration decisions in international commercial matters.[27]

21. Bridgeway Corp. v. Citibank, 201 F.3d 134 (2d Cir.2000); Bachchan v. India Abroad Publications, Inc., 154 Misc.2d 228, 585 N.Y.S.2d 661 (Sup.Ct.1992).

22. Somportex Ltd. v. Philadelphia Chewing Gum Corp., 453 F.2d 435 (3d Cir. 1971); Guardian Ins. Co. v. Bain Hogg Int'l Ltd., 52 F.Supp. 2d 536 (D.Vir.1999); Restatement, Third, Foreign Relations Law § 482.

23. Weintraub, How Substantial Is Our Need for a Judgments-Recognition Convention and What Should We Bargain Away to Get It?, 24 Brook. J. Int'l L. 167 (1998); Enforcement of Foreign Judgments Worldwide (Plato & Horton eds. 2d ed. 1993).

24. Munzer v. Munzer-Jacoby, Cass. 1e civ., Jan. 7, 1964, JCP 1964.II.13,590 (Fr.); Lowenfeld, International Litigation and the Quest for Reasonableness ch. 6 (1996).

25. Brussels Convention on Jurisdiction and Enforcement of Judgments in Civil and Commercial Matters, as amended, 29 I.L.M. 1413 (1990); see also Lugano Convention, 1988 O.J. (L 319) 9.

26. *See* Symposium, Enforcing Judgments Abroad: The Global Challenge, 24 Brook. J. Int'l L. 1 (1998).

27. Convention on the Recognition and Enforcement of Foreign Arbitral Awards, 21 U.S.T. 2517, T.I.A.S. 6997; see 9 U.S.C. §§ 201-08 (implementing legislation).

§ 2.9 Agreements Concerning Jurisdiction

Consent to personal jurisdiction

In the preceding sections we considered the legal limits on the authority of a court when that authority was exercised in the face of a possible objection to its territorial jurisdiction. A court may derive authority to determine a case not only from general law but also by consent of the parties. The idea of "consent" has often been used in a fictitious way to explain certain bases of jurisdiction, for example, in the theory that a foreign corporation "consents" to submit to jurisdiction in consequence of doing local business.[1] Real consent, that is, express or implied assent of the parties, is an independent basis for a court's exercising jurisdiction in a dispute between them.[2]

Parties may not confer subject matter jurisdiction

In this connection, a distinction is drawn between jurisdiction over the subject matter of a dispute and jurisdiction over the parties to it. By well-recognized doctrine, the parties may not by their consent confer subject matter jurisdiction on a court that otherwise lacks such jurisdiction.[3] Thus, persons between whom no diversity of citizenship exists may not agree to "waive" jurisdictional objections and thereby litigate in federal court.[4] A similar problem can arise in state court when it exercises jurisdiction in rem: The subject matter is the *res,* and the parties cannot confer authority to dispose of the res if it is not "before" the court.[5] Personal jurisdiction, by contrast, is subject to waiver, for example when a defendant appears in a case but fails to raise its jurisdictional objection, or when a plaintiff sues in a court and thereby consents to the assertion of the defendant's counterclaim.[6] Hence, the problem we are dealing with is that of a party's consent to the exercise of personal jurisdiction over it.

Arbitration agreements

Parties to a contract or other relationship they create may arrange that disputes arising from the relationship be determined by a certain tribunal. One type of provision is an agreement to arbitrate, whereby the dispute is determined not by a court but by an arbitration panel appointed in some specified way. At one time, the common law courts

§ 2.9

1. *See* § 2.5 note 2 *supra.*

2. *See* von Mehren and Trautman, Jurisdiction to Adjudicate: A Suggested Analysis, 79 Harv. L. Rev. 1121, 1138 (1966).

3. *See* Rose v. Giamatti, 721 F.Supp. 906 (S.D.Ohio 1989).

4. *See* §§ 2.30, 4.3 *infra.*

5. *See* Fall v. Eastin, 215 U.S. 1, 30 S.Ct. 3, 54 L.Ed. 65 (1909). *Cf.* Alton v. Alton, 207 F.2d 667 (3d Cir.1953), *appeal dismissed as moot,* 347 U.S. 610, 74 S.Ct. 736, 98 L.Ed. 987 (1954).

6. *See* § 2.12 *infra*; Adam v. Saenger, 303 U.S. 59, 58 S.Ct. 454, 82 L.Ed. 649 (1938); National City Bank v. Republic of China, 348 U.S. 356, 75 S.Ct. 423, 99 L.Ed. 389 (1955); Adams v. Unione Mediterranea Di Sicurta, 220 F.3d 659 (5th Cir.2000).

viewed such agreements negatively, giving them effect only to the extent of enforcing an award after the parties had submitted their dispute to the arbitrators and the latter had actually decided the controversy. Today, however, agreements to arbitrate are generally enforceable before the arbitration is held by compelling the other party to participate in the arbitration under penalty of the risk that award will go against it by default. Parties to international transactions usually include arbitration clauses in their contracts in order to avoid having to litigate in each others' "home courts," and sometimes in order to control the law that will apply to their transaction.[7]

Stipulation of forum

The parties to a transaction may also agree that a dispute be adjudicated in a specified court. Such an agreement may take one of two basic forms. The parties may directly identify the court and agree to submit to its jurisdiction. Alternatively, one of the parties will appoint an agent for service of process in a specified place, making it possible for it to be sued there when otherwise it might not be subject to service of process in that place. Again, the courts formerly were hesitant to give effect to such agreements on the theory that the normally operative rules for determining jurisdiction are procedural protections that a party should not be allowed to bargain away. But such agreements have generally been upheld when the court selected by the agreement is a reasonably appropriate one and the parties do not have such greatly disproportionate bargaining power that the agreement could be regarded as unconscionable. Thus in *National Equipment Rental v. Szukhent*,[8] the Court held that an agreement between a New York equipment supplier and a Michigan customer providing that the customer designate an agent in New York for service of process did not conflict with the provisions of Federal Rule 4(d) concerning the range of service of process issuing from a federal court and thus rendered the customer amenable to process in New York.

Forum selection clauses

These stipulations, also called forum selection clauses, are an increasingly common feature in contracts involving interstate and foreign

7. *See, e.g.*, Scherk v. Alberto-Culver Co., 417 U.S. 506, 94 S.Ct. 2449, 41 L.Ed.2d 270 (1974); D. H. Overmyer Co. v. Frick Co., 405 U.S. 174, 92 S.Ct. 775, 31 L.Ed.2d 124 (1972); Domke, The Law and Practice of Commercial Arbitration (1968); Craig, *et al.*, International Chamber of Commerce Arbitration (2d ed. 1990); McGonagle, Arbitration of Consumer Disputes, 27 Arb. J. 65 (1972); Sarpy, Arbitration as a Means of Reducing Court Congestion, 41 Notre Dame Law. 182 (1965); Note, Commercial Arbitration in Federal Courts, 20 Vand. L. Rev. 607 (1967).

8. 375 U.S. 311, 84 S.Ct. 411, 11 L.Ed.2d 354 (1964). *See* Annot., 69 A.L.R.2d 1324.*See also* Ehrenzweig, Adhesion Contracts in the Conflict of Laws, 53 Colum. L. Rev. 1072 (1953). *Compare* Atlas Credit Corp. v. Ezrine, 25 N.Y.2d 219, 250 N.E.2d 474, 303 N.Y.S.2d 382 (1969). *Cf.* Annot., 97 A.L.R.2d 934 (contractual stipulations as to venue).

commerce and transportation. *M/S Bremen v. Zapata Off–Shore Co.*[9] involved a contract between companies in West Germany and Texas for towing a drilling rig across the Atlantic, from Louisiana to Italy. A clause in the contract provided that any dispute be adjudicated in London. The Supreme Court held that "a freely negotiated private international agreement, unaffected by fraud, undue influence, or overweening bargaining power, such as that involved here, should be given full effect,"[10] adding that "in the light of present-day commercial realities and expanding international trade we conclude that the forum selection clause should control absent a strong showing that it should be set aside."[11] The Court held that the forum clause was "a vital part of the agreement and [that] it would be unreasonable to think that the parties did not conduct their negotiations, including fixing the monetary terms, with the consequences of the forum selection clause figuring prominently in their calculations."[12]

On the strength of *M/S Bremen*, the Court has upheld a forum selection clause in an adhesion contract. *Carnival Cruise Lines v. Shute*[13] involved a suit by passengers from Washington for negligence against a cruise company for injuries suffered when she fell on shipboard. The cruise contract provided that disputes were to be settled in the courts of Florida, the company's headquarters, although the particular cruise originated in Los Angeles and was bound for Mexican Pacific waters. Even though the forum selection clause was not the subject of bargaining, the court reasoned that it dispelled any confusion as to the proper forum for suits, thus saving the parties time and money, which presumably would be passed on to consumers in the form of lower prices. It is hard to think of a clause designating a plausible forum that could not satisfy this rationale. The Court also construed away a statute that could easily have been read to forbid the result it reached.[14]

Carnival Cruise has been justly criticized because it turns jurisdictional law on its head, allowing a multinational corporation to impose extreme inconvenience on private individuals far less able to bear it.[15]

9. 407 U.S. 1, 92 S.Ct. 1907, 32 L.Ed.2d 513 (1972).

10. 407 U.S. at 12–13, 92 S.Ct. at 1914–1915, 32 L.Ed.2d at 521–522.

11. 407 U.S. at 15, 92 S.Ct. at 1916, 32 L.Ed.2d at 523.

12. 407 U.S. at 14, 92 S.Ct. at 1915, 32 L.Ed.2d at 523. *See* also Stewart Organization, Inc. v. Ricoh Corp., 487 U.S. 22, 108 S.Ct. 2239, 101 L.Ed.2d 22 (1988)(federal court will enforce forum selection clause by transfer under 28 U.S.C. § 1404 notwithstanding contrary state law); Lipcon v. Underwriters at Lloyd's, London, 148 F.3d 1285 (11th Cir.1998)(enforcing London forum selection clause that in effect barred claim under U.S. securities laws).

13. 499 U.S. 585, 111 S.Ct. 1522, 113 L.Ed.2d 622 (1991).

14. 46 U.S.C. App. § 183c. After *Carnival Cruise* Congress amended this statute to reverse its result, but then reinstated the original version. *See* Smith v. Doe, 991 F.Supp. 781 (E.D.La.1998).

15. Purcell, Geography as a Litigation Weapon: Consumers, Forum–Selection Clauses, and the Rehnquist Court, 40 U.C.L.A. L. Rev. 423 (1992); Carrington & Haagen, Contract and Jurisdiction, 1996 Sup. Ct. Rev. 331; Mullenix, Another Easy Case, Some More Bad Law: *Carnival Cruise Lines* and Contractual Personal Jurisdiction, 37 Tex. Int'l L.J. 323 (1992).

Florida is an absurd forum in which to litigate a claim by Washington citizens arising from a Pacific cruise. Unlike the *Bremen* agreement, this one was not negotiated between equals and was not a sensible remedy to problems of international trade. The "consent" of passengers to a small print forum selection clause, which some did not receive before the cruise,[16] was fictitious. So, in all probability, were the reduced prices that the Court promised to passengers. Even if the cruise line did pass its savings to its customers, those savings came at the expense of injured passengers who had to bear the costs of litigating in Florida, or who abandoned any hope of recovery.

Stipulation of inappropriate forum

There are different concepts of the "appropriateness" of the agreed-on court in these cases. The court selected in *Szukhent* is one that would probably have met the "minimum contacts" test, while that in *Bremen* was a forum having no "contacts" with the transaction but having a reputation for disinterestedness and expertise in the type of controversy involved. (It is harder to say what made the Florida court appropriate in *Carnival Cruise* other than its being the headquarters of the cruise company.) If a court selected by the parties failed to meet either of these criteria, the agreement as to forum could well be regarded as violating the protection against an inappropriate forum that is implicit in the rules of jurisdiction.[17]

B. NOTICE AND OBJECTION TO JURISDICTION

§ 2.10 Notice

Service on fictitious agent

A fundamental rule of procedure, now incorporated in the Due Process Clause, provides that persons may not have their rights and obligations determined in a proceeding of which they have no notice.[1] This rule is satisfied in actions commenced by personal service of process because the process is notice.[2] The situation is more complicated when

16. *See* Carnival Cruise Lines, Inc. v. Superior Court, 234 Cal.App.3d 1019, 286 Cal.Rptr. 323 (1991)(another case involving the same cruise).

17. *See* Scoles and Hay, Conflict of Laws §§ 11.2 *et seq.* (1982); *e.g.*, Copperweld Steel Co. v. Demag-Mannesmann Bohler, 578 F.2d 953 (3d Cir.1978).

§ 2.10

1. Mennonite Bd. of Missions v. Adams, 462 U.S. 791, 103 S.Ct. 2706, 77 L.Ed.2d 180 (1983); Greene v. Lindsey, 456 U.S. 444, 102 S.Ct. 1874, 72 L.Ed.2d 249 (1982); Mullane v. Central Hanover Bank & Trust Co., 339 U.S. 306, 70 S.Ct. 652, 94 L.Ed. 865 (1950). Exceptions to this general proposition include representative suits, such as class actions, and situations in which one person's interests are derivative from or in "privity" with another's. *See* § 11.22 *et seq. infra.* Also, a vaguely defined exception is made for emergency public actions against property. *See* Hodel v. Virginia Surface Mining & Reclamation Assn., 452 U.S. 264, 101 S.Ct. 2352, 69 L.Ed.2d 1 (1981).

2. *But see* Aguchak v. Montgomery Ward Co., 520 P.2d 1352 (Alaska 1974) (notice must include information about how to make a defense); Omni Capital Intl. v.

process is served on an agent of the defendant such as the agent of a foreign corporation or of a nonresident motorist, particularly when the "agent" is simply a government official. At one point, this kind of agency was interpreted literally to mean that actual notice did not also have to be sent to nonresidents themselves.[3] Indeed, under the sovereignty theory of *Pennoyer v. Neff*, legally effective process apparently could not run out of state because that would be an invalid extension of the state's authority beyond its boundaries. This theoretical obstacle has long since been overcome, except when process must be delivered in foreign nations that regard this as an infringement of their sovereignty.[4] At any rate, the rule is settled that the ritual of service on a local official agent does not satisfy the requirements of due process; actual notice must be sent to the nonresident at his or her best-known address.[5] The ritual of service on a local official agent still, however, can create its own difficulties. Courts have held that if the ritual is not technically complied with, service of process may be invalid under state law even though the defendant has received actual notice in compliance with the due process requirement.[6]

The requirement of notice applies not only to full-fledged lawsuits, where the complaint puts forward the merits of the plaintiff's grievance, but also to provisional remedies. Such remedies include attachment, sequestration, preliminary restraining orders, and other procedures designed to freeze the status quo pending adjudication of the merits of the controversy. Some of these remedies formerly could be obtained by the plaintiff ex parte, that is, on application to the court without notice to the party whose property was to be temporarily seized or whose conduct was to be temporarily enjoined. But in a series of cases beginning with *Sniadach v. Family Finance Corp.*,[7] such interference with the defendant was held to constitute a denial of liberty or property permissible only on prior notice, except when a showing of urgent necessity was made through specific proof submitted to a judge. In assessing whether notice is required before issuance of a provisional remedy, the Court in *Connecticut v. Doehr* summarized the relevant factors as follows:

> [F]irst, consideration of the private interest that will be affected by the prejudgment measure; second, an examination of the risk of erroneous

Rudolf Wolff & Co., 484 U.S. 97, 108 S.Ct. 404, 98 L.Ed.2d 415 (1987) (notice and authorization of out-of-state service of process required).

3. *Compare* Washington v. Superior Court, 289 U.S. 361, 53 S.Ct. 624, 77 L.Ed. 1256 (1933), *with* Wuchter v. Pizzutti, 276 U.S. 13, 48 S.Ct. 259, 72 L.Ed. 446 (1928).

4. *E.g.,* Umbenhauer v. Woog, 969 F.2d 25 (3d Cir.1992)(overriding Swiss objections). For service abroad, see § 2.11 *infra.*

5. Wuchter v. Pizzutti, *supra* note 3; *cf.* Walker v. City of Hutchinson, 352 U.S. 112, 77 S.Ct. 200, 1 L.Ed.2d 178 (1956).

6. *See, e.g.,* Bond v. Golden, 273 F.2d 265 (10th Cir.1959). *Compare* Clemones v. Alabama Power Co., 250 F.Supp. 433, 435 (N.D.Ga.1966).

7. 395 U.S. 337, 89 S.Ct. 1820, 23 L.Ed.2d 349 (1969). *See* Fuentes v. Shevin, 407 U.S. 67, 92 S.Ct. 1983, 32 L.Ed.2d 556 (1972); North Ga. Finishing, Inc. v. Di–Chem, Inc., 419 U.S. 601, 95 S.Ct. 719, 42 L.Ed.2d 751 (1975); §§ 5.16–18 *infra.*

deprivation throughout the procedures under attack and the probable value of additional or alternative safeguards; and third, ... due regard for any ancillary interest the government may have in providing the procedure.[8]

As the Court noted in *Doehr*, before awarding such a remedy most states require either a preliminary hearing or a showing by plaintiff of exigent circumstances, such as an imminent threat by defendant to abscond with property.

Notice reasonably certain to inform

The more difficult problem has been with notice in in rem and quasi in rem proceedings. Since the basis of jurisdiction is the presence of the property, the authority of the court becomes effective when the property is actually or symbolically "seized" and "brought before" the court. Typical state statutes require that the seizure be accompanied by publication of notice of the proceeding in local newspapers. In *Pennoyer v. Neff*[9] the seizure was held to be effective notice to an owner or claimant of the property on the fictitious assumption that he or she had left a caretaker in charge of the property. Indulgence of this fiction meant that one could have one's rights in property in another state determined without ever having heard about the proceeding, unless one happened to read that state's local newspapers. The Court held in *Mullane v. Central Hanover Bank & Trust Co.* that this did not satisfy the Due Process Clause:

> Process which is a mere gesture is not due process. The means employed must be ... reasonably certain to inform those affected....[10]

In subsequent decisions the Supreme Court has applied the *Mullane* principle rigorously, holding that posting notice at the apartment of a housing project tenant is inadequate notice of proposed eviction proceedings and that a tax foreclosure proceeding against real property must be preceded by mail notice to record holders of interests in the property.[11]

§ 2.11 Technical Requirements as to Notice

Rule 4 requirements

In addition to the constitutional requirement that the person notified be fairly apprised of the pending proceeding, notice must meet the forum's technical specifications concerning its form. A personally served summons, for example, typically must satisfy the following require-

8. 501 U.S. 1, 111 S.Ct. 2105, 115 L.Ed.2d 1 (1991).

9. 95 U.S. 714, 24 L.Ed. 565 (1878).

10. 339 U.S. 306, 315, 70 S.Ct. 652, 657, 94 L.Ed. 865, 874 (1950). *See also* Karl Senner, Inc. v. M/V Acadian Valor, 485 F.Supp. 287 (E.D.La.1980) (admiralty in rem proceeding is subject to the notice requirement).

11. Greene v. Lindsey, 456 U.S. 444, 102 S.Ct. 1874, 72 L.Ed.2d 249 (1982); Mennonite Bd. of Missions v. Adams, 462 U.S. 791, 103 S.Ct. 2706, 77 L.Ed.2d 180 (1983).

ments: it must be accompanied or followed by a copy of the complaint;[1] it must accurately name the person to be served;[2] it must be personally delivered to the person, or left, as the rules may specify, at his or her home or place of business;[3] and it must tell the person when to appear and include a warning that failure to appear may trigger a default judgment.[4] Requirements are similar for notice other than a summons; a general notice containing such particulars may be required to appear periodically in a newspaper of general circulation.[5]

Actual but technically defective notice

Traditionally these requirements were strictly enforced—and still are in some jurisdictions—so that noncompliance rendered some forms of notice legally ineffective.[6] Service by publication was treated with great strictness, perhaps in unstated recognition that it amounted to no notice at all; those who objected to such a defect could be given their day in court after having their objection sustained. Some courts still penalize defects with dismissal when they disapprove of the plaintiff's attitude.[7] More often, now that actual notice is generally required, notice that is technically defective is still sustained so long as it is substantially intelligible.[8]

Notice under the Federal Rules

If the defendant consents, the Federal Rules now permit replacement of service by notice via first class mail, including the complaint and other documents. If the defendant signs and returns the enclosed waiver

§ 2.11

1. *See* Fed. R. Civ. P. 4(d).

2. Schiavone v. Fortune, 477 U.S. 21, 106 S.Ct. 2379, 91 L.Ed.2d 18 (1986); *Compare* Annot., 124 A.L.R. 86 (correction of name of intended individual defendant who was actually served) *with* Annot., 8 A.L.R.2d 6 (correction of name of entity improperly designated). *See generally* Haworth, Changing Defendants in Private Civil Actions Under Federal Rule 15(c), 1975 Wis. L. Rev. 552.

3. *See* Fed. R. Civ. P. 4(d). In Greene v. Lindsey, 456 U.S. 444, 102 S.Ct. 1874, 72 L.Ed.2d 249 (1982), the Court held that posting a notice on an apartment house door did not meet the *Mullane* requirements of reasonable certainty in giving actual notice when evidence showed that such notices were often torn down in the housing project where defendant lived.

4. In Aguchak v. Montgomery Ward Co., 520 P.2d 1352 (Alaska 1974), the court held that a defendant should also be informed of how to defend an action.

5. *See* Note, Constructive Service in New England, 38 B.U.L. Rev. 268 (1958).

6. *E.g.,* Schiavone v. Fortune, 477 U.S. 21, 106 S.Ct. 2379, 91 L.Ed.2d 18 (1986); Feinstein v. Bergner, 48 N.Y.2d 234, 397 N.E.2d 1161, 422 N.Y.S.2d 356 (1979). But see Tuerkheimer, Service of Process in New York City: A Proposed End to Unregulated Criminality, 72 Colum. L. Rev. 847 (1972)(discussing "sewer service").

7. Ayres v. Jacobs & Crumplar, P.A., 99 F.3d 565 (3d Cir.1996)(lawyer plaintiff served unsealed process at wrong place because she thought technical niceties unimportant); Benjamin v. Grosnick, 999 F.2d 590 (1st Cir.1993)(plaintiff failed to explain why wrong complaint was served). With more justification, courts protect the rights of defaulting defendants, who may not have received proper notice. *See* Vives, Requirements for Impeachment of Sheriff Returns as Good Excuse When Setting Aside Domestic Default Judgments, 5 St. Mary's L.J. 318 (1973).

8. *See* Restatement (Second) of Judgments § 3.

of service form, no more is required. To encourage defendants to do so, Rule 4 holds out a carrot consisting of more time to answer the complaint, and a stick consisting of imposition of the costs of service on a defendant who fails without good cause to return the waiver.[9]

The Federal Rules provide for more traditional service if the defendant fails to waive or the plaintiff does not seek waiver. A plaintiff, for example, should use traditional service if suit is brought just before the statute of limitations expires, for fear that the defendant will not waive service and that by the time the plaintiff learns this it will be too late to pursue an alternative. Traditional service can be made by any adult who is not a party, or when appropriate by United States Marshall. Rule 4 specifies where and to whom service must be made. Alternatively, it allows service pursuant to the law of the state where the federal district court is located.[10] A federal court plaintiff may also make use of that state's long arm statute to serve defendants outside the state, or may rely on federal long arm provisions in the limited circumstances in which they apply.[11]

Service abroad

Service outside the United States raises special problems, because many nations object to it as an assertion of foreign power within their territory. Many nations, including the United States, have now joined the Hague Convention on the Service Abroad of Judicial and Extrajudicial Documents,[12] in which participating nations agree to serve within their own boundaries judicial documents emanating from other nations that have been delivered to them through prescribed channels. In cases in which it applies, both federal and state courts must use the Convention's procedures. The Convention does not apply, however, when it is possible to serve the defendant within the United States, for example through an agent for the service of process.[13] When service abroad must be made in a nation not subscribing to the Convention, the Federal Rules provide alternative methods.[14]

§ 2.12 Objecting to Jurisdiction

In considering objections to jurisdiction, a fundamental distinction is drawn between objections to subject matter jurisdiction and objections to personal jurisdiction. In general, an objection to subject matter jurisdiction may be made at any time, even on appeal. And an objection to subject matter jurisdiction may be made by a plaintiff who invoked the jurisdiction but then regretted the choice.[1]

9. Fed. R. Civ. P. 4(d).

10. Fed. R. Civ. P. 4(c, e, g, h, I).

11. Fed. R. Civ. P. 4(k); see § 2.34 *infra.*

12. [1969] 20 U.S.T. 361, T.I.A.S. 6638.

13. Volkswagenwerk Aktiengesellschaft v. Schlunk, 486 U.S. 694, 108 S.Ct. 2104, 100 L.Ed.2d 722 (1988).

14. Fed. R. Civ. P. 4(f); see generally Teitz, Transnational Litigation ch. 4 (1996).

§ 2.12

1. *See* §§ 2.30, 4.3 *infra.*

Failure to object to personal jurisdiction

An objection to personal jurisdiction, in contrast, may be made only by a defendant and must be made immediately, or the objection will be waived. Plaintiffs who invoke the court's jurisdiction are deemed to submit themselves to its authority with respect to personal jurisdiction. As a consequence, they then may be exposed to counterclaims, certainly those that arise out of the transaction originally sued on and perhaps others as well.[2] A defendant who appears in response to a summons and makes no objection to being brought before the court is also deemed to have submitted to the court's authority and consented to its exercise of jurisdiction.[3] This is called a general appearance, as distinct from a special appearance.

What happens if defendants wish to challenge the jurisdiction of the court? One way to do so is to ignore the summons, permit a default judgment to be entered, and raise the objection to jurisdiction when the plaintiff subsequently seeks to enforce the judgment.[4] This method raises the jurisdictional objection by subsequent collateral attack and precludes the risk of consenting to the court's jurisdiction. This method, however, also carries a serious risk: If defendant's subsequent attack on jurisdiction fails, defendant will face a valid judgment whose merits may no longer be contested. An escape from this dilemma is afforded through the procedure called a "special appearance."

Special appearance

A special appearance is the presentation, at the threshold of the proceedings, of the contention that the court lacks jurisdiction over the person making the objection. Under the procedure at common law and under the codes, an appearance was special only if the defendant labeled its appearance "special" and confined its objection to the question of jurisdiction; if defendant did anything else in the proceeding, defendant would be deemed to have made a general appearance.[5] Some authority went so far as to say that if defendant challenged both personal jurisdiction and subject matter jurisdiction, the latter objection became a general appearance and in effect a waiver of the objection to personal jurisdiction.[6] The requirements for making a special appearance are still

2. Adam v. Saenger, 303 U.S. 59, 58 S.Ct. 454, 82 L.Ed. 649 (1938); Adams v. Unione Mediterranea Di Sicurta, 220 F.3d 659 (5th Cir.2000)(waiver by authorizing another to appear); Restatement (Second) of Conflict of Laws § 34, Comment *c*.

3. *See, e.g.*, Everitt v. Everitt, 4 N.Y.2d 13, 148 N.E.2d 891, 171 N.Y.S.2d 836 (1958).

4. *See* § 12.17 *infra*.

5. *See* Restatement (Second) of Conflict of Laws § 81; Note, Developments in the Law—State-Court Jurisdiction, 73 Harv. L. Rev. 909, 991–998 (1960). *See generally* Thode, In Personam Jurisdiction; Article 2031B, the Texas "Long Arm" Jurisdiction Statute, and the Appearance to Challenge Jurisdiction in Texas and Elsewhere, 42 Tex. L. Rev. 279 (1964).

6. *Compare* Goodwine v. Superior Court, 63 Cal.2d 481, 407 P.2d 1, 47 Cal. Rptr. 201 (1965). *See also* Gorfinkle, Special Appearance in California: The Need for Reform, 5 U.S.F. L. Rev. 25 (1970).

treated this way in some states.[7]

Rule 12(b): first appearance

Under the federal rules, however, and in most states, the defendant may raise the question of personal jurisdiction along with other matters, so long as this is done in defendant's first response to the complaint.[8] If, for example, defendant wishes to contend that the court lacks jurisdiction over its person, that venue is improper, and that the complaint fails to state a claim, defendant can do so in a single initial motion to dismiss on these grounds.[9] If, however, defendant first made a motion objecting to venue or to the sufficiency of the complaint, and then made a motion to dismiss for invalidity of process, the second motion would be denied on the ground that defendant had already submitted to the court's jurisdiction.[10]

Adjudicating a challenge to personal jurisdiction sometimes requires a court to resolve disputed issues of fact as well as law. Under current doctrine, the existence of jurisdiction may turn on such facts as a defendant's advertising or sales within a state or the history of the relationship between the parties. Sometimes the jurisdictional issue is hard to distinguish from the merits of the case, as when jurisdiction is based on the defendant's having committed a tortious act within the state and the defendant denies committing the act. Although courts facing such factual disputes sometimes hear the evidence and make factual findings, many inquire only whether the plaintiff has established a prima facie case of jurisdiction and, if so, defer final determination of the jurisdictional issue until the trial of the merits.[11] (Presumably, if the case then settles, the jurisdictional uncertainty affects the parties' appraisals of the plaintiff's chances of prevailing, and hence the amount of the settlement.) The court may allow discovery on the jurisdictional issue, even against a defendant who challenges jurisdiction and therefore maintains that it is not subject to discovery.[12]

Appellate review

The subsequent procedural consequences of having objected to personal jurisdiction should also be noted. If defendant's objection to personal jurisdiction is sustained, the action is dismissed; plaintiff must

7. *E.g.* Harris v. Wally's World of Fun, Ltd., 279 Ill.App.3d 61, 215 Ill.Dec. 927, 664 N.E.2d 324 (Ill.App.1996); C & H Distributors, Inc. v. Cloud Enterprises, Inc., 866 S.W.2d 927 (Mo.App.1993).

8. *See* Fed. R. Civ. P. 12(b), (h).

9. *See, e.g.,* Dragor Shipping Corp. v. Union Tank Car Co., 378 F.2d 241 (9th Cir.1967) (interposition of compulsory counterclaim does not "waive" objection to personal jurisdiction when both were asserted in initial responsive pleading).

10. *See, e.g.,* Tiernan v. Dunn, 295 F.Supp. 1253 (D.R.I.1969). *See also* 5 Wright and Miller, Federal Practice and Procedure § 1391.

11. Boit v. Gar–Tec Products, Inc., 967 F.2d 671 (1st Cir.1992); Brown v. Slenker, 220 F.3d 411 (5th Cir.2000).

12. Insurance Corp. of Ireland, Ltd. v. Compagnie des Bauxites de Guinee, 456 U.S. 694, 102 S.Ct. 2099, 72 L.Ed.2d 492 (1982); see § 2.21 *infra*.

then either appeal from the judgment, hoping to obtain a reversal, or commence another action where valid service of process can be effectuated. If the objection is overruled and defendant refuses to proceed further, a default judgment will be rendered against defendant. The judgment in such circumstances will be incontestably valid because the jurisdictional question will have become *res judicata.*[13] Defendant is therefore well advised not to default. The appropriate course varies, depending on local procedure. In some states defendant can obtain immediate appellate review of the ruling on the jurisdictional question;[14] in others and in the federal system, the ruling on jurisdiction is a nonappealable interlocutory order, which can be reviewed only on appeal from the final judgment.[15] In these latter jurisdictions, therefore, a defendant must go through trial on the merits before it can obtain appellate resolution of the jurisdictional issue (which, of course, defendant will not seek if it wins on the merits).[16]

§ 2.13 Limited Appearance

The special appearance procedure considered in the previous section is associated with in personam jurisdiction. When the court exercises jurisdiction in rem or quasi in rem, to the extent that this is still possible, a twofold problem of somewhat similar character develops. The first is whether the res or status, which is the basis of the court's jurisdiction, is "before" the court. Conceptually, this is a problem of subject matter jurisdiction rather than personal jurisdiction, because by hypothesis the court is purporting to determine interests in the "thing" rather than the rights of persons.[1] It is a close question whether the objection is one that would be waived if not asserted at the threshold by special appearance or one that could be taken—like subject matter jurisdiction questions generally—at any time thereafter. If the court finds that it does have subject matter jurisdiction, a second problem arises: Can a party claiming an interest in the property litigate its interest without thereby submitting to in personam jurisdiction?

Defending the property

The problem arises most clearly in the case of jurisdiction by attachment. Suppose plaintiff asserts a claim for $25,000 but succeeds in

13. Baldwin v. Iowa State Traveling Men's Assn., 283 U.S. 522, 51 S.Ct. 517, 75 L.Ed. 1244 (1931); *cf.* Durfee v. Duke, 375 U.S. 106, 84 S.Ct. 242, 11 L.Ed.2d 186 (1963) (determination of jurisdiction over property res judicata).

14. *See, e.g.,* Buckeye Boiler Co. v. Superior Court, 71 Cal.2d 893, 458 P.2d 57, 80 Cal.Rptr. 113 (1969).

15. *See, e.g.,* Murphy v. Helena Rubenstein Co., 355 F.2d 553 (3d Cir.1965).

16. In the federal system it is possible that in extraordinary circumstances a defendant whose motion to dismiss for lack of personal jurisdiction had been denied on a manifestly erroneous basis could obtain immediate appellate review. *Compare* Thermtron Prods. v. Hermansdorfer, 423 U.S. 336, 96 S.Ct. 584, 46 L.Ed.2d 542 (1976).

§ 2.13

1. *See* Hanson v. Denckla, 357 U.S. 235, 78 S.Ct. 1228, 2 L.Ed.2d 1283 (1958).

attaching local property of the defendant worth only $10,000. If defendant simply appears, he or she will probably be taken as submitting to the court's jurisdiction and thus be subject to a judgment for the full amount of the claim.[2] Defendant, however, wishes neither to litigate the controversy in full by making a general appearance nor to have the property taken by default. May defendant appear and litigate the merits of the plaintiff's claim for the limited purpose of protecting the property without thereby becoming subject to a judgment in the full amount of the claim? The authorities are divided, the apparently more prevalent view being that defendant can make such a limited appearance.[3] But a further question also arises: Is the determination of the *issues* in such a proceeding binding in subsequent litigation? If so, the judgment comes close to being in practical effect an in personam judgment; if not, then the issues may have to be litigated again. The choice between these results, as we have seen, is an unhappy one.[4]

C. JUDICIAL SELF-RESTRAINTS ON EXERCISING JURISDICTION

§ 2.14 Introduction

While modern extensions of jurisdictional concepts have come largely as a response to dissatisfaction with the arbitrary limits of the sovereignty concept and represent considerations of convenience and fairness, these extensions have greatly widened the plaintiff's choice of forum and added new possibilities of abuse in individual cases. The law is not, however, entirely one-sided. For a long time it has had protective rules giving nonresident defendants immunity from service of process when their presence in the state is in the public interest and protecting them from the exercise of jurisdiction when their presence has been procured by force or fraud. The doctrine of *forum non conveniens* may also be available: If the forum chosen by plaintiff is seriously inconvenient and a more appropriate forum is available, the forum chosen by plaintiff will refuse to accept the case. These protective rules are discussed in the following sections.

§ 2.15 Immunity from Service

Most American courts give to nonresidents a privilege or immunity from service of process while they are within the forum state in attendance at trial either as witnesses, parties, or attorneys and during a

2. *See* United States v. Balanovski, 236 F.2d 298 (2d Cir.1956).

3. Cheshire Natl. Bank v. Jaynes, 224 Mass. 14, 112 N.E. 500 (1916); Dry Clime Lamp Corp. v. Edwards, 389 F.2d 590 (5th Cir.1968), with which *compare* United States v. Balanovski, *supra* note 2.

4. *See* Restatement (Second) of Judgments § 32(c) (taking the position that the determination of the issue is conclusive). *But see* Minichiello v. Rosenberg, 410 F.2d 106, 112 (2d Cir.1968) (questioning whether it properly may be).

reasonable time for the journey into and out of the state.[1] "The rule is all but unanimous as to witnesses but there are some decisions which distinguish between nonresident plaintiffs and nonresident defendants," affording immunity to the latter only.[2]

Witnesses attending trial

The rule of immunity is most easily justified, and is generally approved, in the case of witnesses. Absent nonresidents cannot be compelled to attend trials in the forum because the court has no compulsory authority over them. While their depositions may be compelled in the state where they reside, the testimony of witnesses in court is believed to be more valuable to the tribunal than the transcribed testimony of absent witnesses whose demeanor the tribunal cannot observe. Since the attendance of absent nonresident witnesses can be had only if they appear voluntarily, a rule giving them immunity and thereby encouraging their voluntary presence promotes the administration of justice in the forum.[3]

Nonresident defendants

The balance of interests stands differently when the nonresident is a party. A nonresident party's entrance into the state, it is said, serves only his or her selfish advantage and not the administration of local justice. Even a defendant's presence "will not facilitate the progress of the cause" since an effective judgment by default can be entered against such a defendant.[4] But this surely assumes a narrow and provincial view of the administration of justice, which should be concerned with the pursuit of truth on full inquiry and not merely the power to enter an effective default judgment against nonresidents.[5] Hence, it is generally recognized that a nonresident defendant is immune from service of process in other suits unrelated to the principal case.[6]

Nonresident plaintiffs

Immunity is hardest to defend for nonresident plaintiffs. A plaintiff, of course, submits to the forum court's jurisdiction over all counterclaims or cross-claims that may be interposed under the local practice.[7]

§ 2.15

1. Lamb v. Schmitt, 285 U.S. 222, 225, 52 S.Ct. 317, 318, 76 L.Ed. 720, 722 (1932); Stewart v. Ramsay, 242 U.S. 128, 37 S.Ct. 44, 61 L.Ed. 192 (1916); Crusco v. Strunk Steel Co., 365 Pa. 326, 328, 74 A.2d 142, 143 (1950); Note, 12 Vand. L. Rev. 487 (1959); Annot., 74 A.L.R.2d 592.

2. Note, 12 Vand. L. Rev. 487, 488 n.4 (1959).

3. Diamond v. Earle, 217 Mass. 499, 105 N.E. 363 (1914).

4. *See* Keeffe and Roscia, Immunity and Sentimentality, 32 Cornell L.Q. 471, 485 (1947); *cf.* Northern Light Technology v. Northern Lights Club, 236 F.3d 57 (1st Cir.2001) (upholding service on defendant who entered state to contest personal jurisdiction in same case).

5. *See* Crusco v. Strunk Steel Co., 365 Pa. 326, 328, 74 A.2d 142, 143 (1950).

6. Restatement (Second) of Judgments § 9.

7. Adam v. Saenger, 303 U.S. 59, 58 S.Ct. 454, 82 L.Ed. 649 (1938); see National

What about the plaintiff's amenability to service in a new, independent action probably brought by a stranger to the original suit? Here the forum state's interest in affording a forum for the nonresident plaintiff is relatively weak, and its interest in opening its courts to local claimants against nonresidents is relatively strong. Critics of immunity for nonresident plaintiffs point out that the nonresident probably chooses the forum state because he or she cannot get jurisdiction over the (original) defendant in the plaintiff's own state.[8] And surely the forum state has a legitimate interest in affording a forum for claims against persons suable in its courts (possibly residents and citizens) on behalf of nonresidents who cannot use their own courts for this purpose.

Criminal defendant

Immunity from service poses a somewhat different problem when applied to a person who comes into the state as a criminal defendant.[9] If the accused enters the state voluntarily to surrender to the court, there is good reason for immunity, since voluntary appearance furthers the administration of justice and saves the state trouble and expense.[10] The weight of authority confers immunity in such a case. When the nonresident is present within the state as a result of extradition[11] or has been arrested on the criminal charge while within the state and is now present there either in custody[12] or to prevent forfeiture of bail,[13] the weight of authority denies the nonresident any immunity from civil process except when the civil plaintiff has instigated the criminal proceedings in order to bring the defendant within the reach of civil process.[14]

§ 2.16 Sovereign Immunity

The doctrine of sovereign immunity provides that a government may not be subjected to suit without its consent. The rule protects federal,

City Bank v. Republic of China, 348 U.S. 356, 75 S.Ct. 423, 99 L.Ed. 389 (1955)(filing claim waives sovereign immunity as to counterclaim); § 9.13 *infra*. It is important to note how the growing liberality of counterclaim practice affects this problem. The older rules, even under the codes, greatly restricted a defendant's opportunity to interpose claims against the plaintiff in the plaintiff's action against him or her. Modern procedures have swept away all or most restrictions on counterclaims between the original parties to the action. *See* § 9.11 *infra*. It would seem that a counterclaim unrelated to the original action should be treated as a new action for purposes of the problem at hand.

8. *See* Keefe and Roscia, Immunity and Sentimentality, 32 Cornell L.Q. 471, 478–479 (1947); Note, 33 Harv. L. Rev. 721, 723 (1920).

9. Annot., 20 A.L.R.2d 163 (1951).

10. Thermoid Co. v. Fabel, 4 N.Y.2d 494, 176 N.Y.S.2d 331, 151 N.E.2d 883 (1958); Note, 12 Vand. L. Rev. 487 (1959).

11. *See, e.g.,* Adriance v. Lagrave, 59 N.Y. 110 (1874).

12. White v. Underwood, 125 N.C. 25, 34 S.E. 104 (1899). *Cf.* Crusco v. Strunk Steel Co., 365 Pa. 326, 74 A.2d 142 (1950).

13. Netograph Mfg. Co. v. Scrugham, 197 N.Y. 377, 90 N.E. 962 (1910); cases collected in Note, 20 A.L.R.2d 163, 201 (1951). *But contrast* Adamy v. Parkhurst, 61 F.2d 517 (6th Cir.1932); Feuster v. Redshaw, 157 Md. 302, 145 A. 560 (1929).

14. This was the common law and it has been codified in § 25 of the Uniform Criminal Extradition Act, 11 U.L.A. 59.

foreign, and state governments. Growing from obscure English origins, today it is based on the belief that subjecting a sovereign to suit without its permission is disrespectful, if not disruptive and futile.[1] Yet wholly exempting governments from suit would drastically undermine the rule of law, and in many situations frustrate governments' own goals, for example when they seek to enter binding contracts. Statutes and judicial doctrines have therefore recognized many exceptions to sovereign immunity, leaving the law in a highly confusing condition.

Federal immunity

The federal government is immune from suit in both state and federal courts.[2] Although it has consented to be sued in federal court on a variety of constitutional, statutory, contractual and tort claims, some of the consents are limited. For example, the Tucker Act allows some claims to be asserted only in the United States Court of Federal Claims (formerly called the Court of Claims), and the Federal Tort Claims Act bars altogether certain kinds of claims.[3] Because of such restrictions, as well as the rule that the government's consent to suit must be clearly and unequivocally stated,[4] litigation with the federal government is subject to a complex law of its own.

State immunity

The immunity of the states to suit in federal court may have been assumed by the Founders, and was explicitly established by the Eleventh Amendment. Passed in response to *Chisholm v. Georgia,*[5] in which the Supreme Court upheld a diversity suit against a state to collect a debt, the Amendment provides that the judicial power "shall not be construed to extend to any suit in law or equity, commenced or prosecuted against one of the United States by Citizens of another State, or by Citizens or Subjects of any Foreign State." In 1890, the Court held that a state is likewise immune from suit by one of its own citizens, a ruling now held to be constitutionally required.[6] Like the federal government, those of

§ 2.16

1. Jaffe, Suits Against Governments and Officers: Sovereign Immunity, 77 Harv. L. Rev. 1 (1963).

2. *E.g.,* Larson v. Domestic & Foreign Commerce Corp., 337 U.S. 682, 69 S.Ct. 1457, 93 L.Ed. 1628 (1949); Tarble's Case, 80 U.S. 397, 20 L.Ed. 597 (1871); *cf.* 28 U.S.C. §§ 1442, 1442a (allowing the federal government and its agencies and officers to remove to federal court any state court suit arising from acts under color of office).

3. Major consent provisions include: 28 U.S.C. §§ 1346(a)(2), 1491 (Tucker Act); 28 U.S.C. §§ 2401–02, 2671–80 (Federal Tort Claims Act); 5 U.S.C. § 702 (Administrative Procedure Act). *See generally* Lester, Litigation with the Federal Government (3d ed. 1994); § 2.25 *infra.*

4. Lane v. Pena, 518 U.S. 187, 116 S.Ct. 2092, 135 L.Ed.2d 486 (1996).

5. 2 U.S. 419, 1 L.Ed. 440 (1793).

6. Hans v. Louisiana, 134 U.S. 1, 10 S.Ct. 504, 33 L.Ed. 842 (1890). Among the scholarly arguments for a narrower reading of the Eleventh Amendment than the Supreme Court has adopted are Fletcher, A Historical Interpretation of the Eleventh Amendment, 35 Stan. L. Rev. 1033 (1983); Gibbons, The Eleventh Amendment and State Sovereign Immunity: A Reinterpretation, 83 Colum. L. Rev. 1889 (1983).

the states have waived their immunity in many situations, but such waivers are strictly construed and are limited to suit in state courts unless the state explicitly consents to suit in federal court.[7]

State immunity, however, has yielded in part to the need to enforce against the states the rights that the Constitution itself provides. Under the doctrine of *Ex parte Young*,[8] federal courts may enjoin state officials from violating the Constitution even if this imposes expenses on a state, so long as they do not directly order the payment of state funds.[9] This doctrine is based on the fiction that a state officer who exceeds the bounds laid down by the Constitution thereby exceeds any authority granted by the state, so that he or she is acting as a private person unprotected by sovereign immunity. Similar reasoning allows a federal court to hold a state official liable for damages: the judgment does not run against the state, although the state may in fact choose to pay it anyway.[10] Another doctrine states that, for sovereign immunity purposes, municipal and county governments do not count as part of the state, even though as a matter of substantive Constitutional law their acts constitute state action subject to the Fourteenth Amendment.[11] The Court has held that Congress' power to enforce that amendment allows it to subject states violating it to suit.[12] Of the other exceptions to state sovereign immunity, the most important allows the federal government itself to sue a state.[13]

Recently, the Supreme Court has given new breadth to the sovereign immunity of states, overruling earlier precedents to hold that Congress may not subject states to suits by private parties under legislation it passes under the Commerce Clause.[14] This limitation applies to suits in state courts as well as to those in federal courts, a ruling based not on the Eleventh Amendment, which says nothing about state courts, but on

7. *E.g.*, Atascadero State Hospital v. Scanlon, 473 U.S. 234, 105 S.Ct. 3142, 87 L.Ed.2d 171 (1985).

8. 209 U.S. 123, 28 S.Ct. 441, 52 L.Ed. 714 (1908).

9. Edelman v. Jordan, 415 U.S. 651, 94 S.Ct. 1347, 39 L.Ed.2d 662 (1974); Quern v. Jordan, 440 U.S. 332, 99 S.Ct. 1139, 59 L.Ed.2d 358 (1979).

10. Scheuer v. Rhodes, 416 U.S. 232, 94 S.Ct. 1683, 40 L.Ed.2d 90 (1974).

11. Mt. Healthy City School Bd. of Ed. v. Doyle, 429 U.S. 274, 97 S.Ct. 568, 50 L.Ed.2d 471 (1977); Monell v. Department of Social Services, 436 U.S. 658, 98 S.Ct. 2018, 56 L.Ed.2d 611 (1978).

12. Fitzpatrick v. Bitzer, 427 U.S. 445, 96 S.Ct. 2666, 49 L.Ed.2d 614 (1976).

13. United States v. Mississippi, 380 U.S. 128, 85 S.Ct. 808, 13 L.Ed.2d 717 (1965). *See also* South Central Bell Telephone Co. v. Alabama, 526 U.S. 160, 119 S.Ct. 1180, 143 L.Ed.2d 258 (1999)(sovereign immunity to does not bar review by Supreme Court of state court judgment to which state is party); California v. Deep Sea Research, 523 U.S. 491, 118 S.Ct. 1464, 140 L.Ed.2d 626 (1998)(federal court may hear admiralty case concerning ownership of wrecked ship to which state claims title); Nevada v. Hall, 440 U.S. 410, 99 S.Ct. 1182, 59 L.Ed.2d 416 (1979)(state court may hear damage suit against another state).

14. College Savings Bank v. Florida Prepaid Postsecondary Educational Expense Board, 527 U.S. 666, 119 S.Ct. 2219, 144 L.Ed.2d 605 (1999); Seminole Tribe v. Florida, 517 U.S. 44, 116 S.Ct. 1114, 134 L.Ed.2d 252 (1996).

the structure of the federal system.[15] These decisions do not question Congress' power to bind the states by the substantive requirements of Commerce Clause legislation, for example by requiring them to pay minimum wages. State employees remain entitled to minimum wages. They just cannot enforce that right in court, unless they persuade the federal government to sue on their behalf, or the state waives its immunity, conceivably in exchange for federal subsidies. The Court's decisions therefore give the states little substantive autonomy, but impose much procedural obstruction and inconvenience, as well as tempting state officers to violate federal law in the hope that they will not be sued.

How far the Court will proceed to strengthen state sovereign immunity remains unclear. Another of its recent decisions limits the doctrine of *Ex parte Young* under which federal courts have enjoined unlawful acts of state officials, but without establishing any clear majority view.[16]

Foreign government immunity

Yet another branch of sovereign immunity, this one protecting foreign governments, has long been recognized in American law. In 1812 the Supreme Court held that foreign states (sovereigns) are immune from judicial process in the United States.[17] The theory, as Chief Justice Marshall explained, is based on the idea that states, as equal entities under international law, have no authority over one another.

Absolute immunity permitted foreign sovereigns to breach their contractual burdens with impunity. A more restrictive view of the doctrine began to take hold, in the early part of the twentieth century, mainly in response to the inequities engendered under the old rule and the increasing involvement of governments and their agencies in international trade and borrowing. Under the more limited interpretation, sovereign immunity protects a state only from suits arising from the public acts of the foreign state; it does not extend to the strictly commercial acts of the state. The United States formally adopted this restrictive view of sovereign immunity in 1952.[18]

The restrictive theory proved to be difficult to apply. The burden of determining immunity fell on the executive branch, acting through the State Department. Because the difficulty of balancing political, economic,

15. Alden v. Maine, 527 U.S. 706, 119 S.Ct. 2240, 144 L.Ed.2d 636 (1999); see Symposium, Federalism After *Alden*, 31 Rutgers L.J. 631 (2000); Symposium, State Sovereign Immunity and the Eleventh Amendment, 75 Notre Dame L. Rev. 817 (2000).

16. Idaho v. Coeur d'Alene Tribe of Idaho, 521 U.S. 261, 117 S.Ct. 2028, 138 L.Ed.2d 438 (1997).

17. The Schooner Exchange v. McFaddon, 11 U.S. (7 Cranch) 116, 3 L.Ed. 287 (1812).

18. Verlinden B.V. v. Central Bank of Nigeria, 461 U.S. 480, 103 S.Ct. 1962, 76 L.Ed.2d 81 (1983); Vencedora Oceanica Navigacion, S.A. v. Compagnie Nationale Algerienne De Navigation, 730 F.2d 195 (5th Cir.1984); 26 Dept. of State Bull. 984 (1952).

and diplomatic considerations led to inconsistent and confusing rulings, Congress in 1976 enacted the Foreign Sovereign Immunities Act (FSIA)[19] to provide a uniform statutory basis for the determination, thus eliminating the State Department from the process.

The FSIA is couched in terms of broad policy, providing few explicit rules or standards. It states the general rule of immunity from the jurisdiction of the courts of the United States for foreign states, including "a political subdivision of a foreign state or an agency or instrumentality of a foreign state," such as state-owned airlines, shipping, or petroleum companies.[20] The FSIA is the only basis for obtaining jurisdiction over these agencies of a foreign state in the courts of this country.[21]

Under the Act, United States courts may exercise jurisdiction over a foreign sovereign only if an exception to sovereign immunity exists. One of these exceptions is commercial activity, but only if it has a sufficient connection—a "jurisdictional nexus"[22]—with the United States. Three types of acts are identified by the FSIA as sufficiently connected to the United States to satisfy the jurisdictional nexus requirement:

1. a commercial activity carried on in the United States
2. an act performed in the United States in connection with a commercial activity carried on outside the United States
3. a commercial activity carried on outside the United States that has a direct effect on the United States.[23]

The mere existence of commercial operations in the United States, however, does not mean that a foreign sovereign has relinquished all claims to sovereign immunity. There must be not only a jurisdictional nexus but also a connection between the plaintiff's cause of action and the commercial acts of the foreign sovereign.[24] This relationship does not have to be a direct causal connection, but there must be at least a material connection between the cause of action and the commercial acts of the sovereign in the United States.[25] The commercial activities exception will not deprive a foreign state of sovereign immunity for mere "isolated or unrelated commercial actions."[26] To determine whether the

19. 28 U.S.C. §§ 1602–1611.

20. 28 U.S.C. §§ 1603(a),1604.

21. Argentine Republic v. Amerada Hess Shipping Corp., 488 U.S. 428, 109 S.Ct. 683, 102 L.Ed.2d 818 (1989).

22. Stena Rederi AB v. Comision de Contratos del Comite Ejecutivo General del Sindicato Revolucionario de Trabajadores Petroleros de la Republica Mexicana, S.C., 923 F.2d 380, 386 (5th Cir.1991).

23. 28 U.S.C. § 1605(a)(2). *See* Saudi Arabia v. Nelson, 507 U.S. 349, 113 S.Ct. 1471, 123 L.Ed.2d 47 (1993).

24. Vencedora Oceanica Navigacion, S.A. v. Compagnie Nationale Algerienne De Navigation, 730 F.2d 195 (5th Cir.1984); Stena Rederi AB v. Comision de Contratos del Comite Ejecutivo General del Sindicato Revolucionario de Trabajadores Petroleros de la Republica Mexicana, S.C., 923 F.2d 380 (5th Cir.1991).

25. *E.g.*, Republic of Argentina v. Weltover, Inc., 504 U.S. 607, 112 S.Ct. 2160, 119 L.Ed.2d 394 (1992)(issuance of bonds payable in dollars in New York, among other places, and appointment of New York financial agent).

26. America West Airlines v. GPA Group, Ltd., 877 F.2d 793, 797 (9th Cir. 1989); Alberti v. Empresa Nicaraguense De La Carne, 705 F.2d 250, 254 (7th Cir.1983).

commercial activity exception applies, the courts will focus only on the specific acts that form the basis for the suit; the fact of widespread commercial activities is insufficient to support a finding of jurisdiction.[27]

In recent years, federal courts have occasionally moved beyond cases arising from foreign governmental commercial activity to become a force for the protection of international human rights. An old statute bestows federal jurisdiction over actions "by an alien for a tort only, committed in violation of the law of nations."[28] As the law of nations has come to protect individual rights, federal courts have upheld suits under this statute against foreign officials (but not their governments) for torture and other human rights violations.[29] Congress amended the FSIA to allow suits against a foreign nation for torture and terrorism, but only when the President has designated that nation a sponsor of terrorism. A few plaintiffs have obtained large judgments against such nations but have not been able to enforce them, since nations designated as sponsors of terrorism usually keep any assets subject to judicial execution under FSIA out of the United States.[30]

§ 2.17 Cases Involving Force or Fraud

A defendant who has been tricked into coming within the jurisdiction for the purpose of being served process may avoid such process.[1] No doubt the same thing would be true if the plaintiff brought the defendant into the state by force, although the Supreme Court has upheld jurisdiction gained by force in criminal cases.[2] A similar rule prevails when plaintiffs seek to obtain quasi in rem jurisdiction by attachment or garnishment of property that they have tricked defendant into sending within the state for this purpose.[3]

27. Callejo v. Bancomer, S.A., 764 F.2d 1101 (5th Cir.1985).

28. 28 U.S.C. § 1350; see The Alien Tort Claims Act: An Analytical Anthology (Steinhardt & D'Amato ed. 1999).

29. *E.g.*, Filartiga v. Pena-Irala, 630 F.2d 876 (2d Cir.1980); Hilao v. Estate of Marcos, 103 F.3d 767 (9th Cir.1996); Kadic v. Karadzic, 70 F.3d 232 (2d Cir.1995); Wiwa v. Royal Dutch Petroleum Co., 226 F.3d 88 (2d Cir.2000). Such suits parallel recent attempts to impose international criminal liability on government officials for human rights violations. *E.g.*, R v. Bow Street Stipendiary Magistrate, [1999] 2 All E.R. 97 (H.L. 1999)(Eng.).

30. 28 U.S.C. § 1605(a)(7); Flatow v. Islamic Republic of Iran, 76 F.Supp.2d 16 (D.D.C.1999); Slaughter & Bosco, Plaintiff's Diplomacy, Foreign Affairs, Sept./Oct. 2000, at 102.

§ 2.17

1. Wyman v. Newhouse, 93 F.2d 313 (2d Cir.1937); Terlizzi v. Brodie, 38 A.D.2d 762, 329 N.Y.S.2d 589 (1972); Western States Ref. Co. v. Berry, 6 Utah 2d 336, 313 P.2d 480 (1957); Note, 7 Duke L.J. 52 (1957); Annot., 37 A.L.R. 1255 (1925); Restatement (Second) of Conflict of Laws § 82.

2. For civil cases, see dicta in Burnham v. Superior Court, 495 U.S. 604, 110 S.Ct. 2105, 109 L.Ed.2d 631 (1990)(references to voluntary presence); Ex parte Edwards, 99 Cal.App. 541, 278 P. 910, 911 (1929). For criminal cases, see United States v. Alvarez-Machain, 504 U.S. 655, 112 S.Ct. 2188, 119 L.Ed.2d 441 (1992).

3. Forbess v. George Morgan Pontiac Co., 135 So.2d 594 (La.Ct.App.1961); Sessoms Grocery Co. v. International Sugar Feed Co., 188 Ala. 232, 66 So. 479 (1914); Paul Delaney Co. v. Joseph Freedman Co., 93 N.J.L. 456, 108 A. 435 (1919); Pakas v. Steel Ball Co., 34 Misc. 811, 68 N.Y.S. 397

Rationale for immunity

The conceptual basis for the rule is ambiguous. Some courts declare that no jurisdiction is acquired in these cases,[4] others that jurisdiction is acquired but should not be exercised when the force or fraud is present.[5] It will make no practical difference which theory is chosen, except where the force or fraud is exerted by a stranger for whose conduct the plaintiff is not legally responsible. The scant judicial authority holds that service of process is valid even though the person or the property may have been enticed into the jurisdiction by the fraud of a stranger for whose conduct the plaintiff was not responsible.[6] But since due process, in its jurisdictional aspect, is increasingly measured in terms of a state's interest in or contacts with the parties and the subject of the action, it may well be that a defendant's physical presence procured by *anyone's* force or fraud is not alone a sufficient basis for jurisdiction. If, however, the state has sufficient interest in or contact with the parties and the subject of action to form the basis for jurisdiction, perhaps force or fraud should be irrelevant even when perpetrated by the plaintiff.

§ 2.18 Infringement of Constitutionally Protected Activity

Interstate commerce

During the 1920s and 1930s a few Supreme Court decisions forbade state courts to proceed with actions against railroad corporations that had no lines and operated no service within the forum state on the ground that having to defend such actions would be an unconstitutional burden on interstate commerce.[1] In each of these cases the cause of action arose outside the forum state and the plaintiff did not live there when the action accrued.[2] No Supreme Court decision in recent years has found an action to be a burden on interstate commerce, but the doctrine has not been repudiated and may well overlap and complement the more flexible doctrine of forum non conveniens.[3] "[If] the connection of the

(1901). *Cf.* Jaster v. Currie, 198 U.S. 144, 25 S.Ct. 614, 49 L.Ed. 988 (1905).

4. *See, e.g.,* Wyman v. Newhouse, 93 F.2d 313, 315 (2d Cir.1937); Forbess v. George Morgan Pontiac Co., 135 So.2d 594, 596 (La.Ct.App.1961); Ehrenzweig, Conflict of Laws 32 n.1 (1962).

5. *See, e.g.,* Fitelson v. Acuff, 14 Pa. D. & C.2d 486 (Luzerne Co. 1956).

6. Ex parte Taylor, 29 R.I. 129, 69 A. 553 (1908), seems to be the leading case. *See also* Steiger v. Bonn, 4 Fed. 17, 19 (C.C.D.N.J.1880).

§ 2.18

1. *See, e.g.,* Davis v. Farmers' Co-op. Equity Co., 262 U.S. 312, 43 S.Ct. 556, 67 L.Ed. 996 (1923); Denver & Rio Grande W.R.R. v. Terte, 284 U.S. 284, 52 S.Ct. 152, 76 L.Ed. 295 (1932).

2. Barrett, The Doctrine of Forum Non Conveniens, 35 Calif. L. Rev. 380, 385 (1947).

3. *See* Denver & Rio Grande W.R.R. v. Terte, 284 U.S. 284, 287–288, 52 S.Ct. 152, 153, 76 L.Ed. 295, 297 (1932) ("As a practical matter, courts could undertake to ascertain in advance of trial the number and importance of probable witnesses within and without the State and retain or refuse jurisdiction according to the relative inconvenience of the parties"). *Contrast* §§ 2.8, 2.10 *supra.*

forum state with the litigation is too attenuated, the burden on the defendant's business may be unreasonable."[4]

Some lower court decisions held that the First Amendment limits the reach of jurisdiction in actions for defamation,[5] but the Supreme Court has rejected this approach on the ground that the factors weighing for and against jurisdiction are already "counted" in the minimum contacts rule.[6] This analysis would seem also to repudiate giving any special weight to the fact that a defendant's activity is governed by the Commerce Clause.

§ 2.19 Local Action Rule

A rule harking back to English common law, known as the local action rule, required that actions concerning land be brought in the county where the land was located. In this country, the rule has been applied to preclude the courts of one state from entertaining actions concerning land in another state.[1] The rule has been called "jurisdictional." Its origin can be traced to the distinction in English law between local actions (those affecting real property), which had to be brought in the county where the land was located, and transitory actions, which could be brought wherever defendant was subject to service of process.[2] As traditionally formulated, the rule applied not only to actions involving the question of title but also to those involving damages for injury to real property. Insofar as there are still constitutional barriers to one state's rendering a judgment that determines title to property in another state, the local action rule can be regarded as a corollary of the sovereignty theory of state judicial jurisdiction.[3] But no such constitutional limitation exists concerning an action for injuries to property. In this application, and perhaps even with actions concerning title or ownership, the rule is an anachronism.

Convenience of forum

If the problem of actions concerning real property is considered in terms of convenient forum, however, the local action rule can be given a coherent modern form. That is, ordinarily a court should refuse to entertain an action, even one seeking money damages, that concerns use or ownership of land located elsewhere—not because the court lacks

4. Note, Developments in the Law—State-Court Jurisdiction, 73 Harv. L. Rev. 909, 984 (1960). *Cf.* Allenberg Cotton Co. v. Pittman, 419 U.S. 20, 95 S.Ct. 260, 42 L.Ed.2d 195 (1974), referred to in § 2.3 note 12 *supra*.

5. *See* Buckley v. New York Post Corp., 373 F.2d 175 (2d Cir.1967).

6. Calder v. Jones, 465 U.S. 783, 104 S.Ct. 1482, 79 L.Ed.2d 804 (1984).

§ 2.19

1. *See* Livingston v. Jefferson, 15 F. Cas. 660 (C.C.D.Va.1811) (No. 8,411); Reasor-Hill Corp. v. Harrison, 220 Ark. 521, 249 S.W.2d 994 (1952). *Compare* Bigio v. Coca-Cola Co., 235 F.3d 63 (2d Cir.2000) (allowing suit for conversion of foreign land).

2. *See* § 2.23 note 2 *infra*.

3. *See* § 2.8 *supra*.

power to adjudicate such a controversy, but because it is an inappropriate forum for such litigation. If, however, the defendant has injured property in another state and is not amenable to process there (because that state's long-arm statute does not permit it), the application of the local action rule in the state where the defendant can be sued would deny the plaintiff any remedy. One of the few modern decisions on the point has taken this view and sustained its jurisdiction.[4]

§ 2.20 Forum Non Conveniens

The doctrine of forum non conveniens holds that a court has discretionary authority to decline to adjudicate an action whose facts arose in another jurisdiction whenever it appears that the cause may be more appropriately tried elsewhere.[1] The doctrine gained recognition in American law in the early twentieth century and became generally accepted after the Supreme Court adopted it in *Gulf Oil Corp. v. Gilbert.*[2] In the federal courts, the doctrine is now applied primarily when the superior forum is abroad, because when it is in the United States a federal court can simply send the case to the preferred district court under the transfer statute, rather than dismissing the case under the forum non conveniens doctrine.[3] Forum non conveniens differs from a rule of jurisdiction in the following respects:

Court's discretion

1. The forum non conveniens rule explicitly involves an exercise of discretion by the court. The "minimum contacts" concept of

4. *See* Reasor–Hill Corp. v. Harrison, *supra* note 1. *Compare* Still v. Rossville Crushed Stone Co., 370 F.2d 324 (6th Cir. 1966), applying Tennessee law, which the court construed as incorporating the local action rule. The Restatement (Second) of Conflict of Laws § 87 takes the position that a state may entertain an action for injury to land located in another state but that it should not, or may not, entertain one that would determine title.

§ 2.20

1. *See* Piper Aircraft Co. v. Reyno, 454 U.S. 235, 102 S.Ct. 252, 70 L.Ed.2d 419 (1981); Blair, The Doctrine of Forum Non Conveniens in Anglo–American Law, 29 Colum. L. Rev. 1 (1929). *See* Barrett, The Doctrine of Forum Non Conveniens, 35 Calif. L. Rev. 380 (1947); McAllen, Deference to the Plaintiff in Forum Non Conveniens, 13 S. Ill. L.J. 191 (1989); Stewart, Forum Non Conveniens: A Doctrine in Search of a Role, 74 Calif. L. Rev. 1259 (1986); Anderson, What Can the United States Learn from English Anti–Suit Injunctions? An American Perspective on *Airbus Industrie GTE v. Patel*, 25 Yale J. Int'l L. 195 (2000).

2. 330 U.S. 501, 67 S.Ct. 839, 91 L.Ed. 1055 (1947). For state court recognitions of the rule, see, e.g., Price v. Atchison, T. & S.F.R.R., 42 Cal.2d 577, 268 P.2d 457 (1954); Silver v. Great American Ins. Co., 29 N.Y.2d 356, 278 N.E.2d 619, 328 N.Y.S.2d 398 (1972). *See* Annots., 43 A.L.R.2d 774 (FELA actions), 48 A.L.R.2d 800, 850, 90 A.L.R.2d 1109.

3. For transfer, see 28 U.S.C. § 1404(a); § 2.33 *infra*. For a proposal allowing transfer between state courts, *see* Uniform Transfer of Litigation Act, 14 U.L.A. 2001 (Supp. 2000). When federal courts do apply forum non conveniens, they follow federal precedent rather than state law. Ravelo Monegro v. Rosa, 211 F.3d 509 (9th Cir. 2000). Compare American Dredging Co. v. Miller, 510 U.S. 443, 114 S.Ct. 981, 127 L.Ed.2d 285 (1994)(state court need not apply federal precedent in maritime cases).

state court jurisdiction, though it also involves the "weighing" of factors, takes the form of an imperative.

2. The forum non conveniens rule applies only if the court has jurisdiction by virtue of "minimum contacts" or on some other basis. If jurisdictional basis is lacking, the court must dismiss the action for that reason, even if an alternative forum would be more inconvenient.

Conditional dismissal

3. If the court dismisses for forum non conveniens, it may condition the dismissal on the defendant's agreeing to submit to jurisdiction in the more convenient forum, to waive a statute of limitations defense when the new action is brought, and similar equitable considerations. A court that lacks jurisdiction has no authority to impose such conditions.

In early years the courts did not readily embrace the doctrine. Many decisions reflected the notion that a court has the duty to exercise jurisdiction whenever it is properly acquired;[4] other decisions expressed the view that the Privileges and Immunities Clause of the Constitution forbids a state to deny a forum to suitors who are citizens of a sister state.[5] The latter notion has no continuing support. While arbitrary distinctions against noncitizens are forbidden, it is not unconstitutional to decline jurisdiction over cases that have no reasonable connection with the forum state. Litigation between nonresidents over foreign causes of action may have no such connection, while the residence of one of the parties itself "supplies the nexus."[6]

Interests of court and parties

Forum non conveniens represents two strains of policy: public interest and private interest. One is the state's interest in protecting its citizens and taxpayers from the undue expense and congestion that may flow from burdening its courts with litigation having no connection with

4. Barrett, The Doctrine of Forum Non Conveniens, 35 Calif. L. Rev. 380, 394–397 (1947).

5. A dictum by Judge Washington in Corfield v. Coryell, 6 F. Cas. 546, 552 (C.C.E.D.Pa.1823) (No. 3230), reflected the early notion that the right of access to the courts of every state was one of the privileges of the citizens of the several states. *See* Cofrode v. Gartner, 79 Mich. 332, 44 N.W. 623 (1890); Blair, The Doctrine of Forum Non Conveniens in Anglo-American Law, 29 Colum. L. Rev. 1, 3-19 (1929); Barrett, *supra* note 4, at 389–390; Note, Developments in the Law—State-Court Jurisdiction, 73 Harv. L. Rev. 909, 1009, 1010 (1968).

6. *Cf.* Douglas v. New York, N.H. & H.R.R., 279 U.S. 377, 49 S.Ct. 355, 73 L.Ed. 747 (1929) (distinguishing citizenship from residence). It is now well settled that the Constitution does not forbid a state to apply forum non conveniens. Missouri ex rel. Southern Ry. v. Mayfield, 340 U.S. 1, 71 S.Ct. 1, 95 L.Ed. 3 (1950) (repeating the distinction in *Douglas*; four justices dissented, but on the ground that FELA cases enjoyed a special immunity from the rules); Currie and Schreter, Unconstitutional Discrimination in the Conflict of Laws: Privileges and Immunities, 69 Yale L.J. 1323, 1397 (1960) (criticizing the distinction suggested in *Douglas*).

the state. The other is the parties' interest in having litigation between them processed conveniently and in a way most likely to yield a just result. The factors used in applying the doctrine reflect one or both of these policy considerations. Thus, the bona fide residence of the parties is a factor to be weighed for its bearing on both the public and private interest.

The public interest factors include the following:

> the administrative difficulties flowing from court congestion; the local interest in having localized controversies decided at home; the interest in having the trial of a diversity case in a forum that is at home with the law that must govern the action; the avoidance of unnecessary problems in conflict of laws, or in application of foreign laws; and the unfairness of burdening citizens in an unrelated forum with jury duty.[7]

Also relevant are the following factors:

> the relevant ease of access to sources of proof; availability of compulsory process for attendance of unwilling [witnesses], and the cost of obtaining attendance of willing witnesses; possibility of view of premises if view would be appropriate to the action; and all other practical problems that make trial of a case easy, expeditious and inexpensive. There may also be questions of enforceability of a judgment if one is obtained. The court will weigh relative advantages and obstacles to fair trial.... But unless the balance is strongly in favor of the defendant, the plaintiff's choice of forum should rarely be disturbed.[8]

Choice of law

Another factor is choice of law, since the plaintiff often chooses the forum because its law, in many cases its statute of limitations, is more favorable. In *Gulf Oil Co. v. Gilbert*, it was held legitimate for a court to consider whether its law would apply in determining whether to keep the case. The Court said that weight could be given to having "a forum that is at home with the state law that must govern the case, rather than having a court in some other forum untangle problems in conflict of laws, and in law foreign to itself."[9] In *Piper Aircraft Co. v. Reyno*,[10] however, the Court said that a plaintiff's showing of less favorable substantive law in the alternative forum should not be given conclusive or even substantial weight in the forum non conveniens analysis. That would largely exclude from consideration what is evidently an important

7. Piper Aircraft Co. v. Reyno, 454 U.S. 235, 241 n. 6, 102 S.Ct. 252, 258 n. 6, 70 L.Ed.2d 419, 422 (1981). *See also* Lacey v. Cessna Aircraft Co., 932 F.2d 170, 180 (3d Cir.1991). *Compare* Lubbe v. Cape PLC, [2000] 1 W.L.R. 1545 (H.L.2000) (Eng.) (rejecting public interest factors and allowing South African plaintiffs to sue in England because Legal Aid available only there).

8. Gulf Oil Co. v. Gilbert, 330 U.S. 501, 508, 67 S.Ct. 839, 843, 91 L.Ed. 1055, 1062 (1947).

9. 330 U.S. at 509, 67 S.Ct. at 843, 91 L.Ed. at 1063.

10. 454 U.S. 235, 102 S.Ct. 252, 70 L.Ed.2d 419 (1981).

factor–indeed, in international cases, the root of the controversy.[11] The argument for the Court's position is that one forum can still apply the other's law when choice of law rules so dictate.

The alternative forum

Still another factor is whether an alternative forum is available. Forum non conveniens will not be applied if dismissal will deprive the plaintiff of the only available forum for the case or when there is substantial doubt whether any other forum is practically available.[12] One way to handle this difficulty, and mitigate the harshness of dismissal, is to provide for transfer of the case to the convenient forum (or at least to *a* convenient forum). Many states, for example, have venue provisions authorizing transfer of cases within the state in this manner, and provision exists for transferring cases from one federal district to another.[13] The courts of one state, however, may not transfer cases to courts of another state, and dismissal is the only device for implementing forum non conveniens as between states. But the same result can be achieved if the forum court conditions its dismissal on the defendant's stipulation to submit to the jurisdiction of the more convenient forum, the court meanwhile staying the proceedings in the forum and postponing dismissal until after that condition has been fulfilled.[14]

Standard of review

For a court to dismiss a case based on forum non conveniens, the defendant must successfully bear the burden of persuasion in proving all the necessary elements.[15] The court has broad discretion in ruling on the motion to dismiss based on this ground. In the federal system, when a district court "has considered all relevant public and private interest factors, and where its balancing of these factors is reasonable, its decision deserves substantial deference."[16] Accordingly, an appellate court will not perform a de novo review of forum non conveniens issues but will limit itself to a consideration whether the trial court has abused

11. Consider, for example, the dispute whether to try in the United States or in India claims arising from the Bhopal disaster, in which chemicals escaping from a factory killed thousands on Indians. In re Union Carbide Corp. Gas Plant Disaster at Bhopal, 809 F.2d 195 (2d Cir.), *cert. denied*, 484 U.S. 871, 108 S.Ct. 199, 98 L.Ed.2d 150 (1987)(dismissing United States actions); Bi v. Union Carbide Chemicals & Plastics Co., 984 F.2d 582 (2d Cir.1993).

12. *See* Note, Requirement of a Second Forum for Application of Forum Non Conveniens, 43 Minn. L. Rev. 1199 (1959).

13. *See* § 2.33 *infra* regarding transfer of cases within the federal court system.

14. *See* Vargas v. A. H. Bull Steamship Co., 44 N.J.Super. 536, 131 A.2d 39, *aff'd*, 25 N.J. 293, 135 A.2d 857 (1957). *But see* Hill v. Upper Miss. Towing Corp., 252 Minn. 165, 89 N.W.2d 654 (1958).

15. Lacey v. Cessna Aircraft Co., 862 F.2d 38 (3d Cir.1988); In re Air Crash Disaster Near New Orleans, La., 821 F.2d 1147 (5th Cir.1987), *partially vacated on other grounds*, 490 U.S. 1032, 109 S.Ct. 1928, 104 L.Ed.2d 400 (1989); Reid–Walen v. Hansen, 933 F.2d 1390 (8th Cir.1991).

16. Piper Aircraft Co. v. Reyno, 454 U.S. 235, 102 S.Ct. 252, 70 L.Ed.2d 419 (1981).

its discretion.[17] Abuse of discretion generally occurs in two ways: (1) "when [the trial court] fails to consider adequately and to determine the amount of deference due the foreign plaintiff's choice of forum" or (2) "when it clearly errs in weighing the factors to be considered."[18]

Gilbert counsels that courts must also be sensitive to the practical problems of plaintiffs in litigating their claim, especially if the alternative forum is in a foreign country.[19] The ultimate analysis is whether the place of trial will "best serve the convenience of the parties and the ends of justice."[20]

§ 2.21 State Court Jurisdiction in Perspective

Since the Supreme Court constitutionalized personal jurisdiction law more than a century ago, that law has grown steadily more complex and unclear. Even now, basic questions remain unanswered. Is a manufacturer who sells allegedly defective components to another manufacturer subject to suit in the state where the resulting product is sold to a consumer?[1] Will owning land in a state support jurisdiction there over a claim unrelated to that land?[2] Are there any exceptions to the rule that serving a defendant within a state supports jurisdiction over a claim arising elsewhere?[3] Even jurisdictional standards not subject to such basic dispute are often so general and so fact-dependent as to make their application unpredictable. Whether a defendant "purposefully avails itself of the privilege of conducting activities within the forum state"[4] is often hard to determine.

This vagueness, although endemic to law created by judicial precedent if not all law, is especially harmful in jurisdictional law because it undermines that law's goal of protecting defendants from defending suits in inappropriate courts. In theory, a defendant sued in such a court can ignore the suit, knowing that the resulting default judgment against it will be unenforceable because the court lacked jurisdiction. In practice, however, a defendant cannot know this because it is unclear whether or not jurisdiction exists. The only safe course, therefore, is for the defendant to appear and challenge jurisdiction, thus litigating in the very court where (if it is correct) it should not have to defend.

17. Lacey v. Cessna Aircraft Co., 932 F.2d 170 (3d Cir.1991).

18. Lony v. E. I. DuPont de Nemours & Co., 886 F.2d 628, 632 (3d Cir.1989).

19. Wilson v. Humphreys (Cayman) Ltd., 916 F.2d 1239 (7th Cir.1990); Reid-Walen v. Hansen, 933 F.2d 1390 (8th Cir. 1991).

20. Koster v. Lumbermens Mut. Casualty Co., 330 U.S. 518, 67 S.Ct. 828, 91 L.Ed. 1067 (1947).

§ **2.21**

1. Compare the opinions in Asahi Metal Industry Co. v. Superior Court, 480 U.S. 102, 107 S.Ct. 1026, 94 L.Ed.2d 92 (1987).

2. Compare the opinions in Shaffer v. Heitner, 433 U.S. 186, 97 S.Ct. 2569, 53 L.Ed.2d 683 (1977).

3. Compare the opinions in Burnham v. Superior Court, 495 U.S. 604, 110 S.Ct. 2105, 109 L.Ed.2d 631 (1990).

4. Hanson v. Denckla, 357 U.S. 235, 253, 78 S.Ct. 1228, 2 L.Ed.2d 1283 (1958).

This state of affairs also results in the devotion of much time and money to contesting an issue distinct from the merits of the case. One survey discovered 975 reported opinions resolving personal jurisdiction issues during the twenty-five years between 1970 and 1994.[5] This is only the tip of the iceberg, because most motions to dismiss never result in reported opinions. Each jurisdictional dispute that is litigated is likely to involve factual investigation, briefing, and argument. The resulting cost discourages defendants from raising valid objections, and plaintiffs from suing in proper forums.

With all its vagueness and expense, personal jurisdiction law's results are often unfortunate, mainly because of the Supreme Court's recurrent if wavering concern with considerations of interstate federalism that are irrelevant to most litigants' practical concerns, and do little good even to the states whose interests they are meant to protect. Why should the Constitution forbid a mother from litigating her claims for child support in the state where she lives, and where her children live with their father's acquiescence, rather than in the father's state?[6] Why should a defendant's brief presence in a state ground jurisdiction there even if there is no other connection between that state and the plaintiff, defendant or claim?[7] Why should a large national franchisee be able to drag small local franchisees from around the country to litigate its claims in its home state?[8] These examples come from the few cases reaching the Supreme Court; presumably lower courts have reached many equally dubious conclusions. Another indication of personal jurisdiction law's weakness is that lawmakers have felt the need to supplement it with other law--long arm statutes, venue, and forum non conveniens–in the hope of improving the results. This, of course, only adds to the system's cost and complexity.

Legislative solutions

It is easier to criticize than to reform. One way of reforming personal jurisdiction law would be for Congress to pass a statute, under its power to implement the full faith and credit clause,[9] regulating personal jurisdiction in both state and federal courts. This would supercede both constitutional jurisdictional law and state long-arm statutes. Like the Brussels Convention that performs a similar role in the European Union, it could establish different rules for different kinds of cases, for example by allowing consumers to sue a manufacturer at their own

5. Solimine, The Quiet Revolution in Personal Jurisdiction, 73 Tul. L. Rev. 1 (1998).

6. Kulko v. Superior Court, 436 U.S. 84, 98 S.Ct. 1690, 56 L.Ed.2d 132 (1978).

7. Burnham v. Superior Court, 495 U.S. 604, 110 S.Ct. 2105, 109 L.Ed.2d 631 (1990) may not go quite this far.

8. Burger King Corp. v. Rudzewicz, 471 U.S. 462, 105 S.Ct. 2174, 85 L.Ed.2d 528 (1985); see also Carnival Cruise Lines, Inc. v. Shute, 499 U.S. 585, 111 S.Ct. 1522, 113 L.Ed.2d 622 (1991).

9. Const. art. IV, § 1.

domiciles.[10] It would no longer be necessary for the same general standard to cover all parties, regardless of their economic ability or inability to defend in a distant forum. It could also abolish what in Europe are called exorbitant bases of jurisdiction, such as jurisdiction based solely on personal service of a defendant briefly entering a state.[11] If proposals for an international recognition of judgments convention based on the Brussels Convention ever reach fruition, that convention might encourage the passage of such a national statute.[12]

Convenience as basis of forum selection

One might envisage still more drastic reform. The adoption of the doctrine of forum non conveniens, together with the concept of jurisdiction based on minimum contacts, has brought the rules concerning the proper place of trial into a configuration quite different from that created by *Pennoyer v. Neff.*[13] The minimum contacts rule requires either that the defendant have some continuing relationship to the forum, such as residence, or that the transaction sued on have some significant relationship to the forum. The forum non conveniens rule requires, more exactingly, that the forum be not only minimally convenient, as required by the minimum contacts rule, but also relatively convenient compared with other available forums. When the factors of plaintiff's residence and convenience are taken into account, as they should be, the rules together approximate ones of interstate venue in a federal system. It is interesting to note that the federal venue rule in diversity cases defines proper forum in terms alternatively of the residence of the plaintiff, the residence of the defendant, and the place where events giving rise to the claim occurred.[14] Some of the most thoughtful state court decisions applying the concept of minimum contacts emphasize availability of evidence, the possibility of joining additional parties, and relative convenience to the litigants in determining whether such contacts exist—the very factors that go into the question of discretionary change of venue in the federal court system.[15]

10. Brussels Convention on Jurisdiction and Enforcement of Judgments in Civil and Commercial Matters, arts. 13–15, 29 I.L.M. 1413 (1990)(as amended).

11. Other exorbitant jurisdictional grounds barred by the Brussels Convention in suits among nationals of its adhering nations include basing jurisdiction solely on the plaintiff's nationality (as in France) or on the presence in the jurisdiction of the defendant's property (as in Germany). *Id.* at art. 3; see § 2.4 *supra.*

12. Clermont, Jurisdictional Salvation and the Hague Treaty, 85 Corn. L. Rev. 1989 (1999)(proposing an approach resembling that of this paragraph); Borchers, The Death of the Constitutional Law of Personal Jurisdiction: From *Pennoyer* to *Burnham* and Back Again, 24 U.C. Davis L. Rev. 19 (1990); see Symposium, Enforcing Judgments Abroad: The Global Challenge, 24 Brook. J. Int'l L. 1 (1998).

13. 95 U.S. 714, 24 L.Ed. 565 (1878).

14. 28 U.S.C. § 1391(a). *See* § 2.32 *infra.*

15. *See* Buckeye Boiler Co. v. Superior Court, 71 Cal.2d 893, 458 P.2d 57, 80 Cal. Rptr. 113 (1969). *See also* Asahi Metal Indus. Co. v. Superior Court, 480 U.S. 102, 107 S.Ct. 1026, 94 L.Ed.2d 92 (1987).

With this development as a point of departure, the problem of state court jurisdiction can be conceived in a way quite different from the past. Rather than view the states as independent sovereigns between which peaceful relations must be maintained through the Due Process Clause, the state court systems can be considered the primary mechanism for adjudicating cases arising in the country as a whole, other than those based on federal law. As such, they have not only the power but the duty to extend their process, in the form of notice, to all parties who should or might be joined under modern concepts of party joinder. The Due Process Clause could be construed as requiring that a state court refrain from hearing a case in which it could not render as complete or convenient justice as some other state court.[16] The Full Faith and Credit Clause would be given full, rather than equivocal, effect by requiring that the judgment of a court that properly entertained a case, whatever its subject matter, be recognized elsewhere.[17]

The consequence would be not the diminution but the enhancement of the authority of the state courts. The theory of state sovereignty, in elevating the position of the states individually to something like that of independent nations, has had the paradoxical effect of constricting the judicial authority of the state court systems as a whole. A federalist approach would broaden that authority and thereby permit the state courts to perform what seems to be their proper function in our constitutional system.

But the revolution has not yet arrived. As we have seen, the theory of state sovereignty still has life as a theoretical proposition.[18] Moreover, no workable concept of jurisdiction can be based simply on the idea of convenience or efficiency of forum choice. The tasks that civil justice must accomplish are not limited to the adjudication of cases in a convenient forum; on the contrary, the system has to be concerned with rendering judgments that will be enforceable, just as the law at large has to be concerned with both obedience and fairness.

Recognition and enforcement

There are at least two critical aspects of enforcement of a judgment. The first is establishing authority to pronounce a judgment that will be recognized elsewhere if it cannot be enforced within the jurisdiction where it was rendered. The second is being able to enforce compliance with the judgment if the judgment loser refuses to voluntarily comply.

16. *See* Weintraub, A Map Out of the Personal Jurisdiction Labyrinth, 28 U.C. Davis L. Rev. 531 (1995); *cf.* Western Union Tel. Co. v. Pennsylvania, 368 U.S. 71, 82 S.Ct. 199, 7 L.Ed.2d 139 (1961); Korn, Rethinking Personal Jurisdiction and Choice of Law in Multistate Mass Torts, 97 Colum. L. Rev. 2183 (1997); § 2.6 *supra*.

17. *Contra*: Hanson v. Denckla, 357 U.S. 235, 78 S.Ct. 1228, 2 L.Ed.2d 1283 (1958); Fall v. Eastin, 215 U.S. 1, 30 S.Ct. 3, 54 L.Ed. 65 (1909).

18. *See* § 2.5 *supra*.

Ultimately, making judgments enforceable outside the home forum requires an acceptable basis for that forum's own authority. The Constitution's Full Faith and Credit Clause and an implementing federal statute, 28 U.S.C. § 1738,[19] provide generally that the judgments of one state must be recognized by other states. The same principle applies to judgments of federal courts, which must be recognized by the states.[20] But these rules do not by themselves require recognition of American judgments by the courts of other nations, and in today's international economic community that is a significant consideration. Perhaps equally important, according full faith and credit to judgments *within* the United States is a persuasive and therefore effective principle only if the rules of jurisdiction are practically convincing as well as "convenient." Hence, courts have to be concerned that their rules of jurisdiction have an easily intelligible basis while satisfying more subtle considerations of procedural fairness.

The simplest expression of the concept of authority is the bare statement: "Do it because I say so." But saying this in the most insistent and unmistakable form requires saying it in person to defendants themselves. Such an exercise of judicial will intends not only to subordinate the defendant to the law but to remind society at large that subordination to the law is required of everyone. It is in the interest of the law as an institution that such demonstrations be made when necessary to vindicate the law's authority. And the place to do it most effectively is where the defendant is concededly subject to the state's authority.

Presence of defendant

This is the psychological and political basis for the rule of jurisdiction based on domicile, or in this country presence. That is, quite apart from considerations of forum convenience, a defendant who does not peacefully respond when summoned to a convenient court may be compelled to respond in the court of any place where he or she is subject to governmental authority. In a sense, the court in that place is the spokesperson for all courts, and for all legal systems, in saying that a defendant is legally answerable—answerable in a convenient forum if practicable, but above all, answerable. All systems of legal authority, hence all courts, recognize this shared interest in securing compliance with law. Hence, all recognize that, at least when defendants will not answer in any other forum, they are rightly required to answer in the forums where they live. Personal domicile or presence, in other words, is a basis of judicial authority that all legal systems recognize.

19. "The records and judicial proceedings of any court of any . . . State . . . shall have the same full faith and credit in every court within the United States . . . as they have by law or usage in the courts . . . from which they are taken."

20. *See* Restatement (Second) of Judgments 87; Degnan, Federalized Res Judicata, 85 Yale L.J. 741 (1976); § 2.8 *supra*; *e.g.*, Cemer v. Marathon Oil Co., 583 F.2d 830 (6th Cir.1978)

Presence of property

Similar considerations operate at the enforcement end of civil justice. Here the ultimate problem is finding assets of the judgment loser that can be appropriated to pay the winner. With money judgments the object is simple: money or other assets. When the judgment is for an injunction, and the defendant simply refuses to take any action to obey, the court has two alternatives. It can hold the defendant in contempt, ultimately imprisoning him or her, or it can sequester defendant's property to coerce compliance or use defendant's property to pay someone else to take the necessary action to comply with the injunction.[21] These alternatives thus lead back to the presence of the defendant or at least of defendant's property. Because coercing someone to do something is very difficult if he or she really wants to resist, the most practical course is to go after the defendant's property. Hence the presence of a defendant's property is a residual basis of jurisdiction not because it necessarily has anything to do with the merits of a case or convenience in adjudication but because it is the most practical residual basis for enforcing a judgment.

These are considerations that are wrapped up in the term "sovereignty." "Sovereignty" in its simplest definition is "authority." Hence, when the courts refer back to sovereignty they are referring back to the problem of authority of courts and authority of law. Moreover, when courts refer to jurisdiction, they are necessarily invoking an element of sovereignty—bald authority—whether they do or do not so acknowledge. That is, they recognize, even if only tacitly, that procedural law is not simply a matter of fairness but also of enforcement, that jurisdictional rules are part of procedural law, and that jurisdictional rules thus express an element not only of fairness but of expediency in enforcement. At any rate, looking at the problem this way gives coherence to some expressions by the Supreme Court that might otherwise be difficult to fathom.

Jurisdiction to determine jurisdiction

One of these is *Insurance Corp. of Ireland v. Compagnie des Bauxites.*[22] In that case an action was brought in the United States against several foreign insurance companies to recover on policies issued in favor of an American business. The insurance companies moved to dismiss for want of personal jurisdiction, contending that they lacked sufficient contacts or other connection to be subject to process. Plaintiff then invoked discovery procedure to ascertain facts that would show a basis for jurisdiction. The insurance companies responded by saying that they had no obligation to respond to discovery inasmuch as the court had no jurisdiction over them.

21. *See* Pennington v. Fourth Natl. Bank, 243 U.S. 269, 37 S.Ct. 282, 61 L.Ed. 713 (1917).

22. 456 U.S. 694, 102 S.Ct. 2099, 72 L.Ed.2d 492 (1982).

The Supreme Court held that by appearing specially to challenge jurisdiction, the defendant had consented to the court's exercise of jurisdiction to determine whether it had jurisdiction. "By submitting to the jurisdiction of the court for the limited purpose of challenging jurisdiction, the defendant agrees to abide by that court's determination on the issue of jurisdiction."[23] This analysis permitted the court to elude what it seemed to regard as an inescapable trap: How can a court have jurisdiction over a person to determine whether it has jurisdiction over the person, unless it knows whether it has jurisdiction over the person? But in avoiding this trap, the Court fell into two others. First, it found itself compelled to say that personal jurisdiction is not a matter of state sovereignty but only one of a privilege not to be sued in an inconvenient forum; since personal jurisdiction is a privilege, it can be waived. But if that proposition is taken seriously it contradicts much of what the Court has held on the subject of personal jurisdiction.[24] Moreover, the necessary implication is that personal jurisdiction has a lesser constitutional status when it is asserted by special appearance than when it is asserted by suffering a default judgment and later resisting enforcement of the judgment on the ground that the rendering court lacked jurisdiction. That, too, would contradict many of the Court's previous holdings.[25]

But the trap that the Court was seeking to escape is not a serious one at all. If the facts, such as they are, indicate that the court has jurisdiction, it has authority to proceed on the assumption that it does indeed have jurisdiction. Of course, the "true facts" may be such that the court would not have jurisdiction if those facts were made known. But a court works with appearances and it is prepared to work with the best appearances that are practically available. If further evidence would negate the existence of jurisdiction, defendant is at liberty to present such evidence and get a dismissal. Further, the court may as a matter of prudence insist that, where possible, jurisdiction rest on better proof of jurisdictional facts rather than worse proof and hence may require that defendant reveal jurisdictional facts as a condition of going forward on the merits. But a court should not shrink from asserting jurisdiction, and rendering a default judgment if defendant refuses to cooperate, if it appears to the court that it has jurisdiction. The reason why the court should not be inhibited is not because of fairness or because it "has" jurisdiction. It is simply demanding that its authority be recognized by the defendant.

23. 456 U.S. at 706, 102 S.Ct. at 2106, 72 L.Ed.2d at 504 (1982).

24. Thus, the Court itself has repeatedly said that a state's authority to assert jurisdiction over a defendant is a question of "sovereignty." *See, e.g.,* Pennoyer v. Neff, 95 U.S. 714, 24 L.Ed. 565 (1877); World–Wide Volkswagen Corp. v. Woodson, 444 U.S. 286, 100 S.Ct. 559, 62 L.Ed.2d 490 (1980).

25. *E.g.,* Hanson v. Denckla, 357 U.S. 235, 78 S.Ct. 1228, 2 L.Ed.2d 1283 (1958); Shaffer v. Heitner, 433 U.S. 186, 97 S.Ct. 2569, 53 L.Ed.2d 683 (1977).

Jurisdiction to enforce judgments

The same foundation supports the Supreme Court's statements in *Shaffer v. Heitner*[26] to the effect that a court may exercise jurisdiction over property in certain cases even when there is no connection between the forum and the transaction being litigated. The clearest case for exercising such jurisdiction, specifically referred to in *Shaffer v. Heitner*,[27] is when jurisdiction is invoked to enforce a judgment against locally situated property. Unless authority exists to exercise such jurisdiction, wrongdoers could isolate their property in a state where they had no other connections—in effect turning that state into a financial sanctuary. The frustration of enforcement such sanctuaries permit is barely tolerable in the inter-national world. It is intolerable within a socially and commercially integrated society.

That a political community ultimately must insist on compliance with law, even at the price of fairness in procedure, goes to the nature of the law itself. Fairness in procedure can be achieved only under minimal conditions of party compliance. The unavoidable minimum is that the parties accept the authority of the court. The court in self-preservation, for the benefit of society as a whole, ultimately must impose its authority, with or without fairness. At least in this general and minimal sense, *Pennoyer*'s stress on state power is not wholly outdated.

D. STATE SUBJECT MATTER JURISDICTION AND VENUE

§ 2.22 Subject Matter Jurisdiction

As already noted, the authority of state court systems is limited in various important ways by the Due Process Clause of the U.S. Constitution.[1] Subject to these limitations, each state is free to organize its own court system and to prescribe rules of jurisdiction and venue governing them. The present discussion focuses on these state-prescribed rules and assumes that no question is presented as to the authority of the state under the Due Process Clause.

Courts of general and limited jurisdiction

Each state usually has two or more kinds of trial courts in each territorial subdivision.[2] First, there are courts whose authority is con-

26. 433 U.S. 186 nn.35 & 36, 97 S.Ct. 2569 nn.35 & 36, 53 L.Ed.2d 683 nn.35 & 36 (1977).

27. 433 U.S. at 186 n.36, 97 S.Ct. at 2569 n.36, 53 L.Ed.2d at 683 n.36.

§ 2.22

1. *See* § 2.3 *supra.*

2. *See* U.S. Dept. of Justice, Law Enforcement Assistance Administration, National Survey of Court Organization (1973). Now outdated but still illuminating are Pound, Organization of Courts (1940), and Sunderland, Problems Connected with the Operation of a State Court System, 1950 Wis. L. Rev. 585. *See also* President's Commission on Administration of Justice, Task Force Report: The Courts (1967); ABA Standards Relating to Court Organization (1974); Gazell, Lower Court Unification in the American States, 1974 Ariz. St. L.J. 653.

fined to certain types of cases, defined in terms of the amount in controversy or the subject matter of the action. These are referred to as courts of limited, special, or "inferior" jurisdiction and are denominated by such names as municipal court, district court, or probate court. The provisions prescribing their authority typically state that the courts may hear cases in which the amount in controversy does not exceed some stated sum, where the action does not involve title to real property, or where probate jurisdiction is involved. Separate from these courts of limited jurisdiction are the trial courts of general jurisdiction, those whose authority is comprehensive so far as subject matter is concerned—except for all or certain matters within the authority of courts of limited jurisdiction.

Objection to jurisdiction

In any given locality within the state, the coexistence of two or more different trial courts having distinct authority can give rise to problems over whether any particular case is properly brought before one rather than the other. Such a question is one of subject matter jurisdiction or, as it is sometimes called, competence. If an action is brought in the wrong court, the defendant may object and require dismissal of the action or its transfer to the proper court. The traditional rule was that even if the defendant did not object at the outset, he or she could raise the jurisdictional objection later on, even after judgment.[3]

While this rule is still applied in some states when the judgment involved has been rendered by a "very" inferior court, such as a justice of the peace court, the "modernization" of court systems staffed by professionally trained judges has reduced the risk of unauthorized and wholly irregular proceedings and thus has lessened the need for the rule.[4] Modern rules applicable in state courts provide that when an objection based on the court's lack of authority is raised, the remedy is to transfer the case to the proper court, but this does not necessarily mean that if the objection is not raised it is waived and that the court can enter a valid judgment on the merits.[5] The objection to lack of subject matter jurisdiction is thus only slowly coming to be treated like an objection to improper venue.

§ 2.23 State Rules of Venue

Within each state the trial courts at each level of subject matter jurisdiction are organized in separate units along territorial lines. County lines are generally used, but courts of "very" inferior jurisdiction

3. *See* Dobbs, The Decline of Jurisdiction by Consent, 40 N.C.L. Rev. 49 (1961).

4. *See* Dobbs, Beyond Bootstrap: Foreclosing the Issue of Subject–Matter Jurisdiction Before Final Judgment, 51 Minn. L. Rev. 491 (1967).

5. *See* Restatement (Second) of Judgments § 12; 1 Witkin, California Procedure 810–821 (2d ed. 1970); Lynch, Lack of Jurisdiction of the Subject Matter in New Jersey Courts, 6 Seton Hall L. Rev. 1 (1974).

(justice of the peace courts and, in some states, municipal courts) may be organized into smaller geographical units. Among these territorially separate units, rules of venue specify which one is proper. The rules governing trial courts of general jurisdiction are almost always treated as rules of venue; those governing trial courts of "very" limited jurisdiction, however, are sometimes treated as limitations on jurisdiction.[1]

Local actions

The rules of venue in most states preserve a distinction between local and transitory actions, which developed in the course of English common law.[2] Venue originally meant the place from which jurors were summoned for the trial of an action; this was the county in which the land lay in real actions and the place where the disputed transaction took place (or, in debt, also the county in which the defendant "might be best brought to answer") in personal actions.[3] These limitations were associated partly with the fact that jurors were originally chosen for the likelihood that they would have personal knowledge of the facts of the case. Later, as the function of the jury changed, the practice developed through fiction to allow a plaintiff to lay venue in any county in England except in local actions—that is, real actions, ejectment, replevin, and trespass to real estate.[4]

Reflecting these origins, modern venue rules generally provide that certain actions concerning real estate must be brought in the county or district where the land lies.[5] These include actions for possession, partition or foreclosure of a lien, or to quiet title. Statutes and judicial interpretations, however, are not uniform for actions of trespass to land, specific performance of a contract to convey land, or the establishment of a trust in property.

Transitory actions

In transitory actions, state venue rules follow variegated patterns that employ one or more of the following tests: (a) where the cause of action, or part of it, arose or accrued; (b) where some fact is present or happened; (c) where the defendant resides; (d) where the defendant is doing business; (e) where the defendant has an office or place of business, an agent, or representative, or where an agent or officer of defendant resides; (f) where the plaintiff resides; (g) where the plaintiff is doing business; (h) where the defendant may be found; (i) where the

§ 2.23

1. *See* Barquis v. Merchants Collection Assn., 7 Cal.3d 94, 496 P.2d 817, 101 Cal. Rptr. 745 (1972) (justice of the peace court).

2. *See* Blume, Place of Trial of Civil Cases, 48 Mich. L. Rev. 1 (1949); Stevens, Venue Statutes: Diagnosis and Proposed Cure, 49 Mich. L. Rev. 307 (1951). *See also* N.Y. Temp. Commn. on the Courts, Advisory Comm. on Practice and Procedure, First Preliminary Report 497 (1957).

3. Blume, Place of Trial of Civil Cases, 48 Mich. L. Rev. 1, 12, 23 (1949).

4. *See also* Currie, The Constitution and the "Transitory Cause of Action," 73 Harv. L. Rev. 36, 66–69 (1959).

5. *See, e.g.,* Cal. Civ. Proc. Code § 392; N.Y. Civ. Prac. L. & R. 507; § 2.19 *supra.*

defendant may be summoned or served; (j) in the county designated in the plaintiff's complaint; (k) in any county; (1) where the seat of government is located.[6] The tests that give plaintiff the widest choice are often applicable only when defendant is a nonresident of the state.[7] The defendant's residence is the most common provision for venue.[8]

E. FEDERAL JURISDICTION AND VENUE RULES

§ 2.24 Diversity Jurisdiction

As mentioned earlier, the jurisdictional authority of the federal courts may extend no further than Article III of the Constitution and, within that limit, only to the extent authorized by statutes of Congress.[1] Currently, the principal statutory provisions for jurisdiction of the federal district courts are those regarding diversity jurisdiction, "general" federal question jurisdiction, "special" federal question jurisdiction, admiralty, bankruptcy, and actions involving the United States as a party.

The federal district courts have authority to hear actions in which the amount in controversy exceeds $75,000 and the parties to the action are citizens of different states.[2] The Constitution authorized this jurisdiction in order to ensure an impartial forum for litigants from different states and perhaps to encourage interstate commerce by providing expert tribunals sympathetic to business needs. Many observers today, however, doubt that these or other goals justify the preservation of diversity jurisdiction. Among the biases of contemporary jurors, bias against those from other states is probably minimal; and in any event federal court jurors and judges come from the same places and probably share the same biases as their state court counterparts. Proposals for reforming diversity jurisdiction range from forbidding a plaintiff who sues in his or her own state to do so in federal court, to abolishing the jurisdiction entirely except for complex multistate disputes or cases involving aliens.[3]

6. Stevens, Venue Statutes: Diagnosis and Proposed Cure, 49 Mich. L. Rev. 307, 310–315 (1951).

7. *See* Burlington Northern Ry. v. Ford, 504 U.S. 648, 112 S.Ct. 2184, 119 L.Ed.2d 432 (1992)(upholding such a provision against equal protection challenge).

8. Stevens, n. 6 *supra*, at 315.

§ 2.24

1. *See* § 2.1 note 1 *supra*. For subject matter jurisdiction, see also §§ 2.6–2.9, 3.24 (pleading jurisdiction), § 10.10 *infra* (identifying plaintiffs and defendants for diversity purposes).

2. 28 U.S.C. § 1332. *See* Chemerinsky, Federal Jurisdiction § 5.3 (3d ed. 1999); Wright, The Law of Federal Courts ch. 4 (4th ed. 1983); Oakley, Recent Statutory Changes in the Law of Federal Jurisdiction and Venue: The Judicial Improvements Acts of 1988 and 1990, 24 U.C. Davis L. Rev. 735 (1991).

3. On the history of diversity jurisdiction, see Purcell, Litigation and Inequality (1992); Holt, "To Establish Justice": Politics, the Judiciary Act of 1789, and the Invention of the Federal Courts, 1989 Duke L.J. 1421; Friendly, The Historic Basis of Diversity Jurisdiction, 41 Harv. L. Rev. 483 (1928). On possible reform, see American Law Inst., Study of the Division Between State and Federal Courts (1969); Posner, The Federal Courts: Crisis and Reform (1985); Kramer, Diversity Jurisdiction, 1990 B.Y.U.L. Rev. 97.

Complete diversity

Under the rule of "complete diversity"[4] (which applies except in actions under the Federal Interpleader Act),[5] all plaintiffs properly joined must have state citizenship different from that of all the defendants. Hence, an action involving more than $75,000 brought by a citizen of New York could be maintained in federal district court against a citizen of New Jersey but not against citizens of both New York and New Jersey. A case involving the latter set of parties could be maintained only in a state court. The same would be true of a case involving complete diversity in which the amount in controversy did not exceed $75,000 (except for actions under the Federal Interpleader Act).

Jurisdictional amount

Allowing federal courts to hear diversity suits only when the amount in controversy exceeds $75,000 is meant to exclude less important suits, although the connection between importance and monetary amount is plainly controvertible. In a damage suit, a plaintiff meets the requirement by claiming in good faith more than $75,000.[6] When only injunctive relief is sought, jurisdiction exists when the value to the plaintiff of the right sought to be protected exceeds the jurisdictional amount.[7] A plaintiff may reach the jurisdictional amount by adding up several claims against the same defendant. Ordinarily, however, a plaintiff may not aggregate claims against different defendants to reach the amount, nor may several plaintiffs aggregate their claims against a defendant; aggregation is allowed only when all the plaintiffs have a common, undivided interest or all the defendants are jointly liable because, for example, they all joined in borrowing a single sum.[8]

The federal courts' diversity jurisdiction is not exclusive. A suit between diverse parties may be brought in state court, though it may then be removable to federal court.[9]

Federal Interpleader Act

The Federal Interpleader Act creates a special kind of diversity jurisdiction in cases involving parties who have disputed claims to the

4. Strawbridge v. Curtiss, 7 U.S. (3 Cranch) 267, 2 L. Ed. 435 (1806); Note, Diversity Requirements in Multi-party Litigation, 58 Colum. L. Rev. 548 (1958); Note, Developments in the Law: Multiparty Litigation in the Federal Courts, 71 Harv. L. Rev. 874 (1958).

5. 28 U.S.C. § 1335; State Farm Fire & Casualty Co. v. Tashire, 386 U.S. 523, 87 S.Ct. 1199, 18 L.Ed.2d 270 (1967). *See also* § 10.19 *infra*.

6. St. Paul Mercury Indem. Co. v. Red Cab Co., 303 U.S. 283, 58 S.Ct. 586, 82 L.Ed. 845 (1938); *see* 28 U.S.C. § 1332(b) (penalties when plaintiff recovers less than $75,000).

7. Some cases have recognized jurisdiction when the value of the right from the defendant's perspective exceeds the jurisdictional amount. *See generally* 14A Wright, Miller, and Cooper, Federal Practice and Procedure §§ 3703, 3708.

8. *Id.* at § 3704; *see* § 10.22 *infra* (jurisdictional requirements for class actions).

9. *See* § 2.31 *infra*.

same property or fund.[10] Under the Act the federal courts may exercise jurisdiction if diversity exists between any two of the claimants to the property or fund, even if complete diversity does not exist among the rest of the contending parties.[11] The Act illustrates the point that the requirement of complete diversity is a matter of statute and not a constitutional limitation.[12] Hence, Congress could provide for federal jurisdiction in any case in which some diversity exists among the parties, as in a case brought after a mass disaster such as an airplane crash where some victims are of diverse citizenship in relation to the defendant. Congress has not seen fit, however, to provide for federal jurisdiction in such situations.[13]

Citizenship for purposes of diversity

For purposes of diversity jurisdiction, the relevant characteristic of the parties is their citizenship in a U.S. state or, in the case of aliens, their citizenship in another country.[14] The concept is technically distinct from that of a residence or domicile but is determined by essentially the same criteria which are, in short, living in a state and intending to remain there for an indefinite period.[15] For federal jurisdictional purposes, a corporation is deemed a citizen of the state of its incorporation and is also treated as a citizen of the state in which it has its principal place of business.[16] Thus, a Delaware corporation with its principal place of business in New York is, for federal diversity purposes, a citizen of both states. This means that diversity cannot exist between such a corporation and a citizen of either Delaware or New York. If the U.S. corporation has its principal place of business in a foreign country, however, it will probably not be held a citizen of that country and thus an alien for diversity purposes.[17] An unincorporated organization, such

10. 28 U.S.C. §§ 1335 (jurisdiction), 1397 (venue), 2361 (service of process); *see* § 10.19 *infra.*

11. The Federal Interpleader Act, 28 U.S.C. § 1335, provides that "[t]he district courts shall have original jurisdiction of any civil action of interpleader or in the nature of interpleader ... if ... [t]wo or more adverse claimants, of diverse citizenship ... are claiming [the property]." The Supreme Court has held that this section requires diversity between only two claimants without regard to the possibility that other claimants may be co-citizens. State Farm Fire & Casualty Co. v. Tashire, 386 U.S. 523, 87 S.Ct. 1199, 18 L.Ed.2d 270 (1967). *See* § 10.19 *infra.*

12. *See* State Farm Fire & Casualty Co. v. Tashire, 386 U.S. 523, 87 S.Ct. 1199, 18 L.Ed.2d 270 (1967).

13. *Cf.* American Law Inst., Study of the Division of Jurisdiction Between State and Federal Courts (1969); Owen Equip. Co. v. Kroger, 437 U.S. 365, 98 S.Ct. 2396, 57 L.Ed.2d 274 (1978). *See also* Newman-Green, Inc. v. Alfonzo-Larrain, 490 U.S. 826, 109 S.Ct. 2218, 104 L.Ed.2d 893 (1989) (court may dismiss nondiverse party in order to preserve jurisdiction).

14. *See, e.g.,* Sadat v. Mertes, 615 F.2d 1176 (7th Cir.1980); Smith v. Carter, 545 F.2d 909 (5th Cir.), *cert. denied,* 431 U.S. 955, 97 S.Ct. 2677, 53 L.Ed.2d 272 (1977).

15. *See, e.g.,* Krasnov v. Dinan, 465 F.2d 1298 (3d Cir.1972); Janzen v. Goos, 302 F.2d 421 (8th Cir.1962); Wilson v. Pickens, 444 F.Supp. 53 (W.D.Okla.1977).

16. 28 U.S.C. § 1332(c). For the meaning of "principal place of business," see, e.g., Riggs v. Island Creek Coal Co., 542 F.2d 339, 342 (6th Cir.1976). *See also* Cabalceta v. Standard Fruit Co., 883 F.2d 1553 (11th Cir.1989).

17. Cabalceta v. Standard Fruit Co., 883 F.2d 1553 (11th Cir.1989).

as a partnership or association, is treated as having the citizenship of each of its members.[18] Thus, a partnership whose partners are citizens of states *X*,*Y*, and *Z* is for diversity purposes a citizen of all three states and would be correspondingly limited in eligibility for diversity jurisdiction.[19]

Special congressional provisions extend diversity jurisdiction to cases involving citizenship relationships that fall outside the general provision in 28 U.S.C. § 1332, while others deny jurisdiction in some actions that otherwise would come within the general provision. Thus, § 1332(d) provides that for diversity jurisdiction purposes "State" includes the Territories, the District of Columbia, and Puerto Rico.[20] On the other hand, 1332(c) excludes certain actions involving insurance companies sued directly on insurance liability policies.[21] Although § 1332(a)(2) allows diversity suits between a citizen of one of the United States and an alien, it does not extend to suits between two aliens from different nations, and courts have resisted efforts to bring such suits within the jurisdiction by using provisions found elsewhere in the statute.[22]

Parties have resorted to various moves to create or destroy diversity, and courts have had to pass on their effects. One approach is for a party to assign a claim to a resident of an appropriate state, appoint a guardian from that state, or even pack up and move to the state. A statute frustrates some such tactics by barring jurisdiction when a party "has been improperly or collusively made or joined to invoke the jurisdiction of the court."[23] (Note that the statute does not prevent similar methods for destroying diversity.) Sometimes, the existence of jurisdiction turns on whether a party should be classified as a plaintiff or a defendant; the courts may then reclassify parties in accord with the realities of the dispute.[24]

Domestic relations exception

Under what is called the "domestic relations exception," federal courts refuse to hear actions for divorce, alimony or child custody even

18. United Steelworkers v. R. H. Bouligny, Inc., 382 U.S. 145, 86 S.Ct. 272, 15 L.Ed.2d 217 (1965); Labarre Plantation Partnership v. Amoco Prod. Co., 651 F.Supp. 271 (M.D.La.1986).

19. *See* New York State Teachers Retirement Sys. v. Kalkus, 764 F.2d 1015 (4th Cir.1985).

20. *See* National Mut. Ins. Co. v. Tidewater Transfer Co., 337 U.S. 582, 69 S.Ct. 1173, 93 L.Ed. 1556 (1949).

21. *See* Northbrook Natl. Ins. Co. v. Brewer, 493 U.S. 6, 110 S.Ct. 297, 107 L.Ed.2d 223 (1989). For discussion of the qualifications of a "party" for diversity purposes, see § 10.10 *infra.*

22. *E.g.,* Franceskin v. Credit Suisse, 214 F.3d 253 (2d Cir.2000)(alien corporation with U.S. principal place of business still alien); Saadeh v. Farouki, 107 F.3d 52 (D.C.Cir.1997)(alien with permanent U.S. residence still alien).

23. 28 U.S.C. § 1359; Kramer v. Caribbean Mills, Inc., 394 U.S. 823, 89 S.Ct. 1487, 23 L.Ed.2d 9 (1969); see 28 U.S.C. § 1332(c)(2)(executor is treated as having same citizenship as decedent, so that appointing an executor from a different state does not affect jurisdiction).

24. City of Indianapolis v. Chase Nat'l Bank, 314 U.S. 63, 62 S.Ct. 15, 86 L.Ed. 47 (1941); see Wilson v. Republic Iron & Steel Co., 257 U.S. 92, 42 S.Ct. 35, 66 L.Ed. 144 (1921)(dropping party joined just to prevent diversity).

when the requirements for diversity jurisdiction are satisfied. The Supreme Court's creation of this exception reflects disinclination to remove a mass of such cases from the state courts, perhaps based on an assumption that mere family matters are below the dignity of the federal courts. The exception does not forbid ordinary damage suits among family members.[25]

§ 2.25 Federal Question Jurisdiction and Government Litigation

Section 1331, Title 28 of the United States Code authorizes an action "arising under the Constitution, laws, or treaties of the United States" to be brought in the federal district court. This statutory basis of jurisdiction is conventionally known as "general federal question jurisdiction." (The meaning of the phrase "arising under" is considered in § 2.26 *infra.*) The Constitution authorizes federal question jurisdiction in order to ensure the adequate enforcement of federal law and to promote its uniform interpretation. Congress, however, did not provide for general federal question jurisdiction until 1875, and a jurisdictional amount requirement in federal question cases survived until 1980.

Special federal question jurisdiction

The term "special federal question" simply means federal question jurisdiction created by some provision *other* than 28 U.S.C. § 1331.[1] None of these special jurisdictional provisions requires a minimum amount in controversy. Some of them provide, or have been interpreted to mean, that the jurisdiction of the federal courts is exclusive; when this is the case, the action may be brought only in federal court. Normally, however, both state and federal courts have what is called concurrent jurisdiction over federal claims. The plaintiff may therefore sue in either court, subject to the defendant's right to remove a state court case arising under federal law to federal court.[2]

25. Ankenbrandt v. Richards, 504 U.S. 689, 112 S.Ct. 2206, 119 L.Ed.2d 468 (1992); Resnik, Naturally Without Gender: Women, Jurisdiction and the Federal Courts, 66 N.Y.U.L. Rev. 1682 (1991); *see* Dunn v. Cometa, 238 F.3d 38 (1st Cir.2001). A parallel "probate exception" excludes from federal jurisdiction actions to probate a will or appoint an administrator, but not claims against the estate. Markham v. Allen, 326 U.S. 490, 66 S.Ct. 296, 90 L.Ed. 256 (1946); Mangieri v. Mangieri, 226 F.3d 1 (1st Cir. 2000).

§ 2.25

1. *See* Bator, Meltzer, Mishkin, and Shapiro, The Federal Courts and the Federal System 960 *et seq.* (3d ed. 1988); Friendly, Federal Jurisdiction: A General View (1973).

2. Gulf Offshore Co. v. Mobil Oil Corp., 453 U.S. 473, 101 S.Ct. 2870, 69 L.Ed.2d 784 (1981); Note, Exclusive Jurisdiction of the Federal Courts in Private Civil Actions, 70 Harv. L. Rev. 509 (1957); § 2.31 *infra*; *cf.* Chisum, The Allocation of Jurisdiction Between State and Federal Courts in Patent Litigation, 46 Wash. L. Rev. 633 (1971).

Admiralty jurisdiction

The federal district courts have jurisdiction of all actions of "admiralty and maritime jurisdiction."[3] This deceptively simple phrase refers to the transactions of which the court can take cognizance in admiralty jurisdiction, the procedure followed by the court, and the substantive law on which the case is decided.[4] Admiralty jurisdiction extends to contracts whose subject matter is maritime (such as ship charters and maritime liens) and torts that occur on navigable waters. Admiralty procedure was drawn from the procedure followed in England and is largely codified in the Federal Rules of Civil Procedure and the Federal Admiralty Rules.[5] The governing substantive law consists largely of federal law in the form of admiralty and maritime principles originally conceived in England and subsequently elaborated, developed, and modified here by judicial decision and congressional enactment. State law, however, does govern some aspects of maritime transactions.[6] Moreover, to a large extent admiralty jurisdiction is not exclusive. Under the "saving to suitors" clause of 28 U.S.C. § 1333(1), a plaintiff may enforce rights redressable through common law actions by a suit in state court.

United States as a party

Except as otherwise provided by law, the United States, or one of its agencies authorized by statute to bring actions, may bring any civil action it may have in the federal courts.[7] The United States cannot be sued except to the extent that Congress has enacted statutes permitting such suits. Under 28 U.S.C. § 1346, for example, federal district courts have jurisdiction over tax refund suits, contract claims for $10,000 or less, and actions under the Federal Tort Claims Act, which makes the government liable for a "negligent or wrongful act or omission" if a private person "would be liable to the claimant."[8] State courts generally do not have jurisdiction of suits against the United States,[9] but the United States may appear as a plaintiff in state courts.[10] These various provisions protect both the federal government and its legislation from state court adjudications that might be unsympathetic.

3. 28 U.S.C. § 1333.

4. *See generally* Gilmore and Black, The Law of Admiralty (2d ed. 1975).

5. *See* Fed. R. Civ. P. 1 ("These rules govern ... suits of a civil nature whether cognizable as cases at law or in equity or in admiralty, with the exceptions stated in Rule 81"); Supplemental Rules for Certain Admiralty and Maritime Claims.

6. *See, e.g.,* Wilburn Boat Co. v. Fireman's Fund Ins. Co., 348 U.S. 310, 75 S.Ct. 368, 99 L.Ed. 337 (1955); Leather's Best, Inc. v. S.S. Mormaclynx, 451 F.2d 800 (2d Cir.1971); Currie, Federalism and the Admiralty: "The Devil's Own Mess," 1960 Sup. Ct. Rev. 158.

7. 28 U.S.C. § 1345. *See* Lester, Litigation With the Federal Government (3d ed. 1994); Bator, Meltzer, Mishkin, and Shapiro, The Federal Courts and the Federal System 1090 *et seq.* (3d ed. 1988).

8. 28 U.S.C. § 1346(b). *See, e.g.,* Sheridan v. United States, 487 U.S. 392, 108 S.Ct. 2449, 101 L.Ed.2d 352 (1988). *See also* § 2.5 *supra*.

9. An exception is 28 U.S.C. § 2410.

10. *See, e.g.,* County of San Bernardino v. Harsh Cal. Corp., 52 Cal.2d 341, 340 P.2d 617 (1959); Note, 12 Stan. L. Rev. 472 (1960).

The Tucker Act and the Little Tucker Act

The Tucker Act[11] provides for actions against the United States for the recovery of taxes illegally collected, for the unconstitutional taking of property, to recover a fine or penalty, and in similar actions. If the claim is above $10,000, the suit must be brought in the U.S. Court of Federal Claims.[12] The Tucker Act is a jurisdictional statute; it does not create substantive rights, which must be founded in legal sources external to the act.[13] Actions may be based on express or implied in fact contracts with the United States, but not on contracts implied in law.[14]

Claims under $10,000 may be brought either in the Court of Federal Claims or in a district court, according to a provision commonly known as the Little Tucker Act.[15] Appeals from actions based on the Tucker Act or Little Tucker Act are taken to the Federal Circuit Court of Appeals.

Bankruptcy

Article I, Section 8 of the Constitution gives Congress power to establish "uniform Laws on the subject of Bankruptcies." In exercise of this power Congress has created bankruptcy courts as an adjunct to the federal district courts; these courts exercise a broad jurisdiction over proceedings for financial relief of individuals and business organizations who are having difficulty paying their debts.[16] In general, the law governing the obligations in question is state law, but the bankruptcy court has broad authority to rearrange these obligations in consideration of the debtor's financial situation.[17]

§ 2.26 Constitutional Scope of Cases and Controversies and of Federal Question Jurisdiction

The Constitution imposes at least two limits to the federal question jurisdiction: a requirement limiting federal courts to the resolution of "cases" and "controversies," and one allowing jurisdiction only over cases "arising under" federal law.

11. 28 U.S.C. § 1491(a)(3).

12. Chula Vista City School Dist. v. Bennett, 824 F.2d 1573 (Fed. Cir.1987); United States v. City of Kansas City, 761 F.2d 605 (10th Cir.1985); Fitzgerald v. Staats, 429 F.Supp. 933 (D.D.C.1977).

13. United States v. (1)1979 Cadillac Coupe De Ville, 833 F.2d 994 (Fed.Cir. 1987).

14. *Cf.* Hatzlachh Supply Co. v. United States, 444 U.S. 460, 100 S.Ct. 647, 62 L.Ed.2d 614 (1980); A. E. Finley & Assocs. v. United States, 898 F.2d 1165 (6th Cir. 1990).

15. 28 U.S.C. § 1346(a)(2).

16. 28 U.S.C. § 1471(c). Section 151, Title 28 of the U.S. Code created the bankruptcy courts as an adjunct to the district courts. Section 1471(c) delegated the power, vested in the first instance to the district courts, to the bankruptcy courts. *See* 1 Collier on Bankruptcy ¶ 2.01 (15th ed. 1979). In Northern Pipeline Construction Co. v. Marathon Pipe Line Co., 458 U.S. 50, 102 S.Ct. 2858, 73 L.Ed.2d 598 (1982), however, the Supreme Court held this broad delegation of jurisdiction in bankruptcy matters unconstitutional because bankruptcy courts are not Article III courts. *See* 1 Collier on Bankruptcy ch. 3, 1–6 (15th ed. 1979 & Supp. 1983).

17. 11 U.S.C. § 105. For an analysis of this broad authority to rearrange obligation under state law, see 2 Collier on Bankruptcy ¶ ¶ 105.01–105.05 (15th ed. 1979).

Cases and controversies

The Constitution's grants of federal court jurisdiction in Article III use the terms "cases" and "controversies." Although it is unclear what significance the Framers attributed to these terms, courts have developed on their basis various principles to circumscribe the matters federal courts may hear. To an extent that remains uncertain, some of these restrictions are Constitutionally required, while others are prudential limitations laid down by the courts for their own guidance. The case or controversy doctrine is not limited to federal question cases, as its application to declaratory judgment suits demonstrates.[1] But its main use is in such cases, and especially in cases challenging the validity under federal law of federal or state government action.

The doctrine reflects the tradition is that courts exist to settle real, present disputes, not to decide questions on which nothing practical currently turns or to give advisory opinions—although common law courts have sometimes been known to render such opinions.[2] The "case or controversy" requirement promotes both judicial efficiency and sound decisions. It economizes judicial time, limits judicial lawmaking to what is incidental to resolving immediate legal conflicts, and helps insure that cases will be decided in the context of concrete facts between parties who have real and opposing interests arising from those facts. This in turn tends to insure that a court will make narrow and concrete decisions on the basis of what has been developed before it, rather than broad decisions that could affect both situations the court has not fully considered and parties who have not appeared or been represented before it.[3]

The doctrine's proponents have also rooted it in the separation of powers, as an important limit on judicial power.[4] On this view, federal courts resolve Constitutional and statutory issues only when that is required to determine the law applicable to concrete litigation between interested parties that comes before them.[5] Beyond this, they have no

§ 2.26

1. *See* § 1.11 *supra.*

2. *See* Aetna Life Ins. Co. v. Haworth, 300 U.S. 227, 240, 57 S.Ct. 461, 464, 81 L.Ed. 617, 621 (1937). For advisory opinions, see, *e.g.,* McNaghten's Case, 2 Eng. Rep. 718 (H.L. 1843)(Eng.); Fletcher, The "Case or Controversy" Requirement in State Court Adjudication of Federal Questions, 78 Calif. L. Rev. 263, 268 (1990). Constitutional courts in civil law nations often pass on the constitutionality of statutes before they have been applied or, in some nations, passed by the legislature.

3. The underlying issue is how far courts, particularly the highest appellate courts, have scope to make law. *Compare* Brilmayer, The Jurisprudence of Article III: Perspectives on the "Case or Controversy" Requirement, 93 Harv. L. Rev. 297 (1979), *with* Tushnet, The Sociology of Article III: A Response to Professor Brilmayer, 93 Harv. L. Rev. 1699 (1980). *See also* Hazard, The Supreme Court as Legislature, 64 Cornell L. Rev. 1 (1978).

4. *E.g.,* Ashwander v. TVA, 297 U.S. 288, 341, 56 S.Ct. 466, 80 L.Ed. 688 (1936)(Brandeis, J., concurring); Joint Anti–Fascist Refugee Committee v. McGrath, 341 U.S. 123, 149, 71 S.Ct. 624, 95 L.Ed. 817 (1951)(Frankfurter, J., concurring); Lujan v. Defenders of Wildlife, 504 U.S. 555, 112 S.Ct. 2130, 119 L.Ed.2d 351 (1992)(Scalia, J.).

5. Muskrat v. United States, 219 U.S. 346, 31 S.Ct. 250, 55 L.Ed. 246 (1911).

power to strike down illegality or resolve arguments about the law. This view of the courts' role creates some tension with the belief of many that implementing the rule of law and resolving Constitutional disputes is precisely what federal courts should be doing. As conflicting policies and shifting majorities prevail in turn, cases and controversies law has become far too complex to state here except in barest outline.[6]

Standing

A case or controversy exists only if the person raising a federal claim or defense has standing to do so because he or she faces injury in fact, usually to some interest recognized by law.[7] Recently, the Supreme Court has also enforced a requirement that the relief sought would be likely to redress the injury.[8] The Court has also recently shows that it takes its constitutional language seriously, perhaps too seriously, by striking down statutes in which Congress sought to confer standing on citizens that the Court considered to have too little at stake.[9] In some situations, however, the Court will recognize a party's standing to invoke someone else's rights, for example when a white criminal defendant claims that African American grand jurors were denied their Equal Protection rights to be chosen chair of the grand jury that indicted him.[10]

Ripeness and mootness

Other rules control the timing of adjudication. The courts will not consider a claim unless it is "ripe," that is, has reached a stage of development sufficient to focus the legal issues.[11] But if a party waits too long, the claim may become "moot" because the claimant is no longer

6. *See generally* Hart and Wechsler's The Federal Courts and the Federal System (4th ed. 1996); Chemerinsky, Federal Jurisdiction (3d ed. 1999); Monaghan, Constitutional Adjudication: The Who and When, 82 Yale L.J. 1363 (1973).

7. *E.g.,* Raines v. Byrd, 521 U.S. 811, 117 S.Ct. 2312, 138 L.Ed.2d 849 (1997)(member of Congress lacks standing to challenge Line Item Veto Act); Department of Commerce v. U.S. House of Representatives, 525 U.S. 316, 119 S.Ct. 765, 142 L.Ed.2d 797 (1999)(voters have standing to challenge census practice that will reduce impact of their votes).

8. *E.g.,* Steel Co. v. Citizens for a Better Environment, 523 U.S. 83, 118 S.Ct. 1003, 140 L.Ed.2d 210 (1998)(even if manufacturer's failure to file emissions information injured plaintiffs, because manufacturer filed information before suit was filed relief won't redress past violation); Calderon v. Ashmus, 523 U.S. 740, 118 S.Ct. 1694, 140 L.Ed.2d 970 (1998).

9. Raines v. Byrd, 521 U.S. 811, 117 S.Ct. 2312, 138 L.Ed.2d 849 (1997); Lujan v. Defenders of Wildlife, 504 U.S. 555, 112 S.Ct. 2130, 119 L.Ed.2d 351 (1992). But see Vermont Agency of Natural Resources v. United States, 529 U.S. 765, 120 S.Ct. 1858, 146 L.Ed.2d 836 (2000); Department of Commerce v. U.S. House of Representatives, 525 U.S. 316, 119 S.Ct. 765, 142 L.Ed.2d 797 (1999); Federal Election Comm'n v. Akins, 524 U.S. 11, 118 S.Ct. 1777, 141 L.Ed.2d 10 (1998).

10. Campbell v. Louisiana, 523 U.S. 392, 118 S.Ct. 1419, 140 L.Ed.2d 551 (1998).

11. *E.g.,* Abbott Laboratories v. Gardner, 387 U.S. 136, 87 S.Ct. 1507, 18 L.Ed.2d 681 (1967)(pre-enforcement review of regulation); Suitum v. Tahoe Regional Planning Agency, 520 U.S. 725, 117 S.Ct. 1659, 137 L.Ed.2d 980 (1997).

suffering injury that the courts can remedy.[12] Strangely enough, sometimes a suit is unripe and moot at the same time.[13] Even if a claim was alive in the trial court, it must be dismissed if it becomes moot during an appeal; and because the presence of a case or controversy goes to the jurisdiction of the court, the court will raise this issue on its own even if the parties do not.[14] But the courts will hear even a claim otherwise moot if it is likely to recur between the same parties and would otherwise evade review.[15] Ripeness as well can be a flexible concept: the Supreme Court found a way to consider the constitutionality of a statute limiting liability for nuclear disasters without waiting for a power plant to explode.[16]

Arising under federal law

The "arising under" requirement for federal question cases has explicit Constitutional roots that may be more explicit than those of the case or controversy doctrine. Article III, Section 2 of the Constitution provides that "[t]he judicial Power shall extend to all Cases, in Law and Equity, arising under this Constitution, the Laws of the United States, and Treaties made ... under their Authority." Section 1331, Title 28 of the U.S. Code provides that the federal district courts have jurisdiction "of all civil actions arising under the Constitution, laws or treaties of the United States." Although the language of these two provisions is similar, the scope of jurisdiction authorized under Article III is broader than the scope of jurisdiction conferred by 1331 as the latter has been interpreted by the courts. Thus, two basic issues have been presented concerning the meaning of "arising under." First, to what extent *can* Congress invest jurisdiction in the federal courts? Second, to what degree *has* Congress implemented Article III in a statute such as 1331?

Constitutional limits

The earliest interpretations of Article III arose in the context, not of district court jurisdiction, but of the *appellate* jurisdiction of the U.S. Supreme Court in reviewing cases from *state* courts that involved issues of federal law. The seminal case is *Osborn v. Bank of the United States.*[17]

12. Spencer v. Kemna, 523 U.S. 1, 118 S.Ct. 978, 140 L.Ed.2d 43 (1998)(prisoner's challenge to parole revocation moot after final release from custody); Los Angeles v. Lyons, 461 U.S. 95, 103 S.Ct. 1660, 75 L.Ed.2d 675 (1983)(claim of victim of police chokehold practice for injunctive relief is moot because of unlikelihood that police will choke him again).

13. Renne v. Geary, 501 U.S. 312, 111 S.Ct. 2331, 115 L.Ed.2d 288 (1991).

14. *See* Massachusetts v. Oakes, 491 U.S. 576, 109 S.Ct. 2633, 105 L.Ed.2d 493 (1989); Regional Rail Reorganization Act Cases, 419 U.S. 102, 122–25, 95 S.Ct. 335, 42 L.Ed.2d 320 (1974); §§ 2.30, 4.3 *infra.*

15. Norman v. Reed, 502 U.S. 279, 112 S.Ct. 698, 116 L.Ed.2d 711 (1992)(election dispute likely to recur at next election); see Friends of the Earth v. Laidlaw Environmental Services, 528 U.S. 167, 120 S.Ct. 693, 145 L.Ed.2d 610 (2000).

16. Duke Power Co. v. Carolina Environmental Study Group, Inc., 438 U.S. 59, 98 S.Ct. 2620, 57 L.Ed.2d 595 (1978).

17. 22 U.S. (9 Wheat.) 738, 6 L.Ed. 204 (1824).

That decision, authored by Chief Justice Marshall, contained broad but ambiguous dicta:

> If it be a sufficient foundation for jurisdiction, that the title or right set up by the party, may be defeated by one construction of the constitution or law of the United States, and sustained by the opposite construction ... then all the other questions must be decided as incidental to this, which gives that jurisdiction.... On the opposite construction, the judicial power never can be extended to the whole case.... We think, then, that when a question to which the judicial power of the Union is extended by the constitution, forms an ingredient of the original cause, it is in the power of Congress to give the circuit [that is, trial] courts jurisdiction of that cause, although other questions of fact or law may be involved in it.[18]

The last sentence in this passage suggests that "arising under" means a case in which plaintiff's *cause of action* ("the original cause") is based, at least in part, on federal law. The first sentence in the passage, however, suggests that "arising under" also includes a case in which defendant's *defense* is based, at least in part, on federal law, because a "title or right" can be "set up" defensively as well being the basis of an affirmative claim. The middle passage, in which Marshall rejects "the opposite construction," suggests that "arising under" also includes a case in which an issue of federal law is presented in *any way* or *stage*, whatever the procedural context.

In this last interpretation, a case would "arise under" the Constitution if the federal question did not arise until trial, for example, where evidence was objected to on the ground that it was originally procured in violation of constitutional rights. In criminal cases in state courts, federal questions arise this way every day and are subject to review by the Supreme Court in its appellate jurisdiction over the state courts.[19] Moreover, the facts in *Osborn* imply that the Court indeed contemplated a broad scope for Article III. The federal element in that case was the fact that the suit was by a federally chartered corporation, the Bank of the United States. No other federal law was involved in either the plaintiff's claim, the defense, or the evidence.

Various readings have been given this passage in *Osborn*. The scope of Article III remains undetermined, however, because Congress has not attempted to exploit all the possibilities of Marshall's language. The two broadest extensions undertaken by Congress have been, first, a statute the Supreme Court interpreted as conferring authority on the federal courts to develop substantive law in the labor relations field and, second, a statute conferring jurisdiction on the federal district courts in suits between foreign sovereigns. The labor relations statute was considered

18. *Id.* at 822–823.

19. *See, e.g.,* Mincey v. Arizona, 437 U.S. 385, 98 S.Ct. 2408, 57 L.Ed.2d 290 (1978).

in *Textile Workers Union v. Lincoln Mills*,[20] where it was interpreted to give the federal courts authority to develop a federal common law of labor relations. The law defining the cause of action in that case, therefore, was federal law, albeit federal decisional law as distinct from a statute. The foreign sovereigns statute was considered in *Verlinden B.V. v. Central Bank of Nigeria*,[21] which involved litigation between a Dutch commercial corporation and the government bank of Nigeria; the suit was maintained in federal court under the Foreign Sovereign Immunities Act.[22] The Act not only conferred jurisdiction but also redefined the scope of the immunity enjoyed by foreign governments and instrumentalities under international law. The case thus involved elements of federal substantive law as well as a provision for federal jurisdiction. In sum, the cases addressing the scope of Article III have involved either a federal corporate instrumentality created to carry out a federal purpose (as in *Osborn*), or federally prescribed law (as in *Lincoln Mills*), or federally defined incidents of legal claims in a subject area where Congress has authority to regulate the relationship (as in the foreign commerce matter involved in *Bank of Nigeria*).

Nevertheless, major theoretical debate has developed on whether Article III permits Congress to invest the federal courts with jurisdiction over cases where such a jurisdictional provision is the only expression of federal law in the matter. The concept is "protective jurisdiction," whereby the federal courts would protect the parties from supposed unfairness or incompetence at the hands of state courts.[23] The theoretical debate has involved intricate discourse but has little immediate significance. Situations can be imagined in which Congress might wish to invest the federal district courts with jurisdiction of a class of cases without prescribing the rights of the parties. An example is commercial law—transactions involving checks, credit cards, or the sale of goods. If however, Congress wished to give such cases to the federal courts, it would probably proclaim that it was doing so in exercise of its power to regulate commerce, akin to the approach in the Foreign Sovereign Immunities Act. That is, a competent statutory drafter could articulate a federal interest beyond that of providing a federal court as such. This would render moot the issue of "protective jurisdiction." Moreover, as a practical matter, the already existing demands on the federal government, including the federal courts, inhibit Congress from attempting to invest the federal courts with additional jurisdiction except as an aspect of regulating the subject area itself. The controversy over protective jurisdiction thus is likely to remain wholly theoretical.

20. 353 U.S. 448, 77 S.Ct. 912, 1 L.Ed.2d 972 (1957).

21. 461 U.S. 480, 103 S.Ct. 1962, 76 L.Ed.2d 81 (1983).

22. 28 U.S.C. § 1330, 1603 *et seq.*

23. *See* Chemerinsky, Federal Jurisdiction 5.2 (3d ed. 1999); Wright, Federal Courts 20 (4th ed. 1983); *e.g.*, Goldberg–Ambrose, The Protective Jurisdiction of the Federal Courts, 30 UCLA L. Rev. 542 (1983).

The theory is significant, however, as an influence on how the "arising under" jurisdictional statutes are interpreted. If *Osborn* is read with all its implications, statutory grants of federal jurisdiction could be interpreted liberally. Historically, however, jurisdictional statutes have been read as though they reflected congressional reluctance to intrude on the judicial province of the state courts, to which litigants must resort when the federal courts do not have jurisdiction. That tradition helps explain the way in which the arising-under statute, 28 U.S.C. § 1331, has been interpreted.

§ 2.27 "Arising Under": Statutory Scope of § 1331

For purposes of both general federal question jurisdiction under 28 U.S.C. § 1331 and special federal question jurisdictional provisions, the term "arises under" (or "arising under") is a technical one.[1] Its significance can be described as follows:

Plaintiff's claim

- The plaintiff's claim, stated in accordance with pleading rules, must rest on federal law.[2]
- To rest on federal law, the plaintiff's right of action must be expressly conferred by federal statute or implied from a statute or provision of the Constitution creating a duty that benefits the plaintiff. Moreover, if the right of action is not expressly conferred by statute, the court must hold that the breach of duty was intended either by Congress or in the Constitution to give rise to a private federal cause of action.[3] Some decisions treat specific duties established by statute or the Constitution as ones whose breach can be sanctioned only by public authorities and not through actions for private redress; others treat such duties as establishing a standard of conduct but not a cause of action, meaning they can be privately enforced, if at all, only by an action under state law.[4] Only if the federal duty is treated as implying a federal right of

§ 2.27

1. *See* Chemerinsky, Federal Jurisdiction 5.3 (3d ed. 1999); Mishkin, The Federal "Question" in the District Courts, 53 Colum. L. Rev. 157 (1953); Doernberg, There's No Reason for It; It's Just Our Policy: Why the Well–Pleaded Complaint Rule Sabotages the Purposes of Federal Question Jurisdiction, 38 Hastings L.J. 597 (1987); Oakley, Federal Jurisdiction and the Problem of the Litigative Unit: When Does What "Arise Under" Federal Law?, 76 Tex. L. Rev. 1829 (1998).

2. Franchise Tax Bd. v. Construction Laborers Vacation Trust, 463 U.S. 1, 103 S.Ct. 2841, 77 L.Ed.2d 420 (1983); Skelly Oil Co. v. Phillips Petroleum Co., 339 U.S. 667, 70 S.Ct. 876, 94 L.Ed. 1194 (1950); Louisville & Nashville R.R. v. Mottley, 219 U.S. 467, 31 S.Ct. 265, 55 L.Ed. 297 (1911).

3. *See, e.g.*, Metropolitan Life Ins. Co. v. Taylor, 481 U.S. 58, 107 S.Ct. 1542, 95 L.Ed.2d 55 (1987); Bivens v. Six Unknown Named Agents of the Fed. Bureau of Narcotics, 403 U.S. 388, 91 S.Ct. 1999, 29 L.Ed.2d 619 (1971); Bank of America v. Parnell, 352 U.S. 29, 77 S.Ct. 119, 1 L.Ed.2d 93 (1956) (federal common law). *See also* Mowe, Federal Statutes and Implied Private Actions, 55 Or. L. Rev. 3 (1976).

4. *See, e.g.,* Merrell Dow Pharmaceuticals v. Thompson, 478 U.S. 804, 106 S.Ct. 3229, 92 L.Ed.2d 650 (1986); Cannon v. University of Chicago, 441 U.S. 677, 99 S.Ct. 1946, 60 L.Ed.2d 560 (1979); Hazen,

action for redress does an action founded on breach of the duty arise under federal law for purposes of federal question jurisdiction.

Federal defense does not confer jurisdiction

• An action does not arise under federal law if the federal law forms an ingredient of a *defense* rather than plaintiff's cause of action. Whether the federal legal element is allocated to the plaintiff as part of the cause of action or to the defense as a matter of avoidance of the cause of action is usually a matter of decisional law. Plaintiffs may not attempt to transform a federal defense into a part of their pleading by the pleading mechanism of anticipating the defense of their complaint.[5]

The basic rules for resolving this set of "arising under" issues[6] are not consistently applied. The Supreme Court at times has said that not only must the plaintiff's claim be created by federal law, but the lawsuit must involve a question of interpreting the federal law.[7] This would mean that claims clearly well founded on federal law would not be within federal jurisdiction, while debatable ones would be, which is absurd. The Supreme Court at other times has said federal jurisdiction exists if "plaintiff's right to relief necessarily depends on resolution of a substantial question of federal law."[8] Taken literally, this could mean that arising-under jurisdiction exists whenever an issue of federal law *might* determine the outcome of a case even if the issue came up defensively: A plaintiff's "right to relief" depends not only on plaintiff's allegations but also on the defenses interposed.[9] Yet the Supreme Court has emphatically said that 1331 arising-under jurisdiction does not extend to cases where federal law is brought in by way of defense.[10]

Declaratory judgment suits

In some decisions, the Supreme Court has held that a party may not make the suit arise under federal law by framing a complaint as a declaratory judgment rather than allowing the defense to raise a federal legal question. The best example of this proposition is *Skelly Oil Co. v. Phillips Petroleum Co.*[11] There, plaintiff sought a declaratory judgment that its contract with defendant was not rendered invalid by regulatory conditions imposed by the Federal Power Commission, the critical issue

Implied Private Remedies Under Federal Statutes, 33 Vand. L. Rev. 1333 (1980).

5. Pilot Life Ins. Co. v. Dedeaux, 481 U.S. 41, 107 S.Ct. 1549, 95 L.Ed.2d 39 (1987); Skelly Oil Co. v. Phillips Petroleum Co., 339 U.S. 667, 70 S.Ct. 876, 94 L.Ed. 1194 (1950). *Compare* American Law Inst., Study of the Division of Jurisdiction Between State and Federal Courts 1311(a) ("in which the initial pleading sets forth a substantial claim arising under the Constitution, laws, or treaties of the United States").

6. *See* text at notes 2–5 *supra.*

7. *See* Shulthis v. McDougal, 225 U.S. 561, 32 S.Ct. 704, 56 L.Ed. 1205 (1912).

8. Franchise Tax Bd. v. Construction Laborers Vacation Trust, 463 U.S. 1, 28, 103 S.Ct. 2841, 77 L.Ed.2d 420 (1983).

9. *See* the discussion of Osborn v. Bank of United States in § 2.7 *supra.*

10. *See* text at note 12 *supra.*

11. 339 U.S. 667, 70 S.Ct. 876, 94 L.Ed. 1194 (1950).

being the authority of the FPC to impose such conditions. The Court held that plaintiff's claim was "really" for contract enforcement, that the regulatory conditions were an affirmative defense to the claim, and hence that the federal question was not properly part of the complaint. In other words, to determine whether a declaratory judgment action arises under federal law, one must imagine the traditional suit whose validity or invalidity the declaratory judgment proceeding seeks to resolve, and inquire whether that traditional suit arises under federal law. That implies that federal question jurisdiction would exist over a declaratory judgment complaint alleging that the defendant's federal claim is invalid, even though the declaratory judgment plaintiff asserts no federal claim of its own. The Supreme Court, however, has questioned this proposition without actually passing on it one way or the other.[12]

Inconsistencies

In some decisions, the Supreme Court has said that the nature of the claim is determined by examining how the plaintiff has framed the complaint. Thus, in *Fair v. Kohler Die & Specialty Co.*,[13] the Supreme Court said that "[t]he party who brings a suit is master to decide what law he will rely upon and therefore does determine whether he will bring a 'suit arising under'.... "[14] In other decisions, however, the Court has said that the court must, or at least may, "recharacterize ... a complaint [to determine whether it is] an action arising under federal law."[15] The Court has likewise handed down decisions that are difficult to reconcile when faced with cases in which state law provided a cause of action enforcing a federal right.[16]

These differences in formulating what constitutes "arising under" do not involve merely "subtle distinctions"[17] or "*widely perceived*, 'irreconcilable' conflict."[18] They involve actual contradictions—in language, in the means of correlating federal law with state law, in the definition of federal district court jurisdiction, and in fashioning procedural rules to

12. Textron Lycoming Reciprocating Engine Div. v. UAW, 523 U.S. 653, 118 S.Ct. 1626, 140 L.Ed.2d 863 (1998).

13. 228 U.S. 22, 33 S.Ct. 410, 57 L.Ed. 716 (1913).

14. 228 U.S. at 25, 33 S.Ct. at 411, 57 L.Ed. at 717.

15. Metropolitan Life Ins. Co. v. Taylor, 481 U.S. 58, 64, 107 S.Ct. 1542, 1547, 95 L.Ed.2d 55, 63 (1987). *See also* Rivet v. Regions Bank, 522 U.S. 470, 118 S.Ct. 921, 139 L.Ed.2d 912 (1998); Miller, Artful Pleading: A Doctrine in Search of Definition, 76 Texas L. Rev. 1781 (1998).

16. *Compare* City of Chicago v. International College of Surgeons, 522 U.S. 156, 118 S.Ct. 523, 139 L.Ed.2d 525 (1997) *with* Merrell Dow Pharmaceuticals, Inc. v. Thompson, 478 U.S. 804, 106 S.Ct. 3229, 92 L.Ed.2d 650 (1986); Alleva, Prerogative Lost: The Trouble with Statutory Federal Question Doctrine After *Merrell Dow*, 52 Ohio St. L.J. 1477 (1991).

17. Wright, Law of Federal Courts 100 (4th ed. 1983).

18. Merrell Dow Pharmaceuticals v. Thompson, 478 U.S. 804, 814 n. 12, 106 S.Ct. 3229, 3235 n. 12, 92 L.Ed.2d 650, 662 n. 12 (1986).

implement federal jurisdiction. These contradictions cannot be wholly reconciled.

Implied rights of action

The most persistently controverted issue concerning actions arising under federal law is whether a federal statute creating a duty also implies a private right of action. When Congress expressly provides for a civil action by a person injured as a result of another's violation of federal law, such an action certainly may be brought in federal court.[19] When Congress merely prescribes a duty without conferring a civil action for breach of that duty, the situation is ambiguous. On one hand, enforcement through a private remedy gives effect to the congressional substantive purpose, and an intent to create a right of action should be inferred where private enforcement will have such an effect. Since it is hard to conceive how a private remedy would ever *impede* the substantive purpose, the argument is thus always available that a right of action should be implied. On the other hand, since Congress often has expressly conferred private rights of action, it obviously knows how to write a statute that does so. Hence, the argument is always available that Congress's failure to provide for a private right of action implicitly negates an intention to create such a right.

It seems evident that Congress has been aware of this problem since the 1930s, if not earlier. Thus, Congress's failure to deal expressly with the issue whether a private action should be available to enforce a federal duty probably indicates that Congress could not muster a sufficient majority to add or deny a private right of enforcement for the right in question and, therefore, that its will is equivocal on the issue. The Supreme Court has adopted various tests for ascertaining congressional intent. Some tests predispose to finding an implied cause of action, others predispose against doing so.[20] Any such test seems necessarily fictional. The fact is that Congress, where it has not expressly dealt with the matter of a private right of action, has, by implication, deferred the question to judicial resolution. As such, the problem is one of substantive legal policy, like any other common law question, and turns primarily on substantive considerations: Is the federal duty one that injured private parties ought to be allowed to sue to enforce?

This last question—should a federally created duty be enforceable by private right of action—itself involves two issues. The first is whether the duty can be enforced in a private civil suit, be it through state or

19. *See, e.g.,* 45 U.S.C. § 51 (Federal Employer's Liability Act); 46 U.S.C. § 688 (Jones Act).

20. *Compare* J. I. Case Co. v. Borak, 377 U.S. 426, 84 S.Ct. 1555, 12 L.Ed.2d 423 (1964), *and* Merrill, Lynch, Pierce, Fenner & Smith, Inc. v. Curran, 456 U.S. 353, 102 S.Ct. 1825, 72 L.Ed.2d 182 (1982) (finding implied causes of action), *with* Cort v. Ash, 422 U.S. 66, 95 S.Ct. 2080, 45 L.Ed.2d 26 (1975), *and* Merrell Dow Pharmaceuticals v. Thompson, 478 U.S. 804, 106 S.Ct. 3229, 92 L.Ed.2d 650 (1986) (finding no implied causes of action).

federal law. State law may be allowed to recognize a cause of action in which violation of a federal duty is a wrong per se; alternatively, such a cause of action may be regarded as preempted by federal law.[21] This issue is one of substantive policy, but its resolution immediately determines a question of federal district court jurisdiction. If no private cause of action exists, then obviously none arises under federal law.

Assuming that a private right of action predicated on breach of a federal duty is not preempted, the second issue is: Is the private action created by federal cases so that it arises under federal law within the meaning of 1331? Two approaches can be taken in resolving this issue:(1) federal law supplies only the duty, with state law supplying the other elements of the cause of action (proximate cause, damages, and so on);(2) federal law supplies the cause of action itself. If the latter position is taken, then plaintiff can sue on the cause of action in federal court, or defendant can remove it to federal court if the suit is originally filed in state court.[22]

§ 2.28 Supplemental Jurisdiction

The relatively narrow contours of federal district court jurisdiction are to some extent expanded through the concept of supplemental jurisdiction, a new umbrella term comprising such subcategories as ancillary jurisdiction, pendent claim jurisdiction, and pendent party jurisdiction. Ancillary jurisdiction originally referred to bringing additional parties into a case involving claims to specific property. Pendent claim jurisdiction referred to whether the court may adjudicate additional claims between existing parties. Pendent party jurisdiction referred to whether additional parties could be brought in when a suit originally between two parties became a multiparty controversy. The different usages are an historical accident. The term "supplemental jurisdiction" is used by Congress in a 1990 statute seeking to clarify the rules governing this auxiliary jurisdictional authority.[1]

The concepts find their origin in the proposition that a federal court, whatever the basis of its jurisdiction, adjudicates a "case," which can be held to include all legal issues incidental to the main controversy. Counterpoised to this is the proposition that the federal courts have no broader jurisdiction than that expressly conferred by statute; since the

21. *See* Twitchell, Characterizing Federal Claims: Preemption, Removal, and the Arising-Under Jurisdiction of the Federal Courts, 54 Geo. Wash. L. Rev. 812 (1986).

22. On removal jurisdiction, see § 2.31 *infra*.

§ 2.28

1. 28 U.S.C. § 1367; *see* Chemerinsky, Federal Jurisdiction § 5.4 (3d ed. 1999); McManamon, Dispelling the Myths of Pendent and Ancillary Jurisdiction, 46 Wash. & Lee L. Rev. 863 (1989); Miller, Ancillary and Pendent Jurisdiction, 26 S. Tex. L. Rev. 1 (1985); §§ 10.12, 10.17, 10.18 *infra*.

statutes had not provided for ancillary jurisdiction,[2] no such jurisdiction should be exercised.

Over the years the Supreme Court has wavered in its sympathy toward supplemental jurisdiction. In the 1806 decision *Strawbridge v. Curtiss*,[3] the Court held that an additional potential party that was a necessary party could not be joined when doing so would violate the requirement of "complete diversity."[4] This holding is incompatible with the notion that there can be jurisdiction over additional parties. In the 1861 case *Freeman v. Howe*,[5] however, the Court held that jurisdiction could be exercised over a claim by an intervenor whose citizenship did not meet the complete diversity requirement. In *Moore v. Cotton Exchange*,[6] decided in 1926, the Court held that when a district court had jurisdiction over a claim, it could exercise pendent claim jurisdiction over a counterclaim by defendant. In *United Mine Workers v. Gibbs* in 1966, the Court noted that in modern procedure "joinder of claims, parties and remedies is encouraged":

> The state and federal claims must derive from a common nucleus of operative fact. But if, considered without regard to their federal or state character, a plaintiff's claims are such that he would ordinarily be expected to try them all in one judicial proceeding, then ... there is power in the federal courts to hear the whole.[7]

Rationale

In all its forms, supplemental jurisdiction promotes judicial economy by making it possible to try related claims in a single federal action instead of splitting them between federal and state actions. Pendent jurisdiction also protects access to the federal courts; without it a party entitled to sue in those courts would be tempted to proceed instead in a state court where all the claims could be asserted. It protects parties other than the plaintiff from unfairness that might otherwise result from incomplete determination of a controversy in a federal court suit. A defendant who could not assert a state law counterclaim in such a suit, for example, might be forced by a federal judgment to pay the plaintiff even though, in light of the whole transaction, the plaintiff was indebted to the defendant. On the other hand, those concerned to protect the limits on federal jurisdiction worry that litigants relying on supplemental jurisdiction can drag a large controversy into federal court on the basis of a single claim.

2. *But see* 28 U.S.C. § 1338(b) (state law unfair competition claim joined with copyright, patent, or trademark claim).

3. 7 U.S. (3 Cranch) 267, 2 L.Ed. 435 (1806).

4. *See* § 2.3 *supra.*

5. 65 U.S. (24 How.) 450, 16 L. Ed. 749 (1861).

6. 270 U.S. 593, 46 S.Ct. 367, 70 L.Ed. 750 (1926).

7. 383 U.S. 715, 724–725, 86 S.Ct. 1130, 1138, 16 L.Ed.2d 218, 227–228 (1966).

History of the statute

Gibbs suggests that a federal court could exercise supplemental jurisdiction over all claims arising out of the transaction involved in the original claim over which the court had proper jurisdiction. In several decisions in the 1970s, however, the Court backed away from the implications of the broad formulation in *Gibbs,*[8] although in 1988 it reaffirmed the *Gibbs* rationale.[9] Then in *Finley v. United States,*[10] an action brought against the United States under the Federal Torts Claims Act—a claim that could be brought only in a federal court—the Court held that the plaintiff could not join as an additional defendant a private party whose conduct was allegedly also tortious. In doing so the Court repeated language from an 1807 decision that is as hostile to supplemental jurisdiction as the language in *Gibbs* is sympathetic:

> As regards all courts of the United States inferior to this tribunal, two things are necessary to create jurisdiction, whether original or appellate. The Constitution must have given to the court the capacity to take it, and an act of Congress must have supplied it. . . .[11]

Congress reacted promptly to *Finley* by passing the supplemental jurisdiction statute, codified at 28 U.S.C. § 1367. The statute was meant to restore the broader *Gibbs* concept of supplemental jurisdiction by extending jurisdiction to claims sufficiently related to those claims within the federal courts' original jurisdiction to fall within "the same case or controversy under Article III of the Constitution," that is, to press supplemental jurisdiction to its constitutional limits. In particular, the statute allows supplemental jurisdiction over "claims that involve the joinder or intervention of additional parties."[12]

Limits on supplemental jurisdiction

But the statute limited its reach so that plaintiffs would not use it to circumvent the rule requiring complete diversity in diversity jurisdiction cases. The danger feared by the drafters, and previously noted by the Supreme Court,[13] was that a plaintiff would sue those parties over whom diversity jurisdiction existed, anticipating that other parties would then join nondiverse parties or that such parties would intervene, and that the plaintiff could then add its claims against these new parties. Espe-

8. *See* Zahn v. International Paper Co., 414 U.S. 291, 94 S.Ct. 505, 38 L.Ed.2d 511 (1973) (aggregation of class suit claims not permitted to meet minimum jurisdictional amount); Aldinger v. Howard, 427 U.S. 1, 96 S.Ct. 2413, 49 L.Ed.2d 276 (1976) (disallowing joinder of a pendent party to a claim based on 42 U.S.C. § 1983); Owen Equip. & Erection Co. v. Kroger, 437 U.S. 365, 98 S.Ct. 2396, 57 L.Ed.2d 274 (1978) (disallowing plaintiff's assertion of pendent claim against third-party defendant).

9. Carnegie-Mellon Univ. v. Cohill, 484 U.S. 343, 108 S.Ct. 614, 618, 98 L.Ed.2d 720 (1988).

10. 490 U.S. 545, 109 S.Ct. 2003, 104 L.Ed.2d 593 (1989).

11. Finley v. United States, 490 U.S. 545, 109 S.Ct. 2003, 2006, 104 L.Ed.2d 593, 600 (1989) (quoting The Mayor v. Cooper, 73 U.S. (6 Wall.) 247, 252, 18 L. Ed. 851 (1868)).

12. 28 U.S.C. § 1367(a).

13. Owen Equip. & Erection Co. v. Kroger, 437 U.S. 365, 98 S.Ct. 2396, 57 L.Ed.2d 274 (1978).

cially for those who consider diversity cases less central to the purposes of the federal courts than federal question cases, extending the jurisdiction in this way to cases of incomplete diversity would waste the limited resources of the federal court system. The statute therefore forbids plaintiffs in diversity cases to rely on supplemental jurisdiction to assert claims against parties brought into the case by impleader, permissive joinder, intervention, or as indispensable parties.[14]

Unfortunately, the situations in which someone might try to assert supplemental jurisdiction are so numerous that it proved impossible to foresee them all, or to resolve them in a relatively brief statute. The task was made harder because the drafters sought to reverse both the specific holding and the general approach of *Finley* without extending supplemental jurisdiction into areas that might prove controversial enough to block passage of the statute. Case by case development of the doctrine, which had occurred in the past, might well have been a superior approach, had it not been barred by the Supreme Court's intimations in *Finley* that only Congress could bring about future changes. As a result, although experts carefully drafted the supplemental jurisdiction statute, it has created many new questions of greater or less practical significance. Civil procedure scholars have been busy ever since.[15]

Instances of supplemental jurisdiction

The statute preserves the five types of supplemental jurisdiction that existed before it was enacted:

1. A plaintiff asserting a claim arising under federal law may assert what used to be called pendent jurisdiction over state law claims against the federal claim defendant if the state law claims arise out of the same "nucleus of operative fact," that is, the same out-of-court transaction.[16] Thanks to the statute, the plaintiff may now join additional defendants against whom only state law claims are asserted.[17]

2. A defendant may assert a counterclaim arising out of the same transaction as that sued on by plaintiff, even though the court would not have jurisdiction of the counterclaim if it were independently asserted.[18]

14. 28 U.S.C. § 1367(b); see §§ 9.7, 9.8, 10.11–15, 10.17, 10.18 *infra.*

15. For discussions of the statute, see, *e.g.,* Mengler, Burbank, and Rowe, Congress Accepts the Supreme Court's Invitation to Codify Supplemental Jurisdiction, 74 Judicature 213 (1991)(by the statute's drafters); Symposium, 74 Ind. L.J. 1 (1998); Colloquy, 41 Emory L.J. 1 (1992); McLaughlin, The Federal Supplemental Jurisdictional Statute–A Constitutional and Statutory Analysis, 24 Ariz. St. L.J. 849 (1992).

16. United Mine Workers v. Gibbs, 383 U.S. 715, 86 S.Ct. 1130, 16 L.Ed.2d 218 (1966); Hurn v. Oursler, 289 U.S. 238, 53 S.Ct. 586, 77 L.Ed. 1148 (1933); see City of Chicago v. International College of Surgeons, 522 U.S. 156, 118 S.Ct. 523, 139 L.Ed.2d 525 (1997).

17. *E.g.,* Sinclair v. Soniform, Inc., 935 F.2d 599 (3d Cir.1991). *But see* Peacock v. Thomas, 516 U.S. 349, 116 S.Ct. 862, 133 L.Ed.2d 817 (1996)(no jurisdiction over new action seeking to enforce federal question judgment against new party).

18. Moore v. New York Cotton Exch., 270 U.S. 593, 46 S.Ct. 367, 70 L.Ed. 750 (1926). *See* § 9.13 *infra.*

Before the passage of the statute, only a compulsory counterclaim fell within supplemental jurisdiction; it is not clear whether the statute altered this, and if so how.[19]

3. A defendant may implead (bring in) a third party that is liable to the defendant for the relief plaintiff seeks from the original defendant even though the impleader claim by itself would not qualify for federal jurisdiction.[20]

4. A third party may intervene to protect its interest in the subject matter in dispute between a plaintiff and defendant under rules allowing intervention as of right. Under the statute, however, supplemental jurisdiction does not reach an intervening plaintiff's claim in a diversity suit.[21]

5. A defendant may assert a cross-claim against another defendant when it arises out of the same transaction as the original claim against the two defendants, again regardless of whether there would be federal jurisdiction over the cross-claim were it brought separately.[22]

The statute legitimates a sixth type of supplemental jurisdiction that *Finley* had barred, the addition of "pendent plaintiffs" or "pendent defendants" to a federal question action.[23] For example, a plaintiff could join in one suit a federal claim against her employer for sexual harassment and a state law tort claim for assault against a fellow-employee who conducted the harassment but was not subject to federal liability. In a diversity case, however, no such joinder is permissible: a plaintiff may not sue a citizen of another state and then add an additional plaintiff or defendant whose presence would destroy complete diversity.[24]

Effect on diversity class actions

Courts have disputed how the statute affects supplemental jurisdiction over claims whose only jurisdictional defect is failure to meet the $75,000 amount in controversy requirement for diversity claims. Before the statute, the Court refused to allow supplemental jurisdiction over such claims. For example, a federal court could hear a class action based on diversity only if each class member's claim exceeded the jurisdictional

19. *See, e.g.,* Rothman v. Emory University, 123 F.3d 446 (7th Cir.1997)(when counterclaim is so related to claim as to form part of the same case or controversy, supplemental jurisdiction exists even if it is not compulsory counterclaim); Channell v. Citicorp National Services, Inc., 89 F.3d 379 (7th Cir.1996)(no supplemental jurisdiction over unrelated set-off).

20. Owen Equip. & Erection Co. v. Kroger, 437 U.S. 365, 98 S.Ct. 2396, 57 L.Ed.2d 274 (1978). *See* § 10.18 *infra.*

21. Freeman v. Howe, 65 U.S. (24 How.) 450, 16 L. Ed. 749 (1861); § 10.17 *infra.* For the statute's impact, see Development Finance Corp. v. Sower, 54 F.3d 156 (3d Cir. 1995); EEOC v. National Children's Center, Inc., 146 F.3d 1042 (D.C.Cir. 1998); MCI Telecommunications Corp. v. Logan Group, Inc., 848 F.Supp. 86 (N.D.Tex.1994).

22. Owen Equip. & Erection Co. v. Kroger, 437 U.S. 365, 98 S.Ct. 2396, 57 L.Ed.2d 274 (1978); Zurn Industries, Inc. v. Acton Constr. Co., 847 F.2d 234 (5th Cir.1988); *see* § 9.12 *infra.*

23. *E.g.,* Brazinski v. Amoco Petroleum Additives Co., 6 F.3d 1176 (7th Cir.1993); Rodriguez v. Comas, 888 F.2d 899 (1st Cir. 1989).

24. 28 U.S.C. § 1367(b).

amount (or the whole class' claim could be considered a single entity).[25] The legislative history of the statute makes clear that it was not meant to change this principle, and some courts have ruled accordingly.[26] But the language of the statute contains no such limitation, and some courts, refusing to look beyond the language, have held that supplemental claims of this kind are now permitted.[27]

Discretion to dismiss

A federal court having supplemental jurisdiction has nevertheless always had the discretion to dismiss the supplemental claim if it would be more appropriately heard in state court—if, for example, the claim to which it is supplemental is dismissed without trial as lacking in merit.[28] The statute codifies this discretion, specifying that it may be exercised in three stated circumstances, or "in exceptional circumstances" if "there are other compelling reasons for declining jurisdiction."[29]

§ 2.29 Abstention

During the past half-century the Supreme Court has developed doctrines of "abstention" whereby the federal district courts may or must decline to exercise jurisdiction in certain cases involving sensitive issues of state law.[1] The abstention doctrines have been invoked in various types of cases, sustained by a variety of rationales, and applied with much inconsistency. Whatever the diverse formulations, however, three factors are usually involved. First, the plaintiff claims that a provision of state law is invalid by reason of federal law, whether by constitutional invalidity, or federal preemption, or the like. Second, the state legal provision is ambiguous in terms of the allegedly superseding federal provision; that is, the state provision is susceptible of being

25. Zahn v. International Paper Co., 414 U.S. 291, 94 S.Ct. 505, 38 L.Ed.2d 511 (1973); Snyder v. Harris, 394 U.S. 332, 89 S.Ct. 1053, 22 L.Ed.2d 319 (1969); Berman v. Narragansett Racing Ass'n, 414 F.2d 311 (1st Cir.1969); § 10.22 *infra*. Curiously, the same requirement does not apply to diversity of citizenship in federal court class actions: only the citizenship of the named plaintiffs counts. Supreme Tribe of Ben–Hur v. Cauble, 255 U.S. 356, 41 S.Ct. 338, 65 L.Ed. 673 (1921).

26. Meritcare Inc. v. St. Paul Mercury Ins. Co., 166 F.3d 214 (3d Cir.1999); Leonhardt v. Western Sugar Co., 160 F.3d 631 (10th Cir.1998).

27. Stromberg Metal Works, Inc. v. Press Mechanical, Inc., 77 F.3d 928 (7th Cir.1996); Free v. Abbott Laboratories, 51 F.3d 524 (5th Cir.1995), *aff'd by equally divided court,* 529 U.S. 333, 120 S.Ct. 1578, 146 L.Ed.2d 306 (2000).

28. United Mine Workers v. Gibbs, 383 U.S. 715, 86 S.Ct. 1130, 16 L.Ed.2d 218 (1966); *see* Carnegie–Mellon Univ. v. Cohill, 484 U.S. 343, 108 S.Ct. 614, 98 L.Ed.2d 720 (1988).

29. 28 U.S.C. § 1367(c); see Executive Software North America, Inc. v. U.S. District Ct., 15 F.3d 1484 (9th Cir.1994)(reading statute to limit exercise of discretion more than previous law).

§ 2.29

1. *See* Bator, Meltzer, Mishkin, and Shapiro, The Federal Courts and the Federal System (3d ed. 1988); Chemerinsky, Federal Jurisdiction chs. 12–14 (3d ed. 1999); Wright, Federal Courts 52–53 (4th ed. 1983). Abstention may be implemented by dismissing suits for injunctive or other discretionary relief, and by staying other actions. Quackenbush v. Allstate Ins. Co., 517 U.S. 706, 116 S.Ct. 1712, 135 L.Ed.2d 1 (1996).

construed or applied in a way that would not run afoul of federal law. Third, the legal issue thus posed either has already arisen in a pending state proceeding or would so arise in a state proceeding if the legal controversy went forward in the normal course of events. A factor not always mentioned but usually present is that the substantive controversy involved is politically sensitive.

Federal court abstention

The abstention doctrines have come to be known by the landmark cases in which the doctrines evolved. "*Pullman* abstention" derives from *Railroad Commission of Texas v. Pullman.*[2] In that case the Texas Railroad Commission had issued an order prohibiting the operation of sleeping cars within the state unless a conductor was present, apparently in order to eliminate the practice of employing porters, who were black, to be in charge of such equipment. The Pullman company challenged the order in federal court on due process and equal protection grounds, the porters also challenging it on grounds of racial discrimination. The Supreme Court held that the authority of the Texas commission to issue the regulation was unclear and stated that the federal district court should have abstained from considering the constitutionality of the regulation until its interpretation was clarified by the state authorities. If the state courts ruled the regulation improper, the matter would end there; only if they ruled it legal could the federal courts rule on the constitutional issues. The Court offered three justifications for requiring abstention:

1. It would avoid needless friction between state and federal courts. Questionable state laws should first be construed by the state courts.
2. It would reduce the risk of erroneous interpretations of state law.
3. It would avoid "interference with important state functions."[3]

The rationale for *Pullman* abstention remains unconvincing. Friction between state and federal courts is an unavoidable aspect of federal constitutional review of state exercise of authority.[4] Similarly, the meaning of the sleeping car regulation was hardly unclear, and the risk of its misinterpretation was correspondingly remote. Correlatively, *Pullman* abstention entails cost and delay as the case is transferred from state to federal court and back again, with the risk "that valuable federal rights

2. 312 U.S. 496, 61 S.Ct. 643, 85 L.Ed. 971 (1941).

3. *See also* Harman v. Forssenius, 380 U.S. 528, 534, 85 S.Ct. 1177, 1182, 14 L.Ed.2d 50, 55 (1965).

4. *See, e.g.,* Chemerinsky, Federal Jurisdiction 595–599 (1989); Davies, *Pullman* and *Burford* Abstention: Clarifying the Roles of Federal and State Courts in Constitutional Cases, 20 U.C. Davis L. Rev. 1 (1986); Field, Abstention in Constitutional Cases: The Scope of the Pullman Abstention Doctrine, 122 U. Pa. L. Rev. 1071 (1974).

might be lost in the absence of expeditious adjudication in the federal court."[5]

Pullman abstention has been severely circumscribed.[6] The Court has said that abstention is not required merely because the state statute either is being challenged for vagueness, or is patently unconstitutional,[7] or because the state courts have not yet considered the constitutionality of the statute.[8] Although thus undercut, *Pullman* has not been overruled.

"State interest abstention" derives from *Louisiana Power & Light Co. v. City of Thibodaux*,[9] wherein the federal court's jurisdiction was based on diversity, not federal question jurisdiction. In that case the city brought an eminent domain suit to claim property owned by a power company. The case was removed to federal court on diversity grounds, and the federal district court held that it should abstain. The Supreme Court held the abstention proper, noting that eminent domain proceedings are "intimately involved with sovereign prerogative."[10] Yet in *County of Allegheny v. Frank Mashuda Co.*,[11] decided the same day as *Thibodaux*, the Supreme Court reversed a lower court's abstention in an eminent domain case, stating that abstention was proper only in exceptional and unusual cases. It is possible to reconcile *Mashuda* with *Thibodaux* in that the eminent domain statute in *Thibodaux* was said to be ambiguous. Thus, abstention may be proper if both elements—unclear state law and state interests "intimately involved with sovereign prerogatives"—are present.

Administrative abstention

"Administrative abstention" derives from *Burford v. Sun Oil Co.*[12] involving a challenge to the validity of a Texas Railroad Commission drilling permit. The Supreme Court held that federal abstention was appropriate in a case involving extensive state administrative rules and regulations and an important state regulating interest. *Burford* has been characterized as administrative abstention in which federal district court review would unduly intrude into a state administrative apparatus governing an area heavily regulated by state law.[13] But *Burford* was

5. Bolline v. City of New Orleans, 757 F.Supp. 715, 719 (E.D.La.1991).

6. *See* Thornburgh v. American College of Obstetricians, 476 U.S. 747, 106 S.Ct. 2169, 90 L.Ed.2d 779 (1986); Harris County Commrs. Court v. Moore, 420 U.S. 77, 95 S.Ct. 870, 43 L.Ed.2d 32 (1975).

7. Thornburgh v. American College of Obstetricians, 476 U.S. 747, 106 S.Ct. 2169, 90 L.Ed.2d 779 (1986).

8. Wisconsin v. Constantineau, 400 U.S. 433, 91 S.Ct. 507, 27 L.Ed.2d 515 (1971).

9. 360 U.S. 25, 79 S.Ct. 1070, 3 L.Ed.2d 1058 (1959).

10. 360 U.S. at 38, 79 S.Ct. at 1073, 3 L.Ed.2d at 1062.

11. 360 U.S. 185, 79 S.Ct. 1060, 3 L.Ed.2d 1163 (1959).

12. 319 U.S. 315, 63 S.Ct. 1098, 87 L.Ed. 1424 (1943).

13. University of Md. v. Peat Marwick Main & Co., 923 F.2d 265, 267–268 (3d Cir.1991) (quoting Lac D'Amiante du Quebec v. American Home Assurance Co., 864 F.2d 1033, 1043 (3d Cir.1988)).

distinguished in *New Orleans Public Service v. Council of New Orleans*,[14] wherein a utility sought relief from a state rate-making commission's determination that the costs incurred in a nuclear power plant could not be completely reimbursed by rate increases. It is difficult to see how the state interests, administrative complexity, and federal intrusiveness in the *New Orleans Public Service* case were significantly different from those in *Burford.*

Pending state court proceedings

"Pending state proceeding abstention" derives from *Colorado River Water Conservation District v. United States.*[15] In that case, the United States sued numerous defendants in federal district court for a declaration of water rights. A parallel state action had been initiated in which the United States was made a party. The Supreme Court said that in exceptional circumstances federal courts may abstain out of deference to the parallel state action, but "generally ... the pendency of an action in the state court is no bar to proceedings concerning the same matter in the Federal court having jurisdiction.... [T]he circumstances permitting the dismissal of a federal suit due to the presence of a concurrent state proceeding for reasons of wise judicial administration are considerably more limited than the circumstances appropriate for abstention."[16]

In *Colorado River* the Supreme Court upheld deference to the state action, citing the congressional policy to avoid piecemeal adjudication of water rights and stating that a unified proceeding could be best conducted in a state court.[17] In *Will v. Calvert Fire Insurance Co.*,[18] however, the Court held that "a district court is under no compulsion to exercise that jurisdiction where the controversy may be settled more expeditiously in state court."[19]

***Younger* abstention**

There are sound reasons for a federal court to refuse to entertain litigation that raises the central issue of a pending state proceeding involving an important question of the relationship between state and federal law. There may be reasons why the federal courts should abstain from adjudicating controversies involving "unsettled" state law posing "sensitive" issues of state authority. In many of its abstention decisions, however, the Supreme Court has formulated the doctrine in terms that

14. 491 U.S. 350, 109 S.Ct. 2506, 105 L.Ed.2d 298 (1989); *see* City of Chicago v. International College of Surgeons, 522 U.S. 156, 118 S.Ct. 523, 139 L.Ed.2d 525 (1997).

15. 424 U.S. 800, 96 S.Ct. 1236, 47 L.Ed.2d 483 (1976).

16. 424 U.S. at 817, 96 S.Ct. at 1246, 47 L.Ed.2d at 498.

17. *See* Chemerinsky, Federal Jurisdiction 664 (1989); Sonenshein, Abstention: The Crooked Course of *Colorado River,* 59 Tul. L. Rev. 651 (1985). *See also* the McCarran Amendment, 43 U.S.C. § 666, which gave consent for the United States to be sued in State Courts in suits involving the adjudication of water rights.

18. 437 U.S. 655, 98 S.Ct. 2552, 57 L.Ed.2d 504 (1978).

19. 437 U.S. at 662–663, 98 S.Ct. at 2557, 57 L.Ed.2d at 511.

would virtually exclude the federal courts from litigation that would curtail state authority. Thus, in *Younger v. Harris* the Court said that the underlying reason is

> a proper respect for state functions, a recognition of the fact that the entire country is made up of a Union of separate state governments, and a continuance of the belief that the National Government will fare best if the States and their institutions are left free to perform their separate functions in their separate ways.[20]

The strains of "Look Away, Look Away, Dixie Land" may echo through the mind in reading this passage. *Younger* abstention, which began as a restraint on federal injunctions against pending state criminal prosecutions, has expanded to bar injunctions against certain civil law enforcement proceedings as well.[21] Yet the Court has also adhered to ancient doctrine:

> The judiciary cannot, as the legislature may, avoid a measure, because it approaches the confines of the constitution.... We have no more right to decline the exercise of jurisdiction which is given, than to usurp that which is not given.[22]

On this basis the Court has said:

> The federal courts have a "virtually unflagging obligation" to exercise their jurisdiction except in those extraordinary circumstances "where the order to the parties to repair to the State court would clearly serve an important countervailing interest."[23]

The range in these formulations of the abstention doctrine thus runs from leaving state institutions free to perform "their separate functions in their separate ways" to "unflagging ... exercise of jurisdiction" except where an "important countervailing interest" is involved. The proper scope of the abstention doctrines thus remains somewhat uncertain.

§ 2.30 Proof of Jurisdiction

Pleading federal jurisdiction: Rule 8(a)(1)

The tradition in administration of the rules of federal jurisdiction has been one of strict rather than liberal interpretation. One aspect of

20. 401 U.S. 37, 44, 91 S.Ct. 746, 750, 27 L.Ed.2d 669, 675 (1971) (quoted with approval in New Orleans Pub. Serv. v. Council of New Orleans, 491 U.S. 350, 364, 109 S.Ct. 2506, 2516, 105 L.Ed.2d 298, 314 (1989)).

21. Middlesex County Ethics Comm. v. Garden State Bar Ass'n, 457 U.S. 423, 102 S.Ct. 2515, 73 L.Ed.2d 116 (1982)(pending lawyer disciplinary proceeding).

22. Cohens v. Virginia, 19 U.S. (6 Wheat.) 264, 404, 5 L.Ed. 257 (1821) (quoted with approval in New Orleans Pub. Serv. v. Council of New Orleans, 491 U.S. 350, 364, 109 S.Ct. 2506, 2516, 105 L.Ed.2d 298, 314 (1989)).

23. Deakins v. Monaghan, 484 U.S. 193, 203, 108 S.Ct. 523, 530, 98 L.Ed.2d 529, 540 (1988) *quoting* Colorado River Water Conservation Dist. v. United States, 424 U.S. 800, 813, 96 S.Ct. 1236, 1244, 47 L.Ed.2d 483 (1976).

this tradition is the requirement that the jurisdictional basis of an action in federal courts must be affirmatively established. This contrasts with the usual rule in state courts, where the issue of subject matter jurisdiction is raised, if at all, at the instance of a defendant or other party who contends the court lacks jurisdiction. Jurisdiction in federal court is established by allegations in the complaint that disclose the basis of jurisdiction.[1] Thus, if jurisdiction is based on diversity, plaintiff must allege its state citizenship and that of the other parties, and it must appear that the citizenship is diverse.[2] If jurisdiction is based on a federal question, the complaint should refer to the federal law that plaintiffs contend is the basis of their claim.[3] If these allegations are not made, the apparent lack of jurisdiction can be asserted by any party or by the court on its own motion.[4] Such an objection having been made, the plaintiffs must amend their complaint or supply the necessary proof of jurisdiction by affidavits or other supplementary material.

Proof of jurisdiction

The allegations of jurisdiction may be controverted. If the controversy concerns issues of fact, such as the citizenship of the parties, the issues may be tried by affidavit or special hearing, depending on the nature of the proofs.[5] A not uncommon basis for objection to jurisdiction is that the amount in controversy is less than that required under the applicable jurisdictional provision. On such an objection, plaintiffs need not prove their damages as they would at trial on the merits; they need only satisfy the court that there is a legally tenable possibility that they can obtain judgment in at least the minimum amount.[6] If they do so, and the action goes to trial and judgment, the fact that they recover less than the jurisdictional amount does not oust the court of jurisdiction; the judgment is a valid determination on the merits.[7] That is consistent with the principle that jurisdiction is determined as of an action's filing, and is not destroyed by later changes of citizenship or damages.[8]

§ 2.30

1. Fed. R. Civ. P. 8(a)(1).

2. *See* Fed. R. Civ. P. Form 2.

3. *Id.*

4. *E.g.,* City of Kenosha v. Bruno, 412 U.S. 507, 93 S.Ct. 2222, 37 L.Ed.2d 109 (1973).

5. *See* Lake v. Lake, 817 F.2d 1416 (9th Cir.1987) (motion to dismiss proved by affidavit only requires prima facie evidence of jurisdiction). *See also* Note, Trial by Jury of Preliminary Jurisdictional Facts in Federal Cases, 48 Iowa L. Rev. 471 (1963).

6. St. Paul Mercury Indem. Co. v. Red Cab Co., 303 U.S. 283, 58 S.Ct. 586, 82 L.Ed. 845 (1938).

7. *See* 28 U.S.C. § 1332(b), allowing the court in such a case to deny plaintiff recovery of costs. *See* Note, Federal Jurisdictional Amount: Determination of the Matter in Controversy, 73 Harv. L. Rev. 1369 (1960); Note, 71 Colum. L. Rev. 1474 (1971).

8. *E.g.,* Freeport–McMoRan, Inc. v. K N Energy, Inc., 498 U.S. 426, 111 S.Ct. 858, 112 L.Ed.2d 951 (1991). *But see* Caterpillar Inc. v. Lewis, 519 U.S. 61, 117 S.Ct. 467, 136 L.Ed.2d 437 (1996)(lack of complete diversity at time of removal to federal court

A more complicated question is presented when the plaintiff relies on federal question jurisdiction on the basis of a disputable contention about what the federal law is. Plaintiff alleges facts that he or she contends constitute a right of action under federal law; defendant contends that federal law does not create a cause of action on those facts. Thus, the jurisdictional question and the question of the substantive validity of the plaintiff's claim coincide. In such a situation, the federal court has jurisdiction to decide, as it were, the federal law claim that there is a federal law claim. If the court decides that the claim is tenable under federal law, it retains jurisdiction; if it decides the claim is not tenable under federal law, it dismisses on the merits rather than for want of jurisdiction; if it decides the claim was utterly untenable, it dismisses for want of jurisdiction.[9]

Delayed challenge to jurisdiction

The question of jurisdiction occasionally may escape notice in the trial court before rendition of judgment. It may nevertheless be raised by motion after trial; should an appeal be taken, it may be raised before the appellate court, even by the party that first brought the case to federal court.[10] Pursuing this jurisdictional shibboleth a step further, the Supreme Court has ruled that a court must resolve any subject matter jurisdiction issue first, even if it is plain that the case must in any event be dismissed on the merits.[11] If the jurisdictional question has still not been raised, the problem arises whether the judgment can be subsequently attacked by motion to set aside the judgment or by some form of collateral attack. The trend of the law is to treat the judgment at that point as invulnerable unless it was entered on default or unless giving effect to the judgment would offend some transcendent policy of federal law.[12]

§ 2.31 Removal Jurisdiction

An action may be brought into the federal district court not only by being originated there but also by the procedure of removal from state

may be cured by later dismissal of nondiverse party).

9. Wheeldin v. Wheeler, 373 U.S. 647, 83 S.Ct. 1441, 10 L.Ed.2d 605 (1963); Browning–Ferris Indus. v. Muszynski, 899 F.2d 151 (2d Cir.1990).

10. *See* § 4.3 *infra*. *See also* Newman–Green, Inc. v. Alfonzo–Larrain, 490 U.S. 826, 109 S.Ct. 2218, 104 L.Ed.2d 893 (1989), where the court of appeals on its own motion questioned the citizenship of a party and, having found it incompatible with complete diversity, was held properly to have permitted dismissal of that party, thereby validating the court's jurisdiction. *Compare* 28 U.S.C. § 1653 (amending defective allegation of jurisdiction); Fed. R. Civ. P. 21.

11. Steel Co. v. Citizens for a Better Environment, 523 U.S. 83, 118 S.Ct. 1003, 140 L.Ed.2d 210 (1998). *But see* Ruhrgas AG v. Marathon Oil Co., 526 U.S. 574, 119 S.Ct. 1563, 143 L.Ed.2d 760 (1999)(court may sometimes consider personal jurisdiction before subject matter jurisdiction).

12. *See generally* Dobbs, Beyond Bootstrap: Foreclosing the Issue of Subject Matter Jurisdiction Before Final Judgment, 51 Minn. L. Rev. 491 (1967); *cf.* Restatement (Second) of Judgments §§ 12, 69.

court. This procedure is ordinarily permissible only if the action originally could have been brought in federal court.[1] Thus the jurisdictional requirements discussed previously[2] are applicable to removed actions. In particular, an action based on state law may not be removed to federal court on the ground that the defendant has a defense or counterclaim that rests on federal law;[3] it is removable only if the action, as framed by the complaint, would have been maintainable in federal court. The party seeking removal must state, in a notice of removal, why the action is within the federal court's jurisdiction, and the notice must be filed within thirty days of receipt of the complaint or other document from which it may be ascertained that the action is removable.[4]

Diversity removal

Although removal jurisdiction may be invoked in either diversity or federal question cases, a special restriction exists in diversity actions. If any of the defendants in the state court action is a citizen of the state in which the action is brought,[5] then the action may not be removed.[6] If, for example, a citizen of New Jersey brings an action in New York state court against defendants who are citizens respectively of New York and Connecticut, the action may not be removed unless it contains a claim based on federal law. The theory underlying this restriction is that if the plaintiff is willing to choose the defendant's "home court," the locally resident defendant does not need the benefit of the supposedly more neutral federal forum.

If the case is improperly removed, the federal district court is required to remand it to state court.[7] A federal court may not remand

§ 2.31

1. *See* 28 U.S.C. §§ 1441–1452. *See also* Bator, Meltzer, Mishkin, and Shapiro, The Federal Courts and the Federal System 1767 *et seq.* (3d ed. 1988); Chemerinsky, Federal Jurisdiction 5.5 (3d ed. 1999); Wright, Federal Courts ch. 6 (4th ed. 1983); Purcell, Litigation and Inequality: Federal Diversity Jurisdiction in Industrial America, 1870–1958 (1993)(describing strategic use of removal by defendant corporations). On removal of otherwise unremovable actions by federal courts seeking to protect their jurisdiction against state court interference, *see* Steinman, The Newest Frontier of Judicial Activism: Removal under the All Writs Act, 80 B.U.L. Rev. 773 (2000). On proposed expansions of removal, *see* American Law Institute, Complex Litigation: Statutory Recommendations and Analysis (1994).

2. *See* §§ 2.24–27 *supra.* Removal is at the initiative of the defendant, who has the burden of establishing that the claim brought by plaintiff in state court is within the federal court's jurisdiction.

3. Louisville & Nashville R.R. v. Mottley, 211 U.S. 149, 29 S.Ct. 42, 53 L.Ed. 126 (1908); Rivet v. Regions Bank, 522 U.S. 470, 118 S.Ct. 921, 139 L.Ed.2d 912 (1998); *cf.* Wisconsin Dept. of Corrections v. Schacht, 524 U.S. 381, 118 S.Ct. 2047, 141 L.Ed.2d 364 (1998)(suit against state may be removed despite sovereign immunity defense).

4. *See* 28 U.S.C. § 1446(a, b); Murphy Bros. v. Michetti Pipe Stringing, 526 U.S. 344, 119 S.Ct. 1322, 143 L.Ed.2d 448 (1999).

5. 28 U.S.C. § 1441(b). *See also* ITT Indus. Credit Co. v. Durango Crushers, Inc., 832 F.2d 307 (4th Cir.1987); Leonard v. Kern, 651 F.Supp. 263 (S.D.Fla.1986).

6. 28 U.S.C. § 1441(c); Cohen, Problems in the Removal of a "Separate and Independent Claim or Cause of Action," 46 Minn. L. Rev. 1 (1961). On citizenship problems in removal cases, *see* Steinman, Postremoval Changes in the Party Structure of Diversity Cases, 38 U. Kan. L. Rev. 863 (1991).

simply because its calendar is overburdened with other cases.[8] It is uncertain how far a plaintiff can go to reshape the case after removal so as to invite remand to state court. In a leading case the plaintiff, following removal, had reduced the amount of the claim to bring it below the amount in controversy required for federal jurisdiction. It was held that, the case being within federal court's jurisdiction when defendant removed, plaintiff's subsequent reduction of the amount claimed could not "oust" the court of jurisdiction.[9] In *Caterpillar Inc. v. Lewis*,[10] however, the Court held that, even though a case had been improperly removed because complete diversity was lacking, and even though the defendant's timely motion to remand had wrongly been denied, the federal court nevertheless had jurisdiction to decide the case after the nondiverse party had been dismissed from the case. The court thus acquired jurisdiction that had been lacking at the time of removal, and it was not necessary to remand the case and force the plaintiff to start all over again. Perhaps *Caterpillar* marks a first step towards a less rigid and more practical treatment of subject matter jurisdiction issues.

Appellate review of remand

The remand statute, 28 U.S.C. § 1447(c), provides that a case "removed improvidently and without jurisdiction" should be remanded. A district court's remand order ordinarily is not reviewable on appeal,[11] although an exception is made for civil rights cases removed under § 1443. Mandamus likewise is generally unavailable to review remand decisions. Appellate review by mandamus has been afforded, however, when a properly removed case is remanded for reasons not authorized by statute.[12] These rules do not cover a refusal to remand.[13] Since an order denying the motion to remand will be interlocutory, appellate review must usually await the conclusion of the action unless it is allowed by a permissive appeal under the Interlocutory Appeals Act of 1958.[14]

7. 28 U.S.C. § 1447(c).

8. *See* Thermtron Prods. v. Hermansdorfer, 423 U.S. 336, 96 S.Ct. 584, 46 L.Ed.2d 542 (1976).

9. St. Paul Mercury Indem. Co. v. Red Cab Co., 303 U.S. 283, 58 S.Ct. 586, 82 L.Ed. 845 (1938).

10. 519 U.S. 61, 117 S.Ct. 467, 136 L.Ed.2d 437 (1996).

11. 28 U.S.C. § 1447(d).

12. Thermtron Prods. v. Hermansdorfer, 423 U.S. 336, 96 S.Ct. 584, 46 L.Ed.2d 542 (1976); *see* Quackenbush v. Allstate Ins. Co., 517 U.S. 706, 116 S.Ct. 1712, 135 L.Ed.2d 1 (1996)(allowing appeal under collateral order doctrine).

13. *See also* Hansen v. Blue Cross of Cal., 891 F.2d 1384 (9th Cir.1989); Whitman v. Raley's Inc., 886 F.2d 1177 (9th Cir.1989); Air–Shields, Inc. v. Fullam, 891 F.2d 63 (3d Cir.1989);Kolibash v. Committee on Legal Ethics, 872 F.2d 571 (4th Cir.1989); Beard v. Carrollton R.R., 893 F.2d 117 (6th Cir.1989); Rothner v. City of Chicago, 879 F.2d 1402 (7th Cir.1989).

14. Chicago, R.I. & Pac. R.R. v. Stude, 346 U.S. 574, 74 S.Ct. 290, 98 L.Ed. 317 (1954); James v. Bellotti, 733 F.2d 989 (1st Cir.1984).

Mixed cases

Sometimes, a state court action would not be removable as a whole under the main removal statute but contains independent federal claims that would be removable had they been asserted by themselves. For example, suppose both plaintiff and defendant are citizens of the same state, and the plaintiff sues the defendant in state court for breach of the federal trademark legislation and also for breach of an unrelated contract. This case could not be removed under the main removal statute because it could not originally have been brought in federal court. But a special statute allows the defendant to remove not only the federal claim but the whole claim, subject to the federal court's discretion to dismiss or remand the nonfederal claims when appropriate.[15] The court likewise has discretion under the supplemental jurisdiction statute to allow a party to assert new claims falling within the same case or controversy as the removed action.[16]

§ 2.32 Federal Venue Provisions

Party residence

In addition to complying with the requirements of subject matter jurisdiction in federal court, a plaintiff must comply with the rules of federal venue.[1] The federal venue provisions are cast in terms of the federal districts: An action must be brought in the proper district within a state having more than one federal district court.[2] Furthermore, they are cast in terms of the *residence* of the parties rather than, as in diversity jurisdiction, the citizenship of the parties. In the case of individuals, residence and citizenship are ordinarily the same and correspond to the related concept of domicile that is used in the law of conflict of laws.[3] In the case of organizations, however, residence and citizenship are not necessarily the same. A corporation is treated, for diversity purposes, as a citizen of its state of incorporation and of the state wherein it has its principal place of business.[4] For federal venue purposes, however, a corporation is treated as follows: when a plaintiff, it is

15. 28 U.S.C. § 1441(c); City of Chicago v. International College of Surgeons, 522 U.S. 156, 118 S.Ct. 523, 139 L.Ed.2d 525 (1997).

16. 28 U.S.C. § 1367; *see* Carnegie–Mellon University v. Cohill, 484 U.S. 343, 108 S.Ct. 614, 98 L.Ed.2d 720 (1988); Steinman, Supplemental Jurisdiction in § 1441 Removed Cases: An Unsurveyed Frontier of Congress' Handiwork, 35 Ariz. L. Rev. 305 (1993); § 2.28 *supra.*

§ 2.32

1. 28 U.S.C. §§ 1391–1403. *See generally* American Law Inst., Study of the Division of Jurisdiction Between State and Federal Courts 1303, 1314 (1969); Wright, Federal Courts ch. 7 (4th ed. 1983); American Law Inst., Federal Judicial Code Revision Project (Prelim. Draft No. 4 2000).

2. *See* 28 U.S.C. §§ 1392, 1393.

3. *But see* Arley v. United Pac. Ins. Co., 379 F.2d 183 (9th Cir.1967).

4. 28 U.S.C. § 1332(c); Moore and Weckstein, Corporations and Diversity of Citizenship: A Supreme Court Fiction Revisited, 77 Harv. L. Rev. 1426 (1964); Comment, A Corporation's Principal Place of Business for Federal Diversity Jurisdiction, 38 N.Y.U. L. Rev. 148 (1963); Note, Citizenship of a Multi-state Corporation for Diversity Jurisdiction Purposes, 48 Iowa L. Rev. 410 (1963).

deemed a resident of all the districts in the state of its incorporation;[5] when a defendant, it is deemed to reside in any judicial district in which it is subject to personal jurisdiction. In states having more than one judicial district, each district is considered in effect to be a separate state for this purpose.[6] An unincorporated association, whether plaintiff or defendant, is treated as a resident of the districts wherein it is "doing business."[7]

General venue provisions

The federal venue provisions are contained in a general venue statute, 28 U.S.C. § 1391, which applies unless a special venue statute controls, that is, a venue provision governing specified types of actions. The venue rules for actions based only on diversity and for other civil actions are now virtually identical, although they are still stated separately. Either kind of action may be brought in a judicial district where any defendant resides, if all defendants reside in the same state. Alternatively, the plaintiff may choose to bring it in a judicial district in which a substantial part of the events or omissions giving rise to the claim occurred, or a substantial part of property that is the subject of the action is situated.[8]

If and only if neither of these two options is available, there will also be venue in a judicial district in which any defendant is "subject to personal jurisdiction" in an action based solely on diversity jurisdiction, or in which any defendant "may be found" in another action.[9] The difference between the two quoted phrases apparently results from accidents of drafting, but it is possible that "may be found" will be construed to refer to some sort of physical presence in the district, in which case this provision will be narrower than its companion.

Special venue provisions

Many special venue provisions govern certain types of actions, including those against federal officials, against the United States (in suits that have been consented to), interpleader proceedings under the Interpleader Act, those based on copyright or patent infringement, and stockholder's derivative suits.[10] The special venue provisions necessarily

5. American Cyanamid Co. v. Hammond Lead Prod., 495 F.2d 1183 (3d Cir.1974); Manchester Modes, Inc. v. Schuman, 426 F.2d 629 (2d Cir.1970).

6. 28 U.S.C. § 1391(c). *See* 15 Wright and Miller, Federal Practice and Procedure § 3811.

7. Denver & R.G.W.R.R. v. Brotherhood of Railroad Trainmen, 387 U.S. 556, 87 S.Ct. 1746, 18 L.Ed.2d 954 (1967); 15 Wright and Miller, Federal Practice and Procedure § 3812.

8. 28 U.S.C. § 1391(a, b). *See* Bates v. C & S Adjusters, Inc., 980 F.2d 865 (2d Cir. 1992).

9. 28 U.S.C. § 1391(a)(3), (b)(3).

10. 28 U.S.C. §§ 1394–1403. *See* American Law Inst., Study of the Division of Jurisdiction Between State and Federal Courts 498–501 (1969). For a resolution of conflicting provisions of two "special" venue provisions, *see* Radzanower v. Touche Ross & Co., 426 U.S. 148, 96 S.Ct. 1989, 48 L.Ed.2d 540 (1976).

reflect crude approximations of relative convenience as between various classes of litigants.[11] The alternatives, however, are to rely on the relatively indiscriminate rules in the general venue provisions or to confer still broader authority on the trial judges to change venue on the basis of "fairness" or "convenience."

Even when venue exists in a district, personal jurisdiction over each defendant must also be established. Thus, recognizing venue because, for example, one defendant is "subject to personal jurisdiction" does not ensure that the action will be able to proceed against other defendants. Likewise, even if both venue and personal jurisdiction exist, an action may be subject to transfer or to *forum non conveniens* dismissal.[12]

§ 2.33 Change of Venue

If venue in one federal district court is improper but venue in another district is proper, the court may transfer the action to the proper district rather than dismissing it.[1] But the transfer can be made only if the transferee district is one in which the defendants would have been subject to venue and service of process as well as being one specified by the federal venue statutes.[2] As we shall see,[3] the limitations on service of process issuing from the federal courts are of considerable significance, with the result that the potential for curing improper venue is correspondingly limited.

Transfer to more convenient forum

Even if venue is proper, under 28 U.S.C. § 1404(a) the court may transfer the action to some other district if doing so would advance convenient administration of justice and if the transferee district is one in which the action might have been brought initially.[4] Again the defendants must have been subject to service of process and to proper venue in the transferee district, for otherwise it is not a district where the action might have been brought. The provisions of § 1404(a) are a statutory counterpart, in the federal court system, of the principle of forum non conveniens that state courts apply to actions that should have

11. *Compare* Sunstein, Participation, Public Law, and Venue Reform, 49 U. Chi. L. Rev. 976 (1982).

12. *See* §§ 2.20 *supra*, 2.33 *infra*.

§ 2.33

1. 28 U.S.C. § 1406(a). *See* Uniform Transfer of Litigation Act, 14 U.L.A. 201 (Supp. 2000) (proposal for transfer between state courts).

2. Hoffman v. Blaski, 363 U.S. 335, 80 S.Ct. 1084, 4 L.Ed.2d 1254 (1960); Ellis v. Great Southwestern Corp., 646 F.2d 1099 (5th Cir.1981).

3. *See* § 2.34 *infra*.

4. *See* Ferens v. John Deere Co., 494 U.S. 516, 110 S.Ct. 1274, 108 L.Ed.2d 443 (1990); Stewart Organization, Inc. v. Ricoh Corp., 487 U.S. 22, 108 S.Ct. 2239, 101 L.Ed.2d 22 (1988); Van Dusen v. Barrack, 376 U.S. 612, 84 S.Ct. 805, 11 L.Ed.2d 945 (1964); Kitch, Section 1404(a) of the Judicial Code: In the Interest of Justice or Injustice?, 40 Ind. L.J. 99 (1965); Annot., 1 A.L.R. Fed. 15; *see also* Note, Transfer of Quasi in Rem Actions Under 28 U.S.C. § 1404(a), 31 U. Chi. L. Rev. 373 (1964); Note, Transfers of Civil Actions to Districts Where They "Might Have Been Brought" as Permissive Counterclaims, 55 B.U.L. Rev. 465 (1975).

been brought in some other state and that federal courts apply to actions that should have been brought in another nation.[5] As construed, § 1404(a) requires that considerable weight be given to plaintiff's choice of venue and, therefore, that transfer is proper only if other factors of convenience weigh distinctly in its favor.[6]

The statute was intended as a "federal housekeeping measure"[7] to facilitate venue changes within the federal system. Although it was drafted with the principle of forum non conveniens in mind, "the statute was intended to revise rather than merely codify the common law. Courts therefore enjoy a greater discretion to transfer a cause pursuant to § 1404(2) than dismiss the action based on *forum non conveniens.*"[8]

Transfer of related cases

Section 1407 of the Judicial Code authorizes transfer for pretrial proceedings, particularly discovery, for civil actions having related issues of fact. This provision does not authorize *trial* of the transferred cases in the transferee district unless the parties stipulate to that effect, as they often do.[9] Whether to transfer under § 1407 is determined by a special judicial panel on multidistrict litigation.[10] The American Law Institute has endorsed a proposal based on § 1407 that would permit "mass tort" cases, such as those involving airplane crashes and hotel fires, to be consolidated for both pretrial and trial; under the proposal, related cases would be removed from state court into federal court to facilitate such a consolidation.[11]

§ 2.34 Service of Process Limitations

State law limitations

Except where federal law otherwise provides, federal district courts are subject to the limitations on service of process that apply to state courts.[1] Those limitations are explored in previous sections dealing with the constitutional limitations on the personal jurisdiction of state courts.[2] In general, a state court may summon a person before it only if the person is within the state's territorial limits, or has purposely engaged in a transaction in the state, or has some kind of claim or interest in property located within the state. The theory underlying

5. *See* § 2.20 *supra.*

6. *See* authorities cited in note 4 *supra.*

7. Piper Aircraft Co. v. Reyno, 454 U.S. 235, 254, 102 S.Ct. 252, 265, 70 L.Ed.2d 419, 434 (1981).

8. Chrysler Credit Corp. v. Country Chrysler, Inc., 928 F.2d 1509 (10th Cir. 1991).

9. Lexecon v. Milberg Weiss Bershad Hynes & Lerach, 523 U.S. 26, 118 S.Ct. 956, 140 L.Ed.2d 62 (1998). Legislation to reverse this decision is pending.

10. *See generally* Manual for Complex Litigation (3d ed. 1995).

11. *See* American Law Inst., Complex Litigation: Statutory Recommendations and Analysis (1994).

§ 2.34

1. Fed. R. Civ. P. 4(k).

2. *See* §§ 2.3–2.9 *supra.*

these limitations is that each state has legal authority only over matters having some direct relation to it.

State long-arm statutes

No such constitutional limitations confine the federal judicial system, which has legal authority throughout the nation. With the creation of the federal court system, however, statutes and judicial decisions adopted the policy of treating the federal courts like state courts so far as service of process is concerned.[3] Hence, with certain exceptions discussed below, a federal court's process can effectively extend only to persons outside the state whom the state courts could bring before them. This self-imposed limitation considerably restricts the federal courts' authority in cases over which they have subject matter jurisdiction (that is, cases arising under federal law or where there is complete diversity between the parties). The severity of these restrictions has lessened as the scope of state court service of process has widened through relaxation of the constitutional limitations on the states and their passage of long arm statutes.[4] The restrictions can, however, be significant in some situations. Moreover, the limitations on federal court service of process operate cumulatively with the requirements of federal venue: both venue and valid service of process are required to commence a federal court action.

Federal exceptions

Three important exceptions allow a federal court to serve process even when a state court in the same state could not. First, a number of federal statutes such as the securities laws provide for nationwide or even extraterritorial service of process.[5] One of these, the Federal Interpleader Act, is discussed later in this book.[6] Second, a defendant in federal court may, under federal joinder rules, assert a counterclaim or impleader claim that involves a new party and serve that new party within one hundred miles of the courthouse, even though state law would not reach that far. This "bulge service," for example, permits a defendant in the Southern District of New York to bring in a new party through service in Connecticut within one hundred miles of Foley Square in New York City in a case in which New York state courts would not be allow long arm service.[7]

3. Omni Capital Intl. v. Rudolf Wolff & Co., 484 U.S. 97, 108 S.Ct. 404, 98 L.Ed.2d 415; (1987) Barrett, Venue and Service of Process in the Federal Courts: Suggestions for Reform, 7 Vand. L. Rev. 608 (1954).

4. *See* Foster, Long–Arm Jurisdiction in Federal Courts, 1969 Wis. L. Rev. 9.

5. *E.g.,* Board of Trustees, Sheet Metal Workers v. Elite, 212 F.3d 1031 (7th Cir. 2000)(ERISA); Mills, Pendent Jurisdiction and Extraterritorial Service Under the Federal Securities Laws, 70 Colum. L. Rev. 423 (1970);4 Wright and Miller, Federal Practice and Procedure §§ 1118, 1125.

6. 28 U.S.C. §§ 1335, 2361; § 10.19 *infra.*

7. Fed. R. Civ. P. 4(k)(1)(B); Note, Bulge Service Amenability: A Federal Standard, 41 U. Pitt. L. Rev. 801 (1980).

Third, since 1993 a federal court hearing a federal question claim against a defendant who is not subject to the personal jurisdiction of any state court may serve that defendant anywhere in the world if "the exercise of jurisdiction is consistent with the Constitution and laws of the United States."[8] This provision ensures that the limitations of state court personal jurisdiction will not inhibit federal court enforcement of federal law. The plaintiff must still satisfy Constitutional standards, but those are broader than those applicable in state courts. It suffices that the defendant's contacts with the United States as a whole meet due process standards of fair play and substantial justice, even if the defendant lacks adequate contacts with any single state.[9] Presumably, if a plaintiff uses this provision to sue a foreign defendant in a district both inconvenient and unrelated to the claim, the courts will protect the defendant by transferring the case to another district or dismissing it under the *forum non conveniens* doctrine.[10]

F. THE LAW APPLIED BY A COURT

§ 2.35 Introduction

Substance and procedure

In the preceding analysis, we saw that state courts could hear cases involving rights created by federal law[1] and that federal courts could hear cases involving rights created by state law, particularly in diversity cases.[2] This illustrates the general point that a court having jurisdiction of a case may be required to decide the case, or certain issues in it, according to law emanating from some sovereign other than the one that constituted the court itself. Broadly speaking, the requirement is that the court apply the "substantive" law of the sovereign that had legislative authority over the transaction that is the subject of the suit. At the same time, and again speaking in general terms, the court is authorized to adjudicate the controversy according to its own rules of procedure. But "substantive" and "procedural" law interact with each other. Very often, substantive legal provisions are formulated with an eye to procedural aspects of their enforcement—for example, a rule of strict liability may be adopted to avoid the complexities of proving fault.[3] Similarly, rules of procedure, such as those dealing with burden of proof, often are

8. Fed. R. Civ. P. 4(k)(2). On serving process abroad, *see* § 2.11 *supra*.

9. United States v. Swiss American Bank, Ltd., 191 F.3d 30 (1st Cir.1999); *see* Federal Fountain, Inc. v. KR Entertainment, Inc., 165 F.3d 600 (8th Cir.1999)(rejecting more limited jurisdictional views); Casad, Personal Jurisdiction in Federal Question Cases, 70 Tex. L. Rev. 1589 (1992).

10. *See* §§ 2.20, 2.33 *supra*.

§ 2.35

1. *See* § 2.2 *supra*.

2. *Id.*

3. *See* 2 Harper, James, and Gray, Law of Torts §§ 28.12–28.14 (2d ed. 1986). *Compare* Weinberger v. Salfi, 422 U.S. 749, 95 S.Ct. 2457, 45 L.Ed.2d 522 (1975) (definition of marriage for purposes of Social Security benefits).

ultimately related to substantive policies of the enforceability of obligations created by law.[4] Many rules therefore cannot be easily classified within one of these two categories. But some sort of classification has to be made. It would be inappropriate for a court to apply "its own" substantive law simply because the case found its way to that court; further, it would be inconvenient for one court to try to administer several procedural systems in order to accommodate the differing substantive issues presented in different cases.

The problem of distinguishing substantive and procedural rules can be called "vertical," that is, between federal and state law, or "horizontal," between one state and another or between this country and a foreign country.

§ 2.36 Federal and State Law

State court applying federal law

In the "vertical" choice of law in our federal system, part of the problem has long been fairly straightforward. When a state court has before it a controversy governed by federal substantive law, the court is required to apply the federal law under compulsion of the Supremacy Clause in Article VI of the Constitution: "This Constitution, and the laws of the United States which shall be made in pursuance thereof . . . shall be the supreme law of the land." The state's disapproval of the federal policy is not a basis for the state to refuse to enforce the federal law.[1] The state generally may employ its own procedural system in administering the federal law.[2] If, however, a state procedure unduly restricts a litigant's opportunity to assert a federal claim, the state may be obliged to use federal procedure in determining the issue.[3]

The more complicated problems involve two questions: What law does a federal court apply when it decides a controversy not governed by federal law, particularly in cases coming within its diversity jurisdiction? And where should the line(s) be drawn between "substance" and "procedure" when a state court is administering federal law or a federal court is administering state law?

4. *See, e.g.*, Texas Dept. of Community Affairs v. Burdine, 450 U.S. 248, 101 S.Ct. 1089, 67 L.Ed.2d 207 (1981); Cities Serv. Oil Co. v. Dunlap, 308 U.S. 208, 60 S.Ct. 201, 84 L.Ed. 196 (1939).

§ 2.36

1. *See, e.g.*, Hathorn v. Lovorn, 457 U.S. 255, 102 S.Ct. 2421, 72 L.Ed.2d 824 (1982); Testa v. Katt, 330 U.S. 386, 67 S.Ct. 810, 91 L.Ed. 967 (1947); *see also* Redish and Muench, Adjudication of Federal Causes of Action in State Court, 75 Mich. L. Rev. 311, 340–359 (1976).

2. *See* Minneapolis & St. L. R.R. v. Bombolis, 241 U.S. 211, 36 S.Ct. 595, 60 L.Ed. 961 (1916).

3. *See* Dice v. Akron, C. & Y. R.R., 342 U.S. 359, 72 S.Ct. 312, 96 L.Ed. 398 (1952) (jury trial); Brown v. Western Ry., 338 U.S. 294, 70 S.Ct. 105, 94 L.Ed. 100 (1949) (pleading rule). *Compare* Henry v. Mississippi, 379 U.S. 443, 85 S.Ct. 564, 13 L.Ed.2d 408 (1965); Sandalow, Henry v. Mississippi and the Adequate State Ground, 1965 Sup. Ct. Rev. 187.

Federal court applying state law

The first problem—the law to be applied by a federal court when the case is not governed by the Constitution or a federal statute—is generally known as the *Erie* problem, after the leading case of *Erie Railroad v. Tompkins,*[4] decided in 1938; it is associated with diversity cases in federal court but can arise in other cases in federal court.[5]

The legal setting for the *Erie* problem requires reference to the formation of the federal union in 1787.[6] The law governing people's affairs at that time was the law of the several states, for there was no common government (except the Confederation, whose powers were very limited). The Constitution gave the federal government authority to regulate some of these affairs—for example, interstate commerce and foreign relations—but otherwise left their governance with the states in matters such as property ownership, contracts, torts, and family law. State law was, and despite the enormous expansion of federal government regulation still is, the "base line" law in the federal system.

Rules of Decision Act

The first Congress, in the Judiciary Act of 1789, recognized this status of state law by providing, in Section 34 of the Act, that in cases heard in the federal courts "the laws of the several states, except where the Constitution, treaties, or statutes of the United States shall otherwise require or provide, shall be regarded as the rules of decision."[7] This provision came to be known as the Rules of Decision Act.

Swift v. Tyson

The Supreme Court, however, decided in 1842 that the phrase "laws of the several states" had a special meaning. "Laws" meant only statutes and "purely local" subjects of decisional law; the decisional law of a state on other subjects such as commercial law was merely "evidence" of what the proper rule might be; therefore, the federal courts were free to apply their own conception of the law. This interpretation of the Rules of Decision Act, embraced in the case of *Swift v. Tyson,*[8] meant that a case could be decided in one way if in federal court and in another

4. 304 U.S. 64, 58 S.Ct. 817, 82 L.Ed. 1188 (1938).

5. *See* Commissioner v. Estate of Bosch, 387 U.S. 456, 87 S.Ct. 1776, 18 L.Ed.2d 886 (1967); Note, Rules of Decision in Nondiversity Cases, 69 Yale L.J. 1428 (1960).

6. *See generally* Hart, The Relations Between State and Federal Law, 54 Colum. L. Rev. 489 (1954); Hill, The Law-Making Power of the Federal Courts: Constitutional Preemption, 67 Colum. L. Rev. 1024 (1967).

7. *See* 28 U.S.C. § 1652. Along with the Rules of Decision Act, the same Congress adopted the Conformity Act, providing that the procedure in common law actions in federal court should be that used in the state courts where they sat. *See* § 1.8 *supra.* Thus, congressional design provided that the federal courts apply both the substantive law and, except for equity proceedings, the procedural law of the states. *But see* Ritz, Rewriting the History of the Judiciary Act of 1789 (1990), arguing that the Rules of Decision Act was simply not addressed to the problem of choosing between state and federal law.

8. 41 U.S. (16 Pet.) 1, 10 L.Ed. 865 (1842).

if in state court. Only certain parties could get the benefit of the federal court rule: those whose citizenship enabled them to bring the suit in federal court (or, if defendants, to remove the suit there) because of diversity of citizenship.

Swift rested in part on the jurisprudential notion that the common law derived from custom, of which any one precedent was merely evidence. It could also be grounded on the role of the diversity jurisdiction to protect against local prejudice, which could at least occasionally manifest itself in rules of law, such as law unfairly protecting debtors against creditors from commercial states. And of course the *Swift* doctrine also enabled federal judges to implement their own views of what justice demanded.[9]

The rule in *Swift v. Tyson* might have formed the basis for pervasive expansion of federally formulated decisional law. If the state courts had deferred to federal court decisional law, a nationally uniform common law might have developed as it did in Canada. Alternatively, if the "general law" pronounced by the federal courts had been confined to commercial transactions, it might have been sustained by the Constitution's grant of power over commerce to the federal government and become the rule of decision in such commercial cases in state courts as well. As it happened, the doctrine in *Swift v. Tyson* was extended to many matters that seemed "purely local," but the rules involved were applied only in federal court.[10] Such was the situation until 1938 and *Erie Railroad v. Tompkins.*[11]

§ 2.37 *Erie Railroad v. Tompkins*

The facts in *Erie* were simple. While Tompkins was walking along the railroad's right of way, he was struck by something that "looked like a door projecting from one of the moving cars" of a passing train. The accident happened in Pennsylvania. Plaintiff, a Pennsylvanian, sued Erie, a New York corporation, in federal court in New York. Erie insisted that under Pennsylvania law persons who use longitudinal pathways (as distinguished from crossings) were trespassers to whom no duty of care was owed under the circumstances. Tompkins contended that the railroad's duty and liability were to be determined in federal courts as a matter of general law, which imposed a duty of care toward a pedestrian where his presence was foreseeable; the lower courts so ruled, upholding plaintiff's verdict for $30,000. The Supreme Court reversed.

9. *See* Burgess v. Seligman, 107 U.S. 20, 2 S.Ct. 10, 27 L.Ed. 359 (1883); Gelpcke v. Dubuque, 68 U.S. (1 Wall.) 175, 17 L.Ed. 520 (1863); Bridwell & Whitten, The Constitution and the Common Law: The Decline of the Doctrines of Separation and Federalism (1977); Fletcher, The General Common Law and Section 34 of the Judiciary Act of 1789: The Example of Marine Insurance, 97 Harv. L. Rev. 1513 (1984).

10. *See* Bator, Mishkin, Shapiro, and Wechsler, The Federal Courts and the Federal System 694–702 (2d ed. 1973).

11. 304 U.S. 64, 58 S.Ct. 817, 82 L.Ed. 1188 (1938).

The majority opinion, written by Justice Brandeis, overruled *Swift v. Tyson* and reinterpreted the Rules of Decision Act to include the state's common law as well as its statutes and local customs. It recited the former rule's history and pointed out "the mischievous results of the doctrine," particularly the "grave discrimination by non-citizens against citizens" introduced by the former rule, since different substantive rules were often applied by state and federal courts and the noncitizen had the choice of forum.[1] The Court found that the rule of *Swift v. Tyson* was unconstitutional since neither Congress nor the federal courts had the power to "declare substantive rules of common law applicable in a state whether they be local in their nature or 'general,' be they commercial law or a part of the law of torts."[2] Only five of the justices concurred in this opinion. Two dissented; Justice Cardozo took no part; Justice Reed concurred in the conclusion but only on the ground of statutory construction: "If the opinion commits this Court to the position that the Congress is without power to declare what rules of substantive law shall govern the federal courts, that conclusion seems questionable."[3] He suggested the Judiciary Article and the "necessary and proper" clause of Article I as possible sources of such power.

Historically, one can view *Erie* as a Progressive and New Deal move against lawmaking by what had been a conservative federal judiciary, and against the corporations that had gained the benefit of that lawmaking through their access to diversity jurisdiction. Alternatively, one can see the decision as grounded in federalism and protecting the right of states to shape their own law in their own courts, with federal law stepping in only when Congress so decides. Finally, one can read *Erie* as a pragmatic recognition that any hope for using *Swift* to create a national common law had been frustrated by the accumulation of diverging state court precedent, and by the Supreme Court's inability to decide more than a handful of diversity cases, increasingly burdened as it was by the federal statutory and Constitutional issues brought before it. Whatever its original grounds, the decision has become a pillar of contemporary federalism, picking up new meanings in the process.[4]

Erie and the Federal Rules

Erie, as Justice Frankfurter subsequently observed,[5] required a wholly different way of viewing the relations between state and federal

§ 2.37

1. Erie R.R. v. Tompkins, 304 U.S. 64, 75–76, 78, 58 S.Ct. 817, 820, 822, 82 L.Ed. 1188, 1192, 1194 (1938). For colorful details of the litigation giving rise to the decision, *see* Younger, What Happened in *Erie*, 56 Tex. L. Rev. 1011 (1978).

2. *Id.,* 304 U.S. at 78, 58 S.Ct. at 822, 82 L.Ed. at 1194.

3. *Id.,* 304 U.S. at 91–92, 58 S.Ct. at 828, 82 L.Ed. at 1201.

4. *See generally* Purcell, Brandeis and the Progressive Constitution: *Erie*, the Judicial Power, and the Politics of the Federal Courts in Twentieth–Century America (2000).

5. Guaranty Trust Co. v. York, 326 U.S. 99, 101–102, 65 S.Ct. 1464, 1466, 89 L.Ed. 2079, 2082 (1945).

law. The required change in perspective was even greater, because in 1938, the year *Erie* was decided, the Federal Rules of Civil Procedure also went into effect. In simple terms, before 1938 the federal courts in diversity cases applied federal substantive law through state procedure (except in equity cases); after 1938 they applied state substantive law through federal procedure. This basic legal principle remains firmly established.

Given *Erie* and the Federal Rules, however, many subordinate problems have persisted.[6]

Constitutional and statutory grounds of *Erie*

First, is *Erie* a matter of interpreting the Rules of Decision Act, as Justice Reed suggested, or is it a constitutional limitation? Put differently, if Congress prescribed that the federal courts should apply federal decisional law in diversity cases, would such a statute be invalid in some or all of its applications? The answer to this question would be complicated indeed. It would seem valid for federal decisional law to govern transactions that Congress could regulate directly, for example, under the Commerce Clause or the Equal Protection Clause; that covers a lot of ground.[7] Congressional provision for federal law would also seem valid as applied to transactions involving multistate aspects, where the authority of any single state to apply its law could be subject to federal control.[8] Such congressional provisions would seem valid as to *any* aspect of litigation that could be called "procedural" in an even broader sense than suggested by the Federal Rules. Since Congress has not undertaken to enact any such measures but has spoken through the Rules of Decision Act, the *Erie* problem apparently is a matter of interpreting that statute rather than one of constitutional law.[9]

The "outcome" test

Second, does *Erie* require application of state law in matters conventionally categorized as "procedure" and thus question the validity of the Federal Rules of Civil Procedure? For a while after *Erie*, the Supreme Court's decisions suggested that possibility. In *Guaranty Trust Co. v.*

6. The literature is voluminous. *See, e.g.*, Burbank, The Rules Enabling Act of 1934, 130 U. Pa. L. Rev. 1015 (1982); Ely, The Irrepressible Myth of *Erie*, 87 Harv. L. Rev. 693 (1974); Freer, *Erie*'s Mid-Life Crisis, 63 Tul. L. Rev. 1087 (1989); Friendly, In Praise of *Erie*—And the New Federal Common Law, 39 N.Y.U. L. Rev. 383 (1964); Mishkin, The Variousness of "Federal Law," 105 U. Pa. L. Rev. 797 (1957).

7. *See* Textile Workers Union v. Lincoln Mills, 353 U.S. 448, 77 S.Ct. 912, 1 L.Ed.2d 972 (1957) (labor relations); *cf.* Jones v. Alfred H. Mayer Co., 392 U.S. 409, 88 S.Ct. 2186, 20 L.Ed.2d 1189 (1968) (federal statute, 42 U.S.C. § 1982, conferring equal rights to deal with real and personal property).

8. *See* Order of United Commercial Travelers v. Wolfe, 331 U.S. 586, 67 S.Ct. 1355, 91 L.Ed. 1687 (1947); Home Ins. Co. v. Dick, 281 U.S. 397, 50 S.Ct. 338, 74 L.Ed. 926 (1930).

9. Note, The Law Applied in Diversity Cases: The Rules of Decision Act and the *Erie* Doctrine, 85 Yale L.J. 678 (1976).

York[10] the Court held that a state statute of limitations was to be applied by a federal court to limit equitable rights, the decision containing broad language that the state rule must be applied wherever it affected the "outcome of litigation."[11] Since *all* procedural rules can affect outcome, this rationale would leave little room for the Federal Rules where state law was inconsistent with them. The Court confronted this issue in *Byrd v. Blue Ridge Rural Electric Cooperative*,[12] decided in 1958. In that case, a worker sued a company on whose premises he was injured; the defendant company contended that his work was such that he was an "employee" and was therefore limited to a workers' compensation remedy. Defendant further contended that the issue whether Byrd was an "employee" should be decided by the judge rather than the jury because that was the procedure in the state court. Byrd contended that the issue was one of fact and as such was triable by jury under case law that was required, or at least inspired, by the Seventh Amendment's guarantee of jury trial in civil actions.

Federal jury trial procedure

If any rule is determinative of "outcome" in a personal injury action, surely the rule governing jury versus judge trial falls in that category; if any rule is "procedural," surely the rule specifying who decides the facts is included. In *Byrd* the Court held that jury trial applied even if it made an "outcome" difference. This decision in turn led to more general recognition that matters of procedure in federal court can be governed by federal law—statutory and court-made rules, as well as constitutional procedure—even when this practice results in different dispositions between federal and state courts and even if it induces "forum shopping."

Applicability of Federal Rules

This view was expressed in *Hanna v. Plumer*,[13] where the Supreme Court upheld the Federal Rules provisions on service of process in the face of a conflicting state statute. The majority opinion suggested that any court rule that is "rationally capable of classification" as procedural would be valid under the Rules Enabling Act, which empowers the Supreme Court to promulgate rules of procedure.[14] Because Congress has

10. 326 U.S. 99, 65 S.Ct. 1464, 89 L.Ed. 2079 (1945).

11. 326 U.S. at 109, 65 S.Ct. at 1470, 89 L.Ed. at 2086. Other decisions taking this approach include Ragan v. Merchants Transfer & Warehouse Co., 337 U.S. 530, 69 S.Ct. 1233, 93 L.Ed. 1520 (1949) (rule as to when an action is commenced for purposes of statute of limitations); Cohen v. Beneficial Indus. Loan Corp., 337 U.S. 541, 69 S.Ct. 1221, 93 L.Ed. 1528 (1949) (requirement of a bond in prosecuting stockholders' derivative suit); and Bernhardt v. Polygraphic Co., 350 U.S. 198, 76 S.Ct. 273, 100 L.Ed. 199 (1956) (effect to be given arbitration clause).

12. 356 U.S. 525, 78 S.Ct. 893, 2 L.Ed.2d 953 (1958).

13. 380 U.S. 460, 85 S.Ct. 1136, 14 L.Ed.2d 8 (1965). *See* McCoid, Hanna v. Plumer: The *Erie* Doctrine Changes Shape, 51 Va. L. Rev. 884 (1965).

14. 380 U.S. at 472, 85 S.Ct. at 1144, 14 L.Ed.2d at 17. On the Rules Enabling Act, *see* § 1.8 *supra*. For criticism of its broad

broad power to regulate federal court procedure, a rule thus authorized by the Rules Enabling Act would under the Constitution's Supremacy Clause prevail over any conflicting state law. *Hanna v. Plumer*, therefore, suggests that the law's own conventions about what constitutes procedure are determinative.

The *Hanna* doctrine that the Federal Rules prevail over state law has been considerably broadened by two Supreme Court cases, *Burlington Northern Railroad v. Woods*[15] and *Stewart Organization, Inc. v. Ricoh.*[16] These decisions extended the reach of *Erie* to include the Federal Rules of Appellate Procedure as well as federal statutes. More important, they removed the *Hanna* requirement of a conflicting state statute (or a "direct collision," in the language of *Hanna*). As the Court in *Stewart Organization* stated: "It would make no sense for the supremacy of federal law to wane precisely because there is no state law directly on point."[17] Thus, there is a much expanded area in which the *Hanna* doctrine is operative and federal rules displace state law.

Statute of limitations

Third, granted that an applicable Federal Rule prevails over a conflicting state rule, when should the federal rule be construed not to be applicable in order to avoid the conflict? In at least one post-Hanna case, the Supreme Court upheld just such a restrained construction. In effect, the Court, as it had on previous occasions,[18] veered back toward the broad role for state law envisioned in *Guaranty Trust Co. v. York*. In *Walker v. Armco Steel Corp.*,[19] the question concerned the provision of Federal Rule 3 that an action "is commenced by filing a complaint." Plaintiff had filed his complaint in federal court within the period allowed under the applicable state statute of limitations. The state statutory provision on limitations specified, however, that "an action shall be deemed commenced [for purposes of the statute of limitations], as to each defendant, at the date of the summons which is served on him," and plaintiff had effected service of summons only after the limitations period had expired. The Supreme Court held that the action was not commenced in a timely manner, noting that "there is no

reading by the Supreme Court, *see* Burbank, The Rules Enabling Act of 1934, 130 U. Pa. L. Rev. 1015 (1982); Kelleher, Taking "Substantive Rights" (in the Rules Enabling Act) More Seriously, 74 Notre Dame L. Rev. 47 (1998).

15. 480 U.S. 1, 107 S.Ct. 967, 94 L.Ed.2d 1 (1987). *See also* Whitten, *Erie* and the Federal Rules: A Review and Reappraisal after Burlington Northern Railroad v. Woods, 21 Creighton L. Rev. 1 (1987).

16. 487 U.S. 22, 108 S.Ct. 2239, 101 L.Ed.2d 22 (1988). *See also* Freer, *Erie*'s Mid–Life Crisis, 63 Tul. L. Rev. 1087 (1989); Mullenix, Another Choice of Forum, Another Choice of Law: Consensual Adjudicatory Procedure in Federal Court, 57 Fordham L. Rev. 291 (1988); Note, Forum Selection Clauses in Light of the *Erie* Decision and Federal Common Law: Stewart Organization v. Ricoh Corporation, 72 Minn. L. Rev. 1090 (1988).

17. 487 U.S. at 26 n.4, 108 S.Ct. at 2242 n.4, 101 L.Ed.2d at 29 n.4.

18. *See* cases cited in note 10 *supra*.

19. 446 U.S. 740, 100 S.Ct. 1978, 64 L.Ed.2d 659 (1980).

indication that the Rule was intended to toll a state statute of limitations." This is a questionable interpretation of the purpose of Rule 3, but it overcomes the conflict between the Federal Rule and the state law. When the Court later held that Rule 3 *does* govern the tolling of a *federal* law cause of action, it became clear that *Walker*'s construction of the rule was intended to preserve the role of state limitations law.[20]

Conflicting lines of authority

The Court thus has continued to say both that the federal courts may apply federal rules that are "rationally capable of classification" as procedural *and* that the federal courts must try to apply at least some state law by construing the Federal Rules narrowly. In essence, the Court has maintained two conflicting interpretations of the scope of *Erie* while producing results on a case-by-case basis using whatever interpretation supports the conclusion at hand. Moreover, in *Walker v. Armco Steel Corp.* the Court indicated that federal rules such as Rule 3 might be determinative when an action was brought to enforce a *federal* claim as distinct from a state claim.[21] This says, in effect, that whether a federal rule is "procedural" or "substantive" can depend on the substantive context in which that classification is to be made.

Fourth, if no Federal Rule or statute governs a case, when should federal procedural precedents yield to state law? The Supreme Court has propounded two different approaches to answering this question. Unfortunately, it is unclear how they relate to each other. Sometimes courts avoid that problem by squeezing one or the other test so that both will produce the same result in the case at bar.

Outcome determinative test

Under the "outcome determinative test" stemming from *York* and revised in *Hanna,* the court should ask whether using different rules in state and federal court would be likely enough to influence the outcome of a case as to cause litigants contemplating suit to steer their cases to one or the other court. If so--for example, if the state rule imposes sanctions on defendants who refuse reasonable settlement offers while the Federal Rules contain no such provision--that is a reason to apply the state rule in federal court, thus preserving equality among plaintiffs and discouraging forum-shopping. If not–for example, if the federal court follows the practice of assigning each case on filing to a single judge for both pretrial proceedings and trial, while state law mandates a different

20. 446 U.S. at 751 n. 11, 100 S.Ct. at 1985 n.11, 64 L.Ed.2d at 668 n. 11; *see* West v. Conrail, 481 U.S. 35, 107 S.Ct. 1538, 95 L.Ed.2d 32 (1987). For other examples of restrained construction of Federal Rules, *see* Semtek Int'l Inc. v. Lockheed Martin Corp., ___ U.S. ___, 121 S.Ct. 1021, ___ L.Ed.2d ___ (2001); Gasperini v. Center for Humanities, Inc., 518 U.S. 415, 116 S.Ct. 2211, 135 L.Ed.2d 659 (1996)(discussed below); Palmer v. Hoffman, 318 U.S. 109, 63 S.Ct. 477, 87 L.Ed. 645 (1943)(discussed § 3.17 *infra*).

21. S.A. Healy Co. v. Milwaukee Metropolitan Sewerage Dist., 60 F.3d 305 (7th Cir.1995).

procedure–there is no occasion for the federal courts to abandon their own practice. This approach is relatively easy to apply but reduces the goals of *Erie* to the prevention of unequal treatment and forum-shopping, downgrading its ideal of federalism.

Balancing test

Under the competing "balancing test" originating in *Byrd*, the court must embark on the more difficult task of identifying the policies behind a state law rule, and determining whether they are sufficiently strong to prevail over the policies of the federal procedure in question. The Supreme Court recently used this approach in *Gasperini v. Center for Humanities, Inc.*[22] The state law in question there was a New York "tort reform" statute that called on appellate and trial courts to strike down damage awards materially deviating from what would be reasonable compensation, as shown by awards in comparable cases.

The Court believed that failing to apply this statute in diversity jurisdiction tort cases in federal courts in New York would encourage plaintiffs to seek out those courts. It also viewed the statute as a measure of substantive tort law, analogous to a provision stating a cap for damage awards, even though the statute operated through the procedural device of reviewing jury damage verdicts. On the other hand, precedent provided that federal Courts of Appeals can set aside damage awards only if the District Court abuses its discretion in failing to grant the complaining party a new trial. This limit reflects the limited scope of appeals on matters of fact in the federal court system, and hence the division of labor between trial and appellate judges.

To accommodate these conflicting concerns, the Court decided that federal courts should indeed conduct the strengthened review of tort damage awards provided by the New York statute, but that the trial court rather than the appellate court should do so. Appellate review would then be subject to the usual limitations, which the Court proceeded to uphold against arguments based on the Seventh Amendment's provision that facts tried by a jury may not be "re-examined" in any federal court except "according to the rules of the common law." The Court also declined to construe Federal Rule 59 to cover the issue and exclude state law, concluding that the rule provides a procedure for new trials but leaves it to other law to decide when they should be granted.

Gasperini indicates that, even after *Hanna*, state law with procedural aspects will sometimes prevail in federal courts. It also indicates that the balancing test is alive and well, and that it requires courts to identify and give some weight to state provisions that implement policies of

22. 518 U.S. 415, 116 S.Ct. 2211, 135 L.Ed.2d 659 (1996). *See* Rowe, Not Bad for Government Work: Does Anyone Else Think the Supreme Court is Doing a Halfway Decent Job in Its *Erie–Hanna* Jurisprudence?, 73 Notre Dame L. Rev. 963 (1998); Freer, Some Thoughts on the State of *Erie* After *Gasperini*, 76 Tex. L. Rev. 1637 (1998).

substantive law. Finally, it shows that applying *Erie* remains an exercise of judgment rather than the application of mechanical tests, calling for the comparison and in appropriate cases the accommodation of state and federal policies.

In *Gasperini*, at least three policies came into play: New York's policy of limiting tort damage awards; the federal policy, grounded in the Seventh Amendment, of limiting judicial review of jury verdicts; and the federal policy requiring that, when such review does occur, the district courts rather than the courts of appeals should be the primary reviewer. The Supreme Court succeeded in maintaining and reconciling the first and third of these policies, and did its best to construe away the second one.

Finding state law

Fifth, how is a federal court to ascertain the state law it must apply? As would a lawyer or a state trial court, the federal courts look to state statutes and appellate decisions. Although some cases soon after *Erie* bound federal courts fairly strictly by decisions of state intermediate appellate courts, federal judges are now free to predict what the Supreme Court would decide, using all relevant materials.[23] Federal appellate judges as well as trial judges must conduct this investigation; they may not defer to the trial judge's conclusions of law, even if the trial judge is more familiar with the law of the state.[24] Sometimes, in difficult cases, federal courts certify an issue of law directly to a state supreme court. Most state supreme courts now accept and answer such certifications, which provide authoritative rulings, albeit at the cost of some time and money.[25]

Yet one more issue under *Erie* concerns which state's law should be applied in federal court when two or more states are involved. This is a variation of the problem of "horizontal" choice of law and becomes clear if the main problem itself is first described. The problem is that of "choice of law" or "conflict of laws."

§ 2.38 Choice of Law in Multistate Transactions

Substance and procedure

If a New York motorist has a collision in New Jersey with a car driven by a person from Pennsylvania, an action to recover for the injuries involved could under some circumstances be brought in either

23. *Compare* Commissioner v. Estate of Bosch, 387 U.S. 456, 87 S.Ct. 1776, 18 L.Ed.2d 886 (1967) *with* King v. Order of United Commercial Travelers, 333 U.S. 153, 68 S.Ct. 488, 92 L.Ed. 608 (1948).

24. Salve Regina College v. Russell, 499 U.S. 225, 111 S.Ct. 1217, 113 L.Ed.2d 190 (1991).

25. Clark, Ascertaining the Laws of the Several States: Positivism and Judicial Federalism After Erie, 145 U. Pa. L. Rev. 1459 (1997); *see* § 2.29 *supra*.

New Jersey, New York, or Pennsylvania. Wherever it is brought, there could arise "choice of law" problems over which state's law should be applied to specific aspects of the case. If the action were in a New York or Pennsylvania court, New Jersey law on the governing speed limits, rules of rights of way, and so on would doubtless be applied, the theory being (depending on which conflict of laws theory is used) that those rules are "substantive," or govern "primary conduct," or are what the parties may have "expected."[1] At the same time, the New York or Pennsylvania court probably would apply its own rules as to burden of proof and, possibly, its own measure of damages, the theory being that these rules are "procedural."[2] If the action were in a New Jersey court, that court would probably apply New Jersey law on all these issues.

The same kinds of problems can arise in other types of cases—such as contract, property, and family relationship—and not only in multistate transactions but also in international transactions.[3]

State interest theory

Choice of law is a subject unto itself,[4] and only brief notice can be taken here. Until the 1930s the conventional concept of choice of law was based primarily on the same idea of territoriality that was employed in determining the jurisdiction of state courts.[5]

Generally speaking, a court would apply the law of the state where the transaction had occurred. This basic concept was subject to many exceptions and erratic applications because transactions often occur partly in one state and partly in another. In any event, the conventional approach was severely criticized on both theoretical and practical grounds. This criticism led to an alternate approach, signaled in the 1935 case *Alaska Packers Association v. Industrial Accident Commission.*[6] *Alaska Packers* recognized that a state having an "interest" in a transaction, such as when one of its residents was involved, could apply its law in some circumstances even when key aspects of the transaction had not occurred within the state's borders. Judicial doctrine and academic analysis since have endeavored to construct a coherent concept of the "state interest" approach to choice of law.[7] That task remains incom-

§ 2.38

1. *See* Restatement (Second) of Conflict of Laws §§ 156–166.

2. *See* Restatement (Second) of Conflict of Laws §§ 122–144. *See, e.g.,* Kilberg v. Northeast Airlines, 9 N.Y.2d 34, 172 N.E.2d 526, 211 N.Y.S.2d 133 (1961). *Compare* Allstate Ins. Co. v. Hague, 449 U.S. 302, 101 S.Ct. 633, 66 L.Ed.2d 521 (1981).

3. *See, e.g.,* Scherk v. Alberto-Culver Co., 417 U.S. 506, 94 S.Ct. 2449, 41 L.Ed.2d 270 (1974).

4. *See, e.g.,* Leflar, American Conflicts Law (3d ed. 1977); Scoles and Hay, Conflict of Laws (1982); Weintraub, Commentary on the Conflict of Laws (2d ed. 1980).

5. *See* Scoles and Hay, Conflict of Laws § 3.2 (1982); *see also* von Mehren, Recent Trends in Choice-of-Law Methodology, 60 Cornell L. Rev. 927 (1975).

6. 294 U.S. 532, 55 S.Ct. 518, 79 L.Ed. 1044 (1935).

7. *See, e.g.,* Kay, Use of Comparative Impairment to Resolve True Conflicts: An Evaluation of the California Experience, 68 Calif. L. Rev. 577 (1980); Korn, The Choice-of-Law Revolution: A Critique, 83 Colum. L. Rev. 772 (1983).

plete, and choice of law as a practical matter is often determined by where the plaintiff chooses to bring suit.[8]

Choice of law as outcome determinative

Choice of law often has critical significance for the outcome of litigation. A common instance involves a guest passenger in an automobile who sues the driver for personal injuries suffered in a car accident. Under the law of some states, a guest passenger (that is, one not paying for the ride) can recover only on proving that the driver was guilty of gross negligence, as distinct from ordinary negligence. Suppose the driver and passenger are from New York, a state requiring that only ordinary negligence be shown, but the accident occurs in another state where gross negligence is required for recovery.[9] Or suppose that parties to a contract who reside in different jurisdictions agree to arbitrate any disputes under the contract, but such arbitration agreements are unenforceable by the law of one of the two jurisdictions.[10] The outcome of the litigation in either case can depend on the choice of law.

§ 2.39 Choice of Law in Federal Court

The variation of the choice of law problem involving the *Erie* doctrine arises when an action not governed by federal law is brought in federal court and involves multistate elements requiring choice between the law of two or more states. In *Klaxon Co. v. Stentor Electric Manufacturing Co.*,[1] decided shortly after *Erie,* the Supreme Court held that the federal court must apply the conflict of law rules of the state in which it is located. Thus, in the preceding example,[2] the federal district court in New York would apply New York's choice of law rules, while the federal district court in New Jersey would apply New Jersey's choice of law rules. In *Van Dusen v. Barrack*[3] this approach was extended to a change of venue between federal district courts. That case held that the law to be applied is that of the state in which the action is commenced, not the one to which it is thereafter transferred.

8. *See, e.g.,* Allstate Ins. Co. v. Hague, 449 U.S. 302, 101 S.Ct. 633, 66 L.Ed.2d 521 (1981); *cf.* Piper Aircraft Co. v. Reyno, 454 U.S. 235, 102 S.Ct. 252, 70 L.Ed.2d 419 (1981).

9. *See* Scoles and Hay, Conflict of Laws § 17.26 *et seq.* (1982).

10. *See* Scherk v. Alberto–Culver Co., 417 U.S. 506, 94 S.Ct. 2449, 41 L.Ed.2d 270 (1974).

§ 2.39

1. 313 U.S. 487, 61 S.Ct. 1020, 85 L.Ed. 1477 (1941). On *Klaxon, see generally* Bator, Meltzer, Mishkin, and Shapiro, The Federal Court and the Federal System 794–800 (3d ed. 1988); Chemerinsky, Federal Jurisdiction § 5.4 (3d ed. 1999).

2. *See* text at § 2.38 note 1 *supra. See also* In re Air Disaster at Lockerbie, Scotland, 928 F.2d 1267 (2d Cir.1991).

3. 376 U.S. 612, 84 S.Ct. 805, 11 L.Ed.2d 945 (1964).

Effect of transfer on choice of law

The change of venue in *Van Dusen* was made under 28 U.S.C. § 1404, which authorizes such transfers "for the convenience of parties and witnesses, in the interest of justice."[4] The Court listed three reasons for its decision: (1) the statute should not deprive the parties of their advantages under state law; (2) the statute should not create opportunities for forum shopping; and (3) the decision to transfer should turn on the grounds listed in the statute, on convenience, and on the interest of justice rather than possible effects on choice of law.[5]

Van Dusen, which involved a transfer initiated by a defendant, was extended in *Ferens v. John Deere Co.*[6] to allow the transferor's court law to prevail when the plaintiff initiated the change of forum. In *Ferens* a farmer was injured on his farm in Pennsylvania while using a combine manufactured by defendant. After the state statute of limitations had run, a diversity action was filed in Mississippi, where a much longer limitations period was still open. The plaintiff then moved to transfer the action to Pennsylvania on the ground of convenience of parties and witnesses on the assumption that the longer Mississippi statute of limitations would apply.

The court weighed the advantages of having the action tried in a convenient forum against the possible forum shopping advantage available to plaintiffs. The dangers of the latter were downplayed as being inherent in diversity jurisdiction. Thus, the plaintiff, despite conduct the court termed "manipulative," was allowed to have both its choice of law and choice of forum in what might be called a "forum shoppers' paradise."

Choice of law in federal court

The extension of *Erie* into choice of law in the federal courts is perhaps the doctrine's most doubtful application on several grounds. First, it does not seem to be required by the Rules of Decision Act, so that no congressional policy would be offended if the federal courts developed their own choice of law rules. Second, choice of law rules are "procedural" in that they prescribe the way in which a court satisfies itself as to the basis of decision, in this sense being akin to rules of evidence. Third, the purposes of diversity jurisdiction (where federal court choice of law problems most frequently arise) would be served most fully if the federal courts could provide escape not only from possible forensic bias of state courts but also from their proclivity for applying local law. And, finally, choice of law among the states in a federal system is itself a legal problem of federalism and therefore could be regarded as a federal question whenever it arises.[7] But although the

4. 27 U.S.C. § 1404(a).

5. *See also* Piper Aircraft Co. v. Reyno, 454 U.S. 235, 102 S.Ct. 252, 70 L.Ed.2d 419 (1981) (court deciding to dismiss suit for forum non conveniens should ordinarily not consider impact on choice of law).

6. 494 U.S. 516, 110 S.Ct. 1274, 108 L.Ed.2d 443 (1990).

7. *Compare* the Supreme Court's attitude on choice of law in international transactions. Banco Nacional de Cuba v. Sabbatino, 376 U.S. 398, 84 S.Ct. 923, 11 L.Ed.2d

Klaxon rule has been trenchantly criticized on these and other grounds,[8] its authority has been reaffirmed by the Supreme Court[9] and will doubtless remain unimpaired for some time.

§ 2.40 Federal Court Jurisdiction in Perspective

Potential scope of jurisdiction

An enduring question of federal policy is the proper allocation of jurisdiction to the federal courts, with cases not cognizable in federal court being determined in state court. As a matter of constitutional law, it seems clear that the federal courts could be given jurisdiction of every case with diversity of citizenship among the parties,[1] of every case in which a federal issue has arisen, whether at the pleading stage or during the trial or on appeal,[2] and of at least some types of cases in which there is a "federal interest" even though the case is not governed by federal law.[3] Historically, however, the jurisdiction granted by Congress has been far more limited, as we have seen. And the question remains whether the congressional choices represent a wise use of the federal judiciary's limited resources. It might be wiser, for example, to do the following:

Policy alternatives

- provide for nationwide service of process in federal court and regulate place of trial only through the rules of venue and transfer;
- eliminate diversity jurisdiction except when (a) owing to service of process limitations on the states, it would be impossible to join all necessary parties in a single state court proceeding, or (b) the transaction sued on involved significant elements governed by the law of more than one state or of a state and a foreign country, or (c) citizens of another nation were parties;
- eliminate federal jurisdiction of "routine" cases arising under federal law but unlikely to evoke state court hostility to that law,

804 (1967); M/S Bremen v. Zapata Off-Shore Co., 407 U.S. 1, 92 S.Ct. 1907, 32 L.Ed.2d 513 (1972).

8. *See, e.g.,* Hill, The Law-Making Power of the Federal Courts, 67 Colum. L. Rev. 1024 (1967); Horowitz, Toward a Federal Common Law of Choice of Law, 14 UCLA L. Rev. 1191 (1967); Weintraub, The Erie Doctrine and State Conflict of Law Rules, 39 Ind. L.J. 228 (1964); Borchers, The Origins of Diversity Jurisdiction, The Rise of Legal Positivism, and a Brave New World for *Erie* and *Klaxon*, 72 Tex. L. Rev. 79 (1993).

9. Day and Zimmermann, Inc. v. Challoner, 423 U.S. 3, 96 S.Ct. 167, 46 L.Ed.2d 3 (1975).

§ 2.40

1. State Farm Fire & Casualty Co. v. Tashire, 386 U.S. 523, 87 S.Ct. 1199, 18 L.Ed.2d 270 (1967).

2. Osborn v. Bank of the United States, 22 U.S. (9 Wheat.) 738, 6 L. Ed. 204 (1824). For a case involving a federal right arising at the appellate level of state litigation, *see* Anders v. California, 386 U.S. 738, 87 S.Ct. 1396, 18 L.Ed.2d 493 (1967).

3. Textile Workers Union v. Lincoln Mills, 353 U.S. 448, 77 S.Ct. 912, 1 L.Ed.2d 972 (1957).

allowing a federal question case in appropriate categories to be maintained in federal court only when it involves an issue of federal law over which the parties appear to differ substantially;

- subject to the foregoing requirement, afford federal jurisdiction whether the federal issue relates to the plaintiff's claim or to a defense or claim of any other party;
- rather than dismiss a case, authorize a federal court to transfer a case to the state court where it belongs and allow a state court to transfer a case to a federal court.

Although these questions remain open, any change in how they are resolved will come slowly, given the caution of Congress in matters affecting the federal courts and the strong interest that various sectors of the public—and particularly the bar—have in the status quo.[4]

4. *See generally* American Law Inst., Study of the Division of Jurisdiction Between State and Federal Courts (1969); Currie, The Federal Courts and the American Law Institute, 36 U. Chi. L. Rev. 1, 268 (1968, 1969); Friendly, Federal Jurisdiction: A General View (1973); Posner, The Federal Courts: Crisis and Reform (1985).

Chapter 3

PLEADING: THE COMPLAINT

A. THE FUNCTIONS OF PLEADING

§ 3.1 Aims of Pleading

Principal aims of pleading

Before a court can properly decide a case and enter judgment, it must have obtained jurisdiction over both the parties and the controversy to be decided.[1] The adversary must be given fair notice of the case alleged to prepare a response. The controversy must be defined so that the court and the parties may properly direct their efforts and the court may rule on questions of relevancy. The issues of fact and of law must be framed clearly enough so that the tribunal knows what to decide. The scope of the claim(s) should be defined so that a conclusion can be reached—and so that afterward it can be determined what was decided. There is no ironclad time sequence for these steps, except that obtaining jurisdiction and giving notice to the defendant must ordinarily precede a valid judgment.[2] Judgment may sometimes precede trial or hearing, provided the person against whom judgment is rendered is given reasonable opportunity to present his or her case on attacking the judgment after it is entered.[3] Nearly always, however, trial or hearing comes before judgment. Moreover, in a jury trial it is highly convenient to resolve before trial everything except the issues of fact. Otherwise, the trial must be interrupted while issues are framed and the parties given opportunity to meet contentions of which they had no previous notice.

The foregoing list of tasks contains a good deal of overlap and duplication. Ascertaining the court's jurisdiction over a particular controversy, for example, necessarily involves some definition of the controversy, which is also a function of the pleadings. Framing of specific triable issues is a way to both limit the controversy and organize the trial. The framing of issues and the setting of bounds to the controversy give notice to the court and adversary of the subject of trial and the evidence likely to be presented. A court's subject matter jurisdiction is determined by whether a particular case is shown to be within the court's categories of jurisdiction. The pleadings, by indicating what the controversy is, are a means of making this showing. This essentially simple idea can be turned on its head: A court does *not* have jurisdiction of matters *not* presented to it in the pleadings. This inversion formerly was the source of much procedural hypertechnicality.[4]

A legal controversy consists of issues of fact (the parties' contentions as to what happened) and issues of law (the governing rules and how they apply to the facts before the court). A controversy can involve both

§ 3.1

1. *See* Chapter 2.

2. On the requirement that jurisdiction must be first established, *see* Riverside & Dan River Cotton Mills v. Menefee, 237 U.S. 189, 35 S.Ct. 579, 59 L.Ed. 910 (1915); *cf.* Pennoyer v. Neff, 95 U.S. 714, 24 L.Ed. 565 (1878). On the requirement of notice, *see* North Ga. Finishing, Inc. v. Di-Chem, 419 U.S. 601, 95 S.Ct. 719, 42 L.Ed.2d 751 (1975).

3. American Surety Co. v. Baldwin, 287 U.S. 156, 53 S.Ct. 98, 77 L.Ed. 231 (1932). *Compare* Catlin v. United States, 324 U.S. 229, 65 S.Ct. 631, 89 L.Ed. 911 (1945), an eminent domain proceeding under the War Purposes Act of 1917; "judgment" vesting title in the United States was entered prior to hearing or trial pursuant to the Declaration of Taking Act of 1931. A judgment so rendered is not a final judgment. *But see* Fuentes v. Shevin, 407 U.S. 67, 92 S.Ct. 1983, 32 L.Ed.2d 556 (1972).

4. *Cf.* Roberts, Fact Pleading, Notice Pleading, and Standing, 65 Cornell L. Rev. 390 (1980).

fact issues and legal issues, and more than one of each. Boiling down a legal controversy to these components is a complex thought process that involves three steps: (1) setting up the framework of legal rules that govern the facts; (2) gathering, sifting, and fitting the evidence into the legal framework; and (3) fixing the undisputed matters of law and fact so that attention can be directed to the points of disagreement.

Knowledge required to plead

Underlying these procedural objectives are institutional and ultimately substantive considerations. Imposing on a plaintiff a requirement that the claim be articulated in detail means that only claimants who have access to such detail are in a position to state a claim. A pleading rule that does not require detail permits claimants who have such details to assert them or not as they choose. But such a liberal rule also allows other claimants to bring litigation when they may have only suspicions as to the facts. The parties to various types of legal controversies usually have different initial access to the facts. For example, a passenger injured in a train wreck is unlikely to have any knowledge of what caused the wreck, whereas the railroad probably has this information and will ordinarily conduct a field investigation immediately after the event. If a passenger's complaint must state the cause of the wreck in detail, without the benefit of the discovery procedures that become available after the complaint is filed, few passengers will be able to state a viable claim and thereby stay in court. The same would be true of plaintiffs in most products liability and toxic torts cases. And if such claimants generally could not state valid claims because they could not supply the requisite detail, the cumulative effect would be substantial immunity from liability for those who otherwise might be sued.

Discovery and pleading

At common law, principal reliance in defining the scope and issues of litigation was placed on pleadings—the written statements by the parties of their claims and defenses.[5] Indeed, pleadings were nearly the only device that common law procedure afforded for the pretrial disclosure of the parties' claims and evidence.[6] Courts of chancery devised pretrial procedures for interrogating an adversary, obtaining disclosure of documents and other evidence in a party's possession, and taking testimony by deposition.[7] But because these discovery tools were only narrowly available on the common law side of the court,[8] the burden of issue-framing and notice-giving fell on the pleadings.[9]

5. *See generally* Stephen, Principles of Pleading ch. 2 (1824).

6. *See* Millar, Civil Procedure of the Trial Court in Historical Perspective 219 (1952).

7. *See* § 5.1 *infra*; Millar, *supra* note 6, at 201.

8. Millar, *supra* note 6, at 204.

9. *Id.* at 36, 37, 204. *See also* James, Discovery, 38 Yale L.J. 746 (1929).

This is no longer true. In American procedure discovery has now largely supplanted pleadings in performing these functions. But the concepts involved in pleading remain important in three respects. First, many problems that arose in connection with pleading have been carried over to discovery and pretrial motions and orders.[10] Second, the factual and legal issues formerly explained in the pleadings now must be expressed in motions, requests concerning the terms of the pretrial order (governing the matters to be determined at trial), and the parties' plan of proof and motions at trial.[11] Third, dissatisfaction with the heavy costs that discovery entails has led to resurrection of pleading as a device for formulating issues, at least in certain types of cases.[12]

§ 3.2 Common Law Pleading

The process of identifying and resolving the issues in controversy can be conducted largely by oral exchange, with the original written statement of claim serving mostly to initiate the discussion. Such is the procedure in informal dispute resolution, in the civil law system, and in many types of administrative agency adjudication.[1] It also was the procedure of the earliest common law. But later common law procedure—from the fourteenth century onward—placed heavy reliance on written pleadings to identify issues.

The key to common law issue formulation was the sharp distinction drawn between issues of law and issues of fact. This distinction is clear in many, but not all, real-life situations (is "driving too fast" a matter of fact or one of law?). The fact-law distinction was basic to the common law, however, because issues of law and issues of fact were decided by different procedures, and the distinction remains important in American procedure for this reason. Issues of law were decided by the judges, sitting together at the court's headquarters; issues of fact were decided by jury, at a trial held in the county where the transaction occurred. (Jurors originally were fact-reporters or witnesses, rather than neutral and previously uninformed adjudicators; hence, jury trial had to be in a place where jurors would know the facts.) The job of the pleadings was

10. *See, e.g.*, Adickes v. S. H. Kress & Co., 398 U.S. 144, 90 S.Ct. 1598, 26 L.Ed.2d 142 (1970) (sufficiency of a motion for summary judgment); Rigby v. Beech Aircraft Co., 548 F.2d 288 (10th Cir.1977) (scope of issues as defined in pretrial order). *See* Epstein, Pleadings and Presumptions, 40 U. Chi. L. Rev. 556 (1973); Michael and Adler, The Trial of an Issue of Fact, 34 Colum. L. Rev. 1224 (1934).

11. *See* Cleary, Presuming and Pleading: An Essay on Juristic Immaturity, 12 Stan. L. Rev. 5, 15 (1959).

12. *See* Marcus, The Revival of Fact Pleading Under the Federal Rules of Civil Procedure, 86 Colum. L. Rev. 433 (1986); Parness, *et al.*, The Substantive Elements in the New Special Pleading Laws, 78 Neb. L. Rev. 412 (1999); Bockrath v. Aldrich Chemical, 21 Cal.4th 71, 86 Cal.Rptr.2d 846, 980 P.2d 398 (1999).

§ 3.2

1. *See* Davis, Administrative Law Text § 8.02 (3d ed. 1972); Eisenberg, Private Ordering Through Negotiation: Dispute–Settlement and Rulemaking, 89 Harv. L. Rev. 637 (1976), and references therein; Kaplan, Civil Procedure—Reflections on the Comparison of Systems, 9 Buffalo L. Rev. 409 (1960).

to sort the issues into these two categories so that the case could be determined accordingly.[2]

Demurrer

To this end, the plaintiff would state a claim as allegations of facts, together with a demand for judgment. If the defendant thought that, on those facts, the law did not allow a recovery, the defendant would demur, saying, in effect, "so what?." (The second syllables of "demur" and "demurrer" are pronounced to rhyme with "her.") The demurrer took the facts as assumed but raised an issue of law to be resolved by the judges: Assuming x, y, z to be true, as plaintiff alleges, a legally valid claim nevertheless has not been stated. If, however, the defendant acknowledged that the law would give a recovery on those facts but denied that these were the facts, he or she would demand trial. The trial would be held in the county, taking the law as settled and putting the factual questions to the jury. The same process was used regarding fact allegations raised by a defendant.

Pleading to a single issue

In the early stages of common law procedure, it seems clear that a party could raise both issues of law and issues of fact, and more than one of each. But efforts to prevent dilatory tactics apparently led to a rule that a party had to "plead to issue"—not only sort out the issues of law and fact but reduce the case to a single issue, either of law or of fact, with judgment to go according to that issue's resolution.[3]

The insistence that the decision turn on a single issue, while it produced administrative efficiency with a vengeance, too often did so at the expense of substantive justice. It is a characteristic of dispute-settling processes that no one can forecast with certainty what the proof will bring forth in the way of facts, or of issues, or of the possible attitudes toward them that the tribunal may take. Moreover, controversies often present two or more issues—sometimes many—which must all be resolved to reach a judgment.

The common law gradually yielded to these realities. Courts and legislatures attempted to ameliorate the hardship by a series of halfway measures, compromises, and fictions that produced a system lacking both the simplicity of the older dispensation and the elasticity needed for the unfettered examination of a complex controversy. The ideal of singleness of issue—and with it, administrative efficiency—was thus abandoned. But the insistence on the production of issues remained as

2. Stephen, Principles of Pleading 145 *et seq.* (1824). *Compare* Arnold, Law and Fact in the Medieval Jury Trial: Out of Sight, Out of Mind, 18 Am. J. Legal Hist. 267 (1974).

3. *See* Millar, Civil Procedure of the Trial Court in Historical Perspective 33 (1952). *Cf. id.* at 133.

long as did common law pleading, which prevailed in this country until the middle of the nineteenth century.

B. THE COMPLAINT

§ 3.3 Common Law Declaration

Forms of action

Under the common law system the plaintiff's first pleading was a declaration that had to be appropriate to the form of action through which it was asserted.[1] A form of action was a legal document expressing a basic type of claim—trespass, ejectment, and so on. Each form of action had its own distinguishing features so that in most cases the defendant could tell the form of action from the declaration. Since each form of action had a peculiar train of legal consequences, this was important information. The common law's substantive content grew separately under the rubric of each form of action. There were no general theories of liability. Thus, a defendant could know from the first pleading the theory of substantive law that plaintiff was urging. If plaintiff pleaded in trespass, defendant knew that only the legal rules governing liability in trespass could be urged against him or her; the question, in other words, was whether defendant was liable not under the law in general but under the law of trespass. If not, plaintiff could not succeed even though the facts alleged showed that plaintiff was entitled to recover in some other form of action.

Moreover, each form of action had peculiar procedural incidents. The form of action determined, for example, the subject matter jurisdiction of the court, the form of process available to make defendant appear (whether, for instance, there could be a body attachment), the appropriate steps in case of default, the mode of trial (whether by jury or by some older method such as wager of law, ordeal, and so on), the permitted defensive pleas, and the form of judgment and of execution (whether plaintiff could be put in possession of the subject of dispute, whether defendant could be imprisoned or made an outlaw, and so on).[2]

Fact pleading at common law

The initial stage in a common law action (including the declaration) thus gave defendant fairly precise notice of the legal theory and the procedural incidents with which the defendant would be confronted. But

§ 3.3

1. This choice was usually made before any pleading. Each form of action had its peculiar form of original writ. At early common law, actions were usually begun by obtaining such an original writ from the chancery. By the nineteenth century, however, alternative ways of commencing actions (for example, by writs of process or by bill) had become prevalent. Stephen, Principles of Pleading 24–28, 51–60 (1824).

2. Maitland, The Forms of Action 2–4 (1936).

how much did a common law declaration tell the defendant about the *facts* that the plaintiff would rely on at trial?

The answer to this question is not simple. Early common law pleading was oral, and the issue in the case was fixed by a process Morgan has likened to the modern pretrial hearing. When written pleadings were first employed, they tended to follow short, pithy forms and ordinarily were straightforward "statements of the facts." But common law courts expanded their jurisdiction (at the expense of the local courts) by giving new and often fictional effect to the old verbal formulas of the forms of action. These manipulations of the forms of action led to pervasive discrepancies between what was said in the declarations and what was meant.[3] In some forms of action, wholly fictional recitals prefaced the real punch line—that defendant had taken plaintiff's property or failed to pay a debt.[4]

In some types of common law actions the greatest generality of allegation was allowed. A plaintiff could plead a simple capsule formula of liability and recover on proof of quite different facts so long as they had the same legal effect as the stereotyped facts within the formula. This is illustrated by the action in general assumpsit. A plaintiff would declare that defendant "had and received money to the plaintiff's use" and promised to pay the same to plaintiff. On this declaration plaintiff could prove that defendant had stolen or converted plaintiff's goods and sold them, that defendant had fraudulently induced plaintiff to buy some worthless article and that plaintiff had thereafter rescinded the sale, that plaintiff had paid or overpaid money to defendant by mistake, and so on.[5] These were regarded as instances of money "had and received" by defendant.

The common law declaration thus gave a defendant fairly accurate notice of the substantive legal theory and the procedural incidents that plaintiff might use, and it sometimes gave defendant notice of the facts that might be shown at trial. In many situations, however, there was often little or no correspondence between the facts alleged and those that appeared at trial. From the plaintiff's point of view, common law pleading tied the claim down narrowly to a single legal theory and sometimes, with procrustean rigidity, to the facts alleged. In other situations such pleading provided great latitude in matters of fact. From defendant's viewpoint, shrewd surmise was required to discern what plaintiff might seek to prove.

3. Morgan, Some Problems of Proof Under the Anglo-American System of Litigation 28–34 (1956). *See* Milsom, Not Doing Is No Trespass, 1954 Cambridge L.J. 105; Simpson, The Introduction of the Action on the Case for Conversion, 75 Law Q. Rev. 364 (1959).

4. Shipman, Common Law Pleading 254, 258 (3d ed. 1923).

5. *See* New York, First Report of Commissioners 70–71, 145 (1848); Leoni v. Delany, 83 Cal.App.2d 303, 188 P.2d 765 (1948). *Compare* Scott v. Shepherd, 2 W. Black. 892, 96 Eng. Rep. 525; 3 Wils., 403, 95 Eng. Rep. 1124 (C.P. 1773) (trespass).

§ 3.4 Bill of Complaint in Equity

The plaintiff's complaint in equity was originally a narrative statement of grievance, full of detail and imputation of wrongdoing. The formalization of equity procedure by the sixteenth century led to a stylistically intricate pleading system.[1] The complaint was called a "bill" and consisted of three parts: the narrative, the charging, and the interrogative. The narrative stated the facts of the complainant's case for relief. The charging contained a statement of evidence anticipating and rebutting defendant's supposed positions. The interrogative propounded interrogatories calculated to extract admissions and discover evidence from the adversary, who had to respond under oath. All this involved a good deal of repetition and detail. It did not, however, involve the fictions so prevalent in common law pleading. It was to equity pleading that those who drafted the New York Code of 1848 turned for their model.[2]

§ 3.5 Code Complaint

The New York Code of Civil Practice of 1848, known as the "Field Code" after its principal drafter, David Dudley Field, sought to do away with the formulary system of the common law and the distinction between law and equity.[1] Instead it set up a system in which the facts of a grievance would be stated in simple, nontechnical language and the court would be free to apply whatever substantive law it found appropriate to those facts without distinction between the forms of action or between law and equity. No new rights and remedies were meant to be created, and the substantive law still had to be drawn from existing precedents.[2] But the inquiry now focused on whether the facts warranted relief according to *any* of those precedents—not simply according to those associated with a single form of action. The whole substantive law thus was made available to the court in deciding each case.[3]

§ 3.4

1. Pomeroy, Remedies and Remedial Rights § 507, at 535 (1876). *See also* Shipman, Common Law Pleading 11 (3d ed. 1923).

2. New York, First Report of Commissioners 71 (1848).

§ 3.5

1. New York, First Report of Commissioners 67–87 (1848). This title of the report starts out with these words: "The chief object of this title is to declare the leading principles which lie at the foundation of the whole proposed system of legal procedure, and without which, in our judgment, very few, if any essential reforms can be effected in remedial law. We refer to the abolition of the distinction between actions at law and suits in equity, and of the forms of such actions and suits." *Id.* at 67–68. *See also* Clark, Code Pleading §§ 7, 15 (2d ed. 1947); Pomeroy, Remedies and Remedial Rights 28, 67 (1876); Subrin, How Equity Conquered Common Law: The Federal Rules of Civil Procedure in Historical Perspective, 135 U. Pa. L. Rev. 909 (1987).

2. New York, First Report of Commissioners 146, 147 (1849) ("No rule of law, by which rights and wrongs are measured, will be touched, the object and effect of the change being only the removal of old obstructions, in the way of enforcing the rights, and redressing the wrongs").

3. *See* Crary v. Goodman, 12 N.Y. 266, 268 (1855): "[S]ince the enactment of the Code ... the question ... is not whether the plaintiff has a legal right or an equita-

Fact pleading

The medium of expression in pleading under the codes was to be "facts": the complaint was to contain a "statement of facts constituting the cause of action, in ordinary and concise language."[4] This represented a departure from both common law pleading and equity pleading. Common law pleading entailed the recitation of legal formulas expressed in conclusory terms, or a combination of conclusions and fictions; equity pleading consisted of a narrative of evidence. Code pleading was supposed to avoid legal conclusions, for that would reintroduce the common law's formulary system; it was also supposed to avoid the pleading of evidence, because, unlike the bill in equity, code pleading was to be concise. To carry out this scheme, it was necessary to distinguish between "facts," "conclusions of law," and "evidence." Giving effect to the latter distinctions eventually resulted in a whole new corpus of legal technicality at the pleading stage.[5]

§ 3.6 Complaint Under the Federal Rules

Rule 8(a)(2)

The Federal Rules provisions on pleadings use neither the word "facts" nor the term "cause of action." Instead they provide that a claim for relief should contain "a short and plain statement of the claim showing that the pleader is entitled to relief."[1] The intention was to repudiate the gloss which some courts had put on the terms "facts" and "cause of action" and thereby to avoid the semantic quibbling such language had engendered.[2]

The Federal Rules therefore require only very spare allegations: "A short and plain statement of the claim,"[3] thus easing the burden on the pleader. In *American Nurses' Association v. Illinois* the court observed

ble right, or the defendant a legal or equitable defense against the plaintiff's claims; but whether, according to the whole law of the land, applicable to the case, the plaintiff makes out the right which he seeks to establish, or the defendant shows that the plaintiff ought not to have the relief sought for."

4. New York, First Report of Commissioners 120(2) (1848).

5. *See* Clark, Code Pleading § 38 (2d ed. 1947).

§ 3.6

1. Fed. R. Civ. P. 8(a)(2). This rule "was deliberately drafted to avoid this terminology because of the gloss of technical decisions that have grown up in New York and some other code states around the words 'facts' and 'cause of action.' " Tolman, Advisory Committee's Proposals to Amend the Federal Rules of Civil Procedure, 40 A.B.A.J. 843, 844 (1954). The Committee rejected a proposal to reintroduce the omitted language into the rule. Advisory Committee on Rules for Civil Procedure, Preliminary Draft of Proposed Amendments 8–9 (1954). *See also* Wright, Amendments to the Federal Rules: The Function of a Continuing Rules Committee, 7 Vand. L. Rev. 521, 549–551 (1954); 1 Moore, Federal Practice and Procedure ¶ 0.528.

2. Pound, David Dudley Field: An Appraisal, in David Dudley Field Centenary Essays 3, 13, 14 (1949); Clark, Code Pleading and Practice Today, in David Dudley Field Centenary Essays 55, particularly 64–67 (1949). *See also* Tolman, Advisory Committee's Proposals to Amend the Federal Rules of Civil Procedure, 40 A.B.A.J. 843 (1954).

3. Fed. R. Civ. P. 8(a)(2).

that "a complaint is not required to allege all, or any, of the facts logically entailed by the claim."[4]

This ideal of a "short and plain statement" has proved elusive for several reasons. Plaintiffs in federal court often plead claims with the same evidentiary particularity of an old bill in equity, hoping that detailed facts and data will educate the judge and perhaps impress their opponents with a show of the strength of their case. Moreover, it is often difficult to differentiate between the essential and nonessential elements of various claims; rather than omitting some elements at the outset that may prove crucial later on, presenting a fulsome narrative plays it safe. These days, a civil suit often is connected to an ongoing criminal case, such as a suit for damages arising out of the alleged criminal actions of the defendant (industrial pollution, for example), and the form of the civil pleadings may be dictated by the criminal proceedings. Sometimes, too, there is a lack of "client control" on the part of plaintiffs' attorneys. Plaintiffs often wish to assert claims that their attorneys may find unimportant or unpromising; these claims may find their way into the pleadings solely for the purpose of client pacification. Finally, lawyers may be inclined toward overpleading when failure to include an essential element might be grounds for a malpractice suit, whereas the inclusion of superfluous claims would generally be harmless.

Nevertheless, there is risk in prolix pleadings. The judge may react with confusion or even irritation. Worse, the prolixity may reflect the confusion of legal theories in the mind of the plaintiff's lawyer. Still worse, pleading evidence may reveal details showing that plaintiff has no claim. As the court observed in *American Nurses',* "A plaintiff who files a long and detailed complaint may plead himself out of court by including factual allegations which if true show that his legal rights were not invaded."[5]

Discovery as means of giving notice

Intimately related to the idea that pleading of "facts" should not be required under the Federal Rules was the concept that discovery and pretrial hearings would apprise opposing parties of the case they might have to meet. Discovery allows each party to probe the adversary and witnesses for relevant evidence in a manner far more searching than even the strictest pleading. Moreover, discovery yields information from witnesses who actually know the facts, whereas pleadings are merely the statements of the lawyer.[6] Discovery can also be used to unearth facts

4. 783 F.2d 716 (7th Cir.1986).

5. *Id.* at 724. *See also* Fitzgerald v. Codex Corp., 882 F.2d 586 (1st Cir.1989) (a specific theory of recovery need not be pleaded as long as factual allegations are sufficient to show plaintiff was entitled to recover under some theory); Salahuddin v. Cuomo, 861 F.2d 40 (2d Cir.1988) (redundancy and irrelevancy in pleading should be cured by a motion to strike order, Rule 12(f), whereas dismissal is usually reserved for cases where the basis for the claim is so badly stated that it cannot be discerned).

6. *See* statements of Judge Clark in American Bar Association, Proceedings of the Institute on Federal Rules of Civil Pro-

that the party does not know but only suspects, thus helping to develop a case that a pleader is not otherwise in a position to allege. Discovery cannot, however, resolve the legal question whether, if the facts are established (by whatever means), the plaintiff is entitled to relief.[7]

Summary judgment

The Federal Rules likewise implement the view that disposing of baseless claims is usually the task, not of pleadings, but of summary judgment. Summary judgment can get beyond pleaders' allegations to reach the evidence.[8] A party seeking summary judgment, moreover, usually introduces its own evidentiary material, rather than being forced to rely on the allegations pleaded by an opposing party. The Field Code's attempt to assess claims through requiring relatively detailed factual pleading tended not to filter out bad claims so much as to penalize litigants with clumsy lawyers. Even when a motion to dismiss a complaint for failure to state a claim succeeds, the result is often only an amended complaint, not the end of the case. Hence, although a few percent of cases are dismissed on the pleadings,[9] contemporary practice minimizes that function of pleading.

The drafters of the Federal Rules did not directly confront an important point about the code "fact pleading" requirement. This requirement implicitly imposed two related burdens on a pleader that had to be met at the threshold of the litigation. First, the pleader had to have in mind some substantive legal theory that would support some kind of relief on the basis of the supposed claim—otherwise the pleader would not know what to say in the "short and plain statement." Second, the pleader had to have information about the facts going beyond pure conjecture—otherwise no allegations could be made, even with a legal theory. If these threshold requirements were still to apply under the Federal Rules, it was a misplaced idea to refer to discovery as a substitute for pleading because discovery ensues after the complaint has been filed. If the traditional threshold requirements were not to apply, however, it is difficult to see why the pleading should be required to show that the "pleader is entitled to relief." It would have been more appropriate to require only that the pleading state that there is "reason to believe that, upon evidence which may be disclosed by discovery, the pleader may be entitled to relief."

cedure 44, 242, 245 (1939) (quoted in James, The Revival of Bills of Particulars Under the Federal Rules, 71 Harv. L. Rev. 1473, 1474 n.9, 1479 n.32 (1958)).

7. *See* Epstein, Pleadings and Presumptions, 40 U. Chi. L. Rev. 556, 557–560 (1973); Laski, Memorandum for the Committee on Rule 8, 13 F.R.D. 275 (1952).

8. *See* §§ 4.10–16 *infra.*

9. Marcus, The Puzzling Persistence of Pleading Practice, 76 Texas L. Rev. 1749 (1998); n. 13 *infra.*

Conflicting concepts of pleading

The ambiguity of the Federal Rules' purpose has led to two lines of doctrine about pleading. One line, which seems more consistent with the drafters' intent, was that the pleaders did have to allege, if only in sketchy terms, the existence of circumstances that they had reason to believe were true and that, if true, would entitle them to relief of some kind.[10] The other line is that expressed by the Supreme Court in *Conley v. Gibson,* and it asserts that a complaint under the Federal Rules is sufficient unless "it appears beyond doubt that the plaintiff can prove no set of facts in support of his claim which would entitle him to relief."[11]

A fundamental contradiction exists between these approaches. Under the first approach, the pleader can pursue the action into discovery only if the pleading establishes, as it were, probable cause. Under the second approach, the pleader can pursue the action beyond the pleading stage unless the *pleading on its face* shows that the pleader has no cause. This would make pleading requirements rather pointless. Courts and commentators since *Conley v. Gibson* have therefore suggested that the Supreme Court could not have meant literally what it said.[12] No doubt there is agreement that a complaint alleging only that "defendant wronged plaintiff" would not be sufficient, and to this extent *Conley v. Gibson*'s language is hyperbole. But the language is sufficiently undemanding so that the federal pleading rule can be boiled down to the following:

1. The pleader may attempt to state the claim with sufficient clarity and in such detail as to pose at the pleading stage whether there is a legally valid claim on facts he or she supposes to be true. If the pleader does so, and defendant moves to dismiss the claim, the court will give the pleader a ruling on the legal question.[13] This is essentially what code pleading requires.

2. Under *Conley v. Gibson,* the pleader may allege the claim in very general terms without specifying the facts. If the pleader does so, the action will continue into the discovery stage, and the legal sufficiency of the claim will not be determined until discovery is substantially complete.[14]

10. *See, e.g.,* Hoshman v. Esso Standard Oil Co., 263 F.2d 499, 501 (5th Cir.1959) (quoting Moore, Federal Practice and Procedure); *cf.* Decker v. Massey–Ferguson, Ltd., 681 F.2d 111 (2d Cir.1982);Clark, Code Pleading 146–148 (2d ed. 1947).

11. 355 U.S. 41, 45–46, 78 S.Ct. 99, 102, 2 L.Ed.2d 80 (1957). *See also* Ricketts v. Midwest Natl. Bank, 874 F.2d 1177 (7th Cir.1989); Boudeloche v. Grow Chemical Coatings Corp., 728 F.2d 759 (5th Cir. 1984); Dioguardi v. Durning, 139 F.2d 774 (2d Cir.1944); Carbone v. Gulf Oil Corp., 812 F.2d 1416 (Temp.Emer.Ct.App.1987).

12. *See* 2A Moore, Federal Practice and Procedure ¶ ¶ 8.12–8.14; 5 Wright and Miller, Federal Practice and Procedure § 1216. *See also* Marcus, The Revival of Fact Pleading Under the Federal Rules of Civil Procedure, 86 Colum. L. Rev. 433 (1986).

13. A pleader wishing to invite pretrial determination of the legal sufficiency of his or her claim may find it advantageous to use greater detail than the rules require. *See, e.g.,* Dale System, Inc. v. Time, Inc., 116 F.Supp. 527 (D.Conn.1953); Dale System v. General Teleradio, 105 F.Supp. 745 (S.D.N.Y.1952).

14. *See* Covington v. Cole, 528 F.2d 1365 (5th Cir.1976); Dioguardi v. Durning,

There may well be justification for allowing the pleader this second alternative: It avoids the risk of deciding cases on pleading technicalities, and it allows persons who may not know whether, or how, they were wronged to use discovery to find out—as a "fishing expedition." The federal pleading rules as construed by *Conley v. Gibson* clearly have permitted a pleader to go forward on this basis, thus representing a major departure from code procedure.[15] Moreover, as pointed out above, pleaders under the Federal Rules often do what they would do under code pleading as intelligently administered: They make statements of claim that provide the opposing party and the court with a fairly definite picture of the transaction sued on and the legal theories implicitly used. This is the most that can be expected of pleadings.

Allowing a plaintiff to plead in conclusory terms entails costs, sometimes heavy costs. Because the plaintiff can keep his or her action alive on only the skimpiest statement of claim, the defendant cannot get rid of the litigation without first undergoing discovery, which can be time-consuming, aggravating, and expensive. A secondary consequence of this exposure is that defendants have incentives to settle cases before discovery proceeds, even if they think a case has no merit. And a consequence of this set of incentives is that plaintiffs could file suits with little expectation of victory but with the aim of inducing such settlement offers. Such a suit is commonly called a "strike suit."

§ 3.7 Fact–Law Distinction

Logic of a cause of action

The code requirement that the complaint plead facts was not wholly novel, for common law pleading had involved not only the recitation of writ formulary language ("with force and arms," for example) but also a statement of at least part of the particular circumstances. The concept was that this statement furnished the minor premise in a syllogism. The rule of law invoked was the major premise, but that was judicially known to the court and need not be stated. The declaration stated the facts in the case and thereby brought it under the appropriate rule of law. The conclusion was the judgment of the court. The classic example[1] was this:

Major premise:	Against him who hath ridden over my corn, I shall have damages.
Minor premise:	But *A* hath ridden over my corn.
Conclusion:	Wherefore I shall have damages against *A*.

139 F.2d 774 (2d Cir.1944); Garcia v. Hilton Hotels Intl., 97 F.Supp. 5 (D.P.R.1951).

15. *See* § 5.2 *infra.* Any doubt in this respect seems to have been removed by the decision in Hospital Bldg. Co. v. Trustees of Rex Hosp., 425 U.S. 738, 96 S.Ct. 1848, 48 L.Ed.2d 338 (1976), where the Court said: "We have held that 'a complaint should not be dismissed for failure to state a claim unless it appears beyond doubt that the plaintiff can prove no set of facts in support of his claim which would entitle him to relief,' Conley v. Gibson ... And in antitrust cases, where 'the proof is largely in the hands of the alleged conspirators ... dismissals prior to giving the plaintiff ample opportunity for discovery should be granted very sparingly.' " 425 U.S. at 746, 96 S.Ct. at 1853, 48 L.Ed.2d at 345.

§ 3.7

1. 3 Blackstone, Commentaries *396.

This logic is expressed in ancient language but still remains the logic of a legal claim. The applicable law is the major premise, the particular facts are the minor premise, and the conclusion (if both major and minor premises are valid) is that plaintiff should recover.

Conclusions of law

The strictures against pleading "law" that are found among judicial decisions and commentators on code pleading were meant as a prohibition against pleading facts according to their legal effect, or pleading "conclusions of law." But legal analysts came to believe a clear distinction could be made between a statement of "law" and a statement of "fact." In a famous passage Pomeroy stated: "Every attempt to combine fact and law, to give the facts a legal coloring and aspect, to present them in a legal bearing upon the issues rather in their actual naked simplicity, is so far forth an averment of law instead of fact, and is a direct violation of the principle upon which the codes have constructed their system of pleading." According to Pomeroy, "the allegations must be of dry, naked, actual facts."[2]

If this stricture is taken literally it lays down a rule that is virtually impossible to fulfill. Statements in a pleading or other document are not either "law" or "facts." They are statements about legal rules and about real-world events. The application of the law to real-world events is what litigation is all about. In such applications, it is impossible to think of law without regard to particular instances. It is also impossible to think of facts without regard to their legal significance. Only a schizophrenic could maintain the distinction.

Moreover, no good purpose would be served by trying to maintain the distinction. The total number of "facts" about even a simple occurrence or transaction is infinite. Consider all that goes into the signing of a person's name; what myriad facts are connoted by the words "fountain pen," for instance. We select and combine these facts for the purpose at hand. If the fact of signing alone were important, we would say, "he signed the document." If we were concerned with determining whether the signer was right-handed, we would say, "she signed it with her left [or right] hand." If the medium mattered we would say, "the artist signed it in ink."

When we are involved in litigation, we are concerned with legal relations and consequences. Accordingly, what could be more natural than to use words that "give the facts a legal coloring and aspect," and "present them in a legal bearing"? If one sought to describe a situation

2. Pomeroy, Remedies and Remedial Rights § 529, at 566 (1876).

having legal significance entirely in words that were devoid of all legal evaluation the result would be a series of prolix circumlocutions that would serve neither elegance of style nor ease of understanding.[3]

The Field Code commissioners tried to abolish the many fictitious and false allegations of the common law and the practice of pleading the facts according to their legal effect when that did not correspond to the way lay persons would describe them.[4] Fortunately, that is the way the code pleading rules have been interpreted in modern times.[5]

Relative specificity of allegations

The code pleading rules also had another objective—that the other party would be given fair notice of the evidence. This requires reasonable detail in the allegations, not broad, conclusory assertions. For example, the statement that "defendant is legally liable to plaintiff for damages" is in a certain sense a statement of fact. It is certainly not the statement of a legal rule. Yet the statement would not meet the requirements of a complaint under the codes (nor as a declaration under the common law, for that matter). To get a sense of "reasonable detail," let us take a series of statements, starting with the one just analyzed.

1. Defendant is legally liable to plaintiff for damages.
2. Defendant negligently caused plaintiff injury.
3. Defendant negligently caused plaintiff bodily injury through the operation of a motor vehicle.
4. Defendant negligently drove a motor vehicle against plaintiff who was then crossing [named] highway.

   As a result plaintiff was thrown down and his leg was broken.
5. Same as (4) with an added paragraph following the first, as follows:

   The defendant was negligent in that he failed to keep a proper lookout, drove at excessive speed, and so on.
6. Same as (4) with an added paragraph following the first, as follows:

   The defendant was looking at a passenger in the back seat of his automobile and not in the direction in which he was going; he was driving at a speed of 43 miles per hour, and so on.

3. *See generally* Cook, Statements of Fact in Pleading Under the Codes, 21 Colum. L. Rev. 416 (1921); Cook, "Facts" and "Statements of Fact," 4 U. Chi. L. Rev. 233 (1937).

4. New York, First Report of Commissioners 266, 267 (1848) (emphasis added).

5. Dino, Inc. v. Boreta Enters., 226 Cal. App.2d 336, 38 Cal.Rptr. 167 (1964). *See also* Semole v. Sansoucie, 28 Cal.App.3d 714, 104 Cal.Rptr. 897 (1972); Committee on Children's Television, Inc. v. General Foods Corp., 35 Cal.3d 197, 673 P.2d 660, 197 Cal.Rptr. 783 (1983).

What was said in the first statement is true for all the others, but each of the following statements will be satisfied by a progressively narrower, more limited showing of evidentiary facts. All these statements describe facts according to their legal effect and "present them in a legal bearing." Only in the sixth is any attempt made to describe defendant's conduct in words that avoid overt legal evaluation.

Most courts would hold that the first three forms of statement do not suffice because the allegations are mere conclusions of law. Few courts insist, however, on the form of statement found in item (6); some would even characterize it as an improper statement of evidence.[6] Most, if not all, courts would accept the form of statement in (5).[7] The statement in (4) is taken from the common law declaration in an action on the case and is found in Form 9 of the forms set forth in the Federal Rules of Civil Procedure.

The fact-law distinction now has minor importance under the Federal Rules, which permit very general pleadings. But maintaining such a distinction remains a fundamental legal problem. It reappears in distinguishing the functions of the jury from those of the judge in a jury trial, for juries decide "facts" and the judge decides "law," and in distinguishing the function of the trial judge from that of the appellate bench in a case taken on appeal.[8] It also reappears indirectly in defining the scope of discovery.[9] The distinction in the context of pleading suggests that it cannot be generalized, largely because substantive legal considerations are involved in its application in various contexts. As is so often the case, the law has to employ a distinction that is generally workable but that is untenable at the margin.

§ 3.8 Fact–Evidence Distinction

Ultimate facts

As we saw in the preceding section, the distinction between fact and law is conceptually dubious and in practice comes down to a matter of degree of detail. This is also true of the distinction between "fact" or "ultimate fact" (which is to be pleaded) and "evidence" (which under

6. *Cf., e.g.,* Georgia, So. & Fla. Ry. v. Williamson, 84 Ga.App. 167, 65 S.E.2d 444 (1951), wherein plaintiff complained of injury from falling on clinker, coal, or other debris negligently allowed to remain in railroad yard. Defendant by special demurrer attacked the complaint for vagueness in failing to state exactly the kind of debris and its location. Demurrer was overruled. "[T]he pleader is not required to set out his evidence." *See also* Brown v. Western Ry., 338 U.S. 294, 70 S.Ct. 105, 94 L.Ed. 100 (1949).

7. *See, e.g.,* forms in Calif. Continuing Educ. Bar, California Civil Procedure Forms Manual (1967); Connecticut Practice Book Annotated §§ 107 *et seq.* (2d ed. 1979); Illinois Code of Civil Procedure and Rules of Court 24–30 (1990).

8. *See* Pullman–Standard v. Swint, 456 U.S. 273, 102 S.Ct. 1781, 72 L.Ed.2d 66 (1982); Dobson v. Masonite Corp., 359 F.2d 921 (5th Cir.1966).

9. *See* 446 U.S. 997 (1980) (Powell, Rehnquist, and Steward, JJ., dissenting from amendments to discovery rules); Claim or Cause of Action, 13 F.R.D. 253 (1952).

the Field Code should not be pleaded). Again an analytical distinction of sorts is possible. For example, plaintiffs who wish to recover for breach of a written contract must show that a document was executed; they will fail if they do not. Execution of the contract is therefore an ultimate fact to be pleaded. But the plaintiff may show such execution by evidence consisting of defendant's admission, by a witness to the signing of the contract, by opinion evidence to authenticate defendant's signature, or by other means, and the failure to establish execution by any particular line of evidence does not preclude resort to other methods. These methods of proof are evidentiary facts and are not to be pleaded.

Here again, however, the attempted analytical distinction is not as significant as the difference in degrees of specificity or detail. Moreover, the analytical distinction does not meet the real point, which is to avoid unnecessary verbosity in pleading.[1]

Too much detail

The pleading of evidence is not good pleading under the codes, but it is not as serious a defect as the pleading of conclusions of law. Allegations so general as to be "conclusions of law" may be treated as being no allegations at all. If they are so treated, they will be disregarded in determining the sufficiency of the complaint.[2] Hence, a demurrer or motion to dismiss for failure to state a claim may be effective against a complaint stated in such terms. Too much detail, however, will rarely render the complaint vulnerable to such an attack (though it may be stricken on appropriate motion), and will rarely be prejudicial to the pleader's adversary (by failing to give adequate notice of what is to be proved).[3]

§ 3.9 The Degree of Specificity Required

We have now seen that fact pleading under the code boils down to a requirement that the elements of the pleader's claim or defense be stated with sufficient specificity or detail.[1] This raises two questions: (1) What are the elements of claim or defense that a pleader's allegations must cover? (2) What is the requisite degree of specificity for these allegations? These questions also arise in Federal Rules pleading.

Established pleading forms

No satisfactory test of general application can be formulated to mark the degree of specificity required in pleading. The actual decisions cover

§ 3.8

1. Clark, Code Pleading § 38 (2d ed. 1947).

2. Bornhorst v. Lyon, 279 App.Div. 820, 109 N.Y.S.2d 194 (1952); Didier v. Macfadden Publications, 299 N.Y. 49, 53, 85 N.E.2d 612 (1949).

3. Clark, Code Pleading § 38 (2d ed. 1947).

§ 3.9

1. *See generally* Note, Specificity in Pleading in Modern Civil Practice, 25 U. Rich. L. Rev. 135 (1990).

a wide range. There are, however, some guides for the student or the pleader. In any given jurisdiction, forms and judicial precedents exist for many specific situations. The forms set forth in the Federal Rules of Civil Procedure are an example. These official forms and the precedents may be followed, except that they may not always be used with safety in situations different from the specific situation with which they purport to deal. The same words may constitute a proper allegation in one context and yet an impermissible allegation in another.

Degree of detail required

Aside from forms and precedents, there are some guides of a relatively broad nature. There is wide agreement that a pleading must describe at least in a general way the particular conduct (acts or omissions) of the parties charged. Thus, as we have seen, a complaint must indicate generally what defendant was doing (for example, driving an automobile) and how that conduct injured plaintiff (defendant's automobile struck plaintiff, collided with the automobile in which plaintiff was riding, or the like).

Whether greater detail than this minimum will be required depends on a number of factors, which are described below.

Role of pleading

1. The use of such detail will depend on the extent to which the local jurisdiction emphasizes pleading as a means of informing the other side in its preparation for trial, or the extent to which discovery is assumed to perform that function.[2]

Core and peripheral facts

2. The nearer the allegation is to the heart of contentions important to the case, the stronger the insistence on further detail. Thus an allegation that *A* and *B* were married would suffice in a suit for personal injuries negligently caused to one of them by a third party, while the same allegation might well be regarded as an inadequate legal conclusion in a suit by *A* against *B*'s estate to recover a widow's statutory share on the basis of a claimed common-law marriage.[3] Where suit is brought against a trespasser who has no claim of title, a simple allegation that plaintiff was owner of the land in question would be sufficient; the same allegation would be inadequate where a plaintiff out of possession seeks to eject the possessor on the basis of paramount title.

2. *See* Conley v. Gibson, 355 U.S. 41, 78 S.Ct. 99, 2 L.Ed.2d 80 (1957); *see also* Hospital Bldg. Co. v. Trustees of Rex Hosp., 425 U.S. 738, 96 S.Ct. 1848, 48 L.Ed.2d 338 (1976).

3. *Compare* the example given in Morris, Law and Fact, 55 Harv. L. Rev. 1303, 1325 (1942).

Unfamiliar events

3. The more readily the fact alleged corresponds to common experience, the less detail is likely to be required in alleging that fact. In a suit for bodily injuries, for example, the simple allegation that injuries were "caused" by a pedestrian's being struck by an automobile would suffice, while courts dealing with an antitrust claim likely would insist that the causal relation between defendant's antitrust violations and economic injury to plaintiff be spelled out in greater detail.[4]

Other factors

4. Greater pleading detail and precision are likely to be required in actions such as defamation that are disfavored for reasons of policy.

5. The greater the likelihood that defendant has at least equal knowledge of the transaction sued on, the less detail likely to be required.[5]

§ 3.10 The Case For and Against Requiring Detail or Specificity in Pleading

A pleader can rarely be helped by a requirement of detailed pleading. Specific allegations limit proof and therefore tie pleaders down, often preventing them from taking advantage of some unforeseen turn of proof during discovery or trial. At the trial all the witnesses and evidence are brought together for the first time and this itself may act as a catalyst for eliciting new information or revealing new insights into the significance and the relationship of what is already known. The pleader wants not only to avoid being surprised or foreclosed from advantageous development of the evidence but also to show as few cards as possible to the adversary. The pleader may wish to conceal weaknesses in the case with general allegations and thus prolong the period during which the case has a "nuisance value" for settlement.

Adversary's viewpoint

The adversary, in contrast, wants to tie the pleader down by finding out as much detail about the pleader's claims as possible. Since the pleader's case usually depends in part on the adversary's own conduct, the adversary often is aware of facts helpful, but unknown, to the pleader. The adversary also wants to minimize the pleader's chances of recovering on the basis of combinations of fact not yet perceived by either party.

For these reasons, a liberal pleading rule for complaints generally aids plaintiffs, who have the laboring oar in formulating the litigation.

4. *See, e.g.,* Mountain View Pharmacy v. Abbott Labs., 630 F.2d 1383 (10th Cir. 1980). *But cf.* George C. Frey Ready-Mixed Concrete, Inc. v. Pine Hill Concrete Mix Corp., 554 F.2d 551 (2d Cir.1977).

5. *See, e.g.,* Dino, Inc. v. Boreta Enters., 226 Cal.App.2d 336, 38 Cal.Rptr. 167 (1964). *See also* Geringer v. Wildhorn Ranch, Inc., 706 F.Supp. 1442 (D.Colo.1988) (holding that federal and state rules require only that defendant be afforded adequate notice of the claims against him or her).

Only when it comes to pleading a defense is liberality likely to help a defendant.

Public interest

For the judge, detailed pleading facilitates the varied tasks of ruling on relevance of the evidence during pretrial discovery and at trial, charging the jury, and preparing findings when there is no jury.[1] Society presumably has an interest in facilitating the judge's job. Detailed pleading may also help to determine the scope and effect of a judgment, clarifying it for all concerned parties.[2] But there are much better devices for accomplishing this, such as referring to the record of the evidence. Although the balance in pleading has now been clearly established in favor of the pleader, the same question of proper balance arises in other procedural contexts, especially in discovery and summary judgment.

The competing considerations in fashioning pleading rules reflect the general issue all procedural systems must try to resolve: how far to go in the direction of free exploration of a dispute, yet how closely to limit such exploration in the interests of terminating litigation cheaply and expeditiously. Thus, the claims of substantive justice must be balanced with the claims of administrative efficiency and fairness to the adversary; claims of justice in particular cases must be weighed against justice in a system as a whole. Administrative efficiency has great appeal, especially in urban centers where dockets are crowded. This appeal is destined to grow as the population increases and urbanization of our society continues. But unless these pressures are to destroy fundamental values, administrative efficiency should not be bought at the price of substantive justice to the individual. The Federal Rules are designed to ensure wider opportunity to develop a case by the adoption of general pleadings, and the contribution that detailed pleadings can make toward administrative efficiency is limited. A requirement of detail invites cumbersome "shot gun" pleadings and invites motion practice centered on the pleadings.[3]

§ 3.11 The Plaintiff's Burden of Pleading Elements of the Claim

The Federal Rules require a complaint to provide a "statement of the claim showing that the pleader is entitled to relief." Under the codes, the complaint must state facts "constituting the cause of action."[1]

§ 3.10

1. Hazard, Discovery Vices and Transsubstantive Virtues in the Federal Rules of Civil Procedure, 137 U. Pa. L. Rev. 2237 (1989).

2. *See* Chapter 11.

3. *See* statements of Judge Clark in American Bar Assn., Proceedings of the Institute on Federal Rules of Civil Procedure 44, 242 (1939). *See generally* Note, Specificity in Pleading in Modern Civil Practice, 25 U. Rich. L. Rev. 135 (1990).

§ 3.11

1. *See* Clark, Code Pleading § 19 (2d ed. 1947). For a good discussion of the code

Although these terms are not identical, they each require the pleader to describe a specific instance falling within a class of instances that the substantive law recognizes as entitling the injured party to relief, if the facts alleged can be proven. When we later discuss joinder of claims, splitting of causes of action, and amendments of pleadings, we shall consider the limits of the grouping of facts that should be treated as a single unit or claim for each of these various purposes.

Here we are concerned with a more fundamental procedural question: What showing does plaintiff have to make in the complaint in order to be allowed to press the action forward through discovery and trial? This question arises under the Federal Rules as well as the codes. Answering it requires ascertaining the governing substantive law. Suppose plaintiff is injured in an automobile accident and defendant is the driver of one of the automobiles involved. Plaintiff may recover damages from defendant if the following set of statements is true[2]:

- defendant owed plaintiff the duty to use care toward him or her;
- defendant's conduct was negligent toward plaintiff;
- plaintiff suffered actual bodily injury;
- defendant's negligence was a proximate cause of that injury;
- plaintiff's own conduct did not constitute contributory negligence;
- plaintiff did not consent to the injury or assume the risk of defendant's conduct;
- plaintiff has not recovered a former judgment from defendant for this injury;
- plaintiff has not settled the claim with defendant;
- the statute of limitations has not run.

And so on.

Allocation of burden of pleading

Not all these conditions of liability are considered essential elements of plaintiff's cause of action, or claim, and hence matters that plaintiff is bound to plead. Some of them are regarded as defenses that defendant must plead affirmatively if they are to be considered by the court. The question becomes, how does the law allocate the burden of pleading the fulfillment or nonfulfillment of these conditions?

definitions, *see* Elliott v. Mosgrove, 162 Or. 507, 93 P.2d 1070 (1939).

2. *See, e.g.,* Fee, The Lost Horizon in Pleading Under the Federal Rules of Civil Procedure, 48 Colum. L. Rev. 491 (1948); Clark, Simplified Pleading, 2 F.R.D. 456 (1943); Weinstein and Distler, Comments on Procedural Reform: Drafting Pleading Rules, 57 Colum. L. Rev. 518 (1957). There are, of course, other possible sets of conditions. Even if defendant did not owe to plaintiff the duty of ordinary care (for example, under a guest passenger statute), liability might be predicated on willful or wanton misconduct. The set of conditions given in the text is not meant to be exclusive but simply illustrative.

The legislature may specify how this burden is to be borne, and if it does so, this ends the matter, provided the statute does not transgress constitutional limitations. When the legislature creates the right of action, sometimes it also specifically sets forth the conditions that each side must plead, either expressly (this is rare) or by implication from the statutory language in the light of available canons of statutory construction.[3] Again, the legislature may change the allocation that the courts have made through decisional law, as they have in some states on the issue of contributory negligence.[4] But clear legislative direction of either kind is relatively infrequent, and in its absence it devolves to the courts to allocate the burden of pleading.

Efforts have been made to work out a general test for this allocation and specific tests governing particular situations; but in truth no rule of universal and uniform application exists. We shall treat the general test here and some of the specific tests for particular situations in later sections.

Facts showing defendant's duty, breach, causation, and injury

The nearest thing to a general rule is the statement, often found in the cases, that plaintiff must allege facts showing defendant's primary duty toward him or her, defendant's breach of that duty, and actual injury and a causal relation between defendant's breach of duty and that injury.[5] The corollary implied in this rule is that plaintiff need plead only such facts, and if defendant wishes to rely on the nonexistence or nonfulfillment of other conditions of liability, defendant must set them up affirmatively in the answer.

As applied to a negligence case, this analysis would require plaintiff to allege facts showing a duty on defendant's part to use care toward plaintiff (for example, the fact that both were travelers on the highway),that defendant's conduct constituted a breach of that duty (negligence), that plaintiff suffered bodily injury (or property damage, or both), and that the negligence was a cause of that injury. In a simple contract case this rule would require plaintiff to allege defendant's undertaking or promise and the consideration therefor (which together

3. Thus, after the Supreme Court interpreted the Fair Labor Standards Act to provide compensation for time spent between the portal and the worker's job in Anderson v. Mount Clemens Pottery Co., 328 U.S. 680, 66 S.Ct. 1187, 90 L.Ed. 1515 (1946), Congress passed the so-called Portal-to-Portal Act (29 U.S.C. §§ 251–262), which removed the liability unless the activities (between portal and job) were compensable under an express contract or an established custom or practice at the employer's plant. The courts read this statute as requiring plaintiff to plead and prove either the contract or custom as condition precedent to recovery. *See, e.g.,* United States Cartridge Co. v. Powell, 185 F.2d 67 (8th Cir.1950), *modified on other grounds,* 186 F.2d 611 (8th Cir.1951), cert. denied, 341 U.S. 936, 71 S.Ct. 855, 95 L.Ed. 1364 (1951); Medrick v. Textile Mach. Works, 79 F.Supp. 567 (E.D.Pa.1948).

4. *See* 2 Harper, James, and Gray, Law of Torts § 22.10 (2d ed. 1986).

5. *See, e.g.,* Clark, Code Pleading 236–238 (2d ed. 1947).

raise the duty), performance of any conditions precedent to the existence of that duty, and defendant's failure to perform the undertaking.

Complaints drawn according to these general rules would be sufficient in most jurisdictions. The trouble with these generalizations is that they are not helpful in some situations and are positively misleading in others. This trouble comes from three sources, as described below.

Flaws in the above generalization

1. Plaintiff may not be required to plead all these elements. The specific circumstances giving rise to the duty need not be stated in some situations, such as assault and battery, and libel and slander.[6] Beyond that, as we shall see when we discuss burden of proof,[7] considerations of fairness, convenience, and policy sometimes relieve a plaintiff from alleging a fact clearly belonging to his or her claim under the general rule. A plaintiff suing for money lent or for the price of goods sold and delivered, for example, need not prove nonpayment, but defendant is required to allege payment if he or she so contends.[8] And a bailor suing a bailee for negligent injury to the thing bailed need not allege negligence if there is an allegation of delivery in good condition and redelivery in bad condition (or failure to redeliver on demand).[9] While negligence is the very breach of duty sued on, allegation of that fact is not required.

2. Many conditions of liability fall outside the elements of plaintiff's action as defined by the general rules. Sometimes plaintiff is required to plead the fulfillment of such conditions as in contributory negligence. Traditional tort theory held that contributory negligence affords a defense even when defendant has breached a duty of care owed to plaintiff and this breach (negligence) has caused the plaintiff injury.[10] Nevertheless, many jurisdictions once required plaintiff to plead that he or she exercised due care. Again, a statute creating a new primary duty (for example, that a town maintain highways) may condition redress for breach of that duty on the giving of written notice of injury within a specified time. Many jurisdictions require the plaintiff to plead the giving of such notice.[11]

6. *See* § 3.19 *infra.*

7. *See* § 7.12 *infra.*

8. Clark, Code Pleading 610 (2d ed. 1947); Alden, The Defense of Payment Under Code Procedure, 19 Yale L.J. 647 (1910); Reppy, The Anomaly of Payment as an Affirmative Defense, 10 Cornell L.Q. 269 (1925).

9. *See, e.g.,* Berkowitz v. Pierce, 129 N.J.L. 299, 29 A.2d 552 (1943); Annot., 44 A.L.R.3d 171.

10. 4 Harper, James, and Gray, Law of Torts ch. 22 (2d ed. 1986).

11. *Id.* at 1632. *See, e.g.,* Felder v. Casey, 487 U.S. 131, 108 S.Ct. 2302, 101 L.Ed.2d 123 (1988), which held that a state statute requiring notice of a claim before a state-court suit against local governmental entity was inapplicable to a 42 U.S.C. § 1983 federal action brought in state court.

3. Many of the conditions of liability may be viewed either as conditions inherent in one of the elements of plaintiff's claim (such as a condition precedent to the existence of defendant's duty) or as conditions that will defeat liability even when there has been an apparent breach of duty causing injury. If, for example, plaintiff, on defendant's request, performs professional services for defendant with the intent of making a gift of them, then there is no legal liability to pay for the services. If the services were performed in the course of an ordinary business or professional relationship, however, there is an implied obligation to pay for them. The absence of intent to make a gift may reasonably be viewed as a condition of defendant's duty to pay for the services. But because the intent to make a gift of requested professional services may be considered extraordinary, the plaintiff's statement of claim may be viewed as complete without the need to exclude so remote a possibility.[12]

For further example, an actor's duty to refrain from battery on another will usually be defeated (so far as civil liability goes) by the other's consent.[13] Nonconsent, then, may be viewed analytically as a condition on defendant's duty in such a case. This is also true with the defendant, a surgeon, who performs a surgical operation on the plaintiff vis-a-vis a defendant who strikes the plaintiff in the face. It is not surprising that the plaintiff in the surgical operation case will have to plead nonconsent[14] while the plaintiff in the other case will not.[15]

Factors in allocation: convenience

As indicated above, and as we will continue to discover,[16] the analytical test for determining which conditions of liability a plaintiff must include in the complaint is not universally dispositive of the allocation problem.[17] Courts may allocate the pleading burden (and also, as we shall see, the burden of proof) on factors having little to do with the analytical test (primary duty, breach, and so on). Sometimes the allocation is dictated by convenience. The standard rule governing pleading in contract cases requires plaintiff to plead that conditions prescribed in the contract have been fulfilled. In most cases, however, there is no controversy over most of these conditions. Hence, it would be wasteful to call for detailed pleading about matters that will not be litigated. In most jurisdictions plaintiff is therefore permitted to plead generally the perfor-

12. *See* In re Smith's Estate, 202 Okla. 302, 213 P.2d 284 (1949).

13. 1 Harper, James, and Gray, Law of Torts § 3.10 (2d ed. 1986).

14. *See* Kritzer v. Citron, 101 Cal. App.2d 33, 224 P.2d 808 (1950).

15. *See* § 3.11 *infra.*

16. *See* §§ 3.15, 4.5, 4.15, 7.12–17 *infra.*

17. *See also* the problem of statute of limitations, which is ordinarily a defense, when the limitations period is defined as running from the time when plaintiff discovered the injury. Epstein, The Temporal Dimension in Tort Law, 53 U. Chi. L. Rev. 1175 (1986); Kaulbach, A Functional Approach to Borrowing Limitations Periods for Federal Statutes, 77 Calif. L. Rev. 133 (1989); Note, Developments in the Law—Statutes of Limitations, 63 Harv. L. Rev. 1177, 1198–1237 (1950).

mance of all conditions precedent, and the defending party is required in the pleading to specify any conditions the party desires to put in issue.[18]

Unusual course of events

Another factor, related to convenience, is the extent to which a party's claim of what happened deviates from what usually happens. When a lawyer is asked by a stranger to perform legal services, there is usually a mutual expectation that the lawyer will be paid. But when legal services are requested by a member of the lawyer's immediate family the usual expectation is the opposite.[19] The party who claims the unusual occurrence can be required to plead it affirmatively so that the usual assumptions may be indulged as a matter of course when there is no such unusual circumstance.[20]

Access to evidence

Superior access to the evidence on an issue sometimes influences the court in allocating the burden of proof on that issue.[21] The idea is that the one who has the evidence should bear the burden of producing it. This consideration probably underlies the rule requiring that defendant allege payment in many cases in which nonpayment is the breach of contract relied on by a plaintiff. One can integrate the access-to-evidence factor with the unusual-occurrence factor by asking which allocation of the burdens of pleading and proof will minimize litigation costs; this permits sophisticated economic analysis, but is not easy to apply in practice.[22]

Substantive policy

Policy may also play a part in the allocation of burdens, both of pleading and of proof. The law sometimes recognizes claims or defenses that it nevertheless disfavors, and the courts tend to manipulate procedural rules so as to weight the scales against disfavored claims and defenses. Thus a party—plaintiff or defendant—who would charge an adversary with fraud must plead the fraud affirmatively in some detail. One could interpret that rule as reflecting the lawmakers' belief that the harm from baseless fraud claims is greater than the harm of letting some fraud go unrepaired.[23]

18. Fed. R. Civ. P. 9(c); *e.g.*, Cal. Civ. Proc. Code § 457.

19. *See* Johnson v. Johnson, 99 N.H. 392, 111 A.2d 820 (1955) (claim allowed where agreement to pay affirmatively proven); In re Fox' Estate, 131 W.Va. 429, 48 S.E.2d 1 (1948) (agreement to pay not proven).

20. *See* Cleary, Presuming and Pleading: An Essay on Juristic Immaturity, 12 Stan. L. Rev. 5 (1959).

21. *See* §§ 7.15, 7.16 *infra.*

22. Hay & Spier, Burdens of Proof in Civil Litigation: An Economic Perspective, 26 J. Leg. Stud. 413 (1997).

23. *See* Fed. R. Civ. P. 8(c), 9(b); Semegen v. Weidner, 780 F.2d 727 (9th Cir. 1985); Hay, Allocating the Burden of Proof, 72 Ind. L.J. 651 (1997); § 3.19 *infra.*

It has also been suggested that, as a matter of social morality, the law should presume that people have not engaged in serious misconduct, placing the burden of pleading and proof on the litigant claiming that such misconduct has occurred.[24]

As illustrated above, so many variable factors—often working at cross purposes—go into allocating the pleading burden that no satisfactory test of general application can be found. This does not mean, however, that the prospective pleader is altogether without useful guides in specific cases. Any given jurisdiction may have official forms and precedents that will answer the most frequently recurring questions satisfactorily for practical purposes.

§ 3.12 Prayer for Relief

Rule 8(a)(3): the prayer

The declaration at common law[1] and the bill in equity[2] included a demand for relief, sometimes called "prayer for relief" or *ad damnum* clause. Both the codes[3] and the Federal Rules[4] require such a clause in the modern complaint. At common law the relief obtainable in the judgment was limited to the relief demanded;[5] in equity it was not, at least if the bill contained the conventional prayer for such "other and further relief" as might pertain to equity.[6] The chancellor, in other words, was free to do justice between the parties according to the equitable principles the chancellor found appropriate, even where the complainant had misconceived the remedy.

Relief exceeding the prayer

The framers of the Federal Rules adopted the equity rule, except in default cases, as had the Field Code. The basic rule is that "every final judgment shall grant the relief to which the party in whose favor it is rendered is entitled, even if the party has not demanded such relief in his pleadings."[7] If, however, the defendant fails to appear, "judgment by

24. Nance, Civility and the Burden of Proof, 17 Harv. J.L. & Pub. Policy 647 (1994).

§ 3.12

1. Stephen, Principles of Pleading 474 (1824).

2. Clark, Code Pleading 266 (2d ed. 1947); Van Zile, Equity Pleading and Practice 46 (1904).

3. *See, e.g.,* N.Y. Civ. Prac. L. & R. 3017. Some states prohibit the complaint from stating the amount claimed in certain types of actions, *e.g.,* Cal. Civ. Proc. Code § 425.10, apparently to limit sensational publicity on the filing of those kinds of claims.

4. Fed. R. Civ. P. 8(a)(3). How to plead relief is discussed in §§ 3.22–23 *infra.* On pretrial disclosure by the plaintiff of a computation of damages, *see* Fed. R. Civ. P. 26(1)(C); § 5.8 *infra.*

5. Stephen, Principles of Pleading 474 (1824).

6. Sources cited *supra* note 2.

7. Fed. R. Civ. P. 54(c). *E.g.,* Capital Asset Research Corp. v. Finnegan, 216 F.3d 1268 (11th Cir.2000)(defendant may recover contractual attorney fees despite failure to seek them until it prevailed); *see* Metro–North Commuter R.R. v. Buckley, 521 U.S. 424, 117 S.Ct. 2113, 2129, 138 L.Ed.2d 560 (1997)(Ginsburg, J., dissenting).

default shall not be different in kind from or exceed in amount that prayed for in the demand for judgment."[8]

In cases of default, therefore, what a plaintiff asks for still limits what he or she can get. A defendant who does not wish to challenge the plaintiff's claim may therefore default without fear that it will have to pay more than the plaintiff claimed. Some authority even holds that a judgment for relief different from or greater than the relief asked for is void against a defaulting defendant and subject to collateral attack.[9]

In other cases, notwithstanding the usual principle that the prayer for relief does not limit the relief ultimately awarded, the demand for relief may be significant in the following three ways:

1. It is a factor, often determinative, in fixing the amount in controversy to determine whether the case is properly brought in a court whose jurisdiction is defined in terms of an amount, such as in the federal courts.[10]
2. It may be relevant in determining the right to jury trial when plaintiff has a choice of either legal or equitable relief.[11]
3. When a plaintiff's failure to disclose the kind of relief it seeks would substantially prejudice the defendant, the court may deny the plaintiff the additional relief.[12]

§ 3.13 Rule 11: The Lawyer as Gatekeeper

Starting in 1983, in one of the major changes in the Federal Rule of Civil Procedure since their adoption, Rule 11 has been remolded into a stronger deterrent of unconsidered allegations. In effect, lawyers have been recruited to guard the doors of the courthouse, and the easy access to the courts provided by the liberal pleading requirements of the original Federal Rules has been somewhat restricted.

"Easy pleading"

"Easy pleading" meant that a plaintiff could file a complaint on the basis of suspicion and hope that discovery might turn up evidence sufficient to make a case. Since substantial cost could be involved in defending against such a case, a complaint based on mere suspicion could be used to exact unwarranted settlements. Abuses in the form of strike

8. *Id.* For the Field Code, *see* New York, First Report of Commissioners 195 (1848). *See also, e.g.,* Cal. Civ. Proc. Code § 580; N.Y. Civ. Proc. L. & R. 3017, 3215.

9. *See, e.g.,* Reynolds v. Stockton, 140 U.S. 254, 11 S.Ct. 773, 35 L.Ed. 464 (1891); Compton v. Alton SS Co., 608 F.2d 96 (4th Cir.1979); Burtnett v. King, 33 Cal.2d 805, 205 P.2d 657 (1949).

10. Iowa Cent. Ry. v. Bacon, 236 U.S. 305, 35 S.Ct. 357, 59 L.Ed. 591 (1915); Williams v. Rosinsky Motor Co., 133 Cal. App.2d Supp. 798, 284 P.2d 979 (1955); Note, 73 Harv. L. Rev. 1369 (1960).

11. *See* § 8.4 *et seq. infra.*

12. Albemarle Paper Co. v. Moody, 422 U.S. 405, 95 S.Ct. 2362, 45 L.Ed.2d 280 (1975)(plaintiff class that originally sought injunctive relief only may not obtain back pay).

suits and sham pleadings doubtless occurred in some cases, and many targeted defendants thought the abuse chronic. In its original form, Rule 11 had little power to prevent any abuses. It was construed to reach only those cases where it could be shown that the plaintiff's lawyer knew, or had compelling reasons to know, that a claim was baseless. Even then, the rule's weak sanctions discouraged opposing parties from invoking it.[1]

Rule 11

In 1983, the first of two major amendments to Rule 11 added an affirmative requirement that an attorney must investigate the bases of a pleading before filing it. The 1983 additions "in effect changed the standard for finding a violation of the rule from a subjective to an objective standard."[2] The attorney was required to certify that the pleading "is well-grounded in fact and is warranted by existing law or a good faith argument for the extension, modification or reversal of existing law, and that it is not interposed for any improper purpose, such as to harass or to cause unnecessary delay or increase in the cost of litigation." If the pleading did not meet this standard, then "the court . . . shall impose upon the person who signed it, a represented party, or both, an appropriate sanction."[3] The typical sanction was to require the offender to pay the opposing party the expenses that mispleading had imposed, which could include a substantial attorney fee award.

Empirical research has shown that the 1983 amendments caused lawyers to think much more carefully before filing pleadings. Unfortunately, they also caused lawyers to file many rule 11 motions, giving rise to much costly "satellite litigation." During the ten years after the amendments came into effect, federal judges wrote at least 6,000 opinions on Rule 11 issues, and many other motions were filed but decided without opinion. Plaintiffs' lawyers were the target of many more Rule 11 sanctions than defendants' lawyers. Civil rights plaintiffs' lawyers were especially hard hit, although it is not clear if this reflected weak claims, judicial hostility, or other factors.[4]

§ 3.13

1. Nemeroff v. Abelson, 620 F.2d 339 (2d Cir.1980); Risinger, Honesty in Pleading and Its Enforcement: Some Striking Problems with Federal Rule 11, 612 Minn. L. Rev. 1 (1976).

2. Indianapolis Colts v. Mayor of Baltimore, 775 F.2d 177, 181 (7th Cir.1985).

3. 97 F.R.D. 165 (1983); Wiggins & Willging, Rule 11: Final Report to the Advisory Committee on Civil Rules of the Judicial Conference of the United States (1991). For an unusually large award, *see* Avirgan v. Hull, 705 F.Supp. 1544 (S.D.Fla.1989), *aff'd,* 932 F.2d 1572 (11th Cir.1991), *cert. denied,* 506 U.S. 952, 113 S.Ct. 405, 121 L.Ed.2d 330 (1992)(sanctions exceeding $1,000,000).

4. Vairo, Rule 11 Sanctions: Case Law Perspectives and Preventive Measures § 2.02(b) (2d ed. 1992); Marshall, *et al.,* Public Policy: The Use and Impact of Rule 11, 86 Nw. U.L. Rev. 943 (1992); Spiegel, The Rule 11 Studies and Civil Rights Cases: An Inquiry into the Neutrality of Procedural Rules, 32 Conn. L. Rev. 155 (2000).

Revised Rule 11

Responding to widespread discontent in the bar, the rulemakers again adopted important amendments in 1993. These specified more clearly the requirements of Rule 11. More importantly, they tempered the rule's sanctions provisions, increasing the court's discretion, and giving alleged violators the chance to avoid sanctions by withdrawing challenged pleadings. Although these amendments, like their precursors, were controversial, early reports from the field indicate that they have caused no increase in groundless litigation.[5]

In its present form, Rule 11 extends well beyond the plaintiff's complaint: it applies to "every pleading, written motion, and other paper." Every lawyer who submits a written document to a federal court should therefore consider the rule's requirements. The one major exception covers documents relating to pretrial discovery, whether requests, responses, objections or motions. These are exempt from Rule 11, not to leave them unregulated, but because they are subject to sanction under Rule 37.[6]

Duties under Rule 11

The amended Rule 11 imposes on the attorney signing, filing, submitting or advocating a paper two major duties: (1) to make a reasonable inquiry as to the facts in accordance with the requirement that the factual contentions "have evidentiary support," and (2) to make a reasonable evaluation of the law in deference to the parallel requirement that the pleading be "warranted by existing law or by a nonfrivolous argument for the extension, modification, or reversal of existing law or the establishment of new law." These have been referred to as "stop-and-think" provisions. Of course, the lawyer must also read the paper in order to know what factual or legal contentions it contains.[7]

Factual basis

Reasonable inquiry into the facts has been taken to mean more than mere reliance on a client's recitation of facts, unless they are facts as to which the client has the personal knowledge that would entitle him to testify.[8] The signing counsel is not personally required to make the

5. Tobias, The Transmittal Letter Translated, 46 Fla. L. Rev. 127 (1994); Shapard, *et al.*, Report of a Survey Concerning Rule 11, Federal Rules of Civil Procedure (1995). On the continuing controversy, *see* Savage, Supreme Stumpers: The Next President Could Reshape the Court and the Legal Arena, 86 A.B.A.J. 26 (2000)(reporting that the 2000 Republican platform pledged to "strengthen the Federal Rules of Civil Procedure to increase penalties for frivolous suits").

6. Fed. R. Civ. P. 11(a, d). On discovery sanctions, *see* Fed. R. Civ. P. 37; § 5.14 *infra*.

7. Fed R. Civ. P. 11(b)(2,3) & Advisory Committee Notes (1993).

8. Union Planters Bank v. L & J Development Co., 115 F.3d 378 (6th Cir.1997); Southern Leasing Partners, Ltd. v. McMullan, 801 F.2d 783 (5th Cir.1986). Nor can the attorney delegate the responsibility of reasonable inquiry to a forwarding co-counsel. Unioil, Inc. v. E. F. Hutton & Co., 809 F.2d 548 (9th Cir.1986) (failure to inquire about a conflict of interest); Garr v. U.S. Healthcare, Inc., 22 F.3d 1274 (3d Cir.1994)(lawyer relied on another lawyer's pleadings and newspaper article).

inquiry into the facts, but must have sufficient "knowledge, information and belief" to affirm that the pleading has evidentiary support.[9]

Ultimately, the evidentiary support requirement is meant to allow cases that should proceed because there will be evidence supporting their factual contentions, even though those contentions may not prevail. In applying rule 11, lawyers and judges thus act as gatekeepers, determining just how large a likelihood of prevailing should be to warrant starting a suit or filing a motion.[10]

Although compliance with the rule's requirements for factual contentions turns primarily on whether the lawyer made reasonable inquiry and came up with evidentiary support, the lawyer's subjective sincerity does have some relevance.[11] Thus, some courts have taken into account whether the signer was an attorney (being more lenient on *pro se* pleaders) and the attorney's experience in the field, being more exacting on experienced lawyers to determine if something more than lack of knowledge led to the pleading's inadequacy.[12] On the other hand, one court has declined to sanction lawyers who proceeded without adequate investigation because a recent scientific study of which they were ignorant justified filing the suit.[13]

Rule 11 makes a concession to the fact that sometimes a party may need discovery to gather the evidentiary basis for allegations because the evidence is in the hands of others. The Rule allows a litigant to make factual allegations on information and belief, but only if they are identified as such and if they "are likely to have evidentiary support after a reasonable opportunity for further investigation or discovery."[14] The party's lawyer must still conduct whatever investigation is reasonable in the circumstances, and must refrain from advocating the allegation if later discovery reveals it to be baseless.

Denials

Denials of factual allegations are subject to Rule 11, but must obey a slightly different standard: they must be "warranted on the evidence." This provision reflects the assumption that the party making an allegation usually has the burden of introducing evidence to support it, while

9. *See* Schwarzer, Sanctions Under the New Federal Rule 11—A Closer Look, 104 F.R.D. 181, 187 (1985).

10. *See* Yablon, The Good, the Bad, and the Frivolous Case: An Essay on Probability and Rule 11, 44 U.C.L.A. L. Rev. 65 (1996).

11. The requirement that the pleadings are well grounded "to the best of [the attorney's] knowledge, information and belief" is subjective in outlook. Eastway Construction Corp. v. City of New York, 637 F.Supp. 558, 566–567 (E.D.N.Y.1986). *See also* Miller, The New Certification Standard Under Rule 11, 130 F.R.D. 479 (1990).

12. *See* Quiros v. Hernandez Colon, 800 F.2d 1 (1st Cir.1986); Federal Deposit Ins. Corp. v. Elefant, 790 F.2d 661 (7th Cir. 1986).

13. Moore v. Keegan Management Co., 78 F.3d 431 (9th Cir.1996).

14. Fed. R. Civ. P. 11(b)(3) & Advisory Committee Notes (1993). Such an allegation might, for example, begin: "Plaintiff is informed and believes, and therefore alleges, that.... "

the denying party may sit back and let its opponent carry that burden. A denial may therefore be warranted, not only if the denier has evidentiary support for its own version of the facts, but also if reasonable investigation indicates that the party making the allegation has no credible evidence to support it, or if reasonable investigation leaves the denier without information or belief. A party may not, however, deny an allegation it knows to be true.[15]

Legal basis

The requirement that a pleading be "warranted by existing law or by a nonfrivolous argument for the extension, modification, or reversal of existing law or the establishment of new law" has proved more difficult to interpret. Clearly the attorney cannot ignore well-established existing law,[16] but the legal analysis need not necessarily be correct. In determining good faith, the court will usually examine the attorney's circumstances at the time the pleading is prepared and filed to learn "how much time for investigation was available to the signer; ... whether the pleading, motion, or other paper was based on a plausible view of the law; or whether he [the attorney] depended on forwarding counsel or another member of the bar."[17] Some courts will simply make inferences about the attorney's conduct from the submitted papers, while others are more concerned with the adequacy of the attorney's inquiry.[18]

The Rule is not interpreted to require that attorneys behave like judges in reviewing the claims of their clients. The court in *Golden Eagle Distributing Corp. v. Burroughs Corp.* held that "neither Rule 11 nor any other rule imposes a requirement that a lawyer, in addition to advocating the cause of his client, step first into the shoes of opposing counsel to find all potentially contrary authority, and finally into the robes of the judge to decide whether the authority is indeed contrary or whether it is distinguishable."[19] In that case, an attorney misled the court about the law in that he failed to cite contrary controlling authority. Nevertheless, over strenuous dissent, the court stated that "the text of the Rule, however, does not require that counsel differentiate between a position which is supported by existing law and one that would extend it"[20] and reversed the imposition of sanctions. Similarly, courts have held

15. Fed. R. Civ. P. 11(b)(4) & Advisory Committee Notes (1993).

16. Whittington v. Ohio River Co., 115 F.R.D. 201, 207 (E.D.Ky.1987) (an "attorney has not made a reasonable inquiry as to whether a claim or defense is warranted by existing law if he or she hasn't done any research"); Cimino v. Yale Univ., 638 F.Supp. 952 (D.Conn.1986)(on the affirmative duty to shepherdize cases).

17. Fed. R. Civ. P. 11 Advisory Committee Notes (1983).

18. Meyer, When Reasonable Minds Differ, 71 N.Y.U.L. Rev. 1467 (1996).

19. Golden Eagle Distrib. Corp. v. Burroughs Corp., 801 F.2d 1531, 1542 (9th Cir.1986).

20. *Id.* at 1542.

that the inability to cite a single supporting decision for a proposition does not necessarily trigger Rule 11 sanctions.[21]

In examining the legal foundations of a case in applying Rule 11, courts have had little difficulty when the pleader obviously makes no effort to "extend" the law but merely ignores established law.[22] This in itself has been an important gain. Difficulties have been encountered, however, when an imaginative lawyer confronts an unimaginative or unsympathetic judge or when an imaginative judge sees possibilities in a legal argument that most judges would consider beyond the pale.[23] Both judges and lawyers disagree about the proper scope of judicial innovation. In effect, a lawyer making an unorthodox argument has to estimate when unorthodoxy will be regarded as heresy by the judicial authorities. The history of doctrine indicates that this involves an unavoidable element of peril.

Improper purpose

Aside from requiring investigation and support for factual and legal claims, amended Rule 11 continues to contain one frankly subjective standard: a paper may not be presented "for any improper purpose, such as to harass or to cause unnecessary delay" or expense.[24] In practice, this provision is difficult to invoke. It is hard to prove that the opposing party filed a paper for an improper purpose unless one can prove that the paper is baseless; and if one can prove baselessness, that in itself warrants sanctions under the other provisions of the rule. Even when it is shown that a litigant filed a claim that was not groundless for a poor reason, as occurred to one lawyer who wrote a letter threatening to file suit to give the defendant bad publicity, courts have declined to apply Rule 11.[25] This judicial reaction may reflect reluctance to spend time and money investigating the motives of claims with legal and factual foundation, if not tolerance for lawyers' strategic thinking that takes into account economic and public relations consequences.

Safe harbor

Even when a party violates Rule 11, the 1993 amendments allow it to avoid sanctions by withdrawing or correcting the offending paper. This "safe harbor" provision requires a party seeking Rule 11 sanctions to send the opposing party a motion to that effect. Only if the opposing party fails to withdraw or correct within the next 21 days may the

21. Zaldivar v. City of Los Angeles, 780 F.2d 823 (9th Cir.1986); Continental Air Lines v. Group Systems Intl. Far East, 109 F.R.D. 594 (C.D.Cal.1986).

22. *See, e.g.,* In re TCI Ltd., 769 F.2d 441 (7th Cir.1985); Willy v. Coastal Corp., 855 F.2d 1160 (5th Cir.1988) (citation to nonexistent law).

23. *See* Eastway Construction Corp. v. City of New York, 637 F.Supp. 558 (E.D.N.Y.1986).

24. Fed. R. Civ. P. 11(b)(1).

25. Sussman v. Bank of Israel, 56 F.3d 450 (2d Cir.1995); *see* Townsend v. Holman Consulting Corp., 929 F.2d 1358 (9th Cir. 1990).

moving party file its motion in court or present it to the judge.[26] The rule thus seeks to induce compliance rather than to pay victims, if possible without the court's involvement. It follows that a party may not be able to assert a Rule 11 claim when it is too late for the opposing party to retract, for example because the case has been dismissed.[27] The court, however, may impose sanctions on its own initiative when necessary, for example to deal with a repeat offender or blatant violator, without being subject to the safe harbor provision, by directing a party to show cause why it has not violated Rule 11.[28] The court may also postpone hearing a timely Rule 11 motion until the end of the case.

Sanctions

Under the 1993 amendments, sanctions must be "limited to what is sufficient to deter repetition of such conduct [violating the Rule] or comparable conduct by others similarly situated." The goal is deterrence, not compensation. Moreover, the amendments provide that the court "may" impose a sanction, rather than that it "shall" do so as the rule formerly directed.[29] Congress has legislated an exception to these provisions for securities fraud actions, in which the court must sanction Rule 11 violations and an attorney fee award compensating a violation's victim is the presumptive sanction.[30]

The nature and amount of any sanction are in the trial judge's discretion, which is reversible only for abuse of discretion. Under this standard, reversal is appropriate only if a lower court based its ruling on an erroneous view of the law or on a clearly erroneous assessment of the law.[31] If the sanctions are imposed on the attorney, that determination is appealable independent of any appeal by the party.[32] The sanctioned party must receive "notice and a reasonable opportunity to respond" before sanctions are imposed.[33]

The court may choose from among a variety of monetary and nonmonetary sanctions, the latter including such measures as repri-

26. Fed. R. Civ. P. 11(c)(1)(A). This part of the 1993 amendments reverses the ruling in Cooter & Gell v. Hartmarx Corp., 496 U.S. 384, 110 S.Ct. 2447, 110 L.Ed.2d 359 (1990) that a plaintiff's voluntary dismissal of a challenged complaint did not prevent later Rule 11 sanctions.

27. Ridder v. City of Springfield, 109 F.3d 288 (6th Cir.1997).

28. Fed. R. Civ. P. 11(c)(1)(B). The court may not award attorney fees on its own initiative, and may not impose any monetary sanctions on its own initiative unless it issues an order to show cause before any settlement of the case. Fed. R. Civ. P. 11(c)(2).

29. Fed. R. Civ. P. (c). On the pre–1993 situation, *see* Nelkin, Sanctions Under Amended Fed. R. Civ. P. 11—Some "Chilling" Problems in the Struggle Between Compensation and Punishment, 74 Geo. L.J. 1313 (1986).

30. 15 U.S.C. §§ 77z–1(c), 78u–4(c).

31. Cooter & Gell v. Hartmarx Corp., 496 U.S. 384, 110 S.Ct. 2447, 110 L.Ed.2d 359 (1990); Hughes v. City of Fort Collins, 926 F.2d 986 (10th Cir.1991). On sanctions generally, *see* Note, Plausible Pleadings: Developing Standards for Rule 11 Sanctions, 100 Harv. L. Rev. 630 (1987).

32. Hughes v. City of Fort Collins, 926 F.2d 986 (10th Cir.1991).

33. Fed. R. Civ. P. 11(c).

manding the offender, requiring a lawyer to participate in educational programs (a terrifying punishment indeed), or referring the matter to bar disciplinary authorities. Although the court may require the offender to pay the opposing party the attorney fees and other litigation expenses that party incurred as a result of the violation, the 1993 amendments allow that sanction only when "warranted for effective deterrence," so that fines payable into court appear to be the preferred monetary sanction.[34] The authors of the amendments list many factors relevant to the choice of sanction: "whether the improper conduct was willful, or negligent; whether it was part of a pattern of activity ... ; whether it infected the entire pleading ... ; whether the person has engaged in similar conduct in other litigation; whether it was intended to injure; what effect it had on the litigation ...; what amount, given the financial resources of the responsible person, is needed to deter that person from repetition ... ; what amount is needed to deter similar activity by other litigants."[35]

Who may be sanctioned

The court may also have to decide who should receive the sanction. Rule 11 now applies to a lawyer or unrepresented party who presents a paper to the court, "whether by signing, filing, submitting, or later advocating" it.[36] A replacement lawyer may thus be punished for advocating a baseless complaint filed by a previous lawyer, for example if the new lawyer continues to press the claim.[37] A law firm may be sanctioned, absent exceptional circumstances, for misconduct of its lawyers or employees, thus providing a new way to collect monetary sanctions and to press firms to institute proper internal procedures ensuring ethical conduct.[38]

The Rule is not limited to lawyers: parties that violate it "or are responsible for the violation" may be sanctioned.[39] How is a court to choose whether to sanction lawyer or client? To determine which was "responsible" may require an elaborate evidentiary hearing, likely to invade the confidentiality of client-lawyer communications and to create

34. Fed. R. Civ. P. 11(c)(2) and Advisory Committee Notes (1993); Parness, Fines Under New Federal Civil Rule 11: The New Monetary Sanctions for the "Stop-and-Think-Again" Rule, 1993 B.Y.U. L. Rev. 879 (1993). For limits on monetary sanctions, *see* nn. 28, 30 *supra*.

35. Fed. R. Civ. P. 11 Advisory Committee Notes (1993).

36. Fed. R. Civ. P. 11(b).

37. Turner v. Sungard Business Systems, Inc., 91 F.3d 1418 (11th Cir.1996). *Compare* O'Brien v. Alexander, 101 F.3d 1479 (2d Cir.1996)(oral statement in pretrial conference not sanctionable just because it advances contention also found in previous paper).

38. Fed. R. Civ. P. 11(c)(1)(A); *see* Schneyer, Professional Discipline for Law Firms, 77 Cornell L. Rev. 1 (1991). The 1993 amendments thus changed the result in Pavelic & LeFlore v. Marvel Entertainment Group, 493 U.S. 120, 110 S.Ct. 456, 107 L.Ed.2d 438 (1989)(firm may not be sanctioned).

39. Fed. R. Civ. P. 11(c); *cf.* Business Guides, Inc. v. Chromatic Communications Enterprises, Inc., 498 U.S. 533, 111 S.Ct. 922, 112 L.Ed.2d 1140 (1991)(upholding sanctions under pre-1993 Rule 11 against represented party that signed paper).

conflicts of interest for the lawyer by pitting lawyer against client. Sanctioning the lawyer is most likely to deter violations, since lawyers are "repeat players" and are, or should be, familiar with Rule 11's requirements; but perhaps the deterrence will be excessive, frightening lawyers from pressing legitimate contentions for fear of punishment.

In general, courts have responded to this dilemma by assessing the responsibility of clients and lawyers on the basis of apparent facts, without conducting factual inquiries. Rule 11 itself provides that monetary sanctions may not be awarded against a represented party when the basis of the sanction is advancing a claim or defense unwarranted by law. This reflects the view that the lawyer, not the client, is expected to know the law, and to refuse client demands to proceed when there is no legal warrant. On the other hand, a client who backed up false factual allegations with false testimony is clearly subject to sanction.[40] It is conceivable that whoever is sanctioned will be able to shift the sanction to the person truly responsible in another proceeding, a client by suing its lawyer for malpractice, or a lawyer who is free from blame by claiming indemnity from the client.[41]

The harshest way to sanction a party is by dismissal of plaintiff's action or preclusion of defendant's defense. Before using such an extreme sanction, however, a judge should attempt to inquire into the reasons for the violations and consider lesser sanctions. "Consideration of fair play may dictate that courts eschew the harshest sanctions ... where failure to comply is due to a mere oversight of counsel amounting to no more than simple negligence." But where gross professional negligence has been found, "the full range of sanctions may be marshalled."[42]

Beyond the Rule

Notwithstanding the considerable sanctioning power in Rule 11, the courts are not limited to the Rule when improper conduct occurs in the course of litigation. A statute authorizes the courts to require a lawyer who "multiplies the proceedings in any case unreasonably and vexatiously" to pay the attorney fees and other expenses that the lawyer's misconduct caused the opposing party.[43] The courts also have inherent power to impose sanctions, including an assessment of legal fees, for

40. Fed. R. Civ. P. 11(c)(2)(A); Union Planters Bank v. L & J Development Co., 115 F.3d 378 (6th Cir.1997); White v. General Motors Corp., 908 F.2d 675 (10th Cir. 1990).

41. *See* Restatement of the Law Governing Lawyers § 17(2).

42. Cine Forty–Second Street Theatre Corp. v. Allied Artists Pictures Corp., 602 F.2d 1062, 1068 (2d Cir.1979); *see* Shea v. Donohoe Constr. Co., 795 F.2d 1071 (D.C.Cir.1986).

43. 28 U.S.C. § 1927. On the disputed question whether bad faith conduct is a prerequisite to sanctions under this statute, *see, e.g.,* LaPrade, Liddle & Robinson v. Kidder Peabody & Co., 146 F.3d 899 (D.C.Cir.1998); In re 60 East 80th Street Equities, Inc., 218 F.3d 109 (2d Cir.2000).

abuse of the legal process. In *Chambers v. NASCO, Inc.*[44] an owner of a television station agreed to sell it to plaintiff NASCO and then, changing his mind, tried to frustrate the sale by engaging in a series of fraudulent maneuvers in federal court and before regulatory agencies. These acts included both fraudulent behavior out of court and filing of false pleadings and motions. The Court held that the district court had inherent power to sanction both categories of misconduct.

The Court stated that in "narrowly defined circumstances"[45] courts may assess attorney's fees against counsel, even though normally the "American Rule" prohibits fee-shifting.[46] When a party has acted oppressively or in bad faith, the attorney's fees may be assessed against the offending party.[47] However, "when there is bad-faith conduct in the course of litigation that could be adequately sanctioned under the Federal Rules of Civil Procedure, the court ordinarily should rely on the Rules rather than the inherent power."[48]

In the state courts, many states have adopted Rule 11 in either the 1983 or the 1993 version, and a few also make parties that litigate in bad faith pay attorney fees.[49] Some states still require certain pleadings to be verified under oath.[50] And lawyers should not forget that they are subject to professional discipline for asserting frivolous claims or defenses as well as for dilatory practices.[51]

§ 3.14 Miscellaneous Pleading Rules

Code pleading had many auxiliary rules, now obsolete in all but a few jurisdictions. A brief review of them suggests that the imprecision inherent in federal rules pleading is preferable to striving for impracticable precision.

One restriction under code pleading was that "argumentative" allegations were not permitted; this merely became an exercise in semantical distinction between an argument and an assertion.[1] Another

44. 501 U.S. 32, 111 S.Ct. 2123, 115 L.Ed.2d 27 (1991).

45. Roadway Express v. Piper, 447 U.S. 752, 100 S.Ct. 2455, 65 L.Ed.2d 488 (1980).

46. *See* § 1.22 *supra.*

47. Newman v. Piggie Park Enters., 390 U.S. 400, 88 S.Ct. 964, 19 L.Ed.2d 1263 (1968); Universal Oil Prods. Co. v. Roof Ref. Co., 328 U.S. 575, 66 S.Ct. 1176, 90 L.Ed. 1447 (1946).

48. Chambers v. NASCO, Inc., 501 U.S. 32, 111 S.Ct. 2123, 2136, 115 L.Ed.2d 27, 34–35 (1991).

49. *E.g.,* N.Y. CPLR 8303–a; *see* Hess, Rule 11 Practice in Federal and State Court: An Empirical, Comparative Study, 75 Marquette L. Rev. 313 (1992); 1 Mallen & Smith, Legal Malpractice § 10.13 (4th ed. 1996). In some states, concern about defamation suits brought by developers to silence their opponents has led to special legislation. *E.g.,* Calif. Code Civ. P. § 425.16; Pring & Canan, SLAPPs: Getting Sued for Speaking Out (1996).

50. *E.g.,* Calif. C. Civ. P. § 446; Pa. R. Civ. P. 1024. For verification in federal court shareholder derivative suits, *see* Fed. R. Civ. P. 23.1; Surowitz v. Hilton Hotels Corp., 383 U.S. 363, 86 S.Ct. 845, 15 L.Ed.2d 807 (1966).

51. ABA Model Rules of Professional Conduct, rules 3.1, 3.2; *see* Vairo, Rule 11 and the Profession, 67 Fordham L. Rev. 589 (1998).

§ 3.14

1. Under the Federal Rules an argumentative pleading was upheld in Kuenzell v. United States, 20 F.R.D. 96 (N.D.Cal. 1957).

rule precluded the "negative pregnant"—a denial that was so phrased as to be unintentionally infused with affirmative implications—under the rule that an admission in a pleading is construed most strongly against the pleader.[2] Thus, a denial of the allegation that "defendant struck and killed *A*" could be construed as an admission that defendant either struck *A* or killed *A*. There was a requirement of internal consistency, a holdover from the days when it was thought necessary to produce a single issue.[3] On this basis, inconsistent, alternative, and hypothetical pleadings were disallowed, even when plaintiff could not know the precise detail in question. The Federal Rules now explicitly allow alternative allegation.[4] Under the "theory of the pleadings" doctrine, the court had to "decide with certainty what the specific cause of action counted and relied upon" in the complaint was[5] and then confined the plaintiff to recovery under that single theory[6] without regard to the larger question of the merits of the plaintiff's case.[7] Code pleadings were "construed most strongly against the pleader," an onerous burden later repudiated by the Federal Rules.[8]

The Federal Rules opt for a looser construction of the pleadings at the expense of precision. Moreover, the doctrine of aider—that a defective pleading could be "aided" by having its deficiency remedied by matter in an opponent's pleading—is built into Rule 15(b), which allows liberal amendment of pleadings "even after judgment" and provides that "[w]hen issues not raised by the pleadings are tried by express or implied consent of the parties, they shall be treated in all respects as if they had been raised in the pleadings."

C. PLEADING SPECIFIC CLAIMS

Pleading a claim involves, as we have seen, analyzing the substantive legal rules governing the matter sued on, dissecting those rules into factual elements, and describing the facts of the specific transaction in terms of those elements. In selecting the elements to be described, consideration also has to be given to the rules of allocation according to which a specific element properly is either part of the claim or a matter to be raised, if at all, by affirmative defense.

There are as many variations of pleadings as there are legally enforceable obligations—negligence, breach of contract, interference

2. Clark, Code Pleading 588–591 (2d ed. 1947); Shipman, Common Law Pleading 251 (3d ed. 1923); Byard v. Holmes, 34 N.J.L. 296 (1870).

3. *See* James, Objective and Function of the Complaint, 14 Vand. L. Rev. 899, 902–903 (1961).

4. Fed. R. Civ. P. 8(e)(2).

5. Kewaunee County Supervisors v. Decker, 30 Wis. 624, 633 (1872).

6. *See* Albertsworth, The Theory of Pleading in Code States, 10 Calif. L. Rev. 202 (1922); Page, Application of the Derogation Rule to the Code of Civil Procedure, 1955 Wis. L. Rev. 91; Whittier, The Theory of a Pleading, 8 Colum. L. Rev. 523 (1908).

7. *See* James, The Revival of Bills of Particulars Under the Federal Rules, 71 Harv. L. Rev. 1473, 1481–1485 (1958).

8. Clark, Code Pleading § 42 and p. 589 (2d ed. 1947); Fed. R. Civ. P. 8(f).

with property, invasion of privacy, failure to pay taxes, and so on. Their general structure, however, is the same: (1) a description of the relationship or situation of plaintiff and defendant, with respect to which the law creates a duty in defendant; (2) a description of the conduct of the defendant, which the law proscribes as a violation of the duty; (3) the consequences to plaintiff resulting from defendant's conduct that the law recognizes as compensable or justifying other redress (such as injunctive relief); and (4) a demand or prayer for relief. This general structure is illustrated in the pleading of claims for negligence and for breach of contract, which are considered later in this chapter. The Forms that accompany the Federal Rules provide other examples.

§ 3.15 Civil Rights Actions

A plaintiff who believes that a government officer or municipality violated the plaintiff's constitutional rights may seek damages in federal court.[1] These "civil rights act" or "Constitutional tort" actions arise from such alleged misconduct as police brutality, discharge of governmental employees for exercising free speech, and unlawful discrimination.

During the 1980s, many federal courts started to require "heightened pleading" providing factual particularity in these constitutional tort suits.[2] These holdings, which lacked any basis in the language of the Federal Rules, were apparently based on the perception of appellate judges that the federal judges faced an explosion of civil rights claims, most of them baseless. In fact, there has been an increase in constitutional tort claims but no explosion, and (if one leaves out claims brought by prisoners who lack lawyers) these claims are often successful, although less so than other civil actions.[3]

Assuming that the number of baseless civil rights claim does constitute a problem, it is far from clear that requiring more detailed pleadings can solve it. Experience with code pleading indicated that calling for factual detail is less likely to filter out weak claims than to multiply pleading disputes and penalize plaintiffs with less skilled lawyers. Sometimes, even an able pleader cannot provide detail because the defendants control access to significant information, perhaps even the names of the misbehaving officials.[4] It was for just such reasons as these that the drafters of the Federal Rules relied on discovery and summary judgment rather than pleadings to sort out those claims that should go to trial.

§ 3.15

1. 42 U.S.C. § 1983; Bivens v. Six Unknown Named Agents, 403 U.S. 388, 91 S.Ct. 1999, 29 L.Ed.2d 619 (1971); *see generally* Eisenberg, Civil Rights Legislation (4th ed. 1996); Chemerinsky, Federal Jurisdiction (3d ed. 1999).

2. Marcus, The Revival of Fact Pleading Under the Federal Rules of Civil Procedure, 86 Colum. L. Rev. 433 (1986).

3. Eisenberg & Schwab, What Shapes Perception of the Federal Court System?, 56 U. Chi. L. Rev. 501 (1989).

4. *See* § 4.23 *infra*.

When it comes to complaints filed by unrepresented prisoners, the same lack of lawyers which makes it likely that many baseless claims will be filed, also makes pleading requirements less effective. Many prisoners lacking lawyers cannot be expected to produce quality legal drafting. Dismissing the complaints of those who cannot will exclude both bad and good claims. There are other ways besides pleading of dealing with the problem such as providing lawyers or paralegal advisers, asking plaintiffs to respond to questionnaires, and hearings at prisons. Congress has endorsed at least the last of these, as well as some less desirable methods of handling prisoner litigation.[5]

The Supreme Court rejected heightened pleading in *Leatherman v. Tarrant County Narcotics Intelligence and Coordination Unit*,[6] but limited its holding to cases in which the defendant was a municipality, not an individual official. Some but not all lower courts have therefore continued to demand particularized factual allegations in civil rights suits against individuals.[7]

Meanwhile, the focus of concern in constitutional tort cases has shifted to the qualified immunity defense that exempts government officials from damages liability if "their conduct does not violate clearly established statutory or constitutional rights of which a reasonable person would have known" at the time the official acted.[8] Qualified immunity is a defense that the defendant must plead and prove.[9] But the Supreme Court also views the defense as protecting defendants, not just from losing at trial, but from having to defend suits falling within its scope. Thus, a defendant may appeal immediately from a trial court ruling rejecting the defense without waiting for the action to come to an end.[10]

How can defendants be protected from litigating, when deciding whether they are entitled to protection itself requires litigation? The best solution in most cases is encouraging early motions for summary judgment on the qualified immunity issue. Some courts have tried to push up the decision even earlier by calling on the trial court to use its discretion to require the plaintiff to file a detailed reply when the

5. Prison Litigation Reform Act, Pub.L. No. 104–134, 110 Stat. 1321 (1996); *see* Rules Governing Section 2254 Cases in the United States District Court, Appendix of Forms (standard forms for habeas corpus petitions); Comment, Inmates' Civil Rights Cases and the Federal Courts, 28 Creighton L. Rev. 1255 (1995).

6. 507 U.S. 163, 113 S.Ct. 1160, 122 L.Ed.2d 517 (1993).

7. Veney v. Hogan, 70 F.3d 917 (6th Cir.1995); Breidenbach v. Bolish, 126 F.3d 1288 (10th Cir.1997); Moore v. Agency for Int'l Development, 994 F.2d 874 (D.C.Cir. 1993). *Contra*, Castro v. United States, 34 F.3d 106 (2d Cir.1994); Payton v. Rush–Presbyterian–St. Luke's Medical Center, 184 F.3d 623 (7th Cir.1999).

8. Harlow v. Fitzgerald, 457 U.S. 800, 102 S.Ct. 2727, 73 L.Ed.2d 396 (1982).

9. Gomez v. Toledo, 446 U.S. 635, 100 S.Ct. 1920, 64 L.Ed.2d 572 (1980); Crawford–El v. Britton, 523 U.S. 574, 118 S.Ct. 1584, 140 L.Ed.2d 759 (1998).

10. Johnson v. Jones, 515 U.S. 304, 115 S.Ct. 2151, 132 L.Ed.2d 238 (1995); *see* § 12.4 *infra*.

defendant's answer raises the qualified immunity defense.[11] Granted the nature of the defense, such a reply will typically have to set forth the factual basis of the plaintiff's claim, so that it can be ascertained whether the defendant's alleged conduct violated rights that were clearly established when the defendant acted. Requiring the plaintiff to file a detailed reply is hence very like requiring a detailed complaint to begin with, except for being more roundabout. The major difference is that the judge has discretion to require a reply only in those cases in which it is likely that more detail will enable the court to dispose of the case immediately.

§ 3.16 Negligence

The elements of a cause of action or claim for negligence are as follows: (1) a duty to use care must be owed by defendant to plaintiff; (2) there must be a breach of that duty; (3) that breach must be a proximate cause of (4) injury to plaintiff.[1] In general, the plaintiff must include each of these elements in the complaint. A few states also require plaintiffs in negligence cases to allege their own freedom from contributory negligence.

Breach of duty

The principal problem in the pleading of negligence cases concerns the degree of detail or specificity required in the complaint, particularly in pleading defendant's breach of duty. Special problems also arise when breach of a statute, ordinance, or regulation is involved, when custom or usage is relied on, and when last clear chance or *res ipsa loquitur* is claimed as applicable.[2]

Two lines of doctrine developed about pleading in negligence cases. One permitted a plaintiff to describe in general terms the defendant's conduct that caused the injury and to characterize it as negligent or negligently done. This was the method of pleading at common law[3] and seems to have been what the framers of the original codes had in mind.[4]

11. Schultea v. Wood, 47 F.3d 1427 (5th Cir.1995); *see* Fed. R. Civ. P. 7(a); § 4.9 *infra*. Crawford–El v. Britton, 523 U.S. 574, 118 S.Ct. 1584, 140 L.Ed.2d 759 (1998) endorses requiring a reply as one of the court's options.

§ 3.16

1. Kovack, Problems of Plaintiff in Pleading Negligence, 23 Ohio St. L.J. 435 (1962); Prosser and Keeton, Torts 30 (5th ed. 1984). *Compare* Restatement (Second) of Torts § 281.

2. *See* 2 Harper, James, and Gray, Law of Torts §§ 19.5 *et seq.*, 21.0 *et seq.* (2d ed. 1986).

3. Williams v. Holland, 10 Bing. 112, 131 Eng. Rep. 848 (C.P. 1833); Clark, Code Pleading 300 (2d ed. 1947).

The point of view of the general pleaders is expressed, *e.g.*, in 2A Moore, Federal Practice and Procedure ¶¶ 8.02–8.05, 8.12, 8.13; Kovack, Problems of Plaintiff in Pleading Negligence, 23 Ohio St. L.J. 435 (1962).

4. *See* § 3.7 *supra;* Davis v. Guarnieri, 45 Ohio St. 470, 15 N.E. 350 (1887); James, The Objective and Function of the Complaint: Common Law—Codes—Federal Rules, 14 Vand. L. Rev. 899, 914 (1961); Kovack, Problems of Plaintiff in Pleading Negligence, 23 Ohio St. L.J. 435, 439–440 (1962).

It is also the method permitted by the Federal Rules and their state counterparts. An example of this type of pleading is found in Form 9, which is prescribed by the Federal Rules: "On June 1, 1936, in a public highway called Boylston Street in Boston, Massachusetts, defendant negligently drove a motor vehicle against plaintiff who was then crossing said highway." This is sometimes referred to as pleading negligence generally.

The other line of code pleading doctrine required the setting out of the specific acts and omissions claimed to constitute negligence. A good example of the kind of detail required under some interpretations of code pleading rules is described in a Wyoming case:

> Plaintiff was charged with "specific acts and omissions, namely: 1. Failing to keep the truck under control; 2. Operating the truck when its brakes were not in good working order; 3. Failing to keep a proper lookout; 4. Driving the truck onto the pedestrian sidewalk and colliding with plaintiff; 5. Failing to give any warning that the truck was out of control; 6. Failing to turn the truck to right or left so as to avoid colliding with plaintiff; 7. Failing to maintain and keep the truck's brakes in proper mechanical condition; 8. Failing to inspect the truck and determine if the brakes were in good condition."[5]

Causation

Causation may be alleged by a simple statement that defendant's negligence caused or was the cause of plaintiff's injury. This clearly is enough where plaintiff complains of bodily injury or property damage caused in a highway accident. Thus, Form 9 under the Federal Rules, after describing defendant's negligent driving of a motor vehicle against the plaintiff, continues: "As a result plaintiff was thrown down and had his leg broken and was otherwise injured. . . . " In many jurisdictions, it is conventional to use the term "proximate" before "cause" or "result." In other situations, however, the court may have more trouble in accepting the causal connection as a likely explanation of what happened and may insist on greater detail about how defendant's conduct brought about the injury.[6]

Injury

Under the substantive law, negligence is actionable only when it causes actual injury.[7] Pleading injury is not difficult: "bodily harm, emotional suffering, and loss of income," for example, will suffice.

5. McClanahan v. Woodward Construction Co., 77 Wyo. 362, 371, 316 P.2d 337, 339 (1957), *discussed in* Note, 12 Wyo. L.J. 257, 259 (1958).

6. *Cf.* Restatement (Second) of Torts §§ 430 *et seq.*

7. Johnson v. United States, 547 F.2d 688 (D.C.Cir.1976). *Compare* Brown v. Merrow Mach. Co., 411 F.Supp. 1162 (D.Conn. 1976), *with* Bowdach v. Frontierland, Inc., 347 F.Supp. 237 (W.D.N.C.1972).

Problems may develop, however, over the kinds of damages that may be shown under the allegations of injury, particularly over the distinction between "general" and "special" damages. This question is taken up in connection with the rules for pleading damages in contract cases.[8]

§ 3.17 Contributory Negligence

Burden on defendant

At common law, and still in some American states, a plaintiff's contributory negligence bars all recovery in an action for damages caused by defendant's negligence.[1] In an increasing number of jurisdictions, contributory negligence merely reduces the plaintiff's damages.[2] In either event, the question arises as to who has the burden of pleading on this issue. The older rule put the burden on plaintiffs to plead (and also to prove) their freedom from contributory negligence.[3] This pleading burden was sometimes held to be satisfied by an allegation that defendant's negligence was the proximate cause of plaintiff's injury.[4] The prevailing rule today puts the burden on defendants to plead contributory negligence as an affirmative defense or mitigation of damages if they would inject the issue into the case.

Rule 8(c)

The situation in the federal courts, in diversity cases, is somewhat complicated. Rule 8(c) requires that contributory negligence be pleaded as an affirmative defense. But the principle of *Erie Railroad Co. v. Tompkins*[5] requires the federal courts, in adjudicating claims based on state law, to follow applicable state law in allocating the burdens of proof on the issue of contributory negligence.[6] Most states put the burdens of both pleading and proof on defendant so that Rule 8(c) poses no problem in most cases. But when the applicable state rule puts these burdens on plaintiff, what happens to Rule 8(c)? There are three possibilities. Rule 8(c) might have been construed to make the whole matter procedural so that federal law governed throughout. Rule 8(c) might have been construed to govern only the procedural pleading burden, leaving the burden of proof to be governed by state law. Or Rule 8(c) might have been found invalid under *Erie* in states whose pleading rule differs from the Federal Rule.

Diversity cases

8. *See* § 3.22 *infra.*

§ 3.17

1. Restatement (Second) of Torts § 467.

2. *See* Schwartz, Comparative Negligence (1974); Annot., 32 A.L.R.3d 463.

3. *See* Clark, Code Pleading 303 *et seq.* (2d ed. 1947).

4. *See* 2 Harper, James, and Gray, Law of Torts §§ 22.1, 22.2 (2d ed. 1986).

5. 304 U.S. 64, 58 S.Ct. 817, 82 L.Ed. 1188 (1938).

6. Palmer v. Hoffman, 318 U.S. 109, 63 S.Ct. 477, 87 L.Ed. 645 (1943); Sampson v. Channell, 110 F.2d 754 (1st Cir.), *cert. denied,* 310 U.S. 650, 60 S.Ct. 1099, 84 L.Ed. 1415 (1940).

It is defensible to say that the entire problem—burden of proof as well as burden of pleading—is procedural for the purposes of *Erie*. Pleading rules are surely "merely procedural" in some sense; they certainly do not govern the parties' out-of-court conduct. If, however, the federal courts must apply state law when the "outcome" of the litigation will be affected, then the burden of proof rule is "substantial" and state law would have to apply.[7] In *Palmer v. Hoffman*,[8] for example, the Court held that the burden of pleading was validly governed by Rule 8(c) but the burden of proof in diversity cases was determined by state law. Some authorities, notably Professor Moore, have argued that, given the decision in *Palmer v. Hoffman*, Rule 8(c) should be regarded as invalid in diversity cases.[9] According to his analysis, the pleading rule exists only to guide the allocation of burden of proof, and if definitive guidance as to the latter is provided by state law then there is no point in enforcing a discrepant pleading rule. Nonetheless, Rule 8(c) still stands in diversity cases and requires defendant to plead contributory negligence in all cases.[10]

§ 3.18 Pleading Law

The rules of pleading do not call for the pleading of law. Indeed, theoretically pleading of law is positively inappropriate—even though reference in a pleading to the law the pleader has in mind would often clarify not only the legal questions but also the pleader's factual contentions. Rather, a court is apprised of the applicable law by "judicial notice"—the court's taking notice of the law as a universally known event rather than a matter to be proved. Nevertheless, law is sometimes pleaded.

The usual practice in federal court is to plead the specific statutory or constitutional provisions relied on in a "federal claim" action.[1] Such references to the legal basis of the claim are required in the jurisdictional allegations in a federal court action based on federal law.[2] But it is common practice to include them in the statement of claim itself. A similar practice, sometimes obligatory, is followed in state courts in actions based on statutes.[3] Moreover, when the provisions of law in question are not judicially noticeable, they must be pleaded as facts. This is often true of domestic private laws and is generally true of municipal

7. *See* § 2.37 *supra*.

8. 318 U.S. 109, 63 S.Ct. 477, 87 L.Ed. 645 (1943).

9. 2A Moore, Federal Practice and Procedure ¶ 8.27[2]. *See* Sundstrand Corp. v. Standard Kollsman Indus., 488 F.2d 807 (7th Cir.1973).

10. *See* 5 Wright and Miller, Federal Practice and Procedure § 1272. The cases, however, are not so clear. *Compare* Sundstrand Corp. v. Standard Kollsman Indus., 488 F.2d 807 (7th Cir.1973), *with* Glass Containers Corp. v. Miller Brewing Co., 643 F.2d 308 (5th Cir.1981).

§ 3.18

1. *See* § 3.25 *infra*.

2. *See* Fed. R. Civ. P. 8(a).

3. *See* § 3.24 *infra*.

or local ordinances, administrative agency regulations, and the laws of foreign countries.[4]

Federal Rule 44.1 requires that "a party who intends to raise an issue concerning the law of a foreign country shall give notice by pleadings or other reasonable written notice."[5] Some states require the law of foreign countries to be specifically pleaded.[6]

§ 3.19 Pleading Fraud and Other Intentional Torts

Fraud

Greater specificity was required at common law in pleading a charge of fraud than in pleading negligence or assault and battery.[1] This requirement of specificity also holds under the codes[2] and the Federal Rules, presumably to prevent plaintiffs from stating a claim just by adding the word "fraudulently" to a description of a financial transaction.[3] The plaintiff's pleading of such a claim must cover the elements described below.[4]

1. The statement complained of, either verbatim or according to its substance,[5] and the falsity of the statement. The older cases held a blanket statement of falsity defective as a mere conclusion of law and required an allegation of the particular respects in which the statement was false, but this is no longer required.[6] It is required, however, that

4. *See* Cleary et al., McCormick on Evidence § 335 (4th ed. 1999). The Federal Register Act, 44 U.S.C. § 1505, provides for the publication of proclamations, executive orders, and federal administrative regulations; it also provides that "[t]he contents of the Federal Register shall be judicially noticed." *Id.* § 1507. For the effect of this statute in state courts, *see, e.g.,* Mortenson v. McCredie, 1 Ill.App.2d 455, 117 N.E.2d 840 (1954) (federal rent regulations need not be pleaded); Mastrullo v. Ryan, 328 Mass. 621, 105 N.E.2d 469 (1952).

5. *See* Morentin, Failure to Prove Foreign Law in U.S. Courts, 1988 Ariz. J. Intl. & Comp. L. 228; Brown, 44.1 Ways to Prove Foreign Law, 9 Mar. L. 179 (1984).

6. *See* Schlesinger Damaska & Herzon, Comparative Law 108–109 (5th ed. 1988).

§ 3.19

1. Shipman, Common Law Pleading 222 (3d ed. 1923). *See also* Richman, Lively, and Mell, The Pleading of Fraud: Rhymes Without Reason, 60 S. Cal. L. Rev. 959 (1987).

2. Clark, Code Pleading § 48 (2d ed. 1947).

3. Fed. R. Civ. P. 9(b) provides that "[i]n all averments of fraud or mistake, the circumstances constituting fraud or mistake shall be stated with particularity"; Semegen v. Weidner, 780 F.2d 727 (9th Cir. 1985). *See also* Yost v. General Motors Corp., 651 F.Supp. 656 (D.N.J.1986) (holding that because fraud is a conclusion of law, it may not be charged in general terms).

4. *See* 5 Wright and Miller, Federal Practice and Procedure § 1297. *Compare* Pace v. Parrish, 122 Utah 141, 247 P.2d 273 (1952).

5. When the action is based on a simple statement or set of statements, it should be set forth substantially as allegedly uttered. When the action is based on a complicated set of transactions, the requirement of particularity is modified by the general requirement that the pleading be "short and plain" so that all the details of a "fraudulent scheme" need not be alleged. *See, e.g.,* Schlick v. Penn–Dixie Cement Corp., 507 F.2d 374 (2d Cir.1974). *But see* Smith v. Central Soya of Athens, Inc., 604 F.Supp. 518 (D.N.C.1985) (holding that an allegation of fraud must state with particularity the time, place, and content of the false representation; a mere conclusory allegation of fraud is insufficient).

6. *See, e.g.,* Byard v. Holmes, 34 N.J.L. 296 (1870). Contrast the modern approach, *e.g.,* Scervini v. Miles Laboratories, 11

the circumstances described in the complaint show that the statement is one of material fact rather than the kind of opinion or prophecy on which people are not entitled to rely.[7]

2. Knowledge by defendant of the falsity of the statement—*scienter*. This is required by the substantive law of fraud in most jurisdictions[8] in an action for damages for fraud. It is not always required when rescission is sought.[9] When it is required, a simple statement of defendant's knowledge of the falsity should satisfy the pleading requirement.[10]

3. Defendant's intent or circumstances indicating that the statement be relied on by plaintiff or by a class of persons that includes plaintiff.[11]

4. Plaintiff's actual reliance on the statement.[12]

5. Plaintiff's damage.[13]

When fraud claims are brought under state law in a federal complaint, the Federal Rules govern the degree of particularity with which the fraud must be alleged in the complaint.[14]

Securities fraud

As private suits for securities fraud burgeoned, courts elaborated these pleading requirements in an attempt to bar baseless claims at the outset. Class actions have been the main targets of such rulings. The rationale is that the incentives these actions offer to plaintiffs' lawyers, and the pressure on defendants to settle to avoid huge liabilities, result in the filing of class actions whenever a corporation's stock price suffers an unexpected downturn, actions brought in the hope that discovery will reveal plausible fraud claims. The proponents of securities fraud class actions reply that they keep the financial markets honest by sanctioning nondisclosures that corporate executives would otherwise find too tempting.[15]

F.R.D. 542 (S.D.N.Y.1951) (allegation that statements "were false and without basis in law or fact," held sufficient).

7. *See* Restatement (Second) of Torts §§ 538A, 539; 2 Restatement (Second) of Contracts §§ 168–171. *See also* 2 Harper, James, and Gray, Law of Torts § 7.9 (2d ed. 1986).

8. *See* Hill, Damages for Innocent Misrepresentation, 73 Colum. L. Rev. 679 (1973), 74 Colum. L. Rev. 40 (1974).

9. *See* Restatement (Second) of Contracts § 164.

10. Fed. R. Civ. P. 9(b) provides that "knowledge ... may be averred generally."

11. *E.g.*, Lowenschuss v. Kane, 520 F.2d 255 (2d Cir.1975); Prosser and Keeton, Torts § 107 (5th ed. 1984).

12. 1 Harper, James, and Gray, Law of Torts § 7.13 (2d ed. 1986); Prosser and Keeton, Torts § 108 (5th ed. 1984).

13. 1 Harper, James, and Gray, Law of Torts § 7.15 (2d ed. 1986); Prosser and Keeton, Torts § 110 (5th ed. 1984).

14. Stern v. General Elec. Co., 924 F.2d 472 (2d Cir.1991).

15. *E.g.*, DiLeo v. Ernst & Young, 901 F.2d 624 (7th Cir.1990); Semerenko v. Cendant Corp., 216 F.3d 315 (3d Cir.2000); *see generally* Yablon, A Dangerous Supplement: Longshot Claims and Private Securities Litigation, 94 Nw. U. L. Rev. 567 (2000).

Congress has endorsed heightened pleading requirements in securities fraud actions by requiring that the complaint "state with particularity facts giving rise to a strong inference that the defendant acted with the required state of mind." A plaintiff pleading on the basis of information and belief must likewise specify with particularity the information on which the belief is grounded.[16] These provisions apply to all securities fraud actions, both class actions and others. They form just one part of the Private Securities Litigation Reform Act of 1995, which also imposed discovery limitations, a stronger version of Rule 11, and measures intended to ensure better class representation and limit attorney fees. In 1998, Congress responded to assertions that plaintiffs and their lawyers were filing state law fraud actions in state courts in order to avoid the 1995 Act; the new legislation pre-empted a broad range of class actions under state law.[17] These statutes mark a step away from two Federal Rules ideals: a single procedural system for all claims, and rejection of detailed pleading as a means to filter out bad claims.

It seems unlikely that the new legislation will cause claims to be dismissed because plaintiffs' lawyers lack pleading skills. The great incentives that damages class actions offer lawyers, and the prevalence of multiple filings by competing lawyers, make it likely that at least one set of able and motivated lawyers will assert any plausible claim. Indeed, since the passage of the 1995 Act, the number of federal securities class actions filed has substantially increased.[18]

The more serious problem that the 1995 Act creates results from its combination of heightened pleading requirements and stringent restrictions on conducting discovery before challenges to the pleadings have been resolved. The result is that plaintiffs must have fairly detailed information about the fraud before they file suit, and cannot simply rely on discovery.[19] It remains to be seen whether these requirements will prevent baseless claims as their supporters argue, prevent meritorious claims as their opponents argue, or simply add one more stage of procedural maneuvering at the outset of securities fraud class actions.

Other intentional torts

As for pleading requirements for intentional torts other than fraud, these are in general similar to those for fraud: greater specificity is required than in pleading a negligence claim. Although the defendant's

16. 15 U.S.C. §§ 78u–4(b). On conflicting readings of these provisions, *see* Novak v. Kasaks, 216 F.3d 300 (2d Cir.2000). On pleading on information and belief, *see* § 3.13 *supra*.

17. Private Securities Litigation Reform Act of 1995, Pub.L. No. 104–67, 109 Stat. 737 (1995); Securities Litigation Uniform Standards Act of 1998, Pub.L. No. 105–353, 112 Stat. 3227 (1998).

18. Caseload statistics may be found at securities.stanford.edu.

19. 15 U.S.C. §§ 77z–1(b), 78u–4(b)(3); Weiss & Moser, Enter Yossarian: How to Resolve the Procedural Catch–22 That the Private Securities Litigation Reform Act Creates, 76 Wash. U.L.Q. 457 (1998).

mental state may be alleged through the general and conclusory term "maliciously," usually there must be allegations of the circumstances from which the inference can be drawn that the defendant lacked justification for the course of conduct complained of in the statement.[20]

§ 3.20 Pleading in Contract Cases

Substantive elements

The elements of a cause of action or claim for breach of contract are as follows: (1) a contract or agreement involving a quid pro quo (or the presence of some other factor that under substantive law makes an agreement binding), (2) performance by plaintiff of all conditions precedent, and (3) breach of the contract by defendant.[1] Actual damage caused by breach of contract may not be an essential element of a claim,[2] but the injuries suffered should be pleaded.[3]

The common law gave the pleader an option to plead the agreement either verbatim or according to its legal effect, that is, by stating in conclusory terms the obligation assumed by defendant under the contract.[4] Under code pleading a third option came to be used: attaching a copy of the contract to the complaint and incorporating it into the complaint by reference.[5] Modern pleading, including that under the Federal Rules, has preserved all three options.[6]

Consideration

In the parlance of contract law, the term "consideration" refers to the circumstances that make a promise or implied promise legally binding and hence actionable; sometimes it is used in the more limited sense of referring to the performance or return promise in the part of an obligee that can make a promisor's undertaking enforceable.[7] In any event, a contractual obligation may result from not only an agreed exchange but also circumstances such as reliance or unjust enrichment.[8]

20. *See* Prosser and Keeton, Torts §§ 113 (defamation), 117 (right of privacy), 119–121 (misuse of legal procedure) (5th ed. 1984); Annots., 61 A.L.R.3d 984 (wrongful attachment), 76 A.L.R.2d 696 (defamation), 14 A.L.R.2d 264, 326 (malicious prosecution, false arrest); *cf.* Annot., 49 A.L.R.2d 1460 (pleading lack of malice). *Compare* Fed. R. Civ. P. Form 17 (action for patent infringement).

§ 3.20

1. This is the conventional statement of these elements. *See, e.g.,* Marquardt–Glenn Corp. v. Lumelite Corp., 11 F.R.D. 175, 176 (S.D.N.Y.1951); Clark, Code Pleading § 45 (2d ed. 1947); Shipman, Common Law Pleading §§ 113–120 (3d ed. 1923).

2. 11 Williston, Contracts § 1339 (2d ed. 1957); Restatement (Second) of Contracts § 346.

3. *See* § 3.22 *infra.*

4. Joseph v. Holt, 37 Cal. 250, 253 (1869); Fairbanks v. Isham, 16 Wis. 118, 119 (1862); Clark, Code Pleading 277 (3d ed. 1947); Shipman, Common Law Pleading 244 (3d ed. 1923).

5. Clark, Code Pleading § 37 (2d ed. 1947).

6. Fed. R. Civ. P. Form 3, Form 12 n.1; Boulevard Airport v. Consolidated Vultee Aircraft Corp., 85 F.Supp. 876 (E.D.Pa. 1949).

7. Restatement (Second) or Contracts § 71, Comment *a.*

8. Restatement (Second) of Contracts §§ 82–109.

The corresponding pleading rule is that the complaint must contain allegations describing the agreed exchange or the other circumstances recognized by the law as making a promise legally enforceable.[9]

Statute of frauds

If the contract is one within the statute of frauds and hence required to be evidenced by a writing, some states require plaintiff to allege that it was in writing.[10] Other states, and the Federal Rules, put the burden of pleading the statute of frauds on defendant as an affirmative defense.[11]

Conditions precedent

The substantive law of contracts draws a distinction between conditions that must be fulfilled before defendant comes under an immediate duty to perform (conditions precedent) and conditions that will terminate or affect defendant's duty after the duty has already come into effect (conditions subsequent).[12] If substantive law classifies a particular condition as a condition precedent, the plaintiff must plead its fulfillment. Older cases insisted on specific pleading of the fulfillment of each such condition.[13] Under modern rules, it may be alleged only that all conditions have been fulfilled.[14] When plaintiff contends, however, that performance of a condition was waived or otherwise excused, the plead-

9. *See, e.g.,* Bank of St. Louis v. Morrissey, 597 F.2d 1131 (8th Cir.1979). Under "common counts" pleading, however, the allegation of the circumstances creating the obligation may be made in conclusory terms. *See* Fed. R. Civ. P. Forms 5, 6, 8; *compare* Form 7. *See also* § 3.21 *infra.*

10. *E.g.,* Roberts v. Wachter, 104 Cal. App.2d 281, 231 P.2d 540 (1951). *See also* Restatement (Second) of Contracts §§ 138 *et seq.*

11. Fed. R. Civ. P. Rule 8(c); Clark, Code Pleading 278 (2d ed. 1947); 2 Corbin, Contracts §§ 317–320 (1950). This was the common law rule. Shipman, Common Law Pleading 245 & n.27 (3d ed. 1923).

12. 3A Corbin, Contracts § 628 (1960); Restatement (Second) of Contracts §§ 224, 230.

13. Tooker v. Arnoux, 76 N.Y. 397 (1879). *Cf.* Burke v. Gotlieb, 19 Misc.2d 893, 191 N.Y.S.2d 343 (Sup.Ct.1959).

14. The original Field Code in New York had such a provision, which was carried over with modifications into Code Civ. Proc. § 533 (1876). When the Civil Practice Act was adopted in 1921 this provision (again with modification) became New York Civil Practice Rule 92. It permitted plaintiff to plead "in general terms, that he ... duly performed all the conditions of such contract on his part." The courts construed these provisions with excessive strictness, requiring literal compliance with the verbal formula. *See* Prashker, Pleading Performance of Conditions Precedent, 13 St. John's L. Rev. 242, 251–266 (1939). The rule was liberalized in 1948 to read: "The performance or occurrence of a condition precedent in a contract may be pleaded in general terms as a legal conclusion without stating the facts constituting performance or occurrence." The final step was taken by providing: "The performance or occurrence of a condition precedent in a contract need not be pleaded." N.Y. Civ. Prac. L. & R. 3015(a).

Cf. Fed. R. Civ. P. 9(c): "In pleading the performance or occurrence of conditions precedent, it is sufficient to aver generally that all conditions precedent have been performed or have occurred." Plaintiff, however, may still have the burden of proof. *See* McDonough Construction Co. v. McLendon Elec. Co., 242 Ga. 510, 250 S.E.2d 424 (1978) (where *P* alleges compliance with conditions generally, and *D* denies that allegation, *P* still has burden to prove their performance, having failed to insist on a specific denial in the answer).

ing should allege the condition, its nonperformance, and the circumstances justifying the nonperformance.[15]

Breach by defendant

Defendant's breach of contract is an element of plaintiff's claim and must ordinarily be pleaded. The principal question is the degree of detail required in pleading the breach. At common law a simple allegation that defendant "breached" was an insufficient allegation because it was regarded as a conclusion of law.[16] Under the codes the rule remained essentially the same.[17] But an allegation that defendant "failed," "refused," or "failed and refused" to perform the contract was and is regarded as one of fact and therefore sufficient.[18]

When defendant's breach is claimed to be the nonpayment of money due under the contract (as for goods or services or the repayment of a loan), the burden of proof on the issue of payment ordinarily is put on defendant.[19] In such cases, the question arises whether plaintiff must allege nonpayment in the complaint. Most courts hold that plaintiff must plead nonpayment but need not prove it.[20]

§ 3.21 Implied Contracts, Quasi-contractual Obligations, and Common Counts

Common counts at common law

In exchange transactions it is sometimes unclear or disputed whether the parties had an express agreement or only an implied one. At common law an allegation of an express contract to pay a stated price for goods, services, and the like would not support a recovery for their reasonable value on the basis of an implied contract to pay that value.[1] To cover the situations in which the law would find an implied undertaking by defendant to pay money to plaintiff, the common law developed the "common counts"—the *indebitatus* count, the *quantum meruit* count, the *quantum valebant* count, and the count on account stated.[2]

15. Abinet v. Mediavilla, 5 A.D.2d 679, 169 N.Y.S.2d 231 (1957); Williams v. Fire Assn. of Philadelphia, 119 App.Div. 573, 104 N.Y.S. 100 (1907); Prashker, Pleading Performance of Conditions Precedent, 13 St. John's L. Rev. 242, 260–262.

16. Chitty, Treatise on Pleading *343 (16th Am. ed. 1876); Shipman, Common Law Pleading 252 (3d ed. 1923). *Cf.* Maryland Casualty Co. v. Kelly, 3 F.R.D. 28 (E.D.Pa.1943).

17. Jones County v. Sales, 25 Iowa 25 (1868); Clark, Code Pleading 284–286 (2d ed. 1947).

18. *See* United Elec. Workers Local 735 v. Harris–Seybold Co., 8 F.R.D. 422 (N.D.Ohio 1948); Wise v. Southern Pac. Co., 223 Cal.App.2d 50, 35 Cal.Rptr. 652 (1963).

19. *See* § 3.11 *supra;* § 7.16 *infra.*

20. Clark, Code Pleading 286 (2d ed. 1947); Pomeroy, Code Remedies 792 (5th ed. 1929).

§ 3.21

1. *See, e.g.,* Pryor v. York's Executor, 305 S.W.2d 775 (Ky.1957), 47 Ky. L.J. 141 (1958).

Cf. Read v. Smith, 83 Mass. (1 Allen) 519 (1861) (where complaint counts on reasonable value, proof of agreed price constitutes variance).

2. Chitty, Treatise on Pleading *350–357 (16th Am. ed. 1876); Clark, Code Pleading § 46 (2d ed. 1947); Shipman, Common Law Pleading § 61 (3d ed. 1923).

The indebitatus count recited an indebtedness to plaintiff in a specified sum for goods sold and delivered, or for services rendered at defendant's instance and request, or for money had and received by defendant to plaintiff's use; the count then alleged that defendant had promised to pay (*super se assumpsit*) the money in question but had failed to do so. The other counts followed the same pattern and were just as simple. The quantum meruit and quantum valebant counts recited a promise to pay the reasonable value of the services or goods rather than a specified sum. The allegations in the count for account stated were that on an accounting between the parties defendant was found to be in arrears to the plaintiff in a named amount and, being so found, promised to pay the sum but failed to do so.[3]

The common counts recited an express promise by defendant to pay the indebtedness incurred, but this promise was a fiction; it did not have to be proven and could not be traversed.[4] The gist of liability was the obligation to pay imposed by law under the circumstances.[5] The fact that there had been an express contract did not preclude resort to the common counts when the contract had been fully performed by one party and the other party (defendant) could perform only by the payment of money.[6]

Common counts under the Federal Rules

With the advent of code pleading the question arose whether the common counts were still available. Their use was resisted by those who favored more factual detail and deplored the fictitious super se assumpsit.[7] But this manner of pleading was so convenient and so popular within the profession that its use became sanctioned in most jurisdictions,[8] many of them abandoning the requirement that the fictitious promise be alleged,[9] thus streamlining the counts further. This is the solution in the Federal Rules.[10]

3. *See, e.g.,* W.F. Parker & Son v. Clemon, 80 Vt. 521, 523–524, 68 A. 646, 647 (1908), setting forth the form given in Chitty, *supra* note 2.

4. Ames, History of Assumpsit II, 2 Harv. L. Rev. 53 (1888). *See* McKyring v. Bull, 16 N.Y. 297, 300, 301 (1857).

5. Shipman, Common Law Pleading 154, 164 (3d ed. 1923). *See* Restatement (Second) of Contracts § 4.

6. Nugent v. Teachout, 67 Mich. 571, 575, 35 N.W. 254, 256 (1887); Shipman, Common Law Pleading 155 (3d ed. 1923).

7. *See, e.g.,* Moser v. Pugh–Jenkins Furniture Co., 31 Idaho 438, 173 P. 639 (1918); Truro v. Passmore, 38 Mont. 544, 100 P. 966 (1909).

8. Clark, Code Pleading 289–293 (2d ed. 1947); Pomeroy, Code Remedies 27, § 436 (5th ed. 1929).

9. *See* Tuggle v. Wilkinson, 17 Ga. 90, 92 (1855) ("This writ, tested by the Common Law Form, wants only the *super se assumpsit,* and who cares a fig for that?"); Foerster v. Kirkpatrick, 2 Minn. 210, 212 (1858). *See also* cases collected in Clark, Code Pleading 291 (2d ed. 1947).

10. Fed. R. Civ. P. Forms 4–8.

Unjust enrichment

When one businessperson delivers goods or services to another at the latter's instance and request, the recipient usually understands that there is an undertaking to pay for them although nothing is said about it.[11] It is not fictitious, therefore, to imply a promise in such cases. When the concept of implied promise has been used, however, it usually does not in fact correspond to the intentions of defendant or the reasonable expectations of plaintiff about that intention. Here the law imposes liability because of defendant's wrongful conduct or unjust enrichment. Many of these situations came to be remedied at common law by the use of an indebitatus count for money had and received by defendant to plaintiff's use. Thus Lord Mansfield said in a famous case: "[T]his species of assumpsit ... lies for money paid by mistake; or upon a consideration which happens to fail; or for money got through imposition (express, or implied); or extortion; or oppression; or an undue advantage taken of the plaintiff's situation, contrary to laws made for the protection of persons under those circumstances. In one word, the gist of this action is, that the defendant, upon the circumstances of the case, is obliged by the ties of natural justice and equity to refund the money."[12]

The use of common count pleading for this kind of redress obviously puts a strain on the code theory that facts are to be pleaded. Some code courts disapproved its use for this purpose,[13] but this form of pleading is so familiar within the profession that many courts have permitted it.[14] It also is permitted under the Federal Rules.[15]

D. PLEADING DAMAGES AND OTHER RELIEF

§ 3.22 Relief as an Element of the Complaint

A complaint should contain a prayer for relief and should allege the factual basis for that relief. The general nature of this requirement has already been discussed.[1]

Actual and nominal damages

In some instances the showing of actual damage is a necessary element of plaintiff's claim. Examples are negligence actions[2] and actions for damages for misrepresentation.[3] In such cases, the showing of actual damage is needed for a complete statement of the claim. In other situations, however, the law permits recovery of at least nominal dam-

11. *See, e.g.,* Ames, History of Assumpsit II, 2 Harv. L. Rev. 53, 58–59 (1888).

12. Moses v. MacFerlan, 2 Burr. 1005, 1008, 1012, 97 Eng. Rep. 676 (K.B. 1760).

13. Cases cited *supra* note 7. The view that the common counts are improper for this purpose is well expressed in Pomeroy, Code Remedies § 438 (5th ed. 1929).

14. *Compare* Moya v. Northrup, 10 Cal. App.3d 276, 88 Cal.Rptr. 783 (1970).

15. Fed. R. Civ. P. Forms 4–8.

§ 3.22

1. *See* § 3.12 *supra.*

2. *See* § 3.16 *supra.*

3. *See* § 3.19 *supra.*

ages for a breach of duty owed by defendant to plaintiff, even though no actual damages are caused. Examples include assault and battery,[4] trespass to land,[5] and breach of contract.[6] Here no showing of actual damage is required to complete the statement of the claim. Nevertheless, to recover actual damages a plaintiff must allege a basis for such recovery in the complaint. Thus, if an assault and battery causes substantial physical damage entailing expense and loss of earnings, these must be alleged in the complaint if damages are to be allowed for them.[7] In addition, all plaintiffs must disclose soon after filing a complaint a computation of damage claims with any supporting documents, except in cases exempted from the pretrial disclosure rules.[8]

Punitive damages

Exemplary or punitive damages may be recovered for some kinds of wrongs, particularly willful torts. When such damages are sought, the complaint must allege the basis for them—that the tort was willfully committed or the injury intentionally inflicted, for example.[9]

Specific performance

A plaintiff seeking relief through injunction or other equitable decree traditionally could obtain it only by showing that the damages remedy was inadequate. Hence, allegations were required in the complaint to that effect.[10] Thus, specific performance of a contract will not be ordered in all situations but only when the remedy at law is "inadequate."[11] In modern law, courts usually are willing to grant equitable relief when it is more appropriate than damages, especially when damages might be an "inadequate" remedy.[12] But pleading convention calls for plaintiff to allege that damages would be an inadequate remedy.

As we have seen above, in many instances the legal theory employed in pleading damages depends directly on the substantive legal theory on which the claim is based. That is, a specific item of alleged damage may be recovered only if the pleading setting forth the claim contains the elements of wrong or obligation which are a substantively valid predicate

4. Bliss, Code Pleading 438 (3d ed. 1894); Prosser and Keeton, Torts §§ 9, 10 (5th ed. 1984).

5. 1 Harper, James, and Gray, Law of Torts § 25 (2d ed. 1986).

6. *See* § 3.20 *supra.*

7. Clark, Code Pleading 328 (2d ed. 1947), and cases cited therein.

8. Fed. R. Civ. P. 26(a)(C); *see* § 5.8 *infra.*

9. Pruett v. Erickson Air–Crane Co., 183 F.R.D. 248 (D.Or.1998)(discussing state statute requiring evidentiary showing before punitive rights claim may be pleaded); Allman v. Bird, 186 Kan. 802, 353 P.2d 216 (1960); Cays v. McDaniel, 204 Or. 449, 283 P.2d 658 (1955). *See also* Farnsworth, Legal Remedies for Breach of Contract, 70 Colum. L. Rev. 1145 (1970); Louderback, Standards for Limiting the Tort of Bad Faith Breach of Contract, 16 U.S.F. L. Rev. 187 (1982).

10. *See* § 3.10 *supra.*

11. Clark, Code Pleading § 52 (2d ed. 1947). For the bases of specific performance, *see* Restatement (Second) of Contracts §§ 357–369. *See also* Annots., 38 A.L.R.3d 1052, 87 A.L.R.2d 779.

12. *See* Laycock, The Death of the Irreparable Injury Rule (1991).

for that kind of damages. Hence, a close analysis is required of the substantive law in formulating the theory of damages to be asserted in the complaint.

In modern litigation this kind of analysis often must be directed to causes of action created or implied by a statute. Hence, the statute has to be interpreted with an eye to the substantive elements required for damages as well as for establishing liability.

Civil RICO

An example of such analysis is that involved in pleading a "RICO" claim for treble damages. The Racketeer Influenced and Corrupt Organizations Act (RICO)[13] provides severe criminal and civil penalties for persons who engage in a "pattern of racketeering activity" that relates to an "enterprise" affecting interstate commerce. A private civil cause of action is provided to parties injured by such activities, including treble damages along with the costs of bringing suit (including attorney's fees). In order to obtain treble damages, plaintiffs must therefore bring themselves within the statute. This means that they must plead that the defendants engaged in a pattern of racketeering activity relating to an enterprise, which in turn requires pleading at least two specific acts of specified types of fraud within certain time periods, and so forth.[14]

§ 3.23 General and Special Damages

Some problems in pleading damage turn on the distinction between general damages and special damages, a distinction made in both tort and contract cases. Confusingly, these terms stand for different legal concepts in the two fields. In contracts the distinction concerns the substantive conditions of recovery; in torts the distinction usually concerns how damages are to be pleaded.

General damages in contract

Substantive contract law excludes recovery for types of damage that were not "within the contemplation" of the party to be charged at the time the bargain was made.[1] Within the meaning of this rule, "general damages" are such as would generally or normally flow from defendant's breach and are assumed to have been before the minds of the contracting parties. All other damages are "special," and for their recovery it must be shown that defendant assumed responsibility for the risk when the contract was made.[2]

13. 18 U.S.C. §§ 1961–1968 (1970).

14. *See* generally Abrams, The Law of Civil RICO (1991).

§ 3.23

1. Hadley v. Baxendale, 9 Ex. 341, 156 Eng. Rep. 145 (1854); 5 Corbin, Contracts §§ 1007 *et seq.* (1950); 3 Dobbs, Law of Remedies Remedies § 12.2(3) (1993); Restatement (Second) of Contracts § 351. *See, e.g.*, Annots., 11 A.L.R.3d 719 (loss of profits in land purchase contract), 41 A.L.R.3d 1436 (franchise contract), 92 A.L.R.2d 1408 (contract to repair vehicle).

2. The basis for recovery of special damages must appear from the complaint. Parker v. Harris Pine Mills, 206 Or. 187, 291

There is no corresponding substantive rule in tort law generally,[3] although the restriction has been invoked when defendant's negligent act or omission constitutes the breach of a contract between defendant and plaintiff or a third person.[4] Aside from such an exception, the substantive law of torts allows recovery for all damages proximately caused by defendant's negligence.[5] While foreseeability may limit the extent of liability for negligence, plaintiff may recover for damages greater than could have been actually foreseen.[6]

Pleading damages in tort

For the purposes of pleading, however, tort law makes a distinction between "general" and "special" damages. The test here is one of fair notice[7] and involves two questions. The first is whether the specific kind of loss is unusual compared with the kinds that are sought to be proven in the type of tort involved. The kinds of loss in this category are bound to change as concepts of the scope of compensation evolve, gain legal recognition, and become routinely invoked in litigation. The second question is how far the pleadings should go in performing the notice function, given that in modern procedure discovery is an alternative means of doing so. With those questions in mind, the sensible pleading rule would be that particularization of damage elements should be required only to the extent that they are unusual in terms of the law as it stands when the action was commenced.[8] Pleadings conforming to this rule would put defendants on notice that they could not guide their discovery by the existing rules as to recoverable damages.

What actually has happened to the pleading rules, at least in some jurisdictions,[9] is that they have accumulated categories of damages that were once unusual but have long since become standard. Hence, the following items may be required to be pleaded as special damages: expenses incurred in efforts to minimize the loss;[10] loss of use of a

P.2d 709, 56 A.L.R.2d 382 (1955); Note, The Definition and Pleading of Special Damage Under the Federal Rules of Civil Procedure, 55 Va. L. Rev. 542 (1969).

3. On the problem of "special damages" in defamation, *see* Prosser and Keeton, Torts § 116A (5th ed. 1984).

4. 4 Harper, James, and Gray, Law of Torts § 25.5 (2d ed. 1986); Prosser and Keeton, Torts § 92 (5th ed. 1984).

5. Dobbs, Remedies §§ 3.2, 3.3 (1973); 2 Harper, James, and Gray, Law of Torts § 20.5, ch. 20 (2d ed. 1986); Prosser and Keeton, Torts ch. 5 (5th ed. 1984); Restatement (Second) of Torts ch. 47.

6. 2 Harper, James, and Gray, Law of Torts § 20.5(3) (2d ed. 1986); Prosser and Keeton, Torts ch. 7 (5th ed. 1984); Restatement (Second) of Torts § 917.

7. Clark, Code Pleading 350 (2d ed. 1947); McCormick, Damages 34, 35 (1935); Restatement (Second) of Torts § 904.

8. *See* the majority and dissenting opinions in Keefe v. Lee, 197 N.Y. 68, 90 N.E. 344 (1909).

9. *See* Annots., 98 A.L.R.2d 750 (medical expenses), 68 A.L.R. 490 (permanency of injury). *See also* Comment, The Pleading of General and Special Damages in a Personal Injury Action in Pennsylvania, 75 Dick. L. Rev. 325 (1971). *Compare* the analysis in Note, The Definition and Pleading of Special Damage Under the Federal Rules of Civil Procedure, 55 Va. L. Rev. 542 (1969).

10. Sutherland, Damages § 420 (4th ed. 1916).

chattel;[11] past and future loss of income (wages, profits, salary);[12] past and future medical, surgical, hospital, and like costs;[13] other expenses incurred because of personal injury or death (such as the hiring of a substitute, funeral expenses); and unusual physical or mental consequences of the injury alleged, such as epilepsy,[14] disturbance of menstruation,[15] insanity,[16] and the like.[17]

Loss of value of injured property is general damage,[18] but in property claims beyond this, pecuniary loss must be particularly alleged. In personal injury cases, pain and suffering is general damage.[19]

Under the Federal Rules and modern code pleading, it is sufficient to describe the general kinds of injuries or losses sustained and to state the total of their value. In some states, the practice is to describe the injuries, to state that their value exceeded $ ______ (a gross sum), and to "seek leave to amend the amount thereof as the proof may show." In a few jurisdictions claimants are prohibited from alleging the amount of damages in certain types of claims, particularly medical malpractice claims;[20] this is meant to inhibit sensational media reportage of claims in which a large amount is being sought.

E. JURISDICTIONAL ALLEGATIONS

§ 3.24 State Courts

Claim as basis of jurisdiction

The jurisdiction of state trial courts generally depends on the subject matter of the action as revealed by the claim or cause of action pleaded.[1] For this reason the pleading of the claim or cause of action itself

11. J.A. Mahlstedt Lumber & Coal Co. v. Westchester Elec. R.R., 198 App.Div. 1021, 190 N.Y.S. 932 (1921). *Cf.* Ralph N. Blakeslee Co. v. Rigo, 94 Conn. 481, 109 A. 173 (1920).

12. Eckert v. Levinson, 91 Conn. 338, 99 A. 699 (1917); Honaker v. Crutchfield, 247 Ky. 495, 57 S.W.2d 502 (1933); Kennedy v. Van Horn, 77 Okla. 100, 186 P. 483 (1919); McCormick, Damages 37 (1935); Restatement (Second) of Torts § 904, Comment *b*.

13. Honaker v. Crutchfield, 247 Ky. 495, 57 S.W.2d 502 (1933); McCormick, Damages 37 (1935); 4 Restatement of Torts § 904, Comment *b*.

14. Baldwin v. Robertson, 118 Conn. 431, 172 A. 859 (1934) (but held allowable as "a manifestation of the injury to the brain and the loss of brain functioning which is alleged").

15. Kane v. New Idea Realty Co., 104 Conn. 508, 133 A. 686 (1926); City of Hazard v. Combs, 247 Ky. 728, 57 S.W.2d 669 (1933); Powers v. Westchester Elec. R.R., 179 App.Div. 938, 166 N.Y.S. 1110 (1917).

16. McCormick, Damages 37 (1935).

17. Galliaer v. Southern Harlan Coal Co., 247 Ky. 752, 57 S.W.2d 645 (1933) (aggravation of injury by malpractice of doctor).

18. Brodsky v. Red Raven Rubber Co., 111 N.J.L. 453, 168 A. 440 (1933).

19. Smith v. Whittlesey, 79 Conn. 189, 63 A. 1085 (1906); McCormick, Damages 35 (1935); Restatement (Second) of Torts § 904, Comment *a*.

20. *See, e.g.,* Cal. Civ. Proc. Code § 425.10.

§ 3.24

1. *See* §§ 1.13, 2.3 *supra*.

discloses whether the court has jurisdiction.[2] Further allegations that the court has jurisdiction would therefore be surplusage. In a few circumstances, however, allegations may be required concerning jurisdiction rather than the substance of the claim.

Further pleading requirements

A state generally can exercise jurisdiction to grant a divorce only when at least one of the parties is a domiciliary of the state in which the action is brought;[3] an allegation of domicile is therefore necessary or at least customary. Generally, an action may not be brought against a government agency without a claim first having been filed against the agency in a specified time after the claim arose; an allegation that such a claim has been filed and rejected is required and may be regarded as going to the court's jurisdiction.[4] The same rules apply to actions against decedents' estates.[5] A plaintiff seeking to obtain judicial review of administrative agency action may also be required to allege that he or she has previously attempted to obtain redress from the agency itself.[6]

Allegations of the sort just mentioned can be considered simply as matters of condition precedent and a part of the claim itself. Often, however, they are treated as jurisdictional in that the court will require them to be established even if they are not contested by the parties.

§ 3.25 Federal Court

The subject matter jurisdiction of the federal courts is governed by scrupulously enforced limitations.[1] One mechanism of enforcement is the federal pleading rule requiring that the complaint refer to the jurisdictional basis on which the plaintiff proceeds.[2]

Allegations of claim

Certain federal jurisdictional requirements are disclosed by the complaint itself. The amount in controversy in diversity cases is determined by reference to the claim stated and the demand for relief.[3] When

2. *See, e.g.,* St. James Church v. Superior Court, 135 Cal.App.2d 352, 287 P.2d 387 (1955); Brenner v. Sukenik, 410 Pa. 324, 189 A.2d 246 (1963).

3. Clark, Domestic Relations § 11.2 (1968).

4. *Cf.* Annot., 65 A.L.R.2d 1278. *See, e.g.,* California Law Revision Commn., Recommendations and Studies 1 (1958–1959); *id.* at 2–8 (1962–1963).

5. *See* Annots., 34 A.L.R. 362, 22 A.L.R.3d 493; *cf.* Hanna v. Plumer, 380 U.S. 460, 85 S.Ct. 1136, 14 L.Ed.2d 8 (1965).

6. *See, e.g.,* Weinberger v. Salfi, 422 U.S. 749, 95 S.Ct. 2457, 45 L.Ed.2d 522 (1975); McGee v. United States, 402 U.S. 479, 91 S.Ct. 1565, 29 L.Ed.2d 47 (1971); Roadway Express v. Kingsley, 37 N.J. 136, 179 A.2d 729 (1962); 2 Cooper, State Administrative Law 572–585 (1965); Davis, Administrative Law Text ch. 20 (3d ed. 1972).

§ 3.25

1. *See* §§ 2.2, 2.24–2.25 *supra.*

2. Fed. R. Civ. P. 8(a)(1) and Form 2 (giving examples of how to plead jurisdiction). A plaintiff is not required to plead personal jurisdiction, that being a defense for the defendant to raise. *See* § 2.12 *supra* & § 4.2 *infra.*

3. *See* Ilsen and Sardell, The Monetary Minimum in Federal Court Jurisdiction, 29 St. John's L. Rev. 1 (1954); Note, Federal

federal jurisdiction is based on diversity, the amount in controversy must exceed $75,000 exclusive of interest and costs, and a short statement to this effect will satisfy the pleading requirements.[4] If defendant challenges the existence of the jurisdictional amount, under Rule 12(d) a pretrial hearing may be held on the question. When the jurisdiction of the federal courts is invoked on the basis that the claim "arises under" the Constitution, laws, or treaties of the United States, the court will look to the allegations in the claim to determine whether it rests on federal rather than state law.[5] A federal claim may "arise" under federal law either when a federal statute creating a substantive right expressly provides that it is actionable by an injured party or when there is an "implied" right of action.[6] The court will also ask whether, in violation of the rules of allocation, the claim improperly attempts to anticipate a defense based on federal law and thereby to interject a federal question in the complaint when it properly does not belong there.[7] The same type of analysis, directed to the allegations of the claim itself, is used in determining whether there is jurisdiction in admiralty.[8]

Although these elements of federal jurisdiction are determined by reference to the facts alleged in the plaintiff's statement of claim, in practice the pleader seeks to help the court, so to speak, by pleading the federal law on which the plaintiff contends the claim arises.[9]

Allegations of party citizenship

The federal court's diversity jurisdiction depends not on the nature of the claim asserted but on the citizenship of the parties. Party citizenship is generally irrelevant to the merits of a claim and therefore would not be referred to in the statement of claim itself. A mere allegation or claim of diversity jurisdiction will not suffice. For instance,

Jurisdictional Amount: Determination of the Matter in Controversy, 73 Harv. L. Rev. 1369 (1970). If the plaintiff's claimed damages have any possibility of being sustained, the jurisdictional requirement is met: "It must appear to a legal certainty that the claim is really for less than the jurisdictional amount to justify dismissal." St. Paul Mercury Indem. Co. v. Red Cab Co., 303 U.S. 283, 289, 58 S.Ct. 586, 590, 82 L.Ed. 845, 848 (1938). *See, e.g.*, Deutsch v. Hewes St. Realty Corp., 359 F.2d 96 (2d Cir.1966).

4. This amount has been raised from time to time, to keep up with inflation and limit the federal court caseload.

5. If the federal claim is not plainly frivolous, the court has subject matter jurisdiction to determine whether as a matter of federal law a valid claim is stated. Hence, if it concludes that the allegations do not state a claim resting on federal law, dismissal of the claim is on the merits rather than for want of jurisdiction. *See* Wheeldin v. Wheeler, 373 U.S. 647, 83 S.Ct. 1441, 10 L.Ed.2d 605 (1963).

6. On the doctrine of implied causes of action, *see* Thompson v. Thompson, 484 U.S. 174, 108 S.Ct. 513, 98 L.Ed.2d 512 (1988); § 2.27 *supra*.

7. Skelly Oil Co. v. Phillips Petroleum Co., 339 U.S. 667, 70 S.Ct. 876, 94 L.Ed. 1194 (1950).

8. *See, e.g.*, Romero v. International Terminal Operating Co., 358 U.S. 354, 79 S.Ct. 468, 3 L.Ed.2d 368 (1959); Leather's Best, Inc. v. S.S. Mormaclynx, 451 F.2d 800 (2d Cir.1971).

9. *See* Fed. R. Civ. P. Form 2. The failure to refer to a specific provision of federal law is not fatal. 5 Wright and Miller, Federal Practice and Procedure § 1209.

in *Rodriguez v. SK & F Co.*,[10] a wrongful discharge action, plaintiff did not allege his own citizenship but alleged only that of the defendant's corporate parent. The court, in holding that the complaint was insufficient on its face, assumed that plaintiff was a citizen of the jurisdiction of venue; the corporate defendant was also a citizen because its principal place of business was located there; therefore, diversity jurisdiction was lacking. Hence, to indicate the basis of a federal court's jurisdiction in a diversity case, it is necessary to allege the citizenship of the various parties.[11]

10. 833 F.2d 8 (1st Cir.1987). *See also* Laborers Local 938 Joint H. & W. Trust Fund v. B. R. Starnes Co., 827 F.2d 1454 (11th Cir.1987); Randazzo v. Eagle-Picher Indus., 117 F.R.D. 557 (E.D.Pa.1987).

11. 5 Wright and Miller, Federal Practice and Procedure § 1208.

Chapter 4

DEFENDANT'S RESPONSES TO THE COMPLAINT AND OTHER PLEADING PROBLEMS

A. OBJECTIONS TO THE COMPLAINT

§ 4.1 Types of Objection

On the commencement of the action through the complaint and service of summons, defendant may choose from four types of objections or grounds why plaintiff should not obtain judgment: (1) that rules governing the bringing of the action have not been complied with (for example, that service of process was defective, or that the court lacks jurisdiction, or that there was a misjoinder of parties); (2) that the allegations of the complaint do not give enough detail to permit defendant to meet the case; (3) that the substantive law does not authorize recovery on the basis of the facts alleged; and (4) that the facts alleged by plaintiff are not true or that other facts exonerate defendant or mitigate his or her liability.

Devices for asserting defenses

Under common law procedure and most codes, these four types of objection were raised by different procedural devices. Moreover, the objections had to be taken in prescribed sequence of stages, as shown below.

Type of Objection	*Procedural Device*
Preliminary: Misjoinder of parties; another action pending on the same cause; and so on.	Common Law: "dilatory" plea.[1] Codes: motion to dismiss for lack of proper parties, and so on, special demurrer.[2]
Formal defect in complaint.	Common Law: special demurrer.[3] Codes: special demurrer or motion to make more definite and certain.[4]
Complaint fails to state a cause of action.	Common Law: general demurrer.[5] Codes: general demurrer or motion to dismiss for failure to state a cause of action.[6]
Facts alleged are not true; other facts exonerate defendant.	Common Law: traverse or plea in bar. Codes: answer.[7]

Preliminary and formal objections

The sequence made sense in theory and, generally, in practice. Preliminary objections to the bringing of the suit that have nothing to do with the merits should be considered first or they will be waived. Hence, the dilatory plea or equivalent motion had to be made before any other

§ 4.1

1. Shipman, Common Law Pleading ch. 16 (3d ed. 1923); Stephen, Principles of Pleading 63 (1824).

2. Clark, Code Pleading ch. 8 (2d ed. 1947).

3. Shipman, *supra* note 1, at § 148; Stephen, *supra* note 1, at 158–161.

4. Clark, *supra* note 2, at §§ 81, 87. The special demurrer is now obsolete, having been largely superseded by discovery. Lynch v. Patterson, 701 P.2d 1126 (Wyo.1985).

5. Shipman, *supra* note 1, at § 151; Stephen, *supra* note 1, at 175.

6. Clark, Code Pleading §§ 82, 86, 87 (2d ed. 1947).

7. *Id.* at ch. 9.

response. Formal defects in the complaint or declaration should be considered before going to the merits or they will be similarly waived; the special demurrer thus had to be interposed before a general demurrer or answer.

General demurrer

Similarly, if there is objection to the substantive legal sufficiency of the complaint—so that plaintiffs should not recover even if they did prove the facts alleged—that question should be considered before going forward to trial of the facts. A general demurrer made this objection. The facts alleged in the complaint were assumed *arguendo* to be true, and if under the law they did not allow a recovery, the general demurrer was sustained and the action dismissed. If the facts stated would as a matter of law justify recovery but defendants disputed some or all of them, then defendant denied those facts in the answer to the complaint. If defendant wished to assert other exonerating facts, then such statements were set forth as an affirmative defense in the answer. Thereafter, the fact issues would be determined at trial.

There were several practical difficulties with this system. First, rigid adherence to the sequence necessitated that each stage complete the cycle of objection-hearing-ruling before objections assertable in the next stage could be considered.[8]

Additional facts only through answer

Second, it was a general rule that factual matters outside the complaint could be brought to the court's attention only through the answer.[9] Yet perfectly valid preliminary objections often depended on facts not appearing in the complaint.[10] For example, a statute of limitations defense could not be asserted except in the answer unless the complaint itself disclosed the date of the transaction.[11] The need to get the facts before the court without waiting for the answer often led to jockeying in which defendants through special demurrer tried to get the plaintiffs to supply details in the complaint that would make it vulnerable to a general demurrer. It would have been much easier if defendants had some way to supply these facts themselves.

Form and substance

Another difficulty was the impossibility, as we have seen,[12] of distinguishing clearly between the requirements that a pleading be reasonably specific (an objection as to form) and the requirement that it state a cause of action (an objection as to its substantive sufficiency). Yet such a

8. Millar, Formative Principles of Civil Procedure I, 18 Ill. L. Rev. 1, 24–36 (1923); Shipman, Common Law Pleading 221–222 (3d ed. 1923); Stephen, Principles of Pleading 429–430 (1824).

9. Clark, Code Pleading § 514 (2d ed. 1947).

10. *Id.* at § 81.

11. *Id.* at § 522.

12. *See* §§ 3.9–3.11 *supra*.

distinction was the basis of the difference between the special demurrer and general demurrer. The result was that these two devices became almost interchangeable. Special demurrers were allowed to bring out detailed facts so that the court might decide the case on the face of the pleadings instead of sending it to a jury on the evidence. General demurrers became vehicles for requiring very detailed statements of claim, on the theory that a complaint lacking sufficiently specific "facts" in effect alleged no facts at all.

A fourth difficulty arose because the resolution of a fairly simple question might quickly conclude a litigation that would be very complicated if considered in the conventional sequence of stages. Thus, if defendants asserted that plaintiffs had released them from liability, and the release were proven, it would end the lawsuit, whatever the merits might be. But under the stage system, this was a defense on the merits that could only be raised by the answer and then would be tried only as part of the entire case.

Hypertechnical attitude

Finally, the courts under the common law and code systems displayed an internally inconsistent and often perverse attitude toward the insufficiency of a complaint as tested by a general demurrer. On the one hand, they were very exacting as to formalities and thereby encouraged active use of demurrers. On the other hand, they were reluctant to terminate an action merely on the basis of formalities. The net effect was to exalt form over substance in the worst way—by insisting on ritual but not giving it decisive effect.[13]

§ 4.2 Simplifications in the Codes and Federal Rules

Defense by answer or motion

The modern codes and the Federal Rules simplify the procedure for asserting the four basic objections mentioned above. First, the allowable procedural devices are reduced to two: the answer, used as at common law to make denials of factual allegations and to assert affirmative defenses;[1] and the motion, which can ask for whatever remedy is appropriate—dismissal for defect in service of process, want of jurisdiction, failure to state a claim, expiration of statute of limitations, a requirement that plaintiff join additional parties, or a requirement that plaintiff make the complaint more definite and certain.[2]

13. *See* Pike, Objections to Pleadings Under the New Federal Rules of Civil Procedure, 47 Yale L.J. 50 (1937).

§ 4.2

1. Clark, Code Pleading ch. 9 (2d ed. 1947). *See* Fed. R. Civ. P. 7, 8(b), 8(c).

2. Clark, Code Pleading § 87 (2d ed. 1947). *See* Fed. R. Civ. P. 12(b), (c), (e), (f).

Second, the pleadings are compressed into one or two stages. This is done by providing that all objections other than factual denials and affirmative defenses (which are made in the answer) are taken by initial motion or all-purpose demurrer.[3]

Rule 12

Thus the Federal Rules provide that all objections, except a request to make the complaint more definite and certain,[4] can be raised in the answer.[5] Under the Federal Rules the answer may accordingly include denials, affirmative defenses, a demand that the complaint be dismissed for failure to state a claim (the equivalent of the old general demurrer), an objection to service of process, a request for change of venue, and so on.

The Federal Rules also provide that the defendant may have an optional preliminary stage by means of a motion. Such a motion may raise any objection—*other* than factual denials and affirmative defenses, which are made in the answer; filing a timely motion postpones the defendant's deadline for filing an answer until the motion has been resolved. If defendant makes such a motion, however, *all* preliminary or formal objections must be included or they are waived. The preliminary objections in question are lack of personal, jurisdiction or venue and insufficiency of process (the documents that must be served) or in the method of service. These are all matters that can and should be resolved at the outset, before time and money have been invested in the action.[6]

Objections not raised in either the answer or preliminary motion are waived except for the following: failure to state a claim, failure to join an indispensable party, or lack of jurisdiction over the subject matter.[7] This means that under the Federal Rules there is usually only one round of pleadings, and at most two.

Presenting facts by affidavit or testimony

An important advantage of a motion to dismiss is that it can get at the facts necessary to resolve a preliminary question, whereas a demur-

3. Clark, Code Pleading 79 (2d ed. 1947).

4. *See* Fed. R. Civ. P. 12(e).

5. Fed. R. Civ. P. 12(b) provides: "Every defense, in law or fact, to a claim for relief . . . shall be asserted in the responsive pleading thereto . . . except that the following defenses may at the option of the pleader be made by motion" (thereafter listing the matters mentioned in *infra* note 6). *But see* Continental Bank, N.A. v. Meyer, 10 F.3d 1293 (7th Cir.1993)(defendant who pleaded lack of personal jurisdiction in answer lost defense by litigating merits for years without asking court to pass on it).

6. Fed. R. Civ. P. 12(b) allows the following defenses to be made by motion prior to the answer: "(1) lack of jurisdiction over the subject matter, (2) lack of jurisdiction over the person (3) improper venue, (4) insufficiency of process, (5) insufficiency of service of process, (6) failure to state a claim upon which relief can be granted, (7) failure to join a party under Rule 19." Fed. R. Civ. P. 12(g), 12(h)(1) provide that a defendant who does make such a motion waives each of the preliminary defenses mentioned in the text that is omitted from the motion. Fed. R. Civ. P. 12(a)(1), (4) states the times for filing.

7. *See* Fed. R. Civ. P. 12(g), 12(h)(1).

rer could not bring forward any facts on its own. (It was therefore said that a demurrer could not "speak.") Preliminary issues can involve factual matters when, for example, the validity of service of process turns on whether a certain corporate employee is an officer of the corporation, when change of venue depends on determining defendant's place of residence, or when the question arises whether another pending action involves the same controversy. The evidence to resolve these and similar issues can be presented through affidavits (statements signed under penalty of perjury) in connection with a motion or can be heard and determined in a preliminary "mini-hearing" by the court.[8] When a motion is made by one side, with or without supporting affidavits, the other side can bring facts before the court by counter-affidavit; if the evidence thereby presented is in conflict, a mini-hearing may be held.[9] Thus, it is not necessary to hold off determination of such factual issues until a trial on the merits.

The result of these simplifications in modern codes and the Federal Rules is that preliminary objections must be raised and resolved promptly after commencement of the action; otherwise, they are waived. Except when the court may and does allow the defendant to amend the answer, only three objections may be raised at a later stage: lack of jurisdiction over the subject matter, the failure to join an "indispensable" party, and failure to state a claim on which relief may be granted.[10]

Motion to dismiss for failure to state a claim

Modern codes and the Federal Rules allow the defendant defensive devices essentially similar to those available at common law. In place of the common law general demurrer is the motion to dismiss for failure to state a claim on which relief can be granted;[11] under some codes this device is known as the demurrer for failure to state a cause of action.[12] This motion or demurrer challenges the legal sufficiency of the complaint. That is, it treats the facts alleged as true for the purposes of argument and asserts that the action should be dismissed because, under the governing substantive law, no relief should be granted even if the

8. The only express reference in the Federal Rules to use of matters outside the pleadings in connection with determination of motions is in Rule 12(c), which deals with a motion for judgment on the pleadings. By implication this would seem to preclude use of affidavits, testimony in depositions, and the like in connection with any other type of motion, such as a motion to dismiss for improper venue. But the decisional law is clear that such evidentiary material may be used in connection with any type of motion. *See* 5 Wright and Miller, Federal Practice and Procedure § 364.

9. A determination of facts by preliminary trial may be had on such issues as the sufficiency of service of process or other preliminary matters. It may not be used to determine the merits of the controversy if a genuine issue of fact concerns them. *See* § 4.10 *et seq. infra* on the motion for summary judgment.

10. *See* Fed. R. Civ. P. 12(h)(2); §§ 4.3, 4.19–22 *infra*.

11. *See* Fed. R. Civ. P. 12(b)(6).

12. *See* Cal. Civ. Proc. Code § 430.10(f). If there is any reasonable possibility the plaintiff can state a good cause of action, it is error and an abuse of discretion to sustain the demurrer without leave to amend the complaint. Friedman v. Stadum, 171 Cal.App.3d 775, 217 Cal.Rptr. 585 (1985).

facts were proven. This device is found in Rule 12(b)(6). As the Court stated in *Neitzke v. Williams,*[13] "Rule 12(b)(6) does not countenance dismissals based on a judge's disbelief of a complaint's factual allegations."[14] A complaint lacking "an arguable basis in law" or raising an arguable question of law that the court resolves against the plaintiff may be dismissed under Rule 12(b)(6).[15]

In place of the common law traverse and pleas in bar, which raised questions of fact, the modern codes and Federal Rules allow defendant to make these defenses by answer. In answering, defendant may admit some or all of plaintiff's allegations and may affirmatively allege additional facts that have the legal effect of absolving or mitigating liability.[16]

Motion for more definite statement

The special demurrer to exact a more detailed statement of claim is important in some code pleading systems.[17] Its counterpart under the Federal Rules has virtually disappeared from use. The rules provide for a motion for a definite statement if the pleading to which it is addressed is "so vague or ambiguous that a party cannot reasonably be required to frame a responsive pleading."[18] It is hard, however, to imagine many situations in which defendant actually needs particulars in order to draft an answer. To be sure, defendants are required to be fairly specific in their denials, but they need not be any more so than the pleadings they are answering.[19] And they may plead as new matter anything that would amount to a defense to any claim that may be spelled out in the complaint. Nevertheless, courts have occasionally ordered more specific statements. The call for them seems to stem more from a lingering faith in detailed pleading as such[20] than from any demonstrated need for details in order to enable the adversary "to frame a responsive pleading," as the Rule now reads.

Default

Under contemporary practice, a defendant has one final option when served with a complaint: doing nothing. This is usually very unwise. The clerk will enter a default, the plaintiff will move for default judgment, and the case will be lost unless the defendant can show good cause for the default.[21] A defendant might nevertheless default if there is no defense or the defendant does not wish to defend, secure in the knowl-

13. 490 U.S. 319, 109 S.Ct. 1827, 104 L.Ed.2d 338 (1989).

14. 490 U.S. at 327, 109 S.Ct. at 1832, 104 L.Ed.2d at 348.

15. 490 U.S. at 328, 109 S.Ct. at 1833, 104 L.Ed.2d at 348–349.

16. *See* Fed. R. Civ. P. 8(b), (c); Cal. Civ. Proc. Code 431.30(b).

17. *See* 3 Witkin, California Procedure 2409 (3d ed. 1985).

18. Fed. R. Civ. P. 12(e).

19. Fed. R. Civ. P. 8(b).

20. *See, e.g.,* Klott v. Chapman, 191 F.Supp. 484 (N.D.Ind.1961).

21. Fed. R. Civ. P. 55; *see, e.g.,* American Ass'n of Naturopathic Physicians v. Hayhurst, 227 F.3d 1104 (9th Cir.2000).

edge that the default judgment cannot be more than the sum demanded in the complaint.[22] A defendant confident that personal jurisdiction is lacking and having no assets in the state may also default in order to be able to raise that lack of personal jurisdiction as a defense when the plaintiff seeks to enforce the default judgment in another state.[23]

§ 4.3 Objections Not Waived

As noted above, under the Federal Rules several types of objections to the plaintiff's action are not waived by failure to plead them at the pleading stage: lack of jurisdiction over the subject matter, failure to state a claim upon which relief can be granted, and failure to join an indispensable party.[1]

Lack of jurisdiction

Lack of jurisdiction over the subject matter may be raised at any time "by suggestion of the parties, or otherwise." Thus, in *Louisville & Nashville Railroad v. Mottley*[2] neither party raised the question of jurisdiction in the court below, yet on appeal the Supreme Court, on its own motion, found that the suit was not one "arising under the Constitution and laws of the United States" and remanded the case to the trial court with instructions to dismiss the suit for want of jurisdiction. The theory is that a court without subject matter jurisdiction has no authority; hence, the parties cannot "confer" jurisdiction by failing to object. A bit more plausibly, one could regard a federal court's decision of a case beyond its jurisdiction as an injury to the states and their courts, which are not present to object.

This is not the only or the best way to handle the problem. The Court could have held that a court has express authority over cases properly within its jurisdiction and auxiliary authority to enter a valid judgment when the parties and the court have assumed that jurisdiction was valid. That would avoid relitigating the dispute in a different court, and the parties would still have ample incentives to police the jurisdictional limits of the federal courts by challenging subject matter jurisdiction earlier in the case. But in the federal courts the *Mottley* rule has been strictly followed. Indeed, the Supreme Court now flatly forbids federal courts to consider the merits of a claim before passing on their subject matter jurisdiction.[3] Whether such a judgment may be attacked

22. Fed. R. Civ. P. 54(c). On the effect of unclear damage allegations, *see, e.g.*, In re Genesys Data Technologies, Inc., 198 F.3d 128 (4th Cir.1999).

23. *See* § 2.8 *supra.*

§ 4.3

1. Fed. R. Civ. P. 12(h).

2. 211 U.S. 149, 29 S.Ct. 42, 53 L.Ed. 126 (1908).

3. Steel Co. v. Citizens for a Better Environment, 523 U.S. 83, 118 S.Ct. 1003, 140 L.Ed.2d 210 (1998), with which compare Ruhrgas AG v. Marathon Oil Co., 526 U.S. 574, 119 S.Ct. 1563, 143 L.Ed.2d 760 (1999)(court may, but usually should not, consider personal jurisdiction objection before subject matter jurisdiction objection). *See* §§ 2.12, 2.22, 2.28 *supra.*

collaterally for want of jurisdiction is a question we shall treat later.[4]

Indispensable party

As for the objection of failure to join an indispensable party, the rules have a confused history and are still somewhat disoriented. Suffice to say that the objection should be raised by preliminary motion or by answer if the grounds for doing so are then known, but the objection may be raised thereafter and acted on by the court if good reason—notably, protection of the unjoined party—is shown.[5]

Failure to state a valid claim

As for the objection that the complaint fails to state a claim or cause of action, the rule that the objection may be taken after the pleading stage combines two ideas. First, defendants should be allowed to say, after the pleadings are closed, that no legal liability has been established against them in the case made out by plaintiff. Under code procedure and the Federal Rules, this objection may be asserted by motion for judgment on the pleadings,[6] at the pretrial conference,[7] or at trial itself.[8] Second, defendant should be allowed at any time to attack the claim *as pleaded,* even though the evidence at trial discloses that plaintiff has a substantively valid claim. This was the rule at common law and it may have some life under code pleading, but it is abolished by the Federal Rules, under which the sufficiency of a claim at trial is determined by the evidence, not by the pleadings.[9]

B. THE ANSWER AND REPLY

§ 4.4 Denials

At common law, factual issues going to the merits were raised by a defendant through the "pleas in bar." Under the codes and the Federal Rules this is done by the answer. The answer to the complaint may either deny one or more of the allegations, or set forth new facts that avoid the legal effect of the allegations, or both. Denials are sometimes called a "negative" defense; additional facts by way of avoidance are called an "affirmative" defense. Originally, the answering pleader had either to deny the plaintiff's allegations or admit but then avoid them through an affirmative defense.

Common law denial

At common law denials were either general (the general issue), directed to the whole declaration, or specific (the specific traverse),

4. *See* Chapter 12.

5. Provident Tradesmens Bank & Trust Co. v. Patterson, 390 U.S. 102, 88 S.Ct. 733, 19 L.Ed.2d 936 (1968). *See* § 10.11 *et seq. infra* for a full discussion of the problem.

6. *See* Fed. R. Civ. P. 12(c).

7. *See* Fed. R. Civ. P. 16(6); *e.g.,* Newman v. Granger, 141 F.Supp. 37 (W.D.Pa. 1956), *aff'd,* 239 F.2d 384 (3d Cir.1957).

8. *See* § 7.13 *infra.*

9. *See* § 4.18 *et seq. infra.*

directed to a particular allegation. In theory, specific denials were more consonant with the goal of reducing the dispute to a single issue of fact for the jury to resolve: the defendant would deny the plaintiff's weakest material allegation, and the case could be ended without trying all possible issues. But theory yielded, often though not always, to the injustice of forcing a defendant to stake his case on a single fact before even hearing the plaintiff's evidence.[1]

A form of general issue was appropriate to each form of action: for trespass or case, it was *not guilty*; for debt on simple contract, *nil debet*; for assumpsit, *non assumpsit*; and so on.[2] Such a plea enabled a defendant to disprove the existence of any of the essential elements of plaintiff's cause of action.[3] In some forms of action the general issue also allowed defendant to prove certain affirmative defense such as payment or release. The specific or common traverse was addressed to specific allegations in the declaration, usually reciting and denying the challenged statements.[4]

Specific denial

The original codes carried forward these forms of denial.[5] In some code states, defendants have greatly simplified specific denials by denying whole paragraphs of the complaint. Under this practice defendants do not separate the allegations within a paragraph; if a paragraph contains any allegation they are not prepared to admit, they deny the whole paragraph. This does not do much to narrow the issues (unless plaintiffs take care to put in separate paragraphs what they think will be admitted) but it does make for simplified pleading.

General denial

Rule 8(b) permits a general denial when the pleader intends "to controvert all averments [of the preceding pleading] including averments of the grounds upon which the court's jurisdiction depends." But the Rule encourages admissions of uncontroverted facts. If "a pleader intends in good faith to deny only a part or a qualification of an averment, the pleader shall specify so much of it as is true and material and shall deny only the remainder." Alternatively, one "may make denials as specific denials of designated averments or paragraphs." Still alternatively, one "may generally deny all the averments except such designated averments or paragraphs as he expressly admits." For example, suppose a paragraph of the complaint alleges: "3. At all times defendant corpora-

§ 4.4

1. Stephen, Principles of Pleading 184–186 (1824); § 3.2 *supra.*

2. *Id.* at 187–203; Shipman, Common Law Pleading 304–335 (3d ed. 1923).

3. McDonald, Alternative Pleading, 48 Mich, L. Rev. 311, 323–325 (1950).

4. Stephen, Principles of Pleading 283–292 (1824).

5. Pomeroy, Code Remedies §§ 501–561 (5th ed. 1929); Clark, Code Pleading § 92 (2d ed. 1947).

tion was engaged in real estate brokerage and held itself out as a specialist in commercial real estate." Defendant's response to this paragraph in its answer could be: "Defendant denies paragraph 3 except that it admits it was engaged in commercial real estate brokerage." Failure to deny an allegation results in its being admitted.[6]

Lack of information

The codes introduced[7] and the Federal Rules carry forward a form of pleading that is neither an admission nor a denial but has the same legal consequence as a denial. The Federal Rules provide that when one "is without knowledge or information sufficient to form a belief as to the truth of an averment, the party shall so state and this has the effect of a denial."[8] For example, suppose a paragraph of a complaint alleges: "4. Plaintiff was inexperienced in real estate transactions and relied on defendant's expertise therein." Defendant's response to this paragraph could be: "Defendant is without knowledge or information sufficient to form a belief as to the truth of the matters alleged in paragraph 4 and therefore denies the same." It is improper to use this form of pleading when the averment to which it is addressed concerns the pleader's own conduct, or some fact or circumstance presumptively within his or her knowledge, or a matter of public record.[9] And Rule 11 applies to defendants as well as plaintiffs, requiring that "the denials of factual contentions are warranted on the evidence or, if specifically so identified, are reasonably based on a lack of information or belief."[10]

§ 4.5 Affirmative Defenses

Negation by affirmative proof

A defendant seeking to challenge the truth of facts alleged by plaintiff does so by a denial.[1] This is done not only when the credibility of plaintiff's witnesses is to be put in issue but also when defendant will offer an affirmative line of proof that is inconsistent with plaintiff's claim and will thereby tend to negate it. For example, if plaintiff must show ownership of title to recover in a dispute concerning land and has alleged title, defendant may show title ownership in a third person under a denial of plaintiff's allegation.[2] If plaintiff in a tort action alleges that defendant's negligent conduct caused the injuries, defendant may show under a denial that either defendant or plaintiff was elsewhere when the

6. Fed. R. Civ. P. 8(d).

7. Pomeroy, Code Remedies § 531 (5th ed. 1929).

8. Fed. R. Civ. P. 8(b).

9. Pomeroy, Code Remedies § 532 (5th ed. 1929). The consequence of such an improper denial is that the matter alleged will be taken as true. *See* Harvey Aluminum, Inc. v. NLRB, 335 F.2d 749 (9th Cir.1964).

10. Fed. R. Civ. P. 11(b)(4); Divane v. Krull Electric Co., 200 F.3d 1020 (7th Cir. 1999); Bodenhamer Bldg. Corp. v. Architectural Research Corp., 989 F.2d 213 (6th Cir.1993); § 3.13 *supra.*

§ 4.5

1. *See* § 4.4 *supra.*

2. Caldwell v. Bruggerman, 4 Minn. 270 (1860). *Cf.* Denham v. Cuddeback, 210 Or. 485, 311 P.2d 1014 (1957).

accident happened, or that somebody else was the owner and driver of the car that struck plaintiff, or that the injuries resulted from an inevitable accident.[3]

Analytically, lines of proof such as these are not affirmative defenses because the proof does not involve new fact issues. Rather, the proof negates fact contentions made in plaintiff's allegations.

Affirmative defenses

In contrast, suppose in the land dispute the defendant wished to prove that he or she had been given implied permission to use the land in question. This line of proof is an affirmative defense because it avoids the effect of plaintiff's having title to the property rather than controverting that fact. Similarly, in a tort action, a line of proof that plaintiff could have prevented the accident tends to avoid the plaintiff's allegations rather than contradict them. Hence, allegations to this effect must be made in defendant's answer as affirmative defenses.

As applied, this analytical distinction is generally coherent. Occasionally, however, courts have confused the ideas of affirmative defense and negation by affirmative proof. They have sometimes thought that affirmative proof must be in support of an affirmative defense and, hence, that such proof may not be offered unless the affirmation has been pleaded as a defense. There are also instances in which, as a carryover from common law pleading, a denial of plaintiff's allegation will not suffice as a basis for disproving it. Thus, as we have seen, plaintiff must generally aver nonpayment when suing on an obligation to pay money (such as for goods sold or money lent).[4] But defendant's denial of that allegation is not a basis for proof of payment. Payment is an affirmative defense that must be specifically pleaded.[5] Similarly, in an action for defamation, denial of the falsity of the statement traditionally did not allow the defense of truth to be raised; that defense had to be pleaded affirmatively.[6] Further, denial of the date given in a complaint for the accrual of a cause of action is not a basis for showing that the statute of limitations has run.[7] Denials of performance of all conditions precedent may not be enough to require plaintiff to show performance on any given condition or to let defendant show nonperformance.[8]

3. Jolley v. Clemens, 28 Cal.App.2d 55, 82 P.2d 51 (1938); Chesapeake & Ohio Ry. v. Carmichael, 298 Ky. 769, 184 S.W.2d 91 (1944); Pomeroy, Code Remedies § 547 (5th ed. 1929).

4. *See* § 3.20 *supra.*

5. Bank Leumi Le–Israel, B.M. v. Lee, 928 F.2d 232 (7th Cir.1991); Erff v. Mark-Hon Indus., 781 F.2d 613 (7th Cir.1986); Federal Deposit Ins. Corp. v. Siraco, 174 F.2d 360 (2d Cir.1949); Pomeroy, Code Remedies § 535 (5th ed. 1929).

6. *See* § 3.11 *supra.*

7. Atkinson, Pleading the Statute of Limitations, 36 Yale L.J. 914 (1927); Commentary, 3 Fed. R. Serv. 671 (1940).

8. Harty v. Eagle Indem. Co., 108 Conn. 563, 143 A. 847 (1928).

Allocating the burden of pleading

Apart from these analytical and historical anomalies is the question whether a legally significant fact in the dispute must be alleged as part of the complaint, or its converse alleged as an affirmative defense. The question whether a defense must be affirmatively pleaded to be available depends on the same factors that bear on what the plaintiff must plead and on how the burden of proof is distributed. These factors include a formal test, the analytic distinction between negation of a fact and the avoidance of it by other facts, relative accessibility to the evidence, convenience (for example, economy of statement), a desire to place handicaps against disfavored but permitted defenses, and the opposing party's need for special notice.[9]

Deciding whether a particular issue should be required as part of the complaint or as an affirmative defense is sometimes called allocating (between the plaintiff and the defendant) the burden of pleading. The party that carries the burden of pleading usually carries the burden of proof. A good illustration of this is *Gomez v. Toledo.*[10]

Gomez v. Toledo was an action for damages based on 42 U.S.C. § 1983, which allows recovery for "deprivation, under color of any State law . . . of any right, privilege or immunity secured by the Constitution." The plaintiff alleged that he had been employed as a police officer, that he had been discharged by the defendant police superintendent, and that the procedure followed in discharging him was a violation of his due process rights. Under substantive law, the police superintendent is not liable if he acted on the basis of a reasonable belief that his acts were lawful. The question, then, was whether plaintiff had to allege the absence of such a reasonable belief on the part of defendant, so that the matter would be part of the complaint, or whether the defendant had to allege the existence of a reasonable belief, as an affirmative defense.

The Supreme Court, reversing the lower court, held that the matter was an affirmative defense, stating:

> As remedial legislation, 1983 is to be construed generously to further its primary purpose. . . .
>
> By the plain terms of 1983, two—and only two—allegations are required in order to state a cause of action under that statute. First, the plaintiff must allege that some person has deprived him of a federal right. Second, he must allege that the person . . . acted under color of state . . . law.
>
> . . . It is for the official to claim that his conduct was justified by an objectively reasonable belief that it was lawful. . . . [S]uch immunity . . . depends on facts peculiarly within the knowledge and control of the defendant.[11]

9. *See* §§ 3.9–3.11 *supra.*

10. 446 U.S. 635, 100 S.Ct. 1920, 64 L.Ed.2d 572 (1980). On civil rights actions, *see* §§ 3.15 *supra* & 4.15 *infra.*

11. 446 U.S. at 640, 641, 642, 100 S.Ct. at 1923, 1924, 64 L.Ed.2d at 576, 577, 578.

The Court relied on three factors to justify allocating the matter to defendant: the substantive remedial policy of the statute; the literal text of the statute, which is construed as stating the elements of the cause of action; and the supposition, which seems warranted, that the defendant had better access to evidence regarding the matter. The problem is the same as, and the logic of decision the mirror image of, the question whether a matter should be an element of plaintiff's cause of action.[12]

While no simple test can determine what must be affirmatively pleaded, the guidelines for commonly recurring defenses have become fairly well established by precedent, rule, or statute so that the pleader is likely to find a ready answer to most questions in any jurisdiction. The Federal Rules[13] and the Connecticut[14] and New York codes,[15] for example, give lists of affirmative defenses.

A defendant may also follow the safe course of pleading as an affirmative defense any issue whose classification is unclear, although this entails some risk of thereby assuming the burden of proving that issue.[16] In principle, the detail required to plead a defense is the same as that required for a claim, and a defendant sometimes loses a defense by failing to state it specifically.[17] Some defenses, however, are usually asserted briefly, for example, "This action is barred by the statute of limitations."

§ 4.6 Specific Instances of Affirmative Defense

Federal Rule 8(c) provides in part:

> *Affirmative Defenses.* In pleading to a preceding pleading, a party shall set forth affirmatively accord and satisfaction, arbitration and award, assumption of risk, contributory negligence, discharge in bankruptcy, duress, estoppel, failure of consideration, fraud, illegality, injury by fellow servant, laches, license, payment, release, res judicata, statute of frauds, statute of limitations, waiver, and any other matter constituting an avoidance or affirmative defense.

The purpose of Rule 8(c) is to give plaintiff adequate notice prior to trial of the defenses that the defendant intends to assert.[1] Many of these defenses are self-explanatory; others deserve comment.

Contributory negligence

Contributory and comparative negligence have already been discussed.[2] In a few states a plaintiff suing for injuries caused by defen-

12. *See* § 3.11 *supra*; *see also* § 7.16 *infra*.

13. Fed. R. Civ. P. 8(c).

14. 1 Connecticut Practice Book Annotated §§ 164–167 (1989).

15. N.Y. Civ. Prac. L. & R. 3018(b).

16. *See* § 4.7 *infra*.

17. *E.g.*, Woodfield v. Bowman, 193 F.3d 354 (5th Cir.1999).

§ 4.6

1. Fort Howard Paper Co. v. Standard Havens, Inc., 901 F.2d 1373 (7th Cir.1990).

dant's negligence has to plead and prove due care as part of the case. Most states have allocated these burdens to the defendant.

Failure of consideration

Under contract law, the existence of legally adequate consideration for a promise is usually necessary for the promise to be legally binding on the promisor, and plaintiffs must plead consideration as part of their case.[3] Accordingly, *lack* of such consideration may be proven under a denial of the complaint's allegation of consideration. *Failure* of consideration, however, does not mean the *absence* of either consideration or a valid contract; it means, rather, that plaintiff did not perform his or her own undertaking, which was the legal consideration for defendant's promise.[4] Failure of consideration must be affirmatively pleaded as a defense.[5]

Payment

Payment is treated as an affirmative defense to an action in express or implied contract.[6] Although in an action for the price of goods sold, for services performed, or for money lent, nonpayment is the very breach on which plaintiff sues, the prevailing rule is that defendant must affirmatively plead (and prove) payment to take advantage of it as a defense.[7]

Res judicata

Res judicata is a broad term which, as we shall see, is often used to include the effect of a former judgment as a complete bar to any further action on the same claim and as binding the parties to specific findings of fact that may be called into question in a later action on a different claim.[8] At common law a distinction seems to have been made, for pleading purposes, between these two senses in which the term is used. The "prior judgment, to operate as an absolute bar to a subsequent action, had to be specially pleaded," but a former judgment offered for the purpose of establishing issue preclusion on a point at issue in a later action in a different claim was admissible under the general issue, at least in some forms of action.[9] This distinction has largely disappeared today. Res judicata in all its aspects[10] is generally treated as an affirmative defense that must be affirmatively pleaded.[11]

2. *See* § 3.17 *supra.*

3. *See* § 3.20 *supra.*

4. 1 Corbin, Contracts § 153 (1963).

5. *But cf.* Temperato v. Rainbolt, 22 F.R.D. 57 (E.D.Ill.1958).

6. *See* §§ 3.11, 3.20 notes 17–20 *supra.* *See also* § 7.8 *infra.*

7. *See, e.g.,* A.D.E., Inc. v. Louis Joliet Bank & Trust Co., 742 F.2d 395 (7th Cir. 1984).

8. *See* Chapter 11.

9. Williams v. Daisey, 180 A. 908, 911 (Del.Super.Ct.1935); *see also* Piercy v. Sabin, 10 Cal. 22 (1858).

10. Fed. R. Civ. P. 8(c) (specifying *res judicata* without qualification); N.Y. Civ. Prac. L. & R. 3018(b) (expressly specifying both aspects).

Statute of frauds

When a contract is within the terms of the statute of frauds, it is generally unenforceable unless a writing evidences the contract. Hence, the critical issue can be whether a sufficient writing exists to meet the requirements of that statute. Jurisdictions are divided on whether the statute may be raised under a denial of the contract or must be specially pleaded to be available. The modern trend is toward the latter view.[12]

Statute of limitations

In most cases, the statute of limitations was an affirmative defense at common law and under the codes. An exception was commonly made when the time limitation was considered a substantive limitation on the right itself rather than a limitation only on the remedy. The concept of substantive limitation was most frequently invoked where a right was created by a statute that also prescribed the time within which an action might be brought upon it.[13] This was often the case with the action for wrongful death, with tort remedies created against a governmental unit, and other rights and remedies established through legislation. In such actions plaintiff had to show that the action accrued within the statutory period; correlatively, the defense that the action had been brought too late could be raised by demurrer or denial.

Under the Federal Rules, if the complaint recounts the date of the transaction sued on, and that date is more remote than the limitations period, the defense can be asserted by a motion to dismiss for failure to state a claim.[14] Otherwise, the defense should be affirmatively pleaded or raised by a motion for summary judgment.[15]

Other affirmative defenses

Failure to mitigate damages is not mentioned among the affirmative defenses enumerated in the Rule, but most federal courts hold that lack of mitigation is a Rule 8 affirmative defense.[16] Failure to plead it in

11. Lesher v. Lavrich, 784 F.2d 193 (6th Cir.1986).

12. Fed. R. Civ. P. 8(c). *See also* Sound Video Unlimited v. Video Shack Inc., 700 F.Supp. 127 (S.D.N.Y.1988).

13. DeMartino v. Sieman, 90 Conn. 527, 97 A. 765 (1916); Chandler v. Chicago & A.R.R., 251 Mo. 592, 158 S.W. 35 (1913). For criticism of this rule, *see* 4 Harper, James, and Gray, Law of Torts § 24.7 (2d ed. 1986).

14. *See, e.g.,* Wilburn v. Pepsi–Cola Bottling Co., 492 F.2d 1288 (8th Cir.1974).

15. *See, e.g.,* Simon v. United States, 891 F.2d 1154 (5th Cir.1990); Roberts v. College of the Desert, 870 F.2d 1411 (9th Cir.1988); Grant v. Preferred Research, Inc., 885 F.2d 795 (11th Cir.1989); Davis v. Bryan, 810 F.2d 42 (2d Cir.1987). Other affirmative defenses also may be asserted by motion for summary judgment. *See* 5 Wright and Miller, Federal Practice and Procedure § 1277. *Compare* the similar approach in a code system in Kaiser Found. Hosps. v. Superior Court, 254 Cal.App.2d 327, 62 Cal.Rptr. 330 (1967).

16. *See, e.g.,* Sayre v. Musicland Group, 850 F.2d 350 (8th Cir.1988); 999 v. C.I.T. Corp., 776 F.2d 866 (9th Cir.1985).

federal court will normally result in a waiver of that defense and its exclusion from the case.

The final category in Rule 8(c) is "any other matter constituting an avoidance or affirmative defense." This language shows that the list is not meant to be complete and leaves other matters to be determined by judicial decision through the approaches described above.[17]

§ 4.7 Consequences of Failure to Plead Affirmatively an Affirmative Defense

Evidence will be excluded

The general rule under common law, code, and modern pleading is that an affirmative defense is not available to a defendant unless it has been pleaded as such.[1] When the defense has not been so pleaded, evidence offered in support of the defense will, on proper objection, be excluded as constituting a variance from the pleadings.[2] If the defense appears incidentally from evidence that is offered and admitted for other purposes, a defendant is precluded from taking advantage of the defense because it was waived by failure to set it up affirmatively.[3] If, for example, a witness in describing an accident puts its occurrence at a date showing that the statute of limitations had run before the suit was brought, the defense of the statute would nevertheless be unavailable to a defendant who had not pleaded it affirmatively in the answer.

This general rule has been modified by allowing amendments to the answer and by the concept that a variance will usually be regarded as immaterial. This problem is addressed in the discussion of the relation between the pleadings—complaint as well as answer—and the proof. A defendant can never be sure that amendment will be allowed, and should therefore avoid the pitfalls of waiver and variance by pleading affirmatively any defense that might not be available under a denial.[4]

Shift burden of proof

This raises the question whether a defendant runs other risks by pleading an affirmative defense unnecessarily. At common law, affirmative allegation of matters properly constituting a denial was deemed an

17. *See*, § 4.5 *supra*; Clark, Code Pleading § 97 (2d ed. 1947); 5 Wright and Miller, Federal Practice and Procedure § 1271; 3 Witkin, California Procedure 2494–2530 (3d ed. 1985).

§ 4.7

1. Clark, Code Pleading § 96 (2d ed. 1947); Pomeroy, Code Remedies § 548, 567 (5th ed. 1929). *See, e.g.,* Mitchell v. Williams, 420 F.2d 67 (8th Cir.1969).

2. Modern Leasing v. Falcon Mfg., 888 F.2d 59 (8th Cir.1989); Northwest Acceptance Corp. v. Lynnwood Equip., 834 F.2d 823 (9th Cir.1987); Sound Video Unlimited v. Video Shack Inc., 700 F.Supp. 127 (S.D.N.Y.1988).

3. Hunt v. Wooten, 238 N.C. 42, 76 S.E.2d 326 (1953). *Cf.* Schmidtke v. Conesa, 141 F.2d 634 (1st Cir.1944).

4. *See* Harris v. Secretary, U.S. Dept. of Veterans Affairs, 126 F.3d 339 (D.C.Cir.1997)(refusing to relieve defendant from failure to plead defense); § 4.18 *et seq. infra.*

argumentative denial. This was an inadmissible form of pleading and rendered the plea bad on demurrer.[5] A few jurisdictions have held that a defendant who pleads a defense unnecessarily thereby assumes the burden of proving that defense—a burden the defendant would not have otherwise.[6] Because the normal allocation of the burden of proof should reflect weightier considerations, such as access to evidence and convenience, this rule seems indefensible. It barters those considerations for one having the most trivial worth, namely, the imposition of a penalty for an innocent and harmless pleading mistake.[7]

Although alleging a matter as an affirmative defense thus may be treated by the court as "volunteering" for the burden of proof as to that matter, this is a smaller risk than that of being precluded from proving the matter at all. Hence, a defendant usually should resolve a doubt by pleading the matter–always assuming that the basis in fact and law required by Rule 11 is present. This also will preserve the record on appeal, since an affirmative defense that must be pleaded may not be raised for the first time on appeal.[8] In turn, however, this surrenders whatever surprise value is gained by not disclosing a defense until trial. Given the availability of discovery in modern procedure, however, this is rarely a serious tactical consideration, nor is it one that society has any interest in protecting.[9]

§ 4.8 Counterclaims, Cross–Claims, Interpleader

Not only may defendants set up denials and affirmative defenses in their answers, they may also set up claims that they have against the plaintiff. Under code and modern pleading these are called *counterclaims.*[1] Furthermore, persons sued as defendants may assert claims between themselves, called *cross-claims* under the Federal Rules.[2] A defendant claiming a right of indemnification against someone else can implead that other person, that is, assert a claim against that party and summon it as another party to the action.[3] These methods of joining

5. Shipman, Common Law Pleading 410 (3d ed. 1923); Pomeroy, Code Remedies § 517 (5th ed. 1929).

6. Boswell v. Pannell, 107 Tex. 433, 180 S.W. 593 (1915). *Cf.* Boyd v. Geary, 126 Conn. 396, 12 A.2d 644 (1940); Clark, Cases on Modern Pleading 652–653, comment (1952).

Schmitz v. Mathews, 133 Wash. 335, 233 P. 660 (1925), reaches the opposite conclusion from that in *Boswell.*

See Note, Effect of Unnecessary Affirmative Pleading upon the Burden of Proof, 39 Yale L.J. 117 (1929); Comment, 4 U. Chi. L. Rev. 498 (1937).

7. *Cf.* Desjardins v. Desjardins, 308 F.2d 111 (6th Cir.1962).

8. *See* 2A Moore, Federal Practice and Procedure ¶ 8.27[3]; Roberts v. College of the Desert, 870 F.2d 1411 (9th Cir.1988); Great Southwest Life Ins. Co. v. Frazier, 860 F.2d 896 (9th Cir.1988).

9. *See* Jetty v. Craco, 123 Cal.App.2d 876, 267 P.2d 1055 (1954).

§ 4.8

1. Clark, Code Pleading ch. 10 (2d ed. 1947); Pomeroy, Code Remedies 602–684 (5th ed. 1929); Fed. R. Civ. P. 13.

2. *See* Fed. R. Civ. P. 13(g).

3. *See* Fed. R. Civ. P. 14. *See also* Friedenthal, Joinder of Claims, Counterclaims and Cross–Complaints: Suggested Revision of the California Provisions, 23 Stan. L. Rev. 1 (1970).

additional claims and parties involve many complexities and are dealt with later.[4]

Only two points need be treated here. First, the pleading rules governing the complaint and answer apply also to counterclaims, cross-claims, and impleader claims. Thus, a counterclaim or cross-claim must be pleaded according to the same rules of form and specificity and is similarly subject to a motion to dismiss for failure to state a claim (or general demurrer, where that device is still used). It may be attacked for being premature, for defect of parties, or for lack of jurisdiction over the parties or the subject matter.[5] It requires a responsive pleading, which may contain denials and affirmative defenses.[6]

Counterclaim or affirmative defense

The second problem is in distinguishing a counterclaim from an affirmative defense. Both must be pleaded for a defendant to rely on them at trial. But in some situations, the distinction is difficult to make and important consequences may be involved. These include, in some jurisdictions, the availability of jury trial,[7] the application of the statute of limitations (which could apply to a counterclaim but not to an affirmative defense),whether the defendant may obtain affirmative relief,[8] whether the matter can be asserted against a plaintiff who is immune from being sued (such as the government), the application of immunity (which applies to a counterclaim but not to an affirmative defense),[9] and whether the action is subject to transfer to another court where a "counterclaim" is interposed.[10]

In these contexts, the question whether a set of facts is properly a counterclaim or merely a defense is not always an easy one to answer. When the defendant is asking for an affirmative award of money damages rather than simply a reduction of plaintiff's claim, defendant's pleading should be regarded as a counterclaim.[11] But many kinds of relief, though affirmative in form, are in result nothing more than defenses to plaintiff's claim. Common examples of such relief are an injunction against the prosecution of a lawsuit and reformation or cancellation of an instrument. For historical reasons these kinds of relief

4. *See* § 9.9 *et seq. infra.*

5. For instance, in an action in rem, such as forfeiture, in which the property itself is the defendant, a purported owner who may have the status of only a claimant of the property has no status to file a counterclaim. *See e.g.*, United States v. One Lot of United States Currency ($68,000), 927 F.2d 30 (1st Cir.1991).

6. *See* Fed. R. Civ. P. 7(a), requiring a reply to "a counterclaim denominated as such." *See* § 4.9 *infra.*

7. *See* § 8.10 *infra.*

8. *See* § 9.13 *infra.*

9. *See* Casey, Counterclaims Against the United States Under the Tucker Act, 25 Geo. Wash. L. Rev. 315 (1957); Note, Governmental Immunity from Counterclaims, 50 Colum. L. Rev. 505 (1950); Annot., 106 A.L.R. 1241; Annot., 25 A.L.R.3d 322, 366 (liability of foreign sovereign to a counterclaim).

10. *See, e.g.*, Cal. Civ. Proc. Code § 396.

11. *See, e.g.*, Middletown Plaza Assocs. v. Dora Dale of Middletown, Inc., 621 F.Supp. 1163 (D.Conn.1985).

usually could be obtained by an affirmative suit in equity, but they had as their sole object the defeat of a claim that the equity defendant was pursuing as plaintiff in an action at law.[12] There is, then, good historical reason for treating a matter such as cancellation of a contract as a counterclaim, and good analytical reason for treating it as a defense.[13] How it should be treated for the procedural purposes mentioned in the preceding paragraph would seem properly to depend on the policies underlying each of the classifications involved.

Certainly there is no reason to say that a matter that is a "counterclaim" for certain purposes is to be treated as such for all purposes. The Federal Rules allow the court to treat what was mistakenly pleaded as a counterclaim as a defense, and vice versa.[14] The court may, however, protect the plaintiff against prejudice resulting from the mispleader, for example if the defendant's failure to claim affirmative relief deprived the plaintiff of a chance to meet that claim.

§ 4.9 Plaintiff's Response to Answer

Challenge to answer

New matter alleged in the answer is governed by the same pleading rules as apply to a complaint. As a matter of form, affirmative defenses and counterclaims must be alleged with the same specificity as allegations in a complaint and can be objected to by a motion to make more definite and certain.[1] As a matter of substance, an affirmative defense must be one recognized by the governing law. Whether the defense is legally valid can be tested under the codes by a general demurrer to the answer or, under the Federal Rules, by a motion to strike the defense.[2]

At common law the pleadings continued back and forth until an issue of fact or law was produced.[3] An affirmative plea by defendant called for demurrer or replication by plaintiff. If the replication contained new matter, defendant had to demur or file a rejoinder. Plaintiff's plea to new matter in the rejoinder was a surrejoinder. Then came the rebutter and surrebutter, if the occasion called for it.

12. *See* § 1.19 *supra.*

13. *Compare* Hinton, Equitable Defenses Under Modern Codes, 18 Mich. L. Rev. 717 (1920), *with* Cook, Equitable Defenses, 32 Yale L.J. 645 (1923). *See also* Clark, Code Pleading 101 (2d ed. 1947); Restatement (Second) of Judgments 22.

14. Fed. R. Civ. P. 8(c); Reiter v. Cooper, 507 U.S. 258, 113 S.Ct. 1213, 122 L.Ed.2d 604 (1993).

§ 4.9

1. 10 Wright and Miller, Federal Practice and Procedure §§ 2711–2718.

2. Fed. R. Civ. P. 12(f); Ryer v. Harrisburg Kohl Bros., 53 F.R.D. 404 (W.D.Pa. 1971); Cal. Civ. Proc. Code § 430.20. *See also* Note, Motion to Strike Affirmative Defense—The Equivalent of Partial Summary Judgment, 13 Am. J. Trial Advoc. 645 (1989).

3. Stephen, Principles of Pleading 82 (1824); Shipman, Common Law Pleading 31 (3d ed. 1923).

Reply to answer or counterclaim

The codes cut off pleadings with the reply and provide that the parties may present at the trial any defenses or avoidances that would have been available under the eliminated pleadings.[4] In some states a reply is required to a counterclaim and to new matter in the answer.[5] In other states[6] and under the Federal Rules a reply is required to a counterclaim only, except that the court may order a reply to an answer or to a third-party answer.[7] This power to order a reply was sparingly exercised until recently, but some courts are now using it in the hope of disposing of civil rights suits barred by qualified immunity.[8]

Under both systems a reply is required to a counterclaim and operates like an answer to a complaint. In the absence of a reply, the allegations of a counterclaim stand admitted.[9] Under systems that do not require or permit a reply to affirmative defenses in the answer, a question may arise whether matter pleaded in the form of an affirmative defense really constitutes a counterclaim so that its averments are to be taken as admitted if not controverted by a reply. The Federal Rules requires a reply only when the counterclaim is denominated as such (although the label does not determine its nature for other purposes).

C. SUMMARY JUDGMENT

§ 4.10 Introduction

The motion for summary judgment[1] combines certain features of the general demurrer[2] with certain features of the answer. Its aim is suggested by the standard form of the motion: "Defendant moves for judgment in his favor on the ground that there is no genuine issue as to the facts established in the affidavits attached hereto and, on those facts, defendant is entitled to judgment as a matter of law." The plaintiff can make

4. Clark, Code Pleading 688–690 (2d ed. 1947); Pomeroy, Code Remedies § 478 (5th ed. 1929). *See, e.g.,* In re Brandt's Estate, 67 Ariz. 42, 190 P.2d 497 (1948).

5. This was the original provision of the Field Code and had a large following. *See* Clark, Code Pleading § 107 (2d ed. 1947).

6. Clark, Code Pleading § 107 (2d ed. 1947); N.Y. Civ. Prac. L. & R. 3011.

7. Fed. R. Civ. P. 7(a).

8. *Compare, e.g.,* Beckstrom v. Coastwise Line, 13 F.R.D. 480 (D.Alaska 1953); Keller–Dorian Colorfilm Corp. v. Eastman Kodak Co., 10 F.R.D. 39 (S.D.N.Y.1950); Commentary, 4 Fed. R. Serv. 888 (1941) *with* Crawford–El v. Britton, 523 U.S. 574, 118 S.Ct. 1584, 140 L.Ed.2d 759 (1998); Schultea v. Wood, 47 F.3d 1427 (5th Cir. 1995); *see* §§ 3.15, 4.15 *supra.*

9. Clark, Code Pleading 690 (2d ed. 1947); Pomeroy, Code Remedies § 478 (5th ed. 1929). *See* Fed. R. Civ. P. 8(d). See the allowance of leave to interpose a reply to a counterclaim, thereby avoiding admission of its allegations, in Textron, Inc. v. Maloney–Crawford Tank & Mfg. Co., 252 F.Supp. 362 (S.D.Tex.1966).

§ 4.10

1. *See generally* Brunet, Redish & Reiter, Summary Judgment: Federal Law and Practice (1994).

2. And its analogues, including the motion to dismiss for failure to state a claim upon which relief can be granted and the motion for judgment on the pleadings. As to the latter, *see* § 5.21 *infra.*

a comparable motion after defendant has had the opportunity to answer.[3]

Comparison to motion to dismiss

The motion for summary judgment is similar to a motion to dismiss for failure to state a claim in that it invites the court to consider substantive legal grounds for dismissing the complaint without waiting for trial. A summary judgment motion differs from a motion to dismiss in that in the former the court decides whether to dismiss by looking at the facts disclosed in support of the motion, whereas in the latter the court looks only to the facts alleged in the pleadings. Stated in more formal terms, the factual predicate for a motion to dismiss is the statement of claims or defense set forth in the pleadings, whereas in summary judgment the factual predicate is the proof offered in support of and in opposition to the motion. If a motion to dismiss is accompanied by affidavits, the fact predicate becomes those affidavits and the motion thereby becomes one for summary judgment.[4]

Appraising issues of fact and law

That the summary judgment motion is supportable by affidavits or other evidentiary matter has two important effects. First, the evidence supplies specific details that often do not appear in a complaint drafted according to modern rules. These details, if not controverted by opposing evidence, permit the court to see whether as a matter of law there is no possibility of recovery by the party against whom the motion is made. Second, the evidence in support of the motion is taken as establishing the facts in the face of contrary allegations in a pleading unless the nonmoving party controverts that evidence.[5] When the moving party's evidence is uncontroverted, the court enters judgment if the governing law entitles it to judgment on these facts. If the moving party's evidence is controverted, the issues involved must be tried and the motion for summary judgment is therefore denied. The motion is also properly denied if, even though the facts shown in the supporting affidavits are not controverted, the moving party is not entitled to judgment under the governing law.

Effectiveness of summary judgment

In concept, the motion for summary judgment has great potential for resolving controversies in which there is no substantial conflict in the evidence. For many years, the motion was rarely used to terminate litigation because, as administered, the party against whom the motion is made was not rigorously required to meet the evidence offered by the moving party, and a "genuine issue of fact" was regarded as presented if there was the "slightest doubt" as to what the facts were. The decision

3. *See* Fed. R. Civ. P. 56.

4. *See* Fed. R. Civ. P. 12(c).

5. *See* Fed. R. Civ. P. 56(e).

in *Celotex Corp. v. Catrett*[6] reveals a stance much more supportive of summary judgment. The procedure, however, is of practical use only in cases in which documentary or circumstantial evidence is dispositive of critical issues. When the case depends on credibility of testimony or a jury's evaluation of a person's conduct, it cannot be determined summarily.

§ 4.11 The Basics

The weakness of the old demurrer and motion for judgment on the pleadings was that they could only test the pleadings, which had to be taken at full face value. The old motions provided no way to determine whether the pleader could support the allegations by proof or whether anything of substance stood behind a denial. And since no very strong sanction was imposed against groundless pleading or denying, a plaintiff or defendant could easily run the gauntlet of demurrers and motions by tendering paper issues in the pleadings, which would evaporate when proof was made at trial.

Frivolous cases

Why plead groundlessly? Unfortunately, there are strong practical incentives. A defendant from whom payment is sought (for services rendered or goods sold and delivered, for example) often wants delay. Defendant can extend delay by the simple device of denying the debt and, perhaps, by adding a plea of breach of warranty. A plaintiff could gain through a groundless suit by inflicting the costs of defense, thereby establishing a nuisance value for the suit. In addition to the downright dishonest pleader, there are incurable optimists who sue or defend without solid ground in the hope that something may turn up.

Affidavits

The summary judgment motion is an attempt to eliminate paper or sham issues through a procedure that is speedier and less expensive than a full-dress trial.[1] The motion is typically supported by affidavits of witnesses containing statements of fact that would be admissible if testified to at trial. The movant's opponent then has the right to submit

6. 477 U.S. 317, 106 S.Ct. 2548, 91 L.Ed.2d 265 (1986).

§ 4.11

1. *See generally* Childress, A New Era for Summary Judgments: Recent Shifts at the Supreme Court, 6 Rev. Litig. 263 (1987); Collins, Summary Judgment and Circumstantial Evidence, 40 Stan. L. Rev. 491 (1988); Friedenthal, Cases on Summary Judgment: Has There Been a Material Change in Standards?, 63 Notre Dame L. Rev. 770 (1988); Issacharoff and Lewenstein, Second Thoughts About Summary Judgment, 100 Yale L.J. 73 (1990); Nelkin, One Step Forward, Two Steps Back: Summary Judgment After *Celotex,* 40 Hastings L.J. 53 (1988); Robertson, No More Litigation Gambles: Toward a New Summary Judgment, 28 B.C.L. Rev. 747 (1987); Stempel, A Distorted Mirror: The Supreme Court's Shimmering View of Summary Judgment, Directed Verdict, and the Adjudication Process, 49 Ohio St. L.J. 95 (1988); Weakland, Summary Judgment in Federal Practice: Super Motion v. Classic Model of Epistemic Coherence, 94 Dick. L. Rev. 25 (1989).

counter-affidavits of similarly competent witnesses. Sometimes the courts require that notice of the need to file affidavits or evidentiary material be given to the opposing party before a ruling on the motion can be made.[2] Both sides also may use the products of discovery—depositions and interrogatories that establish uncontested facts, admissions made on request to admit, and so on.[3]

If the opponent does not controvert the proofs offered in support of the motion,[4] and the movant's affidavits show facts that would entitle movant to judgment as a matter of law, then summary judgment may be granted. If, however, the proofs fail to exclude all bases on which judgment might be rendered in favor of the person against whom the motion is made, summary judgment must be denied.[5] Likewise, even if the movant's showing is otherwise adequate, the court must deny summary judgment if the party opposing it submits material sufficient to raise an issue as to one of the material facts that the movant sought to establish. The device is not intended to resolve issues that are within the traditional province of the trier of fact, but rather to see whether there are such issues.[6] In deciding whether such issues exists, the court must compare the factual material the parties submit, decide whether there are factual disputes, and resolve whether any such disputes are material–that is, concern facts on which the result may turn under the substantive law.

2. Johnson v. Pullman, Inc., 845 F.2d 911 (11th Cir.1988).

3. Fed. R. Civ. P. 56(c) ("pleadings, depositions, answers to interrogatories, and admissions on file"); 10 Wright and Miller, Federal Practice and Procedure §§ 2721–2724. *See also, e.g.,* Cal. Civ. Proc. Code § 437c(2); Carmen v. San Francisco Unified School Dist., 237 F.3d 1026 (9th Cir.2001) (court may disregard filed material not brought to its attention).

4. Fed. R. Civ. P. 56(e) provides that "[w]hen a motion for summary judgment is made and supported as provided in this rule, an adverse party may not rest upon the mere allegations or denials of his pleading, but his response, by affidavits or as otherwise provided in this rule, must set forth specific facts showing that there is a genuine issue for trial." For the background of this provision, *see* Wright, Rule 56(e); A Case Study on the Need for Amending the Federal Rules, 69 Harv. L. Rev. 839 (1956); Judicial Conference of the United States, Report of Proposed Amendments to Certain Rules of Civil Procedure for the United States District Courts, 31 F.R.D. 621, 648 (1962).

5. Adickes v. S. H. Kress & Co., 398 U.S. 144, 90 S.Ct. 1598, 26 L.Ed.2d 142 (1970).

6. As we have seen elsewhere, the trier of facts may have two distinct and different functions: to find what the facts are and to evaluate those facts in terms of legal consequences. *See* § 7.18 *infra;* 3 Harper, James, and Gray, Law of Torts §§ 15.2–15.3 (2d ed. 1986). Summary judgment should be denied "even where there is no dispute as to the evidentiary facts but only as to the conclusion to be drawn therefrom." Pierce v. Ford Motor Co., 190 F.2d 910, 915 (4th Cir. 1951). *Cf.* Bragen v. Hudson County News Co., 278 F.2d 615, 618 (3d Cir.1960) (whether given facts constituted monopolistic practices); Paul E. Hawkinson Co. v. Dennis, 166 F.2d 61 (5th Cir.1948) (different possible inferences from circumstantial evidence). This does not mean, however, that summary judgment is never available in negligence cases. *See, e.g.,* Berry v. Atlantic Coast Line R.R., 273 F.2d 572 (4th Cir. 1960) (for defendant); American Airlines v. Ulen, 186 F.2d 529 (D.C.Cir.1949) (for plaintiff); Comment, Summary Judgment for Plaintiffs in Negligence Actions in New York, 25 Alb. L. Rev. 278 (1961); *cf.* Annot., 50 A.L.R.2d 1309.

In this connection, it can make a great difference whether the case is to be tried to a jury. As the court observed in *Nunez v. Superior Oil Co.*:

> If the decision is to be reached by the court, and there are no issues of witness credibility, the court may conclude on the basis of the affidavits, depositions, and stipulations before it, that there are no genuine issues of material fact, even though decision may depend on inferences to be drawn from what has been incontrovertibly proved.... A trial on the merits would reveal no additional data....
>
> But, where a jury is called for, the litigants are entitled to have the jury draw those inferences or conclusions that are appropriate grist for juries.[7]

Similarly, in a nonjury case the parties may indicate that they wish the judge to decide the case on the basis of their affidavits, and the judge may then do so.[8]

Reasons to go to trial

In practice, it is often impractical to obtain a summary judgment except in cases that depend on documentary evidence or on determination of a question of law in a case involving undisputed facts that have been brought into sharper focus than is possible with generalized pleadings.[9] For many years–although we shall see that *Celotex* modifies that view-decisions held that the motion was not sustainable if there was any possibility that the factual aspects of the case would look different at trial from the evidence tendered in support of and against the motion.[10]

Such differences can be attributed to several factors. First, an affidavit is made under oath but is made ex parte and without cross-examination. In contrast, cross-examination is a powerful instrument for exposing error and bias. When proof is documentary and witnesses simply authenticate documents, however, the prospect of cross-examination counts for little, and summary judgment is more likely to be appropriate.[11]

7. 572 F.2d 1119, 1123–1124 (5th Cir. 1978).

8. *E.g.*, Garcia–Ayala v. Lederle Parenterals, Inc., 212 F.3d 638 (1st Cir.2000).

9. *See* § 3.6 *supra.*

10. *See* Adickes v. S. H. Kress & Co., 398 U.S. 144, 90 S.Ct. 1598, 26 L.Ed.2d 142 (1970); Louis, Federal Summary Judgment Doctrine: A Critical Analysis, 83 Yale L.J. 745 (1974); Weakland, Summary Judgment in Federal Practice: Super Motion v. Classic Model of Epistemic Coherence, 94 Dick. L. Rev. 25 (1989). Although all state courts adhere to essentially the same verbal formulation of the test for granting summary judgment, and although most of them appear to apply it as the federal courts do, some evidently impose a heavier burden on the party resisting the motion to show that it has evidence to support the allegations of its claim. *See, e.g.*, Fooden v. Board of Governors of State Colleges and Universities of Ill., 48 Ill.2d 580, 272 N.E.2d 497 (1971).

11. Even Judge Frank, leading spokesperson for those who would restrict summary judgment, agreed "that there are cases in which a trial would be farcical," and circumstances in which "cross-examinations of the [adversary] ... would be futile." He gives as an instance the production of a canceled check to plaintiff's order and a written receipt, both signed by plain-

Demeanor evidence

Second, when a case is decided on affidavit and deposition, demeanor evidence is lost. But when the movant's affidavits are uncontradicted and no impeaching facts appear, summary judgment will mean that the affiant's credibility is accepted without a chance to observe his or her demeanor. Whether this is a significant loss depends on whether the trier would be allowed to disbelieve uncontradicted and unimpeached testimony on the basis of demeanor.[12] When a party can show that demeanor evidence could legally affect the result, then summary judgment should be denied.[13] Of course, when the materials on file indicate a conflict in testimony, the case must stand for trial, where the witnesses will appear and their demeanor will be on display.

Third, persons who are willing to perjure themselves in an affidavit or even in the informal atmosphere of a deposition may be impelled to tell the truth by the formal trappings of trial and the personal presence of the judge. When summary judgment is granted, this chance is lost. Whether the chance is significant is highly speculative, but such a chance always exists.[14]

Controversy over summary judgment

Although these considerations explain why summary judgment is unavailing in many types of cases, they do not explain why it has been narrowly operative. It is common ground that the party moving for summary judgment has the burden of showing the absence of any genuine issue of fact and that one party is entitled to judgment as a matter of law, with the material submitted being viewed in the light most favorable to the adversary.[15] Correlatively, summary judgment should be denied whenever a directed verdict would be denied on the same evidence at trial.[16] The Supreme Court has held that "[t]he standard [for granting summary judgment] mirrors the standard for a directed verdict under Federal Rule of Civil Procedure 50(a)."[17] But the

tiff. Arnstein v. Porter, 154 F.2d 464, 470–471 (2d Cir.1946).

12. *See* Dyer v. MacDougall, 201 F.2d 265 (2d Cir.1952).

13. *See* Bauman, A Rationale of Summary Judgment, 33 Ind. L.J. 467 (1958). Empirical evidence suggests, however, that demeanor evidence is not effective because people are generally not able to detect liars at a better rate than pure chance. Wellborn, Demeanor, 76 Cornell L. Rev. 1075 (1991). Some civil law systems, such as those of France and Italy, routinely try cases on written evidence only.

14. *Cf.* Frank, J., in Arnstein v. Porter, 154 F.2d 464, 471 (2d Cir.1946) ("We think that Rule 56 was not designed thus to foreclose plaintiff's privilege of examining defendant at a trial, especially as to matters peculiarly within defendant's knowledge"). For a further discussion of Judge Frank's view of summary judgment in *Arnstein, see* Glennon, The Iconoclast as Reformer (1985).

15. Hunt v. Cromartie, 526 U.S. 541, 119 S.Ct. 1545, 143 L.Ed.2d 731 (1999); Adickes v. S. H. Kress & Co., 398 U.S. 144, 90 S.Ct. 1598, 26 L.Ed.2d 142 (1970).

16. Sartor v. Arkansas Natural Gas Corp., 321 U.S. 620, 64 S.Ct. 724, 88 L.Ed. 967 (1944).

17. Anderson v. Liberty Lobby, Inc., 477 U.S. 242, 106 S.Ct. 2505, 91 L.Ed.2d 202 (1986).

availability of the motions "does not denigrate the role of the jury. It by no means authorizes trial on affidavits. Credibility determinations, the weighing of the evidence, and the drawing of legitimate inferences from the facts are jury functions, not those of a judge."[18]

In concept, summary judgment is proper whenever a verdict would be directed "on the record the parties have actually presented, not on one potentially possible."[19] But some perhaps believe that summary judgment should be denied when the record presented with the motion indicates the possibility that new or different evidence might turn up at trial.[20] As Judge Jerome Frank, the leading advocate of this view, put it: "[T]rial judges should exercise great care in granting motions for summary judgment. A litigant has a right to a trial where there is the slightest doubt as to the facts."[21] This view was stated by two able judges of the same court in *Arnstein v. Porter,*[22] a plagiarism suit against Cole Porter in which the plaintiff's right to recover turned on whether there was proof that Porter had had access to plaintiff's songs. Porter's affidavit flatly and unequivocally denied access and copying. Plaintiff did not show access, but a majority of the court felt that the *possibility* of proof of access at trial was enough to defeat summary judgment.

The standard for summary judgment has nevertheless been held applicable even in large, complex cases such as multiparty antitrust or securities litigation. In *Matsushita Electronic Industrial Co. v. Zenith Radio Corp.,*[23] an antitrust action, the Supreme Court apparently reaffirmed the standard: "When the moving party has carried its burden under Rule 56(c), its opponent must do more than simply show that there is some metaphysical doubt as to the material facts."[24] The Court granted the motion, despite the complex facts and issues, stating that "if the factual context renders respondent's claim implausible ... respondents must come forward with more persuasive evidence to support their claim than would otherwise be necessary."[25]

§ 4.12 Relationship to Discovery

The evidentiary material that may be offered to either support or oppose a summary judgment motion includes not only affidavits but also

18. *Id.,* 477 U.S. at 255, 106 S.Ct. at 2513, 91 L.Ed.2d at 216.

19. Clark, J., in Madeirense do Brasil S/A v. Stulman-Emrick Lumber Co., 147 F.2d 399, 405 (2d Cir.1945).

20. *See* Bauman, A Rationale of Summary Judgment, 33 Ind. L.J. 467 (1958); Louis, Federal Summary Judgment Doctrine: A Critical Analysis, 83 Yale L.J. 745 (1974); Stempel, A Distorted Mirror: The Supreme Court's Shimmering View of Summary Judgment, Directed Verdict, and the Adjudication Process, 49 Ohio St. L.J. 95 (1988).

21. Doehler Metal Furniture Co. v. United States, 149 F.2d 130, 135 (2d Cir. 1945).

22. 154 F.2d 464 (2d Cir.1946).

23. 475 U.S. 574, 106 S.Ct. 1348, 89 L.Ed.2d 538 (1986).

24. 475 U.S. at 586, 106 S.Ct. at 1356, 89 L.Ed.2d at 552.

25. 475 U.S. at 587, 106 S.Ct. at 1356, 89 L.Ed.2d at 552. *Compare* Eastman Kodak Co. v. Image Technical Services, Inc., 504 U.S. 451, 112 S.Ct. 2072, 119 L.Ed.2d 265 (1992).

the product of discovery. An affidavit is simply a sworn written statement by a witness, including a party-witness, averring facts known to the affiant.The product of discovery includes much more: sworn testimony elicited through deposition of the opposing party or nonparty witnesses, documents obtained from the opposing party or from third parties, and expert reports of physical or mental examinations of persons or of the condition of physical objects.[1]

One of the purposes of conducting discovery, therefore, is to obtain from witnesses statements and other evidentiary material that can be used in connection with a summary judgment motion. For example, in a products liability case the employees of the product manufacturer will be asked whether there were any previous incidents involving the same product, and demand will be made on the manufacturer for production of company records concerning such incidents. Positive responses to these discovery demands will not only be helpful in proving plaintiff's case at trial, they also may be offered by plaintiff in support of a motion for summary judgment before trial on the issue of defendant's having notice of the potentially harmful character of the product. Correlatively, if defendant moved for summary judgment on the ground that the product was not defective, such responses could be offered by plaintiff in opposition to the motion to show a genuine issue of fact on the matter. Assuming that the evidentiary submissions showed a genuine issue of fact, defendant's motion would properly be denied. And if the plaintiff had not had adequate opportunity to obtain discovery of the ground in question, it could ask the court to deny or delay the motion until after the plaintiff could obtain discovery.[2]

§ 4.13 Partial Summary Judgment

Under modern procedure, summary determination may be obtained not only of a whole claim or defense but also of specific issues within a claim or defense. The Federal Rules as originally drafted made no provision for such determination of issues. Experience, however, soon showed the usefulness of partial summary judgment, as it came to be called. For example, suppose plaintiff sued on a set of promissory notes issued over a period of time, and the statute of limitations had run on some but not all of the notes. Assuming uncontrovertible evidence to that effect, it would simplify the case to have a summary judgment determination that the earlier-issued notes were time barred. This would leave open for trial any factual and legal questions about the other promissory notes.[1] Another variation of partial summary judgment arises

§ 4.12

1. Fed. R. Civ. P. 56(c). For discovery procedure and the information obtainable thereby, *see* Chapter 5.

2. Fed. R. Civ. P. 56(f).

§ 4.13

1. Fed. R. Civ. P. 54(b), 56(a). The court in Beech Aircraft Corp. v. Superior Court, 61 Cal.App.3d 501, 132 Cal.Rptr. 541 (1976), held that partial summary judgment may be brought "on any single material

when plaintiff can show that there is no genuine issue of fact as to defendant's liability, leaving open for trial the extent of plaintiff's injuries and the damages resulting therefrom.

The amended Federal Rules and most state codes now expressly authorize partial summary judgment.[2] A summary judgment motion may also address some but not all of the claims or counts in a complaint. For example, suppose a complaint alleges liability against an accounting firm based on both fraud and negligence, but under the substantive law no liability for negligence lies unless the accounting report was specifically addressed to the plaintiff. Suppose further that through discovery defendant obtains evidence showing that its accounting report was addressed only to persons other than plaintiff. On this basis defendant could move for summary judgment in its favor on the negligence claim, leaving the fraud claim open for eventual trial.[3]

§ 4.14 Relation to Burden of Proof

Proper administration of the summary judgment motion requires careful consideration of the allocation of the burden of proof at trial.[1] As we have seen, a plaintiff generally has the burden of proof of the allegations in the complaint, and the defendant has the burden of proof only as to matters of affirmative defense.[2] At trial, plaintiff can "get to the jury" by offering evidence supportive of the complaint's allegations that is strong enough to permit the jury reasonably to find in the plaintiff's favor.[3] Such evidence, however, means only that the jury can find for plaintiff; it does not mean that the jury *must* find for plaintiff. At trial, the jury *must* find for plaintiff, and hence a directed verdict be granted in plaintiff's favor, only if plaintiff's evidence is so strong that the jury reasonably could find only for the plaintiff. This can be called evidence sufficient to justify a directed verdict in plaintiff's favor. If the evidence is any weaker than this, then plaintiff will not be entitled to a directed verdict at trial.

issue." *See* Cal. Civ. Proc. Code § 437c(f); 6 Witkin, California Procedure, Proceedings Without Trial §§ 311–312 (3d ed. 1985). *See also* Schwarzer, Summary Judgment: A Proposed Revision of Rule 56, 110 F.R.D. 213 (1986); Comment, Partial Summary Judgments Under Rule 56(a), 32 U. Chi. L. Rev. 816 (1965).

2. *See, e.g.,* Fed. R. Civ. P. 56(d); Cal. Civ. Proc. Code § 437(c); N.Y. Civ. Prac. L. & R. 3212. But "a partial summary 'judgment' is not a final judgment and therefore ... is not appealable ... [it] is merely a pretrial adjudication that certain issues shall be deemed established for the trial of the case," Fed. R. Civ. P. 56(d) Notes (1946).

3. Slobojan v. Western Travelers Life Ins. Co., 70 Cal.2d 432, 74 Cal.Rptr. 895, 450 P.2d 271 (1969).

§ 4.14

1. *See generally* Louis, Federal Summary Judgment Doctrine, A Critical Analysis, 83 Yale L.J. 745 (1974). *See also* Brennan, J., dissenting in Celotex Corp. v. Catrett, 477 U.S. 317, 329–336, 106 S.Ct. 2548, 2555–2560, 91 L.Ed.2d 265, 277–284 (1986).

2. *See* § 3.11 *supra.*

3. *See* § 7.7 *et seq. infra. See also* Adickes v. S. H. Kress & Co., 398 U.S. 144, 90 S.Ct. 1598, 26 L.Ed.2d 142 (1970).

When movant has burden of proof

The summary judgment motion, as we have seen, involves a forecast of the evidence that could be offered at trial. The essential concept in summary judgment is that no trial of facts should be held because there are no genuine issues of fact to try. It can also be forecast that, at trial, plaintiff will have the burden of proof as to all or most of the allegations in the complaint. Accordingly, summary determination of such issues can be properly made in plaintiff's favor before trial only when plaintiff's evidence is so strong that a directed verdict for plaintiff will be required if the case goes to trial. This point can be stated shorthand as follows: A plaintiff moving for summary judgment, as to an issue on which plaintiff has the burden of proof at trial, must offer supporting evidence that would meet the directed verdict standard, not controverted by evidence in defendant's opposition to the summary judgment motion. This is a very heavy burden and shows why summary judgment can be granted to plaintiff (or to a defendant seeking summary judgment on an affirmative defense when the facts are disputed) only in unusual circumstances.

When opposing party has burden of proof

The situation of a defendant in moving for summary judgment is usually very different. The defendant does not have the burden of proof at trial unless the issue in question is a matter of affirmative defense. A party moving for summary judgment who does not have the burden of proof can prevail on either of two bases. One is by offering evidence in support of the motion that negates a material allegation as to which the nonmoving party has the burden of proof. Suppose, for example, plaintiff in a fraud claim must show his or her reliance on the allegedly false representation. A defendant could negate reliance by offering evidence that the plaintiff had already acted in the transaction before the representation was made so that there could have been no reliance. The evidence would have to be only so strong as to permit a jury reasonably to reach that conclusion. If such evidence were offered in support of a motion for summary judgment and were not met with contradictory evidence, it would be a sufficient basis for granting the motion. Of course, if the nonmoving party offered contradicting evidence in opposition to the motion, then a genuine issue of fact would exist and summary judgment properly should be denied.

Showing that opposing party lacks evidence

The other basis on which a party not having the burden of proof can prevail in summary judgment is by showing that the nonmoving party will be unable to prove a critical fact at trial. Here, the moving party is not offering evidence to negate the issue of fact; rather, the moving party seeks to demonstrate that there is no evidence by which such an issue can be presented at trial. For example, the moving party might use interrogatory answers and affidavits to show that neither party knew of any witness to the fact in question. An illustration of this situation is *Celotex Corp. v. Catrett.*[4] The critical issue was whether a worker installing asbestos had been exposed to Celotex asbestos products as distinct from such products made by other manufacturers. Defendant moved for summary judgment, contending that neither plaintiff's own evidence nor the information produced in discovery indicated any exposure to Celotex. The Supreme Court held that the moving party, not having the burden of proof as to the issue at trial, did not have to show affirmatively that the worker was not exposed to Celotex; rather, the moving party had to show only that no proof had been developed showing that the worker had been so exposed. The defendant could do this, for example, by using discovery to show that the plaintiff had found no witness or other evidence to prove exposure. Unless the plaintiff as nonmoving party countered by showing there was such evidence, the defendant's motion should be granted.[5]

The *Celotex* decision clarified a misinterpretation of, or perhaps overruled, an earlier leading decision, *Adickes v. S. H. Kress & Co.*[6] That decision indicated that a party moving for summary judgment was required by affirmative proof to negate facts essential to the nonmoving party's case.

§ 4.15 Quality and Availability of Evidence

The evidence offered for and against a motion for summary judgment must be competent, that is, it must be admissible at trial under the rules of evidence.[1] In *Celotex,* for example, an affidavit by a fellow worker stating that he had heard that the company had been using Celotex asbestos would be inadmissible hearsay as to that fact. But an affidavit that he had seen Celotex products in the plant where the worker was employed would be competent to prove the circumstance that Celotex was available for use, and this would probably be sufficient for a jury to infer that Celotex was actually used.

As stated in *Anderson v. Liberty Lobby, Inc.,* in passing on a summary judgment motion, account must be taken of the fact that at trial "credibility determinations, the weighing of the evidence, and the drawing of legitimate inferences from the facts are jury functions, not those of a judge."[2] Nevertheless, a few decisions have gone so far as to grant summary judgment in the face of a party's contrary affidavit by

4. 477 U.S. 317, 106 S.Ct. 2548, 91 L.Ed.2d 265 (1986).

5. The Court was divided on whether there was such evidence but was not divided on the analysis of summary judgment procedure itself.

6. 398 U.S. 144, 90 S.Ct. 1598, 26 L.Ed.2d 142 (1970).

§ 4.15

1. *See generally* Cleary et al., McCormick on Evidence ch. 6 (3d ed. 1984).

2. 477 U.S. 242, 255, 106 S.Ct. 2505, 2513, 91 L.Ed.2d 202, 216 (1986).

treating that affidavit as "sham" because it contradicted previous statements of the same witness.[3]

Summary judgment procedure also contemplates that the parties will have adequate opportunity to employ discovery before having to deal with an opposing party's summary judgment motion. This is especially important for a party who has poorer access to relevant evidence than the opponent. For example, an employee suing an employer for employment discrimination ordinarily will have much poorer access to information concerning the employer's general employment pattern and practice. It is settled that the parties must have fair opportunity to use discovery procedure to obtain such information before determining whether there are genuine issues to be tried. If a motion for summary judgment is made before that point, the motion will be either denied or postponed to await completion of relevant discovery.

Qualified immunity assertions

A standard more receptive to summary judgment prevails when a public official, sued for damages in a civil suit, asserts a claim of immunity. Such suits may arise when, for instance, a person acting under color of state law deprives another of rights guaranteed under the U.S. Constitution or federal laws.[4] Another instance arises when officials abuse their office or show malice in the execution of their official duties, effectively depriving a citizen of constitutional rights.[5]

Some officials, notably judges, enjoy an absolute immunity from such suits. Others enjoy a qualified immunity, which protects them only if, at the time they acted, their conduct did not violate clearly established rights.

The doctrine of immunity acts as a shield to protect governmental officials so that they will not be discouraged from exercising their powers. Under this doctrine they are protected from the burden of extensive discovery, for example.[6] Thus, a conflict arises between the objectives of full and complete disclosure of a party's case through liberally construed discovery and a desire not to unduly burden the normal functioning of government because of a need to comply with this discovery.

The Supreme Court has taken the position that the qualified immunity question "should be resolved at the earliest possible stage of a

3. *E.g.*, Kalis v. Colgate-Palmolive Co., 231 F.3d 1049 (7th Cir.2000); Margo v. Weiss, 213 F.3d 55 (2d Cir.2000); *see* Fed. R. Civ. P. 56(g) (bad faith affidavits).

4. 42 U.S.C. § 1983; *see* Bivens v. Six Unknown Named Agents of Federal Bureau of Narcotics, 403 U.S. 388, 91 S.Ct. 1999, 29 L.Ed.2d 619 (1971).

5. Martin v. Malhoyt, 830 F.2d 237 (D.C.Cir.1987).

6. *See* Crawford-El v. Britton, 523 U.S. 574, 118 S.Ct. 1584, 140 L.Ed.2d 759 (1998).

litigation."[7] Thus, although the government official must still bear the burden of establishing an immunity defense, he or she may seek to do so by filing an early motion for summary judgment, precluding the commencement or continuation of the discovery process.[8] Likewise, in a *Bivens* action, which requires a showing of malice on the part of the governmental official, an early motion for summary judgment may ensure that evidence of such malice cannot be obtained through discovery, but it would have to be shown independently.[9] This specialized law is just one of the procedural adjustments that some would make to discourage weak civil rights actions.[10]

§ 4.16 Competing Concepts of Summary Judgment

As originally drafted, Rule 56 contemplated that summary judgment would be a readily available procedural device used in conjunction with the broad discovery afforded by the Federal Rules.[1] A series of decisions by the courts of appeals, however, held that the motion could not be granted when there was the "slightest doubt" as to the facts.[2] Since such a doubt about facts almost always exists, even after a jury verdict, this definition of the threshold sharply constricted the use of summary judgment. That view held sway through the decision in *Adickes v. S. H. Kress & Co.*[3]

The trilogy of decisions in *Celotex, Anderson,* and *Matsushita* clearly relocated the standard. They have been criticized for having departed from the earlier interpretation of Rule 56, for correlating the summary judgment standard with the standard for directed verdict, and for bestowing advantages on defendants.[4] While it seems clear that these decisions represent a change in interpretation that favors defendants, their correlation with the directed verdict standard does seem correct. Operatively, the notion of a "genuine issue of fact" refers to an issue that properly can be submitted to a jury. If the nonmoving party cannot show that the evidence is sufficient to be submitted to a jury, then there is no justification for a trial, and the purpose of summary judgment is satisfied.

7. Anderson v. Creighton, 483 U.S. 635, 646 n. 6, 107 S.Ct. 3034, 3042 n. 6, 97 L.Ed.2d 523, 535 n. 6 (1987).

8. Mitchell v. Forsyth, 472 U.S. 511, 105 S.Ct. 2806, 86 L.Ed.2d 411 (1985).

9. Harlow v. Fitzgerald, 457 U.S. 800, 818, 102 S.Ct. 2727, 2738, 73 L.Ed.2d 396, 411 (1982). *See supra* note 4.

10. *See* § 3.15 *supra.*

§ 4.16

1. *See* Chapter 5.

2. *See, e.g.,* Dolgow v. Anderson, 438 F.2d 825 (2d Cir.1970); Arnstein v. Porter, 154 F.2d 464 (2d Cir.1946). *See generally* Louis, Federal Summary Judgment Doctrine: A Critical Analysis, 83 Yale L.J. 745 (1974).

3. 398 U.S. 144, 90 S.Ct. 1598, 26 L.Ed.2d 142 (1970).

4. *See* Issacharoff and Loewenstein, Second Thoughts About Summary Judgment, 100 Yale L.J. 73 (1990); Stempel, A Distorted Mirror: The Supreme Court's Shimmering View of Summary Judgment, Directed Verdict, and the Adjudicative Process, 49 Ohio St. L.J. 95 (1988).

Aside from the advantage this may give the defendant, there is a more fundamental dispute: whether it is right to compare evidence submitted in documentary form prior to trial (as in summary judgment) with evidence submitted by live testimony (as at trial) and, if so, how precise a comparison can be made. People with highly analytic minds probably make the comparison readily and with confidence; others probably think the comparison is one of apples to oranges. Such a difference cannot be resolved by refinement of the formula.

Adjustments of the standard for summary judgment not only regulate procedure but send a message about the substantive law in question. They notify future litigants and their lawyers what evidence they will have to come up in order to keep their cases alive. The institution of summary judgment is like an inner door in the courthouse that bars some of those who have succeeded in rushing into the entrance. And summary judgment decisions determine how easy it will be to pass that door, and thus encourage or discourage different kinds of litigants from asserting their claimed rights.[5]

§ 4.17 Judgment on the Pleadings

We have seen how the common law and early codes provided the demurrer for testing the legal sufficiency of a pleading and how this could permit a case to be decided on the basis of plaintiff's statement of facts.[1] Another device with this effect was the motion for judgment on the pleadings.[2]

This motion was made after the issue was joined. Like the demurrer it could not "speak" but had to rely on allegations of fact well pleaded by the adversary. In the argument on such a motion, the movant could not take advantage of denials in the movant's own pleading (that is, the movant had to take the adversary's allegations as admitted) or of any affirmative allegations in the movant's pleading unless they were admitted by the adversary.[3]

Uses of judgment on pleadings

A defendant can use this motion either as a delayed demurrer to reach a legally insufficient complaint or to obtain judgment when an affirmative defense has been pleaded whose facts are admitted in the reply (a situation that rarely arises when no reply is regularly called

5. *See, e.g.*, Crawford–El v. Britton, 523 U.S. 574, 118 S.Ct. 1584, 140 L.Ed.2d 759 (1998) (civil rights claims); Eastman Kodak Co. v. Image Technical Services, Inc., 504 U.S. 451, 112 S.Ct. 2072, 119 L.Ed.2d 265 (1992) (antitrust claims); Anderson v. Liberty Lobby, Inc., 477 U.S. 242, 106 S.Ct. 2505, 91 L.Ed.2d 202 (1986) (libel claims).

§ 4.17

1. *See* § 4.1 *supra.*

2. Clark, Code Pleading § 87, at 554–556 (2d ed. 1947).

3. *See, e.g.*, Stanton v. Larsh, 239 F.2d 104, 106 (5th Cir. 1957); Cammann v. Edwards, 340 Mo. 1, 100 S.W.2d 846 (1946); 2A Moore, Federal Practice and Procedure ¶ 12.15.

for).[4] A plaintiff can use the motion when the complaint states a good claim that defendant's answer confesses and asserts an affirmative defense, when the attempted defense is insufficient in law.[5] The motion for judgment on the pleadings is useful chiefly when the controversy centers on the legal effect of given facts rather than on proof of the facts themselves. In this respect it is essentially a delayed demurrer or motion to dismiss.[6]

The Federal Rules retain the motion for judgment on the pleadings but expand its usefulness by allowing it to "speak," that is, be supported by affidavits and other evidentiary material.[7] Use of such supporting material transforms the motion into a motion for summary judgment.

D. AMENDED PLEADINGS

§ 4.18 The Doctrine of Variance

The common law and the codes followed the rule that the pleadings limit the proof. Therefore, the proof could not go outside the limits set by the pleadings; evidence constituted a *variance,* and variance was treated as a good ground of objection to the admissibility of evidence. Moreover, the court, in ruling on sufficiency of evidence or in instructing the jury, could allow a claim or defense only if it had been *both* pleaded *and* proved—*secundum allegata et probata.*[1]

Rationales

This idea may have derived from the fact that the common law writs constituting the forms of action originally conferred authority on the court; hence, a variance would result in adjudicating matters outside the court's jurisdiction. That rationale made no sense when the common law pleading system was abolished, but like so many old procedural rules the doctrine took on new and additional justification. The idea of variance under the codes was that the pleadings informed the other side of the matters in dispute and provided the court with its agenda for the trial; variance, therefore, involves problems of fairness of notice and orderliness in administration of the trial.

4. City Bank Farmers Trust Co. v. Liggett Spring Axle Co., 4 F.R.D. 254 (W.D. Pa. 1945).

5. *See* Madregano v. Wisconsin Gas & Elec. Co., 181 Wis. 611, 616, 195 N.W. 861, 863 (1923); Note, 1947 Wis. L. Rev. 422, 424.

6. Moreover, under modern procedure courts approach the motion essentially as they would a motion to dismiss for failure to state a claim in that the motion will not be granted except when it is apparent that the deficiency could not be cured by amendment. *See* Lanasa 82 L.Ed. 422, 424 (1938); *e.g.,* MacIsaac v. Pozzo, 26 Cal.2d 809, 161 P.2d 449 (1945). *See also* Korn and Paley, Survey of Summary Judgment, Judgment on the Pleadings and Related Pre-trial Procedures, 42 Cornell L.Q. 483 (1957).

7. Fed. R. Civ. P. 12(c).

§ 4.18

1. *See generally* Clark, Code Pleading 739–740 (2d ed. 1947); Pomeroy, Code Remedies §§ 447–455 (5th ed. 1929); Stephen, Principles of Pleading 117 (1824). *See also* Farmers Union Coop. Ins. Co. v. Reinwald, 194 Neb. 766, 235 N.W.2d 630 (1975).

Evidence outside scope of pleadings or pretrial order

These problems can still arise under the Federal Rules and modern codes. Evidence at trial is objectionable on the ground that it is outside the issues tendered by the pleadings.[2] This objection is in fact rarely available, however, because pleadings under the Federal Rules serve only a general notice function. More often, the objection can be made that the evidence concerns matters that were outside the scope of the issues developed in discovery. Since under the Federal Rules discovery serves a notice-giving function, this objection is more readily sustainable.[3] Still more important, if a pretrial order has been entered defining the issues, the objection can be made at trial that the evidence goes outside the issues set forth in the pretrial order.

The pretrial conference is now widely used, especially in the federal courts and in complex cases. Ordinarily it follows the discovery stage, when both parties have had full opportunity to develop their own evidence and explore that of their opponent. The pretrial order's specification of the issues to be tried is thus a stipulation made on full information. Hence, an objection made at trial against evidence that goes outside those issues has a very good chance of being sustained.

A good illustration of the problem of variance between evidence offered at trial and the issues framed in discovery and by the pretrial order is *Rigby v. Beech Aircraft Co.*[4] This was an action for wrongful death and personal injury resulting from the crash of a private twin-engine plane manufactured by defendant; the crash allegedly occurred on account of a defect in the fuel system. In the pretrial order, the issues specified for trial were the claimed defects in the "auxiliary fuel cells." At trial, plaintiff sought to offer proof of design defects in the main fuel cells. This evidence was held properly excluded as outside the scope of the pretrial order. Plaintiff was unable to persuade the jury with its proof concerning the auxiliary fuel cells, and lost the case.

The effects of the doctrine of variance can be mitigated by amendment of the pleadings or the pretrial order. The problem is considered in the next section.

§ 4.19 Amendment of Pleadings: In General

At early common law, when pleadings were oral, a good deal of latitude and informality was allowed in framing the issue. An oral statement of position was discussed before the judges and could be withdrawn or modified to meet objections that developed in the discus-

2. Cleary et al., McCormick on Evidence 434 (3d ed. 1984); *see, e.g.,* Annot., 57 A.L.R.2d 485.

3. *See, e.g.,* Anderson v. National Producing Co., 253 F.2d 834 (2d Cir.1958). *See generally* Annot., 4 A.L.R. Fed. 123.

4. Rigby v. Beech Aircraft Co., 548 F.2d 288 (10th Cir.1977).

sion.[1] With the advent of written pleadings, the issues were closed before trial, and discrepancy between pleading and evidence might prove fatal.[2] This rigid formalism gradually relaxed, but it was never possible at common law to change from one form of action to another.[3] The codes more liberally permitted amendment, but introduction of a new cause of action was not permitted.[4]

Rule 15

These restrictions are rejected in the Federal Rules, as Rule 15(a) provides that leave to amend a pleading "shall be freely given when justice so requires." Both plaintiffs and defendants may amend their pleadings. But certain perennial problems inhere in the amendment process, such as protecting the opponent from undue prejudice and preserving the effectiveness of the statute of limitations defense.

§ 4.20 Amendment of Pleadings Before Trial

Court's discretion

Modern pleading systems permit amendment of a pleading within a specified period of time, without leave of court and without the adversary party's consent; after the expiration of this free time, amendments may be made only on the consent of the parties or by leave of court.[1] The matter is widely said to rest in the court's discretion, subject to the general proposition that leave to amend should be liberally extended.[2] In the exercise of discretion, one or more of the following factors may be considered.

1. Whether the amendment embodies a legally valid claim or defense. There is not much point in spending time and effort over a new claim or defense that has no legal merit.[3] If a claim or defense does have merit, however, that is a strong reason to let it be heard.

§ 4.19

1. Hepburn, Historical Development of Code Pleading 60–62 (1897); Morgan, Some Problems of Proof Under the Anglo–American System of Litigation 9–11 (1956).

2. Chitty, Pleading *312 (10th Am. ed. 1847); Morgan, The Variance Problem, 32 Neb. L. Rev. 357 (1953).

3. Clark, Code Pleading 703–705 (2d ed. 1947); Shipman, Common Law Pleading § 163 (3d ed. 1923). *See* Philadelphia, B. & W. R. Co. v. Gatta, 27 Del. 38, 44–45, 85 A. 721, 724–725 (1913); McKay v. Darling, 65 Vt. 639, 27 A. 324 (1893).

4. Clark, Code Pleading §§ 115–116 (2d ed. 1947); Pomeroy, Code Remedies § 329 (5th ed. 1929).

§ 4.20

1. Fed. R. Civ. P. 15(a); Cal. Civ. Proc. Code §§ 472 (of course), 473 (leave of court); N.Y. Civ. Prac. L. & R. 3025(a) (of course) and (b) (leave of court). *See also* Note, Rule 15(a) and "Standing to Amend," 69 Va. L. Rev. 205 (1983).

2. Foman v. Davis, 371 U.S. 178, 83 S.Ct. 227, 9 L.Ed.2d 222 (1962); Nestle v. Santa Monica, 6 Cal.3d 920, 496 P.2d 480, 101 Cal.Rptr. 568 (1972); Campbell v. Ingersoll Milling Mach. Co., 893 F.2d 925 (7th Cir.1990); Eldridge v. Block, 832 F.2d 1132 (9th Cir.1987).

3. *E.g.,* Saul v. United States, 928 F.2d 829 (9th Cir.1991); Commercial Credit Equip. Corp. v. Stamps, 920 F.2d 1361 (7th Cir.1990).

Why amendment not offered earlier

2. The reason why the subject matter of the amendment was not included in the original pleading or offered earlier. For example, the subject matter may not have been in existence when the original pleading was filed, and the amendment may have been offered as soon as there was occasion for it. Thus, the defense of claim preclusion does not arise until a judgment is given in another action; this might occur after the original answer has been filed. It would be an abuse of discretion to deny such an amendment.[4]

At the other end of the scale is affirmative bad faith—for example, an intent to obstruct the proceedings by deliberately withholding allegations in order to offer them by amendment at a strategic time.[5]

Amending party's diligence

Between these extremes, the degree of diligence is a large factor in exercising discretion. Many decisions say, however, that it is an abuse of discretion to deny an amendment on diligence alone when the amendment would work no prejudice to the opponent and no disruption of judicial administration.[6]

Prejudice and delay

3. Prejudice to the opponent. By far the most frequent source of prejudice is the lack of opportunity to prepare and present a case to rebut the amendment. Thus the amendments will not be allowed if they amount to an undue surprise that would prejudice the opposing party.[7] Such opportunity is not usually threatened by pretrial amendments, however, unless they are offered on the eve of trial or unless the needed evidence has been dissipated or impaired by the delay. Usually, the opportunity to take additional discovery will enable the opponent to gather evidence to counter the new allegations of the amendment. If the prejudice to the opponent is measured only by additional expense, the amendment can be allowed on condition that the pleader defray the costs.[8] A party cannot, of course, object that an amendment will cause "prejudice" because it will result in the objector's losing the case on the merits; no one is entitled to be protected from that kind of harm.

4. *Cf.* Kentucky Home Mut. Life Ins. Co. v. Watts, 298 Ky. 471, 183 S.W.2d 499 (1944) (abuse of discretion to deny amendment to answer embodying facts known to plaintiff but first disclosed to defendant on trial).

5. *See* 6 Wright and Miller, Federal Practice and Procedure § 1488.

6. *See, e.g.,* Quaker State Oil Ref. v. Garrity Oil Co., 884 F.2d 1510 (1st Cir. 1989); Cross & Cross Properties v. Everett Allied Co., 886 F.2d 497 (2d Cir. 1989); Nevels v. Ford Motor Co., 439 F.2d 251 (5th Cir. 1971).

7. Snider v. Circle K. Corp., 923 F.2d 1404 (10th Cir. 1991); Campbell v. Ingersoll Milling Mach. Co., 893 F.2d 925 (7th Cir. 1990); Gerli v. G. K. Hall & Co., 851 F.2d 452 (1st Cir. 1988).

8. *Compare* Witcjak v. Allen, 22 F.R.D. 330 (E.D.Pa.1958), *with* Sherrell v. Mitchell Aero, Inc., 340 F.Supp. 219 (E.D.Wis.1971) (nominal costs imposed on court's own initiative).

4. Delay or disruption of judicial administration. If prejudice to the opponent can be prevented only by delay in the progress of the case, the effect is a factor properly considered.[9] Other factors that the courts have considered include a repeated failure to cure deficiencies by amendments previously allowed and the probable usefulness of the amendment.[10] The trial court thus has significant discretion in allowing the amendment, and its decision will be reversed on appeal only for an obvious abuse of discretion.[11]

§ 4.21 Amendments Offered at Trial

Common law rule: variance from pleading

The common law and code rules on amendment at trial were corollaries of their rules concerning pleading: An amendment introducing a new theory or issue was a surprise per se and hence was allowed only in unusual circumstances.[1] At the same time, the offering of unanticipated evidence ordinarily would be not even a basis for a recess during trial because—as there was virtually no pretrial discovery—"surprise" evidence was regarded not as unfair but as a normal part of the trial process.

Modern rule: variance from discovery

Under the Federal Rules the situation is essentially reversed: The pleadings serve the functions of giving general notice and ushering in discovery procedures.[2] Under federal rules of discovery, the opposing parties and witnesses can be examined before trial under oath, and their documents subjected to examination and copying.[3] In addition, a pretrial conference is often held after discovery has been completed, after which a court order specifies the issues to be tried and the evidence to be presented concerning them.[4]

If such a pretrial order has been entered, the interjection of either issues *or* evidence that goes outside its scope is "surprise" and is permitted only on showing of justification.[5] If such a pretrial order has *not* been entered—many courts use the pretrial order only in exceptionally complicated cases—the definition of "surprise" is more ambiguous.

9. *See, e.g.*, Cresswell v. Sullivan & Cromwell, 922 F.2d 60 (2d Cir.1990); Quaker State Oil Ref. v. Garrity Oil Co., 884 F.2d 1510 (1st Cir.1989); One recurring problem is whether an amendment may be conditioned on waiver of an otherwise available right of jury trial. *Compare* Parissi v. Foley, 203 F.2d 454 (2d Cir.1953) (case already partly tried), *with* Local 783, Allied Indus. Workers v. General Elec. Co., 471 F.2d 751 (6th Cir.1973) (trial not yet commenced).

10. Villa v. City of Chicago, 924 F.2d 629 (7th Cir.1991).

11. Stichting Mayflower Recreational Fonds v. Newpark Resources, Inc., 917 F.2d 1239 (10th Cir.1990).

§ 4.21

1. *See* Morgan, The Variance Problem, 32 Neb. L. Rev. 357 (1953).

2. *See* § 3.6 *supra*.

3. *See* Chapter 5.

4. *See* §§ 5.19–5.20 *infra*.

5. *See* Annot., 11 A.L.R. Fed. 786; *cf.* Wright, The Pretrial Conference, 28 F.R.D. 141 (1960).

It is not objectionable to interject a new legal theory or offer additional evidence that is close to the issues implicitly framed in the course of discovery.[6] Counsel is expected to guard against such "surprise" through counter-discovery. If, however, evidence is produced whose existence had been previously denied by the party now producing it or that involved facts wholly novel in time or place, it would probably be regarded as inadmissible.[7]

The policy under modern procedure is aptly summarized in Rule 15(b), which provides in part: "If evidence is objected to at trial on the ground that it is not within the issues made by the pleadings, the court may allow the pleadings to be amended and shall do so freely when the presentation of the merits of the action will be subserved thereby and the objecting party fails to satisfy the court that the admission of such evidence would prejudice him in maintaining his action or defense upon the merits. The court may grant a continuance to enable the objecting party to meet such evidence."

§ 4.22 Amendments to Conform to Proof

Consent by failure to object

Modern systems provide for amendment of the pleadings at trial to conform to the proof.[1] The idea is that by not objecting to the proof, the parties have tacitly consented to try the issues made out by the evidence or have waived their objections by failing to present them when the court could most effectively act on them.

Tactical dilemma in whether to object

Evidence going beyond the pleadings can present the opposing party with a difficult tactical problem. If that party objects that the evidence is outside the issues framed in the case, the objection should be sustained. But the ruling will in turn invite a motion to amend the complaint or pretrial order, and, under the prevailing liberality of attitude, chances are good that such an amendment will be allowed. If the opponent can make a showing of surprise and the need for further time to meet the new allegation, the opponent will be entitled to a continuance and, at most, to some compensation for costs. The party, therefore, cannot expect to keep out the proof unless it is clearly beyond the issues defined before trial.

If the opponent does not object to evidence going beyond the pleadings, then the new issue will be litigated by implied consent as

6. *See* Annot., 20 A.L.R. Fed. 448.

7. If the opposing party had been made aware of the evidence and had an opportunity to marshal opposing evidence, however, then the new evidence could be admissible. *E.g.,* Higgins v. Del Faro, 123 Cal.App.3d 558, 176 Cal.Rptr. 704 (1981).

§ 4.22

1. Fed. R. Civ. P. 15(b); N.Y. Civ. Prac. L. & R. 3025(c); McClure v. Alberti, 190 Cal. 348, 212 P. 204 (1923); Morgan, The Variance Problem, 32 Neb. L. Rev. 357, 371 (1953).

provided in Rule 15(b).[2] Consent can only be implied, however, if the introduction of the evidence or other events at trial put the opponent on notice that the issues were being expanded. Otherwise, the opponent will lack an opportunity to respond to the new matter, and no implied amendment should be recognized.[3] So failing to object may result in the new issues staying outside the case.

§ 4.23 Amendments and Statutes of Limitation

Amended claim or new claim

An additional problem arises when the statute of limitations has run at the time the amendment is presented. If the amendment essentially corrects or amplifies the claim originally presented, it is treated as relating back to the date the action was commenced. Relation back is a legal fiction: we pretend that the amendment was filed at the earlier date because, for reasons of policy, we think that earlier date should be the decisive one for statute of limitations purposes. If, however, the amendment introduces a substantially new claim, the amendment can be considered in effect a new lawsuit and therefore barred if the statute of limitations governing that claim has expired. The problem, then, is whether the amendment will be deemed to present a change in the original claim or a new and different claim.

Narrow approaches

Under the codes, the answer to the question turned on the term "cause of action."[1] If the amendment sought to add a new cause of action, it was barred; if it simply embellished the cause of action already sued on, it was not. When properly interpreted, this test makes sense. A plaintiff should not be allowed to keep alive all claims against a defendant by suing on one of them. A suit on a note given in a business transaction should not prevent the statute from running against an unconnected claim for assault and battery. But the term "cause of action" was sometimes narrowly defined in terms of legal theory of recovery. If plaintiffs mistook their legal ground of action in the original complaint, they could not repair this mistake by amendment after the limitations period had run even though the same underlying transaction or occurrence was involved.[2]

2. *See* Moore v. Moore, 391 A.2d 762 (D.C.App.1978).

3. *E.g.,* Withrow v. Williams, 507 U.S. 680, 113 S.Ct. 1745, 123 L.Ed.2d 407 (1993).

§ 4.23

1. Clark, Code Pleading § 118 (2d ed. 1947); Developments in the Law: Statutes of Limitations, 63 Harv. L. Rev. 1177, 1241 (1950).

2. *See, e.g.,* United States Steel Corp. v. McGehee, 262 Ala. 525, 80 So.2d 256 (1955); Levey v. Newark Beth Israel Hosp., 17 N.J.Super. 290, 85 A.2d 827 (1952); Harriss v. Tams, 258 N.Y. 229, 179 N.E. 476 (1932); Leatherbury v. White, 6 Pa. D. & C.2d 625 (C.P. Philadelphia 1956); Hayes v. Town of Cedar Grove, 128 W.Va. 590, 37 S.E.2d 450 (1946).

A variant of this was the rule, sometimes found, that if the original complaint was defective so that it failed to state a cause of action, then a later amendment curing the defect did not relate back to the time when the suit was begun. This meant that the statute of limitations continued to run even after an action was brought until a technically sufficient complaint was filed.

Policy of the statutes of limitation

These restrictive rules do not serve the legitimate purposes of limitation statutes. The policies underlying such statutes are (1) protection of a defendant from stale claims—"from being put to his defense after memories have faded, witnesses have died or disappeared, and evidence has been lost";[3] (2) protection of defendant from insecurity, which may be economic or psychological or both—"[t]here comes a time when [defendant] ought to be secure in his reasonable expectation that the slate has been wiped clean of ancient obligations";[4] and (3) protection of courts from the burden of stale claims,[5] which as a class probably include a disproportionate share of tenuous claims.

None of these policies is threatened by an amendment that merely adds a ground of recovery or defense arising out of a transaction or occurrence already in suit. This is usually true even when the new ground involves a variation in the facts. A party will likely collect and preserve all the evidence relating to a transaction or occurrence, not just those aspects of it that support or defeat a single legal theory. Moreover, the defendant's sense of security over the transaction or occurrence has already been disturbed by the pending action.

Claim arising out of same transaction

Modern procedure holds that an amendment relates back to the time of the original pleading when "the claim or defense asserted in the amended pleading arose out of the conduct, transaction, or occurrence set forth or attempted to be set forth in the original pleading."[6] The Federal Rules expressly so provide.[7]

3. Chase Sec. Corp. v. Donaldson, 325 U.S. 304, 314, 65 S.Ct. 1137, 1142, 89 L.Ed. 1628, 1635 (1945). *Cf.* Developments in the Law: Statutes of Limitations, 63 Harv. L. Rev. 1177, 1185 (1950).

4. *See supra* note 3.

5. *See supra* note 3.

6. Fed. R. Civ. P. 15(c). *See also* Tiller v. Atlantic Coast Line R.R., 323 U.S. 574, 65 S.Ct. 421, 89 L.Ed. 465 (1945); New York Cent. & Hudson River R.R. v. Kinney, 260 U.S. 340, 43 S.Ct. 122, 67 L.Ed. 294 (1922); Wennerholm v. Stanford Univ. School of Medicine, 20 Cal.2d 713, 128 P.2d 522 (1942); Simpson v. Kansas City Connecting R.R., 312 S.W.2d 113 (Mo.1958); Doyle v. Oklahoma Press Publishing Co., 206 Okla. 254, 242 P.2d 155 (1951); Developments in the Law: Statutes of Limitations, 63 Harv. L. Rev. 1177, 1241 (1950).

7. *See generally* Note, Federal Rule of Civil Procedure 15(c): Relation Back of Amendments, 57 Minn. L. Rev. 83 (1972). *See also* Lewis, The Excessive History of Federal Rule 15(c) and Its Lessons for Civil Rules Revision, 85 Mich. L. Rev. 1507 (1987). N.Y. Civ. Prac. L. & R. 203(e) provides: "A claim asserted in an amended pleading is deemed to have been interposed at the time the claims in the original pleading were interposed, unless the original pleading does not give notice of the transac-

New plaintiff added

When the amendment seeks to add new parties after the limitations period, the statute of limitations policies also come into play.[8] When the change is made on the plaintiff's side to supply an indispensable party or to correct a mistake in ascertaining the real party in interest to pursue effectively the original claim, the defendant will rarely be unfairly prejudiced by allowing the amendment to relate back to the original pleading.[9] When new plaintiffs assert an independent claim on which the statute has run, most courts hold they cannot evade its bar by amendment or intervention[10] unless the original action was a class or representative one.[11]

New defendant added

When a new defendant is sought to be added by amendment, the case may well stand differently. A new defendant who truly has been a stranger to the case should have the benefit of the statute of limitations, and of course is entitled to an opportunity to respond to the claims against it.[12] But in many cases the new defendant is fully aware of the suit from the beginning. This may happen when (1) the process mistakenly describes a nonexistent corporate entity but is served on defendant and is recognized for what is intended, or when (2) the action is brought against the wrong corporate entity (this can occur when substantive liability rests on another entity closely related in financial interest to the first). In the first situation, logic would dictate that the amendment should relate back as the mistakenly described corporate entity would have had actual or constructive notice of the suit. But in the second situation, found in *Schiavone v. Fortune,*[13] the Supreme Court decided that an amendment should not relate back to the suit when a division of a company was mistakenly sued instead of the corporate entity itself, despite the fact that the company had notice of the suit, because the

tions, occurrences, or series of transactions or occurrences, to be proved pursuant to the amended pleading." This was "intended to overcome the effect of Harris v. Tams . . . and related cases." New York, Advisory Comm. on Practice and Procedure, Second Preliminary Report 51 (1958). Harris v. Tams is cited *supra* note 2.

Under the 1993 amendment to Rule 15(c)(1), a federal court may allow relation back either under Rule 15(c) itself or under a rule of the state in which the federal court sits. *E.g.*, Arendt v. Vetta Sports, Inc., 99 F.3d 231 (7th Cir.1996).

8. *See generally* Annot., 8 A.L.R.2d 6. The cases are in hopeless conflict.

9. *See, e.g.*, Wadsworth v. United States Postal Serv., 511 F.2d 64 (7th Cir.1975); Pruitt v. Fontana, 143 Cal.App.2d 675, 300 P.2d 371 (1956).

10. *Compare, e.g.*, Higgins, Inc. v. Kiekhaefer Corp., 246 F.Supp. 610 (E.D.Wis. 1965) (refusing to allow the new plaintiff to assert his claim), *with, e.g.*, Walsh v. Curcio, 358 Mass. 819, 266 N.E.2d 895 (1971) (allowing him to do so).

11. *See* American Pipe & Construction Co. v. Utah, 414 U.S. 538, 94 S.Ct. 756, 38 L.Ed.2d 713 (1974).

12. *See* Nelson v. Adams USA, Inc., 529 U.S. 460, 120 S.Ct. 1579, 146 L.Ed.2d 530 (2000); Annot., 8 A.L.R.2d 6.

13. 477 U.S. 21, 106 S.Ct. 2379, 91 L.Ed.2d 18 (1986).

defendant's correct name was not introduced within the limitations period.[14]

The decision in *Schiavone* was immediately criticized[15] and has led to an amendment to Rule 15(c) intended to accomplish its purpose. The amended Rule gives federal court plaintiffs the benefit of any relation back provisions found in the law providing the applicable statute of limitations, which is often state law. Alternatively, an amendment changing the name of a plaintiff relates back if it arises out of the conduct attempted to be set forth in the complaint, and if–within the limitations period–the correct defendant knew of the suit and knew that, but for the plaintiff's error, it would have been joined as a defendant.[16]

John Doe defendants

Even under the amendment to Rule 15(c), plaintiffs often encounter relation back problems when they join "John Doe" defendants, whose names are absent from the original complaint but added later if the plaintiff succeeds in identifying them. One common situation in which plaintiffs seek to do this is a police brutality action in which the plaintiff does not know the names of the allegedly offending officers. Many states allow John Doe pleadings and some of these allow the amendment inserting a defendant's name to relate back, an allowance that Rule 15(c) then makes available to plaintiffs suing in federal court.[17] When state limitations law is unavailing, most federal courts have refused to construe Rule 15(c) to allow relation back, reasoning somewhat woodenly that the plaintiff's failure to name the defendants resulted from ignorance of their names, not from "a mistake concerning the identity of the proper party" as the Rule requires.[18]

§ 4.24 Supplemental Pleadings

Subsequent events

An amended pleading seeks to correct a pleading or to augment the original pleading's allegations by referring to other aspects of the transaction on which suit originally was filed. A supplemental pleading, in

14. The Court might have followed cases allowing relation back when the substituted party was substantially the same enterprise as the one in the original complaint. Korn v. Royal Caribbean Cruise Line, 724 F.2d 1397 (9th Cir.1984); Montalvo v. Tower Life Bldg., 426 F.2d 1135 (5th Cir.1970).

15. *See, e.g.,* Brussack, Outrageous Fortune: The Case for Amending Rule 15(c) Again, 61 S. Cal. L. Rev. 671 (1988); Lewis, the Excessive History of Federal Rule 15(e) and Its Lessons for Civil Rules Revision, 85 Mich. L. Rev. 1507 (1987).

16. 134 F.R.D. 526, 524–529 (1991).

17. *E.g., see* Saxton v. ACF Industries, Inc., 239 F.3d 1209, 1215 (11th Cir.2001) (citing cases). A plaintiff must identify and serve the John Doe defendants with reasonable diligence to avoid dismissal. Scott v. Hern, 216 F.3d 897 (10th Cir.2000). When a defendant in a state court suit including John Doe defendants seeks removal to federal court, the citizenship of the Does is disregarded in assessing the presence of diversity jurisdiction. 28 U.S.C. § 1441(a).

18. Rice, Meet John Doe: It Is Time for Federal Civil Procedure to Recognize John Doe Parties, 57 U. Pitt. L. Rev. 883 (1996).

contrast, asserts a claim or defense based on events occurring after the filing of the original pleading, which it supplements.[1] For instance, a plaintiff may assert a claim for additional damages occurring since the action was commenced;[2] a defendant may interpose a defense based on events occurring after the original answer was filed.[3] A supplemental pleading may be unnecessary if the matters subsequently occurring were fairly forecast by the original complaint.[4] If a claim involving a somewhat different transaction or different parties is asserted by means of a supplemental complaint,the question of its propriety is essentially the same as that posed by an amended complaint seeking to do so.[5]

The Federal Rules on supplemental pleadings follow the liberal guidelines of *Conley v. Gibson,*[6] in which substance takes precedence over form. As the Court in *Conley* stated, "[t]he Federal Rules reject the approach that pleading is a game of skill in which one misstep by counsel may be decisive to the outcome and accept the principle that the purpose of pleading is to facilitate a proper decision on the merits."[7] Rule 15(d), which governs supplemental pleadings, allows them for additional claims occurring subsequent to the claim presented in the original pleadings. New parties may be added when the subsequent facts make this necessary.[8] The supplemental pleading, however, does not relate back to the original pleadings,[9] unlike amended pleadings under Rule 15(c).

Although the court has discretion to grant leave to amend or supplement the pleadings, *Griffin v. County School Board of Prince Edward County*[10] held that it is an abuse of discretion to deny supplemental pleading for later events that clearly relate to the same cause of action originally pleaded.[11]

Action filed prematurely

A more complicated problem develops if the original complaint was filed prematurely and the supplemental complaint is filed after the

§ 4.24

1. *See* Fed. R. Civ. P. 15(d); N.Y. Civ. Prac. L. & R. 3025(d).

2. *See, e.g.,* McHenry v. Ford Motor Co., 269 F.2d 18 (6th Cir.1959). *Cf.* Annot., 125 A.L.R. 612.

3. *See, e.g.,* Manning v. Hyland, 19 A.D.2d 652, 241 N.Y.S.2d 908 (1963).

4. *Compare* Griffin v. County School Bd. of Prince Edward County, 377 U.S. 218, 84 S.Ct. 1226, 12 L.Ed.2d 256 (1964); *see, e.g.,* Hutcherson v. Alexander, 264 Cal.App.2d 126, 70 Cal.Rptr. 366 (1968).

5. *See* § 4.23 *supra*; 6 Wright and Miller, Federal Practice and Procedure §§ 1506, 1507.

6. 355 U.S. 41, 78 S.Ct. 99, 2 L.Ed.2d 80 (1957).

7. 355 U.S. at 48, 78 S.Ct. at 103, 2 L.Ed.2d at 86. *See also* Foman v. Davis, 371 U.S. 178, 83 S.Ct. 227, 9 L.Ed.2d 222 (1962).

8. Griffin v. County School Bd. of Prince Edward County, 377 U.S. 218, 84 S.Ct. 1226, 12 L.Ed.2d 256 (1964); Keith v. Volpe, 858 F.2d 467 (9th Cir.1988).

9. United States ex rel. Wulff v. CMA, Inc., 890 F.2d 1070 (9th Cir.1989).

10. 377 U.S. 218, 84 S.Ct. 1226, 12 L.Ed.2d 256 (1964).

11. *See also* Intrepid v. Pollock, 907 F.2d 1125 (Fed.Cir.1990); Keith v. Volpe, 858 F.2d 467 (9th Cir.1988); Twin Disc, Inc. v. Big Bud Tractor, 772 F.2d 1329 (7th Cir.1985).

statute of limitations has run. This can occur when, as a condition precedent to maintaining the action, plaintiff is required to file a claim against the defendant and to allow the defendant a specified interval to consider the claim before commencing the action;[12] an action filed before the expiration of the specified interval is premature. If plaintiff has filed the action prematurely and tries to correct that error after the statute of limitations has run by filing a supplemental complaint, some courts have held that plaintiff is barred because the original complaint was too early and the supplemental complaint too late. The better view is that the purposes of neither a claims statute nor a limitations statute is served by such a rule.[13]

12. *See* § 3.24 *supra.*

13. *Compare* Security Ins. Co. v. United States for the Use of Haydis, 338 F.2d 444 (9th Cir.1964), *with* Walton v. County of Kern, 39 Cal.App.2d 32, 102 P.2d 531 (1940). *Cf.* Annot., 125 A.L.R. 612.

Chapter 5

DISCOVERY AND OTHER PRETRIAL DEVICES

A. DISCOVERY

§ 5.1 Historical Background

As we have seen, the common law depended almost entirely on pleadings to give advance notice of the parties' claims and defenses.[1] There were almost no common law devices for probing the adversary's

§ 5.1

1. *See* § 3.1 *supra*; Ragland, Discovery Before Trial 1–5 (1932).

claims or knowledge of relevant information until the trial itself.[2] At the trial, of course, a party could compel witnesses and custodians of documents to appear by serving them with a subpoena. In equity the whole procedure was different. Every bill in equity was said to be a bill of discovery; in addition to the complainant's statements of fact and charges of evidence, the equity bill propounded interrogatories to the defendant that had to be answered under oath. These and other statements of witnesses taken through deposition constituted the evidence on which the chancellor acted. There was no face-to-face trial, no taking of evidence en bloc. Discovery in equity was not a truly *pretrial* device, as we use that term today, but a trial on the basis of documentary evidence.[3]

Discovery in equity

Equity did, however, develop pretrial devices that were the precursors of modern discovery and deposition procedure: the bill of discovery of documents and the bill to take a deposition in aid of an action or defense at law. It was not unusual for equity to implement a legal right in this way, but traditionally it did so only when the remedy at law was inadequate. (Thus, equity would compel a defendant to remove an encroaching structure if it was not feasible for the sheriff to remove it under an execution upon a judgment in ejectment.[4] Equity would subject equitable assets to the payment of a judgment at law if legal execution was returned unsatisfied.[5] And so on.)

Obtaining testimony of opposing party

The principal defect in common law procedure that invited equitable relief through discovery was the common law rule that parties to an action were neither competent nor obliged to testify at trial. Equity sought to fill this evidentiary gap by compelling the defendant in discovery to supply written sworn answers to interrogatories—answers that would be presented in evidence at the trial as admissions against the party making them.[6] Equity did not, however, seek to permit pretrial probing of the evidence; rather it accepted the legal notion that the trial itself was an adequate method for ascertaining the facts of the case. "In short," as Wigmore puts it, "equitable discovery involved no more than a negation of the party's privilege at common-law trials not to testify

2. Ragland, Discovery Before Trial 1–5 (1932); 6 Wigmore, Evidence § 1845 (Chadbourn rev. 1976); James, Discovery, 38 Yale L.J. 846 (1929).

3. Langdell, A Summary of Equity Pleading §§ 55–58, 68, 69 (2d ed. 1883); Ragland, Discovery Before Trial 6, 7, 13–17 (1932); Millar, The Mechanism of Fact–Discovery: A Study in Comparative Civil Procedure IV, 32 Ill. L. Rev. 424, 437–442 (1937).

4. Walsh, Equity 160, 161 (1930).

5. 4 Pomeroy, § Equity Jurisprudence § 1415 (5th ed. 1941).

6. Langdell, A Summary of Equity Pleading § 167 (2d ed. 1883); 2 Story, Commentaries on Equity Jurisprudence §§ 1480–1504 (13th ed. 1886); Millar, The Mechanism of Fact–Discovery: A Study in Comparative Civil Procedure IV, 32 Ill. L. Rev. 424, 440–442 (1937).

against his own cause, and was not intended to give relief against the common-law principle which refused to exact before trial a disclosure of the evidence intended to be given *for* his cause."[7] The fact that equitable discovery preceded the trial at law was a product of necessity—there was simply no other way to provide the party with the needed evidence.

This equitable origin produced limitations on discovery that dominated the scene in America until the adoption of the federal rules in 1938 (although a few states had anticipated something of their liberality). These limitations were as follows: (1) discovery could be had only of facts that pertained to the case of the party seeking discovery (any attempt to pry into the adversary's case was regarded as an improper fishing expedition);[8] (2) the facts sought by discovery had to be either unavailable to the party seeking them[9] or at least helpful in proving that party's case (this seems to have been the rule of the English equity court);[10] (3) discovery could reach only facts or documents that would be admissible in evidence at the trial;[11] and (4) discovery could be had only against the adverse party.[12]

The bill in equity to take a deposition was the main pre-code procedural mechanism for the implementation of these rules. It sought to remedy the possibility that a witness might be unavailable at trial. The deposition in equity would generally be taken only if the witness was beyond the realm or about to depart from it, or was old or infirm or lived at a great distance from the place of the trial.[13]

Discovery under code procedure

Procedural reforms in the mid-nineteenth century removed the rule of incompetence of parties to testify[14] and merged law and equity.[15] These changes did away with the original need for equitable discovery, but the value of pretrial discovery had come to be recognized over and above the need to supply proof for trial.[16] The framers of the New York code,for

7. 6 Wigmore, Evidence § 495 (Chadbourn rev. 1976).

8. *See, e.g.*, Downie v. Nettleton, 61 Conn. 593, 24 A. 977 (1892); Ragland, Discovery Before Trial ch. 15 (1932); 6 Wigmore, Evidence §§ 1846, 1856b and c (Chadbourn rev. 1976); James, Discovery, 38 Yale L.J. 746, 755–760 (1929).

9. *See, e.g.*, Hubert v. New York, N.H. & H. R.R., 90 Conn. 261, 96 A. 967 (1916); Will v. Domer, 134 Wash. 576, 236 P. 104 (1925).

10. Lyell v. Kennedy, 8 App.Cas. 217 (H.L.1883); Green v. Selznick, 220 App.Div. 12, 221 N.Y.S. 63 (1927). For the former equity rule, see 2 Story, Commentaries on Equity Jurisprudence § 1483 (13th ed. 1886).

11. State ex rel. Thompson v. Harris, 355 Mo. 176, 195 S.W.2d 645 (1946); James, Discovery, 38 Yale L.J. 746, 755 (1929).

12. Ragland, Discovery Before Trial ch. 7 (1932); 6 Wigmore, Evidence §§ 1856, 1856a and d (Chadbourn rev. 1976); James, Discovery, 38 Yale L.J. 746, 751–754 (1929).

13. 2 Story, Commentaries on Equity Jurisprudence § 1514 (13th ed. 1886), and *cf. id.* 1508; Weeks, Law of Depositions 14 (1880), and *cf. id.* 11, 12.

14. Allen, The Law of Evidence in Victorian England (1997); Fisher, The Jury's Rise as Lie Detector, 107 Yale L.J. 575 (1997).

15. *See* § 1.6 *supra*; Clark, Code Pleading §§ 6–8 (2d ed. 1947).

16. *See* James, Discovery, 38 Yale L.J. 746, 758 (1929); Millar, The Mechanism of

instance, found provisions for discovery to be "in harmony with the whole spirit of [their] design; which is, to get at the facts in a legal controversy by the shortest possible way."[17]

New discovery devices

The nineteenth century reforms established statutory procedures for discovery and depositions without the need to resort to the cumbersome separate suit in equity. These procedures included written interrogatories addressed to the adverse party, compulsory production of documents prior to the trial by the adverse party, and depositions of specified classes of witnesses (such as the employees of a party) in addition to the parties themselves. These devices have been retained in subsequent procedural reforms[18] and constitute much of the essential framework of modern federal discovery.

Old restrictions on use

The nineteenth century reformers failed to see, however, that the old equity restrictions on discovery would hamstring its usefulness. The early statutes either embodied the old restrictions, expressly or by implication, or failed to repudiate them, thereby leaving the courts free to perpetuate them through conservative interpretation. This probably reflected suspicion of wide-ranging intrusions sponsored by the government into private matters. Thus American discovery in the early twentieth century was not much broader in scope than it had been before the codes. Depositions were still considered, not as a discovery device, but only as a means of perpetuating for the trial testimony that might otherwise be unavailable.[19] Most deposition statutes conditioned the taking of the deposition on the same kind of showing required for the equitable remedy.[20]

§ 5.2 Emergence of Broader Role for Discovery

By the time the Federal Rules were promulgated in 1938, a shift favoring discovery had gathered momentum, at least among academics.[1]

Fact–Discovery: A Study in Comparative Civil Procedure IV, 32 Ill. L. Rev. 424, 448 (1932).

17. New York, First Report of Commissioners on Practice and Pleadings 241 (1848). *See also id.* at 244; Ragland, Discovery Before Trial 16–18, 25, 26 (1932).

18. Millar, The Mechanism of Fact–Discovery: A Study in Comparative Civil Procedure IV, 32 Ill. L. Rev. 424, 446–452 (1932). Ragland, *supra* note 17, contains an excellent description of the discovery provisions in force throughout the United States in 1932; an appendix, at 267–391, sets out verbatim the provisions then in force for the federal courts and each of the states.

19. In re Davis, 38 Kan. 408, 16 P. 790 (1888); Town of Hancock v. First Natl. Bank, 93 N.Y. 82, 86 (1883). *See* Peyton v. Coulson, 190 Misc. 754, 756, 74 N.Y.S.2d 730, 732 (Sup.Ct.1947).

20. *See* statutes set out in Ragland, Discovery Before Trial 267–391 (1932). In a few states some of these limitations persist. N.Y. Civ. Prac. L. & R. 3101(a)(3). *But cf. id.* 3101(a)(4) (the New York limitations apply only to nonparty witnesses).

§ 5.2

1. See Ragland, Discovery Before Trial (1932); Subrin, Fishing Expeditions Allowed: The Historical Background of the

Full investigation of the facts was consistent with Federal Rules' goal of decision on the merits, and with the Progressive Movement's belief in informed decision-making. The bar seems to have shown little interest in the subject. The fear persisted that requiring a party to disclose its evidence would enable the opponent to fabricate other evidence to avoid its thrust.[2] Since the enactment of the Federal Rules, wide mutual discovery has indeed resulted, on balance, in both better marshaling of the available evidence and little fabrication.[3] It has made it possible to prosecute types of claims where relevant evidence is in the hands of defendants, thus shifting the balance of advantage. It has also made some types of litigation much more expensive.

Other sources of information

Discovery is not the only means by which a party may obtain information in civil cases. Speaking to potential witnesses (if they are willing to talk) and similar investigative techniques are often cheaper than discovery and do not require automatic disclosure of the results to other parties. The Freedom of Information Act[4] allows access to federal agency records that may otherwise be unavailable or hard to obtain, and some states have similar statutes.[5]

Purposes of discovery

The main advantage of discovery is that it enables fuller exploration of the facts. Beyond this, proponents of discovery assert that the opportunity to interrogate parties and witnesses before trial and to obtain documents and objects of evidentiary value brings several other benefits.

1. It eliminates fictitious issues. Discovery can show that the evidence on an issue is overwhelming, in which case the issue will usually be uncontested, or that the issue is nonexistent, in which case it will be abandoned or yield to summary judgment. If the issue is a critical one, its elimination can lead to pretrial settlement of the litigation.

2. Discovery can simplify presentation of evidence at trial by eliminating time-consuming objections to innocuous testimony, as discovery usually reveals the critical aspects of a witness's story.[6] Similarly, the party calling a witness knows what questions to ask. In the case of

1938 Federal Discovery Rules, 39 B.C. L. Rev. 691 (1998) See also Federal Judicial Center, Survey of Literature on Discovery from 1970 to the Present (1978); Glaser, Pretrial Discovery and the Adversary System (1968). On the history of the federal discovery rules, see generally 4 Moore, Federal Practice and Procedure ¶¶ 26.00–26.02.

2. 6 Wigmore, Evidence § 1845 (Chadbourn rev. 1976).

3. *But see* Hawkins, Discovery and Rule 34: What's So Wrong about Surprise?, 39 A.B.A.J. 1075 (1953).

4. 5 U.S.C. § 552.

5. On the Freedom of Information Act, see Vladeck and Adler, Litigation Under the Federal Open Government Laws (20th ed. 1997). On state law, *see, e.g.*, Cal. Information Practices Act of 1977, Cal. Civ. Code § 1798 (West 1990).

6. *Compare* Ehrich, Unnecessary Difficulties of Proof, 32 Yale L.J. 436 (1923).

documents, discovery often obviates the time-consuming procedure of authenticating documents at trial ("I show you an item marked Plaintiff's No. 1 for Identification. Do you recognize it?" "Will you tell the court and jury what it is?"). If a document's authenticity is established through discovery, it can be admitted simply by offering it in evidence, a shortcut especially important in cases involving masses of documents.

3. Pretrial deposition of witnesses can secure their testimony when it is fresher, especially if the action is filed relatively soon after the transaction that is the subject of suit.

In concentrating on the costs and complications that broad discovery involves, many of its critics tend to forget these benefits. They can be fully understood only by bringing to mind what trials were like without discovery. In the era before free discovery, much or most of the trial time was spent compensating for ignorance of the opponent's case by such means as hypertechnical objections to the other side's presentation of evidence and painstakingly cautious cross-examination.

Questionable consequences of discovery

Discovery also has effects of a problematic character.

1. It makes possible the prosecution and defense of actions that would be impossible without it. With wide-ranging discovery, an action or defense can be maintained that is dependent on witnesses or documents known only to the opponent—for example, a medical malpractice claim that must be proved through the testimony and records of the treating medical staff, or an antitrust action based chiefly on the records of the alleged offender. Although this intentional result is in one sense more just—indeed, legislatures today may rely on it when they create new claims—it changes the practical effect of the applicable substantive legal rules and thus is not "neutral" in its substantive consequences.

Costs and consequences

2. Discovery increases an important part of the costs of litigation—the time of the attorneys, parties, witnesses, and court reporters consumed in taking the evidence before trial. In effect, a case may be tried twice, once in discovery and once in court, with the first "trial" usually the longer of the two. More cost may be incurred in baselessly seeking or resisting discovery or squabbling about its details. Whether this is offset by reduced trial and social costs is hard to ascertain.

There is much evidence that little discovery or discovery abuse occurs in the great bulk of cases.[7] It is clear, however, that in certain

7. Glaser, Pretrial Discovery and the Adversary System (1968); Willging, *et al.*, An Empirical Study of Discovery and Disclosure Practice Under the 1993 Federal Rules Amendments, 39 B.C. L. Rev. 525 (1998); Trubeck, *et al.*, The Costs of Ordinary Litigation, 31 U.C.L.A. L. Rev. 72 (1983); Federal Judicial Center, Judicial Controls and the Civil Litigation Process: Discovery (1978); see Mullenix, Discovery in

types of litigation the cost of discovery is itself a major factor in a party's decision whether and on what terms to settle. In addition, some question the fairness of requiring one party to bear the burden and cost of helping to prepare another's case; others consider this a desirable instance of cooperation and equalization.

Balancing cost and benefit

Most of the modern law of discovery is an accommodation between affording full and open discovery and safeguarding against unrestrained rummaging through an opponent's files, imposition of oppressive expense, or invasion of the opponent's preparation for adversarial trial. On the whole, a satisfactory balance is struck, but the scope of discovery remains a dilemma in two types of litigation: "big" cases (involving millions of dollars in damages), in which the stakes are so large that the parties have incentive to exhaust every possibility of unearthing or withholding additional evidence;[8] and "little" cases (involving, say, $50,000 or less) in which one party has an incentive to overpower the other by protracting discovery beyond the value of the case and thereby deterring similarly situated persons from maintaining similar litigation.[9]

Over the decades since the Federal Rules came into effect in 1938, many amendments have altered the balance they strike, usually in minor ways. Broadly speaking, two trends have been at work. The amendments up to and including 1970, tended to increase the availability of discovery and simplify its procedure. Since then, although that trend has sometimes prevailed, most of the changes have been meant to prevent discovery abuse by increasing court supervision and sanctions and by establishing presumptive limits on the quantity of discovery.[10]

Notwithstanding these alterations, the federal discovery rules have generally been accepted as establishing an acceptable balance. They have been adopted in whole or substantial part by most states.[11] The following sections are based on the federal discovery machinery.

Disarray: The Pervasive Myth of Pervasive Discovery Abuse and the Consequences for Unfounded Rulemaking, 46 Stan. L. Rev. 1393 (1994).

8. *See* Brazil, Civil Discovery: Lawyers' Views of Its Effectiveness, Its Principal Problems and Abuses, 1980 Am. B. Found. Res. J. 787 (1980). *See* the dictum in Blue Chip Stamps v. Manor Drug Stores, 421 U.S. 723, 741, 95 S.Ct. 1917, 1928, 44 L.Ed.2d 539, 552 (1975). *See also* In re Convergent Technologies Sec. Litig., 108 F.R.D. 328 (N.D.Cal.1985).

9. *Compare* Shuchman, Discovering the Law of Discovery by Low Level Investigations, 38 Geo. Wash. L. Rev. 32 (1969). *See also* ABA, Standards Relating to Trial Courts § 2.74(a)(2).

10. Marcus. Discovery Containment Redux, 39 B.C. L. Rev. 747 (1998); Thornburg, Giving the "Haves" a Little More: Considering the 1998 Discovery Proposals, 52 S.M.U. L. Rev. 229 (1999)(attributing the movement for restrictions to corporate defendants).

11. *Compare, e.g.,* American Law Inst.-American Bar Assn. Comm. on Continuing Legal Educ., Practical Lawyer's Manual of Pretrial Discovery (1973); Practicing Law Inst., Discovery Techniques (1974); Underwood, A Guide to Federal Discovery Rules (2d ed. 1989).

§ 5.3 Mechanics of Discovery: Depositions

Discovery devices include the following: the *deposition,* which may be taken through oral questioning or through written questions and may be taken of either party or a nonparty witness;[1] *interrogatories to a party*, which pose written questions to a party;[2] *production of things* (particularly documents) and entry on property to inspect, make copies or photographs, or conduct tests;[3] *physical or mental examinations* of parties or persons "under the legal control of a party";[4] and *requests for admissions*, which require a party to admit propositions of fact tendered in a written request.[5] In addition, *disclosure* requires parties to transmit certain information and documents to other parties without having been asked.[6] These devices are governed by rules for the scope of discovery.[7] The enforcement of discovery, which helps make these devices practically effective, is governed by sanction rules.[8]

Scope of discovery: Rule 26

The general rule for scope of discovery states that inquiry may be made into "any matter, not privileged, that is relevant to the claim or defense of any party."[9] The matter inquired into need not itself be admissible evidence. For example, a witness may be asked to supply secondhand information that at trial would be inadmissible as hearsay.[10] In a few jurisdictions, the scope of discovery is somewhat more restricted, being limited to matter "necessary" for preparation for trial, but in practice this amounts to nearly the same thing because reasonable trial preparation usually includes inquiring into secondhand information.[11] Because of this broad scope, the operational rule of discovery is that anything concerning the case is discoverable unless prohibited by specific limitations on scope. We will first consider the devices of discovery and then the limitations on scope.

§ 5.3

1. Fed. R. Civ. P. 30, 31. *See also* Fed. R. Civ. P. 27.

2. Fed. R. Civ. P. 33; § 5.4 *infra.*

3. *Id.* 34; § 5.5 *infra.*

4. *Id.* 35; § 5.6 *infra.*

5. *Id.* 36; § 5.7 *infra.*

6. *Id.* 26(a); § 5.9 *infra.*

7. *Id.* 26(b); §§ 5.9–13 *infra.* Rules for the scope of discovery are incorporated in the provisions for specific discovery devices. *See, e.g.,* Fed. R. Civ. P. 33(b), 36(a).

8. Fed. R. Civ. P. 37; § 5.14 *infra.*

9. Fed. R. Civ. P. 26(b)(1). *See also* Haydock and Herr, Discovery Practice § 1.4 (2d ed. 1988); Underwood, A Guide to Federal Discovery Rules (2d ed. 1989) § 5.9 *infra.*

10. Taylor v. Sound Steamship Lines, 100 F.Supp. 388 (D.Conn.1951); see discussion of when court permission is needed in § 5.9 *infra.* Matter is also discoverable even though its potential use is limited to impeaching the testimony of witnesses as distinct from constituting affirmative evidence. *See* Annot., 18 A.L.R.3d 922.

11. *See* N.Y. Civ. Prac. L. & R. 3101(a); 3A Weinstein, Korn, and Miller, New York Civil Practice ¶ 3101.07. It should be observed, however, that in New York the scope of discovery from nonparties is limited by the requirement of "adequate special circumstances." N.Y. Civ. Prac. L. & R. 3101(a)(4).

Oral depositions

The most widely used federal discovery device is the oral deposition,[12] which can be taken of *any* witness, whether a party or nonparty. Even opposing counsel's deposition may be taken, but the courts have viewed this "increasing practice ... as a negative development in the area of litigation, and one that should be employed only in limited circumstances."[13] In contrast to their use in the United States, depositions are infrequent in England and other common law systems and virtually nonexistent in civil law systems, although in the latter their place is taken to some small extent by multiple evidentiary hearings or investigations directed by a judge.[14]

A deposition consists of the questioning of a witness under oath, with other parties permitted to attend and cross-examine. The party taking the deposition pays for its recording and may choose between the traditional court reporter and sound recording or videotape.[15] The deposition may be taken, if within the United States, before "an officer authorized to administer oaths" by federal or local law,[16] usually a court reporter. The officer provides copies of the transcript or other recording to the parties, who do not file them in court until they are used in the proceeding.[17]

A deposition may in most cases be taken simply on notice to the other parties without court order.[18] If the person to be deposed is not a party, however, the witness must be subpoenaed, unless he or she appears voluntarily, and the parties given notice.[19] The lawyer for the party taking the deposition issues the subpoena.[20] If the witnesses are to produce documents or things in their possession, these must be specifically designated and demanded by subpoena *duces tecum*.[21]

The rules governing depositions seek to prevent obstruction while nevertheless providing safeguards against improper inquiries. If a depo-

12. Fed. R. Civ. P. 30. *See* Haydock and Herr, Discovery Practice ch. 3 (2d ed. 1988).

13. Shelton v. American Motors Corp., 805 F.2d 1323 (8th Cir.1986).

14. Sime, A Practical Approach to Civil Procedure 406 (4th ed. 2000) (England); Hazard, Discovery and the Role of the Judge in Civil Law Jurisdictions, 73 Notre Dame L. Rev. 1017 (1998).

15. Fed. R. Civ. P. 30(b)(1, 2); Emerson Electric Co. v. Superior Court, 16 Cal.4th 1101, 68 Cal.Rptr.2d 883, 946 P.2d 841 (1997)(plaintiff may be required to re-enact injury in videotaped deposition); National Bureau of Standards, Potential Uses of Court-Related Video Recording, Report 10-869 (1972). A party taking a deposition may be able to shift its costs to the other party if it wins the case. 28 U.S.C. § 1920(2); U.S.E.E.O.C. v. W&O, Inc., 213 F.3d 600 (11th Cir.2000).

16. *See* Fed. R. Civ. P. 28(a). Rule 30(b)(4) allows the parties to agree to dispense with the presence of such an officer. Rule 28(b) authorizes taking of depositions in foreign countries. *See generally* § 5.15 *infra*; Note, Taking Evidence Outside the United States, 55 B.U.L. Rev. 368 (1975). *See also* Farquhar v. Shelden, 116 F.R.D. 70 (E.D.Mich.1987) (deposition was allowed to shift to the Netherlands, but the requesting party was ordered to pay all its costs).

17. Fed. R. Civ. P. 5(d), 30(f).

18. Fed. R. Civ. P. 30(b)(1); *cf. id.* 30(g)(2).

19. Fed. R. Civ. P. 30(b)(1), 30(g)(1).

20. *Id.* 45(a)(2). On subpoenas, see § 5.5 *infra*.

21. *Id.* 45(a)(1).

nent, whether a party or a nonparty witness, refuses to appear for a deposition or to answer questions propounded in the course of the deposition, an order may be requested compelling an answer.[22] Failure to obey such an order is sanctionable as contempt of court.[23] Lawyers may object to improper questions, but this merely preserves the objection for consideration if the deposition is used as evidence; it does not excuse the witness from answering the question, at which point the cat may be out of the bag.[24] To prevent an answer, a party may use the cumbersome procedure of suspending the deposition and seeking a court protective order.[25] A simpler method is to instruct the witness not to answer but, in the hope of preventing delay, this may be done only to preserve an evidentiary privilege or restriction directed by the court.[26]

Advantages and disadvantages of deposition

The greatest advantage of an oral deposition over other methods of discovery is the flexibility it affords in probing a witness by requiring immediate, on-the-spot answers to oral questions (without the chance to rehearse responses that written interrogatories would afford) and by allowing the examiner to frame successive questions in the light of the answers given. Moreover, the examiner can elicit a preview of the witness's line of testimony as the witness will give it at trial. A deponent who is an adverse party or a hostile witness may be asked leading questions, as on cross-examination.[27]

The greatest disadvantage of the oral deposition is its expense. At least two lawyers are normally present during questioning that often moves slowly, in addition to the witness and the court reporter. In an attempt to reduce costs, the rules allow each party only ten depositions of seven hours apiece unless the court allows more or all parties agree. The court may also grant a protective order restricting the number of depositions even further.[28] In the large majority of cases, neither party comes close to the ten deposition limit.

In some cases the deposition may have a more limited reach than interrogatories addressed to a party, because, as we shall see,[29] interrogatories require a party to respond with any available information—not merely what can be recollected at the time of the question. In depositions, witnesses are required to respond only according to what they can recollect. An exception exists when the named deponent is an organization (such as a corporation or partnership) and the subject matter of the deposition is described with specificity. The organization then must designate appropriate persons to testify who have knowledge of the

22. Fed. R. Civ. P. 37(a)(2), (3).

23. *Id.* 37(b). *See also* § 5.14 *infra.*

24. Fed. R. Civ. P. 30(c).

25. Fed. R. Civ. P. 30(d)(3).

26. Fed. R. Civ. P. 30(d)(1).

27. 4A Moore, Federal Practice and Procedure ¶ 30.58.

28. Fed. R. Civ. P. 26(c), 30(a)(2), 30(d).

29. *See* § 5.4 *infra.*

matters described, and they must provide whatever information is reasonably available to the organization.[30] Aside from this situation, however, a deposition reaches only what the deponent knows.

Another disadvantage of oral deposition is that it may sometimes aid the opponent by preserving testimony that he or she needs and by giving the witness a lesson in how to act under cross-examination.

Deposition of nonparty witness: Rule 45

The Federal Rules limit the distance of the place where a witness may be compelled to attend. A nonparty to whom a subpoena for the taking of a deposition is directed may be required to attend at any place within 100 miles from the place where that person resides, is employed, or regularly transacts business in person.[31] If the deponent is a party or an officer or managing agent of a party, however, he or she must attend the examination at any place designated in the notice unless directed otherwise by order from the court in which the action is pending or from which a subpoena issued.[32]

Use of deposition

While the old equity restrictions on the taking of the deposition have been abolished, restrictions remain on the use of the deposition at trial that reflect the law's preference for the live testimony of a witness with its revelation of demeanor in the presence of the trier of fact and the jury. Because a deposition witness's testimony is delivered out of court, it ordinarily constitutes hearsay. Rule 32 limits its uses to the following:

1. Impeachment. Any deposition—like any other statement of the witness—may be used to contradict or impeach "the testimony of deponent as a witness"[33] at the trial.

2. Deposition in lieu of testimony. The deposition of a party "may be used by an adverse party for any purpose." The main point of this provision is that the whole or any part of a deposition of an opposing party can be introduced as an admission of the facts to which the party testified. The deposition of any other witness "may be used by any party for any purpose" if the court finds the witness to be unavailable or special circumstances justify such use or the rules of evidence allow.[34]

When the adverse party is a corporation, partnership, or association, use of a deposition "for any purpose" is authorized from a deponent who at the time of a deposition was "an officer, director, or managing agent" of the organization. Other procedural consequences turn on this connec-

30. Fed. R. Civ. P. 30(b)(6). *See also* Volz, Depositions of Organizations: The Designation Procedure Under the Federal Rules, 33 S.D.L. Rev. 236 (1988).

31. Fed. R. Civ. P. 45(c)(3)(A)(ii).

32. Fed. R. Civ. P. 26(c), 45(c)(3)(A)(iv). *See* Dickerson, The Law and Ethics of Civil Depositions, 57 Md. L.Rev. 273 (1998).

33. Fed. R. Civ. P. 32(a)(1).

34. *Id.* 32(a)(2). See Fed. R. Ev. 801(d)(2), 804(b)(1).

tion as well, such as sanctions for the witness's refusal to answer question.[35] There is seldom any question whether a deponent is an officer or a director of a corporate party. But controversy has arisen over who is a "managing agent." Courts have tended to adopt a pragmatic test based on the extent of the responsibilities and discretion vested in the agent and the likelihood that the agent will identify with the employer's interests.[36]

Sequence of discovery

The party who can examine its adversary first may thereby obtain a tactical advantage.[37] Before 1970 some courts allowed the party first commencing any discovery to complete all its discovery before the opposing party had its "innings." Rule 26(d), adopted in 1970, repudiates that rule and allows discovery by all parties to go forward simultaneously unless the court orders otherwise.[38] A limited advantage can still be obtained by serving notice to take the opposing party's deposition as soon as possible before one's own deposition is scheduled.[39] Since a defendant ordinarily can "notice" a deposition before the plaintiff can do so,[40] defendants still have whatever edge this may give. It should be noted that pleading deficiencies generally do not affect either party's right to conduct discovery; in fact, this right and corresponding obligation to respond has been held to be especially important to a plaintiff who may need discovery to amend the complaint.[41]

Deposition by written questions

A deposition is usually on oral examination, but the Rules provide that it may be taken on written questions. The questions are asked of the witness and the answers recorded by a court reporter.[42] This is a cumbersome device, for most purposes far inferior to oral examination and not often used. It has, however, the great advantage of being much less expensive and thus may be well suited to certain types of situations, such as when a witness's testimony authenticates a document or establishes a simple fact or when, because the witness is distant, the cost of an oral deposition is disproportionate. Depositions on written questions

35. Under the discovery procedures of some jurisdictions, the right to take a deposition without showing special circumstances depends on the deponent's being an officer or employee of the corporation. *See* N.Y. Civ. Prac. L. & R. 3101(a)(1).

36. *See* Annot., 98 A.L.R.2d 622 ("managing agent"), 56 A.L.R.2d 1108 ("employee"). *Compare* the problem of obtaining information in the hands of a subsidiary corporation, Annot., 19 A.L.R.3d 1134.

37. *See* Younger, Priority of Pretrial Examination in the Federal Courts—A Comment, 34 N.Y.U. L. Rev. 1271 (1959). The New York discovery rule gives priority to the defendant in taking plaintiff's deposition. N.Y. Civ. Prac. L. & R. 3106; 4A Weinstein, Korn, and Miller, New York Civil Practice ¶ 3106.01.

38. Fed. R. Civ. P. 26(d).

39. *See id.* 30(a).

40. *Id.*

41. Mattco Forge, Inc. v. Arthur Young & Co., 223 Cal.App.3d 1429, 273 Cal.Rptr. 262 (1990).

42. Fed. R. Civ. P. 31. *See* Haydock and Herr, Discovery Practice § 2.9 (2d ed. 1988).

are distinguished from interrogatories to parties (examined in the next section), which have their own distinct rules.

§ 5.4 Interrogatories to Parties

Interrogatory procedure

Rule 33 allows a party to serve on any other *party* written interrogatories to be answered by the party served. Each interrogatory must be answered "separately and fully in writing under oath"[1] unless an objection is raised.

If the adverse party is a corporation, partnership, association, or government agency, the answers are to be made "by any officer or agent, who shall furnish such information as is available to the party."[2] The interrogatory, however, is to be addressed to the party, not to an officer or agent. The duty and right to choose the person to make the answers rests with the party interrogated.

Under the Federal Rules, one party may serve on another only twenty-five interrogatories unless the court permits more. This can lead to disputes if the respondent claims that an interrogatory contains "discrete subparts" that should be counted separately. Some states similarly impose restrictions on the use of interrogatories.[3]

If an interrogatory is objected to or not answered, the proponent of the interrogatory may move for a court order compelling an answer. Dispute over whether the interrogatory is proper (for example, whether it calls for privileged information) is resolved on the hearing of the motion.[4] When an interrogatory calls for information contained in the respondent's business records, the burden of searching through the records may be imposed on the proponent by providing the opportunity to examine the records and to make copies or summaries of them.[5]

Advantages and disadvantages

Interrogatories to parties enjoy wide use; the device is almost as popular as the oral deposition. As mentioned previously, it is much less expensive, and, although it lacks the flexibility of the oral deposition, it is often useful to pave the way for more economical and effective use of the deposition procedure (by ascertaining the names and addresses of

§ 5.4

1. Fed. R. Civ. P. 33(a). *See generally* Haydock and Herr, Discovery Practice ch. 3 (2d ed. 1988); Sherman and Kinnard, Federal Court Discovery in the 1980's—Making the Rules Work, 95 F.R.D. 245 (1982). For the special problems presented by discovery against the members of a class in a class suit, see Note, Requests for Information in Class Actions, 83 Yale L.J. 602 (1974).

2. *See* sources cited *supra* note 1.

3. *See, e.g.*, N.Y. Civ. Prac. L. & R. 3130, precluding use of interrogatories in actions "to recover damages for an injury to property, or a personal injury, resulting from negligence, or wrongful death," and also precluding use of both interrogatories and a bill of particulars except by leave of the court.

4. Fed. R. Civ. P. 37(a)(2).

5. *Id.* 33(c). *See* Annot., 96 A.L.R.2d 598.

witnesses) and for the disclosure of documents (by ascertaining their identity and whereabouts). Claims of abuse of the interrogatory procedure, however, are frequent. The questioner can easily frame questions requiring great effort to answer; the answerer can submit vague and evasive answers.

Duty to investigate

As we have seen, an advantage of interrogatories is that they call on the responding party to do at least some investigation in preparing answers, while witnesses on deposition generally need answer only from their personal knowledge and recollection.[6] The duty to investigate has limits. Clearly the respondent must find out what is in its own records and what lies within the knowledge of its own agents and employees concerning the occurrence or transaction in question. The party may be compelled to state facts found as a result of an investigation it has made for trial. But it is not obliged to unearth information outside its direct control, especially if it has no better access to the information than the party who served the interrogatories.[7]

Supplemental answers

Interrogatory procedure raised a vexing question about whether a party had a continuing duty to supply additional information that it acquired after answering an interrogatory. The same problem can arise when a party has given an answer in a deposition and later learns of facts requiring a different or qualified answer. Amended Rule 26(e) requires that a *party* must supplement a response to an interrogatory or request for admission or for production (but not a deposition) if the answer is revealed to be materially incomplete or incorrect and the missing information has not already been made available.[8] The rule also requires supplementation of information provided by a party's expert or pursuant to a party's obligation to disclose certain information without being asked.[9] Responsibility for fulfilling the duty, especially concerning personal knowledge, rests on a party (which probably includes the officers, directors, and managing agents of an organizational party) and its attorney. No duty rests on nonparty nonexpert witnesses to supplement answers they have given in a deposition.[10]

6. A witness nominated by an organization deponent has a duty to collect information. Fed. R. Civ. P. 30(b)(6). *See* § 5.3 *supra*.

7. *See* 8 Wright and Miller, Federal Practice and Procedure §§ 2174, 2177.

8. *See* Slomanson, Supplementation of Discovery Responses in Federal Civil Procedure, 17 San Diego L. Rev. 233 (1980).

9. Fed. R. Civ. P. 26(e)(1); see Fusco v. General Motors Corp., 11 F.3d 259 (1st Cir.1993); Arche, Inc. v. Azaleia, U.S.A., 882 F.Supp. 334 (S.D.N.Y.1995). For disclosure, see § 5.8 *infra*.

10. *But see* Barnes v. St. Francis Hosp., 211 Kan. 315, 507 P.2d 288 (1973), excluding at trial the testimony of a defendant's witness who in his testimony on deposition inaccurately denied the existence of certain medical records.

Use as evidence

Interrogatory answers may be used at trial "to the extent permitted by the rules of evidence."[11] Because they are hearsay, their use is therefore limited. They may, however, be used against the party making them and in certain other circumstances.[12] In practice, however, someone who has made statements under oath in an interrogatory answer can usually be persuaded to testify to the same effect at trial.

§ 5.5 Discovery of Documents and Things

Rule 34

Rule 34 permits a party to obtain inspection of physical objects, including documents and data in a computer, and to enter on land or other property to make inspections.[1] Based on English practice, this form of discovery is now much more extensive in United States courts than in England and other common law systems; most civil law systems have little or no documentary discovery.[2] In connection with the inspection, the party may make copies, photographs, measurements, and tests. Nowadays, parties sometimes seek to inspect computer hard drives in order to retrieve erased messages.[3] The request must describe the things with reasonable particularity and specify the proposed "time, place, and manner of making the inspection and performing the related acts."[4] The opposing party must respond to the request by either consenting or objecting on stated reasons. If the party objects, the proponent may move for an order enforcing the request, and the objections are resolved by the court.[5] Formerly, Rule 34 required a motion for inspection and a showing of "good cause";[6] now, inspection is required as requested unless the respondent objects.

Discovery procedure

This device requires a specification of what is to be inspected. Specification of documents or things may be by category, such as "reports and memoranda concerning injury claims regarding product *X*." If the party seeking discovery lacks information sufficient to make the

11. Fed. R. Civ. P. 33(c).

12. Fed. R. Ev. 801(d)(2).

§ 5.5

1. *See* Haydock and Herr, Discovery Practice ch. 6 (2d ed. 1988); Park, Discovery of Medical Records in a Corporate Negligence Action, 10 Camp. L. Rev. 193 (1987); Note, Right to Independent Testing: A New Hitch in the Preservation of Evidence Doctrine, 75 Colum. L. Rev. 1355 (1975); Annots., 13 A.L.R.3d 657, 4 A.L.R.3d 762, 95 A.L.R.2d 1061.

2. Sime, A Practical Approach to Civil Procedure 271–301, 379–87 (4th ed. 2000) (England); Hazard, From Whom No Secrets Are Hid, 76 Tex. L. Rev. 1665 (1998).

3. Playboy Enterprises, Inc. v. Welles, 60 F.Supp.2d 1050 (S.D.Cal.1999); Comment, The Discovery and Use of Computerized Information: An Examination of Current Approaches, 13 Pepperdine L. Rev. 405 (1986).

4. Fed. R. Civ. P. 34(b); Annot., 8 A.L.R.2d 1134.

5. Fed. R. Civ. P. 37(d).

6. *Compare* Note, The "Good Cause" Requirement of California Discovery Procedure, 20 Stan. L. Rev. 594 (1968).

specification, this information must first be obtained through preliminary use of other discovery devices such as depositions or interrogatories.

Attorneys have an incentive to interpret discovery requests narrowly to avoid damaging disclosures. This in turn requires the requests to be drafted with meticulous care, lest the responder have a basis for avoiding production of a damaging document. But excessively restrictive interpretations of the request invite court-imposed sanctions for misconduct, including an award of attorney's fees[7] and a Rule 37 motion by the opposing party to compel the production of the improperly withheld documents.[8] The rules also seek to prevent a party from mixing up documents before making them available by requiring that the responding party must either produce the documents as they are kept in the usual course of business or organize and label them to match the categories of the request.[9] As already explained, in some circumstances a party must supplement its response to a request for production in light of new information.[10]

Subpoena to nonparty

Rule 34 applies only to documents and things in possession of a party. If a nonparty possesses something portable, it can be compelled to produce it by subpoena duces tecum.[11] Otherwise, and if the nonparty does not willingly surrender the thing, the Federal Rules provide no remedy other than an independent suit for discovery in aid of the original action.[12] In some states, however, the discovery rules provide for compulsory inspection as against nonparties.[13]

The subpoena used to obtain documents or deposition testimony from a nonparty is a judicial command to that nonparty to produce documents or other items, to appear as a witness, or in the case of a subpoena duces tecum to do both.[14] Subpoenas are issued by counsel, and they specify the name of the court, the title of the case, and a time and place for attendance. They may be served by the marshal's office (for a fee in civil cases) or by any nonparty older than 18.[15] A return, or proof of service, is filed with the court clerk describing the details of service.[16]

Failure to comply with a properly served subpoena may be treated as contempt of the court from which the subpoena issued.[17] A party cannot choose to ignore a subpoena on the ground that it or the

7. Sellon v. Smith, 112 F.R.D. 9 (D.Del. 1986).

8. Fed. R. Civ. P. 37.

9. Fed. R. Civ. P. 34(b), 45(d)(1).

10. Fed. R. Civ. P. 26(e); § 5.4 *supra*.

11. *See id.* 30(b), 45(a)(1), (c)(2)("tangible things").

12. *See* Comment, Rule 34(c) and Discovery of Non-Party Land, 85 Yale L.J. 112 (1975).

13. *See* N.Y. Civ. Proc. L. & R. 3120.

14. Fed. R. Civ. P. 45.

15. *Id.* 45(b).

16. *Id.* 45(b)(3).

17. *Id.* 45(e).

documents it seeks are improper, irrelevant, or immaterial, or on Fifth Amendment grounds. The proper procedure is to serve on the issuing attorney written objections to the inspection or copying of the requested materials. The party seeking discovery may then seek an order compelling production, and compliance with the subpoena is then not required until the court grants that motion.[18] The objector may also move to quash or modify the subpoena, for example because it seeks trade secrets or privileged matter, is unduly burdensome, or fails to allow reasonable time for compliance.[19]

Documents outside district

A subpoena for the production of documents is properly addressed to the person who has control over them; ownership is not necessary, nor is actual possession. Tangible items outside the territorial jurisdiction of the court may be obtained as long as the person having control of these documents is within the court's jurisdiction.

If the person to be served is not in the district where the action is pending or within one hundred miles of place within that district where the deposition or production will occur, the party seeking discovery will have to use a subpoena from another district court meeting these requirements, typically the court for a district in which the witness may be served. The person served will then be able to file any motion to quash or modify the subpoena in that district, and will not have to go to the court where the action is pending to have its objections resolved.[20] Thus, when a deposition or production of documents is sought from a nonparty, it may occur anywhere in the United States, or indeed overseas.[21] Parties, by contrast, can be required to produce themselves, their employees, and their documents in the district where the case is pending, although the court after balancing the inconveniences may order that discovery take place elsewhere.[22]

§ 5.6 Physical Examination

Rule 35

Rule 35 provides that in an action in which "the mental or physical condition of a party, or of a person in the custody or under the legal control of a party, is in controversy," the court may order the person involved to submit to a physical or mental examination. The Rule differs from the discovery devices previously discussed in that it requires a motion, notice to the person to be examined, a showing of "good cause," and an order of the court to obtain the examination.[1] These require-

18. *Id.* 45(c)(2)(B).

19. Fed. R. Civ. P. 45(c)(3); Andover Data Servs. v. Statistical Tabulating, 876 F.2d 1080 (2d Cir.1989).

20. Fed. R. Civ. P. 45(b)(2), (c)(3).

21. See § 5.3 note 16 *supra*; § 5.15 *infra*.

22. Fed. R. Civ. P. 26(c), 34(b).

§ 5.6

1. Fed. R. Civ. P. 35(a). *See also* Haydock and Herr, Discovery Practice § 6.2 (2d ed. 1988).

ments reflect a persisting view that examination of a person's physical or mental condition (as distinct from his or her files and correspondence) is a peculiarly sensitive matter. The concern for sanctity of the person, by virtue of which personal examinations were at one time regarded as abhorrent, may also explain why the motion is not a mere formality but requires individual exercise of the court's discretion.[2] It also may explain why Rule 35 does not provide for examination of persons who are neither parties nor "in the custody or the legal control of a party."

"Good cause" required

In operation, the requirement of "good cause" is often a formality. In personal injury litigation, such examinations are arranged by the parties as a matter of course without resort to the court when the plaintiff claims physical injury.[3]

Physical examination of nonparties

A chief problem is whether Rule 35 allows examination of persons other than those specified in the Rule. The scope of the Rule was expanded in 1970, for it formerly allowed examination of "parties" only. In some states, the discovery rules also allow examination of "employees" of a party.[4] A few decisions have held that a court has "inherent power" to order examination of a person whose physical or mental condition is a critical issue, but these seem an unwarranted extension of a device whose scope has been debated and deliberately formulated.[5]

Classes of persons still remain outside the scope of the Rule. For example, in an action for personal injury against the owner of a vehicle but not the driver, the driver's physical condition at the time of the accident may be in issue, but discovery of the physical examination is not available because the driver is not a party. (Plaintiffs usually join the driver as a defendant in order to get such discovery, even when the driver is impecunious.) So also the spouse of a plaintiff seeking damages for loss of consortium is not a "party."[6] The real question is whether the Rule is too narrowly drafted. Now that physical and mental examinations have become routine and nonparties are subject to discovery, the limitation on the scope of examination seems an anachronism, especially in light of the abundant power of the court to prevent examinations that are frivolous or needlessly intrusive.[7]

2. Schlagenhauf v. Holder, 379 U.S. 104, 85 S.Ct. 234, 13 L.Ed.2d 152 (1964); see, *e.g.,* Sacramona v. Bridgestone/Firestone, Inc., 152 F.R.D. 428 (D.Mass.1993)(denying defendant's motion to test plaintiff for HIV in the hope of showing reduced life expectancy).

3. *Cf.* Annot., 135 A.L.R. 883.

4. *See, e.g.,* N.Y. Civ. Prac. L. & R. 3121. *Compare* Annot., 89 A.L.R.2d 1001.

5. *See* Beckwith v. Beckwith, 355 A.2d 537 (D.C.App.1976), relying on a statute authorizing a blood test of a child in a divorce action based on adultery and citing authorities in other jurisdictions.

6. *See* Annot., 89 A.L.R.2d 1001.

7. *See, e.g.,* Vinson v. Superior Court, 43 Cal.3d 833, 740 P.2d 404, 239 Cal.Rptr. 292 (1987).

Designation of doctor

A question occasionally arises over which doctor should conduct the examination. Usually the examining party designates the doctor; this is appropriate, since the examination is meant to furnish the discoverer with a reliable opinion and a potential witness to call at trial. A party's right to choose its own expert witness should not be lightly brushed aside. Nevertheless, the court has discretion to override this choice when objection to the particular doctor is sufficiently strong.[8]

Another question is whether the court should appoint an impartial physician.[9] The argument for the practice, which is routinely used in European jurisdictions, is that an impartial medical examiner is more likely to give a true and unbiased opinion. As one court has said, however, "[i]t is wrong to provide a witness with the [c]ourt's approval where reasonable medical men could disagree as to either the causal connection, the diagnosis, or the prognosis. It seems to be completely at variance with our concept of justice to have one school of thought represented to the jury as the [c]ourt's 'impartial' medical witness, if there is an honest and authoritative difference of opinion."[10] One response is that an honest expert will explain to the jury that there are indeed other schools of thought.

Sanctions

Since physical or mental examination can be compelled by a court order, Rule 37(b)(2) sanctions are available against a party who refuses to obey such an order. In appropriate cases, the court may enter judgment against a recalcitrant party. The contempt of court sanction, however, is not available for such a refusal, reflecting the view that one should not imprison a litigant who refuses to be examined.[11]

Other examination reports

Rule 35(b) provides a form of reciprocal discovery that is triggered by the order for a physical or mental examination. The party against whom the order is made can request a copy of the examiner's report;[12] when that report is delivered, the party initiating the examination can demand a copy of the reports of any "examination, previously or thereafter made, of the same condition."[13] Thus, if defendant obtains an order

8. *See* 4A Moore, Federal Practice and Procedure ¶ 35.04; Barnet, Compulsory Medical Examinations Under the Federal Rules, 41 Va. L. Rev. 1059 (1955); *see also* Annot., 33 A.L.R.3d 1012 and subsequent citations.

9. *See* 8 Wright and Miller, Federal Practice and Procedure § 2239; Comment, The Doctor in Court: Impartial Medical Testimony, 40 S. Cal. L. Rev. 728 (1967). *See also* Fed. R. Evid. 706.

10. Gallagher v. Latrobe Brewing Co., 31 F.R.D. 36, 39 (W.D.Pa.1962).

11. Fed. R. Civ. P. 37(b)(2)(D).

12. A party obtaining an examination of the other party must have the examining expert make a report to avoid evasion of the requirement that a copy of such a report be provided to the examining party. Salvatore v. American Cyanamid Co., 94 F.R.D. 156(D.R.I.1982).

13. Fed. R. Civ. P. 35(b)(1).

for physical examination of a plaintiff who has claimed back injury, plaintiff can obtain a copy of the report by defendant's examining physician, and defendant in turn can obtain a copy of medical records (if any exist) relating to plaintiff's previous back condition and of any examination that plaintiff may have in preparation for trial. This system of exchange is explained partly as a means of equalizing opportunity for discovery and partly as a means of avoiding restrictions on discovery arising from the doctor-patient privilege.[14] It would seem less complicated simply to redefine that privilege as inapplicable in determining a physical or mental condition at issue in litigation.[15] Such an approach, however, might be a doubtful exercise of the rulemaking power of the courts, given the sensitivity of the privilege.

§ 5.7 Request for Admission

Rule 36

Rule 36 allows a party to serve on any other party a written request for the admission of the genuineness of any exhibited document or of the truth of any relevant matter set forth in the request.[1] This can be thought of as a pretrial version of stipulations that often are requested at trial. The purpose is to avoid the often cumbersome process of authentication of documents and other physical evidence whose genuineness is not disputed. In some ways, a notice to admit is a pleading device that narrows the issues to be tried rather than a discovery device to obtain evidence.

A party may request admission of "statements or opinions of fact or of the application of law to fact."[2] A party may file the request without leave of court at any time after the commencement of the action.

Each matter of which admission is requested will be deemed admitted unless the adversary files within 30 days (1) a statement denying the matter or (2) a statement giving "in detail the reasons why the answering party cannot truthfully admit or deny the matter" or (3) written objections to the requests.[3] The responding party is not permitted to deny a matter on the ground that the party lacks information concerning the matter unless it also states that it has made a reasonable inquiry but remains unable to admit or deny the matter.[4] Nor is the responding party permitted to avoid answering on the ground that the issue is central or "ultimate" in the litigation or that it believes the issue is in

14. *Compare* Annots., 21 A.L.R.3d 912, 25 A.L.R.3d 1401.

15. *See, e.g.,* Cal. Evid. Code § 996; *see* Note, 51 Minn. L. Rev. 575 (1967).

§ 5.7

1. *See generally* Fahringer, The Battle for a Bill of Particulars, 26 Crim. L. Bull. 387 (1990); Finman, The Request for Admissions in Federal Civil Procedure, 71 Yale L.J. 371 (1962).

2. Fed. R. Civ. P. 36(a).

3. *Id.*

4. *Id. See* Annot., 20 A.L.R.3d 756.

genuine dispute. If the party later learns that its response was incomplete or incorrect, it must file a timely amendment.[5]

Cost of proving fact not admitted

If the requested admission is admitted or not denied, the proposition is conclusively established, but only for the purpose of the pending action; it may not be "used against the party in any other proceeding."[6] If an objection is made, it is determined by the court, whereupon the respondent must answer or not answer, according to the court's ruling. If the matter is not admitted and the proponent must prove it at trial, the proponent may be awarded "the reasonable expenses of making that proof, including reasonable attorney's fees" unless the respondent had reasonable ground to believe that it might prevail on the matter or other good reason not to admit.[7] The request for admission can thus implement an exception to the "American Rule" that requires a party that refuses to admit a fact without reasonable grounds to pay the proponent's attorney fees.[8]

This device could be useful in avoiding the litigation of matters about which there can be no real dispute, but the extent of its use has been relatively modest.[9] This may be due in part to the fact that counsel in many localities will readily stipulate to facts and the admissibility of documents in cases where the rule would apply, without the need for invoking its rather cumbersome provisions.

§ 5.8 Disclosure

In 1993, a new variant of discovery came into existence: a requirement that litigants disclose certain information without having been asked.[1] It was highly controversial: one Supreme Court Justice described it as "potentially disastrous and certainly premature," and Congress would probably have blocked its implementation had the plaintiffs' lawyers and the defense lobby been able to agree on the terms.[2] Almost half of the District Courts opted out of substantial parts of the new rule, as the rule itself allowed.[3] Subsequently, controversy diminished, and in

5. Fed. R. Civ. P. 26(e)(2).

6. Fed. R. Civ. P. 36(b).

7. *Id.* 37(c)(2).

8. *See* §§ 1.23–24 *supra.*

9. *See* Glaser, Pretrial Discovery and the Adversary System 53 (1968) (tabulating the frequency with which lawyers use the various discovery devices available under the Federal Rules).

§ 5.8

1. Fed. R. Civ. P. 26(a); Symposium, Recent Changes in the Rules of Pretrial Fact Development, 46 Fla. L. Rev. 1 (1994). For comparable state rules, see, *e.g.*, Ariz. R. Civ. P. 26.1(a); Symposium, Innovations in Discovery, 16 Rev. of Litig. 249 (1997).

2. 113 S.Ct. 585 (1993)(Scalia, J., dissenting from adoption of rule); see Carrington,: Learning from the Rule 26 Brouhaha: Our Courts Need Real Friends, 156 F.R.D. 295 (1994).

3. Stienstra, Implementation of Disclosure in United States District Courts, With Specific Attention to Courts' Responses to Selected Amendments to Federal Rule of Civil Procedure 26 (Fed. Judic. Center 1997).

2000 a compromise amendment was promulgated, removing the power of a District Court to opt out but also limiting the information to be disclosed.

Initial disclosure

In its present form, Rule 26(a) requires initial (early) disclosure of two major categories of information, on pain of being unable to use it at trial. First, each litigant must disclose the name, address, and phone number of each witness likely to have discoverable information that the disclosing party may use to support its claims or defenses. Second, it must disclose a copy or description by category of all documents and other things in its control that it may use to support its claims or defenses. Note that a party is not obliged to disclose witnesses or documents that it will not use but that might help the opposing party. In effect, it must disclose its own case, but not its opponent's, although of course the opponent may use discovery to inquire about other witnesses and documents. In addition to these major categories of early disclosure, a party claiming damages must disclose a computation of what it claims with any supporting documentation, and a party that may have to pay damages must disclose any applicable insurance agreement.[4]

The timing for this initial disclosure is governed by a complex series of cross-referencing rules, the overall impact of which is to require disclosure at most eighty-three days after the defendant files its appearance.[5] A party must supplement its disclosures if it learns later that they were incomplete or incorrect, unless the new information has already been made known to the other parties.[6]

Disclosure before trial

All of this applies only to the initial disclosures described above. The rule also requires disclosures, normally ninety days before the trial, of each party's expert witnesses and their reports, so that the opposing party can prepare to cross-examine and rebut their testimony.[7] A final round of pretrial disclosures covers each party's proposed witnesses (whether presented live or by deposition transcript) and exhibits, and must be made at least thirty days before trial.[8]

Exceptions

Like most of the Federal Rules, the disclosure provisions of Rule 26(a) permit a good deal of flexibility. Certain kinds of cases are exempted from initial disclosure altogether, either because they are usually decided on a limited written record (as with review of an

4. Fed. R. Civ. P. 26(a)(1).

5. Fed. R. Civ. P. 16(b), 26(a)(1), 26(f).

6. Fed. R. Civ. P. 26(e). *See* Sheek v. Asia Badger, Inc., 235 F.3d 687 (1st Cir. 2000).

7. Fed. R. Civ. P. 26(a)(2).

8. Fed. R. Civ. P. 26(a)(3).

administrative agency decision), or because they are usually small and simple cases (as with suits by the United States to recover on student loans), or because the litigants cannot reasonably be expected to comply (as with pro se prisoner suits).[9] The parties may agree to modify the scope or timing of disclosure, and the court may order similar modifications.[10] The sanction of excluding evidence is not inflicted if a party has substantial justification for its failure to disclose or the failure was harmless, and the court may impose alternative or additional sanctions.[11]

Perspectives on disclosure

For some, the disclosure rule is a step on the road to the replacement of adversarial discovery contention by spontaneous disclosure of all evidence.[12] In its present form, both the scope and the rationale of the rule are more limited. The information that the parties must disclose is basic information that any sensible adversary would otherwise seek through traditional discovery. Requiring its early disclosure saves time, spares parties the cost of making discovery, and may guard clients from lawyers too incompetent to ask for information. Somewhat similar disclosure has long been required in England, as well as in some state courts that publish uniform sets of interrogatories that all parties in certain kinds of cases must answer as if they had been duly served.[13]

Opponents of disclosure object on principle to being required to help an opposing party without even being asked, and also predict practical problems. They believe that parties will undergo the cost of compliance even when both have good reasons for not seeking discovery, for example because they expect the case to settle soon. (The rule seeks to remove this problem through its provisions for exemption, agreements between the parties, and court modification of the disclosure requirements.) Opponents also predict many wasteful disputes about compliance, excuses and sanctions resulting from the addition of a new set of procedural requirements.[14] So far, surveys have revealed few disclosure disputes, but also no reduction (or increase) of delay or expense.[15]

9. Fed. R. Civ. P. 26(a)(1)(E).

10. Fed. R. Civ. P. 26(a, c), 29.

11. Fed. R. Civ. P. 37(c)(1). *Compare* Klonoski v. Mahlab, 156 F.3d 255 (1st Cir.1998)(excluding evidence) *with* Newman v. GHS Osteopathic, Inc., 60 F.3d 153 (3d Cir.1995)(admitting evidence); see Dixon v. Certainteed Corp., 164 F.R.D. 685 (D.Kan.1996)(failure to disclose as ground for allowing extra deposition).

12. Brazil, The Adversary Character of Civil Discovery: A Critique and Proposals for Change, 31 Vand. L. Rev. 1295 (1978).

13. Fed. R. Civ. P. 26(a), Advisory Committee Note (1993); N.J. Civ. Prac. R. 4:17–1(b); Sime, A Practical Approach to Civil Procedure 271–87 (4th ed. 2000) (England); Winter, In Defense of Discovery Reform, 58 Brooklyn L. Rev. 263 (1992).

14. Bell, *et al.*, Automatic Disclosure in Discovery - The Rush to Reform, 27 Georgia L. Rev. 1 (1992).

15. Willging, *et al.*, An Empirical Study of Discovery and Disclosure Practice under the 1993 Federal Rules Amendments, 39 B.C. L. Rev. 525 (1998); Kakalik, *et al.*, Discovery Management: Further Analysis of the Civil Justice Reform Act Evaluation Data, 39 B.C. L. Rev. 613 (1998).

Disclosure carries forward the commitment of the original Federal Rules to full exploration of the facts, but with some new twists. Its requirements for specified disclosures at specified times reflect the recent belief in judicial management of litigation. Its requirement that litigants disclose their witnesses and documents early in a case could lead plaintiffs to investigate more before filing suit, for fear that the paucity of their disclosures may give rise to sanctions under Rule 11 for filing without evidentiary support.[16]

§ 5.9 Scope of Discovery: In General

Broad scope

As noted earlier, the scope of discovery under modern rules is very broad. Several old limitations have been entirely swept away by Rule 26, which now governs the scope of all discovery devices. It is not an objection to discovery that the matter relates to the case or defense of the respondent rather than to that of the party seeking discovery[1] or that the party seeking discovery may have abundant evidence on the issue being probed, although the latter may warrant court intervention.[2]

Discovery is permitted of any unprivileged matter relevant to the claims and defenses in the case, even if the information would not be admissible at trial, provided it "appears reasonably calculated to lead to the discovery of admissible evidence."[3] It has in the past not been an objection that the matter is irrelevant to the issues under the pleadings as they stand so long as it is relevant to the "subject matter involved in the pending action." For practical purposes, therefore, any matter has been subject to discovery unless: (1) its discovery is categorically prohibited or made conditional by the discovery rules, or (2) the matter is so obviously irrelevant or the mode of discovery so ill-fitted to the issues of the case that it can be said to result in "annoyance, embarrassment, oppression, or undue burden or expense."[4]

The 2000 amendments to Rule 26(b)(1) change one aspect of this by requiring court permission for discovery that is relevant to the subject matter involved in the action but not to a claim or defense. Just what falls into the category requiring permission is unclear. It plainly includes discovery to develop claims or defenses not yet raised by the pleadings.[5]

16. Fed. R. Civ. P. 11(b)(3); *see* § 3.13 *supra.*

§ 5.9

1. Fed. R. Civ. P. 26(b)(1). Discovery is permissible of preliminary matters such as personal jurisdiction. *See* Insurance Corp. of Ireland v. Compagnie des Bauxites de Guinee, 456 U.S. 694, 102 S.Ct. 2099, 72 L.Ed.2d 492 (1982).

2. 4 Moore, Federal Practice and Procedure ¶ 26.59. *But see* Fed. R. Civ. P. 26(b)(1), second para. (added in 1983).

3. Fed. R. Civ. P. 26(b)(1). *See also* St. Joseph Hosp. v. INA Underwriters Ins. Co., 117 F.R.D. 24 (D.Me.1987).

4. Fed. R. Civ. P. 26(c).

5. *See* Hoffmann–La Roche Inc. v. Sperling, 493 U.S. 165, 110 S.Ct. 482, 107 L.Ed.2d 480 (1989) (age discrimination suit; names of potential plaintiffs discoverable).

The drafters of the amendment also refer[6] to discovery about similar incidents - although these are often sufficiently relevant to be admissible in evidence[7] - and about a party's filing system, which is frequently investigated as the prelude to a request for documents. It is to be hoped that courts will continue to allow such discovery in accordance with what the drafters call "the reasonable needs of the action."

The broad overall scope of discovery under the Federal Rules is subject to two kinds of categorical limitations on discovery. First, discovery may not be had of privileged matter, as defined by the "traditional" privileges (such as attorney-client);[8] second, discovery may be had of certain trial preparation material only on a showing of compelling necessity.[9] Beyond these binding limitations, the court has a discretionary power to limit unduly intrusive or burdensome discovery.

Two matters that had been nondiscoverable under some earlier interpretations of the discovery rules are, since 1970, explicitly made discoverable. The first of these is the existence and contents of liability insurance. The other is a statement made by a witness when that witness seeks its discovery.

Insurance coverage

Discovery of insurance coverage is permitted so that the injured party can more intelligently evaluate the settlement value of the case; indeed, a defendant must now disclose its coverage without being asked.[10] In most states, no direct action can be brought against a liability insurer unless and until judgment is rendered against the insured.[11] The fact of insurance is ordinarily not admissible at trial.[12] Hence, the existence and extent of insurance is legally irrelevant while the action involving the insured is still pending. But if an insured party has limited personal assets and disclosure of insurance is not required, the injured

6. Fed. R. Civ. P. 16(b), Advisory Committee Note (2000). On the history of this amendment and previous attempts to reduce the scope of discovery, see Thornburg, Giving the "Haves" a Little More: Considering the 1998 Discovery Proposals, 52 S.M.U. L. Rev. 229 (1999); Marcus, Discovery Containment Redux, 39 B.C. L. Rev. 747 (1998).

7. *E.g.*, Mueller & Kirkpatrick, Evidence §§ 4.8, 4.9, 4.20–25 (1995); Strong, *et al.*, McCormick on Evidence ch. 18 (5th ed. 1999); see Jones v. Clinton, 993 F.Supp. 1217 (E.D.Ark.1998).

8. *Id.* 26(b)(1). *See* § 5.10 *infra*.

9. Fed. R. Civ. P. 26(b)(3) (material "prepared in anticipation of litigation or for trial"), 26(b)(4)(B) ("facts known or opinions held by an expert who has been retained ... in anticipation of litigation or preparation for trial and who is not expected to be called as a witness").

10. Fed. R. Civ. P. 26(a)(1), 26(b)(2). In many states, the existence of insurance covering the defendant is still not discoverable. *See* Annot., 13 A.L.R.3d 822. New York amended its discovery provisions in 1975 to correspond to the Federal Rule. *See* N.Y. Civ. Prac. L. & R. 3101(f). *See also* Simon v. G.D. Searle & Co., 816 F.2d 397 (8th Cir. 1987) (corporate risk management documents that relate to insurance are discoverable in accordance with Rule 26(b)(1)).

11. *See* Note, Direct-Action Statutes: Their Operational and Conflict-of-Law Problems, 74 Harv. L. Rev. 357 (1960).

12. See Strong, et al., McCormick on Evidence § 201 (5th ed. 1999); *e.g.*, Fed. R. Evid. 411.

party has to discount the settlement value of the case in accordance with speculation as to what the insurance coverage might be. It is thought that this uncertainty is an unfair burden in the settlement process. Moreover, liability insurance is now recognized as being not only protection for the insured but also an asset in which the injured party has a contingent interest.[13]

Statements of a witness

A most important item of potential trial evidence is a statement previously made by a witness. It may be used to impeach the witness, that is, to show that the statement conflicts with testimony at trial;[14] it may be used to help a witness's memory of details not remembered on the witness stand;[15] and it is useful in preparing a witness to take the stand, particularly if the trial occurs long after the transaction that is the subject of suit. Moreover, the statement of a *party* may be introduced in evidence as an admission by that party.[16] Following the occurrence of an event that may result in litigation, it is now customary for investigators or attorneys for parties to take the statements of witnesses as soon as possible, sometimes within a few hours or days of the occurrence. These statements can be considered, and were often held to be, part of the trial preparation of the party who took them and therefore discoverable only on a showing of "good cause."[17]

Discovery of witness statements

In the 1970 revision of the federal discovery rules, Rule 26(b)(3) was amended to provide that a *party* may obtain as of course any statement made by it in the possession of another party. Presumably this would extend to a statement by an officer, director, or managing agent of a party, for these persons are generally equated with parties under the Rules. Further, a witness may obtain a statement he or she had made.[18] A party cannot obtain a statement made by a witness other than that party except on the "good cause" showing required for discovering trial preparation materials generally.[19] The witness may, however, obtain a copy of the statement on request;[20] a party may solicit the witness to make such a request and thereby obtain the information. The "good cause" requirement is considered below.

13. *See, e.g.,* Seider v. Roth, 17 N.Y.2d 111, 216 N.E.2d 312, 269 N.Y.S.2d 99 (1966)(no longer good law on the jurisdictional point).

14. Strong, et al., McCormick on Evidence §§ 34–37 (5th ed. 1999).

15. *Id.* at § 9.

16. 4 Wigmore, Evidence §§ 1048–1087 (Chadbourn rev. 1972).

17. *See* 8 Wright and Miller, Federal Practice and Procedure §§ 2027–2028; § 5.11 *infra*. *See also* Annot., 73 A.L.R.2d 12 (obtaining copy of party's own statement).

18. Fed. R. Civ. P. 26(b)(3).

19. *See* Hamilton v. Canal Barge Co., 395 F.Supp. 975 (E.D.La.1974) (also analyzing the elements of "good cause" in production of such statements).

20. *See, e.g.,* Cal. Civ. Proc. Code § 2019.

§ 5.10 Privileged Matter

The discovery rules do not permit discovery of "privileged" matter, but they provide no definition of the applicable privileges. The definition must therefore be sought elsewhere.[1] In state court, the applicable definition is the state law of privilege. In federal court, federal law supplies the definition except when the "element of a claim or defense" is governed substantially by state law (in diversity cases, for example), in which event the privilege is defined by the law of the appropriate state.[2]

Traditional privileges

Most privileges are substantially the same under federal and state law.[3] This is true of privileges given to attorney-client communications, communications between spouses, and priest-penitent communications and the privilege against self-incrimination.[4] Other privileges are less uniform. In litigation involving the U.S. government or one of its agencies or officers, federal law recognizes a cluster of "government" privileges.[5] State law generally does not recognize similar privileges for state agencies and officers, though in some jurisdictions they are immune from some or all kinds of discovery.[6] Most states treat doctor-

§ 5.10

1. On privileges generally, *see* Strong et al., McCormick on Evidence chs. 8 (in general), 9 (marital communications), 10 (client-attorney communications), 11 (patient-physician communications), 12 (government secrets), 13 (self-incrimination) (5th ed. 1999). *See also, e.g.,* Jaffee v. Redmond, 518 U.S. 1, 116 S.Ct. 1923, 135 L.Ed.2d 337 (1996) (psychotherapist); Upjohn Co. v. United States, 449 U.S. 383, 101 S.Ct. 677, 66 L.Ed.2d 584 (1981) (attorney-client); Trammel v. United States, 445 U.S. 40, 100 S.Ct. 906, 63 L.Ed.2d 186 (1980)(dictum) (spousal communications privilege); Carey v. Klutznick, 653 F.2d 732 (2d Cir.1981) (statutory privilege of census returns); Heidt, The Conjurer's Circle: The Fifth Amendment Privilege in Civil Cases, 91 Yale L.J. 1062 (1982); Comment, Plaintiff as Deponent: Invoking the Fifth Amendment, 48 U. Chi. L. Rev. 158 (1981).

2. Fed. R. Evid. 501. Congress refused to adopt a codification of the federal law of privilege, which had been recommended by the Advisory Committee on Rules of Evidence. *See* House Judiciary Committee Report on Federal Rules of Evidence, to accompany H.R. 5463, 93d Cong., 1st Sess. (1973). On nonrecognition of state privileges in federal question cases, see, e.g., Garner v. Wolfinbarger, 430 F.2d 1093 (5th Cir.1970). On application of state law of privilege in federal courts in diversity litigation, see, e.g., Dixon v. 80 Pine St. Corp., 516 F.2d 1278 (2d Cir.1975). *See also* Kaminsky, State Evidentiary Privileges in Federal Civil Litigation, 43 Fordham L. Rev. 923 (1975).

3. *See* Weinstein, The Uniformity–Conformity Dilemma Facing Draftsmen of the Federal Rules of Evidence, 69 Colum. L. Rev. 353 (1969).

4. *See* sources cited *supra* notes 1 and 2.

5. *See* Strong et al., McCormick on Evidence ch. 12 (5th ed. 1999); Duval, Jr., The Occasions of Secrecy, 47 U. Pitt. L. Rev. 579 (1986); Note, The Military and State Secrets Privilege: Protection for National Security or Immunity for the Executive?, 91 Yale L.J. 570 (1982); Note, Discovery of Government Documents and the Official Information Privilege, 76 Colum. L. Rev. 142 (1976); *see also* Annots., 32 A.L.R.2d 391, 85 A.L.R.2d 1105, 1 A.L.R.2d 222.

6. *See, e.g.,* Cal. Evid. Code § 1040 ("information acquired in confidence by a public employee in the course of his duty and not open, or officially disclosed, to the public" is privileged); N.Y. Civ. Prac. L. & R. 3102(f) (state not subject to the devices of interrogatories or admissions); *see* Kaplan v. Kaplan, 31 N.Y.2d 63, 286 N.E.2d 260, 334 N.Y.S.2d 879 (1972).

patient communications as privileged,[7] but a few federal decisions refuse to recognize this privilege except in diversity cases,[8] and the psychotherapist-patient privilege is generally recognized but not everywhere to the same extent.[9]

The courts generally hold that the failure to claim a privilege constitutes a waiver of that privilege as to the document in question and as to the subject of the privilege.[10] This is called "implied waiver" and is a constant risk for the unwary. Problems arise, for example, if a party hands over documents without claiming privilege during discovery and then tries to exclude them from evidence at trial.

New privileges

In some states additional privileges are available, most of fairly recent origin. Some are prescribed by statute, others are the product of judicial decision. For example, some states hold that a party need not produce a file copy of an income tax return as evidence of income level, even though most jurisdictions recognize only a qualified privilege for such a document.[10] In a newspaper shield law case, *New York Times Co. v. Superior Court,*[11] a party attempted to obtain unpublished photos of an automobile accident from a newspaper. It was held that the California Shield Law,[12] which provided a publisher with immunity from contempt for refusal to comply with an evidentiary subpoena, created an absolute immunity from contempt sanctions, and information coming within the scope of a shield law is not discoverable.

This expansion of evidentiary privileges has coincided with the expansion of civil litigation discovery. The availability of wide discovery provides the discovering party with a mechanism for obtaining documents without having to identify them specifically or even to know they exist. Under Rules 26 (scope of discovery) and 34 (demand for production), a party can ask for all documents falling in a reasonably described category, for example: "All reports of defects in the braking mechanism of the *X* type of vehicle."[13] The fact that the discovery mechanisms do not have to be precisely "targeted," and have scope as wide as the action

7. *See* Strong et al., McCormick on Evidence ch. 11 (5th ed. 1999).

8. *See, e.g.,* In re Albert Lindley Lee Memorial Hosp., 209 F.2d 122 (2d Cir. 1953); United States v. Kansas City Lutheran Home & Hosp. Assn., 297 F.Supp. 239 (W.D.Mo.1969).

9. Jaffee v. Redmond, 518 U.S. 1, 116 S.Ct. 1923, 135 L.Ed.2d 337 (1996).

10. *See* Restatement of the Law Governing Lawyers §§ 78–80; Davidson and Voth, Waiver of the Attorney–Client Privilege, 64 Or. L. Rev. 637 (1986); Marcus, The Perils of Privilege: Waiver and the Litigator, 84 Mich. L. Rev. 1605 (1986).

10. *Compare* Sav–On Drugs v. Superior Court, 15 Cal.3d 1, 538 P.2d 739, 123 Cal. Rptr. 283 (1975) *with, e.g.,* Eastern Auto Distribs. v. Peugeot Motors of Am., 96 F.R.D. 147 (E.D.Va.1982).

11. 51 Cal.3d 453, 273 Cal.Rptr. 98, 796 P.2d 811 (1990). Compare In re Farber, 78 N.J. 259, 394 A.2d 330 (1978).

12. Cal. Cons. art. I, § 2, subd. (b); Cal. Evid. Code § 1070.

13. *See, e.g.,* Norman v. Young, 422 F.2d 470 (10th Cir.1970).

itself, means there is little basis for resisting a "fishing expedition" except on the ground of privilege. Also, the general principle of discovery is that the parties' information should be accessible in the name of truth in adjudication.

As discovery has become so wide open it also has become relatively expensive and burdensome, especially in complex cases. These circumstances have impelled some courts to be sympathetic to means of limiting discovery, particularly discovery going into matters that have moral claims to privacy.[14] The simplest means of translating this attitude into a legal limitation is to make the sensitive matter privileged. Thus, the growth of privilege is a concomitant to the growth of discovery. It also reflects the struggle of developing professions for protection and recognition.

Corporate attorney-client privilege

It should not be inferred, however, that the courts have proliferated privilege wholesale. Several Supreme Court decisions indicate the cautious approach that generally prevails. In *Upjohn Co. v. United States*[15] the Court dealt with the attorney-client privilege (considered here) and the work-product privilege (considered in the next section). The Court in *Upjohn* affirmed two important propositions concerning the attorney-client privilege. First, the privilege protects corporate entities as well as individuals. This proposition had been generally but not universally accepted. Second, the scope of the privilege includes corporate communications involving lower echelon employees as well as top management. This branch of the *Upjohn* decision rejected lower court decisions that extended the privilege only to communications involving the "control group" of the corporation.[16] This was an important extension of the rules of privilege, but hardly a quantum leap.

Other privileges

In contrast, the Court has rejected several types of privilege that have been urged on it. The Court rejected a news media privilege for deliberations as to what news matter to include in a published story[17]

14. *See* Valley Bank v. Superior Court, 15 Cal.3d 652, 542 P.2d 977, 125 Cal.Rptr. 553 (1975) (qualified privilege of bank not to disclose financial information about its depositors). *Contra* Rosenblatt v. Northwest Airlines, 54 F.R.D. 21 (S.D.N.Y.1971).

15. 449 U.S. 383, 101 S.Ct. 677, 66 L.Ed.2d 584 (1981). *See also* Sexton, A Post-*Upjohn* Consideration of the Corporate Attorney–Client Privilege, 57 N.Y.U. L. Rev. 443 (1982); Waldman, Beyond *Upjohn*: The Attorney–Client Privilege in the Corporate Context, 28 Wm. & Mary L. Rev. 473 (1987).

16. Some state courts as a matter of state law adhere to the "control group" limitation on the attorney-client privilege. *See* Consolidation Coal Co. v. Bucyrus–Erie Co., 89 Ill.2d 103, 59 Ill.Dec. 666, 432 N.E.2d 250 (1982).

17. Herbert v. Lando, 441 U.S. 153, 99 S.Ct. 1635, 60 L.Ed.2d 115 (1979). A news reporter's "shield" against disclosing sources is recognized by statute in many states. *See* Tofel, "Every Citizen may freely . . . publish": Protecting the Press Under the New York State Constitution, 40 Syracuse L. Rev. 1041 (1989); Rousso, California Newsgatherers' Shield: Inconsistent Inter-

and a privilege for academic peer review,[18] and it refused to recognize an accountant's privilege for documents in which the accountant had estimated the probable income tax liability of a company whose accounts were under audit.[19] The Court also overruled a long-established line of cases by holding that records kept in the ordinary course of business are not protected under the Fifth Amendment.[20]

Competing considerations

Privacy considerations are the core of privilege problems. The constitutionally protected right to privacy, recognized in the seminal case of *Griswold v. Connecticut,*[21] must be weighed in light of the reasonable requests of parties seeking discovery. The courts have held that the filing of a lawsuit may implicitly bring about a partial waiver of one's constitutional right of associational privacy, but the scope of this waiver will be narrowly construed to deter needless intrusion into a party's private affairs.[22] The implicit waiver "encompasses only discovery directly relevant to the plaintiff's claim and essential to the fair resolution of the lawsuit."[23]

The issue frequently arises in cases of sexual harassment. For example, a California statute provides that "any party seeking discovery concerning the plaintiff's sexual conduct with individuals other than the alleged perpetrator must establish specific facts showing good cause for that discovery, and that the inquiry is relevant to the subject matter, and reasonably calculated to lead to the discovery of admissible evidence."[24] Aware that this type of discovery holds the potential for harassment and annoyance and tends to deter lawsuits, the California legislature held that "[a]bsent extraordinary circumstances, inquiry into (these) areas should not be permitted, either in discovery or at trial."[25]

pretation Means Inadequate Protection, 19 Golden Gate U.L. Rev. 347 (1989); notes 11–12 *supra.*

18. University of Pennsylvania v. EEOC, 493 U.S. 182, 110 S.Ct. 577, 107 L.Ed.2d 571 (1990).

19. United States v. Arthur Young & Co., 465 U.S. 805, 104 S.Ct. 1495, 79 L.Ed.2d 826 (1984). But see 26 U.S.C. § 7525 (limited privilege for communications with federally authorized tax practitioner); Armour Intl. Co. v. Worldwide Cosmetics, 689 F.2d 134 (7th Cir.1982) (state accountant privilege in diversity case; choice of law problem as to which state's law to apply); 23 Wright & Graham, Federal Practice and Procedure § 5427 (1980).

20. United States v. Doe, 465 U.S. 605, 104 S.Ct. 1237, 79 L.Ed.2d 552 (1984); Fisher v. United States, 425 U.S. 391, 96 S.Ct. 1569, 48 L.Ed.2d 39 (1976). But see United States v. Hubbell, 530 U.S. 27, 120 S.Ct. 2037, 147 L.Ed.2d 24 (2000).

21. 381 U.S. 479, 85 S.Ct. 1678, 14 L.Ed.2d 510 (1965).

22. Britt v. Superior Court, 20 Cal.3d 844, 143 Cal.Rptr. 695, 574 P.2d 766 (1978); *see also* Vinson v. Superior Court, 43 Cal.3d 833, 740 P.2d 404, 239 Cal.Rptr. 292 (1987).

23. Britt v. Superior Court, 20 Cal.3d 844, 143 Cal.Rptr. 695, 574 P.2d 766 (1978).

24. Cal. Civ. Proc. Code § 2036.1; *see also* Priest v. Rotary, 98 F.R.D. 755 (N.D.Cal.1983).

25. Cal. Civ. Proc. Code § 2036.1. *See also* Vinson v. Superior Court, 43 Cal.3d 833, 740 P.2d 404, 239 Cal.Rptr. 292 (1987). In federal sexual harassment cases, the plaintiff's sexual history is usually inadmissible at trial, which should ordinarily exclude it from discovery. See Fed. R. Ev. 412. A defendant's previous acts of sexual assault or child molestation are usually admissible and discoverable. Fed. R. Ev. 415;

The competing considerations involved in whether to recognize a privilege are always roughly the same. On the one hand is the interest of the public, the courts, and the discovering party in having evidence that could be very relevant to the matters at issue in litigation. On the other hand is the interest of the public and the resisting party in preserving privacy in the matter sought to be discovered, an interest that many European systems protect far more than does ours. Some privileges are entrenched in the Constitution, particularly the Fifth Amendment, and others are almost equally entrenched by tradition, particularly the attorney-client privilege. Others have always been more tenuous. In any given jurisdiction at any given time the question of privilege is likely to be open to new argument.

§ 5.11 Material Prepared for Trial

The basic scheme of pretrial discovery is compatible with the adversary method of trial. Before discovery existed, litigants in Anglo–American systems could subpoena witnesses to appear at trial and question them there, albeit at the risk that their testimony would help the adversary. Discovery procedure simply augments the means by which the parties can develop their evidence in readiness for the competitive demonstration of proof and argument at trial that is the essence of the adversary system. It enlarges the field of competition to the pretrial stage.

In at least two important respects, however, discovery can seriously disturb the adversarial process. First, the evidence for a trial does not simply "exist." Potential evidence must be investigated, sifted, and organized. Some types of evidence are created for trial—photographs, charts, tests, and analyses by expert witnesses. Discovery makes it possible for one side to appropriate the product of the opposing party's efforts to marshal evidence for trial.

Second, because the preparation of a case for trial involves the supervision of the party's attorney and communication between the attorney and other persons, disclosure of material prepared for trial can reveal the attorney's legal strategy, intended lines of proof, and sometimes the strengths and weaknesses of the case.[1]

Access to attorney's files

A conflict of purpose is therefore presented between allowing full pretrial discovery and protecting the integrity of adversary competition. To put the problem simply, it is appropriate to make "the facts"

see Jones v. Clinton, 993 F.Supp. 1217 (E.D.Ark.1998).

§ 5.11

1. *See generally* Clermont, Surveying Work Product, 68 Cornell L. Rev. 755 (1983); Wells, The Work Product Doctrine and Carryover Immunity: An Assessment of Their Justification, 47 U. Pitt. L. Rev. 675 (1986); Thornburg, Rethinking Work Product, 77 Va. L. Rev. 1515 (1991)(proposing the elimination of work product protection).

available to all parties but it is inappropriate to require attorneys to "open their files" to an opponent. This conflict becomes both more intense and more complex as the scope and mechanisms of trial proof and discovery have enlarged to their modern dimensions.

After the scope of discovery was widened with the adoption of the federal discovery rules in 1938, this conflict was initially dealt with through decisional law. Divergent approaches emerged. Some courts attempted to adapt the attorney-client privilege to deal with the problem, but two principal difficulties arose. One was that the attorney-client privilege is framed in terms of communications from the client to the attorney, but many items developed in an attorney's trial preparation simply did not involve such communications. Thus, an interrogation of an independent witness that has been conducted by the attorney or a nonattorney investigator involves communication with the attorney but not between him and his client. The other difficulty was that by its terms the attorney-client privilege is absolute: If an item was found to be within the privilege it could not be discovered under any circumstances. Thus, the attorney-client privilege was at once conceptually inappropriate, too narrow, and too rigid.[2]

Hickman v. Taylor

It was in these circumstances that the Supreme Court, in 1947, decided *Hickman v. Taylor*.[3] In that decision, the foundations were laid for the "lawyer work product" rule, now enlarged to the "trial preparation" rule.

Hickman v. Taylor was an action for the death of a crew member who was drowned when a tugboat sank. Plaintiff's interrogatory asked for production of any statements from witnesses. The defendant admitted that such statements had been taken and recorded by its attorney but declined to produce or summarize them on the ground that the matters called for were privileged since they were obtained in preparation for litigation. In response the Supreme Court created a new privilege but made it a qualified or conditional privilege—one that would ordinarily bar discovery but would yield if the need for discovery were shown to be sufficiently great.

The Court's rationale reveals the conflicting considerations involved.

> We agree, of course, that the deposition-discovery rules are to be accorded a broad and liberal treatment.... Mutual knowledge of all the relevant facts gathered by both parties is essential to proper litigation. To that end, either party may compel the other to disgorge whatever

2. *See, e.g.,* Note, 26 Minn. L. Rev. 744 (1942); Note, 88 U. Pa. L. Rev. 467 (1940); Annot., 22 A.L.R.2d 659. *See generally* 4 Moore, Federal Practice and Procedure ¶ 26.63[3]-[6].

3. 329 U.S. 495, 67 S.Ct. 385, 91 L.Ed. 451 (1947).

facts he has in his possession.... But discovery, like all matters of procedure, has ultimate and necessary boundaries....

[Plaintiff] has sought discovery of right of oral and written statements of witnesses whose identity is well known and whose availability to [plaintiff] appears unimpaired. He has sought production [that] ... would necessarily have included all pertinent information gleaned by [defendant's attorney] through his interviews with the witnesses. We are thus dealing with an attempt to secure ... written statements and mental impressions contained in the files and in the mind of the attorney without any showing of necessity.... Proper preparation of a client's case demands that [the attorney] assemble information, sift what he considers to be the relevant from the irrelevant facts, prepare his legal theories and plan his strategy without undue and needless interferences.... Were such materials open to opposing counsel on mere demand ... the effect on the legal profession would be demoralizing.[4]

The qualifications in this formulation, indeed its internal contradictions, are carried forward into the work-product rule. One major premise is that "mutual knowledge of all relevant facts ... is essential." In principle, this would include anything that a witness said about an event on a prior occasion. A person's statement, whatever was said and to whomever, has an effect on how the person will describe the same event on another occasion. This is because memory is not an implant like a document but rather a transitory process carried out somewhat differently each time it is undertaken. Notoriously, the fact that a witness's narrative was rendered in exactly the same words on a previous occasion could be more significant in assessing its truthfulness than the presence of discrepancies in the two accounts. Hence, if *all* relevant facts were "essential," then every prior statement by a witness should be produced, even if it reflects evaluation by the lawyer who took down the statement.

The other major premise in *Hickman* is that the adversary process should not permit revelation of the lawyer's "mental impressions ... legal theories ... and strategy." According to this premise, the prospect of having to turn over such material to the opposing party discovery would inhibit lawyers' efforts or tempt them to keep inadequate or misleading records. But everything done by a lawyer in handling a case is predicated on these mental processes and therefore reveals them. On this basis, discovery should not be permitted of anything the lawyer has turned up—the identity of witnesses, documents dredged from the client's files, experts consulted, contentions to be made on behalf of the party. Yet all these are discoverable.[5]

4. 329 U.S. at 507–511, 67 S.Ct. at 392–394, 91 L.Ed. at 460–462. Ironically, when *Hickman* was later tried, the defendant sought to introduce the witness statements and the plaintiff successfully objected; the defendant paid about $10,000 to the relatives of four dead crew members. Coady, Dredging the Depths of *Hickman v. Taylor*, 64 Harv. L. Record, May 6, 1977, at 2, in Civil Procedure Anthology 573 (Levine *et al.* ed. 1998).

5. *See* § 5.9 *supra;* see Shapiro, Some Problems of Discovery in an Adversary System, 63 Minn. L. Rev. 1055 (1979). On the

Hence, *Hickman v. Taylor* simultaneously asserts two broad but contradictory premises. It attempted to reconcile these premises by saying:

> [A] burden rests on the one who would invade [the privacy of the attorney's preparation] to establish adequate reasons to justify production through a subpoena or court order.[6]

This statement is the basis of the "good cause" rule: Material prepared by a lawyer or for a lawyer in connection with litigation may not be revealed except on "a showing of substantial need" and then only on protecting against disclosure "the mental impressions, conclusions, opinions, or legal theories" developed for the party.[7]

Rule 26(b)

After *Hickman v. Taylor* these two ideas were elaborated in decisional law.[8] In 1970 they were codified in revised Rule 26(b), particularly subdivisions (3) and (4).[9] The Rule's provisions distinguish four elements of trial preparation, treating each somewhat differently: witness statements, the attorney's analysis of the case, the findings and opinions of experts, and all other material "prepared in anticipation of litigation or for trial."

Witness statements

1. Witness statements (including statements of a party), as mentioned earlier, are *not* protected from discovery. Parties can obtain as of right any statement they have given to someone acting for another party. Nonparty witnesses can obtain any statement they have made; a party can obtain such statements on a showing of good cause.[10] If the statement reflects the analysis of the person taking it and that analysis is protected by the attorney's work-product rule, the protected part can be deleted or "redacted," to use the accepted terminology.[11]

difficulty of deciding what counts as opinion work product, see Waits, Opinion Work Product: A Critical Analysis of Current Law and a New Analytical Framework, 73 Ore. L. Rev. 385 (1994).

6. 329 U.S. at 512, 67 S.Ct. at 394, 91 L.Ed. at 463.

7. Hickman v. Taylor, 329 U.S. 495, 499, 67 S.Ct. 385, 388, 91 L.Ed. 451, 456 (1947).

8. *See* 4 Moore, Federal Practice and Procedure ¶ 26.63[8]; Comment, The Work Product Doctrine in the State Courts, 62 Mich. L. Rev. 1199 (1964).

9. *See* Advisory Committee's Explanatory Statement Concerning Amendment of the Discovery Rules, 48 F.R.D. 487, 500 (1970); Epstein, The Attorney–Client Privilege and the Work–Product Doctrine (3d ed. 1997); Cooper, Work Product of the Rulemakers, 53 Minn. L. Rev. 1269 (1969); Clermont, Surveying Work Product, 68 Cornell L. Rev. 755 (1983); Note, Applying the Attorney–Client and Work Product Privilege to Allied Party Exchange of Information in California, 36 UCLA L. Rev. 151 (1988). See also Calif. C. Civ. P. § 2018.

10. *See* § 5.9 *supra.*

11. Fed. R. Civ. P. 26(b)(3). *See also* Waits, Work Product Protection for Witness Statements: Time for Abolition, 1985 Wis. L. Rev. 305.

Attorney's mental impressions

2. Material consisting of "the mental impressions, conclusions, opinions, or legal theories of an attorney or other representative of a party concerning the litigation" is protected against discovery (unless an opinion given by the attorney is itself at issue in the litigation).[12] The term "other representative" includes an investigator or claims agent who does an investigation in anticipation of possible litigation.[13] In this connection, communications with an expert who is "informally consulted" are similarly protected, seemingly on the theory that such an expert serves as an interpreter of the facts of the case for the attorney.[14] If a report or other document otherwise discoverable (such as an accident report) contains the "mental impressions" of the attorney or other representative, those impressions should be deleted when the material is disclosed.[15]

Although Rule 26(b)(3) treats "other representatives" as on a par with attorneys, a stronger showing would have to be made to discover an attorney's analysis than one by a nonattorney. Some decisions have indicated that an attorney's work product can never be discovered; others, while not going that far, have recognized "special protection" for it. The Supreme Court has let the question remain open, but in doing so it has indicated approval of the standard that an attorney's mental impressions can be obtained only in extraordinary circumstances.[16] The main such circumstance occurs when the lawyer waives the protection of work product by using it to help prepare an expert witness, at which point the court may compel disclosure to permit effective cross examination.[17]

Two other aspects of the work-product rule need to be mentioned. First, if a witness's statement taken by an attorney or investigator records the impressions and conclusions of the interrogator, it may be difficult to separate the witness's statement from these impressions. Hence, the entire statement may be immune from discovery. On the other hand, a witness statement recorded in this form has a sharply

12. *Compare* Duplan Corp. v. Moulinage et Retorderie de Chavanoz, 509 F.2d 730 (4th Cir.1974) (work product prepared for prior case is protected by work-product privilege); see FTC v. Grolier Inc., 462 U.S. 19, 103 S.Ct. 2209, 76 L.Ed.2d 387 (1983); Note, Discovery of an Attorney's Work Product in Subsequent Litigation, 1974 Duke L.J. 799.

13. *See* 8 Wright and Miller, Federal Practice and Procedure §§ 2024, 2026.

14. A distinction is thus drawn between an expert who is "informally consulted" and one who is "employed" to consult but not to testify as a witness at trial, for the opinion of the latter may be discovered on a showing of good cause. *See* text at notes 23–32 *infra.*

15. Fed. R. Civ. P. 26(b)(3); Bogosian v. Gulf Oil Corp., 738 F.2d 587 (3d Cir.1984).

16. Upjohn Co. v. United States, 449 U.S. 383, 101 S.Ct. 677, 66 L.Ed.2d 584 (1981). *Compare* Clermont, Surveying Work Product, 68 Cornell L. Rev. 755 (1983).

17. Fed. R. Ev. 612; Fed. R. Civ. P. 26(a)(2), Advisory Committee Note (1993); Musselman v. Phillips, 176 F.R.D. 194 (D.Md.1997); Waits, Opinion Work Product: A Critical Analysis of Current Law and a New Analytical Framework, 73 Ore. L. Rev. 385 (1994). On waiver of work product protection, see Restatement of the Law Governing Lawyers §§ 91, 92; Marcus, The Perils of Privilege: Waiver and the Litigator, 84 Mich. L. Rev. 1605 (1986).

limited value for impeachment purposes because a memorandum including such impressions does not express the witness's statement as distinctly as a verbatim record of the statement. Thus, the form that these statements take may well be dictated by whether the investigating party's paramount purpose is witness impeachment (verbatim statements) or shielding the material from discovery under the work-product rule (impressionistic memoranda).

In anticipation of litigation

Second, the work-product privilege nominally applies only to material prepared "in anticipation" of litigation. The meaning of "in anticipation" is necessarily somewhat ambiguous.[18] But it is clear that the proposed litigation be readily identifiable;[19] a mere remote possibility of future use in some as yet unidentified lawsuits will not meet the test. A general claim that the materials were prepared "in anticipation of litigation" is not sufficient; the privilege must be delineated with specificity.[20]

In *Upjohn Co. v. United States,* decided in 1981, the Supreme Court discussed the work-product privilege in such a way as to suggest that the requirement of "in anticipation of litigation" might no longer exist.[21] In effect, this would make the work-product privilege much more closely parallel to the attorney-client privilege. However, courts have continued to protect only work product of parties preparing for litigation.[22]

Experts

3. Expert witnesses create special work product problems and receive special treatment in the Federal Rules.[23] Expert testimony is widely used and often indispensable in modern litigation. By definition it involves technical intricacies as to which an opposing party needs to be

18. *See* United States v. American Tel. & Tel. Co., 86 F.R.D. 603, 627 (D.D.C.1979).

19. Southern Film Extruders, Inc., v. Coca–Cola Co., 117 F.R.D. 559 (M.D.N.C. 1987); Simon v. G. D. Searle & Co., 816 F.2d 397 (8th Cir.1987).

20. Toledo Edison Co. v. GA Technologies, Inc., 847 F.2d 335 (6th Cir.1988).

21. 449 U.S. 383, 101 S.Ct. 677, 66 L.Ed.2d 584 (1981). The work product involved in Upjohn Co. v. United States was prepared in anticipation of legal trouble that had not yet materialized into a claim against the client. The Supreme Court did not, however, advert to that fact in holding the privilege to be available. *See* Sexton, A Post-*Upjohn* Consideration of the Corporate Attorney–Client Privilege, 57 N.Y.U. L. Rev. 443 (1982); Waldman, Beyond *Upjohn*: The Attorney–Client Privilege in the Corporate Context, 28 Wm. & Mary L. Rev. 473 (1987).

22. *E.g.*, In re Sealed Case, 146 F.3d 881 (D.C.Cir.1998); National Union Fire Ins. Co. v. Murray Sheet Metal Co., 967 F.2d 980 (4th Cir.1992). *But cf.* United States v. Adlman, 134 F.3d 1194 (2d Cir. 1998). Even when litigation is anticipated, material prepared as part of a client's fraudulent or criminal scheme is unprotected. Restatement of the Law Governing Lawyers § 93.

23. *See generally* McLaughlin, Discoverability and Admissibility of Expert Testimony, 63 Notre Dame L. Rev. 760 (1988); Note, Discovery of the Nontestifying Expert Witness' Identity Under the Federal Rules of Civil Procedure, 37 Hastings L.J. 201 (1985); Day, Expert Discovery in the Eighth Circuit: An Empirical Study, 122 F.R.D. 35 (1988).

prepared in order to meet the testimony effectively at trial. Expert testimony also, however, is ordinarily created at the party's instance and expense for the sole purpose of the litigation; this is essentially attorney work product. Also, a party denied access to an opponent's expert can usually find an equal and opposite expert to retain, albeit at substantial expense. The Rule attempts to balance these considerations by permitting discovery of experts who will testify, permitting discovery on proof of special need of experts who are "specially employed" and denying discovery of experts who are "informally consulted." It also deals with payment of experts' often substantial fees, ordinarily requiring the party seeking discovery to pay the expert's reasonable fees for time devoted to responding, and in some cases to pay as well part of the expert's fees for other time.[24]

The classification system under Rule 33 contemplates that experts fall into four categories, although this four-fold categorization is not explicit in the rule. The categories are as follows: (1) informally consulted experts, whose identity need not be disclosed and who cannot be examined by any discovery device; (2) those specially employed but not expected to be called as witnesses; (3) those employed to give expert testimony at trial; and (4) persons who happen to be experts and who personally observed or participated in the events giving rise to the litigation. Experts in the fourth category are sometimes called percipient or occurrence witnesses and are subject to discovery concerning their knowledge of the matter in essentially the same way as any other witness.[25] That is because their testimony must be available to all parties; a party cannot go out and hire its own occurrence witness, as it presumably can hire an ordinary expert.

Strategy

As a result of this scheme, a party intending to use expert opinion can seek out witnesses without running the risk of adverse discovery. Or to put it more critically: a party can hire the favorable experts while reducing the likelihood that its opponent will hire the unfavorable ones.[26] The technique is as follows:

First, having identified an expert who might be favorable, the party consults the expert informally and elicits the expert's preliminary opinion. If the opinion is unfavorable, the party does not proceed beyond consultation. That makes the expert's identity and opinion nondiscovera-

24. Fed. R. Civ. P. 26(b)(4)(C). In civil cases, indigents may have a right to experts only in extreme cases. *See* Medine, The Constitutional Right to Expert Assistance for Indigents in Civil Cases, 41 Hastings L.J. 281 (1989).

25. Nelco Corp. v. Slater Electric Inc., 80 F.R.D. 411 (E.D.N.Y.1978).

26. Civil law systems usually rely on court-appointed experts, while England is now prodding parties to agree on a single expert. Langbein, The German Advantage in Civil Procedure, 52 U. Chi. L. Rev. 823 (1985); Civil Procedure Rules 1998, rules 35.3, 35.7 (S.I. 1998 No. 3132)(Eng.).

ble.[27] It is even possible that the professional obligations of the expert or of opposing counsel will prevent the opposing party from consulting the expert.[28]

Second, if the opinion is favorable but the expert will not be a very effective or advantageous witness, the expert may be "retained ... in anticipation of litigation." This will make it easier to call the expert as a "back up" if the primary expert witness becomes unavailable to testify at the time of trial. So long as it is not anticipated that the expert will be called as a witness, discovery is permitted only in "exceptional circumstances," for example if the expert examined deteriorating evidence when it was impossible for the opposing party to do so.[29] This leaves the expert probably nondiscoverable.

Third, if the opinion is favorable and it is expected that the expert will be used at trial, the witness is designated as a trial expert. The party must then disclose a written expert report stating the expert's opinions, their basis, the information the expert considered, the expert's credentials and witness experience, the expert's compensation, and other matters. Unless otherwise ordered or agreed, this disclosure must be made at least ninety days before trial, and unexcused failure to provide proper disclosure will lead to exclusion of the expert's testimony.[30] After receiving the report, the opposing party may take the expert's deposition,[31] and of course show the report to its own expert. It will then be prepared to challenge the expert's testimony or to argue that it is inadmissible under the rules of evidence.[32]

Other trial preparation material

4. All other documents and things "prepared in anticipation of litigation or for trial" may be discovered "only upon a showing that the party seeking discovery has substantial need of the materials in the preparation of his case and that he is unable without undue hardship to obtain the substantial equivalent of the materials by other means."[33] This is known as the "good cause" requirement.[34] Examples of such

27. Ager v. Jane C. Stormont Hosp., 622 F.2d 496 (10th Cir.1980); Advisory Committee's Explanatory Statement Concerning Amendment of the Discovery Rules, 48 F.R.D. 487, 504 (1970); 8 Wright and Miller, Federal Practice and Procedure § 2033; Pielemeier, Discovery of Non–Testifying "In–House" Experts Under Federal Rule of Civil Procedure 26, 58 Ind. L.J. 597 (1983).

28. See Restatement of the Law Governing Lawyers § 102 and Reporter's Note.

29. Fed. R. Civ. P. 26(b)(4)(B); Bank Brussels Lambert v. Chase Manhattan Bank, N.A., 175 F.R.D. 34 (S.D.N.Y.1997).

30. Fed. R. Civ. P. 26(a)(2), 37(c)(1); Salgado v. General Motors Corp., 150 F.3d 735 (7th Cir.1998).

31. Fed. R. Civ. P. 26(b)(4)(A).

32. Fed. R. Ev. 702; Kumho Tire Co. v. Carmichael, 526 U.S. 137, 119 S.Ct. 1167, 143 L.Ed.2d 238 (1999) (emphasizing the court's role as "gatekeeper" for expert testimony).

33. Fed. R. Civ. P. 26(b)(3). *Compare* N.Y. Civ. Prac. L. & R. 3101(d).

34. *See* 8 Wright and Miller, Federal Practice and Procedure § 2025; *see also* Note, The "Good Cause" Requirement of California Discovery Procedure, 20 Stan. L. Rev. 594 (1968).

material are photographs taken of a scene that has since changed and the statement of a critical witness given soon after the event in question.[35]

Accident reports

The conditional restriction on discovering "other materials" applies only to materials prepared in anticipation of litigation or for trial. It leaves open for unconditional discovery materials prepared by the party for some other purpose. These include accident or incident reports prepared for ordinary business purposes.[36] One of the purposes of these reports in the business world, however, is anticipation of possible litigation. Operationally the distinction can be drawn in terms of two components—*who* makes the report and *when* it is made. Reports initiated by the persons involved in the accident or incident (such as the bus driver or the driver's supervisor) can be distinguished from reports by employees whose specific responsibility is the investigation of accidents or incidents. Correlatively, a distinction can be drawn between reports made after litigation has been threatened or commenced and those made earlier when it was only a possibility. The tendency in application of the discovery rules is to consider a report as discoverable unless made by someone acting in a direct relation to an attorney after the threat of litigation. Also not protected by either the attorney-client or the work-product privilege are statements made by an insured to an insurer and material in an insurer's files, under the presumption that they were prepared in the normal course of business. If there is a showing that they were prepared at the request or under the supervision of the insured's attorney, they will be protected by the work-product privilege.[37]

§ 5.12 Claims and Contentions of Parties

Bill of particulars

We have seen how pleadings under modern procedural systems may be stated in general terms.[1] Detailed pleadings give a precise blueprint of

35. *See* Annot., 95 A.L.R.2d 1061; 8 Wright and Miller, Federal Practice and Procedure § 2025. It may be noted that the "good cause" that must be shown for discovering such materials is somewhat less than the "exceptional, circumstances" required for discovering the findings and opinion of a "specially employed" expert. *Compare* Fed. R. Civ. P. 26(b)(3) *with* 26(b)(4)(B). The distinction is conceptually tenuous but perhaps practically coherent: Evidentiary material developed by one party often is no longer available in the same form to opponents, but it is unusual for there to be no qualified expert available.

36. *See* 8 Wright and Miller, Federal Practice and Procedure § 2024; Annot., 22 A.L.R.2d 659. In complex litigation, the system for compiling documents is itself an important work product. *See* Sherman and Kinnard, Development, Discovery and Use of Computer Support Systems in Achieving Efficiency in Litigation, 79 Colum. L. Rev. 267 (1979); *cf.* Note, Work Product Protection for Complications of Non-party Documents: A Proposed Analysis, 66 Va. L. Rev. 1323 (1980).

37. *E.g.,* Langdon v. Champion, 752 P.2d 999 (Alaska 1988), unless the insurer was acting "at the express direction of counsel for the insured."

§ 5.12

1. *See* §§ 3.9–3.11 *supra.*

what the pleader intends to prove, thereby narrowing the scope of the issues and the adversary's preparation for trial. When the Federal Rules were adopted, they allowed a motion for bill of particulars and for more definite statement to enable the adversary to prepare a responsive pleading or "to prepare for trial."[2] In 1946, however, this provision was eliminated.[3] Some states still retain the device as a means of testing the opposing party's case.[4]

Nevertheless, many courts allowed interrogatories calling for exactly the same detailed statements of claim that would be compelled in a bill of particulars.[5] If interrogatories asking for legal contentions are propounded before the respondent has opportunity to conduct discovery, they give rise to the same difficulties as special pleading: The respondent risks being trapped into a factual commitment before knowing all the available evidence or being drawn into a game of probe and parry if it tries to avoid committing itself. If the interrogatories are propounded after other discovery is completed, these risks are substantially lessened, and no injustice results by requiring a respondent to "put up or shut up" in advance of trial as to its factual or legal theories of claim or defense.

Specifying contentions after discovery

Requiring a party to particularize its contentions is consonant with the theme of discovery—the cards ought to be on the table once they have all been dealt. In this connection, it must be remembered that the disclosure of a party's contentions can be elicited by two other pretrial devices, the motion for summary judgment and the pretrial conference. The summary judgment motion, if adequately supported by affidavits and other evidentiary matter, requires the party against whom it is made to respond by stating why it thinks the moving party is *not* entitled to judgment as a matter of law.[6] That response necessarily includes at least some reference to the respondent's own legal contentions. In a pretrial conference, the parties are ordinarily required to specify their contentions and outline their contemplated proofs as the court pursues "the formulation and simplification of the issues."[7] Hence, requiring a party to state its contentions by response to interrogatories is simply an alternative to these other procedures for determining the

2. Clark, Code Pleading 342 (2d ed. 1947).

3. Fed. R. Civ. P. 12(e) allows a motion to make more definite and certain only if the pleading to which it is addressed is "so vague . . . that a party cannot reasonably be required to frame a responsive pleading." This is much less exacting than a motion to require clarification of the contentions that will be made at trial. *See* § 4.2 *supra.*

4. *See, e.g.,* N.Y. Civ. Prac. L. & R. 3041: "Any party may require any other party to give a bill of particulars of his claim, or copy of the items of the account alleged in the pleading."

5. *See* James, The Revival of Bills of Particulars Under the Federal Rules, 71 Harv. L. Rev. 1473 (1958).

6. *See* §§ 4.10–16 *supra.*

7. See Fed. R. Civ. P. 16(c)(1); §§ 5.20–21 *infra.*

issues to be tried—if the response to those interrogatories is not required until after discovery is substantially complete.

Rule 33

This view is expressed in Rule 33 as amended in 1970. It provides that an interrogatory is "not necessarily objectionable merely because an answer ... involves [a] contention that relates to fact or the application of law to fact."[8] It also provides, however, that "the court may order that such an interrogatory need not be answered until after designated discovery has been completed or until a pretrial conference or other later time."[9] "Special pleading" thus re-emerges not as a device to define what *will be* the issues but as one to define what *are* the issues once trial is in prospect. To some extent, however, the issues always remain fluid, for the testimony at trial can never be wholly predicted.

§ 5.13 Discovery Controls

The discovery machinery does not operate without friction. Indeed, claims of abuse are frequent, and the Federal Rules have repeatedly been amended to strengthen court controls. The inherent conflict between proponent and respondent is regulated not only by the Rules but also by discretionary and supervisory powers of the court. These powers may be classified under three headings: general power to limit or extend the reach of discovery rights conferred by the Rules, specific powers in supervising use of particular discovery devices, and sanctioning powers to cope with refusal of a party to make required divulgence. The powers of control are explored in this section, sanctions in the next section.

Party agreement

Although court intervention in discovery is no longer regarded as a last resort, the parties are still expected to reduce its necessity. Early in each case, unless excused by a local rule or court order, the parties are to meet and develop a discovery plan.[1] They may modify by agreement virtually every discovery and disclosure provision in the Federal Rules, but not those in court orders.[2] Most discovery matters come before the court only if the parties miss opportunities to reach agreement. Thus, a party seeking discovery must state what it seeks, the opposing party must specify any objections, the seeker must decide to file a motion for an order compelling discovery, and the opponent must oppose the motion before there will be anything for the court to decide. At each stage, agreement or abandonment of a claim or objection may occur.

8. Fed. R. Civ. P. 33(c).

9. *Id. See also* Note, Limiting the Scope of Litigation: Bills of Particulars, Interrogatories, and Requests for Admission in Illinois and Federal Courts, 1979 U. Ill. L.F. 211.

§ 5.13

1. Fed. R. Civ. P. 26(f), 37(g).

2. Fed. R. Civ. P. 26(a)(1, 2), 26(d), 29, 30(a)(2), 30(b)(4, 7), 33(a), 34(b), 35(b)(3), 36(a).

Court supervision

Rather than wait for disputes to reach them, however, courts today routinely set discovery deadlines on their own initiative or bring up the timing and sequence of discovery at any pretrial conference. There is some evidence that active court control of discovery can speed cases and reduce costs.[3] And the court has broad power to control the scope of discovery, for example by regulating discovery of work product, or by determining whether to allow discovery reaching beyond what is relevant to the claim or defense of a party.[4] It may also limit discovery that is unreasonably duplicative, can be obtained more conveniently in some other way, or imposes burdens outweighing its benefits in light of such factors as the size of the case and the parties' resources.[5] Thus, at least if the court so decides, discovery is no longer a matter of right but is subject to the court's discretion in balancing its costs and benefits.

Protective orders

Rule 26(c) contains additional sweeping powers of court control, all guided by the precept that their purpose is to protect against "annoyance, embarrassment, oppression, or undue burden or expense." On motion by a party or witness, the court may order that:

- discovery be had only on specified terms or not at all;
- specified discovery devices not be used or that specified matters not be inquired into;
- outsiders or others designated by the court be excluded while discovery is being conducted, such as in the examination of a witness at deposition, or that a deposition be sealed after having been taken;
- a "trade secret or other confidential research, development, or commercial information" be withheld from discovery or subsequent disclosure;
- the parties exchange documents or information under seal;[6]
- a deposition being conducted in bad faith or in an unreasonable manner be terminated or limited.[7]

The courts have held that Rule 26(c) motions require "the district judge to compare the hardship to the party against whom discovery is sought, if discovery is allowed, with the hardship to the party seeking discovery if discovery is denied."[8]

3. Kakalik, *et al.*, Discovery Management: Further Analysis of the Civil Justice Reform Act Evaluation Data, 39 B.C. L. Rev. 613 (1998).

4. See §§ 5.9, 5.11 *supra;* Minpeco S.A. v. Conticommodity Servs., Inc., 832 F.2d 739 (2d Cir.1987).

5. Fed. R. Civ. P. 26(b)(2).

6. Fed. R. Civ. P. 26(c). *See generally* 8 Wright and Miller, Federal Practice and Procedure §§ 2035–2044; Federal Judicial Center, Judicial Controls and the Civil Litigative Process: Discovery (1978). *See also* Annot., 70 A.L.R.2d 685.

7. Fed. R. Civ. P. 30(d).

8. Marrese v. American Academy of Orthopaedic Surgeons, 726 F.2d 1150 (7th Cir.

Secrecy orders

The Supreme Court has declined to constitutionalize the law of protective orders. It upheld the constitutionality of discovery protective orders that limit public access to discovered information in *Seattle Times v. Rhinehart,* stating that "Rule 26(c) furthers a substantial governmental interest unrelated to the suppression of expression" forbidden by the First Amendment.[9] In this case, one defendant was a newspaper that obtained plaintiff's membership list through discovery and wished to use it in reporting on the plaintiff's activities. The Court upheld the trial court's protective order, ruling that there is no First Amendment right to access to information made available through the discovery process.[10] On the other hand, the fact that discovery may lead to some harmful exposure or reprisals against the complying party has also been held insufficient to guarantee First Amendment protection against discovery or publicity. An organization claiming the publicity will chill its members' exercise of free speech and association must demonstrate that the disclosures themselves would be inherently damaging to them.[11]

The controversy about protective orders limiting public disclosure continues on the nonconstitutional level under Rule 26(c).[12] Some (including plaintiffs' lawyers) claim that protective orders sometimes prevent the public from learning about important health and safety hazards, while others defend them as facilitating discovery and protecting privacy. Courts (and a few state legislatures or rulemakers) have tried to balance these concerns by ruling that a party seeking a secrecy order must show good cause to overcome the presumption that court proceedings are open to the public.[13] In an analogous situation, courts have required would-be John and Jane Doe plaintiffs to make a strong showing before being allowed to conceal their identity from the public.[14]

1984), *rev'd on other grounds,* 470 U.S. 373, 105 S.Ct. 1327, 84 L.Ed.2d 274 (1985).

9. 467 U.S. 20, 34, 104 S.Ct. 2199, 2208, 81 L.Ed.2d 17, 28 (1984). *See also* Note, Fair Trial—Free Press—A State Constitutional Right of Access to Pretrial Hearings, 14 Seton Hall L. Rev. 788 (1984); Note, A Constitutional Right of Access to Pretrial Documents: A Missed Opportunity, 62 Ind. L.J. 735 (1987).

10. *See* Tribe, American Constitutional Law 889, 968–970 (2d ed. 1988); Marcus, Myth and Reality in Protective Order Litigation, 69 Cornell L. Rev. 1 (1983) (critical of public right of access to discovery); Miller, Confidentiality, Protective Orders, and Public Access to the Courts, 105 Harv. L. Rev. 427 (1991).

11. Brown v. Socialist Workers '74 Campaign Committee, 459 U.S. 87, 103 S.Ct. 416, 74 L.Ed.2d 250 (1982); In re Grand Jury Proceeding, 842 F.2d 1229 (11th Cir.1988); Dole v. Local Union 375 Plumbers Intl. Union, 921 F.2d 969 (9th Cir.1990).

12. Hare, et al., Confidentiality Orders (1988); Doré, Secrecy by Consent: The Use and Limits of Confidentiality in the Pursuit of Settlement, 74 Notre Dame L. Rev. 283 (1999); Marcus, The Discovery Confidentiality Controversy, 1991 U. Ill. L. Rev. 457.

13. In re Agent Orange Prod. Liab. Litig., 821 F.2d 139 (2d Cir.1987), *cert. denied,* 484 U.S. 953, 108 S.Ct. 344, 98 L.Ed.2d 370 (1987); Public Citizen v. Liggett Group, 858 F.2d 775 (1st Cir.1988), *cert. denied,* 488 U.S. 1030, 109 S.Ct. 838, 102 L.Ed.2d 970 (1989); Fl. Stat. Ann. § 69.081.

14. Does I Thru XXIII v. Advanced Textile Corp., 214 F.3d 1058 (9th Cir.2000); Doe v. Blue Cross & Blue Shield United,

In practice, secrecy orders are rarely challenged. Parties regularly agree to broad protective orders in sensitive cases, either because both parties prefer privacy or because the party seeking discovery is willing to waive public disclosure in order to encourage the opposing party to provide discovery freely.[15] Any settlement of the case may well continue the protective order.[16] Occasionally, a litigant in another case, newspaper, or public interest organization will seek to obtain the shielded material. When that happens, judges have usually upheld a right of access to court records.[17] But most discovery materials never become court records because a recent amendment to the Federal Rules provides that they are to be filed only when used in the case.[18]

Other protective orders

Protective orders have been issued under Rule 26 to protect a low-income party from undue burden or expense. For example, in *DePetro v. Exxon Inc.*[19] the federal district court found that defendant Exxon's demand for plaintiff's oral deposition would involve undue expense in that her attorney resided in a distant state and that oral discovery by telephone or written interrogatories would have been more appropriate. The court issued a protective order limiting discovery to these alternatives, holding that a "court may be as inventive as the necessities of a particular case require in order to achieve the benign purposes of the rule."[20]

Once a protective order has been issued, the court is generally reluctant to modify it. The party seeking the change in the order bears the burden of showing that it was issued improperly or that some compelling need or circumstance necessitates the disclosure of the information.[21]

Controls in specific rules

Many rules confer on the courts further power to control discovery. Rule 26(a) gives the court extensive discretionary powers of supervision

112 F.3d 869 (7th Cir.1997); Rice, Meet John Doe: It is Time for Federal Civil Procedure to Recognize John Doe Parties, 57 U. Pitt. L. Rev. 883 (1996). For John Doe defendants, see § 4.23 *supra.*

15. *E.g.*, Citizens First Nat'l Bank v. Cincinnati Ins. Co., 178 F.3d 943 (7th Cir. 1999); Procter & Gamble Co. v. Bankers Trust Co., 78 F.3d 219 (6th Cir.1996).

16. *E.g.*, Leucadia Inc. v. Applied Extrusion Technologies Inc., 998 F.2d 157 (3d Cir.1993); § 5.19 *infra.*

17. *See* San Jose Mercury News, Inc. v. U.S. District Court, 187 F.3d 1096 (9th Cir.1999); United States v. Amodeo, 44 F.3d 141 (2d Cir.1995); Grove Fresh Distributors, Inc. v. Everfresh Juice Co., 24 F.3d 893 (7th Cir.1994); Hammock v. Hoffmann–La Roche, Inc., 142 N.J. 356, 662 A.2d 546 (1995); Krahling v. Executive Life Ins. Co., 125 N.M. 228, 959 P.2d 562 (App.1998).

18. Fed. R. Civ. P. 5(d) (as amended 2000). *But see* Tex. R. Civ. P. 76a (presumption against sealing of records includes unfiled discovery materials).

19. 118 F.R.D. 523 (M.D.Ala.1988).

20. Citing 8 Wright and Miller, Federal Practice and Procedure § 2036.

21. Palmieri v. New York, 779 F.2d 861 (2d Cir.1985).

over the various stages of disclosure.[22] Rule 27 gives the court such discretion over whether and on what terms to allow depositions in advance of litigation or pending appeal.[23] Rule 28 allows the court to specify persons before whom a deposition may be taken.[24] Rule 30 allows the court to advance or postpone the date on which a deposition is to be taken, to regulate the technique by which it is recorded, to terminate the taking of a deposition, and to order that the deposition be taken at the courthouse or before the judge.[25] The presumptive limits of Rules 30 and 33 on the number of depositions and interrogatories may be modified by the court.[26] Rule 35, dealing with physical and mental examinations, empowers the court to specify the "time, place, manner, conditions, and scope of the examination and the person or persons by whom it is to be made," to deny opportunity for such an examination, and to specify the terms on which other medical reports are to be exchanged.[27] Rule 37 authorizes the court to determine the sufficiency of answers to interrogatories under Rule 33 or to questions asked in a deposition; the Rule also allows the court to refuse to require answers to all or specified interrogatories or questions.[28]

Potential misuse of discovery controls

Theoretically, these powers could be exercised collectively to shut off discovery or, worse, to make it one-sided. The danger is the greater because most discovery orders are not final judgments and may be immediately appealed only in most unusual circumstances.[29] As a result, discovery decisions by can usually be set aside only if: the case is not settled; the objecting party loses on the merits and appeals; the appellate court not only disagrees with the trial court decision but considers it an abuse of discretion; and the appellate court further concludes that the error may have affected the result, for example by depriving a party of important evidence.

In practice, powerful constraints militate against misuse of judicial discovery powers. The Rules themselves emphasize that full use of the available devices is the norm, restriction the exception. The abundant interpretive case law and commentary elaborates that proposition. The

22. Fed. R. Civ. P. 26(a); see § 5.8 *supra.*

23. Fed. R. Civ. P. 27(a)(3).

24. *Id.* 28(a), (b)(2).

25. *Id.* 30(b)(3)-(4), (d). *See* Kirshner v. Palmer, 7 F.R.D. 252 (S.D.N.Y.1945).

26. Fed. R. Civ. P. 26(b)(2), 30(a)(2), 33(a).

27. Fed. R. Civ. P. 35(a), 35(b)(1).

28. *Id.* 37(a)(2)-(3).

29. In some states discovery orders are appealable. *See* Annot., 37 A.L.R.2d 586. Under federal procedure and that of most states, a discovery order is ordinarily not appealable. But review may be obtainable when the order falls within the "collateral order" category, or when an interlocutory appeal is allowed under 28 U.S.C. 1292(b), or when the trial court's exercise of authority is so unwarranted as to involve a question of "jurisdiction." *See* Annot., 95 A.L.R.2d 1229; 8 Wright and Miller, Federal Practice and Procedure § 2006; Comment, Appellate Review of Discovery Orders in the Federal Courts, 1980 S. Ill. U.L.J. 339. *See also* Chapter 12.

trial bar, moreover, has a professional interest in the stable and even-handed exercise of judicial discretion in supervising discovery. Years of experience with the Rules have left the rulemakers (who include not only judges but also practitioners and professors) with such confidence in this respect that the court's broad powers have repeatedly been confirmed and generalized.

§ 5.14 Sanctions

Because of the frequency of discovery and discovery disputes in contemporary litigation, as well as the complexity of discovery procedures, elaborate sanctions provisions have come into existence. These are meant to discourage discovery abuse, including both improper demands for discovery and improper resistance. In recent decades, increasing judicial management of litigation in general and discovery in particular have brought with them calls for increasing reliance on discovery sanctions.[1]

"Pleading" discovery requests and objections

The possibility of sanctions starts at the very beginning of the discovery process, with the disclosures, requests, responses and objections served by the parties or witnesses. These are exempted from Rule 11, but subject to somewhat similar provisions in Rule 26.[2] Counsel's signing of such a document certifies that, if a disclosure, it is reasonably believed to be complete and correct and, if a request, response or objection, it is reasonably believed to be consistent with the Federal Rules, not interposed for an improper purpose, and not unreasonably burdensome. The court is to impose an appropriate sanction for any violation against the lawyer or party, absent a showing of substantial justification. The main difference between these provisions and those of Rule 11 are that the discovery provision is weaker than Rule 11 because it contains no requirement of evidentiary support for factual contentions, but is stronger in that it provides that the court "shall" sanction any unjustified violation and does not afford violators a "safe harbor" by allowing them to withdraw a challenged paper and thus escape sanctions.[3] Nevertheless, courts can be expected to apply both provisions as part of a consistent sanctioning scheme.

§ 5.14

1. E.g., Chudasama v. Mazda Motor Corp., 123 F.3d 1353 (11th Cir.1997); Brazil, Civil Discovery: Lawyers' Views of its Effectiveness, Principal Problems and Abuses (1980); Ellington, A Study of Sanctions for Discovery Abuse (1979); Renfrew, Discovery Sanctions: A Judicial Perspective, 67 Calif. L. Rev. 264 (1979); Sherwood, Curbing Discovery Abuse: Sanctions Under the Federal Rules of Civil Procedure and the California Code of Civil Procedure, 21 Santa Clara L. Rev. 567 (1981).

2. Fed. R. Civ. P. 11(d), 26(g); see Legault v. Zambarano, 105 F.3d 24 (1st Cir.1997)(sanctions for false interrogatory answer and failure to produce documents); Banco de Ponce v. Buxbaum, 99 F.3d 402 (2d Cir.1995).

3. See § 3.13 *supra*.

Defaults

Another set of rules seeks to ensure that parties from whom discovery is sought will raise any objections in the proper way instead of simply ignoring the request, and that parties seeking discovery will likewise proceed properly. Thus, the court may sanction one who fails to attend a deposition, to answer interrogatories, to respond to a request for inspection of documents or other things, to make proper preparations for a deposition it has scheduled, to attend a pretrial conference, or to participate in preparing a discovery plan.[4] Related sanctions operate automatically unless the court rules otherwise: evidence covered by the disclosure rule is ordinarily inadmissible if not properly disclosed, and a party that fails to deny a request for admissions is ordinarily deemed to have admitted it.[5]

Unreasonable positions

Even if a party follows the discovery procedures, it may sometimes be sanctioned for taking an unreasonable position. When a motion to compel discovery is filed, the court should require the losing party, whether it is the party seeking discovery or the party resisting it, to pay the winner's reasonable expenses for making or contesting the motion unless the loser's position was substantially justified or an award would be unjust.[6] Similarly, a party that refuses without good reason to admit a fact or the genuineness of a document may be required to pay the reasonable expenses of proof.[7] Beyond this, the court has general powers to sanction clearly improper discovery behavior of parties and lawyers.[8]

Violations of court orders

Discovery disputes often lead to a court order, usually an order requiring discovery, a protective order limiting or forbidding it, or an administrative order governing such matters as scheduling.[9] The court may also issue other kinds of order, for example one requiring a party to provide discovery beyond the usual scope.[10] Like other court orders, discovery orders are enforceable by the court's inherent contempt power unless a rule provides otherwise.[11] In addition, Federal Rule 37(b) sets

4. Fed. R. Civ. P. 16(f), 30(g), 37(d, g), 45(e). See Black Horse Lane v. Dow Chemical Corp., 228 F.3d 275 (3d Cir.2000)(witness designated to speak for corporation "fails to appear" when he is totally unprepared).

5. Fed. R. Civ. P. 36(a), 37(c). The latter provision also allows other sanctions for breaches of the disclosure rule.

6. Fed. R. Civ. P. 37(a)(4).

7. Fed. R. Civ. P. 37(a)(4).

8. See 28 U.S.C. § 1927; Chambers v. NASCO, Inc., 501 U.S. 32, 111 S.Ct. 2123, 115 L.Ed.2d 27 (1991); Saldana v. Kmart Corp., 84 F.Supp.2d 629 (D.Vi.1999)(lawyer's profanity at deposition); § 3.13 *supra*.

9. Fed. R. Civ. P. 26 (c, f), 37(a).

10. Fed. R. Civ. P. 26(b)(1); see Harris v. Nelson, 394 U.S. 286, 89 S.Ct. 1082, 22 L.Ed.2d 281 (1969).

11. 18 U.S.C. § 401; Levine v. United States, 362 U.S. 610, 80 S.Ct. 1038, 4 L.Ed.2d 989 (1960)(inherent contempt power). But see Fed. R. Civ. P. 27(b)(2)(no contempt sanctions for failure to comply with medical examination order).

forth a variety of measures that a court may take in response to a violation of a discovery or administrative order.

Types of sanction

Perhaps the most frequently imposed sanction is requiring a party or lawyer to pay the expenses, including attorney fees, that its misconduct has imposed.[12] As with Rule 11 and other sanctions, deciding whether the sanction should fall on lawyer or client raises difficult issues.[13]

Another form of sanction is that of foreclosing a party from advancing or contesting one or more issues. With respect to any claim or defense concerning which discovery has been resisted, the court can do any of the following: order that the facts be deemed established in specified particulars; prohibit the resisting party from introducing evidence, or specified types of evidence, on particular issues; or strike a claim or defense in its entirety.[14] Such measures can be shaped so that the punishment fits the crime. A party may be barred from contesting only the allegations that its recalcitrance hindered the opposing party from proving, or from introducing only the testimony of an expert whose report it failed to disclose.

Contempt sanctions

When a party or witness is held in contempt for violating a court order or failing to comply with a subpoena,[15] further sanctions become available. Setting aside contempt proceedings for courtroom misconduct,[16] these fall into three categories.[17] *Coercive* contempt sanctions order accumulating fines or imprisonment until the contemnor com-

12. Fed. R. Civ. P. 37(a)(4), (b)(2), (c)(1, 2), (d), (g); see, *e.g.*, Roadway Express, Inc. v. Piper, 447 U.S. 752, 100 S.Ct. 2455, 65 L.Ed.2d 488 (1980); Rickels v. City of South Bend, 33 F.3d 785 (7th Cir.1994).

13. See Appeal of Licht & Semonoff, 796 F.2d 564 (1st Cir.1986); Oregon RSA No. 6, Inc. v. Castle Rock Cellular of Oregon Limited Partnership, 76 F.3d 1003 (9th Cir. 1996); § 3.13 *supra*.

14. Fed R. Civ. P. 37(b)(2)(A)–(C). See Insurance Corp. of Ireland, Ltd. v. Compagnie des Bauxites de Guinee, 456 U.S. 694, 102 S.Ct. 2099, 72 L.Ed.2d 492 (1982)(defendant precluded from contesting personal jurisdiction when it denied discovery on that issue); Klonoski v. Mahlab, 156 F.3d 255 (1st Cir.1998)(undisclosed document excluded from evidence); Blumenfeld v. Stuppi, 921 F.2d 116 (7th Cir.1990) (plaintiff's medical expert testimony excluded because expert's findings were not disclosed in a timely fashion during discovery); Coca–Cola Bottling Co. v. Coca–Cola Co., 110 F.R.D. 363 (D.Del.1986) (court ordered some "facts" established against a resisting party).

15. Fed. R. Civ. P. 37(b)(2)(D)(court may treat as contempt violation of any order but one to submit to physical or mental examination), 45(e)(disobedience of subpoena); Waste Conversion, Inc. v. Rollins Environmental Services (NJ), Inc., 893 F.2d 605 (3d Cir.1990).

16. See Fed. R. Crim. P. 42; Taylor v. Hayes, 418 U.S. 488, 94 S.Ct. 2697, 41 L.Ed.2d 897 (1974); Fox, The History of Contempt of Court (1927); Goldfarb, The Contempt Power (1963); Kuhns, The Summary Contempt Power: A Critique and a New Perspective, 88 Yale L.J. 39 (1978).

17. International Union, UMWA v. Bagwell, 512 U.S. 821, 114 S.Ct. 2552, 129 L.Ed.2d 642 (1994); Fiss and Rendleman, Injunctions (2d ed. 1983).

plies.[18] Compliance is thus the goal, and at any time the contemnor can avoid all further sanctions by complying. *Compensatory* contempt sanctions recompense the injured party for the damage that contempt caused, which in the case of discovery disputes usually means assessing attorney fees and other litigation expenses.[19] *Punitive* contempt sanctions impose fines or imprisonment as punishment for the contemnor's violation.[20]

A contempt proceeding leading to punitive sanctions is known as criminal contempt, and is subject to many of the safeguards attending criminal prosecutions.[21] The court designates a special prosecutor, who must prove beyond a reasonable doubt that the defendant willfully violated the court order, and for any imprisonment longer than six months the defendant is entitled to jury trial.[22] If convicted, the defendant may appeal immediately, but may not be allowed to contest the validity of the violated order.[23] By contrast, one found in criminal contempt will be able to challenge the violated order, but will not be able to appeal immediately unless he or she is a nonparty to the action in which the order was entered.[24] Unfortunately for the sake of clarity, trial courts sometimes conduct combine civil and criminal proceedings, and appellate courts sometimes require retrial because the trial court classified as coercive or compensatory sanctions that the appellate court considers punitive.[25] Whatever its complexities, the contempt power is a powerful way of ensuring that litigants take discovery orders seriously.

18. IBM Corp. v. United States, 493 F.2d 112 (2d Cir.1973); Soobzokov v. CBS, Inc., 642 F.2d 28 (2d Cir.1981); Hodgson v. Mahoney, 460 F.2d 326 (1st Cir.1972).

19. Law v. NCAA, 134 F.3d 1438 (10th Cir.1998); Olcott v. Delaware Flood Co., 76 F.3d 1538 (10th Cir.1996)($402,000 award); Jones v. Clinton, 36 F.Supp.2d 1118 (E.D.Ark.1999); Rendleman, Compensatory Contempt: Plaintiff's Remedy When a Defendant Violates an Injunction, 1980 U. Ill. L.F. 971.

20. Smith v. Smith, 145 F.3d 335 (5th Cir.1998); Selletti v. Carey, 173 F.3d 104 (2d Cir.1999); In re Prudential Ins. Co. Sales Practices Litigation, 169 F.R.D. 598 (D.N.J.1997); *see* United States v. United Mine Workers, 330 U.S. 258, 67 S.Ct. 677, 91 L.Ed. 884 (1947).

21. International Union, UMWA v. Bagwell, 512 U.S. 821, 114 S.Ct. 2552, 129 L.Ed.2d 642 (1994); Dudley, Getting Beyond the Civil/Criminal Distinction: A New Approach to the Regulation of Indirect Contempts, 79 Virg. L. Rev. 1025 (1993),

22. Young v. United States ex rel. Vuitton et Fils S.A., 481 U.S. 787, 107 S.Ct. 2124, 95 L.Ed.2d 740 (1987); Codispoti v. Pennsylvania, 418 U.S. 506, 94 S.Ct. 2687, 41 L.Ed.2d 912 (1974); In re Oliver, 333 U.S. 257, 68 S.Ct. 499, 92 L.Ed. 682 (1948); United States v. United Mine Workers, 330 U.S. 258, 67 S.Ct. 677, 91 L.Ed. 884 (1947).

23. Penfield Co. v. SEC, 330 U.S. 585, 67 S.Ct. 918, 91 L.Ed. 1117 (1947); Walker v. City of Birmingham, 388 U.S. 307, 87 S.Ct. 1824, 18 L.Ed.2d 1210 (1967).

24. U.S Catholic Conference v. Abortion Rights Mobilization, Inc., 487 U.S. 72, 108 S.Ct. 2268, 101 L.Ed.2d 69 (1988); Andre, The Final Judgment Rule and Party Appeals of Civil Contempt Orders: Time for a Change, 55 N.Y.U. L. Rev. 1041 (1980).

25. *E.g.,* International Union, UMWA v. Bagwell, 512 U.S. 821, 114 S.Ct. 2552, 129 L.Ed.2d 642 (1994); Law v. NCAA, 134 F.3d 1438 (10th Cir.1998); Mackler Productions, Inc. v. Cohen, 225 F.3d 136 (2d Cir.2000).

Entry of judgment

The ultimate discovery sanction is to dismiss a plaintiff's case or enter judgment against a defendant. In appropriate circumstances, courts have the power to do this when a party violates discovery orders or fails to comply with rules or court orders.[26] In deciding whether to exercise that power, they rely on a number of factors:

1. the extent of the party's personal responsibility;
2. the prejudice to the adversary caused by the failure to meet scheduling orders and respond to discovery;
3. a history of dilatoriness;
4. whether the conduct of the party or the attorney was willful or in bad faith;
5. the effectiveness of sanctions other than dismissal and an analysis of alternative sanctions; and
6. the merit of the claim or defense.[27]

The entry of judgment against a party has been allowed for actions such as the destruction of documents covered by the discovery request or for continuing failure to comply with discovery.[28] Damages may be awarded with a default judgment, but not beyond the amount demanded in the complaint.[29] Such severe sanctions are authorized only in extreme circumstances, and the violations must be due to willfulness, bad faith, or fault.[30] Courts are especially unlikely to end a case for misconduct that appears to be attributable to a lawyer rather than a client.[31]

Judicial discretion

In choosing among the various sanctions available to them, trial courts enjoy considerable discretion.[32] Appellate courts are generally reluctant to overturn a trial court's imposition of sanctions without a

26. Fed. R. Civ. P. 37(b)(2)(C), 41(b), 55; see Link v. Wabash R.R., 370 U.S. 626, 82 S.Ct. 1386, 8 L.Ed.2d 734 (1962).

27. Poulis v. State Farm Fire & Casualty Co., 747 F.2d 863 (3d Cir.1984).

28. *E.g.*, Guex v. Allmerica Financial Life Ins., 146 F.3d 40 (1st Cir.1998); Republic of the Philippines v. Marcos, 888 F.2d 954 (2d Cir.1989); Sig M. Glukstad, Inc. v. Lineas Aereas Nacional-Chile, 656 F.2d 976 (5th Cir.1981); Carroll v. Abbott Laboratories, 32 Cal.3d 892, 187 Cal.Rptr. 592, 654 P.2d 775 (1982).

29. Fed. R. Civ. P. 54(c); Greenup v. Rodman, 42 Cal.3d 822, 231 Cal.Rptr. 220, 726 P.2d 1295 (1986).

30. Refac. Int'l v. Hitachi, Ltd., 921 F.2d 1247 (Fed.Cir.1990); Marshall v. Segona, 621 F.2d 763 (5th Cir.1980); Marx v. Kelly, Hart & Hallman, P.C., 929 F.2d 8 (1st Cir.1991); Webb v. District of Columbia, 146 F.3d 964 (D.C.Cir.1998).

31. See Hillig v. C.I.R., 916 F.2d 171 (4th Cir.1990); Butler v. Pearson, 636 F.2d 526 (D.C.Cir.1980).

32. The attitudes of courts vary considerably and are perhaps the most important variable in the sanctioning process. *Compare, e.g.*, Fox v. Studebaker-Worthington, Inc., 516 F.2d 989 (8th Cir.1975), *with* SEC v. Research Automation Corp., 521 F.2d 585 (2d Cir.1975). *See also* Annots., 4 A.L.R.2d 348 (dismissal of action), 6 A.L.R.3d 713 (default against defendant), 2 A.L.R.2d 811 (exclusion of testimony), 76 A.L.R.2d 953 (imposition of costs); Note, Developments in the Law—Discovery, 74 Harv. L. Rev. 940, 990 (1961); Note, The Second Circuit's Imposition of Litigation-Ending Sanctions For Failure to Comply With Discovery Orders, 62 Brook. L. Rev. 585 (1996).

showing of abuse of that court's discretion.[33] Indeed, most discovery sanctions orders are not final judgments, can therefore not be appealed immediately, and will escape review entirely should the case be settled.[34] An immediate appeal is possible when the court enters judgment against a party or holds it in criminal contempt, and reversals of these sanctions are not uncommon.

Dismissal and due process

Notwithstanding the courts' broad power to sanction, there are limits beyond which it may be unconstitutional for a court to go. In 1897 the Supreme Court held in *Hovey v. Elliott*[35] that due process had been denied by an order striking defendant's answer and entering judgment against him *pro confesso* because of his failure to obey a court order. A few years later, however, in *Hammond Packing Co. v. Arkansas,*[36] the Court upheld a similar order entered against a defendant who had refused to obey an order for pretrial discovery of documents. *Hovey* was distinguished on the ground that it dealt with an attempt simply to punish a party for contempt of court, whereas the order in *Hammond* could be justified by a reasonable presumption that a party who refused to produce evidence lacked a meritorious defense.

A parallel oscillation in sanctions policy is reflected in more recent decisions. On one hand, the Court in *Société Internationale v. Rogers*[37] held it improper to dismiss an action for plaintiff's noncompliance with a discovery order since the plaintiff convinced the court that he had made a good faith effort to comply but could not do so without subjecting himself to criminal penalties under Swiss law. The Court suggested that "substantial constitutional questions"[38] would be involved in dismissing the action in such circumstances. On the other hand, the Court has sustained dismissal of an action for failure of plaintiff's counsel to attend a pretrial conference.[39]

Dismissal upheld

In *National Hockey League v. Metropolitan Hockey Club*[40] the trial court dismissed plaintiff's action for noncompliance with a discovery

33. National Hockey League v. Metropolitan Hockey Club, 427 U.S. 639, 96 S.Ct. 2778, 49 L.Ed.2d 747 (1976); Halaco Eng. Co. v. Costle, 843 F.2d 376 (9th Cir.1988); United States v. $239,500 in U.S. Currency, 764 F.2d 771 (11th Cir.1985).

34. *E.g.*, Cunningham v. Hamilton County, 527 U.S. 198, 119 S.Ct. 1915, 144 L.Ed.2d 184 (1999).

35. 167 U.S. 409, 17 S.Ct. 841, 42 L.Ed. 215 (1897).

36. 212 U.S. 322, 29 S.Ct. 370, 53 L.Ed. 530 (1909).

37. 357 U.S. 197, 78 S.Ct. 1087, 2 L.Ed.2d 1255 (1958).

38. 357 U.S. at 210, 78 S.Ct. at 1095, 2 L.Ed.2d at 1266.

39. Link v. Wabash R.R., 370 U.S. 626, 82 S.Ct. 1386, 8 L.Ed.2d 734 (1962); *see also* Insurance Corp. of Ireland, Ltd. v. Compagnie des Bauxites de Guinée, 456 U.S. 694, 102 S.Ct. 2099, 72 L.Ed.2d 492 (1982).

40. 427 U.S. 639, 96 S.Ct. 2778, 49 L.Ed.2d 747 (1976); see Note, The Emerging Deterrence Orientation in the Imposition of Discovery Sanctions, 91 Harv. L. Rev. 1033 (1978).

order but was reversed by the court of appeals. On further appeal, the Supreme Court reversed the court of appeals' decision as an improper interference with the trial court's discretion and held that dismissal was a proper sanction. The Court stated that this, "the most severe in the spectrum of sanctions provided by statute or rule must be available to the ... court in appropriate cases, not merely to penalize those whose conduct may be deemed to warrant such a sanction, but to deter those who might be tempted to such conduct in the absence of such a deterrent." Thus, the most recent word, but certainly not the last word, is that the sanction of dismissal may validly be imposed for sufficiently serious noncompliance with discovery orders.

New trial

Disputes about discovery never end. Even after a case has been tried, a party discovering that its opponent concealed important information properly sought in discovery may seek sanctions[41] or a new trial.[42] To prevail on the motion for a new trial, the movant must prove by clear and convincing evidence that the verdict was obtained "through fraud, misrepresentation or other misconduct" and that the "conduct complained of prevented the losing party from fully and fairly presenting his case or defense ... but 'when the case involves the withholding of information called for by discovery, the party need not establish that the result in the case would be altered.' "[43]

§ 5.15 Special Problems of Big Cases and Transnational Litigation

Discovery presents additional problems in a large or protracted case[1] such as antitrust and environmental litigation. These kinds of cases may concern the history of a whole industry or an industrywide pattern of activity rather than a single occurrence between individuals. In the ordinary case of the latter kind, the limited scope of the subject matter of the action imposes some limits on discovery, even if discovery is sought of everything conceivably relevant to the action rather than just the issues made by the pleadings. In "big" cases, however, more active management of the discovery process is required.[2]

41. Bush Ranch, Inc. v. E.I. DuPont De Nemours & Co., 99 F.3d 363 (11th Cir. 1996).

42. Fed. R. Civ. P. 59; see § 7.26 *infra.*

43. Jones v. Aero/Chem Corp., 921 F.2d 875, 879 (9th Cir.1990), *quoting* Bunch v. United States, 680 F.2d 1271, 1283 (9th Cir.1982); Advanced Display Systems v. Kent State University, 212 F.3d 1272 (Fed. Cir.2000); see Harr, A Civil Action (1995).

§ 5.15

1. Manual for Complex Litigation Third (1995); Kendig, Procedures for Management of Non-routine Cases, 3 Hofstra L. Rev. 701 (1975).

2. *See generally* Manual for Complex Litigation Third (1995); Brazil, Hazard, and Rice, Managing Complex Litigation (1983).

Big case discovery management

The American Bar Association details this supervision in its Standards Relating to Trial Courts:

> Unusually time-consuming cases generally have two or more of the following characteristics: very large amount in controversy, multiple parties, public notoriety, interconnection with other litigation, and extensive pretrial activity.... Cases identified as potentially protracted should be considered for special supervisory measures, including: ...
>
> —Close supervision of preliminary motions and discovery, including regulation of the sequence and extent of discovery and the time limits within which it is to be completed. Where large volumes of documents are involved, a documents depository should be established....
>
> —Conferences in preparation for trial, in which documents are marked, trial evidentiary questions anticipated and determined, a schedule of witnesses prepared, and the sequence of proof established. Where masses of data or documents are involved, rulings may be made that permit introduction of summaries, tables, charts, and other simplified forms of presentation.[3]

Discovery in large cases generally requires such controls lest it become protracted and riven with disputes over scope, tactics, and whether the parties have honestly fulfilled their duties in responding to discovery demands. The tensions are heightened by the large dimensions of these cases—the stakes involved, the long period in which the lawyers are immersed in a single case, the effects on the lives of the clients and the lawyers. A set of rules to guide the parties, even if precisely drafted, cannot adequately cope with these difficulties. Hence, personal managerial supervision is required of the judge or a judicial officer such as a special master.[4] Such supervision, however, necessarily involves broad discretion that is beyond any effective appellate review. In the hands of a biased or careless judge, these powers can be highly prejudicial, and "managerial judging" has been criticized on this account.[5] There seems no alternative, however, because the complexity of discovery in "big cases" defies governance by simply a set of rules. In effect, these cases are placed on a separate administrative track and treated differently from other litigation, an approach that some reformers would generalize and make more explicit.[6]

3. ABA Standards Relating to Trial Courts § 2.53, Commentary.

4. *See* Schwartzer, Managing Antitrust and Other Litigation (1982).

5. *See* Resnick, Managerial Judges, 96 Harv. L. Rev. 376 (1982); Tornquist, The Active Judge in Pretrial Settlement: Inherent Authority Gone Awry, 25 Willamette L. Rev. 743 (1989).

6. See N.J. Civ. Pr. R. 4:5A; Subrin, Fudge Points and Thin Ice in Discovery Reform and the Case for Selective Substance-Specific Procedure, 46 Fla. L. Rev. 27 (1994). On the tracking recently introduced into English civil procedure, *see* Sime, A Practical Approach to Civil Procedure 229–262 (4th ed. 2000); Access to Justice: Final Report (1996).

Seeking discovery abroad

A whole new set of discovery problems arises when a litigant in the United States seeks discovery abroad, because foreign nations usually regard discovery as a governmental act whose conduct within their boundaries infringes their sovereignty. Even foreign nations with common law procedural systems provide less discovery than exists in the United States, while civil law systems may provide virtually none. These restrictions reflect concern for privacy that have led some nations to pass criminal statutes forbidding banks or other entities to disclose certain information. When one adds that foreign nations sometimes object to litigation that applies United States law to conduct some of which may have occurred abroad, it is not surprising that transnational discovery arising from litigation here has provoked protests and even passage of "blocking statutes" designed to prevent foreign nationals from complying with United States discovery proceedings.[7]

The Hague Convention

The Hague Evidence Convention, a multinational treaty to which the United States and many other nations are parties, seeks to deal with such problems by making it possible to obtain the cooperation of foreign authorities in obtaining evidence.[8] It authorizes a court in one nation to send a letter of request to a central authority in another, the latter then proceeding to collect and transmit the evidence, and if necessary to compel its production. Unfortunately, many subscribing nations excluded all pretrial documentary discovery from their ratifications, and even others have tended to read the Convention narrowly.[9] Perhaps these attitudes will change as globalization increases the need for international cooperation in tracing transnational fraud and other violations.

In the meantime, the Supreme Court has declined to require litigants to use the procedures of the Hague Convention even when they are available. In *Societe Nationale Industrielle Aerospatiale v. United States District Court for the Southern District of Iowa,*[10] the Court held that both the Federal Rules of Civil Procedure and the Hague Evidence Convention are the law of the United States but that the Hague

7. See Lowenfeld, International Litigation and the Quest for Reasonableness chs. 7, 8 (1996);Gerber, Extraterritorial Discovery and the Conflict of Procedural Systems: Germany and the United States, 34 Am. J. Comp. L. 745 (1986); Note, Discovery in France and the Hague Convention: The Search for a French Connection, 64 N.Y.U. L. Rev. 1073 (1989). For discovery in England, *see generally* Sime, A Practical Approach to Civil Procedure 148–56, 271–13, 379–87, 406 (4th ed. 2000).

8. Convention on the Taking of Evidence Abroad in Civil or Commercial Matters, 847 U.N.T.S. 231, 23 U.S.T. 2555 (1970); authorities cited note 7 *supra.*

9. See Rio Tinto Zinc v. Westinghouse Electric Corp., [1978] 2 W.L.R. 81 (H.L. 1978)(Eng.)Norway's Application, [1990] 1 AC 723 (H.L.1989)(Eng.).

10. 482 U.S. 522, 107 S.Ct. 2542, 96 L.Ed.2d 461 (1987). *See also* Restatement, Third, of the Foreign Relations Law of the United States § 442; Martikan, The Boundaries of the Hague Evidence Convention: Lower Court Interest Balancing After the *Aerospatiale* Decision, 68 Tex. L. Rev. 1003 (1990);; Note, The Role of the Hague Convention for Gathering Evidence Abroad, 24 Stan. U.J. Intl. L. 309 (1987).

Convention does not deprive a federal district court of jurisdiction to order a foreign national to produce evidence physically located outside the country. The decision admonished the lower courts to exercise special vigilance to protect foreign litigants against the danger of unnecessary or unduly burdensome discovery.[11] And an advisory committee note to the Federal Rules now advises that a deposition abroad should "ordinarily" be taken under the Hague Evidence Convention or other applicable treaty.[12]

The compulsion game

The main situation in which a United States court can obtain discovery from a foreign national without resort to the Hague Convention occurs when the national is a party to the United States suit or has property or branches here, making it subject to the United States court's coercive jurisdiction.[13] The court can then require the foreign national to produce documents or employees here. Should the national show that doing so would subject it to possible prosecution abroad for violating secrecy or blocking statutes, the United States court may decline to proceed further.[14] Yet if the evidence is important enough, and the party seeking the evidence can afford protracted enforcement proceedings, the United States court has the authority to coerce the foreign national by instituting contempt proceedings or (if it is a party to the suit) entering judgment against it.[15] Eventually, the foreign national usually gives in, and the foreign authorities then drop their threats of prosecution.[16] But this is not the ideal way to run a lawsuit or conduct international relations.

United States discovery by foreign litigants

The opposite situation, in which litigants in foreign courts seek to obtain information in the United States, has produced less conflict. A federal statute allows such litigants to seek the aid of a District Court to obtain documents or testimony.[17] The testimony may be rendered either in a deposition or in some other form consistent with foreign law. The court may grant discovery broader than would be allowed in the foreign

11. In re Anschuetz & Co., GmbH., 838 F.2d 1362 (5th Cir.1988). *See also* Note, Strict Enforcement of Extraterritorial Discovery, 38 Stan. L. Rev. 841 (1986); Riesenfeld, Service of United States Process Abroad: A Practical Guide to Service Under the Hague Convention and the Federal Rules of Civil Procedure, 24 Intl. Law. 55 (1990).

12. Fed. R. Civ. P. 28, Advisory Committee Note (1993).

13. For other alternatives, see 28 U.S.C. §§ 1781, 1783; Fed. R. Civ. P. 28(b); Teitz, Transnational Litigation ch. 5 (1996).

14. *E.g.,* First American Corp. v. Price Waterhouse LLP, 154 F.3d 16 (2d Cir.1998).

15. Société Internationale v. Rogers, 357 U.S. 197, 78 S.Ct. 1087, 2 L.Ed.2d 1255 (1958)(discussed § 5.14 *supra*); Richmark Corp. v. Timber Falling Consultants, 959 F.2d 1468 (9th Cir.1992); see Insurance Corp. of Ireland v. Compagnie des Bauxites, 456 U.S. 694, 102 S.Ct. 2099, 72 L.Ed.2d 492 (1982).

16. Lowenfeld, International Litigation and the Quest for Resaonableness, ch. 7 (1996).

17. 28 U.S.C. § 1782.

court where litigation is pending, but is generally subject to the limits of the Federal Rules and has the discretion to limit discovery further as appropriate.[18]

B. PRELIMINARY RELIEF

Although the procedures described in this book constitute the normal path by which a party may obtain judicial relief, various short cuts allow parties under certain conditions to obtain preliminary or interlocutory relief before the merits of the case have been finally decided. These forms of relief respond to some claimed need for immediate action. For example, the defendant may be ready to chop down a tree where land ownership is disputed or to consummate a corporate merger difficult to disentangle later, or defendant may be using an automobile for which he or she has stopped paying. The defendant, however, often rejoins that the plaintiff's claimed emergency does not exist and that granting the plaintiff immediate relief will infringe the defendant's own rights. The defendant will lose, or at least have to postpone, the chance to complete its merger, drive his or her car, or engage in a protest march.

The fundamental dilemma of preliminary relief is that the court must pass on such claims and rejoinders before it holds a final hearing on the factual and legal issues in dispute. Whether it grants or withholds relief, the court may turn out to have denied one or the other party its legal rights. One way to avoid this dilemma is to decide the merits of the dispute immediately, but the complexity of disputes and the length of court backlogs often discourage this. So, courts often base their decisions concerning preliminary remedies on a rough preliminary assessment of the merits, balanced with the irreparable harm—that is, harm that later relief cannot remedy—that granting or denying relief would inflict.

§ 5.16 Preliminary Injunctions and Temporary Restraining Orders[1]

A preliminary injunction is a court order directing a party to avoid certain conduct or perform specified acts before the court decides the merits of the case. It is issued after a relatively brief hearing, which the judge may sometimes confine to written evidence.

A temporary restraining order (TRO) is a similar but earlier court order limited to a time period that will allow the court to decide whether to grant a preliminary injunction. In the federal courts, that period is ten

18. In re Bayer AG, 146 F.3d 188 (3d Cir.1998); Bayer AG v. Betachem, Inc., 173 F.3d 188 (3d Cir.1999); Metallgesellschaft AG v. Hodapp, 121 F.3d 77 (2d Cir.1997). But see Application of Asta Medica, S.A., 981 F.2d 1 (1st Cir.1992)(U.S. court may grant discovery only of information discoverable abroad).

§ 5.16

1. *See generally* Fiss and Rendleman, Injunctions (2d ed. 1984).

days, with a possible further ten-day extension.[2] Because a temporary restraining order lasts such a short time and should be granted only in an emergency, courts traditionally entered such orders even though the restrained party had received no notice or hearing. Today many jurisdictions require that the restrained party must be given a chance to be heard unless the court finds it impractical to do so. The Constitution has been found to impose this requirement when a temporary restraining order limits the exercise of speech.[3]

Bonds

An enjoined party may be protected against an unwarranted injunction not only by requiring a notice or hearing but also by requiring the party seeking a preliminary injunction or temporary restraining order to post a bond. Such a bond binds the party seeking the injunction to pay the enjoined party for damages suffered from the interruption caused by what turns out to be an improper injunction. Courts have, however, granted preliminary injunctions without requiring a bond. This occurs, for example, in environmental suits in which the plaintiffs seek an injunction in the public interest and have too little of their own at stake to make it worthwhile for them to post a bond.[4]

Standards for relief

Assuming that the procedural requirements for a preliminary injunction or temporary restraining order have been met, whether the court grants relief depends on several factors. These include the plaintiff's likelihood of succeeding on the merits, how much irreparable injury the plaintiff will suffer if relief is denied and plaintiff ultimately prevails, how much irreparable injury the defendant will suffer if relief is granted but defendant ultimately prevails, and the impact of relief on the public interest. Although different courts announce different formulas for combining these factors, the differences do not seem to have much bearing on the results judges reach. In general, a strong showing on one factor will compensate for a weaker showing on another. For example, a plaintiff who persuades a judge that a defendant is almost certainly violating the plaintiff's patent may obtain a preliminary injunction against infringement during the suit on a relatively weak showing that damages will not adequately remedy the infringement—for instance, because the defendant's impact on the plaintiff's share of the market will be hard to compute. A plaintiff less likely to prevail will have to make a stronger showing that denying relief will inflict irreparable injury.

2. Fed. R. Civ. P. 65(b). See Granny Goose Foods, Inc. v. Brotherhood of Teamsters, 415 U.S. 423, 94 S.Ct. 1113, 39 L.Ed.2d 435 (1974),

3. Fed. R. Civ. P. 65(b); Carroll v. President & Commrs. of Princess Anne, 393 U.S. 175, 89 S.Ct. 347, 21 L.Ed.2d 325 (1968).

4. *See generally* Fed. R. Civ. P. 65(c); Dobbs, Should Security Be Required as a Pre-condition to Provisional Injunctive Relief?, 52 N.C.L. Rev. 1091 (1974).

Judges, in short, try to shape relief to minimize the extent to which parties are irreparably injured by what ultimately turn out to be violations of their legal rights.[5]

The Supreme Court recently injected a dose of technicality into this flexible and pragmatic approach by holding that a federal court may not grant preliminary relief preventing a defendant from dissipating assets during an action when the plaintiff's underlying claim is what used to be a claim at law for monetary damages.[6] The Court's reason was that English equity courts traditionally did not grant such relief, and that this limit was a matter of "substantive" law unaffected by the merger of law and equity. As a matter of policy, this makes little sense. Although a preliminary injunction of this sort can raise problems, for example by giving the party obtaining it an advantage over other creditors, it can also be a useful way to prevent an unscrupulous defendant from dispersing its assets while litigation winds its lengthy way.[7] The Court's opinion exaggerates the reluctance of equity courts to protect the right to a money judgment.[8] It can also be argued that, if the right to preliminary relief is indeed substantive, it should be governed by state law, as Federal Rule 64 seems to say.[9] Most importantly, the Court's narrow reading of the merger of law and equity could entangle the courts in antiquarian obscurities, for example those that governed just when an equity court would grant preliminary relief in various kinds of claims.[10]

Contempt and its anomalies

Preliminary injunctive relief has often given rise to controversy, notably in labor cases.[11] Although courts grant such relief without a full hearing on the merits, a violator may be held in contempt of court and

5. *See* Leubsdorf, The Standard for Preliminary Injunctions, 91 Harv. L. Rev. 525 (1978); Zuckerman, Quality and Economy in Civil Procedure: The Case for Commuting Correct Judgments for Timely Judgments, 14 Ox. J. Leg. Stud. 353 (1994). For a controversial attempt to state an algebraic formula for the standard, see American Hospital Supply Corp. v. Hospital Prods. Ltd., 780 F.2d 589 (7th Cir.1986).

6. Grupo Mexicano de Desarrollo, S.A. v. Alliance Bond Fund, Inc., 527 U.S. 308, 119 S.Ct. 1961, 144 L.Ed.2d 319 (1999). *Compare* United States ex rel. Rahman v. Oncology Associates, 198 F.3d 489 (4th Cir.1999)(*Grupo Mexicano* does not apply when plaintiff seeks equitable remedy as well as damages).

7. Wasserman, Equity Renewed: Preliminary Injunctions to Secure Potential Money Judgments, 67 Wash. L. Rev. 257 (1992).

8. See *id.*; Newman, The Effect of Insolvency on Equitable Relief, 13 St. John's L. Rev. 44 (1938).

9. Burbank, The Bitter with the Sweet: Tradition, History, and Limitations on Federal Judicial Power - A Case Study, 75 Notre Dame L. Rev. 1291 (2000).

10. See Eden, A Treatise on the Law of Injunctions (1821). Courts have often rejected attempts to carry forward rules rooted in the distinction between law and equity. *E.g.,* Guaranty Trust Co. v. York, 326 U.S. 99, 65 S.Ct. 1464, 89 L.Ed. 2079 (1945); Laycock, The Death of the Irreparable Injury Rule (1991); see Beacon Theatres, Inc. v. Westover, 359 U.S. 500, 79 S.Ct. 948, 3 L.Ed.2d 988 (1959).

11. *See* Frankfurter and Green, The Labor Injunction (1930). *But see* Fiss, The Civil Rights Injunction (1978), defending final and preliminary injunctive relief that protect civil rights.

receive stringent sanctions.[12] These sanctions include remedial civil contempt sanctions (payment of the damages and attorney's fees incurred by the other party as a result of the contumacious behavior), coercive civil contempt (imprisonment or daily fines continuing until the enjoined party stops violating the injunction), and criminal contempt (imprisonment or fines imposed for past violation). The judge who issued the injunction usually also presides over the contempt proceeding enforcing it. Because an injunction is a remedy traditionally granted by courts of equity, there is no constitutional right to a jury trial in contempt proceedings for violation of an injunction unless criminal rather than civil contempt is charged and imprisoned for more than six months is imposed.[13] A party held in civil contempt while a suit is pending—for violating a temporary restraining order, for example—usually cannot appeal until the suit is finally decided.

These rules and practices, originating in the courts of equity, are often defended today as essential to preserve the power of courts to enforce their interlocutory and final decrees. A striking example is *Walker v. City of Birmingham,* in which the Supreme Court declined to set aside the criminal contempt convictions of associates of Martin Luther King for demonstrating in violation of a temporary restraining order, even though that order violated the First Amendment.[14] The Court reasoned that the demonstrators' remedy was to appeal the order, not to take the law into their own hands. It rejected the argument that a court order inconsistent with the Constitution is no more "law" than an unconstitutional statute.

§ 5.17 Garnishment and Replevin

Garnishment is a court order requiring one who owes a debt to withhold paying it to the original obligee until the court can determine whether the sum should be paid over to a creditor of the original obligee. A familiar example is an order barring an employer from paying an employee all or part of the employee's wages, requiring the amount to be paid instead into the court or directly to someone to whom the employee owes money. Replevin is a court order that requires a defendant to surrender goods to the court or the plaintiff, usually goods that the defendant has bought but assertedly not paid for. In some states, similar remedies are given different names.

Both remedies were formerly readily available to plaintiffs, often on the filing of an affidavit. They were widely used by creditors of workers and by installment sellers. The amounts in dispute were usually small,

12. For the rules stated in this paragraph, see generally Fiss and Rendleman, Injunctions (2d ed. 1984); see § 5.14 *supra.*

13. Bloom v. Illinois, 391 U.S. 194, 88 S.Ct. 1477, 20 L.Ed.2d 522 (1968); *see* §§ 1.4, 1.5 *supra*; 8.1, 8.2 *infra.*

14. Walker v. City of Birmingham, 388 U.S. 307, 87 S.Ct. 1824, 18 L.Ed.2d 1210 (1967).

the defendants were often poor or legally unsophisticated, and the preliminary remedies usually gave plaintiffs all they sought in the litigation. Hence, the supposedly preliminary relief often ended the suit and no tribunal passed on the merits. This led to calls for reform.

Wage garnishment

In *Sniadach v. Family Finance Corp.*[1] the Supreme Court held that wage garnishment before a suit has been adjudicated on the merits violates the Due Process Clause of the Fourteenth Amendment unless the defendant is given prior notice and hearing. The Court reasoned that garnishment deprives the employee of the use of the wages during an action even if the defendant ultimately prevails and the wages are released. Such a deprivation requires the procedural safeguards of notice and opportunity to be heard to insure that the plaintiff is actually entitled to the money. Congress has also regulated wage garnishments, forbidding garnishment of certain basic wages.[2]

Repossession of goods

When the Supreme Court heard cases raising similar due process challenges to replevin, it found them more difficult. A typical case involved an attempt by the seller of a household appliance that had been sold on credit to replevin the appliance when the purchaser failed in making payments. Taking away the defendant's refrigerator without a hearing seems to deprive defendant of his or her property without due process of law; the refrigerator store can reply, however, that the disputed refrigerator is not defendant's property but belongs to the store because the purchaser defaulted on the payments. This is the recurring dilemma of preliminary relief: The court is forced to grant or deny relief before finally deciding which party is in the right.

The Supreme Court responded by allowing replevin for plaintiffs who could make some showing on the merits, but only when an improperly deprived defendant could then obtain speedy and effective relief against the replevin. Thus the Court upheld a statute allowing a plaintiff to obtain replevin when a judge upheld the plaintiff's detailed affidavit, but only on the following terms: The defendant was entitled to a speedy hearing after repossession at which the plaintiff bore the burden of establishing its case, and plaintiff was required to post bond in advance to recompense the defendant for replevin later held improper.[3]

§ 5.17

1. 395 U.S. 337, 89 S.Ct. 1820, 23 L.Ed.2d 349 (1969).

2. 15 U.S.C. §§ 1671–1677.

3. Mitchell v. W. T. Grant Co., 416 U.S. 600, 94 S.Ct. 1895, 40 L.Ed.2d 406 (1974) (remedy called "sequestration"). The Court has invalidated replevin procedures with lesser safeguards. North Ga. Finishing v. Di–Chem, Inc., 419 U.S. 601, 95 S.Ct. 719, 42 L.Ed.2d 751 (1975) (attachment of bank account); Fuentes v. Shevin, 407 U.S. 67, 92 S.Ct. 1983, 32 L.Ed.2d 556 (1972).

State legislatures have rewritten their statutes to provide at least the safeguards required by these decisions.[4] It remains to be seen whether sellers try to bypass due process safeguards by repossessing without a court order or by inserting waivers of the safeguards into sales contracts, and how courts and legislatures react to such waiver contracts.[5]

§ 5.18 Attachment

Another form of preliminary relief is attachment. An attachment is a seizure of defendant's property by the sheriff or similar officer early in an action so that the property will be available to pay the plaintiff's claim. If the defendant's bank account is attached, for example, the defendant cannot use it unless he or she gets the attachment released. This can be done if the defendant provides other assets of equal value or shows that no difficulty will ensue in collecting a judgment. If land is attached and proper notice (often called a *lis pendens*) is inserted in the registry of deeds, the land can be sold to pay for a judgment even though the defendant has already sold the property to someone else. The Supreme Court has held that, in the absence of exigent circumstances, a state may not attach land without notice and a hearing.[1]

Attachment is not only a way to insure that the plaintiff's judgment is collectible; it also is a way for a court to acquire jurisdiction to enter a judgment on a claim against a defendant up to the value of the attached property. Attachment thus raises two kinds of constitutional questions under the Due Process Clause. First, are the procedural safeguards accompanying attachment sufficient to protect the defendant against improper attachments? Second, is the defendant's possession of property in the forum state, together with any other ties to that state, constitutionally sufficient to warrant the state in asserting jurisdiction? This book discusses the second question in connection with the standards governing jurisdiction.[2]

4. *E.g.,* Cal. Civ. Proc. Code §§ 481.010–493.060.

5. *See* Flagg Bros., Inc. v. Brooks, 436 U.S. 149, 98 S.Ct. 1729, 56 L.Ed.2d 185 (1978); D. H. Overmyer Co. v. Frick Co., 405 U.S. 174, 92 S.Ct. 775, 31 L.Ed.2d 124 (1972); Jordan v. Fox, Rothschild, O'Brien & Frankel, 20 F.3d 1250 (3d Cir.1994).

§ 5.18

1. Connecticut v. Doehr, 501 U.S. 1, 111 S.Ct. 2105, 115 L.Ed.2d 1 (1991); see Shaumyan v. O'Neill, 987 F.2d 122 (2d Cir. 1993)(*Doehr* does not apply when facts are simple and plaintiff has interest in attached property). The Supreme Court has applied the constitutional standards applicable to replevin to bank account attachments. North Ga. Finishing v. Di–Chem, Inc., 419 U.S. 601, 95 S.Ct. 719, 42 L.Ed.2d 751 (1975); *see* § 5.17 *supra.*

2. *See* Shaffer v. Heitner, 433 U.S. 186, 97 S.Ct. 2569, 53 L.Ed.2d 683 (1977); §§ 2.15, 2.17, 2.32 *supra.* On the history of attachments, see Millar, Civil Procedure of the Trial Court in Historical Perspective 481–97 (1952).

C. DISPOSITION OF CASE WITHOUT TRIAL

§ 5.19 Alternative Dispute Resolution

Most civil cases are settled out of court. One survey found that only 7 percent of civil cases were resolved through a trial, although some of the rest are not settled but resolved through summary judgment or other means.[1] In addition, many disputes are settled before an action is commenced. Because settlements are usually a compromise, both parties sacrifice a part of their claim in order to avoid the "all or nothing" gamble of a trial.

Pros and cons of ADR

How actions are resolved without court adjudication is thus of practical importance to lawyers. Some lawyers, legislators, and scholars, moreover, have sought to promote alternative dispute resolution (ADR) techniques as better than court litigation. Others oppose that effort as an attempt to shunt less favored disputants into a routinized procedure that weakens their rights.[2]

Most litigants settle before trial in order to avoid its inherent expenses, delays and aggravations.[3] Sometimes, by settling voluntarily, they may be able to preserve a business or relationship or reach a desirable result that a court could not or would not impose. Settlement can be a more considerate and cooperative mode of interaction between litigants than litigation. On the other hand, settlement can deprive parties of an adjudication on the merits, give advantages to the party that is more skilled in negotiation and more willing to risk the costs of trial, and deprive society of valuable precedents.[4]

Settlement negotiations

Settling disputes is an art. Some lawyers take a competitive, hard-line approach, disclosing little and emphasizing their willingness to litigate. Others approach settlement as problem-solving work and try to find solutions advantageous to both sides, discussing the parties' goals and interests more openly. Which works better depends on what ap-

§ 5.19

1. Kritzer, Let's Make a Deal: Understanding the Negotiation Process in Ordinary Litigation (1990); Eisenberg, et al., Litigation Outcomes in State and Federal Courts: A Statistical Portrait, 19 Seattle U.L. Rev. 433 (1996); Gross & Syverud, Getting to No: A Study of Settlement Negotiations and the Selection of Cases for Trial, 909 Mich. L. Rev. 319 (1991).

2. *See generally* Auerbach, Justice Without Law? (1983); Goldberg, Green, and Sander, Dispute Resolution: Negotiation, Mediation and Other Processes (3d ed. 1999); The Politics of Informal Justice (R. Abel ed. 1982).

3. *See* §§ 6.3, 6.4 *infra;* Kritzer, note 1 *supra*; Ross, Settled Out of Court (1970); Genn, Hard Bargaining: Out of Court Settlement in Personal Injury Actions (1987).

4. *See* Fiss, Against Settlement, 93 Yale L.J. 1073 (1984); Menkel-Meadow, For and Against Settlement: Uses and Abuses of the Mandatory Settlement Conference, 33, 485 (1985); Luban, Bargaining and Compromise: Recent Work on Negotiation and Informal Justice, 14 Phil. & Pub. Aff. 397 (1985); NOMOS XII, Compromise in Ethics, Law and Politics (1979).

proach the opposing party is using and on whether the situation permits a problem-solving solution.[5]

A lawyer may not settle the case without the client's consent.[6] The client may consent by approving the settlement, by authorizing the lawyer in advance to settle (perhaps only on specified terms),[7] by behaving so that the opposing party reasonably believes that the client has so authorized the lawyer,[8] or by ratifying a settlement after it has been negotiated.[9] After the parties have consented, they may implement the settlement by asking the court to enter a judgment for money or a consent decree for injunctive relief, which can then be enforced like any other judgment or court order. Alternatively, the parties may agree to dismiss the action with or without prejudice.[10] The terms of the settlement will then not appear in court files accessible to outsiders, and a party may enforce the settlement only by bringing an action on the settlement agreement.[11] Which of these methods is used may itself be a subject of bargaining. In some litigation such as class actions and actions brought by minors, the court must approve any settlement.[12]

Civil procedure and settlement

Although settlement is in a sense a private process, the settling parties often seek to use the court to implement and enforce their agreement. Defendants, for example, often wish to obtain a provision preventing the plaintiff from disclosing the terms of the settlement or information obtained through discovery. Plaintiffs will often accept such a provision in order to obtain a better settlement. If an attempt is later made to challenge or enforce the "gag clause," the court must decide whether the parties' bargain should prevail over any public interest in access to information that might prevent future injuries.[13] Sometimes

5. *See* Mnookin, *et al.*, Beyond Winning: Negotiating to Create Value in Deals and Disputes (2000); Fisher and Ury, Getting to Yes (1981); Gifford, Legal Negotiation (1989); Lax and Sebenius, The Manager as Negotiator (1986); Hyman, Trial Advocacy and Methods of Negotiation: Can Good Trial Advocates Be Wise Negotiators?, 34 UCLA L. Rev. 863 (1987).

6. *E.g.*, Fennell v. TLB Kent Co., 865 F.2d 498 (2d Cir.1989); Model Rules of Professional Conduct Rule 1.2(a) (1983); Restatement of the Law Governing Lawyers § 22. Some authorities adopt a different rule, under which a lawyer has implied or apparent authority to bind a client to a settlement. *See, e.g.*, Lord Jeff Knitting Co. v. Mills, 281 S.C. 374, 315 S.E.2d 377 (App. 1984).

7. *E.g.*, First Fed. Sav. & Loan Assn. v. C.P.R. Construction, 70 Or.App. 296, 689 P.2d 981 (1984).

8. *See, e.g.*, Edwards v. Born, Inc., 792 F.2d 387 (3d Cir.1986).

9. *E.g.*, Nagymihaly v. Zipes, 353 So.2d 943 (Fla.Dist.Ct.App.1978).

10. Fed. R. Civ. P. 41.

11. Kokkonen v. Guardian Life Ins. Co., 511 U.S. 375, 114 S.Ct. 1673, 128 L.Ed.2d 391 (1994).

12. Fed. R. Civ. P. 23(e), 23.1; see, *e.g.*, N.J. Civ. Prac. R. 4:44–3; Hoffert v. General Motors Corp., 656 F.2d 161 (5th Cir.1981); Spaulding v. Zimmerman, 263 Minn. 346, 116 N.W.2d 704 (1962).

13. Leucadia, Inc. v. Applied Extrusion Technologies, Inc., 998 F.2d 157 (3d Cir. 1993); Doré, Secrecy by Consent: The Use and Limits of Confidentiality in the Pursuit of Settlement, 74 Notre Dame L. Rev. 283 (1999); see § 5.13 *supra*.

settlement occurs pending appeal and one party wishes to have the trial court's opinion vacated as part of the settlement in the hope of reducing its issue preclusion or precedential force.[14] Courts disagree about whether implementing such a provision merely facilitates settlement or should be considered to compromise the public interest in declaring the law.[15]

As will be discussed later, courts have increasingly sought to intervene in settlement discussions. In addition, rule-makers have rearranged the expenses of litigation to encourage settlement. Under Federal Rule of Civil Procedure 68, a plaintiff that rejects a settlement offer but does no better at trial loses the right to recover its costs and must pay the defendant's costs incurred after the rejection. Because the costs recoverable in a civil action are small,[16] this rule is limited in effect. It is unclear whether it actually increases the number of settlements or, rather, encourages parties who can least afford the sanctions to settle on less advantageous terms.[17] Proposals to increase the rule's sanctions have so far failed. The Supreme Court has, however, construed the Rule to bar a plaintiff that rejects a settlement offer but does no better at trial from recovering its attorney's fees under a statute providing for recovery of fees by a prevailing plaintiff as part of its costs.[18]

Rule 68 is only applicable to defendants,[19] and, when its terms are met, leaves no room for discretion by the district court.[20] The offer must be made at least ten days before trial and presumably must be made in writing.[21] The offer is invalid unless it specifies "costs then accrued,"[22] although a lump-sum offer will suffice.[23]

14. *See* chapter 11 *infra.*

15. *Compare* U.S. Bancorp Mortgage Co. v. Bonner Mall Partnership, 513 U.S. 18, 115 S.Ct. 386, 130 L.Ed.2d 233 (1994)(vacating decision proper only in exceptional circumstances) *with* Neary v. Regents of the University of California, 3 Cal.4th 273, 10 Cal.Rptr.2d 859, 834 P.2d 119 (1992)(more receptive); see Fisch, Rewriting History: The Propriety of Eradicating Prior Decisional Law Through Settlement and Vacatur, 76 Cornell L. Rev. 589 (1990).

16. *See* § 1.22 *supra.*

17. Miller, An Economic Analysis of Rule 68, 15 J. Legal Stud. 93 (1986); Rowe and Vidmar, Empirical Research on Offers of Settlement: A Preliminary Report, 51 Law & Contemp. Probs., Autumn 1988, at 13.

18. Marek v. Chesny, 473 U.S. 1, 105 S.Ct. 3012, 87 L.Ed.2d 1 (1985); *see* Simon, The New Meaning of Rule 68: Marek v. Chesney and Beyond, 14 N.Y.U. Rev. L. & Soc. Change 475 (1986).

19. Simon v. Intercontinental Transport, 882 F.2d 1435 (9th Cir.1989).

20. Hopper v. Euclid Manor Nursing Home, Inc., 867 F.2d 291 (6th Cir.1989); Johnston v. Penrod Drilling Co., 803 F.2d 867 (5th Cir.1986); Liberty Mut. Ins. Co. v. Equal Employment Opportunities Commn., 691 F.2d 438 (9th Cir.1982).

21. Tyler v. Meola, 113 F.R.D. 184 (N.D.Ohio 1986); Radecki v. Amoco Oil Co., 858 F.2d 397 (8th Cir.1988); Grosvenor v. Brienen, 801 F.2d 944 (7th Cir.1986); Kyreakakis v. Paternoster, 732 F.Supp. 1287 (D.N.J.1990).

22. Fed. R. Civ. P. 68.

23. Marek v. Chesny, 473 U.S. 1, 105 S.Ct. 3012, 87 L.Ed.2d 1 (1985); Kyreakakis v. Paternoster, 732 F.Supp. 1287 (D.N.J. 1990).

Arbitration

Parties that cannot settle disputes through negotiation sometimes resort to arbitration, the resolution of a dispute through the binding decision of a person or panel designated by the parties. Arbitration has a long history and a thriving present.[24] Legislation has swept away most of the court-created legal obstacles to enforcement of arbitration agreements.[25] Parties use arbitration for various reasons—for example, to resolve disputes between stock brokers and their customers[26] or to set up a system for resolving labor-management disputes under collective bargaining agreements.[27]

Arbitration generally is a creature of contract. The parties must agree to arbitrate, either after the dispute to be arbitrated arises or through an arbitration clause in a pre-dispute contract. Employers and others often insert arbitration clauses in their standardized contracts. Courts have refused to enforce some such contracts on the ground that public policy forbids shunting certain claims of public importance into private tribunals that may not enforce the law.[28] But the Supreme Court has become increasingly willing to enforce arbitration clauses even in the face of statutory language that might be read to prohibit waiver of the right to sue in court.[29] This trend reflects a mixture of declining judicial suspicion of noncourt proceedings and increasing enthusiasm for controlling judicial caseloads by encouraging settlement.

An arbitration agreement either designates an arbitrator or panel or designates the way in which one will be chosen. It may also describe the procedure for the arbitration by, for example, adopting the rules of the American Arbitration Association.[30] The parties may thus control such matters as where the arbitration will occur, how much discovery will be permitted, what law the arbitrators will apply, and whether they will issue a written opinion.

A party may go to court to compel arbitration under a contractual arbitration clause or to enforce an arbitral decision. A party may also ask a court to set aside an arbitration agreement or award, but only on very

24. *See* Dawson, A History of Lay Judges (1960); Macneil, American Arbitration Law: Reformation, Nationalization, Internationalization (1992); Macneil, *et al.*, Federal Arbitration Law (1994).

25. *E.g.*, 9 U.S.C. §§ 1–15; Uniform Arbitration Act, 7 U.L.A. 1; *see* Macneil, American Arbitration Law (1992).

26. Fletcher, Arbitrating Securities Disputes (1990).

27. Updegraff, Arbitration and Labor Relations (3d ed. 1970). Labor arbitration poses special problems not treated here.

28. Stempel, Pitfalls of Public Policy: The Case of Arbitration Agreements, 22 St. Mary's L.J. 259 (1990).

29. *E.g.*, Gilmer v. Interstate/Johnson Lane Corp., 500 U.S. 20, 111 S.Ct. 1647, 114 L.Ed.2d 26 (1991)(age discrimination claim); Rodriguez de Quijas v. Shearson/American Express, 490 U.S. 477, 109 S.Ct. 1917, 104 L.Ed.2d 526 (1989)(Securities Act claim); see Circuit City Stores, Inc. v. Adams, 121 S.Ct. 1302 (2001) (Federal Arbitration Act requires enforcement of arbitration clauses in employment contracts). But see Wright v. Universal Maritime Service Corp., 525 U.S. 70, 119 S.Ct. 391, 142 L.Ed.2d 361 (1998)(clause only covers Americans with Disabilities Act claim when that is clearly stated).

30. American Arbitration Assn., Commercial Arbitration Rules (1964).

limited grounds. The challenger, for example, may assert before the arbitration that the arbitration agreement does not embrace the claim in question or, after the award, that the arbitrator did not disclose past connections with the opposing party.[31] The challenger may also resist enforcement on the ground that the arbitrator's decision violated clear public policy or manifestly disregarded the law.[32] Except in extreme circumstances, however, the court will not review the correctness of the arbitrator's procedural decisions, factual findings, contractual construction, or legal rulings.[33]

Arbitration has advantages and disadvantages. It can be quicker than court adjudication. Many believe that it is also cheaper, particularly if frugally conducted (without discovery or without lawyers, for example), but there is some evidence to the contrary.[34] Parties may choose experts as arbitrators and keep their disputes private. On the other hand, when a powerful and sophisticated organization inserts arbitration clauses in its contracts with customers or employees, it may obtain a tribunal more favorable to it than a judge or jury or otherwise manipulate the process.[35] To the extent that one believes in the value of the many procedural safeguards of the judicial process, reducing those safeguards may also reduce the quality of the result.

International arbitration

In international commercial transactions, arbitration clauses are now routinely written and enforced because of their special advantages.[36]

31. *See* First Options of Chicago, Inc. v. Kaplan, 514 U.S. 938, 115 S.Ct. 1920, 131 L.Ed.2d 985 (1995); Commonwealth Coatings Corp. v. Continental Casualty Co., 393 U.S. 145, 89 S.Ct. 337, 21 L.Ed.2d 301 (1968).

32. Merrill Lynch, Pierce, Fenner & Smith, Inc. v. Bobker, 808 F.2d 930 (2d Cir.1986); Sprinzen v. Nomberg, 46 N.Y.2d 623, 389 N.E.2d 456, 415 N.Y.S.2d 974 (1979).

33. *E.g.,* United Paperworkers Intl. Union v. Misco, Inc., 484 U.S. 29, 108 S.Ct. 364, 98 L.Ed.2d 286 (1987); Raytheon Co. v. Automated Business Sys., 882 F.2d 6 (1st Cir.1989). See generall Macneil, *et al.,* Federal Arbitration Law (1994).

34. Kritzer & Anderson, The Arbitration Alternative, 8 Justice System J. 6 (1983)(arbitrations are not cheaper, because a higher percentage of arbitrations is actually tried).

35. *See* Bradford v. Rockwell Semiconductor Systems, Inc., 238 F.3d 549 (4th Cir.2001) (requiring employee to pay half of arbitration costs); Engalla v. Permanente Medical Group, Inc., 15 Cal.4th 951, 64 Cal.Rptr.2d 843, 938 P.2d 903 (1997)(misrepresentations concerning arbitration system's long delays voids agreement); Armendariz v. Foundation Health Psychcare Services, Inc., 24 Cal.4th 83, 99 Cal.Rptr.2d 745, 6 P.3d 669 (2000)(prohibiting arbitration of state law employment discrimination claims when arbitration clause limits damages or lacks specified safeguards); Menkel–Meadow, Do the "Haves" Come out Ahead in Alternative Judicial Systems?: Repeat Players in Alternative Dispute Resolution, 15 J. Disp. Resol. 19 (1999); Thornburg, Going Private: Technology, Due Process, and Internet Dispute Resolution, 34 U.C. Davis L.Rev. 151 (2000).

36. E.g. Vimar Seguros y Reaseguros, S.A. v. M/V Sky Reefer, 515 U.S. 528, 115 S.Ct. 2322, 132 L.Ed.2d 462 (1995); Scherk v. Alberto–Culver Co., 417 U.S. 506, 94 S.Ct. 2449, 41 L.Ed.2d 270 (1974); see Craig, *et al.,* International Chamber of Commerce Arbitration (2d ed. 1990); Dezalay & Garth, Dealing in Virtue: International Commercial Arbitration and the Construction of a Transnational Legal Order (1996).

An multinational treaty known as the New York Convention and its implementing legislation make international arbitration awards enforceable in the courts of the United States and other treaty signatories.[37] Like forum selection clauses that designate the court in which suits will be filed,[38] arbitration clauses in international matters enable the parties to choose a neutral forum, protecting each of them from having to litigate on the other's home turf before judges of the other's nationality. They also give the parties some leeway to choose the law governing their transaction, and according to some decisions sometimes to contract out of one nation's regulatory authority.[39] Courts that enforce arbitration clauses having this effect help to build a global free market in which multinational business can escape regulation.

Other forms of ADR

Many other ways besides arbitration for resolving disputes have been used, ranging over the continuum from the free negotiation of a settlement to the imposition of a decision through court adjudication. They also vary in other respects. A few examples may illustrate the possibilities.[40]

In mediation, a neutral third person helps parties negotiate a solution to their dispute. The mediator may talk with the parties, separately or together, urge them to make settlement offers, or suggest possible terms. The government has long provided mediation for labor-management disputes.[41] Unlike an arbitrator, a mediator does not decide contested issues but merely facilitates agreement by the parties.[42] Some states now require mediation of contested divorce and child custody cases in the hope of reducing the excessive adversariness and recurring litigation of some divorce proceedings.[43] Like other methods of dispute resolution, including court adjudication, mediation works best between equal parties. Otherwise, there is a danger that the weaker and less assertive party will give way, and that the mediator's quest to reach agreement will foster this.[44]

37. Convention on the Recognition and Enforcement of Foreign Arbitral Awards, 21 U.S.T. 2517, 30 U.N.T.S. 38; 9 U.S.C. §§ 201–09.

38. M/S Bremen v. Zapata Off–Shore Co., 407 U.S. 1, 92 S.Ct. 1907, 32 L.Ed.2d 513 (1972); § 2.9 *supra*. For an attempt to work out neutral procedural rules for court proceedings between parties of differing nationality, see ALI, Transnational Rules of Civil Procedure (Prelim. Draft 2000); Special Issue: The Transnational Rules of Civil Procedure, 33 Tex. Int'l L.J. 387 (1998).

39. *E.g.,* Lipcon v. Underwriters at Lloyd's, London, 148 F.3d 1285 (11th Cir. 1998). But see Mitsubishi Motors Corp. v. Soler Chrysler–Plymouth, Inc., 473 U.S. 614, 637 n. 19, 105 S.Ct. 3346, 87 L.Ed.2d 444 (1985).

40. Goldberg, Green & Sander, Dispute Resolution (1985); ADR and the Courts (Fine and Plapinger ed. 1987).

41. *See* 29 U.S.C. §§ 171–173.

42. In a variant of mediation called "med-arb," the mediator does decide disputed issues if mediation does not produce an agreement.

43. *See* Rogers and McEwen, Mediation: Law, Policy, Practice § 5.1 (2d ed. 1994).

44. Grillo, The Mediation Alternative: Process Dangers for Women, 100 Yale L.J. 1545 (1991); Delgado, *et al.*, Fairness and Formality: Minimizung the Risks of Preju-

Complaint procedures are a unilateral form of dispute resolution in which a business, government agency, or other organization invites those with grievances to seek a remedy within the organization. The procedure might involve, for example, an ombudsman,[45] a right to a hearing, or an assertedly impartial outsider. If the complainant is dissatisfied with the result, he or she is free to file suit. The federal government has sought to encourage complaint procedures in certain defective-product disputes.[46]

Parties to legal disputes have resorted to "mini-trials" to resolve complex litigations between wealthy parties such as business corporations. The parties present summaries of their cases, within narrow time limits, before a neutral expert, in a private proceeding in the presence of senior officers of each party. Having thus been educated in the strength and weakness of each side's case, the officers try to work out a settlement. They may, if they wish, ask the expert to render an advisory opinion on the case.[47]

Lawyers and ADR

The lawyers for parties engaging in any of these forms of alternative dispute resolution may be obliged either to write a sort of procedural contract specifying what they contemplate or to adopt an existing set of rules. They must make clear whether the proceeding will be a mediation, an arbitration or something else, what if any kinds of discovery will occur, what if any timetable will be followed, who will pay which expenses, and other matters. To the extent that existing law does not protect the secrecy of the proceedings, they may want to agree that parties will not disclose what goes on during the proceeding and that it will not be admissible in evidence in later litigation between them.[48] Lawyers participating as arbitrators or other intermediaries may also face problems of professional responsibility, such as what future engagements are barred to them because of conflicts of interest.[49] As alternative dispute resolution continues to develop, legislation and professional rules addressing these issues will no doubt multiply.

D. PRETRIAL MANAGEMENT

A major development in twentieth century civil procedure was the increasing power of trial judges. The Federal Rules of Civil Procedure eschewed inflexible rules and trusted judges with wide discretion to

dice in Alternative Dispute Resolution, 1985 Wis. L. Rev. 1359.

45. Gellhorn, Ombudsmen and Others (1966).

46. 15 U.S.C. § 2310(a); 16 C.F.R. pt. 703.

47. *See* Green, Marks, and Olson, Settling Large Case Litigation: An Alternative Approach, 11 Loyola L.A.L. Rev. 493 (1978).

48. *E.g.,* Fed. R. Ev. 408; Calif. Evidence Code §§ 1115–28.

49. In re County of Los Angeles, 223 F.3d 990 (9th Cir.2000); AAA/ABA Code of Ethics for Arbitrators in Commercial Disputes (1997); Menkel–Meadow, Ethics and Professionalism in Non–Adversarial Lawyering, 27 Fla. St. U.L. Rev. 153 (1999).

shape sensible procedures in individual cases. The Federal Rules of Evidence likewise grant trial judges discretion to exclude or admit evidence. Even when a judge violates a rule, appellate courts have applied principles such as the harmless error doctrine to avoid reversal.[1]

In recent decades, judges have increasingly used these powers to implement management techniques in the hope of keeping up with their caseloads and reducing the cost and delay of litigation. Today's judge often does not wait for the parties to submit a matter for decision. Rather, judges actively superintend cases, meeting with counsel, setting schedules, and often urging settlement or proposing alternative dispute resolution techniques.[2] To assist in such matters, federal judges now use auxiliaries: court clerks, law clerks, masters, and magistrate judges to whom many pretrial matters can be delegated.[3] The judicial system organizes such activities through an elaborate system of judicial administration, conferences, and research.[4] The goal for some is to bring scientific and business techniques to bear on the courts.

When case management methods have been empirically tested to see if they in fact reduce cost and delay, the results have usually been negative.[5] Congress itself required a multi-district experiment in case management in the Civil Justice Reform Act of 1990.[6] When the dust cleared, researchers reported little effect on time to disposition, litigation costs, or lawyers' reactions.[7] Broadly speaking, one might trace these disappointing results to two factors: management techniques may require as much time and expense as they save, and judges tend to believe in the methods they introduce and the settlements they see while remaining unaware of the overall impact of those methods. In any event,

1. Yeazell, The Misunderstood Consequences of Modern Civil Process, 1994 Wis. L. Rev. 631.

2. Resnik, Managerial Judges, 96 Harv. L. Rev. 374 (1982); Resnik, Failing Faith: Adjudicatory Procedure in Decline, 53 U. Chi. L. Rev. 494 (1986).

3. 28 U.S.C. § 636; Fed. R. Civ. P. 53, 72, 73; Brazil, Hazard and Rice, Managing Complex Litigation: A Practical Guide to the Use of Special Masters (1983); Seron, The Roles of Magistrates: Nine Case Studies (Fed. Judic. Center 1985); Resnik, Housekeeping: The Nature and Allocation of Work in Federal Trial Courts, 24 Ga. L. Rev. 909 (1990); Hagopian, U.S. Magistrate Judges and their Role in Federal Litigation, 1999 Army Law. 19

4. See, *e.g.,* 28 U.S.C. §§ 601–29; N.J. Rules of Gen. Application 1:30–38; Judicial Conference of the United States, Long Range Plan for the Federal Courts (1995); Resnik, Trial as Error, Jurisdiction as Injury: Transforming the Meaning of Article III, 113 Harv. L. Rev. 924 (2000).

5. Rosenberg, The Pretrial Conference and Effective Justice (1964); Heise, Justice Delayed?: An Empirical Analysis of Civil Case Disposition Time, 50 Case W. Res. L. Rev. 813 (2000)(referring cases to alternative dispute resolution); Dayton, The Myth of Alternative Dispute Resolution in the Federal Courts, 76 Iowa L. Rev. 889 (1991).

6. Pub.L. No. 101–650, Title I, 104 Stat. 5089 (1990); Symposium, Civil Justice Reform, 46 Stan. L. Rev. 1285 (1994); Symposium, Reinventing Civil Litigation: Evaluating Proposals for Change, 59 Brook. L. Rev. 655 (1993).

7. Kakalik, *et al.*, Just, Speedy, and Inexpensive? An Evaluation of Judicial Case Management Under the Civil Justice Reform Act (1997); Symposium, 49 Ala. L. Rev. 17 (1997).

case management continues to flourish and is now being welcomed in England and other nations.[8]

§ 5.20 Pretrial Conference

The Federal Rules[1] and those of most states authorize the court to conduct a pretrial conference, which is a meeting of counsel for the parties (and sometimes the parties themselves) and the judge held before trial and usually after the pleading and discovery stage. The procedure, originating informally in Wayne County, Michigan (Detroit), in the 1920s, was adopted in several metropolitan courts and was given prominence as a procedural mechanism by its incorporation in the Federal Rules as adopted in 1938.[2] In some state jurisdictions, and in many federal districts by local rule, the holding of such a conference is mandatory unless obviated by court order in a particular case. In many courts, however, it is discretionary with the court, which may order a conference on the motion of a party or on its own motion.[3]

Timing

Because a pretrial conference is basically just a meeting, it can be used in many ways. Some courts use it primarily as a technique to encourage settlement, as will be discussed later, and therefore schedule the conference after discovery is complete but before the case is put on the trial calendar. Some courts schedule the pretrial conference early in a case to establish guidelines for discovery; others slate it on the eve of trial to organize the issues and presentation of proofs; others use multiple pretrial conferences, especially in "big" cases.[4] In a sense, extensive use of pretrial conferences moves toward the German system of civil procedure, in which there is no trial at all but rather a series of hearings at any of which the taking of evidence, the clarification of issues, and other matters may be taken up.[5] Many experienced judges and lawyers believe the conference procedure, judiciously administered, can be effective in all these applications. Strong experimental evidence

8. Civil Procedure Rules 1998 (S.I. 1998 No. 3132)(Eng.); Access to Justice: Final Report (1996)(the "Woolf Report"); Civil Justice in Crisis: Comparative Perspectives of Civil Procedure (Zuckerman ed. 1999).

§ 5.20

1. Fed. R. Civ. P. 16.

2. *See* Sunderland, The Theory and Practice of Pre-trial Procedure, 36 Mich. L. Rev. 215 (1937); Shapiro, Federal Rule 16: A Look at the Theory and Practice of Rule-making, 137 U. Pa. L. Rev. 1969 (1989).

3. *See generally* Berger, Pretrial Advocacy (1988); Herr, Haydock, and Stempel, Fundamentals of Pretrial Litigation (1988); Herr, Haydock, and Stempel, Motion Practice chs. 8–20 (2d ed. 1991); Mauet, Fundamentals of Pretrial Techniques (1988); Pretrial Practices, 104 F.R.D. 265 (1985).

4. Manual for Complex Litigation, Third (1995); Brazil, Hazard and Rice, Managing Complex Litigation (1983); Schwarzer, Managing Antitrust and Other Complex Litigation (1982).

5. Langbein, The German Advantage in Civil Procedure, 52 U. Chi. L. Rev. 823 (1985).

suggests, however, that requiring a pretrial conference in routine cases is largely a waste of time.[6]

Conference activities

A pretrial conference may consider many matters.

1. At the outset of a case, federal courts ordinarily establish a schedule for the filing of motions and the completion of discovery. Many judges do this automatically, without first conferring with the parties, but the establishment and modification of deadlines is a frequent topic at conferences.[7]

2. Conferences also deal with discovery. For example, the court may seek to clarify what discovery will be appropriate, establish deadlines for discovery, provide that discovery will occur in "waves" limited to certain issues, grant protective orders, and rule on pending motions. The parties are required to confer about such matters before a scheduling conference is held and to submit a proposed discovery plan unless the court or a local rule exempts them.[8]

3. The court may rule on pending motions.[9] Especially in big cases, rather than let parties schedule each motion for hearing when it is filed, the court may find it more efficient to hold periodic conferences to handle accumulated motions. Indeed, the court may direct the parties to file any motions in a given category at a given time, so that they may be resolved together.

Simplifying issues

4. As the case proceeds, the focus of any conferences shifts either to settlement or to the coming trial. The first and foremost purpose of a trial-oriented conference is the simplification of the issues. That can be done by requiring each party to state what it expects to prove or disprove, indicating what witnesses are to be called, what their testimony is expected to be, and what exhibits will be offered.[10] This will reveal the areas in which no real dispute exists. On the eve of trial and after discovery, counsel are frequently ready to admit many things they were not prepared to admit in the pleading stage. Moreover probing by the judge often yields agreement on areas in which no real basis for dispute exists. The judge may also bring up the appropriateness and timing of summary judgment.

The extent to which individual judges inject themselves into this process varies greatly. On one hand, the success or failure of pretrial

6. *See* Rosenberg, The Pretrial Conference and Effective Justice (1964); Menkel–Meadow, For and Against Settlement: Uses and Abuses of the Mandatory Settlement Conference, 33 U.C.L.A. L. Rev. 485 (1985).

7. Fed. R. Civ. P. 16(a)(2), (b).

8. Fed. R. Civ. P. 16(c)(6), 26(f).

9. Fed. R. Civ. P. 16(c)(11).

10. *See generally* Fed. R. Civ. P. 16(c)(1, 5); Berger, Pretrial Advocacy (1988); Haydock, Herr, and Stempel, Fundamentals of Pretrial Litigation (1988); Mauet, Fundamentals of Pretrial Techniques (1988).

conferences depend in large measure on the judge's skill and interest in "shaping the case to present its actual problems and in leading the counsel to define the issues with him."[11] On the other hand, agreement should come from counsel and not from imposition by the judge.[12]

The success of pretrial conferences (in this and other respects) depends on the attendance of counsel who have authority and responsibility in the trial of the case. The Supreme Court has upheld the severe sanction of dismissal for unexcused nonappearance of counsel at the pretrial hearing.[13]

Trial preparation

5. The judge should insure that the pleadings will accommodate all the claims and defenses revealed at the pretrial conference and thus obviate the need for amendment at trial and possible continuance.[14] A strongly supported school of thought would use the pretrial conference to compel parties to set forth the details of their claims and defenses in much the way that special pleading did. Tying parties down before trial to detailed specifications of claim or defense may, however, foreclose the benefit of unforeseen turns of events at trial.

6. Pretrial conferences also consider the possibility of obtaining admissions of fact and of authenticity of documents which will avoid unnecessary proof.[15]

7. Judges make rulings on evidentiary issues likely to come up at trial such as the admissibility of expert witness testimony,[16] or refer certain issues to a referee or magistrate judge for findings to be used as evidence when the trial is to be done by jury.[17]

8. Shortly before trial, judges often hold a final pretrial conference to formulate a plan for trial.[18] The plan may limit the number of witnesses or exhibits, or the length of each party's time to present evidence. It may regulate the order of the trial, requiring certain matters to be heard first in the hope that they may prove decisive, or ordering a bifurcated trial.

11. Clark, Objectives of Pre-trial Procedure, 17 Ohio St. L.J. 163, 165 (1956); Peckham, The Federal Judge as Case Manager: The New Role in Guiding a Case from Filing to Disposition, 69 Calif. L. Rev. 770 (1981).

12. *See generally* Berger, Pretrial Advocacy (1988); Mauet, Fundamentals of Pretrial Techniques (1988).

13. *See* Link v. Wabash R.R., 370 U.S. 626, 82 S.Ct. 1386, 8 L.Ed.2d 734 (1962), *noted in* 72 Yale L.J. 819 (1963).

14. Fed. R. Civ. P. 16(c)(2).

15. Fed. R. Civ. P. 16(c)(3); see § 5.7 *supra.*

16. *See* Luce v. United States, 469 U.S. 38, 105 S.Ct. 460, 83 L.Ed.2d 443 (1984); Comment, Use of Motions in Limine in Civil Proceedings, 45 Mo. L. Rev. 130 (1980).

17. *See* 28 U.S.C. § 636(b); Fed. R. Civ. P. 16(c)(8), 53; Kaufman, Masters in the Federal Courts, 58 Colum. L. Rev. 452 (1958). *Compare* La Buy v. Howes Leather Co., 352 U.S. 249, 77 S.Ct. 309, 1 L.Ed.2d 290 (1957), holding it improper to refer issues routinely to a master.

18. Fed. R. Civ. P. 16(c)(4, 13–15), 16(d).

§ 5.21 Pretrial Order

Any pretrial conference should culminate in a written or transcribed order embodying the admissions and stipulations of the parties and all other matters settled at the conference. A pretrial order supersedes the pleadings. Amendment or modification of the pretrial order thereafter presents much the same problem as amending pleadings, except that amendment of a pretrial order following completion of discovery is more restricted.[1] If this were not so, the issue-defining and evidence-regulating effect of the pretrial order would be seriously undercut. Rule 15, which governs the amendment of pleadings, expressly states that amendments shall be allowed "freely ... when justice so requires"[2] or "when the presentation of the merits ... will be subserved thereby" and no undue prejudice will result.[3] Rule 16, however, provides that a pretrial order "shall control the subsequent course of the action unless modified by a subsequent order."[4] The different phraseology of the two Rules suggests that the court has somewhat broader discretion to deny amendment of a pretrial order. And if an order was entered after a final pretrial conference, it may be "modified only to prevent manifest injustice."[5] In general, amending the pretrial order at trial to permit interjection of additional issues is allowed only under extraordinary conditions. This follows from the fact that modern discovery usually affords the litigants abundant means of forecasting the eventualities of trial.[6]

§ 5.22 Courts and Settlement

Although case management may have started as an effort to reduce the delay and cost of litigation by riding herd on lawyers, with reduction of judicial backlogs a desirable side effect, it soon became apparent that increasing the settlement rate would promote both these goals. Whether active judicial promotion of settlements is likely to be successful or desirable is another question, whose answer depends on the sort of intervention in question. In any event, fostering settlement has in recent decades become an increasingly important part of the judicial role and the procedural system.[1]

§ 5.21

1. *See* § 4.11 *supra.*
2. Fed. R. Civ. P. 15(a).
3. *Id.* 15(b).
4. Fed. R. Civ. P. 16(e).
5. Fed. R. Civ. P. 16(e).
6. *See, e.g.,* Smith v. Washington Sheraton Corp., 135 F.3d 779 (D.C.Cir.1998); Rigby v. Beech Aircraft Co., 548 F.2d 288 (10th Cir.1977). But see Summers v. Missouri Pac. R.R., 132 F.3d 599 (10th Cir. 1997)(court should have granted pretrial amendment to allow replacement of testimony court had ruled inadmissible).

§ 5.22

1. *E.g.,* Gross and Syverud, Don't Try: Civil Jury Verdicts in a System Geared to Settlement, 44 U.C.L.A. L. Rev. 1 (1996); Galanter and Cahill, "Most Cases Settle": Judicial Promotion and Regulation of Settlement, 46 Stan. L. Rev. 1339 (1994).

What is the judge's role?

Pretrial conferences often lead to settlements. As a result of discussing a case at such a conference, the parties may conclude that they should settle, an appropriate by-product of the procedure. But there has been disagreement about whether the court should schedule pretrial conferences for the express purpose of encouraging settlement or merely pursue the possibility of settlement if and when it arises in a conference.[2]

Some lawyers believe that voluntary settlement can best be reached by the parties themselves, so that judicial involvement accomplishes little. Others object on principle: "Consent is often coerced; the bargain may be struck by someone without authority; the absence of a trial and judgment renders subsequent judicial involvement troublesome; and although dockets are trimmed, justice may not be done ... [S]ettlement is a capitulation to the conditions of mass society and should be neither encouraged nor praised."[3] Many judges and lawyers, however, believe that settlement-oriented pretrial conferences can produce settlements that otherwise would fail or would occur only on the commencement of trial by providing impartial analysis of a case's issues and likely outcome.[4] The difference of view is partly attributable to difference in perspective, particularly the judiciary's concern for the wastefulness of commencing a trial that soon aborts through settlement.

Federal Rule 16(a)(5) now lists "facilitating the settlement of the case" as one purpose of a pretrial conference. It also authorizes the court to "require that a party or its representative be present or reasonably available by telephone" to consider a possible settlement, and to require that whoever is thus present be authorized by the party to enter into any settlement. Indeed, the parties are now required to discuss the possibility of settlement before the first conference occurs.[5] On the other hand, a judge is not required to discuss settlement at a conference, and may not sanction a party for refusing to make a reasonable offer.[6]

Judges vary in their positions toward settlement. Some leave it to the parties. Some urge lawyers to discuss settlement. Some preside over negotiations at settlement conferences, intimating their views of the probable result at trial, proposing terms, noting the expected value of the case, emphasizing the risks of trial, requiring parties to join their lawyers in the courthouse, or urging counsel to avoid a trial.[7] Such

2. *See* Note, Pretrial Conference Procedures, 26 S.C.L. Rev. 481, 506 (1974).

3. Fiss, Against Settlement, 93 Yale L.J. 1073 (1984).

4. *See* Brazil, Settling Civil Suits: Litigators' Views About Appropriate Roles and Effective Techniques for Federal Judges (1985); Menkel–Meadow, For and Against Settlement: Uses and Abuses of the Mandatory Settlement Conference, 33 UCLA L. Rev. 485 (1985).

5. Fed. R. Civ. P. 16(c), 26(f); In re Stone, 986 F.2d 898 (5th Cir.1993); In re Novak, 932 F.2d 1397 (11th Cir.1991); G. Heileman Brewing Co. v. Joseph Oat Corp., 871 F.2d 648 (7th Cir.1989).

6. Hess v. New Jersey Transit Rail Operations, Inc., 846 F.2d 114 (2d Cir.1988); Del Rio v. Northern Blower Co., 574 F.2d 23 (1st Cir.1978).

7. *E.g.,* Schuck, Agent Orange on Trial (1986); *see* Brazil, Effective Approaches to Settlement (1988); Provine, Settlement

methods can lead to unfair pressure to settle and to compromising the judge's neutrality.[8] Perhaps civil cases should be subject to the rule applied in federal criminal cases, under which the judge may not participate in plea bargaining.[9] Some local court rules require such a separation of functions.

Court-annexed ADR

Often, judicial involvement with settlement extends beyond pretrial conferences to the provision of alternative dispute resolution procedures. This dates back at least as far as Elizabethan England, when judges urged parties to submit some disputes to arbitration.[10] It has become far more popular in recent decades; indeed, Congress now requires all federal courts to authorize alternative dispute resolution processes, and litigants (with certain exceptions) to consider using them.[11] Some envision tomorrow's judicial system as a courthouse with "many doors," so that disputants may choose among a variety of procedures of which litigation is only one.[12] Others doubt that devoting public funds to new judicial machinery is worthwhile, or find something of a paradox in governmental prescription of what were supposed to be voluntary and consensual procedures.[13]

The procedures that courts make available are often traditional dispute resolution techniques such as mediation and arbitration.[14] These have sometimes developed new forms. Courts have offered early appraisal of cases by a neutral evaluator, or have required parties to submit to "nonbinding arbitration."[15] California has long offered litigants who can afford it an amalgam of arbitration and adjudication called "rent-a-judge," in which the court refers a case for trial to an adjudicator (usually a retired judge) they select and pay.[16]

Strategies for Federal District Judges (Fed. Judic. Center 1986).

8. *See* Floyd, Can the Judge Do That? - The Need for a Clearer Judicial Role in Settlement, 26 Ariz. St. L.J. 45 (1995).

9. Fed. R. Crim. P. 11.

10. Dawson, A History of Lay Judges (1960).

11. 28 U.S.C. §§ 651(b), 652(a, b); Emerging ADR Issues in State and Federal Courts (Sander ed. 1991); Court ADR: Elements of Program Design (Plapinger and Shaw ed. 1992); Plapinger and Steinstra, ADR and Settlement in the Federal District Courts (1996).

12. Sander, Varieties of Dispute Processing, 70 F.R.D. 111 (1976); see Resnik, Many Doors? Closing Doors? Alternative Dispute Resolution and Adjudication, 10 Ohio St. J. Disp. Resol. 211 (1995).

13. See Bernstein, Understanding the Limits of Court–Connected ADR: A Critique of Federal Court–Annexed Arbitration Programs, 141 U. Pa. L. Rev. 2169 (1993); Menkel–Meadow, Pursuing Settlement in an Adversary Culture: A Tale of Innovation Co–Opted or "The Law of ADR," 19 Fla. St. L. Rev. 1 (1991).

14. Hoeffer, Court–Annexed Arbitration in Ten District Courts (1990); Dayton, The Myth of Alternative Dispute Resolution in the Federal Courts, 76 Iowa L. Rev. 889 (1991); Singer, The Privatization of Family Law, 1992 Wis. L. Rev. 1443 (1992).

15. 28 U.S.C. §§ 654–57; N.J. Civ. Prac. R. 4:21A; Brazil, A Close Look at Three Court–Sponsored ADR Programs, 1990 U. Chi. Leg. Forum 303.

16. Kim, Rent-a-Judges and the Cost of Selling Justice, 44 Duke L.J. 166 (1994).

Court-annexed alternative dispute resolution programs have also given rise to more innovative procedures. Judges have used summary jury trials to give parties a more realistic view of the strengths and weaknesses of their cases. The lawyers present summaries of their cases to groups of jurors chosen from the regular jury pool. The jurors render a verdict, which is not binding but is often used by the parties as a basis for settlement.[17]

Mass settlement techniques

With the rise of mass tort litigation, that is, multiple similar suits such as those arising from the use of asbestos, courts have explored new settlement techniques. Transferring all pending federal cases of a given kind to a single judge for pretrial proceedings,[18] although originally intended to foster judicial efficiency, can also lead to settlements. The lead counsel and executive committee often appointed to coordinate the suits[19] likewise serve both functions. Sometimes the judge will encourage the creation of a class action in the hope of encompassing and settling all pending litigation, an approach that has encountered obstacles.[20]

Judges have also experimented with computer modeling to help reveal the "value" of pending cases and encourage the settlement of mass tort litigation. Experts collect information about cases already tried, investigate which factors influenced the resulting verdicts, and try to develop a formula to predict the result of similar cases. Having such a prediction should make it easier for parties to agree on a settlement.[21] Other procedures can provide encouragement to settle, such as arranging for defendants to offer settlements on standardized terms to claimants submitting specified information. Judges have instituted such procedures in the course of presiding over large numbers of similar cases, over class actions, and over bankruptcy proceedings of corporations against which numerous products liability claims may be brought.[22]

17. Ponte, Putting Mandatory Summary Jury Trial Back on the Docket: Recommendations on the Exercise of Judicial Authority, 63 Fordham L. Rev. 1069 (1995). But see In re NLO, Inc., 5 F.3d 154 (6th Cir.1993)(court may not require party to participate in summary jury trial).

18. 28 U.S.C. § 1407; see Lexecon v. Milberg Weiss Bershad Hynes & Lerach, 523 U.S. 26, 118 S.Ct. 956, 140 L.Ed.2d 62 (1998)(transferee court may not retain case for trial). American L. Inst., Complex Litigation: Statutory Recommendations and Analysis (1994) proposes more far-reaching consolidation techniques; see Special Issue, 1995 B.Y.U.L. Rev. 731.

19. See Manual for Complex Litigation, Third (1995).

20. *E.g.*, Amchem Products, Inc. v. Windsor, 521 U.S. 591, 117 S.Ct. 2231, 138 L.Ed.2d 689 (1997); see §§ 10.20–10.23 *infra*.

21. *See* § 6.4 *infra*.

22. McGovern, Resolving Mature Mass Tort Litigation, 69 B.U.L. Rev. 6599 (1989); Symposium, Claims Resolution Facilities and the Mass Settlement of Mass Torts, 53 L. & Contemp. Probs. No. 4 (Aut. 1990). But see In re Chevron U.S.A., Inc., 109 F.3d 1016 (5th Cir.1997)(court may not use verdicts in 30 selected cases to determine outcome of others); Cimino v. Raymark Industries, Inc., 151 F.3d 297 (5th Cir.1998)(rejecting similar scheme). See generally Advisory Comm. on Civil Rules and Working Group on Mass Torts, Report on Mass Tort Litigation (1999); Symposium, Mass Torts, 148 U. Pa. L. Rev. 1851 (2000); § 10.24 *infra*.

Chapter 6

SOCIAL AND ECONOMIC ASPECTS OF CIVIL LITIGATION

§ 6.1 Introduction

Social conflict

This book is concerned chiefly with the terms, meaning, and legal effect of the rules governing the conduct of civil litigation. It therefore deals with what the law of civil procedure "is" in legal terms. To explain that meaning we employ textual analysis, logical deduction, historical analysis, illustrations of application of rules, and references to court decisions interpreting the rules. All legal rules, however, have sources of meaning beyond their text and have significance beyond their verbal meaning. In this respect the law of civil procedure is no different from any other body of law. The law of civil procedure regulates an activity—civil litigation—that has social, economic, and political dynamics that interact with the legal institutions and ideas governing it. A civil case is not merely the occasion for applying rules, it is a "happening" in the lives of the litigants that can have profound significance for them. Taken in aggregate, these happenings in individual cases have pervasive significance for society. Civil litigation is a social process, one of the techniques by which society adjusts to the conflicts that arise from shortages of resources, misunderstandings and antipathies among members of society, and social change over time.

Litigants and lawyers in an individual case are very aware of the social microcosm in which their case takes place. A lawsuit has practical consequences for the litigants—they want to win. Litigation generally is a vivid and preoccupying part of the litigants' experience while it continues, and sometimes long afterward.[1] The lawyers for the parties tend to be more detached, since litigation is their daily work as professionals; even so, litigation is gripping mentally and emotionally even for

§ 6.1

1. There are many accounts of the experience of being a litigant. The classic narrative is Dickens, Bleak House (1853). See also, *e.g.*, Gaddis, A Frolic of His Own (1994); Harr, A Civil Action (1995)(an account of an actual case).

lawyers of long experience. Partly because of the intensity of this immediate experience, litigants and lawyers often perceive the larger social context of litigation only dimly and with some indifference. They are interested in how the system works for them in the cases in which they are involved, not some larger Olympian view of litigation as a social phenomenon.

Lawyers' viewpoint

For trial lawyers, the perspective of litigation—the relationship between the immediate picture and the larger picture—is skewed in favor of the immediate picture. While the lawyers know best how the system actually works, they have a professional self-interest in the system as it exists at any given time. The legal profession thus has both an intimate but biased knowledge of the system and an ambivalent interest in the larger picture.[2] The task of examining the system therefore becomes primarily an academic process. This also has its limitations. These factors complicate an objective analysis of civil litigation.

Some framework for such analysis, however, is necessary. All cases involving disputed application of procedural rules ultimately, if not immediately, involve factual assumptions about how the legal and social systems work and value preferences for how they ought to work. For example, this text and other analyses of procedure use such terms as "efficient," "fair," and "workable." These terms implicitly compare the various ways in which the system might work. A similar comparison is implicit in every argument over a question of procedure. A practicing lawyer therefore has a critical framework concerning the system, regardless whether he or she is fully aware of it. One must have such a framework simply in order to function. A critical framework is also needed to participate in improving the administration of justice and to understand what is going on in this sector of society.

Since social and economic factors pervade all aspects of civil procedure, there is no specially appropriate place to consider these factors in a text on the subject. We have simply placed this discussion in the middle of the text, after having examined a good part of the law of the subject but before having come to the end.

§ 6.2 Litigation as Coercion

From the viewpoint of the litigants a civil action is a struggle over the coerced resolution of a controversy.[1] A society governed by the rule of

2. Criticism of the legal profession's parochialism is abundant. *See, e.g.,* Auerbach, Unequal Justice: Lawyers and Social Change in Modern America (1976); Lieberman, The Litigious Society (1981); Pound, The Causes of Popular Dissatisfaction with the Administration of Justice, 40 Am. L. Rev. 729 (1906). Professional parochialism, of course, is not unique to the legal profession.

§ 6.2

1. *Cf.* Holmes, J., in McDonald v. Mabee, 243 U.S. 90, 91, 37 S.Ct. 343, 343, 61

law imposes severe limitations on the use of coercion. Indeed, the coercion available through civil litigation is actually so feeble that a person determined to resist can thwart all but the most energetic efforts to enforce a civil judgment. But the fact remains that a court's judgment is effective because of the use or threat of coercion to carry it out—by seizing the loser's property or putting the loser in jail.[2] Furthermore, court decisions ultimately are indisputable not because courts are finally right on the law and the facts but because the courts' final edicts are backed by the police power of the state. As Justice Robert Jackson said of the Supreme Court, "We are not final because we are infallible, but we are infallible only because we are final."[3]

Intellectual coercion

Adjudication is coercive not only in the remedies that follow judgment but also in the intellectual foundations on which an adjudication is based. The law or the facts, or both, in a legal controversy can be reasonably argued both ways unless one side of a controversy is merely frivolous. Therefore, in every nonfrivolous case something very reasonable can be said about the justice of each side's position. In recognition of this, Professor Jerome Michael stated that if an issue is reasonably arguable, it may be that the issue cannot be decided simply by "reason."[4] Hence, the decision of a litigated issue is pre- or post-rational. In any event, a court's decision is not made to "stick" simply on the basis of its reasonableness or persuasiveness. A court may aim to be persuasive in giving judgment and, as we shall see, there are important pragmatic inducements for a court to convince the public, and even the litigants, that its decisions are reasonable. But litigation is not an exercise in pedagogy, a debate, or participatory democracy. Even in the rare system that considers the case only when both litigants assent to the result, the authorities may bring social pressure to bear to secure that assent.[5] Ordinarily, the parties to a lawsuit are obliged to accept the court's results in fact and law. A judicial judgment is an expression of the state's authority.[6]

L.Ed. 608, 609 (1917) ("The foundation of jurisdiction is physical power"); Narrative, Violence and the Law: The Essays of Robert Cover (Minow ed. 1992).

2. *See generally* Rendleman, Compensatory Contempt: Plaintiff's Remedy When a Defendant Violates an Injunction, 1980 Ill. L.F. 971.

3. Brown v. Allen, 344 U.S. 443, 540, 73 S.Ct. 397, 427, 97 L.Ed. 469, 533 (1953) (concurring opinion).

4. Michael, The Basic Rules of Pleading, 5 Record of Assn. Bar City of New York 175, 199 (1950) ("The decision of an issue of fact in cases of closely balanced probabilities, therefore, must, in the nature of things, be an emotional rather than a rational act").

5. French, The Golden Yoke: The Legal Cosmology of Buddhist Tibet (1995).

6. The importance of backing by state authority is clearly revealed in cases where it is absent, such as many international legal controversies. *See, e.g.,* McDougal and Reisman, The Prescribing Function in World Constitutive Process: How International Law Is Made, 6 Yale Stud. in World Pub. Order 249 (1980).

A decision whose ultimate foundation is authority has an anomalous position in a culture, such as ours, that places high value on autonomy of thought, conscience, and action.[7] Both our own and other societies, of course, use means other than authoritative adjudication to resolve many disputes.[8] Thus, tension, if not contradiction, exists between the generally individualistic character of American society and the authoritative position of courts in our form of government, particularly when litigation involves important public policy. Although the social foundation of judicial authority in the United States remains something of a mystery,[9] the pervasive use of litigation as a means of government doubtless is attributable in part to the dearth of alternative repositories of accepted authority. Every large, complex society requires systems of authority to resolve questions too pressing to be determined by unanimous decision of the affected parties. The courts are an especially salient instrument of authority in the American social system. And civil litigation is a principal mechanism, along with criminal procedure, by which that authority is exercised.[10]

Communication between parties

Litigation is coercive in still another way. It interferes with and sometimes monopolizes the terms of communication between the parties to a conflict. The communications between parties to litigation and the communications used in ordinary interpersonal conflict resolution are, of course, very different in the degree to which they manifest cooperation, mutual forbearance, and flexibility of position. From the time that litigation is commenced, the parties ordinarily cease normal, direct communication. Instead, they are obliged to communicate with each other in the language and forms of litigation—charges, countercharges, and denials, "positions," evidence and privilege against revealing evidence, and so on. Other ways of looking at the world must be transformed into narratives consistent with a legal outlook, and those who do so most adeptly gain the advantage.[11] The attorneys become the parties' exclusive spokespersons in court, and often out of court as well. Communicating mainly or exclusively through these legal channels is induced partly by legal restrictions on other forms of communication[12] and partly by the practical risks that arise from using other channels. Informal

7. *See* Vining, The Authoritative and the Authoritarian (1986).

8. *E.g.*, Roberts, Order and Dispute (1979).

9. *See, e.g.*, Choper, Judicial Review and the National Political Process (1980); Ely, Democracy and Distrust: A Theory of Judicial Review (1980); Shapiro, Courts—A Comparative and Political Analysis (1981).

10. Hence, de Tocqueville's classic dictum that "there is hardly a political question in the United States which does not sooner or later turn into a judicial one." De Tocqueville, Democracy in America 248 (Mayer–Lerner ed. 1966).

11. *See* Merry, Getting Justice and Getting Even (1990); O'Barr, Linguistic Evidence (1982).

12. *Cf.* Model Rules of Professional Conduct Rule 4.2: in representing a client, "[a] lawyer shall not communicate on the subject of the representation with a party the lawyer knows to be represented by another lawyer."

communication can result in potentially damaging admissions and disclosures of strategy.

Once the court becomes actively involved in the litigation, through supervising discovery or exploring settlement possibilities, for example, the legal channels of communication become still more dominant. The tendency to preempt other channels is especially strong when temporary injunctive relief is sought, for the crisis atmosphere in such relief usually drowns out any other communication. Some types of permanent injunction, particularly "institutional" decrees, can transform a courtroom into something of a boardroom for conducting the parties' business with each other.[13]

Party coercion

Litigation not only involves the coercive power of the state but also operates through bilateral interaction between the parties, who can exercise coercion on each other. A court ruling involves an implicit threat of coercive sanctions if the ruling is not obeyed. With some exceptions, however, in the adversary system of procedure the court undertakes to rule only on a party's request. Therefore, parties have legally sanctioned authority to invite the court to exercise its coercive powers. As a consequence of this authority, each party has a resource that it can use in "trading" with the opponent. The simplest examples are the threat to bring a lawsuit or a prospective defendant's threat to fight a claim to the bitter end no matter how meritorious the claim may be. Once a lawsuit has begun, there are dozens of lesser potential exercises of coercion or threats, such as whether to make tenable but technical objections or to seek burdensome discovery. Each of these opportunities, and all of them in aggregate, have "trading" value. Such threats, if carried out, inflict a cost on the opposing party, and avoiding that cost is worth something to that party. To put it bluntly, every lawsuit has an element of blackmail. Even when parties settle or turn to alternative dispute resolution, it is often the background threat of litigation that motivates and shapes their behavior.

The fact that the judicial process rests on a foundation of coercion is often obscured in rhetoric to the effect that the adjudicative process, and specifically our version of the adversary system, is a search for truth.[14] There is reason to be skeptical of this hyperbole. It could be assumed that judges and juries have special powers of discovering truth. On that assumption, courts are fair because they comprise uniquely discerning and fair-minded people. But we do not believe such special powers exist, and we know that legal procedure employs ordinary people as arbiters. It

13. *See* Chayes, The Role of the Judge in Public Law Litigation, 89 Harv. L. Rev. 1281 (1976); Diver, The Judge as Political Powerbroker: Superintending Structural Change in Public Institutions, 65 Va. L. Rev. 43 (1979).

14. *See, e.g.,* Frankel, The Search for Truth: An Umpireal View, 123 U. Pa. L. Rev. 1031 (1975).

could be assumed that legal procedures have special power for getting at the truth. On that assumption, courts are fair because of the special procedures they employ. But throughout the civilized world, courts and other tribunals use widely various procedures, some of them quite different from ours. French and Italian courts, for example, provide little discovery or even cross-examination in civil matters. The American adversary system may satisfy many social objectives, but no evidence shows that it is systematically superior to other systems in yielding true or wise decisions.[15]

However that may be, for a party to a legal controversy the alternatives to litigation are either violence (or other form of private coercion) or the status quo. If one's rights have been denied, and the practical consequences are serious, even litigation can be preferable to those consequences. It is in this frame of mind that most litigation is conducted.

§ 6.3 Cost of Litigation

As the economists say, litigation is costly. It involves both private costs to parties and public costs in the form of expenditures to provide judges, court personnel, and courthouses.[1] Nonparties also bear some costs, for example when they must testify or serve as jurors for inadequate compensation. At this point, we focus on the costs to the parties.

Different costs

At minimum, a legal controversy entails the private costs of gathering and exchanging information between the parties about the nature of the claimant's legal demand and the basis of the respondent's refusal to comply with the demand. When the controversy reaches the stage of litigation, parties incur additional cost in their efforts to convey information to the court through pleadings, motions, testimony, and so on. The controversies regulated by the law of civil procedure, and considered in this book, almost always involve lawyers' services,[2] which incur additional and often very substantial costs. Parties must pay court fees, stenographic costs, expert witness fees, and the like. Conducting litigation also preempts time that could be used for other activities. This cost can be crucial in considering how far litigation should be pursued, particularly for participants whose time is very valuable.

Litigation that affects an ongoing activity, such as the management of a school, prison or business, subjects that activity's conduct, environ-

15. *See* Luban, Lawyers and Justice (1988).

§ 6.3

1. Kakalik and Robyn, Costs of the Civil Justice System (1982).

2. *Compare* "small claims" procedure, which at least purports to be manageable without the assistance of a lawyer. *See generally* Steele, The Historical Context of Small Claims Courts, 1981 Am. B. Found. Res. J. 295.

ment, and future to uncertainty. Taking precautions against this uncertainty entails costs, similar to those incurred by a business trying to operate in a locality where the political system is unstable.[3] The costs of legal uncertainty are readily apparent when the controversy affects an ongoing activity or relationship. An example is the uncertainty that American Telephone & Telegraph Co. faced during the pendency of the Government's civil antitrust case against it; resolution of that uncertainty was one element in the company's decision to accept a settlement involving divestiture.[4] On a more personal scale, anyone involved in a pending marriage dissolution is aware of the terrible uncertainty of the family's situation.[5] But there are also "uncertainty costs" during a damage suit that concerns a past transaction for which liability has not yet been assigned. In such a situation, the plaintiff has only a contingent asset—the claim—the value of which must be discounted by the uncertainty of recovery. The resources of the defendant are subject to a corresponding possibility of confiscation to pay the plaintiff's demand. Looking at the parties as though they had joint but indeterminate ownership in the assets available to meet the claim, it can be seen that at least a portion of the value of the assets is effectively frozen. In sum, the "economic costs" of litigation include costs of opportunity and illiquidity, and costs of information processing. At the same time, resolution of a lawsuit may resolve the uncertainty of the parties over their rights and, sometimes, social uncertainty over the state of the law.

Another aspect of the cost of litigation is its psychological toll. Litigants usually find litigation to be not merely a distracting "waste of time" but also intensely aggravating. They suffer worry, loss of sleep, tension, and spasms of rage. There is no legitimate market value for this kind of human suffering, and calculation of its cost is therefore artificial. Moreover, the experience of this cost is highly subjective and varies among individuals; evidently some people even enjoy litigation. The cost for most people is nevertheless real, perhaps especially "real" precisely because the burden of this cost is not readily transferable through the market or through a measure of damages. For this reason it might be better to call litigation's psychological consequences a loss rather than a cost. Be that as it may, it is possible to assign artificially a value to psychological cost, just as the law assigns a value to "pain and suffering" incurred by one who has suffered personal injury. That value can then be made commensurate with the other costs involved.

3. *See, e.g.,* Overholt, Political Risk (1982).

4. Pollack, Uncertainty Gone: Bell Chairman Explains Strategy That Moved Company to Agree, N.Y. Times, Jan. 10, 1982, at 1, col. 5.

5. *See, e.g.,* Spencer and Zammit, Mediation Arbitration: A Proposal for Private Resolution of Disputes Between Divorced or Separated Parents, 1976 Duke L.J. 911.

Injustice of litigation costs?

Collectively these costs can be substantial in any given case and are a classic grievance with the administration of justice. To some extent this grievance results from a naive view of litigation cost. Many people think of litigation cost as the amount paid to the lawyer who handles the case. This view assumes that a party's case has definite facts and law that should result in judgment for the party; it conceives of the lawyer's fee as a processing charge imposed by a monopolizing fraternity for what should be free, that is, true justice. This is a natural interpretation of a legal controversy from the viewpoint of a litigant. It overlooks the fact, however, that the other litigant also has this viewpoint, but from an opposite orientation.

Costs and unpredictability

In simplest terms, if the outcome of a legal controversy could be accurately predicted by both parties, there would be no lawsuit and no litigation cost. That is, if the outcome could be predicted merely by stating the case, it would pay neither side to invest in developing the facts or law of the case in any way.

If I owe $1,000 on a promissory note that has become due, and I can make no defense that a jury or judge would accept, it makes no sense for me to add to my obligations by retaining a lawyer to tell me that I should pay the note. The same would hold if the note were for $100,000 or $10 million. It is not the amount of a claim but the factor of its uncertainty that makes litigation of the claim worthwhile, even though litigation entails expense. And the fundamental question for a litigant, whether plaintiff or defendant, is whether the possibility of success makes litigation of the claim worth the cost that litigation entails.

Notwithstanding this reasoning, it might be worth a party's while not to settle even when the result is known in advance if the process of litigation itself offers advantages. Occasionally, a party may hope to benefit from the publicity a lawsuit inspires. More often, a defendant hopes that litigation will put off the moment when it must pay what it owes, so that it can enjoy the use of that sum in the meantime. The legal system seeks to prevent that motive for delay by requiring a losing defendant to pay prejudgment interest, but does not do so in every case, and in some jurisdictions charges a rate lower than the market's interest rate.[6]

Value of a claim

Leaving this refinement out of the picture, the basic cost analysis equation was simply stated many years ago by attorney Melvin Belli.[7] In

6. See § 1.21 *supra.*

7. Belli, Modern Trials 109 (1954). More sophisticated versions of the analysis employed by Belli appear in Note, An Analysis of Settlement, 22 Stan. L. Rev. 67 (1969); Landes, An Economic Analysis of the Courts, 14 J.L. & Econ. 61, 101 (1971); and Posner, The Behavior of Administrative Agencies, 1 J. Legal Stud. 305, 320 (1972). *See also* Rowe, The Legal Theory of Attor-

this equation, the assumed "true" value of the claim is the amount that the decision maker "would probably award." The amount the court "would probably award" is an informal way of referring to the average of all verdicts that theoretically would be reached if the case were tried an infinite number of times under the same conditions and with the same preparation. Given such an assumed true value of the claim, the net value of the claim for the plaintiff is that true value *minus* what it will cost the plaintiff to try the case; the net value of the claim for the defendant is the true value *plus* what it will cost the defendant to try the case. It is in the parties' interest to settle if the plaintiff's net value is exceeded by defendant's net value. That is, when the true value of the claim can be accurately estimated by both sides, plaintiff can "sell" the claim to defendant at a price defendant is willing to pay in return for dismissal of the litigation—that is, there will be a settlement.

Settlement range

This can be illustrated by using Belli's example. If the true value of the case is $10,000, and it would cost each side $1,000 to try the case, then it is worthwhile to plaintiff to settle for $9,000 (that is, $10,000 minus $1,000) and worthwhile to defendant to settle for $11,000 (that is, $10,000 plus $1,000). Any figure in the range from $9,000 to $11,000 is a reasonable settlement. The same analysis applies to a claim of any size. It also applies to claims seeking an injunction or other "specific" relief, although putting a price tag on an injunction may be difficult, at least theoretically.

If the true value of a claim is similarly estimated by both parties, and if the parties can predict their preparation costs, they could settle every claim on the basis of a fairly simple initial exchange of information. This is in fact what happens in the large percentage of "ordinary" litigation.[8] "Ordinary" litigation refers to cases that fall into typical patterns—typical auto accidents, typical divorces, and so on. These cases occur with enough frequency that experienced lawyers can calculate their value to a reasonably close approximation of the true value that would emerge from trying such cases an infinite number of times.

The relatively narrow variance in the parties' estimate of true value also provides a control on the amount that either side is willing to commit to preparation of the case. That is, generally it would be unwise for either party to make an investment disproportionate to the rate of return implied by the chances of winning, having regard for the opponent's possible countermeasures. The control operates simultaneously on

ney Fee Shifting: A Critical Overview, 1982 Duke L.J. 651; Shavell, Suit, Settlement, and Trial: A Theoretical Analysis Under Alternative Methods for the Allocation of Costs, 11 J. Legal Stud. 55(1982). For material on the settlement process, see §§ 5.21 *supra*, 6.7 note 5 *infra*.

8. *See generally* Trubeck, Sarat, Felsteiner, Kritzer, and Grossman, The Costs of Ordinary Litigation, 31 U.C.L.A. L. Rev. 72 (1983).

both parties so that lawyers on both sides in these cases can fairly accurately predict each other's preparation costs. Hence, "typical" cases can be settled comparatively easily if the litigants accept sound lawyers' judgments of the value of the case. In fact, almost 90 percent of ordinary litigation handled by experienced lawyers is settled, as it is compelled by this practical logic.[9] The logic holds no matter what the true value and the preparation costs may be, so long as both sides can forecast them and neither side has external "strategic" objectives.[10]

One factor that may complicate the prospects of accord is divergence of interests between lawyers and clients. Most parties have little choice but to rely on their lawyers' evaluations of a case's probable result. A lawyer paid by the hour might be tempted to keep the case going as long as possible. A contingent fee lawyer's incentives are more closely aligned with those of the client, but they too can sometimes diverge. For example, going to trial might increase the client's recovery without increasing the lawyer's fee enough to make doing so worth the large amounts of lawyer time that a trial requires. The lawyer might then urge the client to settle by underestimating the probable trial recovery.[11] Other factors tend to reduce the impact of such conflicts of interest. Professional and social standards call on lawyers to pursue their clients' interests rather than their own, and in the long run doing so should promote a lawyer's reputation and financial success. It is not clear how these factors balance out in practice.[12]

§ 6.4 Factors of Uncertainty

Atypical cases

When it is hard to forecast the outcome, appraising the value of a case becomes elusive. Suppose plaintiff thinks the true value of the claim is $250,000 but defendant thinks it is $10,000. The parties virtually cannot settle on the basis of these valuations. Moreover, plaintiff will calculate worthwhile preparation costs in light of his or her estimate—a claim with a value of $250,000 justifies substantial expenditures to present it thoroughly. Defendant will calculate worthwhile preparation on the basis of his or her own estimate—the additional money would be better spent in fortifying the defense than in increasing a settlement

9. *See, e.g.*, Galanter & Cahill, Most Cases Settle: Judicial Promotion and Regulation of Settlements, 46 Stan. L. Rev. 1339 (1994); Eisenberg, et al., Litigation Outcomes in State and Federal Court: A Statistical Portrait, 19 Seattle U.L. Rev. 433 (1996); Gross & Syverud, Don't Try: Civil Jury Verdicts in a System Geared to Settlement, 44 U.C.L.A. L. Rev. 1 (1996).

10. *See* Priest and Klein, The Selection of Disputes for Litigation, 13 J. Legal Stud. 1 (1984), and references therein.

11. Clermont & Currivan, Improving on the Contingent Fee, 63 Cornell L. Rev. 529 (1978).

12. See Kritzer, *et al.*, The Impact of Fee Arrangement on Lawyer Effort, 19 L. & Soc'y Rev. 251 (1985)(reporting little difference between the time invested by hourly and contingent fee lawyers).

offer. The consequence is mutual stonewalling on settlement and mutual escalation of preparation costs.[1] In such an uncertain context, it is also extremely difficult for either side to estimate the expected return on the cost of any additional measure of preparation.

The variance in the parties' estimates of the true value of the case can result from the fact that the case is novel rather than "typical." Since the case is atypical, the lawyers will have difficulty estimating how a jury or court would decide the case. Therefore, they are likely to disagree on its true value. Even if the case is one whose true value most experienced lawyers would agree on, the parties may refuse to accept these estimates. And one or both lawyers may have an idiosyncratic opinion of the value of a case.

High variability

A further complication along these lines is that, even when cases are typical, their outcomes may vary widely. Suppose that one type of case when submitted to various juries would result in outcomes in a range of, say, $20,000 to $30,000. Another type of case, however, results in a range of outcome from, say, $0 to $50,000. The arithmetic means within these two sets of ranges are the same, but the margin of error in estimates of outcome is much wider. The lawyers for the parties, therefore, would have difficulty in being confident of their respective estimates of the case's true value. And the confidence with which the parties would accept their lawyers' estimates might be even less. In the face of divergent indicators of the value of the case, the parties accordingly would be more inclined to invest in going to trial than to accept less and give more in order to settle.

Unnecessary preparation

Another aspect of uncertainty concerns the "payoff" of litigation procedures and techniques. Trial technique is often described as an art, not a science. This means that many different litigation techniques work in that their use is often followed by good results. But it also means that no technique works all the time and, therefore, that a lot of technique must be a waste of time and money. Yet if it remains impossible to predict accurately the effectiveness of specific techniques, then ordinary prudence and anxiety in preparation for litigation will likely generate some unnecessary expense. A good deal of litigation expense is the consequence of doing things because the parties or the lawyers are afraid not to do them. In extreme form, the result is "gold plating"—the ritualistic pursuit of every technical precaution regardless of its probable

§ 6.4

1. The parties theoretically could escalate preparation costs to a point above the amount that either rationally could expect in the way of a verdict. *Compare* Shubik, The Dollar Auction Game: A Paradox in Noncooperative Behavior and Escalation, 15 J. Conflict Resol. 109 (1971). Illustrations of international war escalating in the same way are familiar.

effect on the outcome. The adversarial spirit and financial interests of some lawyers encourage this tendency. Today, sophisticated clients often seek to control the costs of litigation by requiring their lawyers to submit litigation budgets or by using alternative dispute resolution techniques to pursue settlement. Even with careful control of expense, however, litigation involves preparing for eventualities that do not occur. Both sides act with uncertainty when deciding what effects on outcome they "buy" through various levels of preparation expenditure.

Cost escalation

Another dimension of this uncertainty is that one party's costs are determined to an important extent by the costs that the opposing party is willing to run. Both sides may tacitly limit their commitment to some "reasonable" fraction of the amount in controversy; this occurs in much routine litigation. But if one side commits resources that might affect the outcome—by hiring very expensive expert counsel, for instance—then the opposing party can either make a corresponding commitment or accept a reduction in its previous chance of winning. Indeed, a party can compel an opposing party to spend more, for example, by serving interrogatories that the opposing party must answer. Furthermore, the process of competitive investment of resources is interactive, with one side and then the other in a position to increase the stakes in the way of litigation costs. All this occurs in a situation where the outcome is not knowable ex ante but is contingent on the very process in which the expenditures are being committed by the parties.

Litigation as a game

Litigation is thus a game, in the technical sense of that word. Persons concerned with improving the administration of justice tend to deny that litigation is a game and try to restructure procedure to prevent it from being such.[2] But as long as the outcome of litigation cannot be foretold, and can be influenced by maneuver and technique, litigation has the strategic properties of a game, like it or not.[3]

2. *See, e.g.,* Conley v. Gibson, 355 U.S. 41, 48, 78 S.Ct. 99, 103, 2 L.Ed.2d 80, 86 (1957): "The Federal Rules reject the approach that pleading is a game of skill in which one misstep by counsel may be decisive. . . ."

3. LoPucki and Weyrauch, A Theory of Legal Strategy, 49 Duke L.J. 1405 (2000). *Cf.* Jackson, J., concurring in Hickman v. Taylor, 329 U.S. 495, 516, 67 S.Ct. 385, 396, 91 L.Ed. 451, 465 (1947): "Counsel . . . bases his claim . . . on the view that the Rules were to do away with the old situation where a law suit developed into a 'battle of wits between counsel.' But a common law trial is always and should be an adversary proceeding." This is as close as courts get to acknowledging that a trial *is* a game of wits. *See also* Thornburg, Metaphors Matter: How Images of Battle, Sports, and Sex Shape the Adversary System, 10 Wis. Women's L.J. 225 (1995); Note, Discovery Abuse Under the Federal Rules: Causes and Cures, 92 Yale L.J. 352 (1982) (analyzing the position of opposed parties in the discovery stage as a prisoner's dilemma in which both parties could reduce their discovery costs if they could exchange information with each other).

Fact-finder outlook

The game of litigation in the United States has additional uncertainties inherent in the decision maker. Since American courts are relatively activist in redefining the law, in every case lies the possibility that the law will be changed from what it was when the case began. Adding weight to this possibility is the uncertainty of the outlook on which the facts will be determined. Fact determination is to an important extent a function of the outlook or mindset of the finder of fact, whether jury or judge. Predicting the outlook of a contemporary American jury is relatively speculative, even for experienced lawyers, because under today's system a given jury is composed of persons of widely diverse social backgrounds and ideology, and most jurors now sit for such a short time period that they gain no significant common experience in deciding cases.[4] The range of difference in outlook among trial judges is probably less than that among jurors, but trial judges in our system reflect a diversity in political philosophy that expresses the largely political basis of their appointments as judges. In contrast, in most other legal systems the judges are appointed primarily according to traditional professional criteria,[5] and thus are comparatively homogeneous in outlook. Furthermore, in other countries juries either are not used at all or consist of "solid citizens" of conventional outlook.

A great deal of research, both empirical and theoretical, has been done on some of these matters. The theoretical research requires simplifying assumptions to facilitate analysis. Because this simplification often takes the hypothesized cases far from the complexities of reality, the results of theoretical research are suggestive rather than definitive.[6] By a similar token, empirical research has to contend with such a multitude of variables that the inferences and findings of such research are also suggestive rather than definitive.[7] Hence, estimating whether a case ought to be settled at a given price, even if the case is one of a routine type, remains largely a matter of intuition, experience, nerve, and bargaining skill.

Transaction cost of litigation

When a case is not settled, the total costs incurred by the parties, not counting psychological costs, can easily equal the net amount at stake between the parties.[8] The transaction cost of a lawsuit can be 50

4. *See* Dogin and Tevelin, Jury Systems of the Eighties: Toward a Fair Cross-Section and Increased Efficiency, 11 U. Tol. L. Rev. 939 (1980); Graham and Pope, One Day/One Trial or One Week Term of Jury Service, 45 Mo. L. Rev. 255 (1980).

5. *See, e.g.,* Chase, Federal Judges: The Appointing Process (1972); Grossman, Lawyers and Judges: The ABA and the Politics of Judicial Selection (1965). *Cf.* Damaska, Structures of Authority and Comparative Criminal Procedure, 84 Yale L.J. 480 (1975); Sheehan, Criminal Procedure in Scotland and France (1975).

6. *See, e.g.,* Shavell, Suit, Settlement, and Trial: A Theoretical Analysis Under Alternative Methods for the Allocation of Costs, 11 J. Legal Stud. 55 (1982), and references therein.

7. *See, e.g.,* Priest and Klein, The Selection of Disputes for Litigation, 13 J. Legal Stud. 1 (1984), and references therein.

8. *See, e.g.,* Conard, Automobile Accident Costs and Payments (1964); Kakalik,

percent of the total outlay (including the award). For example, when a judgment of $100,000 is awarded on a trial of a personal injury case, it would not be extraordinary for the actual distribution to be as follows:

Plaintiff's lawyer's fee	$ 33,000
Plaintiff's litigation costs (investigation expense, expert witnesses, and so on)	7,000
Plaintiff's net award	60,000
Defense lawyer's fee	15,000
Defense litigation costs	5,000
Total outlay	$120,000

$$\frac{\text{Transaction cost}}{\text{Total outlay}} = \frac{\$60{,}000}{\$120{,}000} = 50\%$$

This relationship can exist whether the amount at stake is $100,000 or $1,000 or $10,000,000, except that the proportion of transaction cost is generally greater the smaller the amount at stake. The above calculation actually underestimates litigation costs because it does not include the costs of running the court system or the administrative costs of the defendant's insurance company.

The critical factor in the cost of litigation, therefore, is not necessarily the absolute cost of a specific procedure or technique, or of the whole trial procedure, at least when the claim is of more than *de minimis* value. Rather, the critical factor is the degree of uncertainty over how the judicial system will assess a case after it proceeds beyond an initial statement of claim. Most discussions of procedural reform for reducing litigation cost ignore the uncertainty factor, apparently presupposing that the unpredictability of outcome has to be taken as a given. In fact, changes in procedure and court organization could significantly reduce uncertainty. For example, jury composition rules could be changed to reduce uncertainty resulting from the unpredictability of jury outlook. Simplifying the law so that assessing claims would involve fewer factual disputes and legal uncertainties would increase the predictability and reduce the cost of litigation, however it might impair sensitivity to the unique features of each case.

Wealth asymmetries

Absolute cost of litigation can influence the result of litigation under some conditions. One such condition would exist when (1) the procedures that the parties normally are allowed to use entail cost not only for the party who uses them but also for the other side, and (2) the parties' economic situations are such that they have greatly different expendi-

et al., Variations in Asbestos Litigation Compensation and Expenses (1984); Trubeck, *et al.*, The Costs of Ordinary Litigation, 31 U.C.L.A. L. Rev. 72 (1983).

ture levels at which they will "go broke." Another way of describing such a scenario is to say that it is a poker game involving a high permissible ante in which one of the players can put up such an ante and the other cannot. In this situation, the party with the greater staying power can force the weaker party out of the game before the latter's chance of winning on the merits can have its effect on the former's self-interest calculations.

This asymmetry of position can favor the party who has more financial resources, such as the "rich corporation." We would expect the richer party to pursue an elaborate scheme of pretrial maneuvers in which the other party is in effect compelled to participate.[9] But the party richer in financial resources may also be more vulnerable to other forms of cost, particularly diversion of its time. Hence we would expect to find the other party using maneuvers that take up the time of the richer party, such as elaborate demands for corporate documents and protracted depositions of high-level corporate officials.

Because courts have been reluctant to shape procedural decisions so as to compensate in any explicit way for economic disadvantage, their decisions have sometimes reinforced wealth asymmetries.[10] Invocations of Constitutional law have had only modest success in dispelling economic barriers to meaningful court access.[11] The main resorts of economically disadvantaged litigants are thus the contingent fee (for plaintiffs with sufficient prospects of recovery to attract a lawyer), attorney fee recovery statutes (for plaintiffs with meritorious claims of the sorts those statutes cover), and the Legal Services Corporation (for litigants who are sufficiently poor, have cases of the sorts that Congress allows the Corporation to accept, and fit within the Corporation's own limited capacity).[12]

9. Purcell, Litigation and Inequality: Federal Diversity Jurisdiction in Industrial America, 1870–1958 (1992); Harr, A Civil Action (1995); Schrag, Counsel for the Deceived (1972).

10. *E.g.*, Carnival Cruise Lines, Inc. v. Shute, 499 U.S. 585, 111 S.Ct. 1522, 113 L.Ed.2d 622 (1991); Helicopteros Nacionales de Colombia, S.A. v. Hall, 466 U.S. 408, 104 S.Ct. 1868, 80 L.Ed.2d 404 (1984); Burger King Corp. v. Rudzewicz, 471 U.S. 462, 105 S.Ct. 2174, 85 L.Ed.2d 528 (1985); Kamilewicz v. Bank of Boston Corp., 100 F.3d 1348 (7th Cir.1996).

11. *Compare* Boddie v. Connecticut, 401 U.S. 371, 91 S.Ct. 780, 28 L.Ed.2d 113 (1971)(indigent may not be required to pay filing fee for divorce); Lindsey v. Normet, 405 U.S. 56, 92 S.Ct. 862, 31 L.Ed.2d 36 (1972)(tenant contesting eviction may not be required to post bond for twice the rent); M.L.B. v. S.L.J., 519 U.S. 102, 117 S.Ct. 555, 136 L.Ed.2d 473 (1996)(indigent mother appealing deprivation of parental rights may not be required to pay $2300 for trial transcript) *with* United States v. Kras, 409 U.S. 434, 93 S.Ct. 631, 34 L.Ed.2d 626 (1973)(indigent may be required to pay bankruptcy filing fee); Ortwein v. Schwab, 410 U.S. 656, 93 S.Ct. 1172, 35 L.Ed.2d 572 (1973)(indigent appealing benefit reduction may be required to pay filing fee); Lassiter v. Department of Social Services, 452 U.S. 18, 101 S.Ct. 2153, 68 L.Ed.2d 640 (1981)(state need not ordinarily provide counsel to indigent facing termination of parental rights). See also Michelman, The Supreme Court and Litigation Access Fees: The Right to Protect One's Rights, 1973 Duke L.J. 1153, 1974 Duke L.J. 527; Note, The Right of Access to Civil Courts Under State Constitutional Law: An Impediment to Modern Reforms, or a Receptacle of Important Substantive and Procedural Rights?, 13 Rut.-Cam. L.J. 399 (1982).

12. See §§ 1.22–23 *supra*. On the Legal Services Corporation, see 42 U.S.C. §§ 2996 *et seq.*; Legal Services Corp. v. Velazquez,

"Repeat players"

Another asymmetry exists when the parties to a suit, whatever their financial resources, have different strategic interests. For example, consider the situation of a consumer creditor asserting a claim against a consumer. For the consumer, the controversy is a "one shot" lawsuit, for he or she is unlikely to be involved in more than one such lawsuit, at least in the short run. Against any single creditor, it makes no sense for the consumer to invest more in defending the case than is indicated by the prospects for winning *that* case. Ordinarily, such a consumer has nothing to gain by fighting a creditor as a deterrent to other creditors.[13] In contrast, the creditor of a consumer has a strategic interest transcending the instant case. The creditor's litigation "investment" decision rationally should take into account the fact that vigorous, if expensive, prosecution of one case will act as a deterrent to other debtors. Thus, the creditor could rationally decide to spend $1,000 to enforce a claim for $1,000, or even one for $500, depending on the estimated value of the enhanced deterrence to others.

The strategic position of repeat players in litigation is thus asymmetrical with that of one-shot players.[14] This difference in position, and perhaps other factors, explains why repeat players are willing, other things being equal, to invest more in one case than are one-shot players, and this has a corresponding effect on prospects for winning at trial and for favorable settlement without trial. There are ways, however, in which this advantage can be offset, at least in part. Various types of one-shot players can be favored by special provisions concerning the award of litigation costs. An example is the federal law providing that citizens can often recover litigation costs if they prevail against the government, but making no corresponding provision in favor of the government.[15] Nevertheless, while the structure of incentives can thus be modified by counterincentives, it cannot be made to disappear.

The varying psychology of litigants creates further asymmetries. Some litigants are more willing than others to gamble, more determined to obtain judicial vindication, or more able to endure courtroom anxieties and exposures. Psychological research suggests that some of these differ-

121 S.Ct. 1043 U.S. ___ (2001); Johnson, Justice and Reform (1974); Tremblay, Acting "A Very Moral Type of God": Triage Among Poor Clients, 67 Fordham L. Rev. 2475 (1999). See also 28 U.S.C. § 1915 (waiving court fees for indigents proceeding in forma pauperis).

13. Of course, if the debtor has lots of creditors, he or she may have something to gain by fighting one very hard, thus compelling the other creditors to recognize that all the debtor's assets may be consumed in litigation. This happened in Jarndyce and Jarndyce in Dickens' Bleak House, and not infrequently happens in contested bankruptcy proceedings.

14. *Compare* Galanter, Why the "Haves" Come Out Ahead: Speculations on the Limits of Legal Change, 9 Law & Soc. Rev. 95 (1974); Special Issue: Do the "Haves" Still Come Out Ahead?, 33 L. & Soc'y Rev. 799 (1999).

15. 28 U.S.C. § 2412(d); *see* Shavell, Suit, Settlement, and Trial: A Theoretical Analysis Under Alternative Methods for the Allocation of Costs, 11 J. Legal Stud. 55 (1982), and references therein.

ences are systematic. Defendants tend to resist paying out a settlement even when refusing to settle exposes them to the risk of greater losses sometime in the future; plaintiffs tend to prefer a cash settlement now to the possibility of larger future gains.[16] When this discrepancy exists, it presumably leads to settlements awarding plaintiffs less than an objective evaluation of their prospects would indicate.

§ 6.5 Lawsuit as Quest for Justice

Even though a lawsuit entails coercion, psychological and social distress, and expense, it is essentially a quest for justice by the parties. Indeed, unless parties are driven by a feeling of having suffered injustice, it seems likely that many disputes would simply be written off as misfortunes, like a flood or a death in the family. If a dispute is to ripen into litigation, a complex process of analysis and evaluation must occur in the mind of the claimant as a preliminary to getting a lawyer or initiating the litigation. This process can be broken down into three elements. The first is "naming" the situation, that is, analyzing the situation as a specific kind of problem. The second is "blaming," that is, attributing the consequences to some specific person rather than to accident or unavoidable circumstances. The third is "claiming," that is, taking the step of charging that other person with legal responsibility.[1]

But there is perhaps a fourth component in a person's mobilizing to seek legal redress. This component is hope. While a "natural" misfortune evokes emotions such as despair or frustration, an act of human injustice also can evoke hope for the restoration of justice, if not for the exact restoration of the status quo ante. This hope is based partly on the law's promise of redress, a promise that the system of government continually reiterates even if it is not completely fulfilled.

Vengeance

The attempt to realize this hope may take the form of a quest for revenge. Lawless societies are often characterized by pervasive blood vengeance. The element of vengeance is not extinguished, however, by the substitution of legal justice; it can manifest itself even in routine litigation. Vengeance is commonplace in domestic relations litigation, but it is also frequently present in litigation arising from failures in business relationships, products liability claims, and even automobile accidents.

Vindication

16. Rachlinski, Gains, Losses, and the Psychology of Litigation, 70 S. Calif. L. Rev. 113 (1996).

§ 6.5

1. For a conceptual analysis and extensive bibliography, see Felstiner, Abel, and Sarat, The Emergence and Transformation of Disputes: Naming, Blaming, Claiming, 15 Law & Soc. Rev. 631 (1980–1981).

Apart from the primordial urge for revenge, the resort to litigation is a quest for vindication of self. A court's favorable judgment is a solemn pronouncement that the victor has acted properly on the basis of a factually accurate understanding of reality. A favorable judgment is an affirmation of the prevailing party's rationality and good citizenship. To a litigant who has suffered the injustice of the original wrong and the further injustice of the antagonist's refusal to settle peacefully on just terms, the law offers much. It offers to be attentive to the litigant's grievance, to conduct an inquiry that is ostentatiously and often genuinely disinterested, to be evenhanded and authoritative in what it says and does, to make definitive pronouncements about basic social values such as the necessity of behaving like a reasonable person and keeping solemn promises, to affirm the facts that the aggrieved party has all along contended them to be, to confer just redress, and to give hope for the future in the example of restoring justice for the past.

All these benefits have a considerable psychological as well as material value. Of course, they can be conferred only on the winner. The yield for the loser is correspondingly bitter.

Final judgments in the real world thus usually have opposite moral outcomes for winners and losers, since the parties of course assess the justice of the result according to their own views. The perspectives of rational litigants therefore oscillate between the vision of victory and vindication and the nightmare of loss and rejection. Both perspectives probably increase in vividness as the date of trial approaches; this may explain in part why many cases settle when the parties reach "the courthouse steps." For those who do not settle, one thing is certain: The judgment results in what the winner may consider justice; for the other litigant, however, the system will have been a failure. The court system can avoid this failure, and save itself time and trouble, by inducing the parties to settle before the verdict. Thus both the parties and the system have an interest in settlements, provided that the methods by which the system encourages settlements do not themselves reduce the system's legitimacy.

Procedural justice

What would a just procedural system look like? Although philosophers have often written about distributive and corrective justice, they have said little about procedural justice. Should the goal be accurate determination of facts and law, or the elucidation and enforcement of social values, or a result acceptable to the parties?[2] Is justice simply a matter of the results reached, or does it also call for process values, such as the opportunity to participate?[3] To what extent should the search for

2. Fiss, Against Settlement, 93 Yale L.J. 1073 (1984); Menkel-Meadow, For and Against Settlement: Uses and Abuses of the Mandatory Settlement Conference, 33 U.C.L.A. L. Rev. 485 (1985).

3. *See, e.g.,* Thibaut and Walker, Procedural Justice: A Psychological Analysis

evidence prevail over the right of litigants and nonparties to protect their privacy? Should the relevant perspective consider civil procedure as part of a governmental system and shape procedure to promote the rule of law and restrain judicial arbitrariness?[4] Or should litigation be appraised as an interaction between human beings, in which sympathy and understanding characterize the true judge and lawyers and litigants eschew today's macho combats?[5] Should mediation and conciliation replace litigation as the central way of resolving disputes?[6]

With all these choices to be made, it is not surprising that systems of civil procedure differ dramatically. For example, the French system, which is similar to those in a number of other nations, in most instances leaves parties to their own resources in gathering evidence.[7] The court rarely requires witnesses to testify, although it may appoint a neutral expert to investigate and report on contested issues. Indeed, even a party's lawyer is supposed to avoid contact with potential nonclient witnesses. In any event, little weight is given to witness statements, because it is assumed that they are far less reliable than documents composed before the suit started. Cases are heard, not by juries, but by panels of judges, and the lawyers present all the evidence to the court in written form. A French trial thus resembles an appellate argument more than a trial in the United States. And a French appeal is very like a French trial, because the appellate panel is free to read the evidence itself and reach its own factual conclusions. This system has endured for hundreds of years, perhaps because it is relatively cheap and reflects social suspicion of governmental intrusion. (French criminal procedure is very different and far more intrusive.) To an American, it seems both strange and unlikely to unearth the truth. Yet one can find other procedural systems that diverge equally strikingly from those of both France and the United States.[8]

(1975); Mashaw, Administrative Due Process: The Quest for a Dignitary Theory, 61 B.U.L. Rev. 885 (1981); Summers, Evaluating and Improving Legal Processes—A Plea for "Process Values," 60 Cornell L. Rev. 1 (1974); Tyler, Citizen Discontent with Legal Procedures: A Social Science Perspective on Civil Procedure Reform, 45 Am. J. Comp. L. 871 (1997).

4. *See* Leubsdorf, Constitutional Civil Procedure, 63 Tex. L. Rev. 579 (1984); Rubin, Due Process and the Administrative State, 72 Calif. L. Rev. 1044 (1984).

5. Resnik, On the Bias: Feminist Reconsideration of the Aspirations for Our Judges, 61 S. Cal. L. Rev. 1877 (1988); Farina, Conceiving Due Process, 3 Yale J.L. & Feminism 189 (1991); Thornburg, Metaphors Matter: How Images of Battle, Sports, and Sex Shape the Adversary System, 10 Wis. Women's L.J. 225 (1995); Symposium, Feminist Jurisprudence and Procedure, 61 U. Cin. L. Rev. 1139 (1993).

6. Menkel–Meadow, The Trouble with the Adversary System in a Postmodern, Multicultural World, 38 Wm. & Mary L. Rev. 5 (1996). But see Grillo, The Mediation Alternative: Process Dangers for Women, 100 Yale L.J. 1545 (1991).

7. See Leubsdorf, Man In His Original Dignity: Legal Ethics in France, ch. 7 (2001); Beardsley, Proof of Fact in French Civil Procedure, 34 Am. J. Comp. L. 459 (1986).

8. See, *e.g.*, Rosen, The Anthropology of Justice: Law and Culture in Islamic Society (1989); Comaroff & Roberts, Rules and Process: The Cultural Logic of Dispute in African Context (1981); French, The Golden Yoke: The Legal Cosmology of Buddhist Tibet (1995); Kaplan, *et al.*, Phases of German

§ 6.6 Civil Justice as a Political Program

Criminal justice

Political parties compete for control of government, among other ways, by offering to provide more or better kinds of government services.[1] Among these services, one of the highest priorities is maintenance of civil order—prevention of murder, mayhem, theft, destruction of property, fraud, and so on. Maintenance of minimal order is a necessary precondition for giving effect to various legal rights, such as rights of personal integrity (including protection against discrimination), family relationship (child custody), contract, property, and relationships with government itself (judicial review of administration action). The immediate mechanism of maintaining order and thus securing legal rights is the "police power," including the police as such and the criminal justice system and the suppression of illegal private coercion. The civil justice system works within the shelter of the system of control established by the police power. Through adjudication, the civil justice system directly provides immediate peaceful resolution of disputes. Indirectly, the civil justice system facilitates negotiated resolution of such disputes through private settlement. It does this by continually reaffirming what the law is and by standing ready to impose legal sanctions when disputes are not resolved by negotiation. In the American legal system more than any other, the courts also act in an important way as a source of legal rules and hence of public policy.

Functions of civil justice

The relationship of civil justice to the social order is complex. It is intertwined with morality at one end, brute police power at the other, and societal values between.[2] It is therefore hard to say what would happen if the system of civil justice atrophied. Most likely, people would increasingly rely on "private" government, such as the extended family and privateering business, and on coercion through police and military force. That in turn would reduce the security, complexity, and variety of transactions that the society could accommodate and would result in a degeneration to "spot markets," black markets, payoffs, and to possession being virtually ten points of the law instead of nine. Society would deteriorate into something nearer the Dark Ages or a civil-war-zone economy. That condition of life is less stable, safe, and productive for

Civil Procedure, 71 Harv. L. Rev. 1193, 1443 (1958); Chase, Legal Processes and National Culture, 5 Cardozo J. Int'l & Comp. L. 1 (1997). For descriptions of civil procedural systems, see Damaska, The Faces of Justice and State Authority: A Comparative Approach to the Legal Process (1974–75); Civil Justice in Crisis: Comparative Perspectives of Civil Procedure (Zuckerman ed. 1999); Access to Justice (Cappelletti ed. 1978–79).

§ 6.6

1. *See, e.g.,* Downs, An Economic Theory of Democracy (1957).

2. *See, e.g.,* Galanter, Justice in Many Rooms: Courts, Private Ordering, and Indigenous Law, 19 J. Legal Pluralism 1 (1981).

most people and is dreaded perhaps beyond anything except total political subjugation. Government therefore offers a comparatively attractive alternative. Indeed, perhaps a primary enduring attraction of government, besides providing common defense against foreign threats, is offering the benefits of domestic legal order. All governments undertake to provide this "public good," at least at a minimum level, and usually promise that all citizens will receive equal justice.

To what degree a government is able or impelled to provide effective civil justice is a different question. The answer obviously varies a great deal from culture to culture, even among nations with modern economies. Japan and New Zealand, for example, both have an apparatus of civil justice that is very modest in scale compared to that in the United States, but for what must be different reasons. In any event, a nation's civil justice apparatus reflects the role in the maintenance of social order that is played by law and legal process as compared with other means of adjusting social conflict. In the United States, law plays an ambiguous role in maintaining social order. Americans seem to have strong motivation to assert legal rights for themselves, but not so ready an inclination voluntarily to recognize legal authority. Perhaps for that very reason, adjustment of social conflict through the claiming and contesting of legal rights plays a very important part in our political culture. This may explain the existence of so much due process and so many lawyers.[3] In recent decades public law litigation and institutional reform litigation have demonstrated another way in which civil justice relates to social order.[4]

Rationing justice

From the government's viewpoint, making the system of civil justice effective is a continuing challenge. There are, of course, perennial calls for speedier and more efficient justice.[5] The government must placate this discontent and respond sufficiently to propitiate serious unrest. But operating the court system is expensive, although the cost is modest compared with that of other social services.[6] Also, providing speedy and efficient justice works to benefit some sectors of society more than others. If civil justice were dramatically improved in its expeditiousness, some political interests would suffer. For example, if loans were more expeditiously collected, it would adversely affect debtors who wish to delay repaying but not to formally reschedule their obligations.[7] Hence,

3. *See* Atiyah, The Lawyers and Rules: Some Anglo-American Comparisons, 37 Sw. L.J. 545 (1983).

4. *See, e.g.,* Cover, Fiss, and Resnik, Procedure (1988); Fiss, The Civil Rights Injunction (1978); Chayes, The Role of the Judge in Public Law Litigation, 89 Harv. L. Rev. 1281 (1976); Fiss, Foreword: The Forms of Justice, 93 Harv. L. Rev. 1 (1979).

5. *See, e.g.,* Pound, The Causes of Popular Dissatisfaction with the Administration of Justice, 40 Am. L. Rev. 729 (1906).

6. *See, e.g.,* Hazard, Rationing Justice, 8 J.L. & Econ. 1 (1965).

7. During much of the nation's history, organized debtors secured statutes obstructing the recovery of debts, which creditors then challenged in the courts. See

the level of effectiveness in civil justice that society actually will tolerate seems to be lower than what the government promises or pretends. Certainly it is lower than even modest reformers might wish.

As the last paragraph suggests, civil procedure is not merely the government's concern. It can effect anyone. Often, however, the effects of any procedural innovation on individuals or social groups are hard to predict. Many people do not know if they will be involved in litigation at all, and if so as plaintiffs or defendants. Many procedures can be invoked by those on either side of a case; discovery, for example, although often thought of as a boon for plaintiffs, is more frequently used by defendants in many cases.[8] Sometimes, the groups benefitting from a procedure change over the years, as when mass tort defendants began trying to use class actions to limit their liability.[9] For these reasons, people rarely organize politically to demand changes in civil procedure. For the most part, procedure is left to lawyers and judges, who of course have interests of their own to advance in proposing or resisting change.[10]

Despite these qualifications, political pressures do impinge on civil procedure. Even the technicalities of removal jurisdiction have been used by groups of litigants, in this case insurance companies and other corporate defendants, to advance their interests, and have thus led to political controversy.[11] Occasionally, a group works successfully to obtain procedural changes, such as federal legislation to help divorced spouses enforce child support orders.[12] In recent decades, the major political players in procedural matters have been the "tort reform lobby" organized by corporate defendants on the one hand, and trial lawyers speaking for themselves and their clients on the other. Because of the general political climate, the former group has usually been more effective in the legislatures than the latter, but sometimes they have cancelled each other out, preventing change in any direction.[13]

Wright, The Contract Clause of the Constitution (1938). Nowadays, creditor-debtor disputes often focus on federal bankruptcy legislation.

8. Glaser, Pretrial Discovery and the Adversary System (1968).

9. *E.g.*, Amchem Products, Inc. v. Windsor, 521 U.S. 591, 117 S.Ct. 2231, 138 L.Ed.2d 689 (1997); Ortiz v. Fibreboard Corp., 527 U.S. 815, 119 S.Ct. 2295, 144 L.Ed.2d 715 (1999).

10. Resnik, Changing Practices, Changing Rules: Judicial and Congressional Rulemaking on Civil Juries, Civil Justice, and Civil Judging, 49 Ala. L. Rev. 133 (1997); Leubsdorf, The Myth of Civil Procedure Reform, in Civil Justice in Crisis: Comparative Perspectives of Civil Procedure 53, 59–63 (Zuckerman ed. 1999).

11. Purcell, Litigation and Inequality: Federal Diversity Jurisdiction in Industrial America, 1870–1958 (1992).

12. *See* 18 U.S.C. § 228; 28 U.S.C. § 1738B; 42 U.S.C. §§ 652 *et seq.*

13. See Mullenix, Hope Over Experience: Mandatory Informal Discovery and the Politics of Rulemaking, 69 N.C. L. Rev. 795 (1991); Koppel, Populism, Politics, and Procedure: The Saga of Summary Judgment and the Rulemaking Process in California, 24 Pepp. L. Rev. 455 (1997); Note, The Lessons of California's Proposition 211: The Ballot Initiative As A Vehicle for States to Sidestep Federal Securities Litigation Reform, 13 J.L. & Politics 965 (1997).

The influences constraining "efficiency" are thus many. These influences are so strong that they can be better analyzed as competing social and political goals rather than as impediments to the achievement of some one overall goal.

§ 6.7 Policy Goals Competing with Judicial "Efficiency"

The English system

If the American system of civil justice were designed for maximum efficiency in deciding cases, presumably it would be patterned after the English system, which many used to regard as a model. The English system has the following characteristics: selection of judges by an essentially nonpolitical authority from among the trial bar (barristers) on the basis of professional assessment of merit as evidenced by experience in practice; admission to the trial bar conditioned on the applicant's ability to afford an extended period of apprenticeship and unremunerative practice, and advancement in the bar on the basis of professional connections and success; a bench and bar that is limited in size, concentrated in location, and professionally close-knit; very restricted use of juries, both in the types of cases that are tried by juries and the scope of the jury's decisional prerogative; limited pretrial discovery as compared with American procedure; limited scope for judicial innovation in decisional law; little use of judicial process to review or restrain government authority; little use of class suits and low incidence of mass tort litigation; relatively narrow admissibility of evidence; relatively parsimonious measures of damage in personal injury litigation; a fee award system compensating the winner for attorney's fees and thus deterring litigants who lack deep pockets; and prohibition of contingent fees.[1] In recent years, complaints about the increasing expense and delay of the English system have led to drastic reforms. Some of these, like increased judicial management, encouragement of settlements, removing the monopoly of barristers on courtroom advocacy, and partially contingent fees, narrow the gap between England and the United States; others, such as the allocation of cases to different "tracks," use of joint instead of partisan experts, and limits on attorney fee recovery plough new ground.[2]

Social values

Even after these changes, the American civil justice system differs markedly from that of England.[3] The differences reflect deeply held

§ 6.7

1. *See* Jackson, The Machinery of Justice in England *passim* (6th ed. 1972).

2. Civil Procedure Rules 1998 (SI 1998 No. 3132); see Access to Justice: Final Report (1996)(the "Woolf Report"); Reform of Civil Procedure: Essays on "Access to Justice" (Zuckerman & Cranston ed. 1995); Grainger and Fealy, The Civil Procedure Rules in Action (2d ed. 2000).

3. *Cf.* Sofaer, Sanctioning Attorneys for Discovery Abuse Under the New Federal Rules: On the Limited Utility of Punishment, 57 St. John's L. Rev. 680 (1983); ABA

American social values, particularly that of open opportunity—that is, the opportunity to be a judge or lawyer, the opportunity for citizens to participate in administering justice by serving on a jury, the opportunity to bring evidence to light regardless of cost, the opportunity to seek changes in the law, and so on. Another characteristic American value is the right to have one's say, specifically, to have one's "day in court." This value translates into the right to a day in court that is not burdened with liability for the costs it may inflict on the other side.[4] Another such value is hope for the future, which translates into hope that justice can be provided in the courts. Yet, as noted earlier, the American ethos is also hostile to authority as such, implementing what might be considered a national commitment to checks and balances. Much of our procedural system seeks to limit the power of all participants. Parties restrain each other through the adversary system; juries and trial judges restrain each other, as do trial and appellate judges; jurisdiction is divided among the courts of different states and between state and federal courts.

Efficiently implementing this set of values would require a peculiar system of civil justice. The system would be wide open to the reception of legal claims and hospitable to giving them elaborate consideration. At the same time, the system would be slow to impose final judgment and would provide relatively weak sanctions to control procedure. It would permit social conflict to be articulated in terms of legal rights but prefer that these conflicts ordinarily be resolved by private bargain. Such a system would accommodate the ideals both of broad formal equality, expressed in legal rights, and broad individual autonomy, expressed in freedom to reach outcomes by contract. The courts would form an arena for compulsory bargaining, with litigation serving to resolve breakdowns in negotiation.[5]

Compulsory bargaining

This may be a correct analysis of the actual, desired goals of the American legal system, as distinct from its professed goals.[6] Of course, different participants in the system have different goals, some seeking to increase judicial efficiency,[7] others to discourage weak claims,[8] and

Standards of Judicial Administration (1977); Summers & Atiyah, Form and Substance in Anglo–American Law: A Comparative Study of Legal Reasoning, Legal Theory and Legal Institutions (1987).

4. *See* §§ 1.23, 6.3 *supra.*

5. *See* Ross, Settled Out of Court (1970); Kritzer, Let's Make a Deal: Understanding the Negotiation Process in Ordinary Litigation (1990); Mnookin and Kornhauser, Bargaining in the Shadow of the Law: The Case of Divorce, 88 Yale L.J. 950 (1979); Gross & Syverud, Don't Try: Civil Jury Verdicts in a System Geared to Settlement, 44 U.C.L.A. 1 (1996).

6. *See* Galanter, Reading the Landscape of Disputes: What We Know and Don't Know (and Think We Know) About Our Allegedly Contentious and Litigious Society, 31 UCLA L. Rev. 4 (1983).

7. Resnik, Failing Faith: Adjudicatory Procedure in Decline, 53 U. Chi. L. Rev. 494 (1986).

8. Quayle, Civil Justice Reform, 41 Am. U. L. Rev. 559 (1992); *see* Mullenix, Discovery in Disarray: The Pervasive Myth of

others to provide a broad range of options for dispute resolution.[9] In addition, the American court system as it exists partially accommodates the authoritative justice exemplified in the English system. Some quotient of authoritative justice—actual adjudication according to the law—is required to make a system of compulsory bargaining work. But the American system is fundamentally one of compulsory bargaining in response to claims of right.[10] On this basis, our system can be considered very efficient. And that would explain why it resists being reformed to yield the more formally respectable but actually less preferred goals of the English system.

Pervsasive Discovery Abuse and the Consequences for Unfounded Rulemaking, 46 Stan. L. Rev. 1393 (1994).

9. Sander, Varieties of Dispute Processing, 70 F.R.D. 111 (1976); Resnik, Many Doors? Closing Doors? Alternate Dispute Resolution and Adjudication, 10 Ohio St. J. on Disp. Resol. 211 (1995).

10. Authorities cited note 5 *supra;* § 6.3 *supra.*

*

Chapter 7

THE TRIAL

A. STRUCTURE OF A TRIAL

§ 7.1 Trial of Issues of Fact

As we have seen, a legal claim involves a factual premise and a legal premise. The factual premise, asserted in the allegations of the complaint, is that a particular set of events occurred, say, that defendant made statements concerning a financial transaction that were inaccurate and that plaintiff relied on the statements. The legal premise of these allegations is that the set of events constitutes a legal wrong for which damages or other relief should be awarded.[1]

Issues of law

The validity of the legal premise may be disputed. If it is, the judge determines the legal issue on the basis of legal argument, set forth in written memoranda or briefs, usually augmented by oral argument. The judge has the authority to determine all questions of law, whether the case is tried to a jury or to a judge without a jury. A ruling on the legal premise of the complaint may be based, for example, on defendant's motion for dismissal[2] or for summary judgment.[3] The judge also determines all incidental questions of law, including those posed by motions before, during, and after trial, and objections to evidence. The trial judge's rulings on questions of law are subject to reconsideration by the appellate court if the case is eventually appealed.[4] Some litigated cases involve issues of law alone, the facts being undisputed.

Issues of fact

Defendant may dispute the facts but accept that the allegations, if proved, would constitute a valid basis for legal relief. Typically, several factual allegations will be disputed. For example, defendant in a fraud case may deny that the representations were made, deny that they were false, deny that any damage resulted, or deny all these allegations. Similarly, a plaintiff may dispute allegations of a defendant's affirmative defense.[5] As a result, an issue of fact or several such issues are presented. Of course, litigation may involve issues of both law and fact.

Types of evidence

Issues of fact are determined on the basis of evidence, including testimony of witnesses, documentary evidence, interpretive testimony by expert witnesses, and other types of proof. Thus, in a typical accident case, causation will be established by the testimony of the injured party and third-person witnesses; the nature and extent of medical expenses and plaintiff's loss of wages will be proved by hospital and employment records, respectively; the extent of the injured party's disability will be determined by the testimony of doctors testifying as medical experts. The defendant will offer contradicting or qualifying evidence of similar kinds on all or some of the issues.

§ 7.1

1. *See* § 3.1 *supra.*
2. *See* § 7.21 *infra.*
3. *See* §§ 4.10–4.16 *supra.*
4. *See* Chapter 12.
5. *See* § 4.5 *supra.*

Special proof requirements

The law prescribes special proof requirements for certain types of factual issues. For example, a contract calling for conveyance of land ordinarily must be in writing; hence, a claim based on breach of such a contract will fail unless plaintiff has the necessary documentary proof.[6] Formerly, the law had similar prescriptions of proof in many types of cases. For example, certain facts had to be proved by the testimony of two witnesses, a requirement going back to medieval canon law and indeed the Bible. At common law, a party to a dispute was disqualified from being a witness.[7] In effect, this meant that in order to prevail a plaintiff needed an admission by the defendant or corroboration from a third-person witness. In modern civil litigation, however, parties are competent to testify and, generally speaking, proof need not meet any peculiar legal requirements.

Ordinary proof

Proof of facts in litigation, therefore, depends on the methods of demonstration and inference used in everyday life. Witnesses say what they saw; the trier of fact has to decide whether a witness had a good opportunity to observe and to remember and whether the witness may be biased. A document has to be authenticated, that is, established by witness testimony or other proof to be what the document purports to be—the particular deed, the hospital record, or the particular correspondence. The trier of fact has to decide the validity of the authenticating testimony, the authenticity of the document, and the accuracy and meaning of the recitations in the document. The thought processes and logic used to deal with these trial assessments are the same as with similar problems outside of court. There is nothing mysterious about legal proof.

Finality

The principal difference between establishing facts in a trial and doing so in everyday life is that a trial is the community's official and final arbitrament of the facts. After the trial court's pronouncement, there is no legal recourse except for a narrow scope of appellate review[8] and an even narrower scope for later reopening on the basis of fraud in the trial, newly discovered evidence, and a few other extraordinary circumstances.[9] A trial, therefore, is ordinarily once and for all. It is this finality of result, indeed, that makes the adjudicative process both authoritative and especially risky and ridden with tension. The presence of these risks and tensions in turn calls for elaborate controls on trial procedure. These include the rules of courtroom procedure and the rules of evidence.

6. *See* § 4.6 *supra;* Fed. R. Civ. P. 8(c).

7. Gibson v. Kennedy Extension Gold Mining Co., 172 Cal. 294, 156 P. 56 (1916); Meyer v. San Diego, 121 Cal. 102, 53 P. 434 (1898).

8. *See* Chapter 12.

9. *See* Fed. R. Civ. P. 60(c).

The following analysis primarily addresses courtroom procedure and only incidentally the rules of evidence. The rules of evidence are chiefly devices through which the court controls the evidence that a jury may be allowed to consider, and secondarily devices through which appellate courts control the evidence that the trial judge may consider.[10] The American law of evidence, being designed primarily to control jury consideration of evidence, is uniquely intricate. It is conventionally treated as a subject in itself and as such is beyond the scope of this work.[11]

§ 7.2 Trial to Judge or Jury

Determination of the facts can be made either by a jury or by the trial judge. In American procedure, there is a right to jury trial in actions at law but not in proceedings in equity.[1] The right to jury trial applies in the typical tort or contract suit for damages. When either party invokes this right, the issues of fact in the case are tried to a jury. If neither party invokes the right, and when there is no right to jury trial, the issues of fact are decided by the judge, unless the judge, as a matter of discretion, impanels an advisory jury,[2] or the parties agree to try their case before a U.S. magistrate.[3]

Waiver

The right to jury trial is waived if not demanded in a timely manner.[4] Under the Federal Rules, the demand must be made within 10 days of the last pleading directed to the issue triggering the demand.[5] Demand procedures under state practice vary.

Common trial procedure problems

Whether the fact issues are tried to the judge or to a jury, several common problems of trial procedure have to be accommodated. One is that of orderly presentation: Which side goes first and how does each side present its evidence? A second problem is the standard of proof: How convincing does it have to be? A third problem is the burden of proof: Which side prevails if the trier of fact is unable to arrive at a conclusion according to the standard of proof?

10. Evidence is construed broadly to uphold, rather than defeat, the trial court's judgment. *See* Grall v. Meyer, 173 N.W.2d 61 (Iowa 1969).

11. *See generally* Strong et al., McCormick on Evidence (5th ed. 1999); Weinstein, Weinstein's Evidence (1975); Wigmore, Evidence (McNaughton rev. 1981).

§ 7.2

1. *See* Chapter 8.

2. *See* Fed. R. Civ. P. 39(c); Annot., 9 A.L.R.4th 1041.

3. 28 U.S.C. § 636(c); Fed. R. Civ. P. 73.

4. *See* Federal Deposit Ins. Corp. v. Palermo, 815 F.2d 1329 (10th Cir.1987) (but a district court may order a jury trial when a party made known its desire for one, even though a demand was not filed in a timely manner).

5. Fed. R. Civ. P. 38(b).

Whether the trial is to a jury or to the judge without a jury, the judge presides. As presiding officer the judge specifies the order of presentation, subject to established rules and traditions. The parties, through their lawyers, present the evidence and argue for its probative significance. In trial to a jury, the standard of proof and the burden of proof are explained to the jury by the judge. The judge also has to explain the legal premises that govern the jury in arriving at its verdict. These explanations are contained in instructions given by the judge to the jury, called a *charge*. In a trial to the court without a jury, the judge is presumed to understand these concepts and to apply them without direct request by the parties.[6]

In the following discussion we first consider the common problems of order of presentation, standard of proof, and burden of proof in both jury and nonjury trial; thereafter we examine the special additional problems involved in jury trial.

§ 7.3 Order of Presentation

Whether a case is tried to a jury or to a judge without a jury, several basic rules govern the order of presentation. These rules have evolved in an institutional context in which most cases are tried to juries. Accordingly, the rules governing procedure at trial are modeled on a jury trial.

Continuous event

The foundational rule is that the trial of issues of fact is a single continuous event. All the evidence on all disputed issues is received day after day and, if necessary, week after week, month after month. No matter how long it can be expected to last, the trial ordinarily is not segmented according to various issues, such as the defendant's fault and the extent of the plaintiff's injuries. This rule responds to the fact that a jury is a set of nonprofessional adjudicators conscripted from the general population for the specific trial.[1] Since this temporary "team" has to be kept together until the game is finished, the game has to be kept going without interruption.

Sometimes, judges exercise their power to bifurcate a trial, typically by trying liability separately from damages.[2] If the evidence relating to these two issues does not overlap, this can save time, because if the defendant prevails in the first part of the trial the second will be unnecessary. In one way, it tends to produce results more favorable to

6. *See generally* Steele, Jr., and Thornburg, Jury Instructions: A Persistent Failure to Communicate, 67 N.C.L. Rev. 77 (1988); Weinstein, The Power and Duty of Federal Judges to Marshall and Comment on the Evidence in Jury Trials and Some Suggestions on Charging Juries, 118 F.R.D. 161 (1988); § 7.22 *infra*. *See also* Slayton v. Wright, 271 Cal.App.2d 219, 76 Cal.Rptr. 494 (1969).

§ 7.3

1. *See* § 8.14 *infra*.

2. Fed. R. Civ. P. 42(b); In re Beverly Hills Fire Litig., 695 F.2d 207 (6th Cir. 1982).

defendants: a jury hearing evidence about liability but not learning about any resulting damages is more likely to find against the plaintiff.[3] In any event, each of the two possible trials occurring with this approach is itself a single continuous event.

Procedural systems that do not use juries are free from this practical constraint. In American administrative adjudication proceedings such as public utility rate hearings, receipt of evidence is noncontinuous—one day this week, two days next week, and so on—and can be segmented according to the issues involved, the convenience of the witnesses, and other practical considerations. The same is true in the civil law system that prevails in Europe and most of the rest of the world, where fact issues are usually tried to judges.[4] The same scheduling flexibility is employed in arbitration and in courts where juries are not used, such as in probate and bankruptcy courts. Traditionally, however, trials to a judge in trial courts of general jurisdiction are continuous, patterned on the jury trial.

Effects of continuous trial

The requirement of continuous hearing imposes severe strains on the trial process. All the participants have to remain as attentive as possible and be in good health. Faltering attention by jurors, judges, lawyers, and witnesses is inevitable, however, in a long trial. So is the risk of mistrial if jurors, judge, or lawyers fall ill. Furthermore, in a continuous trial maintaining strict continuity in receiving evidence is impossible when evidence directly relevant to one issue also is suggestive as to another issue. For example, evidence that the defendant was driving a Mercedes is relevant in describing an automobile accident but also suggests that defendant has plenty of money, which can affect the determination of damages. The requirement of continuous trial also has a feedback effect on trial preparation. Since evidence on all issues will have to be presented if a case goes to trial, discovery and other preparation has to be completed prior to it. In contrast, when trial is segmented into issues going to defendant's liability, with damages considered only after liability is established, then discovery may be correspondingly segmented. The requirement of total preparation inevitably results in unproductive trial and pretrial expense in cases in which resolution of one issue renders other issues moot.

Assignment of judges

When trial is to be held, the first step is the selection of the judge. In the semirural county of yesteryear, this was no problem as there was

3. Zeisel & Callahan, Split Trials and Time Saving: A Statistical Analysis, 76 Harv. L. Rev. 1606 (1963). But see Landsman, *et al.*, Be Careful What You Wish For: The Paradoxical Effects of Bifurcation Claims for Punitive Damages, 1998 Wis. L. Rev. 297 (bifurcation reduces liability findings, but increases damage awards).

4. See, *e.g.*, Kaplan, *et al.*, Phases of German Civil Procedure, 71 Harv. L. Rev. 1193, 1443 (1958).

usually only one judge. Today most trial courts, state and federal, have a number of judges; in large metropolitan centers there are dozens and in Los Angeles County hundreds. Trial courts with multiple judges have assignment rules by which judicial responsibilities are allocated.

Two "calendaring" systems, as they are called, are generally used: the individual calendar and the master calendar. In the individual calendar system, a case, on being filed, is assigned to one judge for all proceedings, including pretrial motions, discovery, and trial. In this system the judge to whom the case is assigned will preside at its trial unless special circumstances require otherwise. The individual calendar is used in most federal courts and in some state courts. It makes it possible for court administrators to check how each judge handles his or her caseload.

In the master calendar system, cases are separated into the pretrial stage and the trial stage. Pretrial, matters such as motions based on the pleadings and disputes over discovery, are heard by a judge holding the pretrial calendar. Other judges handle trials. Cases that do not settle and therefore go to trial are given to these judges. This system may favor efficient handling of large numbers of pretrial motions, but it may also require educating several different judges about the case, and encourages parties to maneuver the timing of motions and trials in order to obtain a favorable judge.

Jury selection

When trial is before a jury, the next step is the selection of the jury. This procedure is considered in detail elsewhere.[5] Suffice to say here that the procedure involves drawing a set of jurors from a list of names, describing to them in general terms what the case is about, interrogating them to find out whether they have knowledge or an opinion about the case, and exercising exclusionary challenges. The jury is then impanelled, that is, officially designated as the jury.

Opening statements

The forum thus constituted, the lawyers for the parties may make opening statements. The party having the affirmative burden of proof is ordinarily entitled to open and close the case, that is, to make the first and last statements to the trier of fact. Sometimes this right may belong to the defendant when, for instance, he or she has admitted the allegations of the petition and pleaded an affirmative defense, counterclaim, or set-off.[6] In a long or complex trial, the right to make a first and last impression on the jury can be important.[7]

5. *See* § 8.14 *infra.*

6. Standridge v. Standridge, 224 Ga. 102, 160 S.E.2d 377 (1968).

7. *See generally* Thibaut & Walker, Procedural Justice: A Psychological Analysis ch. 7 (1975); Lawson, Order of Presentation as a Factor in Jury Persuasion, 56 Ky. L.J. 523 (1968); Wrightsman, The Place of Pri-

The opening statement describes the case and the facts that the party expects to prove.[8] A plaintiff's lawyer will make statements such as: "The evidence will show that the plaintiff in this case was in good health prior to the accident.... The evidence will further show that the defendant operated her car at high speed and lost control as she approached the intersection.... The investigating officer will testify that defendant's car left skid marks more than thirty feet long." A defense opening statement is a counterpart narrative of the evidence defendant expects to offer. Defendant usually has the choice of making its opening statement immediately after that of the plaintiff or reserving it until after all of plaintiff's evidence has been presented. In a multiparty case, each party has a right to make an opening statement. While the length of opening statements may be limited by the court, it is shaped by the speaker's aims of being sufficiently detailed but not boring. An opening statement is not supposed to be "argumentative."[9] This means that the statement may not be cast in overtly exhortative terms. Skillfully done, a party's opening statement is an arresting narrative that gives the trier of fact a clear picture of the case and a disposition to be persuaded by that party's evidence.

A full opening statement is a practical necessity for a plaintiff in a jury case. The plaintiff generally bears the burden of persuasion and will lose the case if the jury cannot reach a conclusion in plaintiff's favor. The risk that the jury will be unimpressed or confused can be overcome by a clear opening statement. A concise opening statement is also usually helpful in a case tried to a judge without a jury, although it may be foregone where the judge has handled the pretrial stage of the case and therefore is familiar with the issues. Defendant usually makes its opening statement after the plaintiff. Defendant's option to postpone its opening statement usually will be exercised only when defense counsel hopes to achieve the advantage of surprise.

Plaintiff's case in chief

Following the parties' opening statements, the plaintiff presents its evidence. The sequence of proof is arranged by plaintiff's counsel with the aim of being clear, logical, and persuasive. This orchestration is constrained, however, by certain ground rules and practical considerations. The primary ground rule is that all testimony from a witness ordinarily must be elicited in one stint on the stand. This rule holds even if the witness is to give testimony on different subjects and even if later witnesses give testimony that could be illuminated by bringing back the

macy in Persuading Jurors: Timing of Judges' Instructions and Impact of Opening Statements, 8 U. Bridgeport L. Rev. 431 (1987).

8. *See generally* Becton and Stein, The Opening Statement, 20 Trial Law. Q. 10 (1990); Snedaker, Storytelling in Opening Statements: Framing the Argumentation of the Trial, 10 Am. J. Trial Advoc. 15 (1986).

9. *See generally* Becton and Stein, The Opening Statement, 20 Trial Law. Q. 10 (1990).

earlier witnesses. A parallel ground rule is that all of plaintiff's evidence must be presented before any of that from the defendant. Another ground rule covers direct examination and cross-examination. Direct examination elicits the witness's testimony through questioning by the counsel for the party presenting the witness. When direct examination is concluded the opposing party has opportunity to cross-examine. All direct testimony must be completed before the witness is turned over to cross-examination, even if more than one subject matter is covered by the witness. When the case has multiple parties, each party is entitled to cross-examine, including witnesses called by a co-party.[10]

A practical constraint in presenting evidence is that the personal schedules of the witnesses have to be taken into account. Hence, testimony often is presented at the point in the trial when the witness is available, regardless whether it logically fits there. This factor, along with the ground rules described above, means that the sequence of the evidence may be very incoherent. Hence, there is both inevitable risk of confusion, especially in a complicated case presented to a jury, and a high premium on the lawyers' explanatory skills.

The plaintiff's evidence as a whole is called plaintiff's case in chief. Plaintiff signifies that its case in chief is complete by stating that plaintiff rests.

Defendant's case in chief

Defendant then has its inning, presenting evidence subject to the same ground rules and constraints. After defendant rests its case in chief, plaintiff may offer rebuttal evidence. Rebuttal is limited to matters newly raised in the defendant's case; plaintiff may not reiterate or reinforce evidence concerning matters in its case in chief.[11] The same principles apply to all parties in a multiparty case.

Closing argument

When all parties have rested, they have opportunity for summations, or "closing arguments" as they are otherwise called. In these arguments counsel seek to persuade the trier of fact that the evidence sustains their respective positions. Wide but not unrestricted rhetorical latitude is permitted. Generally, however, argument is most effective when it highlights evidence that itself was dramatic or very favorable. The art of framing arguments that will persuade a tribunal goes back to antiquity.[12] It requires the advocate to organize the evidence into a story that is both plausible and favorable to the client.[13] The law and the legal profession

10. Fed. R. Ev. 611; Strong, *et al.*, McCormick on Evidence §§ 5–32 (5th ed. 1999).

11. *See id.* § 5.

12. *E.g.*, Quintilian, Institutio Oratoria (Butler transl. 1922).

13. *E.g.*, Bennett & Feldman, Reconstructing Reality in the Courtroom (1981); Burns, A Theory of the Trial (1999); Amsterdam & Bruner, Minding the Law (2000); Feigenson, The Rhetoric of Torts: How Advocates Help Jurors Think About

have developed ethical limitations on permissible advocacy, such as the prohibition against a lawyer's expressing his or her personal view of the merits of the case, appealing to racial prejudice, or relying on factual material that has not been admitted into evidence.[14]

§ 7.4 Recusal of Judge

As described above, each trial court has rules by which judges are assigned to cases. If a judge has a relationship to the parties or to the underlying transaction, he or she should be disqualified from presiding. Disqualification, or "recusal" as it is also called, can be through the judge's own initiative or, if the judge fails to act, on a party's motion. A judge should not, however, be recused on mere surmise. A judge has a "duty to serve" that inhibits him or her from withdrawing except when legal rules require or permit.[1] The basic problems, then, are defining the grounds of recusal and prescribing the procedure by which they can be invoked.

Constitutional standard

Statutes, rules of court, and constitutional law require the judge to be impartial. These requirements apply whatever decisional responsibility the judge may have, whether presiding at a jury trial, ruling on motions, or as trier of fact. The basic rule today is that a judge may not act in a matter in which the judge's "impartiality might reasonably be questioned."[2] As a general principle this has always been the rule. It remains necessary, nonetheless, to define what circumstances "reasonably" impugn a judge's impartiality and to devise procedures that give effect to this principle without unduly harassing the judges or enabling the parties easily to disqualify a judge they dislike.[3]

The common law made it very difficult to disqualify a judge, because it was thought that challenges to judicial impartiality would undermine public respect for the legal system. Although the law required disqualification when a judge had a personal interest in a case, for example because a relative was a party, disqualification for bias was rare.[4] Starting during the nineteenth century, and usually in response to

Causation, Reasonableness, and Responsibility, 47 Hastings L.J. 61 (1995).

14. *E.g.*, ABA Model Rules of Professional Conduct, rules 3.3–.5, 4.4, 8.4 (1983); Cairns, Advocacy and the Making of the Adversarial Criminal Trial 1800–1865 (1998); Note, Restraining Adversarial Excess in Closing Argument, 96 Colum. L. Rev. 1299 (1996); see Weddington v. State, 545 A.2d 607 (Del.1988).

§ 7.4

1. *See generally* Flamm, Judicial Disqualification (1996); Leubsdorf, Theories of Judging and Judge Disqualification, 62 N.Y.U. L. Rev. (1987).

2. 28 U.S.C. § 455. *See also* 28 U.S.C. § 144.

3. *See* Stempel, Rehnquist, Recusal and Reform, 53 Brooklyn L. Rev. 589 (1987); Panel Discussion, Disqualification of Judges (The Sarokin Matter): Is It a Threat to Judicial Independence?, 58 Brooklyn L. Rev. 1063 (1993).

4. 3 Blackstone, Commentaries *361–64.

judicial scandals and controversies, legislatures and judges have imposed stronger disqualification requirements. As a matter of Due Process under the Fourteenth Amendment, the Supreme Court in 1927 held in *Tumey v. Ohio* that it was improper for judges to be compensated by giving them an interest in the outcome of the matters coming before them.[5] In that case, a traffic court judge was paid a share of fines he imposed. The Due Process standard was extended in *Aetna Life Insurance Co. v. Lavoie,*[6] which held it improper for an appellate judge to participate in a case presenting the same legal issue that was involved in trial court litigation in which the judge was a party. This standard requires an objectively provable relationship of the judge to the case before him or her from which bias may be directly inferred.

Statutes and rules

In most jurisdictions, statutes or rules of court impose more exacting requirements governing recusal.[7] The Code of Judicial Conduct, adopted in most states and the pattern for the present federal recusal statute, has a two-level structure. It defines various family and financial relationships between the judge and the parties or the subject matter of the litigation that require the judge to withdraw. For example, recusal is required when the judge or a close relative owns stock in a party, or the judge has personal knowledge of disputed evidentiary facts, or the judge's former law firm was involved in the case while the judge was with the firm.[8]

The Code also has more general and subjective standards. Canon 3E of the Code provides:

> A judge shall disqualify himself or herself in a proceeding in which the judge's impartiality might reasonably be questioned, including but not limited to instances where:
>
> (a) the judge has a personal bias or prejudice concerning a party.[9]

Title 28 U.S.C. § 455 requires judges to disqualify themselves for the above reasons using nearly identical words.[10]

In *Liljeberg v. Health Services Acquisition Corp.*[11] the "impartiality might reasonably be questioned" standard was held violated by a judge who presided in a contract litigation between two parties while at the

5. 273 U.S. 510, 47 S.Ct. 437, 71 L.Ed. 749 (1927).

6. 475 U.S. 813, 106 S.Ct. 1580, 89 L.Ed.2d 823 (1986).

7. *See generally* Shaman, Lubet, and Alfini, Judicial Conduct and Ethics (2d ed. 1995).

8. ABA Code of Judicial Conduct, canon 3(E) (1990 ed.). *See also* Bloom, Judicial Bias and Financial Interest as Grounds for Disqualification of Federal Judges, 35 Case W. Res. L. Rev. 662 (1985).

9. ABA Code of Judicial Conduct, canon 3(E) (1990 ed.).

10. 28 U.S.C. § 455(a),(b)(1). *See also* Matter of Johnson, 921 F.2d 585, 587 (5th Cir.1991).

11. 486 U.S. 847, 108 S.Ct. 2194, 100 L.Ed.2d 855 (1988).

same time being a trustee of a charitable corporation that would have gained from the outcome of the case. The judge claimed, and another judge believed, that he read the papers telling him of the corporation's interest only after deciding the case. The Supreme Court, however, concluded that outsiders not knowing of this might reasonably question his impartiality. (This illustrates how a court may rely on the appearance of justice standard to reduce embarrassment of disqualified judges.) Moreover, the Court held that the verdict could be set aside by motion even after judgment when the judge failed to disclose the problem as soon as he discovered it.

Limits to disqualification

The prevailing standards for recusal do not go as far as many litigants and lawyers think they should. It is not a ground for recusal that a party has a firm belief that a judge is prejudiced against the party personally or is adversely predisposed in the type of case involved. The belief must be based on more than mere conjecture.[12] Getting beyond conjecture to proof may be difficult—the judge, for example, is not subject to discovery—although to some extent the court must accept facts specifically shown by the challenger's affidavits.[13] Usually, the same judge being challenged passes on the challenge with only limited possibilities of immediate appellate review.[14]

Disqualification may not be based on a judge's rulings during a trial, and even opinions based on evidence or events during a past trial involving the same party, unless they show such a commitment to or against a party as would make fair judgment impossible.[15] That is said to be so because forming opinions and making rulings is part of a judge's job. Nor is it a ground for recusal that the judge has exhibited hostility toward the lawyer in other matters.[16] Such sentiments on the judge's part, if they in fact exist, deeply undercut confidence in impartiality. Yet allowing recusal on the basis of the judge's mindset would often reduce to a swearing contest, and it is thought to be too disconcerting to both the judiciary and the parties. Hence, the principle of disinterestedness is mainly symbolic but essential. Most judges, whatever their frailties, take it very seriously.

12. Toth v. Trans World Airlines, 862 F.2d 1381 (9th Cir.1988); Giles v. Garwood, 853 F.2d 876 (11th Cir.1988).

13. See Berger v. United States, 255 U.S. 22, 41 S.Ct. 230, 65 L.Ed. 481 (1921).

14. Redish & Marshall, Adjudicatory Independence and the Values of Procedural Due Process, 95 Yale L.J. 455 (1986); Abramson, Deciding Recusal Motions: Who Judges the Judges?, 28 Val. U.L. Rev. 543 (1994); Note, Judicial Disqualification in the Federal Courts: A Proposal to Conform Statutory Provisions to Underlying Policies, 67 Iowa L. Rev. 525, 540–44 (1982).

15. Liteky v. United States, 510 U.S. 540, 114 S.Ct. 1147, 127 L.Ed.2d 474 (1994).

16. Herrington v. Sonoma County, 834 F.2d 1488 (9th Cir.1987); Matter of Yagman, 796 F.2d 1165 (9th Cir.1986). The 1990 amendments to the Code add bias against a lawyer to the grounds for recusal, but the federal statute contains no such provision.

Peremptory challenge

To avoid the frustrations of proving bias, a number of states give a party the right to peremptorily disqualify a judge. The right, however, may be exercised only once in a case; any subsequently assigned judge may be disqualified only for cause.[17] In the absence of such grounds for disqualification, the judge that hears the case is the judge that the calendaring system assigns.

Other safeguards

Fortunately, there are other safeguards for judicial impartiality. The traditions and ideals of judging encourage judges to strive to play no favorites. The adversary system exposes judges to arguments on both sides, and the possibility of appeals and of professional and public criticism reinforce the requirements of the law. Unlike judges in most European systems, who pursue lifetime judicial careers in which political activities are forbidden, judges in the United States typically come to the bench after careers in which they have dabbled in politics or specialized in representing clients with similar interests. Most states elect judges, in increasingly expensive and partisan campaigns, but the Code of Judicial Conduct prohibits sitting judges from engaging in many biasing extrajudicial activities.[18] In recent decades, the judicial corps has become somewhat more representative of the general population in terms of race and gender than it once was, although (except in justice of the peace courts and the like) judges are still overwhelmingly legally trained and middle or upper class. Federal judges are assured by the Constitution of lifetime tenure "during good Behavior" but, in extreme cases, they may be criminally prosecuted, disciplined by other judges, or impeached.[19]

§ 7.5 Standard of Proof

A trial involves presentations of evidence by the parties and argument as to the significance of the evidence in terms of the legal premises involved in the case.[1] The question, then, is this: What strength of conclusion is required on the part of the trier of fact? This is called the *standard of proof.*

17. *See* Cal. Civ. Proc. Code § 170.6. *See also* Baron, A Proposal for the Use of a Judicial Peremptory Challenge System in Texas, 40 Baylor L. Rev. 49 (1988); Lewis, Systemic Due Process, Procedural Concepts and the Problem of Recusal, 38 U. Kan. L. Rev. 381 (1990); Malarkey, Judicial Disqualification: Is Sexual Orientation a Cause in California?, 41 Hastings L.J. 695 (1990).

18. ABA Code of Judicial Conduct, canon 4 (1990 ed.); Shaman, Lubet, and Alfini, Judicial Conduct and Ethics (2d ed. 1995).

19. U.S. Const. art. III, § 1; 28 U.S.C. § 372; see Symposium, Judicial Election, Selection and Accountability, 61 S. Cal. L. Rev. 1555 (1988); Symposium, Judicial Discipline and Impeachment, 76 Ky. L.J. 633 (1988).

§ 7.5

1. *See* §§ 7.7–7.19 *infra.*

Civil and criminal standards

Ordinarily the standard of proof in civil litigation is proof by a preponderance of evidence. This is in contrast to the standard of proof in criminal cases, which as a matter of constitutional law must be proof beyond a reasonable doubt.[2] Certain issues in civil litigation such as fraud, however, must be proved by "clear and convincing evidence."[3] Thus, there are three generally recognized standards of proof, in ascending order of weight: preponderance, clear and convincing, and beyond a reasonable doubt.[4] The differences in verbal formulation are played out chiefly in jury instructions. A jury trial requires that the jurors, who are new to the task, be given a recitation on the subject. Thus, in a civil case, the judge will say something like:

> A preponderance means the greater part of the evidence you find worthy to be believed. That does not mean the greater number of witnesses.... The phrase refers to the quality of the evidence, the weight and effect that it has on your minds. If the evidence weighs so evenly that you are unable to say that there is a preponderance on either side, then you must resolve the issue against the party having the burden of proof.[5]

When the judge is trier of fact, the judge is required to apply the appropriate standard in the same fashion. A judge is, however, presumed to know the applicable formula. The same holds for the counterpart formulas for "clear and convincing" evidence and evidence "beyond a reasonable doubt." Nevertheless, these terms evidently have different significance to different judges. *United States v. Fatico*[6] set forth results of an informal poll among trial judges in which they indicated their conceptions of the various burdens of proof. "Preponderance" was thought by all the judges to mean a probability greater than 50 percent; "clear and convincing" was thought by some judges to mean a probability of 60 percent and by others a probability up to 75 percent; and "beyond a reasonable doubt" was thought by one judge to mean a probability of 76 percent and by others to be from 85 percent to 95 percent. Similar variance appears among jurors. The fact that the meaning of the standards is somewhat indeterminate, however, should not obscure the fact that they convey distinct impressions to those who apply them.[7]

2. In re Winship, 397 U.S. 358, 90 S.Ct. 1068, 25 L.Ed.2d 368 (1970). *See also* Francis v. Franklin, 471 U.S. 307, 105 S.Ct. 1965, 85 L.Ed.2d 344 (1985).

3. *See* § 7.14 *infra.*

4. *See generally* Clermont, Procedure's Magical Number Three: Psychological Bases for Standards of Decision, 72 Cornell L. Rev. 115 (1987); § 7.14 *infra.*

5. *Cf.* New York Pattern Jury Instructions 1:23 (2d ed. 1974).

6. 458 F.Supp. 388 (E.D.N.Y.1978), *aff'd,* 603 F.2d 1053 (2d Cir.1979).

7. Often, multiple elements such as causation and fault comprise the burden of proof. On the problem of conjunction, see Nesson, The Evidence or the Event? On Judicial Proof and the Acceptability of Verdicts, 98 Harv. L. Rev. 1357 (1985); Cohen, The Probable and the Provable (1977). The problem of burden of proof is further considered in §§ 7.14 and 7.15 *infra.*

§ 7.6 Trial to Judge Without Jury

It is within the preceding procedural and analytic framework that a trial proceeds. A trial to a judge sitting without a jury is procedurally simple. The judge and the lawyers know their accustomed roles as arbiter and advocates, respectively. The lawyers make opening statements, call their witnesses, introduce their documentary and expert testimony, and argue the evidence. Argument may be oral or in writing, or both, according to the lawyers' requests and the judge's preference. In complex cases the parties may have been asked at the beginning of trial to submit trial briefs, outlining in detail the evidence to be presented and its significance under the governing law. The exclusionary rules of evidence, such as the rule excluding inadmissible hearsay evidence, are applied but generally in a more relaxed fashion than in jury trials. The advocates' task is to be persuasive in ordinary and practical terms. The judge's task is to resolve the conflicts in the evidence and to draw the inferences necessary to reach a conclusion. Following the parties' submissions the judge either rules from the bench or, more commonly, takes the case under advisement for later decision.

Written findings and conclusions

On rendering a decision the judge also directs entry of judgment accordingly.[1] Under the Federal Rules and in many states, the judge is required to make findings of fact and conclusions of law.[2] Many judges expect or require counsel for the prevailing party to prepare the findings and conclusions. Of course, their formulation is unlikely to reflect the judge's nuances of thought; to the contrary, counsel's proposed findings and conclusions usually are cast in starkly partisan and nonreversible terms. Appellate courts complain of the practice but are powerless to correct it.[3]

The judge's findings of fact are not reversible on appeal unless "clearly erroneous," with due regard given to the trial judge's opportunity to view the evidence firsthand.[4] This deference to the trial judge's factual determinations applies to the judge's interpretation of documents as well.[5]

§ 7.6

1. Fed R. Civ. P. 58.

2. *Id.* 52(a). *See, e.g.,* Cal. Civ. Proc. Code § 632. *See also* Zuckerman, Law, Fact or Justice? 66 B.U.L. Rev. 487 (1986); Leubsdorf, Constitutional Civil Procedure, 63 Tex. L. Rev. 579, 630 (1984)(proposing a constitutional right to findings of fact).

3. *See, e.g.,* Monroe County Conservation Council v. Adams, 566 F.2d 419, 425 n. 7 (2d Cir.1977) (findings proposed by counsel for the prevailing party adopted by the judge without retyping on the day following argument on a voluminous record that the judge concededly had not read).

4. Fed. R. Civ. P. 52(a).

5. Anderson v. City of Bessemer, 470 U.S. 564, 105 S.Ct. 1504, 84 L.Ed.2d 518 (1985). *See also* § 12.9 *infra*.

B. BASIC CONCEPTS OF JURY TRIAL PROCEDURE

§ 7.7 Introducing the Jury

The United States is now almost alone in entrusting the decision of civil cases to a group of citizens chosen more or less at random from the community. The jury originated in England, but today neither England nor any of the legal systems it spawned uses the jury to any considerable extent in civil cases except for the United States and to some extent Canada. After the French Revolution, some European nations imported the jury because of its relationship to freedom and democracy, but the civil jury did not endure in these nations, although some of them use lay judges who decide cases in conjunction with a professional judge.[1] Here, however, about two-thirds of the roughly six thousand civil trials that take place in the federal courts each year are before juries, as are many trials in state courts.[2]

The influence of the jury extends far beyond the fact that juries rather than judges decide a certain number of cases. The vast preponderance of civil cases settle before trial, but these settlements reflect evaluations by lawyers and parties of how cases will be decided if tried, and in many instances those evaluations necessarily take account of jury trial. Features of our procedural system such as the continuous trial and the limited scope of review on appeal stem in large part from the use of jury trial. So do the many institutions designed to channel and control the jury's power: summary judgment and directed verdicts to keep cases from going to juries, rules of evidence and jury instructions to shape the jury's appraisal of facts and law, new trials to redress jury mistakes and misconduct. In significant part, the history of our civil procedure is the history of the efforts of judges and others to rein in juries without abolishing them.

Ambivalence about juries

The ambivalent attitudes to the civil jury that United States institutions and history reflect continue to struggle today. For some, juries bring diversity of background and knowledge, common sense, and human sympathy to a system otherwise dominated by legalism, chicanery, and political influence. For others, juries undermine consistent, impartial and intelligent application of the law because of their inexperience and incapacity and their susceptibility to emotion and rhetoric.[3] Feminists will note that both admirers and critics of the jury seem to be ascribing stereotyped "feminine" characteristics to it and stereotyped

§ 7.7

1. Dawson, A History of Lay Judges (1960); The Trial Jury in England, France, Germany, 1700–1900 (Schioppa ed. 1987); Symposium, The Common Law Jury, 62 L. & Cont. Probs. 1(1999).

2. Administrative Office of the U.S. Courts, Statistical Tables for the Federal Judiciary December 31, 1999, at 36 (2000).

3. Dooley, Our Juries, Our Selves: The Power, Perception, and Politics of the Civil Jury, 80 Cornell L. Rev. 325 (1995).

"masculine" characteristics to judges,[4] and will relate this to a broader tendency to see litigation as a "masculine" process governed by "reason" from which "feminine" attributes such as "emotion" must be excluded.[5]

Empirical studies tend to rebut the views of both admirers and detractors: whatever the virtues or failings of jurors, the results they reach are remarkably similar to those reached by judges. Indeed, contrary to received opinion, judges may be more sympathetic to plaintiffs than jurors.[6] Jurors are less likely to be influenced by their race, gender or education than by the evidence and by their general views of liability, litigation, businesses and the like.[7] So perhaps some judges and lawyers have been projecting their own characteristics onto jurors.

Jury's political role

What got the civil jury into the Bill of Rights was not its characteristics as an adjudicator but its political role as a representative of the citizenry standing between the government and fellow citizens. That is also what continues to maintain the central role of juries in criminal procedure, not just in the United States but in a number of other nations as well. Admittedly, in its origins the jury was less a democratic institution than a way in which the Norman Kings could conscript local elites to help enforce the law. Even in Colonial times, jury service was restricted to white males owning property. Nevertheless, juries were more democratic institutions than the colonial executive and judiciary. In some colonies, they played a central role in the governmental system because virtually every governmental measure was either enforced through a jury or could be brought before one by means of an action for damages. Until well into the nineteenth century, moreover, it was

4. *E.g.*, Thornburg, Metaphors Matter: How Images of Battle, Sports, and Sex Shape the Adversary System, 10 Wis. Women's L.J. 225 (1995); Grossberg, Institutionalizing Masculinity: The Law as a Masculine Profession, in Meanings for Manhood: Constructions of Masculinity in Victorian America 133 (Carnes & Griffen ed. 1990); Symposium, Feminist Jurisprudence and Procedure, 61 U. Cin. L. Rev. 1139 (1993).

5. *See, e.g.,* Verdict: Assessing the Civil Jury System (Litan ed. 1993); Adler, The Jury (1994); Symposium, The American Civil Trial Jury: Illusion and Reality, 48 De Paul L. Rev. 197 (1998).

6. Clermont & Eisenberg, Trial by Jury or Judge: Transcending Empiricism, 77 Cornell L. Rev. 1124 (1992)(higher win rates for product liability and medical malpractice plaintiffs in judge than in jury trials, although this may reflect litigant choices of trier); Hans, The Illusions and Realities of Jurors' Treatment of Corporate Defendants, 48 De Paul L. Rev. 327 (1998); Wissler, *et al.*, Decisionmaking About General Damages: A Comparison of Jurors, Judges, and Lawyers, 98 Mich. L. Rev. 547 (1999); *see* Vidmar & Rice, Assessment of Noneconomic Damage Awards in Medical Negligence: A Comparison of Jurors with Legal Professionals, 78 Iowa L. Rev. 883 (1993)(jurors and arbitrators make similar awards). *But see* Viscusi, Jurors, Judges, and the Mistreatment of Risk by the Courts, 30 J. Leg. Stud. 107 (2001).

7. Diamond, *et al.*, Juror Judgments About Liability and Damages: Sources of Variability and Ways to Increase Consistency, 48 De Paul L. Rev. 301 (1998); Saks, What Do Jury Experiments Tell Us About How Juries (Should) Make Decisions?, 6 S. Cal. Interdisc. L.J. 1 (1997). See generally Vidmar, The Performance of the American Civil Jury: An Empirical Perspective, 40 Ariz. L. Rev. 849 (1998).

accepted that juries could determine the law as well as the facts, further extending their power.[8]

Because of this history, the omission of a right to jury trial in civil cases from the Constitution led to protests, and to its inclusion in the Seventh Amendment.[9] The Supreme Court has held that guaranty not binding on the states, which are therefore free to deviate from federal jury precedents. They have, however, adopted constitutional and statutory provisions recognizing the right to jury trial in some form.[10]

Helping juries

Granted the existence of civil juries, civil procedure should seek to help them perform their functions. The jury consists of people untrained in law generally, untutored in the applicable substantive law, often unacquainted with the type of transaction involved in the litigation, and unfamiliar with court procedure (except for impressions, many of them misleading, gleaned from the movies and television). Jurors have primary responsibility in the case immediately before them but no responsibility for administration of the law in general. They bring to their task a variety of experience and knowledge as well as competence in the ordinary citizen's common sense and concept of justice. The task for the rules governing jury trial is to bring this competence to bear in a way that adequately takes account of the jurors' amateur status and temporary service with the system of justice.[11]

From this perspective, much could be done to improve the performance of the jury system. Jurors could be allowed to take written notes and propose questions for the judge to ask witnesses, practices to which courts have granted only gingerly approval.[12] Jury instructions could be simplified, presented before jurors hear the evidence rather than just afterward, and given to the jurors in writing.[13] Allowing juries to take videotapes of the trial into their deliberations may be a further step. After all, even highly qualified jurors cannot reasonably be expected to apply accurately highly condensed and abstract legal instructions to their

8. Nelson, Americanization of the Common Law: The Impact of Legal Change on Massachusetts Society, 1760–1830 (1975); Landsman, The Civil Jury in America: Scenes From an Unappreciated History, 44 Hastings L.J. 579 (1993); Harrington, The Law–Finding Function of the American Jury, 1999 Wis. L. Rev. 377.

9. Wolfram, The Constitutional History of the Seventh Amendment, 57 Minn. L. Rev. 639 (1973).

10. Walker v. Sauvinet, 92 U.S. 90, 23 L.Ed. 678 (1876); Blume, American Civil Procedure 370 (1955).

11. *See* Hans and Vidmar, Judging the Jury (1986); Stephens, Controlling the Civil Jury: Towards a Functional Model of Justification, 76 Ky. L.J. 81 (1988).

12. *E.g.*, United States v. Richardson, 233 F.3d 1285 (11th Cir.2000); United States v. Hernandez, 176 F.3d 719 (3d Cir. 1999); People v. Hues, 92 N.Y.2d 413, 681 N.Y.S.2d 779, 704 N.E.2d 546 (1998).

13. See generally Cecil, *et al.*, Citizen Comprehension of Difficult Issues: Lessons From Civil Jury Trials, 40 Am. U. L. Rev. 727 (1991); Jury Reform: Making Juries Work Symposium, 32 U. Mich. J.L. Ref. 213 (1999); Steele & Thornburg, Jury Instructions: A Persistent Failure to Communicate, 67 N.C.L. Rev. 77 (1988).

memories of large quantities of evidence that they heard before learning just what they are to decide.

§ 7.8 Historical Development of the Jury: From Witnesses to Arbiters of Fact

Jurors originally were "chosen as being likely to be already informed" concerning the matters to be tried and were therefore drawn from the neighborhood where the disputed transaction occurred.[1] They were considered witnesses who judged facts within their knowledge but were also authorized to rely on what they had heard from other sources.[2] They could be shown charters and other writings as evidence.[3] Witnesses in the modern sense apparently were not much used before the sixteenth century.[4]

Passive jury

From the beginning, however, parties played an important part in preparing and presenting to the jury relevant data on which to decide the case. Increasingly, the jury took on the function of judging issues of fact on the basis of evidence presented to it. The last vestiges of the older notion of juries as witnesses did not disappear until 1826, but the newer notion had long since come to dominate.[5] Moreover, in eighteenth century England legal counsel were increasingly involved in criminal cases, to the point where they came to control the presentation of facts.[6] A parallel development apparently took place at an earlier stage in civil litigation, in which lawyers had long participated.[7]

As juries lost the power to draw on their own knowledge, they became increasingly dependent on information presented to them at trial. The judges might have assumed all or some of the task of insuring that such material was made available, as they do on the Continent. But English and American judges shunned this responsibility.[8] As a result, almost the entire burden of informing the jury—putting before them the evidence needed for their decision—fell on the parties and their respective counsel.

§ 7.8

1. Thayer, A Preliminary Treatise on Evidence at the Common Law 90–94 (1898) [hereinafter cited as Thayer, Evidence]. *See also* Dawson, A History of Lay Judges (1960).

2. Morgan, Some Problems of Proof Under the Anglo–American System of Litigation 17 (1956).

3. *Id.* at 18; Thayer, Evidence 104–112.

4. 1 Holdsworth, A History of English Law 335 (7th ed. 1956); Thayer, Evidence 122–132, 137.

5. 1 Holdsworth, A History of English Law 332 (7th ed. 1956).

6. Langbein, The Criminal Trial Before the Lawyers, 45 U. Chi. L. Rev. 263 (1978).

7. Yeazell, The New Jury and the Ancient Jury Conflict, 1990 U. Chi. Legal F. 87.

8. 9 Wigmore, Evidence §§ 2483, 2484 (Chadbourn rev. 1981).

Issues of fact and law

In the early history of jury trial, little distinction was made between law and fact. The charge to the jury called for resolution of conclusory questions such as these: "Was a party in possession of something? Did he disseise somebody? . . . What was the . . . custom, of such a place? Was a person legitimate . . . [was he] insane?" These questions often called for "elements of opinion and of law, compounded with those simpler features which catch the eye and ear; questions of 'fact' as we say."[9]

Broadly speaking, the nominal range of the jury's function has not changed very much during the past three or four centuries. Thus, in the typical negligence case the jury is called on to respond to such a conclusory question as this: "Did the defendant use reasonable care in the course of action leading up to the collision?" This is the central point of such a case even though it is embedded in elaborate accompanying instructions. In a typical contract case the key question, again embedded in elaborations, is usually whether the defendant substantially performed or was excused from performing. The basic rule is that the jury decides questions of "fact" and makes application of general legal rules to specific fact situations—what is "due care" in carrying out an activity that resulted in injury to another, for example.

Nevertheless, at various times in the history of the common law, the boundary between "legal issues" (which the judge decides) and "factual issues" (which the jury decides) has been drawn at different places[10] and in different legal contexts. Thus, whether in a breach of contract "remote" losses could be attributable to the breaching party was at one time a decision for the jury as a matter of fact but later was held to be a decision for the court as a matter of law.[11] The scope of jury decision over what constitutes negligence also was, in the late nineteenth century, defined differently from the way it is now.[12] In the latter part of this century the jury's authority to determine the issue of "malice" in defamation cases has similarly been reduced.[13]

The courts draw the boundary between fact and law to determine whether on the evidence an issue of fact exists for the jury to decide. In the earlier common law, the line was drawn partly in contemplation of the rule that a jury returning a "false" verdict could be punished much

9. Thayer, Evidence 184. *See also* Arnold, Law and Fact in the Medieval Jury Trial: Out of Sight, Out of Mind, 18 Am. J. Legal Hist. 267 (1974).

10. *See* Note, The Changing Role of the Jury in the Nineteenth Century, 74 Yale L.J. 170 (1964), with which *compare* Arnold, Law and Fact in the Medieval Jury Trial: Out of Sight, Out of Mind, 18 Am. J. Legal Hist. 267 (1974). *See also* Weiner, The Civil Jury Trial and the Law–Fact Distinction, 54 Calif. L. Rev. 1867 (1966).

11. *See* Danzig, Hadley v. Baxendale: A Study in the Industrialization of the Law, 4 J. Legal Stud. 249 (1975).

12. *See* Green and Smith, Negligence Law, No–Fault, and Jury Trial, 50 Tex. L. Rev. 1093, 1297, 51 Tex. L. Rev. 207, 825 (1973); James, Functions of Judge and Jury in Negligence Cases, 58 Yale L.J. 667 (1949). *See also* Green, Judge and Jury (1930).

13. *See, e.g.,* Bose Corp. v. Consumers Union, 466 U.S. 485, 104 S.Ct. 1949, 80 L.Ed.2d 502 (1984).

as a perjurious witness—a rule that originated when, as we have seen, jurors *were* witnesses.[14] Today, however, legal policies govern whether certain types of issues should be decided by the jury rather than the court. We will consider this problem more fully later.

Freeing and controlling juries

Definition of the jury's province has obvious political overtones.[15] To a certain extent, some believe, judges have reflected the views of government, juries the views of ordinary people; judges the theoretical law and its rational implications, juries the layperson's common sense and the "passional elements in our nature." As Holmes put it: "They will introduce into their verdict a certain amount—a very large amount so far as I have observed—of popular prejudice and thus keep the administration of the law in accord with the wishes and feelings of the community."[16] (The statement suggests that Holmes had his own prejudices, in this instance concerning juries.) Professor Howe has described this conflict, which he calls "basic . . . in the legal history of America," as one "between the people's aspirations for democratic government, and the judiciary's desire for the orderly supervision of public affairs by judges."[17]

During the sixteenth and seventeenth centuries juries were punished for acquitting against the law and the evidence.[18] But this practice did not withstand the famous judgment in *Bushell's Case* (1670)[19] and its clear recognition of the judicial nature of the jury's role. As older methods of controlling the jury became obsolete, new ones quickly took their place. These included the granting of a new trial, mistrial, the motion in arrest of judgment, the judgment notwithstanding the verdict, the demurrer to the evidence, the involuntary nonsuit, and the directed verdict. These devices allowed the judge to assess whether the jury could, on the evidence presented, properly return a verdict in terms of the governing substantive law. In addition, the judges began to give more specific instructions to the jury and to exclude improper evidence. The jury could also be required to render a special verdict, one that answered specific questions. Instructions, the exclusion of evidence, and the special verdict did not directly limit the jury's scope in reaching a verdict, but they did reshape the jury's terms of reference in arriving at their verdict.

14. Thayer, Evidence 187 (1898).

15. *Id.* at 218. *See also* Frederick, The Psychology of the American Jury (1987); Kalven and Zeisel, The American Jury ch. 1 (1966); Kassin and Wrightsman, The American Jury on Trial: Psychological Perspectives (1988). *See also* Wolfram, The Constitutional History of the Seventh Amendment, 57 Minn. L. Rev. 639 (1973).

16. Holmes, Collected Legal Papers 237 (1921).

17. Howe, Juries as Judges of the Criminal Law, 52 Harv. L. Rev. 582, 615 (1939).

18. 1 Holdsworth, A History of English Law 343–346 (7th ed. 1956); Thayer, Evidence 162–164 (1898).

19. Vaughan 135, 124 Eng. Rep. 1006 (C.P. 1670). *See* Green, Verdict According to Conscience (1985).

New trial and mistrial

Judges have long used the remedy of new trial to correct procedural irregularities at trial, such as the jury's verdict being unjustified by the evidence.[20] The mistrial was another device used to withdraw a case from a jury. Historically, a trial infected by error in composition of the tribunal, particularly in composition of the jury, could be declared a mistrial[21]—it counted for nought, as if no trial had been held. A mistrial could be produced by withdrawing a juror, thus decomposing the tribunal, when impropriety had occurred on the part of counsel, parties, witnesses or jurors.

J.n.o.v.

Motion in arrest of judgment was a defendant's procedural weapon for attacking plaintiff's declaration and thereby indirectly attacking the evidence offered in support of the declaration. It could also be used by a plaintiff to attack a defendant's answer in the same way. Thus, if plaintiff's declaration failed to state grounds for recovery, defendant might move to arrest judgment entered on a plaintiff's verdict. If the defendant's answer set up matter in avoidance that—even if true—was insufficient in law to constitute a defense, plaintiff might move for judgment in his or her favor notwithstanding a verdict rendered for defendant.[22] Originally, the defendant's motion in arrest of judgment and plaintiff's motion for judgment notwithstanding the verdict (judgment *non obstante veredicto,* or j.n.o.v.) were addressed to the sufficiency of pleadings and not the evidence produced at trial, but their function increased over time.[23]

Demurrer to evidence

A party wishing to challenge not the pleadings but the sufficiency of the adversary's evidence at trial could interpose a demurrer to the evidence. To do so, however, the demurrant had to make "an express and distinct admission ... of every fact which the evidence of his adversary conduces to prove."[24] On this basis the jury was excused and the judge gave final judgment on the facts shown by plaintiff's evidence. The demurrant had no chance to present evidence if the legal question

20. Thayer, Evidence 169 (1898); 1 Holdsworth, A History of English Law 346 (7th Ed. 1956). *See, e.g.,* Wood v. Gunston, Style 462, 466, 82 Eng. Rep. 863, 864, 867 (K.B. 1655). As Thayer points out, the granting of new trials on such a ground was just as vulnerable to the arguments in *Bushell's Case* as the fine or attaint. The practice described in the text nevertheless did grow and persists today.

21. Arnold and James, Cases on Trials, Judgments and Appeals 617 (1936); Wilbridge v. Case, 2 Ind. 36, 37 (1850).

22. *See* opinion of Van Devanter, J., in Slocum v. New York Life Ins. Co., 228 U.S. 364, 33 S.Ct. 523, 57 L.Ed. 879 (1913).

23. *Id. See also* Bond v. Dustin, 112 U.S. 604, 608, 5 S.Ct. 296, 298, 28 L.Ed. 835, 836 (1884); Van Stone v. Stillwell & Bierce Mfg. Co., 142 U.S. 128, 135, 12 S.Ct. 181, 183, 35 L.Ed. 961, 964 (1891).

24. Slocum v. New York Life Ins. Co., 228 U.S. 364, 388, 33 S.Ct. 523, 533, 57 L.Ed. 879, 890 (1913). *See also* Note, 44 Mich. L. Rev. 468 (1945).

was decided against him or her.[25] This jury control device therefore involved great risk to a party employing it.

Exclusion of evidence

Once it was established that the jury must decide issues on evidence put before it, the court's power to exclude evidence as irrelevant, unreliable or prejudicial developed into an important method of jury control.[26] Exclusion of evidence limits the material jurors can consider and thus may affect the conclusion they are persuaded to reach.[27] Exclusion of evidence may also result in insufficiency of the evidence to support a verdict for the party having the burden of proof.

Instructions to jury

The judge's "charge," or instruction to the jury, was originally an aid to that body in its deliberations. The judge cannot enforce the charge in the same way as the demurrer to the evidence or the directed verdict, for the jury itself must still act on the charge. But ordinarily a jury does not lightly disregard the judge's instruction, and, if its disregard is manifest, then the verdict may be set aside through a motion for j.n.o.v.

Involuntary dismissal

During the eighteenth and early nineteenth centuries new procedural devices were developed.[28] One of these was the compulsory nonsuit, now also called an "involuntary dismissal."[29] Originally the remedy of nonsuit was addressed to a plaintiff who failed to prosecute the action. This device was transformed so that plaintiff could make a voluntary discontinuance when the plaintiff understood the judge was ready to direct an unfavorable verdict.[30] By stages, a defendant also was permitted to suggest such a discontinuance. The nonsuit became "a procedure by which a defendant could put in issue the sufficiency of the plaintiff's evidence to go to the jury"[31] by a motion at the close of the plaintiff's case.[32] If the motion was denied, defendant was free to put in its case and

25. Galloway v. United States, 319 U.S. 372, 403, 63 S.Ct. 1077, 1093, 87 L.Ed. 1458, 1478 (1943).

26. 9 Wigmore, Evidence § 2550 (Chadbourn rev. 1981); Morgan, Functions of Judge and Jury in the Determination of Preliminary Questions of Fact, 43 Harv. L. Rev. 165, 169 (1929).

27. Thayer, Evidence 264–269 (1898). *See also* James, Functions of Judge and Jury in Negligence Cases, 58 Yale L.J. 667, 669 (1948).

28. *See* sources cited *supra* note 27.

29. *See* opinion of McAllister, J., in Hopkins v. Nashville, C. & St. L. R.R., 96 Tenn. 409, 436–443, 34 S.W. 1029, 1035–1037 (1896).

30. Stephen, Principles of Pleading 313 (1824).

31. Galloway v. United States, 319 U.S. 372, 391 n. 23, 63 S.Ct. 1077, 1087 n. 23, 87 L.Ed. 1458, 1471 n. 23 (1943).

32. *See* Di Biase v. Garnsey, 104 Conn. 447, 451, 133 A. 669, 670 (1926); Lewis v. Bowen, 208 Ga. 671, 68 S.E.2d 900 (1952); Thoe v. Chicago, M. & St. P. Ry., 181 Wis. 456, 460, 195 N.W. 407, 409 (1923). *Cf.* Jordan v. Sun Life Assurance Co. of Canada, 366 Pa. 495, 77 A.2d 631 (1951) (error to nonsuit after defendant has introduced evidence).

go to the jury.[33] If it was granted, the judgment of nonsuit ended the case but did not bar the bringing of a new action on the same cause.[34]

Directed verdict

The power of the court to direct a verdict for one party on the ground that the evidence was insufficient to warrant a verdict also came to be recognized.[35] The motion differed from the common law demurrer to the evidence: Although the unsuccessful demurrant necessarily lost the case, the party unsuccessfully moving for directed verdict might still offer evidence, go to the jury, and win.[36]

By the early twentieth century, in many states the motion for nonsuit differed from the motion for directed verdict in two respects:

1. The motion for nonsuit was made at the close of plaintiff's case,[37] and its denial did not preclude defendant from putting on his or her own case; the motion for directed verdict was properly made only at the close of all the evidence[38] so that the movant had to rest his or her case before making such a motion.

2. A directed verdict resulted in a final judgment on the merits, thus binding the parties and precluding further action to the same extent as judgment on any other verdict.[39] Judgment of nonsuit did not bar a new action for the same cause.[40]

Special verdict

Another device for controlling the jury was the special verdict. Ordinarily a jury renders a general verdict: "We the jury find for plaintiff in the amount of $___" or "We the jury find for defendant." In a special verdict, the jury makes more specific findings in response to

33. *See* Eberstadt v. State, 92 Tex. 94, 97, 45 S.W. 1007, 1008 (1898). Note the procedure in Simeone v. Prato, 82 R.I. 496, 111 A.2d 708 (1955).

34. *See* Oscanyan v. Arms Co., 103 U.S. 261, 26 L.Ed. 539 (1880). *See also* Slocum v. New York Life Ins. Co., 228 U.S. 364, 392, 394, 395, 33 S.Ct. 523, 534–535, 57 L.Ed. 879, 891–893 (1913). See the comprehensive opinion of McAllister, J., in Hopkins v. Nashville, C. & St. L. R.R., 96 Tenn. 409, 34 S.W. 1029 (1896).

35. Parks v. Ross, 52 U.S. (11 How.) 362, 13 L.Ed. 730 (1850). For a discussion of the history of the directed verdict, see Hackett, Has a Trial Judge of a United States Court the Right to Direct a Verdict?, 24 Yale L.J. 127 (1914). As the doctrine was originally promulgated, the court could direct a verdict if the proponent offered no evidence whatever. *See* Smith, The Power of the Judge to Direct a Verdict: Section 457a of the New York Civil Practice Act, 24 Colum. L. Rev. 111, 113, 114 (1924); Syderbottom v. Smith, 1 Strange 649, 93 Eng. Rep. 759 (K.B. 1725–1726).

36. Slocum v. New York Life Ins. Co., 228 U.S. 364, 395, 33 S.Ct. 523, 535, 57 L.Ed. 879, 893 (1913).

37. Hopkins v. Nashville, C. & St. L.R.R., 96 Tenn. 409, 34 S.W. 1029 (1896).

38. 9 Wigmore, Evidence § 2495 (Chadbourn rev. 1981). *See, e.g.,* Di Biase v. Garnsey, 104 Conn. 447, 451, 133 A. 669, 670 (1926); Thoe v. Chicago, M. & St. P. Ry., 181 Wis. 456–460, 195 N.W. 407–409 (1923).

39. Smith, The Power of the Judge to Direct a Verdict: Section 457a of the New York Civil Practice Act, 24 Colum. L. Rev. 111, 115 (1924).

40. Oscanyan v. Arms Co., 103 U.S. 261, 264, 26 L.Ed. 539, 541 (1880); Smith, *supra* note 39, at 115.

specified issue formulations: "The plaintiff did (did not) exercise due care for his (her) own safety." In English common law, the special verdict was a protection to the jury to avoid liability for giving false judgment.[41] In America it became a means by which the jury could be required to disclose the basis of its decision.[42] Common law judges not infrequently interrogated juries that brought in special verdicts to amplify the finding of fact on which a judgment would be based. And juries that brought in unanticipated general verdicts were sometimes asked to state their reasons for doing so.[43] The latter practice seems to have become common in New England, where the judges were recognized to have the power to submit written questions to be answered along with the general verdict.[44] Such devices pressure the jury to stick to its fact-finding function as described in the charge.[45] Modern methods for controlling the province of the jury are the descendants or modifications of these common law devices.

§ 7.9 Substantive Error and Procedural Error

Two basic problems arise in controlling the jury's performance of its function. The first stems from the discrepancy in the jury's conception of justice in a particular case from the legal system's conception as defined by the judges. This can produce a verdict radically divergent from the decision that would be rendered by the judges on the same evidence and is considered a problem of substantive jury error. The second problem is that the trial process in a particular case may be contaminated by serious accidental or intentional deviations from proper procedure. This is a problem of procedural error.

Substantive Error

The term "substantive jury error" is conclusory and, in an important sense, question-begging. The underlying question is whether the jury's conception of justice, manifested in a verdict, should prevail over the conception of justice that judges think would be permissible on the basis of the same evidence. The institution of jury trial is founded on the premise that juries decide certain types of cases differently from the way judges would decide them.[1] In terms of politics and efficiency, it would

41. Thayer, Evidence 218 (1898); Green, Judge and Jury 353 (1930).

42. Clementson, Special Verdicts ch. 1 (1905).

43. Walker v. Bailey, 65 Me. 354 (1876); Dorr v. Fenno, 29 Mass. (12 Pick.) 521 (1832); Norris v. Haverhill, 65 N.H. 89, 18 A. 85 (1889); Turon v. J. & L. Construction Co., 8 N.J. 543, 86 A.2d 192 (1952); Clementson, Special Verdicts ch. 2 (1905); Morgan, A Brief History of Special Verdicts and Special Interrogatories, 32 Yale L.J. 574, 591 (1923); Wicker, Special Interrogatories to Juries in Civil Cases, 35 Yale L.J. 296 (1926).

44. Cullum v. Colwell, 85 Conn. 459, 83 A. 695 (1912); Burgess v. Giovannucci, 314 Mass. 252, 49 N.E.2d 907 (1943); Clementson, Special Verdicts ch. 2 (1905).

45. 2 Harper, James, and Gray, Law of Torts 888 (2d ed. 1986).

§ 7.9

1. Kalven and Zeisel, The American Jury (1966); Frederick, The Psychology of the American Jury (1987); Kassin, The

make no sense to preserve jury trial unless such differences were persistent. Jury trial is relatively costly in time and risk of procedural mishap; it is preserved because many believe it has offsetting social gains.[2] The gains are reflected in the attributes of jury justice, embodied in the moral and political viewpoint of ordinary citizens compared with that of legal professionals.

Jury viewpoint

The difference in a jury's moral and political viewpoint can be reflected in various ways. An important one is the assessment of the credibility of witnesses: Is a business or government official more or less believable than a truck driver? Does the race or sex of the official or truck driver make a difference? Do the differences in credibility vary according to the subject matter of the testimony? The difference can also be expressed in assessments of what was reasonable conduct in the circumstances: Did a police officer wait long enough before using force? Did a negotiator adequately disclose facts of which the other side may have been un-aware? Does it make a difference that the negotiator was a real estate broker? That the negotiator was of the same ethnic derivation as the other party? Does the significance of any of these variables change according to the regional, ethnic, gender, and class composition of the particular jury or judge?

Such intertwined issues of what happened and who is responsible form the essence of most civil litigation. The trier of fact assesses these issues in the framework of a legal standard such as "reasonable care," "good faith effort," or "probable cause." The standard will be somewhat indeterminate in any case that goes to trial; otherwise the case would likely have been settled or never brought. The jury's application of the standard may yield a different outcome from one the judge would make.

Legal indeterminacy

At one end of the spectrum, applying a legal standard produces a difference in outcome between one trier of fact and another that is simply a "judgment call." After all, people have various life experiences that influence their factual and normative judgments in the resolution of disputed situations.[3] Jurors as a group differ from judges, and both groups differ among themselves. Differences of outcome on this account simply reflect the limits of law in regulating human affairs precisely. The jury's judgment is as legitimate as a judge's and perhaps more useful in the administration of law. A verdict decides the case but is not prece-

American Jury on Trial: Psychological Perspectives (1988); Kalven, The Dignity of the Civil Jury, 50 Va. L. Rev. 1055 (1964).

2. Lieber, Civil Liberty and Self-Government 234–237 (1874); Higginbotham, Continuing the Dialogue: Civil Juries and the Allocation of Judicial Power, 56 Tex. L. Rev. 47 (1977). *See also* Marcus, Completing Equity's Conquest? Reflections on the Future of Trial Under the Federal Rules of Civil Procedure, 50 U. Pitt. L. Rev. (1988).

3. *Compare, e.g.,* Wright, Black Boy (1945); Gilligan, In a Different Voice (1982).

dent; hence, the system of precedent does not have to take account of jury determinations. The administration of justice accordingly can avoid having to pretend consistency in close cases.

§ 7.10 Legal System Norms and Citizen Norms

At the other end of the spectrum, however, juries may have systematic differences from judges that adversely impact the *general* administration of justice. A jury may consider it inconsequential to award a sympathetic plaintiff damages against a "deep pocket" corporate defendant even when no fault is found; the cost, after all, can simply be taken out of profits or passed on to the consumer. A jury may consider it inconsequential to deny an unsympathetic plaintiff recovery in an employment discrimination case; after all, everyone has to put up with a measure of guff from the boss. By the same token judges may attach significance to formal legal requirements that jurors would consider offensive to common sense. Although empirical research suggests the contrary, it is widely believed that jurors and judges have systematic although marginal differences in their conceptions of justice.[1]

Jury nullification

The difference between legal system norms, as applied by judges, and citizen norms, as applied by juries, results in different outcomes according to who is the trier of fact. In assessing what happened and who was responsible, the jury may go beyond making a "judgment call" within the framework of the law given by the judge. Instead, it may interject its own conception of what the law should be, displacing the judge's instruction of what the law is.

Attitudes toward this power of the jury have varied. Until well after the Revolution, many judges and lawyers accepted the right of jurors to find law as well as fact, and hence to disobey the court's instructions.[2] In criminal cases, "jury nullification" of the law to acquit defendants is widely recognized as a legitimate jury function, although that is certainly not the case when a jury convicts a defendant in the teeth of the law. Nevertheless, courts insist that jurors should not be told of their right to acquit, and sometimes remove jurors who indicate they will do so.[3] The right to nullify the law in civil matters has fewer defenders but, right or no right, juries still have considerable power to do just that.

§ 7.10

1. Kalven and Zeisel, The American Jury (1966); § 7.7 *supra*. *See also* Guinther, The Jury in America (1988); Kassin, The American Jury on Trial: Psychological Perspectives (1988); Feigenson, Legal Blame: How Jurors Think and Talk About Accidents (2000).

2. Harrington, The Law–Finding Function of the American Jury, 1999 Wis. L. Rev. 377. *See* Green, Verdict According to Conscience (1985).

3. *E.g.*, United States v. Thomas, 116 F.3d 606 (2d Cir.1997); United States v. Dougherty, 473 F.2d 1113 (D.C.Cir.1972). See generally Marder, The Myth of the Nullifying Jury, 93 Nw. U.L. Rev. 877 (1999).

Jury displacement of legal rule

An illustration showing the jury's displacement of the legal rule with its own appears in *Simblest v. Maynard.*[4] Plaintiff, a business traveler in his 60s, drove his car through an intersection into the path of a fire truck hurrying to an emergency in Burlington, Vermont. Under the governing statutory rule, an emergency vehicle such as a fire truck with flashing light or sounding siren has the right of way. All witnesses except the plaintiff testified that the fire truck's light was flashing and its siren sounding; on this basis plaintiff would be guilty of contributory negligence in not yielding at the intersection. The plaintiff testified that he did not see the light or hear the siren. From this testimony it could be inferred—if plaintiff were believed and the other witnesses mistaken—that the light and siren were not operating. On this basis the plaintiff would not be guilty of contributory negligence and could be entitled to recover. The jury returned a moderate verdict for plaintiff.

After careful analysis of the physics of the fire truck's flashing light, the court concluded that the plaintiff lacked opportunity, in the split second before the crash, to discern that the light was not flashing. Hence, plaintiff's testimony defied the physical facts and was therefore incredible as a matter of law. Accordingly, his testimony had to be ignored in determining the sufficiency of plaintiff's evidence to establish his case. Since no other evidence supported plaintiff's case, j.n.o.v. for defendant was required.

The conclusion seems inescapable that the jury in *Simblest* was irrational in finding for plaintiff. Yet there was one other fact: About 10 or 15 minutes before the accident, a regional electrical power failure caused a total blackout of the city. With this in mind it would seem that the jury rationally could have thought as follows: The emergency right-of-way rule is fine under normal conditions and, perhaps, even when people have a chance to recover from the shock of an event like a blackout. A fire truck driver, however, is a professional trained to deal with sudden changes in conditions. Given the fire department's special access to news of emergencies, the fire truck driver must have been fully aware of the blackout. On the other hand, the blackout could have disoriented an older person driving a car, and the fire department should have foreseen that effect on people in the town. The right-of-way rule ought to have an exception for such circumstances.

On this interpretation, the jury's determination was perfectly rational, even if it involved making an exception to the pronouncement of the legislature as expressed in the right-of-way statute. The jury had no formal authority to overrule the legislature. The jury as well as the legislature, however, is representative of the people, specifically in the administration of justice. As such, it has some authority to modify the general rules of the law according to its sense of justice. Indeed, the jury

4. 427 F.2d 1 (2d Cir.1970).

might suppose that the legislature would have made a similar exception if it had addressed the problem.

Jury displacement of the legal rule has undoubtedly been involved in myriad cases over the years. Since juries are not required to give explanations for their verdicts, the courts generally cannot discern whether such a displacement of the law or simply a strange "judgment call" is involved. Sometimes, as in *Simblest,* the verdict cannot be rationally reconciled with the legal framework that the jury was instructed to follow. Whether and when the courts should indulge the jury's sense of justice in such cases is profoundly debatable. At stake are two competing aspects of justice according to law: the generality and impartiality achieved in legal rules, and the "equity" and individualization in their application. Also at stake are broader conceptions of justice in the minds of judges and jurors.[5]

These deeper issues are obscured, however, in the terminology with which the jury control rules address problems of jury "substantive error." Instead, as we shall see,[6] the terminology focuses on whether the jury could rationally or reasonably have reached its verdict according to law.

§ 7.11 Procedural Errors in Jury Trial

A trial is an extemporaneous event, whether before a judge or a jury. However well the issues are defined, however comprehensive the pretrial order,[1] however well counsel are prepared, unexpected turns are bound to develop. Some of these will be merely awkward, occasionally funny; most will be normal confusion and therefore bearable. But untoward events can seriously disturb the focus and decorum with which such a serious event as a trial should be conducted. A party or witness can burst out with angry or hysterical irrelevancies; a juror can conceal prior knowledge of the facts or relationship with one of the parties; a lawyer can engage in prejudicial rhetoric or tactics. More mundane but more frequent errors include reception of inadmissible evidence and error in the judge's comments or instructions to the jury.

When the trial is conducted before the judge without a jury, some of these mishaps, such as extravagant testimony by a witness and harassing tactics by counsel, are less likely to affect the decision. Judges usually are unimpressed by conduct that is beyond the bounds of convention; indeed they may consider it counterproductive. Lawyers may restrain themselves accordingly. In any event, experienced trial judges likely will be unperturbed by mishaps at trial; rarely will it be inferred that prejudicial effects resulted.

5. Yeazell, The New Jury and the Ancient Jury Conflict, 1990 U. Chi. Legal F. 87, 103.

6. *See* §§ 7.24 *et seq. infra.*

§ 7.11

1. *See* § 5.21 *supra.*

In a jury trial the problem of procedural error is much more serious. First, jurors do not have a background of trial experience by which to gauge whether particular conduct is out of bounds. Indeed, modern television dramas may have given them misleading impressions of trial court decorum. Hence, it cannot be assumed that juries discount mishaps at trial with the same discrimination as a judge. Second, jurors have to assume that the judge will recognize and control improper conduct. Hence, they can be misled by failure of the judge to take appropriate corrective measures. Third, since the jurors' sense of justice may be somewhat different from that of judges,[2] it is always possible that an irregularity in the trial is a calculated effort by counsel to appeal to that different sense of justice.

Dealing with procedural error in a jury trial necessarily requires balance between the objective of assuring a fair trial according to law and that of doing the job finally, if not perfectly. Striking the right balance has been called the riddle of harmless error.[3] The task is complicated by the interweaving of procedural error and substantive error. It is further complicated by the inevitable temptation for judges to find procedural error when a jury has returned a verdict with which a judge strongly disagrees.

The rules for control of the jury should be read with an eye to these underlying realities.

§ 7.12 Burden of Proof: Two Meanings

For the litigants, the aim in a trial is, of course, to win. Winning in a jury trial means getting a favorable verdict. Getting a favorable verdict means doing what is necessary to persuade the jury on the evidence—and to persuade the judge that this has been accomplished within the rules of substantive and procedural law.

Within the rules of substantive and procedural law, the task of persuasion revolves around the burden of proof. The term "burden of proof" is used to refer to two different concepts. Until the distinction was defined by James Bradley Thayer in 1898,[1] the reasoning of the decisions on this point was hopelessly confused.[2] The two distinct concepts may be referred to as (1) the risk of nonpersuasion, sometimes called the "burden of persuasion," and (2) the duty of producing evidence (or burden of production), sometimes called the "burden of going forward with the evidence."[3]

2. *See* § 7.10 *supra.*

3. Traynor, The Riddle of Harmless Error (1970).

§ 7.12

1. Thayer, Evidence 355–364 (1898).

2. *See generally* McNaughton, Burden of Production of Evidence: A Function of a Burden of Persuasion, 68 Harv. L. Rev. 1382 (1955).

3. *See* Strong et al., McCormick on Evidence ch. 36 (5th ed. 1999); Morgan, Some Problems of Proof Under the Anglo–American System of Litigation 72–73 (1953) [hereinafter cited as Morgan, Some Problems of Proof]; Nesson, The Evidence or the

§ 7.13 Risk of Nonpersuasion

Mind in equipoise

The concept of the risk of nonpersuasion[1] begins with recognition that when a person decides a question of the existence or nonexistence of a fact, there is the possibility that the decider, after deliberation, may be in doubt on the question submitted. That is, on all the evidence submitted, the decider of fact may regard the existence or nonexistence of the fact as equally likely—a matter in mental equipoise. If the trier nevertheless is obliged to decide the question one way or the other, the system must supply a rule for deciding the question—a "default rule," as it is now often called. When the parties to a civil action are in dispute over a material issue of fact, the default rule specifies which party will lose if the trier's mind is in equipoise. Put differently, that party bears the risk that the trier will not be affirmatively persuaded on that issue. This is the risk of nonpersuasion.[2]

The risk of nonpersuasion is more often called "the burden of persuasion."[3] Our system frees the judge and jury of responsibility for investigating and presenting facts and arguments,[4] instead placing that responsibility on the respective parties. But, even in a system where the trier of fact has the job of investigating the facts, doubt or equipoise may still arise when the time for decision comes. A concept of the risk of nonpersuasion is inseparable from any system in which issues of fact are to be decided through rational deliberation on the basis of incomplete knowledge. When the trier of fact is a judge rather than a jury, the same default rules apply as when a jury decides the issue.[5]

When an issue of fact is tried to a jury, it is the members of the jury whose minds may be in doubt or equipoise. Although the judge is not directly concerned with solving the problem, the court formulates standards for the jury's guidance.[6] Through these standards the court allocates the burden of persuasion as to each issue and thereby tells the jury what to do if they cannot decide the question.[7] The court also retains a

Event? On Judicial Proof and the Acceptability of Verdicts, 98 Harv. L. Rev. 1357 (1985).

§ 7.13

1. 9 Wigmore, Evidence § 2485 (Chadbourn rev. 1981).

2. Morgan, Some Problems of Proof 74 (1956); Nesson, The Evidence or the Event? On Judicial Proof and the Acceptability of Verdicts, 98 Harv. L. Rev. 1357 (1985).

3. *See, e.g.,* Texas Dept. of Community Affairs v. Burdine, 450 U.S. 248, 101 S.Ct. 1089, 67 L.Ed.2d 207 (1981).

4. *See* Michael and Adler, Real Proof, 5 Vand. L. Rev. 344 (1952).

5. *See, e.g.,* Preferred Accident Ins. Co. v. Grasso, 186 F.2d 987 (2d Cir.1951); Lecates v. Lecates, 38 Del. 190, 190 A. 294 (1937).

6. "[T]he most important part of the judge's charge relative to the facts—i.e., that of dealing with the burden of proof—ought to be so worded that the jurors can comprehend it." Larson v. Jo Ann Cab Corp., 209 F.2d 929, 935 (2d Cir.1954).

7. Morgan, Some Problems of Proof 71 (1956); Nesson, The Evidence or the Event? On Judicial Proof and the Acceptability of Verdicts, 98 Harv. L. Rev. 1357 (1985).

measure of control over the jury's mental processes by instructing them on the required measure of persuasion.

§ 7.14 Measure of Persuasion in Civil Cases

The measure of persuasion usually applicable in a civil case is a preponderance of the evidence in favor of the party having the burden of persuasion (the proponent) before it is entitled to a verdict.[1] An alternative phrase often used is *greater weight* of the evidence. The general statement is usually explained as referring not to the number of witnesses or quantity of evidence but to the convincing force of the evidence.[2]

Preponderance of evidence

Most courts accept some such formulation of the test. Indeed, in instructing juries on the concept of a preponderance of the evidence, many judges accompany their verbal instructions with a dramatization of the scales of justice, holding their hands out, palms up and level with each other, and then lowering one hand and raising the other. In any event, typical jurors very likely interpret the instruction in a personal and subjective way—in terms of their own feelings and experiences.[3]

A quite different question is whether the preponderance-of-the-evidence test is applied to all types of civil actions and to all issues in them.[4] The Supreme Court has recently answered this question in the affirmative: "Because the preponderance-of-the-evidence standard results in a roughly equal allocation of the risk of error between litigants, we presume that this standard is applicable in civil actions between private litigants unless 'particularly important individual interests or rights are at stake.' "[5]

Clear and convincing evidence

A much stronger degree of belief is required in criminal cases where, as we have seen, guilt must be proved beyond a reasonable doubt.[6] This test is scarcely ever applied in civil actions, but an intermediate standard is applied to many issues in civil controversies when the danger of error seems greater on one side than the other. This test calls for "clear and

§ 7.14

1. *See* Maguire, Evidence, Common Sense and Common Law 180 (1947). *See also* Note, 147 A.L.R. 380 (1943) (examples of jury charges); § 7.22 *infra.*

2. Morgan, Some Problems of Proof 83 (1956); Nesson, The Evidence or the Event? On Judicial Proof and the Acceptability of Verdicts, 98 Harv. L. Rev. 1357 (1985).

3. *Compare* Forston, Sense and Non–Sense: Jury Trial Communication, 1975 B.Y.U. L. Rev. 601.

4. *See* Maguire, Evidence, Common Sense and Common Law 179 (1947).

5. Grogan v. Garner, 498 U.S. 279, 286, 111 S.Ct. 654, 659, 112 L.Ed.2d 755, 764 (1991), quoting Herman & MacLean v. Huddleston, 459 U.S. 375, 389–390, 103 S.Ct. 683, 691, 74 L.Ed.2d 548, 558 (1983).

6. *See* § 7.5 *supra.*

convincing evidence," or evidence that is "clear, precise and indubitable," before the proponent's persuasion burden is met.[7] These formulations reflect notions of both an objective measurement of the weight of proof and the persuasive effect of the proof on the mind of the trier. Imprecise as they may be, they suffice to put the jury in a frame of mind to require more than what is signified by a preponderance. It is doubtful whether any greater clarity can be achieved or is worth pursuing.

§ 7.15 Burden of Producing Evidence

The second meaning that is commonly given to the term "burden of proof" refers to the burden of coming forward with evidence. This is sometimes called "the burden of production." (A more accurate term might be "the risk of nonproduction," but this expression is not in general use.) The burden of producing evidence first comes into play at the very beginning of the trial.[1] We have seen that the judge and jury do not have the responsibility of investigating a case or furnishing the evidence on which the case will be decided; our system imposes that responsibility on the parties. But suppose neither party offers any evidence at the trial; what would happen? The tribunal has no evidence at all, and one party will lose. That party, therefore, bears the risk of nonproduction of evidence.[2] Put differently, that party bears the burden of producing at least some evidence.

Sufficiency of evidence

The next question concerns how much evidence the original proponent needs to produce to satisfy this burden.[3] The proponent must introduce sufficient evidence to justify a verdict in its favor on each of the propositions of fact required to be established as part of the proponent's case.[4] This proposition refers us to the concept of sufficiency of the evidence and the tests for determining which propositions of fact constitute essential elements of the proponent's case rather than the case of the adversary—that is, the tests for allocating the production

7. *See* Clermont, Procedure's Magical Number Three: Psychological Bases for Standards of Decision, 72 Cornell L. Rev. 115 (1987). A widely followed rule is that fraud must be established by "clear and convincing evidence." *E.g.,* Weise v. Red Owl Stores, 286 Minn. 199, 175 N.W.2d 184 (1970). *See also* Santosky v. Kramer, 455 U.S. 745, 102 S.Ct. 1388, 71 L.Ed.2d 599 (1982)(deprivation of parental rights); Addington v. Texas, 441 U.S. 418, 99 S.Ct. 1804, 60 L.Ed.2d 323 (1979)(civil commitment); Woodby v. INS, 385 U.S. 276, 87 S.Ct. 483, 17 L.Ed.2d 362 (1966) (deportation proceeding); Kruse v. Horlamus Indus., 130 Wis.2d 357, 387 N.W.2d 64 (1986) (adverse possession proceeding); § 7.16 *infra.* "Clear and convincing" remains an elusive standard. *See* Slomowitz v. Walker, 429 So.2d 797, 799 (Fla.Dist.Ct.App.1983).

§ 7.15

1. *See* Thayer, Evidence 376 (1898).

2. *See id.* at 357, 376. *See also* 9 Wigmore, Evidence §§ 2487–2488 (Chadbourn rev. 1981).

3. *See* diagram in 9 Wigmore, Evidence § 2487 (Chadbourn rev. 1981). *See generally* McNaughton, Burden of Production of Evidence: A Function of a Burden of Persuasion,68 Harv. L. Rev. 1382, 1384–1385 (1955).

4. *See* Thoe v. Chicago, M. & St. P. Ry., 181 Wis. 456, 195 N.W. 407 (1923); Morgan, Some Problems of Proof 73 (1956).

burden on each issue of fact in the case. These are discussed in later sections.[5]

As we have seen, the consequence of failure to produce evidence—or sufficient evidence—is loss of the case. The mechanisms for precipitating this consequence are the motions for nonsuit, directed verdict, or dismissal.[6] Such a motion is made by the opponent after the proponent has rested its case, indicating that it has put in all the evidence it has on the issue. In ruling on such a motion, the judge determines the sufficiency of evidence and allocates the production burden on each issue.[7] If the proponent has met the production burden, the opponent is entitled to put in controverting evidence. It will then go before the jury to resolve the conflicting evidence.

Directed verdict for proponent

Even if the opponent rests without putting in any evidence, the opponent ordinarily is entitled to have the jury pass on the proponent's evidence.[8] Testimony, even if uncontradicted, usually raises questions of credibility (such as honesty, bias, accuracy of observation, memory, and expression).[9] Circumstantial evidence usually permits more than one possible inference.[10] Admitted conduct may often be evaluated differently (as reasonable or negligent) by different persons.[11] All these matters are proper for the jury to decide.

It will sometimes happen, however, that the proponent's evidence leaves open no question of credibility, of evaluation of conduct, or of choice among competing inferences or which reasonable minds might

5. *See* §§ 7.16, 7.19 *infra.*

6. § 7.21 *infra;* Thoe v. Chicago, M. & St. P. Ry., 181 Wis. 456, 195 N.W. 407 (1923); 9 Wigmore, Evidence § 2495 (Chadbourn rev. 1981).

7. *See* Maguire, Evidence, Common Sense and Common Law 175–176 (1947); 9 Wigmore, Evidence § 2495 (Chadbourn rev. 1981).

8. *See, e.g.,* Sweeney v. Erving, 228 U.S. 233, 240, 33 S.Ct. 416, 418, 57 L.Ed. 815, 819 (1913); George Foltis, Inc. v. City of New York, 287 N.Y. 108, 119–123, 38 N.E.2d 455, 459–463 (1941); Terwilliger v. Marion, 222 S.C. 185, 72 S.E.2d 165 (1952); Texas Employers' Ins. Assn. v. Roberts, 135 Tex. 123, 139 S.W.2d 80 (1940) (plaintiff not entitled to favorable finding as matter of law on issue on which he gave uncontradicted testimony—jury may disbelieve him). *Cf.* Hughes v. Aetna Ins. Co., 261 S.W.2d 942 (Mo.1953) (affirmative defense supported by uncontradicted testimony for jury). *See* Note, Directing the Verdict in Favor of the Party with the Burden of Proof, 50 N.C.L. Rev. 843 (1972).

9. *See, e.g.,* MacDonald v. Pennsylvania R.R., 348 Pa. 558, 36 A.2d 492 (1944) (defendant's uncontradicted evidence exculpating its employees for derailment presents issue for jury); Wyatt v. Moran, 81 R.I. 399, 103 A.2d 801 (1954) (trial court need not accept uncontradicted evidence showing gift inter vivos); Terwilliger v. Marion, 222 S.C. 185, 72 S.E.2d 165 (1952); Knapp v. Holiday Inns, 682 S.W.2d 936 (Tenn.App.1984) (summary judgment not proper when it rests solely on witnesses whose credibility was challenged); Buckner v. Pillsbury Co., 661 S.W.2d 626 (Mo.App.1983).

10. *See* Mahan v. Able, 251 S.W.2d 994, 997 (Ky.1952); George Foltis, Inc. v. City of New York, 287 N.Y. 108, 119–123, 38 N.E.2d 455, 459–463 (1941).

11. *See* Sams v. Albers Super Mkts., 86 Ohio App. 167, 89 N.E.2d 101 (1949); 2 Harper, James, and Gray, Torts §§ 15.3, 16.10, 17.1 (2d ed. 1986); James, Functions of Judge and Jury in Negligence Cases, 58 Yale L.J. 667, 676–679 (1949).

differ. In such a case the proponent is entitled to a directed verdict in its favor if no other evidence is received.[12] At this point the production burden shifts to the party who was originally the opponent. That party then may meet this burden by offering controverting evidence.

Administration by the court

The burden of production thus is a matter for the court to decide, not the jury. It is the analytic device whereby the court determines whether, if the trial were stopped at the given point in the reception of evidence, the court would send the case to the jury. If the evidence is insufficient at that point, the court directs judgment accordingly and the jury has no role to play. If the case is sent to the jury, this signifies that the burden of production has been fulfilled and has no further role to play.[13] The jury's function is defined in terms of the burden of persuasion, that is, preponderance of the evidence or clear and convincing evidence, as the case may be.[14]

Allocation of the burden of production is determined by rules extrinsic to the rules of evidence and trial procedure. These rules are specific to various issues and generally are correlated with the allocation of the burden of pleading.[15] Thus, plaintiff usually is allocated the initial burden of producing evidence on all issues allocated to plaintiff under the pleading rules. By the same token, the defendant usually has the initial burden of producing evidence as to issues involved in affirmative defenses. For example, plaintiff in a negligence case has the burden of initially producing evidence sufficient to permit a jury finding on the issues of defendant's negligence, proximate cause, and the extent of plaintiff's injuries. Defendant has the burden of initially producing evidence on plaintiff's contributory negligence, assumption of risk, statute of limitations, or release.[16]

Once a party with the burden of production has produced evidence sufficient to permit a finding, the opponent must either respond with controverting evidence or take the risk that the trier of fact will be persuaded by the plaintiff's evidence. A classic illustration of such risk-taking appears in *Pennzoil v. Texaco.*[17] Pennzoil sued Texaco for damages arising from Texaco's wrongful interference with Pennzoil's attempt to acquire Getty Oil Co. In its case in chief, Pennzoil offered expert testimony, calculating its damages at $10 billion. Texaco offered no evidence on the damages issue, apparently guessing that the jury would

12. Maguire, Evidence, Common Sense and Common Law 175–176 (1947); 9 Wigmore, Evidence § 2487 (Chadbourn rev. 1981).

13. *See* sources cited *supra* note 12.

14. Morgan, Some Problems of Proof 73 (1956); 9 Wigmore, Evidence § 2487 (Chadbourn rev. 1981).

15. *See* § 7.16 *infra* on allocation of burden of proof; § 3.11 *supra* on allocation of burden of pleading.

16. *See* § 3.11 *supra.*

17. *On appeal,* Texaco v. Pennzoil, 729 S.W.2d 768 (Tex.App.1987), *cert. dismissed,* 485 U.S. 994, 108 S.Ct. 1305, 99 L.Ed.2d 686 (1988).

regard such an astronomical figure as ridiculous and hence find for defendant or at most find minimal damages. But the jury accepted plaintiff's evidence.

Allocation of the burden of production is thus a kind of traffic management rule for the trial when there is evidence on both sides. The allocation rule, in specifying which side loses if no evidence is produced, determines by implication which side goes first with its evidence. Because plaintiff is allocated the burden of production on most issues in a claim, plaintiff goes first in presenting its case.[18]

The allocation of the burden of production also has significance when there is no available evidence on an issue. The party to whom the production burden is allocated will lose on that issue, and often on the whole case.[19] Thus in an action for wrongful death caused by negligence, if there is no evidence of the decedent's own conduct in the incident, the plaintiff cannot recover if the allocation rule imposes on plaintiff the production burden on the issue of contributory negligence.[20]

The concept of burden of production also applies in cases tried to a judge without a jury.[21]

§ 7.16 Allocating Burdens of Proof

There is no a priori test for allocating the burden of persuasion or the burden of producing evidence. The party who must establish the affirmative proposition is sometimes said to have the burden of proof on the issue.[1] But any proposition can be stated either affirmatively or negatively. Breach of a promise, for example, may be termed nonfulfillment; negligence can be described as the failure to exercise due care; a declaration of nonliability is in substance the same as an affirmative defense.[2] Similarly, the burden of proof is sometimes said to rest on the party to whose case the fact in question is essential,[3] and so it is. But

18. *See* § 7.3 *supra.*

19. *See* Texas Dept. of Community Affairs v. Burdine, 450 U.S. 248, 101 S.Ct. 1089, 67 L.Ed.2d 207 (1981); Green Tree Financial Corp. v. Randolph, 531 U.S. 79, 121 S.Ct. 513, 148 L.Ed.2d 373 (2000).

20. Kotler v. Lalley, 112 Conn. 86, 151 A. 433 (1930).

21. *See* City of Memphis v. Greene, 451 U.S. 100, 101 S.Ct. 1584, 67 L.Ed.2d 769 (1981).

§ 7.16

1. Atlantic & Pac. Ins. Co. v. Barnes, 666 P.2d 163 (Colo.App.1983); 1 Greenleaf, Evidence § 74 (16th ed. 1899); Morgan, Some Problems of Proof 75 (1956); Thayer, Evidence 370, 485 (1898); 9 Wigmore, Evidence § 2486 (Chadbourn rev. 1981).

2. *Compare* Preferred Accident Ins. Co. v. Grasso, 186 F.2d 987 (2d Cir.1951) (burden of proof in declaratory judgment action on insured defendant), *and* State Farm Mut. Auto. Ins. Co. v. Smith, 48 F.Supp. 570 (W.D.Mo.1942) (defendant has burden of proof of showing liability), *with* American Indem. Co. v. Davis, 155 F.Supp. 47 (M.D.Ga.1957), *modified,* 260 F.2d 440 (5th Cir.1958) (plaintiff insurer has burden of proof of breach of cooperation clause), *and* Travelers Ins. Co. v. Drumheller, 25 F.Supp. 606 (W.D.Mo.1938) (burden on plaintiff to prove insured did not die as result of accident). *See generally* Note, Developments in the Law—Declaratory Judgments—1941–1949, 62 Harv. L. Rev. 787, 836 (1949).

3. Morgan, Some Problems of Proof 75 (1956); Thayer, Evidence 371 & n.2 (1898); 9 Wigmore, Evidence § 2486 (Chadbourn rev. 1981).

this simply restates the question: To which party's case is the fact essential?

Every jurisdiction has rules of allocation governing most types of claims. As new legal rights are established by decisional law or statute, corresponding decisions have to be made on allocation of the burden of proof.[4] The burden of proof does not follow the burden of pleading in all cases.[5] Many jurisdictions, for example, require plaintiffs to plead non-payment of an obligation sued on but do not require them to prove it.[6] In federal courts defendant must plead contributory negligence as an affirmative defense to an action for injuries negligently caused, but federal courts in diversity cases will follow a local rule that puts the burden of proof on plaintiffs.[7] The burden of pleading is itself allocated on pragmatic considerations of fairness, convenience, and policy rather than on any general principle of pleading.[8] Since the burden of proof is allocated on very much the same basis, an inquiry to determine the pleading rule (absent clear authority) would simply parallel the inquiry needed to determine the burden of proof rule in the first instance.

Access to proof

The burden of proof traditionally is placed on the party having the readier access to knowledge about the fact in question.[9] This consideration, however, has never been controlling. Plaintiff usually has the burden to prove what the defendant's conduct was in negligence and breach of contract. Even more starkly, a plaintiff who has been defrauded has the burden of proving the falsity of the representations and, under classic fraud doctrine, the fact that the falsity was known to defendant but not to plaintiff.[10] If access to facts were a determining factor in allocating the burden of proof, it would be bizarre to require plaintiff to prove in court the facts about which he or she was deceived in the underlying transaction. The alleged wrongdoer's greater access to evidence as a factor in procedural justice is thus offset by another such

4. *See, e.g.*, Texas Dept. of Community Affairs v. Burdine, 450 U.S. 248, 101 S.Ct. 1089, 67 L.Ed.2d 207 (1981).

5. *See* Thayer, Evidence 366–367 (1898).

6. *See* Thomas v. Tygart, 177 Ark. 1195, 6 S.W.2d 827 (1928); Alden, The Defense of Payment Under Code Procedure, 19 Yale L.J. 647 (1910); Reppy, The Anomaly of Payment as an Affirmative Defense, 10 Cornell L.Q. 269 (1925). *But cf.* Conkling v. Weatherwax, 181 N.Y. 258, 73 N.E. 1028 (1905) (action to enforce legacy as lien on realty is not based on instrument for payment of money, so burden of proving nonpayment is on plaintiff). *See also* text at § 3.19 *supra*.

7. Palmer v. Hoffman, 318 U.S. 109, 117, 63 S.Ct. 477, 482, 87 L.Ed. 645, 651 (1943); Ideal Mut. Ins. Co. v. Last Days Evangelical Assn., 783 F.2d 1234 (5th Cir. 1986). *See also* Chapter 3.

8. *See* Clark, Cases on Modern Pleading 610 (1952); Hay, Allocating the Burden of Proof, 72 Ind. L.J. 651 (1997)(burden should be assigned to minimize costs of proof); §§ 3.11, 4.5 *supra*.

9. Maguire, Evidence, Common Sense and Common Law 179 (1947); 9 Wigmore, Evidence § 2486 (Chadbourn rev. 1981); 4 Harper, James, and Gray, Law of Torts § 19.1 (2d ed. 1986). *See, e.g.*, Gomez v. Toledo, 446 U.S. 635, 100 S.Ct. 1920, 64 L.Ed.2d 572 (1980).

10. *See* Prosser and Keeton, Torts 728 (5th ed. 1984).

factor—the sense that a charge of serious wrongdoing should be proven by the person making it.[11]

Access to evidence is a much diminished basis for allocating burden of proof in modern liberal discovery. Whatever testimony is available from an opposing party ordinarily can be elicited through deposition before trial and be at hand for use in evidence.[12] Also, in this era of reporting and recordkeeping, large amounts of relevant evidence are compiled in documents accessible by subpoena duces tecum and, in the case of public records, freedom of information laws.[13] From this perspective, the critical element in allocation is not the burden of coming forward with evidence but the burden of persuasion in the face of evidence of ambiguous significance.

Substantive policy

Finally, substantive considerations are influential in allocation of burden of proof. For real or supposed reasons of policy the law sometimes disfavors certain types of claims and defenses. Burden of proof is often used as a handicap against the disfavored contention.[14] Thus, the defendant in libel or slander formerly was required to prove the truth of the objectionable words to escape liability.[15] The evolved interpretation of the First Amendment, however, requires plaintiff to prove the falsity of a statement in news media about a subject of public interest.[16]

Another substantively influenced rule of allocation is associated with the concept of *res ipsa loquitur* in tort litigation. This concept responds to the injuries suffered by people whose safety is dependent on conditions under the control of others. Res ipsa loquitur, in at least one of its formulations, holds that under certain conditions plaintiff can satisfy the burden of coming forward with evidence to prove negligence without directly proving a specific negligent act. The conditions specify that (1) the injury-inflicting instrument be in defendant's exclusive control in circumstances in which injury does not ordinarily occur without negligence, and that (2) the evidence show no fault on the part of the injured person. This is enough to submit the case to the jury.[17] For somewhat

11. Nance, Civility and the Burden of Proof, 17 Harv. J.L. & Pub. Policy 647 (1994).

12. *See* Fed. R. Evid. 804(a) (admissibility of "testimony given as a witness ... in a deposition ... if the party ... had an opportunity ... to develop the testimony by direct, cross, or redirect examination").

13. *See* Tomlinson, Use of the Freedom of Information Act for Discovery Purposes, 43 Md. L. Rev. 119 (1984); *see also* Lloyd v. American Export Lines, 580 F.2d 1179 (3d Cir.1978) (testimony at government inquest following incident).

14. Clark, Code Pleading 609–610 (2d ed. 1947).

15. *Id.*

16. Philadelphia Newspapers v. Hepps, 475 U.S. 767, 106 S.Ct. 1558, 89 L.Ed.2d 783 (1986). *See* Farragher v. City of Boca Raton, 524 U.S. 775, 118 S.Ct. 2275, 141 L.Ed.2d 662 (1988) (deciding what should be an affirmative defense in sexual harassment cases as a matter of substantive policy).

17. *See, e.g.,* Dermatossian v. New York City Transit Auth., 67 N.Y.2d 219, 492 N.E.2d 1200, 501 N.Y.S.2d 784 (1986).

similar reasons, courts have sometimes thrown the burden on each of several tortfeasors to disprove responsibility for a plaintiff's injuries.[18]

The degree of persuasion required is also sometimes adjusted upward as a handicap against disfavored contentions.[19] Thus if a claim states that a written contract was orally modified, the party claiming the modification must in some jurisdictions prove its contention by clear and convincing evidence.[20]

§ 7.17 Presumptions

The term "presumption" involves a relationship between a proven or admitted fact or group of facts (*A*) and another fact or conclusion of fact (*B*) sought to be proved.[1] The basic idea is that when *A* is established, then through a presumption it may be concluded that *B* occurred. The strength and effect of various presumptions, however, is itself various.

Irrebuttable presumption

At one end of the spectrum is the presumption of law, or conclusive or irrebuttable presumption. If *A* is shown, then *B* is to be conclusively presumed and the court will not accept evidence or entertain argument to show the nonexistence of *B*. As a corollary, if the trier of fact finds *A* it must also find *B*. The conclusive presumption is not really a procedural device but a means of restructuring the substantive law. When the law conclusively presumes the presence of *B* from *A*, the substantive law no longer requires the existence of *B* if *A* is present. A conclusive presumption is not a device of trial procedure but a device for transition in the law itself.[2]

18. *E.g.,* Summers v. Tice, 33 Cal.2d 80, 199 P.2d 1 (1948).

19. *See also* §§ 7.13–7.14 *supra.*

20. *See* Badover v. Guaranty Trust & Sav. Bank, 186 Cal. 775, 200 P. 638 (1921); Clark v. Diefendorf, 109 Conn. 507, 147 A. 33 (1929). *See also, e.g.,* In re Kaminsky's Will, 17 A.D.2d 690, 230 N.Y.S.2d 954 (1962) (proof of inter vivos gift against decedent's estate). Compare Crawford–El v. Britton, 523 U.S. 574, 118 S.Ct. 1584, 140 L.Ed.2d 759 (1998)(rejecting clear and convincing proof requirement in civil rights cases for plaintiff's showing of defendant's unconstitutional motive).

§ 7.17

1. Mueller & Kirkpatrick, Evidence §§ 3.4–10 (1995); Strong, et al., McCormick on Evidence §§ 342–345 (5th ed. 1999); Allen, Presumptions in Civil Actions Reconsidered, 66 Iowa L. Rev. 844 (1981); Ladd, Presumptions in Civil Actions, 1977 Ariz. St. L.J. 275; Louisell, Construing Rule 301: Instructing the Jury on Presumptions in Civil Actions and Proceedings, 63 Va. L. Rev. 281 (1977); Nesson, Rationality, Presumptions and Judicial Comment: A Response to Professor Allen, 94 Harv. L. Rev. 1574 (1981).

2. *See, e.g.,* Usery v. Turner Elkhorn Mining Co., 428 U.S. 1, 96 S.Ct. 2882, 49 L.Ed.2d 752 (1976); 9 Wigmore, Evidence § 2492 (Chadbourn rev. 1981); Bohlen, The Effects of Rebuttable Presumptions of Law upon the Burden of Proof, 68 U. Pa. L. Rev. 307, 311–312 (1920); Gordon and Tenebaum, Conclusive Presumption Analysis: The Principle of Individual Opportunity, 71 Nw. U.L. Rev. 579 (1976). *See also* Comment, California's Tangled Web: Blood Tests and the Conclusive Presumption of Legitimacy, 20 Stan. L. Rev. 754 (1968).

Inference

At the other end of the spectrum, "presumption" refers to an ordinary process of making inferences from proven facts. In this usage the term refers to the logical inference of one fact from the existence of another.[3] The presumption is arbitrary and irrational unless it can be shown, with substantial assurance, that a rational connection exists between the fact proved and the fact presumed and that the presumed fact is more likely than not to flow from the proved fact on which it depends.[4]

Judicial proof usually involves inferences from circumstantial evidence. If Smith mails at a postbox a letter to Jones, with proper address and postage on the envelope, the trier may infer that Jones received the letter.[5] The existence of long skid marks on a pavement permits the inference of great speed on the part of the vehicle.[6] Handwriting similarities permit the inference of identity of authorship of two documents.[7] The possibilities of linkages of facts through inferences is thus as boundless as the diversity of human experience.

As we shall see, courts set limits on the inferences juries may draw. If a court determines that *B* is a rational inference from *A*, then the trier of fact is free to draw that inference as a matter of general reasoning and persuasion without the aid of special procedural rules pertaining to litigation. "Inference" is the word generally and properly used to refer to this process of drawing conclusions of fact on the basis of general reasoning and experience.[8]

Allocating burden of production

The word "presumption" properly refers only to a device for allocating the burden of production.[9] It operates thus: If *B* is presumed from *A*,

3. *See* Amtorg Trading Corp. v. Higgins, 150 F.2d 536, 538 n. 2 (2d Cir.1945); State v. Corby, 28 N.J. 106, 113–115, 145 A.2d 289, 293–294 (1958) (citing 9 Wigmore, Evidence § 2491 (Chadbourn rev. 1981)). *See also* Bohlen, The Effects of Rebuttable Presumptions of Law upon the Burden of Proof, 68 U. Pa. L. Rev. 307, 311–312 (1920).

4. *See* Sanders v. State, 649 S.W.2d 59 (Tex.App.1982). *Compare* Leary v. United States, 395 U.S. 6, 89 S.Ct. 1532, 23 L.Ed.2d 57 (1969) (presumption that possessor of marijuana knows that it was illegally imported).

5. *See, e.g.,* Franklin Life Ins. Co. v. Brantley, 231 Ala. 554, 165 So. 834 (1936); Graybar Elec. Co. v. Sawyer, 485 A.2d 1384 (Me.1985); Williams v. Northeast Mut. Ins. Assn., 51 S.W.2d 142 (Mo.App.1932); 9 Wigmore, Evidence § 2519 (Chadbourn rev. 1981).

6. Pace v. McClow, 119 Ill.App.3d 419, 75 Ill.Dec. 836, 458 N.E.2d 4 (1983); *see* Akers v. Epperson, 172 S.W.2d 512 (Tex. Civ.App.1942); Notes, 23 A.L.R.2d 112, 125 (1952).

7. *See* Flickema v. Henry Kraker Co., 252 Mich. 406, 233 N.W. 362 (1930).

8. *See* Maguire, Evidence, Common Sense and Common Law 183 (1947); 9 Wigmore, Evidence § 2491 (Chadbourn rev. 1981).

9. *See* Fed. R. Evid. 301; Texas Dept. of Community Affairs v. Burdine, 450 U.S. 248, 101 S.Ct. 1089, 67 L.Ed.2d 207 (1981); Legille v. Dann, 544 F.2d 1 (D.C.Cir.1976); Estate of Pfleghar v. Teter, 35 Wash.App. 844, 670 P.2d 677 (1983); Morgan, Some Problems of Proof 77 (1956); 9 Wigmore, Evidence §§ 2490–2491 (Chadbourn rev. 1981); Bohlen, The Effect of Rebuttable Presumptions of Law upon the Burden of Proof, 68 U. Pa. L. Rev. 307 (1920).

then on a showing of *A, B must* be assumed by the trier in the absence of evidence of non-*B*. To put it another way, if *A* is shown, then the party who asserts non-*B* has the burden of production on the issue of *B*'s existence or nonexistence. The word "presumption" will be used here only in this way.

Courts and legislatures have created presumptions in cases in which *B* either (1) would be a permissible inference from *A*, but not the *only* permissible one,[10] or (2) would not even be a permissible inference from *A*.[11] In such situations a presumption has an artificial procedural force and effect (when proponents rest their case) beyond the logical probative effect of the evidence. In the first situation described, a presumption would call for a directed verdict on the issue of *B* or non-*B*[12] if the opponents also rest, while, as we have seen, without the presumption the proponents on that issue would be entitled only to have it go to the jury.[13] In the second situation the presumption has a double effect. It protects the proponents from an adverse directed verdict on the issue (or nonsuit or dismissal), which they would otherwise suffer for want of sufficient evidence.[14] It also entitles the proponents to a directed verdict in their own favor on the issue, absent any countervailing evidence. Later in this section we shall inquire whether a presumption may have further continuing effect after evidence to rebut it has been introduced.

Grounds of presumptions

The preceding discussion shows that presumptions can have important consequences. What, then, are the bases on which courts or legislatures will create presumptions? For the most part they are the same kinds of reasons that influence the allocation of the burden of production generally—convenience, fairness, and policy.[15] What is *likely*, for instance, is often presumed. Most people are sane, as the law reckons sanity; most letters, properly sent, reach their destination. Absent any evidence pointing to an opposite conclusion in the case at hand, it is both convenient and fair to assume that *this* testator was sane when he or she

10. *See, e.g.,* authorities cited *supra* note 2. *See also* McMillan v. Nelson, 149 Fla. 334, 5 So.2d 867 (1942) (that stop sign was erected by proper authority); 9 Wigmore, Evidence § 2515 (Chadbourn rev. 1981) (presumption of ownership from possession).

11. *See, e.g.,* Kusior v. Silver, 54 Cal.2d 603, 354 P.2d 657, 7 Cal.Rptr. 129 (1960) (presumption of child's legitimacy from fact that parents were cohabiting); *Cf.* In re Lisa R., 13 Cal.3d 636, 532 P.2d 123, 119 Cal. Rptr. 475 (1975) (father offering to prove paternity of child born out of wedlock); Conn. Gen. Stat. Rev. §§ 52–182 to 52–183 (1958) (presumption of agency between owner and operator of automobile).

12. *See* Sellers v. Qualls, 206 Md. 58, 110 A.2d 73 (1954); In re Padjan's Estate, 340 Mich. 277, 65 N.W.2d 743 (1954); Ritchie v. Thomas, 190 Or. 95, 105, 224 P.2d 543, 547 (1950); Morgan, Some Problems of Proof 76–77 (1956).

13. *See* § 7.15 *supra.*

14. *See* Thayer, Evidence 336 (1898). *Cf.* O'Dea v. Amodeo, 118 Conn. 58, 170 A. 486 (1934); Morgan, Some Problems of Proof 77 (1956).

15. *See* Fisher v. City of Berkeley, 37 Cal.3d 644, 209 Cal.Rptr. 682, 693 P.2d 261 (1984). *See also* Maguire, Evidence, Common Sense and Common Law 185–186 (1947); § 7.16 *supra.*

made the will,[16] or that *this* person accused of a crime was sane when he or she did the act charged as criminal,[17] or that *this* properly mailed letter reached the addressee.[18] These assumptions will at least save a lot of time and trouble in making ponderous proof of matters that would be controverted in only a small number of cases.

Access to evidence is often the basis for creating a presumption. When goods are damaged in a bailee's possession, for instance, the bailee can more easily find out what happened to them than the bailor, so it is fair to presume the bailee's negligence as an initial matter and put the bailee to the production of exculpatory evidence, if any exists.[19] The owner of an automobile has better means of knowing whether the driver was in his or her service when it struck the plaintiff than has the plaintiff. In this case there is also an increasingly strong policy to make an automobile owner pay for the damage the vehicle causes even where no agency exists in the legal sense. Fairness and policy therefore combine to justify a presumption of agency from the mere fact of ownership.[20] Here, it may be noted, is a presumption (usually created by statute) in a situation in which most courts otherwise would not even permit an inference.

Rebuttal of presumption

If a presumption operates in proponents' favor when they rest their case, two questions arise: What must the opponents do to lift the burden of production then resting on them? If the opponents do lift this burden, what (if any) further effect does the presumption have?

The first question can be rephrased in terms of the symbols we have already used. If from *A* there is a presumption of *B*, and *A* is shown,[21] what must the opponent do to escape a compulsory finding of *B*? The answer is that the opponent must introduce evidence that will justify a finding of non-*B*. This requirement has, to use Maguire's terms, both an extensive and an intensive aspect.[22] To satisfy the extensive aspect, the

16. *See, e.g.,* Panduit Corp. v. All States Plastic Mfg. Co., 744 F.2d 1564 (Fed.Cir. 1984); In re Jamison's Estate, 41 Cal.2d 1, 15, 256 P.2d 984, 990 (1953); Sellers v. Qualls, 206 Md. 58, 110 A.2d 73 (1954); In re Padjan's Estate, 340 Mich. 277, 65 N.W.2d 743 (1954); In re Davis' Will, 14 N.J. 166, 101 A.2d 521 (1953); In re Franks' Will, 231 N.C. 252, 259, 56 S.E.2d 668, 674 (1949); Matter of Estate of Polda, 349 N.W.2d 11 (N.D.1984).

17. *See* Davis v. United States, 160 U.S. 469, 485–487, 16 S.Ct. 353, 357–358, 40 L.Ed. 499, 504–505 (1895).

18. *See* Maguire, Evidence, Common Sense and Common Law 183 (1947); 9 Wigmore, Evidence § 2491 (Chadbourn rev. 1981).

19. Frissell v. John W. Rogers, Inc., 141 Conn. 308, 106 A.2d 162 (1954). *See also* James, Accident Liability: Some Wartime Developments, 55 Yale L.J. 365, 392 n.133 (1946); Morgan, Instructing the Jury upon Presumption and Burden of Proof, 47 Harv. L. Rev. 59, 79 (1933).

20. *See* O'Dea v. Amodeo, 118 Conn. 58, 170 A. 486 (1934); Cebulak v. Lewis, 320 Mich. 710, 32 N.W.2d 21 (1948).

21. Of course, the evidence tending to show *A* may itself fall short of compelling such a finding. If so, the trier will have to decide whether *A* exists.

22. Maguire, Evidence, Common Sense and Common Law 184 (1947).

evidence must cover the whole of *B*. Thus, a presumption of negligence on the part of the charterers of a vessel turned over to them in good condition but sinking while in their control is not met by a showing of care during *part* of the time it was in their control.[23] Such evidence is not enough to lift the burden of production. To satisfy the intensive aspect of the requirement, the evidence must satisfy the qualitative tests of sufficiency of the evidence to show non-*B*.

If the opponent has lifted the burden of production by rebutting evidence that satisfies the above standards, what happens to the presumption? The orthodox view, propounded by Thayer, holds that the presumption is utterly destroyed and disappears, even though the trier disbelieves the countervailing evidence.[24] If, for example, the addressee of a properly mailed letter testifies that he or she never received it, that testimony would, if believed, justify a finding of nonreceipt. Under the orthodox view this testimony would, then, *end the presumption* even if everybody in the courtroom was convinced that the testimony was a lie. In the case put, the destruction of the presumption would not, however, compel a finding of nonreceipt because a properly addressed letter is so likely to reach its destination that a *rational inference* may be drawn that it did so.[25] And although countervailing evidence banishes the artificial procedural effect given by a presumption to the facts proved, *A* (in this case the mailing of the letter), yet it does not destroy the rational probative effect of *A*. If the trier rejects the testimony of nonreceipt as false and believes the testimony of proper mailing, it could and probably would find receipt as an inference from the mailing. On the suppositions here made, this result seems just and proper and the orthodox theory would not prevent it. But in other situations that view presents serious problems.

Persuasive effect of presumption after rebuttal

Suppose, first, that the mind of the trier in the case just described is in equipoise on all the evidence. If the proponents have the burden of persuading the trier of *B*'s existence (that is, that the letter was received), they must lose. Does a presumption of *B*'s existence from proof of *A* have any effect on the persuasion burden? The orthodox doctrine

23. Alpine Forwarding Co. v. Pennsylvania R.R., 60 F.2d 734 (2d Cir.1932); Maguire, *supra* note 23, at 184. *Cf.* Frissell v. John W. Rogers, Inc., 141 Conn. 308, 106 A.2d 162 (1954) (presumption of bailee's negligence arising from redelivery of goods in damaged condition not met by showing they were damaged by fire, without more, since some fires do result from negligence).

24. Thayer, Evidence 346 (1898). *See* St. Mary's Honor Center v. Hicks, 509 U.S. 502, 113 S.Ct. 2742, 125 L.Ed.2d 407 (1993); A.C. Aukerman Co. v. R.L. Chaides Const. Co., 960 F.2d 1020 (Fed.Cir.1992); Sheehan v. Pima County, 135 Ariz. 235, 660 P.2d 486 (App.1982); Gaudreau v. Eclipse Pioneer Div. of Bendix Air Corp., 137 N.J.L. 666, 61 A.2d 227 (Err.& App.1948); Morgan, Some Problems of Proof 77 (1956); 9 Wigmore, Evidence § 2491 (Chadbourn rev. 1981).

25. *See* In re Yoder Co., 758 F.2d 1114 (6th Cir.1985); Southland Life Ins. Co. v. Greenwade, 138 Tex. 450, 456–457, 159 S.W.2d 854, 857–858 (1942); 9 Wigmore, Evidence §§ 2491(1), 2519 (Chadbourn rev. 1981).

says emphatically not—it declares that the effect of a presumption is entirely spent in shifting the burden of production, and it denies that the burden of persuasion ever shifts.[26] But why should this necessarily be so? We have seen that the considerations determining the allocation of the burden of persuasion are of the same kind as those leading to the creation of presumptions.[27] If the developments of a trial bring forth a situation justifying a presumption in the proponent's favor, might not the same considerations (though not necessarily) suffice to call for placing the burden of persuasion also on the opponent?[28] Some courts say frankly that it should, and that a presumption may sometimes shift the burden of persuasion;[29] but on this point the weight of authority indicates that it may not.[30] This problem is important only in cases in which the trier's mind is in equipoise at the end of its deliberations—a situation that may not occur very often.

In another situation the orthodox theory gives more trouble. As we have seen, the fact(s) *A* giving rise to a *presumption* of *B* are often insufficient to warrant an *inference* of *B*. A familiar example is the fairly common presumption of agency from the fact of ownership of an automobile. Suppose that Plaintiff, injured by Owner's automobile driven by Driver, has no available evidence on the issue of agency and therefore rests on a presumption of agency, ownership being proved or admitted. Suppose further that Owner, sole defendant, puts on her own testimony and that of Driver, both of whom deny agency. If this testimony banishes the presumption, you may have the anomaly that the trier must find nonagency, even though it thoroughly disbelieves the denial as self-serving perjury.[31] Such a result does indeed offend common sense and justice, and most courts reject it, although it is hard to reconcile its rejection with the orthodox view.[32] When a presumption comes into play,

26. St. Mary's Honor Center v. Hicks, 509 U.S. 502, 113 S.Ct. 2742, 125 L.Ed.2d 407 (1993); Thayer, Evidence 370, 378 (1898); 9 Wigmore, Evidence § 2489 (Chadbourn rev. 1981).

27. *See* text at note 15 *supra*.

28. Maguire, Evidence, Common Sense and Common Law 185 (1947).

29. Kelly v. Armstrong, 141 F.3d 799 (8th Cir.1998); Page v. Phelps, 108 Conn. 572, 143 A. 890 (1928); Mueller & Kirkpatrick, Evidence § 3.8 note 1 (1995)(listing twelve states in which presumptions shift the burden of persuasion); Morgan, Instructing the Jury upon Presumption and Burden of Proof, 47 Harv. L. Rev. 59, 62 (1933). *See* Maguire, *supra* note 28, at 187. *Cf.* Burr v. Sherwin Williams Co., 42 Cal.2d 682, 268 P.2d 1041 (1954) (res ipsa loquitur said to raise inference rather than presumption, but shifts burden of persuasion to defendant); James, Proof of the Breach in Negligence Cases (Including Res Ipsa Loquitur), 37 Va. L. Rev. 179, 224 (1951). *But cf.* Western & Atl. R.R. v. Henderson, 279 U.S. 639, 49 S.Ct. 445, 73 L.Ed. 884 (1929).

30. *See* Simpson v. Home Petroleum Corp., 770 F.2d 499 (5th Cir.1985); Panduit Corp. v. All States Plastic Mfg. Co., 744 F.2d 1564 (Fed.Cir.1984); In re Marriage of Nagel, 133 Ill.App.3d 498, 88 Ill.Dec. 584, 478 N.E.2d 1192 (1985); Matter of Estate of Mikeska, 140 Mich.App. 116, 362 N.W.2d 906 (1985).

31. *See* McIver v. Schwartz, 50 R.I. 68, 145 A. 101 (1929).

32. *See, e.g.,* O'Dea v. Amodeo, 118 Conn. 58, 170 A. 486 (1934); Cebulak v. Lewis, 320 Mich. 710, 32 N.W.2d 21 (1948); Wyckoff v. Mutual Life Ins. Co., 173 Or. 592, 147 P.2d 227 (1944).

the courts tend to send the matter to the jury unless the evidence to rebut the presumption leaves no reasonable room for the jury's function.

If the issue is sent to the jury, the question arises, as in the illustration involving the mailing of the letter, whether to place the burden of persuasion on plaintiff or defendant. Here again, most courts will probably put it on plaintiff.[33]

Instructions on presumption

A different problem has arisen in connection with presumptions. If a case goes to the jury, what, if anything, should be said to the jury about presumptions that may have come into the case? The orthodox answer is unequivocal: nothing.[34] If a presumption has been met with sufficient evidence, the presumption has vanished and the issue should go to the jury without mention of it.

Even when a court gives a presumption continuing effect after evidence has been introduced to rebut it, there is no need to mention the presumption to the jury and it is probably only confusing to do so. If the burden of persuasion is shifted, that is the only burden the instructions need mention. If it is not, but the jury may find *B* if they disbelieve opponent's evidence of non-*B*, then a simple direction to that effect is all that is needed. The only justification for telling the jury about the presumption would be a desire to implement the policy behind the presumption by inviting the jury to weigh it in some vague manner not easy to understand or articulate, as they would a part of the evidence.

33. *See* Jefferson Standard Life Ins. Co. v. Clemmer, 79 F.2d 724, 729–731 (4th Cir. 1935); authorities cited note 24 *supra;* 9 Wigmore, Evidence § 2491 (Chadbourn rev. 1981).

The two alternative views in the text are not the only ones to attain some judicial support. Morgan, for example, discusses the so-called orthodox view (*see* note 18 *supra* and accompanying text) and lists the following views of presumption: (1) A presumption puts on the opponent the burden of persuading the jury "to believe so much of the evidence against the presumed fact as would justify a reasonable jury in finding against that fact"; the presumption disappears when opponent puts in evidence on which the trier's mind is in equipoise, if that evidence "is of the requisite quantity and quality to justify a reasonable jury in finding the nonexistence of the presumed fact." (2) A presumption puts on opponent "the burden of persuading the jury that the existence of the presumed fact is so doubtful that the jury cannot determine whether it exists." (3) A presumption puts on opponent "the burden of persuading the jury that the presumed fact does not exist." In addition to having one of the foregoing effects, the presumption (a) is to be weighed by the jury together with the evidence in the case; (b) may simply allow an inference of *B* from *A* when the ordinary rules of proof would not allow it; (c) may compel the finding of *B*, unconditionally, if *A* is found (the conclusive presumption). Morgan, Instructing the Jury upon Presumption and Burden of Proof, 47 Harv. L. Rev. 59, 60–62 (1933). A list of possibilities containing fewer refinements is found in O'Dea v. Amodeo, 118 Conn. 58, 170 A. 486 (1934). *See generally* Morgan, *supra,* at 81–86.

34. Thayer, Evidence 337–339 (1898); 9 Wigmore, Evidence § 2491 (Chadbourn rev. 1981). *See also* Fed. R. Evid. 301; Louisell, Construing Rule 301: Instructing the Jury on Presumptions in Civil Actions and Proceedings, 63 Va. L. Rev. 281 (1977). In the context of a criminal trial, the Supreme Court has held that jury instructions imposing mandatory presumptions violate a defendant's due process rights. *See* Carella v. California, 491 U.S. 263, 109 S.Ct. 2419, 105 L.Ed.2d 218 (1989).

But if policy demands additional force to the presumption, better ways than this can be devised to give it.

§ 7.18 Distinction Between Law and Fact in Jury Trials[1]

At least as far back as the time of Coke[2] the distinction between the functions of judge and jury has been phrased in terms of law and fact. But in both a philosophical and a lay sense these terms have never described accurately the line that divides these functions. We shall not here attempt any new or refined definition of terms but rather will examine the kinds of jobs that the tribunal as a whole performs in litigated cases and how they have been assigned by precedent to judge and jury respectively. In this analysis we also shall see the role that policy may play in influencing this assignment.

The word "fact" in the ordinary or lay sense is used "as indicating things, events, actions, conditions, as happening, existing, really taking place."[3] Judges, rather than juries, always have decided many questions of fact in this sense.

Preliminary fact questions

Objections and motions made before trial often turn on the resolution of disputes over such facts. A question may arise, for example, whether process mailed to a defendant ever in fact reached him or her, or whether one of the parties intended to make a new place of abode his or her permanent home. Courts ordinarily decide matters like this as they arise on preliminary motions (for example, to quash service, objections to venue, and jurisdiction) without the aid of a jury.[4] During the trial, objections to offered evidence often raise questions of fact in this sense that must be decided before the matter of admissibility, for example whether a document is a "business record" so as to be admissible under an exception to the hearsay rule. The court ordinarily decides issues of fact that determine the admissibility of evidence.[5]

§ 7.18

1. The classic treatment of this subject is in Thayer, Evidence ch. 5 (1898). *See also* Green, Judge and Jury (1930); 2 Harper, James, and Gray Law of Torts ch. 15 (2d ed. 1986).

2. Thayer, Evidence 185 (1898).

3. *Id.* at 191.

4. Gilbert v. David, 235 U.S. 561, 35 S.Ct. 164, 59 L.Ed. 360 (1915); McNello v. John B. Kelly, Inc., 283 F.2d 96, 99 n. 2 (3d Cir.1960); Southern Photo Material Co. v. Eastman Kodak Co., 224 Fed. 523 (N.D.Ga. 1915); Thayer, Evidence 187 (1898).

5. Fed. R. Evid. 104; Bourjaily v. United States, 483 U.S. 171, 107 S.Ct. 2775, 97 L.Ed.2d 144 (1987); Strong, et al., McCormick on Evidence § 53 (5th ed. 1999); 9 Wigmore, Evidence § 2550 (Chadbourn rev. 1981); Functions of Judge and Jury in the Determination of Preliminary Questions of Fact, 43 Harv. L. Rev. 165, 166, 169, 175 (1929); Maguire and Epstein, Preliminary Questions of Fact in Determining the Admissibility of Evidence, 40 Harv. L. Rev. 392, 412, 413 (1927); Stephens, Controlling the Civil Jury: Towards a Functional Model of Justification, 76 Ky. L.J. 81 (1988).

Events and evaluations

The proposition that the jury decides questions of fact thus has reference only to the ultimate issues of fact litigated in the trial. Here the jury's function may extend to two kinds of questions: first, what were the happenings, occurrences, or conduct of the parties—that is, what did the parties do and what were the circumstances? Second, what are the legal consequences of these "facts"?[6] Such a distinction is crude and not clear-cut, but if we keep its limitations in mind it will be useful for present purposes. The question whether a letter of acceptance was mailed ten or twenty days after the offer is a recognizably different kind of question from whether either period is within a "reasonable time" of the offer. The questions of an automobile's rate of speed before the collision, the condition of the pavement at that time, the visibility, and so on, differ from the question whether that speed (whatever it was) was a reasonable one under the circumstances found to exist. There is the same difference between the question of what a party did and the question (in any form) of what it should have done.

Determinations of what the parties did, particularly where their accounts so differ that an issue of credibility is involved, are prototype questions of fact for the jury. Yet even here the court has important roles to play and opportunities to exercise real control over the jury.

Court decisions on evidence

In the first place, the court limits what a jury may consider by ruling on the admissibility of offered evidence. Questions of admissibility are of two kinds: those involving notions of relevancy and those involving the exclusionary rules.[7] Relevancy is not itself a legal concept, but one invoking logical principles of general application. That is, the question whether a given piece of evidence is relevant in the attempt to prove a proposition and the question of the extent of its probative value both refer to general principles of logical reasoning and concepts of probability, not to any rules of law.[8] Nevertheless, the decision of questions of relevancy invokes the function of the court in the ways described below.

1. The court determines the propositions that must or may be proved, thus limiting and selecting the evidence that will come before the jury for consideration.[9] If, for example, the court rules that defendant's good faith mistake is not a defense to an action for statutory violation, it

6. 2 Harper, James, and Gray, Law of Torts §§ 15.2, 15.3 (2d ed. 1986).

7. Thayer, Evidence 265, 269, 468 (1898); 1 Wigmore, Evidence § 10 (Tillers rev. 1983).

8. "The law furnishes no test of relevancy. For this it tacitly refers to logic and general experience,—assuming that the principles of reasoning are known to its judges." Thayer, *supra* note 7, at 265. *See* 1 Wigmore, *supra* note 7, at §§ 28–29a.

"Is it then really so, that this great multitude of decisions, emerging day by day, and holding that such evidence is or is not admissible, have so little to do with the law of evidence which they are professing to declare? Yes. The greater part of them are really reducible to mere propositions of sound reason as applied to a point of substantive law or pleading." Thayer, *supra,* at 269.

9. Thayer, Evidence 269 (1898).

will not allow evidence to show good faith to be put before the jury. If the court determines that preliminary oral negotiations for a contract may not be considered because the agreement has been completely integrated in a writing, the court will not let the jury hear testimony about the preliminary dealings. In a negligence case, if the court believes that the standard of care is an objective one that takes no account of a defendant's honest but substandard misjudgment, it will not let the jury hear evidence tending to show defendant's good faith belief that the course of action taken was the wisest one.

2. The court determines whether an item of evidence has sufficient probative value to offset objections to admissibility on the ground that it is "remote," or merely cumulative of other evidence, or prejudicial in that it might lead the jury to decide the case on legally impermissible grounds.[10] Thus, the court decides whether a restaurateur may show that the same bean dish was eaten by many patrons without ill effect for the purpose of proving that it was not in fact the cause of plaintiff's sickness.[11] The exclusionary rules of evidence are also administered by the court.[12] Thus, the court determines whether evidence of a conversation is offered for a hearsay purpose and, if so, whether it falls within any exception to the hearsay rule.

In addition to the evidence produced in court, the jury may consider whatever is judicially noticeable, that is, facts of general experience that may be assumed to be true without proof. The court determines when such an assumption may be made. Thus, when no evidence has been presented on whether a given trolley car had a bell, the court decides whether the jury may proceed on the assumption that it did have one.[13] The formula for making this decision in practice gives the courts a good deal of latitude.

Again, the court determines the sufficiency of the evidence admitted (together with whatever relevant facts are judicially noticeable) to show

10. Fed. R. Evid. 403; 1 Wigmore, Evidence §§ 28, 29a (Tillers rev. 1983); Strong, et al., McCormick on Evidence § 184 (5th ed. 1999).

It is true that some questions in the problem that has been called "dependent relevancy" go to the jury. If, for example, the relevancy of fact *A* depends on the coexistence of fact *B*, and if the evidence as to *B*'s existence is in conflict, the jury will determine whether *B* exists and will be told to consider *A* only if this finding is in the affirmative. But here, too, the *court* determines (1) whether there is enough evidence of *B*'s existence to go to the jury, and (2) whether *A* meets the canons of relevancy, if *B*'s existence be assumed. Fed. R. Evid. 104(b); Morgan, Functions of Judge and Jury in the Determination of Preliminary Questions of Fact, 43 Harv. L. Rev. 165, 169 (1929); Maguire and Epstein, Preliminary Questions of Fact in Determining the Admissibility of Evidence, 40 Harv. L. Rev. 392, 419–421 (1927).

11. Landfield v. Albiani Lunch Co., 268 Mass. 528, 168 N.E. 160 (1929).

12. Strong, et al., McCormick on Evidence § 51 (5th ed. 1999).

13. Mills v. Denver Tramway Corp., 155 F.2d 808 (10th Cir.1946) (noted in 60 Harv. L. Rev. 299). *See also* Simblest v. Maynard, 427 F.2d 1 (2d Cir.1970); *cf.* Fed. R. Evid. 201.

the existence of a fact in issue. The concept of sufficiency of evidence is the subject of the next section.

Court's role in evaluation

In the evaluation of facts in terms of their legal consequences, the court's role is at least equally important—and in some cases exclusive.[14] Indeed, the court's role is always exclusive in determining the rules of substantive law applicable to the case at hand. Thus, the court decides whether a contract vests legal rights in a third-party beneficiary, whether an actor's liability for physical damage caused by the actor is absolute or grounded only on negligence, whether the occupier of land owes a duty of care to discover a trespasser's presence at a place where people often trespass, and the like. But each case also involves a more specific evaluation of conduct. The court will declare that an offer must be accepted or a check must be presented within a "reasonable time" for certain legal consequences to follow. It still remains to decide whether the lapse of time shown by the evidence in this case is "reasonable" under all the circumstances. The law requires a motorist to use "reasonable care." It must still be decided whether *this* driver's conduct (speed, lookout, warning, and so on, as found from the evidence) was reasonable.

It is clear that rules of law could be formulated and administered so as to exclude the jury altogether from making these evaluations. A court could decide, for instance, that under a given set of circumstances motorists must blow their horns and that under a different set of circumstances they need not do so. Under such a pair of rules, the theoretical function of the jury would be to decide only whether the circumstances existed and whether the horn was blown, the question whether it should have been blown being decided by the court. By the same token, the rule could be formulated such that the jury decides not only whether the horn was blown but also whether the horn should have been blown.

Deciding who should decide

Whether rules of law shall be administered in either of these two ways is of great importance in many cases; when the facts are not disputed it is, of course, decisive. In deciding whether an issue will be regarded as one of fact or law, courts are deciding whether they think it calls for the community judgment of a jury or for the presumably detached expertise of a judge. The measure of "reasonableness," which recurs at so many points in our law, usually is construed as invoking the community standard of what the reasonably prudent person would do in the circumstances; the application of this standard is committed to the community's representatives on the jury.[15] This is the prevailing rule

14. *See* 2 Harper, James, and Gray, Law of Torts § 15.3 (2d ed. 1986).

15. *See* ABA Standards Relating to Trial Courts § 2.10, Commentary: "The tradi-

today in negligence cases. In malicious prosecution actions, however, a considerable body of authority requires the judge to decide whether the given conduct constitutes reasonable and probable cause.[16]

Trial court versus appellate court

The policy considerations underlying the characterization of an issue as one of fact or law go beyond the roles of jury and trial judge: They also involve the role of the appellate courts. If an issue is treated as one of law, the decision of the issue is finally determinable by the appellate courts, whereas a fact issue as determined in the trial court is conclusive unless the appellate court can say there was insufficient evidence to sustain the finding. The question, therefore, is whether a general rule of law applicable to many cases is desirable and feasible, or whether to rely on more flexible ad hoc judgments. Furthermore, if an issue is one of law, appeal can be taken in every case where that issue is presented in a context slightly different from those in the precedents on that issue. But if an issue is one of fact, the trial court determination terminates the litigation—unless the appellate court can say that it was not sustained by the evidence. One reason for calling the matter of negligence or "scope of employment" an issue of fact is to bar appellate review of determination of such issues;[17] one reason for calling obscenity an issue of law is to make the appellate courts the final arbiters of the kinds of literature that can be suppressed.[18]

Perhaps the clearest case of an appellate court's assumption of authority to decide evaluative questions appears in *Bose Corp. v. Consumers Union of the United States*,[19] an action for defamation of a product that had been adversely evaluated in a consumer magazine. Among the matters that plaintiff had to show was "actual malice" on the part of the publishers. The Court held that having regard for the free speech interests at stake, as to this issue the appellate court must make an independent determination. Indeed, the Court implied that an independent determination is appropriate to the highest court such a case might reach. Such a requirement reflects a deeply held conviction that judges—and particularly members of that Court—must exercise such review in order to preserve the precious liberties established and ordained by the Constitution.[20]

tional province of the jury in civil cases [includes] ... determining standards of conduct that the law itself defines as those that an ordinary reasonable person would observe."

16. Thayer, Evidence 221–232 (1898).

17. *See, e.g.,* Loper v. Morrison, 23 Cal.2d 600, 145 P.2d 1 (1944).

18. *See* Jenkins v. Georgia, 418 U.S. 153, 160–161, 94 S.Ct. 2750, 2754–2755, 41 L.Ed.2d 642, 649–651 (1974). Compare the majority and minority opinions in Pullman–Standard v. Swint, 456 U.S. 273, 102 S.Ct. 1781, 72 L.Ed.2d 66 (1982), and City of Memphis v. Greene, 451 U.S. 100, 101 S.Ct. 1584, 67 L.Ed.2d 769 (1981), both involving whether certain conduct was motivated by a racially discriminatory intent.

19. 466 U.S. 485, 104 S.Ct. 1949, 80 L.Ed.2d 502 (1984).

20. 466 U.S. at 510–511, 104 S.Ct. at 1965, 80 L.Ed.2d at 523.

In tracing a line between issues of fact and law, policy is limited by the constitutional right to jury trial and the history it embodies. Thus, the Supreme Court ruled that judges may assess civil penalties for violations of the Clean Water Act because that is comparable to judges' traditional criminal sentencing function,[21] but felt constrained by history to leave to jurors the somewhat comparable task of awarding statutory damages in copyright suits.[22] In other instances, history and policy coincide, as when the Court concluded that judges and juries should construe technical patent claims in infringement suits.[23]

Lastly, even when the function of evaluation (for example, of what is reasonable) is for the jury, courts have always set the limits within which the jury can perform its function.[24] A jury will be allowed to decide at what points and how often a reasonable pedestrian would look for traffic in crossing a busy street; it will not be allowed to say that a reasonable pedestrian would not look at all.

§ 7.19 Sufficiency of the Evidence

Sufficiency of the evidence concerns the court's function, not the jury's. The court will not submit a case to the jury unless it decides as an initial matter that the proponent has proven each of the propositions essential to the claim by *sufficient evidence* to justify or warrant a *finding in the proponent's favor on it.* This requirement is obviously a corollary of the modern notion that juries must decide cases on the evidence put before them in court and may no longer rely on private knowledge unknown to the judge.[1] Courts pass on the sufficiency of the evidence in response to a motion for directed verdict or for judgment notwithstanding verdict, both of which federal courts now term judgment as a matter of law.

The clearest case of insufficient evidence is presented when proponents offer *no evidence at all* on a proposition essential to their claim. A judicial legend says that there once was a "scintilla rule" under which a verdict could be directed only when there was no scintilla of evidence for proponent;[2] if there ever was such a notion, all that remains of it today is

21. Tull v. United States, 481 U.S. 412, 107 S.Ct. 1831, 95 L.Ed.2d 365 (1987).

22. Feltner v. Columbia Pictures Television, Inc., 523 U.S. 340, 118 S.Ct. 1279, 140 L.Ed.2d 438 (1998).

23. Markman v. Westview Instruments, Inc., 517 U.S. 370, 116 S.Ct. 1384, 134 L.Ed.2d 577 (1996).

24. 2 Harper, James, and Gray, Law of Torts 881–882 (2d ed. 1986). The legal importance of the control exercised through the directed verdict and j.n.o.v. should not obscure the fact that the exercise of such control is statistically infrequent. *See* McLauchlan, An Empirical Study of Civil Procedure: Directed Verdicts and Judgments Notwithstanding Verdicts, 2 J. Legal Stud. 459 (1973).

§ 7.19

1. *See* 9 Wigmore, Evidence §§ 2487, 2494 (Chadbourn rev. 1981); James, Proof of the Breach in Negligence Cases (Including Res Ipsa Loquitur), 37 Va. L. Rev. 179 (1951).

2. *See* 9 Wigmore, Evidence § 2494 n.14 (Chadbourn rev. 1981). This phrase is mentioned, to be repudiated, in the 1800s: Toomey v. R. Co., 3 C.B. (n.s.) 146, 150 (1857); Wheelton v. Hardisty, 8 E. & B. 232, 262,

its universal repudiation.[3]

Direct and circumstantial proof

Before analyzing the requirement of sufficiency of evidence, it will be helpful to briefly describe the kinds of evidence. All proof requires some process of inference before it can be translated into an actual decision by the trier. We are accustomed, however, to divide proof into the categories of direct and circumstantial. When evidence of a fact is in the form of testimony by a purported observer of that fact, we call the evidence direct as to that fact.[4] The only processes of inference have to do with the credibility (including accuracy of observation and memory) of the witness and the accuracy of his or her means of communication. When the thing itself is one of the facts in issue (such as the torn carpet that caused the accident, or the injured limb) and is put before the trier for actual inspection, we call the evidence "real evidence."[5] In all other cases proof is called "circumstantial" and requires further processes of inference. Typically it involves proof of fact *A*, which is not itself a fact in issue, as the basis of an inference of the existence of fact *B*, which is in issue. A word should also be said about what is called "demeanor evidence." This refers to what the trier may actually observe about the witnesses' appearance, conduct, manner, and so on.[6] It may have great bearing on questions of credibility, but it affects the question of sufficiency at only two points, as we shall see.

Sufficiency of testimony

When direct testimony is given on the existence of a simple fact (that is, in the sense of someone's conduct or an item in the circumstances surrounding it),[7] such testimony generally is held in civil cases to satisfy the test of sufficiency—it will justify or warrant a finding by the trier that the fact existed. The concept of sufficiency does not concern the question whether the trier actually will make such a finding, that is, with ordinary questions of credibility or the persuasive effect that evidence will actually have on the mind of the particular jury or judge as trier of fact. It does not ordinarily matter, therefore, that the testimony to the fact may be contradicted or impeached.[8]

277 (1857); Ryder v. Wombell, 4 L.R.-Ex. 32 (1868). It is difficult to find any prior time when the rule was a recognized test in England.

3. 9 Wigmore, Evidence § 2494 n.15 (Chadbourn rev. 1981); Smith, The Power of the Judge to Direct a Verdict: Section 457a of the New York Civil Practice Act, 24 Colum. L. Rev. 111, 114 (1924). *But cf.* Barber v. Stephenson, 260 Ala. 151, 69 So.2d 251 (1953).

4. 1 Wigmore, Evidence § 24 (Tillers rev. 1983).

5. *Id.* Another term is "demonstrative evidence."

6. *See* Hand, J., in Dyer v. MacDougall, 201 F.2d 265, 268–269 (2d Cir.1952); 3 Wigmore, Evidence § 946 (Chadbourn rev. 1970).

7. *See* § 7.18 *supra.*

8. *See* Kircher v. Atchison, T. & S. Fe Ry., 32 Cal.2d 176, 195 P.2d 427 (1948); Taylor v. Corkey, 142 Conn. 150, 111 A.2d 925 (1955); Twohey v. Brown, 246 Iowa 114, 66 N.W.2d 870 (1954); Olney v. Carmichael, 202 Md. 226, 232, 96 A.2d 37, 39

The statements in the last paragraph are subject to two qualifications. First, courts do place outer bounds on credibility, and testimony that is ruled incredible as a matter of law will not be counted in determining sufficiency. If, for example, a witness's testimony is flatly contradicted by indisputable facts or natural laws, it will be disregarded as not capable of belief by reasonable people.[9] Courts have the power to extend the notion of incredibility as a matter of law to contract the jury's function substantially. In fact, however, they have used this doctrine sparingly, extending it only to an occasional extreme set of circumstances beyond the physical fact situation. As one appellate court put it, perhaps overdramatically: "This court and the trial court must ordinarily accept as true the testimony even of a veritable Munchausen in the uttermost stretches of his imaginings."[10]

Corroboration

Direct testimony of a fact's existence may occasionally be regarded as insufficient to warrant a finding of that fact for another reason. The law imposes an artificial requirement of corroboration in a few instances, such as treason[11] or perjury.[12] Such rules were once fairly common but today have almost disappeared from civil cases. A possible exception is found in cases wherein a passenger is injured by the jerk or jolt of a train or other conveyance. Some courts hold, for instance, that the severity of the jolt needed to show negligence is not sufficiently proved by testimony merely describing the jolt as severe by appropriate adjectives; there must be corroboration, such as a showing of its effect on other passengers.[13]

(1953) ("If the testimony of one witness ... is legally sufficient, it matters not that this testimony may be contradicted by ten witnesses for defendant, or even that it may be in conflict with statements before the trial, or testimony in a previous trial or other legal proceeding, of the same witness"); Alvey v. Butchkavitz, 196 Va. 447, 84 S.E.2d 535 (1954); Robben v. Hartford Elec. Light Co., 1 Conn.App. 109, 468 A.2d 1266 (1983).

9. *See, e.g.,* Simblest v. Maynard, 427 F.2d 1 (2d Cir.1970); Ernst v. Ace Motor Sales, Inc., 550 F.Supp. 1220 (E.D.Pa.1982); Curtis v. De Atley, 104 Idaho 787, 663 P.2d 1089 (1983); Bucktown Partners v. Johnson, 119 Ill.App.3d 346, 75 Ill.Dec. 20, 456 N.E.2d 703 (1983).

10. Kuper v. Betzer, 115 F.2d, 842, 844 (8th Cir.1940); *see* Kircher v. Atchison, T. & S. Fe Ry., 32 Cal.2d 176, 195 P.2d 427 (1948); Lutzen v. Henry Jenkins Transp. Co., 133 Conn. 669, 54 A.2d 267 (1947). In *Kircher* a dissenting judge characterized the situation thus (32 Cal.2d at 188, 195 P.2d at 435):

To be expected to believe that the plaintiff could have stumbled over a shallow depression thirteen feet from the westerly rail of the track and been pitched forward and under the train on that track so that his hand was crushed on the easterly rail and his body not injured while under the moving train, taxes credulity to the breaking point.

32 Cal.2d at 188, 195 P.2d at 435.

In *Lutzen* the court held erroneous an instruction that plaintiff would be negligent as a matter of law if she walked into the side of a moving truck in broad daylight.

11. U.S. Const. art. III, § 3. *See* Haupt v. United States, 330 U.S. 631, 67 S.Ct. 874, 91 L.Ed. 1145 (1947). Wigmore calls such requirements "synthetic" or "quantitative" rules. 7 Wigmore, Evidence § 2030 (Chadbourn rev. 1978). *See generally* 7 Wigmore, *supra,* §§ 2030–2075.

12. *See* Weiler v. United States, 323 U.S. 606, 65 S.Ct. 548, 89 L.Ed. 495 (1945); Note, 156 A.L.R. 499; Note, 111 A.L.R. 825.

13. *See* Seidenberg v. Eastern Mass. St. Ry., 266 Mass. 540, 165 N.E. 658 (1929); Norfolk & W. Ry. v. Rhodes, 109 Va. 176,

Circumstantial probability

The question of sufficiency of circumstantial evidence to prove a fact is more complex and subtle. It turns on the concept of legitimacy of the desired inference. If *A* is shown, then the trier may infer *B* from *A* if, but only if, the inference is a rational one.[14] The test of rationality is usually expressed in terms of probabilities. When from the proved facts the nonexistence of the fact to be inferred appears to be as probable as, or more probable than, its existence, then the conclusion that it exists is a matter of speculation, surmise, and conjecture, and a jury will not be allowed to draw it.[15] This test suggests mathematical precision, but the suggestion is spurious. First, we lack the quantitative data about most matters that would be needed to make meaningful statements in terms of probabilities. Of course, some broad generalizations would command general assent; these are the judgments of "common sense," but even they are fallible. How often the science of the morrow makes a fool of today's common sense! Second, there is much room in which thoughtful people who accept today's common sense would either disagree or refuse to guess on which side of the line the greater probability lay.

Another flaw in the test of rationality as usually formulated lies in the possibility that courts may not mean it to be taken literally. One court has said that the test "may be an overstatement of the quantum of proof required."[16] Another, looking in the opposite direction, declared that it is "not enough that mathematically the chances somewhat favor a proposition to be proved; for example . . . the fact that only a minority of men die of cancer [would not] warrant a finding that a particular man did not die of cancer."[17]

It appears then that the test, formulated in terms that suggest objective, scientific precision, is in fact one that gives the courts little guidance and great latitude. It is true that courts today often hear

63 S.E. 445 (1909); Coyle v. Pittsburgh Rys., 149 Pa.Super. 281, 27 A.2d 533 (1942). *But see* Belledeau v. Connecticut Co., 110 Conn. 625, 149 A. 127 (1930). The policy behind such a rule is protection against false claims that may be too easily fabricated. *Cf.* Cardozo, C.J., in Murphy v. Steeplechase Amusement Co., 250 N.Y. 479, 482, 166 N.E. 173, 174 (1929) ("He cannot help himself to a verdict . . . by the . . . facile comment that it threw him with a jerk").

14. *See* 2 Harper, James, and Gray, Law of Torts § 19.4 (2d ed. 1986); James, Proof of the Breach in Negligence Cases (Including Res Ipsa Loquitur), 37 Va. L. Rev. 179, 185–193 (1951). *Cf.* Western & Atl. R.R. v. Henderson, 279 U.S. 639, 49 S.Ct. 445, 73 L.Ed. 884 (1929).

15. *See* Prosser and Keeton, Torts § 39 (4th ed. 1971). *Cf.* Nash v. Raun, 149 F.2d 885, 888 (3d Cir.1945), *cert. denied,* 326 U.S. 758, 66 S.Ct. 99, 90 L.Ed. 455 (1945); Page v. Arnold, 227 Va. 74, 314 S.E.2d 57 (1984).

16. Gutierrez v. Public Serv. Interstate Transp. Co., 168 F.2d 678, 680 (2d Cir. 1948).

17. Sargent v. Massachusetts Accident Co., 307 Mass. 246, 250, 29 N.E.2d 825, 827 (1940). *See also* Houts, From Evidence to Proof (1956); Morgan, Basic Problems of Evidence 183–188 (1961); James, Relevancy, Probability and the Law, 29 Calif. L. Rev. 689 (1941); Tribe, Trial by Mathematics: Precision and Ritual in the Legal Process, 84 Harv. L. Rev. 1329 (1971); Symposium, Probability and Inference in the Law of Evidence, 66 B.U.L. Rev. 377 (1986); Conference, Decision and Inference in Litigation, 13 Cardozo L. Rev. 253 (1991).

evidence concerning probabilities, for example when they are asked to determine the weight of blood type or DNA testing, or when it is argued that the disproportion between the percentage of minority groups or women applying for jobs and those receiving them establishes hiring discrimination. Still, no such evidence is offered in most cases. Instead, courts are constantly asserting or assuming broad generalizations about human behavior and other matters that either rest on their own fallible notions about such things or spring from considerations of policy and expediency. Narrative coherence rather than Bayesian probability theory grounds most judgments of evidentiary sufficiency.[18]

Inference on inference

In addition to the general test for the sufficiency of circumstantial evidence, there is occasionally asserted a proscription against "building an inference on an inference." No such test has ever been applied literally and uniformly, nor is there any rational justification for it.[19] Few cases are tried where inference is not piled on inference two and three deep. A very simple and familiar example will suffice. A person flees the scene of a crime or tort. From this flight we may infer a consciousness of guilt; from the consciousness we may reason to the fact of guilt.[20] If the rule means simply that the jury will not be allowed to draw an inference from proof that does not point to it with sufficient probability, then its meaning is unobjectionable, but the form of the statement is unfortunate and misleading. It has sometimes been applied mechanically to preclude inferences that seem well within the realm of what is reasonable by any rational standard.[21] The rule should be repudiated outright and in its stead should be used a statement such as the incisive one made by a California court: "In a civil case, if the first inference is a reasonably probable one it may be used as a basis for a succeeding inference."[22]

Disbelief as basis for inference

Another proscription often stated is that the disbelief of a denial does not, taken alone, afford affirmative proof that the denied fact existed so as to satisfy the proponent's burden of proving that fact. In one case plaintiff had to prove that his decedent, climbing down the side

18. The Evolving Role of Statistical Assessments as Evidence in the Courts (Fienberg ed. 1988); Statistical Methods in Discrimination Litigation (Kaye & Aikin eds. 1986). On narrative coherence, see, *e.g.*, Bennett & Feldman, Reconstructing Reality in the Courtroom (1981); Hastie, *et al.*, Inside the Jury (1983); Allen, The Nature of Juridical Proof, 13 Cardozo L. Rev. 373 (1991).

19. *See* 1 Wigmore, Evidence § 41 (Tillers rev. 1983); Note, 95 A.L.R. 162.

20. *See* Kotler v. Lalley, 112 Conn. 86, 151 A. 433 (1930); State v. Ford, 109 Conn. 490, 146 A. 828 (1929).

21. *See* cases collected in 1 Wigmore, Evidence § 41, at 1106 n.2 (Tillers rev. 1983); Note, 95 A.L.R. 162, 175 n.22.

22. Vaccarezza v. Sanguinetti, 71 Cal. App.2d 687, 698, 163 P.2d 470, 477 (1945). *See* Daniels v. Twin Oaks Nursing Home, 692 F.2d 1321 (11th Cir.1982). *Cf.* Lemmon v. Paterson Construction Co., 137 Conn. 158, 75 A.2d 385 (1950); Note, 95 A.L.R. 181–196.

of a freight car on a siding, was *actually seen* by the crew of an approaching train in time to sound warning; the fire fighter and engineer testified, however, that they did not see the decedent although they were keeping a proper lookout. The court held that a jury might not infer that decedent was seen from a disbelief of the engine crew's testimony.[23] The jury was not, of course, bound to accept the testimony as true, but its rejection opens up many possibilities that do not include the desired conclusion. The engineer and fire fighter may not have been looking out at all or they may have been talking or joking or distracted by something at the time. It may be argued, therefore, that the probability that the crew did see the decedent does not appear great enough to make the desired inference rational.

This argument overlooks the possibility that demeanor evidence "may satisfy the tribunal, not only that the witness's testimony is not true, but that the truth is the opposite of his story."[24] Moreover, the argument often overlooks, as in the case put, the trier's right to accept part of a witness's testimony (that the witness looked carefully and could see what was obvious) and reject part[25] (that the witness failed to see a person clearly within the line of vision) and the trier's indubitable right to find a fact from circumstantial evidence over the denial of the person who alone has full knowledge of the fact.[26] Furthermore, competing possibilities are often minimized or eliminated in specific circumstances. Such considerations throw doubt on the case just described. Nevertheless, the prevailing rule may be justified in some contexts, since its alternative would enable an unscrupulous litigant to make *any* allegation about the adversary's conduct and get to the jury on the issue with nothing in the way of proof save the possibility that the adversary's denial may be disbelieved.[27]

Evaluation of facts

The preceding discussion has been confined to inferences of the existence of simple facts. As we have seen, many ultimate issues in litigation also involve the evaluation or appraisal of facts in terms of

23. Cruzan v. New York Cent. & Hudson River R.R., 227 Mass. 594, 116 N.E. 879 (1917), *appeal dismissed per stipulation,* 249 U.S. 621, 39 S.Ct. 385, 63 L.Ed. 806 (1919).

24. Dyer v. MacDougall, 201 F.2d 265, 269 (2d Cir.1952).

25. *See* Pandolfo v. Acheson, 202 F.2d 38 (2d Cir.1953); United States ex rel. Leong v. O'Rourke, 125 F.Supp. 769 (W.D.Mo.1954); Foshee v. Wolters, 86 Cal. App.2d 766, 195 P.2d 930 (1948). *But cf.* Olney v. Carmichael, 202 Md. 226, 96 A.2d 37 (1953).

26. *See* Groves v. Webster City, 222 Iowa 849, 270 N.W. 329 (1936); Hamlin v. Roundy, 96 N.H. 123, 124, 71 A.2d 419, 420 (1950); Clark v. Boston & Me. R.R., 87 N.H. 36, 39, 173 A. 368, 370 (1934). *Cf.* Gray v. Southern Pac. Co., 23 Cal.2d 632, 145 P.2d 561 (1944).

27. The kind of situation found in Dyer v. MacDougall, 201 F.2d 265 (2d Cir.1952), presents this possibility (although of course there is no reason whatever to suppose any lack of scruples on the part of plaintiff in that case). The court's reasoning did not stress the point made in the text but rather the impossibility of effective appellate review of any ruling based exclusively on demeanor evidence that could not be brought before the appellate court. 201 F.2d at 269.

their legal consequences, and this evaluation also falls within the jury's province. The issue of negligence in an accident case is a good example. When, however, there is insufficient evidence to warrant a finding for the proponent on an issue involving evaluation, a jury will not be allowed to make that evaluation; no facts legitimately found from the evidence (direct, real, and circumstantial) can be evaluated as negligence or the like.[28] Thus, the concept of insufficiency has a double aspect when used in connection with such an issue. It may involve a lack of proof of what the facts were, so that evaluation is impossible. An example would be a decedent's conduct leading up to his or her unwitnessed death.[29] But evidence may also be called insufficient to show negligence, for instance, when all the relevant facts are fully known—even admitted—but the court is unwilling to let a jury characterize or evaluate those facts in the way that the proponent claims and needs.[30]

All favorable evidence considered

The next question is, what evidence is to be considered in determining sufficiency? The answer is, that part of the reasonably credible evidence most favorable to the proponent, whether it was introduced by the proponent or the opposing party.[31] Sufficiency is not primarily concerned with credibility nor with the choice among competing permissible inferences; sufficiency is a matter for the court to decide, while credibility and persuasive effect are matters for the jury. Thus, all conflicts in the evidence are resolved against the party who challenges the sufficiency of the evidence, including conflicts and contradictions within a witness's or a party's own testimony.[32] And the proponent—such a challenge is always made *against* a party carrying the burden of production—is entitled to the most favorable of competing rational inferences and to have inferences drawn from the most favorable findings.[33] It is the court's function "to determine whether the evidence in

28. *See* 2 Harper, James, and Gray, Law of Torts § 15.2, at 876–877 (2d ed. 1986).

29. *See* Kotler v. Lalley, 112 Conn. 86, 151 A. 433 (1930).

30. *See, e.g.,* Goldberger v. David Roberts Corp., 139 Conn. 629, 96 A.2d 309 (1953) (furnishing young boy with paddle); McDonald v. Fryberger, 233 Minn. 156, 46 N.W.2d 260 (1951) (leaving ordinary kitchen cabinet unfastened to wall); Kimbar v. Estis, 1 N.Y.2d 399, 153 N.Y.S.2d 197, 135 N.E.2d 708 (1956) (failure of boys' camp to light paths in woods at night); Holmes, The Common Law 120–121 (1881).

31. Reeves v. Sanderson Plumbing Prods., Inc., 530 U.S. 133, 120 S.Ct. 2097, 147 L.Ed.2d 105 (2000).

32. *See* Zullo v. Zullo, 138 Conn. 712, 89 A.2d 216 (1952); Stark v. American Bakeries Co., 647 S.W.2d 119 (Mo.1983). *Cf.* Albaugh v. Pennsylvania R.R., 120 F.Supp. 70 (D.D.C.1954), *aff'd,* 219 F.2d 764 (D.C.Cir. 1955); cases cited note 10 *supra.* For historical perspective, see Fisher, The Jury's Rise as Lie Detector, 107 Yale L.J. 575 (1997).

33. *See, e.g.,* Reeves v. Sanderson Plumbing Prods., Inc., 530 U.S. 133, 120 S.Ct. 2097, 147 L.Ed.2d 105 (2000); Interstate Eng. v. Burnette, 474 So.2d 624 (Ala. 1985); Green v. Gowen, 279 Ark. 382, 652 S.W.2d 624 (1983); Gostin v. Scott, 80 Ga. App. 630, 56 S.E.2d 778 (1949); McDonald v. Metropolitan St. Ry., 167 N.Y. 66, 60 N.E. 282 (1901); Szukics v. Ruch, 367 Pa. 646, 81 A.2d 903 (1951). Some courts do not allow parties who later contradict their own favorable testimony to have the advantage of that testimony. Olney v. Carmichael, 202 Md. 226, 96 A.2d 37 (1953). Parties who

its entirety would rationally support a verdict for the plaintiff, assuming that the jury took, as it would be entitled to take, a view of the evidence most favorable to the plaintiff."[34]

Indisputable physical facts

Although this test resolves conflicts in the evidence in favor of the proponent and therefore disregards that part of the evidence favoring the opponent, not *all* conflicts should be so resolved and not *all* evidence unfavorable to the proponent should be disregarded. As we have seen, courts will not let credit be given to testimony that contradicts indisputable physical facts or laws of nature. And that part of the evidence demonstrating such a contradiction (such as that showing beyond doubt the view of highway travelers looking down the tracks as they approached a railway crossing on a clear day) is *not* to be disregarded.[35] While credibility is for the jury, courts set the outer limits of it. In doing so they have the power to make serious inroads into the jury's sphere, but in fact they have exercised this power with marked restraint.[36]

Uncontradicted testimony

The question of credibility is sometimes raised in an entirely different way by a motion to direct a verdict or for judgment as a matter of law. When the proponents, who have the burden of persuasion, offer testimonial evidence that strongly supports their side of the case and the opponents fail to shake it on cross-examination and offer no countervailing evidence, the proponents may move for a directed verdict. If at this point no presumption operates in the proponents' favor, the question may arise whether the jury may reasonably *disbelieve* their evidence. This is not usually described as a problem of the sufficiency of evidence, but it has much in common with that concept, for in the last analysis it comes down to a question of whether demeanor evidence may be sufficient to warrant rejection of an otherwise uncontradicted and unimpeached statement. Some courts answer the question in the affirmative and hold that a directed verdict must be denied for that reason.[37] The

have testified to a fact peculiarly within their knowledge and fatal to their cause of action have been denied recovery although their own unfavorable testimony is contradicted by others. Harlow v. Laclair, 82 N.H. 506, 136 A. 128 (1927).

34. Wilkerson v. McCarthy, 336 U.S. 53, 65, 69 S.Ct. 413, 419, 93 L.Ed. 497, 506 (1949) (Frankfurter, J., concurring); Maskrey v. Volkswagenwerk Aktiengesellschaft, 125 Wis.2d 145, 370 N.W.2d 815 (1985).

35. *See* note 10 *supra*. In Gianotta v. New York, N.H. & H.R.R., 98 Conn. 743, 120 A. 560 (1923), the evidence showing the indisputable physical facts was introduced by defendant. Similarly, much of it was also introduced by defendant in Piscitello v. New York, N.H. & H. R.R., 116 Conn. 638, 166 A. 61 (1933), in which the court upheld a directed verdict for defendant.

36. 2 Harper, James, and Gray, Law of Torts § 15.2, at 877 (2d ed. 1986).

37. Alexander v. Tingle, 181 Md. 464, 30 A.2d 737 (1943); Wooden v. Durfee, 46 Mich. 424, 9 N.W. 457 (1881); Smith, The Power of the Judge to Direct a Verdict: Section 457a of the New York Civil Practice Act, 24 Colum. L. Rev. 111, 121 n.47 (1924); Sunderland, Directing a Verdict for the Party Having the Burden of Proof, 11 Mich. L. Rev. 198 (1913); Note, Directing a Verdict in Favor of the Party with the Burden of

prevailing view, however, regards the clear, uncontradicted, consistent, unimpeached testimony of even interested witnesses as sufficient basis for a directed verdict in favor of the party having both the burden of persuasion and the initial burden of production.[38] This amounts to a holding that reasonable people could not disbelieve such testimony on the basis of demeanor evidence.[39]

Weight of the evidence

The sufficiency of the evidence is different from the *weight* of the evidence, which is for the jury to decide. The weight of the evidence includes questions of credibility and choice among competing inferences. There is also another, more objective sense in which the term "weight of the evidence" (or "clear weight of the evidence") is used. In many jurisdictions a trial court has wide discretion to order a new trial when it believes the verdict is against the weight, or clear weight, of the evidence. In exercising this discretion, courts do appraise credibility—to a greater extent than they are permitted on a challenge to the sufficiency of the evidence, but to a lesser extent than the jury is permitted in making its own rather subjective judgment. Obviously this test is even more vague and more dependent on imponderable factors than is the test of what is not reasonably credible as a matter of law. It must necessarily be addressed largely to judicial discretion.[40]

C. CONTROLLING THE JURY: PREVERDICT DEVICES

§ 7.20 Admission and Exclusion of Evidence

Having examined the concept of sufficiency of the evidence, we next proceed to the various devices available during trial for implementing this concept and for limiting the sphere of what the jury may, and should, consider in cases in which one or more issues are submitted to

Proof, 16 Wake Forest L. Rev. 607 (1980); *see* 1 Wigmore, Evidence § 2495 (Tillers rev. 1983).

38. The cases are reviewed in an excellent opinion by Vanderbilt, C.J., in Ferdinand v. Agricultural Ins. Co., 22 N.J. 482, 126 A.2d 323 (1956). *See also* 9 Wigmore, Evidence § 2495 (Chadbourn rev. 1981); Sunderland, Directing a Verdict for the Party Having the Burden of Proof, 11 Mich. L. Rev. 198 (1913); Note, 62 A.L.R.2d 1191.

39. Or, perhaps, it amounts to a judgment that the chance that a rational verdict will be based on demeanor evidence in such a case, though theoretically possible, is "to the last degree rare," and therefore should be disregarded because of the disadvantages entailed in recognizing it (such as the fact that demeanor evidence cannot be preserved in the record or recaptured on appeal). *Cf.* Hand, J., in Dyer v. MacDougall, 201 F.2d 265, 269 (2d Cir.1952). On jury inability to evaluate demeanor, see Wellborn, Demeanor, 76 Cornell L. Rev. 1075 (1991).

40. *See* § 7.20 *infra;* McBaine, Trial Practice: Directed Verdicts; Federal Rule, 31 Calif. L. Rev. 454 (1943). *See also* Cooper, Directions for Directed Verdicts: A Compass for Federal Courts, 55 Minn. L. Rev. 903 (1971); Schnapper, Judges Against Juries—Appellate Review of Federal Civil Verdicts, 1989 Wis. L. Rev. 237 (finding that the federal courts of appeal have reversed jury fact-finding in almost half of all federal civil appeals).

them. These are the mechanical devices, so to speak, for the court's control of the jury.

Excluded evidence

Courts do, of course, exercise control over juries by deciding what evidence they may hear. In deciding whether to admit expert testimony, for example, courts perform a "gatekeeping" function intended to prevent unreliable but plausible evidence from reaching the jury.[1] The bases for the rules admitting or excluding evidence are related mostly to legal concepts other than the ones we are discussing—concepts usually treated under the heading of evidence rather than under jury control. Several points should, however, be noted here. Evidence that is excluded on objection or struck out on later motion is not counted in measuring the sufficiency of evidence.[2] Evidence that is erroneously admitted over objection will doubtless be counted by the trial judge; a judge who changes his or her mind may thereafter disregard the evidence on a later motion to take the case from a jury, or grant a new trial because of the error.[3] If the erroneous ruling admitting evidence over objection is properly saved for review on appeal, a reversal and new trial may result.[4]

The remaining question concerns how evidence is counted in testing sufficiency when it has been admitted without objection[5] but would have been excluded if objection had been made. The answer turns in part on the ground on which the evidence would have been excluded. If the evidence is irrelevant to the issues in the case, it has no logical probative value and is not entitled to consideration.[6] If, however, the evidence is

§ 7.20

1. *E.g.*, Kumho Tire Co. v. Carmichael, 526 U.S. 137, 119 S.Ct. 1167, 143 L.Ed.2d 238 (1999).

2. *See* Abramowitz v. Abramowitz, 137 N.Y.S.2d 442 (Sup.1954).

3. *See* Jacksonville Paper Co. v. Hartford Accident & Indem. Co., 260 Ala. 132, 69 So.2d 411 (1953); cases collected in Decennial Digest, New Trial at Key number 35.

4. *See, e.g.*, Niedner v. Wabash R.R., 219 S.W.2d 886 (Mo.Ct.App.1949); Dairy & Ice Cream Supply Co. v. Gastonia Ice Cream Co., 232 N.C. 684, 61 S.E.2d 895 (1950). Even if the improperly admitted evidence was the only evidence to support an essential element in plaintiff's case, the disposition should generally be a new trial rather than a judgment for defendant since "but for the court's ruling plaintiff might have offered other proof." 232 N.C. at 686, 61 S.E.2d at 897. *But cf.* Williams v. New Amsterdam Casualty Co., 136 Colo. 458, 319 P.2d 1078 (1957) (trial court reversed finding of Industrial Accident Commission on basis of evidence erroneously received over objection; award of Commission was reinstated).

5. Or, rather, without proper objection. If the objection is not made on the proper ground, it does not count. Thus, relevant but inadmissible hearsay evidence, admitted over an objection that it is "incompetent, irrelevant and immaterial," will be treated as though it came in without objection. *See* Keim v. D. B. Berelson & Co., 105 Cal. App.2d 154, 233 P.2d 123 (1951); In re Estate of Fagin, 246 Iowa 496, 66 N.W.2d 920 (1954).

6. Thus, if the parol evidence rule is viewed as a rule of substantive law rendering parol evidence irrelevant once the agreement has become integrated in a writing, then consideration of parol evidence, though admitted without objection, will be excluded. *See* El Zarape Tortilla Factory v. Plant Food Corp., 90 Cal.App.2d 336, 203 P.2d 13 (1949); Cooper v. Vaughan, 81 Ga. App. 330, 58 S.E.2d 453 (1950); Foster v. Wagner, 337 S.W.2d 485, 492 (Tex.Civ.App. 1960).

relevant and the proper objection would be based on one of the exclusionary rules, the answer may be different. Some of the exclusionary rules are based on considerations having nothing to do with the probative value of the evidence they exclude.[7] If such evidence comes in without objection, there is no reason to be reluctant to consider it. Evidence sufficient to prove a fact under the ordinary canons of logical reasoning and relevancy should not be shorn of that effect simply because it would have been excluded as privileged had the privilege been claimed.[8]

Hearsay

Greater difficulty arises when the rule of exclusion includes some considerations that involve the probative value of the evidence. An example is the hearsay rule. Most of the apposite judicial decisions concern relevant but inadmissible hearsay evidence admitted without objection. When *W*'s testimony of what *X* said is offered to show that what *X* said is true ("to prove the truth of the matter asserted," as the classic phrase has it), then the trier is asked to put faith in *X*'s veracity (used in the broad sense to include accuracy of observation, memory, and expression as well as honesty) even though the adversary has no chance to cross-examine *X* and the trier no chance to observe *X*'s demeanor either in making the statement or under cross-examination on it. The hearsay rule rests on a faith in cross-examination to elicit flaws and defects in the character and powers of the witness and in the statement itself, and to reveal qualifying circumstances that would put the statement in a different light.[9] The exclusion of hearsay, then, rests largely on the lack of guaranty of trustworthiness in extrajudicial statements made without the opportunity to cross-examine. The question is whether this lack is so serious that hearsay statements should not be sufficient basis for finding the fact asserted in such statements when they have been admitted in evidence without objection.

Some courts, perhaps a majority, have taken the broad position that relevant evidence inadmissible under the hearsay or some other exclusionary rule, but admitted without objection, is in the case for all

7. 8 Wigmore, Evidence § 2175 (McNaughton rev. 1981).

8. *See, e.g.,* Burris v. Burris, 75 A.2d 514 (Del.Super.Ct.1950) (in divorce action, affirmative defense of adultery shown by admissions of plaintiff on cross-examination); Stalder v. Stone, 412 Ill. 488, 107 N.E.2d 696 (1952) (in adoption proceeding, grounds for adoption shown by affidavit of natural mother reciting her criminal conduct without claim of privilege); Adams v. State, 200 Md. 133, 88 A.2d 556 (1952) (abortion proven by testimony of women on whom practiced); State v. Desilets, 96 N.H. 245, 73 A.2d 800 (1950) (lascivious acts shown by testimony of accomplice); Bonham v. Bonham, 489 So.2d 578 (Ala.Civ. App.1985) (in divorce action, marital privilege waived unless invoked).

9. *See* Morgan, Some Problems of Proof 106–141 (1956); 5 Wigmore, Evidence §§ 1360–1365 (Chadbourn rev. 1974). This does not necessarily imply that hearsay is worthless, only that live testimony is superior and should therefore usually be required. Nance, The Best Evidence Principle, 73 Iowa L. Rev. 227 (1988).

purposes and that its weight is for the trier of facts.[10] Others, a minority, have declared flatly that admissible hearsay has no probative value and will not support a finding even though admitted without objection.[11]

Perhaps both views are too broad and uncritical, and no single answer should cover all hearsay statements. Not all hearsay is equally untrustworthy, nor does it all possess the same quality. Hearsay ranges from business records on which practical people would rely in lending large sums of money to idle village gossip that responsible people would at once dismiss as worthless.[12] The law of hearsay itself recognizes this diversity; the famous exceptions to the hearsay rule have developed partly because of the guaranties of trustworthiness found in some situations.[13] And whenever hearsay evidence is admitted under one of the recognized exceptions to the exclusionary rule, it is, of course, counted in reckoning sufficiency.[14] The exceptions do not by any means include all the hearsay that people consider reliable; the field of inadmissible hearsay today still covers a wide range.[15] Indeed, England has almost entirely abolished the hearsay rule in civil cases, and civil law systems often rely on hearsay evidence.[16] For such reasons, some courts uphold a finding based on hearsay evidence that has been admitted without

10. *See, e.g.,* Shepp v. Uehlinger, 775 F.2d 452 (1st Cir.1985); Stickel v. San Diego Elec. Ry., 32 Cal.2d 157, 195 P.2d 416 (1948) (conclusion of witness that decedent "must have seen" the bus "because she tried to step on the gas"); Swegle v. State Bd. of Equalization, 125 Cal.App.2d 432, 436–437, 270 P.2d 518, 521 (1954) ("In ordinary civil actions incompetent evidence admitted without objection is sufficient to support a finding"); Pataskas v. Judeikis, 327 Mass. 258, 98 N.E.2d 265 (1951) (authentication of handwriting by witness not shown to have familiarity; case turned on the authorship of these letters and there was no other authentication); Ventromile v. Malden Elec. Co., 317 Mass. 132, 57 N.E.2d 209 (1944) (only evidence to show at trial that plaintiff slipped on wax was plaintiff's testimony that she had so stated on prior occasion; held sufficient); Crampton v. Osborn, 356 Mo. 125, 201 S.W.2d 336 (1947) (inadmissible hearsay, admitted without objection, to be given "its natural probative effect"); Barlow v. Verrill, 88 N.H. 25, 183 A. 857 (1936) (verdict supported by inadmissible hearsay); Clark v. Reynolds, 125 Va. 626, 100 S.E. 468 (1919) (*semble*); Wilson v. Kemp, 7 Ark.App. 44, 644 S.W.2d 306 (1982); Miller v. Rokita, 131 Ill.App.3d, 774, 86 Ill.Dec. 850, 476 N.E.2d 26 (1985).

11. *See* Knox Metal Prods. v. Watson, 100 Ga.App. 832, 112 S.E.2d 295 (1959); Wright v. Dabbs, 220 S.W.2d 681, 685 (Tex. Civ.App.1949).

12. *See* the admirable analysis in Goldthwaite v. Sheraton Restaurant, 154 Me. 214, 145 A.2d 362 (1958). *See also* St. Paul Fire & Marine Ins. Co. v. Ohio Fast Freight, 8 Ohio App.3d 155, 456 N.E.2d 551 (1982); Morgan, Some Problems of Proof 106–195 (1956); Weinstein, The Probative Force of Hearsay, 46 Iowa L. Rev. 331 (1961); James, Book Review, 66 Yale L.J. 160 (1956).

13. In 5 Wigmore, Evidence §§ 1420–1422 (Chadbourn rev. 1974), the author states what he considers the general principles underlying the hearsay exceptions (necessity and circumstantial probability of trustworthiness); in § 1425 he states his intention to take up the application of these principles to each exception, and the succeeding chapters contain the attempts to follow up this intention. *See also* NL Well Serv./NL Indus. v. Flake Indus. Serv., 656 S.W.2d 584 (Tex.Civ.App.1983).

14. *See* Crawley v. Selby, 208 Ga. 530, 67 S.E.2d 775 (1951); United States v. American Tel. and Tel. Co., 516 F.Supp. 1237 (D.D.C.1981).

15. *See* Morgan, Some Problems of Proof 169–195 (1956); James, Book Review, 66 Yale L.J. 160 (1956).

16. Damaska, Of Hearsay and its Analogues, 76 Minn. L. Rev. 425 (1992); Strong, *et al.,* McCormick on Evidence § 326 (5th ed. 1999).

objection if it is the kind on which responsible people would base practical judgments.[17] The test for this type of evidence should be elastic.

§ 7.21 Directed Verdict, or Judgment as a Matter of Law

The major method for testing the sufficiency of the evidence has traditionally been known as the motion for a directed verdict. In the federal courts, it is now known as a motion for judgment as a matter of law, a name it shares with what used to be called judgment notwithstanding the verdict or judgment n.o.v. In some state courts, litigants may move for a nonsuit as well as a directed verdict, but the difference between them seems to be purely one of nomenclature.[1] Challenging sufficiency through a demurrer to the evidence or a motion to dismiss is virtually obsolete, although dismissal does survive for other functions, as when a plaintiff voluntarily dismisses its case as part of a settlement or a judge dismisses it involuntarily for failure to prosecute or misconduct.[2]

Procedure for directed verdict

A party may move for a directed verdict at any time before the case is submitted to the jury, provided that the opposing party has been fully heard on the issues in question.[3] Usually, it is the defendant who seeks a directed verdict, and usually the defendant does so at the close of the plaintiff's evidence. Sometimes, however, either the plaintiff or the defendant seeks a directed verdict at the end of all the evidence.

A judge who grants a motion for directed verdict on the whole case will proceed to enter judgment for the prevailing party. The judge will not actually "direct" the jury to render a specified verdict, or even give them a chance to do so.[4] The jurors will simply be dismissed, there being no case worthy to be submitted to them. That is not what happens, however, if the judge grants a partial directed verdict rejecting a single claim or defense. The case will then go to the jury on the remaining claims and defenses, but the jury will not be instructed about the stricken claim or defense. And of course the party obtaining the partial

17. See the careful appraisals in Shepp v. Uehlinger, 775 F.2d 452 (1st Cir.1985); In re Estate of Fagin, 246 Iowa 496, 66 N.W.2d 920 (1954); Goldthwaite v. Sheraton Restaurant, 154 Me. 214, 145 A.2d 362 (1958); Shepard v. Purvine, 196 Or. 348, 248 P.2d 352 (1952).

Compare the similar problem whether administrative findings may ever be supported by hearsay evidence and, if so, under what circumstances. *See, e.g.,* Consolidated Edison Co. v. NLRB, 305 U.S. 197, 229–230, 59 S.Ct. 206, 216–217, 83 L.Ed. 126, 140 (1938); NLRB v. Englander Co., 260 F.2d 67, 72 (9th Cir.1958); Thompson v. County School Bd., 166 F.Supp. 529 (E.D.Va.1958), *aff'd sub nom.* Hamm v. County School Bd., 263 F.2d 226 (4th Cir.1959); Swegle v. State Bd. of Equalization, 125 Cal.App.2d 432, 270 P.2d 518 (1954); Derrick v. Board of Liquor Control, 98 Ohio App. 97, 128 N.E.2d 239 (1954); Ferguson–Steere Motor Co. v. State Corp. Commn., 63 N.M. 137, 314 P.2d 894 (1957); 1 Wigmore, Evidence §§ 4a–4c (Tillers rev. 1983).

§ 7.21

1. Calif. C. Civ. P. §§ 518c, 630; 7 Witkin, California Procedure, Trial §§ 416–38 (4th ed. 1997).

2. Fed. R. Civ. P. 41; § 7.8 *supra.*

3. Fed. R. Civ. P. 50(a).

4. Fed. R. Civ. P. 50, Advisory Committee Notes (1963).

directed verdict will not submit further evidence on the claim or defense in question.

Standard for directed verdict

A directed verdict will be granted against a party if "there is no legally sufficient evidentiary basis for a reasonable jury to find for that party on that issue."[5] A verdict should be directed when only one reasonable conclusion as to the verdict can be reached. But if "reasonable minds could differ as to the importance of the evidence ... a verdict should not be directed."[6] We have already discussed how courts decide whether this standard is met.[7] In brief, the motion raises the question whether the party having the burden of coming forward with evidence on an issue has carried that burden. If it has not, the opposing party is entitled to a directed verdict. If it has, the proponent may go to the jury, which will decide whether the proponent has persuaded it of the truth of its allegations. The proponent will rarely be able to get a directed verdict for itself, for it is always possible that the jury will not believe its evidence. But there are some situations in which the proponent can indeed obtain a directed verdict, for example because it presents uncontradicted disinterested witnesses to facts susceptible of reliable proof, or because its evidence activates a presumption shifting the burden of coming forward to the opposing party.

Trial by judge

Although a directed verdict, strictly speaking, is available only in a jury trial, a judge sitting as trier of fact may likewise resolve factual issues in appropriate circumstances without waiting until the end of the trial. For example, if the plaintiff fails to carry its burden of producing evidence on an issue essential to its success, the judge may enter judgment as a matter of law without hearing the defendant's evidence. The judge's power to do this is broader than it would be in a jury trial because, as the finder of fact, the judge may decide that he or she does not believe the plaintiff's witnesses when, in a jury trial, that option would have to be left to the jury. In a judge trial, the judge also has discretion to postpone deciding the case until he or she has heard all the evidence even though judgment as a matter of law might have been appropriate earlier. A judge who does grant judgment as a matter of law in a judge trial must enter findings of fact and conclusions of law just as would be done had the trial continued to its conclusions. Such findings of fact, like other findings of fact by judges, may not be overturned by an appellate court unless they are clearly erroneous.[8]

5. Fed. R. Civ. P. 50(a).

6. Anderson v. Liberty Lobby, 477 U.S. 242, 250, 106 S.Ct. 2505, 2511, 91 L.Ed.2d 202, 213 (1986); Porth v. Farrier, 934 F.2d 154 (8th Cir.1991).

7. See §§ 7.12–20 *supra*.

8. Fed. R. Civ. P. 52(c); § 12.9 *infra*. On a judge's power in a case tried without a jury to weigh the evidence and make findings of fact on a motion for dismissal at the close of plaintiff's case. *See* Fed. R. Civ. P. 41(b); Steffen, The Prima Facie Case in

Credibility and directed verdicts

All the devices that take a case from a jury invoke the concept of the sufficiency of the evidence.[9] Some controversy has developed over the questions whether credibility may be considered on some or all of these motions and whether judges may properly direct a verdict whenever they would set aside an opposite one.[10] There may be some shadings in the application of the sufficiency test for the different devices, and among different jurisdictions. And there may once have been wider variations in the test applied. But overall the sufficiency test as described above is used uniformly when any of these devices is invoked,[11] and the doctrinal differences referred to are largely battles of words.[12]

All courts consider credibility on a motion for directed verdict or for judgment as a matter of law to determine, at the least, whether testimony is capable of belief by reasonable people. No court, as we have seen, will let a jury base a verdict on testimony inconsistent with physical facts

Non-jury Trials, 27 U. Chi. L. Rev. 94 (1959).

9. For comprehensive reviews of these various devices, see Galloway v. United States, 319 U.S. 372, 63 S.Ct. 1077, 87 L.Ed. 1458 (1943); Yassoo Enters. v. North Carolina Joint Underwriting Assn., 73 N.C.App. 52, 325 S.E.2d 677 (1985).

When the complaint fails to state a cause of action or claim for relief, and no demurrer or motion to dismiss the complaint was filed in the pleading stage, the question arises whether, on a motion at the trial for directed verdict, the sufficiency of the evidence should be tested by the allegations that the complaint does contain or by those that it ought to contain. This question, primarily one of waiver of defenses, has prompted divergent views from the courts. *See, e.g.,* Buchanan v. Heath, 210 Ga. 410, 80 S.E.2d 393 (1954); Harbin v. Hunt, 151 Ga. 60, 105 S.E. 842 (1921); Bradford v. City of Commerce, 91 Ga.App. 581, 86 S.E.2d 645 (1955); Carlson v. Bankers Trust Co., 242 Iowa 1207, 50 N.W.2d 1 (1951); Coleman v. Whisnant, 226 N.C. 258, 37 S.E.2d 693 (1946); Note, 18 Ga. B.J. 498 (1956); Note, 2 Drake L. Rev. 18 (1952).

10. *See, e.g.,* Kinco, Inc. v. Schueck Steel, 283 Ark. 72, 671 S.W.2d 178 (1984); Winnick v. Nicoli, 185 Conn. 195, 440 A.2d 892 (1981); Blum v. Fresh Grown Preserve Corp., 292 N.Y. 241, 54 N.E.2d 809 (1944); Cooper, Directions for Directed Verdicts: A Compass for Federal Courts, 55 Minn. L. Rev. 903 (1971); McBaine, Trial Practice: Directed Verdicts; Federal Rule, 31 Calif. L. Rev. 454 (1943); Smith, The Power of the Judge to Direct a Verdict: Section 457a of the New York Civil Practice Act, 24 Colum. L. Rev. 111 (1924); Smyser, Rule 50(a) Directed Verdict: Its Function and Criteria in South Dakota, 19 S.D.L. Rev. 39 (1974); Note, The Motion for a Directed Verdict in Indiana: An Evaluation of Present Standards, 32 Ind. L.J. 238 (1957); Note, Appellate Courts of Missouri and the Weight and Credibility of the Evidence, 39 UMKC L. Rev. 87 (1970); Note, Directing the Verdict in Favor of the Party with the Burden of Proof, 50 N.C.L. Rev. 843 (1972).

11. *See* McGowne v. Challenge–Cook Bros., Inc., 672 F.2d 652 (8th Cir.1982); Kingston v. McGrath, 232 F.2d 495 (9th Cir.1956) (same test in jury case whether dismissal or directed verdict sought); Copeland v. Rabing, 110 Cal.App.2d 631, 243 P.2d 119 (1952) (nonsuit); Julien v. Barker, 75 Idaho 413, 272 P.2d 718 (1954) (nonsuit); Schiff v. Oak Park Cleaners & Dyers, 9 Ill.App.2d 1, 132 N.E.2d 416 (1955) (directed verdict or j.n.o.v.); McLeod v. Andrew Murphy & Son, 155 Neb. 318, 51 N.W.2d 620 (1952) (peremptory instruction or nonsuit); Lea v. Bridgeman, 228 N.C. 565, 46 S.E.2d 555 (1948) (nonsuit, prayer for instructions, or objecting to submission of issues); Peterson v. Bober, 79 N.D. 300, 56 N.W.2d 331 (1952) (directed verdict and dismissal); Cooke v. Townley, 265 P.2d 1108 (Okla.1951) (demurrer to evidence or directed verdict); City of Lake Mills v. Veldhuizen, 263 Wis. 49, 56 N.W.2d 491 (1953) (nonsuit).

12. See Note, The Motion for a Directed Verdict in Indiana: An Evaluation of Present Standards, 32 Ind. L.J. 238 (1957), for an excellent treatment of this problem.

or laws of nature;[13] few, if any, courts, however, are willing to go much further than that on such a motion.[14] The real differences arise mostly in the willingness to find contradiction with physical facts or some other basis for declaring evidence incredible as matter of law.[15] Even here courts display a fairly uniform reluctance to go very far in taking matters of credibility from the jury,[16] and usually the jury will pass on disputed factual questions.[17] The apparent differences lie in nomenclature. Some courts consider the problem described in this paragraph a matter of credibility, others do not.

Directed verdict, judgment n.o.v., and new trial

The directed verdict is one of three methods that apply substantially the same standard for deciding whether the evidence warrants submitting a case to the jury. The second is the judgment notwithstanding verdict, which is essentially a postponed motion for directed verdict that is heard after the verdict has been rendered. It uses the same standard to assess the sufficiency of the evidence, and in federal courts is now, like the directed verdict, called judgment as a matter of law.[18] The third is summary judgment, which is considered before the trial. Courts decide summary judgment motions, not on the live testimony presented at trial, but on written materials such as documents, affidavits, and depositions, and they take into account evidence that a party will be able to produce evidence at trial that is not yet available. In other respects, summary judgment tests the same issue and applies the same standard as directed verdict.[19]

Equating the test for directing a verdict or granting judgment as a matter of law to that for setting aside a verdict and granting a new trial is complicated by the wide range of the tests used in different jurisdictions for setting aside a verdict. These will be examined in a later

13. *See* Simblest v. Maynard, 427 F.2d 1 (2d Cir.1970); Winnick v. Nicoli, 185 Conn. 195, 440 A.2d 892 (1981); Cincinnati, N. & C. Ry. v. Johnson, 281 Ky. 565, 136 S.W.2d 769 (1940); Lohmann v. Wabash R.R., 364 Mo. 910, 269 S.W.2d 885 (1954); Cameron v. Goree, 182 Or. 581, 189 P.2d 596 (1948); Lowe v. Preferred Truck Leasing, 528 S.W.2d 38 (Tenn.Ct.App.1975); Morris v. Chicago, M., St. P. & Pac. R.R., 1 Wash. 2d 587, 97 P.2d 119 (1939), *aff'd per curiam on reh'g,* 1 Wash.2d 587, 100 P.2d 19 (1940).

14. *See* Wilkerson v. McCarthy, 336 U.S. 53, 69 S.Ct. 413, 93 L.Ed. 497 (1949); Gunning v. Cooley, 281 U.S. 90, 50 S.Ct. 231, 74 L.Ed. 720 (1930); Jarman v. Philadelphia–Detroit Lines, 131 F.2d 728 (4th Cir.1942); Kostial v. Aero Mayflower Transit Co., 119 Ind.App. 377, 85 N.E.2d 644 (1949). *Cf.* Arms v. State Farm Fire & Casualty Co., 731 F.2d 1245 (6th Cir.1984). Allis Chalmers Mfg. Co. v. Wichman, 220 F.2d 426 (8th Cir.1955), *cert. denied,* 350 U.S. 835, 76 S.Ct. 71, 100 L.Ed. 745 (1955); Kansas City Pub. Serv. Co. v. Shephard, 184 F.2d 945 (10th Cir.1950).

15. *Compare, e.g.,* Pennsylvania R.R. v. Chamberlain, 288 U.S. 333, 53 S.Ct. 391, 77 L.Ed. 819 (1933), *with* Wilkerson v. McCarthy, 336 U.S. 53, 69 S.Ct. 413, 93 L.Ed. 497 (1949).

16. *See generally* 2 Harper, James, and Gray, Law of Torts §§ 15.2, 19.2 (2d ed. 1986).

17. Best v. District of Columbia, 291 U.S. 411, 54 S.Ct. 487, 78 L.Ed. 882 (1934); Porth v. Farrier, 934 F.2d 154 (8th Cir. 1991); Yancey v. Carroll County, 876 F.2d 1238 (6th Cir.1989).

18. Fed. R. Civ. P. 50(b); § 7.30 *infra.*

19. Fed. R. Civ. P. 56; §§ 4.10–16 *supra.*

section, and it suffices here to point out two things: First, the equation is more nearly valid in some jurisdictions than in others, but the differences are attributed to variations in the new-trial test rather than any variation in the directed-verdict test.[20] Second, one formulation of the equation is that a verdict should be directed when "it would be the duty of the court to set aside [a contrary] verdict and grant a new trial."[21] If "duty" refers to what would be sanctioned by reversal on appeal (rather than only by the judge's sense of moral duty), then the equation is largely true but adds nothing, since this duty would exist only where the evidence to support the verdict was *insufficient* in law.[22]

Directed verdicts and the substantive law

The motion for directed verdict or judgment as a matter of law tests not only the factual aspect but also the evaluative aspect of sufficiency.[23] Here, greater differences lie in the availability of this motion than in the matter of credibility. One school of thought (led by Holmes) would have the courts increasingly particularize the rules or standards of conduct for people to follow in recurring situations.[24] This view would manipulate sufficiency of the evidence (for example, no evidence would be sufficient to support a claim unless it showed a deviation from the fixed standard) and would result in more motions for directed verdict being granted. This school of thought has lost ground in the present century, especially in personal injury tort cases. Nevertheless, judicial decisions on the sufficiency of evidence continue to create precedents clarifying and inflecting the rules of substantive law they apply.

§ 7.22 Instructions to the Jury

The judge has the duty to instruct the jury on the substantive law applicable to all the ultimate issues made by the proof.[1] Each party may request instructions, and court rules typically require that such requests be submitted in writing at a specified point before the instructions are given.[2] Nevertheless, the judge is required to give instructions even if not requested.

20. *See* § 7.28 *infra.*

21. Blum v. Fresh Grown Preserve Corp., 292 N.Y. 241, 244, 54 N.E.2d 809, 810 (1944).

22. *See id.*, 292 N.Y. at 245, 54 N.E.2d at 810 (quoting Brown v. Mohawk & H.R.R., 1 How. App. Cas. 52, 66 (N.Y.Ct. App.1847)).

23. 2 Harper, James, and Gray, Law of Torts § 15.3 (2d ed. 1986).

24. *See* Baltimore & O.R.R. v. Goodman, 275 U.S. 66, 48 S.Ct. 24, 72 L.Ed. 167 (1927); Southern Pac. Co. v. Berkshire, 254 U.S. 415, 41 S.Ct. 162, 65 L.Ed. 335 (1921); Lorenzo v. Wirth, 170 Mass. 596, 49 N.E. 1010 (1898); Holmes, The Common Law 110–129 (1881).

§ 7.22

1. Thayer, Evidence 112–114 (1898); Farley, Instructions to Juries—Their Role in the Judicial Process, 42 Yale L.J. 194 (1932); Herron v. Southern Pac. Co., 283 U.S. 91, 51 S.Ct. 383, 75 L.Ed. 857 (1931).

2. Wright v. Farmers Co-Op of Ark. and Okla., 620 F.2d 694 (8th Cir.1980); Missouri Pac. R.R. Co. v. Star City Gravel Co., 592 F.2d 455 (8th Cir.1979); Fed. R. Civ. P. 51.

The judge's power

Because of the judge's prestige and position in the trial, the charge can greatly influence the jury. This influence is enhanced if the judge's charge is given after arguments of counsel and hence is the last significant message before the jury's deliberation. Federal Rule 51, which originally provided that the jury was to be instructed after the arguments of counsel, was amended in 1987 to allow instruction before or after argument, or both, in the discretion of the trial judge.[3] The judge may sum up the evidence and indicate how the legal rules could be applied.[4] The judge may also comment on the evidence, expressing an opinion concerning the credibility of witnesses and the relative strength of competing permissible inferences. The judge must make clear, however, that it is the jury's province to decide such questions of weight and credibility.[5]

These features of instructions to the jury now generally prevail.[6] Populist sentiment in the nineteenth century prescribed a narrower role for the judge. Statutes and constitutional provisions in many states prohibited the judge from commenting on the evidence,[7] required the court to charge only on points covered by specific requests,[8] and required that the judge's charge be given before counsel's arguments.[9] But today, at least in federal court, liberal provisions are made for the judge's role in aiding the jury.[10] Thus, the judge may ask clarifying questions or comments and may also permit the jurors to ask questions of the judge and, through him, of the witnesses and counsel. The judge's role, however, falls short of the traditional English practice in which judges summarize the evidence in detail to the jury, to say nothing of the

3. Fed. R. Civ. P. 51.

4. *See* 9 Wigmore, Evidence § 2551 (Chadbourn rev. 1981); Wright, Instructions to the Jury: Summary Without Comment, 1954 Wash. U.L.Q. 177.

5. *See* Quercia v. United States, 289 U.S. 466, 53 S.Ct. 698, 77 L.Ed. 1321 (1933); Evans v. Wright, 505 F.2d 287 (4th Cir.1974); Sheahan v. Barry, 27 Mich. 217, 226–227 (1873); 9 Wigmore, Evidence § 2551 (Chadbourn rev. 1981); Sunderland, The Inefficiency of the American Jury, 13 Mich. L. Rev. 302, 305 (1915). *See generally* Frederick, The Psychology of the American Jury (1987); Stephens Controlling the Civil Jury: Towards a Functional Model of Justification, 76 Ky. L.J. 81 (1988); Wright, The Invasion of Jury: Temperature of the War, 27 Temp. L.Q. 137 (1953).

6. *See* Hever and Penrod, Instructing Jurors: A Field Experiment with Written and Preliminary Instructions, 13 Law & Hum. Behav. 409 (1989); Wright, Adequacy of Instructions to the Jury, 53 Mich. L. Rev. 505, 813 (1955). *See also, e.g.,* Devitt and Blackman, Federal Jury Practice and Instructions (2d ed. 1970).

7. *See* sources cited *supra* note 6; Sunderland, The Inefficiency of the American Jury, 13 Mich. L. Rev. 302, 307–309 (1915).

8. Wright, Instructions to the Jury: Summary Without Comment, 1954 Wash. U.L.Q. 177, 180–182; Wright, Adequacy of Instructions to the Jury: II, 53 Mich. L. Rev. 813, 821–822 (1955).

9. *See* Wright, Instructions to the Jury: Summary Without Comment, 1954 Wash. U.L.Q. 177, 183–189. *Compare* Blatt, Judge's Charge to Jury Should Precede Arguments of Counsel, 33 J. Am. Jud. Socy. 56 (1949), *with* Hartshorne, The Timing of the Charge to the Jury, 33 J. Am. Jud. Socy. 90 (1949).

10. *See* De Benedetto v. Goodyear Tire & Rubber Co., 754 F.2d 512 (4th Cir.1985). *See also* Annot., 80 A.L.R. Fed. 879; Kassin and Wrightsman, The American Jury on Trial: Psychological Perspectives (1988).

practice in several continental systems that, in those criminal cases tried to a jury, the judges participate in the jury's deliberations.

Scope of instructions

The instructions should state the issues and the rules of substantive law that should be applied to the various possible findings of fact the jury might make under the evidence. They should explain which party has the burden of proof (burden of persuasion) on each issue and the standard of persuasion required.[11] The jury is usually told that it must decide the credibility of witnesses. The jury instructions must relate to the factual circumstances of the case; abstract propositions of law unrelated to the facts of the case are obviously improper and potentially confusing.[12] Judges are not required to single out any particular item of evidence, nor are they required to comment on any part of it, as their restraint is usually needed to maintain impartiality.

Binding instruction

When the evidence presents an issue of law that the judge must decide, the jury is given a binding instruction in that respect. A binding instruction simply tells the jurors the legal premise they must adopt. For example, for the question whether given facts constitute probable cause in malicious prosecution, the court will tell the jury that such and such facts do (or do not) constitute probable cause.[13]

Requests for instructions

Rules or statutes prescribe a time for filing the requested instructions (at the close of the evidence, for example) and require that they be in writing[14] so that the judge and jury may examine them at trial and so that the parties' contentions for possible appeal are preserved.[15] Requests for instructions may be required to follow formal rules such as separately numbered paragraphs and citation of supporting authority. Instructions are given at the end of the case, but the court has discretion, during the course of the trial, to give interim instructions; these are especially useful in long, complicated cases.[16]

11. *See* § 7.12 *supra.*

12. Duke v. Uniroyal Inc., 928 F.2d 1413 (4th Cir.1991); United States v. Holley, 502 F.2d 273 (4th Cir.1974).

13. Carson v. Doggett, 231 N.C. 629, 58 S.E.2d 609 (1950); Patrick v. Wigley, 206 Okla. 194, 242 P.2d 423 (1952); Byers v. Ward, 368 Pa. 416, 84 A.2d 307 (1951). *See* Thayer, Evidence 221–232 (1898).

14. *See* Fed. R. Civ. P. 51. *Compare* Cal. Civ. Proc. Code § 607 *et seq.;* N.Y. Civ. Prac. L. & R. 4017, 5501. *See also* Annot., 91 A.L.R.2d 836.

15. *See* Wright v. Farmers Co-Op of Ark. and Okla., 620 F.2d 694 (8th Cir.1980) (allegations of error in the instructions are not preserved on appeal unless specific instructions are requested); Fisher v. Indiana Lumbermens Mut. Ins. Co., 456 F.2d 1396 (5th Cir.1972).

16. Comment, Memory, Magic, and Myth: The Timing of Jury Instructions, 59 Or. L. Rev. 451 (1981); note 24 *infra.*; § 7.7 *supra.*

The court normally informs counsel of its rulings on the requested instructions before the attorneys commence their arguments to the jury. Instruction conferences are commonly held for this purpose;[17] any objections to the court's proposed instructions should be made part of the record during the conference. It is advisable to have these conferences on the record when disputes regarding the instructions may arise, and a written copy will facilitate appellate review.[18]

Failure to request

An instruction formulated by counsel can emphasize that party's interpretation of the substantive law as well as its theory of the evidence. Failure to request an instruction on an issue is taken as acknowledgment that the issue need not be submitted to the jury. Failure to request instructions, however, does not foreclose the court's duty to give them. As one court put it, even when there are no requests, a federal court must nevertheless charge "on the broad general fundamental rules of law applicable to the principal issues of fact in the case."[19] Failure to do so may be the basis of reversible error. Moreover, under the "plain error" doctrine, an erroneous charge is reversible error even in the absence of objection by counsel when it results in a miscarriage of justice. Counsel, however, cannot rely on being rescued by this rule.[20]

If either counsel wants the jury instructed on a particular matter, counsel must file a request for the instruction as a condition for later claiming that the trial court erred in failing to cover the "particular matter."[21] Thus, in a negligence case the trial judge will be bound to give the general formula for negligence as conduct involving a foreseeable and unreasonable risk of harm to others under the circumstances. But if a party wishes to require the judge to mention any particular circumstance, then it should file a request to charge the jury on that circumstance. The judge is required to indicate, before counsel commence their summations, the subjects on which instructions will be given. In many jurisdictions the instructions to be given must be written and specifically identified.[22] This forecast of the instructions permits counsel's argument to be shaped in accordance with the law as the judge will declare it.[23]

17. *See, e.g.,* Phillips v. Parke, Davis & Co., 869 F.2d 407 (8th Cir.1989); Weir v. Federal Ins. Co., 811 F.2d 1387 (10th Cir. 1987); Estate of Larkins v. Farrell Lines, Inc., 806 F.2d 510 (4th Cir.1986).

18. Dixon v. City of Lawton, 898 F.2d 1443 (10th Cir.1990); King v. Ford Motor Co., 597 F.2d 436 (5th Cir.1979).

19. Turner Construction Co. v. Houlihan, 240 F.2d 435, 439 (1st Cir.1957).

20. *See, e.g.,* Mazer v. Lipschutz, 327 F.2d 42 (3d Cir.1963); Joba Construction Co. v. Burns & Roe, Inc., 121 Mich.App. 615, 329 N.W.2d 760 (1982).

21. DeLong v. Erie County, 60 N.Y.2d 296, 457 N.E.2d 717, 469 N.Y.S.2d 611 (1983).

22. *See, e.g.,* Haw. R. Civ. P. 51(c) (d); Tex. R. Civ. P. 272; Wright v. Farmers Co-Op of Ark., and Okla., 620 F.2d 694 (8th Cir.1980).

23. *See, e.g.,* Keeton, Trial Tactics ch. 6 (2d ed. 1973). *See also* Blackman, Problems of Court and Counsel in Requests and Exceptions, 62 F.R.D. 251 (1974).

Pattern instructions

Instructions by the court, and instructions requested by counsel, must embody a correct statement of substantive law. They should not assume the truth of facts that are in issue. The charge should also be expressed in language the jury can understand. Formerly courts were preoccupied with the technical, legal accuracy of instructions, and they were often couched in nearly incomprehensible language. Today greater emphasis is given to clarity. In most jurisdictions "pattern" instructions have been developed for common types of cases, and these tend to be cast in simple, relatively general language. Even pattern instructions may use legal language and complex sentences that make them hard to follow, especially when the jury does not receive written copies to take into their deliberations. One commentator observes that "judges themselves routinely nullify the law by not communicating the law intelligibly to jurors."[24]

Defective requests

A problem arises when a request correctly identifies an issue on which the party is entitled to a charge but is improper in form or substance. The rules mediate between holding that the judge must give an instruction on a relevant issue, even if the request is irregular, and holding that error cannot be assigned on the basis of an irregular request. Thus, when the meaning of a request is reasonably apparent and its subject matter is significant and not sufficiently covered by a general instruction, abundant authority holds that a court cannot ignore the request merely because its proposition is not absolutely accurate.[25] It is also clear that an appellate court will find no error when the request is inaccurate in substance or is not tendered in conformity with the rules.[26] When a requested charge is refused, the appellate courts will usually not find error unless the "proffered instruction [is] accurate in every respect."[27] Therefore counsel is well advised to frame important requests with precision and care.

24. Saks, What Do Jury Experiments Tell Us About How Juries (Should) Make Decisions?, 6 So. Cal. Interdisc. L.J. 1, 35 (1997). *See* American Jud. Socy., Pattern Jury Instructions (1972); Annot., 49 A.L.R.3d 128 (statutes requiring use of pattern instructions); Charrow and Charrow, Making Legal Language Understandable: A Psycholinguistic Study of Jury Instructions, 79 Colum. L. Rev. 1306 (1979); Steele & Thornburg, Jury Instructions: A Persistent Failure to Communicate, 67 N.C.L. Rev. 77 (1988); Hever & Penrod, Instructing Jurors: A Field Experiment with Written and Preliminary Instructions, 13 Law & Hum. Behav. 409 (1989). *See also* Schwarzer, Communicating with Juries: Problems and Remedies, 69 Calif. L. Rev. 731 (1981).

25. Montgomery v. Virginia Stage Lines, 191 F.2d 770, 772 (D.C.Cir.1951) (request embodying applicable regulations of Interstate Commerce Commission "not entirely correct"). *See also* Readenour v. Marion Power Shovel, 149 Ariz. 442, 719 P.2d 1058 (1986); Annes v. Connecticut Co., 107 Conn. 126, 129, 139 A. 511, 512 (1927) (request embodying applicable last-chance doctrine "of somewhat doubtful accuracy").

26. *See* 1 Reid's Branson, Instructions to Juries 180.

27. Ruggiero v. Krzeminski, 928 F.2d 558, 561 (2d Cir.1991).

Objections to charge

Most jurisdictions require that a party make specific and timely objection to an instruction as a condition to claiming error on appellate review.[28] The rules vary on when and how such objections should be made. In jurisdictions where the counsel are informed before argument of the instructions to be given, objections must be made at that point.[29] In other jurisdictions and under Rule 51, objection has to be made before the jury retires to consider its verdict.[30] Rule 51 should be read in connection with Rule 46, which dispenses with the need for formal exceptions if a party adequately makes known "the objection to the action of the court and the grounds therefore."[31] Thus, taking these two rules together, points clearly raised in proper requests to charge need not be repeated by objection at the close of a charge that does not express the request.[32]

An appellate court will not find error in a trial court judge's refusal to give a proper requested instruction where the substance of the proposed instruction was covered by another instruction which was given.[33] If the refused instruction is not adequately covered by another, most courts follow a three-step test on review:

1. the court will "first inquire as to whether the requested instruction is a correct statement of the law";
2. if it is, then "the next step is to assess whether the instruction addresses an issue that is properly before the jury";
3. even if both of these criteria are met, "there must still be a showing of prejudicial harm that resulted from the failure of the trial court to give the requested instruction before the judgment will be disturbed on that ground."[34]

The general rule is that the trial court has broad discretion to compose the instructions to the jury, provided they are fundamentally accurate and not misleading.[35] The appellate court will uphold the instructions so long as they show no tendency to confuse or mislead the jury on applicable principles of law.[36] A jury-instruction error mandates

28. *See* 1 Reid's Branson, Instructions to Juries 170–175. *See also* Lewis v. City of Irvine, 899 F.2d 451 (6th Cir.1990); Siddiqi v. Leak, 880 F.2d 904 (7th Cir.1989).

29. *See, e.g.,* Cal. Civ. Proc. Code § 607; Tex. R. Civ. P. 274, 275.

30. *See* Fed. R. Civ. P. 51(e); *see, e.g.,* N.Y. Civ. Prac. L. & R. 4110b.

31. *See also* Appeal of Perkinson, 821 F.2d 686 (D.C.Cir.1987); Bowley v. Stotler & Co., 751 F.2d 641 (3d Cir.1985).

32. *E.g.,* Montgomery v. Virginia Stage Lines, 191 F.2d 770 (D.C.Cir.1951); Wright v. Farm Journal, 158 F.2d 976 (2d Cir. 1947); Williams v. Powers, 135 F.2d 153 (6th Cir.1943).

33. Pesaplastic, C.A. v. Cincinnati Milacron Co., 750 F.2d 1516 (11th Cir.1985).

34. Wilkinson v. Carnival Cruise Lines, 920 F.2d 1560, 1569–1570 (11th Cir.1991).

35. Gates v. Northwest Ins. Co., 881 F.2d 215 (5th Cir.1989), *cert. denied,* 494 U.S. 1017, 110 S.Ct. 1320, 108 L.Ed.2d 495 (1990); Landrum v. Goddard, 921 F.2d 61 (5th Cir.1991); Horton v. Buhrke, a Div. of Klein Tools, 926 F.2d 456 (5th Cir.1991).

36. 9 Wright and Miller, Federal Practice and Procedure § 2558; Wilkinson v.

reversal only if the appellate court determines, on its review of the record as a whole, that the error was prejudicial[37] and that the "charge as a whole leaves [the appellate court] with substantial and ineradicable doubt whether the jury has been properly guided in its deliberations."[38] The result is that judges are free to give instructions that have very different impacts on jurors despite being equally accurate statements of legal doctrine. As both lawyers and pollsters know, the way in which one phrases a question often helps determine the answer. That is also true of jury instructions.[39]

§ 7.23 Special Verdicts and Interrogatories

A special verdict is one in which the jury makes findings on specific issues, as distinct from a general verdict of the form "We the jury find for the plaintiff in the amount of $___" or "We the jury find for defendant." The findings in a special verdict usually are "yes" or "no" answers to such questions as "was any statement by defendant materially false?" "Did plaintiff rely on any such statement?" "Did plaintiff have independent information on the subject matter of the statement?"

The special verdict emerged in the old common law as a device by which the jury might protect itself from the risk of attaint for rendering a false verdict.[1] In this country it became transformed into a device for judicial control of juries.[2] It is used infrequently in many jurisdictions because of the requirement that, to support a judgment, a special verdict must include findings on all the material facts in issue. Omission of a finding on an issue later found to be essential renders the judgment erroneous. In contrast, a general verdict is presumed to incorporate a finding by the jury on every issue necessary to the judgment and covered by the instructions.

The Federal Rule on special verdict procedure is not so stringent. Rule 49(a) provides that if, in submitting a case to the jury for special

Carnival Cruise Lines, 920 F.2d 1560 (11th Cir.1991); Gregg v. United States Indus., 887 F.2d 1462 (11th Cir.1989). See Thornburg, The Power and the Process: Instructions and the Civil Jury, 66 Fordham L. Rev. 1837 (1998)(urging more attention to instructions).

37. Street v. Parham, 929 F.2d 537 (10th Cir.1991).

38. Treadaway v. Societe Anonyme Louis-Dreyfus, 894 F.2d 161, 167 (5th Cir. 1990). *See* Bommarito v. Penrod Drilling Corp., 929 F.2d 186, 189 (5th Cir.1991).

39. Brown, Regulating Decision Effects of Legally Sufficient Jury Instructions, 73 S. Cal. L. Rev. 1105 (2000); Solan, Refocusing the Burden of Proof in Criminal Cases: Some Doubt About Reasonable Doubt, 78 Tex. L. Rev. 105 (1999).

§ 7.23

1. Green, Judge and Jury 353 (1930). *See also* Thayer, Evidence 217–219 (1898). *Cf.* Morgan, A Brief History of Special Verdicts and Special Interrogatories, 32 Yale L.J. 575, 588–591 (1923); Note, Using the Special Verdict to Manage Complex Cases and Avoid Compromise Verdicts, 21 Ariz. L.J. 297 (1989).

2. *See* Clementson, Special Vedicts 8 (1905); Green, Judge and Jury 353 (1930); Brodin, Accuracy, Efficiency and Accountability in the Litigation Process—The Case for the Fact Vedict, 59 U. Cin. L. Rev. 15 (1990); Sunderland, Vedicts, General and Special, 29 Yale L.J. 253, 258 (1920).

verdict, "the court omits any issue of fact raised by the pleadings or by the evidence, each party waives his right to a trial by jury of the issue so omitted unless before the jury retires he demands its submission to the jury." The court is then given the power to make findings of fact on the omitted issue, and even its failure to do so is remedied by the assumption of findings "in accord with the judgment on the special verdict."[3]

Interrogatories to jury

A device similar to the special verdict consists of interrogatories to be answered along with a general verdict.[4] This device does not suffer the same impediment as the special verdict because the interrogatories need not cover all issues and are backed by the general verdict. In a few states the practice of submitting such interrogatories has become common.[5]

Inconsistent interrogatories

Rule 49(b) explicitly provides what should be done when the answers to the interrogatories are inconsistent with one another or with the general verdict: The court may (1) direct entry of judgment in accordance with the answers, notwithstanding the general verdict; (2) return the jury for further consideration of its answers and verdict; or (3) order a new trial.[6] In administering these provisions, courts should be astute to reconcile answers with one other and with the general verdict when this is reasonably possible.[7]

In *Gallick v. Baltimore & Ohio Railroad*[8] the Supreme Court held that a case would be remanded for a new trial only if the answers are fatally inconsistent.[9] In *Gallick,* a railroad employee sued his employer for negligence in maintaining on its premises a stagnant pool filled with decaying rats and pigeons. The plaintiff suffered an insect bite on his leg while working near the pool, subsequently fell ill, and had to have his

3. Fed. R. Civ. P. 49(a). *See also* Pau v. Yosemite Park & Curry Co., 928 F.2d 880 (9th Cir.1991).

4. Fed. R. Civ. P. 49(b); Green, Judge and Jury 354–355 (1930); Morgan, A Brief History of Special Verdicts and Special Interrogatories, 32 Yale L.J. 575, 591–592 (1923); Wicker, Special Interrogatories to Juries in Civil Cases, 35 Yale L.J. 296 (1926).

5. *See* Brodin, Accuracy, Efficiency and Accountability in the Litigation Process—The Case for the Fact Verdict, 59 U. Cin. L. Rev. 15 (1990); Frank, The Case for the Special Verdict, 32 J. Am. Jud. Socy. 142, 147–148 (1949).

6. Fed. R. Civ. P. 49(b).

7. *See, e.g.,* Gallick v. Baltimore & O. R.R., 372 U.S. 108, 83 S.Ct. 659, 9 L.Ed.2d 618 (1963); Alverez v. J. Ray McDermott & Co., 674 F.2d 1037 (5th Cir.1982); Safeway Stores v. Dial, 311 F.2d 595, 600 (5th Cir. 1963); Gulf Ref. Co. v. Fetschan, 130 F.2d 129 (6th Cir.1942), *cert. denied,* 318 U.S. 764, 63 S.Ct. 666, 87 L.Ed. 1136 (1943); Morris v. Pennsylvania R.R., 187 F.2d 837 (2d Cir.1951); Tobin v. Van Orsdol, 241 Iowa 1331, 45 N.W.2d 239 (1950); In re Estate of Erwin, 170 Kan. 728, 228 P.2d 739 (1951); Klever v. Reid Bros. Express, 151 Ohio St. 467, 86 N.E.2d 608 (1949); Wicker, Special Interrogatories to Juries in Civil Cases, 35 Yale L.J. 296, 304 (1926).

8. 372 U.S. 108, 83 S.Ct. 659, 9 L.Ed.2d 618 (1963).

9. 372 U.S. at 119–120, 83 S.Ct. at 666–667, 9 L.Ed.2d at 627.

legs amputated. The jury found, in response to a special verdict interrogatory, that the railroad's negligence was the proximate cause of the employee's injuries. It also found that there was no reason to anticipate that maintaining the stagnant pool would result in an injury and, that there was no relation between the maintenance of the pond and the injury to plaintiff. The Court in *Gallick* found, however, that these fact findings were consistent "in light of the jury instructions and in the context of the entire special verdict."[10]

Not all courts would strain so hard to find consistency. In any event, the jury's divergent responses in *Gallick* indicate the difficulties in administering a special verdict. *Gallick* does not prohibit the trial court from resubmitting the special verdict to the jury, but lower federal courts are split on the question whether Rule 49(a) bars resubmission when the answers can be reconciled.[11] As has subsequently been observed:

> *Gallick* implies that, under Rule 49(a), the trial court simply cannot choose to ignore a legitimate finding that is part of the special verdict. The special verdict reflects the jury's findings of fact. The words "reconcile" and "harmonize" imply that the court must treat each legitimate answer as correct and consistent.[12]

Occasionally, a jury, in violation of the trial court's instructions, offers superfluous answers or parenthetical comments on the special verdict form. Generally, these superfluous answers are disregarded as surplusage.[13]

Discretion of court

Strong argument has been made for using special verdicts and interrogatories in complex cases.[14] In most states and in the federal courts, the general rule is that the trial court has complete discretion whether a general or special verdict is to be returned and to answer interrogatories along with a general verdict. This discretion includes the determination of the form of the special verdict, provided it fully and fairly presents to the jury the issues of the case.[15] If a discrepancy exists among the special verdict answers, the trial court has the discretion to

10. 372 U.S. at 121, 83 S.Ct. at 667, 9 L.Ed.2d at 628.

11. *See* Floyd v. Laws, 929 F.2d 1390, 1396 n. 3 (9th Cir.1991).

12. Floyd v. Laws, 929 F.2d 1390, 1397 (9th Cir.1991).

13. *See, e.g., id.;* White v. Grinfas, 809 F.2d 1157 (5th Cir.1987); Tanno v. S.S. President Madison Vessel, 830 F.2d 991 (9th Cir.1987).

14. *See, e.g.,* Skidmore v. Baltimore & O.R.R., 167 F.2d 54, 56, 70 (2d Cir.1948), *cert. denied,* 335 U.S. 816, 69 S.Ct. 34, 93 L.Ed. 371 (1948) (opinions of Frank and Hand, JJ.); United States for Use of Federal Corp. v. Commercial Mechanical Contractors, 707 F.2d 1124 (10th Cir.1982); Green, Judge and Jury 350–374 (1930); Wicker, Special Interrogatories to Juries in Civil Cases, 35 Yale L.J. 296 (1926). *Contrast* the opinions of Clark and Frank, JJ., in Morris v. Pennsylvania R.R., 187 F.2d 837, 843 (2d Cir.1951).

15. Mateyko v. Felix, 924 F.2d 824 (9th Cir.1990); Floyd v. Laws, 929 F.2d 1390 (9th Cir.1991); 5A Moore, Federal Practice and Procedure ¶ 49.03(1).

resubmit the inconsistent answers to the jury for clarification.[16] Jury answers to special interrogatories normally are construed by the court to uphold their validity, as they were in *Gallick,* because of the Seventh Amendment guarantee of jury trial.[17] Only if there is no way to reconcile them are they held to be inconsistent.

Isolation of issues

Special verdicts and interrogatories offer two advantages. First, they isolate error and reduce the necessity for reversal on appeal, whereas the grounds of a general verdict are often not ascertainable.[18] For example, in the typical negligence case the issues made by the pleadings include defendant's negligence, its causal relation to plaintiff's claimed injury, the existence and extent of injury, and the plaintiff's contributory negligence. A general verdict for plaintiff necessarily implies a finding on each one of these issues, but a general verdict for defendant does not, since it may rationally be grounded on any of a number of possible combinations of findings.

If error in the instructions has occurred on only one of the issues, such as contributory negligence, the error may have had no part in producing a verdict for defendant since it could have been based on a finding unrelated to that one issue. If the jury renders a general verdict, so far as appears the error may have contributed to producing the result, and hence reversal would be required.[19] If, however, the jury has made special findings, the record may reveal that the error in instructing on one issue did not contaminate the finding on another issue. The error then will be regarded as "harmless" and a reversal will be unnecessary.[20] On the other hand, using special verdicts can cost as well as save time because of the need to frame clear interrogatories and to untangle procedural snafus and inconsistent answers.

16. *See, e.g.,* Karl v. Burlington N.R.R. Co., 880 F.2d 68 (8th Cir.1989); Santiago–Negron v. Castro–Davila, 865 F.2d 431 (1st Cir.1989); Auwood v. Harry Brandt Booking Office, 850 F.2d 884 (2d Cir.1988). *See also* Annot., 6 A.L.R.3d 438.

17. *See* Smith v. Tidewater Marine Towing, 927 F.2d 838 (5th Cir.1991); Guidry v. Kem Mfg. Co., 598 F.2d 402 (5th Cir.1979).

18. That is, they are not ascertainable even on a theoretical basis. Juries in fact have the *power* to decide cases on grounds they are not supposed to consider—indeed those they have been forbidden to consider. For many purposes, however, the law blandly assumes that juries do what the court tells them to do.

19. *See, e.g.,* Fillippon v. Albion Vein Slate Co., 250 U.S. 76, 39 S.Ct. 435, 63 L.Ed. 853 (1919) (instruction to jury in absence of parties and counsel); Poultryland, Inc. v. Anderson, 200 Ga. 549, 37 S.E.2d 785 (1946) (refusal of a timely request for sequestration of witnesses); Sweeney v. Vierbuchen, 224 Ind. 341, 66 N.E.2d 764 (1946) (erroneous instruction on attorney-client relationship); Gurwell v. Jefferson City Lines, 239 Mo.App. 305, 192 S.W.2d 683 (1946) (erroneous admission of medical opinion); Ferderer v. Northern Pac. Ry., 75 N.D. 139, 26 N.W.2d 236 (1947) (instruction to jury in absence of parties and counsel); Kimball v. Borden, 95 Va. 203, 28 S.E. 207 (1897) (erroneous instruction on negligence).

20. Morris v. Pennsylvania R.R., 187 F.2d 837, 841 (2d Cir.1951). *See* Sunderland, Verdicts, General and Special, 29 Yale L.J. 253, 259; Wicker, Special Interrogatories to Juries in Civil Cases, 35 Yale L.J. 296, 306 (1926).

Focus on issues

A second advantage of special findings is that the instructions may be easier to frame and to understand. Ordinarily the charge must state the law applicable to each of the possible combinations of findings that the jury might make from the evidence. This calls for hypothetical statements that are often repetitious. The special verdict can construct the possibilities in the form of a decision tree that can guide the jury through a point-by-point analysis.

This structure in turn puts psychological pressure on the jurors to adhere to their legally prescribed functions and to prevent them from deciding cases on grounds they are instructed to ignore. This supposed effect is commonly emphasized by protagonists of the special verdict or interrogatories;[21] it can be neutralized, at least to some degree, if the jurors also are instructed on the legal effect of their answers to the special interrogatories. Whether to give such instructions then becomes the subject of controversy paralleling whether the interrogatories should be given at all.[22]

Scope of jury's prerogative

Historically, juries have occasionally taken the law into their own hands and decided a case according to lay notions of what the law ought to be. Lord Coke is reported to have observed "the jurors are chancellors."[23] Holmes said:

> One reason why I believe in our practice of leaving questions of negligence to [jurors] is what is precisely one of their gravest defects from the point of view of their theoretical function: that they will introduce into their verdict a certain amount—a very large amount, so far as I have observed—of popular prejudice, and thus keep the administration of the law in accord with the wishes and feelings of the community.[24]

21. *See, e.g.,* Clementson, Special Verdicts 12 (1905); Brodin, Accuracy, Efficiency, and Accountability in the Litigation Process—The Case for the Fact Verdict, 59 U. Cin. L. Rev. 15 (1990); Frank, The Case for the Special Verdict, 32 J. Am. Jud. Socy. 142, 147 (1949); Sunderland, Verdicts, General and Special, 29 Yale L.J. 253, 262 (1920); Wicker, Special Interrogatories to Juries in Civil Cases, 35 Yale L.J. 296, 306 (1926).

22. *Compare* Note, Informing the Jury of the Effect of Its Answers to Special Verdict Questions, 58 Minn. L. Rev. 903 (1974); Annot., 90 A.L.R. 2d 1040. *See also* the analysis in Smith, Comparative Negligence Problems with the Special Verdict: Informing the Jury of the Legal Effects of their Answers, 10 Land & Water L. Rev. 199 (1975); Comment, Informing the Jury of the Legal Effect of Special Verdict Answers in Comparative Negligence Actions, 1981 Duke L.J. 824.

23. Pound, An Introduction to the Philosophy of Law 133 (1922); see § 7.7 *supra.*

24. Holmes, Collected Legal Papers 237–238 (1920). *See also* Kadish and Kadish, Discretion to Disobey ch. 2 (1973); Pound, Law in Books and Law in Action, 44 Am. L. Rev. 12, 18 (1910); Traynor, Fact, Skepticism and the Judicial Process, 106 U. Pa. L. Rev. 635, 639 (1958); Wyzanski, A Trial Judge's Freedom and Responsibility, 65 Harv. L. Rev. 1281, 1286 (1952).

The relative complexity of some modern types of cases, however, counsels for procedures that give a jury special guidance in resolving abstruse issues outside the ordinary citizen's experience.[25]

D. CONTROLLING THE JURY: POSTVERDICT DEVICES

§ 7.24 New Trial: In General

The most widely used device for correcting a verdict, and thereby controlling the jury after the fact, is by setting aside the verdict and granting a new trial. Granting new trials for judicial errors, jury misconduct, a verdict that is excessive or against the weight of the evidence, and "all sorts of errors and mistakes on the part of the jury" had become fairly well established at common law by the late eighteenth century.[1] This procedure, therefore, is regarded as consistent with the federal and typical state constitutional provisions guaranteeing jury trial.[2] " 'Trial by jury,' in the primary and usual sense of the term at the common law and in the American constitutions, is not merely a trial by a jury of twelve men before an officer vested with authority to cause them to be summoned and empaneled, to administer oaths to them and to the constable in charge, and to enter judgment and issue execution on their verdicts but it is a trial by a jury of twelve men, in the presence and under the superintendence of a judge empowered to instruct them on the law and to advise them on the facts, and (except to acquittal of a criminal charge) to set aside their verdict if in his opinion it is against the law or the evidence." The device may involve the reexamination of a fact tried by a jury, but this is not "otherwise ... than according to the rules of the common law."[3]

Federal Rule 59 outlines the procedures for this motion. It must be filed not later than ten days after entry of the judgment.[4] Thus, a verdict loser may file a new trial motion before the entry of judgment.[5] The district court need not write an exhaustive opinion explaining the

25. *See* In re Japanese Elec. Prods. Antitrust Litig., 631 F.2d 1069 (3d Cir.1980); In re U.S. Fin. Sec. Litig., 609 F.2d 411 (9th Cir.1979), *cert. denied,* 446 U.S. 929, 100 S.Ct. 1866, 64 L.Ed.2d 281 (1980).

§ 7.24

1. Hinton, Power of Federal Appellate Court to Review Ruling on Motion for New Trial, 1 U. Chi. L. Rev. 111, 112 (1933).

2. Gray, J., in Capital Traction Co. v. Hof, 174 U.S. 1, 13–14, 19 S.Ct. 580, 585, 43 L.Ed. 873, 877–878 (1899). *See also* the excellent discussion in Smith v. Times Publishing Co., 178 Pa. 481, 36 A. 296 (1897).

3. See Justice Van Devanter's discussion of the device of "reserving questions of law arising during trials" used for the purpose of reviewing jury verdicts at the time of the adoption of the Seventh Amendment. Baltimore & Carolina Line v. Redman, 295 U.S. 654, 659, 55 S.Ct. 890, 892, 79 L.Ed. 1636, 1639 (1935).

4. Fed. R. Civ. P. 59(b).

5. United States v. Scott, 929 F.2d 313 (7th Cir.1991); Jurgens v. McKasy, 905 F.2d 382 (Fed.Cir.1990). *Cf.* FirsTier Mortgage Co. v. Investors Mortgage Ins. Co., 498 U.S. 269, 111 S.Ct. 648, 112 L.Ed.2d 743 (1991).

granting or denial of the motion; no explanations at all are required, and the motion may be denied out of hand.[6]

§ 7.25 New Trial for Judicial Error

In most jurisdictions the court may grant a new trial either on its own motion or on a party's motion. The trial court may thereby correct its own errors in much the same way that an appellate court does.[1] Thus, a new trial may be granted when the court has improperly denied a jury trial,[2] or committed prejudicial error in its instructions to the jury,[3] or improperly admitted or excluded evidence,[4] provided the error is prejudicial.[5] When the judge's impropriety or error was nonprejudicial, the new trial motion will not be granted.[6] For instance, the jury's misunderstanding of the court's instructions will not in itself justify a new trial.[7]

Scope of discretion

Granting a new trial is commonly said to rest within the trial court's discretion. But this does not mean the trial judge's ruling *either way* will be undisturbed on appeal. The trial court has little or no discretion when asked to grant a new trial on grounds of serious judicial error.

In many jurisdictions an order granting a new trial is not immediately appealable since it is not a final order but contemplates further proceedings.[8] Hence, there is generally no chance for appeal until after

6. Dunn v. Truck World, 929 F.2d 311 (7th Cir.1991).

§ 7.25

1. Bateman v. Roller, 168 Kan. 111, 211 P.2d 440 (1949); Cheswick v. Moorhead, 224 S.W.2d 898 (Tex.Civ.App.1949). *See* Florida Coastal Theatres v. Belflower, 159 Fla. 741, 747, 32 So.2d 738, 741 (1947); National Casualty Co. v. Calhoun, 219 Miss. 9, 67 So.2d 908 (1953); Lyons v. Browning, 170 Or. 350, 353, 133 P.2d 599, 600 (1943).

The common law confined the judge's power to do so during the term when the verdict was rendered. National Casualty Co. v. Calhoun, *supra*. *Cf.* Small v. Connecticut Co., 109 Conn. 481, 146 A. 850 (1929). Current statutes and court rules often prescribe a fixed time limit. *See, e.g.,* Fed. R. Civ. P. 59(d) (ten days).

2. *See* Sulzbacher v. Continental Casualty Co., 88 F.2d 122, 124 (8th Cir.1937). *Cf.* Payton v. Abbott Laboratories, 780 F.2d 147 (1st Cir.1985); Laskaris v. Thornburgh, 733 F.2d 260 (3d Cir.1984); In re N–500L Cases, 691 F.2d 15 (1st Cir.1982).

3. Lewis v. City of Irvine, 899 F.2d 451 (6th Cir.1990); Western Fireproofing Co. v. W.R. Grace & Co., 896 F.2d 286 (8th Cir. 1990); Costilla v. Aluminum Co. of Am., 826 F.2d 1444 (5th Cir.1987).

4. Logan v. Dayton Hudson Corp., 865 F.2d 789 (6th Cir.1989); Petree v. Victor Fluid Power, Inc., 887 F.2d 34 (3d Cir. 1989); Irvan v. Frozen Food Express, 780 F.2d 1228 (5th Cir.1986).

5. Hale v. Firestone Tire & Rubber Co., 820 F.2d 928 (8th Cir.1987); Thweatt v. Ontko, 814 F.2d 1466 (10th Cir.1987).

6. Johnson v. Helmerich & Payne, Inc., 892 F.2d 422 (5th Cir.1990); Kern v. Levolor Lorentzen, Inc., 899 F.2d 772 (9th Cir. 1990); United States v. Killough, 848 F.2d 1523 (11th Cir.1988).

7. D.C. Thompson & Co. v. Hauge, 300 Or. 651, 717 P.2d 1169 (1986).

8. *See* Allied Chemical Corp. v. Daiflon, Inc., 449 U.S. 33, 101 S.Ct. 188, 66 L.Ed.2d 193 (1980); Ford Motor Co. v. Busam Motor Sales, 185 F.2d 531, 533 (6th Cir.1950) (containing a good exposition of this and related problems); Comment, Appellate Review in the Federal Courts of Orders Granting New Trial, 13 Stan. L. Rev. 383 (1961). For an evaluation of the final-judgment rule as applied to new-trial orders, and the trend toward greater appealability among state

the case has been retried and gone to judgment,[9] and by that stage any error in the ruling is likely to have become harmless.[10] If a new trial is denied, the judgment is appealable forthwith, and the trial court's refusal to grant the new trial may itself be assigned as further error in the appellate court. In other jurisdictions, granting of a new trial is an appealable order; if the appellate court finds no judicial error warranting the new trial, then the order will be reversed and judgment ordered on the verdict.[11]

In view of these contingent possibilities, the trial court has discretion in either remedying its supposed judicial error by granting a new trial, thereby preempting appeal, or by refusing to do so, thereby leaving it to the appellate court to determine the seriousness of the error. Thus, there is scope for the trial judge's discretion when there is room for doubt about the prejudicial effect of an error.[12] Moreover, if the original ruling lay within the trial judge's discretion (such as admission of evidence that is relevant but remote from the issue), similar latitude exists in granting a new trial based on that original ruling.[13]

§ 7.26 New Trial for Prejudicial Occurrence

Since a trial is extemporaneous, procedural mistakes can happen. The conduct of a witness, party, counsel, or juror may compromise a fair and impartial verdict. A witness may volunteer a statement that defendant is insured,[1] a party may approach a juror to tell or give him or her something,[2] inadmissible documents may be introduced in evidence or admissible ones concealed,[3] and counsel may ask an inflammatory question or make improper remarks in the course of argument.[4] An extrane-

jurisdictions, see Rabinowitz, Appellate Review of Trial Court Orders Granting New Trials, 8 Rutgers L. Rev. 465 (1954). *See also* Annot., 73 A.L.R.2d 269.

9. American Mfrs. Mut. Ins. Co. v. Wilson–Keith & Co., 247 F.2d 249 (8th Cir. 1957); Pettingill v. Fuller, 107 F.2d 933 (2d Cir.1939). *See also* Altrichter v. Shell Oil Co., 263 F.2d 377, 379 (8th Cir.1959); Ford Motor Co. v. Busam Motor Sales, 185 F.2d 531, 534 (6th Cir.1950).

10. Evers v. Equifax, Inc., 650 F.2d 793 (5th Cir.1981); Lind v. Schenley Indus., 278 F.2d 79 (3d Cir.1960). *But see* O'Rourke v. City of Providence, 235 F.3d 713 (1st Cir. 2001) (reinstating first verdict).

11. Hall v. Chicago & N.W. Ry. Co., 349 Ill.App. 175, 110 N.E.2d 654 (1953); Kessel v. Hunt, 215 Iowa 117, 244 N.W. 714 (1932); Dowell, Inc. v. Layton, 261 P.2d 885 (Okla.1953). *Cf.* Tumlinson v. San Antonio Brewing Assn., 170 S.W.2d 620, 623 (Tex. Civ.App.1943).

12. *See, e.g.,* Nissho–Iwai Co. v. Occidental Crude Sales, 848 F.2d 613 (5th Cir. 1988); Salas v. Wang, 846 F.2d 897 (3d Cir.1988); Simeon v. T. Smith & Son, Inc., 852 F.2d 1421 (5th Cir.1988).

13. *See, e.g.,* State v. Crawford, 96 Minn. 95, 100, 104 N.W. 822, 824 (1905).

§ 7.26

1. M.J. Construction Co. v. Deatherage, 231 S.W.2d 501 (Tex.Civ.App.1950). *Cf.* Gleaton v. Green, 156 F.2d 459 (4th Cir. 1946) (although intentional introduction of such evidence by plaintiff is prejudicial and grounds for mistrial, casual reference by witness was not).

2. *See, e.g.,* Palmer v. Miller, 60 F.Supp. 710 (W.D.Mo.1945).

3. Advanced Display Systems v. Kent State University, 212 F.3d 1272 (Fed.Cir.2000)(concealment during discovery); Threadgill v. Armstrong World Indus., 928 F.2d 1366 (3d Cir.1991).

4. *See, e.g.,* Minneapolis, St. P. & S. Ste. M. Ry. v. Moquin, 283 U.S. 520, 51 S.Ct. 501, 75 L.Ed. 1243 (1931); City of Cleveland

ous event may occur during the trial, although not produced by any one's conscious action, that is likely to be prejudicial.[5]

Corrective measures

Several remedies are available for such mishaps. The least radical and most economical is a curative instruction to the jury. Immediately on the happening of the prejudicial event, or in the final charge, or both, the trial judge may tell the jury to disregard the event.[6] If the judge believes no instruction will wipe out the prejudicial effect, a mistrial may be ordered, thus aborting the trial at that point.[7] The third remedy is to grant a new trial after a verdict is returned. This allows the judge to take into account the verdict itself, indicating whether the improper event was prejudicial.

Mistrial

Waiting and then considering a new trial has two additional advantages over the mistrial: (1) A mistrial will necessarily call for a new trial,[8] while the verdict may indicate that the jury disregarded the prejudicial event so that a new trial is unnecessary;[9] (2) a mistrial must be ruled on in the heat of trial with little time for deliberation and no opportunity to see how the rest of the trial will unfold; a new trial is determined after deliberation and on viewing the prejudicial event in better perspective. On the other hand, a new trial shares with a mistrial the disadvantage of imposing the time and expense of a second trial that will not necessarily be better than the first. Judges therefore tend to rely on curative instructions despite the obvious likelihood that they will have little effect on jurors.

v. Peter Kiewit Sons' Co., 624 F.2d 749 (6th Cir.1980).

5. Examples are Fitzpatrick v. St. L.-S.F. Ry., 327 S.W.2d 801 (Mo.1959) (presence of blind man in courtroom near plaintiff, suing for damage to eye); Hays v. Herman, 213 Or. 140, 322 P.2d 119 (1958) (emotional outburst of defendant in action for wrongful death). The judge's own remarks may be so intemperate as to constitute further error. *Cf.* Note, 62 A.L.R.2d 166. *See also* Note, Pre-deliberations Juror Misconduct, Evidential Incompetence, and Juror Responsibility, 98 Yale L.J. 187 (1988).

6. Price v. H. B. Green Transp. Line, 287 F.2d 363 (7th Cir.1961) (jury properly admonished concerning plaintiff's emotional demonstrations); Ragon v. Day, 228 Ark. 215, 306 S.W.2d 687 (1957) (jury instructed to disregard witness's reference to defendant's insurance). On the ineffectiveness of most corrective instructions, see Kassin & Studebaker, Instructions to Disregard and the Jury, in Intentional Forgetting: Interdisciplinary Approaches (1998).

7. 53 Am. Jur. Trial 967. *See* discussions in Schuttler v. Reinhardt, 17 N.J.Super. 480, 86 A.2d 438 (1952); Ismail v. City of New York, 18 Misc.2d 818, 181 N.Y.S.2d 848 (Sup.Ct.1959) (in which mistrials were not ordered).

8. Unless plaintiff withdraws, the parties settle the case, or the like, possibilities that will remain after the granting of a new trial if a verdict is taken and set aside.

9. Fuentes v. Tucker, 31 Cal.2d 1, 187 P.2d 752 (1947).

Bias

Courts, for example, generally decline to order a new trial on evidence of alleged juror bias unless it fairly clearly implicates the panel's impartiality. For instance, in *McDonough Power Equipment v. Greenwood*[10] plaintiff was injured in an accident involving a power mower manufactured by defendant. On *voir dire* the prospective jurors were asked whether they or any other members of their family had sustained a serious injury. After judgment, it was discovered that the jury foreman's son had been so injured and that the foreman's answer to the question was incorrect. The Supreme Court held that "to invalidate the result of a 3–week trial because of a juror's mistaken, though honest, response to a question, is to insist on something closer to perfection than our judicial system can be expected to give ... to obtain a new trial in such a situation, a party must first demonstrate that a juror failed to answer honestly a material question on *voir dire,* and then further show that a correct response would have provided a valid basis for a challenge for cause. The motives for concealing information may vary, but only those reasons that affect a juror's impartiality can truly be said to affect the fairness of a trial."[11]

The judge has wide discretion in granting new trials for procedural irregularity. The trial judge has a peculiar opportunity to sense the atmosphere of the trial and to observe the characteristics and reactions of the particular jury. Nevertheless, the trial court's discretion is not unlimited. An appellate court may decide that the prejudicial event was so inflammatory that nothing could free the trial from its taint[12]—or so trivial that it would be fanciful to suppose it influenced the jury.

§ 7.27 New Trial for Jury Misconduct[1]

In principle, a new trial should be granted if there has been serious misconduct in the jury's performance of its functions—if, for example, some jurors refuse to discuss their differences of view, or rely on personal knowledge of the events at issue, or are intoxicated during deliberations. The fatefulness of a verdict and the fragility of the jury's cohesion, however, invite the parties or disgruntled jurors to impugn a result with which they disagree. Hence, the law confronts a tension between controlling serious juror misconduct through the device of granting a new trial and protecting the jury's amateur performance from harassing scrutiny. Historically, the prevention of harassing scrutiny

10. 464 U.S. 548, 104 S.Ct. 845, 78 L.Ed.2d 663 (1984).

11. 464 U.S. at 555–556, 104 S.Ct. at 849–850, 78 L.Ed.2d at 671 (1984).

12. *See, e.g.,* Minneapolis, St. P. & S. Ste. M. Ry. v. Moquin, 283 U.S. 520, 51 S.Ct. 501, 75 L.Ed. 1243 (1931); M. J. Construction Co. v. Deatherage, 231 S.W.2d 501 (Tex.Civ.App.1950); Paul v. Drown, 108 Vt. 458, 189 A. 144 (1937).

§ 7.27

1. *See generally* 8 Wigmore, Evidence §§ 2345–2356 (McNaughton rev. 1981); 6A Moore, Federal Practice and Procedure ¶ 59.08(4). *See also* MacCoun, Experimental Research on Jury Decision–Making (1989); Note, Pre-deliberations Juror Misconduct, Evidential Incompetence, and Juror Responsibility, 98 Yale L.J. 187 (1988).

dominated the quest to remedy misconduct. The balance has shifted in favor of wider inquiry, but there are still restrictions, including two rules that have survived from older usage. The traditional rule forbids testimony of the jurors themselves as evidence to show impropriety. The other rule concerns the kinds of improper conduct that will avoid a verdict. The scope given to this rule goes to the very heart of the jury process. An important consideration in all new trial motions for jury misconduct is whether the movant or the movant's counsel has waived the misconduct. Timely objections must usually be made.[2]

Proof of jury misconduct

The evidentiary rule that juror testimony cannot be used goes back to a notion expressed by the Latin maxim *nemo turpitudinem suam allegans audietur* (no one will be heard to assert his own shameful conduct). It was applied by Lord Mansfield to exclude juror testimony in *Vaise v. Delaval*[3] and continues to be invoked.[4] The force of the rule results from the nature of jury deliberations, which are secret and not properly witnessed by any outsider. Hence, the rule seals off the only direct proof of jury misconduct during deliberations but leaves open circumstantial evidence (such as memoranda left by jurors in the jury room or indicia that the jury drew lots).[5] Testimony of an observer[6] sometimes has been accepted notwithstanding the impropriety of eavesdropping on the jury.[7]

Evidence must be found before its admissibility can be considered. Both federal and state trial judges normally have wide latitude in gathering information concerning alleged jury misconduct. But there must be at least a reasonable possibility that the impropriety resulted in prejudice to the plaintiffs.[8] Some states continue to forbid lawyers to question jurors after a trial, and many courts allow such questioning

2. Cooper v. Dyke, 814 F.2d 941 (4th Cir.1987); Dennis v. General Elec. Corp., 762 F.2d 365 (4th Cir.1985).

3. 1 Term Rep. 11, 99 Eng. Rep. 944 (K.B. 1785).

4. 8 Wigmore, Evidence § 2354 n.2 (McNaughton rev. 1961).

5. Central of Ga. Ry. v. Holmes, 223 Ala. 188, 134 So. 875 (1931). *Cf.* McDonnell v. Pescadero, 120 Cal. 476, 52 P. 725 (1898) (circumstantial evidence of quotient verdict considered but found wanting).

6. Reich v. Thompson, 346 Mo. 577, 142 S.W.2d 486 (1940) (eavesdropping clerk's evidence received). *See* Annot., 129 A.L.R. 803.

7. Central of Ga. Ry. v. Holmes, 223 Ala. 188, 134 So. 875 (1931) (eavesdropping counsel's evidence rejected); Bourre v. Texas Co., 51 R.I. 254, 154 A. 82 (1931). Wigmore vehemently opposes the admissibility of such evidence. "Thus, not only does the rule tempt the parties to seduce the bailiffs to tricky expedients and surreptitious eavesdropping, but the law, while with one hand it sanctimoniously puts away the juryman who reports his own misconduct done during the privacy of retirement, yet with the other hand it inconsistently invites to the same witness stand the bailiff whose shameless disregard of his duty in intruding upon that privacy forms his only qualification as a witness and the sole tenor of his testimony. If there cannot be any principle in this rule, it should at least possess logic." 8 Wigmore, Evidence § 2353 (McNaughton rev. 1961).

8. Bolton v. Tesoro Petroleum Corp., 871 F.2d 1266 (5th Cir.1989).

only when the court gives permission.[9] Today, of course, it is often the press that seeks out jurors and broadcasts their accounts of jury deliberations.[10]

Even if there is reason to believe that jury misconduct occurred, courts generally have adhered to the *Delaval* rule, thus rendering jury verdicts invulnerable to attack on the basis of impropriety during the deliberations.[11] This rule of proof survives perhaps because of the prestige of Lord Mansfield,[12] but more likely for pragmatic reasons. In relatively few cases does each juror fully understand and meticulously perform a juror's legal function, observing all its limitations and fulfilling all its affirmative obligations.[13] If the jury room were open to official scrutiny, embarrassing questions would be raised not only about the jury decisional process but also about the counterpart process, when judges decide cases without juries.[14] The jury system can survive, however, despite frank recognition of its shortcomings. If few verdicts actually reflect rigorously correct performance by every juror, then the system should not be preserved by concealing that fact. The point is that the system expresses the values of popular participation in the judicial process, a nontechnical view of the legal dispute shared by a group of laypersons, and giving effect to the community's sense of what the law ought to be and sometimes is not.[15]

Juror testimony

Although a number of jurisdictions now admit juror testimony to prove jury misconduct,[16] three evils could result from doing so. First,

9. Wolfram, Modern Legal Ethics 606–08 (1986); Note, Limitation on Attorney Postverdict Contact with Jurors: Protecting the Criminal Jury and Its Verdict at the Expense of the Defendant, 94 Colum. L. Rev. 1950 (1994); Annot., 19 A.L.R.4th 1209.

10. Marder, Deliberation and Disclosure: A Study of Post–Verdict Interviews of Jurors, 82 Iowa L. Rev. 465 (1997).

11. Fed. R. Ev. 606(b); Comment, Impeachment of Jury Verdicts, 25 U. Chi. L. Rev. 360 (1958).

12. *See* 8 Wigmore, Evidence § 2352 (McNaughton rev. 1961).

13. *See* Green, Judge and Jury ch. 13 (1930); Morgan, Some Problems of Proof 114 (1956) (discussing the traditional distrust of juries).

14. See Perkins v. LeCureux, 58 F.3d 214 (6th Cir.1995)(judge may not impeach his own decision). For an extreme view of this problem, see Frank, Courts on Trial, 115 (1950): "I surmise that the underlying reason for that judicial attitude is this: The judges feel that, were they obliged to learn the methods used by jurors, the actual workings of the jury-system would be shown up, devastatingly. From my point of view, such a consequence would be desirable: The public would soon discover this skeleton in the judicial closet."

Cf. Wigmore, A Program for the Trial of Jury Trial, 12 J. Am. Jud. Socy. 166, 170 (1929): "We want justice, and we think we are going to get it through 'the law,' and when we do not, we blame 'the law.' Now this is where the jury comes in. The jury, in the privacy of its retirement, adjusts the general rule of law to the justice of the particular case. Thus the odium of inflexible rules of law is avoided, and popular satisfaction is preserved."

15. See James, Tort Law in Midstream: Its Challenge to the Judicial Process, 8 Buffalo L. Rev. 315, 342–344 (1959), for collection of authorities favoring such a view. *See also* § 7.23 *supra.*

16. *See* Note, Admissibility of Evidence to Impeach Jury Verdicts, 22 U. Miami L. Rev. 729 (1968); Note, Impeachment of

"[j]urors would be harassed and beset by the defeated party in an effort to secure from them evidence of facts which might establish misconduct sufficient to set aside a verdict." Second, "what was intended to be a private deliberation [would become] the constant subject of public investigation—to the destruction of all frankness and freedom of discussion and conference."[17] Third, new trials granted because of jury misconduct, like other new trials, increase expense and delay without necessarily producing a better product. These considerations have led to an intermediate position.[18]

Jury mental processes

There is general agreement that the mental processes of jurors will not be investigated, nor the effect of those processes on the decision.[19] This precludes inquiring about a juror's failure to understand or to follow the instructions to the jury.[20]

The proposition that a verdict may be set aside for passion, partiality, or prejudice has to be understood in light of this limitation on proving that such emotionalism actually occurred, a limitation that renders the proposition toothless. Even when confronted with evidence of racial or religious prejudice, courts have been reluctant to set aside verdicts.[21] In practice, a verdict may be set aside when the judge infers that the verdict must have been based on a nonrational premise invented by the jury rather than on the law. Characterizing the verdict as the product of passion and prejudice is simply a predicate justification for granting a new trial so that another jury can try the case.

Jury Verdicts by Jurors: A Proposal, 1969 U. Ill. L.F. 388; Note, 10 Ohio St. L.J. 262 (1949); Annots., 40 A.L.R.2d 1119, 18 A.L.R.3d 1132, 32 A.L.R.3d 1356.

17. Lamar, J., in McDonald v. Pless, 238 U.S. 264, 267–268, 35 S.Ct. 783, 784, 59 L.Ed. 1300, 1302 (1915). *See* Brillhart v. Mullins, 128 Mich.App. 140, 339 N.W.2d 722 (1983). *See also* United States Football League v. National Football League, 644 F.Supp. 1040 (S.D.N.Y.1986) (juror testimony of confusion and compromise excluded); Cyr v. Michaud, 454 A.2d 1376 (Me.1983).

18. 8 Wigmore, Evidence § 2354 (McNaughton rev. 1961); 6 Moore, Federal Practice and Procedure ¶ 59.08(4). *Cf.* Morgan, Basic Problems of Evidence 84–85 (1961).

19. Fed. R. Evid. 606(b); Rushen v. Spain, 464 U.S. 114, 104 S.Ct. 453, 78 L.Ed.2d 267 (1983); State v. Kociolek, 20 N.J. 92, 118 A.2d 812 (1955) (noted in 54 Mich. L. Rev. 1003 (1956)); After Hour Welding v. Laneil Management, 108 Wis.2d 734, 324 N.W.2d 686 (1982); 8 Wigmore, Evidence § 2349 (McNaughton rev. 1961). This is true even in Texas, which probably has the most liberal rule in allowing the impeachment of verdicts. Putman v. Lazarus, 156 Tex. 154, 293 S.W.2d 493 (1956). *Cf.* Hasson v. Ford Motor Co., 32 Cal.3d 388, 185 Cal.Rptr. 654, 650 P.2d 1171 (1982)(evidence that jurors read and did crossword puzzles during trial admissible but did not require new trial).

20. Robles v. Exxon Corp., 862 F.2d 1201 (5th Cir.1989); Multi–Service Contractors v. Town of Vernon, 193 Conn. 446, 477 A.2d 653 (1984); Collings v. Northwestern Hosp., 202 Minn. 139, 277 N.W. 910 (1938); Olson v. Williams, 270 Wis. 57, 70 N.W.2d 10 (1955).

21. See Shillcutt v. Gagnon, 827 F.2d 1155 (7th Cir.1987); United States v. Abcasis, 811 F.Supp. 828 (S.D.N.Y.1992). But see United States v. Heller, 785 F.2d 1524 (11th Cir.1986).

Improper outside influence

Proof of an outside influence likely to lead to irrational or biased deliberations is more straightforward. Bribery, private communication with a party, improper remarks made in the jury's presence by a court officer or other outsider, consulting documents not in evidence, and the like, are sufficient grounds for setting aside a verdict.[22] Most jurisdictions will receive juror testimony to show this kind of misconduct. Evidence is also permitted to show that a juror gave false or misleading answers to questions put in voir dire examination, such as acquaintance with either the parties or the facts involved.[23] The Federal Rules of Evidence permit juror testimony to show "whether extraneous prejudicial information was improperly brought to the jury's attention or whether any outside influence was improperly brought to bear upon any juror."[24] According to the Supreme Court, however, jurors who consumer alcohol, marijuana and cocaine are not subject to "outside influence" permitting a challenge to their verdict.[25]

Not every instance of improper outside influence that may be proved warrants granting a new trial.[26] The trial judge has wide discretion to determine whether any particular impropriety was prejudicial, but the judge's decision is subject to review for abuse of discretion.[27]

Erroneous decisional procedure

A third class of improprieties consists of acts that are part of the jury decision-making procedure, such as reaching a verdict by flipping a coin, agreeing to abide by the vote of a majority when a unanimous verdict is required, and determining damages by averaging the sums put down by each juror (the quotient verdict).[28] Some jurisdictions adhere to Lord Mansfield's rule against receiving juror testimony to prove such improprieties.[29] Other jurisdictions allow a verdict to be impeached on grounds of impropriety and receive the juror testimony to do so.

Some courts disallow such proof when it concerns various forms of a compromise verdict. This view may be the soundest, since it recognizes that the opportunity for unexplained compromise may be a justification

22. *See* Jorgensen v. York Ice Mach. Corp., 160 F.2d 432, 435 (2d Cir.1947); 8 Wigmore, Evidence §§ 2348(c), 2354 (McNaughton rev. 1961).

23. *See* Annots., 30 A.L.R.2d 914, 48 A.L.R.2d 971; *cf.* Annot., 64 A.L.R.3d 126. *See also* § 7.26 *supra.*

24. Fed. R. Evid. 606(b).

25. Tanner v. United States, 483 U.S. 107, 107 S.Ct. 2739, 97 L.Ed.2d 90 (1987). *Contra,* Krouse v. Graham, 19 Cal.3d 59, 137 Cal.Rptr. 863, 562 P.2d 1022 (1977); Alschuler, The Supreme Court and the Jury: Voir Dire, Peremptory Challenges, and the Review of Jury Verdicts, 56 U. Chi. L. Rev. 153 (1989).

26. *See, e.g.,* Kritzer v. Citron, 101 Cal. App.2d 33, 224 P.2d 808 (1950); Christ v. Wempe, 219 Md. 627, 150 A.2d 918 (1959).

27. *See, e.g.,* Kilgore v. Greyhound Corp., S. Greyhound Lines, 30 F.R.D. 385 (E.D.Tenn.1962); Bashford v. Slater, 250 Iowa 857, 96 N.W.2d 904 (1959). *Cf.* § 7.26 *supra.*

28. *See* Comment, Impeachment of Jury Verdicts, 25 U. Chi. L. Rev. 360 (1958). *See also* Annot., 32 A.L.R.3d 1356.

29. 8 Wigmore, Evidence § 2354 (McNaughton rev. 1961).

for the jury system. There is a fine line between the give-and-take necessary to reach a fully agreed to composite judgment and an impermissible compromise.[30] Of course, there is nothing good to be said for reaching a verdict by lot.[31]

Private information

Jurors may in their discussion refer to matters of common knowledge among them that they are not supposed to consider, such as the fact that automobile owners usually have liability insurance.[32] They may discuss inferences that they are forbidden to draw, such as the implication of a party's failure to testify when that party has invoked the privilege against self-incrimination.[33] The *Delaval* rule would usually prevent the showing of such misconduct,[34] but some jurisdictions that do allow jurors to testify about such instances may set aside a verdict on such a ground.[35] And it is generally accepted that, whatever the jurors' deliberative procedures, a verdict cannot stand unless the jurors in fact agreed to it. Thus, if a juror expresses dissent from the verdict on being polled by the court when the verdict is rendered, the jury must be returned to reconsider its verdict or a new trial must be ordered.[36]

Circumstantial evidence of impropriety

Absent direct or circumstantial proof of jury misconduct, the court has nothing to go on except its observation of the trial and its assessment of the verdict. If the court considers that the evidence was weak and serious misadventure occurred at trial, then a jury verdict is suspect if it seems aberrant and is likely to entail substantial prejudicial consequences. A common instance is improper inflammatory argument by counsel.[37] An internally inconsistent verdict is also suggestive, such as the verdict being against one spouse but in favor of the other when the

30. Jacobson v. Henderson, 765 F.2d 12 (2d Cir.1985)(jurors screamed, called names, threw chairs); Scogin v. Century Fitness, Inc., 780 F.2d 1316 (8th Cir.1985) (quotient verdict); *see* 6A Moore, Federal Practice and Procedure ¶ 59.08(4).

31. And indeed many states have enacted a statutory exception to the *Delaval* rule in the case of chance verdicts. *See, e.g.,* Turner v. Tuolumne County Water Co., 25 Cal. 397 (1864). Statutes are collected in Comment, Impeachment of Jury Verdicts, 25 U. Chi. L. Rev. 360, 371 n.7b (1958). *But cf.* 8 Wigmore, Evidence 681 (McNaughton rev. 1961).

32. *See, e.g.,* Thomason v. Trentham, 178 Tenn. 37, 154 S.W.2d 792 (1941).

33. *See, e.g.,* Hanes v. State, 170 Tex. Crim. 394, 341 S.W.2d 428 (1960); 39 Am. Jur. New Trial 82.

34. *See, e.g.,* Barrington v. Duncan, 140 Tex. 510, 169 S.W.2d 462 (1943) (insurance); Texas & Pac. Ry. Co. v. Mix, 193 S.W.2d 542 (Tex.Civ.App.1946) (attorney's fees); Harrell v. State, 118 Tex.Crim. 279, 42 S.W.2d 438 (1931) (failure of the accused to testify); Jones v. Sieve, 203 Cal.App.3d 359, 249 Cal.Rptr. 821 (1988) (juror's personal experience).

35. United States v. Tran, 122 F.3d 670 (8th Cir.1997); Andrews v. O'Hearn, 387 N.W.2d 716 (N.D.1986).

36. Bruce v. Chestnut Farms–Chevy Chase Dairy, 126 F.2d 224 (D.C.Cir.1942).

37. *See, e.g.,* Klotz v. Sears, Roebuck & Co., 267 F.2d 53 (7th Cir.1959).

latter claim is derivative for the same injuries.[38] Internal inconsistency may suggest a compromise verdict, as when a personal injury plaintiff receives a verdict so small as to suggest that the jury compromised on the issue of liability.[39] In such situations juror testimony will not be received to impeach the verdict, that is, to undercut its validity.[40] The court will simply draw its own inferences and may set aside the verdict if it finds sufficient impropriety.

Motion to reopen

The motion to reopen a case for additional evidence differs from the motion for a new trial. It does not request a retrial of the entire proceeding but only the right to offer the additional testimony in evidence before the verdict is reached. It is made before the jury has returned or, if the case is tried by a judge, while the case is still under advisement.

The motion is in the court's discretion,[41] and its grant or denial, whether the case is being tried to a judge or jury, will be overturned only on abuse of discretion.[42] The nature of the additional evidence and the timing of the motion are relevant factors for the court to consider. When the additional testimony is presently available and reopening would cause little delay, the trial court may allow the motion even after both sides have rested[43] or after the case has been submitted to the jury.[44] Because of possible prejudice or surprise, the court will more readily grant the motion when the case is tried to a judge rather than to a jury.

§ 7.28 New Trial for Verdict Against Weight of Evidence

As noted earlier, the errors in a jury trial can be procedural or substantive. A procedural error can be corrected by rectifying the error within the trial through a cautionary instruction or by an entirely new

38. As in Lansburgh & Bros. v. Clark, 127 F.2d 331 (D.C.Cir.1942). *See* Annot., 66 A.L.R.3d 472.

39. *See* § 7.29 *infra.*

40. *Compare, e.g.,* Western Cottonoil Co. v. Arnold, 279 S.W.2d 374 (Tex.Civ.App. 1955) (rejecting such testimony), *with* Smith v. State, 205 Tenn. 502, 327 S.W.2d 308 (1959) (accepting it). Of decisions such as the latter, Wigmore said: "There is of course no justification for this, the principle of the present rule accepts the jury's utterance as the final and exclusive expression of their views and declines to investigate for any purpose their prior and preliminary states of mind." 8 Wigmore, Evidence § 2349, at 690–691 (McNaughton rev. 1961). Compare the able treatment by Justice Brennan (later of the Supreme Court) on the distinction between testimony concerning external events and that concerning the effect of these events on the juror's mind in State v. Kociolek, 20 N.J. 92, 98–105, 118 A.2d 812 (1955). *See also* Martin v. Blackmon, 277 Ark. 190, 640 S.W.2d 435 (1982).

41. Zenith Radio Corp. v. Hazeltine Research, 401 U.S. 321, 91 S.Ct. 795, 28 L.Ed.2d 77 (1971); Contempo Metal Furniture Co. v. East Texas Motor Freight Lines, 661 F.2d 761 (9th Cir.1981).

42. Contempo Metal Furniture Co. v. East Texas Motor Freight Lines, 661 F.2d 761 (9th Cir.1981).

43. Skehan v. Board of Trustees of Bloomsburg State College, 590 F.2d 470 (3d Cir.1978).

44. Jianole v. United States, 299 Fed. 496 (8th Cir.1924).

trial for more serious errors. It would be incoherent to redress procedural error by granting judgment in favor of the victim, because the case would not be properly tried on its merits.

Substantive error

A substantive error by the jury, however, is a verdict that in the court's assessment is unsupported by the evidence. Such a situation can be remedied in three ways, depending in part on the nature and degree of the substantive aberration. One remedy is to grant a new trial so that a second jury may examine the evidence. A second jury's verdict will be as valid and, it is hoped, more compatible with the judge's minimum standards of jury rationality. When the verdict is for damages, a second remedy is to increase or decrease the amount, under penalty of granting a new trial. A third remedy is to enter judgment notwithstanding the verdict, thereby granting the verdict loser a favorable determination on the merits. This is appropriate only when such a judgment is clearly warranted on the law and the evidence. In granting j.n.o.v., the court is governed by the same concept of sufficiency and scope of judicial authority as in a motion for a directed verdict, both remedies being forms of judgment as a matter of law.[1]

At common law, when the verdict was based on insufficient evidence the only course of action was to grant a new trial. There the court could direct a verdict if the evidence then presented was the same as in the original trial.[2] In most jurisdictions today this ritual can be foregone and the trial judge can simply order j.n.o.v.[3] It is properly ordered only if the verdict-loser should have been granted a directed verdict. In many jurisdictions, if the judge thinks the verdict was wrong but not so wrong as to require directed verdict, the judge may order a new trial. "How wrong" the verdict is becomes the subject of different tests for granting a new trial.

New trial standards

There are three basic standards for granting a new trial: broad discretion, little discretion, and moderate discretion. In some states the trial court has broad discretion to order a new trial "where there is any evidence which would support a judgment in favor of the moving party."[4] In essence, the trial court acts as a "thirteenth juror."[5] In other states

§ 7.28

1. *See* Fed. R. Civ. P. 50; §§ 7.21 *supra* & 7.30 *infra*.

2. *See* Sunderland, The New Federal Rules, 45 W. Va. L. Rev. 5, 28–29 (1938). *Cf.* discussion in Metropolitan R.R. v. Moore, 121 U.S. 558, 7 S.Ct. 1334, 30 L.Ed. 1022 (1887).

3. *See* § 7.30 *infra*.

4. Hawk v. City of Newport Beach, 46 Cal.2d 213, 219, 293 P.2d 48, 51 (1956). To the same effect are Denney v. Tate, 96 Ga.App. 3, 99 S.E.2d 296 (1957); Oklahoma City v. Drinkwater, 271 P.2d 1108 (Okla. 1954); Cavallaro v. Sharp, 84 R.I. 67, 121 A.2d 669 (1956); McLaughlin v. Broyles, 36 Tenn.App. 391, 255 S.W.2d 1020 (1952).

5. "The rule in this state is—that the trial court shall exercise the function of a thirteenth juror upon hearing of a motion

the test for a new trial is administered so that it approximates the test for directed verdict, though the two are not exactly equated. Most jurisdictions, including the federal courts, take an intermediate position. This is summarized well in a statement by Judge Parker in *Aetna Casualty & Surety Company v. Yeatts*:

> On such a motion it is the duty of the trial judge to set aside the verdict and grant a new trial, if he is of the opinion that the verdict is against the clear weight of the evidence, or is based upon evidence which is false, or will result in a miscarriage of justice, even though there may be substantial evidence which would prevent the direction of a verdict.[6]

"Federal test"

This standard, which may be called "the federal test," does not contemplate the substitution of the judge's judgment for that of the jury. Rather, it admonishes the court to accept jury findings in matters of credibility of testimony and weight of evidence, even if the judge disagrees with them, "unless the verdict is clearly against the general current of the evidence, so that the court can clearly see that they have acted under some mistake, or from some improper motive, bias or feeling."[7] The federal decisions commit the enforcement of these adjurations largely to the self-restraint of the trial judges, and reversals on appeal are rare.[8] Many state courts take the same approach.

Comparison to j.n.o.v.

Although these tests represent differences in degree and may shade imperceptibly into one another, they differ substantially in the extent of control exercised by courts over juries.[9] The standard for granting a motion for j.n.o.v. is more stringent than that required by the standard for a new trial.[10] That is because j.n.o.v. takes the case away from the

for a new trial; that it is his duty to weigh the evidence and independently determine therefrom whether or not it is sufficient to sustain the verdict." McLaughlin v. Broyles, 36 Tenn.App. 391, 397, 255 S.W.2d 1020, 1023 (1952).

6. 122 F.2d 350, 352–353 (4th Cir.1941). This represents the prevailing rule in federal courts. 6A Moore, Federal Practice and Procedure ¶ 59.08(5). It is widely followed in state courts.

7. Fuller v. Fletcher, 6 Fed. 128, 129–130 (D.R.I.1881) (quoting an earlier statement by Justice Story).

8. The granting or denial of a new trial is not an appealable order in the federal system. Montgomery Ward & Co. v. Duncan, 311 U.S. 243, 253, 61 S.Ct. 189, 195, 85 L.Ed. 147, 154 (1940); Dailey v. Timmer, 292 F.2d 824 (3d Cir.1961). Moreover, the granting or denial of such an order on the present ground (if brought before the appellate court by appeal from final judgment) is reviewable only in exceptional cases. 6A Moore, Federal Practice and Procedure ¶¶ 59.08(5), 59.15(3). For instances of reversal, see Occhino v. United States, 686 F.2d 1302 (8th Cir.1982); Spurlin v. General Motors Corp., 528 F.2d 612 (5th Cir. 1976); Lind v. Schenley Indus., 278 F.2d 79 (3d Cir.1960) (two judges dissenting); Kraft v. Kraft, 366 N.W.2d 450 (N.D.1985).

9. Winter v. Brenner Tank, Inc., 926 F.2d 468 (5th Cir.1991); Keeler v. Richards Mfg. Co., 817 F.2d 1197 (5th Cir.1987).

10. *See* Trautman, Motions Testing the Sufficiency of the Evidence, 42 Wash. L. Rev. 787 (1967); Comment, Appellate Review in the Federal Courts of Orders Granting New Trial, 13 Stan. L. Rev. 383 (1961).

jury and ends the case, while a new trial only submits the case to a second jury.[11]

§ 7.29 New Trial for Excessive or Inadequate Verdict

Granting a new trial because of an excessive verdict was a practice well established at common law before the Constitution was adopted.[1] When damages are liquidated or can be easily ascertained, a verdict awarding more than the product yielded by legal rules would be wrong as a matter of law and clearly should be set aside.[2]

Historical situation

Greater difficulty was encountered when the measure of damages was less determinate and required discretion on the part of the jury. In personal injury cases, for example, the fixing of damages has been a principal part of the jury's function.[3] Courts were therefore much more reluctant to interfere with these verdicts.[4] A 1792 review of these cases concluded that a new trial should not be awarded "unless the Damages

11. But see Atlas Food Systems & Services, Inc. v. Crane Nat'l Vendors, Inc., 99 F.3d 587 (4th Cir.1996)(judge did not abuse discretion by granting third trial when jury again awarded excessive punitive damages).

§ 7.29

1. Wood v. Gunston, Sty. 462, 466, 82 Eng. Rep. 863, 864, 867 (K.B. 1655); Clerk v. Udall, 2 Salk. 649, 91 Eng. Rep. 552 (K.B. 1702); Chambers v. Robinson, 2 Str. 691, 93 Eng. Rep. 787 (K.B. 1726). In Bright v. Eynon, 1 Burr. 390, 97 Eng. Rep. 365 (K.B. 1757), Mansfield, J., indicated that at least since 1655 new trials had been granted on the basis of excessive verdicts. "The reason why this matter cannot be traced further back is that the old report books do not give any accounts of determinations made by the courts upon motions." 1 Burr. at 394, 97 Eng. Rep. at 367.

Although the course of decision was clear, it was not uniform. *See, e.g.,* Roe v. Hawkes, 1 Lev. 97, 83 Eng. Rep. 316 (K.B. 1664); Townsend v. Hughes, 2 Mod. 150, 86 Eng. Rep. 994 (C.P. 1677) (Atkins, J., dissenting, citing Wood v. Gunston, *supra*); *compare* cases cited in note 4 *infra*.

Under the eighteenth century English practice such motions were determined, not by the trial judge at *nisi prius,* but by the court sitting en banc at Westminster. Nothing of constitutional significance, however, should turn on this difference from the modern practice, except that perhaps it may justify appellate review of the trial judge's decision. *See* Dagnello v. Long Island R.R., 289 F.2d 797 (2d Cir.1961); Hinton, Power of Federal Court to Review Ruling on Motion for New Trial, 1 U. Chi. L. Rev. 111 (1933).

2. These principles were fully discussed in Duberley v. Gunning, 4 Term Rep. 651, 100 Eng. Rep. 1226 (K.B. 1792), in which a majority of the court felt powerless to interfere, on the ground of excessiveness, with a jury's verdict for £5000 in an action for criminal conversation. *See generally* 3 Graham and Waterman, New Trials 1127–1130 (1855); Graham, An Essay on New Trials 409–410 (1834).

3. *See* Duberley v. Gunning, 4 Term Rep. 651, 100 Eng. Rep. 1226 (K.B. 1792); Mayne, Damages 452 (2d ed. 1872). On the right to a jury determination of damages, see Feltner v. Columbia Pictures Television, Inc., 523 U.S. 340, 118 S.Ct. 1279, 140 L.Ed.2d 438 (1998).

4. *E.g.,* Leith v. Pope, 2 W. Black 1327, 96 Eng. Rep. 777 (C.P. 1780) (malicious prosecution); Fabrigas v. Mostyn, 2 W. Black 929, 96 Eng. Rep. 549 (C.P. 1774) (trespass and false imprisonment); Huckle v. Money, 2 Wils. 205, 207, 95 Eng. Rep. 768, 769 (K.B. 1763) (trespass, assault and imprisonment. "[I]t must be a glaring case indeed of outrageous damages in a tort, and which all mankind at first blush must think so, to induce a court to grant a new trial for excessive damages"); Wilford v. Berkeley, 1 Burr. 690, 97 Eng. Rep. 472 (K.B. 1758). *See generally* 1 Graham and Waterman, New Trials 409–410 (1855).

are such as do appear at the first blush to be quite outrageous."[5] New trials were granted in several tort actions because the verdict was excessive;[6] many more new trials were granted when the court believed the award afforded "internal Evidence of the Prejudice and Partiality of the Jury,"[7] or was "outrageously disproportionate, either to the Wrong received, or to the Situation and Circumstances,"[8] or was "monstrous and enormous indeed."[9] In 1813 it was said that in all types of actions, "if the damages are clearly too large, the Courts will send the inquiry to another jury."[10]

Unlike excessive verdicts, inadequate verdicts did not form a basis for granting a new trial.[11] Sayer found in 1792 that "no case is to be met with, in which a new Trial has in Fact been granted on Account of the Smallness of the Damages."[12] In many American states, however, inadequacy of the verdict became a recognized ground for granting a new trial in actions for tort and breach of contract.[13] Other states denied, sometimes by statute, the propriety of a new trial for inadequacy of the verdict.[14]

5. Sayer, Damages 221 (1792).

6. *See, e.g.,* Wood v. Gunston, Sty. 462, 466, 82 Eng. Rep. 863, 864, 867 (K.B. 1655); Clerk v. Udall, 2 Salk. 649, 91 Eng. Rep. 552 (K.B. 1702); Chambers v. Robinson, 2 Str. 691, 93 Eng. Rep. 787 (K.B. 1726); Jones v. Sparrow, 5 Term Rep. 257, 101 Eng. Rep. 144 (K.B. 1793) (distinguishing Duberley v. Gunning, *supra* note 2, as "a case *sui generis*").

7. Leith v. Pope, 2 W. Black 1327, 1328, 96 Eng. Rep. 777, 778 (C.P. 1780).

8. *Id.*

9. Beardmore v. Carrington, 2 Wils. 244, 250, 95 Eng. Rep. 790, 793 (K.B. 1764). See also Sayer, Damages 210–221 (1792); Mayne, Damages 457–462 (2d ed. 1872); Graham, An Essay on New Trials ch. 12 (1834).

10. Hewlett v. Cruchley, 5 Taunt. 277, 281, 128 Eng. Rep. 696, 698 (C.P. 1813).

11. *See, e.g.,* Barker v. Dixie, 2 Str. 1051, 93 Eng. Rep. 1027 (K.B. 1736); Hayward v. Newton, 2 Str. 940, 93 Eng. Rep. 955 (K.B. 1733). *Compare* Woodford v. Eades, 1 Str. 425, 93 Eng. Rep. 612 (K.B. 1720).

12. Sayer, Damages 201 (1792). *See generally* Grant, Summary of the Law Relating to New Trials 209–211 (1817); Mayne, Damages 455 (2d ed. 1872) ("The alleged reason [that new trials were not granted on the basis of inadequate damages] is, that new trials came only in the room of attaints, as being an easier and more expeditious remedy, and no attaint would lie for giving too small damages"). *Compare* Russel v. Ball, Barnes 455, 94 Eng. Rep. 1001 (K.B. 1745).

13. *See generally* Rawle v. McIlhenny, 163 Va. 735, 177 S.E. 214, 98 A.L.R. 930 (1934); Wilson, The Motion for New Trial Based on Inadequacy of Damages Awarded, 39 Neb. L. Rev. 694 (1960). *See also* Leavitt v. Dow, 105 Me. 50, 53, 72 A. 735, 736 (1908).

14. *See, e.g.,* Colyer v. Huff, 6 Ky. (3 Bibb) 34 (1813); Pritchard v. Hewitt, 91 Mo. 547, 4 S.W. 437 (1887); Edwards v. Missouri Ry. Co., 82 Mo.App. 478, 484 (1900); Shoff v. Wells, 1 Neb. 168 (1871). Statutes forbidding new trials because of low damage awards were once not uncommon but have now largely disappeared. Wilson, The Motion for New Trial Based on Inadequacy of Damages Awarded, 39 Neb. L. Rev. 694, 696, 697 (1960); and *cf.* Smith v. Bailey, 311 Ky. 118, 223 S.W.2d 582 (1949); Dolen v. Beatrice Restaurant Co., 137 Neb. 247, 289 N.W. 336 (1939); Carpenter v. City of Red Cloud, 64 Neb. 126, 89 N.W. 637 (1902). Wilson concludes that the attitude reflected in the earlier cases and statutes "probably was the early American notion that the jury not only possessed the power but the right to decide cases contrary to the trial court's instructions and the feeling that compromise verdicts . . . were not such terrible things after all." Wilson, *supra,* at 696, 697.

Most of the cases cited at the beginning of this note dealt with verdicts for plaintiff

Contemporary approach

With the tremendous growth of personal injury litigation during the twentieth century, the superintending power of the courts over the size of verdicts has increased correspondingly. Some studies show that almost half of certain kinds of verdict are substantially reduced, either by the court or by settlement between the parties.[15] Exercise of judicial authority to modify damages poses several questions.

1. *What formula should be used in exercising this power?* When the rules for measure of damages supply no mathematical formula, the jury necessarily has broad discretion.[16] The court can only delineate the parameters and, in doing so, must itself exercise the same discretionary judgment that the jury has exercised.[17] The standards necessarily are broadly formulated, unlike those used in the eighteenth century.[18]

Appellate review

2. *To what extent is the trial court's ruling reviewable?* In the federal courts, some doubt formerly existed over whether the trial judge's order granting or denying a new trial on account of excessive or inadequate damages is reviewable at all, even when the damages are

in *nominal* amounts (one cent or one dollar). Such cases may be distinguishable from those in which the verdict is substantial but inadequate. *See* note 29 *infra*.

15. *See* Vidmar, *et al.*, Jury Awards for Medical Malpractice and Post–Verdict Adjustments of Those Awards, 48 De Paul L. Rev. 265 (1998); Baldus, et al., Improving Judicial Oversight of Jury Damage Assessments, 80 Iowa L. Rev. 1109 (1995); Schnapper, Judges Against Juries–Appellate Review of Federal Civil Jury Verdicts, 1989 Wis. L. Rev. 237.

16. *See, e.g.,* White v. Chicago, M. & P.S. Ry., 49 Mont. 419, 143 P. 561 (1914); Remmenga v. Selk, 152 Neb. 625, 42 N.W.2d 186 (1950); Simons v. Kidd, 73 S.D. 306, 42 N.W.2d 307 (1950); E.I. Dupont De Nemours v. Taylor, 124 Va. 750, 98 S.E. 866 (1919). *See* note 3 *supra*.

17. *See, e.g.,* Little Beaver Enters. v. Humphreys Rs., 719 F.2d 75 (4th Cir.1983); Humble v. Union Pac. Ry., 90 Cal.App.2d 276, 277, 202 P.2d 791, 792 (1949) ("The trial judge sits as a thirteenth juror"); In re Hollis' Estate, 235 Iowa 753, 16 N.W.2d 599 (1944); Bartley v. Phillips, 317 Mass. 35, 57 N.E.2d 26 (1944).

18. *Compare* Gorman v. County of Sacramento, 92 Cal.App. 656, 667, 268 P. 1083, 1088 (1928) (refusal of appellate court to disturb decision of jury and trial judge "unless the verdict is so plainly and outrageously excessive as to suggest at first blush passion, prejudice, or corruption on the part of the jury"); Dedman v. McKinley, 238 Iowa 886, 892, 29 N.W.2d 337, 340 (1947) (appellate court will not set aside a verdict as excessive and grant a new trial unless the verdict "is so excessive as to shock the conscience"). *See also* Joan W. v. City of Chicago, 771 F.2d 1020 (7th Cir.1985) (verdict must be "monstrously excessive" or no rational connection between evidence on damages and verdict in order for verdict to be set aside).

A distinction should be noted between the standards applied by a trial court and those applied by an appellate court in considering a challenge to a verdict because of excessiveness or inadequacy. *See, e.g.,* Bartley v. Phillips, 317 Mass. 35, 57 N.E.2d 26 (1944). *Compare* also the comments of Hand, J., in Miller v. Maryland Casualty Co., 40 F.2d 463, 465 (2d Cir.1930) ("We must in effect decide whether it was within the bounds of tolerable conclusion to say that the jury's verdict was within the bounds of tolerable conclusion. To decide cases by such tenuous unrealities seems to us thoroughly undesirable; parties ought not to be bound by gossamer strands; judges ought not to engage in scholastic refinements").

ascertainable with some degree of precision.[19] *Fairmount Glass Works v. Cub Fork Coal Co.*[20] illustrates the uncertainties involved in the award of small or nominal verdicts. The evidence showed that if plaintiff was entitled to any recovery for breach of contract, it was for no less than $18,000. The jury brought in a verdict for plaintiff of one dollar. The trial court denied plaintiff's motion for a new trial because of inadequacy of the verdict. In upholding this action, the Supreme Court reasoned that the jury may have found issues for the defendant that would have been permissible under the evidence but returned a verdict designed to free plaintiff from the payment of costs, an error about which *plaintiff* could not complain.

The Supreme Court has now followed the federal appellate courts in upholding review of the lower court's ruling on the new trial motion based on excessiveness or inadequacy of the verdict. This review is based on the theory that the trial judge has abused his or her discretion.[21] Although the appellate courts may rule on the trial court's disposition of the new trial motion, however, they should not themselves determine the proper amount of the verdict. Instead, a new trial should be ordered, and this order may be conditioned on a remittitur when the damages are excessive.[22] Some courts require some evidence that the verdict was a result of bias, passion, or prejudice before they will reverse it.[23] Other courts will uphold the verdict unless it "shocks the court's conscience" or is "grossly excessive" or inadequate.[24]

Most state appellate courts exercise considerably greater supervision over the size of verdicts than do the federal courts. Although judicial review of any kind has been resisted on the ground that it is an invasion of the jury's province,[25] and it is said that the trial court has wide discretion in the matter,[26] the authority of appellate courts to set limits

19. *See* Neese v. Southern Ry., 350 U.S. 77, 76 S.Ct. 131, 100 L.Ed. 60 (1955). *See generally* Dagnello v. Long Island R.R., 289 F.2d 797 (2d Cir.1961), and sources cited therein at 806; Comment, 28 Fordham L. Rev. 500 (1959); Note, 98 U. Pa. L. Rev. 575 (1950).

20. 287 U.S. 474, 53 S.Ct. 252, 77 L.Ed. 439 (1933).

21. Gasperini v. Center for Humanities, Inc., 518 U.S. 415, 116 S.Ct. 2211, 135 L.Ed.2d 659 (1996).

22. Hetzel v. Prince William County, 523 U.S. 208, 118 S.Ct. 1210, 140 L.Ed.2d 336 (1998). On whether the court may itself reduce an constitutionally excessive punitive damage award, *compare* Johansen v. Combustion Engineering, Inc., 170 F.3d 1320 (11th Cir.1999) *with* Rubinstein v. Administrators, 218 F.3d 392 (5th Cir.2000).

23. *See, e.g.,* Auster Oil & Gas, Inc. v. Stream, 835 F.2d 597 (5th Cir.1988); Allstate Ins. Co. v. James, 845 F.2d 315 (11th Cir.1988); Westbrook v. General Tire & Rubber Co., 754 F.2d 1233 (5th Cir.1985).

24. Taylor v. Green, 868 F.2d 162 (5th Cir.), *cert. denied,* 493 U.S. 841, 110 S.Ct. 127, 107 L.Ed.2d 87 (1989) (absent a clearly inadequate or excessive award, an appellate court may not add or subtract from the compensatory or punitive damage awards); Nairn v. National R.R. Passenger Corp., 837 F.2d 565 (2d Cir.1988) (verdict will be vacated as excessive only when it shocks the judicial conscience); Jackson v. Magnolia Brokerage Co., 742 F.2d 1305 (11th Cir. 1984), *cert. denied,* 472 U.S. 1008, 105 S.Ct. 2704, 86 L.Ed.2d 720 (1985).

25. *See* Annot., 11 A.L.R.2d 1217.

26. *See, e.g.,* Fairmount Glass Works v. Cub Fork Coal Co., 287 U.S. 474, 53 S.Ct. 252, 77 L.Ed. 439 (1933); Vanskike v. Union Pac. R.R., 725 F.2d 1146 (8th Cir.1984);

is generally asserted.[27] In *Gasperini v. Center for Humanities, Inc.*,[28] the Supreme Court held that a federal court hearing a claim arising under New York law should follow the standards laid down by a New York statute directing courts to compare damage awards with awards in comparable cases and strike down those deviating materially from what would be reasonable compensation.

Compromise verdicts

3. *Does the trial court have discretion to let a compromise verdict stand?* A verdict for substantially less than plaintiff claims may reflect a rational rejection of some claimed items of damage; therefore, it may not be legally inadequate.[29] But when a verdict fails to cover the plaintiff's clearly proven damages, the inference is strong that the jury compromised.[30] Of course, an inadequate verdict may be the result of prejudice or bias, or some other improper reason, and if that appears to be the case a new trial should be granted.[31] But the most common explanation of the inadequate verdict is that it represents a jury's compromise on the issues of liability and damages. Such a compromise is theoretically improper[32] because the jurors are supposed to divorce considerations of liability from those of damages except when a rule of proportional negligence applies; some courts have held it an abuse of discretion to deny a new trial when the verdict is demonstrably inadequate.[33]

But this point of view seems too doctrinaire. Jury trial is supposed to reflect the community sense of overall fairness, for defendants as well as plaintiffs.[34] Some courts insist that the evidence be examined to see whether a clear preponderance exists for either party on the issue of

Burke v. Reiter, 241 Iowa 807, 42 N.W.2d 907 (1950); Lupi v. Keenan, 396 Pa. 6, 151 A.2d 447 (1959).

27. *See* cases cited in Dagnello v. Long Island R.R., 289 F.2d 797, 799 n. 1 (2d Cir.1961).

28. 518 U.S. 415, 116 S.Ct. 2211, 135 L.Ed.2d 659 (1996); see § 2.37 *supra.*

29. *See, e.g.,* Green Construction Co. v. Chicago, R.I. & Pac. R.R., 65 F.2d 852 (10th Cir.1933); Smith v. Bailey, 311 Ky. 118, 223 S.W.2d 582 (1949).

30. Reisberg v. Walters, 111 F.2d 595 (6th Cir.1940); Smith v. Webber, 282 S.W.2d 346 (Ky.1955); Simmons v. Fish, 210 Mass. 563, 97 N.E. 102 (1912); Dolen v. Beatrice Restaurant Co., 137 Neb. 247, 289 N.W. 336 (1939); Vaughan v. Bartell Drug Co., 56 Wash. 2d 162, 351 P.2d 925 (1960).

31. *See, e.g.,* Rosa v. City of Chester, 278 F.2d 876 (3d Cir.1960); Blacktin v. McCarthy, 231 Minn. 303, 42 N.W.2d 818 (1950).

32. *See* Southern Ry. v. Madden, 235 F.2d 198, 204 (4th Cir.1956); Simmons v. Fish, 210 Mass. 563, 571–572, 97 N.E. 102, 106 (1912). *But see* Coons, Compromise as Precise Justice, 68 Calif. L. Rev. 250 (1980).

33. Hatfield v. Seaboard Air Line Ry., 396 F.2d 721 (5th Cir.1968); Foster v. Dukes, 301 Ky. 752, 193 S.W.2d 159 (1946); Gomes v. Roy, 99 N.H. 233, 108 A.2d 552 (1954); Sherer v. Smith, 85 Ohio App. 317, 88 N.E.2d 426 (1949); Whitney v. City of Milwaukee, 65 Wis. 409, 27 N.W. 39 (1886).

34. Karcesky v. Laria, 382 Pa. 227, 235, 114 A.2d 150, 154 (1955) affirmed the action of the trial court in denying a motion for a new trial when the verdicts for two plaintiffs were manifestly inadequate if liability was found. In the course of an excellent opinion the court said, "[w]here the evidence of negligence or contributory negligence, or both is conflicting or not free from doubt, a trial judge has the power to uphold the time-honored right of a jury to render a compromise verdict."

liability. If it favors defendant, a new trial is not required; if it favors plaintiff, the denial of a new trial will be reversed.[35] In any event, the general adoption of comparative negligence makes every verdict in such cases a compromise. This puts the question of adequacy or excessiveness at one further remove, where conceptual boundaries are virtually indefinable.

Punitive damages

In the opinion of many, serious excessive verdict issues remain over punitive damages, particularly against "deep pocket" defendants. Courts agree that substantial judicial scrutiny is required of punitive damage verdicts, as they are a form of punishment, and legislatures in many states have imposed "caps" on awards. Large punitive damages verdicts usually do not survive trial and appellate court review.[36] The Supreme Court has held that the Due Process Clause of the Fourteenth Amendment imposes constitutional limits (albeit vague ones) on civil punitive damages, and that it requires judicial review of punitive damage awards. This will no doubt spur heightened scrutiny of what juries award.[37]

4. *May a new trial be conditioned on a remittitur or additur?* Because a new trial is costly and time-consuming, in excessive-verdicts cases courts have devised the practice of granting a new trial conditionally—that is, granting it unless the party receiving the verdict consents to the reduction of damages to a specified amount.[38]

35. In Rawle v. McIlhenny, 163 Va. 735, 177 S.E. 214 (1934), the court attempted to classify situations according to the strength of the evidence on the issue of liability. It found five categories, among them the two situations mentioned in the text. In McDowell v. City of Portsmouth, 184 Va. 548, 35 S.E.2d 821 (1945), the court sustained the trial court's refusal to set aside an apparently inadequate verdict where the preponderance of the evidence was clearly against liability "though there [was] evidence to support a finding by the jury that the defendant [was] liable." To similar effect is Young v. Great N. Ry., 80 Minn. 123, 83 N.W. 32 (1900).

In Fischer v. St. Louis, 189 Mo. 567, 88 S.W. 82 (1905), the trial court's refusal to set aside a nominal verdict for plaintiff was reversed on plaintiff's appeal when "there was persuasive evidence of . . . negligence" and "little or no evidence showing a want of due care" on plaintiff's part. To similar effect is Fleming v. Gemein, 168 Mich. 541, 134 N.W. 969 (1912).

36. Rustad, Unraveling Punitive Damages: Current Data and Further Inquiry, 1998 Wis. L. Rev. 15, 40–44; see Eisenberg, The Predictability of Punitive Damages, 26 J. Leg. Stud. 623 (1997).

37. BMW of North America, Inc. v. Gore, 517 U.S. 559, 116 S.Ct. 1589, 134 L.Ed.2d 809 (1996); Honda Motor Co. v. Oberg, 512 U.S. 415, 114 S.Ct. 2331, 129 L.Ed.2d 336 (1994). For proposed approaches to judicial review, see Atlas Food Systems & Services, Inc. v. Crane National Vendors, 99 F.3d 587 (4th Cir.1996); Baldus, *et al.,* Improving Judicial Oversight of Jury Damages Assessments, 80 Iowa L. Rev. 1109 (1995); Eisenberg & Wells, Punitive Awards After BMW, A New Capping System, and the Reported Opinion Bias, 1998 Wis. L. Rev. 387 (1998). Appellate courts must review the constitutionality of punitive awards *de novo.* Cooper Industries, Inc. v. Leatherman Tool Group, Inc., ___ U.S. ___, ___ S.Ct. ___, ___ L.Ed.2d ___ (2001).

38. *See* Annots., 53 A.L.R. 779, 95 A.L.R. 1163.

Remittitur

A remittitur is an action of the court to decrease an excessive jury verdict, usually on the losing defendant's motion for a new trial. The constitutionality of this practice has been questioned because it involves re-examination of a jury's verdict in a manner contrary to the course of common law and the Seventh Amendment, which states that "no fact tried by a jury shall be otherwise re-examined ... than according to the rules of the common law."[39] But the remittitur practice has become so firmly established in both federal and state courts that it probably will not now be overturned on constitutional grounds.[40]

Additur

More recent is the analogous practice of conditioning a new trial on defendant's failure to consent to an additur when plaintiff complains of the inadequacy of the verdict. Some state courts have permitted additur only when the amount of the increase can be established by definite rules of law, as by adding interest omitted from the verdict.[41] Others have awarded additur where the measure of damages is more open-ended, as in personal injury cases.[42]

In 1934 the Supreme Court condemned additur in a 5–4 decision on the ground that it was an unconstitutional invasion of the right of jury trial.[43] Like the Seventh Amendment right to jury trial in civil actions, this ruling binds federal but not state courts. The court differentiated remittitur on two grounds: the existence of English remittitur practice before 1791, and the fact that in remittitur "what remains is included in the verdict along with the unlawful excess—in that sense it has been found by the jury—and the remittitur has the effect of merely lopping off an excrescence."[44] In contrast, an additur is the "bald addition of something which in no sense can be said to be included in the verdict."[45]

39. *See, e.g.,* Carlin, Remittiturs and Additurs, 49 W. Va. L.Q. 1 (1942); Note, 21 Va. L. Rev. 672 (1935), and the misgivings in the court's opinion in Dimick v. Schiedt, 293 U.S. 474, 484–485, 55 S.Ct. 296, 300, 79 L.Ed. 603, 610 (1935). *Compare* Dorsey v. Barba, 38 Cal.2d 350, 240 P.2d 604 (1952).

In Note, 44 Yale L.J. 318 (1934), it is suggested that this constitutional difficulty is not so great under state constitutions that lack the "re-examination" provisions—as most of them do.

40. Dimick v. Schiedt, 293 U.S. 474, 484–485, 55 S.Ct. 296, 300, 79 L.Ed. 603, 610 (1935); see Hetzel v. Prince William County, 523 U.S. 208, 118 S.Ct. 1210, 140 L.Ed.2d 336 (1998); Browning–Ferris Indus. v. Kelco Disposal, Inc., 492 U.S. 257, 109 S.Ct. 2909, 106 L.Ed.2d 219 (1989); Note, Remittitur Practice in the Federal Courts, 76 Colum. L. Rev. 299 (1976).

41. Carr v. Miner, 42 Ill. 179 (1866); Marsh v. Kendall, 65 Kan. 48, 68 P. 1070 (1902); Clark v. Henshaw Motor Co., 246 Mass. 386, 140 N.E. 593 (1923).

42. Gaffney v. Illingsworth, 90 N.J.L. 490, 101 A. 243 (1917); Bachmann v. Passalacqua, 46 N.J.Super. 471, 135 A.2d 18 (1957); O'Connor v. Papertsian, 309 N.Y. 465, 131 N.E.2d 883 (1956); Bodon v. Suhrmann, 8 Utah 2d 42, 327 P.2d 826 (1958). *See also* Annot., 56 A.L.R.2d 213.

43. Dimick v. Schiedt, 293 U.S. 474, 55 S.Ct. 296, 79 L.Ed. 603 (1935). But see Gasperini v. Center for Humanities, Inc., 518 U.S. 415, 433 n. 16, 116 S.Ct. 2211, 135 L.Ed.2d 659 (1996); Liriano v. Hobart Corp., 170 F.3d 264 (2d Cir.1999)(court may itself add to damages liquidated item that jury unaccountably omitted).

44. *Id.,* 293 U.S. at 486, 55 S.Ct. at 301, 79 L.Ed. at 611. (1935). In addition, the court expressed serious misgivings about the constitutionality of remittitur.

45. *Id.*

The Court's history may have been sound, but its economic analysis may not be. In reaching a large verdict, the jurors have rejected all smaller amounts just as they have rejected larger amounts in reaching a small verdict.[46] Furthermore, a jury's conclusion in a given case need not be totally accepted or rejected. If the presiding judge considers that the verdict was generally proper, remittitur or additur may be the sensible way to salvage the good without incurring the expense and delay of a new trial.

Fixing the amount

If one accepts this reasoning, the amount of a remittitur should reduce the verdict to the largest amount a trial court would uphold as not excessive.[47] It would thus let stand whatever part of the award a jury could reasonably award, just as in passing on a motion for judgment as a matter of law the court upholds only a verdict within the bounds of reasonableness. In jurisdictions allowing additur, the same argument would use it to increase the verdict to reflect the smallest amount that the court would allow to stand. The court, moreover, could implement the remittitur or additur directly, not just as an alternative to a new trial.

In practice, however, the court is limited to ordering a new trial if the verdict is inadequate. Such is the governing principle in many jurisdictions;[48] in other states the judge must ascertain the amount that a properly functioning jury would be likely to find and order a remittitur of everything in excess of that amount.[49] This practice seems to be a clear invasion of the jury's sphere, since it calls on the court to fix damages without considering what the jury has actually done.

46. *See* Carlin, Remittiturs and Additurs, 49 W. Va. L.Q. 1, 18, 24, 25 (1942). *Compare* Powers v. Allstate Ins. Co., 10 Wis.2d 78, 88, 102 N.W.2d 393 (1960) (by its verdict "the jury has already indicated that it thinks that the plaintiff deserves the highest figure the evidence will sustain").

47. Since it is a court function to determine whether a verdict is excessive, it is also a court function to determine the point at which a verdict becomes excessive (that is, to fix the limits of tolerable jury discretion). *See, e.g.,* Powers v. Allstate Ins. Co., 10 Wis.2d 78, 91, 102 N.W.2d 393, 400 (1960); Comment, 44 Yale L.J. 318, 320 (1934). The court does not, therefore, invade the jury's function in determining the greatest amount that the evidence would support. The verdict clearly cannot be sustained beyond this point; but up to this point it is either sustainable or so tainted as to affect the whole verdict and merit a new trial.

48. *See* Gorsalitz v. Olin Mathieson Chem. Corp., 429 F.2d 1033 (5th Cir.1970), in connection with a remittitur. *See also* the discussion in Glazer v. Glazer, 278 F.Supp. 476 (E.D.La.1968)

49. *See, e.g.,* Allen v. Giuliano, 144 Conn. 573, 135 A.2d 904 (1957) (in fixing remittitur, "a fair appraisal of compensatory damages, and not the limit of legitimate generosity, is the rule"); Larrissey v. Norwalk Truck Lines, 155 Ohio St. 207, 98 N.E.2d 419 (1951) (trial court may, "with the assent of the plaintiff, reduce the verdict by remittitur to any amount warranted by the evidence"). At least one state statute codifies the authority of the trial judge to add or subtract from the judgment "so much ... as the court in its independent judgment determines ... to be fair and reasonable." Cal. Civ. Proc. Code § 662.5.

Appellate review

A related issue is whether a party who has acquiesced in an additur or remittitur may seek appellate review of the adjusted judgment rather than undergo the new trial. Denial of appellate review is justified on the ground that the party has "elected" to accept the adjustment[50] and should be bound, as if it entered a settlement agreement. But the election is clearly coerced. Furthermore, it is difficult to see why the propriety of the trial judge's determination of the damages should be less reviewable than a determination of liability through a judgment notwithstanding the verdict—the latter being concededly reviewable.[51] Allowing a party to appeal the adjusted verdict, however, allows it to avoid a new trial and raises the possibility that the original verdict may be restored. It has been suggested that a fairer balance would result if the party accepting the adjusted verdict could complain only by cross-appeal—that is, it could seek to have the appellate court reinstate the original verdict only if its opponent sought to obtain reversal of the adjusted verdict.[52]

Partial new trials

When a motion for a new trial is made, the trial court has discretion in both jury and nonjury cases to order a new trial "on all or part of the issues" as to "all or any of the parties."[53] The issues on which the new trial is ordered must be separate and distinct from the rest of the case so that their independent retrial will not result in prejudice. The most common use of partial new trials is to limit the new trial to the issue of damages when the issue of liability is separate and distinct and has already been determined by the jury. A new trial limited to damages obviously will be less complicated, but it may also be less just.

The common law regarded a jury verdict as indivisible. If it were set aside at all, the new trial necessarily had to address all the issues. As Lord Mansfield said, "for form's sake we must set aside the whole verdict."[54] American courts, however, generally have not found an invasion of the jury's function in ordering a partial new trial in appropriate cases. In *Gasoline Products Co. v. Champlin Refining Co.*[55] the Supreme Court held that a new trial limited to damages alone did not offend the Seventh Amendment. The Court added, however, that the practice "may not properly be resorted to unless it clearly appears that the issue to be retried is so distinct and separate from the others that a trial of it alone may be had without injustice."[56]

50. Donovan v. Penn Shipping Co., 429 U.S. 648, 97 S.Ct. 835, 51 L.Ed.2d 112 (1977); Note, 76 Colum. L. Rev. 299, 313 (1976); Note, 1975 Duke L.J. 1150; Annot., 16 A.L.R.3d 1327.

51. *See* § 7.22 *supra*.

52. International Broth. of Elec. Workers, Local 1547 v. Alaska Utility Construction Inc., 976 P.2d 852 (Alaska 1999); Note, 76 Colum. L. Rev. 299, 324 (1976).

53. Fed. R. Civ. P. 59(a).

54. Edie v. East India Co., 1 W. Black 295, 298, 96 Eng. Rep. 166, 167 (K.B. 1761).

55. 283 U.S. 494, 51 S.Ct. 513, 75 L.Ed. 1188 (1931).

56. 283 U.S. at 500, 51 S.Ct. at 515, 75 L.Ed. at 1191. The Court went on to hold that a partial new trial was not appropriate in the case before it.

The point is that a defendant who has been found liable for inadequate damages should usually not be precluded from relitigating the liability issue when its damages exposure has been reopened.[57] When a jury apparently has arrived at a compromise verdict by improperly compounding the issues of liability and damages together, it is an abuse of discretion to order a new trial on the issue of damages only.[58] In a leading case, the Massachusetts Supreme Judicial Court commented on such a situation.

> It is possible that a trial judge might let such a verdict [compromise] stand, for various reasons: as, for instance, if on the whole it should appear to him that a verdict for the defendant ought not to have been set aside. But it would be a gross injustice to set aside such a verdict as to damages alone against the protest of a defendant, and force him to a new trial with the issue of liability closed against him when it appears obvious that no jury had ever decided that issue against him on justifiable grounds.[59]

There may, however, be another explanation for an inadequate award.[60] *Rosa v. City of Chester,*[61] for example, was a wrongful death action in which the jurors' questions showed they had found liability but probably minimized decedent's earning capacity because of improper evidence of his buying whisky on the evening of his death. Most appellate courts seem inclined to accept the trial court's judgment on whether fairness requires a complete retrial.[62]

Unlike an unreasonably low damage award, an excessive verdict surely does not suggest a compromise. Rather, "the excessive verdict suggests that it was a product of mistake, partiality, passion, or prejudice."[63] In this situation, therefore, limiting a new trial to the amount of

57. *See* Annots., 29 A.L.R.2d 1199, 85 A.L.R.2d 19.

58. Rosa v. City of Chester, 278 F.2d 876 (3d Cir.1960); Leipert v. Honold, 39 Cal.2d 462, 247 P.2d 324 (1952); Kinsell v. Hawthorne, 27 Ill.App.2d 314, 169 N.E.2d 678 (1960); Smith v. Webber, 282 S.W.2d 346 (Ky.1955); Simmons v. Fish, 210 Mass. 563, 97 N.E. 102 (1912); Blacktin v. McCarthy, 231 Minn. 303, 42 N.W.2d 818 (1950); Caine v. Collins, 194 Pa.Super. 230, 166 A.2d 675 (1960); Farr v. Fisher, 107 Vt. 331, 178 A. 883 (1935); Zerr v. Spokane City Lines, 58 Wash.2d 196, 361 P.2d 752 (1961).

59. Simmons v. Fish, 210 Mass. 563, 572, 97 N.E. 102, 106 (1912).

60. If liability is conceded, a new trial may of course be confined to the issue of damages. Kovacovich v. Phelps Dodge Corp., 62 Ariz. 193, 156 P.2d 240 (1945); Swartz v. Smokowitz, 400 Pa. 109, 161 A.2d 330 (1960). And if liability is clear enough this may perhaps indicate that the error was confined to the issue of damages even when there is no other affirmative showing that this was the case. *See, e.g.,* Martin v. Donohue, 30 Cal.App.2d 219, 85 P.2d 913 (1938); Whiteside v. Harvey, 124 Colo. 561, 239 P.2d 989 (1951); Vaughan v. Bartell Drug Co., 56 Wash.2d 162, 166, 351 P.2d 925, 928 (1960).

61. 278 F.2d 876 (3d Cir.1960). *Cf.* Blacktin v. McCarthy, 231 Minn. 303, 42 N.W.2d 818 (1950) (liability clear; court believed jury improperly swayed by fact that the plaintiff was unemployed and had spent the "evening with defendant at various night clubs or places of entertainment").

62. Lilly v. Boswell, 362 Mo. 444, 242 S.W.2d 73 (1951); Farr v. Fisher, 107 Vt. 331, 178 A. 883 (1935).

63. Rommell v. United States Steel Corp., 66 N.J.Super. 30, 49, 168 A.2d 437, 447 (App.Div.1961).

damages helps protect the defendant against partiality resulting from the details of its conduct, without depriving the plaintiff of anything to which it is entitled.

§ 7.30 Judgment Notwithstanding Verdict

When a jury verdict is not supported by legally sufficient evidence, rarely is there a substantial chance, in these days of broad discovery, that at the new trial the party with the insufficient case can fill the gap and prevail on the merits. Hence, the new trial will be a waste of everybody's time and money. Of course, the judge could have obviated the need for a second trial by directing a verdict in the original trial in favor of the party who should win as a matter of law. But this course of action has risks. The question of sufficiency of evidence is often close. The trial judge must rule on it in the heat and hurry of trial, usually without a chance to read the transcript; the judge may draw a different conclusion from that reached on the transcript and written briefs. If the trial judge does err in directing a verdict, there must be a new trial, and the first one will have been largely wasted.

Historical evolution

To avoid this dilemma, some ingenious common law judges devised a procedure of "reserving questions of law arising during trials by jury and of taking verdicts subject to the ultimate ruling on the questions reserved; and under this practice the reservation carried with it authority to make such ultimate disposition of the case as might be made essential by the ruling, under the reservation, such as nonsuiting the plaintiff where he had obtained a verdict, entering a verdict or judgment for one party where the jury had given a verdict for the other, or making other essential adjustments."[1] This practice often obviated the need for a new trial. If the appellate court eventually concluded that the case was properly one for the jury, a new trial order would be reversed and judgment entered on the verdict; if not, it would reverse the new trial order.

The procedure fell into disuse by the latter part of the nineteenth century.[2] It was revived in the form of the modern procedure for judgment notwithstanding the verdict, or j.n.o.v.[3] The name is taken

§ 7.30

1. Baltimore & Carolina Line v. Redman, 295 U.S. 654, 659, 55 S.Ct. 890, 892, 79 L.Ed. 1636, 1639 (1935) (citing Carleton v. Griffin, 1 Burr. 549, 97 Eng. Rep. 443 (K.B. 1758); Coppendale v. Bridgen, 2 Burr. 814, 97 Eng. Rep. 576 (K.B. 1759); Bird v. Randall, 3 Burr. 1345, 97 Eng. Rep. 866 (K.B. 1762); Bassett v. Thomas, 3 Burr. 1441, 97 Eng. Rep. 916 (K.B. 1763); Timmins v. Rowlinson, 3 Burr. 1603, 97 Eng. Rep. 1003 (K.B. 1765)). *See also* Thayer, Evidence 241 (1898).

2. *See* Thorndyke, Trial by Jury in United States Courts, 26 Harv. L. Rev. 732, 737 (1913). *Cf.* Schweppe, Judgment Non–Obstante Veredicto in the Federal Courts, 18 Minn. L. Rev. 898, 899 (1934).

3. The abbreviation stands for *judgment non obstante veredicto.* In federal courts, j.n.o.v. is also called "judgment as a matter of law."

from a common law device requiring entry of judgment for a plaintiff when the *pleadings* required a plaintiff's verdict.[4] The newer device authorized judgment for the party entitled to it as a matter of law on the evidence when the verdict was in favor of the other party.[5]

This sensible device, however, was held unconstitutional for the federal courts in *Slocum v. New York Life Insurance Co.*[6] Pennsylvania procedure was employed in that case, it being decided when federal courts followed state procedure under the Conformity Act.[7] The opinion found that the common law afforded no such procedure for the re-examination of a jury verdict. Twenty years later, in *Baltimore & Carolina Line v. Redman,*[8] the Supreme Court upheld j.n.o.v. for a defendant when, under a different state's procedure, the trial court had, prior to verdict, reserved decision on defendant's motion for directed verdict. *Slocum* was distinguished on the ground that the procedure there involved no reservation of decision by the trial court. That, held the Court, was a common law practice compatible with the Seventh Amendment.

Reserved ruling on directed verdict

The Federal Rules on directed verdict and j.n.o.v., the two forms of judgment as a matter of law, were formulated against this background. *Redman* was relied on as a basis for Rule 50(b), which provides that if "the court does not grant a motion for judgment as a matter of law made at the close of all the evidence, the court is considered to have submitted the action to the jury subject to the court's later deciding the legal questions raised by the motion," and may thereafter order j.n.o.v.

The Supreme Court has affirmed the constitutional validity of j.n.o.v. but has required that courts strictly comply with the procedure so that the jury's proper sphere is protected. The party moving for j.n.o.v. must have previously moved for a directed verdict at the close of *all* the evidence. A motion to dismiss at the end of plaintiff's case does not suffice; it should be renewed at the close of all evidence in order for it to serve as a basis for a j.n.o.v.[9] In making the motion for j.n.o.v., the

4. Stephen, Principles of Pleading 129–130 (1824). *See* § 7.4 *supra.*

5. See descriptions of practice under these statutes in Slocum v. New York Life Ins. Co., 228 U.S. 364, 33 S.Ct. 523, 57 L.Ed. 879 (1913); Baltimore & Carolina Line v. Redman, 295 U.S. 654, 55 S.Ct. 890, 79 L.Ed. 1636 (1935). For an analysis of decisional law, see Louis, Post-verdict Rulings on the Sufficiency of the Evidence, 1975 Wis. L. Rev. 503.

6. 228 U.S. 364, 33 S.Ct. 523, 57 L.Ed. 879 (1913).

7. *See* § 1.7 *supra.*

8. 295 U.S. 654, 55 S.Ct. 890, 79 L.Ed. 1636 (1935).

9. Hilord Chem. Corp. v. Ricoh Elecs., 875 F.2d 32 (2d Cir.1989); Mark Seitman & Assoc. v. R.J. Reynolds Tobacco Co., 837 F.2d 1527 (11th Cir.1988); 5A Moore, Federal Practice and Procedure ¶ 50.08; 9 Wright and Miller, Federal Practice and Procedure § 2537.

In many states a prior motion for directed verdict is not a prerequisite to a motion for j.n.o.v., and indeed the trial court may order such a judgment on its own motion. *See* Cal. Civ. Proc. Code § 629; N.Y. Civ. Prac. L. & R. 4404.

movant must expressly ask for that relief; a motion to "set aside the verdict" is insufficient.[10] The motion for j.n.o.v. is also limited to the assertion of issues or grounds specifically raised in the prior motion for a directed verdict.[11]

Federal courts have strictly construed Rule 50(b). In *United States v. Warner,*[12] for example, the government sued an employer for alleged unpaid employment taxes. The jury returned a verdict in favor of the government, and the defendant argued on appeal that there was insufficient evidence to find that the workers were employees rather than independent contractors and that defendant's failure to file tax returns was due only to willful neglect. The court of appeals affirmed the verdict, holding that the taxpayer's failure to move for directed verdict at trial precluded him from challenging the sufficiency of the evidence on appeal.[13]

There are three reasons for requiring the prior motion for a directed verdict. First, courts want to avoid unfair surprise on the nonmovant, who, at the time of the directed verdict, may still cure defects in proof, if any exist. Second, courts wish to avoid second-guessing the jury as much as possible. Third, as already explained, the Supreme Court has held that j.n.o.v. constitutes an infringement on the right of jury trial unless it is merely a postponed version of a directed verdict. On the other hand, once the requisite motion for a directed verdict has been made, the court may wish to delay decision until the jury has spoken, in the hope that the jury will reach the "correct" result, thus obviating the need to decide whether there was enough evidence to go to the jury.

Standard for j.n.o.v.

The standard for granting j.n.o.v. is the same as that for a directed verdict:[14] only one reasonable verdict is possible, regardless of the credi-

10. Johnson v. New York, N.H. & H.R.R., 344 U.S. 48, 73 S.Ct. 125, 97 L.Ed. 77 (1952). The *Johnson* opinion, a 5–4 decision by Justice Black, is widely regarded as hypertechnical. The lower federal courts in more recent years have been less exacting, requiring only that the motion be made when reception of the evidence is substantially complete and that its purpose be fairly intelligible. *See* Pittsburgh–Des Moines Steel Co. v. Brookhaven Manor Water Co., 532 F.2d 572 (7th Cir.1976). It seems probable that this view will in due course be adopted by the Supreme Court.

11. Kutner Buick, Inc. v. American Motors Corp., 868 F.2d 614 (3d Cir.1989); Smith v. Lightning Bolt Productions, 861 F.2d 363 (2d Cir.1988); Morales v. Cadena, 825 F.2d 1095 (7th Cir.1987).

12. 855 F.2d 372 (7th Cir.1988).

13. See also Herrington v. County of Sonoma, 834 F.2d 1488 (9th Cir.1987); Pierce v. Southern Pac. Transp. Co., 823 F.2d 1366 (9th Cir.1987). A narrow exception to the rule requiring a motion for a directed verdict as a prerequisite to j.n.o.v. is made when the jury brings back a special verdict whose answers are "irreconcilably inconsistent" or when the special verdict does not support the judgment. *See* Pierce v. Southern Pac. Transp. Co., 823 F.2d 1366, 1369 (9th Cir.1987).

14. Charles Woods Television Corp. v. Capital Cities/ABC, 869 F.2d 1155 (8th Cir. 1989); Bhaya v. Westinghouse Elec. Corp., 832 F.2d 258 (3d Cir.1987); Newell Cos. v. Kenney Mfg. Co., 864 F.2d 757 (Fed.Cir. 1988); see §§ 7.12–19, 7.21 *supra.*

bility of the witnesses or the evidence.[15] Summary judgment has similar standards. In *Peterson v. Kennedy,*[16] for example, a former football player sued the players' union and its attorneys for breach of duty of fair representation, claiming that they had given him inaccurate advice on which he detrimentally relied in pursuing a grievance against his former ball club. The district judge granted summary judgment for one defendant, issued a directed verdict in favor of another, and granted the union's motion for j.n.o.v. On appeal, the court held that only negligence could be shown, not the arbitrary, discriminatory, or bad faith conduct necessary to prove the breach of duty, and hence the j.n.o.v. and the directed verdict were properly granted and, on review, were subject to the same standards.

As with a directed verdict, when the evidence is conflicting or is insufficient to establish the movant's case, j.n.o.v. should not be awarded.[17] In ruling on the verdict, the court should consider the evidence in the light most favorable to the nonmovant.[18] J.n.o.v. is not appropriate if reasonable minds could differ over the verdict, and all reasonable inferences must be drawn in favor of the nonmoving party.[19]

New trial instead

The standard for a directed verdict or j.n.o.v. differs, as we have already seen, from that for granting a new trial.[20] Even if a party has introduced sufficient evidence to go to the jury, the court still has the discretion to set aside the verdict and require retrial before a new jury if the verdict was against the clear weight of the evidence. Likewise, the court may grant a new trial because of trial error or jury misconduct, which would not warrant j.n.o.v. This is because j.n.o.v. brings the case to an end, while a new trial merely offers the loser a second chance. In these respects, state j.n.o.v. practice resembles that in the federal courts.[21]

15. Ware v. Unified School Dist. No. 492, 881 F.2d 906 (10th Cir.1989); Air–Sea Forwarders v. Air Asia Co., 880 F.2d 176 (9th Cir.1989); National Controls Corp. v. National Semiconductor Corp., 833 F.2d 491 (3d Cir.1987).

16. 771 F.2d 1244 (9th Cir.1985).

17. Larabee v. M M & L Intl. Corp., 896 F.2d 1112 (8th Cir.1990); McNeal v. Hi–Lo Powered Scaffolding, 836 F.2d 637 (D.C.Cir. 1988); Collins v. Illinois, 830 F.2d 692 (7th Cir.1987).

18. Gulbranson v. Duluth, M & I.R. Ry., 921 F.2d 139, 141 (8th Cir.1990); Grant v. Preferred Research, 885 F.2d 795 (11th Cir. 1989); Verdegaal Bros., Inc. v. Union Oil Co. of Calif., 814 F.2d 628 (Fed.Cir.1987).

19. Venegas v. Wagner, 831 F.2d 1514 (9th Cir.1987); Peterson v. Kennedy, 771 F.2d 1244 (9th Cir.1985).

20. 9 Wright and Miller, Federal Practice and Procedure § 2524; §§ 7.24–29 *supra.* The federal courts are divided on whether in a diversity case the standard for the sufficiency of the evidence for a directed verdict or j.n.o.v. is the state standard or a matter of federal law. For the difference between the j.n.o.v. and new trial standards, see, e.g., Bevevino v. Saydjari, 574 F.2d 676 (2d Cir.1978). *Compare, e.g.,* Misco–United Supply v. Petroleum Corp., 462 F.2d 75 (5th Cir.1972), *with, e.g.,* Pittsburgh–Des Moines Steel Co. v. Brookhaven Manor Water Co., 532 F.2d 572 (7th Cir. 1976). *See also* 9 Wright and Miller, *supra,* at § 2525.

21. *See, e.g.,* Senderoff v. Housatonic Pub. Serv. Co., 147 Conn. 18, 21, 156 A.2d 517, 519 (1959); Merlo v. Public Serv. Co., 381 Ill. 300, 311, 45 N.E.2d 665, 672 (1942).

Even if the trial court is warranted in entering judgment as a matter of law it may, in its discretion, order a new trial instead.[22] This discretion should be guided largely by an estimate of the likelihood that the party that received the defective verdict may be able to fill the gaps in its claim or defense in a new trial.[23] When j.n.o.v. is warranted, the trial court's option to grant a new trial does not depend on whether a motion for it is made. A party who makes a motion for j.n.o.v. may couple with it a motion for new trial, but it need not do so, as the court's authority to grant a new trial remains unaffected. If, however, the trial court decides that a j.n.o.v. is not warranted, then it lacks power to grant a new trial[24] unless either a timely motion for new trial has been filed or the court orders the new trial on its own initiative not later than ten days after the entry of judgment.[25] If the trial court grants a motion for j.n.o.v., the party against whom it is granted may then move for a new trial.[26]

New trial and j.n.o.v. in the alternative

Under federal practice the motion for j.n.o.v. is typically, though not invariably, accompanied by an alternative motion for a new trial.[27] The trial court is then required to rule on both motions. The disposition of the action at that point depends on how the motions are respectively decided. The principal variations[28] are as follows:

1. If the trial court denies both motions, the original judgment can be appealed and the rulings on the post-trial motions can be reviewed by the appellate court.[29]

2. If the trial court grants the motion for new trial and denies the motion for j.n.o.v., a new trial is held and the question whether the motion for j.n.o.v. should have been granted becomes moot.

3. If the trial court grants the motion for j.n.o.v., its conditional ruling on the new trial motion (whether grant or denial) is essentially an advisory indication to the appellate court on what course the latter might direct if it reverses the j.n.o.v.[30]

Appellate review

On appeal, the options of the appellate court are as follows:

22. *See* Fed. R. Civ. P. 50(b); Cone v. West Va. Pulp & Paper Co., 330 U.S. 212, 67 S.Ct. 752, 91 L.Ed. 849 (1947). *See also, e.g.,* Masterson v. Atherton, 149 Conn. 302, 316, 179 A.2d 592, 599 (1962).

23. *See* Weade v. Dichmann, Wright & Pugh, Inc., 337 U.S. 801, 69 S.Ct. 1326, 93 L.Ed. 1704 (1949).

24. *See* Peterman v. Chicago R.I. & Pac. R.R., 493 F.2d 88 (8th Cir.1974); Note, 21 U. Kan. L. Rev. 211 (1973).

25. *See* Fed. R. Civ. P. 59(b), (d).

26. *Id.* 50(c)(2).

27. *See id.* 50(c)(1).

28. *See* Note, Post-verdict Motions Under Rule 50: Protecting the Verdict Winner, 53 Minn. L. Rev. 358 (1968); Annot., 69 A.L.R.2d 525.

29. *See* Fed. R. Civ. P. 50(d).

30. *See* Neely v. Martin K. Eby Construction Co., 386 U.S. 317, 87 S.Ct. 1072, 18 L.Ed.2d 75 (1967).

1. If the trial judge granted j.n.o.v., the court affirms if it decides the motion was properly granted. If the appellate court decides that j.n.o.v. was improper, it can order reentry of the original judgment or order a new trial. In considering the latter alternative, the appellate court is strongly guided, but not bound, by the trial judge's conditional ruling on an alternative new trial motion.[31]

2. If the trial court denied j.n.o.v. (or denied an alternative motion for a new trial) so that the original judgment still stands and is appealable, the appellate court in reviewing the original judgment affirms if it concludes that the motions were properly denied. If it finds that the original judgment should be reversed, it can order a new trial; if it further determines that a new trial is inappropriate, it can direct entry of j.n.o.v.[32]

State court variants

In states that have not adopted the Federal Rules, the procedures have several different variations. In some, the trial court has authority to grant j.n.o.v. on its own motion, whether a directed verdict has or has not been previously requested.[33] In some, it may grant a new trial only on motion of a party and not on its motion.[34] In other states, an order granting a new trial is itself appealable.[35] The powers of the appellate courts on review are subject to related variations. Generally, however, appellate courts in the state systems have the same range of choice in the relief to be granted (that is, entering judgment one way or the other or granting a new trial) as the trial judge had, with the qualification that they will overrule a ruling on a new trial motion only if they find that the trial court abused its considerable discretion in so doing.

31. *See* Mays v. Pioneer Lumber Corp., 502 F.2d 106 (4th Cir.1974).

32. Weisgram v. Marley Co., 528 U.S. 440, 120 S.Ct. 1011, 145 L.Ed.2d 958 (2000); Neely v. Martin K. Eby Construction Co., 386 U.S. 317, 87 S.Ct. 1072, 18 L.Ed.2d 75 (1967).

33. *See* Annot., 69 A.L.R.2d 449.

34. *See, e.g.,* Cal. Civ. Proc. Code § 657.

35. *See* Annot., 73 A.L.R.2d 269.

Chapter 8

RIGHT TO A JURY TRIAL

A. THE CONSTITUTIONAL RIGHT

§ 8.1 In General

The federal Constitution guarantees the right to jury trial in civil actions in federal courts,[1] and nearly every state constitution contains a similar guaranty.[2] These provisions, though differing somewhat, "preserve" (but do not extend) the right to jury trial as it existed in English history, either in 1791 when the Seventh Amendment was adopted[3] or, in the case of the states, at the date of the first state constitution.[4] At

§ 8.1

1. U.S. Const. amend. VII. *See* Henderson, The Background of the Seventh Amendment, 80 Harv. L. Rev. 289 (1966); Redish, The Seventh Amendment Right to Jury Trial, 70 Nw. U.L. Rev. 486 (1975); Wolfram, The Constitutional History of the Seventh Amendment, 57 Minn. L. Rev. 639 (1973). *See also* Dawson, A History of Lay Judges (1960); Joiner, Civil Justice and the Jury (1962); Amar, The Bill of Rights: Creation and Reconstruction 89 (1998)(arguing that the Seventh Amendment requires each federal court to follow the jury rules of the state where it sits).

2. *See, e.g.,* Cal. Const. art. 1, § 7; Conn. Const. art. 1, § 21.

3. Dimick v. Schiedt, 293 U.S. 474, 476, 55 S.Ct. 296, 297, 79 L.Ed. 603, 606 (1935); Baltimore & Carolina Line v. Redman, 295 U.S. 654, 657, 55 S.Ct. 890, 891, 79 L.Ed. 1636, 1638 (1935).

4. *See, e.g.,* People v. One 1941 Chevrolet Coupe, 37 Cal.2d 283, 287, 231 P.2d 832, 835 (1951) (the constitutional right to jury trial "is the right as it existed at common law at the time the [state] Constitution was adopted ... and what that right is, is a purely historical question, a fact which is to

such times not all civil matters were tried to a jury. Issues in actions at law were tried to a jury, with some exceptions; issues in suits in equity were not, unless the chancellor in his discretion sent an issue to a jury for an advisory verdict.[5]

New rights and remedies

Many new rights and remedies have, of course, been created since the adoption of the federal and state constitutions. Congress and state legislatures have wide latitude to provide that the new remedies they devise be enforced through administrative agency determinations in which no jury is available.[6] The legislature may even abolish a common law remedy, such as the former action by a servant against his master for injuries caused by the latter's negligence, and substitute for it an entirely new system of compensation for all industrial injuries to be administered by a board or commission that will determine factual disputes without resort to either court or jury.[7] When an administrative scheme is enforced through court civil penalty proceedings, the legislature may entrust to a judge the determination of the appropriate

be ascertained like any other social, political or legal fact.... It is necessary, therefore, to ascertain what was the rule of the English common law upon this subject in 1850").

Some of the states that are not among the thirteen original colonies interpret their constitutional provisions as preserving the constitutional right as it had existed in the territory when identical to the right secured by the Seventh Amendment to the federal Constitution, except as it has been modified by later constitutional provision. *See, e.g.,* Whallon v. Bancroft, 4 Minn. 109 (1860); St. Paul & S.C.R.R. v. Gardner, 19 Minn. 132 (1872). *See also* People v. One 1941 Chevrolet Coupe, *supra.*

In some states, adoption of new constitutions with "preserving" provisions has advanced the date of appropriate historical reference. *See, e.g.,* In re Leary's Estate, 175 Misc. 254, 23 N.Y.S.2d 13 (1940) (relevant date in New York is 1894).

5. Shields v. Thomas, 59 U.S. (18 How.) 253, 262, 15 L.Ed. 368, 372 (1855); Meriden Sav. Bank v. McCormack, 79 Conn. 260, 64 A. 338 (1906); Kimball v. Connor, 3 Kan. 414 (1866); Brown v. Heller, 30 N.M. 1, 227 P. 594 (1924); Crouchman v. Superior Court, 45 Cal.3d 1167, 248 Cal.Rptr. 626, 755 P.2d 1075 (1988)(no jury trial right for small claims). On the distinction between law and equity, see §§ 1.3–1.5 *supra.* In the eighteenth century the chancellor frequently referred issues of fact for jury determination; he may have been compelled to do so at least in certain types of cases. *See* Chesnin and Hazard, Chancery Procedure and the Seventh Amendment: Jury Trial of Issues in Equity Cases Before 1791, 83 Yale L.J. 999 (1974), with which *compare* Langbein, Fact Finding in the English Court of Chancery: A Rebuttal, 83 Yale L.J. 1620 (1974). *See also* Macnair, The Law of Proof in Early Modern Equity 281–89 (1999).

6. *See* Atlas Roofing Co. v. Occupational Safety and Health Review Commn., 430 U.S. 442, 97 S.Ct. 1261, 51 L.Ed.2d 464 (1977); NLRB v. Jones & Laughlin Steel Corp., 301 U.S. 1, 57 S.Ct. 615, 81 L.Ed. 893 (1937); Frank Irey, Jr., Inc. v. Occupational Safety and Health Review Commn., 519 F.2d 1200 (3d Cir.1974); United States v. J. B. Williams Co., 498 F.2d 414 (2d Cir.1974); Kirst, Administrative Penalties and the Civil Jury: The Supreme Court's Assault on the Seventh Amendment, 126 U. Pa. L. Rev. 1281 (1978); Redish & LaFave, Seventh Amendment Right to Jury Trial in Non-Article III Proceeedings: A Study in Dysfunctional Constitutional Theory, 4 Wm. & Mary Bill of Rts. J. 407 (1995).

7. Mountain Timber Co. v. Washington, 243 U.S. 219, 37 S.Ct. 260, 61 L.Ed. 685 (1917); Cunningham v. Northwestern Improvement Co., 44 Mont. 180, 119 P. 554 (1911); State ex rel. Davis–Smith Co. v. Clausen, 65 Wash. 156, 117 P. 1101 (1911).

penalty.[8] But there are limits beyond which a legislature may not go, at least if it provides a judicial rather than an administrative agency forum. If a legislature creates a right to be redressed by an action that is analogous to a common law action (such as those for recovery for a fraudulent conveyance or for compensatory damages caused by wrongful death), it may not deprive the parties to the action of a right to jury trial[9] unless the new right is given against the sovereign and therefore involves a waiver of sovereign immunity.[10] If the legislature does not stipulate how a new remedy is to be tried, the courts fit it into the nearest historical analogy to determine whether there is a right to jury trial.[11]

Actions frequently are referred to alternative dispute resolution proceedings such as mandatory arbitration by the court. This does not violate the right to a jury trial so long as the litigant can demand a trial de novo on completion of the proceeding.[12]

Demanding jury trial

The constitutional guaranty of jury trial has been uniformly construed as a right that may be waived by the parties. Statute or court rule may therefore prescribe reasonable conditions for obtaining jury trial, such as timely demand, and may provide that failure to take steps constitutes a waiver. The Federal Rules, for example, provide that jury trial must be demanded in the pleading in which the jury-triable issue appears or by a demand made not later than ten days after service of the last pleading directed to that issue.[13]

8. Tull v. United States, 481 U.S. 412, 107 S.Ct. 1831, 95 L.Ed.2d 365 (1987). *See* Note, Judicial Assessment of Punitive Damages, the Seventh Amendment and the Politics of Jury Power, 91 Colum. L. Rev. 142 (1991). *But see* Feltner v. Columbia Pictures Television, Inc., 523 U.S. 340, 118 S.Ct. 1279, 140 L.Ed.2d 438 (1998)(right to jury trial on statutory damages issues in copyright case); Murphy, Judicial Assessment of Legal Remedies, 94 Nw. U.L. Rev. 153 (1999).

9. *See* Parsons v. Bedford, 28 U.S. (3 Pet.) 433, 447, 7 L. Ed. 732, 737 (1830). ("By common law, they [the framers] meant . . . not merely suits, which the common law recognized among its old and settled proceedings, but suits in which legal rights were to be ascertained and determined, in contradistinction to those" recognized only in equity or admiralty. "Probably, there were few, if any, States in the Union, in which some new legal remedies differing from the old common law forms were not in use; but in which . . . trial by jury intervened"); Granfinanciera, S.A. v. Nordberg, 492 U.S. 33, 109 S.Ct. 2782, 106 L.Ed.2d 26 (1989); Curtis v. Loether, 415 U.S. 189, 94 S.Ct. 1005, 39 L.Ed.2d 260 (1974); Pernell v. Southall Realty, 416 U.S. 363, 94 S.Ct. 1723, 40 L.Ed.2d 198 (1974). *See also* Damsky v. Zavatt, 289 F.2d 46 (2d Cir.1961).

10. *See, e.g.,* the Federal Tort Claims Act, 18 U.S.C. § 2674 (1958), and the New York Court of Claims Act (29A) pt. 1 (McKinney), both of which provide for determination of fact issues without a jury. *Cf.* Auffmordt v. Hedden, 137 U.S. 310, 11 S.Ct. 103, 34 L.Ed. 674 (1890). The Foreign Sovereignty Immunities Act, 28 U.S.C. § 1330(a), applicable to suits against other national states, precludes jury trial. *E.g.,* Ruggiero v. Compania Peruana de Vapores, 639 F.2d 872 (2d Cir.1981).

11. *See* § 8.7 *infra.*

12. Riggs v. Scrivner, Inc., 927 F.2d 1146 (10th Cir.1991); see § 5.21 *supra.*.

13. Fed. R. Civ. P. 38(b), (d). Some constitutions expressly provide for waiver, *see, e.g.,* the California provisions cited *supra* note 2; others, such as the provisions in the

The federal courts and most state courts hold that there is no constitutional barrier to legislative or judicial extension of jury trial to issues that were formerly equitable.[14] A few state constitutions provide for an extension of jury trial beyond those issues historically allotted to a jury;[15] a few others have construed their constitutions as guaranteeing the right of *nonjury* trial of equitable issues.[16] Barring these legislative or judicial extensions, a jury trial ordinarily is not constitutionally guaranteed to those seeking relief in equity.[17]

§ 8.2 Historical Test

Most constitutions preserve the right to jury trial on what may be called a "historical test."[1] The question then arises whether this freezes the right absolutely as it was in England in 1791 (for example), or whether it can accommodate extensions or contractions of jury trial and, if so, what the limits of such elasticity may be. Some aspects of this

Seventh Amendment and the Connecticut constitution (*supra* note 2), do not. In both cases there seems to be no doubt about the constitutionality of providing for waiver of jury trial unless unreasonable conditions are placed on obtaining it. Bennett v. Hillman, 37 Cal.App. 586, 174 P. 362 (1918); McKay v. Fair Haven & W.R.R., 75 Conn. 608, 54 A. 923 (1903); James, Trial by Jury and the New Federal Rules of Procedure, 45 Yale L.J. 1022, 1024–1025 (1936). For a case holding specific conditions to be unreasonable, see Labow v. Balthazor, 180 Wis. 419, 193 N.W. 244 (1923) ($24 fee in municipal court with civil jurisdiction not to exceed $1,000). The trial court may order a jury trial notwithstanding the failure of a party to demand it. *See* Annot., 6 A.L.R. Fed. 217.

14. *See* Beacon Theatres v. Westover, 359 U.S. 500, 510, 79 S.Ct. 948, 956, 3 L.Ed.2d 988, 997 (1959); Thermo-Stitch, Inc. v. Chemi-Cord Processing Corp., 294 F.2d 486, 490 (5th Cir.1961); Hurwitz v. Hurwitz, 136 F.2d 796, 798–799 (D.C.Cir. 1943). For state cases, see, e.g., Ely v. Early, 94 N.C. 1 (1886); Phillips v. Gorham, 17 N.Y. 270 (1858); Van Hecke, Trial by Jury in Equity Cases, 31 N.C.L. Rev. 157 (1953); Note, The Right to a Nonjury Trial, 74 Harv. L. Rev. 1176, 1179 (1961).

15. Tex. Const. art. 5, 10. North Carolina has so interpreted its constitutional provision. Lee v. Pearce, 68 N.C. 76 (1873). Decisions in Arizona, Massachusetts, and New Hampshire, all now overruled, so construed the constitutional provisions in those states. Georgia and Tennessee have long-standing statutes that provide for jury trial of issues of fact in equity cases. Other states have also experimented with this practice, only to abandon it. The whole subject is admirably set forth in Van Hecke, Trial by Jury in Equity Cases, 31 N.C.L. Rev. 157 (1953).

16. Brown v. Kalamazoo Circuit Judge, 75 Mich. 274, 42 N.W. 827 (1889); State v. Nieuwenhuis, 49 S.D. 181, 207 N.W. 77 (1926); Callanan v. Judd, 23 Wis. 343 (1868); Van Hecke, Trial by Jury in Equity Cases, 31 N.C.L. Rev. 157, 164, 166, 167, 171 (1953) (stating that there were seven such states and one federal circuit); Note, The Right to a Nonjury Trial, 74 Harv. L. Rev. 1176 (1961).

17. *See* 5 Moore, Federal Practice and Procedure ¶ 38.08; Chauffeurs, Teamsters & Helpers Local No. 391 v. Terry, 494 U.S. 558, 110 S.Ct. 1339, 108 L.Ed.2d 519 (1990); Kalish v. Franklin Advisers, Inc., 928 F.2d 590 (2d Cir.1991).

§ 8.2

1. The Seventh Amendment provides that "the right of trial by jury shall be preserved." In the states that have them, "the constitutional guarantees of jury trial in civil cases usually are phrased in strong but not very detailed language. The constitutional authors generally were content to provide that trial by jury 'shall remain inviolate forever,' 'shall remain inviolate,' 'shall be secured,' 'shall remain as heretofore,' etc.... At least implicitly the purport is that the right shall remain in substance as it was when the state constitutional provision was adopted." Hazard, Tait & Fletcher, Cases and Materials: Pleading and Procedure 1120 (8th ed. 1999).

question have not had the attention they deserve and have not received clear answers in judicial decisions. Because the Seventh Amendment right to jury trial in civil actions has not been held binding on the states, each state has been free to work out its own solution to the problem.

Overlap of law and equity

The right to jury trial generally attached to actions "at law" (hence actions within the jurisdiction of the common law courts) but not suits "in equity" (litigation within the jurisdiction of chancery). But, as of 1791, there was no clear division of jurisdiction between law and equity.[2] There were types of suits that once had been maintainable in equity but no longer could be; also, certain types of claims formerly maintainable in equity came to be maintainable also through common law forms of action. An instance of the former may be seen from early petitions asking the chancellor to grant ordinary legal remedies because of the corruption or political impotence of the regular courts, a branch of equity jurisdiction that withered and died in the fifteenth century.[3] An instance of the latter may be seen in the growth of general assumpsit, "especially that implied contract . . . of having undertaken to account for money received to another's use," which had become in Blackstone's time a legal action "almost as universally remedial as a bill in equity."[4] Many matters such as duress, fraud, and illegality, which had once been cognizable only in equity,[5] were familiar defenses to a legal action by the end of the eighteenth century.

On the other hand, chancellors came to try an ever-growing number of issues that they previously had left to be tried at law. There was a time, for instance, when equity was reluctant to grant specific performance if the existence of the contract was disputed; the parties, it was thought, should settle such disputes at law.[6] Later equity courts had no hesitation about deciding for themselves whether there was a contract.[7] Again, the notion developed that if a ground for equitable relief existed, equity would not stop with the granting of equitable relief but would (at

2. *See* § 1.5 *supra*.

3. 1 Holdsworth, A History of English Law 405, 406 (7th ed. 1956); Maitland, Equity 5, 6 (2d ed. 1936); Walsh, Equity ch. 2 (1930).

4. 3 Blackstone, Commentaries *432. Holdsworth thought that Blackstone exaggerated the extent to which law and equity had drawn together. Holdsworth, Blackstone's Treatment of Equity, 43 Harv. L. Rev. 1 (1929). But nothing in Holdsworth's comments impairs Blackstone's authority for propositions in the text.

5. *See* exposition in Cook, Equitable Defenses, 32 Yale L.J. 645 (1923). *Cf.* Hinton, Equitable Defenses Under Modern Codes, 18 Mich. L. Rev. 717 (1920).

6. Huddleston v. Briscoe, 11 Ves. Jr. 583, 32 Eng. Rep. 1215 (Ch. 1805). *Cf.* Colson v. Thompson, 15 U.S. (2 Wheat.) 336, 4 L.Ed. 253 (1817); Waters v. Howard, 1 Md.Ch. 112 (1847).

7. Rash v. Peoples Deposit Bank & Trust Co., 192 F.2d 470 (6th Cir.1951); Canister Co. v. Leahy, 182 F.2d 510 (3d Cir.1950); Mahon v. Bennett, 81 F.Supp. 901 (W.D.Mo.1948); Fraser v. Geist, 1 F.R.D. 267 (E.D.Pa.1940); Altoona Elec., Engg. & Supply Co. v. Kittanning & Ford City St. Ry. Co., 126 F. 559 (C.C.W.D.Pa. 1903).

least if plaintiff wished)[8] decide other aspects of the controversy, and this would often include issues that were ordinarily for the law courts.[9] Thus, if a plaintiff sought reformation of a contract for mutual mistake, the chancellor, if he found mutual mistake, would not only reform the contract but also try any remaining issues that would determine whether damages should be awarded for breach of the contract as reformed and would decree payment of the proper amount.[10] He would thus "clean up" the entire controversy in some circumstances.

Ordinarily, when the ground for equitable relief failed, the bill would be dismissed and the parties left to seek in the common law courts whatever legal remedies remained.[11] In 1786, however, an equity court decided not to dismiss the bill but to retain jurisdiction for the granting of legal relief when the ground for equitable relief (specific performance) failed only because of defendant's wrongful conduct after the suit was begun.[12] This granting of substituted legal relief in equity enjoyed a limited expansion after that.[13] In addition, equity recognized "standing to sue" of persons secondarily interested in enforcement of obligations that, in the law courts, could be enforced only by others. Examples are the right of an assignee to sue on a contract made originally with the assignor[14] and the right of a corporate stockholder to enforce an obligation in favor of the corporation that the directors refused to enforce directly on the corporation's behalf.[15]

The borrowing by each jurisdiction from the other was not accompanied by an equivalent sloughing off of functions.[16] This led to a very large

8. That it was at plaintiff's option seems clear from Whitchurch v. Golding, 2 P. Wms. 541, 24 Eng. Rep. 852 (Ch. 1729); Dormer v. Fortescue, 3 Atk. 124, 26 Eng. Rep. 875 (Ch. 1744); 1 Story, Equity Jurisprudence §§ 71, 82, 83 (14th ed. 1918).

9. Parker v. Dee, 2 Ch. Cas. 200, 22 Eng. Rep. 910 (Ch. 1674); Middletown Bank v. Russ, 3 Conn. 135 (1819); Rathbone v. Warren, 10 Johns 587 (1813).

10. 1 Story, Equity Jurisprudence § 161 (14th ed. 1918); Imperial Shale Brick Co. v. Jewett, 169 N.Y. 143, 62 N.E. 167 (1901).

11. Dowell v. Mitchell, 105 U.S. 430, 26 L.Ed. 1142 (1881); Linden Inv. Co. v. Honstain Bros. Co., 221 Fed. 178 (8th Cir.1915); 1 Pomeroy, Equity Jurisprudence §§ 237d, 237f (5th ed. 1941).

12. Denton v. Stewart, 1 Cox Ch. 258, 29 Eng. Rep. 1156 (Ch. 1786). *See also* Todd v. Gee, 17 Ves. Jr. 273, 34 Eng. Rep. 106 (Ch. 1810); Milkman v. Ordway, 106 Mass. 232, 255 (1870).

13. Gulbenkian v. Gulbenkian, 147 F.2d 173 (2d Cir.1945); Saperstein v. Mechanics' & Farmers' Sav. Bank, 228 N.Y. 257, 261, 126 N.E. 708, 709 (1920); McLennan v. Church, 163 Wis. 411, 158 N.W. 73 (1916); Levin, Equitable Clean-Up and the Jury: A Suggested Orientation, 100 U. Pa. L. Rev. 320 (1951); Jolowicz, Damages in Equity—A Study of Lord Cairns' Act, 34 Camb. L.J. 224 (1975); 1 Pomeroy, Equity Jurisprudence § 237 (5th ed. 1941).

14. *See* Cook, The Alienability of Choses in Action, 29 Harv. L. Rev. 816 (1916).

15. *See* Ross v. Bernhard, 396 U.S. 531, 90 S.Ct. 733, 24 L.Ed.2d 729 (1970).

16. Eyre v. Everett, 2 Russ. 381, 382, 38 Eng. Rep. 379 (Ch. 1826) ("this Court will not allow itself to be ousted of any part of its original jurisdiction, because a court of law happens to fall in love with the same or a similar jurisdiction"); Sweeny v. Williams, 36 N.J.Eq. 627, 629 (1883) ("When courts of law have of their own motion extended their jurisdiction over cases theretofore solely cognizable in equity, the jurisdiction of the latter courts has been in no respect abridged, although when the jurisdiction at law has become well established, the equity jurisdiction has been in some cases declined"); 1 Pomeroy, Equity Jurisprudence

overlap between law and equity. Many facts—fraud in the inducement, for instance—might have been presented and decided either at law or in equity, depending on the context in which they arose. Such overlapping jurisdiction was frequent in the traditional English procedural system, and was associated with competition for business between different courts.

Overlap in the United States

This process of borrowing continued in American jurisdictions, to some extent at least, even after the constitutions were adopted. The issue of fraud in the inducement as a defense to an action on a contract under seal was worked over into law during the nineteenth century.[17] During the same century, courts of equity came to try disputed issues of contract *vel non* (in specific performance),[18] nuisance *vel non* (in suits to enjoin nuisances),[19] and even, in some states, title *vel non* (in suits to enjoin trespasses).[20]

The notion of "cleanup" legal relief in equity enjoyed, as we have seen,[21] a limited extension during the nineteenth century. These steps were taken mostly without any indication that the courts were aware of the constitutional problems the steps involved. But the New York Court of Appeals faced the question squarely when in 1937 the constitutionality of an 1830 statute was challenged.[22] The statute authorized equity courts to enter deficiency decrees in mortgage foreclosure actions, a power that probably had been denied them before the statute. The majority of the court upheld the statute, noting that when equity properly took jurisdiction of a matter it generally decided all issues presented. Since the equity jurisdiction over foreclosures was clear, the former New York law requiring a second suit to get a deficiency decree was a deviation from general equity principles that the legislature might correct. The statute was enacted *after* the constitutional provision for a jury trial was adopted[23] but *before* completion of the union of law and

§§ 276–281a (5th ed. 1941). Pomeroy concludes: "The enlargement of the jurisdiction at law, by the ordinary process of legal development, has not, in general, affected the preexisting jurisdiction of equity." *Id.* at 618.

See also Kemp v. Prior, 7 Ves. Jr. 237, 249, 32 Eng. Rep. 96, 101 (Ch. 1802); Toulmin v. Price, 5 Ves. Jr. 235, 238–239, 31 Eng. Rep. 563, 565 (Ch. 1800); Viele v. Hoag, 24 Vt. 46 (1851).

17. Enelow v. New York Life Ins. Co., 293 U.S. 379, 55 S.Ct. 310, 79 L.Ed. 440 (1935); Prudential Ins. Co. v. Saxe, 134 F.2d 16 (D.C.Cir.1943), *cert. denied,* 319 U.S. 745, 63 S.Ct. 1033, 87 L.Ed. 1701 (1943).

The history of the matter is traced in Abbot, Fraud as a Defence at Law in the Federal Courts, 15 Colum. L. Rev. 489 (1915).

18. *See* note 7 *supra.*

19. Lewis, Injunctions Against Nuisances and the Rule Requiring the Plaintiff to Establish His Right at Law, 56 U. Pa. L. Rev. 289 (1908); Note, Trial by Jury in Suits to Enjoin Nuisances, 25 Colum. L. Rev. 641 (1925).

20. *See* Comment, 32 Yale L.J. 707, 709–710 (1923). *Cf.* Lewis, *supra* note 19.

21. *See* note 13 *supra.*

22. Jamaica Sav. Bank v. M. S. Investing Co., 274 N.Y. 215, 8 N.E.2d 493 (1937).

23. "The trial by jury in all cases in which it has been heretofore used shall remain inviolate forever." N.Y. Const. art.

equity (which made it possible for the two claims to be asserted in the same suit).

Legislative discretion

The decision clearly changes the historical position of jury trial. It can be justified on the ground that it was a proper incident of a legitimate procedural change (avoidance of two suits) rather than a bald contraction of jury trial. In short, the legislature has some latitude to change the scope of the jury trial right if doing so is a reasonably necessary incident to other procedural or substantive objectives and does not withdraw jury trial in an area where historically it has been firmly established. A similar rationale could support the Supreme Court's decision in *Katchen v. Landy,*[24] sustaining a statutory denial of jury trial that was designed to expedite bankruptcy proceedings.

Procedural factors and equity jurisdiction

At no time in history was the line dividing equity from law altogether—or even largely—the product of a rational choice between issues that were better suited to court or to jury trial. There is little to suggest that the chancellor's initial choice of a procedure borrowed from canon law reflected a considered rejection of jury trial.[25] Rather, the choice between law and equity frequently was based on other differences in the procedures of law and equity as they then stood. When equity procedure took shape, it differed from the procedure at law in several important respects.

Evidence in equity was produced largely by sworn pleadings and written depositions taken on written interrogatories,[26] which afforded a

1, § 2. These words have "been part of the fundamental law of the state since the adoption of the Constitution in 1821." Loughran, J., dissenting in Jamaica Sav. Bank v. M. S. Investing Co., 274 N.Y. 215, 224, 8 N.E.2d 493, 496 (1937). The majority took no issue with this statement.

24. 382 U.S. 323, 86 S.Ct. 467, 15 L.Ed.2d 391 (1966).

25. Thus, there is no mention of a desire or choice to reject jury trial in the standard accounts of the origins of equity. *See, e.g.,* 3 Blackstone, Commentaries *50–53, *434–455 (pointing to fact that many early chancellors were clergy); 1 Story, Equity Jurisprudence ch. 2 (14th ed. 1918); Kerly, An Historical Sketch of the Equitable Jurisdiction of the Court of Chancery 81 (1890) (case in 1374 shows the subpoena and the examination of defendant already in regular use by Council, "having been borrowed perhaps by the Chancellors and other Canonists who sat in it from the procedure of the Courts Christian where both had long been established") and ch. 5 (cases on common law side of chancery referred to jury, but cases on equity side so referred only exceptionally). *See generally* 1 Holdsworth, A History of English Law ch. 5 (7th ed. 1956); Maitland, Equity 5 (2d ed. 1936); Plucknett, A Concise History of the Common Law 163–165, 178–181, 675–684 (5th ed. 1956); 1 Pomeroy, Equity Jurisprudence §§ 30–37 (5th ed. 1941); Walsh, Equity ch. 2 (1930).

26. The equity procedure in the eighteenth century is described in 3 Blackstone, Commentaries *442–455. For an account of the taking of evidence in an earlier case, see Kerly, An Historical Sketch of the Equitable Jurisdiction of the Court of Chancery 68–69 (1890). See also Macnair, The Law of Proof in Early Modern Equity (1999).

In New York, the old method was to have testimony in equity cases taken before masters and examiners in chancery, a cumbersome and expensive practice. The Constitu-

measure of pretrial discovery unavailable at law. At law the parties to an action were neither competent nor compellable to testify,[27] whereas in equity each party could offer its own sworn statements and "probe the conscience" of its adversary by propounding written interrogatories, which had to be answered under oath.[28] The chancellor used remedies (notably injunctions) unavailable to the law courts, and the chancellor could handle multiple parties and multiple claims in a way that the law courts had not developed.[29] Trials at law, however, involved oral presentation of testimony, cross-examination, and the jury's capacity to supply standards of "reasonableness" and to assess credibility.

Until the unification of legal and equitable procedure, it was not possible fully to "factor out" these differences and so put squarely the issue whether jury trial was desirable for resolving any given type of factual issue. Thus, even when the allocation of issues between the jurisdictions was based on rational considerations, it would often be dictated by some factor other than jury trial. When the chancellor was faced with a prickly question of credibility of witnesses, his rational desire for the benefits of demeanor evidence could be satisfied only by sending the issue to the law court with its jury.[30] When an accounting between business associates was sought and the inquiry was to include testimony of the parties (the two witnesses who could shed the most—sometimes the only—light on the matter), it would have to be conducted in equity, where the chancellor would decide questions of fact without a jury. The same thing was true when specific performance of a contract was appropriate rather than damages for its breach or when unnecessary multiplicity of suits was to be prevented.[31] To put it colloquially, jury trial (or court trial) was often merely the tail of the dog under a system in which you had to take the whole dog.

Nonprocedural factors and equity jurisdiction

In addition to these considerations, the allocation of a dispute to either law or equity was often made on the basis of considerations

tion of 1846, which paved the way for the Field Code, contained a provision that "testimony in equity cases shall be taken in like manner as in cases at law." Art. 6, § 10. *See* New York, Report of the Debates and Proceedings of the Constitutional Convention of 1846, at 782–785.

27. 2 Wigmore, Evidence §§ 575–577 (Chadbourn rev. 1979).

28. 3 Blackstone, Commentaries *442–451. The bill and answer might be supplemented by affidavits. The bill itself contained not only statements of fact but interrogatories propounded to defendant. 1 Pomeroy, Equity Jurisdiction 191 (5th ed. 1941). "The first answer was ... rarely deemed sufficient, and second, third, fourth and further answers might be ordered on the Master's Certificate, the defendant paying ... costs as ordered...." Kerly, An Historical Sketch of the Equitable Jurisdiction of the Court of Chancery 120 (1890).

29. 1 Pomeroy, Equity Jurisdiction §§ 37, 108–117, 243–275 (5th ed. 1941).

30. For an account of the procedural devices by which this was done, see Chesnin and Hazard, Chancery Procedure and the Seventh Amendment: Jury Trial of Issues in Equity Cases Before 1791, 83 Yale L.J. 999 (1974).

31. Levin, Equitable Clean-Up and the Jury: A Suggested Orientation, 100 U. Pa. L. Rev. 320 (1951).

relevant to the long political struggle between the king and Parliament in England. These considerations had little to do with the efficient administration of justice.[32] And, while the jury occasionally became a symbol and a bone of contention in this struggle,[33] yet here, too, many factors other than the mode of trial often dominated the allocation of subject matter. Indeed, equity sometimes acquired jurisdiction simply because the chancellors rejected on the merits the rules applied to the law courts or were less constrained by precedent than those courts.

It would be a mistake, of course, to suppose that chancellors were never concerned with the jury trial problem in taking or refusing jurisdiction. One reason often given for assuming equitable jurisdiction over an accounting was the difficulty of the case for a jury.[34] The issue of mutual mistake in written instruments may well have been kept from juries out of fear that they might be too ready to upset, on uncritical emotional grounds, the stability that written instruments ought to represent.[35] But when equity courts refused to try disputed questions of legal title in suits to enjoin trespasses, the appropriateness of trying such a dispute to a jury was often stressed.[36]

Although the scope of the jury trial right was not a major issue in England, it has been so in the United States. As previously noted, most state constitutions adopted during the Revolutionary War had express provisions for jury trial, some expanding the right beyond its common law boundaries.[37] The jury trial issue was also a major political controversy in the adoption of the U.S. Constitution. It has been convincingly shown that the Seventh Amendment was a necessary concession by the

32. These struggles are recounted in the sources cited *supra* note 25. *See, e.g.*, Kerly, An Historical Sketch of the Equitable Jurisdiction of the Court of Chancery chs. 4, 7, 10 (1890); 1 Holdsworth, A History of English Law 459–465 (7th ed. 1956); Walsh, Equity 5, 6 (1930). *See also* the majority and dissenting opinions in Parklane Hosiery Co. v. Shore, 439 U.S. 322, 99 S.Ct. 645, 58 L.Ed.2d 552 (1979).

33. Thus, in Heath v. Ridley, Cro. Jac. 335, 79 Eng. Rep. 286 (K.B. 1614), the court reasoned that after a common law judgment "the party ought to be quiet, and to submit thereto" rather than resort to chancery, "for neither writ of error nor attaint can be brought to reverse the decrees [of chancery]; otherwise it is upon trials at the common law; for all matters are there decided either by a jury of twelve men, against whom (if they err in their verdict) an attaint lieth; or by the judges, where if they err in their judgment, the party aggrieved may bring his writ of error." The notion seems to be that the chancellor should not use his extraordinary power to interfere with a composite, appealable judgment representing to some extent the popular and parliamentary side.

34. *See, e.g.*, Bennett v. United Lumber & Supply Co., 110 Conn. 536, 538, 148 A. 369 (1930); Ludlow v. Simond, 2 Cai. Cas. 1, 51–53 (N.Y.Ch.1804). *Cf.* Story, Equity Jurisprudence 425 (14th ed. 1918).*Compare* A Historical Inquiry into the Right to Trial by Jury in Complex Civil Litigation, 128 U. Pa. L. Rev. 829 (1980) *with* Devlin, Jury Trial of Complex Cases: English Practice at the Time of the Seventh Amendment, 80 Colum. L. Rev. 43 (1980).

35. McCormick, The Parol Evidence Rule as a Procedural Device for Control of the Jury, 41 Yale L.J. 365 (1932); 9 Wigmore, Evidence § 2426 at 87 (Chadbourn rev. 1981).

36. Freer v. Davis, 52 W.Va. 1, 43 S.E. 164 (1903). *Cf.* Attorney General v. Cleaver, 18 Ves. Jr. 211, 217–218, 34 Eng. Rep. 297, 299 (Ch. 1811); Appeal of McClain, 130 Pa. 546, 562, 18 A. 1066 (1890) (both nuisance cases).

37. *See* § 8.1 note 15 *supra.*

Federalists in order to obtain ratification of the Constitution.[38] It also seems fair to say that the ambiguity of the Seventh Amendment is at least partly attributable to this political background. The language of the Amendment provides that the jury trial right is "preserved." In the face of the variant and unsettled practice in the states and in England, this language left almost as much unsettled as it resolved. The drafters doubtless could have sought greater precision, but that might have intensified the political conflict and precluded adoption of the compromise.

Ambiguity of history

The Seventh Amendment and state jury-trial guaranties thus are formulated in historical terms, but the historical frame of reference is highly ambiguous. The jurisdiction of law and equity was indistinct in a broad, irregular band of situations. Hence, no distinct boundary marked the province of law and, therefore, the province of jury trial. Moreover, the provinces of law and equity had been undergoing change both before and after 1791. The jurisdictional boundary between law and equity thus was not only indistinct but also shifting. Jury trial was only one feature of procedure on the law side, and in some situations it was less important than other features such as the availability of discovery and the competence of party witnesses. Decisions on whether a matter was at "law" or in "equity," which would carry with them a determination of jury trial right, often were influenced by considerations extraneous to the question of jury trial. And in this country, if not in England, the right to jury trial was politically important both in practice and as a symbol of popular participation in the administration of justice. In a time before large bureaucracies, the jury was a central institution of government before which almost any governmental act could be brought. The question whether a matter was jury-triable of right, while it could be a technical legal issue, always was freighted with these political implications.

A historical test for determining the right to jury trial cannot escape the uncertainties summarized above. Nevertheless, the historical test has compelling attractions. The Seventh Amendment and counterpart state constitutional provisions are framed in historical terms—they "preserve" the right to jury trial. The specific language of a constitutional provision is not always decisive, and is never fully sufficient, in interpreting a constitution. But such language cannot be ignored. At minimum, there has to be very good reason, implicit if not explicit, for reaching a conclusion at variance with the literal meaning. Also, when a court seeks to justify a decision that extends or contracts the scope of the jury trial guaranty, it encounters most of the problems that historically

38. *See* Wolfram, The Constitutional History of the Seventh Amendment, 57 Minn. L. Rev. 639 (1973).

have attended jury trial. Boundaries between procedural systems are difficult to draw, tend to be unstable, involve considerations extraneous to the immediate problem, and often involve sensitive political questions. Using a historical test, or at least purporting to use such a test, can be a welcome refuge when one is struggling with these difficulties.

§ 8.3 Modern Application of Historical Test

Under a merged procedure, few differences between law and equity persist besides the mode of trial. No longer must all the procedures of a litigation be taken as a package, either legal or equitable. A single court is charged with applying the whole law of the land and drawing from it whatever is appropriate to any civil action. All trials are conducted by oral examination of available witnesses in court. Parties are competent and can be compelled to testify on any issue. There is no reason, apart from history, why sharply disputed issues of fact in an action seeking specific performance of a contract should not be tried to a jury if that mode of trial is thought preferable. And there is no reason other than history to keep a court from assigning a complicated construction contract case for court trial if the issues are deemed to be beyond the competence of the jury.

Modified historical approach

The considerations discussed above suggest that the historical test of jury trial right embodied in our constitutions is probably not well adapted to the merged or unified procedures of the present day: The test carries too much deadwood from the past. A critical use of history may be an excellent guide to present problems, but it also takes account of changes in conditions as well as similarities. Moreover, courts are increasingly confronted by causes of action that did not exist when there were separate law and equity courts; applying the law-equity distinction to such claims is an essay in historical fiction. The historical constitutional test is with us, however, and probably will remain because people are unlikely to agree on any formula for restating the right to jury trial.[1] If so, then the above considerations argue in favor of an elastic construction of the historical test by the courts.

Evidence of such an approach appears in the Supreme Court's decision in *Ross v. Bernhard*.[2] That case involved a stockholder's suit (traditionally within equity jurisdiction) in which the claim asserted by the stockholder on behalf of the corporation was jury triable if it had been sued on by the corporation itself. Plaintiff argued that once it was shown that the stockholder properly brought the suit (the equitable component of the claim), the claim itself should be jury triable. The Supreme Court upheld this contention, observing that

§ 8.3

1. *Compare* ABA Standards Relating to Trial Courts § 2.10, Commentary.

2. 396 U.S. 531, 90 S.Ct. 733, 24 L.Ed.2d 729 (1970).

> [a]s our cases indicate, the "legal" nature of an issue is determined by considering, first, the premerger custom with reference to such questions; second, the remedy sought; and, third, the practical abilities and limitations of juries.[3]

Similarly, the Court has decided that a defendant in a civil penalty action has the right to a jury trial on whether a violation occurred but that Congress may designate a judge to fix the appropriate penalty.[4] More questionably, the Court has held that a party could no longer seek a permanent injunction against threats of suit, and hence could no longer bring its case before a judge, because novel legal remedies made equitable relief unnecessary.[5]

Such methods of chopping up and reclassifying claims could radically alter the traditional approach to jury trials. The courts have proceeded thus far with restraint. In *Ross v. Bernhard,* for example, the Court simply allowed in a derivative suit the right to a jury trial that would have existed had the corporation itself sued.[6] But even assuming that traditional claims retain for the most part their classification as legal or equitable, problems arise when new claims are brought or when several claims and defenses are asserted within a single action. Modern procedural systems thus give the jury trial problem a new character.

Admiralty procedures

There is no constitutional right to a jury trial in admiralty suits,[7] with a few exceptions such as maritime claims brought under the "saving to suitors" clause of the Judiciary Act of 1789. This provision saves "to suitors in all cases all other remedies to which they are otherwise entitled."[8] Jury trial also is available in certain statutory maritime actions, notably the Merchant Marine (Jones) Act, which allows sailors to sue their employer for job-related injuries.

B. JURY TRIAL PROBLEMS OF UNIFIED PROCEDURE

§ 8.4 Choice of Mode of Trial at Common Law

The jury trial problem as we know it today is a product of the unified procedure; it had no counterpart under the old system, although

3. 396 U.S. at 538 n.10. The second of these factors has eclipsed the other two. *See* Chauffeurs, Teamsters & Helpers Local No. 391 v. Terry, 494 U.S. 558, 110 S.Ct. 1339, 108 L.Ed.2d 519 (1990); Tull v. United States, 481 U.S. 412, 107 S.Ct. 1831, 95 L.Ed.2d 365 (1987).

4. Tull v. United States, 481 U.S. 412, 107 S.Ct. 1831, 95 L.Ed.2d 365 (1987). But see Feltner v. Columbia Pictures Television, Inc., 523 U.S. 340, 118 S.Ct. 1279, 140 L.Ed.2d 438 (1998), rejecting as unhistorical the argument that a judge should assess statutory damages in a copyright action otherwise tried by jury. See generally Murphy, Judicial Assessment of Legal Remedies, 94 Nw. U.L. Rev. 153 (1999).

5. Beacon Theatres v. Westover, 359 U.S. 500, 79 S.Ct. 948, 3 L.Ed.2d 988 (1959), discussed in § 8.11 *infra.*

6. *See* § 8.6 *infra.*

7. *See* Fed. R. Civ. P. 38(e). *See also* Durden v. Exxon Corp., 803 F.2d 845 (5th Cir.1986).

8. 28 U.S.C. § 1333.

some problems concerning jury trial were presented even before merger. We have seen how chancellors would sometimes decline to take jurisdiction for fear of trespassing on the right to a jury, and how they would at other times take jurisdiction because of the unsuitability of jury trial.[1] But once it was conceded or determined that a case was in the proper court, the mode of trial followed almost automatically. For trial of the issues made by the pleadings, a jury was all a law court had to offer. Except for a discretionary advisory jury, court trial was all that equity would afford. This simplicity was purchased, however, at the price of much hardship and waste through double actions to get complete relief and frequent dismissals of meritorious claims brought to the wrong forum.

Any true merger of law and equity avoids the hardships of the old system. To do so it provides that all relief, legal and equitable, may be sought in a single action—and must be when it arises out of a single transaction or occurrence.[2] Thus, many modern civil actions comprise more than any action could before the merger. But when this aspect of merger is coupled with a constitutional guaranty of jury trial geared to the old system, complex problems arise.

Plaintiff's ability to shape claim

The merger of law and equity had a profound effect on the technical form in which the question of right to jury trial was posed. When the courts of law and equity were separate, the court in any lawsuit could ask whether the action or suit was properly within its jurisdiction.

The answer to that question depended on whether the action, if in a common law court, presented a common law claim, and, if in a court of equity, whether the suit presented a claim within equity's jurisdiction as contemporaneously defined. The answer to this question thus determined whether jury trial was as of right. In this country, particularly in the federal system, law and equity proceedings were held before the same court. But they were conducted according to different procedure, the common law forms of action being used on the law side and modernized chancery procedure being used on the equity side.[3] Hence, the question would still arise whether the suit properly presented a common law action or a claim within equity's "jurisdiction." The answer to this question again would ordinarily determine the question of jury trial. In the area of overlap between law and equity, plaintiffs could

§ 8.4

1. *See* § 8.2 *supra.*

2. Hennepin Paper Co. v. Fort Wayne Corrugated Paper Co., 153 F.2d 822 (7th Cir.1946); Gilbert v. Boak Fish Co., 86 Minn. 365, 90 N.W. 767 (1902); Hahl v. Sugo, 169 N.Y. 109, 62 N.E. 135 (1901); James, Trial by Jury and the New Federal Rules of Procedure, 45 Yale L.J. 1022, 1026 n.29 (1936). *See also* Restatement (Second) of Judgments § 24.

3. *See* § 1.7 *supra.*

frame the claim as they chose and thus influence, if not always determine, whether jury trial would be as of right.

A modern example of this maneuver is *American Life Insurance Co. v. Stewart.*[4] The insurance company issued a life insurance policy; following the insured's death, the beneficiary made a claim for payment, but the company denied payment on the ground that the policy had been procured by fraud. The insurance company brought an action to cancel the policy (historically an equitable remedy) before the beneficiary could bring an action for the proceeds of the policy (historically a common law action). Since the claim first filed was framed as an equitable complaint, the action was treated as in equity and the judge decided the crucial issue of fraud; that issue would have been jury triable had the beneficiary sued first.

With the unification of procedure, however, the situation has changed. Unification involves the use of one form of procedure (jury trial excepted), whatever the basis of the claim. Unification came about in many of the states through adoption of the Field Code in the nineteenth century. Unification came about in the federal court system through adoption of the Federal Rules in 1938. In each situation, the former distinctive procedures of law and equity were replaced by one procedure (jury trial excepted) that operated regardless of the claim being asserted. Hence, after unification it was no longer possible to determine whether the case was at law or in equity simply by looking at the form of the complaint. Rather, using a historical approach it would be necessary to ask whether the nature of the claim—not its pleading form—was legal or equitable.

§ 8.5 Provisions for Mode of Trial in Merged Systems

To meet the jury trial problem the Field Code contained a provision that was widely copied in other early codes:

> Whenever, in an action for the recovery of *money only,* or of *specific* real or personal *property,* there shall be an issue of fact, it must be tried by a jury, unless a jury trial be waived, as provided in section 221, or a reference be ordered, as provided in sections 225 and 226 [emphasis supplied].[1]

This provision essentially treated all claims for money as actions at law for purposes of jury trial—what might be called a "remedy" test.

Another section of this code, also widely copied, provided for waiver of jury trial by written consent of the parties filed with the clerk, by oral

4. 300 U.S. 203, 57 S.Ct. 377, 81 L.Ed. 605 (1937).

§ 8.5

1. N.Y. Sess. Laws ch. 379, at § 208 (1848). The present provision is not greatly different. N.Y. Civ. Prac. L. & R. 4101.

consent in open court entered in the minutes, or by failure to appear at the trial.[2]

Problems with Field Code

These provisions proved faulty. The remedy test was unsatisfactory because it specified the action as the unit to be dealt with rather than the component claim or issue. Also, it overlooked the fact that equity sometimes awarded money only (for example, by imposing a constructive trust) and also sometimes awarded specified property (for example, by granting specific performance). If the New York statute had been construed to include these types of actions, the result would have been a radical expansion of jury trial.[3]

The Field Code provision on waiver of jury trial also was unsatisfactory: It often failed to settle the question of jury trial until the time of the trial, and it required affirmative steps for waiver so that inertia or sloth might yield jury trial even when the parties were indifferent to the question.

Federal Rules approach

Because of the difficulties with the earlier provisions, some of the later codes (notably that of Connecticut)[4] and the Federal Rules of Civil Procedure[5] adopted a different type of provision to govern the mode of trial and the matter of waiver of right to jury trial. The salient features of these later provisions are as follows:

1. They do not set up a self-contained test for matters triable to a jury but instead adopt the constitutional test, that is, that jury trial is "preserved."[6]
2. They specify the issue, rather than the entire action, as the unit to be dealt with in determining the right to jury trial, thus explicitly providing for the trial of some issues to the court and other issues to a jury, all in the same civil action.[7]
3. They require an affirmative demand for jury trial at some pretrial stage in the action and provide for waiver of jury trial if no such demand is made,[8] thus isolating well before trial those

2. N.Y. Sess. Laws ch. 379, at § 221 (1848). *Cf.* N.Y. Civil Practice Act § 426 (1920); N.Y. Civ. Prac. L. & R. 4102.

3. *See* § 8.11 *infra.*

4. *See* Conn. Gen. Stat. § 52–215 (1975).

5. Fed. R. Civ. P. 38(b), (d).

6. *See* McCoid, Procedural Reform and the Right to Jury Trial, 116 U. Pa. L. Rev. 1 (1967); Note, the Right to Jury Trial Under Merged Procedures, 65 Harv. L. Rev. 453 (1952); New York Advisory Comm. on Practice and Procedure, Second Preliminary Report 559–577 (1958).

7. *Compare* Fed. R. Civ. P. 38(b) & (d) *with* Fed. R. Civ. P. 42(b).

8. Fed. R. Civ. P. 38(b); *e.g.,* N.Y. Civ. Prac. L. & R. 4102. *See, e.g.,* Favors v. Coughlin, 877 F.2d 219 (2d Cir.1989); Sound Video Unlimited v. Video Shack Inc., 700 F.Supp. 127 (S.D.N.Y.1988).

cases in which there is to be a jury trial or a problem about jury trial.

The Supreme Court has held that since "the right of jury trial is fundamental, courts indulge every reasonable presumption against waiver."[9] The presumption may operate where a party expresses a desire for a jury trial in a manner not procedurally correct or not fulfilling the requirements of Rule 38. A party objecting to the claimed method of trial may raise the issue in federal court by filing a motion for a new trial in district court or an appeal in an appellate court.[10] If the appellate court finds the method to be in error but the judgment to be correct, it can treat the error as nonprejudicial.[11] The objection to the mode of trial must be timely, and the court will not, on its own initiative, find that the right to a jury trial does not exist.

A party that has requested a jury trial may be held to have waived that right if the party fails to object to an explicit court order specifying trial by a judge.[12] So, too, an implicit waiver of the right to a jury trial may be found when a party fails to object when the jury is discharged and the trial proceeds without it.[13] Because of the decline in jury trial requests and the increasing proportion of cases settled without a trial, only 1 or 2 percent of civil actions ever reach a jury; the jury verdicts that are reached, however, influence settlements in other cases, and in tort litigation the jury still predominates.[14]

Reverting to historical test

Apart from the procedures for demanding jury trial, the provisions of the Field Code and newer Federal Rules were alike in that they both referred to the historical test for the right to jury trial. As was already noted, the New York code used language that would extend jury trial to actions that, like common law actions generally, involved claims for money only or for recovery of specific property.[15] This would have brought actions for accounting, for example, and perhaps for specific performance of land-sale contracts, both formerly equitable suits, within the jury trial right. But the courts in the nineteenth century to a large extent ignored this intention and construed the code provision to be merely declaratory of the constitutional provision.[16] That interpretation returned the question to the historical test.

9. Aetna Ins. Co. v. Kennedy, 301 U.S. 389, 393, 57 S.Ct. 809, 811–812, 81 L.Ed. 1177, 1180 (1937).

10. Perez-Serrano v. DeLeon–Velez, 868 F.2d 30 (1st Cir.1989).

11. Skippy, Inc. v. CPC Intl., 674 F.2d 209 (4th Cir.1982); In re N–500L Cases, 691 F.2d 15 (1st Cir.1982).

12. *See* Royal Am. Managers, Inc. v. IRC Holding Corp., 885 F.2d 1011 (2d Cir. 1989); Sewell v. Jefferson County Fiscal Court, 863 F.2d 461 (6th Cir.1988).

13. *See, e.g.,* Pope v. Savings Bank of Puget Sound, 850 F.2d 1345 (9th Cir.1988).

14. Galanter, The Civil Jury as Regulator of the Litigation Process, 1990 U. Chi. Legal F. 201.

15. *See* New York, First Commissioners Report 185 (1848).

16. *See* Clark, Code Pleading § 16 (2d ed. 1947); 4 Weinstein, Korn, and Miller, New York Civil Practice §§ 4101.04–4101.08. *See also* Walsh, Merger of Law and

A different approach, however, was also possible. This approach began with the observation that merger of law and equity made available in *all* actions the procedural advantages formerly available only in equity—joinder of multiple claims and parties, discovery through interrogatories and depositions, award of both damages and injunctive relief in the same action, and so on. From this premise, the remedy at law would cease to be inadequate in these procedural aspects because these procedures were now available at law. It would follow that the merged procedure of the codes simultaneously reduced the "jurisdiction" of equity and enlarged the "jurisdiction" of law. Jury trial therefore, would be available in all actions under the new merged procedure.[17]

Judicial attitude

The latter approach was not taken by any court until the middle of the twentieth century for two reasons. First, the approach required a strained and simplistic analysis of history, as we shall see more fully in the discussion that follows. Second, it would have been premised on an unequivocal commitment to the virtue of jury trial that the courts of the nineteenth and early twentieth century simply did not share. It is important to keep in mind that beneath all the technical discussion of the historical test was a conscious judicial aversion to jury trial, especially in the federal courts and the court systems of the northeastern states.[18]

There is no evidence, however, that the drafters of either the codes or the Federal Rules intended a wholesale expansion of the right to jury trial. Hence, the problem posed to the courts was this: What is the scope of the jury trial right when that right is "preserved" in terms of a distinction (between law and equity) that has been abolished (by merger)? The problem is unsolvable.[19] The courts for the most part "solved" it piecemeal through rules of thumb purporting to be deduced from the historical test. The commentators have struggled to formulate more generalized resolutions, with only limited success.[20] At least for a while, the federal courts (but not all the states), guided by *Beacon Theatres v. Westover,*[21] solved it by finding a strong, implicit preference for jury trial in the Seventh Amendment.

Equity Under Codes and other Statutes, 6 N.Y.U. L. Rev. 157 (1929).

17. This is the approach taken in Beacon Theatres v. Westover, 359 U.S. 500, 79 S.Ct. 948, 3 L.Ed.2d 988 (1959). *See generally* McCoid, Procedural Reform and the Right to Jury Trial, 116 U. Pa. L. Rev. 1 (1967). *See* §§ 8.8–8.11 *infra.*

18. The literature of the debate is extensive. *See* Kalven and Zeisel, The American Jury 4 n.2 (1966); Symposium, Is the Jury Competent?, 52 Law & Contemp. Probs., Autumn 1989; Symposium, The Role of the Jury in Civil Dispute Resolution, 1990 U. Chi. Legal F. The attitude of the bar seems to have changed in recent years. *See* ABA Standards Relating to Trial Courts § 2.10. See also § 7.7 *supra.*

19. See the highly sophisticated analysis in the majority and dissenting opinions in Damsky v. Zavatt, 289 F.2d 46 (2d Cir. 1961).

20. *See* 5 Moore, Federal Practice and Procedure ¶ 38.16; *compare* 9 Wright and Miller, Federal Practice and Procedure § 2302.

21. 359 U.S. 500, 79 S.Ct. 948, 3 L.Ed.2d 988 (1959). The change in the com-

Special characteristics of jury trial

The deeper difficulty with the historical test is that it tends to foreclose renewed and continuing judicial inquiry into the suitability of different types of issues for jury trial in a modern context. To a certain extent the constitutions themselves foreclose such inquiry. And perhaps it may be assumed that the distinction between law and equity—though it did not to any great extent arise from this consideration—came to reflect, at least in part, the pragmatic judgment of what matters were suitable for jury trial. The question of suitability of jury trial, however, is not simply one of efficiency or procedural policy in the narrow sense. Trial by jury rather than to the court involves a collective decision rather than a decision by a single mind; it applies lay rather than professional concepts of relevance and justice, class differences insofar as jurors on the average have socioeconomic backgrounds and frames of reference that are different from those of the average judge, and, perhaps, differences in the configuration of sympathy and skepticism with which the human mind resolves particular types of conflicts.[22] In short, jury trial often makes a difference, which, of course, explains why it is a constitutional issue.[23]

For the most part, any fundamental argument on the issue must be addressed to either those bodies entrusted with the power to amend constitutions, or to legislatures, or to courts in their rulemaking (rather than their adjudicative) capacity. For good or evil, both the constitutions and the charters of the merged procedure embody the deliberate policy judgment to leave the extent of jury trial where history has come to place it. It may well be doubted whether it lies within the proper sphere of the judicial process to nullify that judgment, although these considerations deserve some room in interpreting statutes and rules (as well as constitutions) and in resolving doubtful lessons of history. But that still leaves many specific situations in which a plausible result could be reached either in favor of or against jury trial.

Time for demanding jury trial

The procedures for demanding a jury trial are specified in Rules 38 and 39. The basic time limit is not later than ten days after the service of

position of the Supreme Court in the 1970s has resulted in a pattern of decisions that is less supportive of jury trial. *See* Atlas Roofing Co. v. Occupational Safety and Health Review Commn., 430 U.S. 442, 97 S.Ct. 1261, 51 L.Ed.2d 464 (1977). For state court decisions rejecting the *Beacon Theatres* approach, see Hiatt v. Yergin, 152 Ind.App. 497, 284 N.E.2d 834 (1972); Lanman Lithotech, Inc. v. Gurwitz, 478 So.2d 425 (Fla.App.1985).

22. The relevance of these considerations becomes clear in the question of the procedures used for selecting jurors. *See* ABA Standards Relating to Trial Courts §§ 2.10, 2.61; McKusick and Boxer, Uniform Jury Selection and Service Act, 8 Harv. J. Legis. 280 (1971); Vanderzell, The Jury as a Community Cross-Section, 19 W. Pol. Q. 136 (1966); Note, Grand Jury Selection: Voter Registration Lists as a Cross Section of the Community, 52 Or. L. Rev. 482 (1973).

23. *See generally* Kalven and Zeisel, The American Jury (1966).

the last pleading directed to such issue.[24] For removal actions, the time limit is within ten days of service of the notice of filing of the removal petition.[25] Failing these deadlines, a party may move under Rule 39(b) that the court in its discretion order a jury trial. Despite the general principle favoring jury trial, an appellate court will not reverse for the denial of a Rule 39(b) motion if the moving party *inadvertently* failed to demand a jury trial.[26] It is said that "waiver [of a jury trial] by failure to make a timely demand is complete even though it was inadvertent, unintended and regardless of the explanation or excuse."[27] A party's knowing participation in a bench trial will be taken as a waiver of a jury trial.[28]

§ 8.6 Civil Actions That Are Counterparts of Former Law Actions or Equity Suits

Many suits today are no more than the counterpart of a former action at law. The typical personal injury suit furnishes a ready example. Other suits present facts and claims that would have been cognizable only in equity. A suit to foreclose a mortgage[1] is a good illustration of a "routine" type of equity suit; suits for injunctions addressed to future conduct, such as those dealing with school desegregation, are likewise readily classifiable as equitable. In cases like these the jury trial problem under merged procedure is no more difficult than it was under a divided procedure.[2] The jury trial right stands where it did before.

Rejecting the historical analogy

Other modern counterparts of old equity suits can be approached in the same way. An important illustration is the stockholder's derivative suit which, as we have seen,[3] was cognizable only in equity even though the claim asserted in behalf of the corporation was one for money damages against someone who allegedly had injured the corporation. In state courts, such a suit is still generally treated as one in equity so that jury trial is not available on the issues concerning injury and damage to the corporation.[4] But the Supreme Court has held that the matter of the

24. Fed. R. Civ. P. 38(b).

25. *Id.* 81(c).

26. *See* O'Malley v. United States Fidelity and Guar. Co., 776 F.2d 494 (5th Cir. 1985); Farias v. Bexar County Bd. of Trustees for Mental Health Retardation Servs., 925 F.2d 866 (5th Cir.1991); United States v. Premises Known as 417 E. Grand Ave., Garland County, Hot Springs, Ark., 761 F.Supp. 657 (W.D.Ark.1991).

27. 9 Wright and Miller, Federal Practice and Procedure § 2321 (quoted in Scharnhorst v. Independent School Dist. No. 710, 686 F.2d 637 (8th Cir.1982)).

28. Royal Am. Managers v. IRC Holding Corp., 885 F.2d 1011 (2d Cir.1989).

§ 8.6

1. *See* § 8.2 notes 22–23 *supra.*

2. *See, e.g.,* Cayman Music, Ltd. v. Reichenberger, 403 F.Supp. 794 (W.D.Wis. 1975). Even here, however, the question of jury trial arises in connection with imposition of sanctions for contempt. *See* Muniz v. Hoffman, 422 U.S. 454, 95 S.Ct. 2178, 45 L.Ed.2d 319 (1975).

3. *See* § 8.2 note 15 *supra.*

4. *See, e.g.,* Rankin v. Frebank Co., 47 Cal.App.3d 75, 121 Cal.Rptr. 348 (1975).

stockholder's standing to sue, formerly recognized only in equity, is an insufficient basis for regarding the issues of injury and damages to the corporation as also equitable; accordingly, jury trial on those issues is available to the plaintiff.[5] Thus, even a clear analogy to a historical equity suit can be rejected in favor of jury trial.

The more difficult problems in a unified procedure are presented by that peculiar product of union, the civil action that contains more in the way of claims or defenses than any suit could have contained in the old days. The plaintiff may inject both legal and equitable claims in the complaint, or an equitable defense or counterclaim may be interposed to an action presenting only legal issues or vice versa. And there may be combinations of these situations in a single action.

§ 8.7 Classification of Claims as Legal or Equitable

Many, if not most, civil actions brought today assert claims that did not exist when constitutional provisions preserving the right to jury trial were enacted. Some of those claims are statutory; others represent new developments in the common law. Because constitutional jury trial provisions apply to claims created by modern law,[1] courts must classify them as legal or equitable.

When the legislature indicates a preference for trial by either jury or judge, courts have almost always implemented that preference. Indeed, they have been alert to seek out a legislative preference.[2] Yet the constitutional trial provisions prevent a legislative preference for trial by judge from prevailing in some instances.[3] Often, moreover, the legislature implies no preference; courts must then classify a claim as legal or equitable.

Remedial test

The remedy sought provides the most straightforward and influential guide to classification.[4] A claim for damages is legal; one for injunctive relief, including specific performance, is equitable.

But the remedial test is not always simple to apply. Courts of equity could grant monetary remedies, usually in the form of restitution for

5. Ross v. Bernhard, 396 U.S. 531, 90 S.Ct. 733, 24 L.Ed.2d 729 (1970).

§ 8.7

1. *See* § 8.1 *supra*.

2. Tull v. United States, 481 U.S. 412, 107 S.Ct. 1831, 95 L.Ed.2d 365 (1987) (legislative history); Lorillard v. Pons, 434 U.S. 575, 98 S.Ct. 866, 55 L.Ed.2d 40 (1978) (references to "legal" relief); Curtis v. Loether, 415 U.S. 189, 94 S.Ct. 1005, 39 L.Ed.2d 260 (1974) (dictum; statutory reference to reinstatement, back pay or "other" equitable relief).

3. Granfinanciera, S.A. v. Nordberg, 492 U.S. 33, 109 S.Ct. 2782, 106 L.Ed.2d 26 (1989); Feltner v. Columbia Pictures Television, Inc., 523 U.S. 340, 118 S.Ct. 1279, 140 L.Ed.2d 438 (1998).

4. *E.g.*, City of Monterey v. Del Monte Dunes, 526 U.S. 687, 119 S.Ct. 1624, 143 L.Ed.2d 882 (1999); Chauffeurs, Teamsters & Helpers Local No. 391 v. Terry, 494 U.S. 558, 110 S.Ct. 1339, 108 L.Ed.2d 519 (1990).

unjust enrichment.[5] Some contemporary courts thus have classified the claim of an improperly discharged worker for back pay as equitable, ordering trial by a judge.[6]

Common law courts, for their part, sometimes granted specific relief. An action at law in replevin began with an impoundment of beasts or chattels in the defendant's possession; one in ejectment ended with the sheriff's restoration of the successful plaintiff to possession of land.[7] Here, too, some decisions have relied on the old anomalies to require jury trial in actions that do not seek damages.[8]

The remedy test, moreover, presupposes that one can ascertain the relief sought at the outset of the case. But every form of specific relief—injunction, specific performance, and so on—can be "monetized" into its damages equivalent.[9] Plaintiffs almost invariably pray for monetary relief in the alternative or as a supplement to such specific relief as restoration to employment or other injunctive relief. Furthermore, under modern procedure monetary relief is deemed to be at issue in any case that is contested. As Rule 54(c) states, "[e]xcept as to or party against whom a judgment is entered by default, every final judgment shall grant relief to which the party in whose favor it is rendered is entitled, even if the party has not demanded such relief in the party's pleadings." Thus, every action under modern merged procedure can be said to "partake" of a legal action. At the same time, however, many kinds of monetary relief can be conceptualized as restitution, a remedial concept originating in equity.[10]

Nature of the claim test

In addition to the remedy test, judges have relied in classifying claims on analogies between the substance of the claim to be classified and claims traditionally asserted in common law or equity courts.[11] This

5. 1 Palmer, The Law of Restitution 1–40 (1978); *see* Cook, The Powers of Courts of Equity, II, 15 Colum. L. Rev. 106 (1915). Remedies against a trustee who breaches trust are another example. Maitland, Equity 171–180 (1926).

6. *Compare* Curtis v. Loether, 415 U.S. 189, 94 S.Ct. 1005, 39 L.Ed.2d 260 (1974) (dictum; judge trial in employment discrimination back-pay case), *with* Chauffeurs, Teamsters & Helpers Local No. 391 v. Terry, 494 U.S. 558, 110 S.Ct. 1339, 108 L.Ed.2d 519 (1990) (jury trial in employee fair representation suit for back pay when defendant is not employer) *with* Wooddell v. International Bhd. of Elec. Workers, 502 U.S. 93, 112 S.Ct. 494, 116 L.Ed.2d 419 (1991)(jury trial for claim based on failure to hire plaintiff).

7. Maitland, The Forms of Action at Common Law 56–61 (1936).

8. Pernell v. Southall Realty, 416 U.S. 363, 94 S.Ct. 1723, 40 L.Ed.2d 198 (1974) (jury trial in landlord's summary eviction action); Department of Transportation v. Kerrigan, 153 Cal.App.3d Supp. 41, 200 Cal. Rptr. 865 (1984)(same). *Contra*, Kredi v. Benson, 1 Conn.App. 511, 473 A.2d 333 (1984).

9. *See* Dairy Queen v. Wood, 369 U.S. 469, 82 S.Ct. 894, 8 L.Ed.2d 44 (1962).

10. *See* Albemarle Paper Co. v. Moody, 422 U.S. 405, 95 S.Ct. 2362, 45 L.Ed.2d 280 (1975).

11. *E.g.*, Wooddell v. International Bhd. of Elec. Workers, 502 U.S. 93, 112 S.Ct. 494, 116 L.Ed.2d 419 (1991); Tull v. United States, 481 U.S. 412, 107 S.Ct. 1831, 95 L.Ed.2d 365 (1987); Damsky v. Zavatt, 289 F.2d 46 (2d Cir.1961).

test is particularly treacherous, for one sufficiently learned in the old law can often find several legal and equitable claims bearing some resemblance—and what resemblances are relevant?—to the new claim to be classified.[12] Nearly every modern legal right is at least analogous to one at common law. Every legal right can be said to involve either tort, contract, or property (concepts expressed in the common law), or life, liberty, or property (interests recognized in the common law). Hence, the common law offers some analogy for every legal right.

Practical or functional test

As a third factor, courts have also sometimes invoked more practical concerns to justify a decision for judge or jury trial.[13] When discretion is needed to shape the remedy, judges may conclude that they are best able to exercise the traditional discretion of the equity courts.[14] Institutional reform cases such as those desegregating public schools require complex remedial orders, based on detailed factual findings and revised as the defendant complies or resists; a jury could scarcely administer such an order. Some urge, but others deny, that jury trial should be denied when the facts of a case are too difficult for jurors to understand.[15] And some decisions may reflect judicial beliefs that jury prejudices may lead to bad results in some kinds of cases or that a popular community judgment is appropriate for others.[16]

Dividing claims

Classifying a claim as legal or equitable presupposes that it must be one or the other; the Supreme Court has, however, divided a claim in two. The Court has held, for example, that assessment of a regulatory penalty may be committed to a judge while upholding the right to jury determination whether the regulation was violated.[17] Similarly, a judge decides whether a corporate derivative suit may be brought, but a jury decides the merits. Such divisibility has some precedent in chancery practice, and of course even in a traditional jury trial some issues are reserved for the judge as questions of law.[18]

12. *E.g.*, Chauffeurs, Teamsters & Helpers Local No. 391 v. Terry, 494 U.S. 558, 110 S.Ct. 1339, 108 L.Ed.2d 519 (1990).

13. *See* Atlas Roofing Co. v. Occupational Safety and Health Review Commn., 430 U.S. 442, 97 S.Ct. 1261, 51 L.Ed.2d 464 (1977); Ross v. Bernhard, 396 U.S. 531, 538 n. 10, 90 S.Ct. 733, 738 n. 10, 24 L.Ed.2d 729, 739 n. 10 (1970); see Markman v. Westview Instruments, Inc., 517 U.S. 370, 116 S.Ct. 1384, 134 L.Ed.2d 577 (1996); § 8.3 *supra*.

14. Tull v. United States, 481 U.S. 412, 107 S.Ct. 1831, 95 L.Ed.2d 365 (1987).

15. See § 8.2 note 34 *supra* & § 8.12 note 8 *infra*.

16. *See* Curtis v. Loether, 415 U.S. 189, 94 S.Ct. 1005, 39 L.Ed.2d 260 (1974) (dictum; judge trial for employment discrimination cases). Compare Lebow v. American Trans Air, Inc., 86 F.3d 661 (7th Cir.1996)(employment discrimination claim under post-*Loether* amendment allowing compensatory and punitive damages subject to jury trial).

17. Tull v. United States, 481 U.S. 412, 107 S.Ct. 1831, 95 L.Ed.2d 365 (1987).

18. Chesnin and Hazard, Chancery Procedure and the Seventh Amendment: Jury Trial of Issues in Equity Cases before 1971, 83 Yale L.J. 999 (1974); Langbein, Fact Finding in English Court of Chancery: A

In any arguable case, in short, relying on the remedy, the substance of the claim, or even practical concerns is susceptible to manipulation to produce the conclusion that the proceeding is legal or equitable. The Supreme Court nevertheless continues struggling to give coherence to the right to jury trial, as two examples illustrate.

Granfinanciera, S.A. v. Nordberg

In *Granfinanciera, S.A. v. Nordberg*[19] a trustee in bankruptcy brought an action seeking to void allegedly fraudulent monetary transfers to Granfinanciera. The Bankruptcy Court denied defendants' request for a jury trial on the ground that "the Seventh Amendment supplied no right to a jury trial because fraudulent conveyance actions are equitable in nature."[20]

The Supreme Court upheld the Seventh Amendment contention. Comparing the statutory action to those in English courts prior to the merger of law and equity, the Court held that actions to recover fraudulent conveyances or preferential transfers were sometimes in courts of law. The remedy sought, monetary damages, was one available at common law. Because there was an "adequate remedy at law," the intervention of equity was not required. By exclusion, the action was therefore at law and jury triable. Of course, the Court could have said that the suit historically was also maintainable in equity and hence that there was no "right" of jury trial for the Seventh Amendment to have "preserved." The Court evidently was guided by preference for jury trial in "gray area" cases. The Court acknowledged that when Congress creates new statutory "public rights" it may assign their adjudication to an administrative agency without a jury, but added that this did not permit nonjury trial in private tort, contract, and property cases. This is one of the rare instances in which a court has struck down an explicit legislative provision for trial by judge.

Chauffeurs v. Terry

In *Chauffeurs, Teamsters & Helpers Local No. 391 v. Terry*[21] the problems of the "right" phase of the right-remedy test become still more apparent. *Chauffeurs v. Terry* was a damages action against a union for violating its duty of fair representation. Quoting *Beacon Theatres v. Westover* that "maintenance of the jury as a fact-finding body is of such importance and occupies so firm a place in our history and jurisprudence that any seeming curtailment should be scrutinized with the utmost care,"[22] the Court sought to apply the twofold right-remedy test enunci-

Rebuttal, 83 Yale L.J. 1622 (1974); see § 7.18 *supra*.

19. 492 U.S. 33, 109 S.Ct. 2782, 106 L.Ed.2d 26 (1989).

20. *See* 28 U.S.C. § 157(b)(2)(H); 492 U.S. at 37, 109 S.Ct. at 2785, 106 L.Ed.2d at 34.

21. 494 U.S. 558, 110 S.Ct. 1339, 108 L.Ed.2d 519 (1990).

22. 359 U.S. 500, 501, 79 S.Ct. 948, 952,

ated in previous cases.[23] The right of action for breach of a union's duty of fair representation, obviously unknown in eighteenth century England, is most closely analogous to an action by a trust beneficiary against a trustee for breach of fiduciary duty, which is an action in equity. But the issue to be tried was held akin to a breach of contract, which the court characterized as a legal issue. Since the remedy sought, compensatory damages, is usually (but not always) legal, the remedy was held to be legal in nature and the union members were entitled to a jury trial.

§ 8.8 Complaint Having Legal and Equitable Claims

In several situations under the former procedure, a suitor needed both equitable and legal relief to get complete redress for an injury; in other situations the suitor had a choice of remedies; in still others the suitor had only one remedy but mistakenly pursued the other. The differences among these were important because different patterns of trial and trial sequence were applied.

Resorting first to equity

In one class of cases a suitor had to resort to equity first to obtain relief. When an instrument to which *A* and *B* were parties did not, as it was written, support any legal claim by *A*, and *A* also claimed that the writing failed by mutual mistake to embody the actual agreement of the parties (which *would* support *A*'s legal claim if it had been embodied in the instrument), then *A* could get nowhere in a court of law unless equity first decreed a reformation of the instrument. This was not the kind of mistake the common law would remedy; it would simply enforce the instrument as written.[1] If the chancellor found mutual mistake, he would not only decree reformation but would also settle any remaining issues pertinent to *A*'s right to relief under the instrument as reformed and award relief.[2] That is, the chancellor would do all that if *A* requested it.[3] If the chancellor found no mutual mistake, he would dismiss the bill, leaving the parties to any remedy they might have at law.[4] In the

3 L.Ed.2d 988, 992 (1959).

23. Tull v. United States, 481 U.S. 412, 107 S.Ct. 1831, 95 L.Ed.2d 365 (1987); Granfinanciera, S.A. v. Nordberg, 492 U.S. 33, 109 S.Ct. 2782, 106 L.Ed.2d 26 (1989).

§ 8.8

1. *Compare* Capital City Bank v. Hilson, 59 Fla. 215, 51 So. 853 (1910) (contract as written supports no legal judgment on facts), *with* Capital City Bank v. Hilson, 64 Fla. 206, 60 So. 189 (1912) (complaint held to show basis for reformation of same contract and for recovery of damages). *Compare also* Franklin Fire Ins. Co. v. Hellerick, 20 Ky.L.Rep. 1703, 49 S.W. 1066 (1899) (no recovery where burned building not within policy description), *with* Hillerich v. Franklin Ins. Co., 111 Ky. 255, 63 S.W. 592 (1901) (amendment presenting basis for reforming same policy held improperly denied).

2. Capital City Bank v. Hilson, 64 Fla. 206, 60 So. 189 (1912); Kelly v. Galbraith, 186 Ill. 593, 58 N.E. 431 (1900); Keith v. Henkleman, 173 Ill. 137, 50 N.E. 692 (1898); Note, 66 A.L.R. 763, 777–787; 1 Pomeroy, Equity Jurisprudence § 237c (5th ed. 1941).

3. *See supra* § 8.2 note 8 and accompanying text.

4. 1 Pomeroy, Equity Jurisprudence § 273d (5th ed. 1941).

illustration put, that would be none; there were cases, however, in which either equity plaintiff *A* or adversary *B* would have some legal remedy under the instrument as written. In this type of case, if *B* sued *A* at law under the instrument as written, the chancellor would enjoin the prosecution of this legal action until the question of mutual mistake had been determined.[5]

Let us call this pattern of behavior "Pattern I." Here, the equitable issue traditionally would be tried first and without a jury.[6] Neither party had a choice about this, nor did the equity court have any real discretion, since a temporary injunction against prosecution of the law action would issue as a matter of course.[7] Moreover, the equitable issue (mutual mistake) was one that law courts did not recognize. Finally, if the equitable issue was decided in favor of *A*, there would be no second suit and thus no jury trial of any issue.[8]

Resorting first to law

At the opposite pole was a class of cases in which equity refused to give relief unless a preliminary legal issue had been determined at law by a jury, yet where equitable relief was needed for plaintiff's complete protection. If *A* claimed that *B*'s structure encroached on *A*'s land but *B* also claimed title to the land under the structure, equity would not order the structure removed until the title dispute was settled at law.[9] If *A* won the law action, equity would order *B* to remove the structure if it was impractical for the sheriff to remove it under a writ of execution.[10] If *A* claimed that *B* owed him a legal debt and wished to reach property conveyed by *B* to *C* to defraud *B*'s creditors, equity would grant no relief if *B* disputed the debt until *A* had reduced his or her debt claim to a judgment at law.[11] Then, at least if execution could not be satisfied,

5. *See, e.g.,* Liberty Oil Co. v. Condon Natl. Bank, 260 U.S. 235, 242–243, 43 S.Ct. 118, 121, 67 L.Ed. 232, 236 (1922). *Cf.* Enelow v. New York Life Ins. Co., 293 U.S. 379, 55 S.Ct. 310, 79 L.Ed. 440 (1935); American Cyanamid Co. v. Wilson & Toomer Fertilizer Co., 62 F.2d 1018 (5th Cir. 1933).

6. Unless, of course, the defendant at law was unaware of the pendency of the lawsuit, or of his own equity, or for some other reason failed to resort to equity before judgment in the action at law. It was the issuance of injunctions in such situations that precipitated the Coke–Ellsmere struggle and finally established the ascendancy of equity. *See* § 1.6 *supra.*

7. Young v. Reynolds, 4 Md. 375 (1853); Hibbard v. Eastman, 47 N.H. 507 (1867); 1 Pomeroy, Equity Jurisprudence 370, 371, 375 (5th ed. 1941); 4 Pomeroy, Equity Jurisprudence §§ 1362, 1363, 1364 (4th ed. 1919).

8. *See* note 2 *supra. But see* text at note 3 *supra.*

9. *See* cases cited § 8.2 note 36 *supra.*

10. *Id.*

11. *See, e.g.,* Case v. Beauregard, 101 U.S. 688, 690–691, 25 L.Ed. 1004, 1004 (1879); Pusey & Jones Co. v. Hanssen, 261 U.S. 491, 497, 43 S.Ct. 454, 455–456, 67 L.Ed. 763, 771 (1923); Southard v. Benner, 72 N.Y. 424, 426 (1878); American Surety Co. v. Conner, 251 N.Y. 1, 166 N.E. 783 (1929) (dealing with change wrought by Uniform Fraudulent Conveyance Act, and also prior law); 5 Pomeroy, Equity Jurisprudence §§ 2294–2318, at 871–895, particularly 2305 at 882 (4th ed. 1919) (this part, which was originally J. N. Pomeroy, Jr.'s Equitable Remedies, does not appear in the fifth edition of Pomeroy, Equitable Jurisprudence).

equitable relief would be forthcoming on a proper showing.[12]

Let us call this pattern of behavior "Pattern II." Here, equity would refuse to try the legal issue, and the legal issue would always be tried first.[13] If *A* won the trial, *A* still would often need a second suit in equity to get complete relief. Thus there would be two trials, one to a jury, and one to a court alone on issues pertaining to the propriety of equitable relief. Neither party had any choice in the matter, and the courts had no discretion.

Plaintiff's choice of tribunal

Between these two fairly clear-cut patterns lay a host of others, in many of which either kind of relief depended on the resolution of an issue that either tribunal would try (with its own mode of trial). Thus, *B*'s violation of *A*'s statutory right (for example, to a patent or copyright) might entitle *A* to an injunction, compensatory damages, and a penalty. The right to any relief would turn on whether *B* violated the statute. *A* might get a determination of that issue without a jury in an equity suit, seeking an injunction and perhaps compensatory damages as incidental to an injunction.[14] Or *A* might obtain such determination in an action at law for damages or for the penalty.[15] Since equity refused to enforce a penalty[16] and the law would not give an injunction, two suits would be required for complete relief. *A* could choose which to bring first, and the first determination of the common issue (violation vel non) would bind the parties in the second action.[17] The plaintiff thus had the power to choose the mode of trial of the common issue, and he or she could so exercise it as to leave no room for judicial discretion.

12. *See supra* note 11.

13. The rules themselves were not without exceptions that warranted equitable relief without first establishing the legal right at law, *see* cases cited *supra* note 11 and § 8.2 note 36. But unless the case could be brought under one of these exceptions, the legal issue always would be tried first.

14. Brady v. Daly, 175 U.S. 148, 20 S.Ct. 62, 44 L.Ed. 109 (1899); Marsh v. Seymour, 97 U.S. 348, 24 L.Ed. 963 (1877). *See* Parklane Hosiery Co. v. Shore, 439 U.S. 322, 99 S.Ct. 645, 58 L.Ed.2d 552 (1979); Barton v. Barbour, 104 U.S. 126, 133–134, 26 L.Ed. 672, 676 (1881); § 11.24 *infra*. *But see* Lytle v. Household Mfg., Inc., 494 U.S. 545, 110 S.Ct. 1331, 108 L.Ed.2d 504 (1990) (when judge erroneously denies jury trial, party is entitled to jury retrial).

15. Bereslavsky v. Caffey, 161 F.2d 499 (2d Cir.1947); Bruckman v. Hollzer, 152 F.2d 730 (9th Cir.1946); Berlin v. Club 100, 12 F.R.D. 129 (D.Mass.1951); Davies v. Allied Indus. Prods., 100 F.Supp. 109 (N.D.Ill. 1951); Pallant v. Sinatra, 7 F.R.D. 293 (S.D.N.Y.1945); Bellavance v. Plastic–Craft Novelty Co., 30 F.Supp. 37, 38–39 (D.Mass. 1939). *But cf.* Chappell & Co. v. Palermo Cafe, 146 F.Supp. 867 (D.Mass.1956). The statutory provision for an "action on the case" for damages for patent infringement was repealed in 1948. 62 Stat. 992. Under the amendment the parties are entitled to jury trial of the issues raised by a claim for damages even when it is coupled with a claim for injunction. Inland Steel Prods. Co. v. MPH Mfg. Corp., 25 F.R.D. 238, 245–246 (N.D.Ill.1959); National Dryer Mfg. Corp. v. Dryer Co. of Am., 130 F.Supp. 912 (E.D.Pa. 1955).

16. Decorative Stone Co. v. Building Trades Council, 23 F.2d 426 (2d Cir.1928).

17. Brady v. Daly, 175 U.S. 148, 20 S.Ct. 62, 44 L.Ed. 109 (1899); Bruckman v. Hollzer, 152 F.2d 730 (9th Cir.1946). *Cf.* Beacon Theatres v. Westover, 359 U.S. 500, 79 S.Ct. 948, 3 L.Ed.2d 988 (1959).

If the statute did not provide for a penalty, *A* might be able to obtain complete relief in a suit in equity.[18] But *A* also would have the option to sue for damages at law and for an injunction in equity separately, in whichever order *A* chose. So, here again, *A* could control the mode of trial of the common issue without leaving room for judicial discretion.

In another class of cases *A* also had a choice, but it was a more limited one. Breach of certain kinds of contracts (such as to convey land) would entitle the injured party to either specific performance[19] (with incidental damages for delay of performance, and the like) or damages for breach[20] (measured on the assumption that the contract would not be performed). Here, *A* could in no case get both forms of relief—*A* had to elect one or the other.[21] This election would govern the mode of trial of issues (the making of the contract,[22] performance of conditions precedent, breach,[23] and the like) that would be presented in a claim for *either* kind of relief.

"Complete justice" in equity

In the case just put, if *A* initially chose equitable relief, the chancellor might find that specific performance was impossible or unsuitable even when there might have been a breach of contract. When equitable relief was denied on this basis, the court would usually dismiss the suit for want of "equity jurisdiction,"[24] leaving *A* free to pursue legal relief in a law court with its jury. The chancellor would not, however, always dismiss a case when specific performance was denied. In *Denton v. Stewart*[25] defendant transferred the subject matter of the contract (a leasehold) to an innocent purchaser after the equity suit was begun. This was held to prevent the granting of specific performance; to save plaintiff from the hardship of a second action, the chancellor determined the issues and awarded damages. This granting of substituted legal relief in equity was exceptional in late eighteenth century England and may not have extended beyond the case of impossibility arising after suit.[26] The

18. *See* note 14 *supra.*

19. 5 Corbin, Contracts ch. 63 (1951).

20. *Id.* 990 and, generally, chs. 55–60.

21. Rushing v. Mayfield Co., 62 F.2d 318 (5th Cir.1932), *cert. denied,* 289 U.S. 750, 53 S.Ct. 695, 77 L.Ed. 1496 (1933). *Cf.* 5 Corbin, Contracts 19, at § 1222 (1951).

22. Rash v. Peoples Deposit Bank & Trust Co., 192 F.2d 470 (6th Cir.1951); Canister Co. v. Leahy, 182 F.2d 510 (3d Cir.1950); Mahon v. Bennett, 81 F.Supp. 901 (W.D.Mo.1948); Fraser v. Geist, 1 F.R.D. 267 (E.D.Pa.1940); Trenchard v. Reay, 70 Utah 19, 257 P. 1046 (1927); Morris, Jury Trial Under the Federal Fusion of Law and Equity, 20 Tex. L. Rev. 427, 428 (1942).

23. *See, e.g.,* Altoona Elec., Engg. & Supply Co. v. Kittanning & Ford City St. Ry., 126 Fed. 559, 561, 562 (C.C.W.D.Pa. 1903) (substantial performance found by court on "a great conflict between the witnesses").

24. Todd v. Gee, 17 Ves. Jr. 273, 34 Eng. Rep. 106 (Ch. 1810); Marks v. Gates, 154 Fed. 481, 484 (9th Cir.1907); Flattau v. Logan, 72 N.J.Eq. 338, 65 A. 714 (1907).

25. 1 Cox Ch. 258, 29 Eng. Rep. 1156 (Ch. 1786).

26. *See* Todd v. Gee, 17 Ves. Jr. 273, 34 Eng. Rep. 106 (Ch. 1810); Milkman v. Ordway, 106 Mass. 232, 253 *et seq.* (1870); Levin, Equitable Clean–Up and the Jury: A Suggested Orientation, 100 U. Pa. L. Rev. 320, 333–334 (1951).

notion has enjoyed considerable growth since then,[27] however, and has even been applied occasionally when specific performance was denied because the contract was unconscionable by equitable standards.[28]

Modern patterns

Pattern II, that is, the situation in which the chancellor would have refused to give relief until a legal issue was first tried, presents no problem under modern merged procedure. The legal issue is tried, to a jury if one is demanded, and any remaining issues then resolved by the judge without a jury.[29]

Pattern I, however, involves more difficulty. This is the situation in which the plaintiff first had to obtain some sort of equitable redress, such as reformation of a contract, before being able to proceed to obtain the related legal remedy, such as damages from breach of the contract as reformed. In some jurisdictions, notably New York, the rule had been that the plaintiff "waives" jury trial by simultaneously asserting a claim in equity and one in law,[30] but this approach is inconsistent with the principle in merged procedure that the plaintiff is obliged to assert such claims in a single action.[31] If waiver is not used as a means of avoiding the problem, then the question of mode of trial has to be resolved by further analysis. If the preliminary equitable issues are separable from the subsequent legal issues, *Ross v. Bernhard*[32] indicates that jury trial is available as to the latter in the federal courts. But if, as is often the case, determination of the preliminary equitable question involves issues that are also involved in the legal claim, it can properly be said that the judge's determination of them precludes any decision by a jury.[33]

The third group of cases falls between Pattern I and Pattern II and is perhaps too heterogeneous to be called a pattern.[34] These cases involve simultaneous presentation of claims within which a common issue, or set of issues, determines both forms of relief and that either law or equity would try under some circumstances. Here again, premerger patterns of

27. *See supra* § 8.2 note 13 and accompanying text.

28. Gabrielson v. Hogan, 298 Fed. 722 (8th Cir.1924). *Cf.* Morgan v. Dibble, 43 Cal.App. 116, 184 P. 704 (1919). *See* Levin, Equitable Clean-Up and the Jury: A Suggested Orientation, 100 U. Pa. L. Rev. 320, 339 (1951).

29. *See* Levin, Equitable Clean-Up and the Jury: A Suggested Orientation, 100 U. Pa. L. Rev. 320, 339 (1951).

30. Di Menna v. Cooper & Evans Co., 220 N.Y. 391, 115 N.E. 993 (1917); Cogswell v. New York, N.H. & H.R.R., 105 N.Y. 319, 11 N.E. 518 (1887).

31. *See* Ring v. Spina, 166 F.2d 546 (2d Cir.1948); Moore v. San Vicente Lumber Co., 175 Cal. 212, 165 P. 687 (1917). The waiver rule has been repudiated, at least in part, by N.Y. Civ. Prac. L. & R. 4102(c).

32. 396 U.S. 531, 90 S.Ct. 733, 24 L.Ed.2d 729 (1970). *See* Brownlee v. Yellow Freight Sys., 921 F.2d 745 (8th Cir.1990) (applying this principle when plaintiff asserts legal and equitable claims against different defendants).

33. *See* Hyde Properties v. McCoy, 507 F.2d 301 (6th Cir.1974).

34. *See* McCoid, Procedural Reform and the Right to Jury Trial, 116 U. Pa. L. Rev. 1 (1967).

judicial behavior are helpful in determining the mode of trial of the common issue.

Cumulative legal and equitable claims

In cases such as patent or copyright infringement plaintiffs were entitled to cumulate legal and equitable remedies and thus had the option to choose the mode of trial; this precluded defendant's option and the court's discretion. Plaintiffs exercised this option by seeking their remedies in separate suits and bringing them in the order they chose. Today, under merger, plaintiffs must seek in a single suit all relief arising out of a single group of operative facts;[35] thus, the traditional manner of exercising their option is no longer available. But it would be inconsistent with the preservation of plaintiffs' jury right to take away the substance of their option for jury trial if that is what they wanted. The problem is simply one of finding a substitute method of exercising the option that is consistent with the other objectives of merger. It has been suggested that the option be exercised by drafting separate counts for legal and equitable relief in the complaint,[36] but this seems to put undue stress on form.[37] The best solution is to let plaintiff express the choice of jury trial by simply claiming it in the way provided by statute or rule.

Historically, the defendant had no choice of trial mode in the situation under discussion.[38] It could be said that plaintiff alone retains the option, or at least that it is within the court's discretion to decide which claim should be tried first. This is to some extent question-begging because the matter to be tried is not the claim as such but the contested issues presented by both claims. It is even more clearly question-begging to inquire which is the "basic" issue or whether the basic issue is by nature equitable or legal: The issues are basic to both claims and their equitable or legal nature has been hybridized beyond differentiation by the law-equity merger. Hence, the question, properly put, is a choice between giving effect to plaintiff's former option and giving defendant a counter-option, and this involves deciding whether jury trial should be preferred when *either* party wants it.

Preference for jury trial

The federal decisions, particularly since *Dairy Queen, Inc. v. Wood,*[39] have held for such a preference, at least in the absence of an expression

35. *See* § 8.4 note 2 *supra.*

36. *See* Russell v. Laurel Music Corp., 104 F.Supp. 815, 816 (S.D.N.Y.1952).

37. *Cf.* McCoid, Right to Jury Trial in the Federal Courts, 45 Iowa L. Rev. 726, 728–731 (1960).

38. American Life Ins. Co. v. Stewart, 300 U.S. 203, 57 S.Ct. 377, 81 L.Ed. 605 (1937); Orenstein v. United States, 191 F.2d 184, 190 (1st Cir.1951). *See also* Tanimura v. United States, 195 F.2d 329 (9th Cir.1952).

39. 369 U.S. 469, 82 S.Ct. 894, 8 L.Ed.2d 44 (1962).

of legislative direction in connection with a specific type of statutory claim. As the Supreme Court said in *Ross v. Bernhard,*

> [w]here equitable and legal claims are joined in the same action, there is a right to jury trial on the legal claims which must not be infringed by either trying the legal issues as incidental to the equitable ones or by a court trial of a common issue existing between the claims.[40]

Alternative legal and equitable claims

Similar problems arise in the specific-performance situations. Formerly, as we saw, plaintiff could have only one of the remedies and had to pursue it in the appropriate forum; plaintiff could not pursue the remedies alternatively in a single suit.[41] And the dismissal of the equity suit because specific performance was inappropriate would not bar a later action at law for damages.[42] The merged procedure has changed this. Plaintiff may still have only one of the remedies[43] but must pursue all the remedies (arising from a single breach of contract) in a single action, and plaintiff may do so alternatively (exercising the necessary choice between the remedies after trial).[44] Further, the court is empowered and directed in most situations to award appropriate relief even when it has not been claimed in the complaint.[45] Question then arises as to any jury trial right on common dispositive issues (such as contract vel non) in the single civil action that plaintiff may bring, when plaintiff expressly pursues both remedies in the alternative or when the court may find appropriate and award a remedy not expressly demanded.

There are at least three ways to approach this situation, and all become operative if either party indicates its desire for a jury trial by timely demand. (Such a demand should have been made in response to plaintiff's claim for specific performance, because the alternative claim for damages is implicitly before the court by reason of the rule that plaintiff is to be given whatever relief is justified by the evidence, even if plaintiff has not requested it.)[46] The three approaches are as follows:

1. Plaintiff has the choice of mode of trial, just as he or she did before merger.[47]

40. 396 U.S. 531, 537–538, 90 S.Ct. 733, 738, 24 L.Ed.2d 729, 736 (1970);see Lytle v. Household Mfg., Inc., 494 U.S. 545, 110 S.Ct. 1331, 108 L.Ed.2d 504 (1990). But see Raedeke v. Gibraltar Sav. & Loan Ass'n, 10 Cal.3d 665, 111 Cal.Rptr. 693, 517 P.2d 1157 (1974); Di Menna v. Cooper & Evans Co., 220 N.Y. 391, 115 N.E. 993 (1917).

41. Rushing v. Mayfield Co., 62 F.2d 318 (5th Cir.1932), *cert. denied,* 289 U.S. 750, 53 S.Ct. 695, 77 L.Ed. 1496 (1933).

42. Logan v. Flattau, 73 N.J.Eq. 222, 67 A. 1007 (1907) (after dismissing bill for specific performance, equity will not enjoin action at law). *Cf.* Pomeroy, Specific Performance of Contracts § 475 (3d ed. 1926).

43. 5 Corbin, Contracts § 1222 (1951) (a party "should not be allowed to enforce and receive specific performance and at the same time get judgment for damages for a total breach").

44. *See, e.g.,* Williams v. Marshall, 37 Cal.2d 445, 235 P.2d 372 (1951); Moon v. Brewer, 89 Idaho 59, 402 P.2d 973 (1965).

45. Fed. R. Civ. P. 54(c); N.Y. Civ. Prac. L. & R. 3017.

46. *See* Gulbenkian v. Gulbenkian, 147 F.2d 173 (2d Cir.1945).

47. *See* Morris, Jury Trial Under the Federal Fusion of Law and Equity, 20 Tex. L. Rev. 427, 432 (1942).

2. Either party may demand jury trial on the common issues (such as contract vel non) because the damages claim is explicitly or implicitly joined in plaintiff's complaint.

3. The court impanels a jury but itself sits as a decider of the facts. If the court decides that specific performance is an appropriate remedy, it resolves the common issues for itself and treats the jury verdict as merely advisory or as surplusage; if it decides that specific performance may not be awarded, it withholds decision on the common issues and treats them as resolved by the jury's verdict.[48]

The third solution is probably the most faithful accommodation to the historical test, but relatively few courts have adopted it. Many, perhaps most, state courts have adopted the first solution.[49] The federal courts have adopted the second, following the mandate articulated in *Dairy Queen v. Wood*: "[T]he legal claims involved in the action must be determined [by a jury] prior to any final court determination of [the] equitable claims."[50]

§ 8.9 Equitable Defense to a Legal Claim

Fraud defense

Historically, certain matters cognizable in equity would defeat a legal claim but were not recognized at law and could not, therefore, be successfully pleaded in an action at law.[1] If *A*, the obligor on a contract under seal, claimed that he or she was induced by fraud to execute it in favor of *B*, *A* could not interpose that fraud in *B*'s legal action on the contract.[2] To get relief, *A* would have to go into equity and seek cancellation for the fraud. Equity would then enjoin the prosecution of the lawsuit temporarily until the question of fraud was determined. If the chancellor found fraud, he would decree cancellation of the contract and make permanent the injunction against *B*'s prosecution of the law

48. *See* Fed. R. Civ. P. 39(c). *See* Hyde Properties v. McCoy, 507 F.2d 301 (6th Cir.1974); *cf.* Bereslavsky v. Caffey, 161 F.2d 499 (2d Cir.1947).*

49. *See* Note, The Right to Jury Trial Under Merged Procedures, 65 Harv. L. Rev. 453 (1952). In some states, the federal courts approach favoring jury trial has apparently had some influence. *See, e.g.,* Cumens v. Garrett, 294 Ala. 535, 319 So.2d 665 (1975).

50. 369 U.S. 469, 479, 82 S.Ct. 894, 901, 8 L.Ed.2d 44, 52 (1962). *See* Lytle v. Household Mfg., Inc., 494 U.S. 545, 110 S.Ct. 1331, 108 L.Ed.2d 504 (1990); Johns Hopkins Univ. v. Hutton, 488 F.2d 912, 916 (4th Cir.1973).

§ 8.9

1. *See* the exposition in Cook, Equitable Defenses, 32 Yale L.J. 645 (1923). *Cf.* Abbott, Fraud as a Defence at Law in the Federal Courts, 15 Colum. L. Rev. 489 (1915); Hinton, Equitable Defenses Under Modern Codes, 18 Mich. L. Rev. 717 (1920).

2. George v. Tate, 102 U.S. 564, 570–571, 26 L.Ed. 232, 233 (1880); Belden v. Davies, 2 Hall 433 (N.Y.Sup.Ct.1829); Franchot v. Leach, 5 Cow. 506 (N.Y.Sup.Ct. 1825); Ames, Specialty Contracts and Equitable Defenses, 9 Harv. L. Rev. 49, 51 (1895).

action.[3] Thus, no jury trial would be held on any issue. The equitable issue would be tried first and would dispose of the whole case, or when there were residual legal issues (as when the instrument was reformed rather than cancelled), equity would dispose of them as incidental to the equitable relief.[4] The equitable relief, though always affirmative in form (cancellation, rescission, and so on), in most cases had only the effect of defeating the law action.[5] If, however, the chancellor found no fraud, he would dismiss the equity suit, dissolve the temporary injunction, and leave the parties to their claims and defenses in the legal action. This pattern is essentially a variant of Pattern I, described above.[6]

One last note should be made before we leave history. Many matters cognizable only in equity in remote times came to be recognized as defenses by courts of law—"worked over into law," as we say.[7] After this process had become complete, equity typically would refuse to enjoin the law action and grant relief, stating that the remedy at law was adequate.[8] The equity plaintiff in our illustration could plead the matter as a defense in the law action.

Defenses in modern procedure

The prevailing pattern in merged procedures faithfully follows the historical pattern, except that all steps occur in a single civil action and there is no injunction. When *B* sues *A* on the legal claim, *A* affirmatively pleads in that action the matter that would have been the subject of a separate suit in equity before the merger. What was accomplished by the temporary injunction under the old procedure can be done under the new by a simple order that the equitable issues tendered by the answer (or counterclaim) be tried to the court and tried first.[9] Since, as we have seen,[10] a temporary injunction would issue as a matter of course in such a situation, there should be no room for judicial discretion today in the matter of trial sequence.[11] And, if the equitable issue is determined in *A*'s

3. *See* Cook, Equitable Defenses, 32 Yale L.J. 645, 649–650 (1923).

4. *See supra* § 8.2 note 10 and accompanying text.

5. *See* Cook, Equitable Defenses, 32 Yale L.J. 645, 650 (1923).

6. *See* text at § 8.8 notes 1–5 *supra*.

7. Abbott, Fraud as a Defence at Law in the Federal Courts, 15 Colum. L. Rev. 489 (1915); Ames, Specialty Contracts and Equitable Defenses, 9 Harv. L. Rev. 49 (1895); Hinton, Equitable Defenses Under Modern Codes, 18 Mich. L. Rev. 717, 721–723 (1920).

8. Cable v. United States Life Ins. Co., 191 U.S. 288, 24 S.Ct. 74, 48 L.Ed. 188 (1903); Abbott, Fraud as a Defence at Law in the Federal Courts, 15 Colum. L. Rev. 489 (1915).

9. Bodley v. Ferguson, 30 Cal. 511 (1866); Weber v. Marshall, 19 Cal. 447 (1861); Davis v. Holbrook, 25 Colo. 493, 55 P. 730 (1898); Penninger Lateral Co. v. Clark, 22 Idaho 397, 126 P. 524 (1912); Piggly–Wiggly Stores v. Lowenstein, 197 Ind. 62, 147 N.E. 771 (1925); Price v. Chambers, 148 Wash. 170, 268 P. 143 (1928). *See* Gegan, Is There a Constitutional Right to Jury Trial of Equitable Defenses in New York?, 74 St. John's L. Rev. 1 (2000). *Cf.* Liberty Oil Co. v. Condon Natl. Bank, 260 U.S. 235, 43 S.Ct. 118, 67 L.Ed. 232 (1922).

10. *See* § 8.8 note 7 *supra*.

11. *But cf.* Crosby v. Scott–Graff Lumber Co., 93 Minn. 475, 101 N.W. 610 (1904).

favor, there is no historical basis for awarding *B* a jury trial on any residual legal issues.

Possible difficulties in applying this simple pattern may arise in the question whether the issue tendered by the defendant had worked over into law by the time of the merger. More important, the whole approach can be jettisoned by arguing that the merger of law and equity transforms all matters of defense into legal issues because the claim itself is "legal."[12]

§ 8.10 Complaint Presenting Equitable Issues and Counterclaim Presenting Legal Issues

In some situations, plaintiff *A* has a claim against defendant *B,* but *B* also has a counterclaim against *A.* When *A*'s equitable claim against *B* had no factual connection with *B*'s legal claim against *A,* then each claim would require a separate action with its own mode of trial.[1] But when the two claims present one or more common issues of fact, the problem is more complicated. This happened in at least two situations.

In one situation, the equity plaintiff *A* sought what we may call "actual" or "substantial" equitable relief, such as foreclosure of a mortgage, specific performance of a contract, or an injunction against conduct (other than prosecuting a lawsuit). In the other situation, *A* sought relief that, though in personam and coercive in form, was in effect a declaration of rights that would dispose of a potential legal claim by *B* against *A* on the ground that would have been available at law to defeat *B*'s claim if *B* pursued it by legal action. In such a case *A* was a putative defendant at law and sought in equity simply to defeat the law action on grounds cognizable at law. Equity jurisdiction was sometimes based on the fact that *A*'s defense (or some other right or interest of *A*) might be prejudiced by delay in the commencement of *B*'s legal action—either because that action was premature or because *B* was free to delay it for tactical reasons.[2] Equity jurisdiction was sometimes based on the desire to prevent a multiplicity of legal actions.[3]

12. *Cf.* Dice v. Akron, C. & Y.R.R., 342 U.S. 359, 72 S.Ct. 312, 96 L.Ed. 398 (1952).

§ 8.10

1. Unless defendants sought to use their damage claims as a set-off against plaintiff's equitable claim, according to the principles formerly prevailing in equity. *See* Savings Bank of New London v. Santaniello, 130 Conn. 206, 33 A.2d 126 (1943).

2. American Life Ins. Co. v. Stewart, 300 U.S. 203, 57 S.Ct. 377, 81 L.Ed. 605 (1937), presented a typical situation in which a life insurance policy would become incontestable, by its terms, "two years from its date of issue," except for nonpayment of premium. The insured had died, but the beneficiary was in a position to postpone her suit until after the policy had become incontestable. The insurance company, claiming fraud by the insured in the application for the policy, sued for its cancellation before it became incontestable. The court cited many federal and state decisions sustaining equitable relief in similar situations. *See also* Enelow v. New York Life Ins. Co., 293 U.S. 379, 384, 55 S.Ct. 310, 312, 79 L.Ed. 440, 443–444 (1935); Prudential Ins. Co. v. Saxe, 134 F.2d 16, 32 (D.C.Cir.1943).

3. *See, e.g.,* Town of Fairfield v. Southport Natl. Bank, 77 Conn. 423, 59 A. 513 (1904); 1 Pomeroy, Equity Jurisprudence sec. IV, particularly §§ 261h *et seq.,* 264a, 264b, 269 (5th ed. 1941).

Defendant choosing whether to counterclaim

In the first situation, under earlier code procedure the defendant could withhold his or her claim and assert it in a subsequent action;[4] if the defendant did so, he or she would have a right to jury trial on it. But this strategy involved both risk and expense. The risk lay in the possibility that if the first action was resolved against the defendant, the issues there determined would be preclusive in defendant's subsequent action.[5] The expense lay in the fact that even if defendant won the first action he or she would have to go through a second action in order to recover the affirmative relief sought on the claim. Hence, there were strong inducements for defendant to assert a legal counterclaim. In the second of these situations, that is, when the plaintiff's action was in effect a trial of the defendant's claim but with the parties inverted, defendant was under similar but even stronger practical compulsion to assert a legal counter-claim.

The question then posed was whether the issues common to the claim and counterclaim would be tried to the court or the jury. Generally, the decisions suggested that they be tried to the court, on one of several theories: that the court of equity, having assumed jurisdiction of the original claim, could determine all claims in the action;[6] that the defendant waived jury trial by asserting a counterclaim;[7] or that the court, in its discretion, could fix the sequence of trials.[8]

Compulsory counterclaim

The context of the problem under modern procedure is rather different. For one thing, the rules of res judicata have expanded the concept of the action so that the defendant is under very strong compulsion to assert the counterclaim, under penalty of not being able to do so in a subsequent action.[9] Moreover, most jurisdictions now have a compulsory counterclaim rule requiring that defendants assert as a counterclaim any claim they may have arising out of the same transaction sued on by the plaintiff.[10] These changes in the procedural context make untenable the theory that a defendant waives jury trial by counterclaim-

4. American Mills Co. v. American Surety Co., 260 U.S. 360, 43 S.Ct. 149, 67 L.Ed. 306 (1922); Reichert v. Krass, 13 Ind.App. 348, 40 N.E. 706, *petition for reh'g overruled,* 13 Ind.App. 348, 41 N.E. 835 (1895); Johnson Serv. Co. v. Kruse, 121 Minn. 28, 140 N.W. 118 (1913); First Natl. Bank v. Erling Bros., 61 S.D. 364, 249 N.W. 681 (1933).

5. *See* Restatement (Second) of Judgments § 22, Comment *c.*

6. *See, e.g.,* Phoenix Mut. Life Ins. Co. v. Conway, 11 N.Y.2d 367, 183 N.E.2d 754, 229 N.Y.S.2d 740 (1962).

7. James, Trial by Jury and the New Federal Rules of Procedure, 45 Yale L.J. 1022, 1033 (1936); Annot., 89 A.L.R. 1391.

8. American Life Ins. Co. v. Stewart, 300 U.S. 203, 57 S.Ct. 377, 81 L.Ed. 605 (1937).

9. *See* Restatement (Second) of Judgments §§ 22, 27.

10. *See* Fed. R. Civ. P. 13(a); Wright, Estoppel by Rule: The Compulsory Counterclaim Under Modern Pleading, 38 Minn. L. Rev. 423 (1954).

ing. And they put more sharply the question why the mode of trial should depend on which of the two parties initiated the litigation.

Many state courts tend to adhere to the proposition that the equitable issues should be tried first, which is to say that the common issues are to be tried to the court rather than the jury.[11] The federal courts, under the rubric of *Beacon Theatres v. Westover,*[12] prefer jury trial of those issues.

§ 8.11 Declaratory Judgment

As we have seen, equity sometimes granted relief that had as its principal substantive effect the binding declaration of the rights of parties.[1] But in many situations equity would not grant such relief. In an action for breach of contract or for negligently causing personal injuries, the putative defendant who claimed to have a good defense could not get equity to determine the validity of the defense. The remedy of interposing this defense to the law action, if and when brought, was considered adequate.

In the 1920s, statutes were passed that provided broadly for actions seeking declaratory judgments with or without coercive relief in all types of situations, including those in which equity had given relief and those in which it had not, and including those in which plaintiff sought simply to establish nonliability under a claim against him or her as well as those in which plaintiff sought some affirmative relief.[2]

Declaratory relief as legal or equitable

The framers of declaratory judgment acts, like the framers of merged systems of procedure, took a neutral position toward jury trial, seeking neither to contract nor to expand it.[3] The courts worked out an essentially simple test for jury trial, consistent with this legislative

11. *See, e.g.,* Veale v. Piercy, 206 Cal. App.2d 557, 24 Cal.Rptr. 91 (1962); Phoenix Mut. Life Ins. Co. v. Conway, 11 N.Y.2d 367, 183 N.E.2d 754, 229 N.Y.S.2d 740 (1962); Annot., 17 A.L.R.3d 1321.

12. 359 U.S. 500, 79 S.Ct. 948, 3 L.Ed.2d 988 (1959).

§ 8.11

1. *See* § 8.10 notes 2 and 3 *supra.*

2. *See* § 1.11 *supra.*

3. *See* Borchard, Declaratory Judgments 399–404 (2d ed. 1941). Borchard had a larger part in promoting and drafting these statutes than any other individual. *See* United States Fidelity & Guar. Co. v. Koch, 102 F.2d 288, 290 (3d Cir.1939), referring to Borchard as the "father" of the declaratory judgment in the United States.

Borchard states: "It may be said that the draftsmen of the Uniform Act included the provision [Section 9] with the sole purpose of refuting any constitutional doubt on the point; it was not intended to indicate that the declaratory action is either equitable or legal or to indicate that jury trial, though demandable in common law cases, is necessary in any case. Declaratory relief is neither strictly equitable nor legal, although ... its historical sources are almost exclusively equitable." Borchard, *id.* at 399.

Section 9 of the Uniform Act reads: "When a proceeding under this Act involves the determination of an issue of fact, such issue may be tried and determined in the same manner as issues of fact are tried and determined in other civil actions in the court in which the proceeding is pending." *See also* Fed. R. Civ. P. 57.

intent. When the declaratory judgment action did not fit into one of the existing patterns for equitable relief, but was, so to speak, an inverted action at law, then the parties had a right to jury trial.[4] When the declaratory judgment was the counterpart of a suit in equity, there was no such right.[5] This simple and consistent pattern has been transformed, for the federal courts, by *Beacon Theatres v. Westover.*[6]

Beacon Theatres v. Westover

In this action Fox, operator of a movie theater in San Bernardino, California, sued Beacon, operator of a drive-in theater eleven miles from San Bernardino, seeking a declaration that Fox was not liable to Beacon for treble damages under the antitrust laws and an injunction to prevent Beacon from suing Fox and its distributors under these acts. Fox alleged that it had long been operating under contracts with distributors granting it exclusive rights to show first-run pictures in the "San Bernardino competitive area"; that when Beacon built its drive-in it notified Fox that it considered these contracts to be violations of the antitrust laws and threatened treble damage suits thereunder; that these notices and threats against Fox and its distributors gave rise to "duress and coercion," which deprived Fox of its valuable property right to negotiate these contracts. Threat of irreparable harm was charged.

Beacon answered and counterclaimed for treble damages. A common issue of the complaint and counterclaim was the reasonableness of the clearances granted to Fox, which depended, in part, on the existence of competition between the two theaters. Beacon made timely demand for jury trial of all the issues. The trial court, however, viewed the complaint as essentially equitable and ordered the issues tendered by it (including the common issue) to be tried by the court before jury trial of the issues tendered by the counterclaim. The court of appeals refused to interfere with this ruling, recognizing that the determination of the issue of clearances by the court would "operate either by way of res judicata or collateral estoppel so as to conclude both parties with respect thereto at the subsequent trial of the treble damage claim."[7] But it concluded that

4. Pittman v. West Am. Ins. Co., 299 F.2d 405 (8th Cir.1962); Johnson v. Fidelity & Casualty Co., 238 F.2d 322 (8th Cir. 1956); Hargrove v. American Cent. Ins. Co., 125 F.2d 225 (10th Cir.1942); Baumgartner v. Schey, 143 Colo. 373, 353 P.2d 375 (1960). *See also* (American) Lumbermens Mut. Casualty Co. v. Timms & Howard, 108 F.2d 497, 499–500 (2d Cir.1939); Aetna Casualty & Sur. Co. v. Quarles, 92 F.2d 321, 325 (4th Cir.1937).

5. Linahan v. Linahan, 131 Conn. 307, 39 A.2d 895 (1944); Hornof v. Klee, 259 Minn. 139, 106 N.W.2d 448 (1960). *See* Annot., 13 A.L.R.2d 777. This method of turning a declaratory judgment suit upside down in order to reveal the traditional action that the party seeking the declaratory judgment wishes to forestall has also sometimes been applied in assessing whether a declaratory judgment action arises under federal law for subject matter jurisdiction purposes. See Textron Lycoming Reciprocating Engine Div. v. UAW, 523 U.S. 653, 118 S.Ct. 1626, 140 L.Ed.2d 863 (1998); § 2.27 *supra.*

6. 359 U.S. 500, 79 S.Ct. 948, 3 L.Ed.2d 988 (1959).

7. Beacon Theatres v. Westover, 252 F.2d 864, 874 (9th Cir.1958).

since the issues tendered by the complaint were equitable, they would have warranted a chancellor in exercising his discretion to enjoin prosecution of the later law action and that the trial judge under the merged system had a similar discretion in ordering trial sequence.[8]

Trying legal issues first

The Supreme Court reversed. The holding itself was not radical. Fox may well have been simply trying to circumvent Beacon's jury right by "jumping the gun" with an equitable action; the district court's exercise of discretion may have been so questionable as to border on abuse. But the Court made two major departures from precedent in the way it analyzed the situation presented. One of these has already been noted: In any action involving both legal and equitable claims or defenses, the issues posed in the legal component of the case were to be tried to a jury if either party so demanded and were to be tried first so that the matters involved in those issues were conclusively established.[9]

Declaratory relief as legal

The other proposition advanced by the Court, having to do with the declaratory judgment remedy, reached much further. The Court held that the declaratory remedy was legal and, hence, that all issues involved in determining that remedy were jury triable. The Court reasoned as follows: (1) An equitable remedy is available in appropriate circumstances only when the remedy at law is inadequate; (2) the declaratory judgment remedy is available on both the law and the equity "sides" of the court because its availability is not limited to situations in which an equitable remedy historically would be available; (3) when the declaratory remedy is available on the law side, legal remedies become "adequate" whenever a declaratory judgment is a sufficient remedy, and equitable jurisdiction need not be resorted to; (4) therefore, an action for a declaratory judgment presents legal issues; (5) because the declaratory action presents legal issues, those issues are jury triable on demand of any party to the action.

All claims as legal

This reasoning is, to say the least, remarkable for several reasons: (1) the adequacy test for determining availability of equitable relief had been in a state of substantial atrophy for two hundred years;[10] (2) there is no evidence that the Declaratory Judgment Act was intended to expand legal, as distinct from equitable, remedies;[11] indeed, if the declaratory remedy were analyzed by historical analogy to the legal-equitable dichotomy in remedies, it most clearly resembled equitable relief; (3) if the reasoning of the case is pushed a step further, *all* actions would be

8. 252 F.2d at 876.

9. *See* § 8.8 *supra.*

10. *See* § 1.5 *supra.*

11. *See* note 3 *supra.*

legal and hence jury triable. The basis for the last conclusion is as follows. First, modern rules of procedure allow courts to give litigants the relief to which they are properly entitled, even if they have not asked for it.[12] Second, in every case in which a party seeks an equitable remedy such as an injunction, the party could have asked instead for a declaratory judgment, foregoing a request for "coercive relief." Therefore, the court in any case in which equitable relief is demanded could, instead, give it declaratory relief, coupled with a "supplementary" injunction if that later proves necessary to secure compliance with the declaration. Thus, declaratory relief is at least implicitly involved in every case in which equitable relief is permitted. Since declaratory relief is legal and jury triable, every case in which equitable (or at least injunctive) relief is sought is jury triable.

Few decisions since *Beacon Theatres v. Westover* have gone this far, and changes in the composition of the Supreme Court make it unlikely that it will go that far in the future. Considered in the light of the subsequent decision in *Dairy Queen v. Wood,*[13] however, the *Beacon* reasoning leaves few if any logical stopping places. The result is that the lower federal courts have wide latitude to find that jury trial is a right in almost any kind of case (by applying *Beacon* liberally, for the most that it implies) or that jury trial is available only in actions in which one of the claims fits the traditional legal mold (by applying *Beacon* only as far as its holding requires). The results have been considerable confusion, the expansion of the jury trial right to some degree, and variant doctrines trying to establish what that degree is.

State courts

In contrast, few if any state courts have followed the lead of *Beacon* to expand jury trial into declaratory judgment actions. The state courts generally handle declaratory actions by analogizing them to various legal and equitable remedies and then deciding the jury trial question in terms of the closest analogy.[14] This usually results in holdings that jury trial is not available.

§ 8.12 Alternatives to Historical Test

Because the use of the historical test in determining the right to jury trial in the modern civil action is perhaps both conservative and difficult to apply, it is natural that competing notions should emerge.

12. *See* Fed. R. Civ. P. 54(c); § 3.12 *supra.*

13. 369 U.S. 469, 82 S.Ct. 894, 8 L.Ed.2d 44 (1962).

14. *See* Annot., 13 A.L.R.2d 777.

"Basic nature" test

One test, proposed by Professor Moore and approved by a number of courts,[1] inquires into the "basic nature" of the issue presented in the action. The trouble with it is that it furnishes no guide for discerning the basic nature of an issue. The distinction between legal and equitable claims reflected not a principled line but a jumble of historical accidents, modified to some extent by practical concerns, some of which are no longer relevant. Some issues, to be sure, would usually (perhaps always) arise only in equity (such as mutual mistake as a basis for reformation, and existence of facts warranting surcharge of an express trustee). Others would always, or nearly always, arise only at law (negligent operation of an automobile).Such issues may well enough be called basically equitable or legal. But they pose no serious problem of trial mode, and no special test need be formulated for them. It is only when an issue was cognizable in either law or equity, depending on the context, that problems are presented and a test needed. Such issues are not inherently legal or equitable. They are like chameleons that take their color from surrounding circumstances. When applied to such issues, the basic nature test amounts to a subjective one, leaving the court free to find either way.[2]

Court discretion

Another approach leaves the decision to the trial court's discretion. Trial courts have, and should have, some discretion in prescribing the order of the business before them. This is confirmed and extended for the federal courts by Rule 42(b), which empowers a court to order separate trials of separate issues. Some courts have suggested that this discretion provides the solution for the problems of jury trial when a tendered issue would be cognizable either at law or in equity and one party claims a jury.[3] But recognizing an express constitutional right cannot properly be made a matter of judicial discretion. That much, at any rate, seems to have been settled by *Beacon Theatres v. Westover* and subsequent decisions.

Functional test

The constitutional issue could be considered one of deciding what types of issues are best fitted for court or jury trial. If all were *tabula rasa,* and some solon were trying to devise an ideal system for the administration of justice, he or she would probably approach the jury trial problems with such an inquiry in mind. This is implied in the statement by the American Bar Association in its Standards Relating to Trial Courts:

§ 8.12

1. *See* 5 Moore, Federal Practice and Procedure ¶ 38.16.

2. *See* Note, 47 Calif. L. Rev. 760, 762 (1959); Note, 45 Iowa L. Rev. 603, 606 (1960).

3. *See, e.g.,* Phoenix Mut. Life Ins. Co. v. Conway, 11 N.Y.2d 367, 183 N.E.2d 754, 229 N.Y.S.2d 740 (1962).

> The traditional province of the jury in civil cases consists essentially of resolving issues of witness credibility, including the resolution of testimonial conflicts between witnesses who may be endeavoring fully to tell the truth; of ascertaining states of mind where the legal significance of conduct depends on state of mind, such as knowledge, intention, or disregard of circumstances; of fixing damages where their calculation necessarily involves a subjective or humanistic judgment rather than reference to market or exchange value; and of determining standards of conduct that the law itself defines as those that an ordinary reasonable person would observe.[4]

This approach may well guide the future course of those charged with amending or recasting constitutions or, within narrower compass, of legislators. But as a guide for judicial decision-making, it creates difficulties because it is not tied to any historical precedent. Such a functional approach should be applied with deference to the scope of jury trial as it existed when the constitutional provisions were adopted; the modern right of jury trial should surely extend to actions that historically could have been maintained only in common law. Even with this limitation, an eclectic test would give the courts great authority in a matter of very great moment. But any tendency of the courts to restrict unduly the scope of jury trial can be changed by legislation.[5] And the exercise of such authority, informed by an appreciation of the jury's value as well as its limitations,[6] seems to hold no greater potential for abuse than attempting to deal with a problem of administering twentieth century justice in terms of a distinction evolved in the quite different procedural context of the eighteenth century. Some recent cases suggest that the courts are moving toward an eclectic approach.[7]

Complex litigation

Perhaps the most dubious case for jury trial is the complex case based on regulatory legislation, such as antitrust or patent litigation. As a practical matter, such a case puts the jury to least advantage. It requires the jury to assimilate large quantities of complex evidence, typically including masses of documents, conflicting expert testimony, and accounts or statistics. The length of trial may make the jurors resentful and thus distracted, and the prospect of a long trial may induce jurors with busy lives to seek excuse from service, thus yielding an unrepresentative jury. The legal and factual issues in such cases are often esoteric and not the kind of everyday problems with which jurors

4. ABA Standards Relating to Trial Courts § 2.10, Commentary.

5. *See, e.g.,* the Jones Act, 46 U.S.C. § 688; Panama R.R. v. Johnson, 264 U.S. 375, 44 S.Ct. 391, 68 L.Ed. 748 (1924); *compare* Dice v. Akron, C. & Y.R.R., 342 U.S. 359, 72 S.Ct. 312, 96 L.Ed. 398 (1952). *But see* § 8.1 note 14 *supra.*

6. *See, e.g.,* Hyde Properties v. McCoy, 507 F.2d 301 (6th Cir.1974); Cumens v. Garrett, 294 Ala. 535, 319 So.2d 665 (1975).

7. *See* Markman v. Westview Instruments, Inc., 517 U.S. 370, 116 S.Ct. 1384, 134 L.Ed.2d 577 (1996); §§ 8.3, 8.6 *supra.*

are most familiar. In sum, practical considerations that in an earlier day militated for the extraordinary relief of equity also militate against jury trial in these cases.[8]

At the same time, the only technical basis for saying that such cases are within the Seventh Amendment guaranty is that they involve the remedy of damages. When an injunction is sought in such cases, the suit can be assimilated to one in equity and the jury trial right is inapplicable.[9] When both an injunction and damages are sought, under the older analysis the suit could be treated as one in equity.[10] It is only the line of cases centering on *Beacon Theatres* that requires such "mixed" actions to be treated as "suits at common law."[11] But they are suits at common law only in remedy, not right. The right is purely a creature of statute and did not exist at common law.

It is therefore technically tenable to say that actions based on statutes are not suits at common law and hence that the jury trial guaranty is inapplicable, even though a damages remedy is sought. In essence, this is the basis on which the Supreme Court decided two important cases in which the claimants sought monetary relief in administrative proceedings that precluded jury trial—*NLRB v. Jones & Laughlin Steel Corp.*[12] and *Atlas Roofing Co. v. Occupational Safety and Health Review Commission.*[13] In *Jones & Laughlin* the Court held that the Seventh Amendment did not apply because the proceeding was a statutory, not a common law, proceeding; in *Atlas* the Court said that a "public right" was involved. Both cases involved statutory proceedings that were adjudicated in administrative agencies rather than in courts. But the Seventh Amendment does not exempt administrative agencies, so as precedents these cases would seem to have application to court proceedings. Furthermore, the Court has held in *Katchen v. Landy*[14] that Congress could exclude jury trial in special court procedures when necessitated by practical considerations of the kind associated with equity.

If these strands of doctrine are put together, it follows that Congress could, if it wished, provide statutory actions for monetary relief in the

8. *See* In re Japanese Elec. Prods. Antitrust Litig., 631 F.2d 1069 (3d Cir.1980); Sanders, Scientifically Complex Cases, Trial by Jury, and the Erosion of Adversarial Process, 48 De Paul L. Rev. 355 (1998); Comment, The Case for Special Juries in Complex Civil Litigation, 89 Yale L.J. 1155 (1980). Many thoughtful analysts think the practical difficulty of jury trial in complex cases is exaggerated. *See* Lempert, Civil Juries and Complex Cases: Let's Not Rush to Judgment, 80 Mich. L. Rev. 68 (1981); In re United States Fin. Sec. Litig., 609 F.2d 411 (9th Cir.1979); Symposium, Is the Jury Competent?, 52 Law & Contemp. Probs., Autumn 1989. On whether denying jury trial in complex cases has an historical basis, see § 8.2 *supra*, note 34.

9. *See* § 8.6 *supra.*

10. *See* § 8.8 *supra.*

11. *See* §§ 8.5 note 17 and 8.11 *supra.*

12. 301 U.S. 1, 57 S.Ct. 615, 81 L.Ed. 893 (1937). *See* § 8.1 note 6 *supra.*

13. 430 U.S. 442, 97 S.Ct. 1261, 51 L.Ed.2d 464 (1977); *see* § 8.1 note 6 *supra.*

14. 382 U.S. 323, 86 S.Ct. 467, 15 L.Ed.2d 391 (1966); *see* § 8.2 *supra.*

courts in which jury trial is precluded.[15] If Congress can so provide, then it cannot be unconstitutional to deny jury trial in such cases. And if that is true, the Court would be free to reach the same result by decisional law. Thus, the Court could hold that the Seventh Amendment does not require jury trial in statutory actions, and that the due administration of justice requires obviating jury trial in cases of extraordinary complexity. The latter proposition can be based on the Due Process Clause of the Fifth Amendment,[16] although this seems an unnecessary buttress to the argument.

This approach may be described as purposeful eclecticism in applying the jury trial requirement. It does not curtail the scope of jury trial in a random manner or because of doubts about the general desirability of jury trial. It simply says that neither constitutional history nor procedural policy require giving the Seventh Amendment the broadest reach permitted by technical analysis when compelling practical considerations militate in the other direction.

§ 8.13 Jury Size

The common law jury consisted of twelve persons who could return a verdict only on reaching a unanimous conclusion. Many states have provisions in their constitution or by statute for a jury of lesser size, ranging down to six; some provide for a jury of twelve in their trial courts of general jurisdiction but a six-person jury in courts of limited jurisdiction.[1] Moreover, many states provide that a civil jury may return a verdict on less than a unanimous vote of its members; for example, a jury may return a verdict on the concurrence of nine of its twelve members.[2] Both a smaller jury size and nonunanimous verdicts are state law provisions, it being settled that neither the Due Process Clause itself nor the doctrine that it "incorporates" various provisions of the Bill of Rights of the U.S. Constitution has the effect of requiring the states to provide civil jury trial.[3]

15. *Cf.* Tull v. United States, 481 U.S. 412, 107 S.Ct. 1831, 95 L.Ed.2d 365 (1987); Albemarle Paper Co. v. Moody, 422 U.S. 405, 95 S.Ct. 2362, 45 L.Ed.2d 280 (1975); Note, Congressional Provision for Nonjury Trial Under the Seventh Amendment, 83 Yale L.J. 401 (1973).

16. In re Japanese Elec. Prods. Antitrust Litig., 631 F.2d 1069 (3d Cir.1980). *Contra* In re U. S. Fin. Sec. Litig., 609 F.2d 411 (9th Cir.1979).

§ 8.13

1. *See* the bibliography in Cooley v. Strickland Transp. Co., 459 F.2d 779, 782 n. 9 (5th Cir.1972). *See also* Institute of Judicial Administration, A Comparison of Six and Twelve Member Civil Juries in New Jersey Superior and County Courts (1972); Developments in the Law-The Civil Jury, 110 Harv. L. Rev. 1408 (1997).

2. *See* Comment, The Case for Retention of the Unanimous Civil Jury, 15 DePaul L. Rev. 403 (1966).

3. Walker v. Sauvinet, 92 U.S. 90, 23 L.Ed. 678 (1876). When, however, a state court entertains an action based on federal law in which federal law prescribes a right to jury trial, the state must use some sort of a jury. *Compare* Dice v. Akron, C. & Y.R.R., 342 U.S. 359, 72 S.Ct. 312, 96 L.Ed. 398 (1952), *with* Minneapolis & St. L.R.R. v. Bombolis, 241 U.S. 211, 36 S.Ct. 595, 60 L.Ed. 961 (1916).

Juries of six

In the federal courts, jury size is governed by federal law. It had long been assumed that the jury trial provision of the Seventh Amendment signified a jury of twelve, following the common law.[4] The Federal Rules, since the adoption in 1938, have provided that the parties could agree to a smaller jury,[5] and such stipulations were strongly invited in many federal districts. But it was taken for granted that if the parties demanded a jury of twelve, it was to be provided as of right.

Smaller juries and nonunanimous verdicts have found many proponents.[6] The theory supporting nonunanimous verdicts predicted that fewer hung juries would result and that the benefits of jury trial could thus be provided at lower cost to litigants and the public. The same considerations of efficiency supported the argument for the smaller jury. It was repeatedly asserted, and often taken to be true, that these variations from the traditional jury of twelve would have no effects on verdict outcomes, or at least that any differences would be inconsequential. Impressive experimental evidence indicates, however, that this is not true.[7]

Be that as it may, in *Colgrove v. Battin*,[8] the Supreme Court held that a jury of six satisfied the requirements of the Seventh Amendment and that adoption of local federal district court rules requiring the use of six-person juries violated neither Federal Rule 48, which at that time plainly contemplated a twelve-person jury, nor the Enabling Act.[9] The Court did not deal with the question of nonunanimous verdicts, although it has upheld them in state court criminal cases,[10] and it may be assumed that the unanimity requirement still applies in the use of federal civil juries.[11] In any event, Rule 48 now allows a jury of six but requires a unanimous verdict unless all parties stipulate otherwise.[12]

As a matter of historical analysis of the Seventh Amendment, the decision in *Colgrove v. Battin* is very unconvincing; its assumption that

4. Capital Traction Co. v. Hof, 174 U.S. 1, 19 S.Ct. 580, 43 L.Ed. 873 (1899).

5. Fed. R. Civ. P. 48.

6. *See* Croake, Memorandum on the Advisability and Constitutionality of Six Man Juries and 5/6 Verdicts in Civil Cases, 44 N.Y. St. B.J. 385 (1972). *Contra*, Arnold, Trial by Jury: The Constitutional Right to a Jury of Twelve in Civil Trials, 22 Hofstra L. Rev. 1 (1993).

7. The matter is thoroughly reviewed in Lempert, Uncovering "Nondiscernible" Differences: Empirical Research and the Jury-Size Cases, 73 Mich. L. Rev. 643 (1975). *See also* Saks, Jury Verdicts: The Role of Group Size and Social Decision Rules (1977).

8. 413 U.S. 149, 93 S.Ct. 2448, 37 L.Ed.2d 522 (1973). See Resnik, Changing Practices, Changing Rules: Judicial and Congressional Rule-making on Civil Juries, Civil Justice, and Civil Judging, 49 Ala. L. Rev. 133 (1997).

9. 28 U.S.C. § 2072.

10. Johnson v. Louisiana, 406 U.S. 356, 92 S.Ct. 1620, 32 L.Ed.2d 152 (1972)(9 out of 12 juror verdict).

11. *E.g.*, Masino v. Outboard Marine Corp., 652 F.2d 330 (3d Cir.1981) (holding that unanimity is required in a federal civil jury).

12. Fed. R. Civ. P. 48 (as amended 1991).

jury size makes no difference is equally so.[13] But the decision is likely to stand and may in the long run aid in preserving the jury trial tradition by attenuating the force of the criticism that jury trial is less efficient than trial to a judge alone.

§ 8.14 Jury Composition

Meanings of "representative"

In theory the jury is representative of the community from which it is drawn. The origin of this concept is not entirely clear. As we have seen, originally the jury was supposed to decide on the basis of its members' own knowledge, as distinct from deciding on the basis of evidence presented to them.[1] A "representative" jury in that context might imply one having the same predisposition to the merits as was held in prevailing sentiment in the community. Later, the jury was conceived as a neutral body.[2] On this theory a jury might be regarded as "representing" the community in the same way as a legislator "represents" his or her electoral district—that is, the jury is supposed to speak for the community, whatever that might entail. But that concept does not necessarily require the jury's composition to correspond exactly or even roughly to the community's social profile. "Represent" can mean "speak for" as well as "correspond to," among many possible meanings. Hence, a jury could be said to represent the community if it consists of responsible people who are seriously concerned with the community's well-being.

Something like the latter concept appears to have prevailed in this country from at least the nineteenth century until the 1940s. Colonial juries, of course, excluded women, African Americans, and men lacking property. Later, the courts spoke in terms of the jury's being "representative." Operationally, however, this meant not a cross section of the community but only that jury selection should not systematically exclude any group.[3] Thus, it was not legally objectionable that the jury was composed primarily of middle class "good citizens" or that the system of jury selection was such as virtually to guarantee that the jury would be so composed.[4] Indeed, as late as 1949 the Supreme Court upheld a New York statute providing for "blue ribbon" juries in certain criminal cases.[5]

13. *See* analysis in Lempert, *supra* note 7.

§ 8.14

1. *See* § 7.8 *supra.*

2. *See* § 7.16 *supra.*

3. *See* Smith v. Texas, 311 U.S. 128, 61 S.Ct. 164, 85 L.Ed. 84 (1940); Annot., 166 A.L.R. 1422; Strauder v. West Virginia, 100 U.S. 303, 25 L.Ed. 664 (1880) (holding that excluding nonwhites violates the equal protection clause).

4. See the procedure held invalid in Thiel v. Southern Pac. Co., 328 U.S. 217, 66 S.Ct. 984, 90 L.Ed. 1181 (1946). *See also* People v. White, 43 Cal.2d 740, 278 P.2d 9 (1954).

5. Fay v. New York, 332 U.S. 261, 67 S.Ct. 1613, 91 L.Ed. 2043 (1947).

Racial discrimination

By the 1940s the courts and legislatures became increasingly receptive to several contentions contrary to previous notions: that juries composed primarily of middle-class persons had a different outlook than other juries might have; that this difference in outlook could affect jury decisions, at least marginally; that this effect wrought a disadvantage to parties who were not middle class and middle aged; and that this kind of difference was a denial either of equal protection or of due process.[6] This reorientation to the problem of representativeness in jury composition was intensified in the legal assault on segregation, in which legal challenge was directed particularly at racial discrimination in jury selection procedure.[7] Most of the cases involving this issue were criminal cases so that the rules for composition of a civil jury were only indirectly implicated. In most jurisdictions, however, civil juries and criminal juries are formed out of the same pool and by the same procedure. Hence, the requirement that a criminal jury selection not be systematically biased in terms of racial composition carried over to civil juries. Furthermore, statutes and other measures to avoid racial bias in jury composition had a considerable effect in reducing unrepresentativeness of juries in terms of economic and social status.[8] Indeed, because of these changes in jury selection, the development of the six-person jury, and the growth of devices to control juries, some would argue that the contemporary jury is an entity entirely different from its medieval or eighteenth century ancestor.[9]

As legal norms have changed, the mechanics of selecting the jury pool have been modernized. Today it is technically feasible to use multiple source lists, including not only the traditional voter list but also lists of licensed drivers, taxpayers, welfare recipients, and so on.[10] The statistical tests for representativeness, which compare the jury pool with the general population, have also become more sophisticated. These statistical techniques have been brought to bear in challenges to jury pools.[11] The generally prevailing rule now is that the jury pool must be representative in the sense that it is not chosen in such a way as to exclude any "recognizable group."[12]

6. Thiel v. Southern Pac. Co., 328 U.S. 217, 66 S.Ct. 984, 90 L.Ed. 1181 (1946).

7. *See, e.g.*, Peters v. Kiff, 407 U.S. 493, 92 S.Ct. 2163, 33 L.Ed.2d 83 (1972).

8. 28 U.S.C. §§ 1861–69; *cf.* Note, Underrepresentation of Economic Groups on Federal Juries, 57 B.U.L. Rev. 198 (1977).

9. Carrington, The Seventh Amendment: Some Bicentennial Reflections, 1990 U. Chi. Legal F. 33; Yeazell, The New Jury and the Ancient Jury Conflict, 1990 U. Chi. Legal F. 87.

10. *See* Kairys, Kadane, and Lehoczky, Jury Representativeness: A Mandate for Multiple Source Lists, 65 Calif. L. Rev. 776 (1977); *see also* McCusick and Boxer, Uniform Jury Selection and Service Act, 8 Harv. L. Legis. 280 (1971). But see Note, Jury Source Lists: Does Supplementation Really Work?, 82 Cornell L. Rev. 390 (1997).

11. *See* Castaneda v. Partida, 430 U.S. 482, 97 S.Ct. 1272, 51 L.Ed.2d 498 (1977); In re Rhymes, 130 Cal.App.3d 232, 181 Cal. Rptr. 764 (1982).

12. *See* In re Rhymes, 130 Cal.App.3d 232, 181 Cal.Rptr. 764 (1982); State v. Porro, 152 N.J.Super. 259, 377 A.2d 950 (1977).

Mechanics of selection

Jury selection procedure begins with a "master list" drawn from source lists of the type mentioned above. From the master list a pool of jurors is summoned at convenient times. Traditionally, new groups of jurors were summoned monthly or bimonthly, sometimes less often. They served for a term equal to that time interval, when they were replaced by a new group. That meant that most jurors would serve on several cases during a term of service. It has been thought that this is an excessive burden, particularly on people who are employed full time. Hence, the trend is to shorten the term of service. In some jurisdictions, the term is shortened to "one day or one trial."[13] That reduces the individual burden of service, but it also means that all jurors are novices, which may affect the way the jury reacts to certain types of cases.

Either before or after they are summoned to become part of the pool, jurors may be examined concerning their qualifications and their eligibility for exemption. Qualifications include adulthood, citizenship, and local residence, and may include the ability to read and write English.[14] Formerly many classes of persons were exempt from jury service because their vocations were thought to be more important (such as teachers) or were conducive to bias (such as police officers). Although there appears to be no constitutional limitation on the legislature's authority to confer exemptions not based on race, gender, or other suspect classifications, modern legislation has tended to restrict exemptions severely to assure better representativeness and to distribute the burden of service more fairly.[15]

Voir dire

Jurors whose eligibility is thus verified convene in court for assignment to courtrooms. When jury selection is ready to begin, a group goes to the courtroom for voir dire examination. The voir dire inquires whether the prospective jurors are acquainted with either the facts or the parties to the cause, or have any predisposition regarding the merits of the case. Jurors are also interrogated, orally or by previous questionnaire, about their general background—vocation, education, family status, and the like. This information may be a ground for challenge for cause if the juror's background suggests an affinity or antipathy to one of the parties. The concept is that of imputed bias, namely that the juror's personal history would ordinarily be expected to result in bias even if the juror denies actual bias. In a suit involving insurance, for example, prospective jurors usually will be asked whether they have an

13. *See* Keilitz and Caviness, Evaluating Jury Selection, Utilization, and Management, State Court Journal, Winter 1980.

14. 28 U.S.C. § 1865(b); United States v. Benmuhar, 658 F.2d 14 (1st Cir.1981).

15. McCusick and Boxer, Uniform Jury Selection and Service Act, 8 Harv. J. Legis. 280 (1971). *See also* the Federal Jury Selection and Service Act of 1968, 28 U.S.C. §§ 1861–1869.

interest in the insurance business.[16] Of course, such an inquiry is intended to make a statement as well as to make an inquiry.

Another subject of questioning is the extent of any bias engendered by media coverage of the case. Trial courts, "in an era of rapid and widespread communications ... must be vigilant to ensure that jurors are not biased and trials are not compromised by media attention surrounding a case."[17] But, at the same time "it is not required ... that jurors be totally ignorant of the facts and issues involved.... It is sufficient if the juror can lay aside his impression or opinion and render a verdict based on the evidence presented in court."[18]

A topic that is especially pertinent and sensitive in challenge for cause is racial identity and attitude. It is clear that these factors may be explored in voir dire and that in criminal cases they must be explored in some circumstances. But what remains unclear is the extent to which an exploration of racial factors, or other bases of imputed disqualification, is mandatory.[19] The general rubric is that the scope and intensity of voir dire rest in the sound discretion of the trial court. The appellate courts disturb that discretion only in what they consider extreme cases, but what might be an extreme case is unsettled.[20] Refusal to make any inquiry about jurors' racial attitudes, if counsel requests such an inquiry, would doubtless be reversible error. It would be difficult to show on appeal, however, that a brief inquiry by the judge was merely perfunctory.[21]

A juror's responses to voir dire questions are on oath and are required to be truthful. Jurors sometimes give false, inaccurate, or misleading answers. The consequences of such answers were addressed in *McDonough Power Equipment v. Greenwood.*[22] In this personal injury case, a juror failed to reveal, in questions related to members of his family, that his son had been injured. The Supreme Court assumed that the parties did not learn the truth until after trial. Nevertheless, it refused to grant a new trial because the juror was found to have acted in good faith and the trial was found to be fair; litigants are "entitled to a fair trial, but not a perfect one."[23]

16. Kiernan v. Van Schaik, 347 F.2d 775 (3d Cir.1965). *See also* McDonough Power Equip. v. Greenwood, 464 U.S. 548, 104 S.Ct. 845, 78 L.Ed.2d 663 (1984); Suggs and Sales, Juror Self-Disclosure in the Voir Dire, 56 Ind. L.J. 245 (1981).

17. United States v. Bakker, 925 F.2d 728, 734 (4th Cir.1991).

18. Irvin v. Dowd, 366 U.S. 717, 722–723, 81 S.Ct. 1639, 1642–1643, 6 L.Ed.2d 751 (1961) (quoted in United States v. Bakker, 925 F.2d 728, 734 (4th Cir.1991)); *see* Dextler, et al., A test of voir dire as a remedy for the prejudicial effects of pretrial publicity, 22 J. Applied Soc. Psych. 819 (1992) (voir dire ineffective).

19. Rosales-Lopez v. United States, 451 U.S. 182, 101 S.Ct. 1629, 68 L.Ed.2d 22 (1981).

20. United States v. Gibbons, 602 F.2d 1044 (2d Cir.1979).

21. Garrett v. Morris, 815 F.2d 509 (8th Cir.1987); Ballard v. Northwestern Natl. Life Ins. Co., 931 F.2d 513 (8th Cir.1991); text at note 37 *infra.*

22. 464 U.S. 548, 104 S.Ct. 845, 78 L.Ed.2d 663 (1984).

23. *Id.*

Challenges for cause

There is no limit to the number of challenges for cause; the limit in their use is inherent in the requirement that good cause be shown for dismissing a juror. Challenges, like motions to disqualify a judge, can raise deep questions about what kind of adjudicator society wants and litigants are entitled to. Few would dispute that a juror should not hear a case in which the juror or a close relative has a financial interest, or in which the juror has already decided how to vote on the basis of pretrial publicity. It is harder to decide whether a juror's disagreement with the law to be enforced indicates unwillingness to enforce that law, or should rather be considered just one of many attitudes that a jury drawn from the community may properly incorporate. Similar questions can be raised about a potential juror's belief that "verdicts are too high" or that "corporations are irresponsible."

Conduct of questioning

Functionally related to the problem of scope and intensity of voir dire is the issue of who conducts the questioning.[24] In the "federal method," followed by most federal judges, the judge conducts the questioning and devises most of the questions, but the judge also explores topics and even uses specific questions proposed by counsel for the parties. The judge may question prospective jurors collectively rather than individually in the federal voir dire system, even in criminal cases.[25]

In the "state method," followed in most states, the lawyers conduct voir dire questioning, the judge monitoring it in the same way as in examination of witnesses at trial. Judges generally prefer the "federal method" because it is more expeditious and because it leads jurors to identify themselves with the court and its neutral purposes. Lawyers generally prefer to do the questioning themselves, on the theory that their questioning will be far more penetrating (which seems true) and also that they can promote sympathy with their clients (which may also be true).[26]

Peremptory challenge

The voir dire examination is also relevant to the exercise of another kind of challenge, the peremptory challenge. A peremptory challenge is a legal privilege to excuse a prospective juror without showing cause. The

24. *See generally* Levitt, Nelson, Ball, and Chernik, Expediting Voir Dire: An Empirical Study, 44 S. Cal. L. Rev. 916 (1971); Hastie, Is Attorney–Conducted Voir Dire and Effective Procedure for the Selection of Impartial Jurors?, 40 Am. U. L. Rev. 703 (1991).

25. *See, e.g.*, United States v. Bakker, 925 F.2d 728 (4th Cir.1991); United States v. Vest, 842 F.2d 1319 (1st Cir.1988).

26. *See* Babcock, Voir Dire: Preserving Its "Wonderful Power," 27 Stan. L. Rev. 545 (1975); Hastie, Is Attorney–Conducted Voir Dire an Effective Process for the Selection of Impartial Jurors?, 40 Am. U.L. Rev. 703 (1991).

connection between voir dire and peremptory challenge is that information obtained in voir dire that falls short of "good cause" nevertheless informs the party in using its peremptories.[27] A party may, however, use any source of information in exercising peremptory challenges.[28] The number of peremptory challenges is limited by statute or court rule.[29] In a federal civil suit, for example, each side is permitted three peremptory challenges.[30] The appropriate procedures for the administration of these challenges generally lie within the trial court's discretion. Usually the court will allow the challenges to be cast alternately, with a replacement juror being drawn on the exercise of a challenge.[31] In the absence of any indication that the jury is unsatisfactory to either party when it was chosen, an appellate court will be reluctant to overturn a verdict based on a challenge to the jury's composition. Usually an objection at trial will be needed to preserve the claim that peremptory challenges were used in a discriminatory manner.[32]

The peremptory challenge is an important but anomalous procedural mechanism. Enormous effort is made to establish and maintain the representative nature of the jury pool and to keep it free from racial prejudice, economic bias, and other influences. Substantial cost is incurred in conducting the voir dire to exclude jurors who are actually biased or to whom bias may reasonably be imputed because of their background. The jury thus painstakingly winnowed is then subject to decomposition by the parties' competing unilateral exercises of privilege. The aim seems to be a jury that is both representative of the community and acceptable to the parties. In some cases this becomes a contradiction in terms.[33] The contradiction is revealed most vividly when one of the parties evidently has employed its peremptories on a basis that is particularly obnoxious—for instance, by excluding all blacks. The courts have not been able to handle this situation very well, because they cannot reconcile the conflicting premises involved.[34]

27. *See* Note, Voir Dire: Establishing Minimum Standards to Facilitate Exercise of Peremptory Challenges, 27 Stan. L. Rev. 1493 (1976).

28. *See* Zeisel and Diamond, The Jury Selection in the Mitchell–Stans Conspiracy Trial, 1976 Am. B. Found. Res. J. 151 (discussing use of sociopsychological "profiles" of prospective jurors).

29. *See, e.g.,* 28 U.S.C. § 1870; Cal. Civ. Proc. Code § 601. *Cf.* Annot., 32 A.L.R.2d 747.

30. 28 U.S.C. § 1870.

31. Kotler v. American Tobacco Co., 926 F.2d 1217 (1st Cir.1990).

32. Anderson v. Cryovac, Inc., 862 F.2d 910 (1st Cir.1988); Real v. Hogan, 828 F.2d 58 (1st Cir.1987).

33. *See* Comment, Peremptory Challenges and the Meaning of Jury Representation, 89 Yale L.J. 1177 (1980).

34. *Compare* Swain v. Alabama, 380 U.S. 202, 85 S.Ct. 824, 13 L.Ed.2d 759 (1965), *with* Batson v. Kentucky, 476 U.S. 79, 106 S.Ct. 1712, 90 L.Ed.2d 69 (1986) (overruling *Swain* and striking down prosecutor's use of peremptories to exclude African Americans from jury trying African American defendant). See Marder, Beyond Gender: Peremptory Challenges and the Roles of the Jury, 73 Tex. L. Rev. 1041 (1995)(urging abolition of peremptories).

Racial and gender discrimination

In *Batson v. Kentucky,* the Supreme Court ruled that the Equal Protection Clause prohibits the states from using peremptory challenges to strike black venire members in a criminal case "on the assumption that they will be biased in a particular case simply because the defendant is black."[35] Prosecutors who challenge black members of the jury venire "must articulate a neutral explanation related to the particular case to be tried." On review, the appellate court will generally uphold a lower court's findings of fact as to whether peremptory challenges of venire members were racially motivated unless such findings are clearly erroneous.[36] In *Edmonson v. Leesville Concrete Co.*[37] the Supreme Court held that private litigants in civil cases may not use peremptory challenges to exclude jurors on account of their race. Challenges based on gender are likewise forbidden, at least when exercised by the state.[38] Whatever the actual impact of jurors' race or gender on the results of civil trials,[39] exclusions on such grounds undermine the ideal of equal justice under law. Forbidding them parallels other efforts to remove racial and gender bias from the judicial system by such means as selecting more diverse judges and educating judges and lawyers.[40]

Although courts thus declare the value of equality in jury selection, they have been less successful in making it a reality.[41] It is hard to determine the true motivation for a peremptory challenge. And if the court rejects a lawyer's stated reason because, although not based on race or gender, it is not much of a ground for a challenge, peremptory challenges will no longer be peremptory but will be subject to a judge's evaluation. Moved by these and other concerns, even in the face of a *prima facie* case of discrimination, courts have accepted very dubious explanations of challenges.[42] Perhaps the most disturbing case is one in

35. 476 U.S. 79, 97, 106 S.Ct. 1712, 1723, 90 L.Ed.2d 69, 88 (1986); see Powers v. Ohio, 499 U.S. 400, 111 S.Ct. 1364, 113 L.Ed.2d 411 (1991)(White criminal defendant can object to exclusion of African Americans). See Underwood, Ending Race Discrimination in Jury Selection: Whose Right Is It Anyway?, 92 Colum. L. Rev. 725 (1992).

36. *See, e.g.,* United States v. Sherrills, 929 F.2d 393 (8th Cir.1991).

37. 500 U.S. 614, 111 S.Ct. 2077, 114 L.Ed.2d 660 (1991).

38. J.E.B. v. Alabama ex rel. T.B., 511 U.S. 127, 114 S.Ct. 1419, 128 L.Ed.2d 89 (1994). See Davis v. Minnesota, 511 U.S. 1115, 114 S.Ct. 2120, 128 L.Ed.2d 679 (1994)(Thomas & Scalia, JJ., dissenting from denial of certiorari, suggesting that peremptory challenges based on religious affiliations are also unconstitutional).

39. See Diamond, Juror Judgments About Liability and Damages: Sources of Variability and Ways to Increase Consistency, 48 DePaul L. Rev. 301 (1998)(finding little impact of race and gender on juror votes).

40. *E.g.,* Report of the Second Circuit Task Force on Gender, Racial, and Ethnic Fairness in the Courts, 1997 Ann. Survey Am. L. 9; Report, Special Committee on Race and Ethnicity, 64 Geo. Wash. L. Rev. 189 (1996); Schafran, Will Inquiry Produce Action? Studying the Effects of Gender on the Federal Courts, 32 U. Rich. L. Rev. 615 (1998); Tobias, The Gender Gap in the Federal Bench, 19 Hofstra L. Rev. 171 (1990).

41. Melilli, *Batson* in Practice: What We Have Learned About *Batson* and Peremptory Challenges, 71 Notre Dame L. Rev. 447 (1996); Charlow, Tolerating Deception and Discrimination after *Batson*, 50 Stan. L. Rev. 9 (1997).

42. *E.g.,* Purkett v. Elem, 514 U.S. 765, 115 S.Ct. 1769, 131 L.Ed.2d 834 (1995)(upholding challenge to African American juror based on his mustache and goatee).

which a court upheld a challenge of jurors because they knew Spanish and might therefore not accept a sworn translator's English translations.[43]

43. Pemberthy v. Beyer, 19 F.3d 857 (3d Cir.1994), cert. denied, 513 U.S. 969, 115 S.Ct. 439, 130 L.Ed.2d 350 (1994). Other cases go almost as far. Hernandez v. New York, 500 U.S. 352, 111 S.Ct. 1859, 114 L.Ed.2d 395 (1991); United States v. Jordan, 223 F.3d 676 (7th Cir.2000).

Chapter 9

JOINDER OF CLAIMS

A. PERMISSIVE JOINDER OF CLAIMS

§ 9.1 In General

Stage

The rules governing the scope of a civil action as to subject matter and parties have several dimensions. The first is the *stage* in the litigation when the rules directly operate. There are some rules, called the rules of joinder of claims and parties, that operate at the commencement of the action or during the action before the final judgment. For example, the modern rule of joinder of claims provides that the plaintiffs in framing a complaint may join all claims they have against a defendant as of the time of commencing the action, even if the claims are unrelated.[1] Other rules, those of res judicata, operate after the final judgment but indirectly affect joinder at the commencement of a lawsuit. These rules prescribe the circumstances under which a litigant is prohibited from asserting a claim or defense when that litigant was a party to litigation in which that claim or defense could have been asserted but was not. For example, under modern rules of res judicata a plaintiff who

§ 9.1

1. Fed. R. Civ. P. 18.

brought an action claiming that a transaction with defendant was a breach of contract, whether that claim was won or lost, is precluded from suing again on the contention that the transaction was a tort;[2] the rules of res judicata treat these two claims as one to determine whether plaintiff can sue a second time.[3] The rules of res judicata therefore operate retroactively on the original action as, in effect, rules of compulsory joinder of claims. In this chapter and in Chapter 10 we refer only incidentally to the rules of res judicata; they are considered comprehensively in a later chapter.[4]

Claims and parties

A second dimension of the rules governing scope of the action concerns the *topic* addressed by the rules governing joinder. Some rules refer to joinder of claims[5] and others refer to joinder of parties,[6] but the two kinds of joinder are not mutually exclusive. Every litigation potentially can entail multiple claims (such as tort and contract), multiple parties (several plaintiffs or several defendants), or both multiple claims and multiple parties. Any given situation therefore may involve the rules of both joinder of claims and joinder of parties. And, since there are both prospectively and retrospectively operating rules, any given situation may involve the prospectively operating rules of joinder of claims and parties and the retrospectively operating rules of res judicata.

Minimum and maximum

The final dimension of the rules governing scope is that of the minimum versus the maximum scope of the action.[7] Some rules *require* that related claims or related parties be brought into the action, if feasible; these specify a minimum scope of the action. Other rules *permit* the plaintiff, or sometimes a defendant or a third party, to expand the litigation to include related claims beyond those required by the rules governing minimum scope.

The concurrent effect of these three dimensions means that joinder of claims and parties can be very complex. Additional complications stem from now obsolete procedural problems, particularly those arising from the dual system of law and equity.[8] Further complexities arise from the interrelationship of joinder rules and rules of jurisdiction, particularly the rules governing the territorial jurisdiction of state courts[9] and the

2. Restatement (Second) of Judgments § 24.

3. *See* § 11.8 *infra.*

4. *See* Chapter 11.

5. *See* Fed. R. Civ. P. 18, 13(b).

6. *See id.* 19, 20, 13(h). *See also* Tobias, Rule 19 and the Public Rights Exception to Party Joinder, 65 N.C.L. Rev. 745 (1987).

7. *See* §§ 10.11–10.15 *infra.*

8. *See* § 9.2 *infra*; *cf.* Fed. R. Civ. P. 18(b).

9. *See* §§ 2.3–2.21 *supra*; *see, e.g.,* World-Wide Volkswagen Corp. v. Woodson, 444 U.S. 286, 100 S.Ct. 559, 62 L.Ed.2d 490 (1980).

subject matter jurisdiction of the federal courts.[10]

To sort out these complexities, two basic concepts of modern procedure should be kept in mind. First, in general, between any pair of adverse parties (such as plaintiff and defendant) any claim, and any defense to a claim, may be asserted regardless of the subject of the out-of-court transactions involved in the claims. Thus, under modern rules a plaintiff could in one litigation sue a defendant for automobile accident injuries and breach of a contract to sell a house. (In real life, of course, it is rare that parties have concurrent legal disputes arising from such wholly unrelated transactions.)

Second, in general, when a litigation involves more than a single plaintiff against a single defendant, the claims that can be asserted must arise from the same out-of-court transaction or from transactions that are closely related in their facts. That is, in a two-party case the claims can concern any subject matter (within the court's jurisdictional limitations, which are particularly important in federal court), but in a multiparty case there must be at least one claim that involves all the parties.

Plaintiff autonomy v. complete justice

As we shall see, the provisions on joinder of parties and claims under the Federal Rules have various inconsistencies and anomalies. These reflect tensions between two basic principles concerning the scope of a civil action. One principle is that the plaintiff should be free to determine which defendants to join and what claims to assert against them. This principle is sometimes expressed by saying that plaintiff should be "master of his suit." The other principle is that when an out-of-court transaction is brought into litigation, all claims involving all parties should be determined, allowing separate trial of peripheral issues if necessary. This principle can be expressed by saying that the court has an interest in doing complete justice in a controversy. The gain to be derived, by the parties and by society, from the broad joinder of claims is "the convenience and utility of settling all differences between parties at once."[11]

Neither objective is fully carried out in the federal joinder provisions. A plaintiff is free to join whatever claims he or she may have against an opposing party, but is not required to do so.[12] A plaintiff is free to join parties so long as the claims against them relate to the same transaction or related transactions, but generally is not required to join

10. *See* §§ 2.2, 2.24–2.28 *supra*; *see, e.g.*, Aldinger v. Howard, 427 U.S. 1, 96 S.Ct. 2413, 49 L.Ed.2d 276 (1976); Stallworth v. City of Cleveland, 893 F.2d 830 (6th Cir. 1990); Manor Healthcare Corp. v. Guzzo, 894 F.2d 919 (7th Cir.1990); 640 Broadway Renaissance Co. v. Cuomo, 714 F.Supp. 686 (S.D.N.Y.1989).

11. Clark, Code Pleading 435 (2d ed. 1947).

12. *See* Fed. R. Civ. P. 18.

all such parties.[13] The principle that all transaction-related claims should be joined is given greater weight in defendant's claims. Thus, a defendant is required to interpose counterclaims arising out of the same transaction.[14] A defendant generally is permitted to cross-claim against a co-defendant[15] and to bring in third parties against whom defendant has a claim for contribution or indemnity.[16] But the joinder rules do not require the assertion of these cross-claims and impleader claims and may not permit them in certain circumstances.[17]

Thus, the fundamental dispute remains unresolved over which principle—inclusiveness or simplicity—should dominate.[18] The reasons for limiting joinder are the fear of confusion and complexity if a lawsuit is allowed to include many diverse issues and perhaps also the possibility of oppression arising from confusion and complexity. The matter comes down to a balance of inclusiveness and simplicity. Fears of confusion, complexity, and oppression have not vanished, although they probably have always been exaggerated. But it is now seen that these evils can be avoided by giving the trial court discretion to order that issues be *tried* separately, where a balance of convenience dictates that course, without forbidding claims to be joined in the same action. A parallel reform authorizes the court to join trial claims filed as separate actions.[19]

§ 9.2 Historical Policies

In common law procedure before the Field Code,[1] very limited latitude was allowed for joinder of claims, and within these limitations even narrower latitude was permitted for joinder of parties. Equity procedure, in contrast, began with the premise that if a controversy was shown to be within the equity court's jurisdiction,[2] the court should draw to itself all related claims and all related parties. The contrast in joinder policy could not have been sharper: Common law procedure precluded assertion of claims based on different legal theories even though the

13. *See id.* 20.

14. *See id.* 13(a).

15. *Id.* 13(g).

16. *See id.* 14.

17. See the careful textual analysis in Greenbaum, Jacks or Better to Open: Procedural Limitations on Co-Party and Third-Party Claims, 74 Minn. L. Rev. 507 (1990).

18. *Compare* Freer, Avoiding Duplicative Litigation: Rethinking Plaintiff Autonomy and the Court's Role in Defining the Litigative Unit, 50 U. Pitt. L. Rev. 809 (1989) (favoring the transaction principle), *with* Transgrud, Joinder Alternatives in Mass Tort Litigation, 70 Cornell L. Rev. 779 (1985) (emphasizing plaintiff autonomy).

19. Fed. R. Civ. P. 42.

§ 9.2

1. New York, First Report of Commissioners (1848); Williams, Pleading Reform in Nineteenth Century America: The Joinder of Actions at Common Law and Under the Codes, 6 J. Legal Hist. 299 (1985). *See also* Subrin, David Dudley Field and the Field Code: A Historical Analysis of an Earlier Procedural Vision, 6 Law & Hist. Rev. 311 (1988).

2. "Jurisdiction" in this context means a showing of justification for an equitable remedy owing to the inadequacy of the action at law or another basis for equitable relief. *See* Rendleman, The Inadequate Remedy at Law as a Prerequisite for an Injunction, 33 U. Fla. L. Rev. 346 (1981).

claims arose out of a single transaction (for example, tort and contract in a products liability situation), while equity could insist on extensive joinder, sometimes to the point of absurdity.[3] In the reforms, first in the Field Code of 1848 and then in the Federal Rules in 1938, equity's extensive joinder policy prevailed, with power reposed in the court to sever claims and parties for separate trial when that was necessary to prevent confusion.[4]

Same form of action

Joinder of separate claims was allowed at common law when there was sufficient *legal similarity* between the claims joined and when all the claims were in favor of the plaintiff(s) and against the defendant(s).[5] The basis for testing the legal similarity of claims was itself historical and not entirely clear,[6] but the concept was that a plaintiff could join claims that were properly presented in the same form of action and not otherwise,[7] except that debt could be joined with detinue[8] and case with trover.[9] Thus, a plaintiff might join two or more counts in trespass[10] or other form of action,[11] but he or she could not join a count in trespass with one in case,[12] or one in assumpsit with either debt or covenant.[13] Moreover, there had to be identity of parties to all the claims joined,[14]

3. *See* Hazard, Indispensable Party: The Historical Origin of a Procedural Phantom, 61 Colum. L. Rev. 1254 (1961).

4. Fed. R. Civ. P. 42(b). *See generally* Subrin, How Equity Conquered Common Law: The Federal Rules of Civil Procedure in Historical Perspective, 135 U. Pa. L. Rev. 909 (1987).

5. See Sunderland, Joinder of Actions, 18 Mich. L. Rev. 571 (1920), for a comprehensive analysis and criticism of common law notions that limited the free joinder of actions.

6. 1 Tidd's Practice 10–12 (2d Am. ed. from 8th London ed. 1828), demonstrating the anomalous theories put forth by common law courts as justification for restrictive joinder rules.

7. Shipman, Common Law Pleading 202 (3d ed. 1923). For the forms of action, *see* §§ 1.3, 3.3 *supra.*

8. Shipman, *supra* note 7. *Cf.* McKelvey, Common Law Pleading § 19 (2d ed. 1917).

9. Beebe v. Knapp, 28 Mich. 53, 58 (1873) (joinder of counts of fraud and trover held proper: "The nature of the causes of action is in legal effect the same: the same plea may be pleaded, and the same judgment given on both counts"). *Cf.* Smith v. Goodwin, 4 Barn. & Adol. 413, 110 Eng. Rep. 511 (K.B. 1833) (on question of misjoinder of case and trespass, court held that controversial count was in trover, hence properly joined with case).

10. Parker v. Parker, 34 Mass. (17 Pick.) 236 (1835) (approved joinder of counts in trespass to realty and trespass to personalty); Bishop v. Baker, 36 Mass. (19 Pick.) 517 (1837) (permitted amendment of trespass claim to realty so as to include count in trespass to personalty); Chicago W.D. Ry. v. Ingraham, 131 Ill. 659, 23 N.E. 350 (1890) (several causes of action, such as injuries to person and property, can be joined when same judgments are required, recoverable in the same form of action between the same parties).

11. *E.g.*, in replevin "he may count of several takings, part at one day and place, and part at another day and place." Fitzherbert, Natura Brevium 68 n.A. (1704).

12. Sheppard v. Furniss, 19 Ala. 760 (1851); Dalson v. Bradberry, 50 Ill. 82 (1869).

13. Guinnip v. Carter, 58 Ill. 296 (1871) (misjoinder, because one of the counts used the word "promised" rather than "agreed," thus sounding in assumpsit and improperly joined with the other counts in debt); Canton Natl. Bldg. Assn. v. Weber, 34 Md. 669 (1871).

14. Sunderland, Joinder of Actions, 18 Mich. L. Rev. 571, 582–583 (1920).

and the parties had to be suing or be sued in the same capacity in all counts.[15]

Claims arising out of the same occurrence thus could not be joined if they required different forms of action for their redress. Slander (case) could not be joined with assault and battery (trespass) even if the words and the beating were parts of a single altercation.[16] This insistence on legal similarity of claims may have served convenience at trial,[17] but the common law limitation on joinder of claims prohibited joinder at the *pleading* stage and thus was not merely a rule governing the trial.[18] Misjoinder was demurrable and was also a ground for a motion in arrest of judgment or a writ of error.[19] Thus the penalties for misjoinder were drastic, and the defect was not waived by a failure to take early objection.[20]

Joinder in equity

The rule permitting the joinder of claims in equity was in principle more flexible and was governed by convenience.[21] Although a concurrent rule provided that a bill in equity (that is, a complaint) could not be *multifarious* with respect either to parties or to subject matter, coherent

15. Shipman, Common Law Pleading 393–399 (3d ed. 1923).

16. *See* notes 6, 7, 12 *supra and compare* § 7.4 *supra. Compare also* Raspaulo v. Ragona, 127 Misc. 160, 215 N.Y.S. 407 (Sup.Ct.1926), decided under then existing Section 258 of New York Civil Practice Act. Section 258 was amended to allow unlimited joinder, subject to the discretion of the court. The significance of this legislation, as "a swing away from a mechanical to a flexible mode of procedure," is noted in 37 Colum. L. Rev. 462 (1937). When it was unclear which form of action would be upheld, a plaintiff could not join both of them in one action.

17. *See* §§ 3.2, 3.3 *supra. Compare* the following statement by Professor Hinton: "The rules themselves were the product of the jury trial, and were based on what appears to be a well founded belief that the capacity of the jury was limited, and that confusion was likely to result from a multiplicity of distinct issues, which would be inevitable if plaintiffs were allowed to join to enforce separate claims against a defendant, or if a plaintiff were permitted to enforce separate claims against different defendants in one action." Hinton, An American Experiment with the English Rules of Court, 20 Ill. L. Rev. 533, 535 (1926) (citing Voorhis v. Childs, 17 N.Y. 354 (1858)). *See also* Blume, Joinder of Causes of Action, 26 Mich. L. Rev. 1, 16 (1927).

18. 3A Moore, Federal Practice and Procedure ¶ 18.02: "[B]oth the common law and the codes (except the more recent innovations) treated the problem of joinder as a pleading problem, while in truth it is solely a trial problem. A score of actions can be pleaded in one complaint as well as in twenty, although it may not be desirable to try them together, and therefore the court should have the power to order separate trials."

19. 1 Chitty, Pleading 206 (1st Am. ed. 1809): "The consequences of a misjoinder are more important than the circumstance of a particular count being defective, for in the case of misjoinder, however perfect the counts may respectively be in themselves, the declaration will be bad on a general demurrer, or in arrest of judgment, or upon error."

20. Sunderland, Joinder of Actions, 18 Mich. L. Rev. 571, 573, 586 (1920). Illustrative cases are Bull v. Mathews, 20 R.I. 100, 37 A. 536 (1897) (objection to misjoinder of causes of action, raised after verdict in form of motion in arrest of judgment, granted); Dean v. Cass, 73 Vt. 314, 50 A. 1085 (1901) (same).

21. "While courts of law were condemning a multiplicity of *issues,* courts of equity were condemning a multiplicity of *suits.*" Blume, Joinder of Causes of Action, 26 Mich. L. Rev. 1, 10 (1927) (emphasis in original).

tests for multifariousness were never worked out.[22] In attempting to formulate guidelines for convenience, equity sometimes used terms that are found in modern rules and statutes—that the claims arise out of the "same transaction" or transactions connected with the "same subject of action," and that a common question of law or fact exist when multiple parties are involved.[23]

§ 9.3 Joinder Under Original Codes

As Professor Moore says, "the early codes failed signally in attacking the joinder of actions problem."[1] The code drafters apparently sought to combine the old law and equity tests without the re-examination of first principles that characterized so much of their valuable work.

Code joinder

Most codes provided for the "uniting" (the term used instead of "joinder") of legal and equitable claims, but only if they (1) fell within one of the classes enumerated in the joinder statute, (2) affected all parties to the action, and (3) did not require separate places of trial.[2] Consistency also was required by a few codes[3] and was added by judicial interpretation to a few others.[4] The first two requirements mentioned above, and the requirement that the allegations be consistent with each other, proved severe and unfortunate limitations on joinder.[5]

22. Brandis, Permissive Joinder of Parties and Causes in North Carolina, 25 N.C.L. Rev. 1, 17 (1946), referring to the equity rules of joinder incorporated in the North Carolina code: "It is quite true that those rules are frequently hard to apply, and the Court has conceded more than once that no general rule has been or can be adopted with regard to multifariousness. But the very vagueness of the rules has enabled the Court to permit joinder which might have been prevented by literal interpretation of the language of the Code provisions. . . ."

First Natl. Bank of Lincoln v. Starkey, 268 Ill. 22, 25–26, 108 N.E. 695, 696–697 (1915): "To lay down any rule universally applicable as to multifariousness, or to say what constitutes multifariousness as an abstract proposition, is, under the authorities, utterly impossible. . . . Under recent decisions it is frequently held that the objection of multifariousness usually raises merely a question of convenience in conducting the suit, and calls for the decision of the court simply upon the question whether, in its discretion, the various causes set forth in the bill should be tried in a single suit or should be divided and tried in two or more separate suits. . . ."

23. *See, e.g.,* Bedsole v. Monroe, 40 N.C. 313 (1848) (discussed in Brandis, Permissive Joinder of Parties and Causes in North Carolina, 25 N.C.L. Rev. 1, 17 (1946)). *See also* Blume, Joinder of Causes of Action, 26 Mich. L. Rev. 1, 16 (1927).

§ 9.3

1. 3A Moore, Federal Practice and Procedure ¶ 18.02.

2. Clark, Code Pleading § 68, at 441–448 (2d ed. 1947).

3. *E.g.,* Minn. Stat. Ann. § 544.27 (West 1946); N.Y. Civil Practice Act § 258 (before 1935 amendment). *Cf.* N.Y. Civ. Prac. L. & R. 601, 602, 3014.

4. Clark, Code Pleading 448 (2d ed. 1947). *Cf.* Seymour v. Chicago & N.W. Ry. Co., 181 Iowa 218, 233, 164 N.W. 352 (1917) ("The statute permits inconsistent defenses. But even that express permission will not permit defenses which are not merely inconsistent with, but destructive of, each other").

5. *See, e.g.,* Ader v. Blau, 241 N.Y. 7, 148 N.E. 771 (1925), where the court declared improper the joinder of counts in negligence against the owner of the fence which caused the injury and the physician who treated the victim.

Joinable classes of claims

The enumerated classes of actions in the early code joinder provisions fell into two groups. One, borrowed from equity, covered causes "arising out of the same transaction or transactions connected with the same subject of action."[6] The other group included a number of classes (ranging from six to ten), each covering claims that were similar in legal theory. This second group of classes roughly corresponded to the common law forms of action,[7] even though the codes sought to abolish the forms of action. Typical was the North Carolina statute,[8] which provided six classes:(1) contract, express or implied; (2) injuries to person or property; (3) injuries to character; (4) claims to recover realty; (5) claims to recover personal property; and (6) claims against a trustee.

The narrowness of these classes is well illustrated in *Bateman v. Wymojo Yarn Mills.*[9] Here, the plaintiff's complaint was held improperly to join "three separate and distinct charges of slander, one for malicious prosecution, one for false arrest and imprisonment, and one for trespass upon his property."[10] The dissenting opinion discloses that these were simply "a number of wrongs arising out of one affair between the plaintiff and the defendants."[11] The court held the claims not joinable since they did not all fall within a single class. "Slander is an injury to character; malicious prosecution is a personal tort, and so are false arrest and imprisonment."[12]

The transaction clause might have been construed to allow joinder when convenience requires it,[13] and indeed it was so construed by a number of courts.[14] But that clause too often received a narrow judicial interpretation,[15] and some authorities confined its operation to equitable claims.[16]

"Cause of action"

The rules on joinder of claims, under the codes or otherwise, presupposed a concept of separate claims or causes of action. That is, if

6. *E.g.*, N.Y. Laws ch. 392, at 167 (1852). This class is discussed in Clark, Code Pleading 452–456 (2d ed. 1947).

7. Clark, Code Pleading 438 (2d ed. 1947).

8. N.C. Gen. Stat. § 1–123 (1953).

9. 155 S.C. 388, 152 S.E. 675 (1930) (criticized in Comment, 25 Ill. L. Rev. 835 (1931)). *Contrast* Harris v. Avery, 5 Kan. 146 (1869).

10. 155 S.C. at 389, 152 S.E. at 675.

11. 155 S.C. at 393, 152 S.E. at 677.

12. 155 S.C. at 390, 152 S.E. at 675–676.

13. Clark, Code Pleading 452–456 (2d ed. 1947).

14. *E.g.*, Boulden v. Thompson, 21 Cal. App. 279, 131 P. 765 (1913); Goggins v. Fawcett, 145 Conn. 709, 147 A.2d 187 (1958); Harris v. Avery, 5 Kan. 146 (1869).

15. Pressley v. Great Atl. & Pac. Tea Co., 226 N.C. 518, 39 S.E.2d 382 (1946); Raspaulo v. Ragona, 127 Misc. 160, 215 N.Y.S. 407 (1926). *See* Carr, Some Aspects of Joinder of Causes, 5 Fordham L. Rev. 452 (1936), discussing the significance of the 1935 amendment to N.Y. Civil Practice Act § 258, with respect to liberalizing construction of the same transactions clause. *Compare* text at § 9.2 note 16 *supra*.

16. Pomeroy, Code Remedies § 369 (5th ed. 1929).

all aspects of a wrong were always one claim, there could not be a problem of joinder of claims.[17] It is impossible to discuss joinder, therefore, without also discussing the dimensions of a "claim" or "cause of action." If a plaintiff was injured in the arm and in the leg in one accident, plaintiff had a single claim for both injuries. Since there was only one claim, no question arose about joinder of claims. Moreover, under the rules of res judicata operating retroactively, the plaintiff would not be allowed to pursue damages for each injury in separate actions.[18]

In other situations, however, it was ambiguous whether one claim was involved. Suppose plaintiff suffered both personal injury and destruction of her automobile in a vehicular collision. In terms of the losses, two claims are involved; in terms of the cause of the losses, one claim is involved. Most courts have come to hold that such a situation gives rise to one claim or cause of action for purposes of res judicata.[19] Thus, the res judicata rules require as minimum scope for the action that the plaintiff include both claims in one action if he or she wants to recover on them, although some courts hold that two causes of action have arisen and thus that two actions would be permitted.[20] But courts agree that plaintiff should be *permitted* to claim for both the personal injury and the property damage losses in one action. Many courts applying the codes, however, would go no further than this in defining "transaction" and thus the scope of permissive joinder.[21]

Alternative theories

Furthermore, courts were reluctant to let a party pursue alternative legal theories for a single loss.[22] This reluctance manifested itself in prohibitions against alternative and hypothetical pleadings, in the theory of the pleadings doctrine, in compelling a party to make an election of remedies, and in various rules requiring consistency in pleading. Collectively these doctrines narrowed the scope of permissive joinder, much as did the restraints of the common law.[23]

Misjoinder

The codes provided that misjoinder of causes was a ground of demurrer if the misjoinder appeared on the face of the complaint, as it

17. *Cf.* Restatement (Second) of Judgments §§ 24–26.

18. *See* § 11.10 *infra.*

19. *See id.*

20. *See, e.g.*, Nationwide Ins. Co. v. Steigerwalt, 21 Ohio St.2d 87, 89, 255 N.E.2d 570, 571 (1970) (in the prosecution of claims under an automobile insurance policy, "the insurer, subrogated to a part of a claim assigned by the insured, may prosecute its claim in a separate action against the tort-feasor" (citing Hoosier Casualty Co. v. Davis, 172 Ohio St. 5, 173 N.E.2d 349 (1961))); *accord*, Rosenthal v. Scott, 150 So.2d 433 (Fla.1961); Sodak Distrib. Co. v. Wayne, 77 S.D. 496, 93 N.W.2d 791 (1958).

21. *See* Clark, Code Pleading 452–456 (2d ed. 1947).

22. *See* § 3.14 *supra.*

23. Clark, Cases on Modern Pleading 684 (1952), and citations therein.

usually would. Failure to raise the objection by demurrer, however, was generally held to constitute a waiver of it.[24] The empty formalism of the code joinder rules is thus suggested by the fact that misjoinder of claims would be meticulously policed if defendants promptly objected, but remorselessly ignored if they did not.

§ 9.4 Modern Joinder Where There Are No Multiple Parties

Under Rule 18 of the Federal Rules of Civil Procedure a party (in a complaint or a counterclaim) may "join, either as independent or as alternate claims, as many claims, legal, equitable, or maritime, as the party has against an opposing party."[1] Under the Rules, the only limitations placed on joinder are those governing the joinder of parties[2] in actions with multiple parties. Thus, a single plaintiff may join all the claims he or she has against a single defendant. The Federal Rules do not *require* a party to join claims, although in some circumstances failure to do so risks that the omitted claims will be barred by claim or issue preclusion.[3]

In addition, in a federal suit the court must have subject matter jurisdiction over all the claims. If there are two claims, this requirement is met if there is diversity of citizenship between the parties and the sum of the amounts in dispute exceeds the jurisdictional amount, or if there is independent subject matter jurisdiction over one claim and the other falls within the court's supplemental jurisdiction.[4]

B. PERMISSIVE JOINDER OF PARTIES

§ 9.5 Background at Common Law and in Equity

At common law there was no permissive joinder of plaintiffs. Those who had a technically joint interest were compelled to join as plaintiffs to enforce a claim concerning the interest;[1] absent such an interest, joinder of plaintiffs was improper. Plaintiffs had a "joint" interest when under the law they together owned a single claim, as opposed to their each owning "several" (separate) but similar claims.

24. Clark, Code Pleading § 72 (2d ed. 1947).

§ 9.4

1. Fed. R. Civ. P. 18.

2. *See id.* 13, 14, 19, 20, 22–24.

3. *See* §§ 11.8–14, 11.17–20 *infra.* One or two states require plaintiffs to join related claims. Mich. Ct. R. 2.203(A); Oltremare v. ESR Custom Rugs, Inc., 330 N.J.Super. 310, 749 A.2d 862 (App.Div.2000).

4. *See* 28 U.S.C. § 1367; United Mine Workers v. Gibbs, 383 U.S. 715, 86 S.Ct. 1130, 16 L.Ed.2d 218 (1966)(federal court's discretion to hear claim arising out of same nucleus of operative fact as claim over which it has subject matter jurisdiction); § 2.28 *supra.*

§ 9.5

1. Thus, plaintiffs were compelled to join when they were (1) joint promisees on the same obligation or instrument, (2) partners at the time of contract, or (3) joint owners of the property that was damaged. Clark, Code Pleading § 56 (2d ed. 1947); Shipman, Common Law Pleading § 226 (3d ed. 1923).

The case stood somewhat differently in joinder of defendants. Joint obligors had to be joined[2] and several obligors had to be sued separately,[3] yet if two or more persons were jointly and severally liable on an obligation, plaintiff had the choice to sue one or more of the obligors.[4] Whether obligations were joint, several, or joint and several depended on conceptual analysis, and in part on the language used in contracts between the parties. Thus, someone lending money to two partners could write into the loan agreement that the partners would be jointly and severally liable to give the lender the option to sue either of the partners separately for the full amount or to sue both in a single action. The plaintiff had a similar choice to sue one or more of those whom the common law regarded as joint tortfeasors.[5]

Equity

The equity rule was broader and more flexible. One could join as a plaintiff if one had an interest in the subject of the action and in the relief demanded.[6] This formulation was not meant to prescribe any hard-and-fast rule but simply to indicate considerations of convenience.[7] Defendants could be joined when the bill against them related "to matters of the same nature, and having a connection with each other, and in which all the defendants are more or less concerned, though their rights in respect to the general subject of the case may be distinct."[8] Equity also allowed a party who should properly be a plaintiff to be brought in as a defendant if he or she refused to join in the suit voluntarily.[9]

§ 9.6 Field Code Provisions

The typical provisions for joinder of parties in the early codes were as follows:

> All persons having an interest in the subject of an action and in obtaining the relief demanded may be joined as plaintiffs.
>
> Any person may be made a defendant who has or claims an interest in the controversy adverse to the plaintiff or who is a necessary party to

2. Shipman, *supra* note 1, at 395. *Cf.* People v. Sloper, 1 Idaho 158, 164 (1867).

3. Register v. Casperson, 3 Del. 289 (1840). *Cf.* Northern Texas Traction Co. v. Clark & Sweeton, 272 S.W. 564 (Tex.Civ. App.1925).

4. *See* Leftwich v. Berkeley, 11 Va. (1 Hen. & M.) 61 (1806) (on joint and several bond, obligors might be sued singly or together; when more than one, but less than all, were joined, this was fatal misjoinder).

5. This was a narrow concept at common law, being confined to those who acted in concert. *See* Prosser, Joint Torts and Several Liability, 25 Calif. L. Rev. 413, 414 (1937).

6. Story, Equity Pleading §§ 279, 279a, 284, 530–540 (10th ed. 1892).

7. *Id.* at §§ 284, 530–540.

8. Brinkerhoff v. Brown, 6 Johns. Ch. 139 (N.Y.Ch.1822).

9. *See* Insurance Co. of N. Am. v. Svendsen, 74 F. 346 (C.C.S.C.1896).

the complete determination or settlement of the question involved herein.[1]

Derivation from equity

Both provisions were borrowed from equity, and it was the apparent purpose of the drafters of the code to apply the flexible equitable principles to all actions.[2] The provisions were often construed, however, to confine their operation within the restrictive rules of the older system.[3]

Joinder of plaintiffs

Perhaps the chief stumbling block to liberal joinder was the joinder of plaintiffs. The code's language suggested that a party must have an interest *both* in the subject of the suit *and* in obtaining the relief demanded. Most courts construed the code to make the requirement double-barreled, at least when they dealt with claims that had formerly been legal rather than equitable.[4] The requirement of interest in the subject of the action did not give much trouble.[5] But the requirement of an interest in the relief demanded was construed to mean that when each of two plaintiffs seeks damages for his or her own injury, neither has an interest in the relief sought by the other. This notion was applied to preclude joinder of several persons injured in the same accident,[6] joinder of husband and wife or parent and child in suing for the injury to the wife or child,[7] and joinder of owners of separate pieces of real or personal property injured by the same wrongful act.[8]

When the plaintiffs' interests were not technically joint, the harshness of results like those above was mitigated by regarding the damages as constituting one lump sum to be divided afterward among the plaintiffs, rather than as separate recoveries.[9] Thus, parties with several interests in the same parcel of land were allowed to join in an action for

§ 9.6

1. Statutes are collected in Clark, Code Pleading 365 n.72, and 382 n.151e (2d ed. 1947); Pomeroy, Code Remedies §§ 111, 185 (5th ed. 1929).

2. New York, First Report of Commissioners on Practice and Pleadings 123–128 (1848).

3. Blume, Joinder of Causes of Action, 26 Mich. L. Rev. 1, 54 (1927).

4. *See, e.g.*, Hellams v. Switzer, 24 S.C. 39, 44–48 (1885); Clark, Code Pleading § 57, at 365–367 (2d ed. 1947). *Cf.* Pomeroy, Code Remedies § 121 (5th ed. 1929).

5. Clark, Code Pleading 366 (2d ed. 1947).

6. Brookside-Pratt Mining Co. v. McAlister, 196 Ala. 110, 72 So. 18 (1916) (husband and wife may not join in action for personal injuries caused to each by flooding of their home).

7. Campbell v. Washington Light & Power Co., 166 N.C. 488, 82 S.E. 842 (1914); Thigpen v. Kinston Cotton Mills, 151 N.C. 97, 65 S.E. 750 (1909).

8. *See, e.g.*, Brandis, Permissive Joinder of Parties and Causes in North Carolina, 25 N.C.L. Rev. 1, 30–32 (1946); St. Louis & S.F.R.R. v. Dickerson, 29 Okla. 386, 118 P. 140 (1911) (different owners of parts of contents of trunk may not join in action against carrier for loss of trunk); Logan Cent. Coal Co. v. County Court of Logan County, 106 W.Va. 578, 146 S.E. 371 (1929) (landlord and tenant may not join in action against tortfeasor for damages to freehold and leasehold caused by same conduct).

9. *See* note 10 *infra*.

damages for injury to it.[10] Moreover, when equitable relief was sought, joinder was more readily allowed since equitable relief often benefited all the plaintiffs indivisibly, as an injunction against the diversion of a stream would protect all lower riparian owners.[11] Even when this was not the case, as when plaintiffs sought rescission of separate sales induced by a common fraud, there was greater readiness to facilitate convenience than in damage cases having a common law background. Essentially, the courts maintained different joinder rules for actions derived from common law and for actions derived from equity.

Occasionally, though all too rarely, a court adopted the purpose of the code's framers "to make available in all cases, whether at law or in equity, the broader equitable rules then prevailing."[12] Thus, in *Bonde v. Stern*[13] thirty bondholders were allowed to join as plaintiffs in a damages action for breach of the bond agreement that set up a method for paying off the bonds. The court found it unnecessary to decide whether the action was equitable or legal.[14]

Two final points on joinder of plaintiffs should be noted. First, if the claims were assignable (such as contract and property damage claims) and if the assignee could sue in his or her own name as real party in interest,[15] then the restriction on joinder of plaintiffs might be circumvented by assigning all claims to a single plaintiff for collection.[16] Second, even when joinder was not permitted, trial convenience might nevertheless be achieved by consolidating separate actions for trial. Many decisions allowed such consolidation even over defendant's objection,[17] a result that throws doubt on the wisdom of the rules forbidding joinder in the first place.

Joinder of defendants

No language in the code provision for joinder of defendants could fairly be construed to preclude such joinder when all defendants were involved in a single harm-producing claim of events. Nevertheless, the decisions limited joinder of defendants to situations in which it had been allowed at common law.

As we have seen, at common law joint tortfeasors could be joined at plaintiff's option.[18] This has remained the rule ever since. Its application

10. *See, e.g.*, Clark v. McClain Fire Brick Co., 100 Ohio St. 110, 125 N.E. 877 (1919); Clark, Code Pleading 366 (2d ed. 1947); Brandis, Permissive Joinder of Parties and Causes in North Carolina, 25 N.C.L. Rev. 1, 40 (1946).

11. Cloyes v. Middlebury Elec. Co., 80 Vt. 109, 66 A. 1039, 11 Law. Rep. Ann. (n.s.) 693 (1907) (collecting cases).

12. Bonde v. Stern, 73 N.D. 273, 281, 14 N.W.2d 249 (1944).

13. *See* note 12 *supra*.

14. 73 N.D. at 279, 14 N.W.2d at 251.

15. *See* Chapter 10.

16. Benedict v. Guardian Trust Co., 58 A.D. 302, 68 N.Y.S. 1082 (1901). *But cf.* Logan Cent. Coal Co. v. County Court of Logan County, 106 W.Va. 578, 146 S.E. 371 (1929) (noted in 36 W. Va. L. Rev. 199 (1930)). *Cf. also* note 8 *supra*.

17. Clark, Code Pleading § 76 (2d ed. 1947).

18. *See* text at § 9.5 note 5 *supra*.

was broadened, not so much from innovation introduced by the codes as by change in the concept of joint tort. Originally only those who acted in concert were considered joint tortfeasors. But the modern American view is that joint tortfeasance includes the case in which the tortious conduct of each defendant contributes to a single indivisible injury, even without concert of action between the defendants. Typical is the situation in which the negligence of each of two automobile drivers brings about a collision that injures a third person.[19] The tortious servant and the vicariously liable master also came to be regarded as joint tortfeasors for the purpose of joining them as defendants.[20]

When, however, the conduct of each of several defendants caused some but not all of the plaintiff's harm, so that each was liable for only the part he or she caused, then joinder generally was not allowed under the codes. Thus, different polluters of the air or of a stream could not be joined in an action for damages,[21] nor could successive converters of the same chattel,[22] nor independent publishers of the same libel.[23] Joinder was even denied when one defendant caused the original injury and another an aggravation of it for which the original tortfeasor would also be liable.[24] These restrictive procedural rules obviously impeded effective enforcement of an injured party's substantive rights, and thus had wealth-distribution effects.

When equitable relief against tortious conduct was sought, the attitude toward joinder was more liberal. Thus, in *Town of Fairfield v. Southport National Bank*[25] the town sought relief against the Southport Bank's wrongful renegotiation of the town's notes, which had been paid but not canceled. Plaintiff joined as defendants the Southport Bank, the bank's receiver, and four other banks to which some of the notes had been transferred, seeking a determination of the rights of the transferee banks in the instruments, cancellation of the notes, and an injunction against negotiation of the notes by each defendant. The court held the defendants properly joined. Even when an injunction was properly

19. Clark, Code Pleading 383–384 (2d ed. 1947); Prosser, Joint Torts and Several Liability, 25 Calif. L. Rev. 413, 416, 432 (1937).

20. *See* Mayberry v. Northern Pac. Ry., 100 Minn. 79, 110 N.W. 356, 12 Law. Rep. Ann. (n.s.) 675 (1907); Brandis, Permissive Joinder of Parties and Causes in North Carolina, 25 N.C.L. Rev. 1, 3 (1946); Prosser, Joint Torts and Several Liability, 25 Calif. L. Rev. 413, 430–431 (1937).

21. *See, e.g.*, Miller v. Highland Ditch Co., 87 Cal. 430, 25 P. 550 (1891); Prosser, Joint Torts and Several Liability, 25 Calif. L. Rev. 413, 437 (1937).

22. Northern Fin. Corp. v. Midwest Commercial Credit Co., 59 S.D. 282, 239 N.W. 242 (1931).

23. Prosser, Joint Torts and Several Liability, 25 Calif. L. Rev. 413, 457 n.158 (1937) (collecting cases).

24. Atkins v. Steed, 208 N.C. 245, 179 S.E. 889 (1935) (discussed in Brandis, Permissive Joinder of Parties and Causes in North Carolina, 25 N.C.L. Rev. 1, 41–42 (1946)). This result is criticized in Prosser, Joint Torts and Several Liability, 25 Calif. L. Rev. 413, 420–421 (1937).

25. 77 Conn. 423, 59 A. 513 (1904).

sought against several defendants to restrain each from maintaining a nuisance, however, courts were divided on the question whether damages might also be recovered in the joined action when each defendant was liable only severally for the damage it caused.[26]

The early codes made no provision for joinder of defendants in the alternative, and such joinder was theoretically improper. As a practical matter, however, joinder could be effective when plaintiff could fairly describe defendants as joint or concurrent tortfeasors. Plaintiffs could join any or all persons who might be liable for his or her single injury and was allowed to have judgment against those found liable by the trier of fact even if the trier found one or some of the defendants not liable.[27]

The code joinder provisions therefore perpetuated some limitations inherited from the common law and were construed narrowly in damages actions. The latter attitude in part reflected judicial lack of confidence in the ability of juries to handle multiclaim, multiparty cases, for the decisions often adverted to potential confusion of the jury. Moreover, the joinder provisions were subject to rather inconsistent interpretations, as is the fate of all legal rules. But the uncertainty in the joinder rules meant that a defendant who objected to misjoinder at the outset always had misjoinder as a ground of appeal, even when it could not have significantly affected the merits. Thus, on the eve of the adoption of the Federal Rules in 1938, the code joinder rules had a deserved reputation for being needlessly technical.[28]

§ 9.7 Modern Joinder Provisions

Federal Rule 20

Dissatisfaction with the restrictive results described in the preceding section led to modifications of the early code rules. Significant reform came first in England and furnished the model for the modern provisions in the Federal Rules and many of the states.[1] The changes ultimately established trial convenience as the guide for joinder. The chief shortcoming of the code joinder provisions was their failure to make clear that they covered joinder of causes as well as joinder of parties. Federal Rule 20 meets this shortcoming by allowing joinder, as plaintiffs or defendants respectively, of all parties (1) by or against whom is asserted any right to relief jointly, severally, or in the alternative arising out of the same transaction, occurrence, or series of transactions or occurrences, and (2) with whom any question of law or fact common to all of them will arise in the action. It is expressly provided that a plaintiff or

26. *See* note 20 *supra*.

27. *See* note 18 *supra*; text at § 9.5 note 5 *supra*.

28. *See* Clark, Code Pleading §§ 57, 60 (2d ed. 1947); 3A Moore, Federal Practice and Procedure ¶ 20.04 (1982).

§ 9.7

1. For pre-Federal Rules statements of dissatisfaction and accounts of the earlier reforms, *see* Blume, Joinder of Action, 26 Mich. L. Rev. 1 (1927); Sunderland, Joinder of Actions, 18 Mich. L. Rev. 571 (1920).

defendant "need not be interested in obtaining or defending against all the relief demanded" and that judgment for or against each party shall be given "according to their respective rights" or liabilities.[2]

This rule sweeps away most of the restrictive rulings at which it was aimed. Indeed, the quoted provisos were intended specifically to abrogate the restrictions under the codes to which they refer. Under Federal Rule 20, for example, all those injured by a single tort may join as plaintiffs.[3] To be sure, separate questions of damage will arise for each plaintiff, and defenses may be available against some and not others, but that is not an objection to the joinder. The rule does not require that *all* questions presented by each plaintiff be common; it is enough if there is any common question, and the tortious quality of defendant's act is a question common to all the claims. Similarly, all distinctions between joint and several rights or obligations on a contract have been abolished.[4]

Subject matter jurisdiction

That plaintiffs or defendants have been properly joined under the Federal Rules or their state court analogues is only one of the requirements that a multiparty action must meet. Personal jurisdiction must have been properly obtained over each defendant (under the standards discussed in Chapter 2), and the court must also have subject matter jurisdiction. Traditionally, in federal court this meant that the claim against each defendant must fall within the diversity, federal question, or miscellaneous category of federal jurisdiction. Under a 1990 statute, however, when a plaintiff has a federal question or other nondiversity jurisdiction claim against one defendant, the court has supplemental jurisdiction to hear that plaintiff's claim against a second defendant arising out of the same transaction or occurrence, even though there would be no independent jurisdiction over the second claim. For example, a plaintiff asserting a claim against a government agency under the Federal Tort Claims Act may join a state tort law claim against another defendant involved in the same accident, even though there would be no independent diversity or federal question jurisdiction over the latter claim.[5] In addition, the statute extends the limitations period when the

2. Fed. R. Civ. P. 20.

3. *See, e.g.*, Franklin v. Shelton, 250 F.2d 92 (10th Cir.1957) (automobile accident); Lansburgh & Bros. v. Clark, 127 F.2d 331 (D.C.Cir.1942) (husband and wife for claims arising out of injury to wife); Dombrovskis v. Murff, 24 F.R.D. 302 (S.D.N.Y. 1959) (deportable alien sailors in action for illegal deprivation of right to be issued special nonquota visas); Comment, Liability Under the Securities Act, 50 Yale L.J. 90, 94 (1950).

4. *See, e.g.*, United States Guar. Co. v. Mountaineer Eng. Co., 12 F.R.D. 520 (W.D.Pa.1952).

5. 28 U.S.C. § 1367; Wilson v. City of Chicago, 120 F.3d 681 (7th Cir.1997); Mengler, Burbank, and Rowe, Congress Accepts Supreme Court's Invitation to Codify Supplemental Jurisdiction, 74 Judicature 213 (1991); § 2.28 *supra*. One purpose of this statute was to overrule Finley v. United States, 490 U.S. 545, 109 S.Ct. 2003, 104 L.Ed.2d 593 (1989), which found no jurisdiction in the circumstances described in the text. The court has discretion under the statute not to exercise its supplemental jurisdiction.

court declines supplemental jurisdiction so that the plaintiff may reassert the state law claim in another court. No such supplemental jurisdiction exists when the court's jurisdiction is based on diversity rather than a federal question, except perhaps[6] when the added claim does not destroy diversity of citizenship and fails to meet the jurisdictional standard only because it falls short of the jurisdictional amount.

Misjoinder

As previously noted, at common law misjoinder of parties was a ground for general demurrer or motion in arrest of judgment if the defect appeared from the declaration, and was a ground for nonsuit when the defect appeared from the evidence at trial.[7] Under the codes misjoinder was a ground for demurrer.[8] Modern procedural systems generally have a statute or rule substantially like Federal Rule 21, which provides as follows:

> Misjoinder of parties is not ground for dismissal of an action. Parties may be dropped or added by order of the court on motion of any party or of its own initiative at any stage of the action and on such terms as are just. Any claim against a party may be severed and proceeded with separately.[9]

Rule 21 relaxes the common law rule that misjoinder is a fatal error subject to a general demurrer. Under the Federal Rules a misjoined party may be dropped at any stage of the proceedings, by motion of either a party or the court itself.[10] The court has the option to proceed separately with the remaining claims (severance) or to dismiss these claims if, for instance, there is no federal jurisdiction over them.[11]

The proper response to misjoinder is a motion to dismiss as to the misjoined party or a motion to sever the misjoined claim, since misjoinder is not a ground for dismissal. The motion to drop a party is at the court's discretion.[12] *Newman-Green, Inc. v. Alfonzo–Larrain*[13] illustrates

6. *Compare* Stromberg Metal Works, Inc. v. Press Mechanical, Inc., 77 F.3d 928 (7th Cir.1996)(upholding jurisdiction) *with* Meritcare Inc. v. St. Paul Mercury Ins. Co., 166 F.3d 214 (3d Cir.1999)(contra). *See* Hirschfeld, The $50,000 Question: Does Supplemental Jurisdiction Extend to Claims Between Diverse Parties Which Do Not Meet § 1332's Amount-in-Controversy Requirement? 68 Temple L. Rev. 107 (1995).

7. Leavet v. Sherman, 1 Root 159 (Conn.1790) (demurrer); Cofran v. Shepard, 148 Mass. 582, 20 N.E. 181 (1889) (error); McNulty v. O'Donnell, 27 Pa.Super. 93 (1904) (arrest of judgment); Ulmer v. Cunningham, 2 Me. 117 (1822) (nonsuit).

8. Clark, Code Pleading 368 (2d ed. 1947). *See* text at § 9.3 note 24 *supra*. While the provisions for amendment were liberal, "[t]he power ordinarily is to be exercised only at the request of the party, and not by the court of its own mere motion." White v. Town of Portland, 67 Conn. 272, 278, 34 A. 1022, 1024 (1896).

9. Fed. R. Civ. P. 21.

10. Newman-Green, Inc. v. Alfonzo–Larrain, 490 U.S. 826, 109 S.Ct. 2218, 104 L.Ed.2d 893 (1989); Continental Airlines v. Goodyear Tire & Rubber Co., 819 F.2d 1519 (9th Cir.1987); Lampliter Dinner Theater v. Liberty Mut. Ins. Co., 792 F.2d 1036 (11th Cir.1986).

11. Aetna Casualty & Surety Co. v. Hillman, 796 F.2d 770 (5th Cir.1986); Duchon v. Cajon Co., 791 F.2d 43 (6th Cir.1986).

12. *See* 3A Moore, Federal Practice and Procedure ¶ 21.03(2); Michaels Bldg. Co. v. Ameritrust Co. N.A., 848 F.2d 674 (6th Cir.1988); Jaser v. New York Property Ins.

the procedure. An Illinois corporation brought suit against a Venezuelan corporation, four Venezuelan citizens, and an American citizen residing in Venezuela. Because the American citizen was domiciled outside the United States, he was not a citizen of any state and therefore was not of diverse state citizenship with the Illinois plaintiff. Complete diversity therefore was lacking. Rather than dismiss the whole action, the lower court dismissed only the American defendant, thus restoring complete diversity.[14] The Supreme Court held that Rule 21 gives district courts the authority at any time to drop dispensable nondiverse parties, including "jurisdictional spoilers" such as the American in this case.[15] It would be a waste of time and judicial resources to dismiss and have plaintiff refile the action minus the "spoiler." Plaintiffs "should not be compelled to jump through these judicial hoops merely for the sake of hypertechnical jurisdictional purity."[16] Courts should, however, consider carefully whether the dismissal of the nondiverse party will prejudice any of the other parties.[17]

Similarly, a misjoined party may be dropped, if necessary, to preserve proper venue.[18] These amendments may relate back, even after a verdict, provided no prejudice results.

Nonjoinder

The rules governing the failure to join an indispensable party (nonjoinder) are similar to those for misjoinder.[19] The issue may be raised in the answer to the complaint or by a motion under Rule 12(b)(7). Leave will usually be granted for the plaintiff to add the necessary party by amendment, if feasible. Rule 12(b)(7) permits the nonjoinder of an indispensable party to be raised at any stage of the proceedings.

A party also may be added at any stage of the proceedings, if this is possible without impairing jurisdiction or prejudicing to the other parties. In *Wilborn v. Escalderon*,[20] for instance, a plaintiff sued several police officers under 42 U.S.C. § 1983, alleging they improperly placed a "hold" on his automobile and its contents. The arresting officer was not named in plaintiff's pro se complaint. The court of appeals held that the district court should have pointed out the deficiency and permitted the

Underwriting Assn., 815 F.2d 240 (2d Cir. 1987).

13. 490 U.S. 826, 109 S.Ct. 2218, 104 L.Ed.2d 893 (1989).

14. 28 U.S.C. § 1332.

15. *See also* Long v. District of Columbia, 820 F.2d 409 (D.C.Cir.1987); Continental Airlines v. Goodyear Tire & Rubber Co., 819 F.2d 1519 (9th Cir.1987).

16. 490 U.S. at 837, 109 S.Ct. at 2225, 104 L.Ed.2d at 905.

17. *See also* Everett Charles Contact Prods. v. Gentec, S.A.R.L., 692 F.Supp. 83 (D.R.I.1988); Varley v. Tampax, Inc., 855 F.2d 696 (10th Cir.1988); Jaser v. New York Property Ins., Underwriting Assn., 815 F.2d 240 (2d Cir.1987).

18. Anrig v. Ringsby United, 603 F.2d 1319 (9th Cir.1978).

19. *See* §§ 10.10–15 *infra.*

20. 789 F.2d 1328 (9th Cir.1986).

plaintiff to add the necessary party.[21] The power of the court to add or drop parties extends to all stages of the proceeding, even after the trial has concluded and on appeal.

Severance

The last sentence of Rule 21 reads: "Any claim against a party may be severed and proceeded with separately." This has the effect of splitting the lawsuit into two or more separate actions. The purpose is to cure defects in the joinder and to simplify complex cases that can be dissected without prejudicing the parties' procedural interests. On the other hand, even if related claims are asserted in different suits, the court may consolidate them when appropriate, either for trial, or for pretrial, or altogether.[22] The rules allowing plaintiffs to join parties thus do not finally determine which claims will be heard together or separately. As in other situations, the Federal Rules rely on the discretion of judges to handle lawsuits efficiently, flexibly and fairly, with only limited appellate review at the end of the case.[23]

C. MULTIPLE CLAIMS WITH MULTIPLE PARTIES

§ 9.8 Modern Party Joinder

As we have seen, the code joinder of parties provisions were often interpreted to require that the claims of each party "affect" other parties in the sense that each plaintiff have an interest in the claims being asserted and each defendant be adversely affected by each claim.

This requirement was met when a contractual or property interest was held by two or more plaintiffs or when defendants were charged as joint tortfeasors. But it was not met when two or more plaintiffs had been injured by the same wrongful act or when two or more defendants were charged in the alternative. This result was often reached by defining "cause of action" to mean the legal right of a claimant against an alleged wrongdoer. Since different individuals suffering personal injury obviously have separate legal rights, any such claimant had a separate cause of action that did not "affect" another claimant. In many code states until amendments were adopted in the twentieth century, if two automobile passengers were injured in a collision with another

21. *See also* Thor Power Tool Co. v. Weintraub, 791 F.2d 579 (7th Cir.1986); Cotton Bros. Baking Co. v. Industrial Risk Insurers, 690 F.Supp. 1541 (W.D.La.1988); Madarash v. Long Island R.R., 654 F.Supp. 51 (E.D.N.Y.1987).

22. Fed. R. Civ. P. 42(a); *see* Cella v. Togum Constructeur Ensemleier en Industrie Alimentaire, 173 F.3d 909 (3d Cir. 1999); Malcolm v. National Gypsum Co., 995 F.2d 346 (2d Cir.1993); 4 Moore's Federal Practice ¶¶ 20.09, 21.06; 8 *id.* ¶¶ 42.10 et seq.; 4 Witkin, California Procedure § 305 et seq. (4th ed. 1997); Steinman, Effects of Case Consolidation on the Procedural Rights of Litigants: What They Are, What They Might Be, 42 U.C.L.A. L. Rev. 717, 967 (1995); *cf.* Lexecon Inc. v. Milberg Weiss Bershad Hynes & Lerach, 523 U.S. 26, 118 S.Ct. 956, 140 L.Ed.2d 62 (1998).

23. *E.g.,* Shump v. Balka, 574 F.2d 1341 (10th Cir.1978).

vehicle, for example, the two would have to sue separately from each other and also would have to bring separate actions against their driver and the driver of the other car. Also, when plaintiff was uncertain which of two potential defendants had done the wrongful act, the claim against one defendant had independent legal footing from a claim against the other.

Federal Rules 18 and 20

The Federal Rules obviated that kind of difficulty by (1) adopting a broad rule for joinder of parties embodying tests geared to trial convenience,[1] (2) abolishing all limitations on joinder of claims,[2] (3) providing that "a plaintiff or defendant need not be interested in obtaining or defending against all the relief demanded,"[3] and (4) permitting a claimant to "state as many separate claims ... as the party has regardless of consistency and whether based on legal, equitable, or maritime grounds."[4]

This combination of provisions afford wide, but not unlimited, possibilities of joinder. It removes the obstacle to joinder of all plaintiffs injured by a single tort and makes clear that the relief sought by or against all parties need not be the same. The provisions, taken together, allow joinder of plaintiffs or defendants in the alternative even when the alternative rights or liabilities would depend on different legal theories, relationships, or facts. They permit joinder of successive tortfeasors when both may be liable for at least part of the damages.

Common question of fact

Even under these broad modern provisions, however, joinder has some limitations. Multiple parties who could sue or be sued separately may join or be joined only "if any question of law or fact common to all of them will arise in the action."[5] This test does not require identity of all questions of law or fact. It has been held, sensibly, it would seem, that the existence of a common question of *law* is not enough for joinder. For example, common questions of law involved in factually unrelated intersection collision cases would not justify their joinder. The rights or obligations of the parties joined must arise "out of the same transaction, occurrence, or series of transactions or occurrences."[6]

§ 9.8

1. Fed. R. Civ. P. 20.

2. *Id.* 18.

3. *Id.* 20(a).

4. *Id.* 8(e)(2). *See generally* Bauman, Multiple Liability, Multiple Remedies and the Federal Rules, 46 Minn. L. Rev. 729 (1962) (written before the modifications in Rule 20 made in 1966); Kaplan, Continuing Work of the Civil Committee: 1966 Amendments to the Federal Rules of Civil Procedure, II, 81 Harv. L. Rev. 591 (1968) (explaining the changes made in 1966).

5. Fed. R. Civ. P. 20(a).

6. *Id.* On the use of similar language in a variety of procedural contexts, *see* Kane, Original Sin and the Transaction in Federal Civil Procedure, 76 Tex. L. Rev. 1732 (1998).

Transaction or occurrence

What, then, will give acts or events unity as a transaction or occurrence or will make them belong to a "series"? The tests suggested are not precise. Ordinarily, if two defendants act entirely independently of each other, the conduct of each is a separate transaction or occurrence and the sum of their acts or activities does not constitute a series. But unity may be added by one of the following:

1. A common scheme, or design, or conspiracy to defraud or to violate the law. Thus, in *Nagler v. Admiral Corporation*[7] thirteen radio and television dealers sued twenty-four suppliers and two retailers, claiming that the suppliers gave the defendant retailers special price concessions in violation of the Robinson–Patman Act and the antitrust laws. On a challenge to the joinder, the court of appeals found it unnecessary to explore various suggestions for finding common questions of law or fact, "since we think that in any event the suggestion of concerted activity because of 'conscious parallelism' of the defendants' acts affords a clear ground of joinder without need of more."[8]

2. The fact that all the acts or the conduct are consciously directed toward or connected with some common core, such as a common purpose, or a common event, or a single claim or item of property. Thus several plaintiff employees can join their claims against an employer implementing a general racially discriminatory policy.[9] In *Rekeweg v. Federal Mutual Insurance Co.*[10] plaintiff was allowed to join (a) a claim against an insurance company and its agent based on fraudulent misrepresentations made to plaintiff's former attorney that induced the attorney to delay suing on a claim, with (b) a claim against plaintiff's former attorney for negligence in failing to sue on the claim within the limitations period.

In *Messelt v. Security Storage Co.*[11] plaintiff was allowed to join (a) a claim for loss and damage against the company that originally agreed to pack and ship goods, with (b) a claim for the same loss against the initial carrier, and (c) a claim for loss of the same goods against their insurer. The court said: "Here the transaction which is the subject matter of the case as it now stands was the shipment and transfer of the plaintiff's furniture ... including claims for damages against the original defendants for goods lost and damaged in transit.... The procuring of the insurance was connected with the transaction...."

3. The fact that completely independent acts converge to cause an injury, for all or for some part of which the actors have a common liability under substantive law. When two or more tortfeasors are liable

7. 248 F.2d 319 (2d Cir.1957).

8. 248 F.2d at 328.

9. *E.g.*, Alexander v. Fulton County, 207 F.3d 1303 (11th Cir.2000).

10. 27 F.R.D. 431 (N.D.Ind.1961). *See also* Great Northern Telegraph Co. v. Yokohama Specie Bank, 297 N.Y. 135, 76 N.E.2d 117 (1947).

11. 11 F.R.D. 342 (D.Del.1951).

for the whole injury, the codes had allowed joinder. The extension under the Federal Rules and modern codes is found when the second defendant is charged with aggravating an injury caused by the first under circumstances that may render both of them liable for the aggravation. Thus, in *Poster v. Central Gulf Steamship Corp.*[12] plaintiff joined successive employers, Sinclair and Gulf, alleging that (a) while in Sinclair's employ plaintiff had contracted a disease (amebiasis) because of Sinclair's negligence in allowing infected persons to prepare food and use the lavatory while its ship was in port in the Suez Canal area, and (b) while in Gulf's employ some three months later plaintiff again became ill with the same disease because of Gulf's similar negligence, also in the Suez area. The court allowed the joinder since plaintiff's "claim for relief is based upon two occurrences, the same in nature, *and the second of which might result in concurrent liability of both companies.*"[13]

A variant of this kind of connection occurs when plaintiff is injured by the act of at least one of two or more defendants but is uncertain which act actually caused the injury. A famous illustrative case is *Summers v. Tice*,[14] in which each defendant fired a shot in plaintiff's vicinity and plaintiff was injured by one of them but did not know which one.

If the transactions or occurrences actually are wholly unrelated, plaintiff has no incentive to attempt joinder, for doing so will only confuse presentation of the case. Thus, plaintiffs have practical disincentives against testing the outer limits of what constitutes a series of transactions or occurrences, and few decisions spell out what those limits may be. One decision finding that those limits were transgressed is *Insull v. New York World-Telegram Corporation*.[15] There, three different sets of authors and publishers independently published statements about Samuel Insull, Sr., who played a conspicuous part in the financial structure that tumbled in the Great Depression. One statement involved a newspaper column published in 1957, which stated that some labor leaders were getting away with the kind of racketeering that sent Insull to jail in the 1930s; one involved Arthur Schlesinger, Jr.'s historical treatment of Insull in The Crisis of the Old Order, also published in 1957; the third involved Trombley's Life and Times of a Happy Liberal, published in 1954. Samuel Insull, Jr. joined these three sets of defendants, claiming that some people took the statements to refer to him and also that he was libeled by the defamation of his father. The court declared that these claims did not have the unity of occurrence needed for joinder, although they did present common questions of law and fact.

12. 25 F.R.D. 18 (E.D.Pa.1960).

13. 25 F.R.D. at 20 (emphasis in original).

14. 33 Cal.2d 80, 199 P.2d 1 (1948). *See also* Sindell v. Abbott Laboratories, 26 Cal.3d 588, 607 P.2d 924, 163 Cal.Rptr. 132 (1980), in which a plaintiff was permitted to join several different manufacturers of a type of drug since she could not identify which manufacturer's product she had actually used.

15. 172 F.Supp. 615 (N.D.Ill.1959).

The court's conclusion in *Insull* is not wholly untenable. But if the statements were false and injurious, their injurious effects at least contributed to one injury—the diminution of Samuel Insull, Jr.'s standing in the community in which he lived—that would seem to be no different from other situations of concurrent tortfeasors. Moreover, if the joinder could be shown by any defendant to be actually prejudicial to defending on the merits—which seems unlikely in the situation presented—the court could direct separate trials. In any event, why should a common liability for the same damage make joinder convenient and expedient, but not a liability for separate but similar damage inflicted on the same plaintiff at the same time? The latter may certainly involve great overlapping of proof. The mere drawing of the line between the damages attributable to one defendant and those attributable to the other involves common proof; the case against each defendant may include proof of total damages (from which a subtraction should be made) and much common proof of cause. Moreover, joinder should, on the one hand, minimize the risk of duplication of damages and, on the other, protect the plaintiff from the risk of falling between two stools.

Justification for joinder limits

Given experience under the joinder provisions of the Federal Rules, a question suggests itself: Why have any limitations on joinder at all? Plaintiffs ordinarily do not want to enlarge their cases to make them unmanageable at the pretrial stage or unintelligible when presented at trial. And in the relatively infrequent situations in which plaintiffs exceed these bounds, the court can pare back the action by exercising its powers of severance.[16] In any event, the operation of the joinder rules in modern practice—questions of service of process and venue aside[17]—makes freedom of joinder almost practically unlimited. And so far as plaintiff is concerned in working with these rules, the practical moral is: When in doubt, join.

D. COUNTERCLAIMS

§ 9.9 Background

The counterclaim is treated at various points throughout this book, but the chief problems it presents are those of joinder of claims, both

16. Fed R. Civ. P. 20(b), 21, 42(b); Arnold v. Eastern Air Lines, 681 F.2d 186 (4th Cir.1982); *see* § 9.7 *supra.*

17. In many situations, the rules of service of process and of venue, the latter particularly in federal court, prevent the plaintiff from joining defendants whom the joinder rules permit to be brought into the action. *See* Chapter 2. The concept of joinder based on trial convenience has, however, been recognized in some quarters as a factor in determining whether a nonresident defendant may properly be subjected to jurisdiction through service of process. *See* Buckeye Boiler Co. v. Superior Court, 71 Cal.2d 893, 458 P.2d 57, 80 Cal.Rptr. 113 (1969); *cf.* Asahi Metal Industry Co. v. Superior Court, 480 U.S. 102, 107 S.Ct. 1026, 94 L.Ed.2d 92 (1987).

permissive and compulsory. How far may defendants expand the dimensions of a lawsuit by injecting their claims into it? And how far must they bring them in or forego them?

The counterclaim, not only the concept but the very word, was introduced into code pleading in 1852.[1] There were two primary antecedents: the *recoupment* in common law procedure and the *set-off* in equity.[2] The Roman law also had a device called *compensation* that has made some mark on the American counterclaim.[3]

Recoupment

In common law actions, a deduction from damages because of part payment, former recovery, or some analogous fact was allowed through recoupment.[4] Later a defendant was also allowed to show, for the purpose of reducing or defeating plaintiff's recovery, facts arising out of the transaction sued on that would have founded an independent action in defendant's favor.[5] Thus, in an action on contract defendants might show failure of consideration,[6] in an action for the purchase price they might show breach of warranty of the goods sold,[7] and so on.

Recoupment had severe limitations. Defendants could use a claim through recoupment only defensively to defeat or diminish plaintiff's recovery; they could recover nothing affirmatively, whether plaintiff's claim stood or fell.[8] Moreover, if defendants used a claim through recoupment, they waived its further use as ground for an independent action; if it exceeded plaintiff's claim, the excess was lost.[9] According to some authority only contract claims could be recouped,[10] but most courts

§ 9.9

1. Lloyd, The Development of Set-off, 64 U. Pa. L. Rev. 541, 563 (1916).

2. *Id.* at 565.

3. Clark, Code Pleading 633–634 (2d ed. 1947); Pomeroy, Code Remedies §§ 607, 611–613 (5th ed. 1929).

4. 2 Sedgwick, Damages § 1034 (9th ed. 1912); Clark and Surbeck, The Pleading of Counterclaims, 37 Yale L.J. 300 (1928).

5. Pennsylvania R.R. v. Miller, 124 F.2d 160 (5th Cir.1941) (noted in 28 Va. L. Rev. 557 (1942), 31 Calif. L. Rev. 210 (1943)); Mack v. Hugger Bros. Construction Co., 153 Tenn. 260, 283 S.W. 448 (1926); Clark and Surbeck, The Pleading of Counterclaims, 37 Yale L.J. 300 (1928). For an interesting brief account of the history of recoupment, *see* McConnell, The Doctrine of Recoupment in Federal Taxation, 28 Va. L. Rev. 577, 579–586 (1942).

6. Wheat v. Dotson, 12 Ark. 699 (1852) (also giving historical analysis of failure of consideration as basis for recoupment).

7. Withers v. Greene, 50 U.S. (9 How.) 213, 13 L. Ed. 109 (1850) (breach of warranty on pedigree of horses). *See* Wheat v. Dotson, 12 Ark. 699, 708 (1852); Pomeroy, Code Remedies § 608 (5th ed. 1929) (illustrations of recoupment).

8. Kingman v. Draper, 14 Ill.App. 577 (1884); Waterman, Law of Set-off § 469 (2d ed. 1872); Pomeroy, Code Remedies § 607 (5th ed. 1929); 3 Sedgwick, Damages § 1049 (9th ed. 1912).

9. Burnett v. Smith, 70 Mass. (4 Gray) 50 (1855); 3 Sedgwick, Damages §§ 1048, 1072 (9th ed. 1912).

10. Recoupment relates "more especially to damages for breach of contract." Slayback v. Jones, 9 Ind. 470, 474 (1857) (*A* sold land and crops to *B*; later *A* trespassed and took *B*'s crops; *A* sues *B* on *B*'s note for land and crops; *B* not allowed to recoup damages for trespass).

probably did not insist on this limitation.[11] In any event, a claim did not have to be liquidated to be the subject of recoupment.[12]

Recoupment was strictly a matter between defendant and plaintiff; no new parties could be brought in.[13] If the defendant's claim did not arise out of the transaction sued on, there was no set-off at common law until the early eighteenth century.[14]

Set-off

Equity would allow set-off of mutual debts[15] when some basis existed for finding or implying an agreement between the parties that the debts be "discounted" or set off against each other.[16] Moreover, such an agreement would be found on very slender evidence,[17] and the requirement of an agreement was essentially a fiction.

Set-off was available only when (1) the debts on both sides were liquidated or easily ascertainable and arose out of contract or judgment,(2) both were due,[18] and (3) the parties to them were identical.[19] As in the case of recoupment, defendants could use their claim defensively only; by setting it off they waived any excess over the plaintiff's claim.[20]

In the American colonies, statutory provisions were more liberal than the English rules in allowing unliquidated contract claims to be set off and allowing defendant an affirmative recovery.[21] Under circumstances not unlike the conditions for set-off, Roman law viewed mutual demands as automatically cancelling each other under the doctrine of compensation.[22]

11. Kingman v. Draper, 14 Ill.App. 577, 578 (1884): "A claim originating in contract may be set up against one founded in tort; and damages for a tort in a suit on a contract."

Accord, Stow v. Yarwood, 14 Ill. 424 (1853); Lee v. Rutledge, 51 Md. 311 (1878).

12. Wheat v. Dotson, 12 Ark. 699, 703 (1852); 3 Sedgwick, Damages § 1047 (9th ed. 1912).

13. 3 Sedgwick, Damages § 1041 (9th ed. 1912): "[T]he claim recouped should be against the plaintiff, and against him alone." This limitation is probably traceable to the fact that recoupment originally was a mere right to a deduction from the amount claimed by the plaintiff, on a showing that the plaintiff's damages were not as great as alleged. *Id.* at § 1034.

14. Waterman, Law of Set-off 11–12 (2d ed. 1872).

15. Lloyd, The Development of Set-off, 64 U. Pa. L. Rev. 541, 547 (1916); 3 Story, Equity Jurisprudence ch. 41 (14th ed. 1918).

16. Waterman, Law of Set-off § 18, at 299 (2d ed. 1872).

17. Jeffs v. Wood, 2 P. Wms. 128, 129, 24 Eng. Rep. 668, 669 (Ch. 1723).

18. Clark, Code Pleading 636 (2d ed. 1947); Waterman, Law of Set-off chs. 6, 7 (2d ed. 1872); Lloyd, The Development of Set-off, 64 U. Pa. L. Rev. 541, 553 (1916). *See* Stooke v. Taylor, 5 Q.B.D. 569, 575 (1880).

19. Lloyd, The Development of Set-off, 64 U. Pa. L. Rev. 541, 553 (1916).

20. Stooke v. Taylor, 5 Q.B.D. 569, 575 (1880).

21. Early laws of Massachusetts, New Jersey, New York, Pennsylvania, and Virginia on this subject are discussed in Lloyd, The Development of the Set-off, 64 U. Pa. L. Rev. 541, 553–562 (1916).

22. *See* the admirable analysis in Comment, Automatic Extinction of Cross Demands: *Compensation* from Rome to California, 53 Calif. L. Rev. 224 (1965).

Equitable cross bills

In a suit in equity, the defendant was allowed to file a cross bill against either the plaintiff or another defendant if the bill dealt with "the matters in question in the original Bill"[23] and did not introduce "new and distinct matters."[24] Within these limits a defendant could assert a claim for affirmative recovery against a plaintiff, the essential concept of a counterclaim.

§ 9.10 Early Code Counterclaim

The Field Code originally contained no provision for counterclaims, but one was added in 1852[1] and came to be widely adopted in other states.[2] This provision required that a counterclaim

> be one existing in favor of a defendant and against a plaintiff, between whom a several judgment might be had in the action, and arising out of one of the following causes of action:
>
> 1. A cause of action arising out of the contract or transaction set forth in the complaint as the foundation of the plaintiff's claim, or connected with the subject of the action.
>
> 2. In an action arising upon contract, any other cause of action arising also upon contract and existing at the commencement of the action.[3]

The parenthood of both clauses is clear—the first is derivative from common law recoupment, the second from equitable set-off. But the offspring had qualities that neither recoupment nor set-off possessed.[4] Defendants under the code might have affirmative recovery if their claim exceeded the plaintiff's[5] or if the plaintiff's claim failed and the counterclaim succeeded.[6] Moreover, contract claims no longer needed to be liquidated.[7] And there was no longer a bar to interposing an equitable claim in a legal action, or vice versa.[8]

Limitations remained, however, on the subject matter of the counterclaim, even when only the original parties to the action were concerned.[9] There was an express limitation that the counterclaim be

23. Story, Equity Pleadings § 289, at 365 (10th ed. 1892).

24. *Id.* § 401, at 375.

§ 9.10

1. *Compare* Act of April 11, 1849, N.Y. Laws ch. 438, at 613 (1849), *with* Act of April 16, 1852, N.Y. Laws ch. 392, at 149, 150, 654 (1852).

2. Clark, Code Pleading § 101 (2d ed. 1947).

3. *See* N.Y. Code of Procedure (1848, with amendments through 1852), *reprinted in* Blume and Reed, Pleading and Joinder 608, 623 (1952).

4. Pomeroy, Code Remedies § 613 (5th ed. 1929); Lloyd, The Development of Set-off, 64 U. Pa. L. Rev. 541, 565 (1916).

5. Stoddard v. Treadwell, 26 Cal. 294, 309 (1864); Lloyd, *supra* note 4, at 565.

6. Pomeroy, Code Remedies § 615 (5th ed. 1929).

7. Stoddard v. Treadwell, 26 Cal. 294, 309 (1864); Lloyd, *supra* note 4, at 565.

8. Pomeroy, Code Remedies §§ 618, 640, and p. 1035n. (5th ed. 1929).

9. The restrictions on the use of counterclaim varied by jurisdiction. *See* Note, 34 Yale L.J. 330 (1925).

maintainable against the plaintiff so that a counterclaim was impermissible if it required joinder of additional parties.[10] In some codes, and judicially implied in others, was a requirement that the counterclaim tend to "defeat or diminish" plaintiff's claim,[11] whatever that meant. And although there were dissenting voices, the prevailing code rule made the counterclaim available to a defendant only; plaintiff could not in his or her reply file a counterclaim to a counterclaim.[12]

"Transaction"

The transaction clause could be interpreted broadly to permit a counterclaim whenever it would be convenient to try plaintiff's and defendant's claim together because of common questions of fact and consequent overlap of proof. Legal classifications of claims as "tort" or "contract" would have no limiting effect on the scope of counterclaims. Some courts interpreted the transaction clause in that way,[13] but there was a tendency to construe it narrowly, as the similar language in the joinder of actions provisions was construed.[14] Thus some courts adopted Pomeroy's view that "transaction" meant a matter of negotiation or business and excluded such occurrences as assault and slander.[15] This approach made it uncertain whether counterclaims were ever permissible in tort actions.[16]

"Contract"

In contract cases, the early code counterclaim appeared to permit only counterclaims based on contract.[17] This could exclude counterclaims based on implied contract or quantum meruit, even though as a practical matter that kind of claim is most likely to have arisen in a controversy

10. Clark, Code Pleading 667 (2d ed. 1947).

11. Bothe v. Noack, 149 Ark. 297, 232 S.W. 606 (1921); Dietrich v. Koch, 35 Wis. 618 (1874); Bliss, Code Pleading §§ 386–389 (2d ed. 1877); Clark, Code Pleading 650–652 (2d ed. 1947).

12. Millar, Counterclaim Against Counterclaim, 48 Nw. U.L. Rev. 671, 677–686 (1954).

13. Commentators have taken opposite views on this subject. *Compare* Clark, Code Pleading § 102 (2d ed. 1947), *with* Pomeroy, Code Remedies § 650 (5th ed. 1929). Some examples of liberal holdings under the older type of statute are Driver v. Gillette, 43 S.D. 62, 177 N.W. 815 (1920); Gentry v. Krause, 106 Wash. 474, 180 P. 474 (1919); Studebaker Corp. v. Hanson, 24 Wyo. 222, 160 P. 336 (1916).

14. *See* text at § 9.3 note 16 *supra*.

15. Earl v. Times-Mirror Co., 185 Cal. 165, 196 P. 57 (1921); Wrege v. Jones, 13 N.D. 267, 100 N.W. 705, 706 (1904); Henrickson v. Smith, 111 Wash. 82, 189 P. 550 (1920); Pomeroy, Code Remedies § 650 (5th ed. 1929). *Contra*, Mulcahy v. Duggan, 67 Mont. 9, 214 P. 1106 (1923).

16. *See* Price v. Kobacker Furniture Co., 20 Ohio App. 464, 467, 152 N.E. 301, 302 (1925). *But see* Kerr, Counterclaim Founded in Tort, 95 Cent. L.J. 27 (1922).

17. *Compare* the classifications in the early joinder of causes provisions (§ 9.3 *supra*), of which Professor Blume justly said: "There is nothing in the English system which corresponds to the arbitrary classifications according to subject matter found in the procedure codes of the various states. How these classifications have so long persisted is hard to understand, unless it be due to the remarkable conservatism which always resists procedural change." Blume, Joinder of Causes of Action, 26 Mich. L. Rev. 1, 24 (1927).

over breach of contract. Interpretation of the contract clause of the counterclaim rule was, however, generally liberal and included all kinds of claims that might formerly have been remedied in covenant, debt, or assumpsit.[18] And even when defendant's claim was based on a tort, he or she could use it as a contract counterclaim if the situation was one in which defendant could have waived the tort and sued in assumpsit at common law.[19]

Although the contract clause did not require that either claim be liquidated, it did require that defendant's claim be one "existing at the commencement of the action."[20] This provision doubtless was designed to prevent a defendant from acquiring contract claims against the plaintiff after commencement of the suit.[21] But it was sometimes construed as barring use of claims that had not *matured* when the suit was brought, although owned by defendant in good faith before that time.[22] Such a result was not needed to further the purpose of the limitation and involved an unduly narrow view of cause of action.[23]

Parties

The code counterclaim had to be one "in favor of a defendant and against a plaintiff, between whom a several judgment might be had in the action."[24] Thus there was no requirement that a counterclaim affect all parties to the action (as in the case of claims joined by plaintiff).[25] A defendant sued with another as concurrent tortfeasors in a personal injury case could, for example, counterclaim for his or her own injuries against plaintiff even though the co-defendant had no legal interest in the counterclaim.[26] If either the principal claim or the counterclaim involved joint rights or obligations, however, then the opposing claim had to be in favor of or against all the joint obligors or obligees.[27] The

18. Clark, Code Pleading 663 (2d ed. 1947). *See, e.g.*, Webster v. Van Allen, 217 App.Div. 219, 216 N.Y.S. 552 (1926); La Grande Natl. Bank v. Oliver, 84 Or. 582, 165 P. 682 (1917).

19. *See, e.g.*, Downs v. Finnegan, 58 Minn. 112, 59 N.W. 981 (1894); Manhattan Egg Co. v. Seaboard Terminal & Refrigeration Co., 137 Misc. 14, 242 N.Y.S. 189 (City Ct.N.Y.1929); Casner v. Hoskins, 64 Or. 254, 128 P. 841, *reh'g denied*, 64 Or. 254, 130 P. 55 (1913).

20. Text at note 3 *supra*.

21. Clark, Code Pleading 665 (2d ed. 1947); Pomeroy, Code Remedies 1091–1092 (5th ed. 1929).

22. Theobold v. Gotham Waist Co., 169 N.Y.S. 498 (App.Term.1918) (counterclaim in suit brought on June 8 for claim maturing on August 14 barred); Pomeroy, Code Remedies 1091–1092 nn.87–88 (5th ed. 1929). *Cf.* Orton v. Noonan, 29 Wis. 541 (1872) (action on a lease for rents due; counterclaim for breaches of covenant occurring after the action was commenced, barred).

23. *See* Fed. R. Civ. P. 13(e), dispensing with this requirement and allowing by supplemental pleading the presentation of a claim that either matured or was acquired by the pleader after serving the pleading.

24. Text at note 3 *supra*. *See* Clark, Code Pleading 642, 667 (2d ed. 1947).

25. *See* Loeb v. Loeb, 24 Okla. 384, 103 P. 570 (1909).

26. *Cf.* Ruby v. Baker, 106 Kan. 855, 190 P. 6 (1920) (suit against joint tortfeasors for assault, counterclaim by one defendant for alienation of wife's affections).

27. Roberts v. Donovan, 70 Cal. 108, 9 P. 180 (1885); Cohen v. Karp, 143 Md. 208, 122 A. 524 (1923).

parties to the counterclaim had to sue or be sued in the same capacities as in the original action. Thus, if plaintiff sued in a representative capacity, the counterclaim must be one against plaintiff in that capacity and not against him or her individually.[28]

§ 9.11 Modern Provisions

When the counterclaim is asserted against an opposing party, modern provisions embody the same policy of unlimited permissive joinder as in modern provisions for joinder of causes by a plaintiff against a single defendant (or set of defendants) and for the same reason.[1] In both situations convenience is served by allowing the entire score between these parties to be settled in a single lawsuit. Indeed, under the Federal Rules and most modern codes, defendants *must* assert as a counterclaim any claim that arises out of the transaction or occurrence that is the subject matter of the plaintiff's claim.[2] They may, at their option, assert against a plaintiff a claim that arises out of an unrelated transaction.[3] As under the codes, however, the parties on both sides must be claiming and claimed against in the same capacity.[4] Protection against confusion of issues is afforded by the trial court's power to order separate trials "in furtherance of convenience or to avoid prejudice."[5]

Compulsory counterclaim

Two important consequences follow when a counterclaim is compulsory rather than permissive. First, if the defendant fails to assert a compulsory counterclaim in the original action, it may not be raised in a later action.[6] This consequence is, in practice, rare. Most defendants are

28. Headington v. Smith, 113 Iowa 107, 111, 84 N.W. 982, 983 (1901) (defendant's counterclaim for malicious assault by plaintiff disallowed because plaintiff had sued in a representative capacity). *Cf.* Thompson v. Sunrise Coal Co.'s Trustee, 181 Ky. 158, 204 S.W. 89 (1918); Mahon v. Harney County Natl. Bank, 104 Or. 323, 206 P. 224 (1922). *See also* Clark, Code Pleading 671–672 (2d ed. 1947); Pomeroy, Code Remedies 1014 (5th ed. 1929).

§ 9.11

1. *See* § 9.4 *supra. See generally* Friedenthal, Joinder of Claims, Counterclaims and Cross-Complaints: Suggested Revision of the California Provisions, 23 Stan. L. Rev. 1 (1970); Kennedy, Counterclaims Under Federal Rule 13, 11 Hous. L. Rev. 255 (1974). *Cf.* Brin, Counterclaims Against the United States Under the Federal Tort Claims Act and the Tucker Act, 28 Ins. Couns. J. 263 (1961); Morris, The Use of Set-off, Counterclaim and Recoupment: Availability Against Commercial Paper, 62 W. Va. L. Rev. 141 (1960).

2. Fed. R. Civ. P. 13(a). *See generally* Clements, Pre-judgment Enforcement of Federal Rule of Civil Procedure 12(a), 74 Cornell L. Rev. 167 (1988); Wright, Estoppel by Rule: The Compulsory Counterclaim Under Modern Pleading, 38 Minn. L. Rev. 423 (1954). Some states lack a compulsory counterclaim rule. *E.g.*, N.Y. C.P.L.R. 3019(a). In a variety of situations, however, the impact of the rules of res judicata and collateral estoppel compels the defendant to counterclaim even in the absence of a rule expressly requiring him or her to do so. *See* Restatement (Second) of Judgments § 22.

3. Fed. R. Civ. P. 13(b).

4. *See* 3 Moore, Federal Practice and Procedure ¶ 13.06.

5. Fed. R. Civ. P. 42(b).

6. *E.g.,* Fox v. Maulding, 112 F.3d 453 (10th Cir.1997); Mohr v. State Bank of Stanley, 241 Kan. 42, 734 P.2d 1071 (1987); § 11.15 *infra.*

only too ready to assert, against those who sue them, any counterclaims—compulsory or permissive, plainly meritorious or questionable—that they may have. Few fail to raise counterclaims and then go to the trouble of starting a new action in order to assert them.

Second, in a federal court the doctrine of supplemental jurisdiction entitles a defendant to assert a counterclaim over which the court would otherwise lack subject matter jurisdiction when it is a compulsory counterclaim arising from the same transaction as the plaintiff's claim. Defendants therefore argue that their counterclaims are compulsory in order to litigate them in the same federal lawsuits that plaintiffs have instituted. Plaintiffs often reply that the counterclaim is merely permissive so that the defendant can assert it only by starting a second suit in another court.

Courts then must determine whether the claim and counterclaim arise from the same transaction. They often do so by inquiring into the factual overlap between claim and counterclaim, the logical relationship, if any, between them, and similar factors.[7] But other questions are also relevant, and more closely related to the purposes of the rule. Is the counterclaim one to which a federal court should devote its limited resources? Does fairness entitle the defendant to litigate the whole dispute in one action rather than being held liable in one court and then seeking in another to recover what he or she has paid out? Alternatively, would joinder be unfair to the plaintiff by entangling the original claim in a complex and embarrassing collateral dispute? If so, will the judge's power to sever cases for trial and pretrial proceedings provide an adequate remedy?

Permissive counterclaim

Modern counterclaim provisions also afford broader scope for counterclaims by foregoing any requirement that a counterclaim defeat or diminish plaintiff's recovery, by allowing new parties to be brought in, by permitting co-defendants or co-plaintiffs to assert cross-claims against each other,[8] and by permitting plaintiff to file a counterclaim to a counterclaim.[9]

The elimination of the requirement that the counterclaim defeat or diminish plaintiff's recovery needs little explanation. In an action to quiet title to real estate, for example, defendant could impose a claim for damages. Federal Rule 13(h) provides for bringing in new parties when their presence is required for the granting of complete relief in the determination of the counterclaim. The rule includes, of course, any

7. *See* Moore v. New York Cotton Exchange, 270 U.S. 593, 46 S.Ct. 367, 70 L.Ed. 750 (1926); Blue Dane Simmental Corp. v. American Simmental Assoc., 952 F.Supp. 1399 (D.Neb.1997); Kane, Original Sin and the Transaction in Federal Civil Procedure, 76 Tex. L. Rev. 1723 (1998).

8. Fed R. Civ. P. 13(c), (g), (h).

9. *See* Millar, Counterclaim Against Counterclaim, 48 Nw. U.L. Rev. 671 (1954).

parties necessary to that determination who are not already in the action, but it is not confined to necessary parties.[10] It also covers those whom defendant might have joined permissively if he or she had brought the counterclaim as a separate action.[11] Thus, when a railroad sues a shipper for freight charges, the shipper may counterclaim for unrelated tort damages arising out of a collision between vessels owned by the respective parties; the shipper may in that counterclaim bring in an alleged joint tortfeasor.[12]

When the action is in federal court, however, jurisdictional difficulties may arise in bringing in an additional party to a counterclaim. This is particularly true when jurisdiction is founded on diversity. Thus, if a New York citizen sues a New Jersey citizen, the defendant can counterclaim and may as a matter of joinder name any proper counterclaim defendant therein. But as a matter of federal jurisdictional law the New Jersey defendant could not add a New Jersey citizen in the counterclaim because no diversity would exist between them.[13] The 1990 statute recognizing supplemental jurisdiction over pendent parties appears, however, to allow the court in its discretion to permit the joinder of such a party.[14] A similar problem can arise in state or federal court when a potential counterclaim defendant is beyond the territorial reach of service of process.[15]

In California, the function of the counterclaim is performed by a pleading called a cross-complaint. The contemporary California cross-complaint is similar to the counterclaim provided for in the Federal

10. Electronic Detection Prods. v. Chapin, 26 F.R.D. 121 (D.Mass.1959); S P A Ricordi Officine Grafiche v. World Art Reproductions Co., 1 Fed. R. Serv. 2d 13h.12, case 2, 22 F.R.D. 312 (S.D.N.Y.1958); Value Line Fund v. Marcus, 1 Fed. R. Serv. 2d 13h.12, case 1, 161 F.Supp. 533 (S.D.N.Y. 1958). *See* United Artists Corp. v. Masterpiece Productions, 221 F.2d 213, 216–217 (2d Cir.1955).

11. In Value Line Fund v. Marcus, *supra* note 10, the counterclaim was permissive and the parties sought to be brought in on it (joint tortfeasors) were proper but neither necessary nor indispensable. It has been said that the test is not whether parties are necessary or indispensable but rather whether the parties' presence is necessary to grant complete relief. Electronic Detection Prods. v. Chapin, 26 F.R.D. 121 (D.Mass.1959). In accordance with its general policy, Rule 13(h) "should be liberally construed and . . . recourse may and should be had to it when necessary to avoid a multiplicity of suits and to dispose of, in one action, all matters arising from the same set of facts." United States v. Milhan, 20 Fed. R. Serv. 13h.12, case 2, 15 F.R.D. 459, 460 (E.D.N.Y.1954).

12. New York, N.H. & H.R.R. Co. v. United States, 25 Fed. R. Serv. 13h.12, case 1, 21 F.R.D. 328 (S.D.N.Y.1958). *Cf.* Value Line Fund v. Marcus, 1 Fed. R. Serv. 2d 13h.12, case 1, 161 F.Supp. 533 (S.D.N.Y. 1958) (joint tortfeasors); S P A Ricordi Officine Grafiche v. World Art Reproductions, 1 Fed. R. Serv. 2d 13h.12, case 2, 22 F.R.D. 312 (S.D.N.Y.1958) (co-conspirators).

13. *See, e.g.*, Hercules Inc. v. Dynamic Export Corp., 71 F.R.D. 101 (S.D.N.Y.1976); Dunbar & Sullivan Dredging Co. v. John R. Jurgensen Co., 44 F.R.D. 467 (D.Ohio 1967), *aff'd on other grounds*, 396 F.2d 152 (6th Cir.1968). *See also* § 9.13 *infra*.

14. 28 U.S.C. § 1367; *see* §§ 2.28, 9.7 *supra*.

15. *See, e.g.*, Cordner v. Metropolitan Life Ins. Co., 234 F.Supp. 765 (S.D.N.Y. 1964); Garfield Gas Gathering Co. v. Indiana–Ohio Pipe Co., 29 F.R.D. 8 (D.Colo. 1961).

Rules and in the codes.[16] Under Federal Rules pleading, a counterclaim should be included in the defendant's answer and captioned as a counterclaim. If the substance of the counterclaim is pleaded instead as an affirmative defense, the opposing party need not file a reply to it, the party pleading the counterclaim may not be able to obtain affirmative relief on it, and other consequences may follow.[17] The court may allow a counterclaim omitted from a pleading to be added by amendment.[18]

§ 9.12 Cross–Claims

A cross-claim is functionally similar to a counterclaim in that it is a claim between parties to the action in addition to the claim or claims asserted in the complaint. Unlike a counterclaim, a cross-claim is between *co-parties*, that is, parties aligned together as co-defendants or co-plaintiffs.

A cross-claim must arise out of the same transaction or occurrence as the original suit or a counterclaim in that suit, or relate to property that is the subject matter of the original action.[1] Thus a cross-claim may not inject matters that are foreign or unrelated to the subject matter already comprehended within the action.[2] This is an important difference between it and a counterclaim. It reflects the danger that defendants may delay a plaintiff's suit by squabbling among themselves about matters unrelated to the plaintiff's claim. But it provides only limited protection against that danger, for once the (related) cross-claim has been filed, the party asserting it may join other and unrelated claims against the same party, who may likewise assert unrelated counterclaims.[3] If these claims are truly unrelated, the court should protect the plaintiff, not by dismissing them, but by severing them for separate preparation and trial.

Because the original cross-claim arises out of the same transaction or occurrence as the underlying suit, it falls within a federal court's supplemental jurisdiction regardless of whether it could have been brought by itself in federal court.[4] That will not be so for unrelated claims that are asserted with or in response to the original crossclaim.

A cross-claim may include the cross-claimant's independent claim, such as a defendant's claim for his or her own personal injuries arising

16. *See* Friedenthal, Joinder of Claims, Counterclaims and Cross–Complaints: Suggested Revision of the California Provisions, 23 Stan. L. Rev. 1 (1970).

17. Fed. R. Civ. P. 7(a), 13, and Form 20; § 4.8 *supra* (discussing difference between counterclaims and affirmative defenses).

18. Fed. R. Civ. P. 13(e), (f).

§ 9.12

1. Fed. R. Civ. P. 13(g).

2. Pacific Mut. Life Ins. Co. v. American Natl. Bank & Trust Co., 110 F.R.D. 272 (N.D.Ill.1986); United States v. DCS Dev. Corp., 590 F.Supp. 1117 (W.D.N.Y.1984).

3. Fed. R. Civ. P. 13(a, b), 18(a).

4. 28 U.S.C. § 1367; Allstate Ins. Co. v James, 779 F.2d 1536 (11th Cir.1986);Zurn Indus., Inc. v. Acton Construction Co., 847 F.2d 234 (5th Cir.1988); §§ 2.28 *supra* and 9.13 *infra.*

out of the accident that caused plaintiff's injuries.[5] It also may include the cross-claimant's claim for indemnity or contribution for all or any part of the claims asserted by plaintiff against the cross-claimant. Thus, co-sureties or joint tortfeasors may cross-claim against each other for contribution when the substantive law gives them such a claim.[6] New parties may be brought in on a cross-claim as well as on a counterclaim and be subject to the same conditions.[7] In California the cross-complaint is used to assert a cross-claim.[8]

§ 9.13 Jurisdiction and Other Problems

Modern rules governing counterclaims and cross-claims in general express the two basic principles of modern joinder rules: (1) two disputing parties may assert all claims between them; (2) in a dispute over a transaction involving multiple parties, all the disputants may be made parties. Rules external to the rules of joinder may, however, complicate or restrict the application of these principles. These external constraints include jurisdictional rules, statutes of limitation, and rules governing identity of parties, particularly when a loss is covered by insurance. In the past, additional complications arose with assigned claims, but these are now mostly obsolete.

Jurisdictional limitations

Rules governing subject matter jurisdiction may prevent assertion of a counterclaim that would be proper under the normal operation of the joinder rules. In state courts the jurisdictional problem typically arises from the fact that most state court systems have two trial court levels, one with jurisdiction over claims of limited dollar amount (up to $10,000,

5. *See* 3A Moore, Federal Practice and Procedure ¶ 13.34. Danner v. Anskis, 256 F.2d 123 (3d Cir.1958) read Rule 13(g) to forbid one coplaintiff to cross-claim against another when no claims have been asserted against them, but this has been disputed. Bickel–Gibson Associates Architects, Inc. v. Insurance Co. of North America, 774 S.W.2d 469 (Ky.App.1989); 6 Wright and Miller, Federal Practice and Procedure § 1432. In federal diversity cases cross-claims may, of course, pose jurisdictional problems, but the question here raised is whether they are available in the absence of such problems.

6. Falciani v. Philadelphia Transp. Co., 4 Fed. R. Serv. 2d 13g.11, case 1, 189 F.Supp. 203 (E.D. Pa.1960) (contribution); Bohn v. American Export Lines, 42 F.Supp. 228 (S.D.N.Y.1941) (same); Brown v. Commerce Trust Co., 13 Fed. R. Serv. 13g.1, case 1, 9 F.R.D. 317 (W.D.Mo.1949) (indemnity). When state law requires a judgment first to be rendered against joint tortfeasor before any right against the other tortfeasor accrues, the cases are split on whether it is proper to render a judgment conditional on compliance with state law. *Compare* Linkenhoger v. Owens, 181 F.2d 97 (5th Cir.1950), *with* Falciani v. Philadelphia Transp. Co., *supra, and* Bohn v. American Export Lines, *supra.*

A cross-claim is not proper when one defendant is seeking to assert simply that he or she is blameless and that his or her co-defendant is solely liable. Washington Bldg. Realty Corp. v. Peoples Drug Stores, 161 F.2d 879 (D.C.App.1947).

7. 3 Moore, Federal Practice and Procedure ¶ 13.39. *See also* Danner v. Himmelfarb, 858 F.2d 515 (9th Cir.1988); Birmingham Fire Ins. Co. v. Winegardner & Hammons, Inc., 714 F.2d 548 (5th Cir. 1983).

8. Cal. Civ. Proc. Code § 428.10 (West Supp. 1983).

for example) and another with general jurisdiction.[1] When a claim of limited dollar amount is brought in a court of limited jurisdiction and defendant wishes to assert a counterclaim for an amount exceeding the court's jurisdiction, the question arises whether the court has jurisdiction over the counterclaim. The reverse situation can also arise, that is, a defendant sued in a trial court of general jurisdiction has a counterclaim below the tribunal's jurisdictional minimum. In the first situation the result in most states, until about the middle of the twentieth century, was that such a counterclaim could not be asserted in the same action, even if it arose out of the same transaction, because the court of limited jurisdiction was held to have no jurisdiction to adjudicate the large counterclaim. A trial court of general jurisdiction, however, usually was permitted to adjudicate a counterclaim involving a claim that was too small to be within its jurisdiction if brought as an independent suit.[2] Whether the two opposed claims could be adjudicated in one action therefore could depend on which party first brought suit, for that would determine the court in which the litigation was initiated. Statutory amendment eventually remedied the situation to provide that when the original action was brought in the trial court of limited jurisdiction, a defendant asserting a large counterclaim could have the action transferred to the trial court of general jurisdiction, where both claims would be adjudicated.[3] That this simple and obvious solution had to be supplied by statute rather than judicial decision illustrates how sound procedural principles often succumb to reverence for even marginal jurisdictional definitions.

Federal jurisdiction

In federal courts, jurisdictional constraints on the scope of counterclaims retain some practical significance. When the counterclaim arises out of the same transaction as plaintiff's claim, no jurisdictional problem arises, because the counterclaim is treated as "supplemental" to the court's original jurisdiction. Thus, when plaintiff asserts a claim based on federal law, a counterclaim arising out of the same transaction but based on state law (and hence not within the federal court's jurisdiction in the absence of diversity between the parties) may be adjudicated on the basis of supplemental jurisdiction.[4] But what happens with a counterclaim based on a different transaction? Although thoughtful analysts

§ 9.13

1. *See* § 1.13 *supra.*

2. *See, e.g.*, Collison v. Thomas, 55 Cal.2d 490, 360 P.2d 51, 11 Cal.Rptr. 555 (1961); Columbus Mills, Inc. v. Dionne, 328 So.2d 467 (Fla.Dist.Ct.App.1976); Andel v. Eastman Kodak Co., 400 S.W.2d 584 (Tex. Civ.App.1966).

3. *See, e.g.*, Cal. Civ. Proc. Code § 396 (West Supp. 1983).

4. *See, e.g.*, Danner v. Himmelfarb, 858 F.2d 515 (9th Cir.1988); Plant v. Blazer Fin. Serv., 598 F.2d 1357 (5th Cir.1979), *reh'g denied*, 605 F.2d 555 (5th Cir.1979). *See also* Fraser, Ancillary Jurisdiction and the Joinder of Claims in the Federal Courts, 33 F.R.D. 27 (1963); § 2.28 *supra* and §§ 10.17, 10.18 *infra* (discussing other aspects of supplemental jurisdiction).

have considered that such a counterclaim ought also to be within supplemental jurisdiction, the clear weight of older authority held that it is not.[5] This strict construction of jurisdictional rules attaches decisive significance to the fact that more than one transaction is involved rather than to the fact that the relationship between the parties has become aggravated to the point of litigation. Once the relationship has reached that stage, it would seem better to construe jurisdictional rules to resolve in one action everything in dispute between the parties.[6] The passage of the supplemental jurisdiction statute offers an opportunity to broaden jurisdiction to cover at least some permissive counterclaims, but it is not yet clear to what extent the federal courts will seize that opportunity.[7]

Federal counterclaim in state court

An even more severe federal jurisdictional limitation on counterclaims exists when defendants are sued in state court but have a claim of their own over which federal courts have exclusive jurisdiction. Suppose that parties to a business transaction fall into a controversy in which one has a state-law contract claim and the other a federal antitrust law claim. If the antitrust claim is brought first in federal court, the state-law contract claim, because it arises from the same transaction, can be asserted as a counterclaim on the basis of pendent jurisdiction—indeed, it must be asserted under the compulsory counterclaim rule—and the whole controversy will be adjudicated in one action.[8] But if the state-law contract claim is first brought in state court, the defendant's antitrust claim cannot be asserted as a counterclaim in that court because federal antitrust claims fall within the exclusive jurisdiction of the federal courts.[9] Furthermore, the defendant in such a situation cannot remove the litigation to federal court, because under the present jurisdictional statute removal depends on there being a federal claim in the *complaint*, as distinct from the counterclaim.[10] Therefore, when the state-law claim

5. *See, e.g.*, By–Prod Corp. v. Armen–Berry Co., 668 F.2d 956 (7th Cir.1982); Federman v. Empire Fire and Marine Ins. Co., 597 F.2d 798 (2d Cir.1979).

6. *See* United States for the Use of D'Agostino Excavators v. Heyward–Robinson Co., 430 F.2d 1077, 1088 (2d Cir.1970) (Friendly, J., concurring); *see also* Green, Federal Jurisdiction over Counterclaims, 48 Nw. U.L. Rev. 271 (1953), and the discussion by Judge Clark in Lesnik v. Public Industrials Corp., 144 F.2d 968, 973–975 (2d Cir.1944).

7. 28 U.S.C. § 1367; Rothman v. Emory University, 123 F.3d 446 (7th Cir. 1997); Channell v. Citicorp National Services, Inc., 89 F.3d 379 (7th Cir.1996); Fletcher, Common Nucleus of Operative Fact and Defensive Set–Off: Beyond the *Gibbs* Test, 74 Ind. L.J. 171 (1998).

8. *See, e.g.*, Cable Vision, Inc. v. KUTV, Inc., 211 F.Supp. 47 (D.Idaho 1962), *vacated and remanded on other grounds*, 335 F.2d 348 (9th Cir.), *cert. denied*, 379 U.S. 989, 85 S.Ct. 700, 13 L.Ed.2d 609 (1965).

9. 28 U.S.C. § 1337; Freeman v. Bee Machine Co., 319 U.S. 448, 63 S.Ct. 1146, 87 L.Ed. 1509 (1943); *see, e.g.,* Classen v. Weller, 145 Cal.App.3d 27, 192, 192 Cal. Rptr. 914 (1983); Rohm and Haas Co. v. Polycast Technology Corp., 297 A.2d 53 (Del.Super.Ct.1972), *aff'd*, 305 A.2d 323 (Del.1973); Azalea Drive–In Theatre v. Sargoy, 215 Va. 714, 214 S.E.2d 131, *cert. denied*, 423 U.S. 940, 96 S.Ct. 300, 46 L.Ed.2d 272 (1975).

10. 28 U.S.C. § 1441(b); *see, e.g.*, Gully v. First Natl. Bank in Meridian, 299 U.S. 109, 57 S.Ct. 96, 81 L.Ed. 70 (1936); Rath Packing Co. v. Becker, 530 F.2d 1295 (9th

is brought first in state court, the antitrust claim will have to be separately adjudicated in federal court even though it arose from the same transaction. In addition to the cost of duplicate litigation there may be confusion and even contradictory results in resolution of issues common to the two claims.[11] The obvious solution would permit removal to federal court of state court actions involving a federal counterclaim arising out of the same transaction as the state court complaint. Congress, however, has not adopted recommendations to that effect.[12]

Personal jurisdiction

Further problems with counterclaims can develop over the issue of personal jurisdiction. When no additional parties are involved in the counterclaim, no problem of personal jurisdiction arises. Plaintiff submits to personal jurisdiction by bringing the action and thereby is vulnerable to any counterclaim that the procedural rules permit. The only exception occurs when the counterclaim arises from a wholly unrelated transaction and ought to be prosecuted in some other clearly preferable forum.[13] If additional parties are involved in a counterclaim, however, personal jurisdictional requirements must also be met as to them. Thus, a defendant asserting a counterclaim against not only the original plaintiff but also a co-wrongdoer of plaintiff must be able to establish personal jurisdiction over the co-wrongdoer, otherwise the counterclaim will not be maintainable against him or her.[14] Furthermore, if that co-wrongdoer is an "indispensable" party in the counterclaim, and if personal jurisdiction cannot be established against him or her, then the counterclaim also will not be maintainable against the original plaintiff.[15]

Thus, in considering the effect of jurisdictional rules on assertion of counterclaims, the situation must be analyzed in terms of both procedural rules governing counterclaims and jurisdictional rules. A counterclaim is maintainable only if it complies with both sets of rules.

Cir.1975), *aff'd on other grounds*, 430 U.S. 519, 97 S.Ct. 1305, 51 L.Ed.2d 604, *reh'g denied*, 431 U.S. 925, 97 S.Ct. 2201, 53 L.Ed.2d 240 (1977); Border City Sav. & Loan Assn. v. Kennecorp Mortgage & Equities, 523 F.Supp. 190 (S.D.Ohio 1981).

11. *Compare* Lyons v. Westinghouse Elec. Corp., 222 F.2d 184 (2d Cir.), *cert. denied sub nom.* Walsh v. Lyons, 350 U.S. 825, 76 S.Ct. 52, 100 L.Ed. 737 (1955), *with* Azalea Drive–In Theatre v. Hanft, 540 F.2d 713 (4th Cir.1976), *cert. denied*, 430 U.S. 941, 97 S.Ct. 1571, 51 L.Ed.2d 787 (1977).

12. *See* Am. Law Inst., Study of the Division of Jurisdiction Between State and Federal Courts 25–26 (1969).

13. *See* National City Bank v. Republic of China, 348 U.S. 356, 75 S.Ct. 423, 99 L.Ed. 389 (1955); Restatement (Second) of Judgments § 9; § 2.15 *supra*.

14. *E.g.*, Garfield Gas Gathering Co. v. Indiana–Ohio Pipe Co., 29 F.R.D. 8 (D.Colo. 1961). The "bulge" service of process provisions of Fed. R. Civ. P. 4(f) apply when a person is to be joined as a necessary party to a counterclaim or cross-claim, so that service may be made within one hundred miles of the courthouse even if that is in another state. *See also* Danner v. Himmelfarb, 858 F.2d 515 (9th Cir.1988).

15. *Compare* H & A Selmer, Inc. v. Musical Instrument Exch., 21 F.R.D. 224 (S.D.N.Y.1957), *with* Dunbar & Sullivan Dredging Co. v. John R. Jurgensen Co., 44 F.R.D. 467 (S.D.Ohio 1967); *see* §§ 10.11–15 *infra*.

Cross-claims

The general analysis of the relationship between procedural rules and jurisdictional rules also applies to cross-claims. With cross-claims, few jurisdictional problems develop. Under the Federal Rules a cross-claim must relate to the transaction sued on in the complaint; this relationship, in turn, is a basis of supplemental federal subject matter jurisdiction.[16] Ordinarily, no problem of personal jurisdiction arises since a cross-claim by definition is against a co-party, that is, one who is already subject to the court's jurisdiction.[17] A cross-claim that involves additional parties, however, poses personal jurisdiction problems similar to those in a counterclaim involving additional parties.[18]

Statutes of limitation

Statutes of limitation may be a bar to a counterclaim. At common law a claim that could be pleaded through recoupment (that is, one that arose out of the same transaction) was available even if a statute of limitations would bar an independent action brought on it. A claim that did not arise out of the transaction that was the subject of plaintiff's claim, however, could not be used through set-off if the statute of limitations had run against it. The prevailing modern rule is basically the same, although the matter is essentially one of statute and statutory construction.[19]

If the use of counterclaims may be barred by the statute of limitations, the question can arise whether the commencement of plaintiff's action stops the running of the statute of limitations or whether the statute keeps running until the counterclaim itself is actually filed. The prevailing American rule holds that the bringing of plaintiff's action stops the running of the statute against defendant's counterclaim.[20]

Identity of parties

Assertion of a counterclaim can be complicated by rules governing identity of parties. In one such situation, the counterclaim affects the plaintiff in a different capacity than that involved in the complaint. For example, a spouse suing as next of kin for wrongful death cannot be subjected to a counterclaim on an obligation of the decedent's estate of which the spouse is the executor, because executor is a different legal capacity than that of next of kin. Here, the technical difference in capacity obscures the substantial identity of economic and social inter-

16. *See, e.g.*, Allstate Ins. Co. v. James, 779 F.2d 1536 (11th Cir.1986); Zurn Indus. v. Acton Construction Co., 847 F.2d 234 (5th Cir.1988); Fairview Park Excavating Co. v. Al Monzo Construction Co., 560 F.2d 1122 (3d Cir.1977). Under 28 U.S.C. § 1367, supplemental subject matter jurisdiction may exist even when the cross-claim adds a new party.

17. Fed. R. Civ. P. 13(g) ("[a] pleading may state as a cross-claim any claim by one party against a co-party").

18. *See, e.g.*, Marine Bank & Trust Co. v. Hamilton Bros., Inc., 55 F.R.D. 505 (M.D.Fla.1972).

19. *See* Annot., 1 A.L.R.2d 630.

20. *See* Annot., 127 A.L.R. 909.

ests in the individual's two legal capacities, which should dictate that the counterclaim be allowed.[21]

At the same time, technical identity of the parties can obscure substantial divergence in the real economic interests involved in a counterclaim situation. The most common instance is a two-car collision in which each driver is injured and is covered by liability insurance.[22] The claim of Driver I is in form against Driver II, but economically the claim is the exclusive or primary concern of Driver II's insurance company, and it is the latter that provides Driver II with legal representation. Correlatively, the counterclaim for Driver II's own injuries is ordinarily of no economic interest to Driver II's insurer or to Driver I, but is of consequence to Driver I's liability insurance. In terms of economic interest, therefore, it would make more sense to consider the situation as involving two separate lawsuits, Driver I v. Insurer of Driver II, and Driver II v. Insurer of Driver I. The procedural rules in most states, however, require that the controversy be regarded as a claim and counterclaim in Driver I v. Driver II. This in turn creates serious complications in such matters as compulsory counterclaim, set-off of the claims, and strategy and tactics in the representation of the parties, all because a four-way transaction is treated as though it were only two-way. Similar problems can arise in cross-claims.[23]

Assigned claims

At common law and under the codes before the Federal Rules, counterclaim problems could become complicated when either the plaintiff's claim or the defendant's counterclaim did not arise from a transaction between them but was based on a claim that had been assigned from another person. Suppose that plaintiff is assignee of a claim for money due from defendant on a contract, but defendant has a claim that the goods supplied by the original party to the contract (the assignor) were defective. Obviously the assignee is not liable for damages for the defect, but is he or she subject to a set-off based on the damages claim? Consider the same situation from defendant's viewpoint: Why should the defendant have to defend one action on the assigned money claim and separately prosecute another action against the original contracting party to recover damages for the defective goods?

The competing underlying policies are meant, on the one hand, to promote assignability and, on the other hand, to prevent an assignment from enlarging the actual scope of the obligation. These two policies

21. *See, e.g.*, Hall v. McDonough, 216 So.2d 84 (Fla.App.1968), *reh'g denied*, 241 So.2d 201 (Fla.Dist.Ct.App.1970); Ellison v. Simmons, 238 S.C. 364, 120 S.E.2d 209 (1961); *see also* Ehrlich v. American Moninger Greenhouse Mfr. Corp., 26 N.Y.2d 255, 257 N.E.2d 890, 309 N.Y.S.2d 341 (1970).

22. *See, e.g.*, Datta v. Staab, 173 Cal. App.2d 613, 343 P.2d 977 (1959).

23. *See, e.g.*, the factual background in Lumbermen's Mut. Ins. Co. v. Massachusetts Bonding and Ins. Co., 310 F.2d 627 (4th Cir.1962).

cannot be fully reconciled, and the case law trying to reconcile them often becomes very confused.[24] In general, the solution reached has allowed the obligor to set off against the assignee any obligation he or she claimed against the assignor, except when the assigned claim was a negotiable instrument.[25] But to obtain affirmative relief against the assignor the obligor has had to pursue an independent action.[26]

24. *See* Restatement (Second) of Contracts § 326; *cf.* Restatement (Second) of Judgments § 55.

25. Restatement (Second) of Judgments § 55, Comment *e.*

26. Restatement (Second) of Contracts § 336, Comment *c.*

Chapter 10

PARTIES TO AN ACTION

§ 10.1 Introduction

To analyze the rules governing parties, we may assume that the action involves a single transaction or a series of connected transactions, because joinder of multiple parties in an action is permitted only if there is such a transactional nexus.[1] Assuming the presence of such a link simplifies consideration of the matter of parties.

§ 10.1

1. *See* Fed. R. Civ. P. 20(a) ("same transaction, occurrence, or series of transactions or occurrences"); Fed. R. Civ. P. 13(h) ("persons other than those made par-

Apart from the required transactional nexus, the rules for parties concern individual party identity and capacity and joinder of multiple parties. The second category is the more complex one. It includes rules of compulsory joinder, defining "necessary parties," and rules of permissive joinder, by which parties permissively can be added to an action. The rules governing multiple parties also include those governing the class action procedure, which entails the concepts of both compulsory and permissive joinder.[2]

The procedural rules governing parties work against a background of other rules considered in more detail elsewhere in this book. Rules governing personal and subject matter jurisdiction can have decisive consequences on joinder of interested parties because they may limit the parties that may be joined.[3] The rules of res judicata can operate in effect as rules of compulsory joinder by threatening a party who fails to raise a claim with the possibility that the claim will be held to be barred if the party ever tries to raise it in a later suit.[4]

A. PARTY IDENTITY AND CAPACITY

§ 10.2 Nominal and Real Parties

As a general principle, the person designated as the plaintiff in an action is the person whose legal right has allegedly been infringed and who will be awarded redress if the action succeeds.[1] This simple concept facilitates notice to the defendant and to the court about the nature of the action, for identifying the aggrieved party often conveys as much information about the dispute as does the complaint's statement of the claim. It also facilitates administration of the rules of res judicata by indicating whose claim has been brought.[2]

Fictitious parties

The designation of a person as a party in an action does not, however, necessarily determine the identity of the litigant. Historically, several common law actions were brought in the name of a fictitious plaintiff or named a fictitious defendant, it being understood that the

ties to the original action may be made parties to a counterclaim or crossclaim in accordance with the provisions of Rules 19 and 20"); Fed. R. Civ. P. 23(a) ("One or more members of a class may sue or be sued . . . if . . . there are questions of law or fact common to the class"). Federal Rules 14 (impleader) and 22 (interpleader) do not explicitly refer to a "transactional nexus" but such a nexus is implicitly required. *See* Kane, Original Sin and the Transaction in Federal Civil Procedure, 76 Tex. L. Rev. 1723 (1998).

2. Fed. R. Civ. P. 23; *see also* §§ 10.20 *et seq.*

3. *See* chapter 2 *supra.*

4. *See* chapter 11 *infra.*

§ 10.2

1. *See* Fed. R. Civ. P. 17; § 10.3 *infra*; *see also* Restatement (Second) of Judgments § 34.

2. *See* Restatement (Second) of Judgments § 37.

real parties were conducting the litigation under *noms de guerre.*[3] Today, litigation involving personally delicate subject matter may be brought under a fictitious name, as in the abortion law case of *Roe v. Wade*[4] ("Roe" is a fictitious name). Thus, the fact that someone's name is used does not invariably mean he or she is the person actually prosecuting and benefiting from the action.[5] Moreover, when one has conducted and controlled a litigation in another's name, one is ordinarily bound to the same extent as if one were a named party.[6]

Uses of fictions

The use of fictional or nominal party identifications has served various practical purposes. One purpose has been to extend a legal remedy to those who under prior law were not entitled to sue—the extension is accomplished by letting such a person sue in someone else's name. Another purpose is to unify management of litigation on behalf of a group interest in the hands of a single representative who sues or is sued on their behalf—this objective is accomplished by treating that representative as the sole party involved. A third purpose is to keep party identity a secret from either the public or the jury. These purposes have arisen in specific substantive contexts and led to specific adaptations of the rules as to party identity. Hence, it is not possible to generalize these adaptations in terms of the procedural rules, even though the courts have sometimes tried to do so.[7]

Common law fictions

Several common law actions involved fictionally designated parties, the best known being the action of ejectment. Originally the action of ejectment was used to litigate rights to leaseholds—whether *P,* who claimed a leasehold of Blackacre, actually had a valid lease. The ejectment action could draw into question the issue of the underlying freehold title to Blackacre (since *P*'s lease is invalid if *P*'s lessor has no title), and it was a more efficient procedure than the traditional "real" actions for trying title to land. The practice therefore developed of pretending that a leasehold was involved when the real controversy concerned the underlying title. To accomplish the pretense, *A,* a person claiming the land, would initiate an ejectment action alleging that there was a leasehold to Doe from *A,* whereupon the defense was that the lease was invalid because *A* had no title.[8] The action was therefore in the

3. *See, e.g.,* Doe ex dem. Carter v. Barnard, 13 Q.B. 945, 116 Eng. Rep. 1524 (1849); *see generally* 1 Chitty, Pleading 209–212 (16th Am. ed. 1879); Clark, Code Pleading § 49 (2d ed. 1947).

4. 410 U.S. 113, 93 S.Ct. 705, 35 L.Ed.2d 147 (1973). *See* §§ 4.23, 5.13 *supra.*

5. *See* § 10.3 *infra.*

6. *See* Restatement (Second) of Judgments § 39; *see, e.g.,* Souffront v. La Compagnie Des Sucreries De Porto Rico, 217 U.S. 475, 30 S.Ct. 608, 54 L.Ed. 846 (1910).

7. *See, e.g.,* Ellis Canning Co. v. International Harvester Co., 174 Kan. 357, 255 P.2d 658 (1953).

8. *See, e.g.,* Doe ex dem. Carter v. Barnard, 13 Q.B. 945, 116 Eng. Rep. 1524

name of a fictitious plaintiff, conventionally called "Doe," and permitted claimants of land to use the ejectment procedure instead of the older, less efficient remedies. To make this possible, the defendant was not allowed to plead that neither Doe nor the lease existed.

Another common law action involving a fictitious party was the action on an assigned claim. The earlier common law gave a remedy for breach to a party to a contract but not to a person to whom rights under a contract had been assigned. Thus, if *A* promised to pay *B* $100, and *B* assigned that right to *C*, and *A* then refused to pay *C*, *C* could not sue *A* through a common law action because *C* was not a party to the contract under which *A*'s obligation arose. *C*'s recourse was to go to the court of equity to require *B* to sue *A*. Eventually equity skipped the involvement of *B* and let *C* as assignee sue *A* directly. Still later, the common law courts, competing with chancery, gave *C* in effect a direct remedy against *A*. They did this by allowing *C* to maintain the action but under the heading *B v. A*, where *B* was a fictitious party.

These and similar evolutions of actions under fictitious names are perfectly intelligible in historical perspective. Indeed, the essence of common law evolution is the stretching of previous categories at the margin until they become new categories. The legacy of such stretching, however, is fiction, in this instance fictional designation of the parties to litigation. Critical minds may call attention to such a discrepancy and point out the "real" situation. Thus, with regard to the assignee of a contract right, the equity courts said that in an assignment suit the "real party in interest" was the assignee.[9]

Actions by representatives

Another arrangement of procedural convenience has to do with actions by or against persons who are representatives of others. Such parties are often called "nominal parties," persons who can be joined to facilitate the recovery of relief without having to bring in a more or less diffuse group of those whose interests are at stake. The nominal plaintiff or defendant can be a trustee, agent, or depositary who has possession of the subject of the litigation. The court will grant relief to or against this person. But nominal parties have no personal interest in which party prevails. Typically, the law requires them to protect the parties who do have personal interests; and without such a requirement it would scarcely be fair to consider those parties bound by the result.

This arrangement is illustrated in several ways. An executor or administrator of an estate can be considered the temporary owner of the decedent's assets, for purposes of paying obligations and collecting and

(1849); Doe ex dem. Greaves v. Raby, 2 Barn. & Adol. 948 (K.B. 1831). *See generally* Clark, Code Pleading § 49 (2d ed. 1947).

9. *See* Atkinson, The Real Party in Interest Rule: A Plea for Its Abolition, 32 N.Y.U. L. Rev. 926 (1957); Cook, The Alienability of Choses in Action, 29 Harv. L. Rev. 816 (1916).

distributing assets; equally, such an official can be considered a representative of the beneficiaries of the estate, acting on their behalf in administering the estate and conducting litigation in connection therewith. So also, a trustee of a trust in relation to the trust beneficiaries, or the guardian of a minor or an incompetent in relation to the ward, can be regarded as an owner with fiduciary duties or as a representative of the beneficiaries. The managers of an unincorporated association can be regarded as representatives of the organization in relation to the organization's litigation.

As an abstract proposition, for procedural purposes these situations could be handled in any of the following ways: (1) as litigation by the beneficiaries (of the estate or trust, the ward, the stockholders or members of the organization) as the "real parties in interest"; (2) as litigation by the fiduciary (the executor or administrator, the trustee), in a representative capacity; or (3) as litigation by a legal entity (the decedent's estate, the trust, the corporation). There is no obvious choice between these forms; any can do the job if it is kept in mind that the litigation concerns the fiduciary-beneficiary group in their group identity and not a set of wholly unrelated individuals. In the case of suits by a minor or an incompetent, in most jurisdictions the plaintiff is styled "*A*, an infant, by his guardian *B*" (the first form above);[10] in suits involving decedents' estates, in most jurisdictions the plaintiff is styled "*A*, as executor of the estate of *D*, deceased" (the second form above);[11] in suits by corporations the plaintiff is now styled "*A Corporation*, a corporation of the state of *X*" (the third form above).[12]

Only historical evolution, often involving accidental decisions, explains why one form is used in one or another situation or jurisdiction.[13] Furthermore, it would make no fundamental difference which form is used because it would be necessary in any case to recognize that the litigation involves the fiduciary-beneficiary set as a bounded interest—essentially, as an entity. But neither the common law courts nor equity ever considered the problem in such general terms. They simply accumulated improvisations.

§ 10.3 Real Party in Interest

The party identification problem as described above drew the attention of the code drafters in the 1840s. Unfortunately, the drafters

10. *See* Fed. R. Civ. P. 17(c); *see, e.g.*, Garrick v. Weaver, 888 F.2d 687 (10th Cir. 1989); Gardner v. Parson, 874 F.2d 131 (3d Cir.1989).

11. *See* Fed. R. Civ. P. 17(a); *see, e.g.*, Lummis v. White, 629 F.2d 397 (5th Cir. 1980), *rev'd on other grounds sub nom.* Cory v. White, 457 U.S. 85, 102 S.Ct. 2325, 72 L.Ed.2d 694 (1982); Byrne v. Shell Oil Co., 295 F.2d 797 (7th Cir.1961).

12. *See* Fed. R. Civ. P. Form 2; *see, e.g.*, Chrysler Credit Corp. v. Superior Dodge, Inc., 538 F.2d 616 (4th Cir.1976), *cert. denied*, 429 U.S. 1042, 97 S.Ct. 743, 50 L.Ed.2d 754 (1977).

13. *See* Navarro Sav. Assn. v. Lee, 446 U.S. 458, 100 S.Ct. 1779, 64 L.Ed.2d 425 (1980); Puerto Rico v. Russell & Co., 288 U.S. 476, 53 S.Ct. 447, 77 L.Ed. 903 (1933).

apparently thought the problem was purely one of form, and even at that failed to appreciate that several different problems of form were involved. After describing the legal and equitable rights of assignor and assignee,[1] they explained: "The true rule undoubtedly is, that which prevails in the courts of equity, that he who has the right, is the person to pursue the remedy. We have adopted that rule."[2] The provision, embodied in two sections, was as follows:

> 91. Every action must be prosecuted in the name of the real party in interest, except as otherwise provided in Section 93.
>
> 93. An executor or administrator, a trustee of an express trust, or a person expressly authorized by statute, may sue without joining with him the person for whose benefit the suit is prosecuted.[3]

Federal Rule 17(a)

A substantially similar provision was widely adopted and appears in the Federal Rules and most states today in order to mystify students who think about it.[4]

One explanation of the rule's purpose is simple and historically perhaps the most accurate: It was intended to abolish the practice of using fictitious names in the caption and the party-identifying allegations of the complaint.[5] Even this purpose of the real party in interest rule has proved to oversimplify the issues, for use of fictional names still persists. But the other problems of plaintiff designation were not addressed in the real party in interest rule, and the courts continued to struggle with them.

Who can enforce the claim?

Some courts seized on the idea that the rule was intended to require that *the* party entitled to enforce the claim should be named as plaintiff.[6] But this approach creates difficulties that also have arisen with the concept of "standing to sue" in modern public question litigation.[7]

§ 10.3

1. *See* § 10.4 *infra.*

2. New York, First Report of Commissioners on Practice and Pleadings 124 (1848) (hereinafter cited as First Report of Commissioners).

This is widely accepted as the origin of the term. Bliss, Code Pleading §§ 45, 47 (3d ed. 1894); Clark, Code Pleading 158 (2d ed. 1947); Pomeroy, Code Remedies §§ 50, 51 (5th ed. 1929).

3. N.Y. Laws ch. 379 (1848).

4. Fed. R. Civ. P. 17(a). In the revision of the New York Civil Practice Laws and Rules, the real party in interest rule was omitted. *Compare* Atkinson, The Real Party in Interest Rule: A Plea for Its Abolition, 32 N.Y.U. L. Rev. 926 (1957).

5. *See* N.Y. Rev. Stat. pt. 3, ch. v, § 6 (1828): "The use of fictitious names of plaintiffs or defendants, and of the names of any other than the real claimants and the real defendants ... are hereby abolished.... "

6. *See* United States v. Aetna Casualty Co., 338 U.S. 366, 70 S.Ct. 207, 94 L.Ed. 171 (1949).

7. *See* Albert, Standing to Challenge Administrative Action, 83 Yale L.J. 425 (1974), and references therein; Kennedy, Federal Rule 17(a): Will the Real Party in Interest Please Stand?, 51 Minn. L. Rev. 675 (1967); § 2.26 *supra.*

Identifying who is entitled to sue may be a complex issue of the substantive law in question.[8] The phrase "real party in interest" tempts courts to assume that the person who will actually benefit if the suit succeeds should sue, but this is not always appropriate: a divorce suit may in practice benefit a spouse's lover or lawyer, who may nevertheless not bring it. To say that the person entitled to bring a claim should be the plaintiff is a tautology that does not help to resolve the real issue: who is so entitled?

Furthermore, this approach assumes that any given interest is invariably enforceable by only one party, when such is not the case. Thus, the loss of property under bailment may be recovered by either the bailee or bailor;[9] the obligor of a contract creating rights in a third-party beneficiary may, under some circumstances, be sued either by the third-party beneficiary or by the promisee who made the contract;[10] the beneficiary of a trust (a situation mentioned in the code) can sue to enforce the trust if the trustee refuses to do so.[11] Much of the caselaw arises from just such situations.

The formulation that "the party entitled to enforce" should be "named as plaintiff" thus raises distinct questions. The first is whether it is ever appropriate, for any purpose, to use fictitious designations of parties. Although the real party in interest rule in the code appears to preclude such fictions, in some situations they seem to be useful.[12] Assuming that the use of fictions is permitted at all, then "who should be named as plaintiff" becomes a relatively trivial question. Yet in terms of the question "who should be named as plaintiff" the courts have struggled to deal with the more fundamental question: Who should be entitled to enforce the claim? That question assumes genuine importance where more than one person has an interest in the claim.

§ 10.4 Assignee of Chose in Action

As we have seen, a principal objective of the real party in interest rule was to enable the assignee of a chose in action (the common law term for a legal claim) to sue in his or her own name in all cases,

8. *See, e.g.,* Warth v. Seldin, 422 U.S. 490, 95 S.Ct. 2197, 45 L.Ed.2d 343 (1975), with which *compare* the problem of actionability in, *e.g.,* Blue Chip Stamps v. Manor Drug Stores, 421 U.S. 723, 95 S.Ct. 1917, 44 L.Ed.2d 539 (1975). *See also* Homburger, Private Suits in the Public Interest in the United States of America, 23 Buffalo L. Rev. 343 (1974).

9. *See* Prosser, Torts 96 (4th ed. 1971); *see also* Restatement (Second) of Judgments § 52.

10. *See* Restatement (Second) of Contracts §§ 133–147; *see also* Restatement (Second) of Judgments § 56.

11. *See, e.g.,* Landis v. First Natl. Bank, 20 Cal.App.2d 198, 66 P.2d 730 (1937); *cf.* Czaplicki v. The Hoegh Silvercloud, 351 U.S. 525, 76 S.Ct. 946, 100 L.Ed. 1387 (1956).

12. *See* §§ 4.23, 5.13, 10.2 *supra*; *e.g.,* Weber v. Stony Brook Hosp., 60 N.Y.2d 208, 456 N.E.2d 1186, 469 N.Y.S.2d 63 (1983) (plaintiff Weber acting as guardian ad litem for "Baby Jane Doe," an infant born with severe physical disorders).

whether formerly denominated legal or equitable.[1] Today assignments of most claims are enforceable, although some states will not enforce assignments of certain "personal" claims on grounds arising from the substantive law in question.[2] Difficulty has arisen when the assignment is for collection only or for security and when there has been assignment of part of a claim. The first of these problems is purely formal, except in federal diversity litigation,[3] but the second is not.

Assignee for collection

A claim is often assigned for the purpose of collection only, with the understanding that the assignee will remit the proceeds to the assignor, either with or without deducting an amount to pay for the service of making the collection. In this case the assignor may be viewed as the one entitled to the fruits of the action, and a few courts have therefore regarded the assignor as the real party in interest and required that the suit be brought in his or her name.[4] Alternatively, the assignee can be viewed as a trustee of a trust, and most decisions hold that the action should be brought in the name of the assignee for collection.[5] Recovery by either method will fully protect the debtor from later recovery by the other.[6]

The same propositions apply when a claim is assigned as security.[7] Since using either name as the plaintiff's has succeeded, and since the action in any event precludes further enforcement of the claim, the choice of nominal plaintiff has depended on extrinsic tactical considerations such as which is the more sympathetic plaintiff.[8]

§ 10.4

1. *See* § 10.3 *supra*; Clark, Code Pleading 155, 164 (2d ed. 1947); Pomeroy, Code Remedies § 63 (5th ed. 1929).

2. On the assignability of legal malpractice claims, *see, e.g.,* New Hampshire Ins. Co. v. McCann, 429 Mass. 202, 707 N.E.2d 332 (1999)(yes); MNC Credit Corp. v. Sickels, 255 Va. 314, 497 S.E.2d 331 (1998)(no); 1 Mallen and Smith, Legal Malpractice § 7.12 (5th ed. 2000).

3. *See, e.g.,* Virginia Elec. & Power Co. v. Westinghouse Elec. Corp., 485 F.2d 78 (4th Cir.1973).

4. *See, e.g.,* Stewart v. Price, 64 Kan. 191, 67 P. 553, 64 L.R.A. 581 (1902); Hoagland v. Van Etten, 22 Neb. 681, 35 N.W. 869, *reh'g denied,* 23 Neb. 462, 36 N.W. 755 (1888); H. S. Leyman Co. v. Piggly–Wiggly Corp., 68 N.E.2d 486 (Ohio Ct.App.1944); Brown v. Ginn, 66 Ohio St. 316, 64 N.E. 123 (1902). *Stewart* and *Hoagland* have been overruled. *See* note 5 *infra.*

5. Titus v. Wallick, 306 U.S. 282, 59 S.Ct. 557, 83 L.Ed. 653 (1939); Leon v. Citizens' Bldg. & Loan Assn., 14 Ariz. 294, 127 P. 721, Ann. Cas. 1914D,1151 (1912); Manley v. Park, 68 Kan. 400, 75 P. 557, 66 Law. Rep. Ann. 967 (1904) (overruling *Stewart,* note 4 *supra*); Saulsbury v. Corwin, 40 Mo.App. 373 (1890); Archer v. Musick, 147 Neb. 1018, 25 N.W.2d 908, 168 A.L.R. 1164 (1947) (overruling *Hoagland,* note 4 *supra*); Eaton v. Alger, 47 N.Y. 345 (1872); Falconio v. Larsen, 31 Or. 137, 48 P. 703, 37 L.R.A. 254 (1897); Citizens' Bank v. Corkings, 9 S.D. 614, 70 N.W. 1059, 62 Am. State Rep. 891 (1897); Note, 64 Law Rep. Ann. 581 (1904); Pomeroy, Code Remedies § 70 (5th ed. 1929).

6. *See* Restatement (Second) of Judgments §§ 37, 39.

7. Wetmore v. City of San Francisco, 44 Cal. 294 (1872); Lawrence v. Congregational Church, 164 N.Y. 115, 58 N.E. 24 (1900); Hilton v. Waring, 7 Wis. 492 (1859); 3A Moore, Federal Practice and Procedure ¶ 17.09.

8. *See, e.g.,* Czaplicki v. The Hoegh Silvercloud, 351 U.S. 525, 76 S.Ct. 946, 100 L.Ed. 1387 (1956).

Subrogation

Subrogation is a kind of assignment that takes place by operation of law under certain circumstances. When an insurer of property (against fire or collision, for example) has paid for an insured loss in whole or in part, the insurer (the "subrogee") becomes subrogated to any claim the property owner (the "subrogor") has against third persons for causing the loss. In other words, the insurer is put in the shoes of the insured owner to the extent of any payment made by the insurer and can sue just as the owner might have done.[9] Frequently a written assignment of this claim is also taken, but subrogation results by operation of law even without the assignment.

Subrogated insurer

The subrogee's right to pursue the subrogor's claims against third parties was recognized in equity before the codes, and the subrogee is generally held to be the real party in interest under the codes and Federal Rule 17(a).[10] This means, of course, that the insurer must sue in its own name. Since the insured commonly is an individual or an ordinary business corporation, the insurer would prefer, for tactical reasons, to have the action brought in the name of the insured, thereby concealing from the jury the fact that collection is being sought by an insurance company rather than by the owner who suffered the loss. To bring about this result and at the same time to facilitate prompt settlement with the insured, who is, after all, their customer, insurance companies often use a "loan receipt" device. This makes the payment to the insured technically a loan, to be repaid only out of proceeds of the claim against the third party, which claim is pledged to the insurer as security for the "loan."[11] The receipt contains a power of attorney appointing the insurer agent to collect this claim, by suit if need be, in the insured's name.

This device has generally been allowed. "The parties [have] the right so to shape their transaction that title would reside wherever they [see] fit."[12] The stratagem is, of course, open to the objection that it sanctions a fictitious denomination of the party whose interest is really at stake, but this only shows that such fictions still have utility. In subrogation situations the fiction may be justified for the plaintiff

9. *See generally* McClintock, Equity 332–335 (2d ed. 1948); 4 Pomeroy, Equity Jurisprudence §§ 1211, 1419 (5th ed. 1941).

10. *See, e.g.,* United States v. Aetna Casualty & Surety Co., 338 U.S. 366, 70 S.Ct. 207, 94 L.Ed. 171 (1949); Cunningham & Hinshaw v. Seaboard Air Line Ry., 139 N.C. 427, 51 S.E. 1029 (1905); Clark, Code Pleading § 24 (2d ed. 1947); Entman, More Reasons for Abolishing Federal Rule of Civil Procedure 17(a): The Problem of the Proper Plaintiff and Insurance Subrogation, 68 N.C. L. Rev. 893 (1990). *See* Annots., 13 A.L.R.3d 140, 229.

11. *See, e.g.,* Phillips v. Clifton Mfg. Co., 204 S.C. 496, 30 S.E.2d 146, 157 A.L.R. 1255 (1944).

12. Sosnow, Kranz & Simcoe, Inc. v. Storatti Corp., 269 App.Div. 122, 126, 54 N.Y.S.2d 780, 783 (1945), *aff'd,* 295 N.Y. 675, 65 N.E.2d 326 (1946);. *See* Note, Loan Receipt and Insurers' Subrogation, 50 Tul. L. Rev. 115 (1975); Annot., 13 A.L.R.3d 42.

because the real defendant in most of these cases is also an insurance company, which cannot be sued directly under prevailing practice and so also hides behind the figure of an insured individual or business corporation.[13]

The use of the device can sometimes result in serious prejudice to the insured if he or she has other claims arising from the transaction in question. If the insured, for example, is driving a car and is injured in a collision, the insurer may give the insured a "loan receipt" in return for paying the property damage to the car, and then sue the other driver to recover that loss, using the insured's name as plaintiff. Under applicable law, however, the insured may be regarded as having only "one cause of action" from the collision; the suit brought in the insured's name may therefore be held to determine that cause of action and, under the claim preclusion rules of res judicata, may bar the insured from bringing an action for personal injuries.[14] This problem is further considered in connection with partial assignments.

A similar problem arises when insurance covers only part of the loss. Fire insurance, for example, is commonly written for a specified amount that may not cover the total value of the property insured. When the insurance payment does not cover the whole amount, the insurer is subrogated only to the extent of the payment, and the balance of any claim rests with the insured owner, with another insurer, or the like. Such a case presents a problem very much like that in partial assignment.

§ 10.5 Partial Assignment and Subrogation

A partial assignment or subrogation results in splitting the claim and is therefore problematic. At common law courts did not recognize the assignment of part of a claim; the reason for this was explained by Justice Story in *Mandeville v. Welch*: "[W]hen [a debtor] undertakes to pay an integral sum to his creditor, it is no part of his contract that he shall be obliged to pay in fractions to any other persons."[1] Equity had a device to protect a debtor from this exposure to multiple suits in its ability to bring all interested parties into a single suit. Since the ability to assign a part, as well as the whole, of a claim was convenient for creditors and the business world generally, the weight of authority allowed partial assignees to sue in equity, provided that they joined with

13. The "loan receipt" device also has other uses. When a shipper insures goods in transit, the carrier's bill of lading often provides that in case of loss or damage for which the carrier shall be liable, it (carrier) shall have the full benefit of any insurance on the goods. This attempt by the carrier to put ultimate liability on the insurer was successfully countered by the "loan receipt" together with a warranty in the policy denying coverage where the carrier was liable for the loss and damage. Luckenbach v. W.J. McCahan Sugar Ref. Co., 248 U.S. 139, 39 S.Ct. 53, 63 L.Ed. 170 (1918). *See* § 10.9 *infra*.

14. *See* Restatement (Second) of Judgments § 37, Comment *d*; § 11.10 *infra*.

§ 10.5

1. 18 U.S. (5 Wheat.) 277, 289, 5 L. Ed. 87, 90 (1820).

them the assignor and any other partial assignee, thus safeguarding the debtor's right to be sued only once.[2] The problem was recognized as one of compulsory joinder.

Joinder of both owners

The weight of modern authority follows the same pattern both for partial assignment and partial subrogation. All who have an interest in the claim, as assignor or assignee, or as subrogor or subrogee, should be joined as plaintiffs, or as defendants if they are unwilling to come in as plaintiffs.[3] If this is not done, a defect of parties results,[4] which the debtor may object to by motion or demurrer, depending on the practice. If objection is not made at the earliest opportunity, however, it is waived.[5] Thus, in partial assignment or subrogation a separate action by each party interested may be maintained unless the debtor, for whose benefit the rule against multiple actions exists, makes suitable objection as soon as it appears that he or she may be "obliged to pay in fractions" in more than one suit.

Not all courts follow the simple and sensible practice just described. Some reject the analogy of partial assignment and deny the partial subrogee's right to sue in his or her own name. Under this rule, suit must be brought in the partial subrogor's name, and the only way the subrogee can recover is "to have its claim included in the plaintiff's claim against the wrongdoer."[6] The harm done by this rule, aside from offense to those who dislike fictions, is that it can result in letting the first to sue cut off the rights of the other through a failure to include the other's claim in the first suit.[7]

Property and personal injury

These difficulties have occurred mainly in the common situation in which plaintiff, an individual who has collision insurance on his or her car, suffers personal injury and has the car damaged in a collision caused by the negligence of another automobile driver, the defendant. When

2. *See, e.g.,* Rogers v. Penobscot Mining Co., 154 Fed. 606 (8th Cir.1907). *See* United States v. Aetna Casualty & Surety Co., 338 U.S. 366, 381–382, 70 S.Ct. 207, 216, 94 L.Ed. 171, 185–186 (1949).

3. *See* cases cited *supra* note 2; State Farm Mut. Liab. Ins. Co. v. United States, 172 F.2d 737 (1st Cir.1949); Yorkshire Ins. Co. v. United States, 171 F.2d 374 (3d Cir. 1948); Hoosier Casualty Co. v. Davis, 172 Ohio St. 5, 173 N.E.2d 349 (1961); Clark, Code Pleading 168–171, 177 (2d ed. 1947). *See also* Annot., 13 A.L.R.3d 140.

4. While all the holders of fractional interests are necessary parties, they are not "indispensable." *See* §§ 10.6, 10.11 *infra.*

5. *See, e.g.,* Grain v. Aldrich, 38 Cal. 514 (1869); Porter v. Lane Construction Corp., 212 App.Div. 528, 209 N.Y.S. 54 (1925), *aff'd,* 244 N.Y. 523, 155 N.E. 881 (1926); 3 Moore, Federal Practice and Procedure ¶ 17.09, at 1345, 1349 (2d ed. 1963); Clark, Code Pleading 170 (2d ed. 1947).

6. Hayward v. State Farm Mut. Auto. Ins. Co., 212 Minn. 500, 504, 4 N.W.2d 316, 318 (1942). *Accord* Van Wie v. United States, 77 F.Supp. 22 (N.D.Iowa 1948); Farmers Ins. Exch. v. Arlt, 61 N.W.2d 429 (N.D.1953).

7. Mims v. Reid, 98 So.2d 498 (Fla. 1957); Saber v. Supplee–Wills–Jones Milk Co., 181 Pa.Super. 167, 124 A.2d 620 (1956); Note, 62 A.L.R.2d 977, 993.

plaintiff's insurer pays plaintiff for the damage to the car, the insurer becomes subrogated to plaintiff's claim for property damage, but not to plaintiff's claim for personal injuries. If at this point plaintiff and the insurer cooperate with each other in bringing suit in plaintiff's name for the whole damage and in making the proper allocation between them of any proceeds, then everyone will get his or her just deserts. The trouble is that this may fail to happen under the rule now being considered.

In some cases the insurance company has sued first, in plaintiff's name, for the property damage alone[8] (this is all the insurer is interested in). In other cases plaintiff has sued first, in his or her own name, for personal injuries[9] (this is all plaintiff is interested in). In either case, when the second suit is brought, also in plaintiff's name, it appears on the face of the pleadings as though the cause of action has been split in a way forbidden by the claim preclusion rules of res judicata. Several courts have therefore held that the second suit is barred by the judgment in the first.[10] These difficulties are avoided by insisting (on defendant's timely objection) that all parties in interest be joined in a single action. In any event, the problem is one of joinder of parties, not denomination of parties.

§ 10.6 Holders of Different Interests in Property and Other Multiple Claimants

More than one person may hold interests in the same property, whether the property is real estate or personal property, tangible or intangible. Thus, there may be mortgagor and mortgagee, landlord and tenant, life tenant and remainderer, tenants in common, and so on. In the evolution of the law, three different rules have existed concerning the proper plaintiff in actions to recover for injury to property in which there are multiple ownership interests. Under one rule, each interest holder sues separately; under a second rule, all interest holders join in suing; under a third, one of the holders sues as a trustee for all, being required to account for the proceeds to the others. The only explanation for these differences is historical, since all of them "work." Again, however, the problem has been framed in terms of denomination of parties, and an answer sought in terms of the real party in interest rule.

Real property

Generally, when such interests are held in real estate, each holder of a legally recognized interest may sue separately to redress any wrong done to his or her interest; the measure of damages in such a suit is the

8. Levitt v. Simco Sales Serv., 135 A.2d 910 (Del.Super.Ct.1957); Sprague v. Adams, 139 Wash. 510, 247 P. 960 (1926).

9. Kidd v. Hillman, 14 Cal.App.2d 507, 58 P.2d 662 (1936); Mims v. Reid, 98 So.2d 498 (Fla.1957); Coniglio v. Wyoming Valley Fire Ins. Co., 337 Mich. 38, 59 N.W.2d 74 (1953); Farmers Ins. Exch. v. Arlt, 61 N.W.2d 429 (N.D.1953).

10. *See* §§ 10.4 note 14 *supra*, § 11.10 *infra*.

amount, if any, necessary to compensate for the injury *to that interest only.*[1] Theoretically, then, there may be several suits but no overlap of recoveries. *Joint* tenants, however, were all required to join in any suit for damage to the property jointly held.

Bailment

The case of bailment of personal property illustrates the third rule, that is, that either holder may sue. A bailment occurs when a bailor who owns a chattel places it in the custody of a bailee—for example, leaving a car in a garage or placing a package with a shipper. If a chattel that was the subject of bailment was converted or damaged by a third party, the law gave the bailee an option to recover for the injury to his or her interest only or for the entire injury.[2] The bailor also had a "general property" interest in the goods, and this was sufficient to give the bailor as well a right of action to recover for the entire injury to the goods.[3] Today either the bailee or the bailor may sue for the whole loss. Defendant is protected by a rule that judgment in favor of or against either bailor or bailee for the whole loss bars any recovery by the other.[4] And each is protected against the other by a rule that the person who recovered the whole loss holds in trust for the other that part of the recovery exceeding compensation for the injury to his or her own interest.[5]

The third rule has been extended by analogy to new relationships opened up by modern methods of financing. Thus, the chattel mortgagors or conditional vendees in possession (that is, installment buyers who have possession of a thing but not yet legal title) are treated as bailees and may sue in their own name for the entire damage done to the chattel by a third-party tortfeasor.[6] Any excess over their own loss must be paid over to the bailor.

A tactical advantage formerly could be gained by suit in the name of the bailor, conditional vendor, or chattel mortgagee. By the weight of modern authority, the bailee's negligence is not imputed to the bailor.

§ 10.6

1. Bliss, Code Pleading § 22 (3d ed. 1894); *cf.* Restatement (Second) of Judgments § 54.

2. *See, e.g.,* Poole v. Symonds, 1 N.H. 289 (1818); Pullman Palace-Car Co. v. Gavin, 93 Tenn. 53, 23 S.W. 70 (1893); Thayer v. Hutchinson, 13 Vt. 504 (1841); Bliss, Code Pleading § 23 (3d ed. 1894); Brown, Law of Personal Property § 90 (2d ed. 1955).

That bailees may sue for injury to their special interest only, *see* Railway Express Agency v. Goodman's New York & Connecticut Express Corp., 129 Conn. 386, 388, 28 A.2d 869 (1942); Bliss, *supra.*

3. Brown, Law of Personal Property 395 (2d ed. 1955); 8 Am. Jur. 2d Bailments §§ 250–252.

4. *See* Restatement (Second) of Judgments § 52.

5. *See* Harris v. Seaboard Air Line Ry., 190 N.C. 480, 483, 130 S.E. 319 (1925); Brown, Law of Personal Property 392–394 (2d ed. 1955).

6. *See, e.g.,* Lacey v. Great N. Ry., 70 Mont. 346, 351, 225 P. 808, 810 (1924); Harris v. Seaboard Air Line Ry., 190 N.C. 480, 130 S.E. 319 (1925).

When, therefore, a third person has negligently damaged or destroyed the thing bailed and the facts suggested that the bailee was also negligent, a defense based on contributory negligence could be circumvented by the bringing of suit in the bailor's name.[7] To the extent that the recovery exceeds the bailor's interest, the bailee obtains that excess even though the contributory negligence would have barred his or her own action. Because of dissatisfaction with this result, statutes or decisional law in some jurisdictions impute the bailee's negligence to the bailor if the latter brings the suit.[8] But the objective could be reached regardless of the procedural rule on the proper plaintiff. This could be done by determining the relative interest of the bailor and bailee in the chattel and applying the bailee's contributory negligence as a bar or diminution of the recovery allocable to the bailee. The courts struggled toward this result, often unsuccessfully, through the indirect mechanism of the rules specifying the proper plaintiff.[9]

Derivative suits

Another kind of division of interest between persons, resulting in difficulties in the rules on the proper party plaintiff, arose in the derivative suit by a corporate stockholder. In such a suit, the claim in question is one in favor of the corporation but is prosecuted by the stockholder because the officers and directors refuse to do so (sometimes because the claim is against them for defrauding the corporation). At common law, the stockholders could not sue. Equity allowed them to do so if they alleged that the directors refused to sue, the corporation was joined as the nominal plaintiff, and the directors were made parties along with the defendant against whom the corporation's claim was asserted. Under modern procedure, stockholders may proceed as they did in equity.[10] Under federal procedure, the matter has been further simplified to reflect its actual character: The stockholder sues as plaintiff, and the corporation, its directors, and the person against whom the corporation's claim is asserted are joined as defendants.[11] Thus, the designation of parties corresponds to what seems to have been the intent of the real party in interest rule.

Fiduciaries and beneficiaries

On this analysis the provision in the Federal Rules and the code that an executor or administrator or a trustee of an express trust may sue

7. Commercial Credit Corp. v. Satterthwaite, 107 N.J.L. 17, 150 A. 235 (1930), *aff'd,* 108 N.J.L. 188, 154 A. 769 (1931).

8. N.J. Stat. Ann. § 2A:53A–6 (Cum. Ann. Pocket Pt. 1963); Motorlease Corp. v. Mulroony, 9 N.J. 82, 86 A.2d 765 (1952).

9. *See, e.g.,* Anheuser–Busch, Inc. v. Starley, 28 Cal.2d 347, 170 P.2d 448 (1946).

10. *See* Henn, Corporations ch. 14 (2d ed. 1970); *e.g.,* Ross v. Bernhard, 396 U.S. 531, 90 S.Ct. 733, 24 L.Ed.2d 729 (1970).

11. Smith v. Sperling, 354 U.S. 91, 77 S.Ct. 1112, 1 L.Ed.2d 1205 (1957); *see* Fed. R. Civ. P. 23.1.

"without joining . . . the person for whose benefit the suit is prosecuted,"[12] adds nothing to the real party in interest provision except illustration. Such is the proper party designation when a fiduciary sues to protect a trust interest. When the trustee defaults or colludes with the wrongdoer, the courts have continued to allow the beneficiary to sue; when the beneficiary brings the litigation by reason of the fiduciary's default, the beneficiary is named as the plaintiff.[13] Similarly, the legatee or distributee of an estate ordinarily may not bring suit to enforce money claims of the estate, but an exception has been recognized parallel to that for beneficiaries of a trust.[14]

Special problems arise over the capacity of a representative appointed in one state to sue in another. These problems, however, result not from the real party in interest rule but from the forum state's policy of protecting local creditors. The general rule is that executors or administrators have capacity to sue only in the state of their appointment and have no capacity elsewhere unless they obtain ancillary appointment in the other state.[15]

Wrongful death and survivor actions

The provision in Rule 17(a) and the code permitting "a party authorized by statute" to sue in his or her own name is also an illustration of, rather than an exception to, the rule that the party suing be named as plaintiff. This provision has received its most frequent interpretation in actions for wrongful death. Recovery on account of wrongful death is purely statutory, and the statutes are essentially of two kinds. One type, patterned on Lord Campbell's Act, gives a remedy to designated beneficiaries for the pecuniary injury done to them by the decedent's death; this is called a "wrongful death statute." The second type of statute provides for the survival of the decedent's own action; this is termed the "survival statute."[16]

Survival statutes pose no peculiar problem so far as parties are concerned. Claims under them are generally part of the decedent's estate and are pursued by the executor or administrator just as any other asset of the estate would be.

Wrongful death statutes usually specify the proper party to an action under them. Some of them name one or more of the beneficiaries; in such a case the party named is, of course, the real party in interest. Many of them require that suit be brought by the personal representa-

12. Fed. R. Civ. P. 17(a); text at § 10.3 note 3 *supra*.

13. Bogert, Trusts § 870 (4th ed. 1963).

14. Buchanan v. Buchanan, 75 N.J.Eq. 274, 71 A. 745 (1909); Clark, Code Pleading 191–192 (2d ed. 1947); 2 Woerner, American Law of Administration 934 (3d ed. 1923).

15. *See* Currie, The Multiple Personality of the Dead: Executors, Administrators, and the Conflict of Laws, 33 U. Chi. L. Rev. 429 (1966).

16. The types of statutes are described in 2 Harper, James, and Gray, Law of Torts § 24.2 (2d ed. 1986). *See also* Restatement (Second) of Judgments §§ 45–47.

tive of the deceased—that is, by the executor or administrator.[17] When the executor or administrator sues under such a statute, however, he or she thus is acting not as a representative of the estate but as a person designated by statute. The difference is more than formal. The judgment or other recovery under such statute is not an asset of the estate but will belong to the statutory beneficiaries, who may not be the same persons who would take as legatees or distributees of the estate; furthermore, the proceeds will not be available to creditors of the estate.[18]

Complications can arise when the decedent's death gives rise to both a survival claim (for the losses sustained by the decedent up until the time of death) and a wrongful death claim (for the losses to dependents resulting from decedent's being no longer alive). In some states, the same person is the proper plaintiff in both actions. Otherwise, the persons designated as the ones to maintain the respective claims can each bring suit—essentially as though they were holders of separate economic interests deriving from the decedent.[19] But the courts sometimes confuse the two actions, with corresponding confusion in the problem of the proper party plaintiff. Further complications can arise if the two actions are governed by different rules under conflict of laws principles.

Actions authorized by statute include those by government agencies for the benefit of persons protected by social legislation. The Fair Labor Standards Act, for example, authorizes the Secretary of Labor to bring an action in his or her own name for the benefit of the employee against an employer who has failed to pay the employee the legally required minimum wage.[20] Similar actions may be maintained for the benefit of victims of discrimination.[21] Sometimes such statutes leave it unclear whether an agency's lawsuit preempts suits by the injured parties themselves. The defendant, therefore, may be subject to two suits, although double recovery is prevented by requiring deduction from the second judgment of amounts previously awarded.[22]

17. This was the provision in Lord Campbell's Act, the first of these statutes, which has been fairly widely copied in America. 9 & 10 Vict. c.93, § 2, set forth in 4 Harper, James, and Gray, Law of Torts § 24.2 n.2 (2d ed. 1986).

18. Harper, James, and Gray, Law of Torts §§ 24.2(1), 25.14 (2d ed. 1986).

19. *See* Restatement (Second) of Judgments §§ 45–47.

20. 29 U.S.C. § 217. *See, e.g.,* Equal Employment Opportunity Commn. v. American Tel. & Tel. Co., 365 F.Supp. 1105 (E.D.Pa.1973), *aff'd,* 506 F.2d 735 (3d Cir. 1974).

21. 42 U.S.C. § 2000b(a); *see, e.g.,* Williamson v. Bethlehem Steel Corp., 468 F.2d 1201 (2d Cir.1972), *cert. denied,* 411 U.S. 931, 93 S.Ct. 1893, 36 L.Ed.2d 390 (1973).

22. *See, e.g.,* Sea–Land Servs. v. Gaudet, 414 U.S. 573, 94 S.Ct. 806, 39 L.Ed.2d 9, *reh'g denied,* 415 U.S. 986, 94 S.Ct. 1582, 39 L.Ed.2d 883 (1974).

§ 10.7 Capacity of Individuals, Corporations, Partnerships, and Unincorporated Associations to Sue and Be Sued

The problem of capacity is whether the persons presenting themselves as plaintiffs are authorized to conduct legally binding litigation.[1] For an individual injured party, the question of capacity is whether he or she has a legal disability; for an injured party that is an organization, the question is whether the organization is legally recognized as a jural person distinct from its individual members.

The legal capacity of an individual or entity to sue or be sued is distinguished from his or her right of action or liability under substantive law.[2] The assignor of an assignable claim, for instance, has no right of action on that claim after the assignment; if the assignor brings suit on it he or she will lose on the merits. Likewise, an assignor or other party may lack "standing" to raise certain claims, for example challenges to the constitutionality of a statute, because the statute does not subject her to actual or threatened injury.[3]

But if suit is brought by the assignee or anyone else who *does* hold a right of action, a further obstacle arises if he or she is a minor or an alien enemy, or is mentally incompetent. Such a status may entail a lack of capacity and require that suit be brought through a representative, a guardian, or the like. The present section deals with this kind of bar—one that is personal to a party plaintiff or defendant and imposed by the law for various reasons of policy usually divorced from the substantive merits of the claim or defense.[4]

A helpful way to approach the problem is to posit as the basic standard of litigating capacity the adult citizen of the forum state who suffers from no mental or legally imposed incapacity. The grounds of incapacity represent deviations from this norm, though by no means do all deviations result in incapacity. The more common ones are discussed below.

§ 10.7

1. *See generally* 3A Moore, Federal Practice and Procedure ¶¶ 17.16–17.26; 6 Wright and Miller, Federal Practice and Procedure §§ 1559–1569; Kennedy, Federal Rule 17(b) and (c): Qualifying to Litigate in Federal Court, 43 Notre Dame L. Rev. 273 (1968); Hazard, Tait and Fletcher, Cases and Materials on Pleading and Procedure 790–96 (8th ed. 1999). *See also* Restatement (Second) of Judgments § 35.

2. *See* Clark, Code Pleading 322 (2d ed. 1947).

3. *See* Allen v. Wright, 468 U.S. 737, 104 S.Ct. 3315, 82 L.Ed.2d 556 (1984); Valley Forge Christian College v. Americans United for Separation of Church and State, 454 U.S. 464, 102 S.Ct. 752, 70 L.Ed.2d 700 (1982); § 2.26 *supra.*

4. These reasons of policy will not be examined here, though a few may be suggested. In the case of infants or incompetents, for instance, the policy to protect them against their own infirmities obviously looms large. In the case of foreign executors and administrators, as we have seen in § 10.6 *supra,* the policy to protect local creditors plays a part. Quite different considerations come in when a convict is concerned. And there are often factors that reflect more of history than of today's practical problems (as in the case of unincorporated associations). Moreover, as should be expected, these are often mixed. *See* Kaplan, Suits Against Unincorporated Associations Under the Federal Rules, 53 Mich. L. Rev. 945 (1955) (suggesting that a policy to protect unions from effective suit sometimes helps to perpetuate archaisms in the law dealing with unincorporated associations).

Former disabilities

Married women could not sue alone at common law, as a result of one of a number of rules that placed their husbands in control of virtually all their economic affairs, but this incapacity has been removed.[5] Similarly, after the slaves were freed, Congress passed legislation forbidding denial of the right to sue based on race.[6] And the former incapacity of imprisoned convicts to sue has been for all practical purposes repealed.[7] Substantive law, of course, may limit the rights of prisoners to engage in certain transactions (for example, to vote) and hence to bring certain kinds of suits (for example, for the denial of the right to vote).

Minors

Special rules apply to minors, and also to those lacking mental competence.[8] Minors may sue or be sued in their own names in many states, but the litigation should be managed by a guardian or next friend. In some states the suit is brought by or against the minor "by his guardian" or next friend.[9] In other states the guardian is treated as the legal representative of the minor and should sue or be sued in his or her own name as guardian.[10] Rule 17(c) is broad enough to accommodate either practice in the federal courts. A failure to observe the proper procedure is usually curable during suit by amendment or substitution of parties, unless this would improperly prejudice the minor's interest.[11]

At one time the plaintiff's incapacity was considered to make any judgment voidable at his or her option. In effect this gave the plaintiff a one-sided option to affirm the judgment if successful or to disaffirm it if not. Modern authority has held that the option of disaffirmance is not available if the plaintiff was adequately represented by counsel, even if no guardian was appointed.[12]

Aliens

Aliens and citizens of sister states are not subject to incapacity because of their status. In the case of citizens of sister states, the

5. *See* Clark, Domestic Relations § 7.2 (1968).

6. 42 U.S.C. § 1981(a).

7. *See* Lewis v. Casey, 518 U.S. 343, 116 S.Ct. 2174, 135 L.Ed.2d 606 (1996); Annot., 74 A.L.R.3d 680. A different result might obtain in the handful of states that still have statutes subjecting prisoners to "civil death."

8. 3 Moore, Federal Practice and Procedure ¶ 17.26 (2d ed. 1963).

9. *See, e.g.,* Cal. Civ. Proc. Code § 373; N.Y. Civ. Prac. L. & R. 1201; Vroon v. Templin, 278 F.2d 345, 349 (4th Cir.1960); 3A Moore, Federal Practice and Procedure ¶ 17.26.

10. *See, e.g.,* Mexican Cent. Ry. v. Eckman, 187 U.S. 429, 23 S.Ct. 211, 47 L.Ed. 245 (1903); Vroon v. Templin, 278 F.2d 345, 349 (4th Cir.1960).

11. *See, e.g.,* Vroon v. Templin, *supra* note 10.

12. *See, e.g.,* O'Neil v. Moore, 118 Ga. App. 424, 164 S.E.2d 328 (1968); Lasquade v. Lippa, 322 Mass. 287, 76 N.E.2d 753 (1948); *see also* Restatement (Second) of Judgments § 35.

Privileges and Immunities Clause[13] requires their being accorded litigating capacity. Aliens, even enemy aliens, likewise enjoy access to the courts, at least in the absence of legislation to the contrary.[14]

Corporations

Corporations have capacity to sue and be sued in the state of their incorporation, although special problems may arise if they have been dissolved or have never completed organization.[15] Just as executors and administrators may ordinarily sue only in a state where they were appointed,[16] foreign corporations (including those of sister states) were originally viewed as creatures of the state of their incorporation, having no legal existence elsewhere and so unable to sue except by grace or comity. This notion has not been repudiated entirely, but it has been drastically limited. Its principal vestige today is the notion that a state may impose some conditions on a foreign corporation's doing business within the state's borders and may forbid access to the state's courts by a corporation that does such business and fails to comply with the conditions.[17]

Unincorporated associations

Partnerships and unincorporated associations were not treated as entities at common law but as individuals having joint rights and joint, or joint and several, liabilities.[18] Accordingly, a partnership or association as such had no capacity to sue or be sued; suit had to be brought by or against all members individually. This created serious practical problems when the membership was large or when some of the members lived outside the jurisdiction; indeed, it sometimes rendered suit impossible. One solution to this problem in some cases was found by equity in the class suit, which we shall examine in a later section. Another solution, promulgated by statute or judicial decision, recognizes a partnership or other organization as a legal entity for the purpose of suing or being

13. U.S. Const. art. IV, 2; Kentucky Fin. Corp. v. Paramount Auto Exch. Corp., 262 U.S. 544, 43 S.Ct. 636, 67 L.Ed. 1112 (1923) (corporation of sister state, while not a "citizen" within Privileges and Immunities Clause, is a "person" within Equal Protection Clause).

14. Ex parte Kawato, 317 U.S. 69, 63 S.Ct. 115, 87 L.Ed. 58 (1942); Sliosberg v. New York Life Ins. Co., 244 N.Y. 482, 155 N.E. 749 (1927); *see* Banco Nacional de Cuba v. Sabbatino, 376 U.S. 398, 84 S.Ct. 923, 11 L.Ed.2d 804 (1964)(foreign government may sue unless at war with United States); Mathews v. Diaz, 426 U.S. 67, 96 S.Ct. 1883, 48 L.Ed.2d 478 (1976) (discussing permissible discrimination against aliens); Neuman, Habeas Corpus, Executive Detention, and the Removal of Aliens, 98 Colum. L. Rev. 961 (1998).

15. *See, e.g.*, MacAffer v. Boston & Me. R.R., 268 N.Y. 400, 197 N.E. 328 (1935); Marcus, Suability of Dissolved Corporations, 58 Harv. L. Rev. 675 (1945).

16. *See* § 10.6 *supra*.

17. *Compare* Eli Lilly & Co. v. Sav-on-Drugs, Inc., 366 U.S. 276, 81 S.Ct. 1316, 6 L.Ed.2d 288 (1961), *with* Allenberg Cotton Co. v. Pittman, 419 U.S. 20, 95 S.Ct. 260, 42 L.Ed.2d 195 (1974).

18. Clark, Code Pleading § 31 (2d ed. 1947); Sturges, Unincorporated Associations as Parties to Action, 33 Yale L.J. 383 (1924).

sued in its common name.[19] In *United Mine Workers of America v. Coronado Coal Co.*[20] the Supreme Court judicially recognized an unincorporated association (labor union) as an entity capable of being sued in its common name on liabilities arising under federal law; this concept was carried over into Rule 17(b).[21] In diversity cases the capacity of such an association is governed by state law,[22] but incapacity of the association does not prevent resort to the class action in federal courts.[23]

§ 10.8 Proper Parties Defendant

The question of who is a proper party defendant is usually a matter of who is liable under substantive law.[1] Whether, for instance, agents who make contracts on behalf of their principals are liable for nonperformance of a contract is a matter of contract law; whether employers are liable for injuries inflicted by their employees is a matter of tort or agency law. There is no rule for defendants that corresponds to the real party in interest rule.[2]

Capacity

Questions of incapacity can arise with a defendant party as well as a plaintiff. Indeed, the rules governing capacity are generally stated in the form "sue or be sued," although some former incapacities, such as alienage, applied only to maintaining litigation as a plaintiff.[3] The defense of incapacity is said to be waived if not asserted in a timely manner, but holdings to that effect generally involve defendants represented by counsel and therefore protected by the functional equivalent of

19. *See, e.g.,* N.Y. Civ. Prac. L. & R. 1025; Revised Uniform Partnership Act §§ 201, 307; Clark, Code Pleading § 31 (2d ed. 1947); 3A Moore, Federal Practice and Procedure ¶ 17.25. *See generally* Ford, Unincorporated Non-Profit Associations (1959); Note, Developments in the Law: Judicial Control of Actions of Private Associations, 76 Harv. L. Rev. 983, 1081–1100 (1963); 8 Calif. L. Rev. Commn. 921, A Study Relating to Suit by and Against an Unincorporated Association (1967).

20. 259 U.S. 344, 42 S.Ct. 570, 66 L.Ed. 975 (1922).

21. Fed. R. Civ. P. 17(b) provides in part that although capacity to sue is in many cases to be determined by the law of the state in which the district court was held, yet "a partnership or other unincorporated association, which has no such capacity by the law of such state, may sue or be sued in its common name for the purpose of enforcing for or against it a substantive right existing under the Constitution or laws of the United States."

22. 3A Moore, Federal Practice and Procedure ¶ 17.25.

23. *See, e.g.,* Oskoian v. Canuel, 269 F.2d 311 (1st Cir.1959). *See also* § 10.20 *infra.*

§ 10.8

1. Thus, while Fed. R. Civ. P. 17(a) prescribes a rule defining the proper plaintiff, there is no corresponding rule defining the proper defendant. Those dealing with defendants concern capacity—Rule 17(b) and (c)—necessary and permissive joinder, and so on—Rules 19, 20, 23(a). The same thing is true of state codes. *See* Clark, Code Pleading § 32 (2d ed. 1947); Hepburn, Historical Development of Code Pleading §§ 50, 52, 54, 125, 230, 231 (1897); Phillips, Code Pleading § 255 (2d ed. 1932).

2. *Cf.* Fed. R. Civ. P. 17.

3. *See, e.g.,* Janusis v. Long, 284 Mass. 403, 188 N.E. 228 (1933).

a guardian. A judgment against an unrepresented incompetent is and should be disaffirmable.[4]

Other questions of who is a proper party defendant concern permissive joinder or compulsory joinder and are explored later in this chapter.[5]

Fictitious defendants

Fictitious denomination of defendants still has some uses. One is the "John Doe" defendant recognized in the practice of California and a few other states. In essence, naming "John Doe" as a defendant allows a plaintiff in these states to extend the statute of limitations as to defendants whose identity is discovered after the action has been filed, on the theory that the subsequently identified defendant was the "John Doe" party.[6] Another common fiction is used in a suit to restrain or compel action by a government agency, nominally designating as defendant the individual who is head of the agency.[7] This fiction also permits suits in federal court challenging the constitutionality of state action notwithstanding the limitations of the Eleventh Amendment, the fiction being that the suit is against a bureaucrat whose usurpation deprives him or her of official capacity.[8] The fiction has to be ignored, however, when inappropriate consequences might be attached to it—for example, when an official sued for damages acted in good faith conformance to apparently valid state law.[9]

Substitution of parties

Substitution of parties may be required when the originally named parties cease to be proper participants because of death, incompetency, transfer of their interest in the case, or the departure of public officials from their office.[10] Strictly speaking, the procedure is an amendment

4. *See* Restatement (Second) of Judgments § 35.

5. *See* §§ 10.11–10.15 *infra.*

6. *See* 28 U.S.C. § 1441(a)(citizenship of unidentified John Doe defendants should be disregarded in assessing whether diversity jurisdiction exists); Hogan, California's Unique Doe Defendant Practice: A Fiction Stranger Than Truth, 30 Stan. L. Rev. 51 (1977); § 4.23 *supra.*

7. *See generally* Cramton, Nonstatutory Review of Federal Administrative Action: The Need for Statutory Reform of Sovereign Immunity, Subject Matter Jurisdiction, and Parties Defendant, 68 Mich. L. Rev. 387 (1970).

8. *See* Ex parte Young, 209 U.S. 123, 28 S.Ct. 441, 52 L.Ed. 714 (1908); § 2.16 *supra. But see* Idaho v. Coeur d'Alene Tribe, 521 U.S. 261, 117 S.Ct. 2028, 138 L.Ed.2d 438 (1997)(limiting *Young*); Pennhurst State School & Hosp. v. Halderman, 465 U.S. 89, 104 S.Ct. 900, 79 L.Ed.2d 67 (1984), holding that the real character of the suit will be recognized under the Eleventh Amendment when the plaintiff's claim is based on state law.

9. *See, e.g.,* Procunier v. Navarette, 434 U.S. 555, 98 S.Ct. 855, 55 L.Ed.2d 24 (1978) (prison officials and guards); Wood v. Strickland, 420 U.S. 308, 95 S.Ct. 992, 43 L.Ed.2d 214 (1975) (local school board members); §§ 3.15, 4.15 *supra.*

10. Fed. R. Civ. P. 25. This rule applies only in federal district court; substitution in the courts of appeals is governed by Fed. R. App. P. 43, and in the Supreme Court by Sup. Ct. R. 35. Substitution does not destroy diversity jurisdiction even if the new party has a citizenship differing from that of the party it replaces. Freeport–McMoRan, Inc. v. K N Energy, Inc., 498 U.S. 426, 111 S.Ct. 858, 112 L.Ed.2d 951 (1991).

referring to the addition of parties—a substituted party replaces a proper, "original party." Rule 25(a) provides that if a party dies and the claim is not thereby extinguished, the court may order a substitution.[11] A motion for substitution may be made by any party or the successors or representatives of the deceased party within ninety days "after the death is suggested upon the record by service of a statement of the fact of the death."[12] If this is not done, the action is dismissed as to the deceased party.

The Rule does not specify what actions survive the death of a party, which is determined by substantive state or federal law. For example, suits by the United States to recover damages survive a defendant's decease and can be enforced against the deceased's estate.[13] When a party transfers its interest in the case during the course of the action, Rule 25 provides that the action may be continued by or against the original party unless the court directs that the person to whom the interest has been transferred be substituted. The court may, in its discretion, refuse the motion for substitution if it finds that the original party is a more appropriate person to continue the case.[14] The court may also order that the additional party to whom the interest has been transferred be joined as an additional party.[15] Even if the additional party is not joined, he or she will be bound by the judgment, as his or her rights are identical to the transferee's.[16]

Rule 25(d) was promulgated to remedy the injustice of the common law rule that an action against a public official is extinguished on the official's departure from office. The substitution is automatic and encompasses "public officers," including federal, state, and local officials.[17] Rule 25(d), however, applies only to suits against public officials in their official capacity.[18]

§ 10.9 Liability Insurer as Defendant

In the typical situation in which the owner or operator of an automobile is covered by liability insurance—or when it is claimed that he or she is so covered—the question arises whether the injured person may bring an action directly against the insurer, either alone or by joining the insurer as a co-defendant with the alleged tortfeasor. In most

11. Fed. R. Civ. P. 25(a).

12. *Id.*

13. *See* Lowe Bros. v. United States, 304 U.S. 302, 58 S.Ct. 896, 82 L.Ed. 1362 (1938).

14. Otis Clapp & Son, Inc. v. Filmore Vitamin Co., 754 F.2d 738 (7th Cir.1985).

15. Hilbrands v. Far East Trading Co., 509 F.2d 1321 (9th Cir.1975).

16. Mobil Oil Corp. v. Linear Films, Inc., 718 F.Supp. 260 (D.Del.1989); Democratic Natl. Comm. v. McCord, 416 F.Supp. 505 (D.D.C.1976).

17. Fed. R. Civ. P. 25(d). *See also* Karcher v. May, 484 U.S. 72, 108 S.Ct. 388, 98 L.Ed.2d 327 (1987); Wright v. Manatee County, 717 F.Supp. 1493 (M.D.Fla.1989); Lawson v. Sheriff of Tippecanoe County, 537 F.Supp. 918 (N.D.Ind.1982).

18. Spomer v. Littleton, 414 U.S. 514, 94 S.Ct. 685, 38 L.Ed.2d 694 (1974).

jurisdictions the injured party may not do so until he or she has recovered a judgment against the insured that remains unsatisfied. In a few states, however, statutes provide for an action against the insurer in the first instance (generally called "direct action" statutes).[1] And in a few other states a similar result is reached when insurance is compulsory[2] (as in the case of public service vehicles).

The original attitude toward the problem was to treat the liability insurance policy as a contract of indemnity only between the insured and insurer, one that gave no rights to an injured party. The only right of action against the insurer was in the insured, and his or her right was conditioned on his or her loss, as by payment of a judgment against him or her in favor of the injured party. If the insured was unable to pay this judgment because of insolvency or the like, no right of action against the insurer could accrue, and the injured party was without effective remedy. The legal insulation of the insurer from claims by the injured person, however, was at war with a growing popular feeling that "the financial protection afforded by the liability policy [should] be made available to the person by whom the loss is actually sustained"[3]—in other words, that at least one function of liability insurance was to help solve the social problem created by automobile accidents and their (otherwise) uncompensated victims.[4] This attitude is reflected by statutes adopted in nearly all states that allow (on varying conditions) the injured person to bring a proceeding against the insurer *after obtaining a judgment against the insured* that remains unsatisfied.[5] The reluctance of most states to go beyond this by permitting a direct action against the insurance in the first instance probably reflects reluctance to display before juries the fact that the judgment will be paid by an insurer, not an ordinary citizen.

Underlying problems

The direct action statutes, whatever their merit as solutions to substantive problems of tort and insurance law, eliminate or moderate several procedural problems that exist when the fiction is maintained that the insurer is not a real party defendant in an action against the insured. These problems include the following:

§ 10.9

1. *See* Note, Direct Action Statutes: Their Operational and Conflict-of-Law Problems, 74 Harv. L. Rev. 357 (1960); Note, Liability Insurer as a Real Party in Interest: Proposed Amendments to the Minnesota Rules of Civil Procedure, 41 Minn. L. Rev. 784 (1957).

2. *See, e.g.,* James v. Young, 77 N.D. 451, 43 N.W.2d 692, 20 A.L.R.2d 1086 (1950); Note, 20 A.L.R.2d 1097; Leigh, Direct Actions Against Liability Insurers, 1949 Ins. L.J. 633, 647–648; Note, 74 Harv. L. Rev. at 358.

3. Leigh, Direct Actions Against Liability Insurers, 1949 Ins. L.J. 633, 634.

4. *See* James, The Columbia Study of Compensation for Automobile Accidents: An Unanswered Challenge, 59 Colum. L. Rev. 408 (1959).

5. Sources cited *supra* note 1. *See, e.g.,* Jackson v. Citizens Casualty Co., 277 N.Y. 385, 14 N.E.2d 446 (1938).

1. the question of discoverability of the insurance policy limits;[6]
2. the situation created by the fictitious "loan receipt," a device that has no justification if the defendant insurer is openly a party;[7]
3. the difficulties of settlement when the policy limits are lower than the potential recovery value of the plaintiff's claim;[8]
4. the issues of collateral estoppel and res judicata that arise if the insurer has subrogation rights after it pays the liability of its insured;[9]
5. the application of the compulsory counterclaim rule when the insured defendant has a claim for his or her own injuries or losses against the plaintiff;[10]
6. the real interests involved when one member of a family sues another, the objective being to have the liability insurer meet the loss that the family has sustained when one of its members has injured another;[11]
7. the duties that a lawyer defending an action in which the insured is the named defendant but the insurer will pay the judgment owes to the insured and the insurer.[12]

These are actual, practical problems that (even when a direct action statute exists) cannot be disposed of by saying simply that the insurer is or is not the "real defendant." Resolution of these problems is sometimes facilitated by focusing on the fact that the primarily interested party is the insurance company. But sometimes, the insurance company's interest is only part of the problem, and in some instances the problem will exist whether the insurance company is or is not called a "party." Thus, whether the plaintiff should be informed of the limits of the insurance coverage would seem to have little to do with whether the insurer is a named defendant; so, too, whether the insurance company should pay for injury to one family member caused by another family member should not depend on the nominal identity of the parties in a

6. Fed. R. Civ. P. 26(a)(D); § 5.8 *supra.*

7. *See* § 10.4 *supra.*

8. *See, e.g.,* Crisci v. Security Ins. Co., 66 Cal.2d 425, 426 P.2d 173, 58 Cal.Rptr. 13 (1967); Keeton, Liability Insurance and Responsibility for Settlement, 67 Harv. L. Rev. 1136 (1954); Annot., 40 A.L.R.2d 168.

9. *Cf.* Czaplicki v. The Hoegh Silvercloud, 351 U.S. 525, 76 S.Ct. 946, 100 L.Ed. 1387 (1956); Spargur v. Dayton Power & Light Co., 152 N.E.2d 918 (C.P. Ohio 1958), *aff'd,* 109 Ohio App. 37, 163 N.E.2d 786 (1959); § 11.10 *infra. See also* Restatement (Second) of Judgments § 37.

10. *See, e.g.,* Rothtrock v. Ohio Farmers Ins. Co., 233 Cal.App.2d 616, 43 Cal.Rptr. 716 (1965). *See also* § 9.11 *supra.*

11. *See, e.g.,* Edwards v. Royal Indem. Co., 182 La. 171, 161 So. 191 (1935), with which *compare* Manning v. Hyland, 19 A.D.2d 652, 241 N.Y.S.2d 908 (1963). *See also* James, Accident Liability Reconsidered: The Impact of Liability Insurance, 57 Yale L.J. 549, 551–557 (1948); James and Thornton, The Impact of Insurance on the Law of Torts, 15 Law & Contemp. Probs. 431 (1950).

12. Restatement of the Law Governing Lawyers § 134, Comment *f.*

suit by one family member against another. Some of these problems are entirely substantive; some of them are partly substantive and partly procedural. None of them is simply a question of the nominal identity of parties, even though the courts sometimes address the problems that way. Put differently, in the insurance situation, as in other party designation situations, the proper designation of parties is a conclusion rather than a premise and is a means of resolving underlying practical problems that have been subsumed under the heading of party designation.

§ 10.10 Problems of Federal Jurisdiction

The provisions governing parties, party identity, and capacity have implications for federal subject matter jurisdiction when such jurisdiction is grounded on the parties' diversity of citizenship. Establishing federal jurisdiction in diversity cases requires ascertaining that the citizenship of the plaintiffs is different from that of the defendants. In ascertaining the citizenship of the parties, the federal courts generally do not permit fictitious party designations that have the effect of creating diversity where it would not otherwise exist.[1] This, in turn, requires determining the identity of those who are "really" involved.

Diversity and real party in interest

The question of party identity for purposes of diversity jurisdiction thus parallels that of party denomination under the real party in interest rule. The fact that the Federal Rules contain a real party in interest rule suggests—and has led many courts to assume—that the same questions are posed under the real party in interest rule and the diversity rule.[2] But they seem different. In some situations the real party in interest rule may require designating as a nominal party someone who is not the real claimant, whose citizenship should count for purposes of diversity jurisdiction—for example, when a stockholder's derivative suit is nominally brought by the corporation as plaintiff but for diversity purposes the corporation is treated as a defendant.[3] In other situations the real party in interest rule may be satisfied but the diversity requirement may not—for example, when a contract claim arises between co-citizens and is assigned to a person of diverse citizenship who then sues as an assignee for collection.[4]

§ 10.10

1. *See* 28 U.S.C. § 1359, providing as follows: "A district court shall not have jurisdiction of a civil action in which any party, by assignment or otherwise, has been improperly or collusively made or joined to invoke the jurisdiction of such court."

2. *See* Virginia Elec. & Power Co. v. Westinghouse Elec. Corp., 485 F.2d 78 (4th Cir.1973).

3. *See* Koster v. Lumbermens Mut. Cas. Co., 330 U.S. 518, 67 S.Ct. 828, 91 L.Ed. 1067 (1947); § 10.6 *supra*.

4. Kramer v. Caribbean Mills, Inc., 394 U.S. 823, 89 S.Ct. 1487, 23 L.Ed.2d 9 (1969).

The differences in the policies involved are clearest in situations involving subrogation of an insurer to the claim for an insured's loss. The policy of hiding this transaction from the jury justifies treating the insured as the real party in interest for purposes of that rule,[5] but this is no reason to ignore the citizenship of the insurer for purposes of diversity. Some cases nevertheless treat the questions as the same, allowing an insurer to "hide behind" its insured not only for the purpose of appearance to the jury but also for the purpose of obtaining adjudication in federal court of a claim that it could not maintain on its own under the diversity of citizenship requirement.[6]

Whose citizenship counts

The rules for party designation that determine whether diversity exists are not wholly consistent. The citizenship of an assignee for collection is disregarded in determining whether diversity of citizenship exists, on the theory that the assignor is the real beneficiary of the action; in a class action, however, the citizenship of the representative determines whether there is diversity even if most of the class members are co-citizens of the opposing litigant.[7] So also, when a claim is vested "in" a trustee for a beneficiary, the trustee is the party for diversity purposes, but when the claim is by a guardian "on behalf of" a ward, or by the representative of a decedent's estate, the ward or decedent's citizenship counts for diversity purposes.[8] A corporation is treated as a citizen of the states where it is incorporated or has its principal place of business, but in a suit by or against a partnership or unincorporated association it is the citizenship of the partners or members that counts.[9] And in a direct action against an insurer, the insurer is deemed to have both its own citizenship as a corporation and the citizenship of its insured.[10] Hence, the pattern is not one of logic but the product of a historical confluence of the procedural rules for identity and capacity and

5. *See, e.g.*, R. J. Enstrom Corp. v. Interceptor Corp., 520 F.2d 1217 (10th Cir. 1975), which also involved the question whether a suit commenced in the name of the insured by the subrogated insurer was properly commenced for the purposes of the statute of limitations. It was held properly commenced so that even if the designated plaintiff should have been changed it would not result in a "new," and hence untimely, action.

6. *See* Virginia Elec. & Power Co. v. Westinghouse Elec. Corp., 485 F.2d 78 (4th Cir.1973). The plaintiff power company, a Virginia corporation, suffered a loss partly covered by insurance issued by INA, a Pennsylvania corporation. Defendant was also a Pennsylvania corporation, but the power company was allowed to assert the claim for the whole loss.

7. Supreme Tribe of Ben Hur v. Cauble, 255 U.S. 356, 41 S.Ct. 338, 65 L.Ed. 673 (1921). *See also* § 10.22 *infra.*

8. *See* 28 U.S.C. § 1332(c) (representative of decedent's estate, infant or incompetent); Navarro Savings Ass'n v. Lee, 446 U.S. 458, 100 S.Ct. 1779, 64 L.Ed.2d 425 (1980)(trustee).

9. 28 U.S.C. § 1332(c)(1)(corporation); Carden v. Arkoma Associates, 494 U.S. 185, 110 S.Ct. 1015, 108 L.Ed.2d 157 (1990)(partnership); United Steelworkers of America v. R.H. Bouligny, Inc., 382 U.S. 145, 86 S.Ct. 272, 15 L.Ed.2d 217 (1965)(labor union); *see* CCC Information Services v. American Salvage Pool, 230 F.3d 342 (7th Cir.2000)(declining to look through corporation to its benefitting members).

10. 28 U.S.C. § 1332(c)(1); *see* § 10.9 *supra.*

the rule that there must be diversity between the parties properly named as such. In these situations there are plausible alternatives, and the choice among them can depend on whether expansion of diversity jurisdiction at the margin is favored or disfavored.[11]

B. NECESSARY PARTIES

§ 10.11 Definitions

The terms "necessary" and "indispensable" parties are technical. Necessary parties are those who must be included in an action either as plaintiffs or defendants unless there is a valid excuse for their nonjoinder.[1] Such parties are sometimes now called "conditionally necessary," but the shorter term will be used here to conform to general usage. Indispensable parties are those whose joinder is so important to a just resolution of the case that, if they cannot be joined, the action should not be allowed to proceed. The necessary party rule, as we shall see, has particular significance in federal diversity litigation because its application can result in adding parties whose citizenship is not properly diverse from those who are already parties.

Two further clarifications are needed in the use of these terms. If *A* alone owes plaintiff a debt, the plaintiff's action cannot go forward unless and until *A* is made a defendant in the action and the court obtains jurisdiction over *A*'s person or property. In a real sense *A* is an indispensable party. But that is not the sense in which the term is used; rather, it refers to compulsory joinder of parties when there are at least two possible defendants (or plaintiffs).

Permissive joinder compared

The second clarification concerns permissive joinder as compared with compulsory joinder. Simply because a prospective party could *properly* be joined under the permissive joinder rules does not mean that it *must* be joined under the compulsory joinder rules. This is true of both plaintiffs and defendants. For example, two persons injured in the same accident may join as plaintiffs in the same action against the alleged

11. *Compare* United Steelworkers v. R. H. Bouligny, Inc., 382 U.S. 145, 86 S.Ct. 272, 15 L.Ed.2d 217 (1965), *with* Navarro Sav. Assn. v. Lee, 446 U.S. 458, 100 S.Ct. 1779, 64 L.Ed.2d 425 (1980). *See also* American Law Inst., Study of the Division of Jurisdiction Between State and Federal Courts (1969); Currie, The Federal Courts and the American Law Institute, 36 U. Chi. L. Rev. 1, 268 (1968–1969); Wright, Restructuring Jurisdiction: The American Law Institute Proposals, 26 Wash. & Lee L. Rev. 185 (1969).

§ 10.11

1. *See generally* 3A Moore, Federal Practice and Procedure ¶¶ 19.01–19.07; 7 Wright and Miller, Federal Practice and Procedure §§ 1601–1611; Freer, Rethinking Compulsory Joinder: A Proposal to Restructure Federal Rule 19, 60 N.Y.U. L. Rev. 1061 (1985); Hazard, Indispensable Party: The Historical Origin of a Procedural Phantom, 61 Colum. L. Rev. 1254 (1961); Reed, Compulsory Joinder of Parties in Civil Actions, 55 Mich. L. Rev. 327 (1957).

tortfeasor or tortfeasors.[2] But this does not mean that they must join; hence, it does not mean that either of them is a necessary party in an action brought by the other. Thus, a parent and child, or spouses, injured in the same accident may bring separate suits for their injuries. It is ordinarily not in their interest to bring separate suits because duplication of effort is involved, and the incentives to join as co-plaintiffs usually result in proceeding through a single suit. But the rules as to joinder of parties generally do not *require* such joinder.

So it is with joinder of defendants. As we have seen, a plaintiff is permitted to join all prospective defendants who contributed to the injury for which plaintiff is suing.[3] Furthermore, a plaintiff ordinarily has strong incentive to join all prospective defendants, for otherwise the one that is sued may defend by "pointing the finger" of responsibility at the absent party. The rules of party joinder, aside from exceptional situations, leave it to these incentives to determine whether all prospective defendants will be joined. They allow plaintiffs to name their defendants but do not require that they join all whom they might under the rules of permissive joinder.[4]

A far broader concept of necessary parties would require all persons potentially liable for a plaintiff's claim to be joined as defendants unless there are practical reasons why this is impossible, such as a specific potential defendant who cannot be served with process. If such a step were taken, consideration would also have to be given to requiring all potential plaintiffs to join in the action—for example, all members of a family injured in a vehicle accident, or all investors in a fraudulent scheme. Such a rule would have to deal with the same difficulties that have been encountered in class actions seeking damages, including the right to opt out.[5] It might also pressure parties into asserting claims that they might otherwise have been content to forgo, and could penalize those who failed to assert a claim later deemed to have been related. For these reasons, the only state supreme court to have experimented with such an approach has now retracted it.[6]

Scope and history of rule

The necessary parties rule thus usually operates not when plaintiff could join all parties involved in the transaction, but when additional parties should be joined in order to permit orderly adjudication of the controversy between those who are already parties. The idea is to bring in third parties without whom it would be awkward for the court to work

2. *See* §§ 9.7–9.8 *supra*.

3. *Id.*

4. *E.g.*, Temple v. Synthes Corp., 498 U.S. 5, 111 S.Ct. 315, 112 L.Ed.2d 263 (1990).

5. *See* §§ 10.20–10.23 *infra*.

6. *See* Olds v. Donnelly, 150 N.J. 424, 696 A.2d 633 (1997); Hazard, An Examination Before and Behind the 'Entire Controversy' Doctrine, 28 Rutgers L.J. 7 (1996); Symposium, The Demise of the Entire Controversy Doctrine, 9 Seton Hall Const. L.J. 755 (1999).

out a judgment between the existing parties. This, in turn, means that the necessary parties rule operates chiefly when there is some connection of property ownership, contract rights, or obligations between those who are initially made parties and those who have not been joined.

The necessary parties rules originated in equity and expressed the principle that a court of equity, once it undertook a case, would not do justice "by halves" but would seek to clean up the whole controversy. In the Field Code of 1848 the rule was combined with a common law rule of compulsory joinder applying to cases of property and contract rights. The code provision has now been superseded by a return, in amended Federal Rule 19, to the original equity principle. We examine that basic principle, and then briefly return to consider the code provision operative from 1848 to 1966.

§ 10.12 Determining Who Is Necessary or Indispensable Party

The concept of necessary and indispensable parties is really a single one denoting the parties who *should* be joined in the action.[1] The difference between a necessary party and an indispensable one relates to what should be done when it is discovered that there is an absentee who should be joined. That person should be served with process or invited to join voluntarily.[2] If the individual cannot thus be made a party (or if, in federal diversity cases, making that person a party would destroy complete diversity), then the question is whether to go ahead without him or her. A decision to go ahead is indicated if it appears that the case can be usefully and fairly decided between the existing parties without joining the individual; that decision signifies that the party is only "necessary." A decision to refuse to go ahead, and therefore to dismiss the action, is indicated if the case cannot be decided without the person except at the cost of seriously prejudicing his or her situation or that of one of the parties; such a decision signifies that the absentee is "indispensable."

Federal and state courts

The decision not to go ahead is more often proper in federal court than in state court, for two related reasons. First, the factor most frequently preventing joinder in federal court—the effect on diversity—is never operative in state court.[3] The federal venue rules can have similar effects, but they, too, are not operative in state court.[4] Hence, the effect of a refusal to go ahead in federal court is generally only to relegate the controversy to state court. Second, the effect of a refusal to go ahead in state court may be that the controversy cannot be adjudicated at all unless there is some other state court that can establish jurisdiction over

§ 10.12

1. *See* Fed. R. Civ. P. 19(a).

2. *Id.*

3. *See, e.g.,* Tell v. Trustees of Dartmouth College, 145 F.3d 417 (1st Cir.1998).

4. *See* 28 U.S.C. § 1391.

all the parties involved.[5] Only in the most extraordinary circumstances, therefore, should a state court reach the conclusion that an absentee is indispensable when he or she cannot be served with process.[6]

A further aspect, often ignored, is the stage of litigation at which the problem of necessary parties is raised. The issue can be raised at any stage in the proceedings.[7] If the question is raised at the threshold, when properly it should be, then the pending case can be compared prospectively with the alternatives—that the absent party be added, or that the action be dismissed with a view to its being maintained elsewhere with the addition of that party. Often, however, the absence of a necessary party is not raised until trial or appeal. At that stage the choice is between letting the proceeding stand in incomplete form or starting again with the addition of the absent party. Each of these alternatives has negative elements. This timing aspect will be considered after application of the rule has been analyzed.[8]

Relevant considerations

The question in administering the rule is, what considerations are relevant in deciding whether absentees should be joined and, if they cannot be, whether the action should be terminated?[9] At least four concerns should be considered: protection of the absent parties from harm resulting from their absence; protection of those present from harm caused by proceeding without the absentees; society's interest in avoiding multiple litigation; and the plaintiff's interest in securing at least one forum where the case can be heard. The rule is administered against the background of an often unstated but very important premise: Persons suffering similar injuries ordinarily do not have to join in seeking to redress their injuries through litigation, and an injured person is ordinarily not required to bring suit against all who might be liable for the injury. The "plaintiff autonomy" premise is the point of departure for the necessary parties rule.[10]

Protection of absentees

A court ordinarily has no jurisdiction over a person who has not been made a party to an action before it; thus, no judgment or decree is binding on nonparties, nor is any finding made in the course of arriving

5. *See* Keene v. Chambers, 271 N.Y. 326, 3 N.E.2d 443 (1936).

6. *See, e.g.,* Csohan v. United Benefit Life Ins. Co., 200 N.E.2d 345, 33 Ohio Op. 2d 36 (1964), where the court refused to permit an action to proceed, appreciating the fact that the matter could be determined in another state with all interested persons being joined there.

7. Provident Tradesmens Bank and Trust Co. v. Patterson, 390 U.S. 102, 88 S.Ct. 733, 19 L.Ed.2d 936 (1968); CP Natl. Corp. v. Bonneville Power Admin., 928 F.2d 905 (9th Cir.1991).

8. *See* § 10.13 *infra.*

9. *See* Fed. R. Civ. P. 19(b).

10. *See* Temple v. Synthes Corp., 498 U.S. 5, 111 S.Ct. 315, 112 L.Ed.2d 263 (1990); § 10.11 *supra*; McCoid, A Single Package for Multiparty Disputes, 28 Stan. L. Rev. 707 (1976).

at the judgment.[11] It does not follow, however, that judgments are always without practical, substantial effects on nonparties. Some of the most obvious and often serious of these effects are usually ignored. One's family and creditors may be greatly affected by a judgment in one's favor or by a judgment against one, but this does not ordinarily give them any standing as parties to the action, much less make their presence necessary or indispensable.

Some practical effects on nonparties are considered, however, in applying the necessary party rule. A judgment under which a fund will be distributed, for example, seriously affects all claimants to the fund.[12] While the claim of a nonparty against the fund is not legally extinguished by the judgment, it may as a practical matter be worthless (for instance, when the obligor is insolvent) unless it can be satisfied out of the fund. A judgment decreeing that the plaintiff is the owner of land will not bind nonparties who claim title or some interest in it, but it doubtless will cast a cloud on their title or other interest.[13] A judgment setting aside a regulatory agency's orders obviously will affect those the orders regulate.[14]

In the above situations the nonparties ought to be joined. But the possibility of an adverse effect on nonparties, even when it is entitled to consideration, should not automatically result in dismissal of the action if they are not joined. In *E.L. Husting Co. v. Coca–Cola Co.*[15] plaintiff alleged that it had a contract with a regional Coca–Cola distributor for the exclusive right to bottle and sell Coca–Cola in the Milwaukee area and that two local bottlers had aided the regional distributor to breach this contract and to make a new exclusive contract with them. The local bottlers were made defendants and served with process; the regional distributor was named defendant but could not be served. The plaintiff asked for damages and an injunction restraining the local companies from performing their contract. They sought dismissal on the ground that the regional distributor was an indispensable party, but the Supreme Court of Wisconsin ruled otherwise. The injunction clearly would have interfered with the distributor's business and probably have

11. *See* Restatement (Second) of Judgments § 34(3).

12. Williams v. Bankhead, 86 U.S. (19 Wall.) 563, 22 L. Ed. 184 (1873); Russell v. Clark's Exrs., 11 U.S. (7 Cranch) 69, 3 L. Ed. 271 (1812); 3A Moore, Federal Practice and Procedure ¶ 19.08. *See also* Carey v. Klutznick, 653 F.2d 732 (2d Cir.1981), holding that, in a suit to revise the census of New York, other states were necessary parties because their representation in Congress could be affected by a recount. "In effect, House membership is a fund in which fifty states have an interest." *Id.* at 736.

13. McShan v. Sherrill, 283 F.2d 462 (9th Cir.1960); Washington v. United States, 87 F.2d 421 (9th Cir.1936).

14. Texas v. ICC, 258 U.S. 158, 42 S.Ct. 261, 66 L.Ed. 531 (1922). In Thomson v. Talbert Drainage Dist., 168 Cal.App.2d 687, 336 P.2d 174 (1959), plaintiff sought to enjoin a drainage district from using its facilities for disposal of waste water from oil wells; the proprietors of the oil wells were held to be indispensable parties.

15. 194 Wis. 311, 216 N.W. 833 (1927). For the subsequent history of this case, *see* 205 Wis. 356, 237 N.W. 85 (1931), *cert. denied*, 285 U.S. 538, 52 S.Ct. 311, 76 L.Ed. 931 (1932).

stopped performance by the local bottlers under their contract; that, in turn, would have injured the regional distributor without its having a day in court to show that the contract involved no invasion of plaintiff's rights. But the regional distributor could have voluntarily become a party, and it is likely that its interests coincided with those of the two local defendants. Given that the alternative was to dismiss the suit, the court properly held that protection of the absentee's interest did not in the circumstances justify treating it as an indispensable party.

Protecting present parties

The absence of *C* as a party to an action may work prejudice to *D*, who is a party, in at least two ways. In the first place it may expose *D* to multiplicity of suits, which is itself something of an evil. Beyond that is the exposure to possible injustice, particularly double liability, if inconsistent results are reached in two or more lawsuits in which the nonparty is not bound by the first judgment.

An example of simple multiplicity is found in partial assignment or subrogation: When debtors have incurred a single obligation they should not be subject to multiple suits for its breach. Partial assignees are therefore regarded as necessary parties.[16] In other situations, however, a party to an action may be exposed to multiple liability as well as multiple suits unless another is also made a party so as to be bound by the judgment. In *Mahr v. Norwich Union Fire Insurance Soc.*[17] the defendant had issued a fire insurance policy to Bartlett on his stock of goods in Iowa. Bartlett then gave the policy to the plaintiff in New York as collateral for a loan, without formally assigning it. The goods were later destroyed by fire. After the loss, Bartlett formally assigned the policy to Kelly of Iowa. The plaintiff sought to restrain the defendant from paying money under the policy to Bartlett or Kelly and to require it to pay to the policy proceeds to the plaintiff. The court ordered Kelly to be made a party, but process could not be served on him. The trial court proceeded without Kelly to grant the relief asked for, but the court of appeals reversed, holding that Kelly was an indispensable party since his absence exposed the insurer to the possibility of double liability. Indeed, as the court pointed out, Kelly had recovered a judgment in Iowa between the time of the New York trial court's judgment and the decision of the appeal.

Other cases, however, find that a defendant's prospective multiple liability does not warrant holding the absent party indispensable. In

16. Grain v. Aldrich, 38 Cal. 514 (1869); Schilling v. Mullen, 55 Minn. 122, 56 N.W. 586 (1893); Verdier v. Marshallville Equity Co., 70 Ohio App. 434, 46 N.E.2d 636 (1940); National Union Fire Ins. Co. v. Denver & R.G.R.R., 44 Utah 26, 137 P. 653 (1913); Clark, Code Pleading 168–171 (2d ed. 1947). While partial assignees and the partial assignor are conditionally necessary parties, they are not indispensable. Resnik v. La Paz Guest Ranch, 289 F.2d 814 (9th Cir.1961); Rogers v. Penobscot Mining Co., 154 Fed. 606 (8th Cir.1907); Hirsch v. Glidden Co., 79 F.Supp. 729 (S.D.N.Y.1948).

17. 127 N.Y. 452, 28 N.E. 391 (1891).

Petrogradsky M. K. Bank v. National City Bank[18] the refugee directors of a bank chartered by the Imperial Russian Government sued after the Russian Revolution, but before recognition of the Soviet government by the United States, to recover a deposit made in a New York bank before the revolution, notwithstanding the Soviet government's expropriation of the Russian bank. The defendant objected to the action on the ground that recovery would subject it to the possibility of double liability, since the Soviet government might enforce its claim against the New York bank's assets in European countries that recognized the legal effect of the expropriation. The New York Court of Appeals, through Chief Justice Cardozo rejected this defense. Cases such as *Mahr* were distinguished because they involved equitable relief and did not govern actions at law. "In actions of that order, a refusal to pay when due is not sustained without more by the presence of an adverse claim. The defendant, if unable to interplead, must respond to the challenge, and defend as best it can.... 'The chance of double payment is a common risk of life.' "[19]

Western Union Telegraph Co. v. Pennsylvania[20] casts constitutional doubt on *Petrogradsky,* at least when both claims are being aggressively pursued so that the threat of double liability is real. *Western Union* suggests that subjecting a defendant to a substantial risk of multiple liability would be a denial of due process. Be that as it may, the necessary party rule in almost all jurisdictions today does not differentiate its operation in legal and equitable actions, as was done in *Petrogradsky.* It would follow that the necessary party rule should protect the defendant from double liability in both the *Mahr* and *Petrogradsky* situations, unless as a matter of substantive policy a bank is required to run risks toward depositors that an insurer is not required to endure toward insureds.[21]

A variant of double liability is the possibility that *D,* who is entitled to indemnity from *C,* may be sued alone and then fail to establish the conditions of indemnity against *C* in a second suit because *C* is not bound by the first judgment. The common law developed a measure of protection for *D* in some such situations through the device of vouching *C* into the first action.[22] Under modern procedure *C* could be made a

18. 253 N.Y. 23, 170 N.E. 479 (1930).

19. 253 N.Y. 23, 39, 40, 170 N.E. 479, 485 (1930) (quoting Coler v. Corn Exch. Bank, 250 N.Y. 136, 145, 164 N.E. 882, 886 (1928)). To the same effect is Steingut v. National City Bank, 38 F.Supp. 451 (S.D.N.Y.1941). The problem presented in *Petrogradsky* is hardly obsolete. *Compare* Alfred Dunhill of London, Inc. v. The Republic of Cuba, 425 U.S. 682, 96 S.Ct. 1854, 48 L.Ed.2d 301 (1976).

20. 368 U.S. 71, 82 S.Ct. 199, 7 L.Ed.2d 139 (1961). *See also* Union Carbide Corp. v. Superior Court, 133 Cal.App.3d 443, 183 Cal.Rptr. 318 (1982).

21. Traditionally, the courts were at least as unsympathetic toward insurance companies as toward banks. *See* New York Life Ins. Co. v. Dunlevy, 241 U.S. 518, 36 S.Ct. 613, 60 L.Ed. 1140 (1916).

22. Degnan and Barton, Vouching to Quality Warranty: Case Law and Commercial Code, 51 Calif. L. Rev. 471 (1963); § 11.30 *infra.*

party by impleader.[23]

Society's interest

Multiplicity of suits is a burden not only on a defendant but also on society, because of the expense to the taxpayers and the burden of crowded dockets on the administration of justice. Curiously, this interest has been given little recognition in joinder of plaintiffs. As expressed in Federal Rule 20, plaintiffs who have claims arising out of the same transaction may join in one action but are not obliged to do so. This reflects the old common law's preference for simple lawsuits, but it often does not make sense in the modern context, especially in two frequently recurring situations. One occurs when several members of a family are injured in an automobile accident. Since their interests are compatible, and often overlap so far as damages are concerned, and since they are usually represented by the same counsel, it would seem that they should be compelled to sue in one action. But the rules do not so require, except that in a few jurisdictions a spouse's claim for loss of consortium by reason of injury to the other spouse can be asserted only if joined in the latter's own action for his or her injury.[24] Plaintiffs may bring separate actions in such situations to avoid the possibility that the jury may be inclined to put a "cap" on defendant's total liability, or to get "two bites" at the issue of defendant's liability—since one family member is not bound by a judgment against another family member.[25]

The other situation in which a single action seems especially desirable arises when many persons are injured in one occurrence, such as a plane crash. As we shall see, defendants in such situations are usually bound in subsequent litigation if they lose, but unjoined plaintiffs are free to sue even if some of their number have lost.[26] Yet the rules do not require joinder; thus, the same issue of liability can be thoroughly litigated more than once, at public expense,[27] unless a class action is allowed.[28]

Closely akin to society's interest in avoidance of unnecessary litigation is its interest in having a judgment or decree be as complete as possible. According to the traditional equitable principle,

> when a decision is made, it shall provide for all the rights, which different persons have in the matters decided. For a "Court of Equity, in all cases, delights to do complete justice, and not by halves," to put an

23. *See* Degnan and Barton, *supra* note 22. On impleader, *see* § 10.18 *infra.*

24. *See* § 10.11 *supra*; Restatement (Second) of Judgments § 48; *e.g.,* Schreiner v. Fruit, 519 P.2d 462 (Alaska 1974).

25. *See, e.g.,* Standard Accident Ins. Co. v. Doiron, 170 F.2d 206 (1st Cir.1948). *Compare* Zaragosa v. Craven, 33 Cal.2d 315, 202 P.2d 73 (1949), involving the effects of a community property law.

26. *See* § 11.24 *infra.*

27. *See, e.g.,* Pan Am. World Airways v. United States Dist. Court, 523 F.2d 1073 (9th Cir.1975).

28. *See* §§ 10.20–10.23 *infra.*

end to litigation, and to give decrees of such a nature, that the performance of them may be perfectly safe to all who obey them.[29]

There are many degrees of incompleteness. The absence of one party may simply prevent the court from putting the last bit of frosting on the cake;[30] the absence of another may render any judgment an altogether futile gesture.[31] Incompleteness of the former kind may be consistent with a judgment that does substantial justice among the parties present and no harm to absentees; its most serious vice may be offending the aesthetic of symmetry. Incompleteness of the latter kind is an entirely different matter. Not only may it invite further litigation and leave present parties unprotected, but it will always have the additional serious vice of propounding a judgment that cannot practically be enforced.[32] An idle decree impairs the moral acceptability of court decisions.

Plaintiff's access to a forum

The plaintiff clearly has an interest in securing some forum, preferably a convenient one, for the adjudication of the claim on the merits. A ruling that a nonparty is indispensable so that the action may not go forward unless it is brought in may, in effect, foreclose all courts to a plaintiff where process cannot be validly served on a person who should be joined.[33] When the action is in a federal court, if federal jurisdiction is based on diversity of citizenship, the diversity must be complete; no plaintiff may be a co-citizen of the same state with any defendant. Even if process can be served on a necessary party, therefore, that party's presence in the action may oust a federal court of jurisdiction over the subject matter. Also, the federal venue rules may mean that the district in which the action is originally brought is not a district in which the new party may properly be sued over its objection to the venue.[34]

These possibilities invite careful attention to whether a jurisdictional basis can be found for joining, through process or notice, all persons

29. Calvert, Parties to Suits in Equity 2, 3 (2d ed. 1847).

30. Such as the formal action by corporate directors in declaring a dividend (on preferred stock) that the corporation is legally bound to pay. *See* Kroese v. General Steel Castings Corp., 179 F.2d 760, 763–765 (3d Cir.1950) (noted in 50 Colum. L. Rev. 997 (1950), 49 Mich. L. Rev. 275 (1950)). *Cf.* Annot., 71 A.L.R.2d 723 (necessary parties in declaratory judgment actions).

31. *See, e.g.,* Warner Valley Stock Co. v. Smith, 165 U.S. 28, 17 S.Ct. 225, 41 L.Ed. 621 (1897).

32. Kendig v. Dean, 97 U.S. 423, 24 L.Ed. 1061 (1878). *See* Underwood v. Maloney, 256 F.2d 334, 338 (3d Cir.1958); *see also* Johnson v. Kirkland, 290 F.2d 440 (5th Cir.1961).

33. This was probably the case in Shields v. Barrow, 58 U.S. (17 How.) 130, 15 L. Ed. 158 (1854); Kroese v. General Steel Castings Corp., 179 F.2d 760 (3d Cir. 1950); Bank of Cal. v. Superior Court, 16 Cal.2d 516, 106 P.2d 879 (1940). *Cf.* Mullane v. Central Hanover Bank & Trust Co., 339 U.S. 306, 70 S.Ct. 652, 94 L.Ed. 865 (1950); Sac and Fox Nation v. Norton, 240 F.3d 1250 (10th Cir. 2001) (unjoined tribe claimed sovereign immunity).

34. *See* Barrett, Venue and Service of Process in the Federal Courts—Suggestions for Reform, 7 Vand. L. Rev. 608, 621–622 (1954); 3A Moore, Federal Practice and Procedure ¶ 19.04.

who ought to be parties. So far as federal subject matter jurisdiction is concerned, the supplemental jurisdiction statute now permits broad joinder of necessary parties whenever the original case falls under federal question jurisdiction (or any other nondiversity jurisdiction).[35] In a diversity case, a plaintiff may not join a nondiverse defendant or assert a claim against one brought in by another party. The statute so provides in order to prevent plaintiffs from dodging the complete diversity requirement by bringing diversity suits to which nondiverse necessary parties must then be added and then claiming against those parties. But supplemental jurisdiction allows a defendant to bring in a nondiverse necessary party, and perhaps even a plaintiff may do so if it asserts no claim against that party.[36] And sometimes a necessary party may be added without destroying complete diversity, as when a Nevada plaintiff sues a California defendant and is later required to add another defendant from any state but Nevada.

Personal jurisdiction over necessary parties

Assuming that any subject matter jurisdiction problems have been resolved, it will still be necessary to establish personal jurisdiction over the new party if that party objects to that jurisdiction. The usual forms of long arm and other jurisdiction may be invoked. In addition, a basis for extending jurisdiction might be found on one of the principles discussed below.

1. It has long been the law that when an action is in rem, the court having jurisdiction over the res has power to adjudicate all interests in and claims to that res. Personal service over the holders or claimants of such interests is not necessary so long as reasonable means are chosen to notify them of the pendency of the action and to give them a chance to come in and present their claims. If, therefore, an action is successfully conceptualized as being in rem, and the action is brought in a state court having jurisdiction over the res, there is no insuperable obstacle to bringing in any party whom a court holds indispensable.[37] Although *Shaffer v. Heitner*[38] cast doubt on the possibility of an in rem action binding persons who lack contacts with the forum, the possibility may still survive in a limited context, such as when ownership of land in the forum state is in dispute. Here the distinction between necessary and indispensable parties loses its significance.

2. Even when an action is regarded as in personam, or not strictly in rem, the requirements for obtaining jurisdiction over a defendant

35. 28 U.S.C. § 1367(a).

36. 28 U.S.C. § 1367(b); McLaughlin, The Federal Supplemental Jurisdiction Statute–A Constitutional and Statutory Analysis, 24 Ariz. St. L.J. 849, 929–31, 952–58 (1992); *see* Sta–Rite Indus., Inc. v. Allstate Ins. Co., 96 F.3d 281 (7th Cir.1996).

37. *See* § 2.7 *supra.*

38. 433 U.S. 186, 97 S.Ct. 2569, 53 L.Ed.2d 683 (1977).

have been substantially liberalized, particularly if the transaction has its "center of gravity" in the forum state.[39]

3. The blow of a ruling that a nonparty is indispensable on the plaintiff's side is softened, to a limited but uncertain extent, by the concept of "involuntary plaintiff." Equity had developed the practice of making an unwilling plaintiff a defendant to bring him or her into the action,[40] and this may be done under the codes and modern procedure. This device will not help, however, when jurisdiction cannot be obtained over the unwilling party since the requirements involved are generally comparable to those concerning defendants.[41]

4. The doctrine of representation and the representative or class suit,[42] where applicable, have enabled parties to overcome the difficulties of indispensability.

5. Congress has used its power to make federal process nationwide. The Federal Interpleader Act has, within limits, greatly increased the availability of parties who may be held indispensable.[43] The Federal Rules now permit an extended range of service of process outside the state to bring in a necessary party (within one hundred miles of the courthouse) so long as the joinder does not destroy complete diversity.[44]

§ 10.13 Weighing Various Factors

The considerations described in the preceding section are the principal, if not the only, ones entitled to weight in determining whether a party is necessary or indispensable. While they are basically few and simple, each may exist in varying degrees, and the different interests represented often compete, so that the total net impact of all the relevant considerations varies infinitely from case to case. Moreover, in many cases a factual inquiry is needed before a realistic decision can be made on the proper weight to give one or more of the factors. Because of all this, the problem does not readily lend itself to solution by fixed and rigid rules. Rather, flexibility and a case-by-case appraisal of the relevant factors are important.[1]

39. *See* §§ 2.4–.6 *supra.*

40. Clark, Code Pleading 354 (2d ed. 1947). *Cf.* Vinson v. Home Ins. Co., 123 W.Va. 522, 16 S.E.2d 924 (1941) (case transferred from law to equity side to permit this practice).

41. Independent Wireless Tel. Co. v. Radio Corp. of Am., 269 U.S. 459, 46 S.Ct. 166, 70 L.Ed. 357 (1926); McAulay v. Moody, 185 Fed. 144 (C.C.Or.1911).

42. *See* Restatement (Second) of Judgments §§ 41–42; §§ 10.20–10.23 *infra.*

43. *See* 28 U.S.C. § 2361. *See also* § 10.19 *infra.*

44. *See* Fed. R. Civ. P. 4(k)(1)(B), (2). Congress has also relaxed federal venue requirements when there is no district where an action could otherwise be brought. 28 U.S.C. § 1391(a)(3), (b)(3).

§ 10.13

1. Confederated Tribes of Chehalis Indian Reservation v. Lujan, 928 F.2d 1496 (9th Cir.1991).

Three-stage analysis

Federal Rule 19 seeks to guide such an appraisal by prescribing three stages of analysis. First, the court should consider any harm that might result from proceeding without the assertedly indispensable party—harm to that party, to a party that might be exposed to double or insistent liability, or to a plaintiff that might be unable to secure complete relief. The last kind of harm should be thought of as harm to the public interest in resolving controversies without multiple litigation, because the plaintiff is presumably willing that the action proceed with whatever parties the plaintiff joined.

Second, if the absence of the assertedly indispensable party is likely to produce one of these harms, the court should seek to join that party under the various joinder provisions discussed here and in the previous chapter. As already noted, this may be impossible in a federal action if joinder would destroy diversity jurisdiction. It may also be impossible, in either a federal or a state court action, if the court lacks personal jurisdiction over the party to be joined. Of course, the party may be invited to join voluntarily as an intervenor, waiving its right not to be sued when personal jurisdiction is lacking.

Third, if the party cannot be joined, Rule 19 calls on the court to decide whether to proceed without the party (treating it as necessary but not indispensable) or to dismiss the action (treating the party as indispensable). The court may consider all relevant factors in making this decision, including, of course, the harms explored in the first stage of analysis. The court also must consider the harms that dismissing the action could cause. These are most grievous when dismissal would leave the plaintiff with no court in which to sue, typically because no forum could obtain personal jurisdiction over all the parties that ideally should be joined. The harm is less severe when federal subject matter jurisdictional rules prevent joinder, for the plaintiff then can usually join the absent party in a state court action. Rule 19, lastly, directs the court to consider ways of shaping relief to reduce or avoid the harms of nonjoinder. Among the ways of doing this are resolving some claims but not others, granting damages but not injunctive relief, delaying relief until litigation elsewhere runs its course, writing a narrowly drawn opinion that makes clear what issues are not being decided, inviting absent parties to intervene, and joining parties likely to protect the interest of the absent party.

Case-by-case evaluation

A few examples of careful judicial appraisal of the relevant considerations may be helpful.

In *Kroese v. General Steel Castings Corp.*[2] a preferred stockholder sued a Delaware corporation in a Pennsylvania federal court to compel

2. 179 F.2d 760 (3d Cir.), *cert. denied,* 339 U.S. 983, 70 S.Ct. 1026, 94 L.Ed. 1386 (1950) (noted in 50 Colum. L. Rev. 997 (1950), 49 Mich. L. Rev. 275 (1950)).

the payment of dividends. Since dividends were payable "when and as declared by the Board of Directors," the district court held a majority of the board members to be indispensable parties. According to the plaintiff's claim there was no state or federal district in which a majority might be served. The court of appeals reversed the ruling, finding that under the allegations of the complaint, affairs had "reached the point where the judgment of the directors is no longer controlling"[3] under substantive law. The directors had been superseded by the court's supervising authority. Further, the decree could be made effective without the directors' being bound by it. The court noted that a chancellor "with legal imagination" could "do a great deal" to corporate property within Pennsylvania, by sequestration, if need be. If the formal act of the directors was necessary to fulfill Delaware law, the court said,

> we cannot think that a receivership or sequestration of a foreign corporation's property will not produce the result. Equity courts have known for a long time how to impose onerous alternatives at home to the performance of affirmative acts abroad as a means of getting those affirmative acts accomplished.[4]

In *Bank of California v. Superior Court*[5] plaintiff sued to enforce the provisions of an alleged contract with the decedent to leave her entire estate (about $225,000) to the plaintiff. The decedent's will "left individual legacies and bequests amounting to $60,000 to a large number of legatees, including charitable institutions and individuals, some residing in other states and in foreign countries."[6] The executor and all beneficiaries under the will were named defendants, but only the executor and the residuary legatee were served. The California Supreme Court held that the trial court had discretion to allow the action to proceed without the missing beneficiaries. Their share of the estate would not be affected at all—the plaintiff would simply get less than she claimed because of their absence.[7] And the objections addressed to inconvenience and possible multiplicity of suits were properly weighed in the exercise of discretion but would not bar the action as a matter of law.

An example of a careful analysis leading to dismissal of a diversity action in federal court is *Haas v. Jefferson National Bank.*[8] Plaintiff, a citizen of Ohio, sued defendant, a Florida bank, in a U.S. District Court in Florida, demanding that the bank issue stock to him. The bank objected that Glueck should be made a party because he also claimed the stock; if Glueck were not joined and plaintiff won, Glueck could still sue the bank, resulting in its being subject to double liability for the same obligation. The bank could not interplead Glueck and the plaintiff under

3. 179 F.2d at 763.

4. 179 F.2d at 764, 765.

5. 16 Cal.2d 516, 106 P.2d 879 (1940).

6. 16 Cal.2d at 518, 106 P.2d at 882 (and left the rest of the estate to a residuary legatee and hospital).

7. *Cf.* Stumpf v. Fidelity Gas Co., 294 F.2d 886 (9th Cir.1961).

8. 442 F.2d 394 (5th Cir.1971).

the Federal Interpleader Act because they were both citizens of Ohio, nor apparently could it get in personam jurisdiction over Glueck to interplead the two claimants under Federal Rule 22. Plaintiff, however, could sue Glueck directly in Ohio and get a judgment establishing which of them owned the stock. Alternatively, it is conceivable that the bank could have deposited the stock in court in a Florida state court, treating it as a res, and sought a determination as to its proper owner.[9]

Provident Tradesmen's Bank

The most comprehensive judicial analysis of the necessary parties problem appears in *Provident Tradesmens Bank v. Patterson*,[10] a case that also illustrates the relevance of timing in applying the necessary parties rule. There, the Supreme Court pointed out that in its original formulation in courts of equity, the necessary parties rule was applied pragmatically with regard to "factors varying with the different cases, some such factors being substantive, some procedural, some compelling by themselves, and some subject to balancing against opposing interests."[11] The rule gradually had acquired a rigidity in formulation and application that was a betrayal of these origins. Rule 19(b) restored the pragmatic orientation, enumerating four relevant considerations to guide a court's judgment:

> first, to what extent a judgment rendered in the person's absence might be prejudicial to the person or those already parties; second, the extent to which, by protective provisions in the judgment, by the shaping of relief, or other measures, the prejudice can be lessened or avoided; third, whether a judgment rendered in the person's absence will be adequate; fourth, whether the plaintiff will have an adequate remedy if the action is dismissed for nonjoinder.[12]

Timing

The Court further held that the weight accorded these factors varied according to the time when the necessary parties question had been raised. If it was raised at the threshold of the litigation in the trial court, dismissal might be more readily indicated than if the action had gone to judgment before the question was raised. When, as in *Provident*, the question is not raised until appeal, only very strong concerns could compel a conclusion that dismissal is appropriate. Indeed, a party that had a chance to raise an indispensable party contention at the outset of a case should be allowed to raise it later only when this is necessary to protect a nonjoined person who had no chance to object. Implicit in the

9. *But see* New York Life Ins. Co. v. Dunlevy, 241 U.S. 518, 36 S.Ct. 613, 60 L.Ed. 1140 (1916); *cf.* Shaffer v. Heitner, 433 U.S. 186, 97 S.Ct. 2569, 53 L.Ed.2d 683 (1977).

10. 390 U.S. 102, 88 S.Ct. 733, 19 L.Ed.2d 936 (1968).

11. 390 U.S. at 119, 88 S.Ct. at 743, 19 L.Ed.2d at 950. *See also* CP Natl. Corp. v. Bonneville Power Admin., 928 F.2d 905 (9th Cir.1991).

12. Fed. R. Civ. P. 19(b).

holding that dismissal was inappropriate is also the proposition that failure to join an indispensable party is not, as was said in some older authorities, a "jurisdictional" defect: The court can decide the part of the case that is before it even if it cannot decide the part of the case that is not before it because the absentee has not been made a party.[13]

Joinder by objecting party

One function of Rule 19(b) is to protect the parties already joined from risk of other claims by parties not joined. Consistent with this policy, the party who objects on the basis of a lack of a necessary party may be obliged to cure this defect itself by joining the required party. For instance, *Associated Dry Goods v. Towers Financial Corp.*[14] involved a tenant who sued a subtenant for failure to pay rent as required by a sublease. The subtenant moved to dismiss for failure to join the primary landlord, the owner of the premises. The joinder of the owner by plaintiff would strip the court of diversity jurisdiction, but joinder through a cross-claim by defendant would be within the court's supplemental jurisdiction. The court held that the motion to dismiss for failure to join an indispensable party would not be granted to a defendant who failed to join that party by a joinder device that it could have employed.[15] As the court stated, the "Rule 19(b) notion of equity and good conscience contemplates that the parties actually before the court are obliged to pursue any avenues for eliminating the threat of prejudice."[16]

§ 10.14 Parties Having Joint or United Interests

Another way of understanding the flexible approach of Federal Rule 19 is by contrasting it to the more categorical approach of the state codes, and to some extent of Rule 19 itself until 1966. Most of the codes required joinder of "parties who are united in interest" as plaintiffs or defendants.[1] This rule was essentially a variation of the necessary parties rule. The full implications of this provision were probably not fully comprehended by the code drafters. Apparently their aim was to incorporate two joinder concepts, one from equity and the other from common law.[2] The equity concept was that of necessary parties, previously discussed. The common law rule held that joint obligees of a contract had to

13. The idea that the defect is "jurisdictional," that is, that the court lacks power to decide the case as between the parties before it because it does not also have other parties before it, still persists in some state courts. *See* Note, 46 U. Colo. L. Rev. 609 (1975).

14. 920 F.2d 1121 (2d Cir.1990).

15. *See* Fed. R. Civ. P. 13(a).

16. Associated Dry Goods v. Towers Fin. Corp., 920 F.2d 1121, 1125 (2d Cir. 1990) (quoting Wright and Miller, 7 Federal Practice and Procedure § 1608, at 112–113). Accord, Viacom Int'l, Inc. v. Kearney, 212 F.3d 721 (2d Cir.2000).

§ 10.14

1. Clark, Code Pleading 358 (2d ed. 1947). Federal Rule 19, before its revision in 1966, provided that "persons having a joint interest should be made parties."

2. *Compare* Clark, *supra* note 1, *with* cases cited in notes 3 and 4 *infra*.

join as plaintiffs[3] and that joint obligors of a contract had to be joined as defendants.[4]

Inflexible joinder requirement under codes

The code provision had two fundamental deficiencies. First, it imported into code procedure the common law's rigid approach to definition of parties who must be joined. The common law held that joint owners of property and joint obligees invariably must join as plaintiffs, a rule that admitted of no reasoned explanation in procedural policy and no flexibility in application. As imported into the code, this rigid concept was applied not only to the old common law joint ownership situation but often also to the infinitely various contexts in which equity had applied the necessary party principle. The result was a definitional nightmare. Courts attempting to distinguish "united" interests from those not united often cited equity precedents in which no such concept had been employed. The second deficiency with the code provision was that it implied, and was interpreted to mean, that the action invariably must be dismissed if the absent party could not be joined.

The necessary parties principle under the codes thus became an often inescapable trap. One could not exactly define what a necessary party *was*, but the absence of such a party meant the action had to be dismissed. It was held accordingly that joinder is required of all who hold interests in land constituting the subject of litigation.[5] Thus, the record title owners of all parcels of land that the plaintiff claims to have acquired by right of accretion must be made parties in the action to have plaintiff's claim declared valid.[6] All tenants in common to land must be joined in an action for its partition.[7] In an action to foreclose a mortgage or other lien, the owner of the equity of redemption and all junior encumbrances were generally regarded as necessary parties.[8] In a partition case, however, a lessee of the property need not, by the weight of

3. Gregory v. Stetson, 133 U.S. 579, 10 S.Ct. 422, 33 L.Ed. 792 (1890); Dewey v. Carey, 60 Mo. 224 (1875).

4. Camp v. Gress, 250 U.S. 308, 39 S.Ct. 478, 63 L.Ed. 997 (1919); Dillon v. Barnard, 328 Mass. 53, 101 N.E.2d 345 (1951); Reed, Compulsory Joinder of Parties in Civil Actions, 55 Mich. L. Rev. 327, 357–367 (1957).

5. McShan v. Sherrill, 283 F.2d 462 (9th Cir.1960); Stewart v. United States, 242 F.2d 49 (5th Cir.1957); Fouke v. Schenewerk, 197 F.2d 234 (5th Cir.1952).

6. McShan v. Sherrill, 283 F.2d 462 (9th Cir.1960).

7. Barney v. Baltimore, 73 U.S. (6 Wall.) 280, 18 L. Ed. 825 (1867); Henry Quellmalz Lumber & Mfg. Co. v. Roche, 145 Ark. 38, 223 S.W. 376 (1920); Gates v. Salmon, 35 Cal. 576 (1868).

8. *See, e.g.,* Black v. London Assurance Co., 122 F.Supp. 330 (W.D.S.C.1954) (judgment lienors junior to mortgage); Auburn Ins. Agency v. First Natl. Bank, 263 Ala. 30, 81 So.2d 600 (1955) (second mortgage); City of Wilmington v. Merrick, 231 N.C. 297, 56 S.E.2d 643 (1949); 4 Am. Law of Real Property 16.188, 16.191 (1952). *Cf.* Kling v. Ghilarducci, 3 Ill.2d 454, 121 N.E.2d 752 (1954). The use of the term "necessary" or "indispensable" here—at least for junior encumbrances—meant not that the action could not proceed in their absence but that their absence would render defective any title based on the judgment. *See* Reed, Compulsory Joinder of Parties in Civil Actions, 55 Mich. L. Rev. 327, 510–517 (1957); 4 Am. Law of Real Property §§ 16.188, 16.191 (1952).

authority, be made a party since the relief affects only the reversion and leaves the tenancy intact.[9] And in foreclosure cases, if liens senior to the plaintiff's will not be disturbed by the judgment sought, then the senior lienors need not be joined.[10]

Impact on class actions

Another serious consequence of the code provision requiring joinder of persons "united in interest" was that the term was also used in connection with the code provisions concerning class actions.[11] The code class-action rule provided that if the parties were united in interest but were too numerous to be joined, then some smaller number of them could sue or be sued as representatives of all. This, in turn, implied that class suits were appropriate only when the members of the class had interests that were united or joint in the same sense as the interests of the obligees or obligors of joint obligation at common law. It thus came to be accepted that a "true" class suit was possible only when such unity or jointness existed among the class.[12] Hence, the effect of employing the term "united in interest" in connection with both the joinder of contract parties and the class suit had the effect of radically narrowing the permissible use of the class suit device under the codes.[13] Only in the revision of Federal Rule 19 in 1966 were the residual effects of the code rule finally abrogated.[14]

§ 10.15 Suits to Review Administrative Action

Suits to review the actions of administrative officials often present problems cast in terms of indispensable parties. In the absence of a statutory procedure for review of an agency's decision, judicial review must usually be sought by a suit to restrain or coerce the appropriate individual in the administrative hierarchy. For all practical purposes, such suits are against the government, but in form they are brought against a specific government official. One line of cases holds, however, that because the suit is actually against the sovereign, the sovereign—that is, the government—is an indispensable party. When the government is indispensable, the action must fail because of sovereign immuni-

9. *See, e.g.,* Fyffe v. Fyffe, 292 Ill.App. 539, 11 N.E.2d 857 (1937); Bethel College v. Gladdish, 204 Ky. 10, 263 S.W. 659 (1924); Thruston v. Minke, 32 Md. 571 (1870); Peterman v. Kingsley, 140 Wis. 666, 123 N.W. 137 (1909). *Compare* Willard v. Willard, 145 U.S. 116, 12 S.Ct. 818, 36 L.Ed. 644 (1892); Finch v. Smith, 146 Ala. 644, 41 So. 819 (1906) (outstanding lease no bar to partition).

10. *See, e.g.,* Mason v. Cathedral Bldg. Corp., 125 F.Supp. 542 (D.Alaska 1954); 4 Am. Law of Real Property § 16.190 (1952).

11. *Compare* the statutory citations in Clark, Code Pleading 358 n.48 (2d ed. 1947), dealing with parties "united in interest," *with* those in Clark, *id.* at 398 n.206, dealing with class suits.

12. *See* §§ 10.21–.22 *infra.*

13. *See, e.g.,* Weaver v. Pasadena Tournament of Roses, 32 Cal.2d 833, 198 P.2d 514 (1948). *See generally* Blume, The "Common Questions" Principle in the Code Provision for Representative Suits, 30 Mich. L. Rev. 878 (1932).

14. *See* § 10.13 *supra* for the discussion of Provident Tradesmens Bank v. Patterson, 390 U.S. 102, 88 S.Ct. 733, 19 L.Ed.2d 936 (1968).

ty unless the government has consented to be sued in that type of claim. In cases in which the first hurdle has been met, a second difficulty arises in the indispensability of a superior officer when a subordinate has originally been sued. A ruling of indispensability here does not foreclose relief altogether, but it may mean that plaintiff must come to the seat of government to pursue a challenge and cannot do so where he or she lives or where his or her business is located.[1] Congress has largely solved the problem, insofar as federal agencies are concerned, by recognizing that such suits are in substance against the government and therefore granting consent to them.[2]

An individual or group may now also challenge an administrative agency's action through statutes such as the Administrative Procedure Act,[3] even though such agencies would normally be immune from suit as government entities. This Act provides judicial review to any person "suffering legal wrong because of an agency action, or adversely affected or aggrieved by agency action within the meaning of a relevant statute" unless the statute precludes review[4] The plaintiffs must establish standing to challenge the administrative agency's action[5] by showing that the action harmed them in some relevant way.[6]

C. OTHER JOINDER DEVICES

§ 10.16 Introduction

Thus far we have examined the concepts of permissive joinder and necessary joinder primarily as they shape the *claimant's* initiatives in fixing the scope of the action for parties. We have seen that the rules of permissive joinder generally authorize the plaintiff to join all parties involved in the transaction being litigated; within that set of potential parties, the necessary parties rule prescribes those that plaintiff is obliged to join. The necessary parties rule is aimed at protecting the interests of the defendant and of absent third parties. But certain procedural devices directly confer joinder initiatives on parties *other* than

§ 10.15

1. The subject is too complex to address effectively in the present context. *See generally* Cramton, Nonstatutory Review of Federal Administrative Action: The Need for Statutory Reform of Sovereign Immunity, Subject Matter Jurisdiction, and Parties Defendant, 68 Mich. L. Rev. 387 (1970).

2. *See* 5 U.S.C. §§ 702–703; 28 U.S.C. §§ 1361, 1391(e); Comment, Sovereign Immunity: A Modern Rationale in Light of the 1976 Amendments to the Administrative Procedure Act, 1981 Duke L.J. 116, 128–131.

3. Administrative Procedure Act § 10(a), 5 U.S.C. § 702.

4. *Id.* This Act does not create a private right of action for damages.

5. Bender v. Williamsport Area School Dist., 475 U.S. 534, 106 S.Ct. 1326, 89 L.Ed.2d 501 (1986); Association of Data Processing Service Organizations, Inc. v. Camp, 397 U.S. 150, 90 S.Ct. 827, 25 L.Ed.2d 184 (1970).

6. United States v. Students Challenging Regulatory Agency Procedures, 412 U.S. 669, 93 S.Ct. 2405, 37 L.Ed.2d 254(1973); Lujan v. National Wildlife Federation, 497 U.S. 871, 110 S.Ct. 3177, 111 L.Ed.2d 695 (1990); Federal Election Comm'n v. Akins, 524 U.S. 11, 118 S.Ct. 1777, 141 L.Ed.2d 10 (1998).

the original claimant. These devices include intervention, impleader, and interpleader, as well as the class action, which has some elements of each of the other joinder devices.

§ 10.17 Intervention

Intervention means essentially what the term implies in ordinary language—a procedure by which one who was not originally a party to an action can enter into litigation commenced between others.[1] By doing so intervenors can protect their interests against possible adverse effects of a judgment; by becoming parties they also become bound by the judgment.[2] Although in retrospect intervention and the necessary parties rule seem to address essentially the same problem, this was not clearly perceived until the 1966 revision of the Federal Rules.[3] Accordingly, both equity procedure and the codes used different terminology, and often reached different results, when considering whether an outsider should be brought in (as a necessary party) or should be allowed to come in (as an intervenor). There are still some vestiges of this conceptual separation.

Intervention had its forerunners in admiralty and equity and even in common law procedure; these, however, were rudimentary and generally confined to cases in which real or personal property was in the custody of the court. For the most part, the notion that third persons might invite themselves into lawsuits between others ran counter to the Anglo–American notion that the plaintiff was master of the suit. The Roman law, in contrast, was much more hospitable to the notion of intervention and such has been the civil law tradition.[4]

Code intervention

The code provisions for intervention took one of two forms.[5] Under the liberal statutes, the prospective intervenor had to have an "interest in the matter in litigation; or in the success of either party, or an interest against both."[6] Other statutes were more limited, allowing

§ 10.17

1. *See* Clark, Code Pleading § 65 (2d ed. 1947); Kennedy, Let's All Join In: Intervention Under Federal Rule 24, 57 Ky. L.J. 329 (1969); Lederleitner and Nolan, Criteria for Intervention, 1967 U. Ill. L.J. 299; Moore and Levi, Federal Intervention, 45 Yale L.J. 565 (1936) (summarizing the federal decisional law prior to adoption of the Federal Rules); Shapiro, Some Thoughts on Intervention Before Courts, Agencies, and Arbitrators, 81 Harv. L. Rev. 721 (1968) (an excellent critical discussion); Annots., 84 A.L.R.2d 1412, 37 A.L.R.2d 1306, 5 A.L.R. Fed. 518.

2. Fishgold v. Sullivan Drydock & Repair Corp., 328 U.S. 275, 66 S.Ct. 1105, 90 L.Ed. 1230, 167 A.L.R. 110 (1946). If the intervenor will be so affected, he or she has standing to appeal from a judgment adverse to his or her interest even if neither of the original parties does so. *Id. But see* Diamond v. Charles, 476 U.S. 54, 106 S.Ct. 1697, 90 L.Ed.2d 48 (1986)(intervenor lacking standing may not appeal).

3. *See* Fed. R. Civ. P. 24, Advisory Committee Notes.

4. 3B Moore, Federal Practice and Procedure ¶ 24.03.

5. Clark, Code Pleading 421 (2d ed. 1947).

6. Cal. Civ. Proc. Code § 387. *See* Clark, *supra* note 5, at 421 n.284, collecting citations to such statutes as of that time.

intervention only in an action for the recovery of real or personal property by one claiming an interest in the property.[7] Most statutes of both types, and the former federal equity rule, also provided that intervention should recognize and be subordinate to the propriety of the main proceeding.[8] This was generally interpreted to require that the intervenor line up with one of the existing parties on the issues already formulated. This interpretation frustrated intervention by one who asserted a position antagonistic to both existing parties and greatly diminished the practical value of the procedure. It has been rejected in modern rules and statutes.

Federal Rule 24

Federal Rule 24 provides for intervention on two bases: as a matter of right and in the discretion of the court. Although no persuasive analytic distinction can be made between the conditions required for intervention as of right and those for permissive intervention,[9] the present rule makes it important to which category an intervention is assigned. (1) Intervention as of right implies that if the conditions for intervention are found to exist, the intervenor must be allowed in, whereas permissive intervention is discretionary with the court.[10] (2) A denial of intervention as of right is appealable, whereas denial of permissive intervention is not.[11] (3) In federal court, intervention as of right has traditionally required no independent basis of jurisdiction.[12] It is bizarre that so much should turn on a distinction that has no substantial basis.

1966 amendment

Intervention as of right is available in the circumstances defined in Rule 24(a) and when a provision of a statute confers that right. Rule 24, as originally formulated in 1938, defined the general circumstances as follows: "The representation of the applicant's interests by existing

7. *See* Clark, *supra* note 5, at 421 n.285, collecting citations to similar statutes. In addition to states that have adopted the Federal Rules since that time, New York has adopted a provision on intervention similar to Federal Rule 24. N.Y. Civ. Prac. L. & R. 1012–1014.

8. Fed. R. Equity 37 (1912); *see* Clark, *supra* note 5, at 424–425.

9. *See* Shreve, Questioning Intervention of Right—Toward a New Methodology of Decisionmaking, 74 Nw. U.L. Rev. 894 (1980).

10. Fed. R. Civ. P. 24(a) ("Upon timely application anyone *shall* be permitted to intervene"); *cf.* Fed. R. Civ. P. 24(b) ("Upon timely application anyone *may* be permitted to intervene").

11. *See, e.g.,* Sam Fox Publishing Co. v. United States, 366 U.S. 683, 688, 81 S.Ct. 1309, 1312, 6 L.Ed.2d 604, 609 (1961) ("If appellant may intervene as of right, the order of the court denying intervention is appealable"); Allen Calculators v. National Cash Register Co., 322 U.S. 137, 64 S.Ct. 905, 88 L.Ed. 1188 (1944) (permissive intervention not reviewable). A court hearing an appeal from denial of intervention as of right may sometimes exercise supplemental jurisdiction over an inextricably intertwined denial of permissive intervention. *See* Steinman, The Scope of Appellate Jurisdiction: Pendent Appellate Jurisdiction Before and After *Swint*, 49 Hastings L.J. 1337 (1998).

12. *See* text at notes 30 *et seq. infra.*

parties is or may be inadequate and the applicant is or may be bound by a judgment in the action," or the applicant might be adversely affected by disposition of property under control of the court. The quoted phrase was given a Catch–22 interpretation: The applicants for intervention had to show that they probably would be bound by the judgment (which could only result if they were in fact adequately represented) and also that their interests were inadequately represented (in which case they would not be bound by the judgment).[13] In 1966, Rule 24 was amended to eliminate this absurdity and to allow intervention as of right essentially on the same principles as those under the necessary parties rule.[14] Rule 24(a) now authorizes intervention as of right when a statute confers that right or when

> the applicant claims an interest relating to the property or transaction which is the subject of the action and the applicant is so situated that the disposition of the action may as a practical matter impair or impede the applicant's ability to protect that interest, unless the applicant's interest is adequately represented by existing parties.

The most important example of a statutory right of intervention is that authorizing the United States to intervene when the constitutionality of an act of Congress is challenged.[15]

Party adversely affected

The first two requirements of Rule 24(a)—that the applicant claim an "interest" and that the action may impair the applicant's ability to protect that interest—call on the court to consider the practical impact of the action on the prospective intervenor. The circumstances in which the rule is satisfied are essentially the same as those that justify classifying the intervenor as a necessary party. Courts often inquire whether the prospective intervenor has a legally cognizable interest, as opposed to a merely ideological one, an inquiry somewhat similar to that pursued in deciding whether a plaintiff has "standing" to raise a claim.[16] Yet no universal catalogue of acceptable interests is possible. Which interests should count depends in part on what the action is about. For example, a property owner's interest in the value of his or her residence may warrant intervention in a zoning dispute, but not in a school desegregation case. The purpose and scope of the intervention may also

13. Sam Fox Publishing Co. v. United States, 366 U.S. 683, 81 S.Ct. 1309, 6 L.Ed.2d 604 (1961).

14. *Compare* §§ 10.12 *et seq. supra.* On the 1966 amendment *see* Kaplan, Continuing Work of the Civil Committee: 1966 Amendments of the Federal Rules of Civil Procedure I, 81 Harv. L. Rev. 356, 400 (1967).

15. 28 U.S.C. § 2403. *See* 18 U.S.C. § 1326(a)(3)(F) (state legislators and certain others entitled to intervene in certain prison cases); Note, Federal Intervention in Private Actions Involving the Public Interest, 65 Harv. L. Rev. 319 (1951).

16. *See* Donaldson v. United States, 400 U.S. 517, 91 S.Ct. 534, 27 L.Ed.2d 580 (1971); Keith v. Daley, 764 F.2d 1265 (7th Cir.1985). On standing, *see, e.g.,* United States v. SCRAP, 412 U.S. 669, 93 S.Ct. 2405, 37 L.Ed.2d 254 (1973); J. Vining, Legal Identity (1978).

be relevant: a newspaper has a sufficient interest to challenge an order sealing court documents, even though it would not be allowed to intervene to dispute the merits of the underlying case.[17]

Drawing on recent caselaw tightening the requirements for a "case or controversy" that federal courts may constitutionally hear,[18] some (but not most) courts have held that an intervenor's "interest" must be substantial enough to meet the Constitutional standing tests, so that the intervenor would be able to assert its claim even if no action were already pending.[19] This makes some sense when the intervenor is in fact litigating an independent claim on its own, as the Supreme Court has held by dismissing an appeal brought by such an intervenor but not joined by any original party.[20] But when an intervenor simply participates in the resolution of claims already before the court, neither the language nor the purposes of Rule 24 support any requirement beyond possession of an affected "interest." Nor does the Constitution. There is already a valid case or controversy before the court. In fact, allowing appropriate intervenors to participate will advance rather than undermine the goals, found by the Supreme Court in the Constitution, of ensuring the concrete adversity that promotes sound decisions and avoiding judicial overreaching.[21] The evidence and argument that intervenors can present will further narrow and improve decision-making, and make less likely unconsidered impacts of court decisions on those who have not been heard.

Inadequate representation

Rule 24(a)'s third requirement—that the applicant's interest be inadequately represented by existing parties—also calls for a flexible judgment. Courts considering the adequacy of representation look at many factors: the overlap between the applicant's interests and those of persons already in the case, the resources and vigor of present parties, the ability of counsel, the number of parties already in the case, the likelihood that intervention will foster delay, and so forth. Sometimes, the court will allow an intervenor to participate in some issues but not in others, or will limit the intervenor's manner of participation by requiring leave of court before the intervenor can take a deposition. A court may also deny intervention but allow the prospective intervenor to submit written or oral argument as an *amicus curiae* (friend of the court), without the right to introduce evidence or to appeal.[22]

17. *E.g.,* Jessup v. Luther, 227 F.3d 993 (7th Cir.2000).

18. *See* § 2.26 *supra.*

19. *E.g.,* Mausolf v. Babbitt, 85 F.3d 1295 (8th Cir.1996). Contra, *e.g.,* Ruiz v. Estelle, 161 F.3d 814 (5th Cir.1998).

20. Diamond v. Charles, 476 U.S. 54, 106 S.Ct. 1697, 90 L.Ed.2d 48 (1986).

21. *E.g.,* Lujan v. Defenders of Wildlife, 504 U.S. 555, 112 S.Ct. 2130, 119 L.Ed.2d 351 (1992).

22. Shapiro, Some Thoughts on Intervention Before Courts, Agencies, and Arbitrators, 81 Harv. L. Rev. 721, 752–756 (1968).

Public law litigation

The flexibility with which courts treat intervention, and their willingness to allow it, are especially marked in litigation involving group interests and "public" question.[23] Because such litigation affects many people, and because judges often have much discretion in shaping remedies, it is important that those affected have a voice in the proceedings. Moreover, if affected groups are not allowed to intervene, they may bring independent suits to relitigate and undermine the court's remedy.[24] Judges must, however, control intervention to prevent unwieldy multiplication of parties and issues, participation by intervenors unwilling or unable to cooperate in the expedition of the case, and collateral quarrels among parties.

Examples

Three cases illustrate the circumstances in which courts have allowed intervention as of right. In *Atlantis Development Corp. v. United States*[25] the government sought to enjoin a claimant to an offshore submerged island from occupying and developing the island, contending that the island was within the government's domain. Another claimant to the island, whose claim was hostile to both the government and the rival private claimant, sought to intervene. The court allowed the intervention under Rule 24(a) on the ground that the determination of the complex legal issue concerning dominion over the island, while not binding in a res judicata sense on the intervenor, would as a practical matter probably be dispositive of the same issue as it might arise in intervenor's dispute with the government. In *Trbovich v. United Mine Workers*[26] a union member opposed to the elected leadership of a union was held entitled to intervene in an action by the Secretary of Labor to set aside the election of the union officers. And in *Cascade Natural Gas Corp. v. El Paso Natural Gas Co.*[27] a state was permitted to intervene in the hearing on a decree of divestiture following an antitrust action against the supplier of natural gas to various users in that state. Although intervention as of right was recognized in all these instances, it should not be inferred that the right is broadly construed or granted. The tradition that the plaintiff ordinarily has the privilege of defining the shape of the action is still strong, particularly in state courts.[28]

23. Yeazell, Intervention and the Idea of Litigation: A Commentary on the *Los Angeles School* Case, 25 UCLA L. Rev. 244 (1978); Symposium, Problems of Intervention in Public Law Litigation, 13 U.C. Davis L. Rev. 211 (1980).

24. *See* Martin v. Wilks, 490 U.S. 755, 109 S.Ct. 2180, 104 L.Ed.2d 835 (1989)(*see* § 11.27 *infra*); Rivarde v. Missouri, 930 F.2d 641 (8th Cir.1991).

25. 379 F.2d 818 (5th Cir.1967).

26. 404 U.S. 528, 92 S.Ct. 630, 30 L.Ed.2d 686 (1972).

27. 386 U.S. 129, 87 S.Ct. 932, 17 L.Ed.2d 814 (1967). *See* Note, Private Participation in Department of Justice Antitrust Proceedings, 39 U. Chi. L. Rev. 143 (1971); *cf.* 15 U.S.C. 16(b) (public notice of proposed antitrust consent decree).

28. *See, e.g.,* Kenny v. George A. Fuller Co., 84 A.D.2d 808, 443 N.Y.S.2d 957 (1981); Estate of Vanderbilt, 109 Misc.2d

Intervention as of right compared

Three other observations can be made concerning intervention as of right. First, its criteria are different in degree rather than kind from those governing intervention on permission of the court. In pragmatic terms, this means that the matter is one of relative urgency and that the appellate court can substitute its judgment for that of the trial court if it regards the urgency as great enough to warrant a determination that intervention should be allowed as of right.[29] Those seeking to intervene usually seek both kinds of intervention.

Second, intervention as of right has a wider scope of application than the necessary parties rule, even on the same set of facts, when the problem at issue is protection of the absentee's interests. When the necessary parties rule is applied in that context, it is the court or one of the existing parties that suggests the propriety of protecting the absentee's interests; in intervention, the *absentee* has shown sufficient concern to take the initiative in becoming a party, and his or her "vote" should count for something.

Federal jurisdiction

Third, in federal court intervention as of right has traditionally been considered ancillary to the main action so that such intervenors need not establish an independent basis of jurisdiction. In permissive intervention, considered below, intervenors have had to show an independent jurisdictional basis.[30] The passage of the supplemental jurisdiction statute has changed but not simplified these rules. Apparently, in all but one situation supplemental jurisdiction now extends to all interventions, whether permissive or as of right, that "are so related to claims in the action ... that they form part of the same case or controversy under Article III of the ... Constitution," which is presumably the case when they arise out of the same nucleus of operative fact.[31]

The one exception is that supplemental jurisdiction does not reach any claim of one who intervenes as a *plaintiff* in a diversity action. This exception is meant to prevent parties from evading the requirement of

914, 441 N.Y.S.2d 153 (1981). The attitude in some states favors intervention. *See, e.g.,* Fireman's Fund Ins. Co. v. Gerlach, 56 Cal. App.3d 299, 128 Cal.Rptr. 396 (1976); Sanders v. Pacific Gas & Elec. Co., 53 Cal.App.3d 661, 126 Cal.Rptr. 415 (1975).

29. Shreve, Questioning Intervention of Right—Toward a New Methodology of Decisionmaking, 74 Nw. U.L. Rev. 894 (1980).

30. 7A Wright and Miller, Federal Practice and Procedure § 1917; Kennedy, Let's All Join In: Intervention Under Federal Rule 24, 57 Ky. L.J. 329, 362–363 (1968); Fraser, Ancillary Jurisdiction of Federal Courts of Persons Whose Interest May Be Impaired, 62 F.R.D. 483 (1974). *See, e.g.,* Gaines v. Dixie Carriers, Inc., 434 F.2d 52 (5th Cir.1970); *cf.* Moosehead Sanitary Dist. v. S. G. Phillips Corp., 610 F.2d 49 (1st Cir.1979); Blake v. Pallan, 554 F.2d 947 (9th Cir.1977) (independent grounds for jurisdiction required under Rule 24(b)).

31. 28 U.S.C. § 1367; *see* United Mine Workers v. Gibbs, 383 U.S. 715, 86 S.Ct. 1130, 16 L.Ed.2d 218 (1966); McLaughlin, The Federal Supplemental Jurisdiction Statute–A Constitutional and Statutory Analysis, 24 Ariz. St. L.J. 849, 929–31, 958–70 (1992).

complete diversity by asserting their claims through intervention.[32] It does not bar intervention in a diversity case when the intervenor is a defendant, or can be reclassified as such, or asserts a claim with an independent basis of federal subject matter jurisdiction, or perhaps if the intervenor seeks no relief for itself and can be said to assert no claim at all.[33]

Permissive intervention

Rule 24(b) provides for permissive intervention when a federal statute confers a conditional right to intervene or "when an applicant's claim or defense and the main action have a question of law or fact in common." The Rule also provides for intervention by a federal or state government "officer or agency" when a statute or regulation administered by that officer or agency is brought into question. The general test for permissive intervention is similar to that for permissive joinder of parties.[34] The trial court's discretion is necessarily broad in administering Rule 24(b), which lays down only one specific caveat for its exercise—that the court "shall consider whether the intervention will unduly delay or prejudice the adjudication of the rights of the original parties."

Timeliness

Intervention either as of right or by permission must be "timely." This term is not specifically defined, so there is room for judicial discretion in passing on questions of timeliness even when intervention is otherwise as of right.[35] Judges consider the harm of denying intervention to the prospective intervenor, any harm to the existing parties from the delay in seeking intervention, and the intervenor's reasons for not seeking intervention earlier. Sometimes intervention becomes appropriate only after the action has proceeded in its development[36]—for example, when a court hearing a legislative reapportionment case receives a proposed reapportionment plan that an intervening group believes would improperly dilute its own votes.

Appeals

An order allowing intervention is not final, and therefore not appealable, until the end of the action.[37] When intervention is sought as

32. 28 U.S.C. § 1367(b); Rowe, 1367 and All That: Recodifying Federal Supplemental Jurisdiction, 74 Ind. L.J. 53 (1998); Freer, Toward a Principled Statutory Approach to Supplemental Jurisdiction in Diversity of Citizenship Cases, 74 Ind. L.J. 5 (1998); see Owen Equipment & Erection Co. v. Kroger, 437 U.S. 365, 98 S.Ct. 2396, 57 L.Ed.2d 274 (1978).

33. Development Finance Corp. v. Sower, 54 F.3d 156 (3d Cir.1995); EEOC v. National Children's Center, Inc., 146 F.3d 1042 (D.C.Cir.1998).

34. *See* Fed. R. Civ. P. 20(a).

35. *Compare* Sokaogon Chippewa Community v. Babbitt, 214 F.3d 941 (7th Cir. 2000) *with* Ruiz v. Estelle, 161 F.3d 814 (5th Cir.1998). *See* Annot., 37 A.L.R.2d 1306.

36. *See* Smuck v. Hobson, 408 F.2d 175 (D.C.Cir.1969)(intervention after judgment so intervenor could appeal); EEOC v. National Children's Center, Inc., note 33 *supra*.

37. *See* 7A Wright and Miller, Federal Practice and Procedure § 1923.

of right, however, an order denying intervention is appealable as a final order.[38] Thus, if the court's discretion is invoked by an application for permissive intervention, it will seldom be possible to get a review of the exercise of that discretion in time for practical effect.

§ 10.18 Impleader

Impleader is a procedural device enabling a defendant to bring into an action a new party who is asserted to be liable to defendant for all or part of the plaintiff's claim.[1] Impleader (also called third-party practice) thus allows defendant to claim against the impleaded third-party defendant any amount for which he or she may be found liable to the plaintiff; it does not permit a defendant to bring in someone he or she contends is actually the one liable to the plaintiff. Impleader is also available to a plaintiff against whom a counterclaim has been asserted.[2]

Indemnity or contribution

Like the other joinder devices under discussion, impleader is aimed at settling in a single lawsuit as many aspects of a controversy as possible. And again, as in the case of other joinder rules, protection against undue trial confusion and prejudice is afforded by judicial discretion to order separate trials of issues rather than by arbitrary limitations on the dimensions of actions. Typical situations covered by impleader are those in which the original defendant, called the "third-party plaintiff" in the Federal Rules, is entitled to indemnity from a third party against loss or liability on account of plaintiff's claim (for example, because the original defendant sold the plaintiff a defective product manufactured by the third party), or is entitled to contribution with respect to it (for

38. *See, e.g.,* Cascade Natural Gas Corp. v. El Paso Natural Gas Co., 386 U.S. 129, 87 S.Ct. 932, 17 L.Ed.2d 814 (1967). In the federal system and apparently in most states, an order denying application for permissive intervention is not appealable. *See* Annot., 15 A.L.R.2d 336; note 11 *supra.* This results in the appealability of the order being dependent on the correctness of the trial judge's decision, which is anomalous, to say the least. *See* Levin v. Ruby Trading Corp., 333 F.2d 592 (2d Cir.1964). It has been suggested that all denials should be reviewable, much as the dismissal of a party's only claim in an action would be appealable. *See* 7A Wright and Miller, Federal Practice and Procedure § 1923.

§ 10.18

1. *See generally,* Clark, Code Pleading § 64 (2d ed. 1947); Ciolino and Roberts, The Missing Direct–Tender Option in Federal Third–Party Practice: A Procedural and Jurisdictional Analysis, 68 N.C.L. Rev. 423 (1990); Feirich, Third Party Practice, 1967 Ill. L.F. 236; Freer, Avoiding Duplicative Litigation: Rethinking Plaintiff Autonomy and the Court's Rule in Defining the Litigative Unit, 50 U. Pitt. L. Rev. 809 (1989); Note, Rule 14: Federal Third–Party Practice, 58 Colum. L. Rev. 532 (1958); Note, Developments in the Law: Multiparty Litigation in the Federal Courts, 71 Harv. L. Rev. 874, 906–912 (1958). *See also* Degnan and Barton, Vouching to Quality Warranty: Case Law and Commercial Code, 51 Calif. L. Rev. 471 (1963); Restatement (Second) of Judgments § 57.

2. Fed. R. Civ. P. 14(b).

example, because the original defendant and the third party worked together to injure the plaintiff). Such rights, whether created by contract or imposed by law, are matters of substantive law.

Rationale and history

Impleader does not create any such substantive right;[3] it is simply an expeditious way to implement the right in the action in which the original defendant's own liabilities are being determined. In this way it avoids multiplicity of actions, and it assures consistency in the determination of issues common to the main claim and the defendant's third-party claim.[4] A defendant otherwise might be held liable to the original plaintiff but fail in a suit against an indemnitor or contributor who successfully contended that the original suit was wrongly decided.

The early codes had no provision for impleader.[5] Later, some codes adopted provisions for bringing in a party who is or will be liable to a defendant,[6] but some of these, notably the New York statute, were narrowly construed.[7] Federal Rule 14 provides broadly that the defendant may bring in a party who "is or may be liable to the third-party plaintiff for all or part of the plaintiff's claim against the third-party plaintiff." There is no requirement that plaintiff have a claim against the third party.

Standards

Several requirements must be met for impleader: (1) The third-party defendant must be liable to the party seeking impleader rather than to the plaintiff;[8] (2) the liability must be for losses suffered by the defendant as a result of plaintiff's claim, not some unrelated liability;[9] and (3) the claim must arise from the same "transaction or occurrence" as the

3. 3 Moore, Federal Practice and Procedure ¶ 14.03.

4. In some situations the common law afforded protection to the original defendant against inconsistency of result. The original defendant might vouch in a person who would be liable to defendant for plaintiff's claim against him or her by giving the third person timely notice of the suit and offering to let him or her conduct its defense. The third person would then be bound by the adjudication of defendant's liability to plaintiff, whether the invitation to conduct the suit was accepted or rejected. A second action might be needed, however, to determine any question about the third party's duty to make indemnity. This practice originated as "vouching to warranty," but it came to be extended to other bases for indemnity. 1 Freeman, Judgments § 454 (5th ed. 1925); 3 Moore, Federal Practice and Procedure ¶ 14.02(1). This device is still available and may be useful today when the third person is beyond reach of the court's process so that impleader is impossible. *See* § 11.30 *infra*; Degnan and Barton, Vouching to Quality Warranty: Case Law and Commercial Code, 51 Calif. L. Rev. 471 (1963). *But see* Comment, Due Process Constraints on Vouching as a Device to Bind Non-parties, 14 Colum. J.L. & Soc. Probs. 189 (1978).

5. Clark, Code Pleading 409 (2d ed. 1947).

6. *Id.* at 410.

7. *Id.* at 411–413.

8. Coleman Clinic v. Massachusetts Mut. Life Ins. Co., 698 F.Supp. 740 (C.D.Ill. 1988).

9. Forum Ins. Co. v. Ranger Ins. Co., 711 F.Supp. 909 (N.D.Ill.1989); National Union Fire Ins. Co. v. Deloach, 708 F.Supp. 1371 (S.D.N.Y.1989).

underlying cause of action.[10] Hence, impleader enforces derivative liability on the part of the person who is impleaded. Impleader under Rule 14 is permissive rather than compulsory, but in some states a claim for such derivative liability will be barred unless asserted by defendant in the original action.

When Rule 14 requires that the third-party defendant "may be liable to the third-party plaintiff for all or part of the plaintiff's claim against the third-party plaintiff," it means that the third-party plaintiff's loss arises from the plaintiff's claim. The rule drops the requirement, imposed under the codes, that there be identity of legal theory between the plaintiff's claim and the defendant's claim against the third party. Nor is complete identity of facts required. Thus, the main claim may be predicted on negligence, the third-party claim on an insurance policy or contract for indemnity.[11] Or, the main claim may be one by a sailor against the ship's master on the latter's strict duty to afford care, cure, and maintenance during disability, while the third-party claim is on the party's common law negligence in causing the sailor's disability.[12] Once a valid third-party claim has been asserted, however, the third-party plaintiff may join with it any other claims against the third-party defendant, provided that if the case is in federal court original or supplemental jurisdiction exists over those claims.[13]

The third-party claim need not be "mature"—that is, there need not be a judgment against the original defendant before the impleader claim can be maintained. Indeed, the typical impleader claim today is conditional: *If* defendant is held liable to plaintiff, *then* the third-party defendant is liable to the defendant/third-party plaintiff.[14]

Substantive right to recovery

Determining whether a defendant may implead a third-party defendant often requires consideration of whether the substantive law gives the defendant a right to recovery, for example under a contribution theory. The common law did not give a right of contribution among tortfeasors who were jointly and severally liable for a plaintiff's injury;[15] where no such right exists under the applicable substantive law, there is no basis for one tortfeasor, sued alone, to implead others.[16] The common law rule has, however, been changed in many states by statute or judicial decision.[17] In some states, however, a defendant may secure contribution

10. Stewart v. American Intl. Oil & Gas Co., 845 F.2d 196 (9th Cir.1988); United States v. One 1977 Mercedes Benz, 708 F.2d 444 (9th Cir.1983).

11. *See, e.g.,* Kirk v. Arc S.S. Co., 21 F.R.D. 293 (S.D.N.Y.1958).

12. *See, e.g.,* Jones v. Waterman S.S. Corp., 155 F.2d 992 (3d Cir.1946).

13. Fed. R. Civ. P. 18(a).

14. *See* Glens Falls Indem. Co. v. United States, 229 F.2d 370 (9th Cir.1955).

15. 1 Harper, James, and Gray, Law of Torts § 10.2 (2d ed. 1986).

16. Roth v. Greyhound Corp., 149 F.Supp. 454 (E.D.Pa.1957).

17. 1 Harper, James, and Gray, Law of Torts § 10.2 (2d ed. 1986).

only if the plaintiff chose to sue both (or all) the tortfeasors and secured a judgment against more than one, and the defendant seeking contribution paid more than his or her share of the judgment. Under this type of statute, impleader may not be had in either the state[18] or federal court.[19] But when the right to contribution is made to arise out of the common liability itself, impleader is available.[20]

Preventing harm

The possibilities of prejudice to the third party and to the plaintiff must be weighed against the benefits of impleader. The Federal Rules guard against possible prejudice to the third party by (1) allowing the third party to plead any defenses that defendant might have against plaintiff's claim[21] and to participate fully in defending against it, and (2) providing for separate trial of any separate issues of the third-party claim if needed to prevent undue confusion or prejudice.[22] Possible prejudice to the plaintiff may take the form of delay or confusion of issues, or both. The additional delay is usually not great, and the very adoption of impleader implies that the routine delay it ordinarily entails is outweighed by other factors. Confusion can be prevented by separate trial of issues if the threat is sufficiently serious.

Jurisdictional problems

Use of impleader can be restricted by jurisdictional requirements. In many cases the defendant can sue the third party in the same court as that in which plaintiff brought the original action; when that is so, no jurisdictional questions arise. Such questions do arise, however, when the defendant cannot sue the third party in that court because requirements of venue, jurisdiction, or service of process are not satisfied. The requirement of personal jurisdiction over the third-party defendant must be met for impleader just as for an independent action.[23] The prevailing interpretation of the federal venue rule is that if venue is properly established for the original action, the third-party defendant cannot

18. Fox v. Western N.Y. Motor Lines, 257 N.Y. 305, 178 N.E. 289, 78 A.L.R. 578 (1931).

19. Brown v. Cranston, 132 F.2d 631 (2d Cir.1942), *cert. denied,* 319 U.S. 741, 63 S.Ct. 1028, 87 L.Ed. 1698 (1943).

20. *See, e.g.,* Bosin v. Minneapolis, St. P. & S. Ste. M.R.R., 183 F.Supp. 820 (E.D.Wis.1960).

21. *See* Fed. R. Civ. P. 14(a).

22. *Id.*; Fed. R. Civ. P. 42(b).

23. Hook v. Hook & Ackerman, 89 F.Supp. 238 (W.D.Pa.1950), *modified on other grounds,* 187 F.2d 52 (3d Cir.1951); Gore v. United States, 171 F.Supp. 136 (D.Mass.1959); 3 Moore, Federal Practice and Procedure ¶ 14.28[1]. However the requirement was slightly relaxed for federal courts by a 1963 amendment of the Federal Rules applicable to impleader and the bringing in of parties under Rules 13(h) and 19. This provides for service outside of the state (but within the United States) "at all places" within 100 miles from the place where the action is commenced or to which it is transferred or assigned for trial. Fed. R. Civ. P. 4(f). This does no more than draw the sting from one arbitrary limit on territorial jurisdiction.

object that venue would have been improper if the action had originally included him or her as a defendant.[24]

In federal courts an impleader claim is within supplemental subject matter jurisdiction.[25] This permits a federal court to entertain an impleader claim even though there is no independent basis for diversity jurisdiction. Thus, the impleader claim may be asserted against a third-party defendant even though that party is a co-citizen of the original defendant; further, the third-party defendant's being co-citizen of the plaintiff does not destroy the diversity established in the original action. In a federal court action in which jurisdiction is based solely on diversity, however, the plaintiff cannot amend the complaint to assert a claim directly against the third-party defendant unless there is diversity of citizenship between them.[26] The third-party defendant, however, may rely on supplemental jurisdiction in asserting cross-claims or counterclaims or in impleading fourth-party defendants, provided that the new claims arise out of the same nucleus of operative facts.[27]

§ 10.19 Interpleader

A stakeholder facing inconsistent claims asserted on the same thing or obligation can use interpleader to bring all the adverse claimants into a single action so that the rights of all parties may be determined. The stakeholder might, for example, be a bank facing two persons claiming the same account, or an insurer facing two persons claiming life insurance benefits under the same policy.[1] An action for this purpose may be initiated by the stakeholder, or interpleader may be set up through a counterclaim to an action brought against the stakeholder by a claimant, with other claimants brought in to respond to the counterclaim.[2] Interpleader thus seeks to avoid double or multiple litigation of the same basic controversy[3] and, like impleader, affords protection against incon-

24. *See, e.g.*, United States v. Acord, 209 F.2d 709 (10th Cir.1954).

25. 6 Wright and Miller, Federal Practice and Procedure § 1444.

26. 28 U.S.C. § 1367(b); Owen Equip. Co. v. Kroger, 437 U.S. 365, 98 S.Ct. 2396, 57 L.Ed.2d 274 (1978).

27. Viacom Int'l, Inc. v. Kearney, 212 F.3d 721 (2d Cir.2000); Northbrook Nat. Ins. Co. v. J & R Vending Corp., 167 F.R.D. 643 (E.D.N.Y.1996).

§ 10.19

1. *E.g.*, State Farm Fire & Cas. Co. v. Tashire, 386 U.S. 523, 87 S.Ct. 1199, 18 L.Ed.2d 270 (1967)(liability insurer holding sum against which many injured persons could claim); New York Life Ins. Co. v. Deshotel, 142 F.3d 873 (5th Cir.1998)(two persons claimed life insurance policy proceeds); Cohen v. Republic of the Philippines, 146 F.R.D. 90 (S.D.N.Y.1993)(art dealer seeking to resolve dispute about ownership of paintings).

2. *See generally* 7 Wright, Miller and Kane, Federal Practice and Procedure §§ 1701–22; Clark, Code Pleading § 66 (2d ed. 1947); Hazard and Moskovitz, An Historical and Critical Analysis of Interpleader, 52 Calif. L. Rev. 706 (1964); Ilsen and Sardell, Interpleader in the Federal Courts, 35 St. John's L. Rev. 1 (1960); Note, Developments in the Law: Multiparty Litigation in the Federal Courts, 71 Harv. L. Rev. 874, 913–928 (1958).

3. *See* Illinois Employers Ins. Co. v. Mihalcik, 801 F.2d 949 (7th Cir.1986).

sistency of results that might impose unfair liability.[4]

Although interpleader had ancient common law roots, these have withered, and the procedure has come to modern times largely as developed by equity. The potentially great usefulness of interpleader was impeded for years, however, by restrictions imposed by two sources—equity jurisprudence and the rules of jurisdiction and venue.

Equitable interpleader

The restrictions developed by equity were usually stated as follows: (1) The same thing, debt, or duty must be claimed by all of the parties against whom relief is demanded; (2) all their adverse titles or claims must be derived from a common source; (3) the person claiming relief by way of interpleader must not have or claim any interest in the subject matter; and (4) the stakeholder must have incurred no independent liability to any of the claimants.[5] These rules often thwarted the remedy.[6]

The fourfold restrictions were not so rigorously applied if the proceeding was characterized as a "bill in the nature of interpleader," but there was hopeless confusion over the difference between such a bill and one for "true" or "strict" interpleader. In fact, there was no difference except in whether these restrictions should or should not be applied.[7] Today, none of these restrictions ought to apply. Interpleader may be brought if the stakeholder has an obligation, acknowledged or contested, that two or more rival claimants threaten to enforce on bases that may subject the stakeholder to double liability for the same obligation.

Jurisdiction over claimants

Restrictions imposed by the rules of jurisdiction severely limited use of interpleader in interstate transactions. When the thing in controversy was realty or tangible personalty, a court having jurisdiction over the res could determine interests in it on notice to claimants without the need for service of process on them within the court's territorial jurisdiction.[8] But when the stakeholder owed, or was asserted to owe, a debt claimed by adverse claimants, the Supreme Court in a leading case in 1917 refused to treat the debt as a res or quasi-res to warrant obtaining

4. In the case of impleader, defendant is threatened with the inconsistency of (1) being held liable to the plaintiff and (2) being unable to hold his or her own indemnitor because of inability to prove in the second action that there was a proper basis for liability in the first suit. *Compare* Restatement (Second) of Judgments § 57.

5. *See* Hazard and Moskovitz, An Historical and Critical Analysis of Interpleader, 52 Calif. L. Rev. 706 (1964), for analysis and critique of the origins of these limitations.

6. Clark, Code Pleading 428–429 (2d ed. 1947). *See, e.g.,* Local Fed. Sav. & Loan Assn. v. Carlock, 194 Okla. 199, 148 P.2d 466 (1944).

7. Hazard and Moskovitz, *supra* note 5.

8. *See* § 2.4 *supra. But see* Shaffer v. Heitner, 433 U.S. 186, 97 S.Ct. 2569, 53 L.Ed.2d 683 (1977).

jurisdiction over the claimants by notice only.[9] The Court held that the claimants' claims could not validly be determined unless they were brought into suit by service of process within a court's jurisdiction.

This meant that if the claimants of money due under an insurance policy live in different states (as they often do), a state court ordinarily would be impotent to grant effective relief since no state can get service on all claimants. The insurance company, however, is usually answerable to suit in each state where a claimant lives so that it is vulnerable to separate suits, which increases the possibility of double liability.[10]

It seems very doubtful that the Supreme Court today would adhere to this interpretation of the jurisdictional problems in interpleader. In any event, one way to handle the problem is to expand the diversity jurisdiction of the federal courts to deal specially with interpleader. Whatever the virtues of diversity jurisdiction in areas of litigation that the states can handle, diversity jurisdiction is at its best where the state courts cannot fill the legitimate needs of suitors and the federal courts can do so. The process of a federal court can by statute be made to reach beyond state lines. Moreover, although general diversity jurisdiction has required complete diversity, this is a statutory rather than a constitutional limitation.[11] Although today venue may be laid in a district in which a substantial part of the property that is the subject of the action is situated, venue provisions were formally much less accommodating.[12]

Federal Interpleader Act

With these difficulties in mind, Congress relieved the situation by enacting a succession of interpleader acts beginning in 1917 and culminating in the Federal Interpleader Act of 1936, the provisions of which were somewhat modified by the Judicial Code Revision Act of 1948.[13] "Statutory interpleader," as it is called, has relaxed the diversity jurisdiction requirement so that there need be diversity of citizenship between only two claimants. If that diversity exists, then the citizenship of the plaintiff-stakeholder and of other claimants is immaterial.[14] For

9. New York Life Ins. Co. v. Dunlevy, 241 U.S. 518, 36 S.Ct. 613, 60 L.Ed. 1140 (1916).

10. *See* Klaber v. Maryland Cas Co., 69 F.2d 934, 937 (8th Cir.1934); Csohan v. United Benefit Life Ins. Co., 33 O.O.2d 36, 200 N.E.2d 345 (1964). For interpleader in state courts, *see, e.g.,* Calif. Code Civ. P. §§ 386, 386.1, 386.5, 385.6; N.Y.C.P.L.R. 1006, 2701, 2702.

11. 3A Moore, Federal Practice and Procedure ¶ 22.04(2).

12. *Id.*; 28 U.S.C. § 1391(a)(2), (b)(2).

13. 28 U.S.C. §§ 1335 (jurisdiction), 1397 (venue), 2361 (service of process). The Federal Interpleader Act was chiefly the result of unrelenting advocacy by Professor Chafee. *See* Modernizing Interpleader, 30 Yale L.J. 814 (1921); Interstate Interpleader, 33 Yale L.J. 685 (1924); Interpleader in the United States Courts, 41 Yale L.J. 1134, 42 Yale L.J. 41 (1932); The Federal Interpleader Act of 1936, 45 Yale L.J. 963, 1161 (1940); Federal Interpleader Since the Act of 1936, 49 Yale L.J. 377 (1940); Broadening the Second Stage of Interpleader, 56 Harv. L. Rev. 541, 929 (1943).

14. State Farm Fire & Casualty Co. v. Tashire, 386 U.S. 523, 87 S.Ct. 1199, 18 L.Ed.2d 270 (1967). *See also* the excellent analysis in Pan Am. Fire & Casualty Co. v. Revere, 188 F.Supp. 474 (E.D.La.1960).

example, an Ohio insurer holding funds claimed by three Ohio citizens and one from Texas may institute a federal interpleader action because one claimant is Texan and another is from Ohio.

The statute also modifies the jurisdictional amount—the amount involved need exceed only $500[15]—and provides that process under the statute reaches throughout the land.[16] Venue may be laid in the district where any claimant resides.[17]

Federal Rule 22

In addition to statutory interpleader, in federal court there may be "rules interpleader." This refers to the interpleader joinder provision in Federal Rule 22, which has a counterpart in almost all state procedural systems. Rule 22 provides that a person who "is or may be exposed to double or multiple liability" through conflicting claims may bring suit against the competing claimants and require them to assert their claims against each other to ensure a consistent determination. Rule 22 abrogates the fourfold restrictions that had grown on the old equitable remedy.

Significant limitations in employing Rule 22 interpleader arise, however, in its use in federal court. Rule 22 can be used just as any of the federal joinder devices can be used, subject only to the usual jurisdictional, venue, and process limitations on the federal courts.[18] Thus, in rules interpleader in a diversity case, (1) the amount in controversy must exceed $75,000;[19] (2) complete diversity must exist between the plaintiff on the one hand and all the claimants on the other;[20] (3) the action must be brought in a state where all the defendants reside or where a substantial part of the events giving rise to the claim occurred;[21] and (4) the defendants must be subject to service of process under the provisions of Federal Rule 4, meaning that they can be served personally within the state or through an applicable "long arm" process provision.[22]

Conduct of interpleader litigation

Both statutory and Rule 22 interpleader involve two stages: a determination of the stakeholder's right to interplead, and the resolution of the claims to the property or debt. If the stakeholder is entirely

15. 28 U.S.C. § 1335(a).

16. 28 U.S.C. § 2361. When a proceeding involving all the claimants can be maintained in state court with jurisdiction over all parties, a federal court could properly refuse to exercise interpleader jurisdiction. *See* NYLife Distributors v. Adherence Group, 72 F.3d 371 (3d Cir.1995); Zellen v. Second New Haven Bank, 454 F.Supp. 1359 (D.Conn.1978); Comment, Deference to State Courts in Federal Interpleader Actions, 47 U. Chi. L. Rev. 824 (1980).

17. 28 U.S.C. § 1397.

18. *See* 7 Wright and Miller, Federal Practice and Procedure §§ 1710–1712. For an example of interpleader in a federal question case, *see* Aetna Life Ins. Co. v. Bayona, 223 F.3d 1030 (9th Cir.2000).

19. 28 U.S.C. § 1332(a).

20. Hunter v. Federal Life Ins. Co., 111 F.2d 551 (8th Cir.1940).

21. 28 U.S.C. § 1391(a).

22. *See* § 2.6 *supra*.

indifferent toward the outcome of the second stage, making no claim to any interest in the subject matter, he or she is entitled to be discharged at the end of the first stage.[23] Thereafter the action becomes one in which the claimants fight out their claims among themselves. Alternatively, the stakeholder may participate in the second stage, disputing the claims of one or all of the claimants. Should a claimant seek relief in another court, the federal court hearing the interpleader action may enjoin the claimant from proceeding elsewhere.[24]

If stakeholders are sued by a claimant, they may counterclaim by way of interpleader either under the Act[25] or under the Rule.[26] In the latter case they may bring in additional parties under Rule 13(h) and, in so doing, are entitled to the benefits of the provision in Rule 4(f) for service outside the state but within 100 miles from the place in which the action is commenced or to which it is assigned or transferred for trial.

§ 10.20 Class Suit: Introduction

The class suit is an action by, or occasionally against, a group or class that sues or is sued through a representative, one who is a party on behalf of the group. The group must be too large to conveniently permit its members to be parties individually; above that minimum the class can include dozens or hundreds or thousands of members. The group can be defined by a bond existing independent of the litigation, such as employment by a common employer or residency in the same neighborhood; it also can be defined in terms of having suffered a common wrong that begets the litigation (for example, all persons suffering from pollution caused by a particular water polluter, or all persons defrauded in a common scheme). The basic idea is that one of the group represents all in litigating a claim that affects the group in some common way.

The antecedents of the class action date back through the equity procedure of the eighteenth and nineteenth centuries to the middle ages. The modern class suit evolved in the civil rights cases of the 1950s and 1960s and in the consumer movement of the 1960s and 1970s. The key legal development in this evolution was the 1966 revision of Federal Rule 23, which eliminated several technical constraints on the class action.

The complexity of class action law reflects, among other things, the different purposes for which class actions have been used. Although a complete survey of that law would require several volumes,[1] surveying the underlying purposes provides a key to the legal principles involved.

23. 3A Moore, Federal Practice and Procedure ¶ 22.14.

24. 28 U.S.C. § 2361; General Ry. Signal Co. v. Corcoran, 921 F.2d 700 (7th Cir.1991); Emcasco Ins. Co. v. Davis, 753 F.Supp. 1458 (D.Ark.1990).

25. *See, e.g.,* Walmac Co. v. Isaacs, 220 F.2d 108 (1st Cir.1955).

26. *See, e.g.,* Guy v. Citizens Fidelity Bank & Trust Co., 429 F.2d 828 (6th Cir. 1970).

§ 10.20

1. *See generally* Newberg and Conte, Newberg on Class Actions (3d ed. 1992).

Judicial economy

1. Although class actions are sometimes said to seek to promote efficiency by reducing multiple litigation, on the whole class actions seem more likely to increase litigation. They are often brought in situations in which each class member's claim is too small to support litigation by itself. When plaintiffs are able to bring independent suits, as in mass tort cases, they and their lawyers usually object to class action treatment. In such situations courts have often resorted to management methods other than recognizing a class action, such as transferring many cases to a district where a single judge can preside over pretrial proceedings.[2] In recent decades, however, class actions have been attempted with some success even in mass tort situations, so that the judicial economy rationale has acquired more foundation.[3]

Enabling litigation

2. A class action can provide access to the courts for a group of persons, none of whom could afford to sue separately. Civil rights and securities fraud class actions have often fulfilled this function.[4] When damages are sought, a plaintiff can finance the class action through the "common fund" doctrine, under which a plaintiff whose lawsuit creates a fund benefitting other people may recover litigating costs out of the fund.[5] In effect, this doctrine enables otherwise unorganized groups to pool their resources to litigate on a more equal footing with institutional litigants such as corporations and government agencies. Some regard this as equalization,[6] while others view it as ganging up to force defendants to settle rather than face bankruptcy.[7]

This pooling of resources is involuntary: The named plaintiff can in effect sign people up as class members (and the plaintiff's lawyer can

2. McGovern, Resolving Mature Mass Tort Litigation, 69 B.U.L. Rev. 527 (1989); Symposium, Claims Resolution Facilities and the Mass Settlement of Mass Torts, 53 L. & Contemp. Probs., No. 4 (Aut. 1990); Symposium, Mass Torts, 148 U. Pa. L. Rev. 1851 (2000).

3. Resnik, From "Cases" to "Litigation," 54 Law & Contemp. Probs. 5 (Summer 1991); Mullenix, Resolving Aggregate Mass Tort Litigation: The New Private Law Dispute Resolution Paradigm, 33 Val. Un. L. Rev. 413 (1999). For analyses that takes the efficiency goal seriously, see Sherman, Class Actions and Duplicative Litigation, 62 Ind. L.J. 507 (1986); Wasserman, Dueling Class Actions, 80 B.U. L. Rev. 461 (2000).

4. *See* Fed. R. Civ. P. 23(b)(2); Hensler, *et al.*, Class Action Dilemmas: Pursuing Public Interest for Private Gain 51–61 (2000); Fiss, The Civil Rights Injunction (1978).

5. Boeing Co. v. Van Gemert, 444 U.S. 472, 100 S.Ct. 745, 62 L.Ed.2d 676 (1980); Dawson, Lawyers and Involuntary Clients: Attorney Fees from Funds, 87 Harv. L. Rev. 1597 (1974); Silver, A Restitutionary Theory of Attorneys' Fees in Class Actions, 76 Cornell L. Rev. 656 (1991). Prevailing class action plaintiffs may also be able to recover their attorney's fees from defendants under statutes such as 42 U.S.C. § 1988. *See* § 1.23 *supra.*

6. *See* Galanter, Why the "Haves" Come Out Ahead: Speculations on the Limits of Legal Change, 9 Law & Socy. Rev. 95 (1974); Hay and Rosenberg, "Sweetheart" and "blackmail" Settlements in Class Actions: Reality and Remedy, 75 Notre Dame L. Rev. 1377 (2000).

7. In re Rhone–Poulenc Rorer, Inc., 51 F.3d 1293 (7th Cir.1995).

sign them up as clients) without consulting them, subject to a class member's right to opt out of certain class actions.[8] Sometimes the lawyer rather than the class members becomes the real motivating force behind the suit.[9] An entrepreneurial class action bar has developed in securities fraud litigation and other fields, serving in its members' opinion to keep the securities markets honest but regarded less hospitably by corporate executives.[10]

Providing a mass production remedy through a class action requires the court to surmount the administrative difficulties of providing relief for hundreds or thousands of people. To help administer the remedy, courts have used devices such as special masters and others, mail, periodical, and television notice to class members, and simplified, standardized claim procedures. In the process these devices often bend the substantive law they enforce. They also entail considerable expense, although less than would individual suits.[11]

Enforcing the law

3. Class actions enforce the law by requiring a violator to bear the costs it inflicts on a class of victims, costs it otherwise could avoid because each victim's injury is too small to warrant suit.[12] This function is achieved when the violator has to pay, even if most of the payment does not reach the victims because it goes to lawyers as fees or because individual damages are unascertainable. To deal with the latter problem, some courts approved a "floating recovery" benefitting members of a group that only roughly coincides with those the defendant injured. For example, one might remedy unlawful overpricing that injured past buyers by requiring the seller to cut prices on future sales.[13] Some criticize such remedies, contending that suits that do not result in meaningful relief to those injured should be brought by the government.[14] The rise of the class action starting in the 1960s reflected the

8. Fed. R. Civ. P. 23(c)(a).

9. Coffee, The Regulation of Entrepreneurial Litigation: Balancing Fairness and Efficiency in the Large Class Action, 54 U. Chi. L. Rev. 877 (1987).

10. Private Litigation Under the Federal Securities Laws: Hearings Before the Subcommittee on Securities of the U.S. Senate Committee on Banking, Housing, and Urban Affairs, 103d Cong., 1st Sess. (1993); Symposium, Class Actions at the Crossroads, 39 Ariz. L. Rev. 407 (1997).

11. Bartsh, A Class–Action Suit That Worked (1978); Hensler, *et al.*, Class Action Dilemmas: Pursuing Public Goals for Private Gain 425–66 (2000); Hazard, The Effect of the Class Action Device upon the Substantive Law, 58 F.R.D. 307 (1973); Wolfram, The Antibiotics Class Actions, 1976 Am. B. Found. Res. J. 251. *See* Basic Inc. v. Levinson, 485 U.S. 224, 108 S.Ct. 978, 99 L.Ed.2d 194 (1988) (upholding substantive legal theory in order to make class actions possible).

12. Kalven and Rosenfield, The Contemporary Function of the Class Suit, 8 U. Chi. L. Rev. 684 (1941); Note, The Cost–Internalization Case for Class Actions, 21 Stan. L. Rev. 383 (1969).

13. *See, e.g.,* State v. Levi Strauss & Co., 41 Cal.3d 460, 715 P.2d 564, 224 Cal. Rptr. 605 (1986).

14. *See, e.g.,* 15 U.S.C. § 15c (antitrust suits by state officials); Berry, Ending Substance's Indenture to Procedure: The Imperative for Comprehensive Revision of the Class Damage Action, 80 Colum. L. Rev. 299 (1980).

contrary view that government agencies cannot adequately enforce certain rights, but some are now similarly skeptical of class actions as well.[15]

Necessary parties

4. Some lawsuits, such as an institutional reform suit in a prison system or a desegregation suit in a public school system, necessarily affect many people. Such persons are, in effect, necessary parties[16] who cannot all be joined because they are too numerous. Providing for their inclusion in a class action[17] places a duty on the court and named plaintiff to protect the absent persons and encourages them to intervene or otherwise submit their views.

Suits by organizations

5. Finally, in some situations class actions perform their traditional function of permitting a suit by or against a group of people who constitute an organization that the law does not recognize as a legal entity.[18] Labor unions, for example, were formerly thus unrecognized in many jurisdictions, although that is no longer so.[19]

As this summary of class action purposes suggests, the modern class action transcends the traditional notion of litigation as a dispute between two persons in which one seeks from the other vindication of preexisting legal rights. Class actions, aside from involving many people, differ from such traditional disputes in many ways: flexibility of remedy, predominance of administrative problems, an expanded judicial role, lawyers who must strive to protect many clients whose interests may diverge, and a greater concern with litigation's effects on the real world.[20] Some of these characteristics will be explored below.

§ 10.21 Background

The class action is an American specialty. It has not been known in civil law systems, although some are striving to introduce group remedies into those systems. Class actions are possible in England and other common law systems but are brought only rarely, perhaps because of the more modest roles of the courts there as well as differing systems of financing litigation. Nevertheless, it is in England that the class action originated.[1]

15. Leubsdorf, Class Actions at the Cloverleaf, 39 Ariz. L. Rev. 453 (1997).

16. *See* §§ 10.11–10.15 *supra.*

17. Fed. R. Civ. P. 23(b)(1).

18. Yeazell, From Medieval Group Litigation to the Modern Class Action (1987); § 10.7 *supra.*

19. *E.g.,* Fed. R. Civ. P. 17(b); United Mine Workers v. Coronado Coal Co., 259 U.S. 344, 42 S.Ct. 570, 66 L.Ed. 975 (1922).

20. *See, e.g.,* Chayes, The Role of the Judge in Public Law Litigation, 89 Harv. L. Rev. 1281 (1976); Eisenberg and Yeazell, The Ordinary and the Extraordinary in Institutional Litigation, 93 Harv. L. Rev. 465 (1980); Feeley and Rubin, Judicial Policy Making and the Modern State: How the Courts Reformed America's Prisons (1998).

§ 10.21

1. Hazard, Gedid & Sowle, An Historical Analysis of the Binding Effect of Class Suits, 146 U. Pa. L. Rev. 1849 (1998); Cappalli & Consolo, Class Actions for Continental Europe, 6 Temple Int'l & Comp. L.J.

Necessary party problems

Although groups of people litigated in the medieval English courts,[2] the more recent class suit had origins in two doctrines of party joinder, the necessary party rule and the rule of permissive joinder of parties involved in the same transaction. The rule requiring joinder of necessary parties was difficult to administer when the set of necessary parties included a large number of individuals.[3] Special difficulty arose when the identity of those parties was indefinite, such as a group of the unborn heirs of a property owner.[4] In applying the necessary parties rule to such situations, the court of equity hit on the device of permitting a member of the class to "stand for" all the class members for purposes of the necessary parties rule. This meant that the action could go forward without individual joinder of all members of the group. The decisions were quite uncertain, however, on whether the unjoined members would be bound by the judgment if it should turn out to be adverse to the class. If the absent members were not bound by an adverse judgment, then declaring that the absentees were somehow parties would nevertheless accomplish two objectives: an escape from the rigor of the necessary parties rule, and the absentees' advantage of a *favorable* judgment, a boon otherwise unavailable under the then-existing rules of res judicata.[5]

Permissive joinder situations

The permissive joinder of numerous individuals through the class suit derived from the principle that equity would act regarding enforcement of legal rights to prevent a multiplicity of suits. Therefore, when it appeared that a large number of people had essentially identical claims or were subject to essentially identical obligations, a court of equity would permit an action by or against one or several of those involved to determine the claims of all in one proceeding.[6] A related use of the class suit involved suits by villagers against a landlord, members of a ship's

217 (1992); Bogart, Questioning Litigation's Role–Courts and Class Actions in Canada, 62 Ind. L.J. 665 (1987); Lindblom, Individual Litigation and Mass Justice: A Swedish Perspective on Group Actions in Civil Procedure, 45 Am. J. Comp. L. 805 (1997); Prichard, A Systematic Approach to Comparative Law: The Effect of Cost, Fee, and Financing Rules on the Development of the Substantive Law, 17 J. Leg. Stud. 451 (1988).

2. Yeazell, From Medieval Group Litigation to the Modern Class Action 132–196 (1987).

3. *See, e.g.,* Attorney General v. Wyburgh, 1 P. Wms. 559, 24 Eng. Rep. 534 (Ch. 1719); Anonymous, 2 Eq. Cas. Abr. 166 (no. 7), 22 Eng. Rep. 141 (Ch. 1709). *See also* Chafee, Some Problems of Equity 200–205 (1950).

4. *See* Roberts, Virtual Representation, 30 Ill. L. Rev. 580 (1936). For a modern judicial description of virtual representation, *see* Matthies v. Seymour Mfg. Co., 270 F.2d 365, 370–371 (2d Cir.1959), *cert. denied,* 361 U.S. 962, 80 S.Ct. 591, 4 L.Ed.2d 544 (1960). *See also* Restatement (Second) of Judgments § 41.

5. *See* Supreme Tribe of Ben Hur v. Cauble, 255 U.S. 356, 41 S.Ct. 338, 65 L.Ed. 673 (1921); Bigelow v. Old Dominion Copper Mining & Smelting Co., 225 U.S. 111, 32 S.Ct. 641, 56 L.Ed. 1009 (1912).

6. *See, e.g.,* Brown v. Vermuden, 1 Ch. Cas. 272, 22 Eng. Rep. 796 (1676); Mayor of York v. Pilkington, I Atk. 282, 26 Eng. Rep. 180 (1737).

crew against the owner, and shareholders in an enterprise against the managers.[7]

Binding the absentees

From the beginning, however, the equity courts were uncertain about the procedural and substantive fairness of the class suit. The procedural uncertainty was twofold: whether the suit could go forward without the absentees (a concern about joinder of necessary parties), and, if it did, whether the judgment ought to be binding on them. These two concerns worked in opposite directions. The suit could be made to go forward without actual joinder of the absentees if it was assured that they would be bound via the class representative. But the unfairness of determining an absentee's rights without his or her having a personal day in court or being represented by someone of his or her own choosing could be avoided only if it was assumed that the absentees would not be bound unless they individually became parties.

In the nineteenth century the courts tried to have it both ways on this key aspect of the class suit. In applying the joinder rules at the commencement of a class suit, the courts proceeded on the assumption that the class members were participants and, therefore, would be bound by the judgment.[8] When confronted by an absentee who claimed to have been unfairly foreclosed without his or her day in court, however, the courts often backed away, saying that an absentee was not bound until he or she joined individually.[9] (Naturally, no absentee would join a suit in which judgment had been entered adverse to the class.) As a result, the courts contradicted the doctrine that a class suit binds the absent class members—one of the central features of a class suit. Worse, this contradiction was not openly recognized, but was concealed in attempts to differentiate between class suits that were binding on absentees and those that were not. Courts attempted to draw a distinction between classes involving "joint" rights, or claims in a specific res, as against classes involving "common" or "several" rights.[10] The result was to obscure the basic doctrinal contradiction and generate confusion that has lasted to this day.[11]

7. *See* Yeazell, From Medieval Group Litigation to the Modern Class Action 132–196 (1987).

8. *See* Smith v. Swormstedt, 57 U.S. (16 How.) 288, 14 L.Ed. 942 (1853).

9. *Cf.* McArthur v. Scott, 113 U.S. 340, 5 S.Ct. 652, 28 L.Ed. 1015 (1885); Hazard, Gedid and Sowle, An Historical Analysis of the Binding Effect of Class Suits, 146 U. Pa. L. Rev. 1849 (1998).

10. *See* Moore and Cohn, Federal Class Actions, 32 Ill. L. Rev. 307, 555 (1938).

11. Fed. R. Civ. P. 23(b)(1), (2), and (3) differentiate "types" of class suits along lines roughly corresponding to the earlier differentiation. The distinctions have important procedural consequences, including the giving of notice and the right of class members to opt out. For an example of the difficulty involved in giving effect to these distinctions, *see* Johnson v. General Motors Corp., 598 F.2d 432 (5th Cir.1979).

The other uncertainty about class suits was of a more substantive character. The common law conception of legal status centered on the individual, as distinct from groups. As late as the early nineteenth century, groups long recognized as legal, such as corporations, were treated as associated individuals rather than as entities distinct from their individual members.[12] Yet treating the group as an entity had obvious convenience when all members had been wronged in the same way. The class suit made it possible for groups to engage in litigation as something like a legal entity, with the concomitant concentration of resources and purpose. At the same time, continued judicial anxiety about such formations was expressed through definitional limitations on the groupings that could constitute a class for class suit purposes.[13] Parallel concerns underlie modern treatment of certain types of class suits.[14]

Code class suit

The class suit sired by equity was taken over by the codes. The codes typically provided that "where the question is one of a common or general interest of many persons or where the persons who might be made parties are very numerous and it may be impracticable to bring them all before the court, one or more may sue or defend for the benefit of all."[15] Strictly interpreted, the code provision would make the class suit available in any litigation involving similar claims affecting a large number of claimants or defendants. But the courts' interpretations of the code provision on class suits generally perpetuated the limitations on class suits that had emerged in equity practice. Thus, the courts said that a group, as defined under the terms of the code, could prosecute a class action only if there was a "well-defined 'community of interest' " among the class members,[16] whatever that meant. In addition, the ambiguity about the binding effect of the judgment was not clarified in the decisions administering code class suits.[17]

Federal equity class suits

Concurrently in the code era of 1848 to 1938, the federal courts continued to employ the equity class suit under traditional equity procedure. The federal decisions concerning class suits in this period also perpetuated the ambiguity about the binding effect of a class suit

12. *See* Laski, The Personality of Associations, 29 Harv. L. Rev. 404 (1916); Horwitz, Santa Clara Revisited; The Development of Corporate Theory, 88 W. Va. L. Rev. 173 (1985).

13. *See, e.g.,* Weaver v. Pasadena Tournament of Roses, 32 Cal.2d 833, 198 P.2d 514 (1948); Yeazell, From Medieval Group Litigation to the Modern Class Action 220–228 (1987).

14. *See* Eisen v. Carlisle & Jacquelin, 417 U.S. 156, 94 S.Ct. 2140, 40 L.Ed.2d 732 (1974).

15. Clark, Code Pleading § 63 (2d ed. 1947).

16. Weaver v. Pasadena Tournament of Roses, 32 Cal.2d 833, 837, 198 P.2d 514, 517 (1948).

17. *See* Hansberry v. Lee, 311 U.S. 32, 61 S.Ct. 115, 85 L.Ed. 22 (1940).

judgment. Justice Story, analyzing the law in the early nineteenth century, found it very uncertain whether a class suit decree had binding effect.[18] The uncertainty in the nineteenth century case law was compounded by a curious combination of determinations by the U.S. Supreme Court. In 1842 the Court promulgated Equity Rules governing the procedure in federal courts. One of them, Rule 48, dealt with class suits. That Rule provided that when the parties were very numerous their joinder could be excused but that the "decree shall be without prejudice to the rights and claims of all the absent parties."[19] Only a decade later, however, in *Smith v. Swormstedt*[20] the Court passed on a federal court class suit case with language plainly implying that the absentees would be bound. The decisions in the federal courts thereafter were, understandably, in profound confusion.[21]

Hansberry v. Lee

Rule 48 (renumbered 38) was revised in 1912 to eliminate the proviso quoted above;[22] the change implied that absent class members would be bound by the judgment. Not long afterward, the Supreme Court squarely held that a class suit decree was binding on absentees, without referring to the character of the relationships among the class before it.[23] In *Hansberry v. Lee*[24] the Court reiterated that, in a state court class action, a decree could be binding on the absentees. The rationale in *Hansberry* referred not to the type of class involved but to the adequacy of representation. Recognizing that "[c]ourts are not infrequently called upon to proceed with causes in which the number of those interested in the litigation is so great as to make difficult or impossible the joinder of all,"[25] the Court said that there is a "failure of

18. Story, Commentaries on Equity Pleading 82–98 (3d ed. 1844).

19. Rule 48, 42 U.S. (1 How.) lxi (1842).

20. 57 U.S. (16 How.) 288, 14 L.Ed. 942 (1853).

21. *See* 1 Street, Federal Equity Practice 344–345 (1909). Street concluded that there were two types of class suits, "true" and "spurious." True class suits were those in which the absentees were bound; spurious class suits were those in which the absentees were nominally parties through representation but were not bound. In this analysis, Street correctly perceived that decisions conflicted over whether a class suit decree was binding. He did not appear to fully appreciate that one source of the conflict was the discrepancy between Rule 48 and Smith v. Swormstedt, *supra* note 20. The tripartite classification of class suits adopted by Professor Moore was derived by combining Story's classification of the cases, *see* note 18 *supra*, with Street's observation about the binding effect of decrees. *See* Moore and Cohn, Federal Class Actions, 32 Ill. L. Rev. 307, 310 n.25 (1937). *See generally* Hazard, Gedid and Sowle, An Historical Analysis of the Binding Effect of Class Suits, 146 U. Pa. L. Rev. 1849 (1998).

22. 226 U.S. 627, 659. *Compare* Rule 39 of the Federal Equity Rules (1912), *id.*

23. Supreme Tribe of Ben Hur v. Cauble, 255 U.S. 356, 41 S.Ct. 338, 65 L.Ed. 673 (1921). That is, the Court did not characterize the suit as "true," "hybrid," or "spurious." The claims in the case were in fact such that arguably they fit into any one of these categories. *See* text at § 10.22 notes 1–3 *infra*.

24. 311 U.S. 32, 61 S.Ct. 115, 85 L.Ed. 22 (1940). On this case's origins in the struggle against housing discrimination, *see* Kamp, The History Behind *Hansberry v. Lee*, 20 U.C. Davis L. Rev. 481 (1987).

25. 311 U.S. at 41, 61 S.Ct. at 118, 85 L.Ed. at 27.

due process only in those cases where it cannot be said that the procedure adopted fairly assures the protection of the interests of absent parties who are to be bound by it."[26] Central to this question was whether there were "potentially conflicting interests"[27] among the representatives and the absentees.

§ 10.22 Modern Suit

In 1938, when the Federal Rules were adopted, the law of class suits remained shrouded in uncertainty on two key issues: (1) the circumstances under which a member of a class could purport to sue or be sued as representative, beyond the fact that "the persons ... are very numerous," and (2) whether a judgment in a class suit was binding on members not made parties. These issues are not only technically complex and confusing but also practically very significant, for social and economic change has vastly expanded the number and kind of situations in which "numerous persons" might be exposed to the same legal occurrence. Unfortunately, the 1938 version of the federal class action rule added to the technical complexity and confusion.

Rule 23 in 1938

The Federal Rules departed from the typical code provision and adopted a tripartite classification based on an analysis done for the Rules Committee. The analysis suggested that such a classification was required by differences in the "jural relationships" among members of the class.[1] The classification, set forth in Rule 23(a) as promulgated in 1938, permitted class suits

> [w]hen the character of the right sought to be enforced for or against the class is
>
> (1) joint, or common, or secondary in the sense that the owner of a primary right refuses to enforce that right and a member of the class thereby becomes entitled to enforce it;
>
> (2) several, and the object of the action is the adjudication of claims which do or may affect specific property involved in the action; or
>
> (3) several, and there is a common question of law or fact affecting the several rights and a common relief is sought.

26. 311 U.S. at 42, 61 S.Ct. at 118, 85 L.Ed. at 27.

27. 311 U.S. at 44, 61 S.Ct. at 119, 85 L.Ed. at 28. On adequacy of representation and on the requirements for binding a class, *see* §§ 10.23, § 11.29 *infra;* Matsushita Electric Industrial Co. v. Epstein, 516 U.S. 367, 116 S.Ct. 873, 134 L.Ed.2d 6 (1996).

§ 10.22

1. Moore and Cohn, Federal Class Actions, 32 Ill. L. Rev. 307 (1937); Federal Class Actions—Jurisdiction and Effect of Judgment, 32 Ill. L. Rev. 555 (1938).

The suits defined by these classifications were dubbed the "true," the "hybrid," and the "spurious" class suits, respectively.[2] Different res judicata consequences were thought to follow, depending on the category in which a particular class suit was placed. If it was a "true" class suit, then all members of the class were bound; if it was a "hybrid" class suit, all members of the class were bound as to the disposition of the property involved; and if it was "spurious," the members were not bound by a judgment adverse to the class but could come in as intervenors, even after judgment, and thereby take advantage of a favorable judgment.[3] This analysis became authoritative to some extent because some courts applying Rule 23 assumed it was sound.[4] It was rejected, however, by several states in administering their class action rules[5] and by the Federal Rules Advisory Committee when it revised Rule 23 in 1966.[6]

1966 Revision

From the adoption of original Rule 23 in 1938 until the revision of the rule in 1966, the use of the class action, particularly in the federal courts, slowly expanded both in numbers and in the types of situation in which its use was permitted. In administering the rule, however, the courts had great difficulty applying the tripartite classification and determining the resultant binding effects on the absentees. To some extent, indeed, the use of the class suit was inhibited by that confusion. The 1966 revision of Rule 23 was designed to overcome these difficulties.[7] Although there have been many proposals for further revision,[8] only one of any significance has been adopted,[9] partly because class actions have become so important and controversial that no consensus for particular changes has emerged.

2. *See* 3B Moore, Federal Practice and Procedure ¶ 23.30; *compare* 7A Wright and Miller, Federal Practice and Procedure § 1789.

3. *See* Moore and Cohn, *supra* note 1.

4. *See, e.g.,* Nagler v. Admiral Corp., 248 F.2d 319, 327 (2d Cir.1957); All Am. Airways v. Elderd, 209 F.2d 247, 248–249 (2d Cir.1954); Pentland v. Dravo Corp., 152 F.2d 851 (3d Cir.1945); Note, Developments in the Law: Multiparty Litigation in the Federal Courts, 71 Harv. L. Rev. 874, 930 (1958).

5. *See* Hamburger, State Class Actions and the Federal Rule, 71 Colum. L. Rev. 609 (1971); Weinstein, Revision of Procedure: Some Problems in Class Actions, 9 Buffalo L. Rev. 433 (1960). *See also* the seminal article Kalven and Rosenfield, The Contemporary Function of the Class Suit, 8 U. Chi. L. Rev. 684 (1941); Chafee, Some Problems of Equity chs. 6, 7 (1950).

6. Advisory Committee Note, 39 F.R.D. 98, 106; Kaplan, Continuing Work of the Civil Committee: 1966 Amendments of the Federal Rules of Civil Procedure, I, 81 Harv. L. Rev. 356, 375 (1967).

7. *See* sources cited in note 6 *supra.*

8. Hensler, *et al.*, Class Action Dilemmas: Pursuing Public Goals for Private Gain 15–37, 51–65 (2000); Symposium, The Institute of Judicial Administration Research Conference on Class Actions, 71 N.Y.U. L. Rev. 1 (1996); Symposium, Mass Torts, 148 U. Pa. L. Rev. 1851 (2000).

9. *See* Fed. R. Civ. P. 23(f)(added 1998 to permit discretionary interlocutory appeals of class certification decisions); §§ 10.23, 12.11 *infra.*

Rule 23(a) requirements

In its current form, Rule 23 first sets forth the preliminary conditions under which a class suit may be maintained:

1. the class is so numerous that joinder of all members is impracticable,
2. there are questions of law or fact common to the class,
3. the claims or defenses of the representative parties are typical of the claims or defenses of the class,
4. the representative parties will fairly and adequately protect the interests of the class.[10]

Plaintiffs bear the burden of demonstrating that the requirements of Rule 23(a) have been satisfied.[11]

Rule 23(b) requirements

If these conditions are met, a class suit may be permitted in the discretion of the court[12] under any one of the three circumstances described below.

1. Separate actions by or against the members of the class would create a risk of "incompatible standards of conduct for the party opposing the class"[13] or of prejudicing the interests of the absent members of the class.[14] These circumstances are essentially the same as those expressed in the necessary parties rule, except that the number of necessary parties is large.[15]

2. The suit involves an injunction or declaratory judgment concerning conduct of the party opposing the class that affects all class members.[16] This category provides a vehicle for institutional reform litigation, such as suits seeking relief against racial or gender discrimination.

3. The claims of the class members have common questions of fact or law that "predominate over any questions affecting only individual members" and a class action "is superior to other available methods of fair and efficient adjudication of the controversy."[17] This third category

10. Fed. R. Civ. P. 23(a). Class suits are also permitted in stockholder's derivative actions, Fed. R. Civ. P. 23.1, and suits by and against unincorporated associations, Fed. R. Civ. P. 23.2. Here, the criteria of adequacy of representation are essentially the same as those specified in Rule 23(a). On the test for associational standing, *see* International Union UAW v. Brock, 477 U.S. 274, 106 S.Ct. 2523, 91 L.Ed.2d 228 (1986).

11. *See* General Tel. Co. of Southwest v. Falcon, 457 U.S. 147, 102 S.Ct. 2364, 72 L.Ed.2d 740 (1982).

12. Fed. R. Civ. P. 23(c). How the trial court's discretion is exercised determines whether the action is a class suit, often a very large one, or simply a suit on an individual claim, often a small one. The criteria for exercising discretion are vague, making the question of appellate review of denial of certification a vital issue. *See* Fed. R. Civ. P. 23(f); Deposit Guar. Natl. Bank v. Roper, 445 U.S. 326, 100 S.Ct. 1166, 63 L.Ed.2d 427 (1980).

13. Fed. R. Civ. P. 23(b)(1)(A).

14. *Id.* 23(b)(1)(B).

15. *See id.* 19(a); §§ 10.11–15 *supra.*

16. Fed. R. Civ. P. 23(b)(2).

17. *Id.* 23(b)(3).

encompasses what is now commonly called the damages class suit, the focus of recent controversies.

Revised Rule 23 provides for court control of the representative's conduct, including allowing absentees to intervene,[18] subdividing the class into subclasses along the lines of their interest, limiting the issues as to which the class proceeding shall be binding on absentees,[19] and requiring court approval of any settlement.[20] The rule requires notice in damages class actions and permits the court to require it in others, leaving open the question of its possible constitutional necessity.[21] In addition, members of a Rule 23(b)(3) class—the damages class suit—may opt out by signifying that they do not wish to have their claims included in the action.[22] Revised Rule 23 thus appears fully to meet the requirements of *Hansberry v. Lee*[23] on adequate protection of the absentees' interests.[24]

Overlapping Rule 23(b) categories

Because the rule requires notice and an opportunity to opt out in Rule 23(b)(3) class actions, parties sometimes try to squeeze class actions into other subdivisions of Rule 23(b). The simplest method is to join claims for damages with claims for class-wide injunctive relief, because the latter can be brought under Rule 23(b)(2). Courts have allowed this, but only when the predominant relief sought is not monetary.[25] An alternative is the "limited fund" theory, under which parties argue that the defendant may not have enough money to pay all the claims of class members, so that they should all be brought into a Rule 23(b)(b)(1)(B) class action in order to protect their interests. The Supreme Court has decided that such an action may be allowed only if the court determines on the basis of adequate evidence that the fund will indeed be inadequate to pay all claims, and that the class action will treat all claimants

18. Fed. R. Civ. P. 23(d)(2). *See* Martin v. Wilks, 490 U.S. 755, 109 S.Ct. 2180, 104 L.Ed.2d 835 (1989); § 10.17 *supra*.

19. Fed. R. Civ. P. 23(c)(4). *See, e.g.,* Pruitt v. Allied Chem. Corp., 85 F.R.D. 100 (E.D.Va.1980); Richmond v. Dart Indus., 29 Cal.3d 462, 629 P.2d 23, 174 Cal.Rptr. 515 (1981). *See also* Note, Class Standing and the Class Representative, 94 Harv. L. Rev. 1637 (1981).

20. Fed. R. Civ. P. 23(e). *See, e.g.*, Amchem Products, Inc. v. Windsor, 521 U.S. 591, 117 S.Ct. 2231, 138 L.Ed.2d 689 (1997); Hazard, The Settlement Black Box, 75 B.U.L. Rev. 1257 (1995); Almond, Settling Rule 23 Class Actions at the Recertification Stage, 56 N.C.L. Rev. 303 (1978).

21. Fed. R. Civ. P. 23(c)(2), (d)(2). On the constitutional issue, *see* § 10.23 *infra*.

22. Fed. R. Civ. P. 23(c)(2).

23. 311 U.S. 32, 61 S.Ct. 115, 85 L.Ed. 22 (1940).

24. *See, e.g.,* Frankel, Some Preliminary Observations Concerning Civil Rule 23, 43 F.R.D. 39 (1967); Note, Collateral Attack on the Binding Effect of Class Action Judgments, 87 Harv. L. Rev. 589 (1974). *See also* Daar v. Yellow Cab Co., 67 Cal.2d 695, 433 P.2d 732, 63 Cal.Rptr. 724 (1967), wherein the California Supreme Court interpolated revised Rule 23 into California class action procedure. *See also* Vasquez v. Superior Court, 4 Cal.3d 800, 484 P.2d 964, 94 Cal. Rptr. 796 (1971).

25. *E.g.*, Bolin v. Sears, Roebuck & Co., 231 F.3d 970 (5th Cir.2000); *see* Thomas v. Albright, 139 F.3d 227 (D.C.Cir.1998)("hybrid" 23(b)(2) class action with notice and right to opt out).

equitably.[26] Some argue that, even if these conditions are met, a bankruptcy proceeding would be a better way than a class action to ensure that all the defendant's assets are collected and that all its debtors (not just those covered by the class action) receive the appropriate priority of payment.[27]

Class action problems

The class action remains a very troublesome procedure. A chief problem is protecting the class members not only from the possibility that their self-appointed representative will act at variance with their interests but also from the often more serious possibility that the class lawyer (also usually self-appointed) has interests that conflict with those of his or her clients.[28] There is no complete solution to this problem, for potential conflicts always exist within any group and some conflict always exists between lawyer and client. Professor Coffee has classified the partial solutions as exit (the right of discontented class members to opt out of the action), voice (the right to participate by intervening or submitting comments), and loyalty (promoting effective representation of all class members by such means as selecting named plaintiffs and lawyers, providing subclasses with their own representation, and imposing fiduciary duties on the representatives).[29] Intensive judicial scrutiny of the conduct of the litigation is necessary to implement and monitor such measures.[30]

Another problem is that the use of the class suit is an invitation to homogenize the legal interests of the members of the class and to simplify their legal relationships with the opposing party in the direction of treating them all as alike.[31] A related problem is whether the class suit

26. Ortiz v. Fibreboard Corp., 527 U.S. 815, 119 S.Ct. 2295, 144 L.Ed.2d 715 (1999).

27. Resnick, Bankruptcy As a Vehicle for Resolving Enterprise–Threatening Mass Tort Liability, 148 U. Pa. L. Rev. 2045 (2000); Roe, Bankruptcy and Mass Torts, 84 Colum. L., Rev. 846 (1984); *see* Report of the National Bankruptcy Review Commission 315–50 (1997). *But see* Hazard, The "Futures" Problem, 148 U. Pa. L. Rev. 1901 (2000).

28. These sources of conflict have been most sharply identified in Rule 23(b)(3) class suits, *see, e.g.,* Handler, The Shift from Substantive to Procedural Innovations in Antitrust Suits, 71 Colum. L. Rev. 1 (1971), but they are no less a possibility in more "traditional" class suits. *See* Saylor v. Lindsley, 456 F.2d 896 (2d Cir.1972) (stockholder's derivative suit); Bell, Serving Two Masters: Integration Ideals and Client Interests in School Desegregation Litigation, 85 Yale L.J. 470 (1976); Rhode, Class Conflicts in Class Actions, 34 Stan. L. Rev. 1183 (1982); Note, Binding Effect of EEOC–Initiated Actions, 80 Colum. L. Rev. 395 (1980); § 10.23 *infra.*

29. Coffee, Class Action Accountability: Reconciling Exit, Voice, and Loyalty in Representative Litigation, 100 Colum. L. Rev. 370 (2000); *see* Issacharoff, Governance and Legitimacy in the Law of Class Actions, 1999 S. Ct. Rev. 337.

30. *See, e.g.,* McGowan v. Faulkner Concrete Pipe Co., 659 F.2d 554 (5th Cir. 1981); Saylor v. Lindsley, 456 F.2d 896 (2d Cir.1972); Developments in the Law—Class Actions, 89 Harv. L. Rev. 1318 (1976); *cf.* Note, Continuation and Representation of Class Actions following Dismissal of the Class Representative, 1974 Duke L.J. 573; § 11.29 *infra.*

31. *See* Hazard, The Effect of the Class Action Device upon the Substantive Law, 58 F.R.D. 307 (1973); Landers, Of Legalized Blackmail and Legalized Theft: Consumer

device has simply become too powerful a litigating weapon to be made available to private litigants in all circumstances, particularly when that is done through the judicial rulemaking power rather than through legislation.[32] For instance, Congress amended the Truth in Lending Act to limit the total liquidated damages recoverable in a class action.[33]

Securities fraud class actions

One area of particular controversy has been the securities fraud class action. Responding to claims by defendants that every dramatic fall in the price of a corporation's stock led to the filing of a fraud class action, often meritless but likely to coerce a settlement enriching the class lawyer, Congress enacted the Private Securities Litigation Reform Act of 1995.[34] This changes the substantive law, requires more particularized pleading, and restricts discovery before class certification.[35] It also limits attorney fee recovery and provides that the stockholder with the largest holdings is presumptively entitled to be class representative, thus seeking to place control of the action in the hands of a party with a sufficient interest to keep class lawyers within bounds.[36] When it was reported that lawyers were evading this act by filing actions in more permissive state courts, Congress preempted many state court securities fraud class actions with the Securities Litigation Uniform Standards Act of 1998.[37] Whatever its other consequences, none of this legislation appears to have reduced the number of securities fraud class action filings.[38]

Mass tort class actions

While securities class actions were thus being regulated, another controversial kind of class action has been showing signs of growth.

Class Actions and the Substance–Procedure Dilemma, 47 S. Cal. L. Rev. 842 (1974); Note, Impact of Class Actions on Rule 10b–5, 38 U. Chi. L. Rev. 337 (1971). *Compare* Vasquez v. Superior Court, 4 Cal.3d 800, 484 P.2d 964, 94 Cal.Rptr. 796 (1971) *and* King v. Club Med, Inc., 76 A.D.2d 123, 430 N.Y.S.2d 65 (1980), *with* Bernard v. First Natl. Bank of Or., 275 Or. 145, 550 P.2d 1203 (1976).

32. *See* Landers, Of Legalized Blackmail and Legalized Theft: Consumer Class Actions and the Substance–Procedure Dilemma, 47 S. Cal. L. Rev. 842 (1974). *See also* Note, Rule 23(b)(3) Class Suits: An Empirical Study, 62 Geo. L.J. 1123 (1974). State class action rules in many instances are legislative in origin. *See* Note, Iowa Uniform Class Actions Rule: Intended Effects and Probable Results, 66 Iowa L. Rev. 1241 (1981).

33. 15 U.S.C. § 1640(a)(1).

34. 15 U.S.C. §§ 77z–1(c), 78u–4(c); *see* Symposium, Class Actions at the Croosroads, 39 Ariz. L. Rev. 407(1997); Private Litigation Under the Federal Securities Laws: Hearings Before the Subcommittee on Securities, U.S. Senate Committee on Banking, Housing, and Urban Affairs, 103d Cong., 1st Sess. (1993).

35. *See* § 3.19 *supra*.

36. *See* Weiss and Beckerman, Let the Money Do the Monitoring: How Institutional Investors Can Reduce Agency Costs in Securities Class Actions, 104 Yale L.J. 2053 (1995).

37. 15 U.S.C. §§ 77p, 78bb(f); Painter, Responding to a False Alarm: Federal Preemption of State Securities Fraud Causes of Action, 84 Cornell L. Rev. 1 (1998).

38. Martin, *et al.*, What Explains Filings and Settlements in Shareholder Class Actions, 5 Stan. J.L. Bus. & Fin. 121 (1999).

Although the drafters of the 1966 amendments to Rule 23 contemplated that mass torts would not ordinarily be appropriate for class actions,[39] during the 1980s courts began to certify such classes.[40] Judicial desire to handle large numbers of related cases more efficiently was a major spur to this development. But courts remain wary of nationwide class actions involving claims governed by the laws of different states, and of the difficulty of assessing the damages suffered by each class member, especially when dealing with "immature" torts that have not been sufficiently litigated to permit estimation of their value.[41]

The most criticized mass tort class actions have been two "settlement class actions" in asbestos litigation. These were promoted by judges seeking to clear dockets and defendants seeking global settlements that would set a single price tag on all their asbestos liabilities, enabling them to put asbestos litigation behind them. They would have funded and established dispute resolution procedures to pay all future asbestos claims against the manufacturers in question. Their supporters argued that they would save administrative costs, leaving more money for injured plaintiffs, and preventing all funds from going to the earlier claimants, leaving nothing for the later ones. Opponents challenged the legitimacy of compensation schemes established by agreement between defendants and certain plaintiffs' lawyers, without basis in legislation, adjudication of the merits, or the consent of those affected. They also argued that the class lawyers could not provide adequate representation because of conflicts of interest within the class, and with the lawyers' own obligations to asbestos claimants not included in the class but simultaneously negotiating for settlement of their own claims. The Supreme Court ultimately vacated both class certifications, primarily on conflicts of interest grounds.[42] Note that, while criticism of securities fraud class actions has come mainly from those sympathetic to the defendants, most critics of settlement class actions have considered them unfair to the plaintiff class members.

39. Fed. R. Civ. P. 23(b)(3)(1996 Advisory Committee Notes); In re Northern Dist. of California, Dalkon Shield IUD Prods. Liability Litigation, 693 F.2d 847 (9th Cir. 1982).

40. In re Agent Orange Products Liability Litigation, 818 F.2d 145 (2d Cir.1987); In re School Asbestos Litigation, 789 F.2d 996 (3d Cir.1986); In re A.H. Robins Co., 880 F.2d 709 (4th Cir.1989); *see* Weinstein, Individual Justice in Mass Tort Litigation: The Effect of Class Actions, Consolidations, and Other Multi–Party Devices (1995); Resnik, From "Cases" to "Litigation," 54 Law & Contemp. Probs. 5 (Summer 1991).

41. *E.g.,* Castano v. American Tobacco Co., 84 F.3d 734 (5th Cir.1996); Valentino v. Carter–Wallace, Inc., 97 F.3d 1227(9th Cir.1996); In re American Medical Systems, 75 F.3d 1069 (6th Cir.1996); *see* Amchem Products, Inc. v. Windsor, 521 U.S. 591, 117 S.Ct. 2231, 138 L.Ed.2d 689 (1997); In re Rhone–Poulenc Rorer, Inc., 51 F.3d 1293 (7th Cir.1995).

42. Amchem Products, Inc. v. Windsor, 521 U.S. 591, 117 S.Ct. 2231, 138 L.Ed.2d 689 (1997); Ortiz v. Fibreboard Corp., 527 U.S. 815, 119 S.Ct. 2295, 144 L.Ed.2d 715 (1999); *see* Symposium, Mass Tortes: Serving Up Just Desserts, 80 Cornell L. Rev. 811 (1995); Coffee, Class Wars: The Dilemma of the Mass Tort Class Action, 95 Colum. L. Rev. 1343 (1995).

State court class suits

The concerns and controversies of class actions, and of damages class actions in particular, may explain the hesitancy of many state courts to give as great effect to the class suit device as its historical possibilities suggest and as the Rule 23 precedent implies.[43] At least until the 1970s state court interpretations of their class action rules tended toward a narrow construction of the permissible use of the device except in situations recognized in equity before the codes;[44] those situations are the necessary party cases in which the number of necessary parties is large[45] and the injunction cases. In the latter, indeed, it is often of little practical importance whether the suit is denominated as a class action; granting the injunction usually will incidentally benefit the whole class, and denying it often may be a deterrent to a later suit.[46] The use of the damages class action formerly was inhibited by determinations that the claims of individual class members were not "united" or "common" so that the initial qualifying requirement under the codes was not met.[47] The more recent decisions have abandoned this conceptual refuge and have directly faced the difficult questions of policy suggested above, including the extent to which the courts should sanction the damages class suit without direct legislative authorization. Although some state courts continue to read statutes and rules restrictively, others provide strong support for the evolving use of the class suit, particularly for relatively small consumer claims. Indeed, a few states have acquired reputations as havens for class actions.[48] In some states these havens are

43. For a historical perspective, *compare* Blume, The "Common Questions" Principle in the Code Provision for Representative Suits, 30 Mich. L. Rev. 878 (1932); Kalven and Rosenfield, The Contemporary Function of the Class Suit, 8 U. Chi. L. Rev. 684 (1941); Hamburger, State Class Actions and the Federal Rule, 71 Colum. L. Rev. 609 (1971); and Dam, Class Action Notice: Who Needs It?, 1974 Sup. Ct. Rev. 97.

44. *See* the Blume and Hamburger articles, *supra* note 43.

45. *See, e.g.,* Heffernan v. Bennett & Armour, 110 Cal.App.2d 564, 243 P.2d 846 (1952); Lichtyger v. Franchard Corp., 18 N.Y.2d 528, 223 N.E.2d 869, 277 N.Y.S.2d 377 (1966).

46. *Compare* Diaz v. Quitoriano, 268 Cal.App.2d 807, 74 Cal.Rptr. 358 (1969), where it made a difference, *with* Murphy v. Erie County, 28 N.Y.2d 80, 268 N.E.2d 771, 320 N.Y.S.2d 29 (1971), where it did not.

47. *See, e.g.,* Weaver v. Pasadena Tournament of Roses, 32 Cal.2d 833, 198 P.2d 514 (1948); *see also* Hall v. Coburn Corp., 26 N.Y.2d 396, 259 N.E.2d 720, 311 N.Y.S.2d 281 (1970).

48. *Compare,* for example, Fletcher v. Security Pac. Natl. Bank, 23 Cal.3d 442, 591 P.2d 51, 153 Cal.Rptr. 28 (1979), *with* Bernard v. First Natl. Bank of Or., 275 Or. 145, 550 P.2d 1203 (1976), and cases cited therein. *See also* the thoughtful analysis in Ratner v. Chemical Bank N.Y. Trust Co., 54 F.R.D. 412 (S.D.N.Y.1972). *See also* Mullenix, Abandoning the Federal Class Action Ship: Is There Smoother Sailing for Class Actions in Gulf Waters?, 74 Tulane L. Rev. 1709 (2000);Note, Determining Class Maintainability in California, 27 Hastings L.J. 293 (1975); Tornquist, Roadmap to Illinois Class Actions, 5 Loy. U. Chi. L. Rev. 45 (1974); Note, Class Actions in New York, 38 Alb. L. Rev. 865 (1974); Donne and Van Horn, Pennsylvania Class Actions, 78 Dick. L. Rev. 460 (1974). *See also* Uniform Class Actions [Act] [Rule] (provision is designed to be either a statute or rule of court), 12 U.L.A. 26, adopted by the National Conference of Commissioners on Uniform State Laws (1976).

in counties where judges are sympathetic to class actions brought by local lawyers.

Problems of federal jurisdiction

Class suits brought in federal court involve two further problems. The first is the determination of citizenship when jurisdiction is based on diversity. The citizenship that "counts" is that of the representatives, not that of each member of the class. Hence, if the representative's citizenship is different from that of the opposing party, it is immaterial that some members of the class have the same citizenship as the latter.[49]

The second problem concerns the minimum-amount-in-controversy requirement, which must be met in diversity jurisdiction. The rule has been that the claims of *each member* of the class must exceed the minimum of $75,000.[50] This means, in effect, that the class in such an action has to be defined as those who have claims of that amount. There are likely to be few situations in which a group of individuals is numerous enough to warrant use of the class suit device and the claim of each person in the group exceeds $75,000. The supplemental jurisdiction statute may perhaps wipe out this requirement so long as one class member meets the $75,000 requirement: the statute can be read that way, but its legislative history shows a contrary intent, and the court decisions are split.[51] As Supreme Court decisions have reined in the damages class actions, some class action enthusiasts have been less eager than formerly to invite them into federal courthouses, while some class action skeptics have become more favorable to keeping them under federal court control. It should be observed that this problem does not arise when the jurisdictional basis of the action lacks a minimum-amount-in-controversy requirement.[52] Thus, the traditional rule allows federal question class actions but excludes from the federal courts most class suits arising under state law.

§ 10.23 Procedural Aspects of Class Actions

When the conditions specified in the class suit rule are met and the action is certified as a class suit, manifold problems arise in its administration. These are the problems alluded to in the provision in Rule

49. Supreme Tribe of Ben Hur v. Cauble, 255 U.S. 356, 41 S.Ct. 338, 65 L.Ed. 673 (1921); *e.g.,* Friedman v. Meyers, 482 F.2d 435 (2d Cir.1973).

50. Zahn v. International Paper Co., 414 U.S. 291, 94 S.Ct. 505, 38 L.Ed.2d 511 (1973). If the members have "joint" ownership of a claim of more than $75,000, the requirement is also met. 7 Wright and Miller, Federal Practice and Procedure § 1756.

51. *Compare* Free v. Abbott Laboratories, Inc., 51 F.3d 524 (5th Cir.1995), *aff'd by equally divided court,* 529 U.S. 333, 120 S.Ct. 1578, 146 L.Ed.2d 306 (2000); Stromberg Metal Works, Inc. v. Press Mechanical, Inc., 77 F.3d 928 (7th Cir.1996)(both holding that supplemental jurisdiction is available) *with* Meritcare, Inc. v. St. Paul Mercury Ins. Co., 166 F.3d 214 (3d Cir.1999); Leonhardt v. Western Sugar Co., 160 F.3d 631 (10th Cir.1998)(contrary).

52. No minimum amount in controversy must be shown in actions arising under federal statutes or the Constitution. 28 U.S.C. § 1331.

23(b)(3) (the damages class suit) that the class procedure be "fair and efficient." Consideration of these administrative problems lies in the court's discretion under Rule 23(c)(1) in determining whether the suit may be maintained as a class proceeding.[1] In the early years of experience with Rule 23 after its 1966 revision, many commentators worried that class suits would necessarily be unmanageable.[2] Much of this concern seems to have been a smokescreen for opposition to the class suit on more substantive grounds. Be that as it may, most class suits are not much more complicated than other "big" cases, such as antitrust or patent litigation, but that is complicated enough. All such suits typically involve complex questions of fact, which beget extensive discovery and often complex and novel issues of substantive law. They also usually involve large stakes and a heavy commitment of lawyers' time, which means that most everything that can be made an issue will be made an issue. Thus, almost all class suits have the characteristics of big lawsuits.[3] They also have some special problems of their own.

Adequacy of representation

The adequacy of class representation is the most important issue. This is true both in legal terms (without legally sufficient representation the class suit is procedurally defective and will not bind the class)[4] and in practical terms (the interest of the absentees rests on representation over which they have no effective supervision). A number of cases approach the adequacy problem by concentrating on the class member who is the designated representative, determining whether that person is a member of the class, whether he or she has conflicts of interest with the class, and related questions.[5] Other cases, however, have given equal or greater attention to the adequacy of the legal counsel who represents the class in terms of competence, experience in general and with the particular substantive issues involved, conflicts of interest, and similar factors.[6] And the Supreme Court has held that when different groups

§ 10.23

1. *See, e.g.,* Philadelphia Elec. Co. v. Anaconda Am. Brass Co., 43 F.R.D. 452, 459 (E.D.Pa.1968); *see generally* 7A Wright and Miller, Federal Practice and Procedure § 1780 (1972).

2. *See, e.g.,* American College of Trial Lawyers, Special Commission on Rule 23, Report and Recommendations (1972); Kirkpatrick, Consumer Class Litigation, 50 Or. L. Rev. 21 (1971).

3. *See* Hensler, *et al.*, Class Action Dilemmas: Pursuing Public Goals for Private Gain (2000); Willging, *et al.*, Empirical Study of Class Actions in Four Federal District Courts: Final Report to the Advisory Committee on Civil Rules (1996); DuVal, The Class Action as an Antitrust Enforcement Device: The Chicago Experience, 1976 Am. B. Found. Res. J. 1021; Kennedy, Securities Class and Derivative Actions in the United States District Court for the Northern District of Texas: An Empirical Study, 14 Hous. L. Rev. 769 (1977); Rosenberg, Class Actions for Mass Torts: Doing Individual Justice by Collective Means, 62 Ind. L.J. 561 (1987).

4. *See, e.g.,* Hansberry v. Lee, 311 U.S. 32, 61 S.Ct. 115, 85 L.Ed. 22 (1940).

5. *See, e.g.,* East Tex. Motor Freight Sys. v. Rodriguez, 431 U.S. 395, 97 S.Ct. 1891, 52 L.Ed.2d 453 (1977); *cf.* Richmond v. Dart Indus., 29 Cal.3d 462, 629 P.2d 23, 174 Cal.Rptr. 515 (1981).

6. *See, e.g.,* McGowan v. Faulkner Concrete Pipe Co., 659 F.2d 554 (5th Cir.1981); Fendler v. Westgate–California Corp., 527

within the class have sufficiently conflicting interests, each group should have its own lawyer.[7] Many, probably most, plaintiff class actions are prosecuted on a *pro bono* or a contingent fee basis, with the lawyer advancing not only time but also litigating expenses. Since financial staying power is often very important, some courts give direct consideration to counsel's adequacy in this respect.

Suits against a defendant class raise special problems of representation, for in such suits the plaintiffs seek to designate the defendant class's representative. That representative may have no incentive to bear the burden of effectively protecting other class members. When the suit seeks damages from the class members, holding them obligated to pay on the basis of a proceeding in which they did not participate would raise significant constitutional problems.[8] Some have challenged even the propriety of a defendant class action seeking injunctive relief, such as a law reform suit seeking to bind a class of state officials.[9] But the language of Rule 23 plainly contemplates a defendant class.

Predominance of classwide issues

In 23(b)(3) class actions, the rule provides that the court may certify the action only if questions common to the class predominate over separate questions such as the extent of each class member's damages, and if a class action is superior to other available methods for fair and efficient adjudication. This sometimes calls for a broad inquiry into such matters as the number of subclasses that will be necessary, variations in state law that may affect the claims of class members from different states, the simplicity or complexity of the class members' individual issues, and the extent of judicial experience with claims of the sort in question.[10] On the other hand. the Supreme Court has discouraged consideration of the merits of the claim.[11] Likewise, when the parties present a proposed settlement together with the motion for certification,

F.2d 1168 (9th Cir.1975); Oxendine v. Williams, 509 F.2d 1405 (4th Cir.1975).

7. Amchem Products, Inc. v. Windsor, 521 U.S. 591, 117 S.Ct. 2231, 138 L.Ed.2d 689 (1997); *see* Ortiz v. Fibreboard Corp., 527 U.S. 815, 119 S.Ct. 2295, 144 L.Ed.2d 715 (1999); Marisol A. v. Giuliani, 126 F.3d 372 (2d Cir.1997).

8. *See* Phillips Petroleum Co. v. Shutts, 472 U.S. 797, 105 S.Ct. 2965, 86 L.Ed.2d 628 (1985) (distinguishing plaintiff class actions from defendant class actions). *See* Willging, *et al.*, Empirical Study of Class Actions in Four Federal District Courts: Final Report to the Advisory Committee on Civil Rules 40–41 (1996)(rarity of defendant class actions).

9. Henson v. East Lincoln Township, 814 F.2d 410 (7th Cir.1987). *But see* 1 Newberg, Class Actions § 4.64 (2d ed. 1985).

10. *E.g.,* Castano v. American Tobacco Co., 84 F.3d 734 (5th Cir.1996); In re Telectronics Pacing Systems, Inc., Accufix Atrial J Leads Products Liability Litigation, 172 F.R.D. 271 (D.Ohio 1997), reversed in some respects, 221 F.3d 870 (6th Cir.2000); *see* Fed. R. Civ. P. 23(b)(3)(listing relevant factors); Wolf, Evading Friendly Fire: Achieving Class Certification after the Civil Rights Act of 1991, 100 Colum. L. Rev. 1847 (2000).

11. *See* Eisen v. Carlisle & Jacquelin, 417 U.S. 156, 94 S.Ct. 2140, 40 L.Ed.2d 732 (1974); Priest, Procedural versus Substantive Controls of Mass Tort Class Actions, 26 J. Leg. Stud. 521 (1997)(urging consideration of merits).

the court's opinion that the settlement is reasonable does not dispense it from considering the adequacy of representation and the predominance of classwide issues: these are independent safeguards for the class, particularly necessary when the parties agree on the settlement and there is no one to challenge its reasonableness.[12]

Appeal of certification

If the suit is certified as a class suit, the action becomes a very big one and the defendant faces increased pressure to settle; if certification is denied, the class aspect of the suit is dismissed and the remaining individual suit may be so inconsequential that it will not be prosecuted. A trial court's decision of the class certification issue is subject to appellate review and reversal at the end of the case.[13] The Supreme Court has held, however, that neither a grant nor a denial of certification is an appealable order;[14] hence, it is not appealable as of right, like a final judgment. The class action status of the suit therefore can remain in limbo until judgment on the merits is rendered in the trial court. In recognition of the practical importance of authoritatively determining whether the suit is a class action, the Federal Rules now grant the Court of Appeals discretion to allow an immediate appeal from a decision granting or denying class certification.[15] Apparently this discretion will be exercised when denial of class action threatens to doom the action, when its grant pressures the defendant to settle, or when important legal issues are involved; these categories seem to include most cases in which certification is seriously disputed.[16] In state courts, the order certifying an action as a class suit, or refusing so to certify it, generally is subject to interlocutory appellate review.[17]

Notice

Some kind of notice to the absent members of the class is required in any kind of class suit. In 23(b)(3) class suits, notice to each member is required to provide the opportunity to opt out. This also gives individuals notice of the pendency of the suit and opportunity to join individually as a party. (In practice, less than one percent of the class usually opts out, because of the impracticality of suing separately and the incompre-

12. Amchem Products, Inc. v. Windsor, 521 U.S. 591, 117 S.Ct. 2231, 138 L.Ed.2d 689 (1997); *see* Hazard, The Settlement Black Box, 75 B.U.L. Rev. 1257 (1995).

13. *See* 7A Wright and Miller, Federal Practice and Procedure § 1802 (1972).

14. Coopers & Lybrand v. Livesay, 437 U.S. 463, 98 S.Ct. 2454, 57 L.Ed.2d 351 (1978).

15. Fed. R. Civ. P. 23(f).

16. Blair v. Equifax Check Services, Inc., 181 F.3d 832 (7th Cir.1999); Waste Management Holdings, Inc. v. Mowbray, 208 F.3d 288 (1st Cir.2000); Prado–Steiman v. Bush, 221 F.3d 1266 (11th Cir.2000); Solimine and Hines, Deciding to Decide: Class Action Certification and Interlocutory Review by the United States Courts of Appeals Under Rule 23(f), 41 Wm. & Mary L. Rev. 1531 (2000).

17. *See, e.g.,* Richmond v. Dart Indus., 29 Cal.3d 462, 629 P.2d 23, 174 Cal.Rptr. 515 (1981); Daar v. Yellow Cab Co., 67 Cal.2d 695, 433 P.2d 732, 63 Cal.Rptr. 724 (1967);N.Y. Civ. Prac. L. & R. 5701 (McKinney 1978); *see also* Uniform Class Action Act 4(c), 12U.L.A. 26.

hensibility of many notices.[18]) In class suits under 23(b)(1) and (2), Rule 23(d)(2) confers discretion in the court to require "that notice be given in such manner as the court may direct to some or all members of the class." It has become standard practice to give some kind of notice, such as mailed notice, to all members of a class who number in the hundreds and to some sample of class members when the class is larger than that, the guiding considerations being cost and the endeavor to provide broad actual notice.[19] Notice not only is given at the outset of litigation but also may be required for a proposed settlement.[20] In a damages class suit in which the court upholds claims for money, further notice may be required so that class members may file their claims. The court may then specify the claim forms to be used, authorize standard damage awards, and otherwise seek to administer the resolution of multiple claims.

Eisen v. Carlisle & Jacquelin

In *Eisen v. Carlisle & Jacquelin,*[21] the Court construed Rule 23(c)(2) to require that actual notice, no less than by mail, be given to all absent members of the class whose addresses are known in Rule 23(b)(3) suits—that is, "consumer" class suits where damages are sought on behalf of a large number of persons. More questionably, payment of the cost of giving notice was held an obligation of the class representative. The practical effect of this ruling is to place a severe cost barrier before mass class actions for damages. It also encourages plaintiffs to delay any decision on class certification and notice until they can negotiate a settlement, which can then be used to fund the notice.

Although the Supreme Court has noted the possibility that the individualized class action notice it ordered under Rule 23(c)(2) in *Eisen* may be constitutionally required,[22] thus far it has found such a requirement only in state court damages class actions with class members from other states who are not within the court's long arm jurisdiction.[23] The

18. Willging, *et al.*, Empirical Study of Class Actions in Four Federal District Courts: Final Report to the Advisory Committee on Civil Rules 45–54 (1996).

19. *See, e.g.,* United States v. Allegheny–Ludlum Indus., 517 F.2d 826 (5th Cir. 1975), *cert. denied,* 425 U.S. 944, 96 S.Ct. 1684, 48 L.Ed.2d 187 (1976); Key v. Gillette Co., 90 F.R.D. 606 (D.Mass.1981); Berman v. Narragansett Racing Assn., Inc., 48 F.R.D. 333 (D.R.I.1969).

20. Fed R. Civ. P. 23(e); *cf.* Almond, Settling Rule 23 Class Actions at the Precertification Stage, 56 N.C.L. Rev. 303 (1978).

21. 417 U.S. 156, 94 S.Ct. 2140, 40 L.Ed.2d 732 (1974).

22. *See* Richards v. Jefferson County, 517 U.S. 793, 116 S.Ct. 1761, 135 L.Ed.2d 76 (1996). The Court has twice accepted, but then not decided, cases raising the claim that a right to opt out is constitutionally required in class actions involving damages. Ticor Title Insurance Co. v. Brown, 511 U.S. 117, 114 S.Ct. 1359, 128 L.Ed.2d 33 (1994); Adams v. Robertson, 520 U.S. 83, 117 S.Ct. 1028, 137 L.Ed.2d 203 (1997).

23. Phillips Petroleum Co. v. Shutts, 472 U.S. 797, 105 S.Ct. 2965, 86 L.Ed.2d 628 (1985) (technically dictum), discussed in text below. *See also* Mullane v. Central Hanover Bank & Trust Co., 339 U.S. 306, 70 S.Ct. 652, 94 L.Ed. 865 (1950)(requiring notice to those whose addresses are known in trust account proceeding to bind beneficiaries throughout the nation); Woolley, Re-

argument for requiring notice, of course, is that a class action may cut off the legal rights of class members, who should therefore have a meaningful opportunity to defend themselves. On the other hand, individualized notice has not traditionally been required in class actions, and is still not required in actions not falling within Rule 23(b)(3) such as actions for injunctive relief.[24] When class members' claims are too small to be individually litigated, the expense of mailing tens of thousands of complex legal documents to bewildered recipients produces less benefit to the class than would other ways of publicizing the action.[25] In such cases, the class members must find their protection in the court, the class representatives and counsel, and other lawyers seeking to participate in order to reap fees under the common fund doctrine[26] by benefitting the class.

Statute of limitations

Since a class suit has the effect of being a suit by all members of the class, the filing of a class suit stops the running of the statute of limitations on the claims of all class members. But suppose a suit denominated as a class suit is refused certification by the trial court. In that case, what happens to the claims of the class members so far as the statute of limitations is concerned? In *Crown, Cork & Seal Co. v. Parker*[27] the Supreme Court established the proposition that the statute is tolled by the class suit, not only for members who elect to present their individual claims in the class action but also for those who prosecute separate actions.

Jurisdiction over nonresidents

When the class includes individuals outside the territorial limits of the state in which the suit is filed, the court's jurisdiction becomes an issue. Weighing against jurisdiction is the fact that such individuals, considered in isolation, lack sufficient contacts to subject them to the jurisdiction of the court. The Supreme Court rejected this argument in *Phillips Petroleum Co. v. Shutts,*[28] ruling that a state court could adjudicate a plaintiff class damages suit with binding effect, provided that class members outside the state received notice and an opportunity to opt out. In part the Court relied on that notice and opportunity as a weaker substitute for consent to jurisdiction. But the Court also emphasized that

thinking the Adequacy of Adequate Representation, 75 Tex. L. Rev. 571 (1997).

24. *See* Hansberry v. Lee, 311 U.S. 32, 61 S.Ct. 115, 85 L.Ed. 22 (1940); Supreme Tribe of Ben Hur v. Cauble, 255 U.S. 356, 41 S.Ct. 338, 65 L.Ed. 673 (1921); Stoetzner v. United States Steel Corp., 897 F.2d 115 (3d Cir.1990); Walsh v. Great Atlantic & Pacific Tea Co., 726 F.2d 956 (3d Cir.1983). *But see* Johnson v. General Motors Corp., 598 F.2d 432 (5th Cir.1979).

25. *See* Dam, Class Action Notice: Who Needs It?, 1974 Sup. Ct. Rev. 97; Note, Developments in the Law: Class Actions, 89 Harv. L. Rev. 1319, 1353 (1976).

26. *See* §§ 1.23, 10.20 *supra.*

27. 462 U.S. 345, 103 S.Ct. 2392, 76 L.Ed.2d 628 (1983).

28. 472 U.S. 797, 105 S.Ct. 2965, 86 L.Ed.2d 628 (1985).

the class members, rather than being deprived of property without due process of law, received the chance to recover, through the efforts of class representatives, on claims that would have been uneconomical for them to assert in individual actions. The opinion thus stirred together considerations of procedural fairness with traditional personal jurisdictional concerns. It raised, but did not answer, constitutional questions on the legitimacy of binding multistate class suits for remedies other than damages, defendant class actions, and multistate damage class suits in which the names and addresses of class members are unknown.[29]

Discovery

Individual members of the class may have relevant information that properly is subject to discovery. In an employment discrimination case, for example, it would be appropriate to discover the data on which applications for employment had been made by various members of the class. Class members are subject to some discovery, but the critical question is whether they should be subject to the more extensive discovery available against parties to an action.[30] On one hand, subjecting the class members to discovery as parties can be justified on the ground that they are indeed parties in some sense. On the other hand, deploying the whole apparatus of discovery against every class member can be an instrument of harassment. Hence, it could be said that class members are not parties to the action in the sense that would subject them to discovery to the same extent as an individual party. Most courts have taken the view that reasonably necessary discovery against individual class members should be allowed as a matter of judicial discretion, but that discovery is not available as of right as it would be against a party to a nonclass suit.[31] In general, the courts seem to have struck a sensible balance in resolving the issue.

Settlement

Most lawsuits are settled before trial, and class suits are no exception. (Contrary to popular rumor, not all class actions settle.[32]) When settlement is in view, however, the tensions within the class suit emerge in sharper perspective. As a package, settlement can include various amounts of monetary compensation and specific relief for the members, such as restoration to seniority in a discrimination case, and compensa-

29. Miller and Crump, Jurisdiction and Choice of Law in Multistate Class Actions after Phillips Petroleum Co. v. Shutts, 96 Yale L.J. 8 (1986).

30. *See* Note, Obtaining Discovery from Absent Class Members in Federal Rule of Civil Procedure 23(b)(3) Class Actions, 30 Drake L. Rev. 347 (1981); *see also* Spoon v. Superior Court, 130 Cal.App.3d 735, 182 Cal.Rptr. 44 (1982).

31. *See, e.g.,* Hoffmann–La Roche Inc. v. Sperling, 493 U.S. 165, 110 S.Ct. 482, 107 L.Ed.2d 480 (1989); Brennan v. Midwestern United Life Ins. Co., 450 F.2d 999 (7th Cir.1971).

32. *E.g.,* Hilao v. Estate of Marcos, 103 F.3d 767 (9th Cir.1996); Willging, *et al.,* Empirical Study of Class Actions in Four Federal District Courts: Final Report to the Advisory Committee on Civil Rules 18–19 (1996).

tion for the attorney for the class. Various "mixes" in the package can affect various members of the class in different ways. For example, a class member in a discrimination case who already has another job is interested in monetary compensation rather than a job offer, while the reverse would be true of a class member still unemployed. For this reason, a settlement proposal should be subject to careful judicial scrutiny and may be the occasion for additional notice to the class and special hearings on the fairness of the proposal.[33] Unfortunately, because the parties that have agreed to a settlement will try not to present its defects to the court, this scrutiny may not be sufficiently searching unless objectors intervene to challenge the settlement.[34] Courts have occasionally appointed a guardian to report on the adequacy of the settlement, and in large cases might appoint an objector to present what can reasonably be said against the settlement.

Obviously, adversarial positions can develop among groups within the class, and there can arise virtually a subsuit among such groups over the terms of settlement.[35] Even when the class has been divided into subclasses, each with its own representatives, those subclasses will rarely be wholly homogeneous. Because the clients' interests conflict, such disputes leave the class lawyer in a difficult situation: withdrawal by the lawyer leaves those clients without representation; advocating the position chosen by a majority of the named plaintiffs may sometimes assist that majority in violating its duty to represent other class members; making an independent choice of a position may result in the lawyer's choice superseding that of the clients whose rights are at stake.[36] Courts have allowed class lawyers to advocate a settlement even though some class representatives and members disagree.[37] But lawyers should remember that they owe duties to all class members and should, for example, inform the court of members' objections that the lawyers consider unfounded.[38]

33. *See* 7A Wright and Miller, Federal Practice and Procedure § 1797; *see, e.g.,* Ace Heating & Plumbing Co. v. Crane Co., 453 F.2d 30 (3d Cir.1971); Plummer v. Chemical Bank, 91 F.R.D. 434 (S.D.N.Y.), *aff'd,* 668 F.2d 654 (2d Cir.1982).

34. *See* Willging, note 32 *supra,* at 56–58; Hensler, *et al.,* Class Action Dilemmas: Pursuing Public Goals for Private Gain 460–63, 486–90 (2000).

35. *See, e.g.,* Schuck, Agent Orange on Trial (1986).

36. *See, e.g.,* In re Agent Orange Prod. Liab. Litig., 800 F.2d 14 (2d Cir.1986); Bell, Serving Two Masters: Integration Ideals and Client Interests in School Desegregation Litigation, 85 Yale L.J. 470 (1976); Rhode, Class Conflicts in Class Actions, 34 Stan. L. Rev. 1183 (1982).

37. *E.g.,* Lazy Oil Co. v. Witco Corp., 166 F.3d 581 (3d Cir.1999); Maywalt v. Parker & Parsley Petroleum Co., 67 F.3d 1072 (2d Cir.1995).

38. Gates v. Cook, 234 F.3d 221 (5th Cir.2000) (removing class counsel); Shapiro, Class Actions: The Class as Party and Client, 73 Notre Dame L. Rev. 913 (1998); Weinstein, Ethical Dilemmas in Mass Tort Litigation, 88 Nw. U.L. Rev. 470 (1994). On the possibility of malpractice actions by class members against class lawyers, *see* Koniak and Cohen, Under Cloak of Settlement, 82 Va. L. Rev. 1051 (1996).

Attorney conflicts of interest

Beyond potential conflicts within the class, there is almost inevitable conflict of interest between the attorney representing the class and the class members. Sometimes the attorney wants the settlement "mix" to consist of a large share of cash from which he or she can recover a fee and the expenses that have been advanced, whereas the class may be interested in specific relief rather than money. Alternatively, the attorney may accept a settlement consisting mainly of discount coupons for class members; such a settlement may cost the defendant little and permit the attorney to claim a fee based on the coupons' face value, although their practical value to the class may be less.[39] Even if the settlement is all in cash, the attorney once paid may have less interest in ensuring its distribution to class members.[40]

To some extent, these conflicts can be controlled by basing the attorney's fee on the benefits actually received by class members,[41] but this may accentuate another conflict. In some situations the class's lawyer has an incentive to settle at the early stages of the litigation before a large investment has been made in preparation, whereas the class, having begun the suit, is interested in the lawyer's committing a major effort to develop the case before settling it. Many class actions now settle early, and sometimes negotiations occur before the action begins, with the complaint and the proposed settlement being filed simultaneously.[42] There has been much controversy over the propriety and treatment of such settlement class actions.[43]

Defendants and their lawyers as well as lawyers representing the class can contribute to these problems. Defendants can seek a settlement beneficial for them but not necessarily for the class by deciding when to pursue settlement negotiations, what attorney fee provisions to accept, and sometimes which plaintiffs' lawyers to negotiate with.[44] Although

39. Miller & Singer, Nonpecuniary Class Action Settlements, 60 L. & Contemp. Probs. 97 (1997); Note, In–Kind Class Action Settlement, 109 Harv. L. Rev. 810 (1996).

40. *See* Boeing Co. v. Van Gemert, 444 U.S. 472, 100 S.Ct. 745, 62 L.Ed.2d 676 (1980)(fee may be paid from whole settlement fund, not just what class members claim); Duhaime v. John Hancock Mutual Life Ins. Co., 989 F.Supp. 375 (D.Mass. 1997)(fees to be paid as claimants are paid); Hensler, *et al.*, Class Action Dilemmas: Pursuing Public Goals for Private Gains 459, 463 (2000).

41. *See* Coffee, Understanding the Plaintiff's Attorney: The Implications of Economic Theory for Private Enforcement of Law Through Class and Derivative Actions, 86 Colum. L. Rev. 669 (1986); Macey & Miller, The Plaintiffs' Attorney's Role in Class Action and Derivative Litigation: Economic Analysis and Recommendations for Reform, 58 U. Chi. L. Rev. 1 (1991); Issacharoff, Class Action Conflicts, 30 U.C. Davis L. Rev. 805 (1997); Resnik, Money Matters: Judicial Market Interventions Creating Subsidies and Awarding Fees and Costs in Individual and Aggregate Litigation, 148 U. Pa. L. Rev. 2119 (2000).

42. *E.g.*, Ortiz v. Fibreboard Corp., 527 U.S. 815, 119 S.Ct. 2295, 144 L.Ed.2d 715 (1999); Willging, *et al.*, Empirical Study of Class Actions in Four Federal District Courts: Final Report to the Advisory Committee on Civil Rules 34–35, 61–62 (1996).

43. *See* Amchem Products, Inc. v. Windsor, 521 U.S. 591, 117 S.Ct. 2231, 138 L.Ed.2d 689 (1997); § 10.22 *supra*.

44. *See* Koniak, Feasting While the Widow Weeps: *Georgine v. Amchem Products, Inc.*, 80 Cornell L. Rev. 1085 (1985); Coffee, Class Wars: The Dilemma of the Mass Tort

some settlements benefit class lawyers at the expense of their clients, the opposite may also occur: defendants have been known to press altruistic class lawyers to waive recovery of the attorney's fee in order to obtain a settlement more beneficial to the class.[45]

Some courts sought to deal with these problems by prohibiting discussion of the attorney's fee until agreement on the rest of a settlement was reached.[46] The Supreme Court, however, rejected such a prohibition as unrealistic, noting that the defendant bargains for a whole settlement, not merely part of one, and that the open discussion of the fee could turn into a discussion conducted through codes and signals between the lawyers.[47] What clearly is possible and proper is close judicial scrutiny of the settlement not only between the class and the opposing party but also between the class and its attorney.[48] Yet this brings us back to the problem from which our discussion of settlement started: once the defendant has agreed in the settlement not to oppose an attorney fee application within stated limits, the court will find it hard to scrutinize that fee unless class members or others appear to challenge it.[49]

Implementing and challenging class action judgments

Even after a class action goes to judgment, it is not necessarily finished. Implementing the judgment so that class members actually receive their shares may be a long process giving rise to further controversy. For example, the settlement fund may prove inadequate, or alternatively there may be money left over.[50] If class members seek to bring independent actions, the extent to which the class action judgment is binding may come into question. This will be discussed below in section 11.29.

Class Action, 95 Colum. L. Rev. 1343 (1995).

45. *E.g.,* Evans v. Jeff D., 475 U.S. 717, 106 S.Ct. 1531, 89 L.Ed.2d 747 (1986).

46. *See, e.g.,* Prandini v. National Tea Co., 557 F.2d 1015 (3d Cir.1977); Wolfram, The Second Set of Players: Lawyers, Fee Shifting, and the Limits of Professional Discipline, 47 Law & Contemp. Probs. 393 (1984).

47. Evans v. Jeff D., 475 U.S. 717, 106 S.Ct. 1531, 89 L.Ed.2d 747 (1986).

48. *See, e.g.,* Saylor v. Lindsley, 456 F.2d 896 (2d Cir.1972); *see also* Dunn v. H. K. Porter Co., 602 F.2d 1105 (3d Cir.1979).

49. Willging, Empirical Study of Class Actions in Four Federal District Courts: Final Reports to the Advisory Committee on Civil Rules 76–77 (1996).

50. *See, e.g.,* Van Gemert v. Boeing Co., 739 F.2d 730 (2d Cir.1984); In re Joint Eastern and Southern District Asbestos Litigation, 78 F.3d 764 (2d Cir.1996); In re A.H. Robins Co., 86 F.3d 364 (4th Cir. 1996); Hensler, *et al.,* Class Action Dilemmas: Pursuing Public Goals for Private Gain (2000); Bartsh, A Class–Action Suit that Worked (1978). Institutional reform class actions may continue for decades after the finding of a violation. *E.g.,* Freeman v. Pitts, 503 U.S. 467, 112 S.Ct. 1430, 118 L.Ed.2d 108 (1992); Rufo v. Inmates of Suffolk County Jail, 502 U.S. 367, 112 S.Ct. 748, 116 L.Ed.2d 867 (1992).

D. JOINDER IN HISTORICAL PERSPECTIVE

§ 10.24 Past and Future Joinder Policy

When viewed in historical perspective, the rules governing joinder of claims and parties have evolved in three eras. The first and longest era began with the early common law writs in the twelfth and thirteenth centuries and continued until the nineteenth century. The second commenced with the Field Code of 1848 and ended with the Federal Rules of Civil Procedure, particularly their revision in 1966. The third is the present era.[1]

Common law and equity joinder

The first era was characterized by the system of common law forms of action and the emergence of equity. The forms of action were predicated not on a theory of civil procedure—that is, how to go about adjudicating civil controversies in general—but on considerations of the political authority of the central government. The legal problem arose in justifying royal court intervention in disputes that ordinarily were matters of local jurisdiction and in limiting royal intervention to cases in which such intervention was politically important. The focus of the common law in its formative stage thus was not on civil disputes as such but on violence that might degenerate into lawlessness and thereby subvert regular adjudication of civil disputes. It was only gradually and incompletely over the centuries that the common law actions were adapted to adjudicate ordinary, peaceful controversies.

Accompanying this development, and partially compensating for the deficiencies of common law procedure, was the emergence of equity. Equity was reactive, ameliorative, and exceptional, providing redress for some of the grosser defects of common law actions. Despite the ameliorative effect of equity, however, Anglo–American civil procedure until the nineteenth century was extraordinarily clumsy. Its common law side was especially ill-adapted to deal with controversies involving more than one substantive legal concept or more than two parties, while its equity side was separately administered according to distinct rules having no direct complement with the common law forms.

The codes and Federal Rules

Procedure in the second historical era, from 1848 to 1966, evolved toward a system free of these deficiencies. Even with the objective of simple adjudication of ordinary legal controversies, however, a century

§ 10.24

1. *See* Clark, Code Pleading 348–392 (2d ed. 1947); Kaplan, Continuing Work of the Civil Committee: 1966 Amendments to the Federal Rules of Civil Procedure I, 81 Harv. L. Rev. 356 (1967); Bone, Mapping the Boundaries of a Dispute: Concepts of Ideal Lawsuit Structure from the Field Code to the Federal Rules, 89 Colum. L. Rev. 1 (1989); §§ 1.3–1.7 *supra*.

passed before many inefficient technicalities were eliminated. Free joinder of claims was finally accomplished only in Federal Rule 18. Joinder of parties and class actions have been somewhat cleared up in the 1966 revisions of the Federal Rules and the 1990 supplemental jurisdiction statute.

Current problems

In the present era, substantial difficulties remain in dealing with controversies that have multistate elements or questions of both state and federal law, since the rules of personal and subject matter jurisdiction have not been fully systematized.[2] In various circumstances the system still cannot determine all aspects of an ordinary civil controversy in one action. There is simply no reason why a multiclaim, multiparty controversy arising within the United States should not be submissible to a single tribunal for a consistent adjudication of the various claims and liabilities.[3] Failure in this objective has multiplied and prolonged litigation, multiplied private and public legal costs, and brought the system of justice into unnecessary disrepute. Only a legal technician could admire the system as it is.

Mass injury litigation

One important subcategory of multiparty litigation is mass injury litigation—the cases arising out of airplane crashes, health injuries such as those resulting from asbestos, employment discrimination, institutional reform litigation, and so on. In this type of case the procedural failures noted above work a costly toll. In addition, many courts remain hesitant to impose massive liability in a single judgment, wondering whether the civil remedial system ought to be put to such use, and to what extent efficiency should limit the right to an individual day in court. The bar is ambivalent, concerned with the costly complexity of the system but also fearful of losing practice should the system be streamlined. Authority and responsibility for procedural reform is divided between the courts, the legislature, and the bar (each of which is itself divided)to the point that the mechanisms for serious reform have been tied in deadlock. In the case of asbestos, for example, attempts to set up fair and workable compensation systems through bankruptcy proceedings, class actions or legislation have all encountered obstacles.[4]

The contending viewpoints are well revealed in a case filed after an airplane crash that killed more than 300 people.[5] The trial judge in effect

2. *See* American L. Inst., Study of the Division of Jurisdiction Between State and Federal Courts (1969); *see also* Hanson v. Denckla, 357 U.S. 235, 78 S.Ct. 1228, 2 L.Ed.2d 1283 (1958).

3. *See* Hazard, Interstate Venue, 74 Nw. U.L. Rev. 711 (1979); *cf.* McCoid, A Single Package for Multiparty Disputes, 28 Stan. L. Rev. 707 (1976).

4. *See* Ortiz v. Fibreboard Corp., 527 U.S. 815, 119 S.Ct. 2295, 144 L.Ed.2d 715 (1999); Symposium, Mass Torts, 148 U. Pa. L. Rev. 1851 (2000).

5. Pan Am. World Airways v. United States Dist. Court, 523 F.2d 1073 (9th Cir. 1975).

consolidated all the claims through joinder, discovery, and class action procedures. The appellate court used the extraordinary remedy of mandamus to undo his work. The dissenting judge observed:

> The majority, in my view, reaches the wrong result because it contemplates the wrong question. The question is not whether some rule permits the action proposed, but whether any rule, statute, or logical concept forbids it.[6]

A reform program

The procedural methods for dealing effectively with these kinds of cases are not mysterious. Indeed, they are familiar and proven. It is only their combination that remains to be accomplished. The combination would include the following:

1. nationwide service of process, and international service of process in cases with significant external elements;[7]
2. venue at the place where the claim arose or where several claimants or defendants reside, with liberal judicial powers of venue transfer;[8]
3. stay of other pending actions involving the same transaction;[9]
4. assignment of the case to an experienced judge who has a record of being firm and levelheaded;[10]
5. representation through class representatives where large numbers of people are involved, and appointment of "lead counsel" for each interest;[11]
6. close judicial supervision of discovery and other aspects of pretrial;[12]
7. severance of the liability issue for separate trial, and individual trials of damages issues when necessary;[13]

6. *Id.* at 1082 (Schnacke, J., dissenting). Resistance to class treatment of mass torts has ebbed somewhat since this decision. Resnick, From "Cases" to "Litigation," 54 Law & Contemp. Probs. 5 (Summer 1991); § 10.22 *supra.*

7. *See, e.g.,* 28 U.S.C. § 2361 (nationwide service of process in interpleader actions); Restatement (Second) of the Foreign Relations Law of the United States § 44, Reporter's Note.

8. *See* 28 U.S.C. §§ 1391(a), (b), 1407. But *see* Lexecon Inc. v. Milberg Weiss Bershad Hynes & Lerach, 523 U.S. 26, 118 S.Ct. 956, 140 L.Ed.2d 62 (1998). American L. Inst., Complex Litigation: Statutory Recommendations and Analysis (1994) makes ambitious proposals for the consolidation and handling of complex litigation; for discussion, *see* Special Issue, 1995 B.Y.U. L. Rev. 731.

9. *See, e.g.,* Archibald v. Cinerama Hotels, 15 Cal.3d 853, 544 P.2d 947, 126 Cal. Rptr. 811 (1976).

10. *See* 28 U.S.C. § 1407(b).

11. Vincent v. Hughes Air W., Inc., 557 F.2d 759 (9th Cir.1977); *see also* Manual for Complex Litigation §§ 1.44, 1.92 (rev. ed. 1982).

12. *See* Brazil, Improving Judicial Controls over the Pretrial Development of Civil Actions: Model Rules for Case Management and Sanctions, 1981 Am. B. Found. Res. J. 873; Peckham, The Federal Judge as Case Manager: The New Role in Guiding a Case from Filing to Disposition, 69 Calif. L. Rev. 770 (1981).

13. *See, e.g.,* Arnold v. Eastern Air Lines, 681 F.2d 186 (4th Cir.1982); Franklin Music Co. v. American Broadcasting Co., 616 F.2d 528 (3d Cir.1979).

8. marshaling insurance resources and apportionment of liability among obligors;[14]
9. judicial supervision of negotiations (perhaps by a judge who will not preside at trial)when there seems to be unreasonable resistance to settlement;[15]
10. facilitation of settlement through decision of test cases, computer modeling of large numbers of comparable cases, and negotiation of standardized claim procedures and settlement terms.[16]

14. *See, e.g.,* Sindell v. Abbott Laboratories, 26 Cal.3d 588, 607 P.2d 924, 163 Cal. Rptr. 132, *cert. denied,* 449 U.S. 912, 101 S.Ct. 285–286, 66 L.Ed.2d 140 (1980); *cf.* State Farm Fire & Casualty Co. v. Tashire, 386 U.S. 523, 87 S.Ct. 1199, 18 L.Ed.2d 270 (1967).

15. *See, e.g.,* Will, Merhige, and Rubin, The Role of the Judge in the Settlement Process, 75 F.R.D. 203 (1977); *see also* Conference for District Court Judges: The Settlement Process, 59 F.R.D. 252 (1973); § 5.19–5.21 *supra.*

16. McGovern, Resolving Mature Mass Tort Litigation, 69 B.U.L. Rev. 659 (1989); Symposium, Claims Resolution and the Mass Settlement of Mass Torts, 53 Law & Contemp. Probs. (Autumn 1990).

Chapter 11

JUDGMENTS

A. RES JUDICATA

§ 11.1 Introduction

On conclusion of the consideration of the issues in an action, the trial court enters a judgment,[1] an order specifying the relief, if any, that plaintiff will receive. If the court determines that plaintiff is not entitled to relief, the judgment is that "plaintiff take nothing." If relief is awarded, it may be one or a combination of three types: an award of a sum of money, the kind of judgment awarded in the usual action for damages; an order directing the defendant to do something or to refrain from doing something, the judgment or decree awarded in a suit for an injunction; or an order specifying the legal relationships between the parties concerning the subject matter of the action, the relief awarded in declaratory judgment actions, in proceedings that determine status such as divorce or parentage, and in actions determining interests in property such as a suit to quiet title to real property.[2]

Single and multiple judgments

Ordinarily, no judgment is entered in an action until the court is ready to enter a single, final judgment.[3] Common law procedure permitted only such a judgment. In equity, a complicated case could be resolved in stages, first determining the parties' rights and then determining the appropriate remedy. The differences were reflected in the rules governing appellate review. At common law, no appeal was available until final judgment. Equity allowed interlocutory appeals from orders granting or denying preliminary injunctions and orders that were final, except for "cleanup" such as accounting.[4] This special treatment of such orders is reflected in modern procedural systems.[5] Furthermore, in equitable proceedings involving multiple parties, a decree could determine the relief for one of the parties while leaving the suit still pending as to other parties. Under most modern procedure systems, if the action involves multiple claims or multiple parties the court is authorized to enter a final judgment on some of the claims or some of the parties while retaining consideration of the action as to the others.[6] Exercise of this authority in effect segments the action for the purpose of determining relief. The final judgment principle applies to a segment of an action.

Consequences of entering judgment

The entry of final judgment has several important consequences. First, it sets in running the time periods for post-trial motions such as those for new trial or judgment notwithstanding the verdict,[7] for an

§ 11.1

1. *See* Fed. R. Civ. P. 54, 55, 58, and Forms 31, 32.

2. *See* §§ 1.8–1.10 *supra.*

3. *Compare* Fed. R. Civ. P. 54(b). *See also* § 12.4 *infra.*

4. *See generally* Crick, The Final Judgment as a Basis for Appeal, 41 Yale L.J. 539 (1932); Restatement (Second) of Judgments § 13.

5. *See, e.g.,* 28 U.S.C. § 1292(a).

6. *See* Fed. R. Civ. P. 54(b). *Compare* Gillespie v. United States Steel Corp., 379 U.S. 148, 85 S.Ct. 308, 13 L.Ed.2d 199 (1964).

7. *See* Fed. R. Civ. P. 59(b), 50(b). *See also* §§ 7.24–7.30 *supra.*

appeal,[8] and for motions for extraordinary relief from the judgment.[9]

Execution

Second, the judgment is a basis on which the winning party can obtain the assistance of public coercive force to realize the benefits of the judgment. A successful defendant is usually entitled to file a "cost bill," which is in substance a money judgment in its favor for the costs awardable to the party obtaining judgment.[10] A successful plaintiff is entitled to present judgment on the award with a cost bill. A party that has obtained a judgment for money may initiate procedure for execution of the judgment through the offices of the sheriff, marshal, or similar official. If plaintiff has obtained an injunctive remedy and defendant fails to comply with it, plaintiff may apply to the court for the sanctions of civil or criminal contempt. When a judgment specifies legal relationships regarding the subject matter of the litigation, the parties may then conduct themselves accordingly. Thus, a plaintiff adjudged the owner of real property may record the judgment in the appropriate land records, much as one would record a deed.[11]

Third, the judgment establishes legal barriers against relitigating the matters involved in the action. These barriers are called the rules of "res judicata" and are addressed in this chapter.[12] "Res judicata" means, roughly, "decided matter." Depending on one's approach to Latin, the first word is pronounced to rhyme with "peace" or "pace" and the first "a" in the second word to rhyme with either "rate" or "rot."

§ 11.2 Policy Considerations

At several points we have noted the conflict between two fundamental goals in the law of procedure. On the one hand, the procedural system aims to permit full development of the contentions and evidentiary possibilities of the various parties so that the case is decided on the merits. On the other hand, the system also aims to bring an adjudication to a final conclusion with reasonable promptness at a reasonable cost. By and large, modern procedure gives greater weight to the first of these objectives during the course of a proceeding. The rules therefore permit assertion of alternative positions, discovery of evidence that goes beyond the issues framed in the pleadings, liberal amendment of contentions prior to trial, and considerable freedom in development of theories of claim and defense during the trial itself.

8. Fed. R. App. P. 4(a). *Compare* Fed. R. App. P. 5(a). *See* § 12.7 *infra.*

9. Fed. R. Civ. P. 60(b). *See* § 12.8 *infra.*

10. Fed. R. Civ. P. 54(d).

11. *Compare* Fed. R. Civ. P. 62.

12. *See generally*, Restatement (Second) of Judgments; Shapiro, Civil Procedure: Preclusion in Civil Actions (2001); Casad and Clermont, Res Judicata (2001).

Scope of finality

There is, in principle, no reason why similar liberality could not be allowed after judgment. Appeal could be—but it is not, as we shall see[1]—an opportunity for a comprehensive reconsideration of the case, including the opportunity to introduce new evidence. Motions for extraordinary relief from judgments could serve a similar function; as we shall see, they have a much more limited scope.[2] Similarly, there is, in principle, no reason why the rules of res judicata could not be limited to the narrow question whether the prior action actually decided the issues necessarily involved in awarding the judgment. This could be called a minimal concept of res judicata; without it, a judgment would not conclusively decide anything. It seems clear that the adjudicative process would fail to serve its social and economic functions if it did not have this minimal effect.

At common law, the scope of the rules of res judicata were almost as narrow. A judgment entered in one case on one form of action did not prevent litigants from pursuing another form of action, although more than one recovery was not permitted for a single loss.[3] The determination of issues was binding only as between parties to the record in the first action.[4] This meant that while a party could not relitigate an issue with a person against whom it had already litigated that issue, it would not be prevented from relitigating the issue against someone else. These rules reflected the concepts underlying common law trial procedure. The common law "action" was a proceeding on a writ, not a comprehensive investigation of responsibility for an alleged injury. And the basis for precluding relitigation of an issue was that a litigant could not contradict a record to which it was a party.[5] More fundamentally, inasmuch as common law procedure required narrow formulation of issues and limited opportunity for joining claims or developing proofs, it accorded a judgment correspondingly limited effects in precluding further litigation.

Wider modern scope

As the rules of litigation have changed in the evolution of modern procedure, so have the rules of res judicata. The changes in the joinder and discovery rules have come about through statutes and rules of court. The corresponding changes in the rules of res judicata have been developed almost entirely through decisional law that evolved in the wake of these legislative reforms. The basic proposition of res judicata, however, has remained essentially the same: A party should not be

§ 11.2

1. *See* Chapter 12.

2. *Id.*

3. *Compare* McCaskill, Actions and Causes of Action, 34 Yale L.J. 614 (1925).

4. *See* Bigelow v. Old Dominion Copper Mining & Smelting Co., 225 U.S. 111, 32 S.Ct. 641, 56 L.Ed. 1009 (1912).

5. Millar, The Historical Relation of Estoppel by Record to Res Judicata, 35 Ill. L. Rev. 41 (1940); Note, Common–Law Incursion into the Civilian Conception of Res Judicata, 64 Tul. L. Rev. 1733 (1990) (describing former Louisiana law).

allowed to relitigate a matter that it already had opportunity to litigate. As the rules of procedure have expanded the scope of the initial opportunity to litigate, they have invited a corresponding expansion of the extent to which that opportunity forecloses a subsequent opportunity.[6] As we shall see, this is the clear tendency of the modern law of res judicata.

Whether the scope of the rules of res judicata is relatively narrow (as it formerly was) or relatively broad (as it has become), the social objectives of the rules have remained much the same. They recognize that the purpose of a lawsuit is not only to do substantial justice but to bring an end to controversy. It is important that judgments of the court have stability and certainty. This is true not only so that the parties and others may rely on them in ordering their practical affairs (such as borrowing or lending money, or buying property) and thus be protected from repetitive litigation, but also so that the moral force of court judgments will not be undermined.

Flexibility is still needed, and, of course, the law does afford procedures for correcting, reversing, reopening, and vacating judgments.[7] Res judicata law itself contains some flexibility to permit relitigation when a party has not had a fair chance to dispute in an appropriate tribunal. In other situations, the policy of finality yields to other policies, as when the tendency to give res judicata effect to administrative adjudications[8] is overcome by indications that Congress wished to assure a judicial forum for certain discrimination claims.[9] But the limitations on relitigation are stricter and more strictly enforced, and the area for discretion is narrower, than is the case with prejudgment procedures.

§ 11.3 Definitions and Distinctions

Claim preclusion

The term "res judicata" refers to the various ways in which a judgment in one action will have a binding effect in another. This includes first the effects of the former judgment when the second action proceeds on all or part of the claim that was the subject of the first action. In traditional terminology, the effects are called "merger" or "bar." In modern terminology both of these effects are called "claim preclusion."

6. *Compare* Schopflocher, What Is a Single Cause of Action for the Purpose of the Doctrine of Res Judicata?, 21 Or. L. Rev. 319 (1942), *with* Restatement (Second) of Judgments 24. *See also* Vestal, Res Judicata/Claim Preclusion: Judgment for the Claimant, 62 Nw. U.L. Rev. 357 (1967). *See also* Premier Elec. Construction Co. v. National Elec. Contractors Assn., 814 F.2d 358 (7th Cir.1987) (because the rules of res judicata developed as a matter of common law, they should yield to a contrary statute or formal rule of procedure).

7. *See* Chapter 12.

8. *See* § 11.21 *infra*.

9. Astoria Fed. Sav. & Loan Ass'n v. Solimino, 501 U.S. 104, 111 S.Ct. 2166, 115 L.Ed.2d 96 (1991).

The "merger" of plaintiff's claim into a judgment in plaintiff's favor extinguishes the entire claim or cause of action and merges it in the judgment.[1] Thereafter plaintiff's rights in that claim or cause of action are confined to proceedings for the enforcement of the judgment—by execution, supplemental proceedings, or, if need be, a new action on the judgment. Plaintiff may no longer sue on the original cause of action or any item of it even if that item was omitted from the original action.

The "bar" of a judgment for the defendant extinguishes the entire cause of action or claim, including items of that claim that were not in fact raised in the former action.[2] The Supreme Court has formulated the concept of claim preclusion in this way: "a final judgment on the merits of an action precludes the parties or their privies from relitigating issues that were or could have been raised in that action."[3] The concepts of bar and merger that make up claim preclusion are sometimes referred to as "the rule against splitting a [single] cause of action."[4]

Issue preclusion

A second effect, traditionally known as "collateral estoppel," is now called "issue preclusion" to distinguish it from claim preclusion.[5] The effect of issue preclusion is that an issue determined in a first action may not be relitigated when the same issue arises in a later action based on a different claim or demand. The most famous formulation of the distinction was made by Justice Field in *Cromwell v. County of Sac*:

> In the former case, the judgment, if rendered upon the merits, constitutes an absolute bar to a subsequent action. It is a finality as to the claim or demand in controversy, concluding parties and those in privity with them, not only as to every matter which was offered and received to sustain or defeat the claim or demand, but as to any other admissible matter which might have been offered for that purpose.... Such demand or claim, having passed into judgment, cannot again be brought into litigation between the parties in proceedings at law upon any ground whatever.
>
> But where the second action between the same parties is upon a different claim or demand, the judgment in the prior action operates as an estoppel only as to those matters in issue or points controverted, upon the determination of which the finding or verdict was rendered.[6]

Full faith and credit

Full faith and credit is another concept that interacts with claim and issue preclusion. Under the Constitution, an implementing federal stat-

§ 11.3

1. Restatement (Second) of Judgments §§ 17(a), 18.

2. *Id.* §§ 17(b), 19.

3. Allen v. McCurry, 449 U.S. 90, 94, 101 S.Ct. 411, 414, 66 L.Ed.2d 308 (1980).

4. *See, e.g.*, Clark, Code Pleading §§ 73–75 (2d ed. 1947).

5. Restatement (Second) of Judgments § 17. *See also* Cooper v. Federal Reserve Bank of Richmond, 467 U.S. 867, 104 S.Ct. 2794, 81 L.Ed.2d 718 (1984); McDonald v. City of West Branch, 466 U.S. 284, 104 S.Ct. 1799, 80 L.Ed.2d 302 (1984).

6. 94 U.S. 351, 352–353, 24 L.Ed. 195, 197–198 (1876).

ute, and precedent, state and federal courts are required to give full faith and credit to the judgments of other state and federal courts, typically by allowing the plaintiff to enforce them against the defendant without having to relitigate the case.[7] The obligation applies when the court entering the original judgment had personal jurisdiction over the defendant. When it does apply, the enforcing court must give the judgment the same faith and credit that it had in the original court. In other words, the enforcing court must apply the original court's law of claim and issue preclusion.[8] That law is very similar in all United States jurisdictions, so usually the enforcing court can simply use the general principles of claim and issue preclusion. But some states have adopted variant versions of these principles, and providing the full faith and credit due to a judgment from such a state will therefore require the enforcing court to explore and implement those variants.[9]

§ 11.4 Requirement of Finality

Both branches of res judicata—claim preclusion and issue preclusion—apply only after a final determination of the claim or issue. The reason is virtually definitional: The rules preclude relitigation of a matter previously determined, and a matter has not been "determined" until a judgment has been rendered. It follows that the rules of res judicata do not ordinarily operate before a final judgment.[1] Thus, an interlocutory order, which is not ordinarily appealable,[2] would not be treated as a final judgment for purposes of res judicata. Similarly, the pendency of a motion that renders a judgment nonfinal for purposes of appeal—such as a motion for j.n.o.v. under Rule 50(b), a motion to amend or make additional factual findings under Rule 52(b), or a motion for a new trial under Rule 59(e)—should also arrest the effect of res judicata on the judgment.[3] There are, however, some important qualifications to this general proposition.

7. U.S. Const. art. IV, § 1; 28 U.S.C. § 1738; § 2.8 *supra*.

8. *E.g.*, Marrese v. American Academy of Orthopaedic Surgeons, 470 U.S. 373, 105 S.Ct. 1327, 84 L.Ed.2d 274 (1985); Burbank, Interjurisdictional Preclusion, Full Faith and Credit and Federal Common Law: A General Approach, 71 Cornell L.J. 733 (1986); § 11.14 *infra*. An arcane principle known as the Rooker–Feldman doctrine also bears on the credit that federal courts owe to state court judgments. See D.C. Court of Appeals v. Feldman, 460 U.S. 462, 103 S.Ct. 1303, 75 L.Ed.2d 206 (1983); Symposium, The Rooker–Feldman Doctrine, 74 Notre Dame L. Rev. 1081 (1999).

9. Semtek Int'l Inc. v. Lockheed Martin Corp., 531 U.S. 497, 121 S.Ct. 1021, 149 L.Ed.2d 32 (2001) (impact of statute of limitations dismissal on suit in another state); St. Paul Mercury Ins. Co. v. Williamson, 224 F.3d 425 (5th Cir.2000)(applying Louisiana preclusion law); Erichson, Interjurisdictional Preclusion, 96 Mich. L. Rev. 945 (1998).

§ 11.4

1. Restatement (Second) of Judgments § 13. The Supreme Court has held that it is "familiar law that only a final judgment is res judicata." G & C Merriam Co. v. Saalfield, 241 U.S. 22, 28, 36 S.Ct. 477, 480, 60 L.Ed. 868, 872 (1916).

2. *See* § 12.9 *infra*; 1B Moore, Federal Practice and Procedure ¶ 0.416(3).

3. *See* 1B Moore, *supra* note 2.

Effect of appeal

One of the most troublesome problems in applying the rule of finality arises when a judgment has been appealed. There are no technically precise, universally recognized rules on the effect of an appeal on the "existence" of a judgment.[4] Certain procedures suspend the enforceability of a judgment or decree during the pendency of the review proceeding;[5] these focus, however, on whether the losing party would have to comply with the judgment pending the appeal. But by inference it could be said that they also suspend the effect of the judgment for purposes of the rules of res judicata.

The state courts are divided on the question. On one hand, it makes little sense to accord conclusive effect to a determination that itself may be nullified through reversal on appeal; on the other hand, it may be a waste of effort to retry an issue simply because an appeal is pending in the case in which the issue was originally determined. Some courts solve the problem through the practical expedient of postponing decision of the res judicata question in the second action until the appeal in the first action has been determined.[6] In the federal courts, the pendency of an appeal does not render a judgment nonfinal for purposes of res judicata.[7] But if the appeal causes the entire case to be removed to the appellate court, and the proceeding hence is de novo, then the appealed federal judgment will be vacated and cannot have res judicata or collateral estoppel effect.[8] A similar difficulty arises when the judgment in the first action is sought to be set aside.[9]

Multiple claims

A somewhat similar problem can develop when an action involves multiple claims or multiple issues. Under modern procedure, when an action involves more than one claim (including a claim that is asserted in identical form against two or more defendants), the court is authorized to determine the claims separately to advance the final conclusion of the litigation. If the court reaches decision on one of the claims and directs entry of judgment on it, the decision on that claim becomes final and the rules of res judicata clearly apply. If the court postpones entry of judgment until the action as a whole is disposed of, however, there is no "judgment" even though there may have been a definite decision on the claim in question.[10] Also, under modern procedure a court can order particular issues to be determined separate from other issues; for example, the court may order the question of liability to be tried while

4. *See* Annot., 9 A.L.R.2d 984.

5. *See* Fed. R. Civ. P. 62; Fed. R. App. P. 7, 8.

6. Restatement (Second) of Judgments § 16, Comment *b*.

7. Wagner v. Taylor, 836 F.2d 596 (D.C.Cir.1987).

8. American Heritage Life Ins. Co. v. Heritage Life Ins. Co., 494 F.2d 3 (5th Cir.1974).

9. *See* 1B Moore, Federal Practice and Procedure ¶ 0.416(3).

10. *See* Fed. R. Civ. P. 54(b).

postponing trial of the question of damages or other relief. In such a situation, an issue can be definitely decided before a judgment based on that decision is rendered.[11]

Traditionally, res judicata would not operate in either situation. The evolving rule, adopted by the Restatement (Second) of Judgments, is that for res judicata purposes the decision should be regarded as final when it is unlikely to be revised in the course of the action in which it was reached.[12] In both this situation and that posed by the appeal of a judgment, the tendency is thus toward using a practical rather than a formal or technical concept of finality in deciding when the rules of res judicata become operative.

§ 11.5 Law of the Case Doctrine

The rules of res judicata are distinguished from a related but distinct rule, the "law of the case."[1] The law of the case rule applies to a question of law that, having been decided in one stage of a case, presents itself again at a later stage. The rule provides that a determination will normally be treated as correct through all subsequent stages of the proceeding except when the question comes before a higher court. Thus, a trial court will treat its own earlier rulings as conclusive in subsequent trial proceedings. If a case is transferred from one trial court to another, the new court should treat the prior rulings of the first court as conclusive. Similarly, an interlocutory appeal that decides a question of law will be treated as conclusive by lower courts, and by the same appellate court if the case later comes before it on appeal from the final judgment. The law of the case rule thus applies to issues of law previously determined in one action and operates prior to final judgment, while the rules of res judicata apply between successive actions and involve preclusion by way of final judgment.

Courts have some discretion to reconsider their own rulings notwithstanding the law of the case doctrine. After all, it would be wasteful for a trial court to adhere to its own previous ruling after it became clear that the ruling would ultimately be reversed on appeal. A court does not have the same discretion to reconsider the prior ruling in the same case of a higher court.

§ 11.6 Stare Decisis

The doctrine of *stare decisis* is a mandate that courts should give due weight to precedent. It holds that an already established point of law

11. *See* Note, Res Judicata and Bifurcated Negligence Trials, 16 UCLA L. Rev. 203 (1968).

12. Restatement (Second) of Judgments § 13, Comment *e*.

§ 11.5

1. *See generally* Vestal, Law of the Case: Single Suit Preclusion, 1967 Utah L. Rev. 1; Steinman, Law of the Case: A Judicial Puzzle in Consolidated and Transferred Caes and in Multidistrict Litigation, 135 U. Pa. L. Rev. 595 (1987); Annot., 87 A.L.R.2d 271; *cf.* Hathorn v. Lovorn, 457 U.S. 255, 102 S.Ct. 2421, 72 L.Ed.2d 824 (1982) (exceptions to law of the case rule).

should be followed without reconsideration, provided that the earlier decision was authoritative. (The first word is pronounced "starry.") Unlike claim and issue preclusion, the effects of stare decisis are not limited to certain persons: courts will apply a precedent to all similar cases, even though the present litigants had no chance to be heard when it was laid down. On the other hand, stare decisis is often applied more flexibly than claim and issue preclusion: precedents can be distinguished, reinterpreted, or even overruled.[1]

The essential principles of stare decisis are as follows:

1. An issue of law must have been heard and actually decided.
2. A decision is stare decisis despite the contention that the argument of counsel was otherwise insufficient.
3. A decision of older vintage may be overruled if it is seriously out of keeping with the development of the law or has proved to be unworkable.
4. There is a heavy presumption that settled issues of law will not be re-examined.[2]

Stare decisis has been described as "of fundamental importance to the rule of law"[3] because it insures that the law does not change erratically and "permits society to presume that bedrock principles are founded in the law rather than in the proclivities of individuals."[4] Departure from precedent is said to require special justification,[5] and a still greater burden must be borne by a party seeking to overrule a point of statutory construction.[6] On occasion, however, the Supreme Court has abandoned constitutional interpretations it concludes to be erroneous. And it is now commonplace for a state supreme court to overrule caselaw that it concludes to be unsuited to contemporary realities, inconsistent with later decisions, or otherwise harmful.

§ 11.6

1. Llewellyn, The Common Law Tradition: Deciding Appeals (1960).

2. Equal Employment Opportunity Commn. v. Trabucco, 791 F.2d 1 (1st Cir. 1986); see Schauer, Precedent, 39 Stan. L. Rev. 571 (1987).

3. Welch v. Texas Dept. of Highways and Pub. Transp., 483 U.S. 468, 494, 107 S.Ct. 2941, 2957, 97 L.Ed.2d 389, 410 (1987).

4. Vasquez v. Hillery, 474 U.S. 254, 265, 106 S.Ct. 617, 625, 88 L.Ed.2d 598, 610 (1986); see Anastasoff v. United States, 223 F.3d 898 (discussing history of stare decisis), vacated, 235 F.3d 1054 (8th Cir.2000).

5. Arizona v. Rumsey, 467 U.S. 203, 104 S.Ct. 2305, 81 L.Ed.2d 164 (1984); see Planned Parenthood of Southeastern Pennsylvania v. Casey, 505 U.S. 833, 112 S.Ct. 2791, 120 L.Ed.2d 674 (1992).

6. Patterson v. McLean Credit Union, 491 U.S. 164 109 S.Ct. 2363, 105 L.Ed.2d 132 (1989).

B. PRECLUSION BETWEEN SAME PARTIES

§ 11.7 Parties

Underlying the rules of res judicata is the notion that persons who have had an opportunity to litigate a matter may justly be denied an opportunity to litigate it on another occasion. Such persons include those who are the named parties to an action and who appear or are validly served with process in the action as well as those who intervene. The rules of res judicata are applied most frequently to parties in this strict sense.[1] The rules pose difficult questions of procedural due process when applied to nonparties who lacked such personal opportunity to participate. We will first consider the rules as they apply between parties and thereafter proceed to the more complex problems concerning nonparties.

Different capacities

A person may have more than one legal capacity in which to appear as a party. Thus, a person who has been appointed a trustee for another can conduct some transactions as trustee and other transactions on his or her own behalf. For legal purposes these are generally treated as the transactions of two different legal personages. The rules of res judicata apply to a person only in the capacity in which the person appeared in the litigation.[2] Accordingly, a trustee who brings or defends a suit in that capacity is not the "same party" as the one involved in a subsequent action brought by or against the same person in an individual capacity. This principle applies to trustees, guardians ad litem, receivers, and the like. Different capacities also can apply when two government agencies are involved in successive actions.[3]

In *Clark v. Amoco Production Co.*,[4] for instance, the plaintiffs, administrators of an estate, sued an oil company and others to establish their mineral rights. Previously the plaintiffs had brought personal actions against some of the same defendants to assert their rights as the heirs to the estate. Defendants asserted res judicata as a defense to the new suit. The defense was overruled on the ground that the capacity in which the plaintiff sued was different in the first case and the prospective beneficiaries of the second action were not all present in the first.

§ 11.7

1. Restatement (Second) of Judgments § 34; see Local 322, Allied Industrial Workers v. Johnson Controls, Inc., 969 F.2d 290 (7th Cir.1992)(intervenor).

2. *See, e.g.,* Freeman v. Lester Coggins Trucking, Inc., 771 F.2d 860 (5th Cir.1985); Farley v. Farley, 19 Utah 2d 301, 431 P.2d 133 (1967); Annot., 170 A.L.R. 1180; Restatement (Second) of Judgments § 36.

3. *See, e.g.,* Commissioners of State Ins. Fund v. Low, 3 N.Y.2d 590, 148 N.E.2d 136, 170 N.Y.S.2d 795 (1958); Note, Res Judicata and Intra-governmental Inconsistencies, 49 Colum. L. Rev. 640 (1949); *cf.* Note, Judicial Resolution of Inter-agency Legal Disputes, 89 Yale L.J. 1595 (1980).

4. 794 F.2d 967 (5th Cir.1986).

Nominal parties

Ordinarily parties to an action are described as such in the complaint and in other pleadings that allege who suffered the legal wrong involved and who is charged with having committed it. The real party in interest rule requires that the action be brought "in the name" of the "real party in interest," and this rule has been generally interpreted to mean the person in whose favor the relief is to be granted.[5] There is no corresponding rule regarding designation of the defendant. The identification of the party defendant is accomplished by the combination of two other rules: (1) The complaint must state a cause of action, which requires that the wrongdoer be identified; (2) summons must be served on the person thus charged.[6]

In a few situations, however, the parties really involved are not those whose names appear as plaintiff or defendant. The most common situation for plaintiffs occurs when the assignee of a claim is permitted to sue in the name of the assignor, one in whose favor the claim originally arose but who thereafter assigned it.[7] Although the judgment in form is for the assignor, the beneficiary of the relief is the assignee; the assignor is therefore only a nominal party. Merely nominal defendants are a rarity; one such situation occurs when an action is brought against a public official to compel the official to do an act that will benefit the plaintiff and operate against the interests of some third party; if the action is actually defended by the third party and the official is only a bystander, the official is a nominal party.[8] A nominal party is ordinarily not bound by the judgment; his or her name is essentially irrelevant decoration. If, however, the nominal litigant has permitted his or her name to be used, leading the opposing party to suppose that he or she is the party actually involved, then the nominal party may be bound by the judgment on the principle of estoppel by conduct.[9]

Person controlling the action

Sometimes a person who is not named a party to the action may actually control the prosecution or defense. This is always the case when the designated party is merely nominal; *someone* is conducting the litigation or it wouldn't be going forward. But the party plaintiff or defendant may sometimes be aided by someone else to the extent that the latter assumes responsibility for the litigation. The most common example is a defendant whose insurer takes over defense of a claim against its insured. Another occurs when the owner of a patent takes over a suit brought by or against a licensee involving the rights allegedly conferred by the patent; a third example is a landlord who takes over a

5. *See* § 10.3 *supra.*

6. *See* § 1.15 *supra.*

7. *See* § 10.4 *supra.*

8. For example, proceedings in which extraordinary writs are used to obtain appellate review of otherwise unappealable orders take the form of a proceeding against the judge. *See, e.g.,* Beacon Theatres v. Westover, 359 U.S. 500, 79 S.Ct. 948, 3 L.Ed.2d 988 (1959).

9. Restatement (Second) of Judgments § 37.

tenant's defense when a third party attempts to oust the tenant from property. In these situations the controlling party's opportunity to litigate is the same as that of a named party and that party is treated as a party for issue preclusion purposes.[10]

Adversarial Position

The rules of res judicata apply only to determinations reached between persons who stand in an adversarial relation to each other. Thus, co-plaintiffs or co-defendants are not bound as against each other on matters litigated with their common opponent. The co-parties have no incentive to present evidence and argument on issues that might arise between them but that have not actually erupted in the litigation in question; indeed, they often have incentives to minimize any such differences in order not to weaken their position against the common adversary. From the court's viewpoint, there is nothing to decide between such parties.

An adversarial relation will arise between co-parties only if they assert claims against each other. In *Davis & Cox v. Summa Corp.*,[11] for instance, plaintiff attorneys sought to recover their fees and defendant corporation counterclaimed for malpractice. The court held that res judicata did not bar to the counterclaim since there was no adversarial position in a prior suit where the attorneys represented the corporation. Also, collateral estoppel did not prevent the litigation of the malpractice issue, since it had not been raised when the corporation tried to set aside a default judgment in the previous action because of the attorneys misconduct.

An adversarial proceeding between co-parties warranting issue preclusion can occur when, although no pleadings have been interjected between the co-parties, each co-party attempts to prove a case adverse to the other concerning the issues presented by the common opponent. This often arises when a plaintiff has sued two defendants alleging that their conduct concurrently produced the loss for which suit is brought. Each defendant may then try to throw the blame on the other. Although the older rule was that a judgment in favor of one of the co-parties but against the other was not determinative between them, the modern rule is that issue preclusion applies between them in subsequent litigation if they had full and fair opportunity to litigate the issue in the first action.[12]

10. *See, e.g.,* Montana v. United States, 440 U.S. 147, 99 S.Ct. 970, 59 L.Ed.2d 210 (1979); Souffront v. La Compagnie Des Sucreries De Porto Rico, 217 U.S. 475, 30 S.Ct. 608, 54 L.Ed. 846 (1910); Annot., 139 A.L.R. 9; Restatement (Second) of Judgments § 39; § 11.27 *infra.*

11. 751 F.2d 1507 (9th Cir.1985); see Durkin v. Shea & Gould, 92 F.3d 1510 (9th Cir.1996)(court approval of settlement does not bar malpractice suit against lawyer for inadequate representation in settling case).

12. *See, e.g.,* Scooper Dooper, Inc. v. Kraftco Corp., 494 F.2d 840 (3d Cir.1974) (co-plaintiffs); Creeco v. Northern Ill. Gas Co., 73 Ill.App.2d 218, 219 N.E.2d 257 (1966) (co-defendants); Annot., 24 A.L.R.3d 318; Restatement (Second) of Judgments § 38. In Hellenic Lines, Ltd. v. The Exmouth, 253 F.2d 473 (2d Cir.1958), the

§ 11.8 Claim Preclusion

As noted earlier, two basic components make up the rules of res judicata: the first deals with the effect of a judgment on the cause of action or claim involved in the first action, the second with the effect on issues determined in the first action. We now speak to the first of these two components. The rule of claim preclusion prevents reassertion of the same claim even though additional or different evidence or legal theories might be advanced to support it.[1] In applying the rule of claim preclusion, the critical question is how broad a definition to give to the term "same claim" or "cause of action." The broader the definition, the broader the scope of preclusion.

Scope of "claim"

At common law, as we have seen, the forms of action were narrow and rigid, and a plaintiff generally could not join one form with another.[2] Since a plaintiff had to choose a single form of action and could prevail only on showing a right of recovery under that form, it occasionally happened that a plaintiff with a good claim on the merits lost the action because it was in the wrong form. Likewise, an equity suitor was sometimes turned out of chancery because an adequate remedy was available at law; a plaintiff at law was sometimes dismissed because the remedy sought was cognizable only in equity. In these cases the unsuccessful plaintiff might pursue the proper remedy in a later action. The new basis of claim was not a matter that "might have been offered" to sustain the claim in the former action, because under the old procedure it was unavailable for that purpose. In such a system the dimensions of the claim or demand closely coincided with the boundaries of the actions or with the boundary dividing law and equity. This allowed for some multiplicity of suits to redress a single grievance or wrong, but it at least did not compound the hardship of the formulary system by piling substantive injustice on procedural technicality.

Under code and modern systems of procedure, however, suitors are no longer confined to a single form of action, legal theory, or set of remedies (legal or equitable). They may usually pursue in a single action all the theories and remedies appropriate to their grievance, and the question naturally arises whether they should not be encouraged and even compelled to do so. There is fairly general agreement today that they should. Such compulsion is administered by giving broad scope to the doctrines of bar and merger; this breadth, in turn, is largely regulated through the definition of the terms "claim," "demand," or

court held that co-defendants were not precluded on issues between them when they were not in a fully adversarial position.

§ 11.8

1. Restatement (Second) of Judgments § 25. *See also* § 11.3 *supra*.

2. *See* §§ 1.3, 3.3 *supra*.

"cause of action." The bar of res judicata "extends not only to the precise legal theory presented in the previous litigation, but to all legal theories and claims arising out of the same 'operative nucleus of fact.' "[3] Similar pressure may be put on defendants by compulsory counterclaim rules or statutes and other devices.[4]

Effect of claim preclusion

Before examining the modern rules for measuring a single cause of action, we should note the mechanics of asserting claim preclusion. The rule is often referred to as one that forbids the splitting of a cause of action or, less often, as one prescribing the compulsory joinder of claims. But these terms carry the suggestion that the compulsion is administered in the first suit as is, for example, the rule that necessary or indispensable parties must be brought into the action before it can proceed over objection.[5] That is not the way the claim preclusion rule works. If a plaintiff splits the cause of action by failing to include all parts of it in the first action, that action will not be abated or subject to demurrer because it is incomplete. The sanction for the rule is, rather, that if the plaintiffs fail to include any part of a single demand or cause of action in the first action, they cannot, after judgment, bring another action to claim the omitted part, whether as an item of damage or a ground of recovery. The entire original cause of action is either barred by or merged in the first judgment—in either event it is extinguished.

Conflicting judgments

By the time claim preclusion is asserted, two or more prior judgments on the same claim may conflict. The courts generally give res judicata effect to the last judgment entered.[6] For instance, one plaintiff sought a stay of arbitration in California state court and simultaneously petitioned a New York federal court for an order compelling defendant to arbitrate the same dispute. Both motions were granted, the California one being issued first. The New York court issued its order 35 days later and stated it was not bound by the California state court ruling. In a third suit, the federal court of appeals gave res judicata effect to the last judgment entered, that of the New York court, and ruled that that court's ruling that it was not bound by a prior judgment was itself binding on a third court.[7]

3. Olmstead v. Amoco Oil Co., 725 F.2d 627, 629 (11th Cir.1984); Dillard v. Crenshaw County, 640 F.Supp. 1347 (M.D.Ala. 1986). This assumes, of course, that the theories could have been asserted in the original suit. *E.g.*, Bank of India v. Trendi Sportswear, Inc., 239 F.3d 428 (2d Cir. 2000); § 11.14 *infra.*

4. Mich. Ct. R. 2.203(A)(party must join all claims against opposing party arising from same transaction); Oltremare v. ESR Custom Rugs, Inc., 330 N.J.Super. 310, 749 A.2d 862 (App.Div.2000); § 9.11 *supra.*

5. *See* § 10.11 *supra.*

6. 1B Moore, Federal Practice and Procedure ¶ 0.405(1).

7. Americana Fabrics v. L & L Textiles, 754 F.2d 1524 (9th Cir.1985). *See also* Balbirer v. Austin, 790 F.2d 1524 (11th Cir. 1986). *Contra* Lesher v. Lavrich, 784 F.2d 193 (6th Cir.1986); Sidag A.G. v. Smoked

§ 11.9 Dimensions of Single Claim or Cause of Action

"Same right"

In the nineteenth century, a fairly narrow definition of "cause of action" was used, reflecting the then-existing limitation on joinder of causes of action. The definition was stated variously as the "same remedial right," the same "substantive" or "primary" right, or the causes of action having involved the "same evidence."[1] A few states still define "cause of action" in comparable terms.[2]

All these definitions begged the question. They did not specify what the remedial right, substantive right, or primary right was, and those terms could be given a wider or narrower meaning in any given case. Thus, one could say in an accident case that the "right" is to recover for physical injury (leaving open a second action for pain and suffering), for personal injury (including the claim for pain and suffering but leaving open a claim for property damage), or for loss resulting from the accident (leaving nothing open for a second action). The "same evidence" test similarly left unspecified the type of evidence—did the cause of action involve evidence of liability, of all losses, or of particular losses? The decisions gave implicit answers in their conclusions, holding that whatever was involved in the second action was or was not within the scope of the claim that had been asserted in the first action. All these concepts, however, defined "cause of action" more narrowly than the limits of permissible joinder of causes; none compelled plaintiffs to join all the claims that they were permitted to join.[3]

How broad should preclusion be?

A good way to begin a critical analysis is to pose the following question: Why should a party not be *compelled* to join all the claims that it *may* join? Surely something is to be gained by wiping a slate clean, and some have urged that the law require this result when parties invoke its processes to settle some of their disputes.[4] If two trials would produce a large overlap of issues or evidence, it is wasteful to society and harassing

Foods Prods. Co., 776 F.2d 1270 (5th Cir. 1985) (first judgment has res judicata effect).

§ 11.9

1. *See* Clark, Code Pleading 127–148 (2d ed. 1947); Pomeroy, Code Remedies §§ 346–356 (5th ed. 1929); Blume, Required Joinder of Claims, 45 Mich. L. Rev. 797 (1947); Schopflocher, What Is a Single Cause of Action for the Purpose of the Doctrine of Res Judicata?, 21 Or. L. Rev. 319 (1942); Vestal, Res Judicata/Claim Preclusion: Judgment for the Claimant, 62 Nw. U.L. Rev. 357 (1967).

2. *E.g.*, Torcasso v. Standard Outdoor Sales, Inc., 157 Ill.2d 484, 193 Ill.Dec. 192, 626 N.E.2d 225 (Ill. 1993); Heiser, California's Unpredictable Res Judicata (Claim Preclusion) Doctrine, 35 San Diego L. Rev. 559 (1998).

3. Under modern pleading rules, a plaintiff may join claims against a defendant regardless of their subject matter and whether they have any connection to each other. *See* Fed. R. Civ. P. 18(a). The rules of claim preclusion have never been formulated or applied to require that a plaintiff exercise the full breadth of this option.

4. Blume, Required Joinder of Claims, 45 Mich. L. Rev. 797 (1947).

to the adversary to have more than one trial. This will often be the case even when the evidence and issues are not identical. Consider the wastefulness of trying in separate actions the alternative theories of breach of express contract to pay for goods or services and breach of an implied undertaking to pay the reasonable value of the same items.

When, however, claims are factually distinct so that no overlap in the supporting evidence will occur, much less is to be gained by either trying them together or including them in a single lawsuit to be tried separately. Indeed, trying them together may cause confusion and prejudice. An insistence that all factually distinct claims be included in one action may have other disadvantages. It will tend to make the parties include possible claims that they may be unwilling to abandon although reluctant to assert. Compulsion might force parties to litigate their potential claims to the utmost.[5]

A relatively broad rule of res judicata can also be a greater trap for the unwary. Criticism is often leveled at the hardship visited on parties whose attorneys overlook some items of their claim or some theory to support it. But unless the res judicata rule has reasonable breadth, a relentless litigant can entrap the opponent in multiple litigation by subdividing legal and factual components of a transaction into separate suits.[6] The rule of claim preclusion attempts to reconcile these competing considerations.

Transactional approach

Since adoption of the Federal Rules, the concept of a "claim" or "cause of action" has been framed in terms of a "transaction." The Restatement (Second) of Judgments uses the following definition of the underlying "claim" or "cause of action":

> 1. When a valid and final judgment rendered in an action extinguishes the plaintiff's claim pursuant to the rules of merger or bar ... the claim extinguished includes all rights of the plaintiff to remedies against the defendant with respect to all or any part of the transaction, or series of connected transactions, out of which the action arose.
>
> 2. What factual grouping constitutes a "transaction," and what groupings constitute a "series," are to be determined pragmatically, giving weight to such considerations as whether the facts are related in time, space, origin, or motivation, whether they form a convenient trial

5. See Hazard, An Examination Before and Behind the 'Entire Controversy' Doctrine, 28 Rutgers L.J. 7 (1996); Erichson, Of Horror Stories and Happy Endings: The Rise and Fall of Preclusion-Based Compulsory Party Joinder Under the New Jersey Entire Controversy Doctrine, 9 Seton Hall Const. L.J. 755 (1999).

6. *Compare* Cleary, Res Judicata Reexamined, 57 Yale L.J. 339 (1948), *with, e.g.,* Federated Dept. Stores v. Moitie, 452 U.S. 394, 101 S.Ct. 2424, 69 L.Ed.2d 103 (1981).

unit, and whether their treatment as a unit conforms to the parties' expectations or business understanding or usage.[7]

Whether "cause of action," "claim," or "demand" is used to denote what a party must include in a single action, the basic problem is not in the terminology. As indicated by the Restatement formulation quoted above, the terminology does not itself determine the proper scope of claim preclusion. That has to be sought in terms of the practical and policy goals that a procedural system should seek to attain.

§ 11.10 Tort Cases

Practical and policy problems can arise in almost any type of tort litigation. Two kinds will be discussed in detail to indicate how the problems arise: an ordinary automobile accident case, and the case of tortious interference with another's use of land (nuisance). Similar problems can arise in other tort actions involving claims for different kinds of injuries, such as injury to real property and to business profits or injury to reputation or to an employment relationship.

Multiple injuries

The most frequently recurring problem in tort cases occurs when defendant's wrong is a single course of conduct but causes more than one type of injury to plaintiff. The most common example is an automobile accident in which defendant's negligence causes personal injury to plaintiff and property damage to plaintiff's car. Authority has split on whether this gives plaintiff one or two causes of action; the majority holds that there is only one.[1]

It would be intolerable to allow plaintiff to sue separately for a broken arm and a broken leg and then still again for the pecuniary losses attendant on each injury, all resulting from a single accident. And, as Chief Justice Coleridge remarked, "it seems . . . a subtlety not warranted by law to hold that a man cannot bring two actions, if he is injured in his arm and in his leg, but can bring two, if beside his arm and leg being injured his trousers which contain his leg, and his coatsleeve which contains his arm, have been torn."[2]

The conclusion, however, is not so simple. The statutes of limitation for the two items may be different; the measures of damages are different; the property damage claim is assignable while the personal injury claim is not; the incidents of the two claims will be different if plaintiff's bankruptcy or death intervenes; sometimes the defendant's

7. Restatement (Second) of Judgments § 24. *See also* Porn v. National Grange Mut. Ins. Co., 93 F.3d 31 (1st Cir.1996).

§ 11.10

1. Mills v. De Wees, 141 W.Va. 782, 93 S.E.2d 484 (1956) (collecting cases); Annot., 62 A.L.R.2d 977.

2. Coleridge, C.J., dissenting in Brunsden v. Humphreys, 14 Q.B. 141, 152 (1884).

conduct may be negligent toward property but not negligent toward the person, and vice versa.[3]

These discrepancies usually pose no serious difficulty. If the statute of limitations has run on one part of the claim but not on another part,this means simply that only the latter part may be allowed as a basis for recovery. There is nothing unusual about part of a claim being barred by limitation; running accounts and temporary continuing nuisances often pose such a problem. The difference in measures of damage means that evidence of more than one kind of inquiry must be received; the evidence on liability will be the same. While it is theoretically possible for defendant's conduct to be negligent only toward property or toward persons, such a possibility is remote.[4] Moreover, it would present no insurmountable problem to a court or jury should it arise.

Assignable claims

The most serious practical difficulties spring from the fact that property damage claims are generally assignable—that is, transferable by the injured party to someone else—while personal injury claims generally are not. This difference comes into play when, for example, plaintiff has collision insurance on his or her automobile so that the collision insurance carrier, on compensating plaintiff for the loss, has become subrogated to plaintiff's property damage claim against the tortfeasor. Plaintiff remains the full beneficial owner of the personal injury claim. If the parties having the beneficial interests (insurer and insured) sue separately, then the single original cause of action appears to have been split. The second action therefore has sometimes been held barred because the personal and property losses are viewed as a single claim. Other courts treat the claims as separate causes of action even when they would treat the situation as involving a single cause of action whenever the same plaintiff has the full beneficial interest in both items.[5]

Thus, the losses can be treated as one cause of action unless there are competing considerations, in which event they can be treated as

3. *See, e.g.,* Reilly v. Sicilian Asphalt Paving Co., 170 N.Y. 40, 62 N.E. 772, 57 Law. Rep. Ann. 176, 88 Am. State Rep. 636 (1902); Vasu v. Kohlers, Inc., 145 Ohio St. 321, 61 N.E.2d 707 (1945). These objections are admirably analyzed in Hinton, Splitting a Cause of Action, 21 Ill. L. Rev. 506 (1927). *Cf. also* Clark, Code Pleading 488–489 (2d ed. 1947).

4. In the famous case Palsgraf v. Long Island R.R., 248 N.Y. 339, 162 N.E. 99 (1928), Judge Cardozo suggested that the defendant's employee may have been negligent only with respect to the *package* of the passenger who was pushed, and not even toward the passenger himself. The push, in other words, foreseeably threatened only the package with harm, not the person who was carrying it. See treatment of this problem in 2 Harper, James, and Gray, Law of Torts § 18.2 (2d ed. 1986).

5. This was recognized in Vasu v. Kohlers, Inc., 145 Ohio St. 321, 338, 61 N.E.2d 707, 716 (1945) ("Indeed, if the plaintiff is the owner of the several causes of action at the time suit is brought, he should so join them, and appropriate legislation could require it"). Rush v. City of Maple Heights, 167 Ohio St. 221, 147 N.E.2d 599 (1958) in effect requires such joinder.

involving two causes of action. The problem is not whether one cause of action "is" involved but whether separate claims should be recognized when there is an additional party (the insurer) with interests that should be protected.[6] The defendant can be protected against multiple actions by requiring that the subrogated claimant join in the action by the original injured party. Arriving at such a sensible accommodation is obstructed if attention is directed only at whether the case presents more than one cause of action.

Similar analysis can be applied when the original claimant dies or becomes bankrupt. These events can result in devolution of the original claim to successors in interest. The structure of the problem is the same as in the case of transfer by assignment or subrogation. The law of succession or bankruptcy has split the cause of action and vested parts of it in different persons, each of whom is thereafter the real party in interest. The claim can be treated as one cause of action unless such change has intervened, in which event two causes of action can be recognized.[7]

Continuing wrong

Some wrongs result from a single event, others from a series of events. If a defendant's conduct culminates in a single event, such as an automobile collision, multiple aspects of defendant's negligence—speeding, failing to look out, and so on—will not permit multiple suits. But if defendant's continuing conduct causes more than one injurious event, then the question arises whether more than one cause of action is involved. In the end, the problem is a matter of degree. If the events are closely connected both temporally and spatially, and the incidents of defendant's conduct are substantially the same so that the evidence supporting them will largely overlap, then there is only a single cause of action. As the overlap in time and elements of injury diminishes, so does the likelihood that the courts will see a single cause of action.[8]

Nuisance

When defendant's conduct consists in maintaining a condition or a continuous operation on his or her land that causes a continuing invasion of the use and enjoyment of plaintiff's land (nuisance), similar problems arise. It is settled that all past damage to the same land must be redressed in a single action.[9] But it is not so clear-cut whether plaintiff can also recover for anticipated future damage and, if so,

6. *See* § 10.5 *supra.*

7. Hinton, Splitting a Cause of Action, 21 Ill. L. Rev. 506, 508 (1927).

8. *Compare* Chicago, I. & L. Ry. Co. v. Ramsey, 168 Ind. 390, 81 N.E. 79, 120 Am. State Rep. 379 (1907), *with* Missouri Pac. R.R. Co. v. Scammon, 41 Kan. 521, 21 P. 590 (1889). *See* Waldman v. Village of Kiryas Joel, 207 F.3d 105 (2d Cir.2000); Clark, Code Pleading 486 (2d ed. 1947).

9. Restatement (Second) of Judgments 826 (Comment on continuing wrongs).

whether he or she is confined to a single action for all damages, past and future, that may result from the nuisance.

Some courts confine plaintiffs to past damages, relegating them to the remedies of injunction or successive suits if the injury continues.[10] Most jurisdictions draw a distinction between "permanent" and "temporary" nuisances. When the nuisance is permanent, plaintiff is allowed only a single action and may recover in it all damages—past and future. When the nuisance is temporary, recovery is limited to past damages only, but successive suits are permitted if the nuisance continues to cause injury.[11]

Other legal consequences flow from the distinction. If the nuisance is classified as temporary, each day's continuance creates a new cause of action, and the statute of limitations begins to run day by day. Plaintiff therefore may recover for the nuisance committed during the statutory period next before the bringing of the action.[12] If the nuisance is classified as permanent, the conduct at once creates a complete and single cause of action for all injury and the statute of limitations runs on this single cause from the time of the beginning of the nuisance.[13] These different consequences make it very important whether a nuisance is classified as permanent or temporary. "[I]f the initial injury is slight and plaintiff delays suit until he has suffered substantial damage and the court then determines that the nuisance was permanent, the defendant may be able to raise the defense that the statute of limitations ran from the time of the initial injury."[14]

Generally, no clear test can distinguish a permanent nuisance from a temporary one. If the condition or operation cannot be legally abated because it is a necessary incident to a public utility, the nuisance (if any) is a permanent one.[15] This means that a single nuisance action for damages is allowed—in effect, an exercise in reverse of the power of eminent domain. Plaintiff is allowed full damages on the assumption that the condition of operation will continue and defendant effectively gets a permanent easement to continue it.[16] But beyond this situation there is uncertainty.

10. *See* Spaulding v. Cameron, 38 Cal.2d 265, 267, 239 P.2d 625, 627 (1952); Note, 26 S. Cal. L. Rev. 338 (1953).

11. Sources cited *supra* note 10; Clark, Code Pleading 486–488 (2d ed. 1947); McCormick, Damages for Anticipated Injury to Land, 37 Harv. L. Rev. 574 (1924).

12. Note, Nuisances—Permanent Injury—Limitations of Actions, 28 Tenn. L. Rev. 433, 434–435 (1961).

13. Robertson v. Cincinnati, N.O. & Tex. Pac. Ry., 207 Tenn. 272, 339 S.W.2d 6 (1960).

14. Traynor, J., in Spaulding v. Cameron, 38 Cal.2d 265, 268, 239 P.2d 625, 628 (1952).

15. Sources cited *supra* note 11; Spaulding v. Cameron, 38 Cal.2d 265, 267, 239 P.2d 625, 627 (1952).

16. Note, 26 S. Cal. L. Rev. 338, 340 (1953). *Cf.* Note, 28 Tenn. L. Rev. 433, 436 (1961).

Plaintiff's option

It seems evident that no conceptual approach to this problem can be satisfactory, because the concept chosen—whether "one" wrong or a "continuing" wrong—will simply suppress the factors that militate in favor of the concept that is rejected. Some courts, and the Restatement (Second) of Judgments, approach the problem by noting that the plaintiff in such a situation rarely has an incentive to litigate the claim piecemeal unless he or she is genuinely hopeful that the wrong will be only temporary or, at worst, episodic. From that premise they reason that it is safe and fair to give plaintiffs an option: They can sue only for accrued damages, thus treating the wrong as continuing, or for future damages as well, thus treating the wrong as permanent. Only if plaintiffs pursue the latter course will they be precluded from maintaining a subsequent action.[17] The same approach can be used with other clusters of tortious conduct that are temporally or spatially connected in only a loose or contingent way. In employing this approach, it is relevant to consider not only the plaintiff's complaint but also the kind of defense asserted by defendant and the matters of discovery pursued by both parties. In other words, in doubtful cases the court's decision on the shape of the claim for preclusion purposes should be guided by how the parties shaped it for litigation purposes in the first action.

§ 11.11 Contract and Other Cases

In theory, every breach of contract gives rise to a right of action. This is true even when the breach is so unimportant that it does not alter the obligations of the parties to fulfill the remaining terms of the contract and when it causes no actual pecuniary loss.[1]

Divisible and indivisible breaches

A plaintiff generally is required to include in a single action all breaches that have occurred before the beginning of the suit. Otherwise, judgment in the action will preclude any later recovery for breaches that occurred before the action began.[2] If the contract is considered "separable" or "divisible," however, then a breach of one part may be sued on separate from breaches of the other part.[3] Only few contracts are treated as separable or divisible for this purpose. The most common case of divisibility is an obligation to pay money in installments, represented by

17. Restatement (Second) of Judgments § 26(1)(e).

§ 11.11

1. Restatement (Second) of Contracts § 346; 4 Corbin, Contracts §§ 946, 948 (1951).

2. 3A Corbin, Contracts § 698 (1951); Restatement (Second) of Judgments § 24, Comment *d. But see, e.g.,* Sawyer v. First City Fin. Corp., 124 Cal.App.3d 390, 177 Cal.Rptr. 398 (1981).

3. 3A Corbin, Contracts § 698, at 303 (1960); 4 *id.* at 955; Clark, Code Pleading 480 (2d ed. 1947); Restatement (Second) of Judgments § 24, Comment *d.*

separate negotiable notes for each installment.[4] The concept does not extend much beyond that. The test for divisibility sometimes hinges on whether the consideration is apportionable to separate items of performance; this concept of apportionability, however, is not applied in the case of the ordinary running account or rental contract, to which divisibility could be most readily applied.[5] Sometimes the matter is said to turn on whether there is physically one contract or two (that is, whether they are on separate pieces of paper). Perhaps the only safe guide is to assume that the obligations under a single contractual transaction are not divisible unless some concrete fact points affirmatively and unequivocally to intent by both parties to have divisibility.[6]

A party generally may treat contractual obligations as continuing even after breach and either (1) maintain successive actions for successive breaches (so long as the rule on divisibility is observed) or (2) wait until the roster of breaches is complete and bring a single action for all of them.[7] If, however, defendant's breach involves a total repudiation of the contract, then plaintiff must treat the contract as at an end and has only a single action for the total breach, including all past and future damages.[8] The judgment in that suit will preclude any other claim arising out of the contract. Some authority holds that if plaintiff performed all consideration and the only remaining obligation is that of defendant to make payment in installments, plaintiff may treat a breach as total or partial even when it is accompanied by a repudiation of the contract.[9] If any uncertainty exists about the characterization of the breach—and it almost always does—plaintiff should sue for total breach or at least seek a declaratory judgment to determine whether the breach is total.

§ 11.12 Alternative Bases of Recovery for Single Injury

Problems of claim preclusion also arise when plaintiff suffers a single injury or set of injuries but alternative grounds of recovery are available for that injury.

4. 4 Corbin, Contracts § 952 (1951).

5. Hare v. Winfree, 131 Wash. 138, 229 P. 16 (1924) (noted in 34 Yale L.J. 677 (1925)); 3A Corbin, Contracts § 698 (1951); Clark, Code Pleading 483–484 (2d ed. 1947).

6. Examples of contracts held divisible may be found in Armstrong v. Illinois Bankers Life Assn., 217 Ind. 601, 29 N.E.2d 415, 131 A.L.R. 769 (1940); Rosso v. New York Life Ins. Co., 157 Miss. 469, 128 So. 343, 69 A.L.R. 883 (1930); Fidelity & Deposit Co. of Md. v. Brown, 228 Mo.App. 164, 65 S.W.2d 1064 (1933). *Cf.* Przyblyski v. Pellowski, 141 Minn. 193, 169 N.W. 707 (1918).

7. 4 Corbin, Contracts § 946, at 811, §§ 948–950 (1951). The plaintiffs need not wait until all performance is due. They may sue after any number of breaches so long as they include all those that have occurred when they bring suit. *Id.*

8. *Id.* § 946, at 811–812, 954; Restatement (Second) of Judgments § 26, Comment *g.* *Cf.* Restatement (Second) of Contracts § 250.

9. Goodwin v. Cabot Amusement Co., 129 Me. 36, 149 A. 574 (1930); Restatement of Contracts § 316; Restatement (Second) of Judgments § 26, Comment *g.*

Different legal theories of recovery may depend on proof of somewhat different factual elements. Moreover, the facts supporting one theory may be inconsistent with those supporting another. Thus, if plaintiff complains that defendant has wrongfully failed to return plaintiff's goods, recovery of damages might be predicated on (1) negligent loss or damage to the goods, (2) breach of a contractual duty to return the goods, or (3) wrongful conversion of the goods. All three bases of recovery may not coexist, and the evidence needed to sustain each is somewhat different. Contemporary pleading rules permit plaintiff to pursue all possible theories in a single action.[1] At common law, plaintiff would have had to resort to three separate forms of action; under modern procedure, the various theories are treated as one cause of action, and the rule of claim preclusion compels plaintiff to assert all forms in one action.[2]

Practical considerations support the modern approach. Evidence showing what happened to the goods will come from the same witnesses and records, whatever the true facts and proper theory may be, and the tribunal will have a better basis for intelligent decision after hearing the whole story with all its conflicts and inconsistencies. No apparent advantage would come from separate trials.

§ 11.13 Legal and Equitable Theories and Remedies

The same considerations compel inclusion in a single action of legal and equitable theories of recovery for the same injury to avoid the bar of res judicata.[1] Thus, if plaintiff contends that a contract (1) as written is properly interpreted to require defendant to perform a certain act, and (2) if not subject to that interpretation as written, should be reformed (in equity) to specify defendant's obligation to perform the act, then plaintiff should be compelled to pursue both theories because of the overlap of evidence and the advantage of sifting the whole matter at one trial.[2] New legal theories do not create a new cause of action.[3]

§ 11.12

1. *See* §§ 3.6, 3.7 *supra.*

2. Federated Dept. Stores v. Moitie, 452 U.S. 394, 101 S.Ct. 2424, 69 L.Ed.2d 103 (1981); *see, e.g.,* Williamson v. Columbia Gas & Elec. Corp., 186 F.2d 464 (3d Cir. 1950), *cert. denied,* 341 U.S. 921, 71 S.Ct. 743, 95 L.Ed. 1355 (1951); Note, Developments in the Law: Res Judicata, 65 Harv. L. Rev. 818, 826–827 (1952); *cf.* Massari v. Einsiedler, 6 N.J. 303, 78 A.2d 572 (1951); Restatement (Second) of Judgments § 25. *Contra* Smith v. Kirkpatrick, 305 N.Y. 66, 111 N.E.2d 209 (1953); Norwood v. McDonald, 142 Ohio St. 299, 52 N.E.2d 67 (1943).

§ 11.13

1. *See* Lytle v. Household Mfg., Inc., 494 U.S. 545, 110 S.Ct. 1331, 108 L.Ed.2d 504 (1990); Pasterczyk v. Fair, 819 F.2d 12 (1st Cir.1987).

2. *See* Hennepin Paper Co. v. Fort Wayne Corrugated Paper Co., 153 F.2d 822 (7th Cir.1946). To similar effect is Ajamian v. Schlanger, 14 N.J. 483, 103 A.2d 9 (1954) (Brennan, J.) (discussed in Note, Problems of Res Judicata Created by Expanding "Cause of Action" Under Code Pleading, 104 U. Pa. L. Rev. 955, 966–967 (1956)).

3. *See* Norman v. Niagara Mohawk Power Corp., 873 F.2d 634 (2d Cir.1989) (holding that a civil RICO action arose out

Breach of a contract may entitle plaintiff to seek either damages or specific performance; in other situations, plaintiff may be entitled to cumulative remedies. If, for instance, defendant's building encroaches on what plaintiff claims to be his or her land, and defendant disputes that claim, legal principles will settle the title dispute and the right to have the sheriff remove any encroachment; if the removal of the building is difficult, under equitable principles the court may order the defendant to remove the encroachment.[4] In any event, the plaintiff is compelled to include the legal and equitable claims.[5]

§ 11.14 Unavailability of Remedy or Theory of Recovery in First Action

By abolishing the distinctions between forms of action and between law and equity, modern procedural systems greatly increase the scope of a single action. Nevertheless, situations remain in which a remedy or ground of action is limited in the first action, for one of several reasons.

Jurisdictional limitations

There may be a limitation on the jurisdiction of the tribunal in which the first action or proceeding is brought. No tribunal may have jurisdiction over both alternative remedies or grounds of recovery, so plaintiff must perforce seek relief in a forum where only one remedy is available. For example, a person injured on the job may have a remedy either under a workers' compensation law or through a common law damage action, depending on the circumstances under which the injury occurred.[1] The injured person cannot have both remedies. The compensation remedy usually must be sought before an administrative tribunal that has exclusive jurisdiction over compensation claims and no jurisdiction over common law claims. The damages remedy must be sought in court, which has no jurisdiction over compensation claims. A judgment by either tribunal that the claim is outside its jurisdiction does not preclude resort to the other.[2] But a judgment in the claimant's favor in

of the same facts as an earlier dismissed action under the civil rights statutes and was therefore barred).

4. Hahl v. Sugo, 169 N.Y. 109, 62 N.E. 135, 61 Law. Rep. Ann. 226, 88 Am. State Rep. 539 (1901), *discussed in* Clark, Code Pleading 475 (2d ed. 1947), which collects citations to many comments on the case, some critical.

5. Views opposed to the position taken here may be found in Cleary, Res Judicata Reexamined, 57 Yale L.J. 339 (1948) as well as in the sources cited in Clark, Code Pleading 475 (2d ed. 1947). *Cf.* United States v. American Heart Research Foundation, Inc., 996 F.2d 7 (1st Cir.1993)(government may bring separate suits for injunction and unjust enrichment because of statutory policy of expediting injunction suits). The Restatement of Judgments makes resolution of the problem dependent on the extent to which the systems of law and equity have been merged. Restatement (Second) of Judgments § 26(c).

§ 11.14

1. *See, e.g.,* Byrd v. Blue Ridge Rural Elec. Co-op., 356 U.S. 525, 78 S.Ct. 893, 2 L.Ed.2d 953 (1958). *Cf.* Carter v. Superior Court, 142 Cal.App.2d 350, 298 P.2d 598 (1956). *But see* Carroll v. Lanza, 349 U.S. 408, 75 S.Ct. 804, 99 L.Ed. 1183 (1955).

2. Restatement (Second) of Judgments § 20(1)(a).

either tribunal does preclude resort to the other on principles of merger.[3]

Another limiting application of these rules arises when plaintiff has arguable claims under both state and federal law arising out of the same transaction, but the federal law claims are within the exclusive jurisdiction of the federal court. There are two possibilities if plaintiff sues in state court (keeping in mind that a federal law claim that is within the exclusive jurisdiction of the federal courts cannot be asserted in state court): (1) If plaintiff wins in state court, the claim probably would be merged in the judgment; (2) if plaintiff loses in state court, subsequent suit in federal court may be precluded by bar, depending on the state's rules of res judicata.

State court suit omitting federal claim

The second situation arose in *Marrese v. American Academy of Orthopaedic Surgeons.*[4] A group of surgeons who were denied membership in the Academy sued first in state court, alleging state antitrust law violation, and then in federal court, alleging federal antitrust law violation. Although most federal claims may be litigated in either federal or state court, only federal courts may hear federal antitrust claims.[5] The Supreme Court pointed out that the Full Faith and Credit Statute, 28 U.S.C. § 1738, requires the federal courts to refer to the state's law in determining the res judicata effect of a judgment of the state court unless contravened by some other federal statute. Hence, if the state law would not make its judgment claim preclusive, then the federal court could not accord it that effect.[6] Thus, if the state court was unable to rule on the issue because of jurisdictional limitations, claim preclusion does not apply unless state law so provides.[7]

Marrese usually will prevent preclusion in similar cases because most states do not apply preclusion to claims beyond the court's jurisdiction (the "prior jurisdictional competency" rule). Therefore, since the states cannot hear cases of exclusive federal jurisdiction, they do not preclude them.[8] The basis for bar in a minority of states would be as follows: Plaintiff could have sued in federal court, asserting the federal claim and the state claim, the latter through supplemental jurisdiction;[9] the election to sue in state court deliberately limited the grounds

3. Chicago, R.I. & Pac. Ry. v. Schendel, 270 U.S. 611, 46 S.Ct. 420, 70 L.Ed. 757, 53 A.L.R. 1265 (1926). *But cf.* Thomas v. Washington Gas Light Co., 448 U.S. 261, 100 S.Ct. 2647, 65 L.Ed.2d 757 (1980) (sister state's workers' compensation award).

4. 470 U.S. 373, 105 S.Ct. 1327, 84 L.Ed.2d 274 (1985).

5. Freeman v. Bee Machine Co., 319 U.S. 448, 63 S.Ct. 1146, 87 L.Ed. 1509 (1943); *see* § 2.25 *supra.*

6. 470 U.S. at 381, 105 S.Ct. at 1332, 84 L.Ed.2d at 274.

7. See Restatement (Second) of Judgments § 26(1)(c); Burbank, Interjurisdictional Preclusion, Full Faith and Credit and Federal Common Law: A General Approach, 71 Cornell L. Rev. 733 (1986).

8. *See generally* Note, The Claim Preclusive Effect of State Court Judgments on Federal Antitrust Claims, 71 Iowa L. Rev. 609 (1986).

9. *See* § 2.28 *supra.*

asserted to the state law theory; a judgment bars bringing an action on another legal theory.[10]

Of course, if the federal claim had been one that could have been but was not raised in state court, most states would consider it precluded, and federal courts would be obliged to give a judgment from such a state the same preclusive force. Because state courts have concurrent jurisdiction over most federal claims, this situation frequently occurs. For example, a plaintiff who asserts a state law claim in state court but neglects to join a parallel federal constitutional claim arising out of the same transaction will not be able to assert the federal claim in a later federal court suit, unless the first suit was filed in one of the few states that take a narrow view of what constitutes a "claim" for claim preclusion purposes.[11]

Federal court suit omitting state law claim

Suppose now that plaintiff sues first in federal court. The federal claim would be asserted; so may the state claim, on the basis of supplemental jurisdiction, because the state claim arises out of the same transaction. Judgment either way in such an action precludes a further suit. If plaintiff failed to include the state law claim, the federal action would still preclude a subsequent suit in state (or for that matter federal) court. Under the federal rule of res judicata, subsequent suit on claims arising out of the same transaction is precluded if such claims could have been asserted in the first federal action. Since the state law claim could have been asserted on the basis of pendent jurisdiction, it is barred. The state court should so rule. But if it erroneously holds that the state claim is still open, the defendant's only remedy is to appeal; otherwise, he or she will be bound by the state court's incorrect decision that claim preclusion does not apply.[12]

Quasi in rem jurisdiction

Analytically similar to these problems are those arising when the court has quasi in rem jurisdiction, or "attachment jurisdiction," to the very limited extent that such jurisdiction may still exist after *Shaffer v. Heitner.*[13] Here too, the court can hear part of what would ordinarily be one case (a claim limited to the value of the property) but has no jurisdiction over the rest of it. Suppose plaintiff has a damages claim in admiralty for $100,000 against a defendant who is not subject to personal jurisdiction but has a boat in the court's territory worth $60,000. Under appropriate circumstances, quasi in rem jurisdiction can still be

10. See Matsushita Electric Industrial Co. v. Epstein, 516 U.S. 367, 116 S.Ct. 873, 134 L.Ed.2d 6 (1996).

11. Migra v. Warren City School Dist. Bd. of Educ., 465 U.S. 75, 104 S.Ct. 892, 79 L.Ed.2d 56 (1984); Restatement (Second) of Judgments § 24, Comment *g*.

12. Parsons Steel, Inc. v. First Alabama Bank, 474 U.S. 518, 106 S.Ct. 768, 88 L.Ed.2d 877 (1986).

13. 433 U.S. 186, 97 S.Ct. 2569, 53 L.Ed.2d 683 (1977); § 2.7 *supra*.

established by attaching the boat. The court can then adjudicate plaintiff's claim as a basis for awarding the $60,000 according to the outcome of that adjudication. But the court's jurisdiction is limited to the value of the property attached.[14] If plaintiff succeeds in the attachment suit, the property is awarded to plaintiff and the balance of the claim can be pursued in a later action.[15] If plaintiff loses, the balance of the claim is not merged and theoretically can still be pursued. As we shall see in a later section,[16] however, issue preclusion may be determinative in any subsequent action if the issues were actually litigated in the attachment proceeding.[17]

Change in applicable law or facts

Because the law changes, often rapidly, legal theories not available during the original action may become available later. Although such a change in the law is not a basis for reopening a damages suit,[18] the courts sometimes respond to such change by manipulating the scope of "cause of action" to permit a renewed claim.[19] When facts occurring after a judgment give rise to a new claim, the plaintiff is of course free to assert it,[20] but may have some difficulty persuading the court that the claim is really new and not just a disguised version of the original claim.[21] An extreme version of the problem is presented by a plaintiff who recovers for a modest injury caused by asbestos exposure, and then years later develops asbestos-related cancer. A number of courts have treated this as a new and distinct claim permitting a second suit.[22]

§ 11.15 Defenses and Counterclaims

When sued on a claim, the defendant must interpose all available defenses in that suit. An omitted defense cannot later be used to attack

14. *See* Restatement (Second) of Judgments § 32.

15. *See, e.g.,* Strand v. Halverson, 220 Iowa 1276, 264 N.W. 266 (1935); Note, 103 A.L.R. 839; Note, Developments in the Law: Res Judicata, 65 Harv. L. Rev. 818, 834 (1952); Restatement (Second) of Judgments § 32, Comment *c.*

16. *See* § 11.22 *infra.*

17. If, however, the forum in which the plaintiffs could have obtained personal jurisdiction over the defendant was one reasonably convenient to the plaintiffs, refusal to avail themselves of that forum should preclude them from later suing to recover the balance of their claim. *See* Minichiello v. Rosenberg, 410 F.2d 106 (2d Cir.1968), *and compare* Restatement (Second) of Judgments § 24, Comment *g.*

18. *E.g.,* Federated Dept. Stores v. Moitie, 452 U.S. 394, 101 S.Ct. 2424, 69 L.Ed.2d 103 (1981); Lim v. Central DuPage Hospital, 972 F.2d 758 (7th Cir.1992) (claim barred even though at time of previous suit court threatened anyone making such a claim with Rule 11 sanctions); *cf.* Restatement (Second) of Judgments § 26, Comment *j.*; § 12.15 *infra* on Fed. R. Civ. P. 60(b). On change of law as a basis for reconsidering continuing injunctive relief, see Miller v. French, 530 U.S. 327, 120 S.Ct. 2246, 147 L.Ed.2d 326 (2000).

19. *E.g.,* Henn v. Henn, 26 Cal.3d 323, 605 P.2d 10, 161 Cal.Rptr. 502 (1980).

20. *E.g.,* Curtis v. Citibank, N.A., 226 F.3d 133 (2d Cir.2000); Baker Group v. Burlington N. & S.F. Ry., 228 F.3d 883 (8th Cir.2000).

21. *E.g.,* Waldman v. Village of Kiryas Joel, 207 F.3d 105 (2d Cir.2000) (new events just additional instances of acts previously challenged); Woods v. Dunlop Tire Corp., 972 F.2d 36 (2d Cir.1992) (plaintiff could have expedited "new" claim).

22. Pustejovsky v. Rapid–American Corp., 35 S.W.3d 643 (Tex. 2000) (citing other cases).

or defeat the operation of the judgment.[1] If defendant has grounds for a counterclaim for affirmative relief, the problem is more complicated. Three situations may be distinguished: (1) when no substantial factual nexus exists between plaintiff's claim and defendant's counterclaim, (2) when the claim and counterclaim arise out of the same transaction and the forum has a rule making "transaction" counterclaims compulsory, and (3) when the claim and counterclaim arise out of the same transaction but the forum does not have a compulsory counterclaim rule.

Unrelated counterclaim

In the first situation, the claim and counterclaim are factually unrelated and no special difficulty arises. The compulsory counterclaim rule does not cover such a claim and hence does not require it to be asserted.[2] Furthermore, since the factual issues in the two claims are distinct, defendant runs no risk that later assertion of his or her claim will be barred by claim or issue preclusion arising out of the first action. Hence, defendant has the choice of asserting the claim by counterclaim (in federal court, only if jurisdictional requirements are satisfied) or asserting it in a separate action.

Counterclaim arising from same facts

In the second situation ("same transaction," counterclaim being compulsory), defendant must assert the counterclaim, for two reasons. First, a strong possibility exists that the issues will be determined in such a way that the rule of issue preclusion will prevent defendant from maintaining the claim in a subsequent action.[3] Thus, if plaintiff sues on a contract, contending that he or she performed the obligation but defendant did not, a judgment for plaintiff will have determined that plaintiff did perform the obligation; under the rule of issue preclusion, defendant cannot relitigate that issue and hence could not succeed in a subsequent action for breach of contract. But, more than this, defendant will be precluded from asserting such an action by the compulsory counterclaim rule.[4] That rule ordinarily applies even if the first action was not decided on the merits; thus, defendant will be barred simply by failing to assert the counterclaim, whatever the resolution of the plaintiff's claim.

§ 11.15

1. Restatement (Second) of Judgments § 18(b). The defense may sometimes be used as a part of a collateral attack on the judgment. *See* § 12.15 *infra*.

2. Fed. R. Civ. P. 13(a), (b). *See* § 9.11 *supra*.

3. Restatement (Second) of Judgments § 27, Comment *a*.

4. *See, e.g.,* Fed. R. Civ. P. 13(a); Fox v. Maulding, 112 F.3d 453 (10th Cir.1997); Mohr v. State Bank of Stanley, 241 Kan. 42, 734 P.2d 1071 (1987); Wright, Estoppel by Rule: The Compulsory Counterclaim Under Modern Pleading, 39 Iowa L. Rev. 255 (1954); Restatement (Second) of Judgments § 22(2).

No compulsory counterclaim rule

The third situation can arise in the minority of jurisdictions that do not have a compulsory counterclaim rule. Two rules are operative that nevertheless make assertion of the counterclaim a practical imperative. The first, referred to above, is the rule of issue preclusion preventing defendant from relitigating any issues determined against defendant in adjudicating plaintiff's claim.[5] The second is that the defendant may not in a subsequent action assert a claim that would nullify or undermine a judgment obtained by plaintiff in the first action.[6] Thus, if plaintiff brings an action to confirm title to property and obtains judgment, defendant may not later assert a claim to an easement, lien, or mortgage on the property—for that would take away from the title already confirmed in the plaintiff. When faced with such a situation, defendant theoretically does not have to assert the counterclaim. Rather, defendant could act on the supposition that he or she will win the first action and hence be able later to sue on his or her own claim. But the risk of losing, and the expense of litigating twice, make such a course of action highly imprudent except under unusual circumstances.

Moreover, defendant may face another problem if he or she tries to withhold the counterclaim when the facts constituting the defense to the plaintiff's action are also components of defendant's affirmative claim for relief. If defendant asserts them through a defense but not through a counterclaim, the court may hold that bringing a separate action on those facts is a "splitting" of defendant's cause of action. If it is held to be a splitting, the rule of claim preclusion will prevent defendant from asserting an affirmative claim in a subsequent action,[7] and there will usually be a preclusive effect barring relitigation of the specific jurisdictional issue already decided.[8] For all these reasons, a defendant who has a counterclaim arising out of the same transaction involved in plaintiff's claim is ordinarily compelled, as a practical matter, to assert it even in the absence of a compulsory counterclaim rule.

Compulsory counterclaims

Two further problems concerning compulsory counterclaims are considered here because of their close relation to the problem of claim preclusion. The first occurs when the forum rendering the judgment in the first action has a compulsory counterclaim rule but the forum in which the second action is brought does not. The general rule on the scope of preclusion is that it is determined by the law of the court in

5. *See* note 3 *supra*.

6. Restatement (Second) of Judgments § 22(2)(b). *See, e.g.,* In re Iannochino, 242 F.3d 36 (1st Cir.2001); Moore v. Harjo, 144 F.2d 318 (10th Cir.1944).

7. *See* Middlesex Concrete Prod. & Excavating Corp. v. Borough of Carteret, 35 N.J.Super. 226, 113 A.2d 821 (1955). *Compare* Restatement (Second) of Judgments § 22, Comment *d*.

8. *See* Magnus Elecs. v. La Republica Argentina, 830 F.2d 1396 (7th Cir.1987); GAF Corp. v. United States, 818 F.2d 901 (D.C.Cir.1987).

which the judgment was rendered.[9] Thus, the first forum's definition of "claim" is determinative for the purposes of subsequent preclusion of the plaintiff. It follows that the first forum's compulsory counterclaim rule, which prescribes the boundaries of the action maintained there, bars a subsequent action on a claim covered by the rule. The better decisions so hold.[10]

The second problem arises when the compulsory counterclaim rule is applied to an insured defendant who is represented by his or her insurer but who also has a separate claim against plaintiff (who, in turn, would be defended by *his* or *her* insurer). Nominally, in such a situation the action is against the defendant-insured, and he or she may thus assert the counterclaim. Actually, the plaintiff's target is usually defendant's insurance coverage, and the counsel provided to defendant is a specialist in defense rather than in prosecution of personal injury claims. The situation may involve considerable conflict of interest between the defendant-insured and his or her insurer in handling defendant's counterclaim for his or her own injuries. This conflict has been assigned as a reason for not adopting a compulsory counterclaim rule.[11] Yet, for the reasons discussed earlier (particularly the risk of issue preclusion), even without a compulsory counterclaim rule it is usually practically imperative that defendant assert his or her claim in plaintiff's action. The compulsory counterclaim rule therefore exacerbates, but does not create, the inherent conflict between defendant-insured and his or her insurer. That conflict could be eliminated only if the plaintiff's claim were required to be asserted against the "real" defendant, the insurance company, which would then simply defend the action unencumbered by the problem of a counterclaim by its insured.[12]

§ 11.16 Judgment on the Merits

Under the rule of claim preclusion as traditionally stated, only a judgment on the merits resulted in merger or bar. The requirement that the judgment be on the merits was significant in two situations. In one, judgment was entered against plaintiff on the sustaining of defendant's demurrer on the ground that the complaint failed to state a cause of action. Many authorities held that such a judgment precluded a subsequent action on the same "theory" but did not preclude an action based on a complaint that had been reformulated so that it did state a cause of

9. Restatement (Second) of Conflict of Laws §§ 94, 95; 28 U.S.C. § 1738. *See also* Casad, Intersystem Issue Preclusion and the Restatement (Second) of Judgments, 66 Cornell L. Rev. 510 (1981); Scoles, Interstate Preclusion by Prior Adjudication, 74 Nw. U.L. Rev. 742 (1979).

10. *Compare* London v. City of Philadelphia, 412 Pa. 496, 194 A.2d 901 (1963) (bars subsequent action), *with* Phoenix Ins. Co. v. Haney, 235 Miss. 60, 108 So.2d 227 (1959) (does not do so).

11. N.Y. Temp. Commn., First Advisory Report of the Advisory Committee on Practice and Procedure 69–70 (1957).

12. *See* § 10.9 *supra*.

action.[1] In the other situation, after plaintiff's presentation of evidence at trial defendant was granted a nonsuit on the ground that plaintiff's evidence was insufficient. Many authorities held that a judgment based on such a nonsuit did not prevent plaintiff from bringing a new action and attempting therein to marshal enough evidence to get the case to the jury.[2]

Opportunity to litigate usually sufficient

Both situations were intelligible under the former prevailing concepts of pleading and trial. Under modern procedure, however, they are not justified. Modern pleading rules allow plaintiffs to allege claim formulations in the alternative and afford liberal opportunity to amend any formulation found insufficient on a demurrer or motion to dismiss a claim.[3] There is no reason not to expect plaintiffs to avail themselves of these opportunities. Similarly, modern procedure, particularly discovery, allows plaintiffs abundant opportunity to develop all available evidence that could be used at trial.[4] These opportunities thus enlarge the scope of what might have been litigated by the plaintiff in the first action and should correspondingly enlarge the scope of claim preclusion. Most of the authorities now hold that a judgment in either of the situations described above precludes a second action based on the same transaction.[5]

The modern rule of claim preclusion does not require that a judgment against the plaintiff be on the merits to be preclusive. It need only be shown that (1) the claims involved in the two actions were based on the same out-of-court transaction,[6] (2) the procedure in the first action (including the possibility of appeal) did not exclude an opportunity to present the matter advanced in the second action,[7] and (3) the judgment was not a dismissal without prejudice or was not based on some other ground that allows the bringing of a second action.[8] The essential concept of the modern rule of claim preclusion is that a judgment against plaintiff is preclusive not simply when it is on the merits but when the procedure in the first action afforded plaintiff a fair opportunity to get to the merits.

§ 11.16

1. *See* von Moschzisker, Res Judicata, 38 Yale L.J. 299 (1929); *e.g.*, Rost v. Kroke, 195 Minn. 219, 262 N.W. 450 (1935).

2. Note, Developments in the Law: Res Judicata, 65 Harv. L. Rev. 818, 838 (1952).

3. *See* § 4.19 *supra.*

4. *See* Chapter 5.

5. *See, e.g.,* Fed. R. Civ. P. 41(b); EFCO v. U.W. Marx, Inc., 124 F.3d 394 (2d Cir. 1997); Glick v. Ballentine Produce, Inc., 397 F.2d 590 (8th Cir.1968); Elfman v. Glaser, 313 Mass. 370, 47 N.E.2d 925 (1943); Restatement (Second) of Judgments § 9.

6. *See* Restatement (Second) of Judgments 24, 25. *But see* Keidatz v. Albany, 39 Cal.2d 826, 249 P.2d 264 (1952).

7. Restatement (Second) of Judgments § 26.

8. Restatement (Second) of Judgments § 20.

Dismissal without prejudice

The third requirement mentioned above takes into account the fact that judgment against a plaintiff may not purport to foreclose him or her from bringing a subsequent action. The court may, for example, dismiss the action without prejudice. In the federal courts, a dismissal requested by the plaintiff is ordinarily without prejudice while an involuntary dismissal ordinarily operates as a judgment on the merits, in each case subject to the power of the court to order otherwise.[9] The court may also dismiss the action for lack of personal or subject matter jurisdiction, for improper venue, or for having been brought prematurely. In such circumstances, the judgment does not preclude a subsequent action free of the first one's defect.[10]

§ 11.17 Issue Preclusion: In General

When an action between two parties terminates in a valid judgment, a later action between the parties may be affected even though it involves a different claim or cause of action. Even if the actions are on different claims, the former judgment "operates as an estoppel as to those matters in issue or points controverted, upon the determination of which the finding or verdict is rendered."[1] The prior litigation does not, however, preclude inquiry into matters that might have been but actually were not put in issue and determined in the former action.[2] This more limited effect of a judgment, formerly called "collateral estoppel," is now called "issue preclusion."[3]

The difference between these two kinds of preclusion has been defined this way by the Supreme Court: "Under res judicata, a final judgment on the merits of an action precludes the parties or their privies from relitigating issues that were or could have been raised in that action.... Under collateral estoppel, once a court decides an issue of fact

9. *See* Fed. R. Civ. P. 41(a, b); 9 Wright and Miller, Federal Practice and Procedure §§ 2373, 4436. Even when a federal court dismisses an action on the merits, a new suit elsewhere may be possible, for example when the dismissal was based on the local statute of limitations. See Semtek Int'l Inc. v. Lockheed Martin Corp., 531 U.S. 497, 121 S.Ct. 1021 149 L.Ed.2d 32 (2001).

10. Fed. R. Civ. P. 41(b); Restatement (Second) of Judgments § 20; 1B Moore, Federal Practice and Procedure ¶ 0.405(5). *See also* Winslow v. Walters, 815 F.2d 1114 (7th Cir.1987); American Natl. Bank v. Federal Deposit Ins. Corp., 710 F.2d 1528 (11th Cir.1983) (res judicata does not apply to a dismissal for want of jurisdiction even when the former action was brought in bad faith).

§ 11.17

1. Cromwell v. County of Sac, 94 U.S. 351, 353, 24 L.Ed. 195, 198 (1877). *See also* Parklane Hosiery Co. v. Shore, 439 U.S. 322, 99 S.Ct. 645, 58 L.Ed.2d 552 (1979).

2. *See generally* Scott, Collateral Estoppel by Judgment, 56 Harv. L. Rev. 1 (1942); Polasky, Collateral Estoppel—Effects of Prior Litigation, 39 Iowa L. Rev. 217 (1954); Note, Developments in the Law: Res Judicata, 65 Harv. L. Rev. 818, 840–850 (1952); Restatement (Second) of Judgments §§ 27, 28; Shell, Res Judicata and Collateral Estoppel Effects of Commercial Arbitration, 35 UCLA L. Rev. 623 (1988).

3. The federal courts have preferred the use of the terms "claim preclusion" and "issue preclusion" over the use of the terms "merger," "bar," and "collateral estoppel." *See* Robi v. Five Platters, Inc., 838 F.2d 318, 321 & n. 2 (9th Cir.1988); Wade v. City of Pittsburgh, 765 F.2d 405, 408 (3d Cir. 1985).

or law necessary to its judgment, that decision precludes relitigation of the same issue on a different cause of action between the same parties."[4]

When issue preclusion is involved between the same parties as those to the original suit, the one who claims its benefit (proponent) must show that the very fact or point now in issue was, in the former action, (1) litigated by the parties, (2) determined by the tribunal, and (3) necessarily so determined.[5] When these conditions are met, issue preclusion may also apply to persons who were not parties to the former action. This we shall take up in later sections;[6] the first part of our discussion will assume identity of parties.

§ 11.18 Matter or Point Must Have Been Litigated

Parties often do not raise every matter or point that might conceivably be relevant to the claim or defense. The reasons why they do not do so cover a wide range; examples of them are given in a famous opinion: "the smallness of the amount or the value of the property in controversy, the difficulty of obtaining the necessary evidence, the expense of litigation, and his own situation at the time."[1] Another reason may be the fear of diverting the tribunal's attention from a good claim or defense by injecting a weak, confusing, or unpopular issue.

Difference between claim and issue preclusion

If a party omits some matter or point from the first action, as we have seen, the party is precluded by the judgment from later raising that matter or point either to promote or to defeat the original claim.[2]

Claim preclusion, in precluding the litigation of issues that should have been raised in the first suit, but for some reason were not, has the effect of setting up a "due diligence" standard. For instance, in *McWilliams v. McWilliams*[3] Mrs. McWilliams filed a 42 U.S.C. § 1983 civil rights claim, alleging that the record a previous action was replete with racial references intended to prejudice the judge and jury against her in her divorce action and causing her to lose custody of her children. Her attorney made no objections to the remarks, although they were impermissible. The court in the second action found her allegations to be true but held she was barred by claim preclusion because her attorney should have known that the remarks were improper.

4. Kremer v. Chemical Construction Corp., 456 U.S. 461, 467 n. 6, 102 S.Ct. 1883, 1889 n. 6, 72 L.Ed.2d 262, 271 n. 6 (1982).

5. Polasky, Collateral Estoppel—Effects of Prior Litigation, 39 Iowa L. Rev. 217, 222 (1954); Restatement (Second) of Judgments §§ 27, 28; James, Consent Judgments as Collateral Estoppel, 108 U. Pa. L. Rev. 173, 177–178 (1959).

6. *See* §§ 11.23 *et seq. infra.*

§ 11.18

1. Cromwell v. County of Sac, 94 U.S. 351, 356, 24 L.Ed. 195, 199 (1877).

2. *See* §§ 11.8–11.17 *supra.*

3. 804 F.2d 1400 (5th Cir.1986).

To this extent, then, a party is under pressure to litigate the first action to the utmost. The collateral effect of a judgment is limited, however, to issues actually decided therein. Thus, the pressure to litigate in the first action will not be carried so far as to make omissions from the first action fatal to raising the omitted point in all possible contexts in which it may become relevant in future disputes between the parties.[4]

Scope of issues

As Professor Polasky pointed out, the breadth of collateral estoppel depends on how broadly or narrowly the issue decided is conceived. If, in a negligence case, the issue is considered broadly as whether negligence existed, then a finding of no negligence will preclude plaintiff from showing the opposite (that is, negligence) in a later action even on an item (such as failure to look out) that was not urged in the first action. But if pleadings raise specific items of negligence, so that the issue is whether defendant was negligent in failing to blow his horn, for example, then a finding for defendant in the first action might not preclude showing other items of negligence in the second.

Issues not litigated

Economy of litigation is not necessarily promoted by using issue preclusion to eliminate or limit the scope of the second action. An impending threat of issue preclusion could so increase the dimensions of the first action that more judicial effort is expended than would be the case in the two potential actions.[5] The extent of a single claim usually can be appreciated in the first action so that the parties have a basis for calculating with fair accuracy the risks of omissions and the worth of litigating to the utmost. The potential contexts in which collateral estoppel may apply in the future, however, are often more difficult to foresee. An unduly broad rule of issue preclusion might generate undue pressure to make every petty claim a "federal case," so to speak.[6] Of course, when an issue simply goes by default in the first action, there is no duplication of effort if the issue is drawn into contest in the second action.

Stipulated matters

Matters may be put in issue by the pleadings, the pretrial order, or by the evidence without being reflected in the pleadings or pretrial order.[7] If a defendant over whom jurisdiction has been obtained defaults

4. *See* Polasky, Collateral Estoppel—Effects of Prior Litigation, 39 Iowa L. Rev. 217, 222–224 (1954). *See also* Restatement (Second) of Judgments § 28, Comment *i.*

5. Various strategic objectives may induce a litigant not to raise issues that could be raised. Such issues are not precluded in subsequent litigation. *See, e.g.,* Haring v. Prosise, 462 U.S. 306, 103 S.Ct. 2368, 76 L.Ed.2d 595 (1983).

6. *Cf.* Hand, J., in The Evergreens v. Nunan, 141 F.2d 927, 929 (2d Cir.1944), *cert. denied,* 323 U.S. 720, 65 S.Ct. 49, 89 L.Ed. 579 (1944).

7. *See* § 4.22 *supra.*

by failure to appear or otherwise fails to defend, nothing is put in issue.[8] Hence, the judgment determines no issue and does not become binding in later actions on different claims.[9] Matters or points put in issue may still be abandoned or withdrawn before judgment, as when a case is settled by a consent judgment for plaintiff or a judgment of dismissal on stipulation. Similarly, facts established by stipulation or otherwise admitted in the first action have not been put in issue.[10] The party's change of position as to the issue of fact may be used in the second case to impeach its evidence or as a basis for disallowing a contrary contention. But these effects hinge on the inconsistency of the party's position, not on the preclusive effect of the judgment in the first action.[11]

Showing issue was raised

The party who claims the benefit of issue preclusion has the burden of introducing evidence to show that the matter or point now at issue was also put in issue in the former action.[12] The proponent may show what was put in issue by any part of the record in the former action, including a transcript of the proceedings.[13] Evidence not included in the record also may be used, usually limited to matters that occurred during the course of the first action.

§ 11.19 Matter or Point Must Have Been Determined

Not only must the matter or point have been put in issue but it must also have been determined by the tribunal in the first action.[1] It is

8. The court has the duty on its own motion to ascertain the existence of the facts as to subject matter jurisdiction; therefore, the facts may be said to be "in issue" even though defendant has not done anything to make them so. To this extent the adversary system is qualified.

9. Restatement (Second) of Judgments § 27, Comment *e*; Benjamin v. Traffic Executive Assn., 869 F.2d 107 (2d Cir.1989); Matter of Cassidy, 892 F.2d 637 (7th Cir. 1990).But see Bay Area Factors v. Calvert, 105 F.3d 315 (6th Cir.1997) (applying California preclusion law, under which default judgment does support issue preclusion). Some states give guilty pleas in criminal cases issue preclusive effect. *Compare* State Farm Fire & Cas. Co. v. Fullerton, 118 F.3d 374 (5th Cir.1997); Colorado Farm Bureau Mut. Ins. Co. v. Snowbarger, 934 P.2d 909 (Colo.App.1997) *with* Bower v. O'Hara, 759 F.2d 1117 (3d Cir.1985); see Shapiro, Should a Guilty Plea Have Preclusive Effect?, 70 Iowa L. Rev. 27 (1984).

10. *See* Arizona v. California, 530 U.S. 392, 120 S.Ct. 2304, 147 L.Ed.2d 374 (2000)(consent judgment); Gall v. South Branch Natl. Bank, 783 F.2d 125 (8th Cir. 1986); Jackson Jordan, Inc. v. Plasser Am. Corp., 747 F.2d 1567 (Fed.Cir.1984). On the possibility of wiping out a judgment's issue preclusive effects by conditioning a later settlement on vacation of the judgment, *see* § 5.19 *supra*.

11. *See* James, Consent Judgments as Collateral Estoppel, 108 U. Pa. L. Rev. 173, 183 (1959); Restatement (Second) of Judgments § 27, Comment *c*.

12. Fay v. South Colonie Cent. School Dist., 802 F.2d 21 (2d Cir.1986) (where the basis of the decision is too ambiguous to determine if it was put in issue, there is no preclusion); Norfolk & W. Ry. v. United States, 768 F.2d 373 (D.C.Cir.1985); Restatement (Second) of Judgments § 27, Comment *f*. *See also* In re Real Estate Title & Settlement Servs. Antitrust Litig., 869 F.2d 760 (3d Cir.1989).

13. Wheeler v. Laudani, 783 F.2d 610 (6th Cir.1986); Dozier v. Ford Motor Co., 702 F.2d 1189 (D.C.Cir.1983).

§ 11.19

1. Polasky, Collateral Estoppel—Effects of Prior Litigation, 39 Iowa L. Rev. 217, 222 (1954); Note, Developments in the Law: Res

not always easy to ascertain whether a particular issue was actually determined.

Multiple issues presented

If the first case was tried to the court without a jury, the court often will have made findings of fact and conclusions of law to support its judgment;[2] these may show what matters and points were determined as the basis for the decision in that action. In contrast, the general verdict of a jury will often be ambiguous. A verdict for defendant in a negligence case, for example, may have been based on plaintiff's contributory negligence, on the absence of defendant's negligence, on the lack of a causal connection between negligence and injury, or on a combination of more than one of these findings.

Unless such ambiguities are resolved by admissible evidence, the party who seeks the benefit of issue preclusion will fail[3] unless *any* of the possible grounds for the former decision is a sufficient factual basis for judgment in favor of the proponent of issue preclusion in the second action.[4] Juror testimony, moreover, will not be allowed in an effort to determine what the jury actually decided,[5] as that would be contrary to the policy considerations of the Federal Rules of Evidence.[6] Likewise, an appellate court will not take evidence from the trial judge to determine the meaning of his or her findings.[7]

Ultimate and mediate facts

When it has been satisfactorily established that the issue in question was determined in the first action, two further problems sometimes arise: (1) Does the finding on the issue imply also a conclusive finding on all the evidentiary issues leading up to the finding, or, as it is sometimes expressed, does the finding of the "ultimate issue" signify that the "mediate data" leading to it were also determined? (2) Is a finding on an ultimate issue in the first action conclusive in the second action not only on that issue but also as a mediate datum (that is, a step in the process of evidentiary inference) in that action?

Answers to these questions vary. Some courts have held that an ultimate finding does not imply a finding on the facts on which it seemingly was based. Other courts have held that an ultimate finding

Judicata, 65 Harv. L. Rev. 818, 840 (1952); Restatement (Second) of Judgments § 27.

2. *See* Fed. R. Civ. P. 52(a).

3. Steel v. United States, 813 F.2d 1545 (9th Cir.1987); Davis v. West Community Hosp., 786 F.2d 677 (5th Cir.1986).

4. Myhra v. Park, 193 Minn. 290, 258 N.W. 515 (1935).

5. Kazan v. Wolinski, 721 F.2d 911 (3d Cir.1983); Ohio–Sealy Mattress Mfg. Co. v. Kaplan, 90 F.R.D. 11 (C.D.Ill.1980).

6. *See* Fed. R. Evid. 606(b); § 7.27 *supra*. *But see* Katz v. Eli Lilly & Co., 84 F.R.D. 378 (E.D.N.Y.1979) (testimony of juror in first action received to prove verdict was a compromise).

7. Grip-Pak, Inc. v. Illinois Tool Works, 694 F.2d 466 (7th Cir.1982); Eaton v. Weaver Mfg. Co., 582 F.2d 1250 (10th Cir.1978).

should be carried over into the second action for the purpose of establishing either an ultimate issue or a subordinate evidentiary step in the latter action.[8]

These answers, or even opposite ones, are logically coherent, but they seem casuistical. The supposed difference between an ultimate and a mediate fact can be made to appear or disappear depending on how the factual issue itself is described. Moreover, in deciding whether to carry the determination into the second action, it seems less important to characterize it in these terms than to inquire whether the issue was central rather than peripheral in the first action, whether the chain of inference leading to it was direct rather than circuitous, whether the fact-finder apparently focused on the issue, and whether the context in which the issue arises in the second action is the same as it was in the first. The point, in other words, is that the syllogistic position of the finding is less important than whether it was fully litigated and necessarily decided.[9]

§ 11.20 Determination Must Have Been Necessary to Result

"Dictum" not binding

The requirement that the determination must have been necessary to the result in the first action is well illustrated by a Massachusetts decision. The first action sought relief for personal injury caused by *C*'s negligence under the then-prevailing substantive law that a plaintiff's contributory negligence is a complete bar to recovery in a negligence action. Hence, a finding that plaintiff was contributorily negligent made it unnecessary to decide whether *C* was negligent. Nevertheless, the case ended in a defendant's judgment pursuant to an explicit finding that plaintiff's conduct constituted contributory negligence and an equally explicit finding that *C* was negligent. This second finding was held not binding in a later action because it was unnecessary to support the judgment.[1]

Three considerations support this ruling. First, the parties' attention and efforts are likely to be focused on points and matters that are necessary to the result. Second, the tribunal's attention is likely to be focused on the grounds necessary for its decision. Findings that are

8. *Compare* Yates v. United States, 354 U.S. 298, 338, 77 S.Ct. 1064, 1087, 1 L.Ed.2d 1356, 1386 (1957); The Evergreens v. Nunan, 141 F.2d 927 (2d Cir.1944), *with* Dobbins v. Title Guar. & Trust Co., 22 Cal.2d 64, 136 P.2d 572 (1943). *See* Comment, 36 N.Y.U. L. Rev. 522 (1961); Annot., 142 A.L.R. 1243.

9. *Compare* Restatement (Second) of Judgments § 27, Comment *c*. *See* SEC v. Monarch Funding Corp., 192 F.3d 295 (2d Cir.1999); Hyman v. Regenstein, 258 F.2d 502, 509–512 (5th Cir.1958); Hinchey v. Sellers, 7 N.Y.2d 287, 165 N.E.2d 156, 197 N.Y.S.2d 129 (1959).

§ 11.20

1. Cambria v. Jeffery, 307 Mass. 49, 29 N.E.2d 555 (1940). *See also* Restatement (Second) of Judgments § 27. *Compare* Vestal, Preclusion/Res Judicata Variables: Nature of the Controversy, 1965 Wash. U.L.Q. 158.

unnecessary partake of *obiter dicta.* Third, unnecessary findings are usually not subject to appellate review. While the availability of appellate review is not an essential predicate of res judicata,[2] its absence is a consideration in determining whether the prior judgment should be given issue-preclusive effect in subsequent litigation.[3]

Alternative basis

A related problem arises when determination of the issue was an alternative basis for the judgment in the first action. This problem is illustrated by a variation on the case mentioned above. Suppose the trier of fact in the first action finds both that defendant was not negligent and that plaintiff was contributorily negligent. Either finding is sufficient to justify the judgment, so either could be essential to the judgment or be obiter dictum. The reasons for not applying issue preclusion to a "dictum," suggested above, also appear pertinent to an alternative finding. But it seems absurd that defeated litigants can relitigate because they lost on two grounds rather than one.

The cases are divided.[4] The Restatement (Second) of Judgments reluctantly takes the position that neither finding is subsequently binding because it cannot be clearly ascertained that it was necessary to the first judgment, unless the issue was isolated by being reviewed on appeal in the first action and its determination there affirmed.[5] This seems sound as far as it allows the affirmed finding to be binding. Perhaps a better approach would be to ask whether the two issues were actually distinct (negligence and contributory negligence, for example, can be compressed into the issue of relative fault), whether they were fully litigated, whether their context in the two actions is about the same, and whether there is any reason to suppose the trier of fact in the first action would have reached a different conclusion if the issue in question had been presented alone rather than in company with another issue.

In *Deweese v. Town of Palm Beach,*[6] for instance, the municipality, in state court litigation, appealed the trial judge's ruling that an ordinance prohibiting people from appearing in public without a shirt was a violation of the Ninth Amendment. But the municipality had acquiesced

2. Schellong v. Immigration and Naturalization Serv., 805 F.2d 655 (7th Cir. 1986); Stewart v. National Shopmen Pension Fund, 730 F.2d 1552 (D.C.Cir.1984); Wickham Contracting Co. v. Board of Educ. City of N.Y., 715 F.2d 21 (2d Cir.1983).

3. Bell v. Dillard Department Stores, Inc., 85 F.3d 1451 (10th Cir.1996); Restatement (Second) of Judgments § 27, Comment *i*; Note, Developments in the Law: Res Judicata, 65 Harv. L. Rev. 818, 846–847 (1952). An added problem arises when an appeal has been dismissed as moot. Scott, Collateral Estoppel by Judgment, 56 Harv. L. Rev. 1, 16–17 (1942), as well as the sources cited *supra.*

4. *See* Halpern v. Schwartz, 426 F.2d 102 (2d Cir.1970), reviewing the decisions. *Compare* Magnus Electronics, Inc. v. La Republica Argentina, 830 F.2d 1396 (7th Cir.1987) *with* Connors v. Tanoma Mining Co., 953 F.2d 682 (D.C.Cir.1992).

5. Restatement (Second) of Judgments § 27, Comment *o*; see In re Baylis, 217 F.3d 66 (1st Cir.2000).

6. 688 F.2d 731 (11th Cir.1982).

in the judge's alternate ruling that the ordinance was fatally vague and overbroad. Hence, it had no motive or incentive to pursue the appeal vigorously on the Ninth Amendment issue. In subsequent federal court litigation involving a revised ordinance again challenged on the basis of the Ninth Amendment, it was held unfair to preclude the town from relitigating that issue in federal court.

§ 11.21 Questions of Law

In its older formulation, collateral estoppel applied only to issues of fact, not to issues of law.[1] Relitigation of issues of law was constrained, not by a rule that the *parties* could not reassert a legal contention that previously had been rejected, but by the rule of stare decisis, under which the *court* would not re-examine a question of law that it had previously decided.[2] Ordinarily, the refusal to apply issue preclusion to an issue of law makes sense. There seems no reason why a party who has litigated an issue of law should be under greater disability to invite a court to depart from precedent than a party who has not litigated the issue. The law, whatever the content of its rules, governs all litigants alike and generally should be applied to all.

In many applications, however, the distinction between issues of fact and issues of law is artificial. This is especially true when the rule of law has been previously defined in essentially the same factual context as is presented in the second action, and between the same parties. Some courts have held, for example, that "an expansive definition of 'issue' may be used to encompass any legal theory or factual assertion put forward in a second action that is relevant to the subject matter and relevant to the issues actually adjudicated in the initial action."[3] Hence, issue preclusion is applied to issues of law as well as fact, subject to some special qualifications.[4]

Government litigation

One qualification is that issue preclusion should not be applied if doing so would place the party who won on the issue in a favored position in the general administration of the law. This problem is illustrated by tax cases and others involving government agency administration of the law. Suppose a taxpayer litigates whether certain income

§ 11.21

1. *See* Shell Oil Co. v. Texas Gas Transmission Corp., 176 So.2d 692 (La.App.1964).

2. Note, Developments in the Law: Res Judicata, 65 Harv. L. Rev. 818, 843–845 (1952); § 11.6 *supra.*

3. Purter v. Heckler, 771 F.2d 682, 689–690 n. 5 (3d Cir.1985).

4. *See* United States v. Stauffer Chemical Co., 464 U.S. 165, 104 S.Ct. 575, 78 L.Ed.2d 388 (1984); Burlington Northern R.R. v. Hyundai Merchant Marine Co., 63 F.3d 1227 (3d Cir.1995); Restatement (Second) of Judgments § 27; *id.* § 28, Comments *b, c. See also* Buckley, Issue Preclusion and Issues of Law: A Doctrinal Framework Based on Rules of Recognition, Jurisdiction, and Legal History, 24 Hous. L. Rev. 875 (1987); Hazard, Preclusion as to Issues of Law: The Legal System's Interest, 70 Iowa L. Rev. 81 (1984).

in a particular tax year is attributable to him or her, and obtains a determination that it is not. Suppose that in subsequent tax years, the same question comes up as to this taxpayer and as to another taxpayer, but is resolved against the latter in separate litigation. If the determination reached in the first action is preclusive against the government, the taxpayer in that action will have a perennial special tax exemption (unless the tax statute itself is changed).The policy against relitigation of issues does not seem strong enough to overcome the policy in favor of equal treatment of similarly situated taxpayers.[5]

Unappealed ruling

A second qualification is that opportunity to obtain reconsideration of a legal question might be afforded when the first determination was not carried up through the appellate process to the extent that it might be in the second litigation. For example, an important issue of law may have been resolved in an intermediate appellate court in the first litigation and then arise again in litigation that could be carried to the Supreme Court. If opportunity is not afforded for relitigation in the second action, every case becomes a "test case" for a litigant who is likely to confront the issue with some frequency—such as a government agency administering a statute or a financial enterprise continually involved in litigation governed by the Uniform Commercial Code.[6]

Administrative agency rulings

A variation of this problem arises in the question whether administrative adjudications should be given preclusive effect. The procedures of many administrative agencies differ significantly from court procedures. Hence, there has been some reluctance to foreclose litigation on the basis of prior administrative adjudication. In *University of Tennessee v. Elliott* the Supreme Court held that "giving preclusive effect to administrative fact finding serves the value underlying general principles of collateral estoppel: enforcing repose. This value ... is equally implicated whether fact finding is done by a federal or state agency."[7] In *Astoria Federal Savings & Loan Association v. Solimino,*[8] however, the Court denied

5. Commissioner v. Sunnen, 333 U.S. 591, 68 S.Ct. 715, 92 L.Ed. 898 (1948).

6. *Cf.* United States v. Mendoza, 464 U.S. 154, 104 S.Ct. 568, 78 L.Ed.2d 379 (1984), *and* United States v. Stauffer Chem. Co., 464 U.S. 165, 104 S.Ct. 575, 78 L.Ed.2d 388 (1984); Restatement (Second) of Judgments § 29, Comment *i. See also* Estreicher and Revesz, Nonacquiescence by Federal Administrative Agencies, 98 Yale L.J. 679 (1989); Diller and Morewitz, Intracircuit Nonacquiescence and the Breakdown of the Rule of Law: A Response to Estreicher & Revesz, 99 Yale L.J. 801 (1990); Kuczynski, Administrative Res Judicata and the Age Discrimination in Employment Act, 89 Colum. L. Rev. 111 (1989).

7. 478 U.S. 788, 798, 106 S.Ct. 3220, 3226, 92 L.Ed.2d 635, 646 (1986). See Allen v. McCurry, 449 U.S. 90, 101 S.Ct. 411, 66 L.Ed.2d 308 (1980); Restatement (Second) of Judgments § 83; Carlisle, Getting a Full Bite of the Apple: When Should the Doctrine of Issue Preclusion Make an Administrative or Arbitral Determination Binding in a Court of Law?, 55 Fordham L. Rev. 63 (1986).

8. 501 U.S. 104, 111 S.Ct. 2166, 115 L.Ed.2d 96 (1991).

issue preclusion to state agency findings in a discrimination case that had not been subject to judicial review.

Change of law

A third qualification is that preclusion should not be applied to an issue of law that is part of a body of law that has undergone substantial change since the first litigation. It is one thing to preclude litigants from relitigating a legal issue that was decided two or three years ago; it is quite another to hold them to an interpretation that is obsolete or now superseded though not yet overruled.[9]

§ 11.22 In Rem and Quasi in Rem Proceedings

Issue preclusion is most frequently applied in cases involving what are traditionally denominated actions in personam—those in which the basis of the court's authority to adjudicate is presence of the defendant or the fact that the defendant was involved in a transaction occurring within the court's territorial jurisdiction.[1] The rule of issue preclusion also is applied in actions in rem—those in which the basis of the court's authority to adjudicate is the presence of property in which the defendant has a claim of interest. If, for example, the defendant should appear in an in rem action and litigate an issue in a suit to quiet title, the determination of the issue is conclusive in a subsequent action in which the same issue arises again.[2]

A difficult problem occurs in actions quasi in rem, when the basis of the court's authority to adjudicate is the seizure of property owned by the defendant[3] (this exercise of jurisdiction is often called "attachment" jurisdiction). The court assumes to adjudicate a claim that has nothing to do with the property as such; instead, the court holds the property as security for payment of the plaintiff's claim if that claim is found legally valid. In a few situations, quasi in rem jurisdiction may survive *Shaffer v. Heitner*.[4]

Limited appearance

It is clear that the court must allow the defendant an opportunity to defend the claim asserted in connection with the attachment.[5] If defen-

9. Restatement (Second) of Judgments § 28(b)(ii).

§ 11.22

1. For the distinction between jurisdiction in personam and jurisdiction in rem, *see* § 2.4 *supra.*

2. Restatement (Second) of Judgments § 30; *e.g.,* Durfee v. Duke, 375 U.S. 106, 84 S.Ct. 242, 11 L.Ed.2d 186 (1963).

3. See Carrington, The Modern Utility of Quasi In Rem Jurisdiction, 76 Harv. L. Rev. 303 (1962); § 2.7 *supra.*

4. 433 U.S. 186, 97 S.Ct. 2569, 53 L.Ed.2d 683 (1977). For possible survivals, *see* § 2.7 *supra*; Banco Ambrosiano, S.P.A. v. Artoc Bank & Trust, Ltd., 62 N.Y.2d 65, 476 N.Y.S.2d 64, 464 N.E.2d 432 (1984)(litigant may use quasi in rem statute when defendant is constitutionally subject to jurisdiction but state long arm statute does not apply).

5. *Cf.* Fuentes v. Shevin, 407 U.S. 67, 92 S.Ct. 1983, 32 L.Ed.2d 556 (1972).

dant appears without reservation, he or she becomes a party in an unqualified sense and is bound by the rules of res judicata.[6] Most authorities indicate that a defendant may make a "limited" or "special" appearance to defend against the claim for the purpose of defending the property.[7] Suppose defendant makes such an appearance and litigates the merits of the claim asserted by the plaintiff-garnisher. Since the basis of the court's authority is the property itself, the court cannot purport to determine the claim itself; the judgment determines only whether defendant retains the property (if defendant wins) or plaintiff takes it (if plaintiff wins).[8] But what about the determination of the issues that are litigated?

If the determination is treated as conclusive under the rule of issue preclusion, it gives the judgment an added "bootstrap" effectiveness in subsequent litigation. That is, although the court lacks authority to adjudicate the cause of action as such, giving its determinations of issues conclusive effect comes fairly close to being such an adjudication. If, however, the determinations are not given conclusive effect, then the issues involved may have to be tried twice. There is no good solution to the problem, which arises from the anomalous character of attachment jurisdiction itself.[9]

Assuming that attachment jurisdiction remains a valid basis for adjudication, some conclusion has to be reached on the issue preclusion problem. The Restatement (Second) of Judgments suggests that the rule of issue preclusion ordinarily should apply. The theory is that if the value of the property seized is enough to induce defendants to defend it, it is also enough to induce them to litigate the issues with sufficient vigor to make it fair that the litigation be conclusive.[10]

C. PRECLUSION INVOLVING NONPARTIES

§ 11.23 Due Process

In this and the following sections we consider the circumstances in which a judgment may have preclusive effects for nonparties. This discussion proceeds from an important major premise: As a general rule, a person's legal rights may not be concluded without an opportunity to litigate them. The protection of this opportunity is a matter of due

6. *See* Frumer, Jurisdiction and Limited Appearance in New York: Dilemma of the Nonresident Defendant, 18 Fordham L. Rev. 73 (1949); *cf.* United States v. Balanovski, 236 F.2d 298 (2d Cir.1956).

7. Note, "Special" Appearance to Contest the Merits in Attachment Suits, 97 U. Pa. L. Rev. 403 (1949); Note, Developments in the Law: Res Judicata, 73 Harv. L. Rev. 900, 953 (1960).

8. *See* § 11.14 *supra.*

9. *See generally* Minichiello v. Rosenberg, 410 F.2d 106 (2d Cir.1968).

10. Restatement (Second) of Judgments § 32. *Cf.* Note, Limited Appearances and Issue Preclusion: Resetting the Trap?, 66 Cornell L. Rev. 595 (1981).

process under the Constitution.[1] Because protection of this opportunity is a matter of constitutional right, the exceptions to the general rule are carefully defined.

"Privity"

The exceptions fall into two broad categories. First, a nonparty's rights may be concluded when that person's interests have been represented by another who is authorized to act as a party on his or her behalf. Second, a nonparty's rights may be concluded when his or her substantive legal right is so defined that it stands or falls according to a judgment involving another who was a party to prior litigation. Persons falling within either category were traditionally referred to as being in "privity" with the party to the judgment. This remains useful as a general descriptive term but it must be used with great caution. To say that a person is in "privity" with a party signifies only that the relation between them is such that the judgment involving the party may justly be conclusive on the one who is not a party. The problem remains: What relationships justify that consequence?

Before considering these relationships, it is appropriate to consider two important implications of the due process basis for the general rule that a person is not bound by a judgment to which he or she is not a party. The first implication is that one can be affected in a practical way by a judgment without thereby having had one's legal rights foreclosed; put differently, there are some practical effects of a judgment that one has no legal right to ignore simply because one was not a party to the judgment. These follow from what is described below as the transformational effect of a judgment.

The second implication is that a judgment may operate *in favor of* a nonparty even though it could not operate against the nonparty because that person has not had his or her day in court. Specifically, a party who has fully litigated an issue against one opponent is ordinarily precluded from relitigating that same issue against another opponent in subsequent litigation. The subsequent opponent thus becomes a "free rider" on the outcome of the first litigation. In the terminology of the law of res judicata, the latter is referred to as the "mutuality" problem.[2]

§ 11.24 Transformational Effect of Judgment

There is no generally used term to describe one important kind of consequence that a judgment may have. Holmes called it the "legislative

§ 11.23

1. *See, e.g.,* South Central Bell Tel. Co. v. Alabama, 526 U.S. 160, 119 S.Ct. 1180, 143 L.Ed.2d 258 (1999); Richards v. Jefferson County, 517 U.S. 793, 116 S.Ct. 1761, 135 L.Ed.2d 76 (1996); Martin v. Wilks, 490 U.S. 755, 109 S.Ct. 2180, 104 L.Ed.2d 835 (1989); Blonder–Tongue Laboratories v. University of Ill., 402 U.S. 313, 329, 91 S.Ct. 1434, 1443, 28 L.Ed.2d 788, 800 (1971); Zenith Radio Corp. v. Hazeltine Research, 395 U.S. 100, 110, 89 S.Ct. 1562, 1569, 23 L.Ed.2d 129, 140 (1969); Postal Telegraph Cable Co. v. Newport, 247 U.S. 464, 38 S.Ct. 566, 62 L.Ed. 1215 (1918).

2. *See* § 11.25 *infra.*

effect" of a judgment;[1] a better term seems to be "transformational effect." A judgment transforms or confirms legal relations between the parties to the action in a way that others must recognize, at least until they come forward to assert their own claims through litigation. Thus, if a plaintiff recovers judgment and obtains execution against defendant's property, another person having a claim against defendant ordinarily may not contest the property transfer effectuated by the execution (except, for example, when a bankruptcy proceeding may be used to set aside such a transfer). If a married couple is divorced, the change in their marital status ordinarily may not be contested by others. If *A* obtains an injunction against *B* directing that *B* cease dealing with *C*, *C* ordinarily may not ignore the injunction if he or she has knowledge of it; although *C* is still free to litigate the issues involved, and thereby obtain a judgment that might supersede the injunction, until *C* does so *C* is ordinarily required to observe the obligation the judgment imposes on *B*.[2]

These effects on the nonparty are not the result of res judicata rules as such. They flow from the fact that a judgment not only determines issues and claims but also may redefine the relationships of the parties to the litigation with respect to each other, to property, and to their future courses of conduct. For nonparties, the judgment thus operates much like a privately negotiated contract or conveyance. Because such transformational effects affect legal relationships, they are distinguishable from the purely practical effects of a judgment. Practical effects may also reach nonparties, as when the payment of a heavy damages judgment has a financial impact on the dependents of the plaintiff and defendant.

§ 11.25 Mutuality Rule

A judgment, as we have seen, determines both claims and, if based on actual litigation, issues. The same issue may arise in subsequent litigation involving another claim. If that subsequent litigation is between the same parties, the determination in the first action is conclu-

§ 11.24

1. Brigham v. Fayerweather, 140 Mass. 411, 413, 5 N.E. 265, 266 (1886): "If a competent court declares a vessel forfeited, or orders it sold free from all claims, or divorces a couple, or establishes a will . . . a paramount title is passed, the couple is divorced, the will is established as against all the world, whether parties or not, because the sovereign has said that it shall be so." Like so many of Holmes' aphoristic dicta, this obscures more than it enlightens, for there are limitations on the extent to which a court can clear property of all claims, or give effect to a status determination, or establish a will. *Compare* Mullane v. Central Hanover Bank & Trust Co., 339 U.S. 306, 70 S.Ct. 652, 94 L.Ed. 865 (1950); *cf.* Armstrong v. Manzo, 380 U.S. 545, 85 S.Ct. 1187, 14 L.Ed.2d 62 (1965).

2. *See* Fed. R. Civ. P. 65(d); Fiss and Rendleman, Injunctions (2d ed. 1983); Rendleman, Beyond Contempt: Obligors to Injunctions, 53 Tex. L. Rev. 873 (1975).

sive in the second action under the rule of issue preclusion or "collateral estoppel," as it was formerly called.[1]

Mutuality rule

The determination traditionally was not conclusive if the second action involved different parties, even though one of them had been a party to the first action and had unsuccessfully litigated the issue on that occasion. Thus, if *A* was injured as the result of *B*'s operation of a car owned by *C*, and *A* sued *C*, contending that *B* acted negligently, and *A* lost on a finding that *B* had not been negligent, *A* was not prevented from suing *B* and therein relitigating the question of *B*'s negligence. The reason offered to support this conclusion was that if *A* had won the first action, the determination would not be binding on *B* because *B* was not a party to that action; since *B* was not bound, the estoppel resulting from the first action was not mutual, that is, it was not a two-way street as between *A* and *B*; therefore, *A* should not be bound. This was the "mutuality" rule.[2]

Bernhard v. Bank of America

The rule was subject to many exceptions, but it remained almost universally recognized, though often criticized, until 1942, when it was repudiated in the leading case of *Bernhard v. Bank of America.*[3] In that case the first judgment approved an account filed by an executor in probate proceedings for the estate of a decedent. The beneficiaries under the will filed objections to the account, and, after a hearing on the objections, "the court settled the account, and as part of its order declared that the decedent during her lifetime had made a gift to ... [the executor] of the amount of the deposit in question."[4]

After the executor's resignation and discharge, Bernhard, one of the beneficiaries, was appointed administrator. She brought a second action against defendant bank for some money earlier withdrawn by the executor, contending that this withdrawal was not authorized. The Supreme Court of California, in an opinion written by Justice Traynor, held Bernhard and her fellow beneficiaries bound by the finding that the decedent had given the deposit to Cook during her lifetime, which of course cut the ground from under the claim against the bank. The Traynor court thus allowed the bank to invoke the probate judgment as preclusive on the issue of the ownership of the money even though the bank would not have been bound by a finding the other way because it was not a party to the earlier litigation. The court said: "In determining

§ 11.25

1. *See* § 11.17 *supra.*

2. Bigelow v. Old Dominion Copper Mining & Smelting Co., 225 U.S. 111, 32 S.Ct. 641, 56 L.Ed. 1009 (1912); *see* Restatement of Judgments § 93(b).

3. 19 Cal.2d 807, 122 P.2d 892 (1942).

4. 19 Cal.2d at 809–810, 122 P.2d at 893.

the validity of a plea of res judicata three questions are pertinent: Was the issue decided in the prior adjudication identical with the one presented in the action in question? Was there a final judgment on the merits? Was the party against whom the plea is asserted a party or in privity with a party to the prior adjudication?"[5] The Traynor court found no compelling reasons sustaining the mutuality rule and therefore held that it should not impede issue preclusion. *Bernhard* gradually gained adherence from other courts.

Spread of one-way issue preclusion

Thus in *Israel v. Wood Dolson Co.*[6] a real estate broker sued Wood Dolson Co. for a commission on the sale of real property to Gross, allegedly due under a brokerage contract. Gross was also made defendant and a claim was asserted against him for wrongfully inducing Wood Dolson to breach the brokerage contract. The claims were severed for trial. In the first trial Israel lost on a finding that he had not been instrumental in obtaining the sale (in effect, that there had been no breach of contract). This was then held to preclude Israel's recovery against Gross. The New York Court of Appeals found that a common thread of principle ran through the exceptions to mutuality: "Where a full opportunity has been afforded to a party to the prior action and he has failed to prove his freedom from liability or culpability on the part of another, there is no reason for permitting him to retry those issues."[7] Moreover, "the fact that a party has not had his day in court on an issue *as against a particular litigant* is not decisive."[8] The court stated that its holding was "merely the announcement of the underlying general principle which is found in the cases classed as exceptions."[9]

By 1971 many jurisdictions, though probably not a majority, expressed approval of what had become known as the "*Bernhard* rule," or "one-way issue preclusion."[10] In that year, the U.S. Supreme Court adopted the *Bernhard* rule or, perhaps more precisely, rejected the "mutuality" rule. In *Blonder-Tongue Laboratories v. University of Illinois*[11] it held that a patent holder who had brought an action to enforce the patent but lost on the ground that the patent was invalid was bound by the determination of invalidity in a subsequent action against another alleged infringer. Under the influence of that decision, all but a few states have now accepted the *Bernhard* rule and it has now been adopted in the Restatement (Second) of Judgments.[12] As one court has said, "it

5. 19 Cal.2d at 812, 122 P.2d at 895.

6. 1 N.Y.2d 116, 134 N.E.2d 97, 151 N.Y.S.2d 1 (1956).

7. 1 N.Y.2d at 119, 134 N.E.2d at 99, 151 N.Y.S.2d at 4.

8. *Id.* (emphasis in original).

9. 1 N.Y.2d at 120, 134 N.E.2d at 99, 151 N.Y.S.2d at 5.

10. *See* Note, 35 Geo. Wash. L. Rev. 1010 (1967); Annot., 31 A.L.R.3d 1044.

11. 402 U.S. 313, 91 S.Ct. 1434, 28 L.Ed.2d 788 (1971).

12. Restatement (Second) of Judgments § 29; Wright, Miller, and Cooper, Federal Practice and Procedure § 4464. Some states still hold out. *E.g.*, Stogniew v. McQueen, 656 So. 2d 917 (Fla.1995); Angstadt v. At-

has come to be widely accepted that usually little good and much harm can come from allowing a determined plaintiff to retry the same issues in exhausting fashion against successive defendants.''[13]

Offensive preclusion

A number of problems remain, and the law of issue preclusion developed from *Bernhard* is still somewhat fluid. One of the most difficult problems is encountered when the prior determination is sought to be used *offensively* against a defendant who was held liable to one of several persons injured in a common accident. Applying issue preclusion is troublesome because persons injured as the result of one act are ordinarily not required to become plaintiffs in, or otherwise made parties to, a single action.[14] If one of them sues and loses, then the others are still free to bring their own actions and attempt to convince the trier of fact in the second action that the defendant was liable. As soon as one of them wins, however, and the *Bernhard* rule is applied, then the defendant's liability is effectively established as to all the remaining claimants.

This means that each case is essentially a test case for the defendant but not for the claimants who are not parties. The result is great disparity in litigating risks.[15] In one instance, for example, the New York Court of Appeals upheld a $40,500 judgment against an electric company for damages resulting from a power blackout, and then held that this precluded the company from relitigating whether it had been grossly negligent in other blackout suits claiming more than $200 million in damages.[16] A further consequence of this disparity of risks is that it puts great pressure on a defendant who faces multiple claimants to settle with each one rather than risk an adverse determination by going to trial.

These potential consequences of the *Bernhard* rule have led most commentators and courts to suggest that issue preclusion not always be applied offensively when it might appropriately be applied defensively. *Bernhard*, *Israel*, and *Blonder-Tongue*[17] each involved defensive applications. A few commentators and courts believed that preclusion should never be applied offensively when the second action involved a different claimant.[18] But a complete refusal to apply the rule offensively would

lantic Mut. Ins. Co., 249 Va. 444, 457 S.E.2d 86 (1995).

13. McLaughlin v. Bradlee, 803 F.2d 1197, 1201 (D.C.Cir.1986).

14. *See* § 10.12 *supra.*

15. *See* Currie, Civil Procedure: The Tempest Brews, 53 Calif. L. Rev. 25 (1965); Note, Exposing the Extortion Gap: An Economic Analysis of the Rules of Collateral Estoppel, 105 Harv. L. Rev. 1940 (1992); *see, e.g.,* Humphreys v. Tann, 487 F.2d 666 (6th Cir.1973).

16. Koch v. Consol. Edison Co., 62 N.Y.2d 548, 479 N.Y.S.2d 163, 468 N.E.2d 1 (1984); *cf.* Green, The Inability of Offensive Collateral Estoppel to Fulfill Its Promise: An Examination of Estoppel in Asbestos Litigation, 70 Iowa L. Rev. 141 (1984).

17. *See* text at notes 3, 6, and 11 *supra,* respectively.

18. *See* United States v. Mendoza, 464 U.S. 154, 104 S.Ct. 568, 78 L.Ed.2d 379 (1984)(no nonmutual offensive issue preclu-

result in its being withheld in at least three "offensive" situations in which preclusion does not seem unfair.

Proper uses of offensive preclusion

In one situation only two or three claimants have filed claims, and the stakes in the action first tried are substantively similar to those in the other two.[19] In a second situation there are many claimants, most or all of whom have filed actions that are pending, and a trial is held on the claims of one or several of them in which the defendant makes a full dress effort to defeat the contention that his or her conduct was wrongful.[20] In a third situation, the first suit is brought by the government to enforce a statute or regulation and the second is a suit by a private party who was injured by the conduct in question. That was the case in *Parklane Hosiery Co. v. Shore.*[21] In the first action the SEC had obtained an injunction against continuation of the conduct for which the private claimant, Parklane Hosiery, was seeking damage in the second action. On the question of offensive use of issue preclusion, the Supreme Court said:

> We have concluded that the preferable approach ... is not to preclude the use of offensive collateral estoppel, but to grant trial courts broad discretion to determine when it should be applied. The general rule should be that in cases where a plaintiff could easily have joined in the earlier action, or where ... for other reasons, the applications of offensive estoppel would be unfair to a defendant, a trial judge should not allow the use of offensive collateral estoppel.
>
> In the present case, however ... the petitioners received a "full and fair" opportunity to litigate their claims.... [They] are collaterally estopped from relitigating the question of whether the proxy statements were materially false and misleading.[22]

In such cases, it is clear that the defendant has had adequate incentive to defend; unless there were some peculiar procedural limitations in the case, such as restricted discovery, defendant has had a full opportunity to try the issue of liability. Moreover, if the defendant wins on this issue, the judgment is of considerable value in dealing with the other claimants. While such claimants are not bound by the determination, the settlement value of their claims is obviously reduced. This is particularly true if the issue of liability is a complex and expensive one to try, as it often is in the mass tort cases.

sion against United States); Annot., 31 A.L.R.3d 1044.

19. *See, e.g.,* Bahler v. Fletcher, 257 Or. 1, 474 P.2d 329 (1970).

20. *See, e.g.,* Zdanok v. Glidden Co., 327 F.2d 944 (2d Cir.1964); United States v. United Air Lines, 216 F.Supp. 709 (E.D.Wash. & D.Nev.1962), *aff'd,* 335 F.2d 379 (9th Cir.1964).

21. 439 U.S. 322, 99 S.Ct. 645, 58 L.Ed.2d 552 (1979).

22. 439 U.S. at 331–334, 99 S.Ct. at 651–652, 58 L.Ed.2d at 562–563.

Nonjury determinations

The operation of issue preclusion also has been questioned when the first adjudication involved a nonjury determination and the second action was triable to a jury. The argument against preclusion is that it denies the party the right to jury trial on the issue in question. The Supreme Court rejected this argument in *Parklane Hosiery Co. v. Shore*,[23] and that view has also prevailed in state courts. Therefore, issue preclusion can operate to foreclose a litigant's right to a jury trial. When, however, the denial of a jury trial was the result of an erroneous ruling in the trial court, the findings made by the trial judge are not conclusive when the same issue is thereafter tried to a jury.[24]

Avoiding one-way preclusion risks

Defendants faced with multiple claimants may sometimes reduce the risks of one-way issue preclusion by bringing a single declaratory judgment action against them to determine liability.[25] Defendants rarely do this, however, apparently because it is in their interest not to stimulate assertion of claims that might otherwise remain dormant. So the no-win situation defendants confront when facing multiple claimants may be one they have brought on themselves by failing to use the declaratory judgment device.

§ 11.26 Exceptions to One-Way Issue Preclusion

The offensive use of issue preclusion is only one of several uses that have prompted the courts to consider the appropriateness of applying issue preclusion in favor of a person who was not a party to the first action. As it has been refined through experience, the *Bernhard* rule has come to involve a two-step inquiry. The first step inquires whether the person against whom preclusion is to be applied had a full and fair opportunity to litigate the issue in the first action—an opportunity at least equivalent to that available in the second action. If so, issue preclusion presumptively applies—that is, the party against whom the issue was resolved cannot relitigate the issue unless it can show a good reason why it should be allowed to do so.[1]

Reasons for nonpreclusion

The reasons that may justify giving a party an opportunity to relitigate, as catalogued by the Restatement (Second) of Judgments, include the following:

23. 439 U.S. 322, 99 S.Ct. 645, 58 L.Ed.2d 552 (1979); see Shapiro and Coquillette, The Fetish of Jury Trial in Civil Cases: A Comment on Rachal v. Hill, 85 Harv. L. Rev. 442 (1971).

24. Lytle v. Household Mfg., 494 U.S. 545, 110 S.Ct. 1331, 108 L.Ed.2d 504 (1990).

25. *See* Pennsylvania R.R. v. United States, 111 F.Supp. 80 (D.N.J.1953); *cf.* Chafee, Some Problems of Equity 149–198 (1950) (bill of peace in equity). *But see* In re Northern Dist. of Cal., Dalkon Shield Litig., 693 F.2d 847 (9th Cir.1982).

§ 11.26

1. McLaughlin v. Bradlee, 803 F.2d 1197 (D.C.Cir.1986); Tole S.A. v. Miller, 530 F.Supp. 999 (S.D.N.Y.1981).

- the law governing the administration of the claims involved in the two actions indicates that the rule of preclusion should not be applied;
- the party invoking the benefit of the rule could have joined in the prior action but refrained from doing so;[2]
- the prior determination is of dubious reliability in that it was inconsistent with another determination of the same issue, was affected by the peculiar relationship between the parties to the first action, was based on a compromise verdict, or is indicated by incontestable evidence to have been plainly wrong;
- treating the issue as conclusive would prejudice another party involved in the second action;
- the issue is one of law rather than fact and the party should have an opportunity to obtain a reconsideration of the issue;
- other compelling circumstances justify relitigation.[3]

As refined, the *Bernhard* rule has proved to be a reasonable accommodation of the relevant considerations governing issue preclusion. Because the rule has a substantial degree of flexibility, the question of preclusion now depends to a large extent on "sound judicial discretion." Many lawyers understandably find this uncomfortable because it makes issue preclusion somewhat unpredictable. Yet this unpredictability seems no greater than before *Bernhard*, when the mutuality rule was subject to unpredictable exceptions in which preclusion was applied under the rubric of privity. The modern formulation of the *Bernhard* rule at least makes explicit the factors that ought to govern the exercise of discretion. Moreover, the point of departure remains that issue preclusion ordinarily should operate.[4]

Exception for change in the law

One exception to the general rule of issue preclusion occurs, as mentioned above, when "[t]he issue is one of law and ... a new determination is warranted in order to take account of an intervening change in the applicable legal context or otherwise to avoid inequitable administration of the laws."[5] This does not mean that "an issue, once

2. *See, e.g.*, Howell v. Vito's Trucking & Excavating Co., 386 Mich. 37, 191 N.W.2d 313 (1971). But see Collins v. Seaboard Coastline R.R., 681 F.2d 1333 (11th Cir. 1982).

3. Restatement (Second) of Judgments § 29(1)-(8).

4. *See* Allen v. McCurry, 449 U.S. 90, 101 S.Ct. 411, 66 L.Ed.2d 308 (1980). *But see* Flanagan, Offensive Collateral Estoppel: Inefficiency and Foolish Consistency, 1982 Ariz. St. L.J. 45.

5. Restatement (Second) of Judgments § 28(2)(b). *See, e.g.*, United States v. Mendoza, 464 U.S. 154, 104 S.Ct. 568, 78 L.Ed.2d 379 (1984), holding that the United States is not subject to offensive issue preclusion invoked by a nonparty to the previous decision, because allowing preclusion would bind the government nationwide to a possibly erroneous reading of the law proclaimed by a single court, at least when the Supreme Court declined to review that decision. See also Note, Nonmutual Issue Pre-

litigated and resolved, may be reopened whenever the governing law changes or clarifies. Such a broad exception would swallow the general rule, greatly undermining the twin goals of collateral estoppel—the avoidance of repetitive litigation and the promotion of finality of judgments."[6] Nor does the exception allow relitigation of an issue arising out of the same transaction or set of facts that formed the basis of the first action.[7] Rather, the exception allows for application of an intervening change in the governing law in an action arising out of a new incident.[8] This is designed to prevent the inequality of treatment that would result, particularly in the regulatory context, if collateral estoppel were applied to prevent the application of changes in the law to similarly situated individuals.[9]

§ 11.27 Preclusion Resulting from Representation

As we have seen, issue preclusion applies to a person who was a party in the first litigation; it prohibits the relitigation of an issue that was previously litigated. The requirements of due process present no inhibitions because the party has had a day in court on the issue.

Preclusion of nonparties

Very different problems arise when preclusion is applied against a person who has not been a party to the judgment in the first action. As noted earlier,[1] the bases on which a judgment can be given a preclusive effect against a nonparty can be grouped into two categories: preclusion by representation, and preclusion by reason of substantive legal relationships. These two categories are in many respects related because, as we shall see, the substantive legal relationships that result in preclusion have an element of representation. Broadly speaking, the question posed in applying preclusion on either of these bases is whether the relationship between the person who was a party and the person whom the party is treated as representing is such that the absentee's interests can be regarded as having been fairly represented by the party.

As mentioned, a prior judgment precludes a nonparty when the nonparty is in privity with the parties bound by the judgment. A nonparty will be considered in privity with the parties in the prior suit in three situations:

clusion Against States, 109 Harv. L. Rev. 792 (1996).

6. O'Leary v. Liberty Mut. Ins. Co., 923 F.2d 1062, 1069 (3d Cir.1991); see Burlington Northern R.R. v. Hyundai Merchant Marine Co., 63 F.3d 1227 (3d Cir.1995).

7. Montana v. United States, 440 U.S. 147, 99 S.Ct. 970, 59 L.Ed.2d 210 (1979); Cole v. Greyhound Lines, 220 Mont. 503, 716 P.2d 611 (1986).

8. O'Leary v. Liberty Mut. Ins. Co., 923 F.2d 1062, 1069 (3d Cir.1991).

9. *See, e.g.,* Restatement (Second) of Judgments § 28, Illustrations 3–4; § 11.21 *supra.*

§ 11.27

1. *See* § 11.23 *supra.*

> First, a nonparty who has succeeded to a party's interest in property is bound by any prior judgments against that party....
>
> Second, a nonparty who controlled the original suit will be bound by the resulting judgment....
>
> Third, federal courts will bind some nonparties whose interests were represented adequately by a party in the original suit.[2]

Control

The second situation requires actual control, defined as "effective choice as to the legal theories and proofs to be advanced in behalf of the party to the action."[3] Some examples of participation in the lawsuit that do not amount to control are representation by the same law firm, helping finance the litigation, appearance as amicus curiae, testimony as a witness, participation in pretrial proceedings, or the making of some limited presentations to the court.[4]

Virtual representation

"Adequate representation" is relatively straightforward. "[It] refers to the concept of virtual representation, by which a nonparty may be bound because the party to the first suit is so closely aligned with his (the nonparty's) interests as to be his virtual representative."[5] Virtual representation has been narrowly applied. In *Freeman v. Lester Coggins Trucking, Inc.*[6] plaintiff brought an unsuccessful suit in a state court for injuries in a car crash; he then brought a federal suit on behalf of himself and as representative for his wife and children for the wrongful death of his daughter killed in the same crash. Collateral estoppel blocked plaintiff's claim but did not preclude those of his wife and children. Thus, he was not the virtual representative of the other family members so as to preclude their claims, based on the reasoning that they were entitled to assert separate claims in court.

The question whether the absentee's interests have been fairly represented is especially acute because *claim preclusion* can apply. Because of the rules of merger and bar, if the representative relationship is found to exist the absentee not only is bound to issues litigated but also is precluded from asserting the claim or cause of action involved in

2. Freeman v. Lester Coggins Trucking, Inc., 771 F.2d 860, 864 (5th Cir.1985). *See also* Benson and Ford, Inc. v. Wanda Petroleum Co., 833 F.2d 1172 (5th Cir.1987).

3. Hardy v. Johns–Manville Sales Corp., 681 F.2d 334, 339 (5th Cir.1982); § 11.7 note 10 *supra.*

4. Becherer v. Merrill, Lynch, Pierce, Fenner & Smith, 131 F.3d 580 (6th Cir. 1997); 18 Wright, Miller, and Cooper, Federal Practice and Procedure § 4451.

5. Freeman v. Lester Coggins Trucking, Inc., 771 F.2d 860, 864 (5th Cir.1985). *See also* Monfils v. Taylor, 165 F.3d 511 (7th Cir.1998); Tyus v. Schoemehl, 93 F.3d 449 (8th Cir.1996); Shaw v. Hahn, 56 F.3d 1128 (9th Cir.1995) Benson and Ford, Inc. v. Wanda Petroleum Co., 833 F.2d 1172 (5th Cir.1987); Bone, Rethinking the "Day in Court" Ideal and Nonparty Preclusion, 67 N.Y.U. L. Rev. 193 (1992).

6. *See supra* note 5. See also Tice v. American Airlines, Inc., 162 F.3d 966 (7th Cir.1998); Bittinger v. Tecumseh Prods. Co., 123 F.3d 877 (6th Cir.1997).

the first action. Moreover, in some circumstances the determinations in the representative's action are also binding under issue preclusion in a second suit on a different cause of action. Hence, to analyze the problem of preclusion through representation, it is necessary to ask the following questions: (1) Did a relationship exist between the absentee and the party to the previous action such that a rule of preclusion applies against the absentee? (2) If a rule of preclusion does apply, is it claim preclusion alone or does issue preclusion also apply?

Due process

The scope of preclusion applied to nonparties is constrained by due process considerations, as suggested in *Martin v. Wilks.*[7] Here, the Supreme Court considered whether a nonparty to a prior lawsuit could be bound by the decision because he had purposely relinquished an adequate opportunity to intervene. In this case, white firefighters sued the city, alleging that they were being discriminated against by being denied promotions in favor of less qualified blacks. The city claimed that earlier litigation, in which the white firefighters had chosen not to participate, resulted in consent decrees that included minority hiring and promotion goals governing the fire department. A divided Supreme Court held that the nonparty white firefighters could challenge the employment provisions of the consent decrees.

> [J]oinder as a party, rather than knowledge of a lawsuit and an opportunity to intervene, is the method by which potential parties are subjected to the jurisdiction of the court and bound by a judgment or decree. The parties to a lawsuit presumably know better than anyone else the nature and scope of relief sought in the action.... It makes sense, therefore, to place on them a burden of bringing in additional parties where such a step is indicated, rather than placing on potential additional parties a duty to intervene when they acquire knowledge of the lawsuit.[8]

The decision did not resolve the Constitutional issue or consider whether the white firefighters could be regarded as represented by or in privity with the city. It is familiar law that citizens of a city may be in privity with the city so that they are bound by litigation in which the city is a party. This situation is considered below.[9]

§ 11.28 Representative Parties

Trustees and similar representatives

A party can be invested with authority to represent a person who is not a party in two ways. One is investiture through some private

7. 490 U.S. 755, 109 S.Ct. 2180, 104 L.Ed.2d 835 (1989); *see* Symposium, 78 Iowa L. Rev. 965 (1993); § 11.32 *infra.* On the due process issue, see Richards v. Jefferson County, 517 U.S. 793, 116 S.Ct. 1761, 135 L.Ed.2d 76 (1996); § 11.23 *supra.*

8. 490 U.S. at 765, 109 S.Ct. at 2186, 104 L.Ed.2d at 846.

9. *See* § 11.30 *infra.*

transaction;[1] the represented person may or may not be a party to that transaction. The simplest case of such investiture occurs when a trust is established in which a trustee undertakes to manage property for the benefit of beneficiaries. The trust can be established through a transaction between the settlor of the trust and the trustee, to which the beneficiary is not a party; for example, parents may establish a trust for the benefit of their children, to be administered by a bank. The bank, as part of its duties as trustee, is the party to bring and defend suits with third parties concerning affairs of the trust.[2] Other cases of private investiture include a transaction in which the owner of a claim assigns it to another for purposes of collection, allowing the assignee to sue in the assignee's own name but for the benefit of the assignor,[3] and a transaction in which a member of an organization (such as a labor union) permits that organization to appear in litigation determining the member's rights.[4]

A judgment in an action in which a trustee or other representative participates in its capacity as representative is conclusive on the beneficiary (1) as to the claim involved in the action, under the rule of claim preclusion, and (2) as to the issues determined, if those issues should arise in subsequent litigation concerning the trust, under the rule of issue preclusion.[5]

Guardians

Investiture of representative authority can also occur by operation of law. In the simplest cases a guardian is appointed to manage the property of a minor or other incapacitated person, or an administrator or executor is appointed to manage the affairs of an estate, including bringing and defending suits concerning the estate. A judgment for or against the guardian, administrator, or executor is conclusive on the estate beneficiaries in the same way as is a judgment involving a trustee. The existence of some care-taking responsibilities does not, however, necessarily entail authority to conduct binding litigation. In *Virginia v. Johnson*,[6] for instance, a child's mother brought a paternity action against the alleged father, and the child then brought an action making the same claim. The child's suit was not barred because the interests of the mother and child were not identical. Had the child been represented by a guardian ad litem in the mother's suit, the later suit would have been precluded. A similar situation occurs when a government official is

§ 11.28

1. *See* Restatement (Second) of Judgments § 41.

2. *See* § 10.2 *supra.* See Nevada v. United States, 463 U.S. 110, 103 S.Ct. 2906, 77 L.Ed.2d 509 (1983)(Native American tribe bound by United State's litigation on its behalf).

3. *See* § 10.4 *supra.*

4. *See, e.g.,* Corey v. Avco–Lycoming Div., Avco Corp., 163 Conn. 309, 307 A.2d 155 (1972); *cf.* Aluminum Co. of Am. v. Admiral Merchants Motor Freight, 486 F.2d 717 (7th Cir.1973) (member of trade association).

5. *Compare* Restatement (Second) of Judgments § 41 *with id.* § 42(1)(b).

6. 7 Va.App. 614, 376 S.E.2d 787 (1989).

authorized to bring or defend suits for "the public" as a whole or for some specified class of individuals.[7]

It is established doctrine that a suit by a person in his or her own behalf, whether successful or unsuccessful, precludes a later suit by a representative on that person's behalf. In *Equal Employment Opportunity Commission v. United States Steel Corp.*[8] individual employees brought unsuccessful age discrimination claims against the employer. The EEOC then brought a suit on behalf of a group of employees that included these individuals. The court held that the EEOC was proceeding in a representative capacity on behalf of the employees, not to enforce an independent governmental right, and hence the right to recover was precluded.

§ 11.29 Class Suits

An increasingly common form of representative suit is the class suit.[1] In a class suit one or more of a large group of similarly situated persons may, with the permission of the court, maintain or defend an action on behalf of the entire group. Until the twentieth century it was unclear whether a judgment in a class suit could be binding under any circumstances against the absent members of the class. Although it is now clear that it can be, judicial wavering has not ended, with some confusion remaining over whether this binding effect is permissible only in class suits in which the "jural relations" among the members of the class are of some particular kind.[2] As indicated in the previous discussion of class suits, the sounder view holds that a class suit can bind the members of the class, regardless of the nature of the "jural relations" among its members, if, first, members of the class were designated as representatives and had interests compatible with those whom they purported to represent, and, second, the representatives managed the litigation with faithfulness and adequate aggressiveness. When these conditions are met, the judgment can be conclusive as to both the claim involved in the first action and the issues determined in it.[3]

Representation problems

Although the res judicata effect of a class suit judgment is now clearly established, the nature of a class suit requires that res judicata be applied with special caution. The groups that may be represented through the class suit device sometimes have a continuing cohesion fostering confidence in the representatives' adequate representation of

7. *See, e.g.,* Rynsburger v. Dairymen's Fertilizer Coop., 266 Cal.App.2d 269, 72 Cal.Rptr. 102 (1968). *See* Restatement (Second) of Judgments § 41(1)(d).

8. 921 F.2d 489 (3d Cir.1990).

§ 11.29

1. *See also* §§ 10.20–10.23 *supra.*

2. Hazard, Gedid & Sowle, An Historical Analysis of the Binding Effect of Class Suits, 146 U. Pa. L. Rev. 1849 (1998).

3. *See* Matsushita Electric Indus. Co. v. Epstein, 516 U.S. 367, 116 S.Ct. 873, 134 L.Ed.2d 6 (1996); Restatement (Second) of Judgments §§ 41(1)(e), 42(1)(e).

the whole group. Such is the case, for example, of the representation through officers of an unincorporated association such as a union, a club, or a church. Other groups, however, have only the transitory unity resulting from its members having been injured by a course of conduct affecting them all. Such is the case of the group involved in a suit on behalf of taxpayers, persons charged excessive rates by a public utility, or stockholders whose corporation has been injured by the wrongful acts of the corporate directors.

In such situations, the members of the class who come forward to represent the entire class are self-appointed. They may be only a subgroup whose interests conflict with other members of the class whom they purport to represent; they may be dominated by, or indeed be virtually the creature of, the attorneys who act for them—and the attorneys may be chiefly interested in conducting the action in such a way that they are assured of their fee. Indeed, on occasion the attorneys for the class have themselves brought the action on the suggestion of defendants hoping to obtain a settlement binding on the class.[4]

Judicial caution

The courts are generally cautious in applying preclusion against individual claims on the basis of a prior class action of which the individual may not either have had full knowledge or have fully accepted the adequacy of its representation of his or her claims. In *Wright v. Collins*,[5] for instance, prisoners sought declaratory and injunctive relief against conditions in the Maryland prison system. The class won on a declaratory claim concerning overcrowding, but the court awarded no monetary damages. An individual prisoner then brought suit for damages. The court held that the suit was not barred and that before a member of a class may be barred from an individual damage claim, the notice of the class action must give clear warning that individual claims may be lost. Similarly, courts have held that an individual suit for damages is not precluded by the individual's membership in a class action that seeks no monetary relief.[6]

In *Federated Department Stores v. Moitie*,[7] however, the Supreme Court held that res judicata would bar the relitigation of one unappealed adverse judgment when other similarly situated plaintiffs bringing parallel suits had already prevailed on appeal. The Court thus explicitly

4. *E.g.*, Amchem Prods., Inc. v. Windsor, 521 U.S. 591, 117 S.Ct. 2231, 138 L.Ed.2d 689 (1997); *see* § 10.21 *supra*.

5. 766 F.2d 841 (4th Cir.1985).

6. Norris v. Slothouber, 718 F.2d 1116 (D.C.Cir.1983). *See also* Cooper v. Federal Reserve Bank of Richmond, 467 U.S. 867, 104 S.Ct. 2794, 81 L.Ed.2d 718 (1984) (class action judgment construed not to include individual claims); Martin v. Wilks, 490 U.S. 755, 109 S.Ct. 2180, 104 L.Ed.2d 835 (1989)(bystander not bound); Bronson v. Board of Educ., 525 F.2d 344 (6th Cir. 1975)(scope of previous judgment rejecting claims of unconstitutional segregation); 18 Wright, Miller, and Cooper, Federal Practice and Procedure § 4455.

7. 452 U.S. 394, 101 S.Ct. 2424, 69 L.Ed.2d 103 (1981).

rejected the argument that res judicata should not be applied if it will result in injustice:

> Simple justice is achieved when a complex body of law developed over a period of years is evenhandedly applied. The doctrine of res judicata serves vital public interests beyond any individual judge's ad hoc determination of the equities in a particular case. There is simply no principle of law or equity which sanctions the rejection by a federal court of the salutary principle of res judicata.[8]

In a similar vein, courts have upheld the preclusive effects of complex consent decrees resolving unemployment discrimination claims, against individual claims by employees hired after the judgment for acts occurring postjudgment.[9]

Notice

The looseness of the bonds among a class whose only connection is their common victimization has led to the development of several procedures for assuring protection of the class's interests. First, under the Due Process Clause as interpreted by the Supreme Court, a state court class suit for damages cannot proceed unless notice has been given to at least all out-of-state members of the class to be represented.[10] Some form of individual notice may be constitutionally required in other class suits[11] or may be given pursuant to rules or judicial discretion.

Court supervision

Second, under Rule 23 and class suit rules similar to it, a class action can be settled only if the court approves the settlement. Notice of a proposed settlement must be given to members of the class before the court can approve it.[12] More broadly, the court has an obligation to ensure that class members receive proper representation, for example by certifying proper representatives.

8. 452 U.S. at 401, 101 S.Ct. at 2429, 69 L.Ed.2d at 110. *See also* Dillard v. Crenshaw County, 640 F.Supp. 1347 (M.D.Ala. 1986).

9. *E.g.*, Equal Employment Opportunity Commn. v. Children's Hosp. Medical Center, 695 F.2d 412 (9th Cir.1982).

10. Phillips Petroleum Co. v. Shutts, 472 U.S. 797, 105 S.Ct. 2965, 86 L.Ed.2d 628 (1985). *See also* Miller and Crump, Jurisdiction and Choice of Law in Multistate Class Actions After Phillips Petroleum Co. v. Shutts, 96 Yale L.J. 383 (1986). In federal courts, Rule 23(c)(2) similarly requires notice and an opportunity to opt out in Rule 23(b)(3) class actions.

11. Eisen v. Carlisle & Jacquelin, 417 U.S. 156, 94 S.Ct. 2140, 40 L.Ed.2d 732 (1974); Richards v. Jefferson County, 517 (1996); Dam, Class Action Notice: Who Needs It?, 1974 Sup. Ct. Rev. 97; Reno, Notice and Due Process in Federal Class Actions: A Requiem for Revised Rule 23?, 2 Hastings Const. L.Q. 479 (1975). The Supreme Court has twice agreed to pass on whether notice and an opportunity to opt out are constitutionally required, but each time failed to reach that issue. Adams v. Robertson, 520 U.S. 83, 117 S.Ct. 1028, 137 L.Ed.2d 203 (1997); Ticor Title Ins. Co. v. Brown, 511 U.S. 117, 114 S.Ct. 1359, 128 L.Ed.2d 33 (1994).

12. *See* Fed. R. Civ. P. 23(e).

Collateral challenge to adequacy of representation

Third, after judgment has been entered and subsequently is invoked against the class, the adequacy of representation is open to examination, particularly regarding the possibility of conflict of interest among the class. If a conflict exists such that some or all of the absentees could not fairly have been represented by those who appeared as parties, the judgment is not binding on them.[13] Although similar scrutiny is required in other types of representative suits (such as a judgment in a suit by a guardian),[14] a class suit judgment is subject to a more searching appraisal, and doubts over the adequacy of representation are more readily resolved in the direction of withholding res judicata effects from the judgment.[15]

The test of the adequacy of representation may be applied during the course of the class action itself to avoid res judicata. In *O'Brien v. Sky Chefs, Inc.*,[16] for example, the federal district court decertified the class because it found no evidence of classwide discrimination. This course was found "more appropriate than summary judgment against the class. Since plaintiff's failure to produce evidence may have been due to inadequate representation of the class interests rather than to absence of classwide discrimination, decertification avoided any res judicata effect against the class."[17]

Future claimants

As class actions have become a possible way to deal with mass torts,[18] there have been attempts to include "future" claimants within the class, that is, claimants who may have claims in the future, for example because they have been exposed to a defendant's product, but have not yet suffered any legally cognizable injury. Some may be aware that they face possible injury while others may not. Some, indeed, may not even have been born. Defendants want future claims included in a class action in order to obtain a "global settlement" that will protect them from all future claims by setting aside a fund from which they may be paid. Because the members of the class do not yet know that they will have claims, they can usually participate or be represented in the action only in the sense that guardians and lawyers can be designated to

13. *See* Hansberry v. Lee, 311 U.S. 32, 61 S.Ct. 115, 85 L.Ed. 22 (1940); Koniak and Cohen, Under Cloak of Settlement, 82 Virg. L. Rev. 1051 (1996); Woolley, The Availability of Collateral Attack for Inadequate Representation in Class Suits, 79 Tex. L. Rev. 383 (2000); Note, Collateral Attack on Binding Effect of Class Action Judgments, 87 Harv. L. Rev. 589 (1974); see Richards v. Jefferson County, 517 U.S. 793, 116 S.Ct. 1761, 135 L.Ed.2d 76 (1996).

14. Restatement (Second) of Judgments § 42(1)(e).

15. *Id.* § 42, Comments *e, f.* But see Epstein v. MCA, Inc., 126 F.3d 1235 (9th Cir.1997)(class members who intervened bound by decision that representation was adequate); Kahan and Silberman, *Matsushita* and Beyond: The Role of State Courts in Class Actions Involving Exclusive Federal Claims, 1996 S.Ct. Rev. 219. On attempts by the class action court to enjoin relitigation in other courts, see Monaghan, Antisuit Injunctions and Preclusion Against Absent Nonresident Class Members, 98 Colum. L. Rev. 1148 (1998).

16. 670 F.2d 864 (9th Cir.1982).

17. 670 F.2d at 869.

18. *See* § 10.22 *supra.*

protect their interests. It is hard to see how they can be given meaningful notice of the action.[19] A class action judgment can give them the option to waive their right to sue in order to obtain the benefits available under the judgment. Whether they can be bound by the judgment if they decline to do this remains open to serious question.[20]

§ 11.30 Substantive Relationships Resulting in Preclusion

Substantive legal relationships exist that make a judgment for or against one of the parties to the relationship conclusive on the other party to the relationship. Such relationships fall roughly into four categories: family, contract and property, organizational affiliation, and indemnity. The applicable rules are complex and sometimes arbitrary. In part, they reflect a balancing of such factors as efficiency, the autonomy of litigants, the likelihood that one kind of litigant will adequately protect the interests of another, and the need to protect defendants from repeated claims. They also reflect appraisals of whether two litigants are asserting a "single right" so that a decision involving one of them should bind the other.

Not all types of relationships within these categories carry with them consequences under the rules of res judicata; only some of them do, and these are to some extent explainable only on historical grounds. If, for example, a husband sues for his own injuries and loses the action, that judgment precludes the wife from suing for her loss of consortium (that is, loss of his companionship) resulting from the husband's injury;[1] the judgment does not, however, preclude the wife from suing for bodily injuries to herself suffered in the same accident.[2] The wife's claim for loss of consortium is considered derivative from the husband's claim, while her claim for bodily injuries is considered one that she has independent of the husband. The children likewise have independent claims for any bodily injuries. The law might have developed differently: Either parent could have been considered the proper party plaintiff to sue for losses to minor children of the family, and the judgment in that action treated as conclusive as to all the claims of the family members. Indeed, if the law had developed that way, some might say it would have made a lot more sense. But such has not been the law. The rules determining which relationships have preclusive effects and which do not are to an important degree arbitrary.

19. See Amchem Products, Inc. v. Windsor, 521 U.S. 591, 117 S.Ct. 2231, 138 L.Ed.2d 689 (1997)(noting but not resolving the problem); see also Ortiz v. Fibreboard Corp., 527 U.S. 815, 119 S.Ct. 2295, 144 L.Ed.2d 715 (1999).

20. See Hazard, The Futures Problem, 148 U. Pa. L. Rev. 1901 (2000) and the comments following it.

§ 11.30

1. *See, e.g.,* Sisemore v. Neal, 236 Ark. 574, 367 S.W.2d 417 (1963).

2. *See, e.g.,* Standard Accident Ins. Co. v. Doiron, 170 F.2d 206 (1st Cir.1948).

Family relationships

When a family member is injured, two kinds of losses result that may be recoverable in a suit by another family member. One type of loss is the medical expenses paid by a family member other than the injured person, such as the medical expenses of children paid by their parents or the medical expenses of one spouse paid by the other spouse. In most jurisdictions, this kind of loss can be recovered *either* by the injured person or by the family member who paid the expenses. Under the rules of claim preclusion, a judgment for or against the injured party precludes a second action by a parent or spouse to recover the medical expenses; correlatively, a judgment in an action by the parent or spouse to recover the medical expenses precludes recovery of those expenses in a subsequent action by the injured person.[3] The latter action does not, however, preclude the injured person from suing for physical impairment or pain and suffering.

The second kind of loss is a family member's loss of companionship resulting from a physical injury to a spouse, child, or parent. Under the rules of issue preclusion, if the person who was physically injured loses an action to recover for his or her injuries, then the family member is bound by that determination in a subsequent action to recover for loss of companionship.[4]

Similar rules apply to another set of claims arising out of family relationships. These result when a person is injured by an act eventuating in his or her death. The injured person has a claim for the injuries suffered to the point of death—that is, medical expenses, loss of income, pain and suffering; if the person dies, a separate claim arises in favor of the family members (or, in many jurisdictions, the estate) for the losses resulting from the person's death. If the injured person brings a personal injury claim while alive and loses, the judgment has preclusive effects on the persons entitled to bring the wrongful death action later. Claim preclusion prevents them from suing the person in whose favor the previous judgment was entered; by a rule of issue preclusion, they are bound by the determinations made against the injured person in that action. Furthermore, in most jurisdictions, if the injured person brought an action and won, the potential claims for his or her wrongful death are merged into that judgment so that no wrongful death claim thereafter may be maintained.[5]

Contract and property

Certain types of contract relationships empower more than one person to enforce the contract obligation of another. An assignable contract right can be enforced by the original obligee until the obligee

3. Restatement (Second) of Judgments § 48(1).

4. *Id.* § 48(2).

5. *Id.* §§ 45–47. But see Sea-Land Services, Inc. v. Gaudet, 414 U.S. 573, 94 S.Ct. 806, 39 L.Ed.2d 9 (1974).

assigns his or her interest in it, and thereafter by the assignee if the latter gives the obligor notice of the assignment; a contract that creates an obligation jointly in favor of two promisees may be enforced by either one. In each situation, the person entitled to enforce the promise can bring an action on it for that purpose. The judgment in such an action, whether for or against the plaintiff, is usually conclusive on the other person who could enforce the promise.[6] A somewhat similar situation exists with a contract creating a third-party beneficiary. The contract may be enforced by either the promisee or the third-party beneficiary; a judgment for or against the third-party beneficiary in his or her action precludes the promisee from enforcing it on his or her own behalf; a judgment for or against the promisee precludes an action by the third-party beneficiary if, under the law of contracts, the promisee had power to discharge the promisor at the time the judgment was rendered.[7]

The situation with concurrent owners of property is more complicated. Usually, when two or more persons have interests in property, a judgment affecting one of them has no effect on the other. Thus, an action by a joint tenant or cotenant is not preclusive in a subsequent action by the other co-owner; so also an action by a mortgagor is not preclusive against a mortgagee. In these relationships, the co-owner must be made a party in order to be bound by the litigation.[8]

There are, however, two co-ownership relationships in which res judicata applies. One is that of community property; here, the husband was traditionally recognized as a kind of managing partner in the property who could maintain or defend actions that would be conclusive on the wife. This rule is now changing to treat the wife as equal co-owner so that a judgment concerning the property is not conclusive on her unless she is a party to the action.[9] The other relationship is that of bailment, where property owned by one person is in the possession of another with the owner's consent. In a rather fortuitous way, the rule developed that either the owner of the property (the bailor) or the person having its possession (the bailee) could bring an action for loss or damage to the property resulting from the act of a third party. The rules of res judicata were shaped accordingly. Thus, a judgment for or against the bailor or bailee in an action asserting a claim for loss or damage to the bailed property precludes the other from subsequently suing for the loss.[10]

Finally, and perhaps most important, is the rule concerning successors in interest in property. An action between rival claimants to property will determine the extent of their respective ownership inter-

6. Restatement (Second) of Judgments §§ 53, 55.

7. *Id.* § 56.

8. *Id.* § 54.

9. *See* Annot., 58 A.L.R.2d 701; *e.g.*, Dulak v. Dulak, 496 S.W.2d 776 (Tex.Civ.App. 1973), with which *compare* Note, 52 Tex. L. Rev. 1410 (1974).

10. Restatement (Second) of Judgments § 52.

ests in the property. That is, it operates as an involuntary conveyance between them. If, following the judgment, either conveys his or her interest to a third party, that third party receives only what the transferor has to convey. In this way, the rights of a successor in interest as to one who has been a party to an action concerning property are concluded by the judgment in the action.[11] A somewhat similar rule applies to one who receives a transfer of property while an action concerning the property is pending.[12] These are classical instances of the traditional notion of privity: the right of one property owner is considered to pass along with the property to a new owner, so that the new owner is bound by an adjudication to which the previous owner was a party.

Organizations

Members of formally constituted organizations ordinarily are bound, so far as their interests in the organization are concerned, by judgments in actions conducted by the managers of the organization. We refer here to corporations, partnerships, and unincorporated associations. The clearest case is that concerning judgments for or against a corporation or a similar entity such as a limited liability company. Such a judgment may greatly affect the value of a stockholder's interest, but so, of course, can other transactions engaged in by the corporation. The theory of corporate organization is that the directors and officers operate the corporation, for better or worse, for the benefit of the stockholders. A corollary of this theory is that, in the absence of collusion in the proceedings, a judgment to which the corporation is a party is conclusive on the stockholders; they may not through a derivative suit seek to relitigate the matters that were adjudicated.[13] Shareholders are generally held to be in privity with the corporation. Privity is determined on the basis of whether the shareholder's rights are adequately protected, a test that is essentially circular.

A somewhat similar theory is beginning to govern partnerships and unincorporated associations. At common law, a partnership did not exist as an entity; it was simply a small group of persons acting together for business purposes. Associations were treated the same way.[14] Thus, all partners had to join in suits on partnership transactions; if partners were sued, the judgment was conclusive only on those actually joined as defendants. Modern courts, however, tend to treat some types of associations, particularly labor organizations, as entities similar to corporations.[15] The tendency in the law of partnerships is the same way.[16] When

11. *Id.* § 43.

12. *Id.* § 44.

13. *See, e.g.,* Amalgamated Sugar Co. v. NL Indus., 825 F.2d 634 (2d Cir.1987); *cf.* Doe v. Urohealth Systems, Inc., 216 F.3d 157 (1st Cir.2000); (corporation and wholly owned subsidiary); Reconstruction Fin. Corp. v. Central Republic Trust Co., 128 F.2d 242 (7th Cir.1942); 1B Moore, Federal Practice and Procedure ¶ 0.411(10).

14. *See* § 10.7 *supra.*

15. *Id.*

16. *See* Revised Uniform Partnership Act §§ 201, 307; Crane and Bromberg,

an association is treated as an entity, an action for or against the association is managed by its officers; the judgment is binding on the organization as such and does not result in individual liability of its members. At the same time, as in the case of a corporation, the members cannot bring an action on their own to relitigate matters determined in the judgment for or against the association.

Indemnitee/indemnitor

The relationship of indemnitee and indemnitor gives rise to a complex set of claim-and issue preclusion problems. This relationship exists when one person (the indemnitee) who has been held liable to an injured party is entitled to be recompensed for his or her liability by payment from another (the indemnitor). The most common indemnity relationship is that between one who is insured under a typical liability insurance policy and the insurer under such a policy. The insured as indemnitee is entitled to be repaid by the insurance company as indemnitor for any amount, up to the limits of the policy, by which the insured becomes liable to the injured person. The relationship of indemnitee and indemnitor can arise in other circumstances. Indeed, it is the general rule that when one person is vicariously responsible for the acts of another (for example, an employer's being vicariously responsible for the acts of an employee), the person with the vicarious responsibility has by law a right of indemnity against the active wrongdoer. Thus, if judgment is entered against an employer for a tort committed by an employee, the employer has a right of indemnity against the employee for the amount of the judgment.

In any such indemnity relationship, two claims are involved. One is the claim by the injured person against the indemnitee; the other is the claim by the indemnitee against the indemnitor. The issues involved in the two claims generally coincide to an important extent, for the obligation to indemnify necessarily refers to the original claim for which indemnity is sought. Moreover, the indemnitor, who runs the risk of bearing the ultimate loss, is recognized as having a legitimate interest in the defense of the action by the injured person against the indemnitee. Accordingly, the law allows the indemnitee to call on (or "vouch in") the indemnitor to defend the action by the injured party. If the indemnitor then takes over the defense of the indemnitee, the indemnitor is bound in two ways if judgment is awarded to the injured person. First, the indemnitor is bound to the indemnitee's being liable to the injured person. Second, the indemnitor is bound to issues determined in the action, at least if there is no conflict of interest between the indemnitor and the indemnitee as to those issues. The theory is that the indemnitor, in controlling the defense, had opportunity to litigate the issues in

Partnership ch. 6 (1968). *See also* Restatement (Second) of Judgments §§ 60, 61.

question and should not be allowed to relitigate them when the indemnitee seeks recovery against the indemnitor.

The burden on the indemnitor goes even further. If the indemnitor is called on to defend the action by the injured person but declines to do so, and the judgment is in favor of the injured person, the judgment is conclusive on the indemnitor as to the indemnitee's liability to the injured person. Thus, if an insurer declines to defend its insured, it cannot later dispute the insured's liability. The theory is that the indemnitor, having had opportunity to defend the action, should be estopped to dispute the matters established in the judgment. The indemnitor is still free, however, to contest whether he or she has an obligation to indemnify. Thus, if the insurance company does not defend its insured but is bound by the insured's liability to the injured person, the insurance company can litigate whether the loss was within the terms of the policy or whether the policy had lapsed by reason of nonpayment of premiums.[17]

The judgment in the injured person's action against the indemnitee can have another effect. If the judgment is *against* the injured person, the results reached in that action are conclusive in favor of the other obligor.[18] Thus, if an injured person sues an employer for a tort committed by an employee and loses, the injured person cannot relitigate the claim in a subsequent action against the employee.

An indemnitor is not precluded by determinations in the action against the indemnitee in which they have conflicting interests. Illustrative is *State Farm Fire & Casualty Co. v. Garrity*,[19] in which the insured was sued in the first action for wrongful death. The indemnitor-insurer provided defense counsel under a reservation of rights agreement, whereby it agreed to provide defense but did not admit the loss was covered by the policy. A judgment was awarded to plaintiff in the state court action based on a finding that defendant was negligent. The appellate court held that this finding did not preclude the insurer from showing that the death was an intentional killing that would not be covered by the policy. The court reasoned that the issue of intentional killing did not arise in the state court and the insurer could not have become a party to the state court action. Hence, the insurer should not be bound "to the result of a proceeding in which it was not in true privity with its insured and its unique interests were not represented."[20]

§ 11.31 Ameliorating Rigors of Preclusion

The rules of claim preclusion (merger and bar) and issue preclusion (formerly collateral estoppel) rest on policies so important to the effective administration of justice that they are ordinarily applied as a matter

17. *See* Restatement (Second) of Judgments §§ 57, 58; §§ 10.9, 10.12, 11.7 *supra*.

18. Restatement (Second) of Judgments § 51.

19. 785 F.2d 1225 (4th Cir.1986).

20. 785 F.2d at 1228.

of course. This is true particularly when the party to be bound itself participated in a prior proceeding that afforded it ample opportunity to develop its contentions of fact and law. But there are limits to every legal principle, certainly one that prevents a person from litigating a matter that seems to have substantial merit. We have noted some of the limits on claim preclusion already:

Limits on claim preclusion

- the rigors of the rule of claim preclusion can be ameliorated by defining narrowly, rather than broadly, the scope of the "claim" involved in the first action;[1]
- a judgment that dismisses an action for want of jurisdiction does not preclude the plaintiff from bringing a subsequent action in a court that does have jurisdiction;[2]
- the rule of issue preclusion does not apply if it cannot be definitely ascertained that the issue was necessarily decided in the first action;[3]
- the rule of issue preclusion does not apply when the losing litigant takes on a new adversary and can show good reason why he or she should be allowed to relitigate the issue in question;[4]
- the rules of preclusion do not apply to a person represented by another when it can be shown that the representation was manifestly inadequate.[5]

There are still other limitations. One, considered more fully in the discussion of attacks on judgments,[6] relates to the effect of a judgment when a question arises whether the court rendering it had personal or subject matter jurisdiction over the defendant. A plaintiff is not precluded from maintaining a second action on a part of the claim involved in the first action (or, in other words, is permitted to split the claim) if the splitting was sanctioned by agreement of the parties, by order of the court in the first action, or by governing rules that permitted or required the claim to be split.[7] Litigants may be relieved from claim preclusion if they can show extraordinary circumstances warranting opportunity to reassert their claim, such as a change in the governing law that they could not fairly have anticipated, the fact that the prior judgment left the parties in a situation of continuing and unresolved conflict, or the fact that the prior judgment was obtained as a result of fraud or the overreaching of a fiduciary.[8]

Moreover, the claim may be based on a statutory remedial scheme that provides an opportunity for adjudication of the claim in a specified

§ 11.31

1. *See* § 11.9 *supra.*
2. *See* § 11.16 *supra.*
3. *See* §§ 11.19–.20 *supra.*
4. *See* § 11.26 *supra.*
5. *See* § 11.29 *supra.*
6. *See* Chapter 12.
7. Restatement (Second) of Judgments § 26.
8. *Id.* § 26(f); §§ 11.21 *supra*, § 12.15 *infra.*

procedure even though it involves issues, or the very claim, that had previously been determined in another forum.[9] In other words, the legislature may provide that litigants will have more than one chance to litigate certain kinds of claims.

Limits on issue preclusion

Similar considerations moderate application of the rule of issue preclusion. We have seen that an important element of discretion is involved in deciding whether a party should be precluded from relitigating an issue with a new adversary.[10] A comparable, but narrower, range of discretion exists in determining whether issue preclusion should be applied when the parties to the two successive actions are the same but the second action involves a different cause of action. Thus, issue preclusion may be withheld if (1) the legal and factual contexts of the two actions are different, (2) the burden of proof is significantly different in the second action, (3) the issue is one of fact and the procedures of discovery and decision of fact in the two actions are substantially different, or (4) the issue is one of law and the governing legal authorities have undergone change since the first action.[11] The most familiar example of varying burdens of proof is the discrepancy between the requirement of proof beyond a reasonable doubt in criminal prosecutions and the preponderance of the evidence standard in civil cases, and of course courts will not use preclusion to prevent a party that has failed on the more stringent test from trying to meet the more lenient one.[12]

The number and variety of these qualifications of the rules of res judicata should not be taken as suggesting that they have frequent application. The courts require a showing of very good reason before preclusion will not be applied. Under modern law, it is not the kind or category of "good reason" that makes a difference, but rather the quality of the reason judged by the character of all the circumstances. The underlying idea harks back to the old concept of estoppel: A party ought not to be allowed to assert claims or contentions that it has already made or had fair opportunity to make.

The law has, however, generally limited this rule of estoppel to claims and contentions that can be asserted against the persons actually

9. *E.g.,* Barrentine v. Arkansas–Best Freight Sys., 450 U.S. 728, 101 S.Ct. 1437, 67 L.Ed.2d 641 (1981). *Compare* Kremer v. Chemical Construction Corp., 456 U.S. 461, 102 S.Ct. 1883, 72 L.Ed.2d 262 (1982) (state court judgment against state remedy for discrimination precludes federal action under Title VII for same conduct), *with* Astoria Fed. Sav. & Loan Assn. v. Solimino, 501 U.S. 104, 111 S.Ct. 2166, 115 L.Ed.2d 96 (1991) (state agency findings not issue preclusive).

10. *See* § 11.26 *supra.*

11. Restatement (Second) of Judgments § 28.

12. United States v. One Assortment of 89 Firearms, 465 U.S. 354, 104 S.Ct. 1099, 79 L.Ed.2d 361 (1984)(acquittal does not bar government from seeking property forefeiture); City of Detroit v. Qualls, 434 Mich. 340, 454 N.W.2d 374 (1990)(criminal defendant not bound by previous civil judgment); see Dowling v. United States, 493 U.S. 342, 110 S.Ct. 668, 107 L.Ed.2d 708 (1990).

joined as opponents. It has not required that plaintiffs join as defendants all persons to whom they might look to recovery of the loss involved in their action.[13] Nor does the law now require, or in many instances even permit, a defendant to bring in other persons who might have liability for the loss.[14] Here the rules of res judicata still leave the plaintiffs to a large extent the "master of the action." It seems possible, however, that the trend of the law, partly through the medium of the rules of res judicata, will enlarge the scope of required joinder of parties in much the same way as it has enlarged the scope of required joinder of claims and contentions.[15] This trend seems implicit in the concept of equitable preclusion.

§ 11.32 Equitable Preclusion

Some decisions have denied opportunity to maintain an action on grounds other than those already discussed. They involve the following circumstances: (1) There had been a prior action involving the same claim or affecting the same property as is involved in the second action; (2) the party seeking to maintain the second action knew of the first action and could then have asserted the claim it now seeks to assert, either by intervening in the first action or by bringing in as a party the person against whom it now asserts its claim; (3) the person against whom the claim is asserted in the second action was apparently relying on the first action to be dispositive of the controversy out of which the claim arises; and (4) the party asserting the claim in the second action knew, or reasonably should have known, of that reliance.

Party reliance

Two cases are illustrative. In *Aerojet-General Corp. v. Askew*[1] the plaintiff sought specific performance of a contract that it contended gave it a right to purchase certain lands from a state agency. After judgment for the plaintiff, an agency of local government came forward to restrain conveyance of the land on the basis that a state statute gave the local agency an absolute prior right to purchase the land. This contention had not been advanced by the state in the original litigation, nor had the local agency intervened to assert its claim even though it was well aware of the pending action. It was held that the local agency was concluded by the judgment. The court asserted that the two agencies were in "privi-

13. *See* § 10.12 *supra.*

14. *See* § 10.18 *supra.*

15. *Compare* McCoid, A Single Package for Multiparty Disputes, 28 Stan. L. Rev. 707 (1976), *with* George, Sweet Uses of Adversity: *Parklane Hosiery* and the Collateral Class Action, 32 Stan. L. Rev. 655 (1980).

§ 11.32

1. 511 F.2d 710 (5th Cir.1975). This case, and the concept suggested in the text of this section, is criticized in Note, The Expanding Scope of the Res Judicata Bar, 54 Tex. L. Rev. 527 (1976), which also contains a number of decisions supporting the analysis herein; *cf.* Note, Preclusion of Absent Disputants to Compel Intervention, 79 Colum. L. Rev. 1551 (1979).

ty," an assertion that is unsupported by any recognized version of that concept. Considered as a matter of inequitable delay on the part of the local agency, however, the result seems fully justified.

In *Fleming v. Cooper*[2] a farm tenant brought an action to determine the share between himself and his landlord of the proceeds of crops grown on the land. Named as landlord and defendant was the husband of the couple with whom the tenant had dealt. After judgment for the tenant, the wife of the original defendant brought an action asserting that she was the actual landowner and that the proper share was otherwise than determined in the first action. It was held that she was bound by the determination in the first action, having stood "idly by with full knowledge of ... the pendency and progress of the suit."[3]

The Supreme Court's decision in *Martin v. Wilks*,[4] however, casts a shadow on these decisions. The opinion in that case, without considering the question of estoppel by acquiescence on which others have relied, has broad language suggesting that a bystander to a prior action may always bring his or her own lawsuit, no matter how similar the issues and how great the reliance. It seems unlikely that this broad dictum will survive hard cases in which it would have to be applied, such as in *Aerojet-General.* The doctrinal contradictions may be resolved by saying that *Martin v. Wilks* decided an issue of preclusion by judgment whereas *Aerojet-General* and similar cases involve estoppel by conduct taking the form of litigation.

In any event, shortly after the decision in *Martin v. Wilks,* Congress reversed the decision as it applies to employment discrimination cases, the legislative history expressly stating an intention to overrule the Supreme Court's decision.[5] *Martin v. Wilks* still casts doubt on the estoppel principle as it would apply in other contexts. Yet estoppel seems justified when a person stands "idly by" while another is investing time and energy into an undertaking that the bystander's legal claim will frustrate. The process of settling legal rights through adjudication is simply another form of such an investment, whose value a bystander should not be allowed to destroy knowingly by silence and inaction.

2. 225 Ark. 634, 284 S.W.2d 857 (1955).

3. 225 Ark. at 638, 284 S.W.2d at 860. *See also* Provident Tradesmens Bank & Trust Co. v. Patterson, 390 U.S. 102, 114, 88 S.Ct. 733, 740, 19 L.Ed.2d 936, 947 (1968) (Harlan, J.: "It might be argued that Dutcher should be bound by the previous decision because, although technically a nonparty, he had purposely bypassed an adequate opportunity to intervene"); Tyus v. Schoemehl, 93 F.3d 449 (8th Cir.1996); Gonzalez v. Banco Central Corp., 27 F.3d 751 (1st Cir.1994); Garcia v. Wilson, 63 Wash.App. 516, 820 P.2d 964 (1991). *Compare* Restatement (Second) of Judgments § 62.

4. 490 U.S. 755, 109 S.Ct. 2180, 104 L.Ed.2d 835 (1989); see Symposium, 78 Iowa L. Rev. 965 (1993). See also Richards v. Jefferson County, 517 U.S. 793, 116 S.Ct. 1761, 135 L.Ed.2d 76 (1996); South Central Bell Tel. Co. v. Alabama, 526 U.S. 160, 119 S.Ct. 1180, 143 L.Ed.2d 256 (1999).

5. 42 U.S.C. § 2000e–2; see Rutherford v. City of Cleveland, 137 F.3d 905 (6th Cir.1998); Catania & Sullivan, Judging Judges: The 1991 Civil Rights Act and the Lingering Ghost of *Martin v. Wilks*, 57 Brook. L. Rev. 995 (1992).

Chapter 12

POST-TRIAL ATTACKS ON JUDGMENTS

§ 12.1 Introduction

This chapter addresses the procedures for challenging a judgment entered in a trial court. A judgment that is not subjected to such a challenge, or that survives it, has the res judicata effects described in Chapter 11. The analysis of res judicata revealed the two conflicting policy objectives of all adjudications—to insure that substantial justice is done on the merits and to bring the controversy to a final conclusion. The same conflict of objectives also presents itself in appellate procedure and other postjudgment attacks on the trial court's determination of a civil action.

Policies sustaining finality

We have seen this conflict before and noted that modern courts tend to afford liberal opportunity for presentation of cases on their merits through the stages of pleading, pretrial, and trial. No matter how liberal that opportunity may be, however, judgments are rendered that can plausibly be questioned on the ground that they were procedurally irregular or erroneous on the merits. If a judgment were subject to invalidation whenever such a question could be raised, few legal controversies could ever be brought to final conclusion. And if judgments did not, in general, have finality, the consequences would be at least as serious as the fact that injustice had been done. These consequences include the disturbance of the parties' reliance on judgments and the erosion of the moral authority of the judicial system as final arbiter of legal disputes. A further consideration supporting finality is that additional investment in litigation, by the parties and the court, is generally subject to diminishing returns. The likelihood is small that the additional time and expense would result in a clearly more just verdict. This is particularly true in modern procedure, where abundant opportunity is afforded for full inquiry in the proceedings leading to judgment.

The essential problem considered in this chapter is, therefore, how serious an alleged deficiency in a proceeding must be before the objective of achieving finality will yield to that of achieving substantial justice. Related to this is how promptly the objection is raised, for the parties' reliance on a judgment and the strength of the judgment's moral authority are to an important degree a function of the length of time during which a judgment's finality remains in limbo.

Appeals

Appellate review has a public and systemic aspect extending beyond its effects on the parties. It is through appellate decisions that legal issues are definitively resolved, and discordant lower court decisions are brought into some kind of uniformity. Hence the familiar pyramidal pattern of contemporary court systems, in which cases and issues from numerous trial courts are gradually filtered through intermediate appellate courts until a few of them reach a supreme court.

This hierarchical system is not inevitable. Traditional Islamic law and some other traditional systems did not provide for appeals. The old English common law system only gradually developed procedures for appellate review. Although today almost any case that is not settled can eventually be appealed under applicable legislation, precedent on the books declares that there is no constitutional right to appeal.[1] On the other hand, many civil law systems allow at least one appeal that is not limited to issues of law but provides a complete reconsideration of the case, sometimes including the reception of additional evidence.

In our own system, the scope if not the availability of appellate review is under pressure from the increasing numbers of appeals. Most

§ 12.1

1. *E.g.*, Lindsey v. Normet, 405 U.S. 56, 77, 92 S.Ct. 862, 31 L.Ed.2d 36 (1972)(dictum); see Leubsdorf, Constitutional Civil Procedure, 63 Tex. L. Rev. 579, 628–31 (1984); Resnik, Tiers, 57 S. Cal. L. Rev. 837 (1984). On appeals in other legal systems, see 16 International Encyclopedia of Comparative Law §§ 8–13 to 8–18 (1982).

state court systems have moved toward a three tier system modeled on that of the federal courts, in which litigants may appeal as of right to an intermediate appellate court, but the state supreme court hears relatively few cases, selected because of their importance to the law. The thirteen federal Courts of Appeals now receive 55,000 new matters each year, of which more than two thirds are civil appeals.[2] As a result, virtually no parties receive more than fifteen minutes to present oral argument, and almost half of federal appeals are decided without any oral argument at all. Likewise, in most cases the federal courts now deliver abbreviated opinions that are not published, although available through Lexis and Westlaw.[3] (Few lawyers, however, are complaining of a lack of precedents.) Requiring appellants to post bond or penalizing them for baseless appeals discourages some appeals.[4] Prehearing conferences and other case management techniques designed to promote expedition, economy and settlement have appeared in appellate as well as in trial courts.[5]

Procedures for challenging judgments

The procedures for challenging a judgment are, to say the least, untidy when viewed either historically or conceptually. For purposes of clarity, they have three aspects. The first is "standard" or "normal" challenge, referring to the procedures for obtaining review that are employed most frequently; these include ordinary post-trial motions and review through appeal of a judgment. The second is appellate review of a trial court determination at some point prior to the rendition of a final judgment, with a view to forestalling an erroneous trial court determination before it becomes a final judgment. The third is extraordinary relief by proceedings occurring after the judgment has become final and the time for appeal has expired.

In considering these procedures, it is important to keep in mind the time limits on their availability. The ordinary post-trial motions are those for j.n.o.v. or for a new trial. These motions must be made very shortly after judgment is rendered; under the Federal Rules the period is ten days.[6] An appeal from a final judgment must be taken in a somewhat longer period after the judgment (thirty days in federal procedure, which

2. Administrative Office of the United States Courts, Statistical Tables for the Federal Judiciary, December 31, 1999, at 7 (2000).

3. Fed. R. App. P. 34(a); Case Management Procedures in the Federal Courts of Appeals 11, 21 (Fed. Judic. Center 2000); Posner, The Federal Courts: Challenge and Reform (1996); T. Baker, Rationing Justice on Appeal: The Problems of the U.S. Courts of Appeal (1994); see Anastasoff v. United States, 223 F.3d 898, vacated, 235 F.3d 1054 (8th Cir.2000).

4. *E.g.*, Bankers Life & Cas. Co. v. Crenshaw, 486 U.S. 71, 108 S.Ct. 1645, 100 L.Ed.2d 62 (1988); Adsani v. Miller, 139 F.3d 67 (2d Cir.1998); § 12.8 *infra*.

5. *E.g.*, Managing Appeals in Federal Courts (Fed. Judic. Center 1988); ABA Standards of Judicial Administration, Appellate Courts (1976); Comment, Minnesota Supreme Court Prehearing Conference: An Empirical Evaluation, 63 Minn. L. Rev. 1221 (1979); note 3 *supra*.

6. Fed. R. Civ. P. 59(b) (new trial), 50(b) (j.n.o.v.).

is fairly typical),[7] and the period for appealing is extended if a post-trial motion is pending.[8] Extraordinary relief after judgment, depending on the grounds on which it is based, is available within a specified period, such as one year under Federal Rule 60(b)(1)-(3), or without specific limit as to time.

Although this chapter will focus on appeals from trial courts, other sorts of appeals do exist. When a federal District Judge delegates matters to a Magistrate Judge, parties may be able to secure various forms of review of the magistrate's decisions in the District Court or, sometimes, the Court of Appeals.[9] Many decisions of federal administrative agencies may be appealed directly to a Court of Appeals.[10]

A. POST-TRIAL MOTIONS

§ 12.2 Postverdict Motions

We have already extensively considered the ordinary post-trial motions that may be employed for challenging a judgment based on a jury verdict. These are the motions for new trial[1] and for judgment as a matter of law notwithstanding the verdict.[2] As established in that discussion, the motion for j.n.o.v. is available when (1) the case has been determined on a hearing of evidence before a jury and (2) the evidence is such that judgment on the merits should be entered against the verdict-winner. The motion for new trial following a jury trial has a broader range. The verdict-loser may gain a new trial instead of j.n.o.v., thereby giving the verdict-winner a second chance in the new trial to establish a sufficient case on the merits. But a new trial may also be granted even if the evidence was sufficient to support the verdict. This may be done when the judge believes the verdict was against the clear weight of the evidence or when procedural errors were committed (such as erroneous admission or exclusion of evidence or misconduct of a party or counsel) that, in the trial judge's estimate, may have seriously contaminated the proceeding.[3]

7. Fed. R. App. P. 4(a). This rule, however, allows 60 days to appeal in civil cases in which "the United States or its officer or agency is a party."

8. The motions that have the effect of extending the time for appeal under Fed. R. App. P. 4(a)(4) are as follows: motion for j.n.o.v. under Fed. R. Civ. P. 50(b); motion to amend the judgment or the findings on which it is based in a case tried to a judge without a jury under Fed. R. Civ. P. 52(b); motion for attorney fees under Fed. R. Civ. P. 54 if the court so provides; motion to amend a judgment under Fed. R. Civ. P. 59(e); and motion for a new trial under Fed. R. Civ. P. 59, when that motion is denied. When the time for appeal is so extended, its full length begins to run from the date of entry of the order disposing of the motion. For a general treatment of post-trial motion procedure, see Herr, Haydock, and Stempel, Motion Practice §§ 22, 23 (2d ed. 1991).

9. 28 U.S.C. § 636(b)(1), (c)(3); Fed. R. Civ. P. 72, 73; Fed. R. App. P. 3.1.

10. See Fed. R. App. P. 15–20; Jaffe, Judicial Control of Administrative Action (1965).

§ 12.2

1. *See* § 7.24 *supra.*

2. *See* § 7.30 *supra.*

3. *See* §§ 7.26, 7.27 *supra.*

Motion for new trial and appeal

An order denying a new trial is not appealable in itself, although it is reviewable in an appeal from the judgment to which it pertains.[4] If the new trial motion is granted, no appeal may be taken because such an order is not final; the further proceedings in the trial court must be had first.

The j.n.o.v. is essentially a part of the original trial because its grant or denial is determined by reference only to the evidence offered at trial. The motion for new trial, however, may invite not only a reconsideration of the matters adduced at trial but also consideration of new matter, such as newly discovered evidence or misconduct not previously evident.[5] In addressing alleged errors during the adjudication, the motion for new trial can serve the same function as an appeal from the judgment. Furthermore, because this motion is available before either appeal or subsequent extraordinary relief, a party is ordinarily obligated to use it in preference to these other means of review if it will accomplish the same purpose. In a few jurisdictions, a motion for new trial is a prerequisite to taking an appeal if the appeal concerns errors at the trial itself.[6] In all jurisdictions, a party taking an appeal must show that the error of which it complains on appeal is not one that could have been effectively remedied by a new trial motion. And in all jurisdictions, a party seeking extraordinary trial court relief must show that the grounds on which it seeks the relief were not ones that it reasonably could have discovered in time to have sought a new trial.[7]

§ 12.3 Postjudgment Motions in Cases Tried to a Judge

In cases tried to a judge without a jury, a motion similar to a motion for new trial may be used to set aside or revise the judgment.[1] A case may be decided by a judge without a jury in two situations. One occurs when a question of law is posed at the pretrial stage that is determinative of the action and that may be resolved without a trial of factual issues going to the merits. Such a situation arises, for example, when a party moves for dismissal for lack of jurisdiction or for summary judgment on the ground that no genuine issue of fact is involved. The other situation occurs when issues of fact are tried to the court without a jury. In such a case, under the Federal Rules and the rules of most states the judge is required to make findings of fact and thereupon to direct entry of judgment.[2]

4. Osterberger v. Relocation Realty Serv. Corp., 921 F.2d 72 (5th Cir.1991); Youmans v. Simon, 791 F.2d 341 (5th Cir. 1986).

5. 11 Wright and Miller, Federal Practice and Procedure §§ 2808, 2810.

6. *See, e.g.,* Evans v. Wilkinson, 419 P.2d 275 (Okla.1966).

7. *See* Fed. R. Civ. P. 60(b)(2).

§ 12.3

1. *Id.* 52(b), 59(a), (b). *See generally* Cooper, Civil Rule 52 (a): Rationalizing the Resources of Appellate Review, 63 Notre Dame L. Rev. 628 (1988).

2. Fed. R. Civ. P. 52(a). *Compare* Cal. Civ. Proc. Code § 632 (findings required only if requested by a party); N.Y. Civ. Prac. L. & R. 4214(a).

In either event, after the judgment has been entered on the basis of the judge's decision, a party may within a limited time move to amend the judgment or, when a trial of fact issues has been held, move for a new trial. Assuming that such a postjudgment motion is timely, there are virtually no limitations on the relief that the court can give; the judge can fully reconsider the decision.[3] Judges, however, are not supposed to reach a decision in the first place until their conclusion is firm. Hence, such a motion is rarely granted, and for this reason infrequently made, unless it presents some factual or legal matter that had not earlier been adduced.

The motion is not a prerequisite for taking an appeal, nor does the failure to have made it invariably preclude the possibility of subsequent extraordinary relief from the judgment. But, as with the postverdict motion in a case tried to a jury, the availability of the motion in a case tried to a judge is an important factor in determining whether redress through appeal or through subsequent extraordinary relief from the trial court will be granted. In *Osterneck v. Ernst & Whinney*,[4] for instance, the Supreme Court held that a postjudgment motion for discretionary prejudgment interest constituted a motion to alter or amend the judgment, as contemplated by Rule 59(e), and thus a notice of appeal filed before the disposition of the motion was ineffective.

B. APPEAL

§ 12.4 Final Judgment Rule

Generally, appellate review of a trial court determination may be had only on appeal from a final judgment in the trial court.[1] This requirement has been strictly construed by the Supreme Court; a final judgment is one that "ends the litigation on the merits and leaves nothing for the court to do but execute the judgment."[2] In determining whether a judgment ends the litigation, the language of the judgment itself is controlling. Judgment is final when a court "hands down a judgment couched in language calculated to conclude all claims"[3] before

3. *See* 6A Moore, Federal Practice and Procedure ¶ 59.06.

4. 489 U.S. 169, 109 S.Ct. 987, 103 L.Ed.2d 146 (1989).

§ 12.4

1. *See, e.g.*, 28 U.S.C. § 1291; Cal. Civ. Proc. Code § 904.1; Cobbledick v. United States, 309 U.S. 323, 60 S.Ct. 540, 84 L.Ed. 783 (1940); Crick, The Final Judgment as a Basis for Appeal, 41 Yale L.J. 539 (1932); Note, Appealability in the Federal Courts, 75 Harv. L. Rev. 351 (1961). *See generally* Herr, Haydock, and Stempel, Motion Practice § 25 (2d ed. 1991). New York does not require a final judgment as a prerequisite to an appeal. *See* § 12.12 *infra*. For exceptions to the final judgment rule, *see* §§ 12.10–13 *infra*.

2. Lauro Lines S.R.L. v. Chasser, 490 U.S. 495, 109 S.Ct. 1976, 1978, 104 L.Ed.2d 548, 551 (1989). *See also* Budinich v. Becton Dickinson & Co., 486 U.S. 196, 108 S.Ct. 1717, 100 L.Ed.2d 178 (1988); Zink v. United States, 929 F.2d 1015 (5th Cir.1991).

3. Armstrong v. Trico Marine, Inc., 923 F.2d 55 (5th Cir.1991); Vaughn v. Mobil Oil Exploration and Prod. Southeast, 891 F.2d 1195, 1197 (5th Cir.1990).

it. As we shall see, there are important exceptions to this general principle.

Putting the exceptions aside for the moment, the final judgment rule means that only after final judgment has been entered may a party resort to an appellate court.[4] This limitation applies whether the ground of appeal is error in the judgment itself or in the proceedings leading to it. Thus, a party ordinarily may not obtain appellate review of a trial court's ruling on joinder of claims or parties, change of venue, permissible discovery, or admissibility of evidence at trial until after final judgment has been rendered in that court.[5] A party appealing from that judgment will then be able to challenge all rulings that contributed to it.

In contrast to the trial court's final judgment are its interlocutory rulings. An interlocutory ruling is one made within ("inter") the stage when the procedural dialogue ("locution") in the trial court is still continuing. Thus, the term includes all rulings prior to final judgment. Broadly speaking, interlocutory rulings can be put in two categories: pretrial rulings (on matters such as discovery) and rulings during trial (on matters such as disqualification of a juror or exclusion of evidence).

Final judgment rule and policy

The final judgment rule is usually defended for its efficiency. One appeal will consume less time and money than several and will prevent parties from using appeals as delaying tactics. Although this is a sound argument against unlimited appeals, whether a specific appeal will waste or save time and expense depends on the answers to several questions. How much time and expense will it save if the appellant prevails and thus prevents the trial court from proceeding further down an erroneous road? How likely is it that the appellant will so prevail? Is there some reason to consider the time of some participants (such as appellate judges) more valuable than that of others (such as trial judges)? Unfortunately, some of these questions cannot easily be answered, especially before the merits of the appeal have been decided. Thus, legislators and judges must rely on guesswork and common sense when deciding whether an interlocutory appeal or class of appeals is justifiable.

4. It can be difficult to identify, in a purely mechanical sense, the final judgment. *See* United States v. F. & M. Schaefer Brewing Co., 356 U.S. 227, 78 S.Ct. 674, 2 L.Ed.2d 721 (1958), which led to the revision of Fed. R. Civ. P. 58, requiring that the "judgment" be a "separate document." *See also* 53 A.L.R. Fed. 595. This created further problems when the court neglected to enter the separate judgment, see Acosta v. Louisiana Dep't of Health & Human Resources, 478 U.S. 251, 106 S.Ct. 2876, 92 L.Ed.2d 192 (1986), which have been addressed by Fed. R. App. P. 4(a)(2). Beyond this mechanical problem, questions can arise as to whether a particular disposition is actually final. *See* Gerson, The Appealability of Partial Judgments in Consolidated Cases, 57 U. Chi. L. Rev. 169 (1990); Note, Appealability Problems in Nebraska, 53 Neb. L. Rev. 73 (1974); 9 Witkin, California Procedure § 43–55 (3d ed. 1985); *cf.* Annot., 10 A.L.R.2d 1075 (effect of motion for rehearing).

5. *See* 9 Moore, Federal Practice and Procedure ¶ 110.08.

The final judgment rule does make sense when the ground of appeal is that the judgment is substantively erroneous, for this question is ordinarily impossible to answer intelligently until judgment has actually been rendered. It also usually makes sense as applied to interlocutory rulings during trial (such as on the admissibility of evidence) because allowing appeal during trial would disrupt the trial process. But as applied to rulings in the pretrial stage, where the final judgment rule is more problematic, interlocutory appellate review (that is, review prior to final judgment) has become more widely available.[6] It is unusual, however, for a ruling at the pretrial stage to have decisive effects that cannot be remedied by appeal after the trial court has finally disposed of a case. Hence, appeal from the final judgment, while no longer the nearly exclusive means of obtaining appellate review of a trial court order, is still the usual means of doing so.

Settlements and stipulations

Certain judgments having elements of finality may nonetheless not be subject to appeal. A settlement is generally not appealable because it normally constitutes an agreement to resolve a dispute without trial court or appellate adjudication.[7] Courts have allowed an exception to this when the parties have explicitly entered into the settlement agreement without waiving their rights to appeal. In *Bash v. Firstmark Standard Life Insurance Co.*,[8] for example, the court stated that one way a party could appeal a partial summary judgment was by "negotiating a settlement agreement that was expressly conditional on the order of partial summary judgment being upheld on appeal. Then it would have been clear that he was not waiving his right to appeal by consenting to the entry of a final judgment."[9] The appealability of a stipulated judgment is more doubtful; some federal courts allow it, others do not. When the parties' stipulation expressly states an intent or the reservation of the right to appeal, it will usually be allowed.[10] Thus, a party who consented to a dismissal of the case as moot, so as to appeal a district court's order, was not barred from appealing the case, as the consent did not imply waiver of appellate review.[11] Also appealable would be a stipulated judgment resolving one issue between the parties but recognizing their continued disagreement on other issues already decided by the court.[12] With or without an appeal, a party generally will not be granted relief

6. *See* § 12.11 *infra.*

7. Geaney v. Carlson, 776 F.2d 140 (7th Cir.1985). See Digital Equipment Corp. v. Desktop Direct, Inc., 511 U.S. 863, 114 S.Ct. 1992, 128 L.Ed.2d 842 (1994)(order vacating settlement and allowing case to proceed not immediately appealable).

8. 861 F.2d 159 (7th Cir.1988).

9. *Id.* at 162–163. *See also* Hudson v. Chicago Teachers Union, Local No. 1, 922 F.2d 1306, 1312–1313 (7th Cir.1991).

10. Dorse v. Armstrong World Indus., 798 F.2d 1372 (11th Cir.1986). *But see* Amstar Corp. v. Southern Pac. Transp. Co., 607 F.2d 1100 (5th Cir.1979).

11. Greenhouse v. Greco, 544 F.2d 1302 (5th Cir.1977).

12. Hudson v. Chicago Teachers Union, Local No. 1, 922 F.2d 1306 (7th Cir.1991).

from a consent judgment unless there is some showing of fraud or mutual mistake of fact.[13] The best guideline on these matters may be that given by the Supreme Court in *Newman-Green, Inc. v. Alfonzo–Larrain*,[14] where the Court stated that jurisdictional issues in appellate procedure ought to be analyzed pragmatically.

Collateral order doctrine

There has always been need for escape from the rigors of the final judgment rule. Interlocutory orders of various kinds can have practically decisive effects on continuation of the trial court proceeding or have adverse consequences that could not be remedied by subsequent appeal. For example, an order sustaining service of process over a nonresident compels the defendant to litigate through to final judgment in a forum that may, on appeal from the judgment, be held to have lacked jurisdiction.[15] So also a party whose claim of evidentiary privilege is denied faces loss of confidentiality of the information, or an adverse judgment for failure to yield the information, if immediate appellate review cannot be obtained.[16] Some, though not all, such decisive interlocutory orders are appealable under various theories.

A traditional route of escape was the proposition that interlocutory orders claimed to be erroneous could be reviewed by an appellate court through extraordinary writ procedure (prohibition or mandamus) when the order was so erroneous that it exceeded the trial court's "jurisdiction."[17] The predicate of decisions along this line was a distinction between errors going to the court's jurisdiction and those that did not. A reading of the decisions suggests, however, that the distinction is not clear at all, indeed that it begs the question. It has been easier for courts to state the distinction as a basis for their decisions than for others to foresee how the distinction will be applied.[18]

Perhaps out of frustration with the concept of "excess of jurisdiction," the Supreme Court articulated another concept for escaping the final judgment rule: the collateral order doctrine. The doctrine was announced in *Cohen v. Beneficial Industrial Loan Corp.*[19] The Court, in permitting appeal, said that the order in question

13. *See* 7 Moore, Federal Practice and Procedure ¶ 60.19. *See also* Mallory v. Eyrich, 922 F.2d 1273 (6th Cir.1991); Brown v. County of Genesee, 872 F.2d 169 (6th Cir.1989).

14. 490 U.S. 826, 109 S.Ct. 2218, 104 L.Ed.2d 893 (1989). *See also* Hudson v. Chicago Teachers Union, Local No. 1, 922 F.2d 1306 (7th Cir.1991).

15. *See, e.g.,* Insurance Corp. of Ireland v. Compagnie des Bauxites de Guinee, 456 U.S. 694, 102 S.Ct. 2099, 72 L.Ed.2d 492 (1982).

16. *See, e.g.,* Upjohn Co. v. United States, 449 U.S. 383, 101 S.Ct. 677, 66 L.Ed.2d 584 (1981) (attorney-client and work-product privileges).

17. *See* § 12.13 *infra.*

18. *Compare, e.g.,* United States Alkali Export Assn. v. U.S., 325 U.S. 196, 65 S.Ct. 1120, 89 L.Ed. 1554 (1945), *with* Roche v. Evaporated Milk Assn., 319 U.S. 21, 63 S.Ct. 938, 87 L.Ed. 1185 (1943).

19. 337 U.S. 541, 69 S.Ct. 1221, 93 L.Ed. 1528 (1949).

> appears to fall in that small class which finally determine claims of right separable from and collateral to rights asserted in the action, too important to be denied review and too independent of the cause itself to require that appellate consideration be deferred until the whole case is adjudicated.[20]

This definition is the basis of an arcane jurisprudence expounding the concept of "collateral order." But the definition itself is almost empty. The phrase "too important to be denied review" covers any kind of ruling that might be rendered moot by other developments in a case before it reaches final judgment. Thus, almost any ruling except a final judgment could have this effect. The phrase "too independent of the cause itself to require that appellate consideration be deferred" covers any kind of ruling that involves a principle of law that has importance beyond its context in the specific case. Almost any ruling could have that kind of significance. The phrase "separable from and collateral to rights in the action" covers everything except the legal merit of the cause of action, which is determined only by final judgment. Hence, the definition amounts to this: A collateral order is dispositive of an important issue separable from the merits that a court believes to warrant immediate review. The phrase, therefore, could arguably include any order except the final judgment.

The order in *Cohen v. Beneficial* around which this definition was fashioned required the plaintiff to post a bond for costs before continuing the prosecution of a Rule 23.1 stockholder's derivative suit. The requirement of a bond had long been discretionary; the state statute in question simply made it a mandatory aspect of derivative litigation. Hence, the order could be described as "integral" rather than "collateral." Immediate review, however, enabled the Supreme Court to pass on the validity of such a mandatory bond requirement without waiting until a plaintiff refused to post bond and received a judgment dismissing his or her case.

Such as it is, the collateral order concept recognizes that certain types of determinations relating to a litigation in the trial court can be considered as independent from it; since these matters are independent, an order determining them is, in and of itself, a final resolution of a separate proceeding and therefore appealable. The collateral order concept permits adherence to the letter of the final judgment rule but makes it possible for an appellate court to accept jurisdiction of an appeal on the issues involved in the order while the litigation in the trial court is pending. The concept is not susceptible of infinite manipulation but it has a lot of play.

Different collateral orders

Since there is no clear demarcation between collateral orders and noncollateral orders, classification turns on deciding when and how far

20. 337 U.S. at 546, 69 S.Ct. at 1225–1226, 93 L.Ed. at 1536.

to permit departures from the final judgment rule. Courts tend to be restrictive, thereby maintaining the finality principle.

The most generally recognized type of order coming within the collateral order doctrine is the holding of a party in criminal contempt for conduct in the course of a trial court proceeding.[21] A variety of other types of orders have also been so classified in some circumstances.[22] The collateral order doctrine permits appellate review of district court orders that "pose a risk of important and probably irreparable loss if an immediate appeal is not heard."[23] For example, a denial of a claim of sovereign immunity under the Foreign Sovereign Immunity Act[24] is immediately appealable under the doctrine.[25] So is an order rejecting a state officer's qualified immunity defense to a damage suit for violation of constitutional rights.[26] In both of these instances, the Court has been concerned to protect the defendant not just from losing an action but also from having to defend one. Allowing an immediate appeal promotes this goal.

Motions to stay

The indeterminacy of the collateral order concept is revealed in recent Supreme Court decisions. One set concerns whether the doctrine applies to a ruling on a motion to stay trial court proceedings. Such a motion may ask for the stay of a suit in federal district court in deference to an action involving the same dispute and parties in another court. If the stay is granted, then the litigation will be determined in the other court; if the stay is denied, then the litigation will go forward in

21. *See, e.g.*, United States v. Ryan, 402 U.S. 530, 91 S.Ct. 1580, 29 L.Ed.2d 85 (1971); Law v. National Collegiate Athletic Assoc., 134 F.3d 1025 (10th Cir.1998). But a party may not appeal a civil contempt order. Byrd v. Reno, 180 F.3d 298 (D.C. Cir. 1999); Andre, The Final Judgment Rule and Party Appeals of Civil Contempt Orders, 55 N.Y.U. L. Rev. 1041 (1980); § 5.14 *supra*.

22. *See* 9 Moore, Federal Practice and Procedure ¶¶ 110.10–110.13; Redish, The Pragmatic Approach to Appealability in the Federal Courts, 75 Colum. L. Rev. 89 (1975); Comment, The Collateral Order Doctrine in California, 15 Hastings L.J. 105 (1963); Annot., 3 A.L.R.2d 342. *Cf.* Annot., 54 A.L.R.3d 595 (class action determinations); Annot., 18 A.L.R.3d 400 (orders staying proceeding in trial court); Annot., 95 A.L.R.2d 1361 (pretrial orders); Note, 44 Fordham L. Rev. 433 (1975) (orders consolidating cases); Annot., 19 A.L.R.2d 640 (attachment orders); Annot., 37 A.L.R.2d 586 (discovery orders); Note, 1973 Duke L.J. 1063 (orders denying claim of privilege not to disclose information).

23. Acosta v. Tenneco Oil Co., 913 F.2d 205, 208 (5th Cir.1990).

24. *See* § 2.16 *supra*.

25. *See, e.g.*, Rush-Presbyterian–St. Luke's Medical Center v. Hellenic Republic, 877 F.2d 574 (7th Cir.1989), *cert. denied*, 493 U.S. 937, 110 S.Ct. 333, 107 L.Ed.2d 322 (1989); Compania Mexicana De Aviacion v. United States Dist. Court, 859 F.2d 1354 (9th Cir.1988); Gould, Inc. v. Pechiney Ugine Kuhlmann & Trefimetaux, 853 F.2d 445 (6th Cir.1988).

26. *E.g.*, Behrens v. Pelletier, 516 U.S. 299, 116 S.Ct. 834, 133 L.Ed.2d 773 (1996); see Puerto Rico Aqueduct & Sewer Authority v. Metcalf & Eddy, Inc., 506 U.S. 139, 113 S.Ct. 684, 121 L.Ed.2d 605 (1993)(claim of Eleventh Amendment immunity). But see Johnson v. Jones, 515 U.S. 304, 115 S.Ct. 2151, 132 L.Ed.2d 238 (1995)(no appeal when denial of immunity summary judgment based on presence of genuine issue of fact).

the court where the motion is made, perhaps in both courts. The Supreme Court has held that a federal district court order granting a stay in deference to a pending state case is a collateral order that may be immediately appealed, but an order denying such a stay is not.[27] Likewise, the Court has allowed an appeal from an order remanding to state court on abstention grounds a case that the defendant had removed to federal court, even though a federal statute appears to forbid appeals from remand orders.[28] The Court also has held that an order refusing to give effect to a forum selection clause, hence retaining the case in the court where it was filed, is not a collateral order.[29] These holdings allow an immediate appeal when a case is in effect sent to another court but not when it is kept in the federal court, even though neither measure brings the litigation to an end or imposes a greater burden than the other on the losing party.

Class suit rulings

Another set of decisions, now partly modified by rule, concerns rulings at the threshold of class suits. In *Coopers & Lybrand v. Livesay*[30] the Court held that an order denying certification of a class suit is not appealable as a collateral order, even though a refusal of certification is the "death knell" of a class suit. Yet *Cohen v. Beneficial Industrial Loan Corp.*[31] had held that an order requiring a plaintiff in a stockholder's derivative suit to post a bond was collateral and appealable; in another case the Court held that an order requiring defendant to pay expenses of notice to the class also was collateral.[32] Hence, it would appear that rulings on important incidents of a class suit are collateral orders, but the ruling determining whether the proceeding is a class suit in the first place is not a collateral order. Fortunately, although there is still no appeal as of right, an amendment to the Federal Rules now allows an appeal in the Court of Appeals' discretion of a decision to certify or not to certify a class.[33]

27. *Compare* Moses H. Cone Memorial Hosp. v. Mercury Construction Corp., 460 U.S. 1, 103 S.Ct. 927, 74 L.Ed.2d 765 (1983), *with* Gulfstream Aerospace Corp. v. Mayacamas Corp., 485 U.S. 271, 108 S.Ct. 1133, 99 L.Ed.2d 296 (1988).

28. 28 U.S.C. § 1447(d); Quackenbush v. Allstate Ins. Co., 517 U.S. 706, 116 S.Ct. 1712, 135 L.Ed.2d 1 (1996).

29. Lauro Lines S.R.L. v. Chasser, 490 U.S. 495, 109 S.Ct. 1976, 104 L.Ed.2d 548 (1989).

30. 437 U.S. 463, 98 S.Ct. 2454, 57 L.Ed.2d 351 (1978). *Compare* Amato v. General Motors Corp., 67 Ohio St.2d 253, 423 N.E.2d 452 (1981) (orders certifying or refusing to certify are orders in a "special proceeding" and as such are appealable).

31. 337 U.S. 541, 69 S.Ct. 1221, 93 L.Ed. 1528 (1949). *See* text at notes 19–20 *supra*.

32. Eisen v. Carlisle & Jacquelin, 417 U.S. 156, 94 S.Ct. 2140, 40 L.Ed.2d 732 (1974).

33. Fed. R. Civ. P. 23(f); *see* Blair v. Equifax Check Services, Inc., 181 F.3d 832 (7th Cir.1999); § 12.11 *infra*.

Disqualification and contempt orders

Also incongruous is the disparate treatment of an order disqualifying counsel and a contempt of court order against a nonparty in the trial court. The Supreme Court has held that an order disqualifying counsel for conflict of interest is not a collateral order.[34] But such an order surely meets the definition in *Cohen v. Beneficial.* A disqualification order is final in itself; it does not involve the merits of the main case, it affects the interests of a distinct party (the disqualified lawyer), it imposes a legal liability, and it often involves important questions of law. Such an order almost certainly cannot be shown to have been prejudicial in an appeal from the final judgment, because the disqualified lawyer will have been replaced by other counsel. Yet these are said to be the characteristics of a collateral order.

The Supreme Court has, however, reaffirmed the rule that an order of civil or criminal contempt of court against a nonparty is collateral, and as such is immediately appealable,[35] because the order ends the litigation for the nonparty. (That, of course, is equally true for a disqualified lawyer.)

Official immunity

Similar criticisms cover the Court's decisions applying the collateral order doctrine to a denial of a government official's threshold claim of qualified official immunity from being sued.[36] The rationale was that the immunity is designed to avoid the burden of unwarranted litigation, not merely the burden of liability. But that rationale would apply to every rule that defines the means and scope of litigation in the trial court. The point of the final judgment rule is that the burden of litigation has to be borne until the trial court has arrived at final judgment.

Judicial approach

As a further example, a district court order granting permissive intervention but denying intervention as of right has been held not immediately appealable under the doctrine.[37] So too was the denial of a motion to dismiss based on an extradited person's claim to immunity from service, and an order denying a motion to dismiss on the ground of forum non conveniens.[38] The only conclusion one can draw is that since

34. Richardson-Merrell, Inc. v. Koller, 472 U.S. 424, 105 S.Ct. 2757, 86 L.Ed.2d 340 (1985); see Cunningham v. Hamilton County, 527 U.S. 198, 119 S.Ct. 1915, 144 L.Ed.2d 184 (1999)(no appeal from order sanctioning lawyer). *Compare* Annot., 5 A.L.R.4th 1251 (1981) (appealability of disqualification orders in state court).

35. United States Catholic Conference v. Abortion Rights Mobilization, Inc., 487 U.S. 72, 108 S.Ct. 2268, 101 L.Ed.2d 69 (1988). A *party* may appeal a criminal but not a civil contempt sanction. *See* note 21 *supra.*

36. Mitchell v. Forsyth, 472 U.S. 511, 105 S.Ct. 2806, 86 L.Ed.2d 411 (1985); note 26 *supra*; *see* § 3.15 *supra.*

37. Stringfellow v. Concerned Neighbors in Action, 480 U.S. 370, 107 S.Ct. 1177, 94 L.Ed.2d 389 (1987). But a simple order denying intervention is appealable. *See* United States v. South Fla. Water Management Dist., 922 F.2d 704 (11th Cir. 1991).

38. Van Cauwenberghe v. Biard, 486 U.S. 517, 108 S.Ct. 1945, 100 L.Ed.2d 517 (1988).

Cohen the Supreme Court has been generally hostile to expansion of interlocutory appeal through the collateral order concept and has arbitrarily selected exceptions to it. As an exercise in judicial lawmaking the performance has not been distinguished in either explications or results. Because Congress has now given the Court, acting in its capacity as promulgator of the Federal Rules, the power to specify what judgments will count as final and to authorize interlocutory review, some further delineation of the circumstances in which a party may appeal may occur through rule-making.[39]

Scope of appeal

Assuming an order is collateral and appealable, a further question is the extent to which the appeal can consider other issues in the case. Different approaches have been taken by the lower federal courts in determining the scope of their authority in reviewing a collateral order. Some circuits, having accepted an interlocutory order for review, will confine their review to that order.[40] Other circuits hold that once an order is before them on appeal, they may address additional orders of the trial court, including ones that may not meet their criteria for immediate appeal.[41] This expansionary interpretation of interlocutory review is called pendent appellate jurisdiction.[42]

Further doctrinal intricacies involved in the collateral order rule are avoided when interlocutory appeals are expressly allowed as exceptions to the final judgment rule. As we shall see,[43] such provisions are limited in the federal courts and more liberal in many state courts systems. Another device for escape from the final judgment rule is the use of extraordinary writs to obtain interlocutory review, a matter considered later in this chapter.[44]

§ 12.5 Attorney's Fee Awards

Confusion has developed over the appealability of awards of attorney's fees in connection with trial court litigation. To an important

39. 28 U.S.C. §§ 1292(e), 2072(c).

40. The First, Third, Fourth, and Ninth Circuits, and probably the D.C. Circuit. *See, e.g.*, Cunningham v. Gates, 229 F.3d 1271 (9th Cir.2000); Kershner v. Mazurkiewicz, 670 F.2d 440 (3d Cir.1982) (denial of preliminary injunction in prisoner's civil rights suit did not allow review of the denial of class certification included in the same order). See Swint v. Chambers County Comm'n, 514 U.S. 35, 115 S.Ct. 1203, 131 L.Ed.2d 60 (1995)(no appellate jurisdiction over "pendent party").

41. The Second, Fifth, Sixth, Eighth, and Eleventh Circuits. *See, e.g.*, Showtime/The Movie Channel v. Covered Bridge Condo., 881 F.2d 983 (11th Cir.1989) (in review of summary judgment order, appellate court could address an issue that went to the merits of this order); McKnight v. Blanchard, 667 F.2d 477 (5th Cir.1982) (in an order staying prisoners' civil rights suit, denial of other motions and orders are reviewable on appeal).

42. Steinman, The Scope of Appellate Jurisdiction: Pendent Appellate Jurisdiction Before and After *Swint*, 49 Hastings L.J. 1337 (1998); Note, The Proper Scope of Pendent Appellate Jurisdiction in the Collateral Order Context, 100 Yale L.J. 511 (1990).

43. *See* § 12.13 *infra*.

44. *See* § 12.12 *infra*.

extent this is a product of substantial legislative changes in the law governing these fees. Increasingly, provision is made for award of attorney's fees to the prevailing party but without auxiliary provisions concerning appellate review of such awards. Courts must therefore struggle to fit fee awards into the traditional appellate scheme.

Traditional costs

As noted earlier,[1] the baseline American rule is that a prevailing party is entitled to "costs," which includes various incidental expenditures in the trial court but not attorney's fees.[2] Recoverable costs normally are modest in amount and easily calculable. Ordinarily they are totaled when the litigation concludes and then added by the clerk to the final judgment.[3] Given this normal procedure, the corresponding rule concerning appeal from such determinations is that costs are part of the judgment and hence reviewable on appeal from the final judgment, not reviewable by separate appeal from the cost determination.[4] Even in the old days this simple arrangement did not always govern. In certain types of proceedings one of the parties might be entitled to a provisional award of attorney's fees at the beginning of the litigation. This rule commonly applies in divorce cases.[5]

Attorney fee awards

In modern adjudication there are many circumstances in which the trial court may award attorney's fees separate from the judgment and, in some situations, before the final judgment. Many remedial statutes provide for award of attorney's fees to a prevailing plaintiff in civil rights and employment discrimination cases.[6] Some statutes define recoverable damages to include attorney's fees.[7] In addition, Rule 11, 28 U.S.C. § 1927, and similar state procedural rules provide for imposition of attorney's fees in favor of a party subjected to ill-founded or harassing litigation.[8]

Enforcement of these fee award provisions involves two related requirements relating to appealability. One requirement is that of a separate hearing, or separate segment of the main trial, to receive evidence in many cases and arguments on whether attorney's fees are due and, if so, in what amount. Such a hearing can be a substantial trial

§ 12.5

1. *See* §§ 1.22, 6.3 *supra.*

2. Tanker Management, Inc. v. Brunson, 918 F.2d 1524 (11th Cir.1990).

3. *See* Fed. R. Civ. P. 54(d).

4. Wetzel v. Ohio, 371 U.S. 62, 83 S.Ct. 111, 9 L.Ed.2d 26 (1962).

5. *See, e.g.,* In re Marriage of Zannis, 114 Ill.App.3d 1034, 70 Ill.Dec. 545, 449 N.E.2d 892 (1983). *See also* Annot., 22 A.L.R.4th 407.

6. *See* §§ 1.23, 3.22–3.23 *supra.* See generally Derfner & Wolf, Court Awarded Attorney Fees (1998).

7. *Id. See also* People ex rel. Cooper v. Mitchell Brothers' Santa Ana Theater, 165 Cal.App.3d 378, 211 Cal.Rptr. 501, *cert. denied,* 474 U.S. 948, 106 S.Ct. 347, 88 L.Ed.2d 293 (1985).

8. *See* § 3.13 *supra. See also* Carnal v. Dan Coleman, Inc., 727 P.2d 412 (Colo.App. 1986).

in itself. The other requirement is that the separate hearing come at an appropriate time in relation to the main case. The appropriate time may be before the main case gets under way (as in the provisional award of attorney's fees at the beginning of a divorce case), midway in the litigation (for example, attorney's fees sought for a Rule 11 violation of discovery to forestall further abuse),[9] or after the issue of liability has been determined in plaintiff's favor in the main litigation, along with determination of other damages.[10] The appropriate time may be even after the judgment has been entered in the main litigation, as an award supplementing the judgment.[11]

Is fee decision separate from merits?

When evidence concerning attorney's fees is received along with other damages evidence in the main case, it seems clear that the attorney's fee award should be considered an element of the final judgment and reviewable only in connection therewith.[12] Except for this situation, however, the attorney's fee determination can be viewed either as a separate proceeding or as an incident of the main proceeding.

It can be viewed as a separate proceeding because, ordinarily at least, it will have been heard at a separate stage and time from the main case, either before, midway, or afterward. When the main case is tried to a jury, the attorney's fee determination usually will also be separate because it will be made by the judge without a jury. Rule 11 awards may be separate in the further sense that they are against the lawyer, or both lawyer and party, rather than against the party alone, as is the judgment in the main case.[13] Also, the fee award ordinarily will be recorded in a separate document. Indeed, fee awards are often given in lengthy, institutional reform suits in which the court enters many different appealable orders over the years. If the fee award follows by weeks, months, or years what looks like a final judgment, courts must either treat it as a second appealable judgment, hold it completely unappealable, or require the entry of a new, all-embracing judgment. All these factors incline toward regarding the attorney's fee award as a separate proceeding leading to a separate judgment or collateral order that is itself appealable.

The attorney's fee determination can alternatively be viewed as an incident of the main proceeding. Often the determination is made in a provisional way, indicating that it is to be later incorporated in the final

9. *See, e.g.*, Schiff v. Simon & Schuster, Inc., 766 F.2d 61 (2d Cir.1985).

10. *See, e.g.*, Wells v. Dallas Indep. School Dist., 576 F.Supp. 497 (N.D.Tex. 1983).

11. *See, e.g.*, Morley v. Cohen, 888 F.2d 1006 (4th Cir.1989) (motion for attorney's fees twenty days after judgment).

12. *See, e.g.*, Mills v. Electric Auto-Lite Co., 396 U.S. 375, 90 S.Ct. 616, 24 L.Ed.2d 593 (1970); Leubsdorf, Recovering Attorney Fees as Damages, 38 Rutgers L. Rev. 439 (1986).

13. *See, e.g.*, Golden Eagle Distrib. Corp. v. Burroughs Corp., 801 F.2d 1531 (9th Cir.1986).

judgment. Sometimes the only record of the determination is its incorporation in the final judgment. Usually the fee amount depends on the size and basis of the judgment in the main case, as the reasonableness of the award cannot be coherently determined independent of that judgment. This usually suggests the appropriateness of a joint appeal; but sometimes it suggests to a trial court that it should wait for appellate resolution of the main case before considering a fee award.

Hence, the basis of the attorney's fee award, the procedure by which it was determined, and the circumstances under which the determination was recorded all determine whether the fee award is a separately appealable order. Such a case-by-case approach, however, encourages continuing litigation of appealability issues and raises problems of unfairness concerning the timing of the appeal challenging the attorney's fee award. If the aggrieved party seeks immediate appeal, it may suffer a dismissal of the appeal on the ground that the determination is not separate from the final judgment and hence not separately appealable.[14] If the aggrieved party holds off appealing the award until final judgment is rendered, it may suffer dismissal of the appeal on the ground that the determination was separate and that the time to appeal from it has expired.[15] Similar dilemmas arise when a judgment comes first and a fee award follows.

Rulings on appealability

White v. New Hampshire Department of Employment Security[16] adopted a fairly broad interpretation of the appealability of fee awards. The Supreme Court held that a filing of claims for fees was not a motion to alter or amend under Rule 59(e) and therefore was not subject to the ten-day deadline. The Court held that the award is independently appealable, as it is not inherent in or necessarily subsumed by the decision on the merits. *Budinich v. Becton Dickinson & Co.*[17] made clear that this analysis holds even when for other purposes the fee award is considered part of the damages, so long as it is adjudicated after the judgment.

White, Budinich and a subsequent amendment to the Federal Rules provide guidance for cases in which a party who has prevailed in an action seeks an attorney fee award from the court. The party's motion for an award must be filed no later than fourteen days after entry of judgment, unless otherwise provided by court order or statute. If this deadline is met, the court may (but need not) direct that the time for

14. *See, e.g.*, Wetzel v. Ohio, 371 U.S. 62, 83 S.Ct. 111, 9 L.Ed.2d 26 (1962).

15. *See, e.g.*, White v. New Hampshire Dept. of Employment Sec., 455 U.S. 445, 102 S.Ct. 1162, 71 L.Ed.2d 325 (1982); Terket v. Lund, 623 F.2d 29 (7th Cir.1980).

16. 455 U.S. 445, 102 S.Ct. 1162, 71 L.Ed.2d 325 (1982); see Green, From Here to Attorneys' Fees: Certainty, Efficiency, and Fairness in the Journey to the Appellate Courts, 69 Corn. L. Rev. 207 (1984).

17. 486 U.S. 196, 108 S.Ct. 1717, 100 L.Ed.2d 178 (1988).

appealing the underlying judgment will be extended until the attorney fee motion is decided, at which time both may be appealed together.[18] If the court does not so direct, the underlying judgment and the attorney fee award will each be appealable, and a party wishing to appeal either the judgment or the award must do so within the time limit applicable to it.

Whether an attorney fee order entered before judgment in the main case is immediately appealable is another issue. Most probably, it is not, but circumstances may make a difference.[19] By way of further complication, some courts distinguish between a fee award for legal services in the same case in which the award is made and damages for the expense of other legal services, with the latter considered inseparable from the rest of the judgment.[20]

In miniature these problems of appealability of attorney's fee awards repeat the technical procedural problems of appeals generally. The causes of the confusion include inattention of legislators to the special problems of appealability posed by fee determinations, the piecemeal way in which courts confronted the problem, and the diversity of fee award provisions. Above all, the decisions reflect the tension between the objective that a case be resolved in the trial court before any part of it is examined on appeal and the objective that case-stopping interlocutory orders be subject to appellate scrutiny before disastrous injustice results.

§ 12.6 Parties

The basic rule is that a party to an appeal must have been a party to the judgment from which the appeal is taken. Thus, a judgment between two parties in the trial court cannot be appealed by a nonparty who believes that the judgment was unfair or erroneous.[1] This is true even if the nonparty was substantially affected by the judgment.[2] Correlatively, if a party in the trial court is not made a party to the appeal, the judgment cannot be reviewed or reversed as to that party even though the appeal may ultimately be successful as to other parties.[3]

18. Fed. R. Civ. P. 54(d)(2)(B), 58; Fed. R. App. P. 4(a)(4)(A)(iii).

19. See Cunningham v. Hamilton County, 527 U.S. 198, 119 S.Ct. 1915, 144 L.Ed.2d 184 (1999)(order sanctioning lawyer not immediately appealable); Petties v. District of Columbia, 227 F.3d 469 (D.C.Cir. 2000).

20. Justine Realty Co. v. American Nat'l Can Co., 945 F.2d 1044 (8th Cir.1991); Ragan v. Tri–County Excavating, Inc., 62 F.3d 501 (3d Cir.1995).

§ 12.6

1. *See, e.g.*, Microsystems Software v. Scandinavia Online AB, 226 F.3d 35 (1st Cir.2000); Hispanic Socy. of the New York City Police Dept., Inc. v. New York City Police Dept., 806 F.2d 1147 (2d Cir.1986); Balcom v. Lynn Ladder & Scaffolding Co., 806 F.2d 1127 (1st Cir.1986).

2. Marino v. Ortiz, 484 U.S. 301, 108 S.Ct. 586, 98 L.Ed.2d 629 (1988). *See also* Walker v. City of Mesquite, 858 F.2d 1071 (5th Cir.1988) (holding that non-named class members lack standing to appeal); Note, The Nonappealability of Class Action Consent Decrees by Nonnamed Class Members, 63 Tul. L. Rev. 1732 (1989).

3. See Swint v. Chamber County Comm'n, 514 U.S. 35, 115 S.Ct. 1203, 131 L.Ed.2d 60 (1995). In many states it is necessary for the appellant to serve notice on the parties against whom it takes the appeal. Under the Federal Rules of Appel-

Persons who were not parties in the trial court have only two avenues of recourse if they wish to participate in the appeal. One is to become a party to the proceeding below by intervention after judgment or to obtain permission, granted only in unusual circumstances, to intervene as a party to the appeal even though the applicant was not a party below.[4] The other is to obtain permission from the appellate court to appear amicus curiae (as a friend of the court), with authority limited to arguing on behalf of the position of one of the parties.[5]

Nonparties

Bender v. Williamsport Area School District[6] illustrates the rule that only a party may appeal. Here, the issue was whether an individual member of a school board had standing to appeal from a judgment against the board. Since the judgment was not against the appellant in his personal capacity but against the board as a whole, the school board member had no personal stake in the outcome of the litigation and could not appeal the judgment.

Similarly, in *Karcher v. May*[7] the Supreme Court held that if a party at the time of judgment is a party only in an official capacity, then that person may lack standing to appeal in an individual capacity. In this case, two presiding officials of a state legislature intervened as defendants on behalf of the legislature. After subsequently losing their presiding positions they appealed the case. The Supreme Court held that since they had become parties only in their official capacity as representatives of the legislature and not as individual legislators, they lacked standing to appeal.

Participating nonparties

A few courts have allowed persons who have challenged the settlement of a class or derivative action to appeal even though they have not

late Procedure, the appellant files the notice of appeal with the clerk of the trial court, who then notifies all the parties to the proceeding. *See* Fed. R. App. P. 3(a), (d). this means that all parties to the trial court proceeding become parties to the appeal. But the appellant must designate the part of the judgment from which it appeals. *See* Fed. R. App. P. 3(c). If it omits any part, such as that involving one of several opposing parties, then that part of the judgment cannot be reversed or modified. *See* Ruckman & Hansen, Inc. v. Contracting & Material Co., 328 F.2d 744 (7th Cir.1964). The parties appealing must be specifically mentioned in the notice of appeal. *See* § 12.8 *infra.*

4. *See, e.g.*, Sanguine, Ltd. v. United States Dept. of Interior, 736 F.2d 1416 (10th Cir.1984); Meridian Homes Corp. v. Nicholas W. Prassas & Co., 683 F.2d 201 (7th Cir.1982); United States v. G. Heileman Brewing Co., 563 F.Supp. 642 (D.Del. 1983). *Cf.* Annot., 15 A.L.R. 2d 368. Even an intervenor may not appeal if no one else does and if it does not meet the constitutional requirements for standing (see § 2.26 *supra*) because the judgment does not sufficiently affect it. Diamond v. Charles, 476 U.S. 54, 106 S.Ct. 1697, 90 L.Ed.2d 48 (1986).

5. *See* Note, The Amicus Curiae, 55 Nw. U.L. Rev. 469 (1960).

6. 475 U.S. 534, 106 S.Ct. 1326, 89 L.Ed.2d 501 (1986).

7. 484 U.S. 72, 108 S.Ct. 388, 98 L.Ed.2d 327 (1987).

intervened.[8] Formally, one can argue that filing objections, which the Federal Rules encourage in such cases by providing for notice to those affected,[9] should be considered the equivalent of intervention. Practically, this would seem a reasonable recognition of the facts that these actions determine the rights of many persons, that multiple interventions would be burdensome for all, and that the lawyers and parties who have represented a class during an action may not continue to do so adequately once they have agreed to a settlement that is likely to be profitable for the lawyers. Of course, such an appealing challenger, like any other appellant, may only argue to the appellate court points that were presented to the trial court.

Aggrieved parties

A final limitation on parties is that only an *aggrieved* party may appeal. This includes any party against whom judgment was entered and anyone who has sought relief (a plaintiff or, for example, a counterclaimant) but has been denied the full extent of the relief requested. A party who has obtained judgment in its favor ordinarily may not appeal merely because the trial court based the decision on a ground other than one the party may have wished.[10] Thus, if a litigant seeks to enjoin the enforcement of a statute and obtains an injunction on the ground that the statute does not apply to its situation, the litigant may not appeal on the ground that the statute does apply but is unconstitutional. The underlying theory is that, although an appellate court has authority to resolve questions of law, it may exercise that authority only when necessary to correct an improper disposition of the controversy, apart from the basis on which the disposition may have been made.[11]

Substitution

The Federal Rules permit the substitution of parties in the event of death and other "good reason." If a party dies after the notice of appeal is filed, the representative of the deceased may be substituted on filing of a timely motion.[12]

§ 12.7 Jurisdiction of Appeal

In general, appellate review of a state trial court judgment is conducted through the state's appellate court system. Correspondingly, appellate review of a federal district court judgment is conducted through the federal courts of appeals, and then the Supreme Court. The

8. Powers v. Eichen, 229 F.3d 1249 (9th Cir.2000); Kaplan v. Rand, 192 F.3d 60 (2d Cir.1999); Rosenbaum v. MacAllister, 64 F.3d 1439 (10th Cir.1995); *see* S.E.C. v. Forex Asset Management LLC, 242 F.3d 325 (5th Cir.2001). *Contra, e.g.*, Felzen v. Andreas, 134 F.3d 873 (7th Cir.1998).

9. Fed. R. Civ. P. 23(d)(2), (e), 23.1, 23.2.

10. *See* Annot., 69 A.L.R.2d 701.

11. *See, e.g.*, N.Y. Civ. Prac. L. & R. 5511; De Korwin v. First Natl. Bank of Chicago, 235 F.2d 156, 159 (7th Cir.1956); 9 Moore, Federal Practice and Procedure ¶ 203.06.

12. Fed. R. App. P. 43.

Supreme Court also has appellate jurisdiction to consider federal questions that have been adjudicated in state courts.

State and federal appellate courts

Appeal has not been held a constitutional right under the Due Process Clause. All jurisdictions nonetheless make appellate review from the judgments of trial courts generally available in some form. The rules determining the court to which an appeal may be taken are usually prescribed by statute and sometimes by constitutional provision or by rule of court.[1] In many states, the judgments of trial courts of limited jurisdiction are appealable to the trial court of general jurisdiction, where they maybe considered either by trial de novo or by review of the lower court record.[2]

A few states have no intermediate appellate court, so appeals from the trial court of general jurisdiction go directly to the state supreme court. In most states, the judgments of trial courts of general jurisdiction are appealable to the intermediate appellate court and only thereafter to the highest court.[3] There are many provisions, however, that permit direct appeal from the trial court to the state's highest court. In systems having an intermediate appellate court, a second appeal from that court to the highest court is ordinarily permitted only on leave of the higher court, given through a writ of certiorari or a procedure involving similar discretion.[4] In some jurisdictions, however, the discretion of the highest court is restricted in that only certain specified decisions of the lower courts may be entertained on appeal, and in other types of cases an appeal is mandatory.[5]

Federal review of state court decisions

Restrictive jurisdictional rules govern the reviewability of state court judgments by the federal courts. In very limited circumstances, state court proceedings may be subject to review by a federal district court

§ 12.7

1. *See, e.g.*, 28 U.S.C. §§ 1291 (appeals from the district courts to the courts of appeals), 1252 (direct appeal from district court to Supreme Court), 1254 (appeal and certiorari review of courts of appeals by Supreme Court), 1257 (appeal and certiorari review of state court judgments by Supreme Court). *Cf.* McGarity, Multi-party Forum Shopping for Appellate Review of Administrative Action, 129 U. Pa. L. Rev. 302 (1980).

2. *See, e.g.*, O'Brion, Russell & Co. v. LeMay, 370 Mass. 243, 346 N.E.2d 861 (1976) (record in lower court treated as prima facie evidence of facts); State v. Stacey, 25 Or.App. 97, 548 P.2d 527 (1976) (trial de novo).

3. *See, e.g.*, Korn, Civil Jurisdiction of the New York Court of Appeals and Appellate Divisions, 16 Buffalo L. Rev. 307 (1967); Sales and Cliff, Jurisdiction in the Texas Supreme Court and Courts of Civil Appeals, 26 Baylor L. Rev. 501 (1974).

4. *See, e.g.*, Hayes, Certiorari Review of District Court of Appeal Decisions by the Supreme Court of Florida, 28 U. Miami L. Rev. 952 (1974); Poulos and Varner, Review of Intermediate Appellate Court Decisions in California, 15 Hastings L.J. 11 (1963). *See also* American Jud. Socy., Intermediate Appellate Courts (1976).

5. Scheinkman, Civil Jurisdiction of the New York Court of Appeals: The Rule and Role of Finality, 54 St. John's L. Rev. 443 (1980).

through the mechanism of extraordinary relief, such as habeas corpus in a criminal case or an injunction.[6] Such review is not, however, an appeal but a de novo proceeding based on the extraordinary grounds asserted. A federal court may also be the forum for considering the effect of a state court judgment relied on under the rules of res judicata.

Aside from these possibilities, a state court judgment is reviewable in the federal courts only under the narrowly defined conditions under which the U.S. Supreme Court may accept an appeal or grant certiorari for that purpose. The judgment must have been finally determined by the highest state court to which an appeal could be taken, and the judgment must have involved a federal question. The Supreme Court's review is limited to consideration of the federal issues.[7]

Appeals in the federal court system are governed by 28 U.S.C. §§ 1253–1295. An appeal from a district court ordinarily is taken to the Court of Appeals for the circuit in which the district is located.[8] Review of a Court of Appeals decision may be sought in the Supreme Court.[9]

The evolving expansion of constitutional clauses, such as those guaranteeing due process and equal protection, and the expansion of federal legislation into fields previously regulated by the states have greatly enlarged the incidence of federal questions in state court cases and, hence, the availability of Supreme Court review of state court judgments. The jurisdictional limitations stated above nevertheless still apply. Further, given that the Supreme Court's authority to review is discretionary and that its docket is heavy, the possibility of its reviewing a state court judgment is statistically remote.[10] Thousands of litigants ask the Court to hear their cases each year, but the Court accepts fewer than two hundred, typically because the lower court decision conflicts with other decisions or decides a new and important federal question.[11]

6. There are important statutory limitations on the authority of a federal court to enjoin state court proceedings. *See* 28 U.S.C. § 2283; Comment, Federal Court Stays of State Court Proceedings, 38 U. Chi. L. Rev. 612 (1971); *see generally* Bator, Mishkin, Shapiro, and Wechsler, The Federal Courts and the Federal System 1230 *et seq.* (3d ed. 1988). A federal court may not entertain an appeal from a state court decision. See District of Columbia Court of Appeals v. Feldman, 460 U.S. 462, 103 S.Ct. 1303, 75 L.Ed.2d 206 (1983); Symposium, The Rooker-Feldman Doctrine, 74 Notre Dame L. Rev. 1081 (1999).

7. *See* 28 U.S.C. § 1257; Dyk, Supreme Court Review of Interlocutory State Court Decisions: "The Twilight Zone of Finality," 19 Stan. L. Rev. 907 (1967); Cox Broadcasting Corp. v. Cohn, 420 U.S. 469, 95 S.Ct. 1029, 43 L.Ed.2d 328 (1975).

8. 28 U.S.C. § 1294, which refers to the exceptions provided in 28 U.S.C. §§ 1292(c), (d), and 1295.

9. 28 U.S.C. § 1254.

10. *See* Hellman, The Supreme Court, the National Law, and the Selection of Cases for the Plenary Docket, 44 U. Pitt. L. Rev. 521 (1983); Hellman, Error Correction, Lawmaking, and the Supreme Court's Exercise of Discretionary Review, 44 U. Pitt. L. Rev. 795 (1983).

11. See S. Ct. R. 10; Estreicher and Sexton, A Managerial Theory of the Supreme Court's Responsibilities: An Empirical Study, 59 N.Y.U. L. Rev. 681 (1984); Hartnett, Questioning Certiorari: Some Reflections Seventy-Five Years After the Judges' Bill, 100 Colum. L. Rev. 1643 (2000).

§ 12.8 Procedure

The particulars of appellate procedure vary not only between jurisdictions but, to some extent, between the various appellate levels within each court system. The essential elements, however, are much the same.[1]

An appeal presupposes that a judgment has been properly entered. An oral indication of the judge's decision is not a judgment. What is properly required is a separate document designated "judgment."[2]

Notice of appeal

The appeal is commenced by a notice of appeal.[3] For the federal courts, the Federal Rules of Appellate Procedure prescribe the contents of the notice, requiring that it specify the party taking the appeal, the judgment or portion of it appealed from, and the court to which the appeal is taken.[4] The appellant need not list the appellees, which is the responsibility of the clerk. The purpose of the rule is to provide notice of the appeal to the other side by naming the judgment from which the appeal is taken.[5]

Strict compliance

Appellants proceed at their peril in complying with the procedural requirements for taking an appeal. Although Rule 2 allows the court of appeals to "suspend the requirements ... of any of these rules,"[6] the notion persists that various procedural steps are "jurisdictional" and may not be waived.[7] Hence, failure to take one of the steps can result in failure to invest the appellate court with jurisdiction, ending the appeal before it begins. Arguably, however, procedure is a different matter than

§ 12.8

1. Martineau, Modern Appellate Practice—Federal and State Civil Appeals (1983); Stern, Supreme Court Practice (6th ed. 1986); Stern, Appellate Practice in the United States (2d ed. 1989); Wiener, Briefing and Arguing Federal Appeals (1967). Pound, Appellate Procedure in Civil Cases (1941), is now dated but is very valuable for historical purposes. *See also* Hazard, After the Trial Court: The Realities of Appellate Review, *in* The Courts, the Public and the Law Explosion (Jones ed. 1965); Carrington, The Function of the Civil Appeal: A Late-Century View, 38 S.C.L. Rev. 411 (1987).

2. *See* Fed. R. App. P. 4(a)(1, 2); Fed. R. Civ. P. 58; § 12.4, note 4, *supra.*

3. *See* Fed. R. App. P. 3. Both sides may appeal. *See* Stern, When to Cross-Appeal or Cross-Petition: Certainty or Confusion, 87 Harv. L. Rev. 763 (1974).

4. Fed. R. App. P. 3(c). *See also* Torres v. Oakland Scavenger Co., 487 U.S. 312, 108 S.Ct. 2405, 101 L.Ed.2d 285 (1988).

5. Chathas v. Smith, 848 F.2d 93 (7th Cir.1988).

6. Fed. R. App. P. 2: "In the interest of expediting decision, or for other good cause shown, the court of appeals may, except as otherwise provided in Rule 26(b), suspend the requirements or provisions of any of these rule in a particular case on application of a party or on its own motion and may order proceedings in accordance with its direction."

7. The Supreme Court has referred to Rule 3 (how to take an appeal) and Rule 4 (when to take it) as a single jurisdictional threshold. Torres v. Oakland Scavenger Co., 487 U.S. 312, 315, 317, 108 S.Ct. 2405, 2408, 2409, 101 L.Ed.2d 285, 290 (1988). *See also* State Trading v. Assuranceforeningen Skuld, 921 F.2d 409 (2d Cir.1990).

jurisdiction, which should depend on whether, in form and content, the papers on file look like an appeal.

In some instances, departure from the rules has been indulged. In *Houston v. Lack*[8] the Court held that a prisoner's *pro se* appeal was not too late when the notice of appeal, although not filed with the clerk of court within the time required, had within that time been given to the prison authorities for filing with the clerk. This was in the teeth of the recognized rule that timeliness of filing an appeal is jurisdictional.[9] Similarly, in *Smith v. Barry*,[10] the Court allowed a prisoner's brief to be treated as a notice of appeal when it was filed within the time limit for such a notice, albeit in the wrong court.

But in *Torres v. Oakland Scavenger Co.*,[11] decided the same day as *Houston v. Lack*, the Court held that omission of the plaintiff-appellant's name from the notice of appeal, through secretarial mistake, resulted in his appeal not being before the court. The Court held that the phrase "et al." did not identify the appellants, and thus the court of appeals never had jurisdiction. This overly technical ruling compelled lower courts to dismiss many appeals during the following years. Fortunately, an amendment to the rules now allows "et al." and similar phrases.[12]

Timeliness

In any event, the notice of appeal must be timely. In many states the procedure requires filing with the trial court, accompanied by service on other parties to the appeal. Timeliness is usually strictly required, much as compliance with a statute of limitations is required in commencing an action in the trial court.[13] It is also commonly held that the time to file an appeal cannot be extended by waiver or estoppel.[14] Certain motions, such as a motion for a new trial, do provide additional time to appeal, since the appeal time begins to run only when they are decided.[15]

Federal Rule of Appellate Procedure 4(a) permits federal district courts to extend the time for filing the notice of appeal providing there is "a showing of excusable neglect or good cause." The courts strictly interpret excusable neglect: "[W]ith the exception of 'extraordinary cases

8. 487 U.S. 266, 108 S.Ct. 2379, 101 L.Ed.2d 245 (1988).

9. *See, e.g.*, Griggs v. Provident Consumer Discount Co., 459 U.S. 56, 103 S.Ct. 400, 74 L.Ed.2d 225 (1982); *cf.* United States v. Locke, 471 U.S. 84, 105 S.Ct. 1785, 85 L.Ed.2d 64 (1985).

10. 502 U.S. 244, 112 S.Ct. 678, 116 L.Ed.2d 678 (1992).

11. 487 U.S. 312, 108 S.Ct. 2405, 101 L.Ed.2d 285 (1988).

12. Fed. R. App. P. 3(c)(1)(A).

13. *See* Fed. R. App. P. 4(a), allowing the trial court to grant an extension of time of up to thirty days. *Compare* Fed. R. App. P. 26(b). *See also* Adams, The Timing of Appeals Under Rule 4(a)(4) of the Federal Rules of Appellate Procedure, 123 F.R.D. 371 (1989); Hall, The Jurisdictional Nature of the Time for Appeal, 21 Ga. L. Rev. 399 (1986). *See also* Osterneck v. Ernst & Whinney, 489 U.S. 169, 109 S.Ct. 987, 103 L.Ed.2d 146 (1989) (strict attitude on timeliness).

14. 9 Witkin, California Procedure § 408 (3d ed. 1985).

15. Fed. R. App. P. 4(a)(4).

where injustice would otherwise result,' few cases will ordinarily qualify"[16] under this standard. Examples that qualify include unforeseen delays in the delivery of the mail and illness of counsel, and Congress in 1990 gave the district courts power to extend the time for appeal on those grounds.[17] "Excusable neglect" and "good cause" are often interpreted as overlapping standards rather than mutually exclusive categories.

The need to ameliorate technical noncompliance with the procedure for taking an appeal is further illustrated in *FirsTier Mortgage Co. v. Investors Mortgage Insurance Co.*[18] The trial court had ruled favorably on defendant's motion for summary judgment, requesting defendant to submit proposed findings and conclusion and saying: "The Court then will modify, add to it, delete and write its own findings of fact and conclusions of law and judgment. . . . " Plaintiff then filed a notice of appeal, designating this order as the judgment appealed. Thereafter, defendant submitted proposed findings and conclusions and the court entered judgment in a separate document as required by Federal Rule of Civil Procedure 58. Plaintiff did not file a new notice of appeal. The Supreme Court held that the notice of appeal was effective under Federal Rule of Appellate Procedure 4(a)(2), which provides that a notice of appeal "filed after the announcement of a decision or order shall be treated as filed after such entry and on the day thereof." If such a defect of prematurity can be cured by rule, it is difficult to see why indulgence of similar errors could not be permitted by case law.

Record on appeal

After a notice of appeal is filed, the record on appeal must be prepared. The appealing party must designate the trial court materials to be included in the record; these may be documents filed in the trial court (such as pleadings and motions) and a transcript of oral proceedings, particularly testimony.[19] Other parties have the privilege of cross-designating other matter if they believe its inclusion necessary to present the case below fully and accurately. Designation is important, for an appellate court is ordinarily required to regard the case as wholly encompassed in the record and will not go beyond it to ascertain what happened in the court below. In older appellate procedure, the appellant was also required to prepare a list of grounds of appeal, variously

16. Reinsurance Co. of Am. v. Administratia Asigurarilor de Stat, 808 F.2d 1249, 1251–1252 (7th Cir.1987) (quoting Advisory Committee Comment to 1966 amendment to Rule 4).

17. 28 U.S.C. § 2107(c). See, *e.g.*, Doctor v. Seaboard Coast Line R. R., 540 F.2d 699 (4th Cir.1976); Islamic Republic of Iran v. The Boeing Co., 739 F.2d 464 (9th Cir. 1984), *cert. denied*, 470 U.S. 1053, 105 S.Ct. 1755, 84 L.Ed.2d 819 (1985).

18. 498 U.S. 269, 111 S.Ct. 648, 112 L.Ed.2d 743 (1991).

19. Fed. R. App. P. 10(a) provides that "[t]he original papers and exhibits filed in the trial court ... and a certified copy of the docket entries" shall be included in the record, together with such part of oral proceedings that may be designated by the parties under Rule 10(b). *See* Annot., 2 A.L.R. Fed. 545.

denominated as a "bill of exceptions," "assignments of error," or the like. Under modern practice, this particularization of the issues is often postponed until the briefs.

Briefs

The parties then submit their briefs. The appellant has a specified time, typically thirty to sixty days from completion of the record, to submit a written brief in support of the appeal.[20] The brief contains a description of the proceedings below, a statement of the questions presented by the appeal, a narrative of the case with references to the record as documentation, the propositions advanced as grounds for reversal or modification of the judgment, and legal authorities and argument believed to support those propositions.[21] Other parties have similar opportunity to submit briefs, also exercisable within specified time limits.

The court then sets the case down for oral argument, unless it finds that unnecessary.[22] Ultimately, it affirms the judgment below, remands for entry of a different judgment, or orders further proceedings. Its decision is embodied in a judgment, and in a mandate that issues to the trial court.[23]

Stay of judgment

A judgment from which an appeal is taken remains in effect until reversed or modified. Accordingly, in most states a judgment may be enforced by execution of a money judgment or by proceedings for contempt to secure compliance with an injunction, unless the judgment's effectiveness is suspended.[24] In a few states, commencing the appeal automatically stays the judgment. Barring this, suspension of a money judgment may ordinarily be obtained by the appellant's posting a bond (called a *supersedeas bond*) to secure payment of the judgment if it is subsequently affirmed, or as otherwise ordered by the court.[25] In the case of an injunction, suspension requires an order of either the trial or appellate court and may be conditioned on a similar bond.[26] In a few extreme cases, courts have held heavy appeal bonds unconstitutional.[27]

20. Fed. R. App. P. 31 allows the appellants forty days after the record is filed in which to serve and file their brief; the appellees have thirty days thereafter in which to file their reply brief.

21. *See* Fed. R. App. P. 28. These and other rules are supplemented by rules applicable in each of the circuits.

22. Fed. R. App. P. 34(a).

23. Fed. R. App. P. 36, 41.

24. *Cf.* Annot., 90 A.L.R.2d 483.

25. Fed. R. Civ. P. 62. As the bond must cover the judgment and interest costs, in large cases it may be prohibitively expensive. *See, e.g.*, Pennzoil Co. v. Texaco, 481 U.S. 1, 107 S.Ct. 1519, 95 L.Ed.2d 1 (1987), where the required bond would have been in excess of $13 billion.

26. *See* Fed. R. App. P. 8; 9 Moore, Federal Practice and Procedure ¶¶ 208.03 *et seq.*; 9 Witkin, California Procedure §§ 323–326 (3d ed. 1985).

27. Lindsey v. Normet, 405 U.S. 56, 92 S.Ct. 862, 31 L.Ed.2d 36 (1972); O'Day v. George Arakelian Farms, Inc., 536 F.2d 856 (9th Cir.1976); see M.L.B. v. S.L.J., 519 U.S. 102, 117 S.Ct. 555, 136 L.Ed.2d 473 (1996).

§ 12.9 Scope of Review

Appellate review is not a retrial of the case, but rather a review of the trial court's determination to discern whether prejudicial error occurred. The rules on scope of review are discussed below.

Error in the record

Review is limited to considering errors revealed in the record.[1] An appellate court will not consider matter that may have been received in the trial court unless it is included in the record on appeal. Ordinarily the appellate court will also refuse to receive evidence of events outside the proceedings below—for example, evidence of jury misconduct that was not presented to the trial court through a vehicle such as a motion for a new trial.[2] The main exception is evidence that a case has become moot. This limitation on the evidentiary matter that an appellate court may consider is one reason why application for relief in the trial court is usually an essential precondition to seeking relief by way of appeal.

Asserted at trial

Apart from the evidentiary problem just considered, the general rule is that a party may not complain to an appellate court of an occurrence in the trial court unless it had objected in the trial court at or promptly after the time of the occurrence.[3] Failure to raise the issue with the trial court precludes any review except for the most manifest error.[4] The underlying concept is that a party should take measures in the trial court that will avoid the commission or consequences of an error so that an appeal will be necessary only insofar as such measures have failed. Arguments raised in a lower court in a perfunctory or underdeveloped manner similarly may be lost on appeal.[5] Sometimes, however, appellate courts will consider issues that were not argued in the trial court. Analysts of the decisions find little pattern in the exceptions, save that they involve issues that appear important at the appeal stage but were neglected by counsel at the trial stage.[6]

§ 12.9

1. *See, e.g.*, Stone, The Scope of Review and Record on Appeal, 2 F.R.D. 317 (1943). *See also* Martineau, Modern Appellate Practice—Federal and State Civil Appeals (1983).

2. *See* Louisell and Degnan, Rehearing in American Appellate Courts, 44 Calif. L. Rev. 627 (1956); Millar, New Allegation and Proof on Appeal in Anglo-American Civil Procedure, 47 Nw. U.L. Rev. 427 (1952). *Compare* Fed. R. App. P. 10(e) (supplementation of the record); 9 Moore, Federal Practice and Procedure ¶ 210.08.

3. *See* Fed. R. Civ. P. 46; Fed. R. Ev. 103.

4. Roberts v. Madigan, 921 F.2d 1047 (10th Cir.1990). *See also* Huddleson, Preserving Your Record on Appeal, 2 Prac. Litigator 71 (1991).

5. Kensington Rock Island Ltd. Partnership v. American Eagle Historic Partners, 921 F.2d 122 (7th Cir.1990).

6. *See* Martineau, Considering New Issues on Appeal: The General Rule and the Gorilla Rule, 40 Vand. L. Rev. 1023 (1987); Martineau, Subject Matter Jurisdiction as a New Issue on Appeal: Reining in an Unruly Horse, 1988 B.Y.U. L. Rev. 1; Dennerline, Pushing Aside the General Rule in Order to Raise New Issues on Appeal, 64 Ind. L.J. 985 (1989).

Asserted on appeal

The principle of adversarial presentation applies in appellate review as well as in trial court proceedings. Accordingly, an appellate court will not ordinarily consider errors not presented in the appeal[7] or arguments belatedly raised after appellee has filed its brief.[8] It usually will not on its own initiative search the record for error. Issues or claims presented in the trial court that are unargued or not raised on appeal will be considered waived or abandoned.[9]

Perhaps the most notorious instance of autonomous decision by an appellate court is the Supreme Court's 1938 decision in *Erie Railroad v. Tompkins.*[10] That case decided an issue neither briefed nor raised at trial or in the court of appeals or in the Supreme Court itself, but one that Justice Brandeis evidently wanted to resolve before his retirement that year.[11] The authority to consider issues not raised by the parties has been justified on the basis of the appellate court's responsibility to notice errors that "affect the fairness, integrity, or public reputation of public proceedings."[12] It is difficult to think of any serious and obvious error that could not be said to come within this definition, but the courts give it a narrow application.

Discretionary rulings

Trial judges have a wide range of discretion in many matters vitally affecting the decision of a case—for example, the scope of discovery, the severance or consolidation of issues for trial, the order of presentation of evidence at trial, and the admissibility of evidence that is not clearly admissible or inadmissible. The appellate court will reverse such discretionary decisions only when it is satisfied that the trial judge was clearly and prejudicially wrong.[13] In practice, the willingness of appellate courts to find an abuse of discretion is likely to vary with the impact of the trial court's ruling: a preliminary injunction delaying a corporate merger receives more appellate attention than a judge's decision to reschedule a trial.[14] Sometimes, moreover, a court will break down a discretionary

7. *See* Vestal, Sua Sponte Consideration in Appellate Review, 27 Fordham L. Rev. 477 (1959); Annot., 42 L.Ed.2d 946 (1976); Jones v. Aero/Chem Corp., 921 F.2d 875 (9th Cir.1990).

8. Najarro v. First Fed. Sav. and Loan Assn. of Nacogdoches, Tex., 918 F.2d 513 (5th Cir.1990).

9. *See, e.g.*, Bhan v. NME Hosps., 929 F.2d 1404 (9th Cir.1991); Cooper v. Sheriff, Lubbock County, Tex., 929 F.2d 1078 (5th Cir.1991).

10. 304 U.S. 64, 58 S.Ct. 817, 82 L.Ed. 1188 (1938).

11. Other decisions reached on the court's own motion include Bender v. Williamsport Area School Dist., 475 U.S. 534, 106 S.Ct. 1326, 89 L.Ed.2d 501 (1986) (issue of standing, therefore considered jurisdictional); Gardiner v. A. H. Robins Co., 747 F.2d 1180 (8th Cir.1984) (trial judge's improper comments noticed).

12. *See* United States v. Atkinson, 297 U.S. 157, 160, 56 S.Ct. 391, 392, 80 L.Ed. 555, 557 (1936).

13. *See* Cooter & Gell v. Hartmarx Corp., 496 U.S. 384, 110 S.Ct. 2447, 110 L.Ed.2d 359 (1990); Rosenberg, Judicial Discretion in the Trial Court, Viewed from Above, 22 Syracuse L. Rev. 635 (1971).

14. Friendly, Indiscretion About Discretion, 31 Emory L.J. 747 (1982).

decision into its components, reviewing rulings of law and findings of fact under the standards usually applicable to them, and reserving the abuse of discretion standard for the trial judge's ultimate balancing of the relevant interests.[15] In addition, once an appellate court has found error infecting a judgment, it enjoys some discretion of its own in determining what procedures should be followed, for example whether the plaintiff should be given a second chance to make its case, or whether on remand the case should be assigned to a different judge.[16]

Prejudicial error

Even when the error is clear, erroneous determinations in the trial court do not warrant reversal unless the appellate court concludes that they materially affected the outcome or involved an important issue of procedural justice.[17] This harmless error principle, like other barriers to appellate reversal, tends to increase the power of trial judges at the expense of appellate judges,[18] or (from another perspective) to protect the latter from too many appeals. In general, the task of the appellate court is to determine whether the judgment can justly be allowed to stand, despite error. Whether an error probably affected the result is the central concern, but it is often hard to know what would have happened had the trial court acted otherwise. Other factors are likely to influence the appellate court's decision as well, for example the impact of the error on the fairness of the trial.

Invited error

A party may not raise on appeal an error that the party invited or provoked the court or the opposite party to commit. Known as the doctrine of "invited error," this has been applied to a wide range of conduct and has been referred to as "a cardinal rule of appellate review."[19] Thus, a plaintiff who "invited" witnesses to make references to inadmissible evidence was not allowed to complain on appeal that the evidence should have been excluded.[20] Similarly, when a plaintiff requested a jury trial on his racial discrimination claim, he could not complain on appeal that it was error to allow the jury to consider it.[21] Invited error

15. *E.g.*, Lawson Products, Inc. v. Avnet, Inc., 782 F.2d 1429 (7th Cir.1986).

16. *E.g.*, Weisgram v. Marley Co., 528 U.S. 440, 120 S.Ct. 1011, 145 L.Ed.2d 958 (2000); United States v. Jacobs, 855 F.2d 652 (9th Cir.1988).

17. 28 U.S.C. § 2111; Fed. R. Civ. P. 61. *See, e.g.*, McDonough Power Equip., Inc. v. Greenwood, 464 U.S. 548, 104 S.Ct. 845, 78 L.Ed.2d 663 (1984); Traynor, The Riddle of Harmless Error (1970); Wright, The Doubtful Omniscience of Appellate Courts, 41 Minn. L. Rev. 751 (1957); *cf.* Kornstein, Bayesian Model of Harmless Error, 5 J. Legal Stud. 121 (1976); Note, Principles for Application of the Harmless Error Standard, 41 U. Chi. L. Rev. 616 (1974).

18. See Yeazell, The Misunderstood Consequences of Modern Civil Process, 1994 Wisc. L. Rev. 631.

19. Crockett v. Uniroyal, Inc., 772 F.2d 1524, 1530 (11th Cir.1985).

20. All Am. Life & Casualty v. Oceanic Trade Alliance Council Intl., Inc., 756 F.2d 474 (6th Cir.1985).

21. Harvis v. Roadway Express, 923 F.2d 59 (6th Cir.1991).

is "a branch of the doctrine of waiver by which courts prevent a party from inducing an erroneous ruling and later seeking to profit from the legal consequences of having the ruling set aside. It is based on reliance interests similar to those that support the doctrines of equitable and promissory estoppel."[22]

These are basic concepts of appellate procedure, not invariable rules. Federal appellate courts, for example, must dismiss a case when subject matter is lacking even though the party seeking dismissal raised no objection below and in fact itself brought the case to federal court.[23] In every jurisdiction, moreover, lines of cases ignore or distort the usual rules, as appellate courts reach for outcomes they consider just notwithstanding the constraints on their legal role. From a litigant's viewpoint, however, these principles must be regarded as rigorous rules because in any given case they may be applied as such.

Limited review of fact issues

Even more fundamental is the principle that an appellate court reviews questions of law and may not substitute its own view of the facts or make new fact findings. Since the effect of a legal principle depends on what the facts are taken to be, this limitation sharply restricts the scope of appellate review. Whether the fact issues in the trial court are determined by a jury or a judge, the appellate court limits itself to inquiring whether they rest on a substantial evidentiary basis. This means, for example, that a lawyer arguing an appeal may not simply state the evidence supporting the client's position; he or she must start with the facts found in the trial court, challenging them to the extent that they lack an evidentiary basis.

Jury findings

The scope of review of factual determinations by a jury has always been limited to whether, on the evidence, the jury "might reasonably" have found as it did—essentially the same test as for a directed verdict, but with the further limitation that the appellate court will ordinarily accord some weight to the trial judge's conclusion on whether the verdict should stand.[24] This scope is based on the belief that those who saw the witnesses testify are best able to appraise their testimony, on the appellate courts' central function of promoting uniformity in the law, and on the role of the jury. In the federal courts, indeed, limited review reflects the Seventh Amendment's mandate that "no fact tried by jury, shall be otherwise re-examined in any Court of the United States, than according to the rules of the common law." Because juries usually render general verdicts that do not specify just what facts they found,[25] the

22. *Id.* at 61.

23. See Martineau, Subject Matter Jurisdiction as a New Issue on Appeal: Reining in an Unruly Horse, 1988 N.Y.U.L. Rev. 1; §§ 2.30, 4.7 *supra*.

24. *See* § 7.3 *supra*.

25. See § 7.23 *supra*.

appellate court will in effect assume that the jury made all factual findings consistent with its verdict and with the judge's instructions that had evidentiary support.[26] This constitutes a further obstacle to reversal. The jury's damage award, if not set aside by the trial court, is particularly resistant to appellate review, except perhaps in the case of punitive damages.[27]

Judge findings

The rule is more complicated when applied to facts found by a judge sitting without a jury. A trial judge sitting "at law" has often been regarded as a surrogate for the jury, and his or her findings have then received corresponding weight. Before the merger of law and equity, however, a trial judge sitting in equity was in some jurisdictions regarded essentially as a special master or hearing officer whose findings were entitled to no special weight except as they rested on assessments of witness credibility (the trial judge having the opportunity, not available to the appellate court, to see and hear the witnesses). Under modern procedure, the rules on the weight of facts found by a judge reflect various combinations of these historical antecedents. Depending on the jurisdiction, the weight of the judge's findings may be equal to the weight of a jury verdict in all cases or only in "law" cases, or it may be somewhere between the weight accorded a verdict and that accorded the findings of a special master.

Federal Rule 52(a)

The widely accepted formula is found in Federal Rule 52(a):

> Findings of fact, whether based on oral or documentary evidence, shall not be set aside unless clearly erroneous, and due regard shall be given to the opportunity of the trial court to judge the credibility of the witnesses.[28]

Prior to its revision in 1985, Rule 52(a) was taken to mean that factual findings based on documentary evidence were accorded the same treatment as legal issues, that is, they were subject to plenary review by

26. E.g., Molnar v. Booth, 229 F.3d 593, 597 (7th Cir.2000); see City of Monterey v. Del Monte Dunes at Monterey, Ltd., 526 U.S. 687, 119 S.Ct. 1624, 143 L.Ed.2d 882 (1999); Chicago & Nw. Ry. v. Bower, 241 U.S. 470, 36 S.Ct. 624, 60 L.Ed. 1107 (1916); Jacobs v. Marks, 182 U.S. 583, 21 S.Ct. 865, 45 L.Ed. 1241 (1901).

27. Gasperini v. Center for Humanities, Inc., 518 U.S. 415, 116 S.Ct. 2211, 135 L.Ed.2d 659 (1996). On punitive damages, see Honda Motor Co. v. Oberg, 512 U.S. 415, 114 S.Ct. 2331, 129 L.Ed.2d 336 (1994); BMW of North America, Inc. v. Gore, 517 U.S. 559, 116 S.Ct. 1589, 134 L.Ed.2d 809 (1996); § 7.29 *supra*.

28. Fed. R. Civ. P. 52(a). *See* Cooper, Civil Rule 62(a): Rationing and Rationalizing the Resources of Appellate Review, 63 Notre Dame L. Rev. 645 (1988); Howard, Rule 52 and the Appellate Process; Appellate Review of Fact Finding in Nonjury Cases, 40 Ala. L. Rev. 575 (1989); Sunderland, A Simplified System of Appellate Procedure, 17 Tenn. L. Rev. 651 (1943); Weiner, The Civil Nonjury Trial and the Law–Fact Distinction, 55 Calif. L. Rev. 1021 (1967); Note, Federal Rule of Civil Procedure 52(a): Applicability of the "Clearly Erroneous" Test to Findings of Fact in All Nonjury Cases, 29 How. L.J. 639 (1986).

the appellate court. But since the trial court was recognized to be a better judge of oral testimony and witness credibility, its rulings on such issues were not to be overturned lightly. In 1985 Rule 52(a) was revised to afford documentary evidence the same standard of review on appeal as witness testimony.

The meaning of "clearly erroneous" in Rule 52(a) is, of course, the nub of the question. The Supreme Court said in *Anderson v. Bessemer City*:

> [A] finding is "clearly erroneous" when although there is evidence to support it, the reviewing court on the entire evidence is left with the definite and firm conviction that a mistake has been committed.... In applying the clearly erroneous standard to the findings of a district court sitting without a jury, appellate courts must constantly have in mind that their function is not to decide factual issues de novo.... If the district court's account of the evidence is plausible in light of the record viewed in its entirety, the court of appeals may not reverse.... [29]

The Court in *Anderson* made clear that such deference was required even when the district court's findings are based on physical or documentary evidence, not just credibility determinations. The Court gave three reasons for this deference to the trial court's findings: 1) The trial court is an expert determiner of fact; 2) duplication of the trial court's efforts in the appellate courts would contribute only negligibly to the accuracy of the fact determination, at a large cost; and 3) the parties have already focused their energies and resources on the trial court's determination.[30]

What was not said is that an appellate court can read documents as well as a trial judge, perhaps better. Moreover, all appeals involve duplication of effort by design, and the focus of effort of the trial court, however intense, was obviously in vain if the trial judge gave the crucial documents an untenable reading. Furthermore, even under the clearly erroneous formula an appellate court's inclination to accept a trial judge's findings can also depend on the extent to which the findings rest on witness credibility (where the trial judge has an obviously superior vantage point) and on the court's unstated degree of confidence in the trial judge's fairness.

"Law" and "fact"

An escape from the restriction of the rule is to call the issue one of law.[31] In *Bose Corp. v. Consumers Union*[32] the Supreme Court stated:

29. 470 U.S. 564, 573–574, 105 S.Ct. 1504, 1511, 84 L.Ed.2d 518, 528 (1985).

30. 470 U.S. at 574–575, 105 S.Ct. at 1512, 84 L.Ed.2d at 529. *But see* Hunt v. Cromartie, ___ U.S. ___, 121 S.Ct. 1452, ___ L.Ed.2d ___ (2001) (using closer review for clear error of findings based mainly on documents and expert testimony).

31. Matsushita Elec. Indus. Co. v. Zenith Radio Corp., 475 U.S. 574, 106 S.Ct. 1348, 89 L.Ed.2d 538 (1986).

32. 466 U.S. 485, 104 S.Ct. 1949, 80 L.Ed.2d 502 (1984).

> Rule 52(a) applies to findings of fact, including those described as "ultimate facts" because they may determine the outcome of litigation.... But Rule 52(a) does not inhibit an appellate court's power to correct errors of law, including those that may infect a so-called mixed finding of law and fact, or a finding of fact that is predicated on a misunderstanding of the governing rule of law ... nor does Rule 52(a) furnish particular guidance with respect to distinguishing law from fact.[33]

The classification of the issue as one of "fact" rather than "law" can be decisive. If the issue is designated as "fact," then the appellate court has the narrow scope of review accorded by Rule 52(a) or by similar standards in state appellate practice. If the issue is classified as one of "law," then the appellate court has plenary and superior authority to determine the question for itself.[34] The court's anticipation of the outcome can affect how it classifies the issue.

The consequences of classification extend beyond a single appeal, as we have already seen when discussing the allocation of fact issues to juries at the trial level.[35] Judges sitting as triers of fact (and sometimes juries) will have broad power to decide issues classified as factual on the facts of each future case, without regard to other cases. Legal issues, in contrast, will be decided by appellate judges seeking to follow uniform rules. How an appellate court classifies an issue depends in part on which of these approaches it considers preferable. Is it possible and desirable to lay down acceptable rules governing an issue, or should it be left to case by case determination?

Pullman-Standard v. Swint

The problem of classification is well illustrated in *Pullman-Standard v. Swint*.[36] That action was brought under Title VII of the Civil Rights Act of 1964 by black employees challenging the validity of a seniority system under a collective bargaining agreement. The system operated by departments rather than on a company-wide basis, and those departments coincided with the lines of job segregation that existed before the Civil Rights Act. The question was whether the seniority system not only had a discriminatory effect but also was the product of an "intention to discriminate because of race." The evidence was entirely documentary, being essentially the various collective bargaining agreements in force before and after the enactment of the Civil Rights Act. The trial judge found no intent to discriminate. The court of appeals reversed:

> An analysis of the totality of the facts and circumstances surrounding the creation and continuance of the departmental system at Pullman–

33. Salve Regina College v. Russell, 499 U.S. 225, 111 S.Ct. 1217, 113 L.Ed.2d 190 (1991).

34. 466 U.S. at 514, 104 S.Ct. at 1967, 80 L.Ed.2d at 525–526.

35. See § 7.18 *supra.*

36. 456 U.S. 273, 102 S.Ct. 1781, 72 L.Ed.2d 66 (1982). *See also* § 7.18 *supra.*

> Standard leaves us with the definite and firm conviction that a mistake has been made.... The obvious principal aim of the [white union] in 1941 was to exclude black workers from its bargaining unit.[37]

The Supreme Court in turn reversed the court of appeals:

> Rule 52 broadly requires that findings of fact not be set aside unless clearly erroneous. It does not make exceptions or purport to exclude certain categories of factual findings.... It does not divide facts into categories; in particular it does not divide findings of fact into those that deal with "ultimate" and those that deal with "subsidiary" facts.
>
> ... [W]hether the differential impact of the seniority system reflected an intent to discriminate on account of race ... as we see it, is a pure question of fact.... It is not a question of law and not a mixed question of law and fact.[38]

Justice Marshall in dissent pointed out that the departmental seniority system in fact isolated the blacks and that in the trial court no legitimate explanation was offered for perpetuating two separate tool and die departments and two separate maintenance departments, and the trial court's error therefore must have been an erroneous understanding of the controlling legal principles. On that basis, the reversal by the court of appeals would have been proper under Rule 52(a). Justice Marshall also could have said, contrary to the majority's opinion, that the courts have recognized a broader scope of review in "certain categories" of facts, such as free speech,[39] as well as distinctions between "ultimate" and "subsidiary" facts[40] and a more liberal test of "clearly erroneous" than that in *Pullman-Standard.*[41]

The Court itself has acknowledged

> the practical truth that the decision to label an issue a "question of law" a "question of fact," or a "mixed question of law and fact" is sometimes as much a matter of allocation as it is of analysis.... [W]here the relevant legal principle can be given meaning only through its application to the particular circumstances of a case, the court has been reluctant to give the trier of fact's conclusions presumptive force and, in

37. Swint v. Pullman–Standard, 624 F.2d 525, 533 (5th Cir.1980).

38. 456 U.S. at 287–289, 102 S.Ct. at 1789, 72 L.Ed.2d at 78–79.

39. *E.g.*, Bose Corp. v. Consumers Union, 466 U.S. 485, 104 S.Ct. 1949, 80 L.Ed.2d 502 (1984); Monaghan, Constitutional Fact Review, 85 Colum. L. Rev. 229 (1985).

40. *E.g.*, Baumgartner v. United States, 322 U.S. 665, 64 S.Ct. 1240, 88 L.Ed. 1525 (1944).

41. *E.g.*, United States v. United States Gypsum Co., 333 U.S. 364, 68 S.Ct. 525, 92 L.Ed. 746 (1948). *See* Goettel, Appellate Fact Finding—and Other Atrocities, 13 Litigation 7 (1986); Nangle, The Ever Widening Scope of Fact Review in Federal Appellate Courts—Is the "Clearly Erroneous Rule" Being Avoided?, 59 Wash. U.L.Q. 409 (1981); Schnapper, Judges Against Juries—Appellate Review of Federal Civil Jury Verdicts, 1989 Wis. L. Rev. 237. *See also* Cooter & Gell v. Hartmarx Corp., 496 U.S. 384, 110 S.Ct. 2447, 2458, 110 L.Ed.2d 359, 378–379 (1990).

so doing, strip a federal appellate court of its primary function as an expositor of the law.[42]

Mixed questions

In *Pullman-Standard* the Supreme Court defined mixed questions of law and fact as "questions in which the historical facts are admitted or established, the rule of law is undisputed, and the issue is whether the facts satisfy the statutory standard, or to put it another way, whether the rule of law as applied to the established facts is or is not violated."[43] Federal courts are divided over the proper standard of review for these mixed law and fact questions. Some circuits apply a clearly deferential standard of reversing only when the lower court decision is "clearly erroneous." Other circuits apply a plenary (de novo) standard of review; the remainder follow a variable standard from case to case.[44]

The deferential standard is exemplified in Judge Posner's language in *Mucha v. King*:[45]

> [T]he main reason for appellate deference to the findings of fact made by the trial court is not the appellate court's lack of access to the materials for decision but that its main responsibility is to maintain the uniformity and coherence of the law, a responsibility not engaged if the only question is the legal significance of a particular and nonrecurring set of historical events.... Review is deferential precisely because it is so unlikely that there will be two identical cases; the appellate court's responsibility for maintaining the uniformity of legal doctrine is not triggered.[46]

The de novo standard, by contrast, has been justified as a necessary review of "ultimate" facts that "entails an examination for legal error of the legal components of those findings."[47]

Remedies for trial court error

The variant standards of review applicable to issues of fact, law, and mixed law and fact require different responses by the appellate court when it finds error. In *Icicle Seafoods v. Worthington*[48] the Supreme

42. Miller v. Fenton, 474 U.S. 104, 114, 106 S.Ct. 445, 451, 88 L.Ed.2d 405, 413 (1985). *See* Buford v. United States, ___ U.S. ___, 121 S.Ct.1276 ___ L.Ed.2d ___ (2001).

43. 456 U.S. at 289 n.19, 102 S.Ct. at 1790 n.19, 72 L.Ed.2d at 80 n.19. *See also generally* Lee, Principled Decision Making and the Proper Role of Federal Appellate Courts: The Mixed Questions Conflict, 64 S. Cal. L. Rev. 235 (1991); Louis, Allocating Adjudicative Decision Making Between the Trial and Appellate Levels: A Unified View of the Scope of Review, the Judge/Jury Question, and Procedural Discretion, 64 N.C.L. Rev. 993 (1986).

44. Lee, Principled Decisionmaking and the Proper Role of Federal Appellate Courts: Mixed Questions Conflict, 64 So. Cal. L. Rev. 235 (1991); Cooper, Civil Rule 52(a): Rationing and Rationalizing the Resources of Appellate Review, 63 Notre Dame L. Rev. 645 (1988).

45. 792 F.2d 602 (7th Cir.1986).

46. 792 F.2d at 605–606.

47. Universal Minerals v. C. A. Hughes & Co., 669 F.2d 98, 102 (3d Cir.1981).

48. 475 U.S. 709, 106 S.Ct. 1527, 89 L.Ed.2d 739 (1986).

Court reversed the court of appeals for independently determining a historical fact—the question whether the respondent's employment was predominantly related to maritime work. The court of appeals had applied a de novo standard of review to that issue, reviewing the record independently and finding that the nature of the predominant task was industrial maintenance, not maritime. The Supreme Court held such independent fact-finding improper:

> If the Court of Appeals believed that the District Court had failed to make findings of fact essential to a proper resolution of the legal question, it should have remanded to the District Court to make those findings. If it was of the view that the findings of the District Court were "clearly erroneous" within the meaning of Rule 52(a), it could have set them aside on that basis. If it believed that the District Court's factual findings were unassailable, but that the proper rule of law was misapplied to those findings, it could have reversed the District Court's judgment. But it should not simply have made factual findings on its own.[49]

Sometimes the Supreme Court has referred to a "substantial basis" test of review[50] without equating it to the "clearly erroneous" standard. The Court may be using these standards interchangeably, but it should not be concluded that they mean the same thing.[51] It is clear that the Court has not abandoned the "clearly erroneous" standard.[52]

C. INTERLOCUTORY APPELLATE REVIEW

§ 12.10 Introduction

Under the final judgment rule, a determination in the course of a trial court proceeding is not reviewable by appeal until judgment has been entered. Longstanding exceptions to the rule have permitted certain types of orders to be treated as the equivalent of a final judgment for purposes of appeal.[1] Modern courts tend to enlarge the category of orders for which interlocutory review may be obtained but to provide that such review may be had only on permission of the court rather than as a matter of right. This trend accepts the final judgment rule as a sound working premise but recognizes that (1) no type of order other than a final judgment is invariably of such importance that it should be appealable as of right, and (2) almost any type of order can be, under

49. 475 U.S. at 714, 106 S.Ct. at 1530, 89 L.Ed.2d at 744–745.

50. *See, e.g.*, New York v. P. J. Video, Inc., 475 U.S. 868, 876, 106 S.Ct. 1610, 1615, 89 L.Ed.2d 871, 881 (1986) ("duty of reviewing court is simply to ensure that the magistrate had a substantial basis"); Massachusetts v. Upton, 466 U.S. 727, 104 S.Ct. 2085, 80 L.Ed.2d 721 (1984).

51. United States v. McKinney, 919 F.2d 405, 409 (7th Cir.1990).

52. *See, e.g.*, Citibank v. Wells Fargo Asia, 495 U.S. 660, 110 S.Ct. 2034, 2040, 109 L.Ed.2d 677, 688 (1990); *cf.* Michigan v. Mosley, 423 U.S. 96, 96 S.Ct. 321, 46 L.Ed.2d 313 (1975).

§ 12.10

1. *See* § 12.4 *supra*.

certain circumstances, an appropriate occasion for corrective action through appellate review.[2]

§ 12.11 Discretionary Interlocutory Appeal

Many jurisdictions have procedures by which some or all types of interlocutory orders may be made appealable on the exercise of judicial discretion.[1] The discretion may be that exercised by the trial court or the appellate court or both.

Federal Rule 54(b)

Rule 54(b), for example, gives the trial court discretion to make an order appealable. Under that rule, when the trial court has determined some of the claims involved in an action and further trial proceedings are in prospect for the remainder, the trial judge may direct entry of judgment on the resolved claims without waiting to include them in a single final judgment later on. If the trial judge does direct entry of a separate judgment, that judgment becomes immediately appealable.[2] This rule does not allow a judge to pluck out any appealworthy issue from a case for immediate review: only a decision resolving a "claim" may be certified.[3] If such a decision has been rendered, the judge must then consider whether there is no just reason for delay, or whether on the contrary an immediate appeal would simply multiply the proceedings.[4]

Interlocutory Appeals Act

Provisions requiring the exercise of discretion by both the trial and appellate court are set forth in 28 U.S.C. § 1292(b), known as the Interlocutory Appeals Act. Under this section, the trial judge may certify that resolving a controlling issue of law as to which there is ground for disagreement may advance the termination of the case, and the appellate court may then agree to accept an appeal from the order.[5] If the trial judge refuses to certify the order, the aggrieved party's only remedies are

2. *See* ABA Standards Relating to Appellate Courts § 3.12.

§ 12.11

1. *See, e.g.*, 28 U.S.C. § 1292(b). *See* Note, Interlocutory Appeals in the Federal Courts Under 28 U.S.C. § 1292(b), 88 Harv. L. Rev. 607 (1975); Tuchler, Discretionary Interlocutory Review in Missouri, 40 Mo. L. Rev. 577 (1975); Note, 42 Tenn. L. Rev. 584 (1975); *cf.* Korn, Civil Jurisdiction of the New York Court of Appeals and Appellate Divisions, 16 Buffalo L. Rev. 307 (1967).

2. *See* Curtiss-Wright Corp. v. General Elec. Co., 446 U.S. 1, 100 S.Ct. 1460, 64 L.Ed.2d 1 (1980); *cf.* Gillespie v. United States Steel Corp., 379 U.S. 148, 85 S.Ct. 308, 13 L.Ed.2d 199 (1964). *See* Comment, Appealability Problems in Nebraska: Advantages of Federal Rule 54(b), 53 Neb. L. Rev. 73 (1974).

3. Liberty Mut. Ins. Co. v. Wetzel, 424 U.S. 737, 96 S.Ct. 1202, 47 L.Ed.2d 435 (1976); Sears Roebuck & Co. v. Mackey, 351 U.S. 427, 76 S.Ct. 895, 100 L.Ed. 1297 (1956).

4. Curtiss-Wright Corp. v. General Electric Co., 446 U.S. 1, 100 S.Ct. 1460, 64 L.Ed.2d 1 (1980); Cold Metal Process Co. v. United Engineering & Foundry Co., 351 U.S. 445, 76 S.Ct. 904, 100 L.Ed. 1311 (1956).

5. *See* references in note 1 *supra*.

to seek an extraordinary writ, contend that it is a collateral order, or await final judgment.[6]

Class certification

A final option, appeal in the discretion of the appellate court alone, now exists for decisions granting or denying class certification.[7] This provision responds to complaints that certification decisions, although not appealable as final judgments,[8] often have an immense impact. If certification is denied, the named plaintiffs may not have the resources to proceed through the case in the hope of ultimately securing reversal, with the result that thousands of class members may in effect lose their rights. If certification is granted, a defendant faces the possibility of immense liability and is therefore likely to settle, so that again ultimate appellate review will never happen. Courts of appeals may use their discretion to allow appeals when one of these prospects looms, and in other situations raising important issues that have in the past eluded review.[9]

In general, these provisions for interlocutory review have worked satisfactorily, moderating the rigors of the final judgment rule without loosing a flood of interlocutory appellate litigation. There is much to be said, however, for a procedure in which trial judges could indicate whether they believe interlocutory appeal would be appropriate for specific orders but in which their adverse views would not foreclose the appellate court from granting review. Such a procedure would combine the elements of § 1292(b) and the California extraordinary writ procedure to represent a better balance of the practical considerations that should govern allowance of interlocutory review.[10] Recent legislation enables the writers of the Federal Rules to provide for immediate appeals in these or other situations without waiting for Congress to act.[11]

§ 12.12 Orders Appealable as of Right

Some orders other than final judgments have been treated as appealable as of right on two bases. One is statutory.[1] Many state statutes provide that an order granting a new trial after a jury verdict is

6. *But see* Gillespie v. United States Steel Corp., 379 U.S. 148, 85 S.Ct. 308, 13 L.Ed.2d 199 (1964).

7. Fed. R. Civ. P. 23(f); § 10.23 *supra*; see Bolin v. Sears, Roebuck & Co., 231 F.3d 970 (5th Cir.2000).

8. Coopers & Lybrand v. Livesay, 437 U.S. 463, 98 S.Ct. 2454, 57 L.Ed.2d 351 (1978).

9. Blair v. Equifax Check Services Inc., 181 F.3d 832 (7th Cir.1999); Prado–Steiman v. Bush, 221 F.3d 1266 (11th Cir. 2000); Solimine and Hines, Deciding to Decide: Class Action Certification and Interlocutory Review by the United States Courts of Appeals under Rule 23(f), 41 Wm. & Mary L. Rev. 1531 (2000).

10. *See* ABA Standards Relating to Appellate Courts § 3.12, Commentary.

11. 28 U.S.C. § 1292(e).

§ 12.12

1. *See, e.g.*, 28 U.S.C. § 1292(a); Cal. Civ. Proc. Code § 904.1. *See also* Stern, Appellate Practice in the United States 79–101 (2d ed. 1989).

appealable, on the theory that the cost and delay of an appeal is ordinarily less burdensome than a retrial that an appellate court may later deem unnecessary.[2] In various jurisdictions other types of orders, such as those sustaining a demurrer or granting a change of venue, are made appealable. In New York many kinds of orders are appealable.[3]

Under 28 U.S.C. § 1292(a)(1), and similar statutes in many states, an order granting an injunction is appealable on the theory that its practical consequences may be severe. The statute is broad enough to include preliminary injunctions, interlocutory orders granting a permanent injunction, and changes or extensions of an existing injunction.[4] Orders denying any of these forms of relief also fall within the statute.[5] The granting of a permanent injunction is immediately appealable, of course, as it is a final decision in the case.

Not every court order, however, counts as an appealable injunction. A temporary restraining order does not qualify, because of its short duration.[6] Ancillary orders, such as those compelling discovery, are not within § 1292(a)(1).[7] The Supreme Court has said that the decision whether an order is an injunction for purposes of appealability should be made by looking at the effect of the order and the potential harm to the parties. *Carson v. American Brands*[8] held that an order refusing to approve a consent decree in an employment discrimination suit pleaded as a class action was appealable as an injunction denial because of its practical effect. "Serious, perhaps irreparable consequences" would follow if an immediate appeal were not allowed.[9]

The other basis on which interlocutory orders have been treated as appealable is decisional law. The decisions proceed from the premise that a particular type of order is either effectually final or that it has been entered as the final disposition of an aspect of the trial proceeding that is

2. *E.g.*, Cal. Civ. Proc. Code § 904.1(d).

3. *See* N.Y. Civ. Prac. L. & R. 5701.

4. *See, e.g.*, Bernard v. Air Line Pilots Assn. Intl., 873 F.2d 213 (9th Cir.1989) (grant of a temporary injunction); Cohen v. Board of Trustees of the University of Medicine, 867 F.2d 1455 (3d Cir.1989) (order reinstating allegedly tenured professor); Adams-Lundy v. Association of Professional Flight Attendants, 792 F.2d 1368 (5th Cir.1986)(extension of injunction);Continuum Co. v. Incepts, Inc., 883 F.2d 333 (5th Cir.1989)(termination of injunction). *See also* Silberman, Injunctions by the Numbers: Less Than the Sum of its Parts, 68 Chi.-Kent L. Rev. 279 (1987).

5. Keyes v. School Dist. No. 1, Denver, Colo., 895 F.2d 659 (10th Cir.1990); Sperry Corp. v. City of Minneapolis, 680 F.2d 1234 (8th Cir.1982).

6. Sampson v. Murray, 415 U.S. 61, 94 S.Ct. 937, 39 L.Ed.2d 166 (1974); § 5.16 *supra*.

7. Gardner v. Westinghouse Broadcasting Co., 437 U.S. 478, 98 S.Ct. 2451, 57 L.Ed.2d 364 (1978)(denial of class certification not denial of injunction even though it reduces scope of any final injunctive relief). See 9 Moore, Federal Practice and Procedure ¶ 110.20(1), for a list of orders not considered to be injunctive in nature, that is, discovery orders, orders denying remand, and orders granting an attachment.

8. 450 U.S. 79, 101 S.Ct. 993, 67 L.Ed.2d 59 (1981).

9. *See also* Gulfstream Aerospace Corp. v. Mayacamas Corp., 485 U.S. 271, 108 S.Ct. 1133, 99 L.Ed.2d 296 (1988).

separate from or "collateral" to the main litigation.[10] An example of this is the well-settled case law that treats an order denying a motion to intervene as a matter of right as a final, appealable order.[11]

The procedure for appealing an interlocutory order subject to appeal as of right is generally the same as that for appealing a final judgment. An appeal from the grant or denial of a preliminary injunction does not stay the underlying action unless the trial or appellate court decides otherwise.

§ 12.13 Extraordinary Writ Review

Prohibition and mandamus

Another device for escape from the final judgment rule, and one that has been used with increasing frequency, is review by a writ of mandamus or prohibition emanating from the appellate court. The English court of King's Bench used these writs to control inferior courts and administrative bodies. The theory of the writs is that by issuing an order the trial court has exceeded its jurisdiction (thus making prohibition appropriate), or by refusing to issue an order it has failed to fulfill a mandatory judicial obligation (making mandamus appropriate). In form the writ proceeding used to begin with a petition in the appellate court naming the trial judge as defendant, but that is no longer done, and it is the opposing party who responds to the petition and argues that the writ should not issue.[1]

When available

The Supreme Court has described the remedy of mandamus as "a drastic one to be invoked only in extraordinary situations. Only exceptional circumstances amounting to a judicial 'usurpation of power' will justify the invocation of this extraordinary remedy."[2] Mere doubt of the trial court's subject matter jurisdiction is insufficient to invoke the appellate court's writ power.[3] It must be shown that the lower court's jurisdictional usurpation was "clear and indisputable" and that no other adequate means exist to obtain relief.[4]

Although mandamus is disfavored and used rarely and reluctantly by the federal courts, under some circumstances it is proper. Five

10. *See* § 12.4 *supra*.

11. United States v. South Fla. Water Management Dist., 922 F.2d 704 (11th Cir. 1991); United States Envtl. Protection Agency v. City of Green Forest, Ark., 921 F.2d 1394 (8th Cir.1990); Sellers v. United States, 709 F.2d 1469 (11th Cir.1983); *see* § 10.17 *supra*.

§ 12.13

1. Fed. R. App. P. 21.

2. Will v. United States, 389 U.S. 90, 95, 88 S.Ct. 269, 273, 19 L.Ed.2d 305, 309 (1967). *See* 28 U.S.C. § 1651; Gulfstream Aerospace Corp. v. Mayacamas Corp., 485 U.S. 271, 108 S.Ct. 1133, 99 L.Ed.2d 296 (1988); Berger, The Mandamus Power of the United States Courts of Appeal, 31 Buff. L. Rev. 37 (1982).

3. In re School Asbestos Litig., 921 F.2d 1310 (3d Cir.1990).

4. *Id.* at 1314.

guidelines are used by the federal courts to determine whether mandamus is the appropriate remedy in a given case:

1. whether the party seeking the writ has no other adequate means, such as direct appeal, to attain the relief desired;
2. whether the petitioner will be damaged or prejudiced in a way that is not correctable on appeal;
3. whether the district court's order is clearly erroneous as a matter of law;
4. whether the district court's order is an oft-repeated error or manifests persistent disregard for the Federal Rules;
5. whether the district court's order raises new and important problems or issues of law of first impression.[5]

Careful comparison of these standards with the definition of "collateral order"[6] reveals overlap. This is not surprising, since both concepts are devices for escaping the final judgment rule. The careful practitioner seeking to obtain appellate review of a trial court interlocutory ruling therefore may use both devices. Review will be sought by the procedure for an appeal, asserting that the ruling is a collateral order. Concurrently, review will be sought by petition for writ of mandamus, asserting that the ruling is in excess of jurisdiction and meets the definition in formulations such as the one stated above. Even when the exceptional circumstances under which the writ may be issued are found to exist, the party seeking mandamus bears the burden of demonstrating a clear and indisputable right to the issuance of the writ.[7]

Flexibility

Beyond this, it is difficult to generalize the circumstances under which such a writ may be granted.[8] Any serious procedural misadventure can be characterized as "jurisdictional," and the proclivity for resorting to this characterization varies widely from one jurisdiction to another. Under the practice in California, and to a lesser degree in a few other

5. In re Cement Antitrust Litig., 688 F.2d 1297, 1301 (9th Cir.1982). *See also* Mallard v. United States Dist. Court, 490 U.S. 296, 109 S.Ct. 1814, 104 L.Ed.2d 318 (1989); In re Blodgett, 502 U.S. 236, 112 S.Ct. 674, 116 L.Ed.2d 669 (1992).

6. *See* § 12.4 *supra.*

7. United States v. Noriega, 917 F.2d 1543 (11th Cir.1990).

8. *See, e.g.*, Schlagenhauf v. Holder, 379 U.S. 104, 85 S.Ct. 234, 13 L.Ed.2d 152 (1964) (discovery order requiring medical examinations); Dairy Queen, Inc. v. Wood, 369 U.S. 469, 82 S.Ct. 894, 8 L.Ed.2d 44 (1962)(denial of jury trial); La Buy v. Howes Leather Co., 352 U.S. 249, 77 S.Ct. 309, 1 L.Ed.2d 290 (1957) (order referring case for hearing before master). *But see* Kerr v. United States Dist. Court, 426 U.S. 394, 96 S.Ct. 2119, 48 L.Ed.2d 725 (1976) (circumstances insufficient for review of discovery order by mandamus); Allied Chem. Corp. v. Daiflon, Inc., 449 U.S. 33, 101 S.Ct. 188, 66 L.Ed.2d 193 (1980) (order granting new trial not appealable and "rarely, if ever, will justify the issuance of a writ of mandamus"); 9 Moore, Federal Practice and Procedure ¶¶ 110.26 *et seq. See also* Thornburg, Interlocutory Review of Discovery Orders: An Idea Whose Time Has Come, 44 Sw. L.J. 1045 (1990) (discussing use of mandamus).

states, the writ procedure has become a routine method of seeking interlocutory appellate review; the writ is ordinarily allowed whenever the question presented is either of great practical importance in a particular case or of general importance as a matter of procedural law.[9] In other jurisdictions, including the federal system, the writs are much more sparingly granted and are available only when the need for immediate appellate review is both obvious and extreme.[10]

The use of extraordinary writs for interlocutory review involves little less than a perversion of the concept of "jurisdiction"; certainly the concept has a far broader meaning in this context than when it is used to refer to the authority of the trial court to enter a valid judgment in the case pending before it.[11] The writ procedure has, however, introduced into appellate practice a device of great flexibility and practical utility. The procedure is bounded by much stricter time limits than an appeal, involves a relatively simple record, concerns almost purely legal issues, and permits the appellate court to consider giving relief only in cases in which the application shows a strong justification for doing so. Nevertheless, the writ procedure would be unnecessary if "ordinary" interlocutory review were less restricted in its availability.

D. EXTRAORDINARY RELIEF FROM JUDGMENT

§ 12.14 Introduction

Direct and collateral attack

The problem considered now is that of obtaining relief from a judgment when neither a "normal" postjudgment motion[1] nor an appeal will avail. This problem most often arises when the time has expired within which those remedies may be pursued. It can also arise when the effect of a judgment is called into question in a subsequent action. The "normal" postjudgment motions and appeal are usually termed "direct attack" on a judgment, while the procedures considered below are often collectively referred to as "collateral attack." The latter term is imprecise, however, for it includes some obsolete procedures as well as modern procedures that are no less direct than a motion for a new trial.[2]

Historically, the common law court had several procedures to modi-

9. *See, e.g.*, Buckeye Boiler Co. v. Superior Court, 71 Cal.2d 893, 458 P.2d 57, 80 Cal.Rptr. 113 (1969). In California, mandamus is called "mandate."

10. In Allied Chem. Corp. v. Daiflon, Inc., 449 U.S. 33, 101 S.Ct. 188, 66 L.Ed.2d 193 (1980), the Supreme Court summarily reversed an attempt by the court of appeals to provide appellate review, by means of extraordinary writ, of an order granting a new trial.

11. *See, e.g.*, Abelleira v. District Court of Appeal, 17 Cal.2d 280, 109 P.2d 942 (1941).

§ 12.14

1. *See* §§ 12.2–12.3 *supra*.

2. Comment, The Value of the Distinction Between Direct and Collateral Attacks on Judgments, 66 Yale L.J. 526 (1957).

fy, reopen, or vacate a judgment.[3] Another remedy was the suit in equity whereby a party could avoid a common law judgment on the basis of matter that could not be pleaded in a common law action, such as fraud or mistake in the transaction that was the subject of suit.[4] A third remedy was the interposition of a plea of invalidity against a judgment that had been set up by an adverse party in a subsequent action.[5] These devices were relatively remote in time and forum from the original judgment and were denominated collateral attack. There were, so to speak, degrees of collaterality; to some extent there still are.

§ 12.15 Rule 60(b) Relief

Although rarely successful, some parties seek to continue litigating even after final judgment and appeal. As exemplified by Federal Rule 60(b), modern procedural rules authorize a postjudgment motion, made in the court that rendered the judgment, through which relief can be obtained that previously had to be sought through one of the devices mentioned above.[1] The grounds for relief under Rule 60(b) include three that must be asserted within one year: mistake and excusable neglect, newly discovered evidence, and fraud. There are also three grounds on which no time limit is imposed: when the judgment is void, when the judgment has been satisfied or ought no longer to have prospective effect, and "any other reason justifying relief from the judgment." The 60(b) motion supersedes all but two of the older devices for obtaining relief from a judgment. The first is the independent suit in equity to set aside a judgment; the other is the interposition of a contention that a judgment is void when that judgment is relied on in a second action.[2]

This remedial scheme poses two basic problems. The first arises from the categorical system of Rule 60(b) itself: if the motion is made more than one year after the judgment, do the circumstances relied on fall within one of the first three categories (in which event relief may not be obtained) or within one of the second three categories? The other

3. *See generally* Orfield, The Writ of Error Coram Nobis in Civil Practice, 20 Va. L. Rev. 423 (1934); Harris v. Hardeman, 55 U.S. (14 How.) 334, 14 L. Ed. 444 (1852).

4. *See* § 1.5 *supra*.

5. *See* Fraser, Reopening of Judgments by the Plaintiff, 42 Iowa L. Rev. 221 (1957); Klingbiel, Relief from Judgments, 1951 U. Ill. L.F. 121; Comment, The Value of the Distinction Between Direct and Collateral Attacks on Judgments, 66 Yale L.J. 526 (1957); Note, Post-Term Vacation of Judgments Obtained by Perjury, 54 Colum. L. Rev. 403 (1954).

§ 12.15

1. Fed. R. Civ. P. 60(b) was derived from Cal. Civ. Proc. Code § 473. *See* Note, History and Interpretation of Federal Rule 60(b), 25 Temp. L.Q. 77 (1951); Restatement (Second) of Judgments ch. 5, Introductory Note; Note, Relief from Final Judgment Under Rule 60(b)(1) Due to Judicial Errors of Law, 83 Mich. L. Rev. 1571 (1985). When a case has been appealed, parties occasionally move for recall of the appellate court's mandate instead of filing a Rule 60(b) motion in the trial court, usually with no greater success. See Calderon v. Thompson, 523 U.S. 538, 118 S.Ct. 1489, 140 L.Ed.2d 728 (1998).

2. *See, e.g.*, Durfee v. Duke, 375 U.S. 106, 84 S.Ct. 242, 11 L.Ed.2d 186 (1963) (prior judgment set up defensively); Conn v. Whitmore, 9 Utah 2d 250, 342 P.2d 871 (1959) (prior judgment sued on in sister state).

problem is whether, and in what circumstances, resort may be made to one of the other remedies, that is, the independent suit in equity or interposing the "voidness" of a judgment when the judgment is relied on in a second action. These problems are to some extent intertwined. The artless system of categories in Rule 60(b) leaves in doubt when relief can be obtained pursuant to that Rule; that doubt, in turn, can be a reason for affording relief through one of the other remedies.[3] The discussion that follows will first consider Rule 60(b).

Prerequisites

Rule 60(b) does not explicitly state that an applicant for relief must show anything more than the existence of one of the circumstances referred to in the Rule. Except when the judgment is "void," however, the decisional law, much of it derived from administration of the older collateral attack remedies, requires that the following conditions be satisfied:

1. The moving party must have acted with reasonable promptness and diligence after having discovered the grounds on which the motion is based. Diligence after discovery is required even within the one-year limit imposed on the first three categories of 60(b) relief.[4]
2. The moving party must have a claim or defense of substantial merit that can be asserted if the judgment is set aside.[5]
3. Granting the motion must not unfairly jeopardize interests of reliance that have taken shape on the basis of the judgment.[6]
4. The grounds advanced must not have been previously adjudicated in the original action[7] or in some previous effort to obtain relief from the judgment and must not be grounds the applicant could have asserted by appeal from the judgment.[8]

Rule 60(b) and appeals

Rule 60(b) states that "a motion under this subdivision (b) does not

3. *See generally* Kane, Relief from Federal Judgments: A Morass Unrelieved by a Rule, 30 Hastings L.J. 41 (1978); Comment, Rule 60(b): Survey and Proposal for General Reform, 60 Calif. L. Rev. 531 (1972); Note, Relief from Final Judgment Under Rule 60(b)(1) due to Judicial Errors of Law, 83 Mich. L. Rev. 1571 (1985).

4. *See* 11 Wright and Miller, Federal Practice and Procedure § 2866.

5. *See, e.g.*, Assmann v. Fleming, 159 F.2d 332 (8th Cir.1947); *cf.* Handley v. Mortland, 54 Wash.2d 489, 342 P.2d 612 (1959).

6. *See, e.g.*, Collins v. City of Wichita, 254 F.2d 837 (10th Cir.1958); Menashe v. Sutton, 90 F.Supp. 531 (S.D.N.Y.1950); Shammas v. Shammas, 9 N.J. 321, 88 A.2d 204 (1952).

7. *See* Durfee v. Duke, 375 U.S. 106, 84 S.Ct. 242, 11 L.Ed.2d 186 (1963).

8. *See* Ackermann v. United States, 340 U.S. 193, 71 S.Ct. 209, 95 L.Ed. 207 (1950); *e.g.*, Flett v. W. A. Alexander & Co., 302 F.2d 321 (7th Cir.1962). On all of these points, see also Restatement (Second) of Judgments §§ 67–72, 74.

affect the finality of a judgment or suspend its operation."[9] Hence, a Rule 60(b) motion does not toll the time for appeal from the final judgment,[10] and an appeal from a denial of a Rule 60(b) motion brings only that ruling up for review, not the entire final judgment.[11] Because Rule 60(b) provides a forum for raising the issues it covers in the trial court, they cannot be asserted for the first time in the appellate court;[12] when appropriate, the appellate court can be requested to remand the case to the trial court.[13] During the pendency of an appeal, however, the trial court is divested of jurisdiction and cannot grant relief under Rule 60(b) (although some courts say that it may deny relief) except with permission of the appellate court or on remand.[14]

A Rule 60(b) motion applies only to final judgments, orders, or proceedings. It does not govern relief from interlocutory orders, which are left to the trial court that rendered them.[15] Hence, an adjudication of one or more, but not all, of the issues in a lawsuit, or an adjudication as to less than all the parties, is interlocutory, since it is subject to revision at any time before all issues of all parties have been adjudicated, and thus is not susceptible to a Rule 60(b) motion for relief.[16]

Default judgments

Rule 60(b) and the analogous rules of some states do not formally differentiate between relief from a default judgment and relief from other judgments. Rule 60(b) might well have been better drawn if it had done so, because relief from default judgments constitutes the most frequent occasion for resort to the Rule and because the courts consistently show solicitude to these applicants. Furthermore, the problem of default judgments clearly reveals the ambiguity of the Rule's categorical structure.

Default can result when a plaintiff fails to prosecute the action by failing to complete pretrial preliminaries or to appear on the day of trial; default also can occur when a defendant is guilty of similar failures or fails to make any appearance at all.[17] Default can be the consequence of

9. Fed. R. Civ. P. 60(b).

10. 7 Moore, Federal Practice and Procedure ¶ 60.29.

11. Center for Nuclear Responsibility v. United States Nuclear Regulatory Commn., 781 F.2d 935 (D.C.Cir.1986).

12. Weisman v. Charles E. Smith Management, 829 F.2d 511 (4th Cir.1987); Lasky v. Continental Prods. Corp., 804 F.2d 250 (3d Cir.1986).

13. *See* 7 Moore, Federal Practice and Procedure ¶ ¶ 60.20, 60.28; Long v. Bureau of Economic Analysis, 646 F.2d 1310 (9th Cir.1981); *cf.* Calderon v. Thompson, 523 U.S. 538, 118 S.Ct. 1489, 140 L.Ed.2d 728 (1998).

14. Venen v. Sweet, 758 F.2d 117 (3d Cir.1985); SEC v. Johnston, 143 F.3d 260 (6th Cir.1998); Boyko v. Anderson, 185 F.3d 672 (7th Cir.1999). *See also* 7 Moore, Federal Practice and Procedure ¶ 60.30.

15. Fed. R. Civ. P. 60(b). *See also* Adams v. Lever Bros. Co., 874 F.2d 393 (7th Cir.1989); United States v. Baus, 834 F.2d 1114 (1st Cir.1987).

16. 7 Moore, Federal Practice and Procedure ¶ 60.20.

17. There is a distinction between a default, which occurs when the court notices that the time has expired in which the party involved should have taken a procedural step but has not, and a default judg-

several other eventualities: the party or its attorney may not actually have received notice of the action or the scheduling of one of its stages, such as the pretrial conference or the trial itself; the party's attorney may have failed to act in a timely manner on behalf of his or her client; the party may have relied on some third person, such as the insurer, to take care of representing it, but the third party failed to do so; the party may have relied on a technical defect in the proceedings, such as invalid service of process, which it supposed would render the proceedings void.

Void judgments

If the Rule 60(b) motion is made within one year of the judgment and the conditions stated above have been met, relief from unintentional default is readily granted under the provision in Rule 60(b)(1) governing "excusable neglect."[18] But what can be done if the motion is made after the year has passed? One possibility is to consider the judgment void and hence within Rule 60(b)(4). Although a judgment ordinarily is considered void only if it is rendered without service of process or perhaps by a court whose lack of subject matter jurisdiction is plain, in the context of default judgments the decisions strain to find voidness when equitable considerations militate in favor of setting aside a default.[19] If the circumstances are extreme, another option is to find "any other reason justifying relief" within Rule 60(b)(6). The difficulty is that default, even in extreme circumstances, is necessarily the result of inaction and, therefore, is in some sense "neglect." Since "neglect" is referred to in Rule 60(b)(1), which is governed by the one-year limitation, the problem comes down to distinguishing defaults that are excusable within one year and defaults that are excusable thereafter.[20]

Beyond the difficulty of formulating criteria for such a distinction lies a further anomaly: If the motion must be denied because it was made more than one year after the default, the applicant may still succeed if he or she proceeds not by a Rule 60(b) motion but by independent suit in equity,[21] perhaps even in the same court.

ment, which is the order disposing of the action that may thereafter be entered. *See* Fed. R. Civ. P. 55(a), 55(b). Only when a judgment has been entered can Rule 60(b) become operative. *See* Fed. R. Civ. P. 55(c).

18. *See* In re Cendant Corp. Prides Litigation, 234 F.3d 166 (3d Cir.2000) (minor lateness); Restatement (Second) of Judgments § 67; Comment, Relief from Default Judgments Under Rule 60(b), 49 Fordham L. Rev. 956 (1981).

19. *See, e.g.*, Robinson Engineering Co. v. George, 223 F.3d 445 (7th Cir.2000)(improper service); Newball v. Offshore Logistics Intl., 803 F.2d 821 (5th Cir.1986) (excusable neglect); *cf.* Bass v. Hoagland, 172 F.2d 205 (5th Cir.1949) (failure to give notice of trial date). The most thinly adorned way of setting aside a default judgment is to say that the complaint on which it was based had failed to state a cause of action. *See, e.g.*, C & H Transp. Co. v. Wright, 396 S.W.2d 443 (Tex.Civ.App.1965); *see* Comment, 1 UCLA L. Rev. 195 (1954). *But see* United States v. Cirami, 535 F.2d 736 (2d Cir.1976) (denial of relief against default judgment against neglectful party).

20. *See* United States v. Karahalias, 205 F.2d 331 (2d Cir.1953); *cf.* Pioneer Investment Services Co. v. Brunswick Associates Limited Partnership, 507 U.S. 380, 113 S.Ct. 1489, 123 L.Ed.2d 74 (1993).

21. *Compare* Bass v. Hoagland, 172 F.2d 205 (5th Cir.1949).

Judgment procured by fraud

Motions for Rule 60(b) relief often make claims of fraud. Traditional doctrine distinguishes between "intrinsic" and "extrinsic" fraud, and "fraud upon the court." Intrinsic fraud includes use of perjured testimony or forged evidentiary documents. It was not regarded as a basis for setting aside a judgment since procedures of discovery and cross-examination were considered sufficient protections against this kind of procedural injustice and since a claim of perjury could be the basis for setting aside any judgment based on conflicting testimony. Extrinsic fraud includes bribery of the judge or jury, fraudulently inducing the party not to appear in court, and other stratagems that corruptly frustrate a party's opportunity to have a fair day in court.[22] "Fraud upon the court" refers to conduct that misleads the court, as distinct from misleading the opposing party.[23]

The preceding distinctions have proved just as elusive in applying Rule 60(b) as they were in administering the old equity suit to set aside a judgment. The distinction between intrinsic and extrinsic fraud has long been criticized as unintelligible and anachronistic.[24] The distinction between intrinsic fraud on an opposing party and fraud upon the court assumes that there can be a situation in which false proof is knowingly employed in such a way as to deceive the court but not the opponent. This is difficult to imagine.

Fraud under Rule 60(b)

Rule 60(b) recognizes the distinction among the three types of fraud but deals with them in a way that only compounds the confusion. On one hand, Rule 60(b)(3) now allows a judgment to be set aside within one year on the basis of fraud, whether intrinsic or extrinsic. On the other hand, Rule 60(b)(4) allows a judgment to be set aside after one year if the judgment is void, and some decisions have considered extrinsic fraud as rendering a judgment void.[25] Furthermore, Rule 60(b) expressly recognizes the power of a court to set aside a judgment procured by fraud upon the court through an independent action, though not by motion. Thus, fraud of any kind can be remedied by motion within one year,

22. *See, e.g.*, Kulchar v. Kulchar, 1 Cal.3d 467, 462 P.2d 17, 82 Cal.Rptr. 489 (1969). The leading Supreme Court case is United States v. Throckmorton, 98 U.S. 61, 25 L.Ed. 93 (1878). But see Marshall v. Holmes, 141 U.S. 589, 12 S.Ct. 62, 35 L.Ed. 870 (1891), which seems plainly inconsistent with *Throckmorton*. *See also* Restatement (Second) of Judgments §§ 68, 70. *See also* Note, Relief from Fraudulent Judgments in the Federal Courts: Motion to Vacate or Independent Action—Opposite Sides of the Same Coin, 86 Drake L. Rev. 389 (1987).

23. Hazel-Atlas Glass Co. v. Hartford-Empire Co., 322 U.S. 238, 64 S.Ct. 997, 88 L.Ed. 1250 (1944). *See also* In re Genesys Data Technologies, Inc., 198 F.3d 128 (4th Cir.1999); 7 Moore, Federal Practice and Procedure ¶ 60.33.

24. *See, e.g.*, Shammas v. Shammas, 9 N.J. 321, 88 A.2d 204 (1952). *But see, e.g.*, Schwartz v. Merchants Mortgage Co., 272 Md. 305, 322 A.2d 544 (1974).

25. *See, e.g.*, McKinney v. Boyle, 404 F.2d 632 (9th Cir.1968).

extrinsic fraud perhaps by motion at any time, and fraud upon the court by independent suit.

No procedural policy reason is apparent for this scheme of remedies. The most important variables for determining whether relief from the judgment will be granted are the strength of the proof of fraud (however denominated), the opportunity for having detected it, and the consequences of its commission. It seems fair to suggest that a rule governing fraud cast in these terms would be more easily administered, and no more subversive of the finality of judgments, than the current Rule 60(b).

Difficulty of securing relief for fraud

The standards that must be met in a showing of fraud of any kind in a Rule 60(b) motion are stringent. Rule 60(b) "provides for extraordinary relief which may be granted only upon an adequate showing of exceptional circumstances."[26] Clear and convincing evidence is required. The fraud or misconduct must be so serious that it prevents the appellant from "fully and fairly"[27] presenting his or her case. In *Paige v. Sandbulte,*[28] for example, there were allegations that a personal injury plaintiff perjured himself at trial on the extent of his postaccident work activities. The court held that even if such perjury were committed, the defendant would not be entitled to a vacation of the adverse judgment unless he could show that he was prevented from "fully and fairly" presenting his case.[29]

A similar standard was applied in *Anderson v. Cryovac, Inc.,*[30] involving the intentional concealment of materials requested in discovery. Failure to disclose or produce these materials, even if accidental, may constitute misconduct within the meaning of Rule 60(b)(3). But to obtain a retrial, "the moving party must demonstrate misconduct—like fraud or misrepresentation—by clear and convincing evidence, and must then show that the misconduct foreclosed full and fair preparation or presentation of its case."[31] The misconduct need not alter the result to merit Rule 60(b)(3) relief.[32] The court recognized that "lack of access to *any* discoverable material forecloses 'full' preparation for trial since the material in question will be missing," but "the concealed evidence may turn out to be cumulative, insignificant, or of marginal relevance."[33] The proposed solution was that, as a consequence of the discovery miscon-

26. United States v. Young, 806 F.2d 805, 806 (8th Cir.1986), *cert. denied,* 484 U.S. 836, 108 S.Ct. 117, 98 L.Ed.2d 76 (1987).

27. E. F. Hutton & Co. v. Berns, 757 F.2d 215, 217 (8th Cir.1985).

28. 917 F.2d 1108 (8th Cir.1990).

29. *Id.* at 1111.

30. 862 F.2d 910 (1st Cir.1988).

31. *Id.* at 923. *See also* In re M/V Peacock, 809 F.2d 1403 (9th Cir.1987); Harre v. A. H. Robins Co., 750 F.2d 1501 (11th Cir. 1985).

32. Wilson v. Thompson, 638 F.2d 801 (5th Cir.1981).

33. Anderson v. Cryovac, Inc., 862 F.2d 910, 924 (1st Cir.1988) (emphasis in original).

duct, "the challenged behavior must *substantially* have interfered with the aggrieved party's ability fully and fairly to prepare for and proceed at trial."[34] It would be sufficient to show that the "concealment precluded inquiry into a plausible theory of liability, denied access to evidence that would have been probative on an important issue, or closed off a potentially fruitful avenue of direct or cross examination."[35] It may be presumed that the suppressed evidence was damaging to the party who suppressed it, but this is a rebuttable presumption.

Newly discovered evidence

Newly discovered evidence is another commonly used basis on which to seek relief from a judgment. Under Rule 60(b)(2), newly discovered evidence may be relied on only by a motion made within one year of the judgment. But even within this time limit the chances of obtaining relief on this ground are usually remote. The court must be convinced not only that the conditions mentioned above have been met but also that the new evidence would likely lead to a different decision on the merits and that the evidence could not have been uncovered through normal discovery procedures or within the time allotted for a new trial motion immediately after trial. Under Rule 60(b)(2), it is the *discovery* of the evidence that falls within the time limit of one year; the evidence itself must have existed at the time of the judgment.[36] In view of the abundant armory of modern discovery devices, these conditions are rarely present.[37]

Change in law

A somewhat similar ground on which to seek relief from judgment is a decisive change in the governing law after the judgment has become final. Neither the traditional doctrine of collateral attack nor the scheme of Rule 60(b) deals with this problem. The courts have generally undertaken to subsume it under Rule 60(b)(6)—"other reason justifying relief"—but so far have had difficulty formulating criteria for deciding what kind of change in the law is "reason" enough. The importance of the problem rises in proportion to the rate of change in the law; it therefore promises to be far more troublesome in the future than it has been in the past. Little imagination is required to foresee that if much latitude were given to change in the law as a basis for setting aside a judgment, judgments depending on questions of law would be effectively final only in static areas of the law. One proposed solution would inquire whether the judgment was "based" on a decision that has changed.[38] In

34. *Id.* (emphasis in original).

35. *Id.* at 925.

36. New England Mut. Life Ins. Co. v. Anderson, 888 F.2d 646 (10th Cir.1989).

37. *See* 11 Wright and Miller, Federal Practice and Procedure ¶ 2859.

38. *See* Comment, Federal Rule of Civil Procedure 60(b): Standards for Relief from Judgments Due to Changes in Law, 43 U. Chi. L. Rev. 646 (1976). *See also* Annot., 53 A.L.R. Fed. 558.

practice, courts tend to limit this ground for relief to judgments that have continuing effect, such as long-term injunctions (discussed below) and determinations of status, and even then to impose additional requirements.[39]

Modifying injunction

Courts are far more willing to reconsider an injunction or other equitable decree having continuing effects because of new legal or factual developments than they are a money judgment. It is one thing to say that, once a money judgment has been paid and appeals have been exhausted, the transaction is over, and quite another to say that a party may be required under threat of contempt sanctions to continue complying with an injunction that no longer makes legal or factual sense. Likewise, there seems little reason why a court should devote its resources to enforcing such an injunction. Hence Rule 60(b)(5) allows relief when "it is no longer equitable that the judgment should have prospective application." Even so, there is a danger that dissatisfied litigants will seek to relitigate matters that have already been decided on the basis of more or less implausible claims of new developments, with resulting waste of time and money. A balancing of interests is therefore called for.

Sometimes, resort to Rule 60(b) is unnecessary because a case is still in a remedial phase during which the court is seeking to shape fair and effective injunctive relief. Especially in institutional reform litigation, relief frequently has an experimental character and must be modified because it does not work or gives rise to new problems or to new forms of resistance. The court has considerable discretion to do this.[40] Ultimately, however, at least in school desegregation cases, the court will conclude that relief has succeeded in eliminating the unlawful condition and its consequences, the case will be closed, and any live injunctions may be terminated.[41]

Increased willingness to modify injunctions

When final injunctive relief remains in effect, however, parties may seek Rule 60(b) relief to modify or end it because of changed conditions.

39. *See* Federated Dept. Stores v. Moitie, 452 U.S. 394, 101 S.Ct. 2424, 69 L.Ed.2d 103 (1981); DeWeerth v. Baldinger, 38 F.3d 1266 (2d Cir.1994); Restatement (Second) of Judgments § 73, Comment *c*; compare *id.* § 28, Comments *b* and *c*; Note, Relief from Final Judgment Under Rule 60(b)(1) Due to Judicial Errors of Law, 83 Mich. L. Rev. 1571 (1985).

40. *E.g.,* United States v. Paradise, 480 U.S. 149, 107 S.Ct. 1053, 94 L.Ed.2d 203 (1987); Hutto v. Finney, 437 U.S. 678, 98 S.Ct. 2565, 57 L.Ed.2d 522 (1978); Wright v. Council of the City of Emporia, 407 U.S. 451, 92 S.Ct. 2196, 33 L.Ed.2d 51 (1972); Griffin v. County School Bd., 377 U.S. 218, 84 S.Ct. 1226, 12 L.Ed.2d 256 (1964).

41. Board of Educ. of Oklahoma City Public Schools v. Dowell, 498 U.S. 237, 111 S.Ct. 630, 112 L.Ed.2d 715 (1991); Freeman v. Pitts, 503 U.S. 467, 112 S.Ct. 1430, 118 L.Ed.2d 108 (1992); see Parker, The Future of School Desegregation, 94 Nw. L. Rev. 1157 (2000). See also 18 U.S.C. § 3626(b)(limiting duration of relief in prison reform cases).

The standards for such relief have changed over the decades. *United States v. Swift*,[42] held that a continuing decree should remain in effect until the bound party can show "a grievous wrong evoked by new and unforeseen conditions."[43] As a result, in the *Swift* case itself several meatpacking companies were prevented for decades from reentering the grocery business, which they were forbidden to do under an antitrust decree to which they had consented, despite claims that any threat to competition had vanished.[44]

There are, however, softer and more recent statements of the required showing. Clear changes in law, such as a new statute, warrant relief from an injunction against conduct that is no longer unlawful.[45] In *United States v. United Shoe Machinery Corp.* the Court observed: "*Swift* teaches ... [that] a decree may be changed upon an appropriate showing, and it holds that it may not be changed ... if the purposes of the litigation as incorporated in the decree ... have not been fully achieved."[46] Although this leaves open what the "purposes" were, it suggests that achieving them is more likely to warrant relief than would protecting defendants from unexpected burdens. But if the burdens were truly unforeseeable when a consent decree in an institutional reform case was originally entered, a significant factual change that makes "compliance with the decree substantially more onerous" may warrant Rule 60(b) relief, and the *Swift* test does not apply.[47] The Supreme Court's greater willingness to grant such relief reflects the flow and ebb of institutional reform litigation as well as the practical problems caused by complex and continuing injunctive relief.

Void judgments

One final ground for relieving a party from a final judgment under Rule 60(b) is that "the judgment is void." The term "void" in this context usually refers to a judgment that is defective because the court

42. 286 U.S. 106, 52 S.Ct. 460, 76 L.Ed. 999 (1932).

43. 286 U.S. at 119, 52 S.Ct. at 464, 76 L.Ed. at 1008. See Jost, From *Swift* to *Stotts* and Beyond: Modification of Injunctions in the Federal Courts, 64 Tex. L. Rev. 1101, 111 (1986).

44. The courts rebuffed several attacks on the *Swift* decree. Swift & Co. v. United States, 276 U.S. 311, 48 S.Ct. 311, 72 L.Ed. 587 (1928); United States v. California Co-operative Canneries, 279 U.S. 553, 49 S.Ct. 423, 73 L.Ed. 838 (1929); United States v. Swift & Co., 286 U.S. 106, 52 S.Ct. 460, 76 L.Ed. 999 (1932); United States v. Swift & Co., 189 F.Supp. 885 (N.D.Ill.1960), aff'd, 367 U.S. 909, 81 S.Ct. 1918, 6 L.Ed.2d 1249 (1961). But see United States v. Armour & Co., 402 U.S. 673, 91 S.Ct. 1752, 29 L.Ed.2d 256 (1971). Finally, sixty years after the consent decree was entered, the United States agreed to its termination. United States v. Swift & Co., 1983–1 Trade Cas. ¶ 65,250 (N.D.Ill.1980).

45. *E.g.*, Agostini v. Felton, 521 U.S. 203, 117 S.Ct. 1997, 138 L.Ed.2d 391 (1997); System Federation No. 91, Ry. Emp. Dept., AFL-CIO v. Wright, 364 U.S. 642, 81 S.Ct. 368, 5 L.Ed.2d 349 (1961); see Miller v. French, 530 U.S. 327, 120 S.Ct. 2246, 147 L.Ed.2d 326 (2000).

46. 391 U.S. 244, 248, 88 S.Ct. 1496, 1499, 20 L.Ed.2d 562, 566 (1968). See Chrysler Corp. v. United States, 316 U.S. 556, 62 S.Ct. 1146, 86 L.Ed. 1668 (1942).

47. Rufo v. Inmates of Suffolk County Jail, 502 U.S. 367, 112 S.Ct. 748, 116 L.Ed.2d 867 (1992).

rendering it lacked jurisdiction.[48] This kind of defect can also be asserted either by an independent suit to set aside the judgment or by seeking to avoid the effect of the judgment when it is relied on in a subsequent proceeding. Jurisdictional defects that render a judgment void are considered below in the discussion of the latter remedy.

§ 12.16 Independent Suit in Equity

Given the wide scope of relief available under the Rule 60(b) motion, the independent suit in equity[1] has lost its former significance. One technical obstacle to such a suit is that when a party can resort to a Rule 60(b) motion, it has a remedy at law that, under conventional doctrines of equity jurisdiction, precludes resort to equity.[2] The independent suit must be employed, however, if the situation in question does not fall within Rule 60(b). And in at least two situations, the suit has a function.

Attack by nonparty

The independent suit is a proper remedy for an attack on the judgment by a person who was not a party to it.[3] Ordinarily, a nonparty has no legal interest in a judgment in an action between others.[4] Such a judgment does not determine the nonparty's rights and obligations under the rules of res judicata, and the nonparty may so assert if the judgment is relied on against him or her. But in some situations a nonparty's interests, especially personal legal status or claims to property, may be placed in practical jeopardy by a judgment between others. In such circumstances a nonparty may seek the aid of a court of equity, but the grounds on which that person may rely are severely limited.

The general rule is that a nonparty must show either that the judgment was void for lack of subject matter jurisdiction or that it was the product of fraud directed at the petitioner.[5] The Supreme Court recently described relief as available only to prevent a grave miscarriage of justice.[6] In *Houck ex rel. United States v. Folding Carton Administra-*

48. 11 Wright and Miller, Federal Practice and Procedure § 2862; § 12.17 *infra.*

§ 12.16

1. *See* Fed. R. Civ. P. 60(b)(rule does not limit court's power to entertain independent action); Comment, Equitable Relief from Judgments, Orders, and Decrees Obtained by Fraud, 23 Calif. L. Rev. 79 (1934); Restatement (Second) of Judgments § 79; *see also* Moore and Rogers, Federal Relief from Civil Judgments, 55 Yale L.J. 623 (1946).

2. *E.g.*, Taft v. Donellan Jerome, Inc., 407 F.2d 807 (7th Cir.1969); Poulos v. Cimini, 86 R.I. 401, 135 A.2d 618 (1957).

3. Restatement (Second) of Judgments §§ 75, 76.

4. In some jurisdictions a nonparty may use a motion similar to that under Rule 60(b) to attack the judgment. *See, e.g.*, Carden v. Otto, 37 Cal.App.3d 887, 112 Cal. Rptr. 749 (1974).

5. *See, e.g.*, Griffith v. Bank of N.Y., 147 F.2d 899 (2d Cir.1945); Shapiro v. DiGuilio, 95 Ill.App.2d 184, 237 N.E.2d 771 (1968). *See* Restatement (Second) of Judgments §§ 69–72.

6. United States v. Beggerly, 524 U.S. 38, 118 S.Ct. 1862, 141 L.Ed.2d 32 (1998)(newly discovered evidence did not warrant reopening judgment quieting title to island).

tion Committee,[7] for example, a complex antitrust litigation produced a large fund in excess of what was needed to fulfill all filed claims. A district court entered a settlement agreement between the parties under which the excess funds would be distributed to the plaintiffs on a pro rata basis. A nonparty who had been helping tardy claimants file their claims thereupon sued on the ground that the agreement was procured through fraud upon the court. On appeal, the court held that the nonparty was without standing to sue under Rule 60(b) because he did not complain of any injury he had suffered as a result of the agreement to distribute the funds. The court stated that there are occasions when a nonparty may attack a fraudulently obtained judgment through an independent action, but the grievant must show a legal interest that was adversely affected by the judgment.

Defense to enforcement proceeding

The other situation involving an independent action arises when the person who obtained the judgment sues on it in another jurisdiction.[8] A defense to the action on the ground that the judgment is void or was procured by fraud is, under merged procedure, allowed without having to commence a new action, but the basis of defense is essentially the same as that asserted by the independent suit in equity.

§ 12.17 Attacking a Void Judgment

A void judgment may be attacked in several ways: (1) by Rule 60(b) motion, regardless whether the motion is made in one year or later;[1] (2) by an independent suit in equity, if for some reason the Rule 60(b) motion would not provide adequate relief;[2] (3) by a denial of the validity of the judgment when it is relied on in a subsequent action; (4) by a Rule 59 motion for a new trial, or by appeal; or (5) by a Rule 50(b) motion for j.n.o.v. The advantage of attacking the judgment under Rule 60(b) is the longer time permitted for the action; the mover must still, however, be diligent. For instance, if new evidence is discovered, or should have been discovered by due diligence, in the ten days after entry of judgment required in time to move for a new trial under Rule 59(b), relief must be sought under that Rule.

Fraud

Many decisions characterize a judgment that has been procured by fraud as void, though more often such a judgment is characterized as voidable. The distinction, and the purpose of making it, has never been clearly or consistently articulated. One purpose of the distinction is to

7. 881 F.2d 494 (7th Cir.1989).

8. Restatement (Second) of Judgments §§ 81, 82; *e.g.*, Britton v. Gannon, 285 P.2d 407 (Okla.1955); Annot., 31 A.L.R.4th 706 (on the application of the Uniform Enforcement of Foreign Judgments Act).

§ 12.17

1. *See* Fed. R. Civ. P. 60(b)(4); Restatement (Second) of Judgments §§ 65, 69.

2. *See* § 12.16 *supra*.

emphasize that the person seeking to nullify the judgment should ordinarily do so by going into the court that rendered the judgment rather than by filing an independent suit. Hence, it has been said that a void judgment can be attacked in an independent suit, but a voidable one must be attacked by a motion similar to that under Rule 60(b). But if the applicant for relief is always required to use a Rule 60(b) motion unless it would not provide adequate relief,[3] then the distinction is unnecessary.

Lack of personal jurisdiction

At any rate, a judgment rendered by a court that lacks jurisdiction is universally characterized as void.[4] Traditionally, such a judgment is a legal nullity. In modern decisions, however, the problem is more complicated.[5] In some situations a court lacking jurisdiction has rendered a judgment that should nevertheless be given effect. Here it is important to distinguish between personal and subject matter jurisdiction.

Personal jurisdiction may be lacking for several reasons: adequate notice may not have been given to the person against whom judgment was rendered;[6] the court may have lacked the required contacts with the case;[7] or, although jurisdiction was secured over a party purporting to represent the person, the representation may have been inadequate.[8] Unless the party somehow learned of the action and made an appearance to contest the exercise of jurisdiction over his or her person,[9] the judgment is void on due process grounds in all these circumstances. Many decisions also hold a judgment void when the party obtained actual notice from a court that had sufficient contacts with the case but the process was not in technical compliance with the rules governing the mechanics of service.[10] Inasmuch as the party had actual notice and could have raised the technical objection by special appearance, however, it is not clear why the judgment should be treated as void, particularly if

3. *See* § 12.16 *supra.*

4. *See* 11 Wright and Miller, Federal Practice and Procedure § 2862. *But see* Honneus v. Donovan, 691 F.2d 1 (1st Cir. 1982) (federal court's mistaken assumption of diversity jurisdiction renders a judgment only erroneous, not void).

5. *See* Restatement (Second) of Judgments §§ 65, 69; Boskey and Braucher, Jurisdiction and Collateral Attack, 40 Colum. L. Rev. 1006 (1940).

6. *E.g.*, Walker v. City of Hutchinson, 352 U.S. 112, 77 S.Ct. 200, 1 L.Ed.2d 178 (1956). *See also* United States v. Brand Jewelers, Inc., 318 F.Supp. 1293 (S.D.N.Y. 1970) (injunction by the United States against procuring judgments on the basis of "sewer service"); *see* Tuerkheimer, Service of Process in New York City: A Proposed End to Unregulated Criminality, 72 Colum. L. Rev. 847 (1972).

7. *E.g.*, Hanson v. Denckla, 357 U.S. 235, 78 S.Ct. 1228, 2 L.Ed.2d 1283 (1958).

8. *See* Restatement (Second) of Judgments § 71(2)(c).

9. *Id.* 65. If the defendant made an appearance and contested jurisdiction, the determination of that issue is res judicata. *See* Durfee v. Duke, 375 U.S. 106, 84 S.Ct. 242, 11 L.Ed.2d 186 (1963); Baldwin v. Iowa State Traveling Men's Assn., 283 U.S. 522, 51 S.Ct. 517, 75 L.Ed. 1244 (1931); § 2.8 *supra*.

10. *See,. e.g.*, Central Operating Co. v. Utility Workers of Am., 491 F.2d 245 (4th Cir.1974). *But see* Restatement (Second) of Judgments § 3.

the statute of limitations has run on the claim by the time the judgment is attacked.

Subject matter jurisdiction

The problem of lack of subject matter jurisdiction involves different considerations. The old rule was that a judgment of a court lacking subject matter jurisdiction was a legal nullity.[11] This rule was subject to various saving qualifications—for example, jurisdiction was presumed if the rendering court was one of general jurisdiction, and evidence outside the record was inadmissible to prove lack of jurisdiction. But the rule made judgments potentially vulnerable when a substantial question of subject matter jurisdiction arose.

The modern view takes a different approach, at least when the lack of jurisdiction is not entirely obvious. In this approach the critical questions are, first, whether the party against whom the judgment was rendered had opportunity to litigate the question of jurisdiction in the original action, and, if so, whether there are strong policy reasons for giving a second opportunity to do so. The questions arise in three contexts: if (1) the question of jurisdiction was raised in the original action, (2) the party charged with the judgment appeared in the action but did not raise the jurisdictional question, and (3) the judgment was rendered by default.

Jurisdictional ruling as res judicata

If the question of jurisdiction was raised and adjudicated in the original action, the modern view is that the judgment is not subject to subsequent attack, on the premise that a court has auxiliary jurisdiction to determine its jurisdiction.[12] Although some authorities suggest that this rule is inapplicable to courts of limited jurisdiction, there seems no reason why it should be. An erroneous determination of the jurisdictional question can be remedied by review through appeal or extraordinary writ, and failure to pursue such a remedy should foreclose subsequent disputation of the issue.

Opportunity to challenge in original action

If the party charged with the judgment appeared in the action, there is almost equally strong reason for holding that the question of subject matter jurisdiction may not be raised by subsequent attack on the judgment.[13] By hypothesis the party had opportunity to raise the jurisdic-

11. *See* Dobbs, The Decline of Jurisdiction by Consent, 40 N.C.L. Rev. 49 (1961).

12. Durfee v. Duke, 375 U.S. 106, 84 S.Ct. 242, 11 L.Ed.2d 186 (1963).

13. *See* Restatement (Second) of Judgments § 69; Dobbs, Beyond Bootstrap: Foreclosing the Issue of Subject-Matter Jurisdiction Before Final Judgment, 51 Minn. L. Rev. 491 (1967); *e.g.*, Gschwind v. Cessna Aircraft Co., 232 F.3d 1342 (10th Cir.2000); Moffat v. Moffat, 27 Cal.3d 645, 612 P.2d 967, 165 Cal.Rptr. 877 (1980). *Compare* Moore, Collateral Attacks on Subject Matter Jurisdiction: A Critique of the Restatement (Second) of Judgments, 66 Cornell L. Rev. 534 (1981).

tional defense. There is little reason for saying that defense should survive the judgment when defenses on the merits would not. Moreover, the party who obtained the judgment may be assumed to suppose it is valid and justifiably conduct itself accordingly. Nevertheless, some authorities still adhere to the view that the jurisdictional question can be subsequently raised, by motion under Rule 60(b) or its analogues, by separate suit in equity, or by attacking the judgment when it is relied on by an opponent. Most such cases, however, have involved no intervening reliance interests and have involved either a judgment of a tribunal of limited jurisdiction or an attack on constitutional grounds.[14] Even in these situations courts tend to sustain the judgment except when its enforcement would affect the government itself or the administration of a remedial scheme having significance beyond the immediate parties.

Jurisdictional challenge to default judgment

When the judgment has been entered by default, it is usually regarded as open to attack if rendered without subject matter jurisdiction. When the default was entered without constitutionally adequate notice, the judgment is infirm on due process grounds.[15] If notice was adequate, however, the party can be said to have had opportunity to raise the question of subject matter jurisdiction and should be foreclosed from subsequent opportunity to do so. In any case, however, default judgments are disfavored,[16] especially if the rendering court apparently lacked the authority it purported to exercise. The better rule would hold such a judgment void except when it has given rise to substantial interests of reliance of which the person against whom it was rendered was aware.[17] Binding the person to the judgment in the latter situation can be justified not so much on a principle of res judicata as on one of equitable estoppel,[18] for a judgment is not the only basis on which one's rights may be treated as finally concluded.

14. *See* sources cited *supra* note 13. *See, e.g.*, United States v. United States Fidelity & Guar. Co., 309 U.S. 506, 60 S.Ct. 653, 84 L.Ed. 894 (1940); Jordon v. Gilligan, 500 F.2d 701 (6th Cir.1974).

15. *See* notes 6–8 *supra.*

16. *See* § 12.15 *supra.*

17. *See* Restatement (Second) of Judgments § 69, 74.

18. *See* § 11.32 *supra.*

*

TABLE OF CASES

References are to Pages.

Agostini v. Felton, 521 U.S. 203, 117 S.Ct. 1997, 138 L.Ed.2d 391 (1997), 790
Aguchak v. Montgomery Ward Co., Inc., 520 P.2d 1352 (Alaska 1974), 96, 99
A.H. Robins Co., Inc., In re, 86 F.3d 364 (4th Cir.1996), 666
A.H. Robins Co., Inc., In re, 880 F.2d 709 (4th Cir.1989), 655
Air Crash Disaster Near New Orleans, La. on July 9, 1982, In re, 821 F.2d 1147 (5th Cir.1987), 117
Air Disaster at Lockerbie, Scotland on Dec. 21, 1988, In re, 928 F.2d 1267 (2nd Cir.1991), 175
Air–Sea Forwarders, Inc. v. Air Asia Co., Ltd., 880 F.2d 176 (9th Cir.1989), 488
Air–Shields, Inc. v. Fullam, 891 F.2d 63 (3rd Cir.1989), 157
Ajamian v. Schlanger, 14 N.J. 483, 103 A.2d 9 (N.J.1954), 694
Akers v. Epperson, 172 S.W.2d 512 (Tex. Civ.App.-San Antonio 1942), 424
Alaska Packers Ass'n v. Industrial Acc. Com'n, 294 U.S. 532, 55 S.Ct. 518, 79 L.Ed. 1044 (1935), 174
Albaugh v. Pennsylvania R. Co., 120 F.Supp. 70 (D.D.C 1954), 441
Albemarle Paper Co. v. Moody, 422 U.S. 405, 95 S.Ct. 2362, 45 L.Ed.2d 280 (1975), 205, 512, 533
Alberti v. Empresa Nicaraguense De La Carne, 705 F.2d 250 (7th Cir.1983), 110
Albert Lindley Lee Memorial Hosp., In re, 209 F.2d 122 (2nd Cir.1953), 310
Alden v. Maine, 527 U.S. 706, 119 S.Ct. 2240, 144 L.Ed.2d 636 (1999), 109
Aldinger v. Howard, 427 U.S. 1, 96 S.Ct. 2413, 49 L.Ed.2d 276 (1976), 146, 545
Alexander v. Fulton County, Ga., 207 F.3d 1303 (11th Cir.2000), 563
Alexander v. Tingle, 181 Md. 464, 30 A.2d 737 (Md.1943), 442
Alfred Dunhill of London, Inc. v. Republic of Cuba, 425 U.S. 682, 96 S.Ct. 1854, 48 L.Ed.2d 301 (1976), 82, 614
All American Airways v. Elderd, 209 F.2d 247 (2nd Cir.1954), 650
All American Life and Cas. Co. v. Oceanic Trade Alliance Council Intern., Inc., 756 F.2d 474 (6th Cir.1985), 768
Allegheny County v. Frank Mashuda Co., 360 U.S. 185, 79 S.Ct. 1060, 3 L.Ed.2d 1163 (1959), 151
Allegheny–Ludlum Industries, Inc., United States v., 517 F.2d 826 (5th Cir.1975), 661
Allen v. Giuliano, 144 Conn. 573, 135 A.2d 904 (Conn.1957), 482
Allen v. McCurry, 449 U.S. 90, 101 S.Ct. 411, 66 L.Ed.2d 308 (1980), 676, 711, 721
Allen v. Wright, 468 U.S. 737, 104 S.Ct. 3315, 82 L.Ed.2d 556 (1984), 598
Allenberg Cotton Co., Inc. v. Pittman, 419 U.S. 20, 95 S.Ct. 260, 42 L.Ed.2d 195 (1974), 62, 113, 600
Allen Calculators v. National Cash Register Co., 322 U.S. 137, 64 S.Ct. 905, 88 L.Ed. 1188 (1944), 627
Allied Chemical Corp. v. Daiflon, Inc., 449 U.S. 33, 101 S.Ct. 188, 66 L.Ed.2d 193 (1980), 463, 780, 781
Allis Chalmers Mfg. Co. v. Wichman, 220 F.2d 426 (8th Cir.1955), 450
Allman v. Bird, 186 Kan. 802, 353 P.2d 216 (Kan.1960), 230
Allstate Ins. Co. v. Hague, 449 U.S. 302, 101 S.Ct. 633, 66 L.Ed.2d 521 (1981), 60, 174, 175
Allstate Ins. Co. v. James, 845 F.2d 315 (11th Cir.1988), 478
Allstate Ins. Co. v. James, 779 F.2d 1536 (11th Cir.1986), 574, 579
Alpine Forwarding Co. v. Pennsylvania R. Co., 60 F.2d 734 (2nd Cir.1932), 427
Alton v. Alton, 207 F.2d 667 (3rd Cir.1953), 93
Altoona Electrical, Engineering & Supply Co v. Kittanning & F C St R Co, 126 F. 559 (C.C.W.D.Pa.1903), 495, 518
Altrichter v. Shell Oil Co., 263 F.2d 377 (8th Cir.1959), 464
Aluminum Co. of America v. Admiral Merchants Motor Freight, Inc., 486 F.2d 717 (7th Cir.1973), 725
Alvarez–Machain, United States v., 504 U.S. 655, 112 S.Ct. 2188, 119 L.Ed.2d 441 (1992), 86, 111
Alverez v. J. Ray McDermott & Co , Inc., 674 F.2d 1037 (5th Cir.1982), 458
Alvey v. Butchkavitz, 196 Va. 447, 84 S.E.2d 535 (Va.1954), 437
Amalgamated Sugar Co. v. NL Industries, Inc., 825 F.2d 634 (2nd Cir.1987), 733
Amato v. General Motors Corp., 67 Ohio St.2d 253, 423 N.E.2d 452 (Ohio 1981), 751
Amchem Products, Inc. v. Windsor, 521 U.S. 591, 117 S.Ct. 2231, 138 L.Ed.2d 689 (1997), 358, 380, 652, 655, 659, 660, 665, 668, 727, 730
Americana Fabrics, Inc. v. L & L Textiles, Inc., 754 F.2d 1524 (9th Cir.1985), 685
American Airlines v. Ulen, 186 F.2d 529, 87 U.S.App.D.C. 307 (D.C.Cir.1949), 260
American Ass'n of Naturopathic Physicians v. Hayhurst, 227 F.3d 1104 (9th Cir. 2000), 243
American Cyanamid Co. v. Hammond Lead Products, Inc., 495 F.2d 1183 (3rd Cir. 1974), 159
American Cyanamid Co. v. Wilson & Toomer Fertilizer Co., 62 F.2d 1018 (5th Cir. 1933), 516
American Dredging Co. v. Miller, 510 U.S. 443, 114 S.Ct. 981, 127 L.Ed.2d 285 (1994), 114

*

INDEX

References are to pages.

†